United States Department of State

Papers Relating to Foreign Affairs

accompanying the Annual Message of the President to the First Session Thirty-Ninth Congress - Vol. 3

United States Department of State

Papers Relating to Foreign Affairs
accompanying the Annual Message of the President to the First Session Thirty-Ninth Congress - Vol. 3

ISBN/EAN: 9783337960414

Printed in Europe, USA, Canada, Australia, Japan

Cover: Foto ©Suzi / pixelio.de

More available books at **www.hansebooks.com**

PAPERS

RELATING TO

FOREIGN AFFAIRS,

ACCOMPANYING THE

ANNUAL MESSAGE OF THE PRESIDENT

TO THE

FIRST SESSION THIRTY-NINTH CONGRESS.

PART III.

WASHINGTON:
GOVERNMENT PRINTING OFFICE.
1866.

PAPERS

RELATING TO

FOREIGN AFFAIRS.

AUSTRIA.

AUSTRIA—Continued.

PRUSSIA.

PRUSSIA—Continued.

PRUSSIA—Continued.

BELGIUM.

BELGIUM—Continued.

BELGIUM—Continued.

PORTUGAL.

PORTUGAL—Continued.

PORTUGAL—Continued.

No.	From whom and to whom.	Date.	Subject.	Page.
		1865.		
348	Mr. Harvey to Mr. Seward.	July 5	Relative to instructions to the admiral of the United States squadron in European waters.	131
176	Mr. Seward to Mr. Harvey.	July 24	Receipt of despatches	132
353	Mr. Harvey to Mr. Seward.	Aug. 8	Relative to hospitalities extended to insurgent cruisers in European waters.	132
357	......do..........	Sept. 6	Ministerial crisis	134
358	......do..........	Sept. 10	Proposed establishment of a coal depot at the Cape de Verd islands.	134
178	Mr. Seward to Mr. Harvey.	Sept. 13	Relative to hospitalities extended to insurgent cruisers in European waters.	136
366	Mr. Harvey to Mr. Seward.	Nov. 21	Relative to the death of José Manuel, killed in an affray with American seamen.	136

ITALY.

No.	From whom and to whom.	Date.	Subject.	Page.
		1864.		
109	Mr. Marsh to Mr. Seward.	Nov. 22	Relative to the temporary establishment of a naval depot of the United States at Cagliari.	139
		1865.		
111	......do..........	Jan. 16	Removal of the court from Turin to Florence. Reception of the news of the re-election of President Lincoln.	140
125	Mr. Seward to Mr. Marsh.	Feb. 7	Acknowledgment of the above despatch	141
114	Mr. Marsh to Mr. Seward.	Feb. 13	Removal of the court from Turin to Florence.	142
117	......do..........	April 28	The same subject	142
118	Mr. Marsh to Mr. Hunter.	April 29	Receipt of the news of the assassination of the President and attempted assassination of the Secretary of State.	143
119	......do..........	May 15	Assassination of the President. Rumored alliance for the maintenance of an imperial dynasty in Mexico.	144
121	......do..........	June 5	Mexican question	145
122	......do..........	June 10	Relative to the treatment of United States vessels-of-war in foreign ports.	146
123	Mr. Marsh to Mr. Seward.	June 29	Proposed treaty of commerce and navigation between the United States and Italy. Mexican question.	148
135	Mr. Seward to Mr. Marsh.	July 24	Acknowledgment of the above despatch	149

ROME.

DENMARK.

DENMARK—Continued.

SWEDEN AND NORWAY.

SWEDEN AND NORWAY—Continued.

SWITZERLAND.

SWITZERLAND—Continued.

JAPAN.

JAPAN—Continued.

JAPAN—Continued.

TURKEY.

TURKEY—Continued.

EGYPT.

EGYPT—Continued.

TUNIS.

TANGIERS.

TANGIERS—Continued.

MEXICO.

MEXICO—Continued.

MEXICO—Continued.

MEXICO—Continued.

MEXICO—Continued.

MEXICO—Continued.

MEXICO—Continued.

MEXICO—Continued.

MEXICO—Continued.

MEXICO—Continued.

MEXICO—Continued.

MEXICO—Continued.

MEXICO—Continued.

MEXICO—Continued.

MEXICO—Continued.

MEXICO—Continued.

MEXICO—Continued.

MEXICO—Continued.

MEXICO—Continued.

No.	From whom and to whom.	Date.	Subject.	Page.
		1864.		
83	Mr. Koerner to Mr. Seward.	Mar. 20	Movements of Maximilian	780
85	......do..........	Mar. 27	Alleged treaty between Spain and Maximilian.	780
90	......do..........	April 2	Resolutions of Congress protesting against the establishment of a monarchy in Mexico.	781
81	Mr. Seward to Mr. Koerner.	April 7	Course to be pursued towards the envoys of Maximilian.	781
82	......do..........	April 18	Pretended diplomatic agents sent to Mexico by the insurgents.	781
92	......do..........	May 17	Assumption of imperial authority by Maximilian in Mexico.	782
95	......do..........	May 19	Spanish-Peruvian difficulties	782
66	Mr. Seward to Mr. Motley.	April 18	Policy of the United States regarding Mexico.	783
78	......do..........	July 14	Influence of events in the United States on its relations with Austria.	783
		1863.		
34	Mr. Motley to Mr. Seward.	Sept. 21	Rumored offer of the throne of Mexico to Maximilian. Reported secret understandings between agents of the insurgent States and the Emperor of France.	784
36	......do..........	Oct. 5	The same subject	786
38	......do..........	Nov. 24	The same subject	788
		1864.		
72	Mr. Seward to Mr. Judd.	May 9	Mexican affairs	788
62	Mr. Judd to Mr. Seward.	April 16	Departure of Maximilian for Mexico	789
148	Mr. F. W. Seward to Mr. Sanford.	Sept. 26	Enlistment of Belgians for military service in Mexico.	789
	Mr. Seward to Mr. Sanford.	Oct. 4	Probabilities of a special mission to be sent to Mexico by Belgium.	789
199	Mr. Sanford to Mr. Seward.	July 6	Enlistment of Belgians for military service in Mexico.	790
214	......do..........	Sept. 7	The same subject	790
215	......do..........	Sept. 15	The same subject	791
220	......do..........	Oct. 24	The same subject	791
228	......do..........	Nov. 21	The same subject	792
230	......do..........	Nov. 28	Debate in the Belgian house of representatives on Mexican affairs.	792

MEXICO—Continued.

MEXICO.—Continued.

MEXICO—Continued.

MEXICO—Continued.

No.	From whom and to whom.	Date.	Subject.	Page.
		1866.		
169	Mr. Motley to Mr. Seward.	May 6	The same subject	840
	Mr. Motley to Count Mensdorff.	May 6	The same subject	840
37	Mr. Canisius to Mr. Seward.	May 8	The same subject	843
174	Mr. Motley to Mr. Seward.	May 15	The same subject	844
177	......do	May 21	The same subject	845
184	Mr. Seward to Mr. Motley.	May 26	Receipt of despatch No. 169	846
185	......do	May 26	Reception of despatches	846
186	......do	May 30	Enlistment of Austrian troops for service in Mexico.	846
189	......do	June 9	The same subject	847
325	Mr. Bigelow to Mr. Seward.	May 25	The same subject	848
469	Mr. Seward to Mr. Bigelow.	May 31	Receipt of despatch No. 320	848
474	......do	June 4	Receipt of despatch No. 316	848
476	......do	June 6	Receipt of despatch No 325	849
330	Mr. Bigelow to Mr. Seward.	June 4	Withdrawal of French troops from Mexico	849

CORRESPONDENCE.

AUSTRIA.

Mr. Motley to Mr. Seward.

No. 78.] LEGATION OF THE UNITED STATES,
Vienna, October 23, 1864.

SIR: I have the honor to acknowledge the receipt of your despatches, Nos. 87, 88, 89, 90, 91, 92, 93, 94, and 95, of dates August 26, (two,) 29th, September 19, (two,) 24, 26, October 4, (two,) respectively, and a circular of date September 12.

I thank you very earnestly for the full and authentic intelligence they convey as to political and military events, the general character of which is certainly most encouraging to all those who sincerely love their country and have an abiding faith in the noble destiny of the commonwealth of the United States.

I have nothing especially new to report of European affairs. There has been a lull of considerable duration in the long agitation of the political surface.

The peace between the German powers and Denmark has not yet been signed, but it is thought that no obstacle exists to its signature in the immediate future. The treaty, when concluded, will doubtless be published, and as there is probably nothing in the details of any especial interest to us on the other side of the Atlantic, I have not thought it desirable to call your attention to such portions of them as might become known during the progress of the negotiation. After the scission of the provinces from the Danish monarchy has been consummated, the question of the sovereignty will press very strenuously for its solution, and there will probably be much animated debate before the succession question has been settled by the diet at Frankfort.

I am not in possession of any state secrets, and certainly should never affect in this correspondence to enjoy such an advantage, even supposing it to be an advantage to a representative of the United States government, and supposing that there were really very many profound mysteries in the diplomatic world to be discovered. I have, therefore, always abstained from attempting to cast any horoscope as to European politics, save to give the result of my observations from time to time as to the general question of peace or war in the immediate future, always an important one to us.

At the beginning of the year a war between Denmark and Germany seemed inevitable, as I ventured to state. During its progress it appeared probable, from the menacing language and attitude of other powers, that the local war would expand into a more general one. That fear has since been dispelled, and it is even possible that Denmark may now be more tranquil, deprived of provinces which it was unable or forbidden to incorporate, than during that period of struggle against an inexorable conclusion which has been terminated by the war and the consequent triumph of the German powers.

The "personal union," which at a certain stage of the proceedings might probably have been secured by Denmark, would hardly have been more than a very temporary arrangement.

I am not able, therefore, to inform you who is to be the sovereign of the duchies, although I suppose it to be probable that Lauenburg will be annexed to Prussia.

As to the future settlement of the "burning questions" of Europe I pretend to no power of prophecy. I doubt, too, whether there are many European statesmen who would be willing to hazard predictions with confidence. There is logic in events, but the syllogisms can with difficulty be comprehended until they have been fairly propounded by time. Academic dissertations about Prussian ambition and its possible schemes of annexation and mediatization, the chronic dualism between the great kingdom and the great empire of Germany, and their historic rivalry for the hegemony of the great people by which central Europe is mainly occupied, the embodiment of the German state-right principle in the policy pursued by the middle and lesser powers, the remodelling of the maps of Europe, and, in general, the possible future of the world in this century or the next, are interesting and important themes for philosophical and historical speculation, but have surely no place in a diplomatic correspondence, especially in that of a transatlantic power. I shall only say, therefore, that, so far as my observation can reach, no political changes seem very imminent, and the immediate future can be best expressed by negations.

It does not seem to me very probable at present that Schleswig Holstein will be annexed to Prussia, or that the German confederation will be strengthened or weakened or essentially modified in any way, or that France will extend her frontiers, or that the King of Italy will reign at Rome, or that an independent Poland will be reconstructed, or that Venetia will cease to be a part of the Austrian empire. At present it appears that the instinct of the governments, if not of the nations, is for peace, for the husbandry of state resources, and for the development of internal industry.

I have nothing to say of the famous French-Italian convention of September. Two years hence is a long way into the future. It is not probable that this government would look with satisfaction on the downfall of the Pope's temporal power, even supposing that such an event were a possible result of the treaty. It is very certain that Austria would abstain from any unprovoked attack upon Italy, or upon any power, and I suppose it to be equally certain that she would resist to the utmost any attempt to deprive her of Venice and the Lombard quadrilateral. I neither comment nor moralize, but give you objectively what seem to me the actual facts.

Austria is sincerely desirous of peace with all the world. Her financial condition is not very satisfactory at present, and there is a varying, but considerable deficit. The rate of taxation is very high. In Vienna, one-third of the rents of real estate goes to the tax-gatherer, and there is an income tax of seven per centum. The debt is about three thousand millions of florins, including the fund for disencumbering the soil from feudal charges (greindentlastungs steuer.) Nevertheless, the resources of the empire are very great, and with a long period of peace, and a more thorough development of liberal institutions, there is no reason why the wealth of the empire should not be vastly increased.

The statesmen of Austria are well aware that the least profitable item of national expenditure is war-making. There is a strong party, too, who believe that the old system of exclusive tariffs, and of what it is the fashion in many parts of the world to call protection of native industry—that is to say, taxation of the mass of the consumers of a country for the benefit, not of the national treasury, but of a certain class of producers—is an error, and a very expensive one. But the production of beet-root sugar, of native tobacco, of spirits, wines, and many other articles, which could be purchased far more cheaply, and of better quality, in foreign countries, has been immensely stimulated by protection, and the classes interested are too powerful not to be able to oppose with success any sacrifice of their vested interests.

The new Zollverein, which will be formed on the basis of the recent French-

Prussian treaty at the expiration of the original one after next year, will include nearly all the states of Germany, excepting the Austrian empire, and the tariff of duties will be considerably lower than those of the present Zollverein, and of course than those of this empire. There is much negotiation, I believe, between Austria and Prussia on this subject, and it is supposed some bitterness, as the political as well as commercial advantages ensuing to Prussia through the new customs union are thought to be great.

As you are well aware, the direct trade between the United States and Austria has sunk to an almost imperceptible amount. The direct exportation from the United States to Austria in the year 1862 was $35,615, although, of course, a considerable portion of the exports to Bremen, Hamburg, and the Zollverein, which in the same year amounted in all to nearly thirteen millions of dollars, was sent to Austria. Nevertheless, it will at some future day seem most astonishing that the traffic direct and indirect of seventy millions of people—about equally divided between the republic and the empire—could be kept within such infinitesimal proportions, mainly owing to the prohibitory legislation of both countries. There is a kind of panic in the Vienna bourse, and there has been a rise in the gold agio of a few per cent.—a very trifling matter in comparison with the spasmodic oscillations of our own exchange, but one which, nevertheless, causes uneasiness. The premium on specie is now about 17 per cent. The panic is partly ascribed to the large purchases going on in financial centres, like Frankfort, of United States bonds, and a corresponding sale of Austrian securities. Certainly, to those who believe in the continued existence of the United States in the family of nations, the prices of our stocks are tempting. It is not often that the obligations of a great commonwealth pay an interest of 15 per cent. to the purchaser. When one recollects that the nation whose credit stands thus low adds one-third to its population and doubles its capital every ten years, and has never been delinquent to its plighted faith since its government was established, it may be supposed that there are individuals hardy enough to venture upon such a speculation, notwithstanding the enormous falsehoods and calumnies which have been sown broadcast through the world by our enemies.

I should say that a considerable change in the public opinion of Europe in regard to our affairs had taken place of late. It begins to be thought possible that the republic of the United States may, after all, prove to be the fact, and the slaveholders' confederacy the fiction; and the world of late has been somewhat less favored than before with school-boy declarations about the horrors of war and the blessings of peace. Writers or speakers who imagine that the American people, in defending their national existence and their free institutions against the revolt of the slaveholders, were simply inspired by a love of carnage in the abstract, and by a desire to sacrifice themselves, their children, and their worldly goods, for the mere amusement of carrying on a terrible war, are, perhaps, a little less admired than they have been.

Those Europeans, on the other hand, who could understand from the first the great purpose, the high resolve, the steady progress, and the unfaltering energy of a great people, when engaged in a work which Providence had imposed upon this generation of Americans, rejoice at the result, which now seems to them secured—that negro slavery and the oligarchy based upon it are to be numbered with the things of the past—they have seen that no war of which history has preserved a record was ever more definite or more logical in its object, more humane in its details, or more thoroughly justified by reason and the highest considerations of humanity.

For the American republic to have accepted the political annihilation threatened by the slaveholders, from a base fear of the perils and sacrifices of war, would have been to proclaim itself unworthy to be the guardian of popular freedom and free institutions in the western world.

The Reichsrath has been summoned by his Imperial Royal Majesty to assemble on the 12th of November.

I have the honor to remain, sir, your obedient servant,

J. LOTHROP MOTLEY

Hon. WILLIAM H. SEWARD,
Secretary of State, Washington.

Mr. Motley to Mr. Seward.

No. 79.] LEGATION OF THE UNITED STATES,
Vienna, October 31, 1864.

SIR: I have the honor to state that, upon the 26th of October, his Imperial Royal Majesty accepted the resignation by his excellency Count Rechberg of his functions as minister of foreign affairs and of the imperial household. The fact was communicated on the same day by circulars to the various foreign legations at Vienna. On the following day a circular from Count Mensdorff Ponilly announced his appointment to the functions resigned by Count Rechberg.

I have the honor to remain, your obedient servant,

J. LOTHROP MOTLEY.

Hon. WILLIAM H. SEWARD, *&c., &c., &c.*

Mr. Motley to Mr. Seward.

No. 82.] LEGATION OF THE UNITED STATES,
Vienna, November 8, 1864.

SIR: I have the honor to acknowledge the receipt of your despatch No. 99, enclosing a copy of a despatch from Mr. Jackson, United States consul at Halifax, in which certain reports are given from Charleston and Halifax newspapers in regard to a supposed scheme for shipping thirty or forty thousand Polish soldiers for the rebel armies. I shall not neglect your instructions to use due vigilance towards thwarting the scheme referred to, but I would observe that so far as Austrian Poland is concerned the state of siege in that country still exists, and it would be extremely difficult for any recruits for this Polish confederate army to cross the frontier in any direction, except with permission of the government, which assuredly would not be given.

I have the honor to remain, sir, your obedient servant,

J. LOTHROP MOTLEY.

Hon. WILLIAM H. SEWARD,
Secretary of State, Washington.

Mr. Motley to Mr. Seward.

No. 86.] LEGATION OF THE UNITED STATES,
Vienna, December 12, 1864.

SIR: I have the honor to acknowledge the receipt of your despatch No. 103, of date November 14, giving an account of the ceremonies performed at New York in honor of the deceased imperial royal minister resident at Washington, Count Giorgi, in conformity with the instructions issued by the State Department, and enclosing copies of two letters from the United States district attorney, E.

Delafield Smith, esquire—the one to the Department of State; the other to the imperial royal consul general at New York, Mr. Loosey.

I have further to state that, immediately upon the receipt of the documents, I addressed a note to his excellency Count Mensdorff, imperial royal minister of foreign affairs, communicating the substance of your despatch, together with a copy of Mr. Smith's letter to the department.

I also took the opportunity to express my own sympathy for the loss sustained by the imperial royal government in the death of Count Giorgi, and to add my own tribute to his personal worth.

I now enclose the translation of a note just received from his excellency Count Mensdorff, in which, as you will perceive, I am requested to express the high appreciation by the imperial royal government of the friendly and becoming spirit in which the United States government has thus paid these last and well-merited honors to the lamented deceased.

I have the honor to remain, sir, your obedient servant,

J. LOTHROP MOTLEY.

Hon. WILLIAM H. SEWARD,
Secretary of State, Washington.

Count Mensdorff to Mr. Motley.

[Translation.]

VIENNA, *December* 7, 1864.

The undersigned, minister of the imperial household and of foreign affairs, has the honor to acknowledge the receipt of the esteemed note of the envoy extraordinary and minister plenipotentiary of the United States of America, Mr. Lothrop Motley, of date the 2d instant, and to express his thanks for the official communication therein made in relation to the decease of the imperial Austrian minister resident at Washington, Count Giorgi, and to the solemn ceremonies at his funeral.

The undersigned takes the liberty also of expressing to the United States minister the great satisfaction with which he has perceived in that esteemed note and its accompanying documents, that the sincere grief which the imperial government feels at the loss of its representative at Washington is shared by the government of the United States, and that the latter issued such comprehensive directions in relation to the last honors to the deceased as exhibit a striking proof of its sympathy.

The imperial government values all the more highly the confirmation upon this occasion of the friendly sentiments of the United States government, since it recognizes therein a purpose to do honor to the power of which the deceased was a representative, and to give a worthy expression to the friendly relations between the two states.

The undersigned has the honor also to request the United States minister to express the sincere thanks of the imperial royal government to the United States government for its proceedings upon the occasion of the obsequies, so honorable both to the deceased, Count Giorgi, and to the Austrian imperial states, and embraces the opportunity to renew to the minister the assurance of his high and distinguished consideration.

MENSDORFF PONILLY.

Mr. LOTHROP MOTLEY,
Envoy Extraordinary and Minister Plenipotentiary of the United States of America.

Mr. Motley to Mr. Seward.

[Extract.]

No. 87.] LEGATION OF THE UNITED STATES,
Vienna, February 13, 1865.

SIR: * * * * * * * * * * * * *

There has been for a period of two or three months a remarkable lull in the European atmosphere. In this empire an indisposition on the part of the government to depart from the circle of its domestic cares and duties is more and more apparent. The Reichsrath is occupied—in committees chiefly—with projects for retrenchment and economy, and it is supposed that the budget for 1866 may possibly be laid before the Chambers previously to the final disposition of the estimates for 1865.

Projects exist of assembling the diets in Hungary, and hopes are entertained even of obtaining deputations from that kingdom to the Reichsrath before the expiration of the term for which the present assembly was chosen, but the projects would seem to be premature and the hopes over-sanguine.

At present matters remain in much the same condition as that which has existed for the last two years. The passive opposition of Hungary to any plans for merging its separate existence in the constitutional empire still continues.

The close political intimacy between Austria and Prussia seems unbroken, so far as can be judged from any outward signs, and this combination, which a few years ago would have been an impossibility, has already become one of the commonplaces of European politics. Yet there is no doubt that a vague feeling of uneasiness on the subject exists both in Germany and in the rest of Europe.

Prussia and Austria combined are an enormous military force, capable of neutralizing any manifestation in the centre of Europe, to which it should be hostile. External movements against the Rhine or against Venetia, rising in Poland or Hungary, would be utterly futile so long as this alliance remains.

Whether the Schleswig-Holstein matter is to cement the compact, or whether, on the contrary, it is to fall asunder as soon as a decision of that question is reached, must soon be seen.

There is much impatience felt here as to the masterly Prussian procrastination through which the interim still continues. The diplomatic correspondence between the two powers has not yet been published, nor has it yet come to an end, but the general opinion would seem to be that a present scheme for annexing the duchies to Prussia does not exist. It is observable, however, that while the liberal party is loud in denouncing all such projects, and in calling for the installation of the prince of Augustenburg as rightful sovereign of the duchies, the more ministerially inclined appear almost indifferent as to the possibility of annexation, and are lukewarm in regard to Augustenburg. But the matter cannot be protracted much longer, and a decision as to the sovereignty must soon be made.

In regard to our own affairs, I should say that a decided change in what is called the public opinion of Europe is manifesting itself. In this empire we have never had to combat with the malice, the calumny, and the treacherous and perfidious "neutrality" by which some other nations have succeeded in injuring us almost as much as by direct hostilities.

We have not often been brought into actual contact with the government on exciting questions, but its attitude towards us has been uniformly loyal, frank and unequivocal. The sovereign of the country has, on more than one occasion, done me the honor to express in energetic language his admiration of the steadiness, the courage, and the vast resources by which the United States government had maintained its authority, and his sympathy with our military successes; and certainly not a word has ever emanated from the imperial royal Foreign Office, or from any statesman or public speaker, that could offend the dignity or wound the susceptibility of the American people, engaged as it is in a life and death contest with the demon of slavery.

The tone of the journalism in this capital in regard to our affairs has been, in general, respectful, friendly, and intelligent, while articles have been occasionally published manifesting a thorough acquaintance with the subject, and much breadth and depth of reflection as to the consequences of our great revolution. At present the opinion seems to have pervaded every channel of public thought in Europe that the war is drawing to a close, that the cause of the confederacy is lost, and that the united republic is to rise superior to all the powers of domestic treason and foreign malice, and to be more conspicuous and formidable than ever.

I shall not endeavor to analyze the materials of which this opinion is compounded. I only state it as a fact, and as a new one. The very opposite opinion has been until lately the prevailing one; and those who have maintained the certainty of the continued existence of our undivided commonwealth, and the ultimate extinction both of the mutiny and of slavery, have been met with a smile of incredulity. For my own part, as I have never faltered for one instant since the beginning of the war in my faith that Jefferson Davis and his fellow conspirators had undertaken an impossible task, and that a government founded like ours, on the broad basis of the popular will, and a widely extended suffrage, was immovable and impregnable, I do not feel any more encouraged now that the whole European world accepts than I was disturbed when it denounced and ridiculed such convictions.

On the contrary, I should say that Europe in its impatience is again going too fast. Four years ago it was in a great hurry for the United States government to abdicate, and for the American nation to get itself decently buried without further delay. Now it is equally hasty in giving short shrift to the rebellion, and in expecting by every day's steamer to hear that it had given up the ghost. Especially an importance which seems inexplicable has been attributed to certain reported negotiations which it was supposed were at once to bring the war to a close. As if the very term negotiation were not in itself an absurdity and a recognition of the rebellion, and as if the United States government were about to make itself an accomplice in one of the darkest crimes ever recorded by history, by proposing to compound the gigantic felony with the chief criminals.

Certainly there seem unequivocal symptoms of a coming counter revolution by the people of the slaveholding States against the oligarchs. The palingenesis of Missouri, of Maryland, and (as it now seems probable) of Tennessee, makes the heart of every loyal American and every hater of slavery leap for joy, and it would seem to require only a wider expansion of the movement—to expect which in the early future seems not over sanguine—to cause the whole commonwealth of the United States to be born again into a newer and a higher life.

But we cannot disguise from ourselves that we have a long road to travel before the end of this war is reached. Rebellion still maintains great armies in the field, and defies the lawful government from its intrenched capital.

Until those true peace negotiators, our great generals and admirals and our magnificent armies and fleets, have destroyed the military power of the rebellion, we can hardly dare to hope for an effective counter revolution in the insurgent States.

The European public is, however, already busy with speculations as to the series of events likely to follow the reconstruction of the Union, prominent among which, of course, are tremendous military movements by the combined veteran armies of the loyal and of the lately insurgent sections.

The invasion of Canada and of Mexico without an instant's delay, the sweeping off from the American continent of every vestige of European dominion, from Behrings Straits to the Isthmus, the revolutionizing of Ireland—a war with France and England, and I know not what besides—these are the phantoms made to dance about to appal the souls of fearful politicians. It is superfluous to say that such tricks to inveigle the rulers of Europe into rendering assistance at the last moment to the sinking rebellion are too shallow to have a chance of success.

I have the honor to remain your obedient servant,

J. LOTHROP MOTLEY.

Hon. WILLIAM H. SEWARD, *&c.*, *&c.*, *&c.*

Mr. Motley to Mr. Seward.

No. 88.] LEGATION OF THE UNITED STATES,
Vienna, February 26, 1865.

SIR: I have the honor to acknowledge the receipt of your despatches Nos. 123 and 124, of dates of January 30 and February 7, both reaching me by the same post.

The subject which, perhaps, more than any other is causing excitement in the European world at this moment is the late conference between the United States government and the insurrection. The rumors concerning these negotiations, as they are called, have been various, and the comments upon them in many organs of public opinion in Europe occasionally very laughable. For my own part, I have been waiting very patiently for an authentic account, never having an atom of fear that the President could contemplate any compromise on the integrity of the nation and the abolition of slavery, and not entertaining a hope that the ringleaders of the insurrection were yet ready to abandon their attempt to destroy our great republic.

As it is not possible for me to imagine any third result to the war—the only alternative being the absolute success of the insurgents, or their subjugation—I have always believed that the sword must continue to be the only instrument to effect a solution of the terrible problem, which has been given the Americans of the present generation to solve. Four years is a long time in the life of an individual, but it is a mere moment in the life of a great nation; and although every heart is sick with the bloodshed and the sufferings—worse than death— which this slaveholders' insurrection has brought upon our once prosperous country, no man capable of thought on great subjects can doubt that the only way to avoid eternally recurring warfare on our continent in future is to make thorough work now.

It is very heroic, no doubt, to talk of resisting subjugation by the United States government, but as you and I and all of us are also subjugated in the same way without much discomfort, and as twenty-five millions of Americans are willingly obedient to the law, there does not seem any great tyranny in enforcing it on a minority who happen to prefer anarchy.

If our fundamental law, the United States Constitution, violates the eternal principles of reason and justice, rebellion against it, with a reasonable prospect of success, would be most virtuous. But as no man ever yet had the hardihood to make such an assertion, it is clearly the duty of the President to maintain the Constitution until rebellion is beaten down, or until bloody treason has trampled out the government of our fathers.

Neither result has as yet been reached, and, therefore, peace seems still impossible. In this empire, as I have always informed you, we have never had to contend with the calumny and malevolence with which America has been so profusely indulged by some other countries.

Here there is an honest desire, I think, both on the part of the government and of a majority of the population, that the insurrection should be suppressed, slavery abolished, and the Union restored. It is not necessary on this occasion to analyze very closely these sentiments, but there is a feeling that the growth of the United States in power and prosperity is not, necessarily, a misfortune for the Austrian empire; and there is also a general conviction that the United States government represents law, order, and civilization, while the slaveholders' rebellion means barbarism and anarchy.

There is a strong wish expressed here that peace should be restored in America, and the contrast is very great between this sentiment and the panic which raged in England and France at the moment when there seemed a probability that peace was to be suddenly restored in our country.

There is something almost diverting at first sight, and yet, in reality, very melancholy in the public explosions of fear, of hatred, and of irritation at such a possible result on the part of those who have so long been howling over our "wicked, causeless, hopeless war."

Nothing will suit the American people, when its government is once restored in its integrity, it appears, but an instantaneous onslaught upon Canada on the one side, and upon Mexico on the other.

The American mob, dripping in gore and domineering over a feeble government, (which, however, has become so entirely tyrannical as to have obliterated every vestige of popular liberty,) is about to rush forward to a war with France and England at once, not being half satisfied with the bloodshed of the last four years.

As it is not possible to discover in our own country any respectable source of any such dire forebodings, one is forced to ascribe them to the guilty imaginations of public writers and stump-speakers on this side of the Atlantic. It is thought natural, perhaps, that the Americans, whose national character, public men, current history, whose noblest deeds and highest aspirations, have been during the last four years the object of calumny, hatred, and persistent falsification, altogether without example in history in what used to be called "our mother country," stung by the memory of those insults and by the material injury inflicted upon their commerce by English pirates, may be disposed to avenge themselves when they feel themselves strong enough. And because the destruction of an unfortunate republic—our next-door neighbor—by the fleets and armies of the first military power in the world, does not seem exactly consonant to our ideas of right and to our national traditions, it is supposed that we shall consider it our duty to dethrone the new emperor by force of arms, even although the Mexicans should unequivocally manifest their desire to be governed by him. I need not say that I have on proper occasions combated all these hysterical suggestions; and until I am otherwise instructed, and until I see very different indications of the national tendencies from such as are now evident to me, I shall continue to maintain that the dearest object of the people and of the government—which are one in the United States—is to preserve peace with all the world, and to have no more bloodshed during this century if it can be avoided.

We shall have enough to do when our civil war is over in cultivating the arts of peace; and as to our European enemies, whose name is legion, it is to be hoped, so long as they refrain from passing from words to blows, that we shall astonish them by a great indifference.

I am glad to see the termination of the Fort Monroe conference and cannot help believing that its result will be to strengthen the government by making manifest the fact—which has, however, always seemed evident enough—that until there is a counter revolution in the insurgent States against the leaders of the rebellion, the idea of peace must be renounced.

The report of the President, together with your despatch to Mr. Adams of February 7, reached me yesterday as published in the New York journals, and I need not say with how much interest I have read them.

I send you a bit of European comment on these various "negotiations" with the Richmond cabal, printed in a great variety of continental journals, and coming originally from an English source. If you have not seen it, it may cause you a laugh in the midst of your labors to see the solemnity with which such childish gabble is uttered by the public instructors of Europe. I cut the slip from a Belgium paper, never having seen the English original. The facts of President Lincoln's having abandoned the emancipation proclamation, and of the coming incorporation of the rebel army with that of the United States for foreign war, are very refreshing.

Our volunteers by the terms of enlistment being disbanded on peace being made with the insurgents, the United States army will prove but a slender nucleus for the great invading force contemplated.

I have the honor to remain, sir, your obedient servant,

J. LOTHROP MOTLEY.

Hon. WILLIAM H. SEWARD, *&c.*, *&c.*, *&c.*

[Translation.]

NEWS FROM ENGLAND.

LONDON, *February* 17, 1865.

The Morning Post vouches for the truth of the following news, which it borrows from the Owl, which appeared on Wednesday:

We have it in our power, from information through a special channel, to give positively the conditions transmitted by President Lincoln, through the intervention of Mr. Blair, to President Davis, as bases of pacification. They are as follows:

1st. The abolition of slavery shall be determined by the legislatures of the States as to time and circumstance, but slavery must be abolished.

2d. The Confederate States shall re-enter the Union with the same rights and privileges which they had when they left it.

3d. The confederate army shall not be disbanded, but shall be incorporated with the federal army for foreign war.

4th. In the Union re-established, the past shall be forgotten.

The second of these propositions having been immediately rejected by President Davis, it became useless to discuss the others.

In publishing this document we shall call the special attention of our readers, first, to the fact that we know, upon incontrovertible authority, that if Mr. Blair had not been invested with full power by President Lincoln, he would not have been received by President Davis; secondly, to the fact that President Lincoln abandons emancipation by his own proclamation, leaving the question to the separate action of the States; thirdly, to the fact that the policy of his government tends directly to foreign aggression.

Mr. Seward to Mr. Motley.

No. 129.] DEPARTMENT OF STATE,
Washington, March 13, 1865.

SIR: I thank you for your very interesting despatch of the 13th of February, which relates exclusively to German affairs. Although there is no immediate connexion between those matters and the now ruling interests in the United States, it is nevertheless certain that a knowledge of the political and financial condition of the continental European countries, and of their neutral relations, is necessary to enable us to determine what policy, in regard to ourselves, we may at any time expect at the hands of the principal maritime powers.

At present, these powers are so far easy in regard to European questions, that they remain at liberty to co-operate, as they have generally done, in a policy which is unfair and illiberal towards the United States and the other American republics.

Harmony among the European nations is not likely to increase, while, happily for us, our military and political situation seems to be steadily and decidedly improving.

It was the chief responsibility of our administration during the last four years to preserve the integrity of the Union against the assaults of faction. The next four years may well be occupied, so far as this department is concerned, with lawful efforts to restore its prestige among the nations.

I am, sir, your obedient servant,

WILLIAM H. SEWARD.

J. LOTHROP MOTLEY, Esq., *&c., &c., &c., Vienna.*

Mr. Motley to Mr. Seward.

No. 89.] UNITED STATES LEGATION,
Vienna, April 2, 1865.

SIR: The debates in the Reichsrath for the past few days have been of unusual interest. The subject of the budget has been under discussion, and the finance committee of the Reichsrath, after having obtained a concession for government of twenty millions of florins as a reduction of the appropriations, has insisted on still further subtractions in detail, amounting in gross to some five or six millions. This the government opposes, and there has been for a time a good deal of talk, both in the papers and in various circles of society, about what it is the fashion to call a "ministerial crisis." As it seems certain that on the question of reduction the government would be in a minority, it was supposed that the ministry would resign.

The speeches in the Reichsrath have been very able; for, as I have often had occasion to remark in this correspondence, it is for no lack of forensic talent that Austria is not among the leading parlimentary governments of Europe; but I cannot venture to ask your attention, occupied so intensely as it is with our own most weighty affairs, to the debates in general; but I would recommend you to read the able and luminous exposition of the policy and principles of the present imperial administration, especially in regard to internal affairs, made by the minister of state, M. de Schmerling, the most pregnant passages of which I have just translated.

I abstain from all comment, because the speech itself will give you a clearer idea of the position of parties in and out of the Reichsrath than I could possibly do, even by a long despatch. You who are so familiar with the *certaminis gaudia* of great legislative assemblies, and are yourself so consummate a master of debate, will not fail to observe the passages which called forth the angry retorts of opponents, and those which gave most satisfaction to the supporters of government.

The conclusion you will perceive to be that the ministers have no intention of resigning.

(SPEECH OF THE MINISTER OF STATE.)

"The debate on the address and the discussion of the budget," said the minister of state, "are commonly the moments in parliamentary life when the contest is carried on on both sides in the most vigorous manner, and where the weightiest forces are summoned into action either for or against the government. We had the one contest—that on the address—months ago. The second is now begun; and although I maintain that, perhaps, under our present circumstances, it is not entirely justifiable to bring on a contest for or against the government on the occasion of the budget discussion, yet I cannot conceal from myself the fact that the contest is taking place.

"If I say that, according to my individual view, this should not be the object of an excited contest in the present condition of Austria, I may be permitted to express myself somewhat more definitely. Above all, there is no doubt on the part of the government and of the Reichsrath that the greatest possible economy should be practiced, that every possible effort should be made to restore the equilibrium in the state accounts, while in regard to the measure there may indeed be a difference.

"Still less, in my opinion, is there any reason to make a so-called act of confidence or of distrust in the government out of the question whether one votes for a greater or a lesser sum. This may have full justification in other parliaments, and, in fact, we have seen that the votes given in a budget discussion have been of necessity interpreted into a vote of confidence or want of confidence in the government. But in other countries—for in other countries we have, after all, totally different arrangements in the composition of the budget, quite different arrangements in the appropriation of the voted sum, quite different arrangements in the calculations of the same. There, where it is permissible to make a general appropriation for the whole of one department (ministerium;) there, where it is even permissible to make one general appropriation for all the departments—there, indeed, this act is of such a nature that it implies confidence or distrust in the government. For where a vast power of dealing with money is given to the departments, there certainly is a possibility of misuse of the sums voted, there certainly corruption is possible; but of all this there is no possibility in Austria.

"I say this quite openly. Any man who reads the five volumes of our state computations; who sees with what exactness the salary of the minister as well as the humblest servant, the residence of the stadtholder as of the gamekeeper on any domain, is settled; who sees the thousand and thousand sets of figures, and, on the other hand, looks through the finance laws in which the government is bound not only to the separate chapters but to the particular titles and paragraphs—that man I will ask, What minister, even if a much larger sum is accorded to him than to many may seem proper, will find that a special confidence is reposed in him, when it is pefectly clear in what way the money is to be spent, and when the ministers are not in the position to spend the money for anything else than the objects for which it was voted? * * * * * * * * * * * During the debate on the address there was a very loud cry to us ministers in particular—for you we have one warning—self-recognition and conversion. Now, as regards self-recognition, we can openly confess that we have it sufficiently. It is very conceivable that we should possess it; for if one looks into our circumstances, if one observes what is written and spoken, one will indeed admit that there has been no lack of warnings, rebukes, and tuition for the ministers. The days in which it could be said that men flattered princes and ministers are long since passed away. Certainly, the ministers are not much flattered at present. [Universal and continued merriment.] * * * * * * And, first, of external policy. I shall say but a few words of this, as I doubt not my honored colleague, the minister of foreign affairs, will be able within a few days to speak circumstantially on the subject. * * * * * * * * Doubtless, one demands of us the greatest energy in our foreign policy, in order to strengthen and maintain the position of Austria as a great power. This is doubtless what is wished, what is justly required of him in whose hands the direction of our foreign affairs is placed. What is offered to him now for support of this vigorous policy? On the one side, that we cannot possibly maintain anything else than a perpetual peace—that we, at least, should not think of ever following any other policy than that of peace, that is to say, the abstinence from every active proceeding, even should such active proceeding be, after all, very much demanded. And what further is offered us? Perpetual representations that we are an entirely broken-down, dilapidated, creditless, ruined state.

"I think, gentlemen, that these are not the elements out of which to create for us a powerful position in foreign lands, and to make it possible for the minister of foreign affairs to bring his word as a weighty one into the councils of Europe. [Bravo in the centre.]

"Look, gentlemen, at the way in which they deal with such matters a little to the northward of us. We have in a northern capital the truly melancholy and unrefreshing spectacle of ruinous internal constitutional circumstances, an earnest conflict carried on by the house of deputies against the government, and the fierce and animated debates are brought to us in every newspaper. But have you, gentlemen, heard from one single deputy in that northern capital, during the debate on the military reorganization, an intimation that Prussia should give up her position as a great power—should reduce herself for a time, and keep quietly at home in politics, and let things roll over her as they might? * * * * * * * *

"No deputy has so spoken. * * * * * * Not one intimation has there been that the state was a broken-down and a ruined one, and that one must, therefore, renounce any vigorous movements in the external world. [Commotion on the left.]

"I come now to that which most concerns me, and about which I have been obliged, both yesterday and to-day, to hear many reproaches—namely, the management of our internal policy. The reproach is always made to the government that the interior constitutional circumstances are not yet arranged; in other words, that the constitution is not yet carried out, or, as it is the fashion to say, the Hungarian question is not yet solved. * * * * * * * For us there is but one solution, whether a resultless one or not the future must show, that we hold on inviolably to the constitution, and put everything in motion to bring about its recognition in Hungary. We are by far not so sanguine as one thinks, if one assumes that we flatter ourselves that the next Hungarian diet (Landtag) will bring the constitution question to a pacific solution, and that, a few weeks after it has assembled, deputies will be chosen from Hungary for the Reichsrath, and come here to take their seats among us. We are not so sanguine as that; and if from some parts of the house there is always the greatest value attached to the summoning of the Hungarian Landtag, while then the constitutional question is to be at once solved, we are not disposed to believe that the question will be at once solved.

"But we flatter ourselves thatby a quiet and consistent forward movement of the government at last this question will also come to a settlement. We expect that very many, even in Hungary, who have the inner conviction that a close annexation (Anschluss) must be carried out, and that the imperial constitution must at last become a truth for Hungary; that they at last will take courage to stand up for their convictions by speaking out, and that we shall thus at last reach the goal towards which we have so long been striving.

"That this aim is a great one no man will deny; that great aims are not reached in a very short time is quite as certain; and if you will look back, gentlemen, to the period when it was at last possible for an English parliament to carry the Catholic bill, the corn bill, the reform bill, you will not stigmatize this government as careless and inefficient if it has not in four years found it possible to bring the Hungarian question to its solution. At any rate, we have the honest will to take hold of the question. We can only manifest that will by declaring, in the name of the government, that all preparations are made to convoke in the shortest time the Croatian and Hungarian diets, and that at last it will only depend on this high assembly to hasten the period, because those bodies can only be assembled when the larger Reichsrath (Gesamntreichsrath) has concluded its session. * * * * * * * * * In regard to the financial condition of the empire, the finance minister has already spoken, and I have, therefore, but little to say. But this I will say, that if our financial circumstances are such as they have been depicted—if the distress is so great throughout the empire as we have here been told, then is our position an entirely desperate one, and then one had better take counsel how to apply radical remedies for the calamity; I say radical remedies, because that it is not a radical measure, whether twenty or twenty-five millions are struck off from a budget of more than five hundred millions, seems to me tolerably clear.

* * * * * * * *

"A few words, in conclusion, as to the position of this administration in regard to this house and the different parties in it.

"I have repeatedly said, and say it now, that a true constitutional life is only thoroughly possible when there is as harmonious a co-operation as is practicable of the government with the representative body. I have repeatedly said that the government and the representative body are not two different parties, inasmuch as that both have one object before their eyes, namely, the welfare of the empire, and, perhaps, can only be of different opinions in regard to the means. I have already declared that conflicts between the government and the repre sentative body are to be lamented, and to be as much as possible avoided, for the very simple reason that they are not two opposing parties, and because, if even that were the case, there is no superior judge to decide between the parties, that therefore prudence and necessity drive government and representatives into the way of working as harmoniously as possible together.

"This is the view which I have ever taken, and which I now express again, because it brings me to declare whether the government deserves the reproach that it is one-sided, obstinate, self-willed, because it does not conform itself in all directions to the votes of the representative body. On this I have to observe as follows; I leave out of view whether or not a strong parliamentary government is a possibility in Austria; whether it be possible or not to govern exactly according to the majority, and if it be possible or not to form so-called majority administrations.

"I will only indicate the moral effect of the so-called majority of a house on the resolutions of the government. I can well understand that a government which is opposed by a closely-formed party, a party which has a fixed programme, a party in the midst of which are men with a sufficient knowledge of affairs (Sachkenntnisz) and equipped with a competent gift of administration to take the reins of power if they are called upon to do so. I can well understand that a government is morally bound to be accountable to such a party and to accommodate itself to it as far as possible.

"I beg to be excused, however, if I adhere to the opinion of a deputy who has said that such parties do not exist in this house, and that, in particular, the party which calls itself his Majesty's faithful opposition cannot be considered by us as a party with a fixed programme. The relation is rather that many men, doubtless guided by conviction, have temporarily found themselves together, who, in the most important questions, have quite divergent views, and whom we cannot, therefore, regard as a party, because it is only a party in that it makes opposition to government.

"And to this party we cannot concede that decisive weight which, according to our opinions, ought to fall into the scale as the moral weight of a fully organized party. This must not be taken ill of us, and therefore offence should not be taken, if when here and there the votes of this house go against the government we still find it consistent with our honor, our duty, and our constitutional principles, to continue to place our services at the disposition of his Majesty. * * * * * * If we are—however we may lament it—not always in accordance with the views of this honorable house, it is not from a contradictory spirit; it is the expression of the feeling that the government is an independent factor in the constitutional life, and, therefore, must act according to its convictions, as it is assumed to be the case with the other factors of the constitutional life.

"For us is the same device as that which has often been announced by members of this honorable house: true to the Emperor, but also to the constitution, and true obedience to duty."

You are aware that a new step is about to be taken in the Schleswig-Holstein affair. A motion has been made in the Diet, and will be voted on the 6th of this month, to establish the prince of Augustenburg in the government of Holstein, the question *de jure* being reserved for future decision. This so-called Saxon-Bavarian-Hessian proposition is to this effect, the diction being important:

"That the high assembly of the Bund would, under reservation of a further and final decision, (Beschlusz fassung,) express the confident expectation that it will please the high governments of Austria and Prussia to give now to the hereditary prince of Schleswig-Holstein Sondesburg-Augustenburg into his own administration, the duchy of Holstein; in regard, however, to the arrangements made between them as to the duchy Louenburg, to cause communications to be made to the Diet."

I have reason to believe that this proposition is favored by the Austrian government, and that it will be opposed by Prussia.

The matter was, of course, much alluded to in the debates in the Reichsrath, and you will see by extracts from the speech of Count Mensdorff, which I append, that the position which Austria means to take will be very clearly laid down in the Diet. You will observe that the minister attaches the highest importance to the good understanding with Prussia, but expresses himself as hopeful of a satisfactory solution of the Schleswig-Holstein question.

If the Austrian declaration to the Diet be of the nature indicated, it is difficult to see how it can be otherwise than unpalatable to Prussia.

COUNT MENSDORFF'S SPEECH.

* * * * "Very far from regarding diplomacy," said the minister of foreign affairs, Count Mensdorff, "as an exclusive guild, mystery, only attainable by the elect, I entirely share in the opinion expressed in this house, that it is possible for every educated man of average capacity, without having been at a regular diplomatic school, to form a correct judgment in questions of foreign policy. But I also permit myself to hold to my modest view, that the handling of these foreign questions requires the greatest discretion when one is not intending to quit the diplomatic field and to go over to that of deeds. The word which falls into publicity from the lips of the foreign minister of a great power must be closely and wisely pondered, because it imposes upon the state the obligation, in case of necessity, with its whole power to makeit good. That may be the reason why in all times and places the observance of reserve has always formed and still forms one of the first rules of diplomacy.

"After the gloomy picture painted in this house of our interior circumstances, it is a doubly sacred duty for him who has the honor of conducting our foreign affairs to lend all his energies to the maintenance of peace, of which the empire seems in every respect to stand so much in need. We believe ourselves to have never left this aim out of view, and to have attained it through the course pursued by the imperial cabinet, so far as that an earnest danger of war is not threatening us from any quarter.

"In a rapid solution of so complicated a question as that of Schleswig-Holstein probably no one ever seriously believed. Were the legal question as indisputably clear and indubitable as it is represented here to be on many sides, there would not be so many various conceptions concerning it, and the affair would have long since found its solution. The imperial cabinet will have an opportunity on the 6th of April to indicate in Frankfort the stand-point which it means to take on the question. By the co-possession in the duchies, Austria is in a position to prevent a solution detrimental to itself, and to guard the justifiable claims of the German Bund.

"Prussia enjoys the same advantage with equal justification, and we entertain the conviction that this much-decried diplomacy will succeed in making a solution possible without endangering that good understanding with Prussia which, notwithstanding all arguments to the contrary, has thus far, according to my inmost conviction, prevented any interference by foreign powers in German affairs. I see therein still the basis for a greater unifiction of Germany, and therefore of an elevation of our prestige (auschen) in respect to foreign countries. A less circumspect policy would probably have involved us in a war, as to the dimensions and consequences of which I shall refrain from giving any opinion. If thereby financial difficulties have been lessened, and the development of our institutions furthered, are questions which answer themselves.

You may be sure that the imperial government will do its best to further the industrial interests of the empire. * * * * * *

"The relations with Italy have great difficulties. The hostile attitude comes not from Austria alone, but it is maintained in those regions perpetually, and on all public manifestations nothing is neglected to depict our possessions in Italy as an unjustifiable one, and as an attack upon Italy. That this is no small difficulty for the minister of foreign affairs to find a way consistent with the honor and dignity of Austria for furthering Austrian commercial interests in this direction, you will surely, gentlemen, admit." * * * *

I have the honor to be, your obedient servant,

J. LOTHROP MOTLEY.

Hon. WILLIAM H. SEWARD, &c., &c., &c.

Mr. Motley to Mr. Seward.

No. 92.] LEGATION OF THE UNITED STATES,
Vienna, April 9, 1865.

SIR: I have the honor to acknowledge the receipt of your despatch No. 129, of date 13th of March, containing very interesting reflections on the close connexion of the political condition of Europe with the development of our great revolution.

You observe that the principal maritime powers of Europe are so far easy in regard to European questions that they remain at liberty to co-operate as they have generally done in a policy which is unfair and illiberal towards the United States and the other American republics. You add that the next four years of the present administration may well be occupied in restoring the prestige of our republic among the nations. No expression could certainly be more just or more moderate than those thus employed to characterize the conduct of the great western powers towards the American republic throughout her great contest with the slave power. It is difficult to speak with calmness of that unfairness and illiberality on the part of two governments which have not unfrequently affected at somewhat earlier periods of our history to hold the institution of African slavery in horror. That their whole moral influence, besides very considerable material support, has been given to the insurgent slaveholders in their efforts to destroy the United States, and to establish an independent state avowedly based upon slavery as its corner-stone, and that whenever in the course of our great struggle to maintain the national life disasters seemed most to thicken upon us, the danger of direct or indirect foreign interference in our domestic affairs has always become most imminent, are facts which history will forever hold fast, and which the American people are not likely soon to forget. If there remain to us any illusions that the tie of a common language and origin between ourselves and the subjects of the one power, or any hereditary friendships and traditional kind feeling towards us on the part of the other great nation, were likely to influence their combined policy towards us, these illusions have been rudely dispelled. This effect will be salutary if it impresses upon us the important truth that in international affairs, liberality and justice are freely manifested by great powers towards others as great as themselves, and that the Union, if true to itself, and to the great principles of human freedom on which it is founded, will be always strong enough to dispense with political friendships, which experience has shown to be impossible.

As to the recovery of our prestige among the nations, that process seems already to have begun. Several long debates in the English House of Commons on transatlantic subjects, with hardly one insulting or calumnious expression towards the United States, are certainly refreshing and novel phenomena.

The slaveholders' conspiracy must indeed be considered in a desperate condition by its European patrons.

In regard to the attitude of this government towards the United States and of the general tone of public opinion in this empire, I have only to repeat what it has so often been my pleasure to state, that nothing could be more frank and high-minded than they have been from the beginning. Now that the hours of our trial are numbered, and that the great republic is seen to be emerging more prosperous and powerful than ever, the feeling towards us has not diminished in cordiality.

I have so recently addressed you on the subject of German politics that I shall say nothing more to-day, save to observe that the Saxon-Bavarian-Hessian motion before the Diet has obtained, as you doubtless have noticed, the expected majority. The opposition of Prussia, and the fixed resolution of Austria to preserve its intimate relations with that kingdom, deprive the vote, I suppose, of much practical significance.

I have the honor to remain, sir, your obedient servant,

J. LOTHROP MOTLEY.

Hon. WILLIAM H. SEWARD,
Secretary of State, &c., &c., &c.

Mr. Motley to Mr. Seward.

No. 93.] LEGATION OF THE UNITED STATES,
Vienna, April 9, 1865.

SIR: I have the honor to acknowledge the receipt of your despatch No. 130, of date 13th of March, containing military news, especially in relation to Major General Sheridan's magnificent expedition, which certainly seems to be one of the most remarkable exploits of this or of any war.

We are looking with intense anxiety, but with highest hope, upon the development of our vast military drama, of which the details, obviously prearranged by the hand of a great master in the art of war, seem rapidly bringing about the catastrophe for which the whole world has so long been almost breathlessly waiting.

The exposition of the political situation of Richmond, referred to in your despatch, has also reached me, and I have read it with very great interest. Of course the importance of such pictures depends upon their accuracy, and upon the opportunities of the artist who paints them. As you seem to have been satisfied as to their fidelity, I need not say how closely I have studied them.

I have the honor to remain, sir, your obedient servant,

J. LOTHROP MOTLEY.

Hon. WILLIAM H. SEWARD, &c., &c., &c.

Mr. Motley to Mr. Seward.

No. 95.] LEGATION OF THE UNITED STATES,
Vienna, April 16, 1865.

SIR: I have the honor to acknowledge the receipt of your despatch No. 132, of date 21st of March, containing military intelligence, especially concerning General Sheridan's splendid successes, of which the importance can scarcely, I think, be exaggerated.

The details of General Sherman's wonderful campaign reach us slowly, but are studied with intense care, and it would be difficult for me to describe the emotions of pride and patriotic exultation with which we follow the career of this daring and most sagacious chieftain. Who can doubt that the cause of civilization and of human freedom must triumph under the guidance of such military genius as it now possesses?

I have the honor to remain, sir, your obedient servant,

J. LOTHROP MOTLEY.

Hon. WILLIAM H. SEWARD,
Secretary of State.

Mr. Hunter to Mr. Motley.

No. 140.]

DEPARTMENT OF STATE,
Washington, April 22, 1865.

SIR: Your despatch of the 2d instant, No. 89, has been received. For the very interesting summary which it presents of the recent debates in the Reichsrath, you will please accept the thanks of the department.

I am, sir, your obedient servant,

W. HUNTER, *Acting Secretary.*

J. LOTHROP MOTLEY, *&c., &c., Vienna.*

Mr. Motley to Mr. Seward.

No. 100.]

LEGATION OF THE UNITED STATES,
Vienna, April 24, 1865.

SIR: It would be quite impossible for me to express the joy with which every American heart abroad, as well as at home, has been filled at the recent tidings of the occupation of Richmond and the destruction or capture of the whole of Lee's army. The first emotion must naturally be one of intense and humble gratitude to God, that our terrible expiation is nearly accomplished. Certainly no one can now doubt that the four years' war by which an oppressed race has been redeemed from slavery and the great republic secured upon well-nigh impregnable foundations, is rapidly approaching its end.

No thinker in any part of the world, no one accustomed to ponder the meaning of daily events and to estimate moral and political forces, can ever have doubted as to the ultimate result of this great struggle. Nowhere more than in America have the moral forces a direct and visible effect upon political affairs, and never were the moral forces of humanity exerted on so prodigious a scale and in so unequivocal a direction as in this contest of principles which the profane and vulgar of Europe have been in the habit of denouncing as our "wicked, causeless, and hopeless" war. Certainly, those who have so firmly hoped for the success of a conspiracy ostentatiously founded on perpetual negro slavery as its corner-stone, must have been brought up in a different school of morals from that in which the majority of Americans have been educated. And if the preservation of a great commonwealth like ours, resting on wider foundations of popular liberty, and offering better hopes for the general progress of humanity than any political organization yet attempted by mankind, did not justify the vast and voluntary expenditure of blood and treasure with which the American people has startled the world, then was bloodshed never authorized on earth. In my own humble judgment, there has never seemed a chance of success for the rebellion even in the darkest hours, for to contend against the democratic principle in America was like struggling against any of the elemental and inexorable laws of nature. But while the supremacy of the republic and the destruction of the rebellious oligarchy were predestined events, there was ever a terrible uncertainty as to the number of years during which the sacrifice of human life and the outpouring of national wealth might go unchecked; and it was not until the final destruction of Hood's army by Thomas, and the magnificent march of Sherman from Atlanta to Wilmington, that the downfall of the so-called confederacy within the current year became inevitable. I confess, however, that I, for one, was not prepared for the most dramatic and complete catastrophe which the genius of the Lieutenant General had so quietly ordained. It is an additional cause of national gratitude to that great soldier that the decisive crushing of the rebellion against American liberty has been effected in so sudden and startling a manner.

The haters of popular freedom everywhere who have been praying so fervently for the success of the slaveholders cannot but be more vividly impressed by such a termination than if Lee had withdrawn his army intact from an untenable position, and had thus, perhaps, been enabled to continue the struggle in some other stronghold until the rebellion perished of exhaustion. And the moral effect upon after ages will thus be the more distinct, for the method taught by Grant of trampling out sedition against the majesty of the people will assuredly be a lesson to be studied in the schools of states unborn and nations yet to be.

I do not think it exaggeration to say that this ten days' work will always rank among the most consummate of military achievements.

Not often in history have we read of a stronghold like Richmond—besieged, but not invested—being taken by assault, and the whole defending army of seventy thousand men, killed, wounded, or captured within less than a fortnight of time. And the modesty and patience of the general-in-chief awaiting with the steadiness of fate the issue of his vast combinations, and the utter indifference to the common joys of the conqueror, in abstaining from taking formal possession of the captured city that he might the more rapidly intercept the flying but not yet annihilated rebels, are as impressive in a moral point of view as are the wisdom of his strategy and the vigor of his blows when the long foreseen hour to strike had come.

I am trespassing too much on your time, having nothing especial to communicate, and it is superfluous for me to dwell any longer upon this victory of Grant, upon the splendor of Sheridan's exploits, which will live as long as we have a history, and upon the steadiness, courage, and sagacity of all our other leaders, and of the whole noble army of the Potomac from corps commanders to privates. But what is most likely to strike the foreign observer, and to be most pregnant in useful lessons to mankind, is the magnanimity exhibited by the American people in the hour of its triumph, the absence of a thirst for vengeance, the yearning for reconciliation with our opponents which mingled with the rapture of success; above all, the spontaneous outburst of devout thanksgiving to the Almighty for the preservation of our united republic.

Military and naval triumphs as signal as those which have made the names of Grant and Sherman, and Farragut, and of others, immortal might prove a curse instead of a blessing to the nation if we forgot that they had been achieved over our own brethren, and if they should foster in our people a love of war for its own sake, a passion for a national military renown which at best, in this age of the world, is a poor thing, and which for us would be fatal as well as vulgar.

Of this we need entertain no fear, I think; and it seems to me the duty of every American representative abroad to combat the very prevalent theory that our success in crushing a domestic sedition by force of arms foreshadows war with foreign nations, and that it will be necessary to seek new fields of action for the great fleets and armies which the rebellion has called into existence. There is no need of my dwelling now on the very obvious arguments, so familiar to every American, by which I endeavor to prove the unsoundness of these fears, the certainty that the American people has had enough of bloodshed for a century, and that it has far too much common sense not to perceive that a future of prosperity and of a higher life is opening before it by cultivating the arts of peace such as never lay before any nation until now.

I ought to add, that on reading the telegraphic news of the surrender of Lee with the remains of his army I had an interview with the Count Mensdorff, and nothing could be more cordial or genial than the felicitations with which he greeted me on my entrance, for the news had already reached him.

"You know," he said, "that our wishes have always been for your success, and that his Majesty has always frankly desired the suppression of the rebellion." It was a pleasure to me to respond that ever since my residence here I had never heard a word from any one connected with the imperial royal government except of friendship and cordiality to the American Union. I take pleasure in adding that the language of the Austrian press, so far as I have observed, and of all circles of Vienna society, is one of very sincere congratulations.

Europe is ringing with the news almost to the exclusion of other topics, but the voice of detraction and of impotent malice is unheard in these regions.

In concluding, I beg to express my most fervent congratulations on these auspicious events to the President, who during this eventful period has so well represented the American people in its unsophisticated wisdom, its courage, its patience, and its generosity.

I have the honor to remain, sir, your obedient servant,

J. LOTHROP MOTLEY.

Hon. WILLIAM H. SEWARD,
Secretary of State, &c., &c., &c.

Mr. Motley to Mr. Seward.

No. 101.]

LEGATION OF THE UNITED STATES,
Vienna, April 30, 1865.

SIR: The news of the great tragedy, which has brought desolation upon our country in the very moment of our highest joy, reached this place on the 26th. This is the first post which leaves Vienna since the receipt of the intelligence.

I shall not even attempt to picture the consternation which the event has caused throughout the civilized world, nor to describe the anguish which it has excited in my own heart, as in that of every loyal American, whether at home or abroad.

The European public spontaneously expresses in every public way its admiration for the character of the murdered President, and its horror at the vile assassin who has taken his life. And if the inhabitants of foreign and distant lands are giving expressions to such deep and unaffected sentiments, what must be the emotions now sweeping over our own country? I confess that I shudder at the thought of the despatches and journals now on their way to Europe. As yet we have nothing but the brief telegraphic tale of horror published by the Secretary of War to Mr. Adams, in London, and by him transmitted to the United States legations on the continent.

Not often in human history has a great nation been subjected to such a sudden conflict of passions. In the midst, not of triumph nor vulgar exultation, but of deep, religious, grateful joy at the final suppression of a wicked rebellion, the redemption of the land from the perils of death, and the certainty of its purification from the great curse of slavery, blessings brought about under God by the genius of our great generals, the courage of our armies, and the sagacity of our statesmen, the American people has seen its beloved and venerated Chief Magistrate murdered before its eyes.

The eminent statesman who, with such surpassing ability, has guided our foreign relations during the most critical and dangerous period of our history seems, thank God, to have escaped death, if we may trust the recent telegrams received last night; but we must wait with intense anxiety the arrival of more than one post before we can feel confidence that the cowardly and murderous assault upon him in his sick bed has not after all been successful. May God grant that his invaluable life may be spared, and that the country may long have the benefit of his wise and faithful counsels. May the life of that excellent son, who has so nearly perished in the attempt to defend his father, also be preserved. What may be the effect of this sudden revulsion in the national feeling I hardly dare to contemplate.

The benignant heart of the late President was filled, as we have reason to believe, with thoughts of peace and reconciliation and reunion; with the feelings of compassion for the criminal, mingled with detestation of the crime, becoming the chief of a great, free, and magnanimous nation, in the hour of its victory, when the assassin took his life. And the country itself, conscious of its strength, seemed fully to respond to these sentiments of the President.

Will not these gentler feelings give way to a desire to vengeance, to a conviction of the necessity of terrible severity, now that the great treason has just accomplished its darkest crime, now that the most illustrious of all the innumerable victims of the slaveholders' rebellion has been so basely and wantonly sacrificed?

I should apologize for giving expression to these thoughts, not suitable to a formal despatch, but in such days as these, and in the midst of such a national sorrow, it is difficult to be formal, and impossible to be calm. Nor can I resist the impulse to add my humble contribution to the universal eulogy which I know is pouring forth at this moment from so many more eloquent tongues than mine, and out of so many millions of sorrowing and affectionate hearts, now that the most virtuous of chief magistrates is no more.

I know that one should avoid the language of exaggeration of over-excited enthusiasm, so natural when a man, eminent in station, mental abilities, and lofty characteristics, is suddenly taken away, yet I am not afraid to express the opinion that the name of Abraham Lincoln will be cherished so long as we have a history as one of the wisest, purest, and noblest magistrates, as one of the greatest benefactors to the human race, that have ever lived. I believe that the foundation of his whole character was a devotion to duty. To borrow a phrase from his brief and simple, but most eloquent inaugural address of this year, it was "his firmness in the right as God gave him to see the right" which enabled him to discharge the functions of his great office, in one of the most terrible periods of the world's history, with such rare sagacity, patience, cheerfulness, and courage. And God, indeed, gave him to see the right, and he needs no nobler epitaph than those simple words from his own lips.

So much firmness with such gentleness of heart, so much logical acuteness with such almost childlike simplicity and ingenuousness of nature, so much candor to weigh the wisdom of others, with so much tenacity to retain his own judgment, were rarely before united in one individual.

Never was such vast political power placed in purer hands; never did a heart remain more humble and more unsophisticated after the highest prizes of earthly ambition had been obtained.

Certainly, "government of the people, by the people, for the people"—to quote again his own words—shall never perish from the earth so long as the American people can embody itself in a character so worthy to represent the best qualities of humanity—its courage, generosity, patience, sagacity, and integrity—as these have been personified in him who has been one of the best of rulers, and is now one of the noblest of martyrs.

If it seems superfluous and almost presumptuous that I, a comparative stranger to Mr. Lincoln, although honored with his commission, should speak of him thus at length to those who shared his counsels and enjoyed his intimacy, I can only reply that the grief which, in common with every loyal American, I most profoundly feel at his death demands an expression, and that at this distance from my country it is a consolation for me to speak of his virtues to those who knew him best.

I have followed his career and have studied every public act and utterance of his with an ever-increasing veneration for a character and an intellect which seemed to expand and to grow more vigorous the greater the demand that was made upon their strength.

And this feeling, I believe, is shared not only by all Americans worthy of the name, but by all the inhabitants of foreign lands, who have given themselves the trouble to study our history in this its most eventful period.

I wish to conclude this despatch by requesting you to convey my most respectful compliments to President Johnson, together with my prayers for his success in administering the affairs of his great office. That he is animated with the warmest patriotism, and by a determination to meet wisely and manfully the great responsibility which has devolved upon him, we are all convinced; and I am sure that the best wishes of every patriotic heart, and the counsels of the wisest minds will be ever ready to support him in the great task of reconstructing that blessed Union which traitor hands have failed with all their efforts to destroy.

I have the honor to remain, respectfully, your obedient servant,

J. LOTHROP MOTLEY.

Hon. WILLIAM H. SEWARD,
Secretary of State, Washington.

Mr. Motley to Mr. Seward.

No. 102.] LEGATION OF THE UNITED STATES,
Vienna, April 30, 1865.

SIR: The impression created in this capital by the horrible murder and attempts to murder just committed in Washington has been intense.

The whole diplomatic corps, with scarcely an exception, have called upon me, as representative of the United States, and their warm and sincere expressions of sympathy at our national loss, of cordial good will for the Union, and, more important than all, of decided respect and admiration for the character of our lamented President, have been most grateful to my heart.

The journals of the capital—all of them, as I have often had occasion to remark, conducted with great ability—have vied with each other in eloquent tributes to the virtues of Mr. Lincoln, in expressions of unaffected sympathy for the great cause of which he was the impersonation, and of horror at the accursed crime by which one of the best of men has been taken from the world.

I enclose (marked A and B) the correspondence between the minister of foreign affairs and myself in relation to this event. I send, further, a translation (marked C) of the report, taken from the journals of the day, of the action taken on the subject in the Reichsrath. Dr. Berger, the member who pronounced the brief but feeling eulogy upon Mr. Lincoln, is one of the most distinguished and eloquent members of the house.

I have the honor to remain, sir, your obedient servant,

J. LOTHROP MOTLEY.

Hon. WILLIAM H. SEWARD, *&c., &c., &c.*

A.

The undersigned, envoy extraordinary and minister plenipotentiary of the United States of America, deems it his duty to state to his excellency Count Mensdorff, imperial royal minister of foreign affairs, and through him (if such a course be considered proper) to his Majesty the Emperor, that official intelligence has been received by telegraph at this legation of the assassination of Abraham Lincoln, President of the United States, in his box at the theatre at Washington, on the evening of the 14th April. The President died on the morning following.

The extent of this calamity can hardly now be duly measured.

No President of the United States, since Washington, has so thoroughly possessed the confidence and the veneration of the great majority of the American nation as did Mr. Lincoln. No man doubted his purity of character, his patience, his firmness of purpose, his benignity, his wise cheerfulness in the darkest hours, and his transparent honesty.

His love of his whole country was perfect. To restore the blessed Union which the rebellion of a vast number of misguided individuals, acting in the interest of negro slavery, had attempted to destroy, was the object of his administration. That object had been secured after four years of terrible warfare, by the capture of all the strongholds of the insurrection, the capitulation of its principal armies, and by due legal provisions for the emancipation of the slaves.

The President was on the point of issuing an address to the people of the insurgent States, doubtless with the intent of expressing the terms of that amnesty and pardon which Congress, relying upon his wisdom and generosity, had already empowered him, at his discretion, to grant, when the hand of the assassin took his life.

The undersigned will not even allude to the universal distress which this tragic termination to the virtuous career of their Chief Magistrate must cause in the hearts of the whole American people. Words are too weak to depict such a universal sorrow as this; but if an excuse be thought necessary on the part of the undersigned for thus dwelling upon the events which have just overwhelmed him with grief, it must be found in the fact that the imperial royal government has ever so frankly and so nobly manifested its sentiments towards the United States government in its contest with this iniquitous rebellion, as to justify the hope of its sympathy at this tragic moment. It is a consolation to the undersigned to remember that one of the last public utterances of the lamented President in regard to foreign affairs was a recent acknowledgment of the magnanimity and friendly attitude of his imperial royal Majesty towards the United States throughout the course of the great contest.

No details as to the condition of the United States minister of foreign affairs, Mr. Seward, has yet been received, but the critical state of his health, caused by a severe accident a very little while before the murderous attempt upon his life, makes it but too probable that the United States may soon be called on to mourn also for the loss of this most eminent and accomplished statesman.

The undersigned seizes the opportunity to renew to Count Mensdorff the expression of his most distinguished consideration.

J. LOTHROP MOTLEY.

His Excellency COUNT MENSDORFF,
Imperial Royal Minister of Foreign Affairs.

B.

VIENNA, *April* 28, 1865.

The undersigned has the honor to acknowledge the receipt from the Hon. J. Lothrop Motley, envoy extraordinary and minister plenipotentiary of the United States of America, of the esteemed note concerning the frightful act perpetrated against the President, Mr. Abraham Lincoln, and to state that he at once laid the said note before his most gracious Majesty the Emperor.

The imperial government could not receive the news of this horrible event without the deepest indignation, which has made upon it the more painful impression, as shortly before it had seen reason to instruct its minister at Washington to express to the government there its sincere congratulations upon the brilliant results which promised a speedy end of the bloody contest in the States of the Union.

The horrid crime of which Mr. Lincoln was the victim could not but inspire the government of his Majesty the Emperor with the more sincere grief, as at no time have the relations between Austria and the United States borne a more friendly character than during the official term of Mr. Lincoln.

The imperial government cannot but cherish the liveliest desire that the hopes of a happy future for the United States, which in this country it was believed might be confidently based on the distinguished characteristics, the wisdom and moderation of the lamented President, may be fulfilled under his successor, and the peaceful relations between the United States and foreign powers be preserved undisturbed.

In conclusion, the undersigned feels it his duty to give expression to the sincere wish of the imperial government, that it may please Providence to preserve to the country still further the eminent Secretary of State, whose life has also been in danger from murderous hands.

The undersigned avails himself of this occasion to renew to the honorable minister the assurance of his distinguished consideration.

In the absence of the minister of foreign affairs,

MEYSENBUG,
The Under Secretary of State.

His Excellency J. LOTHROP MOTLEY,
Envoy Extraordinary and Minister Plenipotentiary of the U. S. of America.

C.

SESSION OF THE HOUSE OF DEPUTIES, *April* 29, 1865.

The session opened at 10. 40. Deputy Dr. Berger spoke as follows:

GENTLEMEN: The news of the tragical fate which has befallen the President of the United States, Abraham Lincoln, through a murderous hand, at the very moment in which the cause of the northern States, and with it the cause of freedom and civilization and humanity, was victorious, has, I believe I may announce, deeply moved all circles and all classes of society in our fatherland also.

From the very beginning of that eventful and bloody struggle, which has lasted several years, Austria was always on the side of the north, and on the day on which the news of the last victory of the northern States reached Washington, the man who now stands at the head of the United States declared that the sovereign of the state to which we belong, from the beginning an enemy of every rebellion, had always stood on the side of the north.

I think that it becomes this house, which represents the population of Austria, to express its sympathy for the cause of the northern States, its sympathy for the tragic fate of Abraham Lincoln, the plain, simple man, who has risen out of the people to be placed at the head of the greatest state, and I move that the president should summon the house to signify, by rising from their places, this its double sentiment—sympathy for the tragic fate of President Lincoln—sympathy for the cause of the northern States.

The PRESIDENT. I doubt not that the house shares the views and feelings which the deputy, Berger, has expressed, and will be ready to give proper evidence thereof by rising from their seats.

(The assembly rises. During this ceremony the ministers are in their places as deputies)

Mr. Motley to Mr. Hunter.

No. 103.] LEGATION OF THE UNITED STATES,
Vienna, May 8, 1865.

SIR: I have the honor to acknowledge the receipt of despatch No. 136, of date April 10, signed by F. W. Seward, Acting Secretary of State, and giving official intelligence of the great events which would seem to have nearly destroyed the military power of the insurrection—the battles before Petersburg, the capture of Richmond, and the capitulation of Lee.

As this intelligence had already reached me, and had already been made the subject of more than one congratulatory despatch on my part, I refrain from further allusion at this moment to this memorable campaign, which has rarely been surpassed in consummate military ability and success in the annals of our own or of any other nation.

I have the honor to remain, sir, your obedient servant,

J. LOTHROP MOTLEY.

Hon. WILLIAM HUNTER, *&c., &c., &c.*

Mr. Motley to Mr. Hunter.

No. 105.] LEGATION OF THE UNITED STATES,
Vienna, May 8, 1865.

SIR: I have the honor to acknowledge the receipt of your circular, of date April 17, giving official intelligence of the horrible crimes committed at Washington on the night of the 14th April, and of the great national bereavement in the death of our wise, courageous, and virtuous President.

As I have already, both in official despatches and private letters, expressed my emotions upon this awful calamity, and alluded to the intense and universal sympathy which it has excited throughout this country and the civilized world, I confine myself to-day simply to acknowledge your despatch.

You further inform me that Andrew Johnson has formally entered upon the duties of President, and I beg through you to offer my most respectful good wishes to the new Chief Magistrate of the nation, together with an expression of entire confidence in the zeal, patriotism, and great ability with which he seems assuredly destined to carry out the great work of the national redemption from the horrors of treason and slavery.

Already there is a general feeling of respect, not unmixed with astonishment, felt throughout Europe for the steadiness and tranquillity with which this change in the executive head of the government has been effected in the midst of a tragedy almost unparalleled in history, and of a popular emotion hardly ever known before.

The world's faith in the stability and beneficence of democratic institutions is not likely to be diminished by so noble a spectacle of national anguish, tempered by national self-reliance.

You likewise notify me that you have been authorized temporarily to act as Secretary of State, and I shall accordingly have the honor to address my despatches to you in that capacity.

I have the honor to remain, sir, your obedient servant,

J. LOTHROP MOTLEY.

Hon. WILLIAM HUNTER,
Acting Secretary of State.

Mr. Motley to Mr. Hunter.

No. 106.] LEGATION OF THE UNITED STATES,
Vienna, May 8, 1865.

SIR: I have the honor to acknowledge the receipt of your despatch No. 139, of date April 18, by which the news is officially confirmed of the capture of Selma and of Mobile, and of the proposed surrender by Johnston, Mosby, and Imboden, of the insurgent armies.

You further inform me that "Mr. Seward, senior, is decidedly improving, and that Mr. F. W. Seward's case has shown more favorable symptoms."

For this most consoling intelligence I am sincerely grateful, and I beg through you to offer to our eminent statesman and his excellent son my congratulations and my fervent hopes for their complete recovery.

You instruct me in the same despatch to notify all United States consuls within the Austrian dominions that all the usual forms of national mourning for the President are to be observed, and I beg to say that this instruction has already been complied with.

I have the honor to remain, sir, your obedient servant,

J. LOTHROP MOTLEY.

Hon. WILLIAM HUNTER,
Acting Secretary of State.

Mr. Hunter to Mr. Motley.

No. 144.] DEPARTMENT OF STATE,
Washington, May 16, 1865.

SIR: I have the honor to acknowledge the receipt of your despatches from No. 90, of the 9th ultimo, to No. 100, of the 24th of the same month, with the exception of No. 98, which has not yet come to hand.

Your observations upon the fall of Richmond, and the military events which immediately succeeded the occupation of the insurgent capital, are extremely interesting and instructive.

I am, sir, your obedient servant,

W. HUNTER.

J. LOTHROP MOTLEY, Esq., *&c., &c., Vienna.*

Mr. Motley to Mr. Seward.

No. 107.] LEGATION OF THE UNITED STATES,
Vienna, June 5, 1865.

SIR: I have the honor to acknowledge the receipt of your despatches Nos. 140 to 144, from April 22 to May 16, containing summaries of political and military events.

In No. 143, of date 16th May, were enclosed two copies of the President's proclamation relative to insurgent cruisers, one of which, in accordance with your instructions, I have communicated to the imperial royal government, accompanied by a brief note, of which the following paragraph is an extract:

"The undersigned is glad to make use of this occasion to express his satisfaction and that of his government with the fact that, so far as the Austrian empire is concerned, this proclamation has no practical application, inasmuch as the insurgent cruisers in question have never, so far as known to the undersigned, been harbored or countenanced within the dominions of his Imperial Royal Majesty."

I have the honor to remain, sir, your very obedient servant,

J. LOTHROP MOTLEY.

Hon. WILLIAM HUNTER,
Acting Secretary of State, Washington.

Mr. Motley to Mr. Hunter.

No. 108.] LEGATION OF THE UNITED STATES,
Vienna, June 5, 1865.

SIR: It seems to me that the time of the department must be too much absorbed by the grave duties of reconstruction at home, and of directing our relations abroad with those foreign states whose conduct during the four years' war has been less straightforward and loyal than that of the Austrian government has been, to leave many leisure moments at present for attending to less important correspondence.

I shall only say, therefore, in regard to the affairs of this country, that nothing very important has occurred since my last writing. The Emperor is about to make a visit to Hungary, and hopes are entertained that the personal presence of the sovereign may exercise a fortunate influence on the relations between the countries beyond the Leitha and those other parts of the empire which have already accepted the constitution of 1861.

I believe it is expected that before the close of this year the Diet of Hungary will be convoked, during the sessions of which vigorous attempts will be made to overcome the passive resistance hitherto offered by that kingdom to the constitutional union. I should not think, however, that sanguine hopes were entertained of very soon seeing Hungarian deputies elected to take the seats provided for them in the Reichsrath.

The Schleswig-Holstein affair drags its slow length along. The imperial government has consented to the Prussian proposition, that the provincial Diets of the Elbe duchies should be summoned according to the electoral law of 1854, rather than the more liberal one of 1849.

The sovereignty of those provinces still remains in the joint possession of the Emperor of Austria and the King of Prussia, and no very rapid steps seem likely to be taken on the part of those potentates to vacate their condominium in favor of any of the rival claimants to the dukedoms. There will be much tedious, legal, and historical disquisition before Prussia will avow herself convinced on the subject, and meanwhile her able and indefatigable prime minister will see to it that the naval and military requirements of that kingdom receive no detriment.

The question of Mexico occupies a very large part of public attention in Europe, and the probable dangers impending over her new order of things, so far as established in that country, is a very fruitful topic of discussion in the journals. I have had no conversation, official or informal, on the subject with the imperial government. My personal views as to this adventure have been long ago expressed whenever fitting occasions offered, and the position of the government of the United States has been fully set forth by my communication of the despatches of the Secretary of State according to his instructions. As I have often had occasion to observe, the imperial government has ever held itself aloof from the whole Mexican enterprise, and disavows responsibility for its results. I suppose that the United States government continues its diplomatic relations with the Mexican republic, and has no present intention of departing from the line of strict neutrality which it has laid down between the contending parties in that country, nor any intention of lending assistance by underhand means to either belligerent. In case any change of attitude is contemplated, I beg to receive as early instructions as possible, and I should be much gratified to be informed, if such a course be not inconvenient, as to any important communications that may have been had on this subject at Washington or elsewhere. It is obvious that my position requires me to be at least as well instructed in this matter as other diplomatic representatives of the United States may be.

I have the honor to remain, sir, your obedient servant,

J. LOTHROP MOTLEY.

Hon. WILLIAM HUNTER,
Acting Secretary of State, Washington.

Mr. Seward to Mr. Motley.

No. 148.]

DEPARTMENT OF STATE,
Washington, June 13, 1865.

SIR: I have received and have read with deep interest your despatches from No. 101, of April 30, to No. 106, of the 8th ultimo. Your accounts of the feeling with which the news of the assassination of the late President of the United States was received throughout the Austrian empire, as well as elsewhere in Germany, are very gratifying. Your own proceedings upon the case are approved.

I am, sir, your obedient servant,

WILLIAM H. SEWARD.

J. LOTHROP MOTLEY, Esq., *&c., &c., Vienna.*

Mr. Motley to Mr. Seward.

No. 111.] LEGATION OF THE UNITED STATES,
Vienna, June 27, 1865.

SIR: I have no startling events to record since my last writing. Nevertheless it cannot be denied that the attention of the Austrian statesmen is absorbed by very grave matters. Whether the position of the administration or of any members of it is seriously compromised or not I am not prepared to decide; but it is certain that defeats have been sustained by the government on vital questions, which, in a regularly organized parliamentary system on the English model, would necessarily lead to a resignation or to a dissolution. A few days ago there was a warm debate upon the question whether, according to a certain article (No. 13) in the February constitution, ministers were not bound to obtain the sanction of the Reichsrath to measures taken during its recess. A resolution to the effect that such measures were unconstitutional and void unless subsequently confirmed by the representative body was carried against the ministers by a majority of two-thirds. I have not learned that there are to be any steps taken in consequence of this vote.

This week the minister of finance has announced that a loan of 117 millions of florins will be necessary to cover the estimated deficit for the years 1865 and 1866. The house of deputies refused to sanction at present a loan of more than 13 millions, or one-ninth of the whole amount, a sum immediately required for the protection of the July coupons on the existing debt, and reserves the further authorization of the loan demanded until the finance laws for 1865 and 1866 shall have been constitutionally passed.

The effect of these sentiments and discussions has been very perceptible on the exchange and in the public feeling. There is a sentiment, amounting almost to conviction in some quarters, that the empire is on the high road to national bankruptcy; that it is impossible to raise any more revenue from taxation, as the people are not able to bear the existing burden, and that some means must be discovered without delay for reducing the expenses at least to an equilibrium with the present revenue, and for putting an end to the annual deficit which has assumed a frightful regularity.

Those means have not yet been found, and I refer you to extracts appended to this despatch from remarkable speeches just made in the house of peers, by some distinguished members of that body, as proofs that very great alarm is felt, and that the alarm is not without cause.

In previous despatches I have given you sufficient details as to the annual budgets of the empire, and as to the amount of the national debt.

In round numbers, for general purposes, it may be said that Austria owes to-day about as many florins as the United States government owes dollars.

The annual interest, exclusive of that upon the "Grund Entlastung," (a debt of about 500 millions, contracted for the emancipation of the peasants,) is not far from 120 millions of florins. The market price of the Austrian loans, bearing 5 per cent. interest in specie, is quoted to-day in Frankfort at 66⅞, and that of the United States six per cent. five-twenties at 75.

Thus, at this moment of our emerging from a terrible civil war of four years' duration, which has cost 3,000 millions of dollars, our credit is about equal to that of the Austrian government, although our actual indebtedness is about double theirs, (a florin being nearly half a dollar,) while the population, respectively, of the empire and of the republic is almost exactly the same.

As United States stocks have been sold as low as 36 in Frankfort, or at less than half their present market value, you perceive how rapid has been the advance, in the belief that the American government is not rushing very rapidly upon that national bankruptcy which our excellent friends in England have so steadily predicted.

After all, it is felt that a nation which has a vested capital of at least 21,000 millions of dollars, or seven times its debt, whose population doubles every quarter of a century, whose wealth doubles every ten years, and whose annual production may be fairly stated at 4,000 millions, or considerably more than that of any other country, is not in danger of insolvency unless the character of its people, both for industry and good faith, should suffer some astounding metamorphosis.

The instant disbanding of a large part of those armies and navies, (as soon as the last shot in the civil war was fired,) with which it was considered so certain abroad that we were at once to attack England and France, and the world in general, in order to find occupation for our warriors, and to slake the persistent thirst for blood which the war against the slave power was supposed to have engendered, has astounded Europe—for Europe always knows that we are going to do exactly the reverse of what we really do—but it has benefited our credit.

The rapid disappearance of those tremendous forces seems as prodigious to the European mind as their sudden apparition when required to save our national life, while the vanishing into space of the "nation" created by Jefferson Davis, and so warmly welcomed by the haters of our republic, without leaving one solid fragment of itself in existence, ought to furnish a lesson to politicians in future in the art of distinguishing exhalations from organized bodies.

But it is hardly possible for the Austrian empire, or for any of the great or little powers of the continent, to effect such sweeping retrenchments as our geographical position and our democratic institutions allow. Of the four millions of soldiers always kept on foot in Europe, this empire has from 320,000 to 613,000, the latter figure being that of its army on a war footing, while the total number (active and reserve) of the army of Hesse Cassel, with its population of 740,000, is 15,000, or two thousand more than the whole United States army—officers, musicians, and privates—in 1860.

It is true that the expense of the imperial army has just been reduced, as was well put by Minister von Schmesling in his speech to the peers, from 135 million florins to 95 millions, being a saving of 40 millions; but the exposed condition of the empire, the troops of enemies ever ready to take advantage of any momentary weakness, and the constant possibility of external wars, great or little, or of disturbances in some portion of its very heterogeneous population, render it doubtful whether such a diminution can be sustained, and almost certain that it could be carried no further.

That the exigency of diminishing the imperial expenditure is very great, and that there is a frank determination, both of the ministry and of the opposition, to effect such retrenchments, seem to be certain, but the road to them does not seem so clear.

It was wittily observed by Count Rechberg, ex-minister of foreign affairs, that the opposition was very loud in shouting fire, but they did not come forward with the engines to put it out; and it was quite as wittily replied, by Count Auersperg, that the key of the engine-house was not in their hands, but in that of the authorities.

Thus far I have not seen any very promising indications of large economies to be effected in the future; and, after all, a great empire in Europe must, under the universal system which now prevails in this hemisphere, look rather to increased national production than to very great savings of expenditure to relieve its embarrassments.

I suppose it to be as well established a fact as any in human history, that the largest individual liberty of action consistent with due security to life and property will give the largest national production, other things being equal.

It is for this reason that in the United States the same amount of capital, land, and labor yields more wealth than can be expected in any European country.

No doubt the resources of Austria are great, almost inexhaustible; but this, after all, is but a phrase. The resources of Mexico are boundless, so are those of Turkey, while the national resources of Holland are almost null; yet Holland has been at times one of the richest and most productive states in the world.

The more Austrian industry is freed from its fetters; the sooner the emancipated serf finds himself able to earn more than twenty kreuzers, or ten or twelve cents per diem, which is about the daily wages of the laborer in many of the most populous and important provinces, the sooner will the deficit which now perpetually stares the country in the face, suggesting horrid visions for the future, begin to withdraw his disagreeable visage.

Certainly democratic institutions are not possible, scarcely conceivable, or desirable in Austria; but so long as protection, legislation, class privileges and general administrative interference with the individual prevent the mass of the people, by whom the resources of a state must be worked, from having any better prospect in life than that of earning, by twelve hours of daily toil, about one-tenth of what can be earned by an American laborer of the lowest class in the same time, certainly a very largely increased productiveness of the empire cannot be expected.

To perpetually look upward to government for assistance, direction, instruction, advice, and commands in daily affairs is not a habit which inspires a people with the spirit of self-confidence and of self-help, out of which is born national wealth, and which gives the deathblow to deficits. But I am not writing an essay on political economy.

I have the honor to be, sir, your obedient servant,

J. LOTHROP MOTLEY.

Hon. W. Hunter,
Acting Secretary of State.

[Extracts.]

Session of the House of Lords, *June* 23, 1865.

Count Anton Auersperg. * * * * It would be before all things desirable to expect that the official upholders of the constitutional principle should be those who would feel bound to work most earnestly for the removal of those financial troubles. * * * * At the beginning of the so-called *new era* the old figures were retained as a result of the old system remaining unaltered. I know that thorough and lasting reforms cannot be effected in a moment's time, but in these five years there has certainly been too little upward movement, and even an impulse towards a spring has not been given. * * * * Louder and louder rise to us voices from the provinces, partially from the over-burdened provinces—voices of taxpayers crying for relief from taxes hardly longer to be borne. In Hungary, owing to exceptional circumstances, a payment of taxes in natural products has been granted and an attempt made in this direction. Out of Styria, a country which, under its regular conditions, enjoys a quiet and secure prosperity, a wish for similar favors reaches us through official organs. I will not even speak of my poor home, Krain (Carniola,) where it has been allowed as a favor that executions should not be proceeded with, after the object for the execution has ceased to exist. * * * * I should call attention to the fact that from these circumstances results a certain amount of demoralization. If any one succeeds in spite of these melancholy circumstances in laying up a fortune by dint of industry and economy, does he know what he possesses? What can he really call his own? If the father of a family invests his aquired capital in real estate, he receives from it either no revenue at all, or a comparatively small one. If he invests it in stocks, he does not know what would remain to his heirs to-morrow if he were to close his eyes to-day. He allows that the fruits of his earnings should be squandered in the enjoyment of life, even if he does not share in them. The phantasmagoria of an almost exaggerated enjoyment of life and pleasure must not blind us to what lurks behind; there is in them the sting of resignation, if not of despair. This is certainly a position of things far removed from that which we had in view, and on which we placed our hopes, when the celebrated circular of the minister of state opened a vista to us into a new future when we were informed that "Austria would find in the constitution the means to rise to that height of power which is the necessary foundation of material prosperity and intellectual aspiration." But I look vainly around for this prosperity, for this increase of elasticity. The conditions in which we live, and the causes which have brought them about, were prophetically indicated to a certain extent by another Austrian statesman when he said, "I consider it a destructive measure, the exclusive covering of the wants of the state by a perpetual new increase of the debt; it makes the cultivation of order in the domestic affairs of the state an impossibility; it undermines general confidence because every one loses confidence in himself and gives way to despair." * * * * * *

If I meet the father of a family regularly at a pawnbroker's door, if I see a husbandman regularly mortgage his still ungathered harvest, without laying up these most urgently required means against a day of want, I know what sort of order I have to expect in the household of such a man. It is not to be denied, in the channel which has been entered upon, the ship of state is rushing inevitably into the whirlpool of a financial catastrophe, and we must try with all our strength to save her, for we have reached that point when the two levers which have been used to assist us in the still increasing need have ceased to perform their service. It is certainly impossible to go any further in the augmentation of taxes. * *

The loan system, too, has its limits. The eventual creditor is generally a good reckoner, and if he holds up to himself a domestic interior of the state, in which the interest of the state debt and the army budget consumes half the revenues, and of the other half, twenty-six millions are consumed by arrears of taxes, he will not be very impatient to place his capital at the service of such a state. * * * * * I believe that this is understood in the other house. I believe that it is also understood in this house, under these conditions the finance budget was laid before the Reichsrath with a total appropriation of five hundred and forty-eight millions, and with a deficit which, according to government figures, must be estimated at thirty millions. A species of permanent declaration of deficit seems on the point of taking place, if an energetic opposition is not made. This has already been made in the other house, and the result has been that the government itself, at the first serious attack, has reduced its own budget twenty millions and a fraction. I regret that the government on the presentation of the first budget has not won for itself these laurels; that it made these important reductions only after the pressure of the representatives of the people. In the crown lands this proceeding has not had a favorable result; the conclusion has been drawn that the original budget was not put together with that earnest care which the position and necessity of the state demanded; it was further concluded—and I hardly believe that this was a mistaken inference—that if twenty millions could thus be saved, one could also have saved in a greater or less degree in former years.

* * * * * * * * * *

COUNT LEO THUN. The detailed reports had made upon men the impression of an attempt at fine coloring; and even the principal report was not free from this, for it mentioned, for instance, that the end could only be reached gradually, and not by a single effort. The committee indicates that a steady diminution of the deficit had taken place, but it was not only a diminution—it was an entire removal of the deficit, that was urgently required. In this way (the speaker continued) we shall never reach that end. That no further increase of taxes is possible every one will admit to me, but I am justified in my question, why, in this increase of taxes, a sudden impulse was not avoided? If all those last farthings which are brought in by means of the tax execution are put into circulation and a deficit still remains, in consequence of which the weight of interest rises to a sum which is still greater than that which is brought in by the executions, then those last farthings have been collected in vain. [Bravo!] What is wanted is not a gradual change, but an immediate radical cure; for I am firmly convinced that if the balance is not soon successfully restored, this task will in a short time become impossible. Our position can be characterized in a few propositions, the indisputable truth of which, according to the report of the minister of state, has received full recognition in government circles. The first proposition is this: that every household which is so arranged that the yearly returning expenditure is greater than the receipts, while the difference has to be covered by new and ever more disastrous loans, must necessarily come at last to bankruptcy. The second proposition is this: that our receipts cannot be increased by tax laws; a tax reform is ever hinted at. The sanguine hopes, however, which are based upon this, are only that by this means the amount from taxation as it exists at present, can be made permanent for the future. A good deal of this is in no event to be expected. [Applause.] Consequently the equilibrium in the state accounts can only be obtained by a diminution of the expenditure at least to that figure at which the receipts are now estimated. [Bravo!]

To the result which the house of deputies, led by this view, have already reached, I must on one side still oppose the fact that even the figure at which the House of Deputies has arrived does not seem to me sufficient. * * * * * * I cannot think that the first speaker has painted with too black a pencil, and I should consider it serious at such a time as this to bring such a reproach against anybody, for I admit frankly that the state of affairs with regard to finance is so black that it would be difficult to paint blacker than the reality.

This fact is so well known that an avowal of it, in this house, cannot bring about discouragement on the part of the population. [A voice: Quite right.] Those who have any knowledge of financial affairs know our situation, and it is not by an open exposition of them that we shall injure a credit which is only to be helped by the conviction that we are fully alive to the danger, and by inspiring the conviction that we mean to seek for a remedy. [Bravo!]

As far as regards the population, it feels through its own interests the consequences of the position; and certainly what it feels works more deeply than anything that is said in this house or written in the newspapers. The tax-payer, whose house is sold over his head, will not look around him to be told by the newspapers what is the condition of financial affairs. * * * *

The MINISTER OF STATE, v. Schmerling. * * * * It is an undoubted fact that we have a deficit in this year of 1865, and we can hardly deny the fact that we shall hardly get through 1866 without a deficit. This is certainly a serious and melancholy circumstance, but I must permit myself to throw a little glance on the past year in order to show that the requisitions of the present year and of the coming year are very different from those that existed in former years. Whoever will throw a glance at the requisitions of a former year, and compare them with those rates that have their present expression in the state proposition of 1865 and 1866, will not be able to avoid the conclusion that a decided retrogression has taken place in the requisition.

I shall only point to the one fact that the war budget, which has been so often drawn into consideration, has experienced a reduction of more than forty millions. It is certainly said, however, why is this saving just now? Why not in former years? If the conviction has been attained that a round sum of 95 millions is sufficient for the war budget, why were 135 millions required in former years? Well, to-day we enjoy the certainty of a European peace; to day, in great and important things, we enjoy security in our interior. That this was not the case in former years will be clear to all who will throw a glance into the past. * * * * * * * * * *

I go further into the question. The government of his Majesty, and certainly not the finance minister alone, but the assembled advisers of the crown, are penetrated and moved by the conviction that in all branches of the administration thorough reforms are necessary, particularly in the direction simplifying the administration, and therefore necessarily making it less expensive. [Bravo!]

The government will be, however, in the position to lay before the lesser Reichsrath, as well as before the Diets in the provinces of the eastern half of the empire, propositions which will give the desired aid exactly in the right direction. [Bravo!]

But there is another very important question which must be kept in view, and that for the present is only to be touched upon. It is necessary to increase the income of the state, not by augmenting taxes, for the government is as thoroughly convinced as this high assembly; but, in the present condition of the empire, there can be no further augmentation of taxes. But we must take into consideration the maxim repeated so often, that in Austria there are still many resources which now lie dormant. They must be utilized, not in augmenting the taxes, but by creating new sources of revenue, and, as in this way the state will indirectly obtain the means of imposing taxes which will not be burdensome, for the future we may look to this as a source of help. That the government of his Majesty have already turned their attention to this purpose, this high assembly must believe from one slight indication, that it is endeavoring in all directions to give every possible assistance to institutions of credit which have the purpose of animating commerce, traffic, and industry, as well as to influence those individuals who are devoted to commerce. When, therefore, through the untiring activity to which the government is pledged and supported by the lively participation of this high assembly, and by the high House of Deputies, we shall have succeeded in working in the double direction, that on one side a total reform of the administration shall diminish the requirements, that, on the other, new sources of national prosperity shall be developed, then we shall have attained what we all wish to attain, and the deficit will be permanently covered. [Bravo!]

Mr. Motley to Mr. Hunter.

No. 112.] LEGATION OF THE UNITED STATES, *Vienna, June 28, 1865.*

SIR: As postscript to my despatch of yesterday, which will probably go by the same mail which takes this, I have to state that important changes in the cabinet have just taken place.

It is officially announced that the Archduke Regnier, president of the council of ministers, has received, at his own request, a long leave of absence, and that the minister of foreign affairs and of the imperial household, Count Mensdorf, will act provisionally as president.

It is further announced that his Majesty has accepted the resignation of Count Hermann Zichy, aulic chancellor of Hungary, and of Count Nadasdy, director of the aulic chancery of Transylvania.

Mr. George Von Maylath has already taken the oath of office as chancellor of Hungary.

It is further understood that State Minister von Schmerling, Police Minister Baron Mescery, Finance Minister von Plener, and the ministers von Hein and von Lasser, have likewise resigned, and that they are now holding office, at the request of the Emperor, only until their successors can be appointed.

In short, the Schmerling administration, identified with the February constitution and with the idea of the parliamentary centralization of the imperial dominions, has come to an end.

The principal and immediate cause of this change of policy is undoubtedly the Hungarian question, and the appointment of Mr. De Maylath, one of the leaders of the conservative party in Hungary, as chancellor of that kingdom, points to an attempt at a compromise.

The statesman most prominently mentioned as successor to Mr. De Schmerling is Count Beleredi, at present statthalter of Bohemia, belonging to the anti-centralization and aristocratic party.

I have not time to add anything more, save that the changes would seem to be in the direction of a federal and aristocratic, as opposed to a centralizing and more popular policy.

Before the next post day it is probable that the various rumors now circulating as to the new cabinet will have given place to facts.

I have the honor to remain, sir, your obedient servant,

J. LOTHROP MOTLEY.

Hon. W. HUNTER,
Acting Secretary of State, Washington.

Mr. Motley to Mr. Seward.

No. 115.] LEGATION OF THE UNITED STATES,
Vienna, July 10, 1865.

SIR: I have the honor to acknowledge the receipt of the circular of date June 7, ultimo, signed by yourself, giving notice of the departure of Admiral Goldsborough to take command of the European squadron, and communicating certain orders of the Navy Department to that officer.

As you are well aware, those orders have no particular application, so far as the ports of this empire are concerned, the imperial government never having extended belligerent rights to United States rebels.

I have the honor to remain, sir, your obedient servant,

J. LOTHROP MOTLEY.

Hon. WILLIAM H. SEWARD, *&c., &c., &c.*

Mr. Motley to Mr. Seward.

No. 118.] LEGATION OF THE UNITED STATES,
Vienna, July 24, 1865.

SIR: I confine myself to-day to the simple statement that the new ministry is formed, although not yet formally announced.

Count Larisch, a noble of large fortune and high character, who has not been hitherto much employed in the public service, is to succeed M. De Plener as minister of finance. Like the other leading members of the new cabinet, Count Mensdorff, Count Maurice Esterhazy, Count Beleredi, and M. De Maylath, who are all between 40 and 50 years of age, he is in the prime of life for political labor.

This is also true of the new Travernicus of Hungary, Baron Seunyey, whose appointment is also settled. This post, which answers in some respects to that of a minister of the interior for Hungary, (*Tavernicoumere regalium magister,*) is of special importance at this moment, and I understand that M. De Seunyey, like M. De Maylath, the new Hungarian chancellor, belongs distinctly to the "old conservative" party.

It would seem obvious, therefore, that the effort to bring about a reconciliation of the kingdom of St. Stephen with the "hereditary provinces" is to be founded on a good understanding between the conservatives in all parts of the Austrian dominions.

It is not worth while to add any further conjectures to those already made in this correspondence as to the probable policy of the new adminisrration. The budget for 1865 has been voted, and the Reichsrath will adjourn on the 27th instant. The lesser Reichsrath will probably not assemble before the new year.

Meantime, the Hungarian diet will be convoked in October, the measures of the government will then be developed, and the great practical questions, how to establish a united Austria for imperial purposes, how to reconcile the legal continuity of the Hungarian constitution with the February patent, and how to modify that organic law in a constitutional manner, will press for solution.

The Schleswig-Holstein matter is no nearer a settlement, and it cannot be denied that the fair days of the Austro-Prussian alliance have been succeeded by a somewhat threatening atmosphere.

I have the honor to remain, sir, your obedient servant,

J. LOTHROP MOTLEY.

HON. WILLIAM H. SEWARD,
Secretary of State, Washington.

Mr. Motley to Mr. Seward.

No. 120.] LEGATION OF THE UNITED STATES,
Vienna, July 31, 1865.

SIR: The session of the Reichsrath was closed on Thursday, the 27th instant, with the usual formalities, in the hall of ceremonies of the imperial palace, the speech from the throne being read by the Archduke Lewis Victor, the Emperor's youngest brother, as "*alter ego*" of the sovereign.

The speech was as follows:

"HONORED MEMBERS OF THE REICHSRATH: The honorable charge is conferred upon me of solemnly closing, in the name of his Imperial Royal Apostolic Majesty, the present session of the Reichsrath. In doing this, I greet you, archdukes, princes of the imperial house, illustrious and honored gentlemen of both houses of the Reichsrath. Before all, it is incumbent on me to discharge an agreeable duty in expressing our most gracious Emperor's entire appreciation of the patriotic zeal and the unwearied activity which has been displayed, as well in the committees as in the assemblies of both houses, during the discussion of many important subjects.

"Recognizing the influence which the stimulation of traffic and of industry exerts on the universal welfare, a great part of your activity was devoted to the discussion of such projects as had for their object the furtherance of industrial activity in the interior, the establishment of the legal protection necessary for the same, and the auxiliary support on the part of the government for undertakings which are to be regarded as the most effective means for promoting industrial and natural production, trade and manufacture.

"The reasons which have induced you, after a careful and intelligent examination, to adopt the new commercial treaty with the states of the German Zollverein have guided likewise the decision of his Majesty in signing it. We may indulge the hope that, with a fresh and courageous exertion of the industrial energy and intelligence of the country, and by rapidly and prudently making use of the advantages presented by the treaty, this work will conduce essentially to the augmentation of the prosperity of the empire.

"Through laudable and mutual harmony of action in both houses, many laws necessary for the requirements of the national household have been passed, especially the finance law for 1865. The determination exhibited during the discussion of this law to observe, in the appropriation of the means at command for the necessities of the state, an economy reaching to that limit which cannot be overstepped without weakening the strength of the monarchy, and its position towards the external world, deserve a thorough appreciation.

"The maintenance of the universal European peace, which was always the task of the imperial government, will continue to be the object of its earnest endeavor.

"In the Schleswig-Holstein question, his Majesty, in harmony with his Majesty's illustrious ally, the King of Prussia, will seek to bring the same to a solution such as is required by the interests of Germany and the position of Austria.

"Weighty reasons, which touch the general interests, and which, on that account, have found patriotic and eloquent expression in the assembly of both houses, demand the speedy convocation of the legal representatives of the people in the eastern parts of the empire, and bring with them the necessity of pretermitting the discussion of the finance law for the year 1866 in this session.

"Most serene, most worthy, illustrious, highly honored gentlemen: The satisfaction created by the thought of your intelligent, patriotic labors does not diminish the deeply cherished aspiration that a common discussion of the laws, duties, and interests which are common to all the kingdoms and provinces, may in the near future throw a firm bond of union around all the peoples of this empire. This hope is rooted in a recognition of the vital conditions of the monarchy; it is rooted in the noble feelings of true love and attachment to the throne and the fatherland.

"Where a hope rests on such firm ground, that which now finds expression as a warm wish will, with the aid of God, soon ripen to the glad announcement of a completed fact."

It would be superfluous to make comments on the foregoing speech, further than to call your attention to the fact that it contains no distinct indication of the future policy of the government, while, perhaps, as significant a criticism as any other could be derived from the absence in it of any allusion to the "constitution."

It has also not escaped notice that among the new ministers—whose appointment was officially announced on the day after the prorogation of the Reichsrath—no name is to be found that has been identified with the February patent.

I subjoin the list of the incoming administration, so far as published:

Count Mensdorff, foreign affairs and imperial household.

Count Belcredi, minister of state and president of the council of ministers.

Count Larisch, minister of finance.

Mr. De Komers, minister of justice for all the kingdoms and provinces not belonging to the Hungarian crown.

Mr. De Franck, minister of war.

Mr. De Maylath, chancellor of Hungary.

Count Haller, chancellor for Transylvania.

Count Maurice Esterhazy, minister without portfolio.

What would seem thus far to be certain is, that the theory of forfeiture by the Hungarians and the other people beyond the Leither of their old constitutions, in consequence of the troubles of 1848, has been abandoned, and that the known political opinions of the new ministers furnish a guarantee of as large a measure of autonomy to those kingdoms as is consistent with any form of substantial imperial union.

The cabinet has obviously been constructed upon what is here called a federal, as opposed to a centralistic basis.

I say nothing to-day of Schleswig-Holstein. There is a general feeling, however, that affairs between Austria and Prussia are at last approaching a crisis, and the result of the special mission of Count Bloome, Austrian minister at Munich, to the King of Prussia, now at the bath of Gastein, in Styria, is looked forward to with some anxiety. It would be useless to deny that there is a wide and deep dissatisfaction felt in this empire at the position of things in the Elbe duchies, and the bitterness between Austria and Prussia is increasing every day.

I have the honor to remain, sir, your obedient servant,

J. LOTHROP MOTLEY.

Hon. WILLIAM H. SEWARD, *&c., &c., &c.*

Mr. Motley to Mr. Seward.

No. 122.]

UNITED STATES LEGATION,
Vienna, August 8, 1865.

SIR: The relations between Austria and Prussia upon the Schleswig-Holstein question have become so very much embittered that I think it my duty to write a line by to-day's steamer, although there are but few new facts to communicate.

The mission of Count Bloome to the King of Prussia, at Gastein, to which I referred in my last, has not produced a distinct result. I am informed that he reports his Prussian Majesty and his prime minister as not disposed to concessions, and as maintaining very firmly the propositions of February last, which have already been distinctly rejected by the Austrian cabinet.

Those propositions which relate to the conditions to be laid down before any one of the candidates for the position of Duke of Schleswig-Holstein can be installed in that dignity, are regarded here as inadmissible, because they give the virtual sovereignty, both military and political, in those provinces to Prussia, and would reduce the nominal duke to a state of vassalage.

On the other hand, no compensation, as I understand, is offered to Austria.

The answer of the imperial government has always been—let us decide the question between the rival claimants of the sovereignty first, and then prescribe such conditions as may seem proper.

Prussia insists on laying down the conditions first; and those conditions are regarded by Austria as incompatible with any sovereignty but that of the King.

The provinces, as you are aware, have been, since the termination of the war with Denmark, under the condominium of Austria and Prussia, as represented by two commissioners, and sustained by detachments of troops from both armies.

This condominium, as might be supposed, has led to much wrangling and to many unpleasant incidents, the result of which has been great exacerbation of feeling between the empire and the kingdom. Yet the only means of avoiding an immediate rupture, to be followed by a war between these two great German powers, is a continuation of that condominium.

As well as I can learn, Count Bloome will go back this week to Gastein, instructed to propose this prolonged condominium under new conditions, and with new commissioners.

Obviously, this arrangement is but little better than an armed truce preliminary to a war which, although it yet may be averted, is now regarded as at least probable.

Austria, believing the Prince of Augustenburg to be the sovereign desired by a majority of the inhabitants of the provinces, and most acceptable to Germany in general, has supported and continues to support his claim.

Prussia insists, as I understand, upon his expulsion from the duchies, together with all his adherents, and refuses to hear of him as a candidate.

As the Prince of Augustenburg has for some time been residing in the duchies, and will probably not withdraw voluntarily, it seems almost inevitable that his violent expulsion during the condominium would lead to an armed conflict between Austria and Prussia within those provinces.

If diplomacy succeeds in arranging this question without bloodshed, it will achieve a triumph, of which, at present, I am sorry to say there are no strong indications.

It is considered almost certain by Austria that Prussia is bent upon annexing the provinces in question. This is not possible for the imperial government to permit, for it would be equal to an abdication on the part of Austria of her position of first German power. Even now that rank, and the consequent precedency of the Diet at Frankfort, is regarded by Prussia as an assumption, because Prussia has already more German subjects than the empire has. Should she now place half a million more Germans under her sceptre this argument would be irresistible.

Austria is in no position to go to war. Her internal affairs, and especially the condition of her budget, (on all which subjects I have fully dilated in my recent despatches,) make peace almost indispensable to her, and most earnestly is she striving to avert a conflict.

Nevertheless, the annexation she will, I think, prevent if possible, even at the cost of a war. Every effort, however, will be made to keep the peace, and it is fervently to be hoped that those efforts will be successful.

I have the honor to remain, sir, your obedient servant,

J. LOTHROP MOTLEY.

Hon. WILLIAM H. SEWARD, *&c., &c., &c.*

Mr. Seward to Mr. Motley.

No. 153.] DEPARTMENT OF STATE,

Washington, August 14, 1865.

SIR: Your despatch of the 24th of July, No. 118, has been received. I shall follow with much interest the development of the imperial policy for obtaining an effective and yet liberal national system of financial administration in Austria. While the steps that have been taken thus far appear to have been attended by much discouragement, it must be conceived that the government is exercising extraordinary patience and assiduity.

I am, sir, your obedient servant,

WILLIAM H. SEWARD.

J. LOTHROP MOTLEY, Esq., *&c., &c., Vienna.*

Mr. Motley to Mr. Seward.

No. 125.] LEGATION OF THE UNITED STATES,
Vienna, August 22, 1865.

SIR: I write a few lines just as the mail for this week's steamer is closing, to say that a convention was signed at Salzburg on Sunday last, 20th August, by which the governments of Austria and Prussia continue for the present their condominium in the Elbe duchies, and the chance of conflict between those two powers is averted, or at least postponed.

The treaty is not to be made public until the 24th of this month, but I am able to state to you that the essential conditions are, that Austria will exclusively administer the affairs of Holstein, while Prussia will govern Schleswig—each for an indefinite period.

Nothing has been settled as to the eventual sovereignty of those provinces, so that the arrangement is merely a continuation of that state of suspense which has already caused much anxiety.

The most obvious criticism upon the present modification in the arrangements is, that the two provinces are now separated, whereas one of the leading motives in the agitation which brought about the war with Denmark was the supposed necessity of their perpetual union with each other.

Whether this same necessity will ultimately cause the junction of Holstein with Schleswig, under the sceptre of Prussia, time will show, but it would not seem probable that Austria could remain in Holstein for a very long period.

I have the honor to remain, very respectfully, your obedient servant,

J. LOTHROP MOTLEY.

Hon. WILLIAM H. SEWARD, *&c., &c., &c.*

Mr. Seward to Mr. Motley.

No. 154.] DEPARTMENT OF STATE,
Washington, August 30, 1865.

SIR: The despatch which you addressed to Mr. Hunter on the 29th of June, No. 111, was duly received, and the very suggestive parallel between the Austrian financial situation and that of the United States deserves especial acknowledgment and appreciation. It is, however, hardly necessary for me to mention how uncertain any continuing foothold in the department has been rendered for me during the summer, by ill health and other casualties. It seems to me that the encouraging view which you take of our fiscal prospect is quite correct. We have been able already, since the capitulation of the rebels, to disband, pay and discharge a force of eight hundred thousand men. We still retain a force believed to be adequate for any domestic or foreign exigency that can be reasonably apprehended. But this force is far less than the standing army which Austria maintains in time of peace. It surprises many of our countrymen that thus far no great financial reaction has resulted from the sudden change we have made from civil war to what, as yet, continues to be profound peace. While political economy is so very imperfectly understood as a science, prudence in regard to expenditures is very obvious policy.

Like yourself, I find it difficult to conceive how Austria is effectually to reorganize her financial system, and yet at the same time reduce the large military force upon which she depends for securing the integrity of the empire. But, in this respect, her situation differs only in degree from that of other transatlantic powers; it seems probable that the whole system of armed independence, which prevails throughout the European continent, must at no distant day receive a shock which may open the way for beneficent modification of government.

I am, sir, your obedient servant,

WILLIAM H. SEWARD.

J. LOTHROP MOTLEY, Esq., &c., &c., &c., *Vienna.*

Mr. Motley to Mr. Seward.

No. 128.] LEGATION OF THE UNITED STATES,
Vienna, October 8, 1865.

SIR: Having been staying for a few weeks in the country at a few hours' distance from the capital at the time of the promulgation of the imperial manifesto and patent of the 20th of September, I neglected to transmit translations of those important documents.

As they have, however, been printed in various versions in all the European and (doubtless) American journals, I content myself now with forwarding an official copy of the manifesto and the patent as part of the history of the time.

As I have said so much concerning the internal politics of Austria in my recent despatches, especially Nos. 111, 112, 113, 116, 118 and 120, in all of which the steps leading to the present position were described, and the catastrophe has now occurred clearly indicated, I abstain to-day from any superfluous reflections; I say catastrophe, because, although there is no violent upheaval of the social and political elements, yet the constitution of February 7, 1861, under which the empire has been administered for the last four years, seems to have come to an end, and an interim of chaos to have returned.

The new patent of September, 1865, is brief; it consists, as you will observe, of two articles.

Article first contains one important word, *sistirt*—suspended. Article second provides that during said suspension the government will take all indispensable financial measures.

How and when this period of suspended animation will terminate time must soon show. The new manifesto holds fast to the principles of October, 1860, by which some kind of constitutional existence was promised to his people by an absolute monarchy. It declares, however, the February experiment to be a failure.

That the new attempt to breathe the breath of life into the constitutional embryo will prove more successful, we must be rather sanguine to believe without any hesitation. Meantime not only the centrifugal forces of magyarism and czechism are in full play, but movements for independent national existence are rife in Croatia, Dalmatia, Illyria, and elsewhere, to say nothing of the Italian portions of the imperial dominions.

To unite such vast and heterogeneous groups of nationalities as compose this empire, ten kingdoms (not counting Jerusalem) and at least thirty duchies and principalities under one sceptre by the coercive force of absolutism was possible. But is a constitutional *E pluribus unum* conceivable, now that the February Reichsrath has confessedly failed?

The very best that can be hoped for it is an *E pluribus duo*; for the realms of Saint Stephen, after their recent victory, can hardly be expected to send members to an imperial parliament at Vienna.

The Transleitha diets are convoked, and will be in session before the end of the year, and it will then be seen what propositions for legislative union the government has to lay before them, and how such projects are to be received; meanwhile the said imperial parliament is *sistirt*.

I have the honor to remain your obedient servant,

J. LOTHROP MOTLEY.

Hon. WILLIAM H. SEWARD, *&c.*, *&c.*, *&c.*

[Translation.]

IMPERIAL MANIFESTO.

To my People:

To strengthen the monarchy by reciprocal action in highest state matters, and to preserve the integrity of the country in its various and manifold constituents, was my chief design in my diploma of the 20th of October, 1860, and will hereafter continue to be my guide in trying to promote the welfare of my subjects.

The right of the people to participate in legislation and management of the finances, through their legal representatives, as security for the advancement of the interests of the empire and its provinces, is solemnly guaranteed and irrevocably established.

The forms for the execution of these laws is indicated in my patent of 26th February, 1861, promulgated with the fundamental laws concerning representation; and in the sixth article of the same patent I have revised the entire code, and pronounced it to be the charter of my empire.

The revival of this form, with harmony in all its parts, I leave to the free management of my people.

I warmly acknowledge the readiness with which a large portion of the monarchy sent representatives to the capital for a number of years, at my invitation, for the purpose of solving certain highly important questions.

But my design for the formation of a durable and constitutional charter of rights for the empire, which would receive strength and importance from the free participation of all the subjects of the empire, is yet unaccomplished.

The people of a large portion of the empire, though warmly patriotic their hearts may throb, have firmly refused any legislative action, perhaps, because the various laws now composing the imperial code, in their judgment, appear inconsistent.

My duty forbids me to disregard a fact that hinders the realization of my good intentions, and threatens the foundation of popular rights, for legislative action is only authorized in those lands not belonging to the Hungarian crown, which were specified as part of the empire in article VI of the patent of 26th February, 1861. So long as the principles of fundamental law of clear intelligence are wanting, there remains an important work for an imperial constitutional assembly.

Now, to keep my imperial promise, and not to sacrifice the sense of the letter, I have determined to enter upon the way leading to an understanding with the legal representatives of my people in the eastern portions of the monarchy, and to lay for acceptance before the Hungarian and Croatian diets the diploma of 20th October, 1860, and the fundamental law promulgated by the patent of the 26th of February, 1861, concerning the representation of the empire.

As, however, it is legally impossible to make one and the same constitution the subject of negotiation in one part of the empire, while it is simultaneously treated in another part as a fundamental law, generally binding, I find myself compelled to suspend the validity of the constitution and the actual representation, with the express declaration and reserve that the result of the deliberations of the diet in each eastern kingdom, in case they comprehend a modification of existing laws compatible with the unity of the empire, and its position as a great power, shall be laid for ultimate approval before the legal representatives of the other kingdoms and provinces, to receive and worthily estimate their expression of opinion. I can but regret that this imperatively required step also brings with it a suspension in the constitutional working of the lesser Reichsrath, as the unity and equivalency of all legal principles for the deliberation of the council makes a distinctive and partial effect of the laws impossible.

So long as the representatives of the empire shall not be assembled, it will be the duty of my government to forward all measures that cannot be postponed, and among them, especially, such as are required by the financial and commercial interests of the empire.

The course leading to an understanding, while taking into consideration legitimate rights, is now open, if, as I expect with full assurance, a sacrificing and conciliatory spirit and ripe insight guide the views of my faithful subjects, to whom this imperial word is addressed in thorough confidence.

FRANZ JOSEPH, M. P.

VIENNA, *September* 20, 1865.

[Translation.]

IMPERIAL PATENT.

We, Francis Joseph the First, by the grace of God Emperor of Austria, King of Hungary and Bohemia, King of Lombardy, &c., &c., make known, to wit:

In consideration of the unavoidable necessity of forming a durable and constitutional charter of rights for the empire which shall receive strength and importance from the free participation of all its subjects, the legal representatives of the lands of the Hungarian crown included, and of proposing to the diets for their acceptance the diploma of 20th October, 1860, and the patent of the 26th February, 1861, concerning the representation of the empire:

In further consideration, as these laws are forbidden to be considered generally binding in every part of the empire, with the advice and counsel of our ministers, we decree as follows:

First. The effect of the fundamental laws concerning the representation of the empire, with certain exceptions, is suspended, and the deliberations of the Hungarian and Croatian diets, in case they comprehend a modification of the existing laws, compatible with the unity of the empire, and its position as a great power, shall be laid for our ultimate approval before the legal representatives of the other kingdoms and provinces, to receive and worthily estimate their expression of opinion.

Second. So long as the imperial representatives do not assemble, it is the duty of our government to forward all measures that cannot be postponed, and among these, especially, such as are required by the financial and commercial interests of the empire.

Given in our capital and place of residence, the 20th of September, 1865, and in the 17th year of our reign.

FRANZ JOSEPH.
BELCREDI.
MENSDORFF.
ESTERHAZY.
FRANK.
MAJLATH.
LARISCH.
KOMERS,
MAZURANIĆ.
HALLER.

By supreme command:

BERNHARD RITTER V. MEYER.

PRUSSIA.

Mr. Judd to Mr. Seward.

No. 80.] LEGATION OF THE UNITED STATES,
Berlin, January 12, 1865.

SIR: Late events at home, beginning with Mr. Lincoln's re-election, followed by the opening of Congress and the President's firm and unflinching message regarding the war and the question of slavery, together with the glorious success of General Sherman's wonderful campaign, and the brilliant victories of General Thomas, have not failed to affect most powerfully public opinion throughout Germany and Europe, and it affords me satisfaction to lay before you some editorial extracts from articles that have lately appeared in the German press. I have selected the three foremost German papers, the "Berlin National Zeitung," the "Kolnische Zeitung," and the "Augsburg Allgemeine Zeitung." The ability with which they are edited, no less than the numbers and class of their readers, put them widely ahead of all other papers in Germany. Their views, as expressed in the articles from which I have selected the following extracts, cannot fail to exercise a wholesome influence. I now proceed to quote as follows:

"There are two features running through this year's message of Mr. Lincoln, which raise it far above the average value of his former state papers. It is full of the consciousness that a tribunal, even higher than Congress, has approved of his administration, and that the people have accepted and sanctioned the principles which will impart to the statesmen of the north unity of purpose, and stamp the war with the sanctity of high aims worthy of the greatest sacrifices. The chosen leader of the people may well discard, as he has done, the petty arts which subserve to represent events and expectations in a more pleasing light than a faithful record of the actual state of affairs would show them in. During the election campaign, all the deeds and shortcomings, successes and failures, causes and effects, on the part of the administration, have been sifted through, and been painted in the most varying colors. The President need not add his version to the manifold and widely differing representations of the great political parties. He does not court the favor of Congress, nor approbation from abroad. In his re-election he has received a testimonial, that in his person he far more embodies the will and the views and aims of the people, than the present Congress assembled in its last session.

"In the message, the unmistakable voice of the American people speaks to us, and that people has nothing to conceal, and need not soften a line of the stern picture of the present aspect of affairs. The north of the Union has searchingly surveyed all the events since the breaking out of the rebellion, and has arrived at the conviction that slavery has ceased to be legitimate in that civilized portion of the globe which in the future is destined to perpetuate the name of the United States of America. This is the great stream of light, the rays of which reach us across the Atlantic. From that source the whole picture rolled up before us receives its wonderful light, and over all the surrounding groups that were heretofore wrapt in dark and gloomy shade is poured the clear light of day.

"Now the goal is found, which no possible measure of sacrifice can purchase at too great cost, and success is assured. The reign of human slavery has ceased in the United States; therein lay the real significance of Mr. Lincoln's re election, and from this consciousness flow the noble and simple words of his message."

Another article contains the following:

"The American people can contemplate the close of the year with satisfaction. With that practical instinct that has always characterized that nation, they have re-elected Abraham Lincoln as President; and as at the ballot-box, so on the field of battle they have won a great victory. General Sherman has accomplished his march through the very heart of the rebellious States, from Atlanta to the Atlantic ocean, a march which in conception, spirit, and execution recalls Hannibal's crossing of the Alps. The south, it is true, is still possessed of a valiant army and able generals, but Sherman has proved that the southern colossus rests on feet of clay, and that the rebels have no power to place against the warriors and free laborers advancing from the west."

The following was penned on receipt of the news of the capture of Savannah:

"Every day the Union comes out more powerfully, more giant-like, from this dreadful civil war. She has no need to plead for friendships; her own citizens are the pillars of her free States. A few more months and Davis with his friends and rebel companions will seek an asylum at the shores of the British lion. There triumphal arches will be built for them, addresses made, and dinners given to them, until, a few months later, they, like so many others before them, will be handed down to obscurity."

I might add many others equally strong and expressive, but I content myself for the present, and have the honor to be,

Your obedient servant,

N. B. JUDD.

Hon. WILLIAM H. SEWARD,
Secretary of State, Washington.

Mr. Judd to Mr. Seward.

No. 81.]

UNITED STATES LEGATION,
Berlin, January 16, 1865.

SIR: The legislative body of this kingdom assembled in pursuance of the royal proclamation on the 14th instant. The ceremonies were held in the large hall of the palace, called "der weisse saal," and were unusually imposing. A large assembly had gathered, and by the great display of uniforms afforded a fine spectacle. The galleries for the court, the diplomatic corps, and the public were largely filled. Besides the members of the two chambers, there were assembled the generals of the monarchy, with field-marshal Count Wrangel at their head; the minister of the royal household, Herr von Schlemitz, and all the high court officials, and very many of the privy councillors and chief functionaries of the civil service. At the appointed time the state ministers took their places at the left of the throne, and after her Majesty the Queen and her royal highness the Crown Princess had made their appearance in the royal gallery, his Majesty entered the hall, followed by the Crown Prince and all the other princes of the royal house. His Majesty was received with the cheers of the assembly, and after having bowed his thanks and placed the helmet on his head—he wore a general's uniform—he received from the hands of the president of the state ministry, Herr von Bismarck, the manuscript of the crown speech, which he proceeded to read in a loud, and at times an elevated tone of voice. The close of the reading was followed by renewed cheers, and when the King had retired,

Herr von Bismarck, in the King's name, declared the Chambers of the monarchy opened.

I annex hereto a copy of the opening address. It corresponds in the main with the expectations which persons familiar with the condition of internal affairs in Prussia had conceived. The government inflexibly maintains its stand-point on the question of the reorganization of the army. This is expressed in the speech in terms not to be mistaken. The tone is rather conciliatory, and the King at the close expresses the hope that the differences now existing between his government and the House of Deputies may be removed. But it is difficult to see how this is to be brought about, when the very question upon which that difference arose is maintained with even more emphasis than ever before. It requires no prophetic gift to foretell that the present session bids fair to lead to no other result than the three preceding ones. No understanding is likely to be reached on the army question, and as this is the condition precedent of a settlement of the constitutional and budget controversy, matters so far as regards that issue, too, will remain *in statu quo*.

The part of the speech relating to Schleswig-Holstein is so worded that no definite prognostic can be given regarding the policy of Prussia in that matter. The language is intentionally non-committal, and so framed as to leave to the government freedom of action. It is no secret that Herr von Bismarck really means to annex them if Austria can be induced to consent thereto.

The finances and commercial relations as well as the industrial and agricultural interests of the monarchy are reported to be in a most gratifying and flourishing condition. The war has been carried on without the necessity of resorting to a loan, and notwithstanding the extraordinary expenses, the budget for the current year will show a balance of receipts over expenditures.

The enlargement of the navy is warmly advocated, and in connexion therewith, the building of the ship canal between the Baltic and the North sea is insisted on in a manner as if that great enterprise was but an internal affair of Prussia.

Foreign relations are represented to be in a particularly satisfactory condition.

Of course the army comes in for its due share of the royal eulogium and approbation for its prowess and success in the war with Denmark. This is the topic upon which his Majesty ever loves to dwell and enlarge.

The foregoing constitute the leading points in the King's address. As it yields nothing in principle, the House of Deputies, while grateful for the conciliatory tone of the speech, will maintain its position as unflinchingly as before. An impression has prevailed that the military excitement consequent upon the successes in Schleswig-Holstein, the satisfaction of the nation at the separation of the duchies from Denmark, and the prospective gain territorially on the part of Prussia, as well as the increase of external influence and position already by the Prussians as a nation, would be strong enough to compel submission on the part of the house to the demands of the ministry, and that indemnity for the ministry for the past, governing without a budget voted by the house, and a grant for the future, to meet the King's military views, would be the result of the present session. From all that I can as yet hear as to the temper of the house, the ministry will be disappointed in these expectations as before stated. No official action has yet taken place in the house beyond its organization. Herr Grabon has been re-elected president almost unanimously, and if that fact and his opening speech are indications of the temper of the house, no agreement between it and the ministry is probable. The following extract from his opening speech expresses in fewer words than I can find, the interior administrative policy of the present ministry:

"When we were last dismissed, the hope of an agreement with this house was renounced. Since, prosecutions of the liberal press and of liberal officials, non-confirmations of the elections of liberal muncipal officers, aspersions, accusations, and slandering of all liberal citizens, have prevailed in a greater degree than before. Liberal views and opinions are under the ban. Fidelity to their convictions, the fairest ornament of the Prussian official of old, is prescribed by the Prussian regime of to-day. But the King's motto, 'He who plants himself on the rock of justice stands on the rock of honor and victory,' is ours too. Under this banner we can find the agreement with the government which we too desire and have hitherto endeavored in vain to bring about in a way alone which does not involve the sacrifice of the rights the people have confided to us, and we have sworn to uphold."

I abstain from speaking of the House of Lords. That body is in full accord with the government, and will sanction all the measures which may be brought before it by the ministry.

Herr von Bismarck's policy of postponement and "masterly inactivity" in settling the question of succession in the duchies of Schleswig-Holstein yet prevails, and no arrangement between Austria and Prussia has been reached. In the mean time they are governed by Prussia and Austria jointly, the real power and influence being on the side of Prussia.

I am, sir, your obedient servant,

N. B. JUDD.

Hon. WILLIAM H. SEWARD,
Secretary of State, Washington.

Speech from the throne.

Illustrious, noble, and dear lords and gentlemen of the two chambers: A year fertile in events has passed away. In concert with his Majesty the Emperor of Austria we have succeeded in acquitting ourselves of a debt of honor which had been frequently recalled to our recollection, and with regard to which sentiments traditional in the memory of the entire country had been called forth. An honorable peace has been won by the brilliant valor of our united armies.

Encouraged by the satisfaction with which our people cast a retrospective glance upon this success worthy of Prussia, we turn our hearts with humility towards God, whose blessing has enabled me to give thanks, in the name of the country, to my army, for its exploits, which equal those of its most glorious military annals. After fifty years of peace, broken only by honorable but short campaigns, the education and discipline of my army, the utility of its organization and of its armament, have been brilliantly tested by the war of last year, which the inclemency of the season and the valiant resistance of the enemy will render forever memorable. Owing to the existing organization of the army, the war was enabled to be carried on without our being compelled, by calling out the Landwehr, to inflict injury upon the relations of labor and of family among the people. After such experience it is more than ever my duty as a sovereign to maintain the present arrangements and to develop them upon the existing basis, so as to impart to them greater perfection. I may expect that both houses of parliament will afford me their constitutional assistance in accomplishing this duty.

The development of the navy also creates special obligations. By the part it has taken in the war the navy has acquired just rights to my gratitude, and has proved its high importance to the country. If Prussia desires to fulfil the high mission imposed upon her by her geographical situation and her political position, it is requisite for her to give her navy the fitting development, and not to refrain from making considerable sacrifices for this purpose. Acting upon this conviction, my government will lay before you a bill for the augmentation of the fleet.

The duty of providing for those soldiers whose health has been impaired in the field, and for the families of those who have fallen, will find legitimate expression in the presentation of a bill for the pensions of invalids, which I hope will meet with a favorable reception at your hands.

I have been enabled to put an end to the concentration of troops upon the Polish frontier after the suppression of the insurrection in the adjoining country. The moderate but firm attitude of my government has sheltered Prussia from the encroachments of the insurrection, while the competent tribunals have sentenced persons guilty of isolated participation in tendencies aiming at the separation of a portion of the monarchy.

The prosperous state of our finances has enabled us to carry on the war against Denmark without being compelled to have recourse to a loan. This result must arouse great satisfaction. It has been obtained by economical and far-sighted administration, and above all by the considerable surplus of the public revenue during the last two years.

After striking the balance of last year, my government will lay before you a complete report upon the subject of the costs occasioned by the war and the sums from which they have been met.

The budget of the current year will be laid before you immediately. It includes the increase of revenue expected to arise from the new land and industrial tax. While confining itself to the tried limits of a prudent estimate, my government has also been able to place the other branches of revenue at an augmented amount. It has thus been enabled, not only to re-establish equilibrium between the revenue and the expenditure in this budget, but also to allot considerable sums to meet the new requirements in all branches of the administration. Besides the general accounts respecting the budgets of 1859, 1860, and 1861, which will be again laid before you, you will also receive the accounts for 1862, in order that the government may be released from the same.

The labors for the ulterior regulation of the land-tax have been completed within the prescribed period and in a satisfactory manner. I am happy to acknowledge that this result is solely due to the zeal and efforts which have been made in all quarters to arrive at a solution of this difficult and laborious question. The preparatory labors of the tax upon buildings are also very greatly advanced, and only now require definitive approval.

My government does not cease its efforts that the same progress should be realized in the different branches of production, and that care should be taken to extend and improve the method of communication. The bill for a general regulation of roads will again form an important item of your deliberations. Several bills will also be laid before you for the extension and completion of the railway system.

My government has had the preparatory technical works executed for the construction of a canal between the North sea and the Baltic, across Holstein and Schleswig, which should be constantly navigable for merchantmen and vessels of war of all dimensions. In view of the importance of this great undertaking to the interests of commerce and of Prussian shipping, my government will endeavor to guarantee its execution by a participation of the state in the expenses it will occasion. More detailed communications will be made to you upon this subject at the close of the preliminary deliberations.

The working of mines, being freed from harassing restrictions, relieved from taxation, and developed by increase of the markets, acquires a more and more satisfactory position. You will have to examine the bill of a new general mining code, intended to regulate the legal position of this branch of industry.

The ordinance dictated by the interests of our commerce and our maritime ports, pending the duration of the war, relative to extraordinary duties upon the flag, will be laid before you in virtue of an ulterior authorization. My government has succeeded in removing the obstacles which threatened to compromise the existence of the German Zollverein at the expiration of the period fixed by treaty. The treaties concluded with the government of his Majesty the Emperor of the French have obtained the adhesion of all the governments constituting the Zollverein, and the customs treaties have been renewed with some modifications justified by experience. These treaties, together with the arrangements upon the subject of the wishes expressed by one of our allies in the Zollverein, will be laid before you for the purpose of obtaining your assent. The negotiations which, in consequence of these treaties and in accord with the governments of Bavaria and Saxony, have been entered into with Austria with the view of facilitating and reciprocally developing business, permit the hope of a speedy result. The work commenced by these treaties with France in August, 1862, and the execution of which has been pursued since that time with equal perseverance by my government and that of his Majesty the Emperor of the French, is thus approaching a conclusion which will open a vast field to commerce, and, by the common development of prosperity, will afford a fresh guarantee for the amicable relations of neighboring nations.

I cannot allude to the exploits of my army without expressing my satisfaction with, and cordial acknowledgment of, the deeds of the Austrian troops. As the soldiers of the two armies have shared their laurels together in the fraternity of arms, so the two courts have continued united in the complications that have ensued by a close alliance, which has found a solid and durable basis in my German sentiments and in those of my august ally. In these sentiments and in fidelity to treaties is to be found the guarantee for the preservation of the tie which connects the German states and secures them the protection of the confederation.

The peace with Denmark has given back to Germany her disputed northern frontier, and has restored to the inhabitants of those countries the possibility of taking an active part in our national life. The task of my policy will be to secure this conquest by institutions which shall facilitate the honorable duty of protecting this frontier, and allow the duchies to employ and turn to account their resources in the interest of developing the land and sea forces of the common country.

In the maintenance of these legitimate claims, I shall seek in their fulfilment to combine both the well-founded demands of the country and of the sovereigns. In order, therefore, to gain a secure basis to judge of the legal questions in dispute, I have requested the law officers of the Crown, conformably with their duties, to give a legal opinion upon the subject.

My convictions on the legal side of the question, and my duty towards my country, will assist me in my endeavors to come to an understanding with my illustrious ally, with whom I at present share the occupation and the care of a regular administration of the duchies.

It affords me lively satisfaction that the complications of the war have been confined within a narrow compass, and that the dangers which might have threatened European peace have been averted. The re-establishment of diplomatic relations with Denmark has commenced, and I entertain firm confidence in the formation of those more friendly and more profitable relations which so thoroughly conduce to the natural interests of the two countries.

Our relations with all the other powers have not been in any way troubled, and continue to present the most agreeable and most satisfactory character.

Gentlemen: It is my earnest wish that the difference which has arisen within the last few years between my government and the Chamber of Deputies should be brought to reconciliation. The memorable events of 1864 will have assisted to enlighten the public mind upon the necessity of improving a military organization which has passed through the test of a successful war.

I am resolved still to respect and uphold the rights the constitution has granted to the representatives of the country, but if Prussia is to maintain her independence and the rank to which she is entitled among European states, her government must be firm and strong, and a good understanding with the representatives can only be secured by the maintenance of the organization of the army, which guarantees its military efficiency, and, consequently, the security of the country.

All my efforts and all my life are devoted to the happiness and the honor of Prussia. By pursuing the same object, I have no doubt you will find the way leading to a complete agreement with my government, and your labors will thus conduce to the welfare of the country.

Mr. Seward to Mr. Judd.

No. 85.] DEPARTMENT OF STATE,
Washington, February 1, 1865.

SIR: Your despatch of January 12, No. 80, has been received. I thank you for the very agreeable information it gives concerning the favorable impression which recent political and military events here has made upon the popular mind in Germany.

I am, sir, your obedient servant,

WILLIAM H. SEWARD.

NORMAN B. JUDD, Esq., *&c., &c., Berlin.*

Mr. Judd to Mr. Seward.

[Extract.]

No. 85.] UNITED STATES LEGATION,
Berlin, February 24, 1865.

SIR: * * * * * * * *

There is no immediate prospect yet that the *status* of the duchies of Schleswig-Holstein and Lauenburg will soon be settled. Prussia and Austria cannot come to an understanding, and the question is more than ever a matter of agitation and apprehension throughout Germany.

An interismistic flag for the shipping of the duchies has been agreed upon between Prussia and Austria, consisting of three horizontal stripes of blue, white, and red, with a yellow field in the blue stripe, on the top near the flagstaff, and foreign maritime nations will be asked to recognize that flag, and accord to the shipping of the duchies the rights and privileges as provided in the commercial and maritime treaties of Denmark with those nations, and which it enjoyed when the duchies constituted a part of Denmark.

I am, sir, your obedient servant,

N. B. JUDD.

Hon. WILLIAM H. SEWARD,
Secretary of State, Washington.

Mr. Judd to Mr. Seward.

No. 87.] UNITED STATES LEGATION,
Berlin, March 13, 1865.

SIR: Your despatch No. 85, dated February 7, 1865, is received. The differences between the Prussian administration and the house of representatives, so far from being compromised or adjusted, increase in their intensity, and the hope of a return to constitutional rule and to a condition in which the representatives of the people shall exercise some influence and control over the expenditures of the government is exhausted.

At the last court ball Herr von Bismarck said to me that he saw no prospect of an agreement between the ministry and the house. That body is at present debating the budget for the purpose, as I suppose, of diffusing information among the people, and the result of the vote, when that is taken, will be its rejection in the form presented by the government, and the ministry will continue to carry on the affairs of state according to their own will and pleasure, its only responsibility being to his Majesty.

The negotiations between Prussia and Austria, in relation to the Schleswig-Holstein question, "drag their slow length along," apparently no nearer a termination than they were six months since. Herr von Bismarck's "masterly inactivity" still leaves the administration of the duchies in his hands, and the Prussianizing process is going on, not apparently with much success. A favorable result could hardly be expected with the known feelings of a majority of the people of the duchies. Still this entire Schleswig-Holstein business has been from the beginning a series of lucky accidents in aid of Prussian experimental policy. There are those that believe the finality will place the duchies substantially and really under the control of Prussia, although formal annexation may not be proclaimed. It is true, Austria has just refused to agree to propositions made by Herr von Bismarck to that effect, but this will not preclude further transaction, and not occasion a rupture, as Austria fears a total disagreement with Prussia in the present attitude of Italian affairs, and Herr von Bismarck knows it. As long as that continues, the negotiations can end in only one way, and that is, by the concession of all that Prussia desires.

I am, sir, your obedient servant,

N. B. JUDD.

Hon. WILLIAM H. SEWARD,
Secretary of State, Washington, D. C.

Mr. Judd to Mr. Seward.

No. 92.] UNITED STATES LEGATION,
Berlin, April 18, 1865.

SIR: On Saturday I hung out of the legation our "star-spangled banners," and thus notified the people of Berlin that rebellion and slavery had met their doom; that their fortified capital had been taken; that their executive was a fugitive, and the rebel army of Richmond for the most part killed, wounded, and prisoners. No details reached us on that day except such as a rebel subsidized news company, located in London, chose to despatch to the continent. I knew enough, however, to warrant unfurling the flags, and to-day the happiness is increased by the cordial congratulations of true friends. The well-informed have expected the "collapse" ever since Sherman entered the "shell;" but, notwithstanding, the actual occurrence produced impressions as enthusiastic and exciting as though the result had not been expected.

The number of "I told you so's" on the streets is rather remarkable. Still, the genuine reactionary and feudalist consoles himself with the wise belief that the nation, although successful in armed contest, is bankrupt, and that the finances will bring ruin to the (by him detested) republic. We can laugh at his "divine right," ignorance, and conceit.

Your serenade announcement of non-intervention was a happy inspiration for the moment, as it accompanied the message of our triumph, and will soothe the alarms of those that know they deserve chastisement for their past conduct towards us during our depression.

The European rebel sympathizers, who for four years have gloated over the anticipated ruin of the republic, and have believed to see in this ruin the final end of all hope for that form of government in any part of the world, feel somewhat easier in the presence of the "armed democracy" successful at your assurances that justice and honor only are to be sought for and protected in its future career, and that the nation reinstated can afford to forget slights given us in times of affliction, however meanly it may think of the manhood of those who have sought the protection of such circumstances to utter their contumelies. I have only a short telegraphic synopsis of your remarks, and as construed by me they only laid aside thoughts of vengeance, but yield not a jot of justice and honor.

I am awaiting to hear that you have demanded of other nations that pirates and piracy shall be called by their right names, and treated according to the laws of the civilized world, and the honeyed phrase of "belligerent rights" should cease to be used, and the protection of neutral harbors for such craft should be withdrawn.

I am, sir, your obedient servant,

N. B. JUDD.

Hon. WILLIAM H. SEWARD,
Secretary of State, Washington.

Mr. Judd to Mr. Seward.

No. 93.]

UNITED STATES LEGATION,
Berlin, April 27, 1865.

SIR: Intelligence of the assassination of President Lincoln, and of the murderous attack upon yourself and many members of your household, reached Berlin at about two p. m. yesterday. The statement had such an aspect of horror that I did not believe it. At the exchange, where it was first received, it was pronounced a stockjobbing report. I telegraphed immediately to Mr. Adams, and his reply was a confirmation of the dreadful tidings. Your condition, as reported, gives occasion for the most intense anxiety, and no words can express the feelings with which I await further despatches. The report states that your son, Frederick W. Seward, was killed in defending the life of his invalid father. A noble death of one so young and promising, though sad and mournful to surviving relatives and friends to know that he died by the hand of an assassin. The terrible and tragic death of Mr. Lincoln, and the calamities that befell your household in that fearful night, are heavy blows for one enfeebled by previous illness. May He who saved your life amidst all its horrors give healing to your wounds, and restore you again to health and usefulness.

I cannot realize that Mr. Lincoln has been assassinated. He was saved from the Baltimore demons, when on his way to Washington, to be slain now in the midst of friends, and just at the moment when public affairs have assumed their brightest aspect, and peace and order are about to return to the country he loved so well.

All the afternoon and evening yesterday the legation was thronged with anxious and inquiring friends, and many tears fell from the eyes of strong men. Berlin talks of nothing else to-day. Expressions of horror and indignation at the foul murder of our great and good President, and of deep sympathy and condolence for our stricken people, mingled with fervent wishes that you may recover and survive this terrible affliction, are on the lips of all—on the lips of foreigners and strangers, who see in you the trusted friend and counsellor of our martyr President, and the man who, for four years so fraught with dangers and trials, has preserved peace with Europe.

The legation is draped in black, and the passing world beholds that this is a house of mourning.

I am, sir, your obedient servant,

N. B. JUDD.

Hon. WILLIAM H. SEWARD,
Secretary of State, Washington.

Mr. Judd to Mr. Seward.

No. 94.] UNITED STATES LEGATION,
Berlin, April 28, 1865.

SIR: I have to-day received a communication from the minister president and minister of foreign affairs, Herr von Bismarck-Schoenhausen, expressing the deep sympathy of his Majesty's government with the government of the United States at the death of Mr. Lincoln, and the attempt on your life, and desiring me to convey the expression of their sympathy to my government. Herr von Thile, under-secretary of state for foreign affairs, was charged with delivering the note in person, and came to the legation with it. In doing so he expressed in the warmest terms, for himself and his government, the deep feeling the sad occurrences have occasioned.

I annex, marked A and B, copies of that communication and my response to it. Herr von Bismarck's note has been in turn delivered in person to Herr von Thile by the secretary of this legation, Mr. Kreisman.

My colleagues of the diplomatic corps are all calling to express their sympathy with us in this affliction, and their abhorrence of the foul deed.

I am, sir, your obedient servant,

N. B. JUDD.

Hon. WILLIAM H. SEWARD,
Secretary of State, Washington.

A.

[Translation.]

BERLIN, *April* 27, 1865.

The royal government is profoundly moved by the intelligence, which reached here yesterday, of the assassination of President Lincoln, and the simultaneous attempt on the life of the Secretary of State, Mr. Seward.

In view of the so happily existing friendly relations between Prussia and the United States, the undersigned cannot forbear to express to their government the sincere sympathy of the royal government with the great loss that this crime has inflicted upon them. He therefore requests the envoy extraordinary and minister plenipotentiary of the United States of America, Mr. Judd, that he will convey the expression of these sentiments to his government, and he avails himself of this occasion, too, to renew to Mr. Judd the assurance of his distinguished consideration.

V. BISMARCK.

Mr. N. B. JUDD, &c., &c., &c.

B.

LEGATION OF THE UNITED STATES OF AMERICA,
Berlin, April 28, 1865.

The undersigned has the honor to acquaint his excellency the minister president and minister of foreign affairs, Herr von Bismarck, that he will not fail to transmit at once to his government the expressions of sincere sympathy with the great loss the United States have sustained in the assassination of their President, Abraham Lincoln, and the prostration of the Secretary of State, Mr. Seward, which his excellency, on behalf of his Majesty's government, has been pleased to address to the undersigned, in the note of the 27th of April, 1865, and which was delivered in person, by his excellency the under-secretary of state, Herr von Thile.

In the midst of their great affliction, it will afford the government of the undersigned, as it does him, a sincere satisfaction to receive a renewed and so marked a token of the happily existing friendly relations between the United States and Prussia.

The undersigned but anticipates the directions of his government in assuring his excellency that the expressions of sympathy and condolence of his Majesty's government will be received with due appreciation and acknowledgment, and he avails himself of this occasion, too, to renew to his excellency the assurance of his distinguished consideration.

N. B. JUDD.

His Excellency HERR VON BISMARCK, *&c., &c., &c.*

Mr. Judd to Mr. Seward.

No. 95.]

UNITED STATES LEGATION,
Berlin, April 29, 1865.

SIR: Telegra[illegible] advices from the United States by a later steamer reached here at noon to[illegible] and it affords me sincere pleasure to learn that the first report of the death [illegible] Mr. F. W. Seward has been erroneous, and that although in a critical condition [illegible] still lives; and that notwithstanding the cruel and strange wounds inflicted on [illegible]u by a cowardly assassin, in addition to the severe injuries sustained by your late accident, your condition was considered hopeful.

All of the members of the diplomatic corps have paid me their visits of regard and condolence. So have the King's chiefest officials, and many of the distinguished men of science and letters.

As the details of the horrible crime become known, the interest and excitement in every circle and among every class of men increases. It is the one theme of conversation and discussion. The public journals here and elsewhere are entirely filled with it. O[illegible]e intense and spontaneous burst of sorrow and indignation is [illegible]nging throughout Germany, and every one, high and low, great and humble, is [illegible]er to bear testimony of his admiration and grief for a great and good man d[illegible]

Yesterday [illegible]as brought before the House of Deputies by one of its most distinguis[illegible]rs, Dr. William Lœwe, well known among our German citizens in the Uni[illegible]es, from his long residence in New York, as a political exile from his fathe[illegible]. In eloquent and feeling terms he paid a warm tribute to President L[illegible]ln, and at the close of his remarks called upon the house to unite with him [illegible] an address appropriate to the occasion, to be presented to the American [illegible]nister here. Nearly the whole house rose in token of concurrence, and the a[illegible]ress, as drawn up by the speaker, is receiving numerous signatures. It is to [illegible] presented to me by a deputation of members, headed by the president and the [illegible]wo vice-presidents of the house. Dr. Lœwe has conferred with me, and it is [illegible] arranged that the address is to be presented on the afternoon of Monday next[illegible]

At my invitation the A[illegible]nericans at present at Berlin have met at the legation, and it has been decided to [illegible] have divine services, in memory of the late President, on Tuesday next, May 2, a[illegible]t 4½ o'clock p. m., in the "Dorothea church," the use of which for that purpose has been kindly granted us by the city authorities and the pastors of the church. President H. P. Tappan, formerly of Michigan university, will conduct the services for us.

I am, sir, your obedient servant,

N. B. JUDD.

Hon. WILLIAM H. SEWARD,
Secretary of State, Washington.

Mr. Judd to Mr. Seward.

No. 96.]

UNITED STATES LEGATION,
Berlin, May 1, 1865.

SIR: This forenoon Captain von Lucadon, personal aide-de-camp of his royal highness the Crown Prince of Prussia, presented himself at the legation and informed me that he was charged by their royal highnesses the Prince and Princess Royal of Prussia to request me to transmit on their behalf, to the government of the United States, their condolence at the sad event that had transpired, and desiring me also to convey to Mrs. Lincoln their kind sympathies in her affliction. I enclose herewith a copy of my letter of condolence written to Mrs. Lincoln. I shall send the original through the State Department, sealed.

I am, sir, your obedient servant,

N. B. JUDD.

Hon. WILLIAM H. SEWARD,
Secretary of State, Washington.

(For accompaniment see Appendix, separate volume.)

Mr. Judd to Mr. Seward.

No. 97.]

UNITED STATES LEGATION,
Berlin, May 2, 1865.

SIR: In my despatch No. 95, you were informed, that I had named Monday, the first day of May, as the time to receive from the members of the Prussian House of Deputies their address of condolence on account of the death of President Lincoln, and the attempt to assassinate yourself. A note, received in the morning of that day, appointed five o'clock p. m. as the hour at which the deputation would be at the legation for that purpose.

I had concluded, from some casual remark of a m[illegible] the deputation would be composed of some six or eight members. [illegible] pleasurable surprise on its arrival, I found it numbered twenty-six [illegible] most talented, celebrated and influential men of the Chamber, headed [illegible] venerable President Grabow, First Vice-President Herr von Unruh, and [illegible]nd Vice-President Herr von Backum Dolffs. The additional names of th[illegible] members of the committee were as follows: Deputy Dr. William Loewe, deput[illegible] Prof. Dr. Virchow, deputy Baron von Vaerst, deputy Stavenhagen, deputy D[illegible]ur Waldeck, deputy Parrisius, deputy von Bonin, (ex-minister,) deputy B[illegible]ssenge, deputy Schroeder, deputy Dr. Ziegert, deputy Duncker, deputy Lent, [illegible] deputy Baron von Zedlitg and Kurzbach, deputy Riebold, deputy Schneider, d[illegible]puty Dr. Johann Jacoby, deputy Raffauf, deputy von Saucken-Tarputschen, [illegible]eputy Dr. Liemens, deputy Dahlmann, deputy Dr. Krebs, deputy Dr. Von Bun[illegible]sen.

The title of doctor repeatedly recurring indicates [illegible] a university degree, and not that of a physician, as used in our country. Dr. L[illegible]ewe, who had the honor of your personal acquaintance when he resided in New York, the political troubles of 1848 and 1849 having caused his temporary absence from Prussia, as stated in a former despatch, presented the address with a few remarks in German expressive of the deep feeling in all Germany at the death of Mr. Lincoln, and your narrow escape from the same fate, at the hand of an assassin, which he followed by reciting the address in full. After apologizing in German for my imperfect use of that language, and asking to be allowed to respond in English, I expressed the thanks of the government and the people of the United States for this sympathetic manifestation of interest in our affliction, assuring them that the latest advices happily stated your improving condition, although the danger had not yet fully passed. That they might rest under the certain conviction that the object sought to be accomplished by the conspirators in these horrible and murderous attacks would not succeed. The government would not be paralyzed, but move stoutly and firmly forward in the political and social regeneration of the communities in rebellion. That the experience of the last four years had demonstrated beyond question the power of a people under a republican form of government to resist and overcome interior commotion and rebellion. That the administration of public affairs had passed to a new President, habituated to public life and to deal with national questions, and whose talents and firmness of purpose would speedily bring into submission what little remained of the rebellious spirit. That revenge was no part of our national character, but security for the future was the essential element that would control and guide the conduct of public affairs. That the people of the United States appreciated the sympathy of the German people during this terrible rebellion, and that the soldiers of German birth, many of whom not even citizens, would be held in lasting remembrance by a grateful people, and that their memory would be bound with the laurel common to all who had fought this battle of freedom, without distinction as to nativity or color. One member of the committee, Mr. Schneider Sagan, was then in mourning for an only son, killed at Petersburg, Virginia, and another, Deputy Raffauf, has now a son serving in the army of the United States. The German heart has been more moved by these awful occurrences than by any event in their own history since the year 1813. In the minds of the great mass of German readers Mr. Lincoln had come to symbolize the republic in all its attributes of the liberty and equality of all men, and their aspirations and hopes turned to him with admiration and affection. They feel that in him all humanity has lost a pure and noble champion.

After the close of my remarks, some time was spent in friendly conversation with the various members of the committee, and I parted with them at last, deeply gratified and consoled by this mark of generous and noble sympathy with our people and our cause.

I enclose herewith the original address, with an English translation thereof, by the secretary of this legation, Mr. Kreismann, who was present during the interview. It is signed by two hundred and thirty-eight members of the chamber, and I feel persuaded that a fit place will be assigned by you for this interesting document in the archives of the State Department.

Your old acquaintance and friend, Professor Tellkampf, a member of the upper house, sought and obtained leave to add his signature. You will readily find his to you familiar handwriting.

I am, sir, your obedient servant,

N. B. JUDD.

Hon. WILLIAM H. SEWARD,
Secretary of State, Washington.

[Translation.]

ADDRESS OF THE MEMBERS OF THE PRUSSIAN HOUSE OF DEPUTIES.

SIR: We, the undersigned, members of the Prussian House of Deputies, beg you to accept the expression of our profoundest sympathy in the severe loss the government and the people of the United States have suffered in the death of President Lincoln, and alike the expression of our deepest horror at the shocking crime to which he fell a victim. We are the more deeply moved by this public calamity, inasmuch as it occurred at a moment when we were rejoicing at the triumph of the United States, and as the simultaneous attempt upon the life of the faithful partner of the President, Mr. Seward, who, with the wisdom and resolution of true statesmanship, supported him in the fulfilment of his arduous task, betrays the object of the horrible crime to have been, by the death of these great and good men, to deprive the people of the United States of the fruits of their protracted struggle and patriotic self-sacrificing devotion at the very moment when the triumph of right and law promises to bring back the blessings of a long desired peace.

Sir, living among us, you are a witness of the heartfelt sympathy which the people have ever preserved for the people of the United States during this long and severe conflict. You are aware that Germany has looked with pride and joy on the thousands of her sons who in this struggle have placed themselves so resolutely on the side of law and right. You have seen with what joy the victories of the Union have been hailed, and how confident the faith in the final triumph of the great cause, and the restoration of the Union in all its greatness, has ever been, even in the midst of adversity.

This great work of the restoration of the Union will, we confidently hope, not be hindered or interrupted by this terrible crime. The blood of the great and wise chieftain will only cement the more firmly the Union for which he has died. This the inviolable respect for law and love of liberty, which the people of the United States have ever evinced in the very midst of the prodigious struggles of their great war, abundantly guarantees.

We request your good offices for giving expression with your government to our sincere condolences, and our sympathies with the people and government of the United States, and proffer to yourself, sir, the assurance of our distinguished consideration.

(Follow two hundred and thirty-eight signatures.)

REMARKS OF DEPUTY DR. WILLIAM LOEWE IN THE PRUSSIAN HOUSE OF DEPUTIES.

GENTLEMEN: I have ventured to request the president to permit me to make a communication, for which I claim your sympathy. That which I wish to request of you does not indeed belong to the immediate field of our labors, but it goes so far beyond the narrow circle of private life that, in union with a number of our colleagues, [illegible] ave ventured to call your attention to it. A considerable number of our colleagues fee[illegible]e need, under the dismay produced by the shocking news of the unhappy death of President Lincoln, to give expression to their feelings in regard to his fate, and their sympathy with the nation from whom he has been snatched away. Abraham Lincoln has fallen by the hand of an assassin in the moment of triumph of the cause which he had conducted, and while he was in hopes of being able to give to his people the peace so long desired.

Our colleagues wish, in an address, to express the sympathy, not of this house—this I say in order to remove all apprehension of a violation of the rules of the house—but the sympathy of the individual members of the house in this great and unhappy event. This address we desire to present to the minister of the United States. Gentlemen, I will lay the address on the table, and I beg those of my colleagues who share with me the feelings of warm and heartfelt sympathy in the lot of a nation which is united by so many bonds with our own people to give expression to these feelings by appending their signatures to the address. These sympathies I regard as all the more justified, as the United States have won a new and splendid triumph for mankind, through the great struggle which they have been carrying on for the cause of true humanity, and which, as I confidently hope, in spite of this murder of their chief, they will conduct to a successful termination. In expr[illegible]ing our feelings of pain, we desire at the same time to prove our hearty sympathy with the [illegible]merican nation, and those of our brothers who have taken part in the struggle for their cau[illegible] The man, gentlemen, who has fallen by the murderous hand, and whom I seem to see [illegible]h his simple, honest countenance—the man who accomplished such great deeds from th[illegible]mple desire conscientiously to perform his duty—the man who never wished to be more or [illegible] than the most conscientious and most faithful servant of his people—this man will find h[illegible]wn glorious place in the pages of history. In the deepest reverence I bow my head before t[illegible] modest greatness, and I think it is especially agreeable to the spirit of our own nation, wit[illegible]s deep inner life, and admiration of self-sacrificing devotion, and effort after the ideal, t[illegible]y the tribute of veneration to such greatness, exalted as it is by its simplicity and mod[illegible] I beg you, gentlemen, accordingly, to join in this expression of veneration for the g[illegible] dead, which, without distinction of party, we offer to him as a true servant of his state [illegible]f the cause of pure humanity.

Mr. Judd to Mr. Seward.

No. 98.] UNITED STATES LEGATION,
Berlin, May 2, 1865.

SIR: To-day, at 1 o'clock, a deputation, composed of Count Joseph Potulreki and Mr. St. Motty, both members of the Prussian Chamber of Deputies, presented to me an address on the subject of the late terrible calamity to our nation, signed by the Polish members of the Prussian Chamber of Deputies, with a request to have the same laid before the government and people of the United States. I assured them of our full appreciation of this act of sympathy, and that I would not fail to immediately forward the address to my government. The address is herewith enclosed.

I am, sir, your obedient,

N. B. JUDD.

Hon. WILLIAM H. SEWARD,
Secretary of State, Washington.

[Translation.]

ADDRESS OF THE PRUSSIAN CHAMBER OF DEPUTIES.

The Polish members of the Chamber of Deputies of Prussia, at this moment present in Berlin, join their German colleagues in expressing all the grief and indignation they have experienced on learning of the abominable crime to which the illustrious President Lincoln has fallen a victim—a martyr to the great cause of the abolition of slavery.

(Follow the signatures.)

Mr. Judd to Mr. Hunter.

No. 99.] UNITED STATES LEGATION,
Berlin, May 4, 1865.

SIR: Your official circular, dated 17th April, is received. The intelligence of the assassination of President Lincoln, and the attempt upon Mr. Seward, accompanied by the wounding of Mr. F. W. Seward, official notice of which is contained in your circular, reached Berlin on the 26th of April. I need not repeat again the grief and horror felt on receiving the tidings of the sad event.

The Americans in Berlin met at this legation and resolved to hold appropriate divine services, in memory of the lamented President. The original intention of meeting in the little chapel, ordinarily used by us for religious worship, had to be abandoned, on account of the almost universal desire of men of all classes here to afford them an opportunity of participating in the services, and mingling their grief with ours in paying a last tribute to the great and good man departed. We therefore sought and readily obtained of the Berlin city authorities the use of the Dorothea church, one of the most spacious buildings of public worship here. It was arranged that the Rev. H. P. Tappan, D. D., of New York, now temporarily in Berlin, should conduct the services and deliver an address, and the German part of the exercises was intrusted to the very distinguished author and divine, Rev. Dr. Krummacher, chaplain to his Prussian Majesty at Potsdam, who kindly had consented to officiate on the occasion. We also obtained the services of the choir of the Royal Cathedral; the church was draped in black, and the American flags hung in mourning.

The services were among the most significant and solemn ever held in Berlin. The attendance was so large that many persons were unable to obtain admission, and remained standing outside in the church yard. His Majesty the

King was represented by Major General Von Boyen, his aide-de-camp. The president of the ministry of state, and minister of foreign affairs, Herr von Bismarck, was also present. So were the members of the diplomatic corps in full, a large number of the Prussian house of deputies, and very many of the distinguished men of science, letters, and art. It was indeed a noble tribute to our martyr President, and the cause in which he had died. I beg leave to enclose the order of exercises as printed for the occasion.

The addresses by Dr. Tappan and Dr. Krummacher were eloquent and feeling tributes to the public and private virtues of the deceased, and to the genius of our institutions in developing character, as illustrated in the life of Mr. Lincoln. Throughout the whole of the exercises the audience remained absorbed and profoundly touched by the simple solemnity and impressiveness of the scene, which will be long remembered by the people of Berlin.

There is no abatement as yet of the intense excitement and heartfelt sympathy in all classes of society, here and elsewhere in Germany, over the sad event, and the possible and probable consequences thereof. All are moved, and seeking words and modes to show us their deep emotion and genuine sympathy.

The first feeling of many here and elsewhere, on learning of the assassination of President Lincoln, was one of alarm and apprehension lest his death might be followed by anarchy and confusion, and our government be paralyzed. The quiet and undisturbed assumption of office by President Johnson, his speeches at his inauguration, and on other occasions, have now removed all fear, and convinced all persons that the people, and not dynasties, rule in the United States; that our government and our institutions do not depend upon any man's life, however great and good that man may be. The American people stand forth greater than ever in the eyes of Germany and Europe.

Whatever may have been done in the United States, Mr. Lincoln is being canonized in Europe. A like unanimity of eulogy by sovereigns, parliaments, corporate bodies, by the people, and by all public journals, was never before witnessed on this continent. The most truthful and eloquent testimonials are now given by some of those that belied him most while living.

I am, sir, your obedient servant,

N. B. JUDD.

Hon. WILLIAM HUNTER,
Acting Secretary of State, Washington.

Mr. Judd to Mr. Hunter.

No. 100.]

UNITED STATES LEGATION,
Berlin, May 8, 1865.

SIR: On the 6th instant a deputation from the "Berlin Workingmen's Union," consisting of Messrs. A. Korig, L. Hoff, R. Krebs, Robert Nouvel, and Lœhmann, presented an address of condolence in relation to the death of Mr. Lincoln.

That Union is composed of nine hundred members, and is one of the influential clubs of Berlin.

I thanked them for their kind sympathies, and promised to forward the address to the government of the United States, to be laid before the people.

Annexed is a translation into English, made by the secretary, Mr. Kreismann.

I am, sir, your obedient servant,

N. B. JUDD.

Hon. WILLIAM HUNTER,
Acting Secretary of State, Washington, D. C.

(For accompaniment see Appendix, separate volume.)

Mr. Judd to Mr. Hunter.

No. 101.]

UNITED STATES LEGATION,
Berlin, May 28, 1865.

SIR: Accompanying this I have the honor to forward an address to the President, presented to me for transmission by a committee of the "Berlin Artisans' and Mechanics' Union," a very large and respectable association of men for mutual advancement and benevolence. I have properly responded to and thanked the gentlemen who delivered me the address, and I herewith enclose it with an English translation thereof, made by the secretary of this legation, Mr. Kreismann.

I also beg to enclose an address to the President, presented by a committee of the Berlin branch of the "Allgemeiner Deutscher Arbeiter-Verein," an association of German workingmen, extending in branches, with a central organization at Leipzig, throughout all Germany.

These are but additional tokens of the deep and universal sympathy prevailing among the Germans of all classes for our cause and our people, and are entitled and will receive our grateful acknowledgments.

I am, sir, your obedient servant,

N. B. JUDD.

Hon. WILLIAM HUNTER,
Acting Secretary of State, Washington.

(For enclosures see Appendix, separate volume.)

Mr. Judd to Mr. Hunter.

[Extract.]

No. 105.]

UNITED STATES LEGATION,
Berlin, June 2, 1865.

SIR: Prussian politics, internal and external, remain as unsettled as ever. Negotiations still continue between Prussia and Austria, in relation to the final disposition to be made of the duchies of Schleswig-Holstein. The peculiar views and desires of Prussia I have mentioned in previous despatches, and thus far masterly inactivity is having its influence in her favor. So sure was she of accomplishing her objects, that a short time since her fleet was ordered to the harbor of Kiel, and the initiatory steps entered upon, to establish a permanent navy yard and a depot of naval stores and supplies at that port, to be accompanied by fortifications permanently armed and manned by Prussian troops. This was done without saying even "by your leave," to the duchies or to Austria. The interference of the Austrian commissioner in the duchies has so far checked that action. Propositions are now pending between Prussia and Austria for the assembling of the estates of the duchies, and this seems to be assented to by both the governments, but they are still separated by the questions as to what are the constituent parts of said estates under existing laws; by what law the composition is to be regulated, and when assembled, who is to have the initiative in the measures [illegible] be acted upon, and other points of a like nature. Certain it is, that neither [illegible] the governments intends to permit the estates to settle the succession, a[illegible] egulate such other matters as may to them seem necessary. The peo[illegible] the duchies are treated as of no importance, and are to be finally dispos[illegible] ording to the interests and wishes of the conquerors of Denmark, to w[illegible] chies were ceded as the spoils of victory.

The differences [illegible] e government and the Chamber of Deputies continue as decided and ir[illegible] as ever. The military budget has been overwhelmingly rejected. The annual budget has shared the same fate. In fact every measure of the government, having for its object a grant of money beyond the points of the most restricted ordinary expenditure, is peremptorily rejected. The debates are bolder and freer than ever before in the history of this kingdom. The charges of corruption and despotism against the minister of justice, in the composition of the courts for the trial of political offences, are boldly uttered, and, that too, by members who themselves are judges. Unfortunately, the charges of using the judicial power to punish political opinions are too true to be denied, and the minister of justice has no other defence than that of saying "I protest," without meeting one of the specifications with even a plausible explanation. The truth is, that Prussia is to-day as thorough a despotism as exists in Europe; the excesses of the despotism being, however, restrained by the really good heart of his Majesty.

The debates in the chamber have created a profound sensation among the people. They are permitted to appear in full in the newspapers, but a pamphlet edition thereof, intended for general circulation, has been confiscated by the government. Repression, according to the system now in vogue in France, is being carried out in this kingdom.

The influence of the United States at the present time upon the masses in Europe, and especially in Germany, cannot be estimated by a person not living among them. The brilliant military success, the putting down of the rebellion, the quiet transfer of the government from one man to the other, as the result of the horrible tragedy in Washington, the stern and steady onward march of public affairs under the new President, have convinced the masses of the steadiness of power in a self-governed people, and European rulers look to-day with more interest at what shall emanate from your department than all the other diplomatic bureaus in Europe. The system of the repression of liberal ideas that now prevails in all the governments of Europe, with the exception of Russia and Italy, must break down, and no influence does or will operate so strongly to produce this result as the universal discussion in every circle of the affairs of the United States, and the successful progress of events there, grander and more powerful for humanity than any that have yet occurred in the political or military history of this continent.

The rebel cause has now no longer any friends in Europe. The murder of President Lincoln, and the attempt upon the lives of the Secretary and Assistant Secretary of State, so filled the public mind with horror and indignation that all its advocates and sympathies here are thoroughly silenced. And now the capture of the redoubtable rebel chief, Davis, in his wife's petticoats, has covered him and his ruined cause with withering ridicule. What a fall there was! A shout of homeric laughter went forth all over Germany at the ridiculous plight in which that worthy was taken prisoner. His capture, it is plainly felt, removes the last obstacle to a permanent and lasting peace. Kirby Smith and his bushwhackers will not long stand in the way thereof. The fourth of July next will see the nation restored, slavery abolished, and our land not only in song, but in fact, "the land of the free, and the home of the brave."

United States bonds here and elsewhere in Germany are quite buoyant. They are now quoted at 73. Permanent investments therein continue to be made quite largely, although the speculating mania which h[illegible] seized upon them, and was crowding out all other funds, has perceptibly aba[illegible]d. The attempt which was lately made by the enemies of our cause to stop [illegible] sale of our bonds, by starting rumors of the circulation of large numbers [illegible] counterfeit bonds, has utterly failed. A letter from the Secretary of the Tr[illegible], which was received here in Berlin, and published in the daily journals, h[illegible] removed all apprehensions regarding the existence of any counterfei[illegible] bonds whatever. The article on our finances, and ability to pay our [illegible]ebt, prepared by Dr. William Elder, under the auspices of Jay Coo[illegible]ise done much good. I deemed it of sufficient importance to seek its insertion in substance in the "Berische Zeitung," the journal of the largest circulation here.

* * * * * * * * *

Yesterday, the first of June, pursuant to the President's proclamation, was duly observed at this legation in memory of our late beloved President.

I am, sir, your obedient servant,

N. B. JUDD.

Hon. WILLIAM HUNTER,
Acting Secretary of State, Washington.

Mr. Seward to Mr. Judd.

No. 91.]

DEPARTMENT OF STATE,
Washington, June 13, 1865.

SIR: Your despatches from No. 93, dated April 27, to No. 100, dated May 8, have been received, and have been attentively read. Your narratives of the public and private demonstrations of sympathy in Prussia, occasioned by the tragic occurrence of the 14th of April last, are very interesting as well as highly gratifying.

I am, sir, your obedient servant,

WILLIAM H. SEWARD.

NORMAN B. JUDD, Esq., *&c., &c., Berlin.*

Mr. Judd to Mr. Seward.

No. 109.]

UNITED STATES LEGATION,
Berlin, July 3, 1865.

SIR: Your despatch No. 91, dated June 13, 1865, is received, and contents duly noted. I am deeply gratified that a kind Providence has restored you to health, and preserved your invaluable services to our country, that stands so much in need thereof. May you soon have the happiness of seeing your son Frederick also entirely recovered.

The department circular, relating to Admiral Goldsborough's squadron in European waters, is likewise received, and I shall not fail, as occasion may require, to make the subject of the circular known to the proper persons here.

Berlin at this time is entirely deserted by all prominent official and diplomatic personages. His Majesty the King has gone on his annual tour to Karlsbad, accompanied by M. de Bismarck, and he is not expected to return to Berlin before September next.

Affairs in the United States continue largely to engross the attention of the press and people of Germany, and hopes are indulged that the reconstruction of the States on the basis of the total and final abolition of slavery will be successfully carried out. Public sentiment here is strongly in favor of seeing the right of suffrage conceded to the colored population of the rebellious States.

The demand for United States bonds is still very active, so much so that at this time they are from 2 to 3 per cent. higher than in New York. They are quoted to-day at $77\frac{5}{8}$ *a* $77\frac{7}{8}$.

I am, sir, your obedient servant,

N. B. JUDD.

Hon. WILLIAM H. SEWARD,
Secretary of State, Washington.

Mr. Seward to Mr. Wright.

No. 2.]

DEPARTMENT OF STATE,
Washington, July 18, 1865.

SIR: Information has been received at this department, from the United States consul at Bremen, of the shipment from that port to the United States of two sentenced criminals from Prussia. I enclose a transcript of the consul's despatch upon the subject, from which it appears that the convicts referred to were sent to Bremerhafen by the local authorities at Wandersleben, in Prussia, under the escort of a Prussian officer, in order to be shipped to this country at the cost of the said local authorities. It further appears that one of the criminals has already sailed, and that the other, having committed a fresh offence at Bremerhafen, has been sentenced to three months' imprisonment, at the expiration of which he will also probably be sent to the United States, his passage thither having already been paid.

You are requested to make a representation of the above facts to the Prussian government, and to express the expectation that prompt measures will be taken to prevent a repetition of such unfriendly proceedings on the part of any of the local authorities of that government. You will also state that the criminals referred to will, in case of their detection on arrival here, be promptly returned to the port whence they departed.

I am, sir, your obedient servant,

WILLIAM H. SEWARD.

JOSEPH A. WRIGHT, Esq., *&c., &c., Berlin.*

CONSULATE OF THE UNITED STATES OF AMERICA, AT THE
FREE HANSEATIC CITY OF BREMEN, *Bremen, June* 21, 1865.

SIR: With reference to my despatch No. 159, I have to inform you of a new case of shipment of criminals to the United States. In this case the culpability of the local authorities in Prussia has been fully proved in a Bremen court, and reclamations, if you deem them necessary, can be based upon positive facts. It appears from the proceedings in the Bremen assizes, of June 15, that in the first days of March two criminals from Prussia, named Ernest Roediger and Krumholz, both incorrigible criminals, and already many times sentenced for larceny to the penitentiary, have been sent by the local authorities of Wandersleben, Prussia, to Bremerhafen, escorted by a public officer, in order to be shipped to the United States at the cost of the above local authorities. Kumholz sailed with the Bremen ship Laura, but Roediger committed another larceny at Bremerhafen, and was sentenced to three months' imprisonment, after the expiration of which he will probably be sent to the United States, as his passage is already paid. I subjoin the full evidence in the reports of two different newspapers for further use. I cannot believe that these local authorities are acting without the consent of their government; and even if they do, a diplomatic reclamation from our government would probably put a stop to this daily increasing mal-practice.

I am, sir, your obedient servant,

HENRY BOERNSTEIN,
United States Consul.

Mr. Judd to Mr. Seward.

[Extracts.]

No. 115.]

UNITED STATES LEGATION,
Berlin, August 9, 1865.

SIR: Allow me earnestly to call your attention to the question of the impressment of adopted citizens of the United States into the armies of Prussia and other German states. It is now assuming such importance, by reason of the numbers returning to Germany, that I would respectfully suggest that the restrictions placed upon this legation in your despatches, and particularly in those numbered 29, 49, and 92, should be removed, and liberty given to the representative here to exercise his discretion in the cases as they arise.

With the closing of our civil war, the reasons for the prohibitions contained in those despatches have ceased. Citizens of the United States, Germans by birth, who have boldly followed the flag of the Union for the last three years and more, are now returning to visit their relatives, and they are threatened with compulsory military service here. And this will apply to many who have acquired the right of citizenship in accordance with the act of Congress conferring such right for actual service in our army. Every steamer brings more or less of these young men to the land of their nativity. * * * *

I suppose that the government of the United States intends to protect its citizens. It surely should do so, and not permit this state of things to continue, even if extreme measures should have to be resorted to. If this is not to be done, good faith to our adopted citizens, at least, requires that they be notified that they are not to be or cannot be protected when they return to Germany, and that the claims for the free right of expatriation, which we have always made on foreign governments, should cease. I hold there is no occasion for the latter course, and that a positive and earnest demand for the adjustment of the question would be successful. Hiding from the military authorities of Prussia and other German states, by a man who has worn our uniform during the last four years' struggle, is not the course a citizen of the United States should be required to take, and is not in accordance with the prestige of our nation. * * * * * *

I am, sir, your obedient servant,

N. B. JUDD.

Hon. WILLIAM H. SEWARD,
Secretary of State.

Mr. Wright to Mr. Seward.

[Extract.]

No. 1.] UNITED STATES LEGATION,
Berlin, September 7, 1865.

SIR: In answer to the request of Mr. Judd, the minister of foreign affairs, Baron Von Bismarck replied the King would receive Mr. Judd and myself in audience at Baden Baden on the 3d instant at 11 o'clock a. m. The day previous I met the King with his brother, Prince Carl; they both greeted me with words of compliment; his Majesty remarking in English, "I am most happy to welcome you again to Prussia." At the appointed hour Mr. Judd and myself were presented by the minister of foreign affairs, (Mr. Judd preceding me.) The interview was brief. The King spoke highly complimentary of Mr. Judd's course at Berlin, and bade him an affectionate adieu. His Majesty said, among other things, he was rejoiced at the termination of our war, and the prospect of the restoration of law and order. I had remarked on this subject, that during the last four months we had discharged eight hundred thousand soldiers, and paid out more than two hundred millions of dollars; yet, amid all this, there was no perceptible change in society except the labor of the soldier being transferred to his ordinary avocations of life. I assured the King of the sentiments of friendship and esteem entertained for him and his subjects by the President, and the ardent desire of the President and people of the United States that the two nations might become more and more closely united in the bonds of friendship. To this his Majesty warmly responded, most fully reciprocating the sentiment, and closed by saying to me personally

"I trust your future residence at Berlin will be as happy and productive of good feeling as the past." The day before this interview with the King I was introduced to the minister of foreign affairs. In the course of our conversation he alluded, with some feeling, to the subject of military duty of Prussian citizens, and to the position of the Prussian government. I hear every few days of cases of arrest throughout Prussia. Some of these purchase their way out of the country; others leave in a manner not very creditable to an American. The consul general at Frankfort (Mr. Murphy) writes me as follows: "I have before me four new cases in Cassel and Nassau. One of the parties is too old to serve in the military; he has no money to procure a substitute or pay a fine, and he lies in jail now. He emigrated to America when he was seven years old, and has lived there twenty-one years, and now for the first time visits his old home." There is a great increase in the number of our German adopted citizens returning this year, many of whom have been soldiers of our army. In this connexion the views of our government on this subject, as expressed from time to time, are well known to Prussia, and hence I have no doubt the subject is now attracting the attention of the Prussian government. I have no evidence of any change in the police of the government. Yet I do believe good will result from a direct and firm issue on this subject. Prussia desires our friendship and good will; her ministers fully comprehend what is to be the condition of things resulting from the past, present, and future emigration to our country. I am not mistaken in saying some of them are anxious to settle this vexed question. A despatch from you at this hour may be of incalculable benefit.

I enclose copies of correspondence with P. F. Von Rhein, of San Francisco, California, on the subject of his return to Prussia. I deem it my duty to call the attention of the government to the probable demand for our agricultural productions on this side of the Atlantic. In some portions of the country the drought has entirely destroyed the grass crop, and farmers are shipping their stock away or making hurried sale. Already there have been some heavy importations of American rye into Hamburg at a good profit. I believe this is only the commencement of large importations from our side to supply the wants of many portions of the country on this side of the Atlantic. It should be known also that during the past year a considerable business was done in importing corn to Hamburg, (called here the white horse tooth-corn,) for seed. They cut the plant green and use it for fodder, so that every year the demand for the seed is renewed, and constantly increased.

Emigration to our country is on the increase; every berth on steam or sailing vessel from Hamburg (and I hear the same is true of Bremen) is taken up to the last of October, and the companies are sending out extra vessels.

We have some German papers which are willing to publish articles giving a correct condition of things at home. I shall not fail to furnish such papers and pamphlets, or items sent from the department or may come to my notice, which are adapted to the German mind. * * * * * *

I have the honor to be, most respectfully, your obedient servant,

JOSEPH A. WRIGHT.

Hon. WILLIAM H. SEWARD,
Secretary of State.

Mr. O. F. Von Rhein to Mr. Wright.

SAN FRANCISCO, *July* 18, 1865.

SIR: It is not unlikely that circumstances will make it desirable for me to reside in Berlin for some length of time, or it may be permanently. You would, therefore, confer a great favor if you will kindly reply to one or two questions which I shall take the liberty to ask. Your answer must in some measure decide whether I return to my native city or not. I am as captain in the royal army. I left Berlin sport which entitled me to remain abroad for wever, for over five years, when, having become , I returned to Germany on a visit to my mother, two weeks, being, during that time, in hourly fear the army. With the exception of these two weeks, I my sixteenth year. The question, then, to which I crave merican citizen, permanently reside in Berlin without dan- in the Prussian army? In order that your honor may under- perhaps be well to add that on my return from my former visit what annoyed at being obliged to make my stay in Berlin very uld have done had it not been for fear of the army, I addressed a rk Herald, to which, contrary to my expectations, the editor attached

lect the exact words I used; but they were about as follows: "To the York Herald. Sir: I am by birth a Prussian; by adoption a citizen of the n a recent visit to Berlin, finding myself in danger of being forced into the called on Governor Wright, the American minister in Prussia, for protec- man, after examining my passport, told me that while he had the wish and ked the power to protect me. Governor Wright, therefore, advised me to as soon as possible. Such being the case, Mr. Editor, would it not be better to a passport from naturalized citizens than to consign them to the very grasp of a with no better protection than a worthless piece of paper?"

The appearance in the New York Herald of a notice something like the above aroused some little discussion, through the public press, by parties who were strangers to me personally, but felt interested in the principle involved. It is, therefore, not impossible that the fact that I have written and published a notice similar to the above may have come to the knowledge of the Prussian government; and if so, can I be held responsible on the ground that I have formerly been a Prussian subject?

I am a married man, having a wife (a native of New Orleans) and two young children, and, if I decide to reside in Berlin any length of time, not being rich enough to live on the interest of my money, shall be obliged to do something towards the support of my family. I should either engage in some mercantile pursuit or establish myself as a teacher of languages; (I speak French, English, Spanish, and German.)

The subject is to me a very important one. I have for this reason been more lengthy than I at first intended, at the risk even of trespassing on your honor's patience.

Be kind enough to address your reply to the undersigned at San Francisco, California.

Very respectfully, your honor's most obedient servant,

O. F. VON RHEIN.

The Hon. UNITED STATES MINISTER *to Prussia.*

Mr. Wright to Mr. Von Rhein.

BERLIN, PRUSSIA, *August* 26, 1865.

SIR: Yours of the 18th of July, dated San Francisco, is just at hand. I am not yet the accredited minister to Prussia, but shall be in a short time. I hasten, however, to say, in reply to your note, that no change has been effected on the subject of expatriation and the rights of citizenship between our government and Prussia since you called upon me in 1858. The subject is now being agitated on account of the great number of German soldiers from our army and others returning to the land of their fathers. I will advise you if any change occurs. Under all the circumstances you name, I cannot at present deem it advisable for you to change your residence.

In haste, yours truly,

J. A. WRIGHT.

O. F. VON RHEIN, 105 *Montgomery street, San Francisco.*

Mr. Wright to Mr. Seward.

[Extract.]

No. 6.]

UNITED STATES LEGATION,
Berlin, October 25, 1865.

SIR: Immediately on receipt of the news of Lord Palmerston's death, I called upon Lord Napier e English ambassador at this court and expressed to him my profound sy hy and regret, in which my country would join, at

the loss his government had sustai
country. His lordship responded with
pathy, and desired me to convey to m
this mark of respect and sympathy, and he
cially remembered to you.

I forward with this despatch the reply of Bar
foreign affairs, to the application of Jacob Carl Bre
Prussia with a view of settling his family affairs.
Mr. Judd, December 27, 1864, in despatch No. 79. T
is certainly without any precedent. The idea of a child
charged of having left his country with a view of avoiding
to me most absurd. After making this statement, as connect
of the court at Newstadt, he says: "Under the peculiar cir
case, the government will permit the said Breiger a short stay
the condition that he submits to the judgment, by the payment
imprisonment for one month;" and then adds, most generous
must pay the cost." This language is applied to a young ma
country when a child with his brother, having committed no offe
whom no liability had accrued of any kind, and who is now only ask
mission to return to adjust and settle his family matters with a government which have, by solemn treaty with us in 1828, stipulated and agreed, among other things, that "the inhabitants shall be at liberty to sojourn and reside in all parts of said territories, in order to attend to their affairs," &c. Having written so much on this subject, I do not propose to take your valuable time with a repetition of my views, but would most respectfully refer you to my despatches Nos. 50 and 56, as also No. 13, with the accompanying documents connected with the case of Eugene Dullye.

The Minister Baron von Bismarck is not expected to return for some days. I am most anxious to see him before replying to your despatch No. 4. I will, however, say we have everything to gain and nothing to lose by taking a decided and firm stand on this subject; not by attempting to enforce our views by threats, nor by the way of menace, but by argument. The condition of things in Prussia at this time is most favorable for us. All is not quiet and secure. Much dissatisfaction exists in many portions of the country. Great discontent is to be found among the working classes, not only on account of the question of wages, but on political questions. The agitation is greatest in the Rhenish provinces. The questions connected with Schleswig-Holstein and Lauenburg provinces are not settled. Prussia has a popular legislature, called the Landtag, elected by the people, who are at variance with the King, and have been for years. Taxes are levied and collected for the payment of the army without appropriations made by law, although she has a written and liberal constitution. Large bodies of her leading men have been prohibited from meeting together to discuss political questions.

At this time our commerce and trade with Prussia is very great. We purchase five times the amount of Prussia that she does of us. The emigration is constantly increasing, consequently the communication and correspondence are daily becoming more frequent by the cheap and weekly steamers by the way of Bremen and Hamburg.

There have been at least five hundred American citi[illegible]s in Prussia the present year, liable to perform military duty according to [illegible]ir laws and regulations. They do not succeed in placing in the army one [illegible] hundred. I believe the arrest of any American citizen by Prussia, which n[illegible]ssarily becomes the subject of discussion in the papers, with the consequ[illegible] agitation that follows, is productive of great evil to Prussia. All these thi[illegible] are beginning to be fully understood by the Prussian cabinet; they will not [illegible] the subject lie over from year to year, becoming, as it must, more and more [illegible]plicated and formidable.

But the initiative should come from Prussia. In my opinion it will come if we take our position with firmness, for they desire the continuance of our good will and friendship. Prussia acknowledges the right of men to expatriate themselves, as she is constantly admitting citizens of other countries to become citizens of Prussia; acknowledging thereby she is opposed to the doctrine of perpetual allegiance, and thus favoring the right of men everywhere to form new political associations. * * * * *

I have the honor to be, sir, most respectfully, your obedient servant,

JOSEPH A. WRIGHT.

Hon. WILLIAM H. SEWARD,
Secretary of State.

[Translation.]

BERLIN, *October* 21, 1865.

In reply to the memorandum of the 4th of April last, the undersigned has the honor to inform Mr. Wright, envoy extraordinary and minister plenipotentiary, that the former Prussian subject, now citizen of the United States, Jacob Carl Breiger, who desires to return temporarily to Prussia on account of family matters, was condemned to a month's imprisonment or a fine of fifty R. (fifty thalers) by the circuit court of the district of Newstadt, on the 10th of February, 1858, for having left the country with the intention of avoiding the performance of military service. In consideration of the peculiar circumstances of the case, the government will permit the said Breiger a short stay in Prussia, upon the condition that he submits to the judgment which was passed upon him, and he pays besides the costs. It is in this sense that the authorities have been instructed to act.

The undersigned takes this occasion to renew to Mr. Wright the assurances of his most distinguished consideration.

The minister for foreign affairs, by authority,

THILE.

Mr. WRIGHT, *&c.*, *&c.*, *&c.*

Mr. Wright to Mr. Seward.

No. 7.]

UNITED STATES LEGATION,
Berlin, November 8, 1865.

SIR: I forward with this despatch the reply of Baron Thile, acting minister of the Prussian government, to your despatch, No. 2, dated July 18, 1865, which refers to the sending by the authorities of Erfurt two condemned criminals from Prussia to the United States. The answer of the minister evades the main question, by attempting to show it was the act of individual citizens, and not of the Prussian authorities. I quote his language: "This request, according to existing laws, could not be refused, and, in consequence, the authorities at Erfurt gave them permission to emigrate." This is the very act of which we complain. They were condemned criminals. They could not leave Prussia without the consent of the legal authorities. This consent was given, and from this reply of the minister of his Majesty's government there is to be found no condemnation of the act of the public authorities at Erfurt, but a distinct approval. If such is the existing laws of Prussia, they should be repealed at once. The answer of the minister, to use his own language, may present this case in its true light, but I cannot believe it will be satisfactory to the government of the United States. If so, this will form a precedent for sending to our country the condemned criminals of other countries whenever philanthropic individuals can be found to raise the necessary means for the accomplishment of this purpose. I do not believe the minister for foreign affairs, Baron von Bismarck, would have made such a reply. I shall know in a few days.

The views of the President in reference to the protection of our adopted citizens, if expressed in his annual message, will do much good. No document from our country is so generally published and read by the Germans as the message of the President. In this way the German people can be made to understand our views on this subject. I do trust it will be alluded to in the forthcoming message.

I have the honor to be, most respectfully, your obedient servant,

JOSEPH A. WRIGHT.

Hon. WILLIAM H. SEWARD,
Secretary of State.

[Translation.]

BERLIN, *November* 1, 1865.

The legation of the United States of America, in a note dated 19th of August last, complains that two condemned criminals, George Simon Krumbholz and Ernst Frederick Rödiger, from Wandersleben, province of Erfurt, had been forwarded by a steamer to America, under the conduct and costs of the local authorities. The undersigned has the honor to inform Mr. Wright, envoy extraordinary and minister plenipotentiary of the United States of America, in reply to this note, that, from the inquiries which have been made concerning this affair, the complaint seems to rest upon erroneous suppositions. Krumbholz and Rödiger, who are in truth condemned subjects, had expressed the desire to seek in America a new home, thinking a continued existence in Wandersleben doubtful. To put this plan into execution, a manufacturer, Lilienthal, living in the vicinity, animated by philanthropic sentiments, had given a considerable sum, and the citizens of Wandersleben had furnished an equal amount for this purpose. These two individuals ask now, in order to accomplish this purpose, their liberation as Prussian subjects. This request, according to existing laws, could not be refused, and, in consequence, the authorities of the province of Erfurt gave them permission to emigrate. Only, in order to see that the money given by Lilienthal and the citizens of Wandersleben should be employed for the purpose proposed, a member of the local authorities of Wandersleben accompanied the two individuals as far as Bremerhafen. This conduct was not in the character of police; it took place only in the peculiar and private interest of Lilienthal and the citizens of Wandersleben, who, in a very generous manner, had offered to these two emigrants the means of seeking a new existence.

In asking Mr. Wright to make this affair known to the government of the United States, the undersigned has no doubt but that this explanation of the case will be sufficient to make the affair appear in its true light.

The undersigned takes this occasion to renew the assurance of his most distinguished consideration.

The minister for foreign affairs, by authority,

THILE.

Mr. WRIGHT, *&c., &c., &c.*

Mr. Wright to Mr. Seward.

No. 8.]

UNITED STATES LEGATION,
Berlin, November 15, 1865.

SIR: I have had an interesting conversation with Count Bismarck, minister of foreign affairs. My opinion is, he will in a few days modify and change the views as expressed in Baron Thile's communication, forwarded to you by my last despatch, in reference to the two sentenced criminals designed to be sent to the United States by the authorities at Erfurt.

The minister's attention was called to the case of Jacob Carl Breiger. It was evident he had no knowledge of this case, it being acted upon during his absence. This brought up the whole subject of Prussian laws as connected with military service, and the difficulties in the way of adjusting the same with the United States. He said it would be almost impossible to change by legislation the Prussian laws, in view of the prejudice among the German peasants, that, as all Prussians are subject to military duty, the returning adopted citizens would be exempt. After some conversation, during which the count exhibited the most earnest desire to adjust the whole subject—admitting it was becoming more formidable and complicated every year, as the numbers returning from the United States were increasing—he agreed with me that not one in fifty liable under the Prussian laws were brought into the army, and, to use his own language, "There was no desire on the part of his Majesty's government to arrest any American citizen returning to his native land on business; but when a case was presented to the government by the police authorities, giving the name, place of birth, age, &c., the law was imperative, and the government compelled to act." He remarked, "The subject could only be adjusted by some treaty arrangement with the United States; at least, in his opinion, this would be the proper way to commence its adjustment, and, if it was successful, no doubt the principles agreed upon would be carried out by the legislative authorities of both countries."

My anxiety was to hear his plan for the settlement of this vexed question in detail. It was substantially this: "Exemption to all Prussian subjects returning to their native land who had left before their seventeenth year, and exemption also to all other persons who were not in the army or notified to enter at the time of leaving, and who shall have been out of the country for ten years."

Allusion was then made to the difficulty in arresting and bringing to trial persons charged with criminal offences in either of the two countries under the present extradition laws. While on this subject, he remarked the progress in the commercial world since the date of our treaty, in 1828, showed the propriety of some additional guards and restrictions of a summary character, whereby a more prompt enforcement of the criminal laws may be had, and he hoped there would be some modification of the extradition laws between the two countries.

I left Count Bismarck with the understanding that he would communicate with Baron Gerolt on this subject, and the military authorities of his Majesty's government in Prussia. If they should concur in his views, he would then, through this legation, communicate to the United States government his views upon the propriety of making some changes in our present laws on the subject of surrendering criminals; expecting the government of the United States, if receiving the same favorably, would reply with an allusion to the military law of Prussia, asking for some modification of the existing law by which the settlement of this question might at least be entered upon, and which, he trusted, would result in its satisfactory adjustment. I heard all; gave no assent to his proposals, but remarked, I would communicate the same to the government of the United States, believing they would be favorably received. I believe Count Bismarck is in earnest and desires the settlement of this question. He promises to look into the case of Mr. Breiger, and I am more confirmed in my opinion that if this subject is referred to in the forthcoming message of the President, it will accelerate the settlement of this question.

The Paris correspondent of the Czas, a Polish paper published at Cracow, who derives his Mexican intelligence from the Polish generals and colonels in the service of the emperor Maximilian, and whose trustworthiness has been repeatedly tested by gentlemen in whom I place implicit confidence, states that the French government have opened negotiations with the imperial government of Mexico on the subject of the withdrawal of the French troops from Mexico within one or two years. The emperor Maximilian (the correspondent adds) is very unwilling to accede to the proposal, but the French Emperor insists upon his assent, giving him, however, to understand, if, at the time of the contemplated withdrawal of the troops, the state of things in America and Europe should render it proper for France to leave her troops in Mexico, arrangements will be so modified as to suit the then existing state of things. In the opinion of the same writer, this arrangement will be perfected in time for Napoleon to announce this fact at the opening of the next French Chambers, and it is intended to pacify the United States, on the one hand, leaving Napoleon, on the other, full liberty for the future. A few weeks will test the truth of this writer's prediction. I should say many of the diplomats at this court place full confidence in his statements.

I have the honor to be, most respectfully, your obedient servant,

JOSEPH A. WRIGHT.

Hon. WILLIAM H. SEWARD,
Secretary of State.

Mr. Seward to Mr. Wright.

No. 13.]

DEPARTMENT OF STATE,
Washington, November 30, 1865.

SIR: Your despatch of November 15, No. 8, has been received. I shall be glad to hear that the Prussian government has reconsidered the decision which was announced here by Baron Von Gerolt, in the case of the convicts exported to the United States. Directions have been given in that case to refuse the convicts a landing, and to cause them to be returned to Prussia. The expense, if any, which may attend that proceeding, we think will be a fair ground of claim against the Prussian government.

You will read this despatch to Count Bismarck, and leave a copy with him if he shall desire it. It is the President's wish that it may be understood as a respectful protest against any future proceedings by which the Prussian government might direct or consent to the transportation of convicted criminals to the United States.

I am, sir, your obedient servant,

WILLIAM H. SEWARD.

JOSEPH A. WRIGHT, Esq., *&c., &c., Berlin.*

Mr. Seward to Mr. Wright.

No. 15.]

DEPARTMENT OF STATE,
Washington, December 2, 1865.

SIR: Recurring to your despatch No. 8, which has already been acknowledged, I have now the honor to give you the President's views in regard to the proceedings in Prussia, by which natives of Prussia who have voluntarily exchanged allegiance from that government for the rights and privileges of citizens of the United States, and have been duly naturalized as such, are nevertheless arrested and held liable to perform military service on occasions of their transient visits to their native country. The question involved in these proceedings is an old one, and was a subject of elaborate discussion between the two countries before the occurrence of our late civil war. Considerations of ease and policy prevailed with this department to allow the subject to rest during the continuance of the war. We became even less anxious upon the subject when it was seen that worthless naturalized citizens fled before the requirement of military service by their adopted government here, and not only took refuge from such service in their native land, but impertinently demanded that the United States should interpose to procure their exemption from military service exacted here. Those circumstances, however, have passed away, and the question presents itself in its original form. The United States have accepted and established a government upon the principle of the rights of men who have committed no crime to choose the state in which they will live, and to incorporate themselves as members of that state, and to enjoy henceforth its privileges and benefits, among which is included protection. This principle is recommended by sentiments of humanity and abstract justice. It is a principle which we cannot waive. It is not believed that the military service which can be procured by any foreign state in denial of this principle can be important or even useful to that state. The President desires that you will present the subject to the serious consideration of Count Bismarck. In doing so, you will assure the minister for foreign affairs that we are animated by sentiments of sincere friendship and good will to Prussia, and that, therefore, we shall be ready to receive and consider with candor any opinions upon the subject that the Prussian government may think proper to communicate.

You will also assure Count Bismarck that any suggestions that he may think proper to make relative to the extradition laws of the two countries will receive just and friendly attention.

I am, sir, your obedient servant,

WILLIAM H. SEWARD.

JOSEPH A. WRIGHT, *&c., &c., Berlin.*

BELGIUM.

Mr. Seward to Mr. Sanford.

No. 150.] DEPARTMENT OF STATE,
Washington, October 15, 1864.

SIR: I call your attention to the enclosed copy of a despatch from Mr. M. A. Jackson, United States consul at Halifax, and of an extract from a late Charleston paper by which it was accompanied, in regard to the proposed building in England of a number of fast-sailing steamers for the purpose of running the blockade of Wilmington with troops from Poland to the number of thirty thousand.

You will exercise your usual vigilance towards thwarting the scheme referred to.

I am, sir, your obedient servant,

WILLIAM H. SEWARD.

HENRY S. SANFORD, *&c., &c., Brussels.*

(For enclosures see despatch No. 1130 to Mr. Adams, Diplomatic Correspondence 1864, Part 2.)

Mr. Seward to Mr. Sanford.

No. 155.] DEPARTMENT OF STATE,
Washington, December 21, 1864.

SIR: Your despatch of November 25, No. 229, has been received, and I thank you very sincerely for the full account it gives of newspaper opinion in Europe concerning the probable influence of the recent presidential election. I regret with you that Europe does not see American facts more clearly, and reason upon them more wisely. I can well believe that a newspaper in Europe which should speak in the name and with the authority of the government would in many respects be useful. But, on the other hand, I remain of the opinion I have heretofore expressed to you, that there is no need that the United States should compromise their just dignity by employing other than the customary diplomatic defenders in any part of the world. The rebels naturally subsidize presses in Europe, for they seek favor and aid there. We stand or fall not by means of foreign love or hate, but exclusively by reason of our own physical and moral strength. We wish only good to all Europe. We get in return for this benevolence mingled love and hate. This results from the nature of our institutions, and our unusually elevated aspirations. Let us be content with this situation. We shall thus get through our troubles all the sooner, and be all the safer when they are passed.

I am, sir, your obedient servant,

WILLIAM H. SEWARD.

HENRY S. SANFORD, Esq., *&c., &c., Brussels.*

Mr. Sanford to Mr. Seward.

No. 234.] LEGATION OF THE UNITED STATES,
Brussels, December 29, 1864.

SIR: The message of the President has been widely republished here, and has confirmed and deepened the profound impression produced by the elections. Its compactness has also contributed to assure it a more general circulation than has been usually given to such documents.

Its unyielding position with regard to slavery has destroyed effectually the only remaining argument of our enemies, which had much influence on the popular mind abroad—that slavery had nothing to do with the war, and would be protected even if the south would not yield.

The impression on all sides, so far as I can observe, is, that the rebellion is approaching its end, and that the cause of the Union must triumph.

It would have been of great utility if there had been sent abroad, at the same time with the message, copies of the departmental reports. They excite a good deal of interest, are much sought after, and could have been very effectually employed among public men and the organs of public opinion before they came emasculated in substance and spirit, through the medium of a hostile press.

I have the honor to be, with great respect, your most obedient servant,

H. S. SANFORD.

Hon. WILLIAM H. SEWARD,
Secretary of State, &c., &c., &c.

Mr. Seward to Mr. Sanford.

No. 158.] DEPARTMENT OF STATE,
Washington, January 16, 1865.

SIR: Your despatch of the 29th of December has been received.

We learn with pleasure that on the continent the President's message is generally accepted as proving the confidence of the people of the United States in their ability to overcome the resistance of slavery, and to preserve their national Union.

The military and political incidents which have occurred since the message was transmitted to Congress tend to confirm the favorable impression which has thus been made.

I am, sir, your obedient servant,

WILLIAM H. SEWARD.

HENRY S. SANFORD, *&c., &c., Brussels.*

Mr. Seward to Mr. Sanford.

No. 159.] DEPARTMENT OF STATE,
Washington, January 20, 1865

SIR: I have received a despatch from Mr. Crawford, United States consul at Antwerp, communicating a congratulatory address to the President from the "Free Speech Society," on the occasion of his late re-election. The interesting paper has been submitted to the President, who desires that you will make an acknowledgment of its receipt. In doing so you will state that so far as the sentiments expressed by the society are personal, they are accepted by the President with a sincere and anxious desire that he may be able to prove himself not unworthy of the confidence which has been recently extended to him by his fellow-citizens, and by so many of the friends of humanity and progress throughout the world.

I am, sir, your obedient servant,

WILLIAM H. SEWARD.

HENRY S. SANFORD, Esq., *&c., &c., Brussels.*

Mr. Sanford to Mr. Seward.

No. 236.] LEGATION OF THE UNITED STATES,
Brussels, February 1, 1865.

SIR: M. de Balan delivered his letter of credence to the King as envoy extraordinary and minister plenipotentiary of Prussia near this court, on the 25th ultimo; Prince de Reuss, who had been previously designated for this post, having been appointed to Munich.

I have had the honor to receive in due course your despatches Nos. 154 to 158 inclusive.

I have the honor to be, with great respect, your most obedient servant,

H. S. SANFORD.

P. S.—Another detachment of the Belgo-Mexican Legion, and, I believe, the last, numbering about two hundred men, sailed for Vera Cruz, *via* Saint Nazaire, on the 14th ultimo.

H. S. S.

Hon. WILLIAM H. SEWARD,
Secretary of State, &c., &c., &c.

Mr. Sanford to Mr. Seward.

No. 237.] LEGATION OF THE UNITED STATES,
Brussels, February 2, 1865.

SIR: I have the honor to transmit herewith, from the Moniteur, tabular statements prepared at the department of finance, showing the movement of trade and commerce of Belgium with foreign countries for the year 1864.

By reference to these it will be seen that the augmentation of imports and exports over the year 1863 is ten per cent. and nine per cent. respectively.

The importations of wool, linen, hides, and woollen fabrics have been in round numbers to the amount of four and a half, three, one, and one million of dollars, respectively, over the importation of 1863. The imports of grain, salt meats, &c., and cotton have diminished respectively by three, one and a quarter, and half a million dollars.

The augmentation of exports are on manufactures of linen, woollen, and iron, and on coal; and the diminutions fall principally on refined sugars, butter, and fire-arms.

Petroleum has become the most important article among our exports to Belgium; the importation from all countries the past year, according to these tables, amounts to about six millions of dollars, of which it is fair to presume that over five-sixths is of American origin. I learn from another source that the importations from the United States of this article at Antwerp the past year are about nine millions of gallons.

These tables give evidence of the steady growth in wealth and prosperity of this country.

I have the honor to be, with great respect, your most obedient servant,

H. S. SANFORD.

Hon. WILLIAM H. SEWARD,
Secretary of State, &c., &c., &c.

Mr. Sanford to Mr. Seward.

No. 239.] LEGATION OF THE UNITED STATES,
Brussels, February 6, 1865.

SIR: I have the honor to transmit herewith, from the Moniteur, the reports of an interesting debate in the House of Representatives upon the war budget. The general discussion of that appropriation bill, commencing on the 19th ultimo, closed on the 28th, the debate up to the vote on the 1st being confined thereafter to the articles in detail.

Free expression was given therein to the different shades of opposition to the military system of Belgium, whether in favor of abrogation of a standing army altogether or of its reduction; and on the other hand, in defence of this system, which, upon a nominal army of 100,000 men, keeps up a peace establishment, in round numbers, of 40,000 men under arms, and with a war budget of seven million dollars.

Instead of an analysis of the debate, which would exceed the limits usually given to a despatch, I would refer you to the speeches of Mr. Hardy de Beaulino and of Mr. Coomans, the one opposed to standing armies, the other opposed to the present system; and on the other side, to that of the minister of war, General Chazal, and of Mr. Vanoverloop. The very able speeches of the minister of war, while showing a much more profound knowledge of military affairs in Belgium than in the United States, are an interesting exposé and defence of the military system in this country.

The bill was passed on the 1st by 64 to 27 votes and 9 abstentions, 10 of the liberal members voting against it.

I refer particularly to this debate as being probably a point of departure of a systematic opposition to the large military establishment of this country, and as likely to have an important bearing, unless political events come in meanwhile, to change the growing popular feeling on this subject on the next general election.

I have the honor to be, with great respect, your most obedient servant,

H. S. SANFORD.

Hon. WILLIAM H. SEWARD,
Secretary of State, &c., &c., &c.

Mr. Sanford to Mr. Seward.

No. 241.] LEGATION OF THE UNITED STATES,
Brussels, February 20, 1865.

SIR: I have had the honor to receive your despatch No. 159, and, in accordance with its instructions, have addressed a letter to the Free Speech Society, in reply to its congratulatory letter to the President upon his re-election, of which I enclose a copy herewith.

I have the honor to be, very respectfully, your most obedient servant,

H. S. SANFORD.

Hon. WILLIAM H. SEWARD,
Secretary of State, &c., &c., &c.

LEGATION OF THE UNITED STATES,
Brussels, February 15, 1865.

GENTLEMEN: Your congratulatory address of the 26th November to the President on the occasion of his late re-election, and forwarded through the United States consul at Antwerp, has been submitted to him.

I am desired by the President to acknowledge its receipt, and to say to you that, in so far as the sentiments expressed by the society are personal, they are accepted by him with a sincere and anxious desire that he may be able to prove himself not unworthy of the confidence which has recently been extended to him by his fellow-citizens and by so many of the friends of humanity and progress throughout the world.

I have the honor to be, gentlemen, your obedient servant,

H. S. SANFORD.

To the MEMBERS OF THE FREE WORD SOCIETY, *Antwerp*.

Mr. Sanford to Mr. Seward.

[Extract.]

No. 246.] LEGATION OF THE UNITED STATES,
Brussels, March 13, 1865.

SIR: I had the honor to enclose to you in my despatch No. 214 the report of the debate in the House of Representatives on recruiting in this country for the Belgo-Mexican legion, and the result, viz., a vote on Mr. Bara's motion that "the House, in view of the formal declaration that the government has remained, and will continue to remain, completely aloof (*étranger*) from the formation of a corps destined to serve in Mexico, passes to the order of the day."

On the 24th ultimo the debate was again opened upon the subject, which is a thorn in the side of the government that the extremes of both parties appear to delight in vexing, upon the report of the committee to whom were referred two petitions touching the legality of these enlistments; one of the petitions is by Mr. Vandenkerkhove, a lawyer here, being a pamphlet of considerable volume, invoking on this subject the action of the laws, and more especially the 92d article of the penal code, against recruiting in Belgium for foreign service.

Five of the ministers of the government took part in the discussion, which was quite animated, and which served to bring forward the fact of the personal sympathies in this enterprise of several of them, including the minister of foreign affairs, while at the same time all insisted that the government had not, as such, taken any part in it. A request was made of the minister of war for the documents bearing upon the formation of this legion, and these appear in the Moniteur of yesterday.

After a day's discussion, the report of the committee, referring the petition to the minister of justice and of the interior, was adopted.

* * * * * * * * *

The first, under date of the 25th of July, is a circular, signed in behalf of the minister, addressed to the generals commanding territorial divisions or army corps, "to give, without delay, to Lieutenant General Chapelie, *pensionné*, all the facilities which he may ask for the accomplishment of the mission with which he is charged."

The second, under date of 3d September, (the day after the vote before mentioned,) is a circular to the same authorities, as follows: "The intervention of the government, in accordance with the desire expressed by the House of Representatives, being to remain aloof from the said organization of a Mexican corps, I have to recall to you that you can execute no act which can engage the responsibility of the government."

These are accompanied by the royal decrees of 8th October and 19th November, 1864, and 10th February, 1865, authorizing officers and soldiers "to serve temporarily in the armies of his Majesty the Emperor of Mexico," and continue to them their Belgian nationality.

According to the minister's statement in the House, 875 authorizations were given to officers and soldiers to enlist; and according to statements made in the course of the debate, it would seem that the whole number recruited in the Belgo-Mexican legion was from 1,200 to 1,500.

There have been difficulties, before referred to, growing out of the want of means and dissatisfaction of the soldiers, which have prevented the raising the 2,000 originally contemplated, and complaints of the soldiers from Mexico, and their parents here, which are now beginning to be heard, will probably make this a sore subject for some time to come.

I have the honor to be, with great respect, your most obedient servant,

H. S. SANFORD.

Hon. WILLIAM H. SEWARD,
Secretary of State, &c., &c., &c.

Mr. Sanford to Mr. Seward.

No. 247.] LEGATION OF THE UNITED STATES,
Brussels, March 14, 1865.

SIR: I have the honor to enclose herewith, from the Moniteur, the text for a convention ratified by this government on the 14th November last, entered into by Belgium, Baden, Denmark, Spain, France, Hesse, Italy, the Netherlands, Portugal, Prussia, Switzerland, and Wurtemberg, for ameliorating the condition of soldiers wounded in armies in campaign, and by which military ambulances and hospitals are, together with their attendants, recognized as neutrals.

The various provisions for mitigating, so far as is consistent with the rules of warfare, its rigors, will be read with interest.

This convention, signed at Berne the 22d of August last, only appeared in the Moniteur of 8th January, and was at the time mislaid, or it would have been forwarded to you more promptly.

I have the honor to be, with great respect, your most obedient servant,

H. S. SANFORD.

Hon. WILLIAM H. SEWARD,
Secretary of State, &c., &c., &c.

Mr. Sanford to Mr. Seward.

No. 248.] LEGATION OF THE UNITED STATES,
Brussels, March 16, 1865.

SIR: I have had the honor to receive your despatch (unnumbered,) under date of 7th of February, relative to the peace conference near Fortress Monroe.

This despatch has since been published in the public press from documents communicated to Congress, has had wide circulation, and attracted much attention.

So far as my observation extends, it seems to have made a most favorable impression, and to have come very opportunely in aid to counteract a wide-spread apprehension of ulterior foreign aggression on our part.

The earnest endeavors of the agents of the insurgents abroad to convey the belief that the extrinsic policy referred to therein did not originate with or was favored by them, seem to have failed. People are beginning to remember that the aggressive spirit and language on our side, which so frequently excited apprehension abroad before the rebellion, almost invariably emanated from southern influences, and that the moderation displayed by our government, amid the trials which have beset it for the past four years, are indications that our future course will continue to be equally just and conservative.

There exists still, however, a very general but diminishing feeling of distrust touching our foreign policy after the peace which all now anticipate. It is assumed that our great armies cannot safely be disbanded, and will require employment, which popular sentiment will favor in the direction of Canada or Mexico.

My reply to the expression of these apprehensions is, that if our past course towards foreign states is no guarantee to them for the future, our interests are also opposed to other wars than in defence of our nationality; that we have now all the territory that we can well govern, and the sentiment of the country is opposed to further acquisitions; and that our practical people, having learned now that war means debt, taxation, draft, and deranged trade and finances, will not be able to favor any "extrinsic policy" likely to renew such costly experience.

I have the honor to be, with great respect, your most obedient servant,

H. S. SANFORD.

Hon. WILLIAM H. SEWARD,
Secretary of State, &c., &c., &c.

Mr. Sanford to Mr. Seward.

No. 250.] LEGATION OF THE UNITED STATES,
Brussels, March 20, 1865.

SIR: Important modifications have been lately made, and are likely hereafter to be introduced, in various of our departments of administration; and these, as time and experience shall test them, will, doubtless, require further changes and adaptations.

It has occurred to me that much useful information in aid thereof might be procured abroad expeditiously and without expense to the government through its public agents in Europe; especially in matters connected with the department of our finances, where a new revenue system has been introduced, and where a knowledge of the machinery and workings of similar branches of administration in Europe would be likely to be valuable. Their system of collection of internal revenue, and of accountability of collectors and receivers in particular, perfected by the experience of centuries of taxation, could not but be a profitable study to us.

It would afford me real pleasure to furnish any facts on these subjects likely to be useful at home; and I would suggest that the best method to procure them would be by a series of questions on specific points where information is needed.

I have at different times, looking forward to our future requirements in this field, made reports upon the systems and workings of different branches of administration abroad. In Ex. Doc. 68, 33d Congress, in the same volume with my report upon the Penal Code of Europe, is an extended paper of mine upon the administrative changes introduced in France by the republic and the empire. My despatches Nos. 68 and 177 (the former published in Diplomatic Correspondence of 1862) accompanied, respectively, reports upon the revenue system of this country, and the recruiting systems of this and other countries. I have also prepared for a congressional committee a paper upon the legislation of European states touching bankruptcy, and for another a paper upon the military schools of this country, and this experience has convinced me that much of the labor in preparing such documents might be saved if attention could be directed to the precise points upon which information is most needed. Hence the suggestion which I have taken the liberty to make to you.

We have now nearly passed the phase of war, and of solicitude touching the action or opinion of Europe with respect to it and its consequent labors, and we are about entering upon the important one of reorganization and consolidation; and it seems to me that our agents abroad could materially aid in laying and strengthening the bases of the modified administrative system which the wants and changes of the past four years have rendered necessary.

If I can be of assistance in that work, the department has but to command my services.

I have the honor to be, with great respect, your most obedient servant,

H. S. SANFORD.

HON. WILLIAM H. SEWARD,
Secretary of State, &c., &c., &c.

Mr. Seward to Mr. Sanford.

No. 165.] DEPARTMENT OF STATE,
Washington, March 25, 1865.

SIR: I enclose for your information a copy of a late instruction addressed to Mr. Bigelow, and also to Messrs. Adams, Perry and Wood, relative to the pirate Stonewall, otherwise Olinde or Stoerkodder.

I am, sir, your obedient servant,

WILLIAM H. SEWARD.

HENRY S. SANFORD, Esq., *&c., &c., Brussels.*

(For enclosure see despatch No. 1302 to Mr. Adams.)

Mr. Seward to Mr. Sanford.

No. 166.] DEPARTMENT OF STATE,
Washington, April 4, 1865.

SIR: Your despatch of the 16th of March, No. 248, has been received.

The politicians in Europe who anticipate aggressive wars by the United States as a consequence of the expected return of our domestic peace, reason rather from European than American principles. We must insist on the freedom of the seas for our commerce and the safety of our borders against external violence. These rights will doubtless be yielded to us, although not without regret and possible reluctance. Beyond that there are no questions which may not be safely and wisely left to the province of diplomacy.

I am, sir, your obedient servant,

WILLIAM H. SEWARD.

HENRY S. SANFORD, *&c., &c., Brussels.*

Mr. F. W. Seward to Mr. Sanford.

No. 167.] DEPARTMENT OF STATE,
Washington, April 8, 1865.

SIR: Your despatch of the 20th of March, No. 250, has just been received. The subject to which it relates is an important one, and the suggestions you have offered are valuable. I have submitted the despatch for perusal to the Secretary of the Treasury.

I am, sir, your obedient servant,

F. W. SEWARD,
Acting Secretary.

HENRY S. SANFORD, Esq., *&c., &c., Brussels.*

Mr. Sanford to Mr. Seward.

No. 252.]

LEGATION OF THE UNITED STATES,
Brussels, April 12, 1865.

SIR: I transmit herewith from the Moniteur the report of another debate which took place in the House on the 4th and 5th instant, upon *interpellations*, by M. Delaet, a member of the opposition from Antwerp, touching the organization of the Belgo-Mexican corps of volunteers for the service of Mexico.

No new facts of special moment were elicited during a discussion marked by considerable bitterness and violence of language.

The following motion proposed by M. Coomans, of the opposition—"The House, regretting that the government has not remained completely aloof from the Belgo-Mexican expedition, passes to the order of the day"—was rejected by 27 to 44 votes. The motion of M. Bara, that "the House, in view of the explanations given by the government, persists in its decision of the 2d September, and passes to the order of the day," was adopted; the portion of the liberal party opposed to the Mexican expedition being evidently unwilling to aid the opposition in weakening or overthrowing the ministry.

The most notable event in connexion with this debate is that it appears to have led to a duel between M. Delaet and the minister of war, in which the latter was slightly wounded.

I have the honor to be, with great respect, your most obedient servant,

H. S. SANFORD.

Hon WILLIAM H. SEWARD,
Secretary of State, &c., &c., &c.

Mr. Sanford to Mr. Seward.

No. 254.]

LEGATION OF THE UNITED STATES,
Brussels, April 24, 1865.

SIR: I telegraphed you on the 23d instant, *via* Queenstown, as follows:

"Moniteur announces an indisposition, not without gravity, of the King."

Yesterday's bulletin at the palace states: "The King contracted in England a severe bronchitis; great prostration has followed; condition this morning more satisfactory."

This morning's bulletin announces "less prostration of strength, but the cough was more frequent during the night."

The bulletins since have stated that his condition has ameliorated, but he has been in a very critical state, and cannot yet be considered out of danger. His natural robust health has carried him through an attack which would have proved fatal to most men.

I believe it is expected that the Duke de Brabant will reach Suez this week on his return from China.

I have the honor to be, with great respect, your most obedient servant,

H. S. SANFORD.

Hon. WILLIAM H. SEWARD,
Secretary of State, &c. &c., &c.

Mr. Sanford to Mr. Seward.

No. 255.] LEGATION OF THE UNITED STATES,
Brussels, April 24, 1865.

SIR: The news of the capture of Richmond and rout of Lee is generally received here as a certain indication of the collapse of the rebellion.

A deputation consisting of the chairman, M. Picard, officers and other participants of a public meeting of Belgians held in this city, preceded by music and the flags of the United States and Belgium and followed by a large procession with torchlights, came to this legation on the evening of the 22d to present an address of congratulation upon this event.

I enclose a copy of the address, and also of my reply (A) and rough translations of each, (B and C.)

In response to the serenade which followed, and the enthusiastic cheers of the immense crowd which had accompanied the deputation, I appeared at the balcony and thanked them for their congratulations. Although what I said would appear too insignificant to bear repetition, I annex D, in accordance with general instructions—verbatim in translation—the few words I said to the assembled multitude.

I have the honor to be, with great respect, your most obedient servant,

H. S. SANFORD.

Hon. WILLIAM H. SEWARD,
Secretary of State, &c. &c., &c.

B.

SIR: Deputed by a large number of our fellow-citizens assembled in public meeting, we come to congratulate you upon the brilliant triumphs gained by the people of the United States, and to evince at the same time the lively sympathies which we ever entertain for them.

We are happy and proud to be near you, sir, who represent here the great American republic, the organ of this manifestation.

During the days of trial which the Union has traversed we have not ceased to pray for its triumph. To-day, when that noble cause is victorious, permit us to associate ourselves with the joy of the people of the United States, and to salute them as brothers.

The capital of the rebels is taken; the star-spangled banner floats over the walls of Richmond. It may be asserted henceforth that the revolt is conquered, and that the Union will subsist in its integrity.

These facts represent more than material victories, and therefore we could not remain indifferent to them.

When a country enjoys, as yours does, every liberty; when every part of its territory, when every individual, has its share in the national sovereignty, resistance to the laws of the majority is an attack upon right; armed rebellion becomes a crime.

The revolt of the south against the north was unjustifiable. It could not be that right, desperately struggling with blind interests, was to issue mutilated from this great combat.

War, often an iniquitous scourge, has been elevated with you to a mission of justice and of humanity. It was, in fact, the arm, the mailed arm, of civilization.

The blood which has been shed will not flow in vain. The dead have freed the living. Two hundred and fifty thousand men of the north have perished, but, in falling, they have given liberty, and admitted to the common law, four millions of slaves, and with them a whole race up to this day oppressed and despised.

Doubly fruitful sacrifice! It suppressed slavery at the same time that it strengthened the American Union.

The whole people of the United States will again enter upon the tranquil current of works of peace, and give us the blessed example of the complete development of its liberties.

The whole world has been deeply moved by your successes, for it feels that beyond the seas you are a harbor to it.

It knows that the United States represent the aurora of a new policy, which is caused to replace everywhere the ancient law. It knows that, after having repudiated governments based upon force or divine rights, you have, since a long time, proclaimed the principle of the autonomy of every nation. It knows that with you every man is really a citizen in the true acceptation and grandeur of that word, and in the whole reality also it knows that with you all the powers emanate from the nation. These principles are not only inscribed in your Constitution—the practice of each day reaffirms them.

You have the veritable sentiments of democracy, and this sentiment has caused American society to tend constantly towards the most perfect realization of self-government, that political ideal of society. Hence, what marvellous results have everywhere been obtained by you! Human invention, extending each day its limits; your system of railroads and telegraphs, vaster than that of all Europe, carrying the conquest of civilization from the shores of the Pacific to those of the Atlantic; popular instruction, that vivifying well-spring, penetrating from strata to strata, till it reaches the home of the poorest citizen, and from prairie to prairie across your immense territories to the most distant hamlets; the participation in public affairs of all the citizens formed in the double school of a vigilant press, which spreads abroad everywhere the opening idea, and of immense popular assemblies, where came, and whence issue in every direction, the great currents of opinion; the constant accord of the administration with the nation it represents, and of which it is proud to be the simple organ; finally, even in the midst of the severest trials, this admirable spectacle of order always maintained in the midst of agitation, and of liberty ever respected.

Such noble efforts, such noble conquests, will bear their fruits for humanity.

Your entire continent will be gradually drawn into the current of your expansive civilization.

These teachings which Young America gives us will not be lost on Old Europe.

You have thus paved the way for universal brotherhood. You have strengthened the Union at home; we count upon you to cement the union of peoples.

C.

GENTLEMEN; I thank you for this manifestation of your sympathies for the American Union and for your congratulatory address to the people of the United States by your fellow-citizens without party distinction, on the occasion of the victories which assure the end of the slaveholders' rebellion.

It is natural that the friends of civilization, humanity, and progress everywhere, should celebrate an event of such great influence upon the world's affairs. The triumph of this formidable but now expiring rebellion would have been a retrograde of civilization and a perpetual menace for public peace. It was, indeed, devised by a class for its own selfish and criminal purposes, not only to overthrow the republic but to make itself, while destroying universal suffrage, an oligarchy of slaveholders and fillibusters, and it believed with the monopoly of cotton to be able to dictate laws to the universe. And our victories are not alone the defeat of a class of slaveholders; they complete emancipation, strengthen the Union, elevate the nation, abase our enemies, and consolidate American liberty. The rebel chiefs will seek to escape by flight from the vengeance of their fellow-citizens whom they have destroyed, as much as from the penalties of the laws they have violated; and the world will see how a great people, which to crush the rebellion and to defend its cherished institutions has made unheard-of sacrifices, will be generous and magnanimous towards its erring brethren. Those who think that the Union will not come out intact from this last great trial, deceive themselves; there will be, it is true, a change in the Constitution; the stain of slavery will disappear from its pages; but with that respect for legality which is one of the most striking characteristics of our people, and which they have constantly maintained during this crisis of civil war, it will be done legally and in accordance with the provisions of that venerated charter.

We shall soon enter, I hope, upon an era of peace. Certainly it will not be the people of the United States which will desire to see it disturbed; they comprehend, and hope that others will comprehend, that every State has the right to, discuss, vote, and, if need be, to fight out its own internal questions, without interference on its part against others, or on the part of others against it.

I thank you again, gentlemen, and I pray you to thank, in my name, those you represent, for their sentiments towards the people of the United States and their sympathies for our cause, which you have expressed to me; they cannot but tighten the bonds of friendship and of brotherhood which so visibly draw together the two peoples.

D.

My voice cannot command this vast crowd; but, although I have just thanked your deputation, I cannot omit to thank you personally for this imposing manifestation of your sympathies for the cause of the American Union, and your congratulations upon the defeat of the slaveholders' rebellion.

I am happy to salute the flag of Belgium which I see here by the side of that of my country. Again I thank you.

Mr. Sanford to Mr. Seward.

No. 257.] LEGATION OF THE UNITED STATES,
Brussels, April 28, 1865.

SIR: The tragic tidings from Washington of the assassination of the President, and murderous assault upon the Secretary of State, has caused a deep impression here of horror and indignation at the cowardice and cruelty of the confederate plotters. Following so rapidly upon the excitement created by our late victories, and the public demonstrations on account of them, the announcement has aroused unusual agitation in this city, and through the country.

The King, from his sick bed, sent to me one of his aides-de-camp, Major General Boarman, to express in his name his deep feeling at this tragic event, and for the great loss we have sustained. The minister of foreign affairs and the other members of the cabinet, the president of the House of Representatives, the high dignitaries of the court, most of the foreign legations, and a very large number of persons of every rank and station, have come personally to offer their condolence, and to express their horror at this crowning atrocity of the rebellion.

M. Rogier informed me he had sent a despatch to the Belgian chargé d'affaires at Washington to offer directly to the government the expression of their sympathy at the sad event. Immediately on receipt of Mr. Adams's telegram I addressed a circular to our consuls, of which I annex a copy.

The shock caused by this news is too great to permit me to appreciate calmly its influence on public sentiment touching our affairs abroad. It cannot fail, I think, to cause a far-reaching reaction in the sympathies heretofore entertained by the so-called "better classes" in Europe for the rebels and their cause, and to stimulate, on the other hand, a more friendly feeling toward us and the cause of the Union.

The fact that the confederate loan at the London exchange yesterday rose 3 per cent. upon the news is a significant indication of the effect which the instigators of this dreadful crime imagined it would have upon their cause.

The calm transition of the executive power to other hands at Washington, contrasted with what would be likely to occur on a similar occasion in most European states, cannot but help to strengthen the conviction already becoming general by the influence of the success which has crowned this trial under the strain of the rebellion of the power, fitness, and durability of our system of government.

I have the honor to be, with great respect, your most obedient servant,

H. S. SANFORD.

Hon. WILLIAM H. SEWARD,
Secretary of State.

LEGATION OF THE UNITED STATES,
Brussels, April 26, 1865.

SIR: Another dreadful crime has signalized the slaveholders' rebellion. After having been marked by barbarities which could only emanate from the influence of a barbarous cause, its overthrow has culminated in a crowning atrocity; the President, whose assassination was attempted through the same influences at the outset, has been murdered; a merciful God has weakened the arm of the assassin, who sought to murder, in his sick bed, the Secretary of State, and add another affliction to the country, another foul crime against society.

Elevated by his own worth from the humblest sphere to a position of power and responsibility unequalled in the world, Abraham Lincoln has given to mankind a rare example of unselfish patriotism, integrity, and singleness of purpose, in working for the country's good and carrying out the behests of the people. The denomination of "honest," which popular sentiment had affixed to his name, will pass to history, as his well-earned distinction with that of patriot and martyr. What a bright example he leaves for those who follow after him!

Providence spared him to see the virtual accomplishment of the great work to which he had been called; the rebellion and slavery, its cause, are at an end; and the Union is not alone preserved, but has gathered new strength and vitality as a nation. Thank God, its safety or peril can depend on the life of no one man; its government is but an emanation of the popular will, and the passing away of the elect of the people at another time than the limit of his presidential term can cause no perturbation in the state. The people remain, and their will is continued by his successors.

Called upon to mourn the death of a great and good man, and the loss of an eminent Chief Magistrate, I have to request you to display your flag on the day, and for the three following days, after the receipt of this communication, at half-mast; also, that you will cause the masters of the American shipping in your port to hoist their flags for the same period at half-mast.

I have further to request that you wear the usual band of mourning for thirty days.

Respectfully, yours,

H. S. SANFORD.

TO UNITED STATES CONSUL *at Antwerp, Brussels, Ghent, Liege.*

Mr. Sanford to Mr. Seward.

No. 258.] LEGATION OF THE UNITED STATES,
Brussels, April 28, 1865.

SIR: The bulletin of the King's health issued at the palace to-day is the same as that of yesterday, and is as follows: "The night has been more tranquil. The general condition of the King is more satisfactory."

I do not consider he is yet out of danger. He has been much debilitated and prostrated, mentally as well physically, from want of food and sleep, and these tell additionally upon his advanced age. His physicians, I understand, finally induced him, not without difficulty, to partake of some nourishment on the day before yesterday, and sleep followed, and he has since improved, but not without one relapse of the suffocating attack which caused so much alarm a few days since. One lung seems to be seriously affected. There is a good deal of apprehension touching the result still entertained, but he is in a much less critical condition than he has been.

The Duke de Brabant, if he connects with the various steamers from India, will arrive here about the 8th proximo.

I have the honor to be, with great respect, your most obedient servant,

H. S. SANFORD.

Hon. WILLIAM H. SEWARD,
Secretary of State, &c., &c., &c.

Mr. Sanford to Mr. Seward.

No. 261.] LEGATION OF THE UNITED STATES,
Brussels, April 30, 1865.

SIR: His royal highness the Count de Flanders sent to me yesterday one of his officers of "ordnance" to express in his name his condolence on the untimely death of the President. I also received in the afternoon a private note from M. Rogier, expressive of his sentiments, of which, as he refers to it in public debate, I venture to enclose a copy, A. I replied to it by a few lines of thanks.

In the House of Representatives, this afternoon, M. Hardy de Beaulieu, a member of the extreme left, moved, in accordance with previous notice, for an expression of feeling at the late tragic event at Washington. He was followed and warmly seconded by the late Canon de Hearne, of the "conservative" party, who is the author of a widely disseminated pamphlet on our war, and is an ardent friend of the cause of the Union, and by M. Rogier, who announced that he adopted on the part of the government the views just expressed, and that he hoped the House would join in the expression of his desire for the recovery of the eminent statesman, Mr. Seward, to whose existence was attached, in so great a degree, the definitive pacification of the country for too long a time desolated by war; and, after rendering homage to the moderation which he had displayed, the minister expressed the hope "that they might one day rejoice over the restoration of his health, at the same time with the re-establishment of peace between the fractions of a great people whom they admired, and who had always had their sympathies, and which he hoped would take again in the world the great part which is assigned to it." All which, interrupted by frequent marks of approval by the members, was declared by the president to be the unanimous sentiment of the House.

I enclose the report of the same from the Moniteur, (B.)

I wrote to thank M. Hardy de Beaulieau and the Canon de Hearne for initiating this expression of opinion by the House, and transmit (C) copies of my letters to them.

I have the honor to be, with great respect, your most obedient servant,

H. S. SANFORD.

Hon. WILLIAM H. SEWARD,
Secretary of State, &c., &c., &c.

A.

[Translation.]

MY DEAR MINISTER: While I transmit to Washington the expression of the sentiments of the government of the King, on account of the horrid crime perpetrated upon your venerable President, I must inform you of our astonishment at the sad news that has resounded through the entire country, and beg you to be the medium of our sentiments to your government.

I also take the liberty of asking you to have the kindness to be my interpreter with the family of Mr. Seward, for whom I have always professed a particular regard. The news given by the papers leave some hope for the recovery of the eminent statesman; and it is my dearest wish that he may be restored to perfect health, and give peace to a country so long desolated by the calamities of a war greatly to be deplored by all friends of liberty.

Accept, my dear minister, the new assurance of my very high and affectionate consideration

CH. ROGIER, *Minister of Foreign Affairs.*

BRUSSELS, *April* 29, 1865.

B.

[Translation.]

Motion in order.

Mr. LE HARDY DE BEAULIEU. Gentlemen: You were all horrified three days ago on hearing of the assassination of the President of the United States. You all felt that it was not only the chief of a free nation that was struck down, but at the same time it was law, the safeguard of all, and I may say civilization itself; for there is no longer any personal security when political passion substitutes brutal action for the protective power of law. I have thought it becoming, gentlemen, for us not to let this occasion pass without the expression of our painful sentiments.

I will not give you the history of the eminent man who is no more: he sprung from the humblest ranks of society, and elevated himself by labor and industry, when the American nation, with that acumen that rarely fails an intelligent people in important emergencies, chose him as a guide to direct it through a dangerous situation, where a formidable insurrection had placed it.

You all know, gentlemen, what difficulties Mr. Lincoln had to overcome.

Confronted by a portion of the nation that rebelled against the laws they themselves had made, he did not falter once in his patriotic duty. In the most perilous circumstances, in face of all kinds of dangers, external and internal, he was always calm, and, I may even say, benevolent to his bitterest enemies.

After gigantic efforts, after a struggle of four years, Mr. Lincoln at last reached the close of that most bloody contest on American soil, and the greatest troubles of his life seemed over.

He had already expressed the sentiments of conciliation that animated him—it was in his last message, his political testament—when the assassin's bullet struck him in the back of the head, and laid him low.

I cannot foretell the consequences of that crime, so horrid that no terms are strong enough to condemn it; all I can say is, that the parliament of a free nation like Belgium would fail in its duties of international confraternity, if it did not express its feelings of horror and regret at a crime that has robbed a great and generous nation of its eminent Chief Magistrate.

In expressing these sentiments, we confirm the unanimous wishes that the deplorable loss may not deprive the American nation of that calmness which is necessary to finish the great work of conciliation and pacification which Mr. Lincoln had so nobly begun. I am done.

Mr. DE HEARNE. I agree with my honorable colleague in the sentiments he has expressed, and I am persuaded that the feeling of horror produced by this sad news from America is felt not only in this house, but in every quarter of the globe. Yes, gentlemen, we feel the greatest indignation at this political crime that has plunged a great people in the deepest mourning, but has not discouraged it, we must hope; for the great President, who was the victim of the barbarous and cowardly act, has set an example which his successors should follow for the good of the nation they represent and the enlightenment of a free people.

The dreadful catastrophe that has thrown America into the greatest consternation and has appalled the world contains a great lesson for the people, particularly when contrasted with the victories that had rejoiced the American Union only a few days before.

On Palm Sunday the news of General Lee's capitulation was announced in most of the cities of the United States—on that day consecrated to the Prince of Peace, as an American paper expresses it—and on Good Friday Mr. Lincoln and Mr. Seward were attacked by barbarous assassins. And this recalls a profound remark of the august and holy pontiff Pius IX, who, speaking of the many vicissitudes of his reign, said: "Truly, Good Friday is very near to Palm Sunday!"

The people of the Union who were identified with their chief, particularly after the last presidential election, were morally immolated with him, after enjoying the national triumph, to which Mr. Lincoln added glory by his moderation.

The nation is plunged in grief, but hope will resurrect her from the gloom, like the Prince of peace and glory. This grand and terrible lesson of misfortune to the people and their governments will prove a valuable instruction by the spirit of conciliation bequeathed them by their worthy President, as a mysterious pledge of future prosperity, the secret of which is hidden in their past glory.

If there is a nation that ought to sympathize with America in its grief on this occasion, that nation is Belgium; for we are the only nation that has remained faithful in spirit to traditional rights, and followed America from the foundation of her political establishment and her liberal institutions. Yes, gentlemen, we looked upon England, on the one hand, as worthy of imitation in the march of progress, in the path of true and practical liberty; but, at the same time, we were conscious that there were certain customs in the institutions of that country we could not adopt, and we cast our eyes beyond the Atlantic, where we found a great people worthy of entire imitation; and it is the institutions of that people we have chiefly inscribed upon our organic charter. We have followed their example in all that regards public liberty, the distribution of power, the election of representatives, and decentralization of rule. For that reason, I say that Belgium ought to sympathize with America by expressions of horror and indignation, such as all civilized nations feel, and protest against the act of barbarism that has stained the soil of America with the last mournful trace of expiring slavery, which has now vanished before the vivifying breath of modern civilization.

The sentiments manifested in this house are felt throughout all Europe: England has protested through Parliament; France has spoken by the mouth of her Emperor; Prussia by her legislative assembly, where all the members rose to declare that the infamy of the horrid act deserved the condemnation of all civilized nations. We must also do homage to the man who was the victim of that atrocious crime—to the man who, as the honorable Mr. de Beaulieu has truly said, sprung from the people to adorn a nation, and, like certain popes, came from the lowest ranks of society to be the greatest honor to the church.

Lincoln was a self-made man; he drank from the spring of liberty; he was guided by the light of a democratic nation; and merit elevated him to the highest dignities of the country.

He has set a worthy example, which his successor ought to follow, relying on the support of public opinion, which should be his constant guide, never to be abandoned or opposed.

That, gentlemen, should be his greatest honor, which, united with his firmness and wise impartiality, will mark him a place in history.

In joining other civilized nations in our protest against this political crime, we do a good deed; by our participation in the sentiment of universal indignation, we help to arrest the contagion of an abominable example that might attack other nations.

By outlawing monsters guilty of such crimes, we terrify those who might be tempted to commit them.

Mr. ROGIER, minister of foreign affairs. It is useless for me to say, gentlemen, that the government participates in the sentiments so eloquently expressed by the two honorable members of this assembly, entertaining different political sentiments. Our government sympathizes with the bereaved nation, and has transmitted the expressions of its sorrow to the government of the United States and their honorable representative in Brussels.

The motion just made is new to Belgium: but it has been made elsewhere, and the importance of the event justifies it. I consider the sympathy expressed in the speeches of the honorable Mr. de Beaulieu and Mr. l'Abbé de Hearne as the unanimous opinion of the House; and thus the legislative assembly joins the government in the regrets felt and expressed on the occasion of a crime that has filled Belgium and the rest of the world with dismay.

We must also express our wishes for the recovery of the eminent statesman who was attacked at the same time with the venerable President of the republic. His life must be preserved to insure the final pacification of a splendid country too long desolated by the calamities of a war afflicting to all friends of true liberty.

May that great statesman, now burdened with a heavy duty, persevere in the sentiments of moderation he has always shown through the excitement of the great struggle, and may we soon hear of the restoration of his health and the return of peace between the factions of a great people whom we admire, who have always had our sympathies, and who will soon resume their exalted station in the world.

The PRESIDENT OF THE HOUSE. Gentlemen: As no objection is offered, it is now decided that this house is unanimous in its approval of the sentiments just expressed by the two honorable members, whose speeches you have just heard.

C.

Mr. Sanford to M. de Beaulieu.

LEGATION OF THE UNITED STATES,
Brussels, April 30, 1865.

MY DEAR SIR: I write to thank you for initiating in the House of Representatives, yesterday, the expression by it of its horror and regret at the last rebel atrocity which has brought to an untimely end our loved Chief Magistrate. I could not doubt that the national representatives of liberal Belgium would give public token to its appreciation of this crime, and of its sympathy for a sister nation, and I thank you again for having elicited it.

Yours truly,

H. S. SANFORD.

Monsieur HARDY DE BEAULIEU,
Representant de Peuper, &c., &c.

D.

Mr. Sanford to M. le Chanoine.

LEGATION OF THE UNITED STATES,
Brussels, April 30, 1865.

CHER MONSIEUR LE CHANOINE: I cannot allow the words you uttered in the House of Representatives yesterday, in the reprobation of the last infamous act of an expiring rebellion, and of sympathy for the cause of the United States, to pass without writing to thank you for them. I have known you too long as one of the most ardent and best-informed defenders of the cause of right, justice, and liberty, against this atrocious attempt to overthrow free institutions in America for the benefit of slavery, not to be certain that your voice would be raised on such an occasion, and that your words would find echo not only in the chambers, but in the country. Certainly, as you say in your speech, if there is any nation which ought to associate itself with our mourning in these circumstances, it is Belgium, whose institutions have been in so large part formed upon our own; and I am happy to testify to you, as one of the originators of this expression of horror, regret, and sympathy by the House, the satisfaction it has given me, and which I know will be shared by all loyal people in my country: and I pray you at the same time to accept the assurance of my cordial regard.

H. S. SANFORD.

Monsieur LE CHANOINE DE HEARNE,
Representant du people, &c., &c., &c.

Mr. Sanford to Mr. Seward.

No. 262.]

LEGATION OF THE UNITED STATES,
Brussels, May 1, 1865.

SIR: The Moniteur of yesterday contains a note touching the expression of [th]e sentiments of the King, of the Count de Flanders, of the minister of foreign affairs, and the cabinet, as well as the House of Representatives, with respect to the murderous attacks upon the life of the President and the Secretary of State. I enclose it herewith.

I have this day called upon the minister of foreign affairs to express my gratitude for the condolences of the King, and of the Count de Flanders, and to ask him to convey to his Majesty, and to his royal highness, the expression of it; I took occasion at the same time to offer my thanks to him and his colleagues for the evidence they had given for their sympathy on this occasion.

I have the honor to be, with great respect, your most obedient servant,

H. S. SANFORD.

Hon. WILLIAM H. SEWARD,
Secretary of State.

(For enclosures see Appendix, separate volume.)

[Note from the Moniteur of the 30th April, 1865.—Translation.]

The King ordered one of his aides-de-camp to go to Mr. Sanford's and express to him the sorrow his Majesty felt at the news of the attacks on the President and Secretary of State of the United States of America. His highness the Count of Flanders also sends one of his aids to the minister, on the same mission. The minister of foreign affairs and other members of the cabinet, on their part, hastened to call on Mr. Sanford, and instructions were sent to the Belgium legation in Washington to express to the American government the sentiments of regret and condemnation excited by such odious acts.

In the House session of yesterday Mr. Hardy de Beaulieu spoke in the most moving terms of the emotion produced in Belgium by the news of the tragic event which has just occurred in the United States. He called general attention to all the eminent virtues of President Lincoln.

Mr. de Hearne joined Mr. de Beaulieu in a eulogy of much beauty upon the character of the lamented President.

The minister of foreign affairs added, that the government sympathized sincerely in the sentiments just expressed by the honorable members, and that he had already despatched a communication of that effect to the government of the United States, and to their honorable representative in Brussels. He expressed the most fervent wishes for the recovery of the distinguished statesman, Mr. Seward, whose life was necessary to the final pacification of a country that had been so long ravaged by the desolation of war, and the prosperity of which was greatly desired by all friends of liberty.

Mr. Sanford to Mr. Hunter.

No. 266.] LEGATION OF THE UNITED STATES,
Brussels, May 5, 1865.

SIR: The voice of hostility to the Union is hushed by the universal sentiment of horror and sympathy which has been aroused by the tragic events at Washington. Under the cloak of condolence, however, is a general outcry on the part of those most opposed to us heretofore for "moderation, conciliation," &c. It would seem as if our enemies, assured that this rebellion was to be a failure, were seeking, under the plea of humanity, to prevent the thorough eradication of treason from our land, in order that its roots may remain and bring forth a new crop of rebels, to again attempt our destruction.

My reply, in my limited sphere, to these officious people, is that the treatment of those who plotted and carried on this rebellion is an internal matter which concerns ourselves solely, and is the business of those charged to execute our laws, and of nobody else; that the masses who have been led astray, I doubt not, will be treated as erring brethren, who have already been punished severely enough by the calamities of the war into which their chiefs betrayed them, but that their political leaders will, doubtless, receive the same punishment, if captured, that would be meted to treason in any other country.

I have the honor to be, with great respect, your most obedient servant,

H. S. SANFORD.

Hon. W. HUNTER,
Acting Secretary of State, &c., &c., &c.

Mr. Sanford to Mr. Hunter.

No. 267.] LEGATION OF THE UNITED STATES,
Brussels, May 5, 1865.

SIR: I desire to supply an omission in my despatch No. 257.

The compliments of condolence and of sympathy addressed to me on the part of the King, as I have since learned from his aide-de-camp, applied also to the crime which nearly cost to the state the life of Secretary Seward.

I have the honor to be, with great respect, your most obedient servant,

H. S. SANFORD.

Hon. WILLIAM HUNTER,
Acting Secretary of State, &c., &c., &c.

Mr. Sanford to Mr. Hunter.

No. 269.] LEGATION OF THE UNITED STATES,
Brussels, May 6, 1865.

SIR: I have the honor to acknowledge the receipt of despatch No. 169, enclosing copies of three proclamations of the President, under date of 11th April, relating to the closing of certain ports of entry, and reciprocal hospitalities to the vessels of foreign navies in the ports of the United States, and to our vessels-of-war in foreign ports. I am heartily rejoiced at the steps taken with respect to the unjust and humiliating treatment to which our national ships have been subjected, and I doubt not it will lead to a return to that courtesy which is due to a friendly power. I have also had the honor to receive despatches Nos. 166, 167, and 168.

I have the honor to be, with great respect, your most obedient servant,

H. S. SANFORD.

Hon. W. HUNTER,
Acting Secretary of State, &c., &c., &c.

Mr. Sanford to Mr. Hunter.

No. 270.] LEGATION OF THE UNITED STATES,
Brussels, May 6, 1865.

SIR: I have had the honor to receive this day your circular despatch of the 17th ultimo, announcing the assassination of the President and the attempt to murder the Secretary of State.

I have already informed you of the profound sentiment of indignation and sympathy it had excited here.

Unusual interest has been manifested with respect to the new President, and never, perhaps, in Europe, have accounts of the past life and public record of the incumbent of that high office been sought for with more interest or been more widely disseminated.

I am happy to state that the result has been to create a most favorable impression in the public mind, which has been augmented by the conservative tone of the President's reply to the British minister on presenting his credentials.

Public sentiment here, somewhat incredulous at first, owing to the malignant aspersions of enemies, now is, that the succession has fallen into capable and worthy hands. However much the late tragic events may have caused sadness, there is one feature in connexion with them abroad which cannot but cause a melancholy pride, and that is, the conviction created thereby in classes heretofore incredulous in the permanency of our system of government, which, uninfluenced by what would shake any European government to its foundations, moves calmly on in its great work, amid the most formidable difficulties with which a government has ever had to deal.

I have the honor to be, with great respect, your most obedient servant.

H. S. SANFORD,

Hon. W. HUNTER,
Acting Secretary of State, &c., &c., &c.

Mr. Sanford to Mr. Seward.

No. 274.] LEGATION OF THE UNITED STATES,
Brussels, May 19, 1865.

SIR: Mr. Mann, the commissioner of the late insurgents, has, I understand, taken his departure from Brussels and returned again to obscurity. His action and influence here seem to have been mainly limited to furnishing his version of the news from the United States to a small journal here, which was finally compelled, under the pressure of events and the indignant sentiment of the party to which it belonged, to throw him and his cause overboard.

I am not aware that we have any extradition treaty with Belgium. In view of the probability that many of the accomplices in the assassination at Washington will seek refuge here, I would respectfully call the attention of the department to this fact.

I have the honor to be, with great respect, your most obedient servant,

H. S. SANFORD.

Hon. WILLIAM H. SEWARD,
Secretary of State, &c., &c., &c.

Mr. Sanford to Mr. Seward.

[Extract.]

No. 277.] LEGATION OF THE UNITED STATES,
Brussels, May 29, 1865.

SIR: Mourning has been brought to many families here by the news from Mexico of the destruction of a detachment of the Belgian legion in a combat at Tamcaburo, in the State of Michoacan, on the 11th of April. It is stated in the published reports that the whole detachment of about 300 men were either killed, wounded, or taken prisoners. Among the killed is a son of the minister of war, General de Chazal, who was a captain, and seven other officers. * *

I have the honor to be, with great respect, your most obedient servant,

H. S. SANFORD.

Hon. WILLIAM H. SEWARD,
Secretary of State, &c., &c., &c.

Mr. Sanford to Mr. Hunter.

No. 283.] LEGATION OF THE UNITED STATES,
Brussels, May 31, 1865.

SIR: I enclose a copy of a letter of condolence on the occasion of the assassination of President Lincoln from the Septentrion Lodge of Masons, of Ghent, and translation of my reply.

I have the honor to be, with great respect, your most obedient servant,

H. S. SANFORD.

Hon. WILLIAM HUNTER,
Acting Secretary of State, &c., &c., &c.

(For enclosure see Appendix, separate volume.)

LEGATION OF THE UNITED STATES,
Brussels, ——, ——.

SIR: I have received the letter which you addressed me on the 20th instant, informing me of the regrets and sympathies of the Septentrion Lodge, of Ghent, on the occasion of the assassination of our venerable President, Linçoln, and also of the satisfaction at the triumph of the United States over the slaveholders' rebellion.

I cannot but subscribe to the touching manifestation of fraternal sentiment, and beg to offer through you to the Septentrion Lodge my sincere thanks for this new proof of the sympathy of Belgians for my country and for the cause of the Union.

Accept the assurance of my distinguished sentiments.

H. S. SANFORD.

The PRESIDENT OF THE SEPTENTRION LODGE, GHENT.

Mr. Sanford to Mr. Hunter.

[Extract.]

No. 284.] LEGATION OF THE UNITED STATES,
Brussels, May 31, 1865.

SIR: The order of the day to the army, of the minister of war, upon the late disaster to a portion of the Belgian corps in Mexico, of which mention was made in my despatch No. 277, appeared in the Moniteur yesterday, and was the subject of *interpellations* by M. Coomans in the House, who expressed his regrets at this association of the Belgo-Mexican legion with the army of Belgium.

M. Rogier replied that the minister of war had communicated the account received direct from the military cabinet at Mexico to the army and to the journals, for the information of all. A sentiment of pride in the gallant conduct of Belgians had, doubtless, influenced him in bringing it thus officially to the knowledge of their former companions-in-arms; he insisted anew that the departure for Mexico of Belgian volunteers was not a government enterprise; that the Belgian legion, although for the most part going from the army, was not a part of it—did not serve under the Belgian flag or wear a Belgian cockade. There was nothing in this, he thought, to compromise the government.

He was followed by M. D'Hane-Steenhuyse, who insisted anew upon the enrolment of the Belgian legion, composed, he said, in great part of soldiers of the army, who had left it for the purpose, under the express authority of the government, and who might be considered as on leave, as compromising the neutrality of Belgium, likely to expose its commerce to the attack of Juarez's privateers, and in the end to cause difficulties with the United States.

M. Rogier, in reply, treated as absurd the possibility that, in case of an intervention by the United States in Mexico, Belgium would be held responsible for the presence of a thousand Belgians under the Mexican flag; those Belgians had, moreover, he continued, contracted an engagement not to compromise the foreign relations of Belgium, and in the event of a regular war, could return home. As many Belgians, he affirmed, had served in the United States under the American flag during the late war as were now under the Mexican flag.

M. Haymans considered the discussion useless; that the Mexican question had been long ago decided by the chambers, and on three occasions in the sense that there was no Belgian expedition in Mexico, and that if any power could find fault with Belgium under this head, it would be, least of all, the United States, which, according to him, had enrolled recruited soldiers everywhere; and he again insisted upon the charges he had made, in a newspaper which he edits, that Belgians had been enrolled by force into the army of the United States after having been engaged here as laborers.

* * * * * *

I regret not having been supplied by the department with the refutation of these charges to which M. Haymans referred, and which were brought to your knowledge in my despatch No. 222, accompanying the letter of M. Rogier on the subject.

A copy of the "answer of the governor of Massachusetts to inquiries respecting certain emigrants who have arrived in this country from Europe, and who are alleged to be illegally enlisted in the army of the United States, &c.," printed at the Government Printing Office, came into my hands a short time since, through a private source, and appears to be a complete refutation of these charges. I immediately, on reading the debate referred to, took it to the Foreign Office and left it for M. Rogier, who was out, with the request that, if it had not already been brought to the attention of the government by its own agents in the United States, he would take cognizance of it; and I propose seeing him to-morrow to repeat the hope I expressed to the secretary general, that he would have the justice to correct the impression which his silence on the occasion of M. Haymans's assertions would seem likely to make on the public as indorsing these scandalous statements.

I have the honor to be, with great respect, your most obedient servant,

H. S. SANFORD.

Hon. W. Hunter,
Acting Secretary of State, &c., &c., &c.

Mr. Sanford to Mr. Hunter.

[Extract.]

No. 289.] Legation of the United States,
Brussels, June 12, 1865.

Sir: The Moniteur of yesterday contains a note announcing that this government has been officially informed that war has been declared between Brazil and Paraguay, and that the ports of the latter have been blockaded by the Brazilian navy. Recalling the fact that Belgium had adhered to the principles laid down in the declaration of the congress of Paris, of April 16, 1856, it gives warning that all persons subject to the laws of the kingdom who shall fit out or take place in privateers, or do any act contrary to the duties of neutrality, will be liable to be prosecuted before the Belgian courts, independently of any other measure of rigor which they may incur in other countries. * * * * * *

I have the honor to be, with great respect, your obedient servant,

H. S. SANFORD.

Hon. W. Hunter,
Acting Secretary of State, &c., &c., &c.

Mr. Sanford to Mr. Hunter.

No. 288.] LEGATION OF THE UNITED STATES,
Brussels, June 13, 1865.

SIR: With reference to that part of my despatch No. 284 touching assertions by M. Haymans, in the House of Representatives, relative to alleged compulsory enrolment in the United States of Belgian emigrants, I called upon M. Rozier the following day to repeat what I had said to the secretary general. He said that he regretted the incident; that he had himself called out, "You are wrong," to M. Haymans, but that his remark had not been reported in the official journal. He would look into the matter, he continued, and thought he would seek an occasion to bring the subject up in the House, in order to make correction if found advisable after looking into the reports of their agents in the United States upon the subject. I expressed the hope that he would make such correction.

I have the honor to be, with great respect, your most obedient servant,

H. S. SANFORD.

Hon. W. HUNTER,
Acting Secretary of State, &c., &c., &c.

Mr. Sanford to Mr. Seward.

[Extract.]

No. 293.] LEGATION OF THE UNITED STATES,
Brussels, June 24, 1865.

SIR: The Moniteur of the 15th instant publishes the census of the population of Belgium for the year 1864. According to the statistics furnished by the "commercial" administrations, under the direction of the minister of the interior, the population of the kingdom on the 31st of December, 1864, was 4,940,570, showing an increase over 1863 of 47,549, five-sixths of which is due to excess by births over deaths. * * * * *

The resumé shows that the ratio of births to the population is one to 31.7; of deaths, one to 42.6; of marriages, one to 133.7. There is one still-born in 19.9 births. The ratio of female births is one to 1.06 male. The proportion of illegitimate births is one in eight in the cities, and one in eighteen in the country; and there is an average of four legitimate births to one marriage.

I have the honor to be, with great respect, your most obedient servant,

H. S. SANFORD.

Hon. WILLIAM H. SEWARD,
Secretary of State, &c., &c., &c.

Mr. Sanford to Mr. Seward.

No. 303.] LEGATION OF THE UNITED STATES,
Brussels, July 31, 1865.

SIR: The Niagara left the Scheldt yesterday on her return to the United States. It is my pleasing duty on the occasion of her departure from these shores to bear testimony to the good impression which her commander and officers have left upon the authorities and people of this country. Commodore Craven has won the respect and esteem of all with whom he has come in conact here, and carries with him their good wishes.

The presence of the Niagara in these waters has had an excellent effect.

While in Antwerp she was visited by many thousand citizens, who came from all parts of the country for that purpose, and the courteous reception and kind attention extended to them have done much, I doubt not, to stimulate the cordial good feeling which exists on the part of this government and people for the United States. Both ship and commander have done us credit, and have left favorable impressions in Belgium.

I have the honor to be, with great respect, your most obedient servant,

H. S. SANFORD.

Hon. WILLIAM H. SEWARD,
Secretary of State, &c., &c., &c.

Mr. Sanford to Mr. Seward.

[Extract.]

No. 309.] LEGATION OF THE UNITED STATES,
Brussels, September 13, 1865.

SIR: The cattle plague, which is causing such great ravages in England, has appeared in this country, having spread from Holland, where it was brought by some Dutch cattle sent to London for sale, and reimported. A commission of Belgian veterinary surgeons was sent to Holland to examine into and report upon this malady, and the cattle on the farms where it has appeared have been destroyed and the importation or transit of cattle, fresh hides, meat, and tallow have been prohibited by royal decree; and stringent regulations for the immediate slaughter of cattle infected, and the proceedings with regard to those suspected of or liable to infection, have been promulgated—indemnity to the amount of two-thirds of the value being allowed to the owners of cattle destroyed by order of the authorities. * * *

I have the honor to be, with great respect, your most obedient servant,

H. S. SANFORD.

Hon. WILLIAM H. SEWARD,
Secretary of State, &c., &c., &c.

Mr. Sanford to Mr. Seward.

No. 311.] SPA, *September* 30, 1865.

SIR: I have the honor to transmit herewith, in translation, some data I have procured touching the attributions of the court of accounts of this country, and which I owe, for the most part, to the obligingness of one of its counsellors, M. Misson, and which I think may be useful for reference.

I do not send the laws referred to therein, as I have not all in my possession; but if desired by the department, I will forward them on so far as I can procure them.

In my despatch No. 250 to the department, in the month of March last, I suggested that, in view of the probability of an early termination of the war, and the changes in the various departments of the government, required to meet the new condition of things caused by it, series of questions touching the system, organization, and workings of similar departments in Europe be prepared and sent to our public officers abroad, in order that our government might be able to profit by the experience of other countries, and our agents be able to labor intelligently to that end. I still think that most valuable information, especially in respect to systems of revenue and taxation, collection of accounts, &c., &c., can be obtained, of the highest importance in forming a definite legislation for ourselves on these vital subjects.

I have the honor to be, with great respect, your most obedient servant,

H. S. SANFORD.

Hon. WILLIAM H. SEWARD,
Secretary of State, &c., &c., &c.

The great principles which govern public accounts in Belgium are derived from the constitution and from the law of the 15th of May, 1846.

The court of accounts was created by the constitution of 1831, and organized by the law of the 29th October, 1846; it is charged with the examination and the liquidation of the accounts of the general administration, and of those of all having accounts with the treasury; it sees to it that no article of expenses of the budget is exceeded, and that no transfer takes place; it audits the accounts of the different administrations of the state, and is charged to this end to collect all necessary information and vouchers.

The court judges and passes upon the accounts of the state and provinces.

No requisition is paid by the treasury except with the visa of the court, which visa is only given by that body after having examined and verified that the payment asked for is really destined to acquit a debt of the treasury; that it is applied for the time and for the purpose specified in the appropriation; that it is due to the parties in whose favor it is drawn; that the conditions of the contracts or bargains have been faithfully and exactly executed; in fine, that it is a regular debt, which is due and has to be paid.

When the court deems it proper not to give its visa, the motives of its refusal are examined by the cabinet; and when it decides that the payment shall be made upon its responsibility, the court *visas*, but renders an account of its course and the reasons thereof in its annual report to the chambers.

The justification of a credit can be made subsequently to the visa in two cases only, to wit: when the nature of the service demands the opening of credits for an outlay to be made, and where the continuation of a service carried on from motives of economy requires advances to the agent of said service.

These advances cannot exceed 20,000 francs ($4,000,) and their employment must be accounted for to the court within the delay of four months.

The opening of a credit for outlays to be made is by an ordinance *ad hoc*, which is submitted for the preliminary visa of the court, and this credit is disposed of by drafts upon the agents of the treasury in favor of the creditors of the state. The payments are audited monthly by the court of accounts, which, after examination of the vouchers annexed to the ordinances of *regularization*, visas them.

A duplicate of the great book of public debt is deposited with the court of accounts, which sees to it that the transfers and payments, as well as the new loans, are duly inscribed therein; it also sees that each accountable functionary furnishes the caution money provided for as a guarantee for the faithful performance of his official duties.

All bonds whatever, of loans or of conversions, and certificates of caution money must have the visa of the court.

The court keeps a duplicate of the pension register. The pension certificates are visé and registered by it after examination and payment.

The inventories of furniture furnished by the state are deposited in its office, and it receives from the head of the ministerial departments a detailed statement of the property and revenue of the state.

The court of accounts corresponds with the ministers direct; it corresponds also with the accounting officers in what relates to the rendering of their accounts; it fixes the delays within which their accounts must be deposited at its office. It can condemn those who are behindhand to a fine to the profit of the state, not to exceed half of the salary, independent of suspension or loss of office, which it can cause if there is ground therefor. Every condemnation to a fine is pronounced upon the demand of the youngest counsellor, who acts as public prosecutor.

The court judges and passes upon accounts, it establishes by definitive decisions whether or no the accounts of accounting officers are balanced, are in advance or in debt; in the two first cases it pronounces a final discharge, and orders a restitution of the caution mo[illegible] if need be, the raising of injunctions and mortgages upon their property by re[illegible] functions incident to the account passed upon. In the third case it condem[illegible] their debt to the treasury within a delay which it prescribes. In each ca[illegible] proceedings is addressed to the minister of finance, that he may see to thei[illegible] years after the cessation of his functions the accounting officer has a d[illegible] the court of accounts has not otherwise provided. The court, notwithstanding a decision which has definitively passed upon an account, can proceed to its revision, either upon the demand of the accounting officer, supported by vouchers recovered since the decision or *proprio motu* for error, omission, or double entry, discovered in the verification of other accounts.

The decisions of the court against accounting officers are carried into effect, unless within three months appeal is made to the court of cassation for violation of form, or of the law. In case of cassation, the affair is sent before a commission *ad hoc* from the House of Representatives, and judged without appeal.

The court of accounts is composed of a president, six counsellors, and a clerk.

The president and the counsellors must be at least thirty years old, and the clerk twenty-five years; the latter has no vote; they are named every six years by the House of Representatives, but can be dismissed at its pleasure. The members of the court cannot be related or connected with each other by marriage within the fourth degree inclusive, nor at the epoch of their first appointment related or connected within the same limit to a minister; they cannot be members of either house, nor fill any office salaried by the treasury, nor be interested, directly or indirectly, in any enterprise liable to accountability to the state; they cannot exercise by themselves, or in the name of a wife or any other intermediary, any kind of commerce, or be business agents, or participate in the administration of a company or industrial enterprise. They cannot deliberate upon affairs which concern them personally, or in which their relations or connexions to the fourth degree inclusive are interested.

For its ordinary labors the court is divided in two sections of three counsellors each; every six months changes are made in the composition of the sections in such way that every counsellor shall sit in both sections every year. The first section is occupied with auditing accounts; the duties of the second comprise the functions of comptroller, and the care of all that relates to the public debt; the accounts are closed and passed upon in general assembly of the court.

The court of accounts has no vacation.

No tax for the benefit of the state can be established save by laws; such taxes are voted annually.

No privilege can be established in levying taxes.

No exemption or moderation of a tax can be established save by law.

Exception in cases formerly specified by law; no citizen can be constrained to pay money save under the head of taxes for the state, province, or commune.

The chambers pass every year the law of accounts, and vote the budget, in which must be included all the receipts and expenses of the government. The vote upon the budget is by chapter and by article. By this means the chambers exercise a real and efficacious control upon the finances of the state.

Every law relating to receipts and expenses of the government must, in the first place, be voted by the House of Representatives.

The collection of state dues can only be effected by an agent of the treasury, whose mission it is, under the supervision of superior officers, to liquidate and compute the amount due from tax-payers, (excepting in case of direct taxes, which are confided to special agents,) to notify to them the amount thereof, to collect the same, and to prosecute therefor, in accordance with the laws and regulations laid down for that purpose.

These agents, before entering into their functions, must take oath and deposit the amount of their bonds, or caution money, which is regulated according to the importance of the collections which they are employed to make.

They are responsible for the full amount of the taxes which collection is confided to them, and they are not discharged from this responsibility with respects to sums not collected except upon proof that the non-collection did not proceed from their negligence, and that all necessary prosecutions had been made.

Every collector, depositary, or agent whatsoever, in charge of the public moneys, must obtain, in case of robbery or loss of funds, proof that it was the result of superior force, and that the precautions prescribed by the regulations were taken, or he is held accountable for the same.

The amount of collections made by these agents must be paid to the treasurer-general once or twice a month, according to the importance of the receipts, orders, and necessities of the service.

On the 31st December every year their papers and books are passed upon by functionaries or agents appointed for that purpose, and in a detailed minute the amount of money and the cash and bills on hand, which is annexed to the account of their stewardship, and which they are required each year to render to the court of accounts. This account presents all acts in connexion with their office during the year, whatever their nature, and to whatever service, publ[illegible] individual, they may relate.

[illegible]ts—1st. A list of moneys on hand in cash or in bills, and of bills receivable at the [illegible]ent of the year. 2d. The receipt and expenses of every nature made during this [illegible]d in detail. 3d. The amount in cash and bills on hand, and the amounts re[illegible]ted, or the sum which the agent is in advance.

[illegible]ounts have annexed to them statements showing by article and by sub[illegible] [illegible]maining uncollected at the close of this fiscal term, with the reasons fo[illegible] non-collection, the justification of the agent, and the observations and opinions of the provincial directors.

The minutes of the condition of the cash account and of bills receivable drawn up at the end of each year by agents of the administration, specially appointed for that purpose, are also annexed to the individual accounts of the agents; they enable the court not alone to verify the amount in cash and bills reported in the general account of finances, but also to examine into the character of the bills.

The public treasury has prior lien upon the property of its agents, and the officers specially and directly charged with the supervision and control of their accountability are responsible for any deficit which may have been occasioned by a remissness in verifying the conduct of the functions of the defaulting agent. The degree of responsibility of these functionaries is decided by an administrative inquest before which they are examined, and after inspection of all the papers, books and documents of accountability, this inquest is ordered by the minister to whose department these functionaries belong.

If it results that these functionaries are in fault, and as such declared responsible, the recovery of the sum charged to them is prosecuted as provided for by law, and if need be, for withholding their salary, without prejudice to disciplinary measures to be taken in the interest of the service.

The heads of the ministerial departments send to the courts all documents serving to show a right required to the State. These documents enable it to verify the annual accounts of the agents.

After being culled by the court, these documents become themselves the elements of verification to arrive at the correctness of the results stated in the accounts of budgets or fiscal period.

The above accounts serve the court, therefore, for the successive examination of the account of the past fiscal year, and of the provisary account of the succeeding year, concurrently with the following documents:

1st. The books of payments made for account of budgets and of special funds voted for the wants of corresponding fiscal years. (These books are kept in the bureaus of the court.)

2d. The discharges delivered by the court for payments made and justified.

3d. The statements of payments made as verified by the duplicates of the receipts which receive the visa of the agents of the treasury in the provinces, in conformity with article 4 of the law of the 15th of May, 1846. (These duplicates or minutes—talons—of receipts, which are transmitted to the court quarterly, enable it to exercise a control in comparing the funds whose payment is announced, with those receipted for in the account of the treasurer, and to thus verify the regularity of the accounts, the one by the other.)

4th, and finally. The statement of receipts and expenses as shown by the *virements* of accounts in the general *comptabilité*.

These operations of *virements* of accounts in the general *comptabilité* of the finances apply to articles of receipt and expense which only represent changes of designation, movements of accounts current, and other operations which give rise to no material entry or outgo of money.

To the general account of the finances is annexed an account of the treasury, showing the movement of funds the issue and payment of bills payable as well as the receipts and expenses in account current, and which have for object as much to maintain the equilibrium between the resources and wants of the State, as to assure everywhere the punctual payment of the public expenses. This account has annexed to it the balance-sheets of the administration of finances, showing the situation, on the 31st of December of the year which has expired, the operations of the current year, and the situation on the 31st of December.

By the aid of the account of the treasury, the court of accounts can follow every movement of the public moneys, and assure itself as to the employment of the funds of the state from the receipt of the taxes up to the payment of the public indebtedness.

Public debt.—The special account of the public debt is also joined to the general account of the finances; it gives the situation of the different kinds of debts, and makes known by means of tables annexed thereto, the amount of the capital of each of them and the amount of the interest money at the different periods when it falls due, the situation of the sinking fund and that of credits granted by the budgets. The said tables make known, finally, the amount and the number of existing pensions, the movements and the motives of increase or decrease thereof.

Sinking fund.—The resources destined for the extinguishment of the national debt are placed at the disposition of the bureau of the sinking fund semi-annually, by orders having the visa of the court, and the employment thereof is justified subsequently to it, by the accounts of the bankers who have made the purchases in the markets.

After having published in the Moniteur notice of the same, the *titres* brought in are destroyed by an officer of the department of finances in the presence of the delegate of the commission of supervision, of a member of the court of accounts, and of the lenders when their intervention is demanded by the terms of the loan.

These operations are ratified by a minute (*procés verbal*,) the duplicate of which is sent to the court of accounts.

Floating debt.—When it is foreseen that the ordinary resources of the government will not suffice to meet all its expenses, a provision of the yearly loan of wages and means authorizes the government to issue treasury bonds up to a certain sum. When it reaches a large amount and can embarrass the government it is transferred into consolidated debt.

These treasury notes are *visé* by the court of accounts, and those paid are returned to it every fortnight.

The bureau of the sinking fund and that of the *depôt et consignations* (where caution money is deposited by public officers or their bondsmen) were organized by the law of 15th of November, 1847. The royal decree which provided definitively for the execution of this law is of the 2d November, 1848.

The law which organizes the service of treasurer of the state is dated May 10, 1850. The bases of the organization of the service of the treasury in the provinces were determined by royal decree 28th October, 1850. See, also, the instructions of the minister of finances, dated 5th and 21st of December, 1850.

A royal decree, dated December 27, 1847, regulates the service of expenses payable by the agents of the treasury in the provinces.

Another royal decree of December 27, 1847, provides for the application of the articles of the law of accountability which relate to the duration of the *exercice*, the accounts of the state, of the ministers, and of the agents with the treasury, and the accountability of the provinces.

The decree which regulates the form of the budgets and their relations with the accounts to be rendered is dated February 19, 1848.

The royal decree of November 15, 1849, brings together the provisions in vigor touching the *comptabilité* of the state, and regulates the application thereof.

A royal decree, dated December 6, 1853, regulates the accountability touching objects of consumption and of transformation belonging to the state in every department of the public service.

A royal decree to assure the regular and uniform execution of article 47 of the law of accountability touching furniture, provided by the state, was published March 26, 1858.

Public revenues.—The budget of ways and means is divided into four chapters:

Taxes, tolls, capital and revenue, payments.

Taxes, properly so called, are divided into direct and indirect. Of these two fiscal sources, the first, which is derived upon real and personal property, licenses the sale of spirituous liquors, and tobacco is fixed annually, and is consequently certain, foreseen, and obligatory. The second, the indirect revenue, is, from its nature, essentially variable, having its source in consumption—changes, in a word, in all that constitutes social activity.

The branches of revenue which compose the three last chapters are derived from services carried on by the government, or from payments made to the treasury from divers sources.

Owing to the moderation of the taxes, as well as to the comparatively easy circumstances of the people, the revenues of the state are collected with remarkable regularity.

The budget of ways and means increases each year by the single fact of the development of public prosperity and the progressive increase of the population.

The direct taxes comprise the real estate tax, the personal licenses, dues from mines, retail of spirituous liquors, retail of tobacco.

The real estate tax is based upon cadastral valuation.

The bases of the "personal" tax are the following:

Renting value, (*valeur locatiff.*) doors and windows, fireplaces, furniture, domestics, horses.

The license tax comprises trades, commerce, and the professions in general.

The dues from mines reach directly those working mines, and according to their degree of prosperity.

The principal aim of the law of March 18, 1838, creating a tax upon the sale of distilled liquors, was moral rather than financial.

The tax upon the sale of tobacco was established by the law of December 20, 1851.

Vouchers of receipts.—These are documents going to show a right acquired by the state, the reports of revenue, and receipts.

Vouchers of expenses.—Every draft upon the public treasury, in order to be admitted for payment by the court of accounts, must be sustained by documents which show that the object is to pay in whole or in part a debt of the state.

Thus for the *personnel* expenses there must be produced statements setting forth the grade, character of employment, the position as to presence or absence, the service done, the duration thereof, the deductions to be made in favor of the *caisse* of widows and orphans, and the net amount to be paid.

And for the expenses of the *matériel:* 1st, copies or extracts, duly certified, of royal decrees, or ministerial decisions, of contracts of sale, orders or minutes of acceptance, of leases, agreements, or bargains; 2d, detailed statements of the deliveries, of regulation, and of liquidation, showing the service rendered and the sum due on account or in full.

If need, be the court demands other vouchers to verify the credit to the persons in cause.

Vouchers of payments.—The drafts which are paid are transmitted quarterly to the court, by the director general of the public treasury; after examination and admission of the same they remain deposited at the court with a copy of the statements concerning them; the other copy, clothed with the visa of reception and admission, is sent back to the director general of the public treasury, to be annexed to the public account.

Mr. Seward to Mr. Sanford.

[Extract.]

No. 179.] DEPARTMENT OF STATE,
Washington, October 2, 1865.

SIR: Your interesting despatches Nos. 309 and 310, both dated September 13, and your private notes, dated, respectively, August 29 and September 12, have been received.

The subject of the communication addressed to you by Baron de Rothschild will be duly considered.

* * * * * *

I am, sir, your obedient servant,

WILLIAM H. SEWARD.

Mr. Sanford to Mr. Seward.

No. 313.] LEGATION OF THE UNITED STATES,
Brussels, October 21, 1865.

SIR: The Moniteur of to-day contains a report to the King by the minister of finance, accompanying the annual statement of the trade and navigation of Belgium for the year 1864. It shows increase of trade as compared with previous years. The general commerce (of importations and exportations) amounted to nearly $500,000,000, being an increase of 18 per cent. upon 1863, and 24 per cent. upon 1862.

The importations from and exportations to the United States have increased 10 per cent. upon 1863.

The exportations to Mexico, it will be observed, continue to augment in notable proportion, being 356 per cent. increase upon 1863.

The statement gives evidence of the steady increase of wealth and prosperity of the country.

I have the honor to be, with great respect, your most obedient servant,

H. S. SANFORD.

Hon. WILLIAM H. SEWARD,
Secretary of State, &c., &c., &c.

Mr. Sanford to Mr. Seward.

No. 315.] LEGATION OF THE UNITED STATES,
Brussels, October 30, 1865.

SIR: I have the honor to inform you that the Moniteur of yesterday contains a convention additional to the postal convention of 30th December, 1857, between Belgium and France. The postages on letters between the two countries is reduced by it from 8 cents to 6 cents for the single rate of 10 grams ($\frac{1}{3}$ oz.) when prepaid, and is to be 10 cents when not franked. Business papers and other manuscripts not having the character of correspondence can be forwarded prepaid for 10 cents the single rate of 200 grams—about 7 oz. Newspapers are to pay $1\frac{1}{3}$ cent coming from, and $1\frac{3}{5}$ cent going to France.

Another convention provides for the safe transmission of moneys, &c. in registered letters. In additional to the usual charge for such letters, they can be insured up to $400, by paying 4 cents for every $20 or fraction thereof of amount transmitted, and in case of loss the same to be refunded by the post offices.

The date of entering in force of these conventions is not fixed, and is to be announced later.

I have the honor to be, with great respect, your most obedient servant,

H. S. SANFORD.

Hon. WILLIAM H. SEWARD,
Secretary of State, &c., &c., &c.

Mr. Seward to Mr Sanford.

No. 183.] DEPARTMENT OF STATE,
Washington, November 17, 1865.

SIR: Your despatch of the 30th ultimo, No. 315, has been received.

I shall take great pleasure in submitting a copy of the new postal treaty between Belgium and France, which accompanies it, to the Postmaster General, for the information of that department.

I am, sir, your obedient servant,

WILLIAM H. SEWARD.

HENRY S. SANFORD, Esq., *&c., &c., Brussels.*

Mr. Sanford to Mr. Seward.

No. 318.] LEGATION OF THE UNITED STATES,
Brussels, November 30, 1865.

SIR: I cannot give a better idea of the sentiments generally prevailing here touching the administration of our government, than by an extract from a toast given by the Canon de Hearne, a member of the House of Representatives, to the minister of the United States, at a dinner at his house on the 28th instant, where the large party assembled was composed of conservatives, members of both houses of Parliament, and of the clergy.

Although the dinner was a private one, the character of the guests present, representing a class which has not been noted for its sympathy for our cause, and the very warm reception given to the sentiments expressed, prompted me to communicate it to you as an interesting indication of the drift of feeling concerning the President and our country, and I accordingly asked permission of my host to do so.

I have honor to be, with great respect, your most obedient sevant,

H. S. SANFORD.

Hon. WILLIAM H. SEWARD,
Secretary of State, &c., &c., &c.

[Translation.]

* * * To the representative of the great American nation; to the envoy of President Johnson, that distinguished statesman, of whom we admire the wisdom, the moderation, as well as christian, patriotic, and truly liberal sentiments:

Worthy successor of the wise Washington, of Madison, that great promoter of religious liberty, and of Lincoln, that noble victim of the purest patriotism, Mr. Johnson has given a striking proof of those sentiments in the proclamation which he published one month ago, setting apart, as a day of national thanksgiving, the first Thursday of December, for religious exercises, in which all generous and Christian hearts should be associated. In that memorable document, the President of the United States renders thanks to the Almighty for the increase of civil liberty. He invites people to render thanks to the Creator of the universe for the benefits and blessings which they have received at his hands. He recommends the whole people to make a confession of national sins against the infinite goodness of God, and to implore with one heart and spirit the Divine guidance to walk in the paths of national virtue and holiness. He resumes these beautiful ideas by a phrase worthy of the greatest men of ancient or modern times: "Righteousness exalteth a nation, while sin is a reproach to any people." Such principles as these are indeed the basis of the grandeur and veritable power of a nation.

PORTUGAL.

Mr. Seward to Mr. Harvey.

No. 157.] DEPARTMENT OF STATE,
Washington, December 2, 1864.

SIR: Your despatch of the 2d ultimo, No. 301, has been received. I thank you for the information it conveys relative to the affair at Bahia, and commend the vigilance and diligence practiced by you on this as on other occasions affecting the interests of your government.

I am, sir, your obedient servant,

WILLIAM H. SEWARD.

JAMES E. HARVEY, Esq., *&c.*, *&c*, *Lisbon.*

Mr. Seward to Mr. Harvey.

No. 158.] DEPARTMENT OF STATE,
Washington, December 5, 1864.

SIR: Herewith I enclose for your information a transcript of a letter of the 3d instant from the Secretary of the Navy, on the subject of your despatch No. 296, which was submitted to him for perusal, and in which you suggest the expediency of a readier mode of communication between the ministers of the United States and our naval officers on foreign stations.

I am, sir, your obedient servant,

WILLIAM H. SEWARD.

JAMES E. HARVEY, Esq., *&c.*, *&c.*, *Lisbon.*

NAVY DEPARTMENT, *December* 3, 1864.

SIR: I have the honor to return herewith despatch No. 296, from Mr. Harvey, United States minister at Lisbon, which you transmitted to me on the 29th ultimo, and commended to my attention the suggestion contained therein concerning the expediency of a readier mode of communication between the ministers of the United States and our naval officers on foreign stations.

It is in contemplation to establish at an early day a squadron in European waters, and place it in charge of an experienced officer, who will feel authorized to make such arrangements as may appear to him advisable and expedient regarding communication with our ministers within the limits of his command.

Very respectfully, &c.,

GIDEON WELLES,
Secretary of the Navy.

Hon. WILLIAM H. SEWARD, *Secretary of State.*

Mr. Harvey to Mr. Seward.

No. 308.] LEGATION OF THE UNITED STATES,
Lisbon, December 23, 1864.

SIR: Reports have reached me from different quarters, written within the last few days, that two suspicious steamers have appeared off the southern part of this coast, under circumstances which have excited the apprehension on my part that they are destined for hostile service, and that they design, if practicable, to enter one of the secluded harbors with which the Algarve district is indented at various points, and from that base to operate against our commerce.

That region, as I have had reason to represent on former occasions, offers peculiar advantage to piratical cruisers, from its natural formation, its geographical position, the character of its population, and the comparative impunity with which depredations may be committed, unless it be strictly guarded.

This government is not able to maintain the supervision which is required by our exposed interests, but I was able to effect an understanding a year ago that still continues in force, by which the duty of the required vigilance was to be performed by our special agent, with such assistance as he could procure, while the government agreed on its part to expedite a war steamer to the spot whenever the agent should report to me a sufficient reason for that purpose. In fact, that was done on two occasions with effect.

His Majesty's government is really anxious to avoid any form of complication which might possibly arise from the arming, equipping, or harboring of hostile cruisers in the ports of this kingdom or its colonies, and that disposition has been manifested very positively and beneficially at the mid-ocean islands, but its means are limited, and the suggestion is not unreasonable that we should co-operate in preventive measures which look exclusively to the protection of our own commerce.

I have to-day adopted the best expedient which this emergency permits, by sending the special agent heretofore employed down to the Algarve upon my own responsibility, hoping for an approval in view of the imperative necessity of that proceeding. He is active, faithful, and understands the people, their language, and their habits. But as I consider any discretion in this matter on the part of the legation wholly terminated by your despatch No. 142, of the 30th of June last, I beg leave to ask for a particular instruction upon the subject, so as to protect myself while making the endeavor to discharge my duty with efficiency and benefit. Should there be another mode more agreeable to the department, whereby the desired object may be attained, I shall not fail to adopt it with alacrity and zeal.

If the remote and secluded harbors of a sparsely populated portion of this kingdom are used to our injury, as has been repeatedly threatened, against the best efforts of the government, the sufferers will find but cold comfort in the prospect of subsequent reclamation and redress by diplomatic intervention. Such issues ought to be avoided, if possible; and although the suggested co-operation on our side is necessarily attended with expense, it is worthy of consideration whether that cost is not, after all, a real and valuable economy. That question is, however, to be determined by the more enlightened judgment of the department.

The United States steamer Sacramento, which had been in port for several weeks undergoing repairs to her machinery, went out yesterday, at my suggestion, to the succor of an American ship reported to be in distress. I shall request her commander, upon his return, to proceed to the Algarve, and endeavor to establish a means of communication between him and the special agent now on his way there.

I have the honor to be, sir, your obedient servant,

JAMES E. HARVEY.

Hon. WILLIAM H. SEWARD,
Secretary of State.

Mr. Seward to Mr. Harvey.

No. 162.] DEPARTMENT OF STATE,
Washington, December 27, 1864.

SIR: Your despatch of the 3d of December, No. 305, has been received. The proceedings which you took on the occasion of the birth-day of the Emperor of Brazil were proper and commendable.

This government does not feel serious embarrassment in regard to the affair at Bahia. It reposes confidence enough in the public strength and virtue to insist on its own rights, and to recognize the just rights of other nations.

I am, sir, your obedient servant,

WILLIAM H. SEWARD.

JAMES E. HARVEY, Esq., *&c., &c., &c., Lisbon.*

Mr. Harvey to Mr. Seward.

No. 312.] LEGATION OF THE UNITED STATES,
Lisbon, January 8, 1865.

SIR: I have had the honor to receive your No. 155, instructing me to make a representation to his Majesty's government in regard to the equipment of another pirate in Portuguese waters.

As that instruction is predicated, apparently, upon the belief that a British steamship called the Sea King had, by preconcert and collusion with another British steamer called the Laurel, been converted into a rebel cruiser at the Desertas, near Funchal, I have deemed it prudent to suspend action until the explicit information, which I have heretofore sought in vain upon this subject, can be obtained.

There are various conflicting reports, none of which are quite satisfactory to my mind. Our vice-consul at Funchal seems in much doubt as to the real facts, and has not been able to answer distinctly the various inquiries made from this legation.

Had it not been for special official causes, demanding my constant presence here for some time past, I should have gone personally to Madeira, and to the spot, to make a thorough investigation of the matter, under the authority conferred for that purpose by your No. 133. It may be still necessary for me to adopt that course, and no personal convenience will be allowed to interfere with its execution if further reflection and a sense of duty should require it.

I have heretofore explained that we must look mainly for the protection of American commerce in these waters to our own resources; and it was for that reason that I ventured frequently within the last two years to urge with much earnestness upon the proper department the absolute necessity of placing upon a more efficient footing than has all along existed whatever naval force could be spared for European service. Those suggestions, derived from actual experience and from anxious observation, failed to attract attention, doubtless because of more pressing cases, so that we have paid a costly penalty for the want of plain and effective organization.

This government has a very limited navy, which is not equal to the protection of its own exposed interests, and is but little available for those duties which other nations may claim under circumstances such as now embarrass the United States. An unusually prompt and good disposition has been manifested on various occasions to arrest the intended equipment and preparation of rebel cruisers, but the means are not always at hand when most needed, and consequently we are thrown back upon our own naval resources to prevent depredations and to punish the depredators.

There is no other reliable mode of security; and if our ships-of-war now

Europe, or to be sent to these waters, are judiciously devoted to this important object, there will soon be less injury to regret, and little cause for serious complaint. But as long as there is no system, and nothing but indifferent concert of action between the civil and military agents of the government abroad, commerce will be comparatively at the mercy of the corsairs which roam the ocean, seeking what they may plunder and destroy.

I have the honor to be, sir, your obedient servant,

JAMES E. HARVEY.

Hon. WILLIAM H. SEWARD,
Secretary of State.

Mr. Harvey to Mr. Seward.

No. 316.] LEGATION OF THE UNITED STATES,
Lisbon, February 5, 1865.

SIR: Information from various sources and directions has reached this legation within the last ten days, all tending to show that several rebel cruisers are afloat in these and the neighboring waters, and that a serious hostile demonstration against our commerce is meditated. Copies of the notes and telegrams on this subject are communicated herewith, in the order that they were received.

The United States steamer Sacramento left here about a month ago for Cadiz, principally to take in stores deposited there, and at the same time to make some necessary repairs. As soon as I was made aware of the facts above stated, a telegram was sent to her commander, inquiring if the ship was ready for efficient service, and upon receiving an affirmative reply, he was requested to come here immediately. It is to be presumed he is now on his way to this port.

The United States steamer Niagara is supposed to be in one of the ports of Belgium or Holland, and as her services are not needed in that quarter, but are imperatively required hereabouts, I deemed it proper to telegraph Mr. Sanford at Brussels yesterday, requesting him to give that information to Commodore Craven.

The steamer Ajax, referred to in Mr. Moran's note, put into the Tagus on the 3d instant, owing to stress of weather. From inquiries made yesterday, I am led to believe that she is an intended blockade-runner and not a cruiser.

The ram mentioned in Mr. Montagnie's despatch has not yet appeared here.

Immediate steps will be taken in regard to the representations made by Mr. Bayman at Funchal, but it will be necessary to proceed with a certain degree of prudence, as this government, under any pressure, might be inclined to follow the example of the larger powers, and apply a rule to our vessels-of-war which, under existing circumstances, would be far more injurious to the public interest than the impertinent proceedings to which attention has been called.

My first endeavor and duty, in the midst of these complications, and with but a single ship-of-war at hand, must be to protect our exposed commerce, and, if possible, to punish the armed depredators.

I venture to suggest, as Lisbon is a much more available point than Cadiz for the information by which the movements of our ships-of-war in these waters must be to a great extent determined, that it would be a material economy of time and of money if the supplies intended for them were stored here, so as to be quite at hand in case of emergency. Whatever naval force can be spared for Europe should be so disposed in all respects as to give it the fullest vigor and efficiency. The want of systematic organization has been and is still seriously felt

I have the honor to be, sir, your obedient servant,

JAMES E. HARVEY.

Hon. WILLIAM H. SEWARD, *Secretary of State.*

Mr. Moran to Mr. Harvey.

LONDON, *January* 19, 1865.

MY DEAR SIR: I write privately to say that there is a double screw propeller now in the harbor of Kingstown, Ireland, which is, no doubt, intended to be used as a rebel gunboat. She is called the Ajax, has but one funnel, painted white, and a black hull. She has iron beams, and is very strong. I cannot learn her tonnage. She has eighty berths, with tables to let down from the ceiling of saloons to accommodate that number of persons; and although she has no guns on board, she has ample room at the bows and stern for pivot guns; and though she has no portholes, her bulwarks are low enough for guns to range over them, and she is a three-decker. Her crew are all in a state of mutiny, and say she is going to Madeira. There are two or three rebel officers on board. She has two masts, but no yards, as she only uses mainsails. She has four boats swung on davits painted white. Her coal is in bags. Her engineer says she is to be used as a gunboat. If we should not stop her I will telegraph to you. She took arms and iron plating on board at Glasgow.

I give you these facts for your own use, so that you may have one of our vessels on the lookout for the Ajax about Madeira. The rebels recently sent away a large number of men from London on a screw steamer of theirs called the City of Richmond. She may be intended to meet the Ajax.

Ever truly,

BENJAMIN MORAN.

Hon. J. E. HARVEY.

[Telegram.—Lisbon, January 27, 1865.]

Benjamin Moran, Esq., Legation of the United States, London:

Your letter has been received. You should notify Niagara, which is probably at Antwerp. Mr. Sanford, perhaps, knows her whereabouts.

JAMES E. HARVEY.

[Telegram.—Nantes, January 30, 1865.]

American Minister, Lisbon:

Ram Olinde, built at Bordeaux, and transferred by Danes to rebels at Houat island, here sailed for Lisbon on Saturday.

MONTAGNIE, *Consul.*

[Telegram.—Lisbon, January 31, 1865.]

Captain Walke, war steamer Sacramento, Cadiz:

Have your repairs been completed, and is your ship ready for efficient service?

JAMES E. HARVEY.

[Telegram.—Cadiz, February 1, 1865.]

United States Minister, Lisbon:

Sacramento is ready for efficient service. Have answered by letter.

CAPTAIN WALKE.

[Telegram.—Lisbon, February 2, 1865.]

Captain Walke, war steamer Sacramento, Cadiz:

Your letter just received. Come here immediately.

JAMES E. HARVEY.

[Telegram.—Madrid, February 4, 1865.]

Minister of the United States, Lisbon:

The confederate cruiser Shanandoah is in the harbor and asks for repairs. Notified our ships.

PERRY.

[Telegram.—Lisbon, February 4, 1865.]

Hon. H. S. Sanford, United States Minister, Brussels:

Inform Commodore Craven that several vessels, reported to be rebel cruisers, are hereabouts, and, unless restricted by orders, his services are urgently needed.

JAMES E. HARVEY.

[Telegraph.—Lisbon, February 5, 1865.]

E. S. Eggleston, Consul of the United States, Cadiz:

Has Sacramento started? If not, tell Captain to come here immediately.

JAMES E. HARVEY.

Mr. Bayman to Mr. Harvey.

UNITED STATES CONSULATE,
Madeira, January 31, 1865.

SIR: On the 3d instant the steamer Alice arrived, five days from Cork; burden, 450 tons; forty-seven men, all told; bound to Nassau; took 150 tons of coal, and sailed the 6th instant. This vessel came in under the rebel flag, afterwards lowered by order of the governor. I enclose copy of my correspondence upon the subject.

On the 28th instant the steamer Fannie arrived, ten days from Glasgow; 390 tons, fifty men, all told, two passengers; took 200 tons of coal, and sailed to-day. Also under the rebel flag, which was ordered to be lowered, as well as that of the steamer Confederate States, just arrived, thirteen days from Nassau, 279 tons, fifty crew, twelve passengers; reports in ballast, bound to Liverpool.

These three steamers are paddle-wheeled, painted white, and said to go 15 knots the hour.

Have had no correspondence with the government regarding the Fannie and Confederate States, as the policy pursued towards the rebel vessels will not be altered without orders from Lisbon.

If there be any vessels of war within reach of your telegram, it is well to let them know that this place is likely to be frequented by the rebel ships bound to and from Nassau.

I should state that the steam power of the Alice was 200 horse; the Fannie, 250; and Confederate States, 140.

I have the honor to remain, sir, very respectfully, your obedient servant,

ROBERT BAYMAN.

His Excellency JAMES E. HARVEY,
United States Minister, Lisbon.

Mr. Harvey to Mr. Seward.

No. 317.]

LEGATION OF THE UNITED STATES,
Lisbon, February 6, 1865.

SIR: Inasmuch as sufficient time has elapsed for the United States steamer Sacramento to come here from Cadiz, in response to my urgent request of the 2d instant, and as she had not appeared, and no reply had been received to my telegram, I made inquiry of our consul at that port yesterday, and was surprised to learn that she had started on Saturday, (the 4th instant,) at 2 p. m., for Vigo.

Without having any information upon the subject, I presume this movement has been made in consequence of the cruiser Shenandoah being reported at Corunna, seeking repairs. I find myself, therefore, without any resource to confront the various emergencies to which reference was made in my despatch yesterday.

Superadded to the causes of anxiety already stated, a telegram in the Spanish papers received this morning contains the following information:

"FERROL, *1st.*—The confederate war steamer Stonewall has just entered this port in distress, with damages, from Copenhagen."

As Ferrol is a little to the northward of Corunna, it is possible that the vessel named in the foregoing telegram may be the same referred to in Mr. Perry's despatch, (communicated in my No. 316 yesterday,) of the 4th instant, under the name of the Shenandoah; for, according to previous accounts, the steamer Shenandoah was committing depredations along the coast of Brazil.

A telegram from our minister at Brussels, in reply to mine of Saturday, the 4th instant, requesting him to notify the United States steamer Niagara of the state of facts hereabouts, informs me—

"Niagara sailed yesterday morning. Copy of your despatch forwarded to Craven, at Dover.

"SANFORD

"BRUSSELS, *February* 5, 1865."

In view of the actual situation, and of the disappointment occasioned by the departure of the United States steamer Sacramento in another direction, I have just now addressed the following telegram to Mr. Adams at London:

"LISBON, *February* 6—11½ a. m.

"Hon. CHARLES FRANCIS ADAMS,
"*Minister of the United States, London:*

"Please inform Commodore Craven immediately that several rebel cruisers are in these waters, and that his presence is urgently needed. Niagara is at Dover.

"JAMES E. HARVEY."

It will thus be seen that every precaution has been taken to provide for the pressing exigency, which never would have existed if the suggestions derived from positive and costly experience that have been presented, urged, and repeated time and again during the last three years, had been regarded as worthy of attention by the proper department.

Efficient steps have been taken for a thorough investigation in regard to the suspicious steamer Ajax, now in the Tagus.

I have the honor to be, sir, your obedient servant,

JAMES E. HARVEY.

Hon. WILLIAM H. SEWARD,
Secretary of State.

Mr. Harvey to Mr. Seward.

No. 318.] LEGATION OF THE UNITED STATES,
Lisbon, February 9, 1865.

SIR: The United States steamer Sacramento put into this port yesterday with her engine in a disabled condition, having started from Cadiz for Vigo on Saturday last in consequence of information communicated from our legation at Madrid; it is yet uncertain when the necessary repairs will be completed, though her commander, who has just left me, will urge them forward with all possible expedition.

It is now positively ascertained that the opinion ventured in my last despatch was correct, and that the rebel cruiser supposed by Mr. Perry to be the Shenandoah at Corunna, is in fact the French ram Olinde under the name of Stonewall, which entered Ferrol in a damaged state on the 1st instant.

If the Sacramento can be got ready for sea in time, she will be despatched without delay to the vicinity of Ferrol, in the hope of capturing or destroying the ram in question. Or, if the Niagara should appear in these waters, as is remotely hoped, in consequence of my telegram to Mr. Adams on the 6th instant, (to which no reply has yet been received,) that duty will be assigned to her, also, in concert with or independent of the Sacramento, as circumstances may render necessary.

There is no other resource that can be invoked for this urgent occasion, but every pains will be taken to employ our limited means to the best advantage.

I have the honor to be, sir, your obedient servant,

JAMES E. HARVEY.

Hon. WILLIAM H. SEWARD,
Secretary of State.

Mr. Harvey to Mr. Seward.

No. 319.] LEGATION OF THE UNITED STATES,
Lisbon, February 11, 1865.

SIR: The following telegram reached me yesterday morning:

"MADRID, *February* 9.

"Has the Sacramento sailed? Send her. Lose no time. I am afraid the ram will be off to-morrow.

"PERRY."

The only answer which I could give was, that the repairs to the Sacramento were proceeding, and it was uncertain when they would be completed. Not satisfied, however, with the reports which had reached me on that subject, I determined to go on board immediately and make an investigation on the spot which should clear away all doubt.

That purpose was at once put into execution, and Captain Walke summoned the chief engineer, at my request, to a conference in his cabin. I interrogated him as to the nature of the injury to the machinery, the possibility of its being properly repaired here, and the time that would be absolutely necessary to complete the work. Without going into details, it may be said, in brief, that the engineer stated ten days were required for this labor. That reply necessarily precluded all hope of employing the Sacramento for the capture of the rebel ram at Ferrol; and, upon returning on shore, I notified Mr. Perry by telegraph of the result of my inquiry, so that he might shape his proceedings upon a certain knowledge of the unpleasant fact.

I received his answer an hour ago, substantially as follows, so far as it can be made out, for the telegram is confused in the transmission:

"MADRID, *February* 10—10.50 p. m.

"If that ship (Sacramento) cannot move forward immediately, ought to have help of Commodore Craven on the scene of action. This is certainly a most unfortunate condition.

"PERRY."

I have not been able to put myself in communication with the Niagara, and, indeed, am wholly ignorant of her whereabouts. Upon the suggestion of Mr. Sanford's telegram of the 5th instant, I supposed she was at Dover, and therefore telegraphed Mr. Adams, informing him of the urgency of her presence in these waters. As he has not replied, I must infer that the Niagara was not at Dover, or within reach of notice from him.

This state of things is not only unfortunate for the public interests, but is most mortifying in every respect, for, with means to capture or destroy the vessels which have recently been set afloat to depredate upon our commerce, we are wholly unable to employ them; in one case, because of an unlucky accident; and in the other, because, for the want of a proper system, there is no mode of ascertaining where to find a substitute.

Every ship-of-war is provided with a clerk to the commander, whose ordinary duties are easy and light. If the commanders now in Europe were simply required to notify the United States' ministers when starting out on a cruise, long or short, of their intended movements and destinations, much confusion would be avoided, and some degree of efficiency would be given to the service. Under the imperfect arrangements which have heretofore existed, it is quite impossible, except by mere chance, to assure the presence of any ships-of-war for the exigencies which are constantly occurring. This experience is by no means new or recent, and it has involved most serious and costly consequences.

I avail myself of this opportunity, without making a special despatch on the subject, to state that the Portuguese government has withdrawn its offer of mediation between Brazil and England, and, therefore, that the original *status* of the question which complicates these two powers is necessarily resumed.

I have the honor to be, sir, your obedient servant,

JAMES E. HARVEY.

Hon. WILLIAM H. SEWARD,
Secretary of State.

Mr. Harvey to Mr. Seward.

No. 320.]

LEGATION OF THE UNITED STATES,
Lisbon, February 12, 1865.

SIR: It was a great relief to my anxiety to receive the telegram which is given below, last evening, when nearly all hope of being able to make any effective opposition to the exit of the rebel ram at Ferrol had been abondoned:

"CORUNNA, *February* 11—2 o'clock p. m.

"Am here with the Niagara. Please send the Sacramento here immediately.

"CRAVEN."

Necessity compelled the answer of which you are already informed, and which I repeat for a more perfect understanding:

"LISBON, *February* 11—7½ o'clock p. m.

"Commodore CRAVEN, *United States Steamer Niagara, Corunna:*

"Sacramento is disabled and cannot be repaired under ten days. Please keep me informed of your movements.

"JAMES E. HARVEY."

I shall make it a point to go on board the Sacramento again to-day with the intention of hastening the repairs if that be at all practicable.

As yet I am not informed whether the Niagara has appeared at Corunna in response to the urgent requests contained in my telegrams to Mr. Sanford and Mr. Adams or not, though it appears quite probable from the dates of the two facts. In any event, the presence of that ship at such a time is a cause of much gratification.

I have the honor to be, sir, your obedient servant,

JAMES E. HARVEY.

Hon. WILLIAM H. SEWARD,
Secretary of State.

Mr. Harvey to Mr. Seward.

No. 322.] LEGATION OF THE UNITED STATES,
Lisbon, February 19, 1865.

SIR: Anticipating yesterday that the United States steamer Sacramento would be in a condition to leave this port without much further delay, and that there would be anxiety on that account owing to the presence of a rebel ram at Ferrol, I addressed the following telegraphic despatch to my colleague at London, with a view of having the information transmitted to the department by the Cunard packet which sailed yesterday:

"LISBON, *February* 18—1 o'clock.

"Hon. CHARLES FRANCIS ADAMS, *Minister of the United States, London:*

"Please inform department immediately that Sacramento will start to-night or to-morrow to join Niagara at Ferrol, where rebel ram is still reported.

"JAMES E. HARVEY."

The repairs to the Sacramento were pushed forward night and day, and whatever influence I could exert personally to urge expedition was applied. I have now the satisfaction of announcing that she has just left the Tagus, bound for Ferrol, which place ought to be reached within two days. This fact is now on the way to Commodore Craven, of the Niagara, who has been anxiously calling for the aid of the Sacramento.

There were other duties which claimed attention in these waters, and for which I should have requested the service of the Sacramento under a different condition of things; but as the case at Ferrol seemed to be regarded as the most urgent, all the resources at command have been turned in that direction, though at the hazard of some exposure elsewhere. There are but two United States ships-of war in Europe, and they are both at one spot.

If the reports which have reached me from various sources are to be credited, the "ram," which has excited so much apprehension, is effectually disabled, and cannot be made seaworthy without going into dock and being entirely overhauled.

I have the honor to be, sir, your obedient servant,

JAMES E. HARVEY.

Hon. WILLIAM H. SEWARD,
Secretary of State.

Mr. Harvey to Mr. Seward.

No. 326.] LEGATION OF THE UNITED STATES,
Lisbon, March 18, 1865.

SIR: A British steamer, known as the Amy, put into this port some time ago in a disabled condition, and has remained here since then evidently waiting for instructions. That vessel was strictly observed by my direction, because her appearance, and the reports which attached to her, excite suspicion.

Since the capture of Wilmington the Amy has received orders to return to Glasgow—a fact which points almost conclusively to her original destination. A pending controversy between the crew and commander has developed a fact which is worthy of notice by the Navy Department, since it may serve to guide the instructions to be given to officers afloat, on blockade or other duty, concerning the papers of ships which they may examine.

The actual captain of the Amy is not the person named in her papers, and he holds no certificate, such as the British law requires, entitling him to command. His explanation is that he took charge of the steamer at the last moment, because the regular commander refused to make the voyage. It may be assumed that many such cases have occurred, and, perhaps, have escaped seizure as lawful prizes upon the faith of papers which covered international fraud.

I have the honor to be, sir, your obedient servant,

JAMES E. HARVEY.

Hon. WILLIAM H. SEWARD, *Secretary of State.*

Mr. Seward to Mr. Harvey.

No. 168.]

DEPARTMENT OF STATE,
Washington, March 28, 1865.

SIR: Your despatches No. 323, of February 28, and No. 324, of March 6, have been received. The explanation given in the former is entirely satisfactory, and leaves happily nothing to censure or regret in any quarter. The information communicated in your No. 324, relative to the resignation and the subsequent reappointment of the Duke de Loulé, is very interesting.

I am, sir, your obedient servant,

WILLIAM H. SEWARD.

JAMES E. HARVEY, Esq., *&c., &c., Lisbon.*

Mr. Harvey to Mr. Seward.

No. 327.]

LEGATION OF THE UNITED STATES,
Lisbon, March 28, 1865.

SIR: I have the honor to inform you that the rebel cruiser Stonewall, a most formidable iron-clad ship, entered this port on Sunday evening, the 26th instant, having left Ferrol the previous day. As the flag which was flaunted from her mast-head was entirely unknown here, and somewhat resembles that of the Russian service, she was generally supposed to belong to that navy. And, in fact, the real character of the vessel was not ascertained positively until the next morning, when certain individuals, calling themselves officers, published their disloyalty in the streets in gray uniforms and arrogant language.

As soon as I was informed of the identity of the craft, immediate steps were taken, personally, to have her ordered out of port, and they were followed later in the day by a formal note to Duke de Loulé, now enclosed, (marked A,) which will explain itself.

Assurances were given without hesitation that the vessel would be required to depart within twenty-four hours, and I have occasion to know that the orders were at once made, and the notice officially communicated to the Stonewall.

The Niagara and Sacramento arrived last evening, having been delayed on the way from Corunna many hours, by the deranged condition of the latter's engines. Their presence created great excitement in the city, from the absurd apprehension of a naval combat in the harbor, which it was very difficult to allay, and the contagion of which seized even those who should have been better informed. As an accident delayed the departure of the Stonewall until this morning, the alarm became greatly magnified, although our ships had remained, at the friendly request of the authorities, off Belem, some few miles down the river. At an early hour I despatched a messenger to request Commodore Craven, the superior officer, to call at my residence to consult with him as to the measures which duty and wise policy required to be adopted. While we were in conference, the under-secretary for foreign affairs came in with a verbal reply to my note, and perhaps with a view of getting an assurance that no collision would be permitted. Indeed, the King himself had previously sent an aide-de-camp on board the Niagara to express his solicitude on that point. A few words soon relieved any misgiving, but I improved the occasion to say emphatically, that if our ships desired to go out they should go out, because the time for the departure of the Stonewall had elapsed, and because the rule applicable to an armed pirate, in no legal sense recognized as a belligerent by this government, should not be applied to a regular ship-of-war carrying the honorable flag of my country.

A brief consultation with Commodore Craven soon satisfied me—for I did not feel at all qualified to judge a professional question of such moment and serious importance—that in the present condition of fine weather and smooth sea, to seek a combat with this powerful iron ship would be to invite almost certain and wanton destruction of life and property. There was another reason bearing directly upon a decision in a different form, which necessarily attracted attention. By referring to the letters marked B and C, of our consul at Liverpool, it will be seen that two vessels are now on their way to this port with cannon, munitions of war, and large military supplies for the Stonewall. They may be expected hereabouts from one day to another. It is very important to cut off and capture these sinews of war, without which the intended hostile operations of the cruiser cannot be successfully prosecuted. Our ships will address their efforts directly to that duty.

According to my information derived from careful inquiries and investigation, the Stonewall is in perfect sea-going condition; has all the improvements of modern art, science and experience adapted to the objects for which she was constructed; received all the necessary repairs which were required, during a stay of seven weeks at the naval station of the Spanish government at Ferrol, and succeeded also while there in enlisting numbers of seamen and others for her piratical service. She is of remarkable speed for a heavy iron-clad, having made the voyage from Ferrol to Lisbon in some thirty hours, which compares favorably with the running time of the best steamers of the commercial marine.

Large inducements were held out to procure enlistments in Lisbon. As much as £10 sterling monthly wages and £15 bounty were offered, but only one misguided and dissipated victim was secured, and he by a process of kidnapping. The fact only came to light too late to be visited with the penalty which I should certainly have assisted in seeing enforced.

Inasmuch as anxiety will naturally be felt at Washington in regard to the movements of the Niagara and Sacramento, and the Stonewall, I deem it proper to communicate to Mr. Adams the fact stated in the telegram, marked D, herewith, in order that he might transmit them immediately to the department.

I also communicate herewith, marked E, a copy in translation of the note of the Duke de Loulé, in reply to mine of yesterday's date.

These papers and this general statement concerning the cruiser Stonewall since her presence in the Tagus will enable the President and the department to appreciate understandingly the official proceedings which were adopted to meet an exceptional and vexatious emergency.

I have the honor to be, sir, your obedient servant,

JAMES E. HARVEY.

Hon. WILLIAM H. SEWARD, *Secretary of State.*

A. 1.

Mr. Harvey to the Duke de Loulé.

LEGATION OF THE UNITED STATES,
Lisbon, March 27, 1865.

SIR: A piratical steamship called the Stonewall entered the harbor of Lisbon yesterday (Sunday) under a flag not recognized by any civilized nation. That vessel quitted the port of Ferrol, Spain, on Saturday, the 25th instant, at 11 o'clock, after having remained there since the 4th of February, that is to say, during a period of seven weeks, the pretext for claiming hospitality being serious injuries previously suffered at sea.

Attention is called particularly to the two facts above stated—first, to show that the excellent condition of the ship is attested by the short passage from Ferrol; and secondly, to demonstrate that upon no pretended plea of humanity can any claim be justified for furnishing coals and supplies after a voyage of little more than twenty-four hours, and after a continuous stay in port of nearly two months.

The Stonewall is a formidable iron-plated armed ship, commanded and officered by persons representing themselves as in the service of a factious insurgent force, who have revolted against the authority and laws of the United States. The open and avowed aim of this piratical craft is to burn and destroy and ravage the property of citizens of the United States on the high seas, and to embroil, if possible, the friendly relations now happily subsisting between Portugal and the United States.

In addition to these grave and undoubted facts, information has just been received from the United States consul at Liverpool, which gives the most serious importance to the presence of the Stonewall here and to the purposes of those concerned in a hostile conspiracy against the commerce and interests of the United States, for which it is proposed to make the ports and islands of this kingdom the base of *military* operations. The consul's letter to me, dated March 19, says: "The English brig Fairline, now lying at this port, has taken forty bales of clothing, blankets, supplies and the like, marked C, and numbered from one to twenty; eight large guns, weighing eight and a half tons, each with equipment or fixtures; a quantity of small-arms, and a large quantity of shot and shells suitable and no doubt intended for the guns; also enough coal to supply a large steamer. The shot and shell are computed to weigh one hundred tons. The vessel is ostensibly entered for Rio de Janeiro, but the crew say she is to go actually to Lisbon. There can be no doubt but these guns and supplies are intended for a war steamer, and most probably the Stonewall. The crew of the Fairline was shipped yesterday, but it is not probable that she will sail before Wednesday."

In another letter, dated March 21, the consul says: "I wrote you on Sunday last about the schooner Delgada taking anchors and cable for two steamers at Ferrol. I learn this morning that the Delgada had proved too small, and that the schooner Merton Castle is to be substituted in her place. The captain of the former told one of my men that a part of the anchors and cables, together with the stores, were for the rebel iron-clad *Stonewall*, now at Ferrol. She is to take ten large anchors and two hundred fathoms of large and heavy chain cable. * * * * * The English brig Fairline, in command of Captain Savage, mentioned in my last letter, cleared and sailed this morning for Lisbon."

The evidence of a collusive intention to outrage the territory of his Majesty and the obligations of the public law are too clear to admit of any reasonable doubt, as is also the design of this audacious conspiracy to wage a piratical warfare against citizens and commerce of the United States.

I have reason to know, positively, that the Stonewall has entered this port to obtain a large stock of coals and provisions, and with a view of increasing her hostile equipment by enlisting seamen and firemen. Such proceedings are forbidden by the royal proclamation of July 29, 1861, by good faith, and by the law of nations applicable to the existing circumstances.

It becomes my duty, therefore, to ask in the name of the United States—

1st. That his Majesty's government will immediately adopt the necessary measures by which this piratical vessel, now flaunting in an insulting manner, a flag not recognized by any nation, shall forthwith leave the port.

2d. That no supplies of coal shall be allowed.

3d. That all enlistments of seamen, firemen, or others, shall be strictly prohibited.

The urgency of this occasion is such as to admit of no delay, and therefore I permit myself to hope that the decisions of his Majesty's government will be made known in sufficient time to be telegraphed to-morrow, so as to be forwarded to the United States by the Liverpool packet of Wednesday, the 29th instant.

If supplies and enlistments are in any way permitted here or elsewhere within Portuguese jurisdiction, the government of the United States will be constrained to accept such a proceeding as a most unfriendly act, and to claim the fullest indemnity for every species of depredation that may be committed by this pirate.

I avail myself of this occasion to renew the assurances of my most distinguished consideration.

JAMES E. HARVEY.

His Excellency the DUKE DE LOULÉ,
Minister and Secretary of State for Foreign Affairs.

B.

Mr. Dudley to Mr. Harvey.

UNITED STATES CONSULATE, TOWER BUILDING,
South Water street, Liverpool, March 19, 1865.

DEAR SIR: The English brig Fairline, now lying at this port, has taken forty bales o clothing, blankets, supplies, &c., marked C, and numbered from one to twenty; eight large guns, weighing eight and a half tons each, with equipment or fixtures; a quantity of small-arms, and a large quantity of shot and shells suitable and no doubt intended for these guns, and enough coal to supply such a steamer as the Alabama. The shot and shell are computed to weigh one hundred tons. The vessel is entered for Rio de Janeiro, but the men say she is to go to Lisbon. There can be no doubt but what these guns and supplies are intended for some war steamer. There is everything to fit her out for a cruise. I fear they are intended for some piratical craft to destroy our commerce. Her crew were shipped yesterday, but it is not probable that she will sail before Wednesday. It would be well to communicate this information at once to our consuls in the islands, and to tell them to keep a lookout for the suspicious steamers.

Very respectfully yours, &c., &c.,

THOMAS H. DUDLEY.

Hon. JAMES E. HARVEY.

N. B.—The schooner Delgada has taken ten large anchors and chains for steamers, as she says, now at Ferrol, in Spain.

C.

Mr. Dudley to Mr. Harvey.

UNITED STATES CONSULATE, TOWER BUILDING,
South Water street, Liverpool, March 21, 1865.

SIR: I wrote you on Sunday last about the English schooner Delgada taking anchors and cable for two steamers at Ferrol. I learn this morning that the Delgada has proved to be too small, and that the schooner Merton Castle is to be substituted in her place. The captain of the former vessel told one of my men that a part of the anchors and cable, together with the stores, were for the rebel iron-clad Stonewall, now at Ferrol, and that another vessel was to be there, to which the balance is to be transferred. I learn from other sources that this is true. She will sail, so far as I learn, on purpose to supply this vessel and some other rebel vessels which she is to meet. She is to take ten large anchors and two hundred fathoms of large and heavy chain cable. I infer from what the captain says, as well as from the quantity of anchors and cable, that there is another iron-clad somewhere afloat intended for the rebels. The English brig Fairline, in command of Captain Savage, also mentioned in my letter of Sunday last, cleared and sailed this morning for Lisbon. She has eight large guns, with equipments, fixtures, &c., each weighing eight and a half tons—I think one-hundred-pounders—and about fifty cases of clothing, small-arms, and supplies; one hundred tons of shot and shell intended for the guns, and a quantity of coal, all intended for some war vessel. The man who had the charge of shipping them told one of my men they were for the Spanish government. If this is so, why do they clear her for Lisbon? From what I learn from outside sources, I think they are intended for some piratical vessel built in Europe for the confederates. I have but little doubt about it. Look out for her, and inform our consuls at all seaport towns.

I am, sir, very respectfully, your obedient servant,

THOMAS H. DUDLEY.

Hon. JAMES E. HARVEY.

D.

Mr. Harvey to Mr. Adams.

[Telegram.—Lisbon, March 28, 1865.]

Hon. CHARLES FRANCIS ADAMS, *American Minister, London:*

Please inform department immediately that cruise Stonewall arrived here Sunday evening, and left this morning, ordered out by government on my application. Niagara and Sacramento arrived last evening, and remain temporarily on special and important service.

JAMES E. HARVEY.

E.

Duke de Loulé to Mr. Harvey.

DEPARTMENT OF STATE FOR FOREIGN AFFAIRS,
March 28, 1865.

I received the note which you were pleased to address me under yesterday's date, regarding the entry in this port of the steamer Stonewall, wherein, after sundry considerations on this occurrence, you make the following requests:

1. That his Majesty's government shall immediately take the necessary steps to order that vessel away.

2. That she be not allowed to receive supplies of coal.

3. That the enlistment of seamen, firemen, or any other individuals be prevented.

In reply, I have the honor of informing you that, so soon as his Majesty's government was made aware of the arrival of said vessel, and that the cause thereof was the want of coal, intimation was given to the respective commander that, on completing his supply, and within twenty-four hours, he should proceed to sea. Said term expired this afternoon. On perceiving this morning that the vessel was still at her anchorage, a naval officer was sent on board to ascertain the reason why she had delayed her starting. The said officer, on his return, stated that if the Stonewall had not started within the prescribed time, it was owing to her not having taken in all the coal, and that there being to-day a strong current, the commander was afraid that a slight derangement in his capstan might prevent his weighing anchor; and the latter further declared that as soon as the current might diminish its intensity he would quit the port, and this he effected about 10.50 a. m.

Regarding the supply of coal, against which you insist, allow me to observe that the vessel being a steamer, his Majesty's government could not avoid, with good foundation, that she should be provided with that article, for the same reason that it could not deny to any sailing vessel in a dismantled state to provide itself with the needful sails. In reply to your third request, and to what you say regarding the English brig Fairlihe and the schooner Merton Castle, which were about sailing for Lisbon with munitions of war, chains, and anchors, supposed to be destined for the Stonewall, I hasten to assure you that his Majesty's government, having greatly at heart not to give any motive which might alter the friendly relations and the good harmony which happily subsists between Portugal and the United States, has not hesitated in adopting all necessary measures, through the departments of marine, interior and finance, to put a stop to all such plans.

I avail myself of this opportunity to renew the assurances of my most distinguished consideration.

DUKE DE LOULÉ.

JAMES E. HARVEY, Esq., *&c., &c., &c.*

Mr. Harvey to Mr. Seward.

No. 328.] LEGATION OF THE UNITED STATES,
Lisbon, March 31, 1865.

SIR: The enclosed copy of a note which I had occasion to address to the Duke de Loulé on the 29th instant, and the papers which accompany it, will bring to your notice a vexatious incident, which has excited much interest and feeling in this community. It is not necessary now to repeat the details, since the complete history of the case is related in the note to the minister of foreign affairs. It may be observed, however, that no moral doubt was entertained that the offence complained of originated in the inexcusable mistake or excessive zeal of the imprudent officer in command of Belem castle, which, though bearing a very imposing name, is really little more than a beautiful architectural ornament to the harbor, and of no consequence in a military point of view.

The government of his Majesty served no notice of any kind upon me, applying to our ships what is known as the 24-hour rule, and I feel authorized to state, from that fact and others, that there was no intention on the part of the responsible authorities to impose any such restraint upon their movements.

In the midst of the confusion and alarm which prevailed during the presence of the Stonewall in port, and the apprehension that a collision might occur in the Tagus, verbal orders were probably passed among military officers, without definite instructions from their superiors, which led to this untoward circumstance;

still the event was of itself of a character which could not be passed by in silence, and, after a lapse of 24 hours, I addressed the Duke de Loulé in such terms as seemed to be appropriate to the occasion, keeping in view the propriety of a dignified calmness, and not forgetting that our own government had been recently compromised by a similar indiscretion. That note was not delivered in point of fact at the Foreign Office until yesterday at 12.20 p. m., and was sent from there to the royal palace of the Ajuda, where the Duke de Loulé was attending the King in a council of ministers. It was kept back in order that there might be no appearance of precipitancy, and in the hope that the government would anticipate the necessity of any communication whatever.

At the usual audience of the diplomatic body later in the afternoon of yesterday, the Duke de Loulé stated to several of my colleagues that he was gratified with the moderation and tone of my representation, and that he would respond to it by ample reparation for the wrong. I permit myself to hope that this proceeding may merit the approval of the department.

The shots which struck the Niagara did not inflict the least injury, or I should have required the repairs to have been made.

I have the honor to be, sir, your obedient servant,

JAMES E. HARVEY.

Hon. WILLIAM H. SEWARD,
Secretary of State.

No. 1

Commodore Craven to Mr. Harvey.

UNITED STATES FRIGATE NIAGARA,
Lisbon, March 28, 1865.

SIR: With the object of shifting her berth further up the river, so as to be nearer the usual landing straits, at about 3.15 p. m., the Niagara was got under way with a regularly authorized Portuguese pilot on board, and was about being turned head "up stream," when three shots were fired in rapid succession directly at her from Castle Belem. Supposing that the officer commanding the fort might have been under the impression that I was in the act of following the pirate Stonewall out to sea, and had fired those guns as a warning not to proceed, I immediately ordered our flag to be dipped, or hauled part way down, a signal that his warning was understood and that I did not intend to pass the fort.

But, to my astonishment, so soon as those guns could be reloaded, they were again fired at my ship, and this too when my flag was at half-mast and the ship's head being rapidly turned up stream. The firing having been ceased for some few minutes, my flag was run up to its place at the "peak," when almost immediately a third volley of three shots was fired at us. At the moment this last round was fired at us the port quarter of the Niagara was presented to the castle, and no one but an idiot could have imagined for a moment that there was any appearance of intention on my part to quit the port.

The officer who perpetrated this gross outrage upon our flag cannot invent the least possible excuse for his conduct, and I feel that I have only to submit this statement for your consideration, in order that the whole case may be presented to the Portuguese government.

I have the honor to be, sir, with great respect, your obedient servant,

THOMAS T. CRAVEN.

Hon. JAMES E. HARVEY,
Minister Resident of the United States of America at Lisbon.

No. 2.

Mr. Ivens to Mr. Munro.

RUA DA EMENDA, *March* 29, 1865.

MY DEAR SIR: In reply to your request to be informed of anything I know regarding the affair between the United States ship Niagara and Belem castle, I beg to say that I went on board said steamer between 3 and 4 o'clock yesterday afternoon with my two sons, for the purpose of ascertaining what coals she might require; when I spoke to Mr. Roberts, the chief engineer, he told me that he could only state the quantity exactly, when she got to her anchorage near the city; and as she was then under steam, and about to leave her moorings, he told us we had better get into our boat at once, which we did. I then steered for the Sacramento, and after a few minutes I heard a gun, followed immediately by another, and looking round I saw a shot or two strike the water, and in a short time two or three, or more, one of which passed the Niagara and struck on the shore, on the south side, near Porto Brandao, or the Lazaretto, when the Niagara's head was that way far over on the south side, viz., her head and stern across the river; this was the last shot I saw fired.

I must mention also that at the second or third shot the Niagara dipped her colors; I must also state that, as the tide was coming in, her head was necessarily turned down river, therefore she could not make the turn without steaming a little way ahead.

I remain, my dear sir, faithfully yours,

ARTHUR H. IVENS.

CHARLES MUNRO, Esq.

No. 3.

Mr. Tufnell et al. to Mr. Harvey.

LISBON, *March* 29, 1865.

SIR: In compliance with your request, we have to state that we were visiting the castle of Belem yesterday afternoon about 3 o'clock, when suddenly a shotted gun was fired at the United States ship-of-war Niagara. which was then in motion, and immediately after three others were discharged in quick succession. Meanwhile the Niagara was plainly turning towards the city, and after her bow was pointed in that direction, two other guns were fired at her.

WILLIAM TUFNELL, London.
AUGUST ARNAUD, 48 Boulevard Picalle, Paris.
GEORGE W. WURTS, of Philadelphia.
Attaché a la Legation des Etats Unis a Madrid.

His Excellency JAMES E. HARVEY,
Minister Resident of the United States at Lisbon.

Mr. Harvey to Count de Loulé.

LEGATION OF THE UNITED STATES,
Lisbon, March 29, 1865.

SIR: The unpleasant duty is imposed upon me of bringing to the attention of his Majesty's government an event which is officially reported by the letter of Commodore Craven, communicated herewith, (marked No. 1,) and which, unexplained, assumes the nature of an act of war on the part of the Portugese against the United States, without notice, cause or provocation of any sort. The facts of this case are so extraordinary that it is difficult to believe they could have occurred in a community governed by the laws and usages of civilized society.

The United States steamers Niagara and Sacramento arrived in this port on Monday afternoon, the 27th instant, and upon entering the harbor were verbally requested by some officer claiming to represent the naval authorities to anchor near Belem, as much anxiety and apprehension were entertained, owing to the presence in the Tagus of the piratical cruiser Stonewall. Although that request involved considerable inconvenience, and was in no manner obligatory, it was at once respected and obeyed.

The two ships remained off Belem until about three o'clock yesterday afternoon, some five hours after the departure of the Stonewall. Commodore Craven then ordered them to be moved to the usual place of mooring of vessels-of-war, which is more convenient for intercourse with the city. The Niagara was under the charge of a regularly licensed Portuguese pilot in making this change of position, and he alone directed her movements. As soon as the ship got under way to be turned, Belem castle discharged three shotted guns in quick succession directly at the Niagara, without previous warning of any kind. As Commodore Craven supposed that this hostile and unwarrantable act proceeded from some misapprehension on the part of the officer commanding at Belem, the flag of the Niagara was immediately dipped or hauled partly down, a signal which is universally understood to express submission to the governing authority. The guns were reloaded and fired in flagrant disregard of this token. The national flag of the United States was then hoisted at the peak, and while the bow of the ship was actually turned to the city, the guns of the castle again opened fire. These proceedings were witnessed by numbers of persons and are verified in detail by the statements marked Nos. 2 and 3, which accompany this note.

Three of the shots struck the Niagara at different parts of the ship, and if no life was sacrificed, it was not because the gunners at Belem castle did not do their best regardless of consequences. If the Niagara did not respond to this warlike demonstration, as she was, and is still, entitled to do, it may be attributed to the singular prudence and forbearance of

Commodore Craven, who with becoming humanity wished to avoid the effusion of blood, and to spare innocent persons from the penalty which they would have inevitably shared with the authors of this crime, if the broadside of the Niagara had been once opened upon Castle Belem. A state of actual war would have then been inaugurated, the consequences of which I do not permit myself to contemplate.

It is assumed with entire confidence that his Majesty's government has in no way authorized or sanctioned the acts which are now presented to notice, though it is not easy to reconcile the fact of a military officer at all competent to command a post proceeding to such violent extremities without the knowledge or consent of his government. But whether that officer acted with or without instructions, the actual responsibility is the same, though the moral aspect of it may be modified by explanation.

The facts of the case admit of no dispute, and of no extenuation, whether the plea be misapprehension, hot zeal, or ignorance of duty. The amicable relations between governments and the grave questions of peace and war are too momentous in themselves to be committed to the keeping of a caprice, passion, prejudice or partiality.

The conviction is entertained that his Majesty's government will regard this matter in the only light that it can be viewed with due respect to legal and moral obligations, and will be glad of the opportunity to disavow at once all responsibility for the wrong, accompanied by proper acknowledgment and atonement, to require the flag of the United States to be saluted in form with a national salute by Belem castle, and the national fortifications and ships in harbor at a day and hour to be named for that purpose, and to visit the officer who directed the firing upon the Niagara with the most exemplary punishment.

As it is desirable for both parties that a question of this character should not be allowed to hang in suspense, and as there is no necessity or reason for discussion since the proof is conclusive, the hope is indulged that his Majesty's government will find it convenient to signify its pleasure within forty-eight hours after the delivery of this note, in order that the decision may be made known to my government, by the British packet which can be intercepted in Ireland on Sunday next by the telegraph.

In closing this communication, I beg to assure your excellency of a sincere and earnest desire on my part to avoid any and every form of complication, and to strengthen friendly relations between the two countries in the most enduring manner.

I avail myself of this opportunity to reiterate the sentiments of my highest consideration and respect.

JAMES E. HARVEY.

His excellency the DUKE DE LOULÉ,
Minister and Secretary of State for Foreign Affairs.

Mr. Harvey to Mr. Seward.

No. 331.]

LEGATION OF THE UNITED STATES,
Lisbon, April 7, 1865.

SIR: I have now the honor to communicate a copy of the note of the Duke de Loulé in reply to the representation regarding the indignity and violence offered to the United States steamer Niagara, by the governor of Belem castle, on the 28th of March, and of my acknowledgment and acceptance of the same.

It should be stated in this connexion that the flag of the United States was raised above the main tower of Belem castle yesterday at noon, and formally saluted with twenty-one guns. The Niagara returned the salute as an act of courtesy. This was the first occasion upon which the flag of a foreign nation ever floated over the tower of Belem, it being reserved exclusively for the royal standard. A flagstaff is erected upon the lower part of the castle for salutes of ceremony.

I have the honor to be, sir, your obedient servant,

JAMES E. HARVEY.

Hon. WILLIAM H. SEWARD,
Secretary of State.

The Duke de Loulé to Mr. Harvey.

DEPARTMENT OF STATE FOR FOREIGN AFFAIRS,
March 31, 1865.

I received yesterday the note which you were pleased to address to me under date of the 29th instant, calling attention of his Majesty's government to the disagreeable occurrence which on the previous day had taken place with the United States ships Niagara and Sacramento.

You observe—

1. That these two vessels having entered the port of this capital on Monday, the 29th instant, it was virtually requested of them by a naval officer, in the name of the respective authority, that they would anchor near Belem, seeing there existed apprehensions and fears owing to the steamer Stonewall being then in the Tagus, a request which Commodore Craven respected and obeyed, notwithstanding that it implied great inconvenience, and was not in any way obligatory.

2. That both vessels remained at the point thus indicated to them until near 3 p. m. of the day before yesterday, near five hours after the starting of the Stonewall, the said commodore issuing then his orders to weigh anchor and proceed to the usual mooring ground of men-of-war, which is less inconvenient for communicating with the shore; but that as soon as the Niagara commenced moving, so as to turn round, three shots in succession were fired directly at her, without any previous warning of any kind from Belem fort.

3. That Commodore Craven, supposing this hostile and unjustifiable act to proceed from some misapprehension on the part of the commander of the tower, immediately lowered his flag as a signal universally acknowledged to express submission to the constituted authority; but that, notwithstanding, they continued to fire on him in flagrant disregard of said signal; and that hoisting then the national flag of the United States at the peak, and when the bows of the Niagara were already turned towards the city, the firing was continued, three of the shots striking that ship in different points.

You add that you have full faith in the fact that his Majesty's government in no way authorized or sanctioned the acts to which your said note refers, but that whether said officer acted under instructions or not the responsibility is all alike, however much its moral aspect may be modified by means of explanations; and you conclude by declaring that you confide in his Majesty's government that it will not deny that prompt and complete reparation which may be due, and will hasten to make known its disapproval of the conduct of whosoever may have thwarted its good intentions, and have offended the flag of the United States.

Taking into due consideration all that you have exposed, and assuring you that his Majesty's government preserves unaltered its desire to maintain and strengthen every day more and more its friendly relations with the United States, it is my duty to add that the facts treated of in the note you were pleased to address to me yesterday shall not put a stop to this desire in presence of the following frank and loyal reply:

With respect to the first of the three above-mentioned points, it is my duty to say that in Portugal, as in all other civilized countries, it is the exclusive attribute of the national authority to regulate the police of its ports in such manner as may be judged most convenient.

To Commodore Craven were indicated, by the competent authority, the points in the Tagus where the two men-of-war, Niagara and Sacramento, should anchor. On this occasion Commodore Craven did not manifest the slightest wish to select any other anchorage, and nobody could have supposed that he did not consider as obligatory in the port of Lisbon that which is so in all other military ports. Further, if Commodore Craven entertained any doubts on this head it would have been natural for him to have requested information thereon from the authority who communicated to him said information, but no information was asked for, which shows that the point indicated and accepted as anchorage was considered obligatory.

With regard to the second point, it occurrs to me to say that the authority who transmitted to Commodore Craven the indication as to the anchorage ground, informed him at the same time that the Niagara and Sacramento, having entered the port of Lisbon, should not leave until after the lapse of twenty-four hours from the starting of the Stonewall, which was then in the Tagus waters.

Five hours had not yet elapsed since the Stonewall had weighed anchor and quitted the port, when the Niagara and Sacramento began to move, keeping their bows turned towards the bar.

The Niagara gradually approached the tower of Belem, and always with her bows in the same direction.

Notwithstanding that this vessel had anchored near the Portugese corvette Sagores, whence had emanated the above-mentioned communications, Commodore Craven did not intimate either to the corvette or to the competent authorities the movement which he intended to execute. It must be further added, that if the Niagara had kept her moorings for a very short time longer, the turn of the tide to the ebb would have placed her in a position to proceed to the new anchorage grounds, and to avoid the movements which gave rise to the shots from Belem tower.

Through this concurrence of circumstances it was to be supposed that the movements of the United States ships indicated the purpose of quitting the port of Lisbon.

I must call your attention very particularly to this point, because, if Commodore Craven had manifested his desire to change his anchorage, the authorities would not have opposed themselves to the carrying out of his wish, and all the subsequent events would have been avoided.

With reference to the last part of your note, I must bring under your consideration that in conformity with international rights, his Majesty's government could not, and ought not, to abstain from its duty of issuing the necessary orders to prevent, by every means, the sailing of the Niagara and Sacramento before the stipulated time.

In consequence of the first movement of the Niagara it became the duty of the governor of Belem tower to order the firing so long as the ship did not indicate that her movements had not for their object the quitting of the port of Lisbon, but immediately that Commodore Craven showed that he had not such an intention, and hastened to make a signal indicating submission to the warning given him, the governor of Belem tower ought immediately to have ceased firing.

This did not happen, as the firing still continued after the Niagara had changed her direction, and receiving the last shot when she was already steering with her bows turned towards the city of Lisbon.

Commodore Craven's prudence displayed in this last period is worthy of praise.

With that frankness and loyalty which guide the conduct of his Majesty's government, and from which it never swerves, it is my duty to declare to you that the shots fired from the tower of Belem subsequently to the moment in which the Niagara lowered her flag constitutes a fact which his Majesty's government deeply deplores—a fact which was completely independent of its will, and which is deserving of its disapproval; the conduct of the governor of Belem tower, who went beyond the instructions communicated to him, being in this part worthy of reprimand.

Under these circumstances his Majesty's government considers that a reparation is due to the United States, and in conformity the governor of Belem tower shall be dismissed without delay; his dismissal shall be published in the first order of the day of the army, and subsequently in the *Diario*.

This categorical explanation precludes any idea that, on the part of his Majesty's government there existed the remotest intention of offence to the flag of the United States.

But a very short time ago, in its conduct towards the Stonewall, did his Majesty's government, give evident proof to the United States of how much it has at heart the acting with justice and loyalty.

In virtue of the foregoing considerations his Majesty's government thinks that no doubt can exist regarding the sentiments which have always animated it in continuing in good and amicable relations with the United States, and which it desires to strengthen more and more.

I avail of this opportunity to renew the assurances of my most distinguished consideration.

DUQUE DE LOULÉ.

JAMES E. HARVEY, Esq., *&c.*, *&c.*, *&c.*

Mr. Harvey to the Duke de Loulé.

LEGATION OF THE UNITED STATES,
Lisbon, April 6, 1865.

SIR: I have the honor to acknowledge the receipt of your note of the 31st March, and to say that the explanations and reparation made for an act of unjustifiable violence towards the United States steamer Niagara are accepted, though it would have been more agreeable to my government if they had come spontaneously and without the necessity of an official representation, since the facts were notorious to the whole public, and their serious character demanded a prompt and thorough investigation by his Majesty's government. The privilege is reserved for another occasion of demonstrating, as can be done without the least difficulty, that the views advanced by his Majesty's government, in regard to the international rights involved in this question, are in conflict with all the accepted principles of public law as applied to the *status* of Portugal.

And it is my duty to add, that when your excellency assumes that, "in consequence of the first movements of the Niagara, it became the duty of the governor of Belem Tower to order the firing so long as the ship did not indicate that her movements had not for their object the quitting of the port of Lisbon," a grave responsibility is accepted, and a doctrine is asserted, which, with less moderation and prudence than were manifested on that particular occasion by Commodore Craven, might have provoked a very different state of facts from that which now happily exists; for, had it been understood that his Majesty's government considered the governor of Belem in "duty" bound to fire shotted guns at a ship-of-war of the United States without warning, precaution, or injury of any kind, it is quite sure that those shots would not have been accepted as evidence of the friendly assurances which have been protested so strongly. On the high seas when a ship-of-war desires to examine a suspicious vessel a blank cartridge is fired as the first notification of the intended purpose. If that notice be disregarded, then at least one and sometimes two shotted guns are discharged across the bows, and, as a last alternative, a shot may be fired at the hull. The practice of all civilized nations has sanctified this usage as law. If this be the rule for the sea, how much more ought it to be the rule inside harbors, and especially towards the ships-of-war of friendly nations, having rights to claim and responsibility to protect them against unworthy suspicion?

As a mere matter of practice the firing of shotted guns is forbidden as a mode of warning.

even when there is good reason to suppose a meditated wrong; and, in the case of the Niagara, taking in view the position which Portugal and the United States occupy towards each other under the law of nations, that firing would be an act of deliberate and flagrant war according to the doctrine described as a "duty" by his Majesty's government in the paragraph already cited from your excellency's note.

The complete power of his Majesty's government to regulate the police of the ports of the kingdom has in no manner been questioned. That power is a natural attribute of sovereignty, but police regulations may not discriminate partially and to the prejudice of friendly nations. Ships-of-war of the United States do not enter Portuguese ports upon mere sufferance, subject to the caprice, convenience, or orders of local subordinates. They come clothed with the rights guaranteed by treaty and by the public law, which are fully reciprocated on the part of the United States. They carry with them wherever they go the ensign of nationality, and represent the dignity and honor of a government which respects the rights of others, and is competent to maintain its own. Those ships-of-war are specially instructed to manifest, and have always shown, the utmost respect and courtesy towards the authorities of her Majesty's government, giving a most signal proof of that disposition in the very case under consideration, by accepting and obeying the verbal request of an unknown subordinate to anchor at Belem, in the presence of the fact that a pirate or privateer was allowed to proceed without objection or restriction to the anchorage assigned to regular vessels-of-war. The United States claim the same privileges that are conceded to other nations in this respect, and when they involve indisputable rights they will be asserted.

I permit myself to hope that measures will be taken to prevent the recurrence of any such incident as that which has recently engaged attention, because it is not always possible to assure the same calm demeanor in presence of such great and serious provocation.

I avail myself of this opportunity to renew the assurances of my most distinguished consideration.

JAMES E. HARVEY.

His Excellency the DUKE DE LOULÉ,
Minister and Secretary of State for Foreign Affairs.

Mr. Seward to Mr. Harvey.

No. 170.]

DEPARTMENT OF STATE,
Washington, April 22, 1865.

SIR: Your despatches Nos. 325, 326, 327, and 328, dated respectively March 12, March 18, March 28, and March 31, have been received. Nos. 326, 327, and 328 have been submitted for perusal to the Secretary of the Navy. Your proceedings relative to the rebel ram Stonewall and the firing upon the United States frigate Niagara from Castle Belem are approved.

I am, sir, your obedient servant,

WILLIAM H. SEWARD.

JAMES E. HARVEY, Esq., *&c., &c., Lisbon.*

Mr. Harvey to Mr. Seward.

No. 335.]

LEGATION OF THE UNITED STATES,
Lisbon, April 28, 1865.

SIR: I communicate herewith the copy of a note which I addressed to the Count de Avila on the subject of the recent royal decree regarding the admission of cereals into the ports of this kingdom, which decree affects injuriously the interests and the rights of the United States under the treaty with Portugal.

I have the honor to be, sir, your obedient servant,

JAMES E. HARVEY.

Hon. WILLIAM H. SEWARD,
Secretary of State.

Mr. Harvey to the Count de Avila.

LEGATION OF THE UNITED STATES,
Lisbon, April 26, 1865.

SIR: A royal decree, issued under date of the 11th instant, and countersigned by the late ministry, assumes to establish provisionally the rates of duty that shall be paid in this kingdom for the admission of various cereals, discriminating between ports on the sea and what are called *portos seccos*—dry ports. This discrimination not only draws invidious discrimination between countries standing upon the same footing by commercial treaties with Portugal, but it does so with a prejudice on the one side and a partiality on the other that are inconsistent with those obligations.

For example, a duty of six hundred reis per hundred kilogrammes is imposed on wheat in grain and eight hundred reis on wheat in flour in the sea ports, while but two hundred and four hundred reis, respectively, are imposed on the same articles in the dry ports. It is very well known that the only dry ports are those along the Spanish frontier, which are wholly inaccessible to all other nations, and consequently the effect of the decree in its existing form is to give a preference to the productions of Spain, at the expense of other countries enjoying the same rights.

Article three of treaty between Portugal and the United States declares as follows:

"No higher or other duties shall be imposed on the importation into the kingdom and possessions of Portugal of any article the growth, product, or manufacture of the United States of America, and no higher or other duties shall be imposed on the importation into the United States of America of any article the growth, product, or manufacture of the kingdom and possessions of Portugal, than such as are, or shall be, payable on the like article, being the growth, product, or manufacture of any other foreign country."

It has been shown that the terms of the decree are in conflict with the article of the treaty by a large discrimination in favor of Spanish grains and flour, to the injury of those of other countries.

At this time there are, at least, ten American ships at Porto loaded with grain, the growth and product of the United States, and others are daily expected to arrive here and there.

Those cargoes are not fairly subject to the prejudicial distinction which the decree assumes to make for the exclusive advantage of one nation over all others, and, therefore, this representation is now made in the expectation and belief that his Majesty's government will take immediate measures to correct an error so manifest in itself, so urgent in its operation, and so violative of the spirit of the treaty.

The hope is entertained, inasmuch as there are large interests at stake and an important commerce may be seriously affected, that this matter may at once engage attention. The cargoes in question will not be discharged from the ships until the decision of his Majesty's government is known.

I avail myself of this occasion to renew the assurances of my most distinguished consideration.

JAMES E. HARVEY.

His Excellency the COUNT DE AVILA,
Minister and Secretary of State for Foreign Affairs.

Mr. Harvey to Mr. Seward.

No. 336.]

LEGATION OF THE UNITED STATES,
Lisbon, April 28, 1865.

SIR: Mr. Adams telegraphed me last night from London the terrible news of the assassination of President Lincoln, and of the atrocious attempt upon the life of Mr. Seward on the same evening—the result of which is not yet known here—by the hand of another assassin. These events have excited the profoundest emotions in all the circles of Lisbon, and have called out general and particular expressions of sympathy and respect from the government, the diplomatic body, and the community.

I do not trust myself to speak of this great crime at a moment of mingled sorrow and prostration, but I may be allowed to say, that after the grief natural to such an occasion, the sense of humiliation at the thought that an atrocity so awful could by possibility be perpetrated in a country like ours is that which most masters and overwhelms me.

Christian charity may, with the blessing of God, teach us to bow down before this stern trial, but the stain which it inflicts cannot soon be wiped out from a name heretofore untarnished by any such act of infamy.

If there was anything wanting to complete the fame of Mr. Lincoln, it may be found in the crown of martyrdom with which an eventful career in a most eventful epoch has been closed, to the regret of a whole people who shared his convictions, honored his virtues, and lamented his taking off.

I have the honor to be, sir, your obedient servant,

JAMES E. HARVEY.

Hon. WILLIAM H. SEWARD,
Secretary of State.

Mr. Harvey to Mr. Seward.

No. 337.] LEGATION OF THE UNITED STATES,
Lisbon, May 8, 1865.

SIR: I have had the honor to receive your No. 169, with the proclamations referred to therein.

Attention is specially called to the one which very properly prescribes that the measures of hospitality which foreign nations may extend to national ships of the United States shall be reciprocated by the United States to the ships-of-war of those nations.

No exception can be taken to a rule so just in itself, and so necessary to the dignity and position of our government before the world.

I am proud to say that no diplomatic action will be needed here in regard to this particular instruction. Portugal never declared neutrality during the war now happily terminated, and never conceded belligerent rights to communities which revolted against the constituted authority in the United States. Our ships-of-war have used these ports with the same freedom and entire absence of restriction as their own, and have been welcomed with a generous and friendly hospitality throughout.

Efforts were made at the outset of our sad struggle to induce his Majesty's government to adopt the policy and the proclamations of the principal powers, but it declined to go beyond the declaration of the treaty of Paris, of 1856, prohibiting the equipment of privateers, and the sale of prizes made by such vessels. And the royal proclamation to that effect was made at my own instance, and with an object which has served an important purpose.

I have the honor to be, sir, your obedient servant,

JAMES E. HARVEY.

Hon. WILLIAM H. SEWARD,
Secretary of State.

Mr. Harvey to Mr. Seward.

No. 338.] LEGATION OF THE UNITED STATES,
Lisbon, May 11, 1865.

SIR: The papers herewith enclosed will bring to your view the proceedings of the Cortes in regard to the recent melancholy event which has so much shocked the civilized world.

The note of the minister of foreign affairs only communicates the action of the chamber of deputies, because the motion in that body specially required it to be done, while that in the peers did not do so. I have thought it best, however, to send a translated copy of the full proceedings in both branches of the

Cortes, in order that their spirit may be the better appreciated. The tardy publication of the official journal does not permit at this time (on the eve of the departure of the mails) such a translation as I desired to furnish, but the general tone of the speeches is fairly reported. That of Mr. Rebello da Silva, in the peers, was remarkably eloquent and touching, and has received very imperfect justice at the hands of the translator. In the pressure of the moment it has been found impracticable to translate one of the addresses, which is communicated in the original.

It seemed to me only becoming to make an acknowledgment of the note of the chamber of deputies, and I beg to enclose a copy of my letter to that effect.

Every manifestation of respect to the memory of the late President Lincoln which could be expected or desired has been made by this government and people, both in an official and in a private manner. His Majesty the King, immediately upon being informed of the sad event, sent me the kindest words of sympathy and regret. Every member of the government called in person to express similar sentiments, and when our ships-of-war, the Niagara and Kearsarge, exhibited the customary signs of mourning on Sunday, Monday, and Tuesday last, the Portuguese national ships not only united in a similar observance, but Castle Belem also responded to all the salutes by order of the authorities, and without any notice or request on our part.

While upon this subject, I may be permitted to remark, as quite worthy of notice, that the popular legislative bodies of the different states of Europe have taken the initiative in nearly all the expressions of public sympathy. Such a tribute was not only fitting in itself towards our lamented President, but the fact is significant of a mighty change and progress in ideas and usages, as it is of a coming time in the near future when the peoples of Europe will claim the right to assert those great principles of political and personal liberty which Abraham Lincoln illustrated so well, and for which he may be said to have even made a sacrifice of his life.

I have the honor to be, sir, your obedient servant,

JAMES E. HARVEY.

Hon. WILLIAM H. SEWARD,
Secretary of State.

HOUSE OF PEERS,

Session of May 5, 1865.

Mr. REBELLO DA SILVA. Mr. Speaker, I desire to bring forward some considerations in an affair which I deem of importance; my object is to present my reasons for the motion which I shall presently introduce.

The house is aware, by official documents published in the foreign papers, that a criminal event has plunged in grief and mourning a great nation on the other side of the Atlantic—the powerful republic of the United States.

The COUNT D'AVILA. I desire to speak on this incident on the part of the government.

Mr. REBELLO DA SILVA. President Abraham Lincoln has been assassinated in the theatre, almost in the very arms of his wife!

The perpetration of this cruel act has caused profound pain in America and in every court of Europe. Every cabinet and every parliament have given vent to their deep feelings on such a painful event. It behooves all civilized societies, it becomes almost the duty of all constituted political bodies, to cause their manifestations to be accompanied by the sincere expression of horror and profound pain with which they deplore acts so grave and criminal. [Hear, hear.]

It very often happens, apparently through fatality or through the sublime disposition or unfathomable mysteries of Providence, which is the most Christian historic law, that in the life of nations as in that of individuals, after attaining the highest position; after consummating the most eventful destiny, and even having reached the very highest steps in the scale of human greatness, when the road appears suddenly easy and smooth, when all clouds disappear from the horizon and the brightest light enlivens every object around, it is then that an invisible hand raises itself up from darkness, that an occult and inexorable force arms itself in silence, and brandishing the poignard of a Brutus, pointing the cannon of a Wellington, or presenting the poisoned cup of the Asiatic kings, dashes down from the heights the triumphant and laurelled victor, and casts him at the foot of Pompey's statue like Cæsar, at the feet of exhausted fortune like Napoleon, at the feet of the Roman colossus like Hannibal.

The mission of all great men, of all heroes, who are looked upon almost as demigods, while receiving, as they do, from above, that short-lived omnipotence which revolutionizes society and transforms nations, passes away like the tempest's blast in its fiery car, and moments afterwards dashes itself against the eternal barriers of impossibility, those barriers which none can go beyond, and where all the pride of their ephemeral power is humbled and reduced to dust. God alone is immutable and great.

Death strikes the blow, or ruin attains them in the height of their power, as an evidence to all princes, conquerors, and nations, that their hour is but one, and short; that their work becomes weak, as all human work, from the moment that the luminous column which guided them is extinguished and darkness overtakes them on their way; the new road which they have carved out, and whereby they expected to proceed undaunted and secure, have turned into abysses where they have fallen and perished from the moment that the Most High numbered the days of their empire and their ambition. [Hear, hear.]

This has been witnessed as a terrible example, as an admirable lesson, in the catastrophes which have overtaken the most conspicuous men in history; and thus do we this day see the recent pages of the annals of the powerful republic of the United States spotted with the illustrious blood of one of its most remarkable citizens.

At the close of the first four years of a government, during which war became his motto, the President of the republic is suddenly struck down at the moment of his triumph, and his now inanimate and paralyzed hands let fall those reins of administration which the force and energy of his will, the co-operation of his countrymen, the prestige and sublimity of the grand idea which he personified and defended, have immortalized with the acclamations of millions of arms on the battle-fields and of voices in the popular elections. Re-elected, carried a second time on the popular bucklers to thes upreme administration of affairs at the moment when the ardor of a civil contest was subsiding, when the union of that immense dilacerated body seemed to foreshadow the healing up of the wounds whence had gushed forth for so many months and in such torrents the generous blood of the free, almost in the arms of victory, in the midst of that populace who loved him most, in the centre of his popular court, he suddenly meets with death, and the bullet of an obscure fanatic closes and seals up the golden volume of his destiny at the very hour when success promised a new life and was welcoming peace with joyful acclamations.

This is no king who disappears in the darkness of the tomb, burying with himself, like unto Henry the IVth, the realization of great hopes. He is the chief of a glorious people, leaving a successor in every citizen who shared his ideas and who sympathized with his noble and well-founded aspirations. It is not a purple-covered throne which has been covered with crape; it is the heart of a great empire which has been cast into mourning. That cause of which he was the strenuous champion has not ceased to exist, but all weep at his loss, in horror at the crime and the occasion, and for the expectations which his pure and generous intentions had inspired.

Lincoln, a martyr to the prolific principle which he represented in power and in strife, now belongs to history and to posterity. Like unto the name of Washington, whose example and principles he followed, his own name shall be allied with the memorable era to which he belonged and which he appreciated.

As the champion of freedom in America, Lincoln drew without hesitation the sword of the republic, and with the point thereof erased from the code of a free people that anti-social stigma, that blasphemy against human nature, the sad, shameful, infamous codicil of antiquated societies, the dark and repugnant abuse of slavery, which Jesus Christ was the first to condemn from the height of the cross when he proclaimed the equality of men before God, and which nineteen centuries of a civilization enlightened by the Gospel has proscribed and condemned as the opprobrium of these our present times. [Hear, hear.]

At the moment that he cast away the chains of an unfortunate race of men, and when he contemplated millions of future citizens in the millions of emancipated men; at the very moment that the echo of Grant's victorious cannon proclaimed the emancipation of the soul, of conscience, and of labor; when the lash was about to drop from the hand of the task-master; when the former hut of the slave was about to be converted into a home; at the moment that the stars of the Union, bright and resplendent with the gladdening light of liberty, waved triumphant over the fallen ramparts of Petersburg and Richmond, it is then that the grave opens its jaws, and the strong and the powerful falls to rise no more. In the midst of triumphs and acclamations a spectre appeared unto him, and, like that of Cæsar in the ides of March, said, Thou hast lived!

Far be it from me to enter into the appreciation of the civil questions which have disturbed the brotherhood of the same family in America; I am neither their judge nor their censor. I bow down to a principle, that of liberty, whenever I see it respected and upheld; but at the same time I have learned to love and cherish another, not less sacred and glorious, the principle of independence. May the force of progress in our days bind again those who have been separated by differences of opinion, and may it reconcile the ideas which exist in the heart, the aspirations, and in the desire of all generous-minded men.

In this warfare, the proportions of which have exceeded everything that has ever been seen or heard of in Europe, the vanquished of to-day are worthy of the great race from which they descend. Grant and Lee are two giants, whom history will in future respect in an inseparable manner. But the hour of peace was perhaps about to strike, and Lincoln desired it as the reward of his pains, as the great result of summary sacrifices. After the exhibition of strength comes toleration; after the bloody fury of battle comes the fraternal embrace of citizens.

Such were his manifested intentions—these were the last and noble wishes which he had formed. And at this very instant, perhaps the only one in which a noble mind is so powerful in doing good, and when the soul rises above whole legions as a pacificator, that the hand of the assassin rises up in treachery and cuts off such mighty and noble purposes. [Hear! Hear!]

Were not the American nation a people grown old in the painful strifes and experiences of government, who is there that could foresee the fatal consequences of this sudden blow?

Who knows but that, in such a case, the fiery torch of civil war, in all its horrible pomp and terror, would spread itself to the furthermost States of the federation? But happily no such calamity is to be apprehended. At the time that the press and public opinion have, with justice and severity, condemned this event, and given expression to their horror at the fatal crime, sentiments and feelings which are common to the whole of Europe, they pay homage to the ideas of peace and conciliation just as if the great man who first invoked them had not disappeared from the great scene of the world. And I purposely repeat the expression *great man*, because, in truth, great is that man who, confiding alone in his own merits, rises from profound obscurity to the greatest heights, like Napoleon, like Washington, like Lincoln. Who elevate themselves to the heights of power and of greatness, not in virtue of the chances of birth or of a noble descent, but by the prestige of his own actions, by that nobility which begins and ends in themselves, and which is solely the work of their own hands. [Cheers; hear, hear.]

The man who makes himself great and famous by his own acts and by his own genius is more to be envied than he who was born among inherited escutcheons of nobility.

Lincoln belongs to that privileged race, to that aristocracy. In infancy his energetic soul was tempered in poverty; in youth, labor inspired him with the love of liberty and respect for the rights of men. Up to the age of 22, educated in adversity, with his hands hardened by honorable labor, while resting from the fatigues of daily toil, drinking in from the inspired pages of the Bible the lessons of the Gospel, and in the ephemeral leaves of the public journals which the morning brings forth and the evening disperses, the first rudiments of that instruction which is subsequently ripened by solitary meditation. Light gradually and gently illuminated that soul. The wings with which it took its flight then expanded and strengthened, the chrysalis felt one bright day the rays of the sun which called it into life, it broke through its bonds, and rose up from its humble condition to those luminous spheres where a higher destiny was awaiting its approach. The farmer, the laborer, the shepherd, like Cincinnatus, abandoned his plough half buried in the earth, and as a legislator in his native State, and subsequently in the national Congress, he prepared in the public tribune to become one day the popular chief of many millions of people, the defender of the whole principle which Wilberforce inaugurated. What strifes, what agitated scenes, what a series of herculean works and incalculable sacrifices are involved and represented by their glorious results in these four years of warfare and government!

Armies in the field, such as ancient history speaks not of; immense battles, during which the sun rises and sets two and three times before victory declares itself on either side. Heavy marches, where thousands of victims, whole legions, cover with their dead every foot of the conquered ground. Invasions, the daring and dangers whereof far surpass the records of Attila and the Huns!

What awful obsequies for the scourge of slavery! What a terrible and salutary lesson has this people, still rich and vigorous in youth, given to the timid scruples of ancient Europe, now the battle-field of principles likewise sacred!

These were the beacons, the land-marks, which guided his grand career. If the sword was the instrument in his hands, yet liberty, inspiration, and the courage, which were the outgrowth of his principles, were equally effective. Trampling down the thorns in his path, guiding his steps amidst the tears and the blood of so many holocausts, he still lived to see the promised land. He was not permitted to plant on that soil the auspicious olive branch of peace and concord. When he was about to reunite the loosened bond of the Union, when he was about to infuse into the body of his country the vivifying spirit of free institutions, after collecting and reuniting its dispersed and bloody members; when the standard of the republic, its funeral dirges ended, its agonies of pride and defeat silenced and subsided, was about to rise again, and to spread its glorious folds over a reconciled people, purified and cleansed from the stain of slavery, the great athlete tripped in the ring and fell, thus proving that, after all, he was but mortal. [Hear, hear. Applause.]

I think this brief and hurried sketch is quite sufficient for the occasion. The chamber being, by its nature, by duty, and by orgnizaton, not only the conservator, but the faithful warden of traditions and principles, will not hesitate to take part in the demonstration which the elective chamber has already adopted, thus following the example of all the enlightened parliaments of Europe. Silence, in the presence of such criminal attempts, can only be maintained by such senates as are dumb and void of elevated sentiments and aspirations. [Hear, hear.]

By voting the present motion the chamber of peers takes a part in the feelings of pain now experienced by all civilized nations. The crime which has closed the career of Lincoln—a martyr to the noble principles of which this epoch has reason to be proud—is almost, is essentially, a regicide, and a monarchical country cannot but abhor and condemn it. The descendants of those men who were the first in the 16th century to reveal to Europe the new road which, across stormy and unknown seas, opened the gates of the eastern world, must not be the last to bow down before the grave of a great citizen and a great magistrate, who himself piloted his people through terrible tempests, and succeeded in leading them in triumph over the fallen ramparts of slavery's stronghold. Let each people and each era have its task and its share of glory. Let each illustrious citizen have his crown of laurel, or his civic crown. [Hear, hear. Applause.]

The MINISTER OF FOREIGN AFFAIRS, Count d'Avila. As a peer of the realm, he takes part in this noble manifestation. As minister of the crown he had already done as much, in his own name at first, when mere rumors were circulated that the crime had been committed; and again, after having received the order of his Majesty, as soon as no doubt, unfortunately, existed on the subject, in order to show what were the sentiments of the Portuguese government.

Mr. REBELLO DA SILVA. Mr. Speaker, I am rejoiced to hear the words of the minister of finance and of foreign affairs. They give evidence that the government has acted in this affair with that propriety and promptitude which its duty indicated, and which are inspired by noble feelings. I shall now lay on the table my motion of order, as follows:

"The chamber of peers deplores, with the most sincere feelings of pain, the criminal act which has just thrown into mourning the sons of a great nation, by the death of the President of the United States of America, Mr. Lincoln, who died a martyr to his duty."

L. A. REBELLO DA SILVA, the speaker. The chamber has heard the reading of this motion. I do not consider it necessary to have it again read from the table, as it would not have a better effect than when read by its author. [Hear, hear.]

Mr. REBELLO DA SILVA. The Count d'Avila has likewise signed the motion.

The SPEAKER. All the worthy peers who approve of the motion will be pleased to indicate as much.

It was unanimously approved.

The COUNT D'AVILA. I request that it be recorded in the minutes that the voting was unanimous. [Hear, hear.]

[Translation.]

HOUSE OF DEPUTIES,
Session of May 3, 1865.

The PRESIDENT. The proposal just placed on the table by the deputy, Mr. Medeiros, will now be read; it is as follows:

Proposal: I move that the house do insert in its minutes a significant expression of the profound emotion with which it received the news of the barbarous assassination committed on the person of Mr. Lincoln, the President of the United States of America, and that the worthy representative of that republic at this court be respectfully informed of the deliberation of the house on this subject.

House of sessions, May 3, 1865. The deputy Henrique Medeiros de Paula Medeiros.

The minister of public works, (Mr. CARLOS BENTO.) I do not know whether the motion is admitted, but it appears to me that from its very nature, it is of an urgent and exceptional character. On my part I do not hesitate, in the name of the government, in sharing such a noble and feeling manifestation as the one contained in the proposal.

We are all unanimous, in common with the civilized nations of Europe, in condemning an act which has excited the indignation of the whole people, without respect to party distinctions. All and every individual reprobates the fatal deed which has taken place in the United States.

I willingly take part in the expression of the vote contained in the proposal. I feel convinced that the Portuguese parliament will not hesitate one moment in adopting the manifestation of such becoming sentiments. [Hear, hear.]

Mr. SANT'ANNA E VASCONCELLOS. I thank the illustrious deputy, the author of the motion, for having brought it forward, and I do so from my whole heart.

Mr. PAULA MEDEIROS. I thank the noble deputy for his expressions.

Mr. SANT'ANNA E VASCONCELLOS. If the disastrous war which has existed in America during the last three or four years has a justification, it is to be found in the one grand and noble motive which has dominated throughout the—abolition of slavery. The man who has just fallen a victim to the assassination which we all deplore maintained that noble and sub lime idea. In view of the fact which is in itself so much to be deplored and in presence o the great and persistent idea of that great citizen, we cannot refrain from being unanimous in voting the motion.

The MINISTER OF PUBLIC WORKS. I spoke in the name of the government, and I can assure the house that the government has already tendered those manifestations which its duty and its feelings clearly indicated. I congratulate myself on the fact that the parliament was allowed the opportunity, by a spontaneous initiative, of manifesting its sentiments.

In putting the motion to the vote it was carried unanimously.

I have the honor of handing you copies, inclosed, of a communication addressed to me by the secretary of the chamber of deputies, under yesterday's date, and of the motion referred to in said communication, which was presented in the session of the 3d instant and voted unanimously; manifesting the sentiments of said chamber in regard to the horrible deed committed on the person of Mr. Abraham Lincoln, late President of the United States of America.

While requesting you to bring these documents before your government, it is my duty to inform you that his Majesty's government, immediately that it was informed of an event which has saddened a nation whose destinies had been confided to such an illustrious magistrate, issued the needful instructions to his Majesty's minister in the United States, with a view to express to the American government the profound regret with which his Majesty the King and his government received the news of that event.

I avail of this opportunity to reiterate the assurances of my most distinguished consideration.

CONDE D'AVILA.

DEPARTMENT OF STATE FOR FOREIGN AFFAIRS, *May* 6, 1865.

LEGATION OF THE UNITED STATES,
Lisbon, May 10, 1865.

I have received, with deep emotion, the expression of sympathy and condolence uttered by the honorable chamber of deputies in a manner so touching and marked, in reference to the deplorable event which now saddens the hearts of the American people.

In the very hour when peace had spread her benignant wings over a distracted country, he, who by his virtues, gentleness, and public worth had inspired everywhere a generous confidence, was struck down by the criminal hand of passionate resentment.

The martyrdom with which an eventful career was crowned becomes the legacy not only of a nation but of humanity; for his life was a sacrifice on the altar of duty.

A great and a good man has fallen, but the principles which he represented and defended so uprightly and well survive to honor his memory, and will continue to live and be cherished wherever constitutional government, liberty, and justice are respected.

The people of the United States, who had learned to value the good will and honorable conduct of Portugal during a period of strife now happily terminated, will welcome her voice of sympathy in this hour of universal grief as a token of friendship which should bind them more closely together.

It will be my duty to communicate immediately to the government of the United States the sentiments expressed by the honorable chamber of deputies, but I cannot permit this occasion to pass without conveying, on behalf of the constituted authorities and for myself individually, a united appreciation of this high mark of consideration and respect.

JAMES E. HARVEY.

Mr. Harvey to Mr. Hunter.

No. 339.] LEGATION OF THE UNITED STATES,
Lisbon, May 13, 1865.

SIR: A Russian squadron of four ships, bearing the remains of the late Duc Héritier, entered the Tagus on the morning of the 10th instant. The United States ships Niagara and Kearsarge were then in port. The Russian minister, Mr. de Kondriaffsky, had previously informed me of the intention of the squadron to come in, and of the ceremonies proposed by the Portuguese authorities when it should appear and during its stay here. The Niagara had just returned from a cruise to Madeira, and I at once addressed a note to Commander Craven, requesting him to consult and co-operate with the Portuguese authorities, and to superadd to their action any peculiar tribute of respect permitted by the naval service of the United States on such occasions.

Commodore Craven called upon me soon afterwards to say, that as he was going to Antwerp, he proposed to offer his ship as an escort to the Russian squadron. The suggestion struck me as a very proper and becoming expression of our sympathy, and at the same time as a manifestation of friendship towards a great power which, from first to last, had borne itself kindly and considerately to the United States during our whole struggle.

I fully concurred, therefore, in the view of Commodore Craven, and made the intention known to the Russian minister, in order that he might accept or decline the offer, according to the wishes of his government. He at once expressed the greatest satisfaction and gratitude for the courtesy, and made the purpose known to the Emperor, now at Darmstadt. I received a formal visit from him yesterday, being instructed, as he said, by the Emperor to express his acknowledgments for this act of considerate and welcome attention.

It occurred to me as proper for the Kearsarge to accompany the said cortege a certain distance to sea; first to render our respect the more imposing, and next in order that the progress of the voyage up to a particular point might be reported to the imperial court.

I feel quite confident that no manifestation of good feeling or of sympathy on this melancholy occasion could be made here which would not be acceptable to the President and the department, and therefore I have had no hesitation whatever in obeying my own impulses, because they responded, as I believe, to the wishes and sentiments of our people.

And if there had been no other reason to guide me, the expression and conduct of the Russian government at the great affliction which has recently been deplored by our people, and the language of friendly attachment addressed to the United States by the official press at Saint Petersburg, in the presence of the world, would have been sufficient to have determined any little responsibility on my part, if a doubt as to the plain course of duty had ever crossed my mind.

The Russian squadron is now about leaving the Tagus, under the convoy of the Niagara and Kearsarge, her Majesty's ship Defence, detailed from the fleet recently here to escort the squadron to Plymouth, and the Portuguese ship Sagree, which will attend it ceremoniously a short distance.

I have the honor to be, sir, your obedient servant,

JAMES E. HARVEY.

Hon. WILLIAM HUNTER,
Acting Secretary of State.

Mr. Harvey to Mr. Hunter.

No. 340.] LEGATION OF THE UNITED STATES,
Lisbon, May 15, 1865.

SIR: A royal decree was communicated to the Chamber of Deputies to-day, dissolving the Cortes and convoking the chambers, after the elections, for the 30th of July.

The new ministry found it wholly impracticable to carry on the government with a majority in the popular assembly, which had been instrumental in causing the abandonment of power by its own friends.

Parties are now in a state of fusion, and the chiefs of opposing divisions have banded together in the hope of carrying into office a coalition which contains the seeds of its own dissolution, even in the event of a temporary triumph.

Both sides profess confidence in their ability to secure a majority in the Chamber of Deputies, but the actual ministry has an advantage in the organized machinery of official patronage which quite counterbalances if it does not exceed the combination of strange elements which form the temporary opposition.

The ministry of the Marquis de sa da Bandeira attracts the sympathy of the substantial interests of the country, and deservedly enjoys the confidence and respect of the representatives of foreign governments.

I have the honor to be, sir, your obedient servant,

JAMES E. HARVEY.

Hon. WILLIAM HUNTER,
Acting Secretary of State.

Mr. Harvey to Mr. Hunter

No. 341.] LEGATION OF THE UNITED STATES,
Lisbon, May 16, 1865.

SIR: The note from the Count d'Avila which accompanies this despatch communicates officially the proceedings of the Chamber of Peers in reference to the assassination of the lamented President Lincoln. It will be observed that the count was associated in the motion which was passed unanimously in that body.

The eloquent speech of the distinguished orator Rebello da Silva—the author of the proposition—was included in the note of the minister of foreign affairs, having been recorded as a part of the minutes of the chamber; but I do not now enclose it, as my No. 338 has already put the department in possession of a copy published in the official paper.

I have the honor to be, sir, your obedient servant,

JAMES E. HARVEY.

Hon. WILLIAM HUNTER,
Acting Secretary of State.

Count d'Avila to Mr. Harvey.

DEPARTMENT OF STATE FOR FOREIGN AFFAIRS,
May 12, 1865.

In addition to my note dated 6th instant, I have the honor to hand you enclosed a copy of the communication which, under date of 9th, was sent to me by the vice-president of the chamber of peers of the realm as well as of the document, a copy of which accompanied it, containing the motion made in the session of the 5th instant by the worthy peer Luiz Augusto Rebello da Silva, a motion in which I took part as a peer of the realm, and which was carried unanimously, to the effect of having it recorded in the minutes how deep was the pain experienced at the news of the horrible crime perpetrated on the person of Mr. Lincoln, President of the United States.

In the aforesaid document you will find that part of the minutes which refer to the subject, and I have to request that you will be pleased to make known to your government the manifestations of said chamber on an event which all so deeply deplore.

I avail of this opportunity to renew the assurances of my most distinguished consideration.

COUNT D'AVILA.

JAMES E. HARVEY, Esq., *&c., &c., &c.*

CHAMBER OF WORTHY PEERS OF THE REALM.

MOST EXCELLENT SIR: The chamber of peers of the realm having unanimously resolved, in its session of 5th instant, and on motion of the worthy peer Luiz Augusto Rebello da Silva, in which the worthy peer Count d'Avila took part, to record in its minutes the expression of great pain which the chamber felt at the news of the horrible crime committed in the United States of America on the person of Mr. Lincoln, their illustrious President, I have now the honor of handing your excellency the enclosed copy containing the aforesaid motion and that part of the minutes which relates to the subject, in order that your excellency may, through such channel as may be deemed most appropriate, cause the same to be made known to the government of the United States.

May God preserve your excellency. Palace of the Cortes, May 9, 1865.

COUNT DE CASTRO, *Vice-President.*

His Excellency the COUNT D'AVILA,
Minister and Secretary of State for Foreign Affairs.

EMILIO ACHILLES MONTEVERDE.
DEPARTMENT OF STATE FOR FOREIGN AFFAIRS, *May* 12, 1865.

Mr. Harvey to Mr. Hunter.

No. 342] LEGATION OF THE UNITED STATES,
Lisbon, May 18, 1865.

SIR: I have the honor to communicate herewith the copy of a note from the Count d'Avila, with the proceedings of the chamber of deputies, in regard to the reply which I addressed to that distinguished body on the 10th instant in answer to their expression of sympathy on the occasion of President Lincoln's death.

I have the honor to be, sir, your obedient servant,

JAMES E. HARVEY.

Hon. WILLIAM HUNTER,
Acting Secretary of State.

DEPARTMENT OF STATE FOR FOREIGN AFFAIRS,
May 16, 1865.

I have the honor of handing you for your information the enclosed copy of a despatch which the secretary of the chamber of deputies, now dissolved, addressed to me under date of 13th instant, and likewise of the motion which accompanied the same, made by one of its members, and unanimously voted, on the occasion of communicating to the said chamber the note which you addressed to the house on the 10th instant.

I avail of this opportunity to renew the assurances of my most distinguished consideration.

COUNT D'AVILA.

JAMES E. HARVEY, Esq., *&c., &c., &c.*

BUREAU OF THE SECRETARY OF THE CHAMBER OF DEPUTIES.

MOST EXCELLENT SIR: I have the honor of transmitting to your excellency, for your information, the enclosed copy of the motion presented in this chamber by one of its members, and voted unanimously on the occasion of communicating to the house the note from the legation of the United States of America at this court, in reply to the manifestation of feeling and regret addressed to said legation on the atrocious assassination of the President of that republic.

May God preserve your excellency. Palace of the Cortes, May the 13th, 1865.

JOAQUIN XAVIER PINTO DA SILVA,
Deputy and Secretary.

His Excellency the MINISTER AND SECRETARY OF STATE
for Foreign Affairs.

True copy: EMILIO ACHILLES MONTEVERDE.
DEPARTMENT OF STATE FOR FOREIGN AFFAIRS, *May* 16, 1865.

I move that it be recorded in the minutes that the chamber has heard with every demonstration of true respect and profound sympathy the note which has just been read at the table, and addressed to the house by the minister resident of the United States of America at this court.

I further move that the government be informed of this deliberation, in order to communicate the same to the distinguished minister, Jacintho Augusto de Sant'Anna e Vasconcellos.

Correct copy: POSIDONIO A. P. PICALUGA.
BUREAU OF THE SECRETARY OF THE CHAMBER OF DEPUTIES, *May* 13, 1865.

True copy: EMILIO ACHILLES MONTEVERDE.
DEPARTMENT OF STATE FOR FOREIGN AFFAIRS, *May* 16, 1865.

Mr. Harvey to Mr. Hunter.

No. 344.] LEGATION OF THE UNITED STATES,
Lisbon, June 5, 1865.

SIR: The Russian minister, Mr. de Kondriaffsky, called upon me this morning and brought with him the last number of the "Journal de Saint Petersbourg," (the official paper,) containing an article describing the manner in which the Russian squadron, bearing the remains of the lamented archduke, had been received in the port of Lisbon, and the part taken by this legation and our ships-of-war.

As the semi-official note which I addressed to the minister on that occasion had also been published, he desired to explain to me that he had transmitted it at the time to the Emperor, who, being pleased with the sentiments therein expressed, had personally directed the note to be embodied in the official document of the proceedings.

This is all the information I have regarding the publication in question, and in case it should happen to attract your attention, I have thought it proper to make this statement, in order to correct any possible misapprehension.

I permit myself to believe that the sentiments of that hasty but sincere note express the real feelings of our government and people towards a country which never wavered in friendship or fidelity when those terms had a practical and valuable signification.

I have the honor to be, sir, your obedient servant,

JAMES E. HARVEY.

Hon. WILLIAM HUNTER,
Acting Secretary of State.

Mr. Seward to Mr. Harvey.

No. 172.] DEPARTMENT OF STATE,
Washington, June 13, 1865.

SIR: Your several despatches from No. 330, dated April 6, to No. 339, of the 13th of May, inclusive, (with the exception of No. 332,) have been received, and have been read with great interest. Your proceedings as therein set forth are approved.

I am, sir, your obedient servant,

WILLIAM H. SEWARD.

JAMES E. HARVEY, Esq., *&c., &c., Lisbon.*

Mr. Harvey to Mr. Seward.

No. 346.] LEGATION OF THE UNITED STATES,
Lisbon, June 16, 1865.

SIR: The accompanying address was delivered to me a few days ago by a special committee delegated by an association for the improvement of the working classes of Lisbon. I replied verbally at the time, promising a more formal acknowledgment afterwards, which is now also enclosed.

The presentation of this address was delayed by the illness of the president of the society.

I have the honor to be, sir, your obedient servant,

JAMES E. HARVEY.

Hon. WILLIAM H. SEWARD,
Secretary of State.

(For address see Appendix, separate volume.)

LEGATION OF THE UNITED STATES,
Lisbon, June 16, 1865.

GENTLEMEN: The address which you did me the honor to deliver personally, in behalf of the "Centro Promotor dos methoramentos das classes laboriosas de Lisboa," expressive of sympathy and regret on the occasion of the death of President Lincoln, will be immediately communicated to my government, and will be received as an utterance at once worthy in itself, and acceptable from its touching and appropriate sentiments.

Among the many sympathetic expressions which this sad occasion has called forth, none have been more welcome than the voices of associations like yours, whose aim is to elevate and dignify man by enlarging his intelligence and usefulness, and whose ambition is thus to promote the prosperity and happiness of the people at large.

However much the political institutions of the New and Old World may differ, these are objects upon which all men may agree, since they are the necessary foundations of stable and successful government. Enlightened progress marches forward in proportion as popular education is diffused, and it stops and stagnates where free instruction is denied. The civilization of a state can only be measured by the intelligence of its people.

Abraham Lincoln was a striking illustration of this idea, and his career furnishes an example and an honorable incentive which will endure in all history. Humble in origin, unfavored in fortune, self-reliant, and upright, he rose from obscure beginnings to a position which attracted the gaze of the world. How bravely and well he bore himself; how unselfish and noble was his conduct; how fervent and patriotic were his aspirations; how gentle and guileless was his heart; how simple and yet how grand was his nature, are qualities and virtues for the future historian to describe. It is our pride to point to him as a type of American civilization.

None sympathize more strongly than he with every effort to improve the condition of labor; to educate its children, and to raise it up to a higher dignity. His hands had been hardened by honest toil, and his youth had been disciplined by stern necessity. Therefore his sympathies were ever earnest and practical.

Hence it is fitting that associations with kindred aims to those which illustrated the life of our lamented President should linger over and leave offerings upon his grave, and that we, who in foreign lands witness these voluntary tributes, should feel our hearts swell with mingled emotions of gratitude and manly pride.

I am, with high respect,

JAMES E. HARVEY.

Messrs. FRANCISCO VIEIRA DA SILVA,
President,
And MIGUEL JUSTINIANO CORREA EL SILVA,
ALFREDO AUGUSTO CORREA,
Secretaries.

Mr. Harvey to Mr. Seward.

No. 348.]

LEGATION OF THE UNITED STATES,
Lisbon, July 5, 1865.

SIR: I have the honor to acknowledge the receipt of your No. 172, together with various circulars recently issued relating to the public service, to which proper attention will be given.

There is no necessity for communicating with his Majesty's government in regard to the squadron under command of Rear-Admiral Goldsborough, as no concession of belligerent rights was ever made by Portugal, and no restriction of any kind was ever imposed upon our ships-of-war, during the existence of the civil strife now happily terminated. That squadron will be cordially welcomed here by the public authorities, whenever and under whatever circumstances it may appear.

I avail myself of this occasion to offer my sincerest felicitations upon your return to the department, and to express the hope that you may be spared, not only to consummate the great work of pacification, but to enjoy long and well the fruits of that noblest of victories.

I have the honor to be, sir, your obedient servant,

JAMES E. HARVEY.

Hon. WILLIAM H. SEWARD,
Secretary of State.

Mr. Seward to Mr. Harvey.

No. 176.] DEPARTMENT OF STATE,
Washington, July 24, 1865.

SIR: Your despatch of June 8, without number, and your two subsequent ones Nos. 346 and 347, dated the 16th and 18th of June, respectively, have been received. The address which accompanied your No. 346, and which was delivered to you by a special committee, delegated by an association for the improvement of the working classes of Lisbon, together with your interesting acknowledgment in reply, will be carefully preserved in the archives of the department.

I am, sir, your obedient servant,

WILLIAM H. SEWARD.

JAMES E. HARVEY, Esq., *&c., &c., Lisbon.*

Mr. Harvey to Mr. Seward.

No. 353.] LEGATION OF THE UNITED STATES,
Lisbon, August 8, 1865.

SIR: Immediately upon the receipt of your despatch, enclosing the President's proclamation in regard to the harboring or giving hospitality to insurgent cruisers, I transmit a copy of the same with a note, of which a copy is herewith enclosed, to the minister of foreign affairs, stating at the same time that the proclamation of July 29, 1861, if properly enforced, would give the necessary protection in this respect.

Count d'Avila, in order, as he supposed, to comply fully with the wishes of our government, directed a new portaria or decree to be issued, enjoining the strict and continued execution of the proclamation, as will be seen by his note to me and its enclosure.

As the proclamation of 1861 did nothing more than reaffirm the adhesion of this government to that clause of the treaty of Paris of 1856, by which the arming and equipment of privateers and the sale of prizes made by them in Portuguese ports was prohibited, I have not thought it necessary to ask for its revocation, which I am sure would be at once granted, if desired. But if the department entertains any other view upon this subject, I will be most happy to carry out its instruction, or to adopt whatever policy may be considered as most wise and proper.

It may be observed in this connexion, that the proclamation of 1861 was issued at my own instance, and was suggested as a means of preventing a concession of belligerent rights, such as had been then just proclaimed by nearly all the maritime powers, and the example of which Portugal was then and afterwards hard pressed to follow. That proceeding kept the ports open and unrestricted to our ships-of-war, avoided any application of the 24-hours rule, and was materially serviceable in arresting the schemes of public enemies who expected to use the mid-ocean islands and the secluded harbors of the coast for hostile enterprises.

The government co-operated to the extent of its ability, and with sincere good-will, in efforts to stop all abuses of hospitality, and often seconded my endeavors when there were no United States ships-of-war at hand, by despatching their own vessels to exposed points in order to protect our commerce and to prevent intended depredations.

Considering the relation of this country to other powers, and its peculiar circumstances, it is barely justice to say, that the conduct of Portugal towards the United States, during the whole period of the late civil strife, was exceptionally friendly and stands out in marked contrast to that of various states, which seem to claim and receive credit for rescinding concessions, that largely contributed to the moral and material support of the rebellion during its existence. And this is the more proper to be said, since there appears to be a disposition to depreciate and disparage that conduct by those who are either ignorant of or indifferent to the facts.

I have the honor to be, sir, your obedient servant,

JAMES E. HARVEY.

Hon. WILLIAM H. SEWARD,
Secretary of State.

Mr. Harvey to Count de Avila.

LEGATION OF THE UNITED STATES,
Lisbon, June 8, 1865.

SIR: I am directed to communicate to his Most Faithful Majesty's government the enclosed copy of a proclamation by the President of the United States, in regard to the harboring or giving of hospitality to insurgent cruisers which have heretofore depredated and still threaten to commit further depredations upon the commerce of the United States.

The proclamation of his Majesty, dated 29th of July, 1861, if properly enforced, would exclude all such vessels from Portugese ports, and it is hoped that the necessary measures will be adopted to give it full vigor in this kingdom and all its possessions. I avail myself of this opportunity to renew the assurances of my most distinguished consideration.

JAMES E. HARVEY.

His Excellency the COUNT D'AVILA,
Minister and Secretary of State for Foreign Affairs.

Count d'Avila to Mr. Harvey.

[Translation.]

DEPARTMENT OF STATE FOR FOREIGN AFFAIRS,
August 5, 1865.

I acknowledge the receipt of the note which you were pleased to address me under date of the 8th of June last, transmitting, by order of your government, a proclamation from the President of the United States, regarding hospitality and asylum granted to insurgent cruisers, which have caused and still cause so much damage to the commerce of the United States, and manifesting the desire that the decree of the 29th of July, 1861, be continued in full force in the ports of Portugal, as well as in those of the adjacent islands and colonial provinces.

Having taken due note of your said communication and of its enclosure, I have now the honor of informing you that through the marine and colonial department, under yesterday's date, was published, as you will please observe, by the enclosed number of the "Diario de Lisboa" of this day, a royal order to all the governors of the colonial provinces, to the major general of the navy, and to the navy inspectors, directing them to observe in the most stringent and punctual manner the execution of the aforesaid decree, whereby full satisfaction is thus given to your representation.

I avail myself of this opportunity to reiterate the assurances of my most distinguished consideration.

COUNT D'AVILA.

JAMES E. HARVEY, Esq., *&c., &c., &c.*

[Translation from the "Diario de Lisboa" of August 5, 1865.]

DEPARTMENT OF STATE FOR MARINE AND COLONIES,
Royal Palace, August 4, 1865.

It being possible that doubts may arise on the part of some of the authorities, whether the dispositions of the decree of the 29th of July, 1861, are to be considered in full force, in view of the present position of the United States of America, his Majesty the King, through the marine and colonial department, is pleased hereby to declare unto all the governors of the colonial provinces, to the major general of the navy, and to the inspectors of the navy, that the said decree of the 29th of July, 1861, continues to subsist in full force, and that it is their duty to execute the same in the most punctual and stringent manner.

SD. DA BANDEIRA.

Mr. Harvey to Mr. Seward.

No. 357.]

LEGATION OF THE UNITED STATES,
Lisbon, September 6, 1865.

SIR: The ministry of the Marquis de Sa da Bandeira resigned office on the 2d instant without any formal expression on the part of the Cortes. After a close contest for the choice of presidents of the chamber of deputies, in which the ministry barely succeeded, it became evident that a sure working majority could not be relied upon, and that to prolong the struggle would only involve additional embarrassments. Under these circumstances it was considered proper to withdraw from an irksome and thankless responsibility, and to leave to an opposition of mixed materials, which had united for a given purpose, the task of administering the government in the difficult circumstances which it had brought about.

His Majesty the King then summoned Mr. de Aguiar and the Duke de Loulé, the two chiefs of the coalesced opposition, and committed to them the duty of organizing a cabinet. After various conferences the interest represented by the Duke de Loulé confided the organization exclusively to Mr. de Aguiar, and he announced to the chambers yesterday the new ministry, composed as follows:

President of council and minister of interior, J A. de Aguiar; minister of foreign affairs and public works, Conde de Castro; minister of finance, Fontes Pereira de Mello; minister of justice and worship, Barjona de Freitas; minister of war, Conde Torres Novas; minister of marine and colonies, Visconde Praia Grande.

No confidence is entertained that this ministry will succeed any better than the one which it succeeded in ousting from office; and so far as respects the practical conduct of affairs, and especially the diplomatic relations, it is less acceptable that its predecessor.

It was announced in the chambers to-day that the Cortes would be adjourned till November. This recess may enable the new cabinet to recruit some additional strength, but there are certain elements of discord which cannot be easily reconciled, and chronic causes of complaint which a mere change of ministers will not remedy.

The public men, generally, have either neglected or failed in the courage to apply the stern treatment which the situation demands, or, in other words, to confront the necessity, as it presents itself to every careful observer.

In compliance with the terms of the constitutional charter the King has obtained leave from the Cortes to absent himself temporarily from the country, and intends to make a voyage with the Queen, soon after the opening of the exposition at Porto, on the 16th instant, to include visits to England, France, and Italy, travelling in comparative incognito under the title of Duke and Duchess of Braganza.

I have the honor to be, sir, your obedient servant,

JAMES E. HARVEY.

Hon. WILLIAM H. SEWARD, *Secretary of State.*

Mr. Harvey to Mr. Seward.

No. 358.]

LEGATION OF THE UNITED STATES,
Lisbon, September 10, 1865.

SIR: The accompanying communication is enclosed for information, as it is of interest to our vessels-of-war which may touch at the Cape de Verd islands for supplies of coal and water.

The present supplies of those necessities, for the national and commercial marine, are to be obtained at the Cape de Verd group of islands, only from the

British consul at St. Vincent, whose undisguised sympathy and partial proceedings during the existence of the late rebellion were frequently made the subject of complaint to this legation by those who had experienced exceptional treatment at his hands.

I have the honor to be, sir, your obedient servant,

JAMES E. HARVEY.

Hon. WILLIAM H. SEWARD,
Secretary of State.

Messrs. Burnay and Martins to Mr. Harvey.

LISBON, *August* 23, 1865.

SIR: We, the undersigned, ask permission to lay before your excellency certain facts concerning the establishment of a coal depot in the Cape de Verd islands, which facts we most respectfully pray your excellency to make known to the proper authorities in the United States.

For more than a year we have been engaged in the preliminary arrangements for establishing a coal depot at Porto Praya, a safe and excellent harbor of St. Jago, the capital island of the group known as the Cape de Verd. We obtained from the Portuguese government, in the month of June this year, in the name of one of the undersigned, the enclosed grant, from which your excellency will see that we have every desirable privilege as to wharves, coal, depot, &c. We ought here to remark, that though the present concession is in the name of but one of us, we are, nevertheless, partners in the enterprise, and the Portuguese government will before long cause the documents to be duly amended.

To one acquainted with the Cape de Verd islands it would be superfluous to say that St. Jago is the most fertile of the group. It contains about 25,000 inhabitants; abounds in vegetables, fruit, and excellent water, and is, moreover, the seat of government. Only once in the memory of man has St. Jago been visited by the dreadful dry season which has frequently been so disastrous to the other islands. * * * * *

We intend to keep a constant supply of the best American anthracite, Cardiff, and New Castle coal, at a uniform rate, not varying with the necessities of the steamers, or the whim of our agents or employés. By the end of January we shall be able to supply vessels-of-war and merchant steamers on the African coast, or those bound to the Cape of Good Hope, or from southern Europe to the Brazils. There is but one other coal depot in the Cape de Verd, at the barren island of St. Vincent. Till now this has been a monopoly, and sometimes a burdensome one, enabling the proprietors to take advantage of the necessities of steamers.

A few considerations will show the desirableness as well as superiority of a coal depot at Porto Praya:

1. The competition of the new will be a wholesome check on the old establishment.

2. The water at St. Vincent, according to the testimony of every captain, is of very inferior quality, having often proved unfit for cooking after it has been brought on board; so that men-of-war, after coaling at St. Vincent, have frequently gone to Porto Praya for water. On the other hand, the water at Porto Praya is of the best quality, and can be put alongside ship for $1 per hogshead, that of St. Vincent costing from $1 50 to $2 per hogshead.

3. St. Vincent is a barren, volcanic island, obtaining all its supplies either from Europe or from some other more favored islands. All stores, therefore, are high. Porto Praya, on the contrary, has had at all times (except the one dry season referred to) plenty of vegetables—as sweet potatoes, turnips, cabbage, squashes, pumpkins, &c.; and abundance of fruit—as oranges, lemons, bananas, &c.

4. Porto Praya is no further out of the way than St Vincent in the voyage from America to Africa or China.

5. At first, coals will be shipped with the same rapidity as at St. Vincent, but when our machinery (for which one of us will go to America, the other to England) is all in operation we shall be enabled to do it much quicker.

In conclusion, we may say that one of us (J. B. Burnay, from Belgium) is a merchant of long standing in this city, and your excellency can easily be satisfied of his capabilities and responsibility. The other partner (C. Martinez) is a naturalized American, of the State of Massachusetts, though a native of Porto Praya, and speaks English fluently. Mr. Martinez was for a long time on the coast of Africa, as agent of Charles Hoffman, esq., of Salem, Massachusetts, the well-known merchant in the hide trade; he was also American consul at Bissau, west coast of Africa.

Submitting this memorandum to your excellency's judgment, and hoping that your excellency may see no objection to laying these facts before the government of the United States, we remain your excellency's most obedient servants,

JEAN BTA. BURNAY.
CLARIMUNDO MARTINS.

His Excellency JAMES E. HARVEY, Esq.,
Minister of the U. S. of America at the court of his Majesty the King of Portugal.

Mr. Seward to Mr. Harvey.

No. 178.] DEPARTMENT OF STATE,
Washington, September 13, 1865.

SIR: Your despatch of August 8, No. 353, has been received. The course pursued by you on receiving my instruction enclosing the President's proclamation in regard to the harboring or giving of hospitality to insurgent cruisers and the proceedings of the Portuguese government in relation thereto were doubtless sufficient, and they are satisfactory. It is for the government of Portugal to decide whether it desires to be undemonstrative in the matter. We ask nothing.

I am, sir, your obedient servant,

WILLIAM H. SEWARD.

JAMES E. HARVEY, Esq., *&c., &c., Lisbon.*

Mr. Harvey to Mr. Seward.

No. 366.] LEGATION OF THE UNITED STATES,
Lisbon, November 21, 1865.

SIR: The correspondence communicated with this despatch will bring to your notice the material facts connected with a lamentable event which occurred here on the evening of the 24th October, resulting in the death of a Portuguese subject, named José Manuel.

As the consul is charged with questions relating to American seamen, the authorities necessarily addressed themselves to him in the preliminary proceedings, but he at once consulted with me as to the steps to be taken, and fully concurred in my earnest wish to have the criminal discovered and delivered up.

All efforts at detection have thus far failed, probably from the indisposition of the seamen to make any revelations on the subject which might criminate one of their own body; and the investigation before a mixed commission, informally organized for the purpose, while in some degree complicating one of the sailors, did not warrant his surrender, for the testimony only excited a misgiving, and was not of a nature to be regarded as judicially or even morally sufficient against a person of established good character.

Rear-Admiral Goldsborough, and indeed all the officers, manifested a proper and becoming disposition to advance the ends of justice, and vigilance will not be relaxed because the case has assumed its present form. His Majesty's government is fully satisfied that every desire is entertained, and that every energy has been exerted to trace the offender, as also that these endeavors will be continued so long as there is a reasonable possibility of discovery.

As the unfortunate victim of the affray was the sole support of aged and infirm parents, I suggested the propriety of a subscription for their immediate relief, which was handsomely responded to by the officers and crews of the ships now in port.

I have the honor to be, sir, your obedient servant,

JAMES E. HARVEY.

Hon. WILLIAM H. SEWARD,
Secretary of State.

Count de Castro to Mr. Harvey.

The civil governor of Lisbon, in a communication under date of October 26, made known to the department of interior that, on the 24th of said month, about 6 o'clock p. m., a boatman, named José Manuel, residing in Rua da Silva, No. 37, was mortally wounded, with two stabs, by one of the seamen belonging to one of the American men-of-war now in the Tagus, said occurrence having taken place on the Caes do Sodré, from whence the wounded man was carried to St. Joseph's hospital, where he died shortly after. The aforesaid magistrate further adds, that the aggressor managed to escape on board one of the boats without its having been possible to identify him.

In bringing this serious affair to your notice, his Majesty's government expresses the hope that you will not fail to adopt such necessary measures as may lead to the punishment of the criminal, assuring you that, as communicated to me by the minister of interior, the civil governor of Lisbon has caused to be drawn out the requisite form of declaration, with all the attending circumstances and investigations regarding the crime and its perpetrator, in order that proper proceedings may be instituted, and that communication has been made to the United States consul of all that has taken place, at the same time requesting him to have the criminal given up.

I renew on this occasion the assurance of my most distinguished consideration.

CONDE DE CASTRO.

DEPARTMENT OF STATE FOR FOREIGN AFFAIRS, *November* 7, 1865.

Mr. Harvey to Count de Castro.

LEGATION OF THE UNITED STATES,
Lisbon, November 14, 1865.

SIR: I have the honor to acknowledge the receipt of your note of the 7th instant, which was only delivered at this legation at 6 o'clock last evening, six days after its date.

The general facts relating to the unfortunate event, to which your excellency invites attention, had already been brought to my notice by the consul of the United States, and the measures taken by him and by the officers of the United States ships-of-war in port, for the purpose of investigating the alleged crime and tracing out the criminal, were adopted with my knowledge, privity, and co-operation.

It appears from the inquiries made through this legation, that a seaman belonging to th United States transport ship Guard was badly maltreated by some of the boatmen who pursued their calling at the Caes do Sodré, in the afternoon of the 24th of October, and that subsequently, when one of that ship's boats reached the quay at about 6 o'clock, and while its crew were in the act of transporting their disabled and wounded comrade to the boat, a general broil ensued between the Portugese boatmen and American sailors, during which one José Manuel was stabbed by some unknown hand, and subsequently died of the wounds.

As it was alleged that the fatal blow had been struck by one of the sailors of the Guard, the commanding officer of that ship, upon being made aware of the charge, immediately and of his own accord ordered all the seamen attached to two boats which had been on duty, and five others who had been ashore on liberty, under strict arrest to await judicial examination, and he proceeded to make an inquiry himself, with a view of discovering the criminal, if he was on board the ship. That inquiry made no disclosure affecting any of the seamen in question, but the arrest was nevertheless continued.

Inasmuch as a report had gained currency that the offender could and would be promptly identified by various witnesses, if all the seamen said to be implicated were produced, the consul of the United States, at the instance of the commander of the Guard, addressed a note to the civil governor on the 2d instant, stating his readiness and desire to furnish that opportunity, and to have instituted the most searching investigation.

Accordingly an appointment was made for an examination at the arsenal on the 4th instant, which was attended by his Majesty's administrador, the United States consul, the commander of the Guard, and other officials designated for that purpose. The fifteen seamen were ranged in line, subject to the fullest scrutiny of four witnesses who were brought forward; not one of them had been engaged in the melee, and of whom two were boys. The recorded evidence establishes that there is not a particle of proof to criminate any particular individual, or to fix the responsibility of this grave crime. In the absence of such proof or of any evidence that would be recognized in a court of law to hold a person charged to answer for crime, it is necessarily impossible to make delivery of a criminal who is not known, and who as yet has avoided all efforts at discovery, if he really be one of the seamen suspected. But there is every disposition on the part of this legation, and of the officers of the ships-of-war, to promote the course of justice, and to that end every aid will be given for further investigation, in any proper form that may be indicated by his Majesty's government. Although there is no treaty of extradition between Portugal and the United States, all questions of form will be waived in order that the criminal may be brought to a speedy trial, if he is within the jurisdiction or under the protection of the American flag. And with a view of leaving no duty undischarged, the whole case will be at once presented to the notice of Rear-Admiral Goldsborough, who arrived in the Tagus this morning, so that such additional measures may be adopted as his superior authority over the fleet will authorize.

Without the least desire to avoid responsibility, or to depreciate the seriousness of this crime, it may be suggested as worthy of consideration, whether in the confusion of a broil at nightfall, in which a large number of persons were engaged, there can be any reasonable certainty without clear and convincing testimony, as to the individual who may have inflicted the fatal wound, or whether the blow was struck intentionally or accidentally. The Portuguese boatmen largely outnumbered the American sailors, and it is very remarkable that not one of those engaged in the affray should have appeared at the arsenal, to testify at the examination which they were notified was to take place. There is no doubt but their cruel treatment of one of the seaman was the provoking cause of the quarrel and of its lamentable consequence.

The occasion is a fitting one to call the attention of your excellency to the imperfect police at the Caes do Sodré, and to suggest the propriety of designating a special landing for boats belonging to foreign ships-of-war, or at least of establishing some regulation, by which they may be protected against the constant outrages of boatmen who throng that quay and obstruct free communication.

Since writing the foregoing, Admiral Goldsborough has called at the legation and been informed of this note. He fully concurs in its suggestions and stands ready to afford every facility for the most thorough investigation, and to assist personally in any manner that will best promote that object.

I avail myself of this opportunity to renew the assurances of my most distinguished consideration.

JAMES E. HARVEY.

His Excellency the COUNT DE CASTRO,
Minister and Secretary of State for Foreign Affairs.

Count de Castro to Mr. Harvey.

I have had the honor of receiving the note which you were pleased to address me under yesterday's date, informing me that notwithstanding all the efforts employed, it has not been possible to discover the perpetrator of the crime attributed to one of the seamen belonging to the American transport ship Guard, and declaring that there exists both on the part of the legation under your charge and of the commanding officers of the United States ships-of-war, the utmost desire to aid the Portuguese authorities in forwarding the ends of justice.

Thanking you for this communication, which I shall immediately make known to the minister of the interior, and appreciating in a high degree the good offices tendered by the worthy commander, and other officers of said ship, with the approval of Admiral Goldsborough, in the case in question, I shall avail myself of the first opportunity to make known to you any resolution which may be adopted, with regard to your suggestion as to the designation of a special point for the landing of the crews of foreign ships-of-war.

I avail of this opportunity to renew the assurances of my most distinguished consideration.

COUNT DE CASTRO.

DEPARTMENT OF STATE FOR FOREIGN AFFAIRS, *November* 15, 1865.

Mr. Harvey to Rear-Admiral Goldsborough.

LEGATION OF THE UNITED STATES,
Lisbon, November 20, 1865.

SIR: I have the honor to furnish you with copies of a correspondence between his Majesty's government and this legation, in regard to a charge of crime made against some unknown seaman alleged to belong to the transport ship Guard, attached to the squadron under your command.

It appears that his Majesty's government is entirely satisfied with the disposition shown and the efforts made by all of the officials of the United States, not only to discover the criminal in question, but to purge themselves of all responsibility connected with the crime, and that no further investigation seems to be desired.

In view of these facts, there is no good reason for detaining the transport ship longer in port, as you had properly and promptly directed should be done pending the investigation.

I have the honor to be, sir, your obedient servant,

JAMES E. HARVEY.

Rear-Admiral L. M. GOLDSBOROUGH,
Commanding U. S. European Squadron now at Lisbon.

ITALY.

Mr. Marsh to Mr. Seward.

No. 109.] LEGATION OF THE UNITED STATES,
Turin, November 22, 1864.

SIR: I mentioned in a recent despatch that I had applied to the Italian government to permit the temporary establishment of a depot for naval stores of the United States at Cagliari.

I have received a reply, a translation of which is enclosed herewith. The decision of the Navy Department to defer for the present the employment of storehouses on shore, renders it unnecessary to prosecute the subject further, and I have notified the Italian government accordingly.

I have the honor to be, sir, your obedient servant,

GEORGE P. MARSH.

Hon. WILLIAM H. SEWARD,
Secretary of State.

[Translation.]

TURIN, *November* 1, 1864.

MR. MINISTER: I have communicated to the ministry of marine the contents of your note of the 26th September last, in relation to having magazines in the port of Cagliari to receive the United States naval stores, which are to be removed from the depot at Spezia, on account of the transformation of the gulf of Spezia into a military establishment for the royal marine of Italy.

In view of the amicable relations existing between the two countries, and in consideration of the exceptional circumstances that the United States of America have no possession in Europe, and their great distance from the Mediterranean does not permit them to provision directly and opportunely their ships in that sea, the government of the King has no objection to granting the permission desired. But you will recognize, Mr. Minister, in making this concession we are obliged to return to the King's government that liberty of action which its own interests and the maintenance of maritime neutrality demand. It is my duty then to fix the following conditions:

The privilege accorded to the United States to rent magazines at Cagliari for the stores of their naval station in the Mediterranean can at any time be revoked by the government of the King, and the marine of the United States will be held to evacuate the aforesaid magazines within a delay of three months after notice given to the legation of the United States at the court of Italy.

In case of a rupture between the United States and any European power, the magazines of Cagliari must be evacuated immediately after the declaration of war.

The United States will not be entitled to indemnity for the evacuation of their naval magazines at Cagliari.

Ships-of-war of the United States marine will conform to the provisions of the royal decree of 6th of April, 1864, hereunto annexed, in regard to the neutrality of the ports of the Italian Kingdom.

In case that ships-of-war of the United States should have to remain in the port of Cagliari beyond the time fixed by article 12 of the said decree, they will be required, except in case of forced stoppage or of damage, to obtain the authorization of the King's government.

The provisions of the before mentioned decree relating to belligerent ships will be applicable to the military marine of the United States, whenever the United States shall be at war with any other power, or in case ships-of-war or privateers (armis en course) of the separatists should make their appearance in the Mediterranean.

I shall be glad, Mr. Minister, if, while appreciating the necessity of these conditions, you should find no difficulty in accepting them.

I hasten to add that the government of the King will be happy to be able to give proofs of its friendship towards the United States in according to the federal marine all facilities that may be consistent with its duties.

I take with pleasure, Mr. Minister, this occasion of renewing to you the assurances of my high consideration.

ALPHONSO LA MARMORA.

Mr. MARSH, *Envoy Extraordinary and Minister Plenipotentiary of the United States of America.*

Mr. Marsh to Mr. Seward.

[Extract.]

No. 111.] LEGATION OF THE UNITED STATES, *Turin, January* 16, 1865.

SIR: * * * * * * * *

The removal of the seat of this government to Florence is to take place on the first of May next, and the necessary alterations and constructions of public buildings for the accommodation of the different departments of the ministry and other branches of public service are now in progress at that city.

The excitement which the sudden announcement of this change produced having subsided, the measure has now become a subject of calm reflection, and is by no means regarded, even at Florence, with the favor which welcomed the first intelligence of the convention. On the contrary, while it has gained no new friends, as a wise or necessary step, the convictions of those who originally opposed it have been strengthened, and if the question were now to be tried upon its merits, I do not think the ministry could command a majority of either branch of the national legislature in its favor; that it was intended by some of the parties to the negotiation as a renunciation of the claim to Rome as the national capital would now be scarcely denied; but however that may be, the effect of it will be to renew the agitation of the Roman question, and it will soon present itself to the people in a shape more imperiously demanding a satisfactory solution than ever.

Hitherto the desire to retain the seat of government at the ancient capital of its kings has, in a great measure, stifled the voice of Piedmont on this question, and, therefore, the most powerful national influence which could be brought to bear upon it has been, to a certain extent, paralyzed. The moral strength of the nation resides in Piedmont, and the whole influence of all classes, with the exception of the clergy, throughout the old provinces, will now be directed to the accomplishment of an end to which the population of the former Sardinian kingdom has been hitherto comparatively indifferent. Jealousy of Florence and of Tuscan influence in the government will combine to rouse the spirit of other parts of Italy in the same direction, and the peninsula will be better united on this point than it has hitherto been on any other.

Happily for the interests of Italian liberty, the recent encyclical letter of Pope Pius IX is likely to frustrate the various schemes of conciliation which have been dreamed of as effectually as the madness of our own southern pro-slavery politicians has dispelled the visions of a new compromise between the spirit of slavery and the spirit of freedom in our own commonwealth.

One of the mose important measures now under discussion in the Italian parliament is the bill for the suppression of monastic corporations. It is unfortunate that the measure had not been proposed and sustained on moral rather than financial grounds; for its advocates have thus deprived themselves of their strongest argument, and at the same time furnishes their opponents with the most powerful weapons of resistance. Considered as a question of expediency in a moral point of view, independently of religious prejudice, the reasons for the suppression of the conventional establishments are overwhelming, and their force is much increased by numerous recent disclosures of a turpitude and depravity among the members of many monastic institutions which are happily unimaginable in countries not familiar with the history of similar establishments in former periods. Four or five monastic schools have recently been closed by the government for reasons similar to those which led to the suspension of the school of the Gynorantelli at Turin, in 1863. * * * * *

The fate of the bill is doubtful, but it is thought probable that it will pass the chamber of deputies, in a modified form, and then perhaps fail altogether in the senate.

But while the political condition of Italy is in many respects unsatisfactory, there are in some directions some tokens of at least material progress. The readiness with which the proposal to anticipate the taxes for 1865 has been met by the people, is a very favorable indication of the pecuniary condition of the people; and the improved well-being of the laboring classes, and especially the great reduction in the number of mendicants, are circumstances which very forcibly strike the attention of all strangers who knew Italy fifteen years ago. The sale of the railroads and of the public domain, though at prices far below their probable value, will serve to relieve the treasury, and, in fact, the financial embarrassments of the government are among the least of its real difficulties.

The re-election of President Lincoln has, as you have heard from all quarters, been received with the greatest satisfaction by the friends and the greatest disappointment by the enemies of European liberty. The issue presents itself on the continent in two aspects; first, as a question of the abolition of domestic slavery, and, secondly, as a question of the power of popular government to maintain themselves against domestic as well as against foreign hostility. The present administration of the American government enjoys, I believe, the confidence of our European well-wishers—that is to say, of all the popular masses on this side of the Atlantic, on both points. I have no reason to doubt that most of the members of this government are friendly to us, though I regret to say that it allows the ministerial journals to indulge in a tone of malevolence and misrepresentation of fact against us, which it certainly would not permit in the case of states whose good will it valued at a high rate.

I have the honor to be, sir, your obedient servant,

GEORGE P. MARSH.

Hon. WILLIAM H. SEWARD, *Secretary of State.*

Mr. Seward to Mr. Marsh.

No. 125.] DEPARTMENT OF STATE,
Washington, February 7, 1865.

SIR: Your despatch of the 16th of January, No. 111, has been received, and your proceedings therein mentioned are approved.

I thank you for the information you have given me concerning the political affairs of Italy.

The United States rejoice in everything that contributes to the stability of the Italian government, or tends to promote the welfare and happiness of the Italian people. If, as you suppose, these sentiments are not fully reciprocated by the government of Italy at the present moment, we may regret the circumstance without allowing it to affect our settled policy in regard to that very interesting country. Once we enjoyed the general respect of European states, some of them became unfriendly when we entered the ways of adversity. We shall always gratefully remember that Italy was not one of these nations. However unfriendly any of its governing statesmen may regard us, we do not cease to remember that the fate of the civil war in which we are engaged is little dependent on foreign favor; that if we fail we cannot expect friends, and if we continue to be successful, it will be less necessary than it has been hitherto to plead for friendship.

I am, sir, your obedient servant,

WILLIAM H. SEWARD.

GEORGE P. MARSH, Esq., *&c., &c., Turin.*

Mr. Marsh to Mr. Seward.

No. 114.] LEGATION OF THE UNITED STATES,
Turin, February 13, 1865.

SIR: As the public journals have already informed you, the King of Italy left Turin for Florence on the third day of the present month, and the latter city will henceforth be the royal residence. The immediate occasion of the King's departure was the absence of any representation of the municipality of Turin at a court ball given on the evening of January 30, and the refusal of that body to disclaim or apologize for popular manifestations of dissatisfaction in the streets and public squares of the city on that evening.

These manifestations, it appears, were specially provoked by the neglect of parliament to pass resolutions implying some censure of the ministry for their conduct during the disturbance of September 21 and 22, and to make any provision for the relief of the widows and children of innocent persons killed on that unhappy occasion.

The departure of the King was extremely sudden. No previous notice of his intention to remove to Florence was given, nor, in fact, was that intention even generally suspected at Turin before it was carried into effect; no public announcement of his change of residence has been since promulgated, nor has any communication yet been made to the diplomatic corps on the subject. The King, however, was accompanied by General La Marmora, president of the council and minister of foreign affairs, by some others of the ministry, and by the principal officers of the court, and many of the public journals declared that the personal removal of the King and court was held to involve the removal of the seat of government, and to be, in fact, an execution of the act of parliament and the royal decree for transferring the capital to Florence.

In order to inform myself on this point, I visited the minister of foreign affairs at Florence on Monday last, and learned from him that Turin is still considered the official capital of the kingdom, and will continue to be so regarded until the actual removal of the public offices and their archives and *personnel.*

This it is understood will not take place until April, or more probably May, and in the mean time most, if not all, of the foreign diplomatic representatives will remain here, visiting Florence from time to time, if occasion shall require.

I shall, unless otherwise instructed, pursue the same course, and hope that this decision will meet your approbation.

I have the honor to be, sir, your obedient servant,

GEORGE P. MARSH.

Hon. WILLIAM H. SEWARD, *Secretary of State, &c., &c., &c.*

Mr. Marsh to Mr. Seward.

No. 117.] LEGATION OF THE UNITED STATES,
Turin, April 28, 1865.

SIR: I have received from the minister of foreign affairs official notice that the office of that ministry will be transferred to Florence on the fifteenth day of

May next, but I have been since informed by the secretary general that it is doubtful whether the minister of foreign affairs will be at that city in person before the end of the month.

It is understood that the King leaves Turin for Florence to-day, but no formal announcement of his change of residence has been made.

I shall remain at Turin until the removal of the public offices actually takes place, and shall then proceed to the new capital.

I have the honor to be, sir, your obedient servant,

GEORGE P. MARSH.

Hon. WILLIAM H. SEWARD,
Secretary of State.

Mr. Marsh to Mr. Hunter.

No. 118.] LEGATION OF THE UNITED STATES,
Turin, April 29, 1865.

SIR: Two days since a telegraphic message forwarded to this city for transmission to Constantinople brought us the first announcement of the fearful crime to which the Chief Magistrate of the Union has fallen a victim. The want of direct intelligence and the brevity of the telegram led many to suspect that it was a false rumor, invented for purposes of speculation, but it was confirmed by later messages, and the post of this morning brings us many of the details of the assassination, as well as a notice of your appointment as Acting Secretary of State.

Upon the reception of the first message members of the Italian senate and chamber of deputies, which were then there in session, called at my house for information as to the truth of the report. This, in consequence of the accidental failure of telegrams to and from Mr. Adams, I was unable to give, but knowing, as I do, the character of the enemies with whom the late President had to contend, and remembering the threats of which he was often the object, I have long thought such an event probable, and did not hesitate to say that I so considered it.

You will receive from nearer sources abundant evidence of the reprobation and horror which this enormous offence against humanity has excited throughout Europe, and I am happy to say that the most eminent friends of Italian liberty are not behind the foremost in condemnation of the crime and in regret for the sudden removal of a public officer who, at the moment of his death, enjoyed the reverence of the civilized world in a higher degree than any other man of our times.

The minister of foreign affairs has requested me to assure my government of the special regret and sympathy of the King of Italy and of the present administration of the kingdom, and most of the foreign ministers at this court have expressed to me similar sentiments. The senate and the chamber of deputies have passed appropriate resolutions on the occasion, but as these will be officially communicated to the government through the Italian minister at Washington I forbear to transmit them. I, however, enclose herewith, at the request of respectable persons, two series of resolutions from masonic associations, which have just been communicated to me.

Great interest is naturally felt and expressed respecting the probable policy of Mr. Lincoln's successor, and the effect of the President's death on the political interests of the United States. It has been a great satisfaction to me to be able to testify, from personal acquaintance with the present incumbent of the presidential office, to the purity and elevation of his character, and to his soundness, ability, and integrity as a statesman, and at the same time to profess a confidence in the stability of our institutions which excludes all fear either of a dangerous shock to them or of a temporary derangement of their normal functions from even so calamitous an event as this.

It would be ungracious at this moment to inquire jealously into the sincerity of the official expressions of European regret, or into the probable effects of Mr. Lincoln's death on the policy of foreign powers towards us. Happily the progress of our arms has secured us from all visible danger of European intervention, and if there are governments which, in earlier stages of the rebellion, might have availed themselves of such a conjuncture as this for evil ends, it is now too late to make it an occasion of successful wrong-doing by any European state to the people of the United States.

We are yet without definite information as to the condition of the Secretary of State and of his son and assistant; but the telegraphic intelligence seems favorable to the life and complete restoration of both of them. The great wisdom and ability with which Mr. Seward has conducted the foreign relations of the United States are universally acknowledged, and are, indeed, so deeply felt that his decease at this moment would be regarded by Europe as a loss to his country hardly less than that of the President himself, and I most earnestly trust both that his life may be saved and that he may be spared the heavy affliction of the loss of a distinguished son.

I am, sir, with high respect, your obedient servant,

GEORGE P. MARSH.

Hon. W. HUNTER,
Acting Secretary of State.

(For enclosure see Appendix, separate volume.)

Mr. Marsh to Mr. Hunter.

[Extract.]

No. 119.] LEGATION OF THE UNITED STATES,
Turin, May 15, 1865.

SIR: I have the honor to acknowledge the receipt of your instruction of April 17, 1865, with the official announcement of the assassination of the President of the United States. I immediately communicated a copy of this announcement to the minister of foreign affairs, and have received a reply, of which a translation is annexed.

I have received a considerable number of addresses, resolutions, and other expressions of condolence with the people of the United States on this sad event, which I shall forward to Washington by the first private conveyance. I retain them in the mean time, because they would form a package somewhat bulky for the mails.

* * * * * *

There are in circulation many rumors of a projected alliance between France, Austria, Italy, and Spain for the maintenance of the new imperial dynasty in Mexico, at a cost, even, of a war with the United States; and a visit of General Cialdini to Spain, at this moment, is suspected by some to be connected with a negotiation for this end. The whole thing seems extremely improbable as to some of the powers in question, and supremely absurd as to the best interests of all of them. In such a crusade I can hardly believe that this or any other European government, except, perhaps, England, would have the support of its own people; and so transparent an attempt to put down republicanism in America as this would be, might very probably teach European statesmen that democracy is a much more powerful element of opposition to measures of despotic policy than they, at this moment, consider it.

The session of parliament is not yet closed, and the minister of foreign affairs is still here, but the transfer of all the public offices to Florence will probably be completed before the month of June, and I intend to go to that city in the course of the present or the next month.

I am, sir, respectfully, your obedient servant,

GEORGE P. MARSH.

Hon. WILLIAM HUNTER,
Acting Secretary of State.

[Translation.]

TURIN, *May* 6, 1865.

Mr. MINISTER: I have received the note which you have done me the honor to address me under date of May 5, transmitting to me a copy of a circular of the Department of State at Washington, which conveys the official announcement of the assassination committed on the person of the President of the United States and of the accession of Mr. Andrew Johnson to the Presidency.

On the 28th of April last, I hastened to transmit to the minister of Italy at Washington the address which the Italian parliament had voted to the Congress of the Union, in order to express to that body its sentiments of lively sympathy and the indignation which the execrable crime of which Mr. Lincoln has been the victim has excited in Italy.

The King, my august sovereign, and his government, fully concur in this manifestation, and I renew to you, Mr. Minister, the warmest expression of the sentiments they have felt, in common with the whole Italian nation, on this sad occasion.

In forming sincere wishes for the prosperity of the States of the Union and of their worthy President, Mr. Andrew Johnson, I beg you to accept, Mr. Minister, the assurance of my high consideration.

ALPHONSE LA MARMORA.

Mr. Marsh to Mr. Hunter.

No. 121.] LEGATION OF THE UNITED STATES,
Florence, June 5, 1865.

SIR: I left Turin on Tuesday last and came immediately to this city. I shall make my arrangements for a permanent residence here as rapidly as possible, though, for reasons stated in a former despatch, I shall be obliged to make occasional visits to Turin, until I can secure proper apartments for my family, and the convenience of the legation, which is by no means an easy task. Mr. Clay preceded me by a few days, and has taken lodgings which will serve as an office until a better provision is made.

The Foreign Office is now established at Florence, although one branch of it, the diplomatic council, as well as some other public offices, still remain at the former capital.

I saw General La Marmora on Saturday. He inquired into our present and probable future relations with Mexico, with no small interest, and I know from various sources that this subject is now occupying the serious attention of Italian statesmen of all shades of political opinion. In case the Emperor Napoleon shall decide to send large re-enforcements to Mexico, I have no doubt whatever that Italy will be called upon to furnish a contingent, and the leading article in the Opinione, a semi-official organ, which I sent to you by the last post, was doubtless intended to prepare public opinion in Italy for such an event.

The pending negotiations with Rome are looked to with much anxiety. Nothing authentic has transpired as to the character of the instructions of the Italian envoy. * * * * * * * *

I have the honor to be, sir, your obedient servant,

GEORGE P. MARSH.

Hon. WILLIAM HUNTER,
Acting Secretary of State.

Mr. Marsh to Mr. Hunter.

No. 122.] LEGATION OF THE UNITED STATES,
Florence, June 10, 1865.

SIR: On the receipt of the three proclamations of the President of the United States, dated April 11, 1865, relating, respectively, to the treatment of vessels-of-war of the United States by foreign powers, in the ports and waters of such powers, to the closing of certain ports of the United States, and to the port of Key West, I enclosed copies of them all to the minister of foreign affairs, with a note, a copy of which, marked A, is hereto annexed.

On the 29th of May I addressed to the minister a note, of which a copy, marked B, is hereto annexed, together with a copy of the proclamation therein referred to.

I have received from the minister two notes, dated June 6th and June 9th, translations of which, marked, respectively, C and D, are annexed.

I shall go to Turin to-day, partly for reasons of personal convenience, and partly to finish the draught of the treaty which I am authorized to negotiate with this kingdom. The library and archives of the legation still remaining at Turin, I can perform this labor much more conveniently at that city than at this, and I hope to complete it in a few days.

It is now announced that the archives and offices of the Italian parliament will remain at the old capital for some weeks, or even months longer, and, as the expected dissolution of the national legislature has not yet taken place, it is suggested that a new session may be convoked at Turin for the purpose of sanctioning a convention with Rome, or, possibly, of acting on the question of furnishing an Italian contingent to the French army of occupation in Mexico. The latter supposition is less probable than it seemed a few days since; but the present chambers would go with France and the Italian ministry on either point. The next parliament may prove less pliable.

I have the honor to be, sir, your obedient servant,

GEORGE P. MARSH.

Hon. WILLIAM HUNTER,
Acting Secretary of State.

A.

LEGATION OF THE UNITED STATES,
Turin, May 5, 1865.

YOUR EXCELLENCY: I have the honor to enclose to you copies of a proclamation by the President of the United States, dated April 11, 1865, relating to the treatment of vessels-of-war of the United States by foreign powers in the ports and waters of such powers; a proclamation by the President of the United States, dated April 11, 1865, relating to the closing of certain ports of the United States enumerated in said proclamation, and a proclamation by the President of the United States, dated April 11, 1865, declaring that the port of Key West, inadvertently included in the terms of the last-mentioned proclamation, shall remain open.

Your excellency is aware that the government of the United States has never admitted the validity of the reasons which have induced various foreign powers, during the rebellion of a portion of the lawful territory of the Union, to deny to the armed vessels of the United States the hospitalities reciprocally usual between friendly nations.

It is also known to your excellency that by recent victories of the arms of the Union, the federal government is once more in undisputed possession of nearly the whole of the territory lately occupied by the rebel forces, and that the so-called Confederate States are now without a political capital, without an army, without seaports, and, in fact, without a government recognized even by themselves.

The alleged reasons for the refusal of the usual international comity to our ships-of-war, never, as I have said, sufficient in the eyes of the federal government to justify such refusal, have now, therefore, altogether ceased to exist, and my government confidently expects that all foreign powers, and especially the kingdom of Italy, in whose waters no vessel bearing the rebel flag has ever appeared, and which has always manifested the most amicable sentiments towards the United States, will acquiesce in the justice and propriety of restoring to the armed vessels of the Union the enjoyment of the hospitalities which has been granted by each of the two nations to the navy of the other.

It is proper that I should admit, on this occasion, that the United States have had no occasion to complain of the enforcement, in practice, of the rules prescribed by his Majesty's government respecting the treatment of foreign armed vessels, and I take pleasure in acknowledging a comity on the part of the Italian government, of which my own is by no means insensible, and which may justly be regarded as a proof that the friendship so long manifested by his Majesty's government for the government of the United States is in no degree impaired.

I pray your excellency to accept the renewed expression of my high consideration.

GEORGE P. MARSH.

His Excellency General A. LA MARMORA,
Minister of Foreign Affairs.

B.

LEGATION OF THE UNITED STATES,
Turin, May 29, 1865.

YOUR EXCELLENCY: I have the honor to enclose herewith a printed copy of a proclamation by the President of the United States in relation to the treatment of cruisers acting under the pretended authority of the so-called Confederate States in the ports of foreign powers.

It is certainly not to be expected that vessels under the rebel flag will seek an asylum in the ports of his Majesty the King of Italy, but in such case the liberality with which his Majesty's government has treated the armed ships of the United States in Italian waters, and the notorious fact that no shadow of a confederate government now exists, justify the expectation that no manner of recognition, aid, or comfort will be extended to ships claiming to belong to this illegal organization.

I pray your excellency to accept the renewed expression of my high consideration.

GEORGE P. MARSH.

His Excellency General A. LA MARMORA
President of the Council and Minister of Foreign Affairs.

C.

[Translation.]

FLORENCE, *June* 6, 1865.

MR. MINISTER: The transfer of the capital to Florence has not allowed me to reply sooner to the note you did me the honor to address me, under date of May 5, communicating to me proclamations of the late President of the United States, Mr. Lincoln, relating to the treatment of ships-of-war of the Union in foreign waters and to the closing of certain ports of the United States.

You are aware, Mr. Minister, that the King's government has never concealed its sympathies for the just cause which has obtained so decisive successes, and you have yourself admitted that if we have been obliged to apply, in principle, to the armed vessels of the United States in the waters of Italy the conditions which our regulations impose upon belligerent vessels, we have taken care to mitigate their enforcement in practice, so as to embarrass as little as possible the entrance of Union ships-of-war into our ports and roads and their stay at such points.

Now that the civil war may be considered at an end, we are happy to be able to give to the government of the United States new pledges of our continued friendship.

I hasten, then, to announce to you that all the restrictions provisionally adopted with reference to the armed vessels of the United States are rescinded, and that hereafter these vessels will be treated in our waters on the footing of the ships-of-war of other friendly powers in time of peace.

As to the armed vessels of the separatists, we hope that none of them will appear on our coasts. But if, contrary to all probability, any such should present themselves, they would not be received into our ports except in case of urgent necessity, under circumstances where the laws of humanity would not allow us to reject them; and in that event, our authorities will take all necessary precautions to prevent any inconvenience from resulting therefrom.

Accept, Mr. Minister, the assurance of my high consideration.

A. LA MARMORA.

Mr. GEORGE P. MARSH,
Envoy Extraordinary and Minister Plenipotentiary of the United States of America.

D.

[Translation.]

FLORENCE, *June* 9, 1865.

MR. MINISTER: The decisions which I had the honor to announce to you by my despatch of June 6, having anticipated the communication, which by your note of May 29 you have made me, of a proclamation by the President of the United States relative to the treatment of armed vessels of the separatists, it only remains for me to discharge the duty of acknowledging the receipt of that document.

I avail myself of this occasion to offer you the assurance of my high consideration.

For the minister, M. CERRUTI.

Mr. GEORGE P. MARSH,
Envoy Extraordinary and Minister Plenipotentiary of the United States of America.

Mr. Marsh to Mr. Seward.

[Extracts.]

No. 123.] LEGATION OF THE UNITED STATES,
Florence, June 29, 1865.

SIR: Although I am not officially informed that you have so far recovered as to be able to resume the discharge of your functions as chief of the State Department, I infer from the newspaper accounts that you are again at your post, and I accordingly address this despatch to you. I beg you, sir, to accept for yourself and our common country my sincere congratulations on your return to duties which, if less arduous than heretofore, are still of a character to demand the utmost powers of an intellect which has been exerted with such commanding ability and such signal success in the direction of our foreign affairs during the eventful administration which has lately closed.

The transfer of the official capital of the kingdom of Italy to Florence is now substantially effected, though some public offices still remain at Turin. The work of reorganization is, however, not completed, and it will be some months before the engine of state is again in regular operation. The King has gone to Piedmont for the summer, and the minister of foreign affairs is at present at Turin.

I have left a draught of the proposed treaty of commerce and navigation between the United States and Italy at the Foreign Office for examination, and shall proceed with the discussion of its provisions as soon as the ministry is ready to enter upon it.

By the letter of my instructions I am authorized to negotiate a treaty or treaties. I suppose this expression would include a consular convention as well as an ordinary commercial treaty, but I am not clear as to the expediency of concluding a separate convention for this purpose. A consular convention much resembling ours with France was negotiated between that power and Italy in 1862. Great Britain has no consular convention with this kingdom, and the British government has contented itself with inserting in the treaty of commerce and navigation of 1863 a general clause securing to the consuls of the two countries respectively the powers, privileges, and exemptions granted by each to consuls of the most favored nations.

As I view the question, the principal motive for negotiating an independent convention for defining the power and privileges of consuls would be to limit the exemption of consular officers from liability to attendance in courts as witnesses. To invest consular pupils, or vice-consuls who may be American citizens, or commercial representatives of insignificant powers, with privileges which may occasion great inconvenience to American legal tribunals, as we appear to have done in our convention with France, seems to me a subordination of the judicial authority to mere commercial interests, which is inconsistent with the dignity properly belonging to what American and English law regards as so exalted a department, and I should propose to exempt only consuls general and consuls, citizens of the states they represent and not engaged in commerce, from compulsory attendance in courts of justice.

You have certainly better means than I can have of judging of the intentions of the French Emperor with regard to Mexico and the United States, but I cannot help attaching some importance to the tone of the Italian ministerial press, and of all the Italian journals in the French interest, in regard to this question. They are evidently still aiming to prepare the public mind for a call from France for a contingent to the French army of occupation in Mexico, and for a possible rupture with the United States. How far these journals speak from ministerial inspiration, and how far from French suggestion, it is hard to say. * * *

The negotiations with Rome will be resumed as soon as the preliminary elections are over; and if the present ministry remains in power new concessions will be offered, provided it suits the policy of France to require them. Many suppose the settlement of the Roman question to be especially desired at this moment by Napoleon in order that both his troops and those of Italy be less embarrassed in their Mexican movements, but I shall be much disappointed if a Gallo-Italic transatlantic war does not end in a Gallo-Italic revolution at home.

I am, sir, your obedient servant,

GEORGE P. MARSH.

Hon. WILLIAM H. SEWARD,
Secretary of State.

Mr. Seward to Mr. Marsh.

No. 135.] DEPARTMENT OF STATE,
Washington, July 24, 1865.

SIR: Your despatch of June 29, No. 123, has been received. I thank you for the interesting information which it communicates. It is not deemed important that you should make at present any proposition to the Italian government relative to the negotiation of a consular convention. You will, therefore, confine yourself, under the authority that has already been given you, to the negotiation of a commercial treaty.

I am, sir, your obedient servant,

WILLIAM H. SEWARD.

GEORGE P. MARSH, Esq., *&c., &c., Florence.*

ROME.

Mr. King to Mr. Seward.

No. 29.] LEGATION OF THE UNITED STATES AT ROME,
December 24, 1864.

SIR: I have the honor to acknowledge the receipt of your despatch No. 20, of November 18, in answer to mine of October 24, and am gratified to learn that the contents of the communication to which it refers were satisfactory to the government.

Since my last, of November 24, nothing has occurred at Rome calling for special mention. Political quiet continues to prevail throughout the papal dominions. The health of his Holiness, somewhat impaired by a cold during the past week, is now fully restored.

The intelligence of Mr. Dayton's sudden death in Paris was received here by all who knew him with feelings of profound regret. The country loses in him an able, faithful and zealous public servant, and his family one whose place cannot be supplied.

The impression produced in Europe by the ever-memorable result of the recent presidential election, and the firm self-reliant unyielding attitude assumed by the American people in vindication of the national authority and honor and in defence of the national life, continues to strengthen and extend. It is the ardent hope of all loyal Americans abroad, and of the millions in Europe who sympathize with them, that the progress of our arms may speedily complete the triumph of law, liberty and Union which the popular verdict of November 8 so gloriously inaugurated.

I avail myself of the occasion to tender to our honored President and his faithful cabinet ministers the good wishes and congratulations appropriate to this festive season.

I am, sir, with great respect, your obedient servant,

RUFUS KING.

Hon. WILLIAM H. SEWARD, *&c., &c., &c.*

Mr. King to Mr. Seward.

[Extract.]

No. 30.] LEGATION OF THE UNITED STATES AT ROME,
January 7, 1865.

SIR: * * * * * *

In accordance with diplomatic custom, I paid an official visit to the Pope and cardinal secretary of state, during the Christmas week, to tender the good wishes and congratulations appropriate to the season; I enjoyed with each a pleasant and satisfactory interview, and availed myself of the opportunity to direct their attention to the gratifying character of the recent intelligence from America. They both appreciated in its full force the significance of the news and joined in the hope, which I expressed, that the steady progress of the federal arms would speedily restore to our country the inestimable blessings of peace and union.

Bishop Lynch, of Charleston, South Carolina, returned from Paris to Rome a few days since. I know of no reason to suppose, however, that he is at all more likely to be received and acknowledged as an official representative of the rebel government than at his previous visit.

I have the honor to be, with great respect, your obedient servant,

RUFUS KING.

Hon. WILLIAM H. SEWARD, *&c., &c., &c.*

Mr. King to Mr. Seward.

No. 31] LEGATION OF THE UNITED STATES AT ROME, *January* 14, 1865.

SIR: I have the honor to acknowledge the receipt of despatch No. 21, of December 16, from the State Department, in reply to mine of November 12, and conveying instructions as to the disposition to be made of sundry volumes in the archives of the United States legation in Rome.

The intelligence of the capture of Savannah by the federal forces, under command of General Sherman, reached us on Monday last, and was received with the utmost enthusiasm by the Americans in Rome. I attended a state dinner at the Austrian ambassador's on the same day, and had the pleasure of receiving from various members of the diplomatic corps their hearty congratulations upon the favorable complexion of the news. The Russian chargé d'affaires, Baron Meyendorf, and the newly appointed minister from Venezuela, Signor Pullido, were especially earnest in their felicitations. Baron Meyendorf remarked that Russia sympathized deeply with the United States in this hour of our national trouble, and that not only the Emperor but the people of Russia had been inexpressibly touched by the warm and generous welcome extended to the Russian fleet, during its visit last year to different ports in the United States. I cordially assented to the hope which he expressed that the relations between our two governments might become more and more kindly and fraternal as the years rolled on. The Venezuelian minister was even more emphatic in the expression of his good wishes. He said that for years past the predominance of the pro-slavery interests in the councils of the great American republic had exerted a baneful influence upon the new-born governments of the south American states; that in their early struggles and later development they had met with little sympathy from the quarter to which they had naturally looked for encouragement, as well as example, but that now, happily, all was changed, and from the United States of North America, under their present rulers, they had met with the kindest recognition; therefore it was, he added, that the progress of the federal arms and the impending overthrow of the slaveholders rebellion was hailed with delight by the people and states of South America, as it held out to them the bright promise that the system of free government and republican institutions, inaugurated and vindicated by the people of the United States, was to be the common heritage and proud boast of the entire western continent.

The telegraphic despatches yesterday gave us the substance of the note addressed by the State Department to the government of Brazil in reference to the capture of the Florida in the harbor of Bahia. I thought it a good occasion to converse with the Chevalier de Figuereido, the Brazilian chargé d'affaires, on the subject, and was glad to find that he was equally pleased with the spirit and tenor of the communication, as calculated to allay all ill feeling between the two governments, and to satisfy the authorities and people of Brazil that the United States would do justice in the premises.

I had an official interview yesterday morning with the cardinal secretary of state; he too expressed his satisfaction with the action of our government in the matter of the Florida, and remarked that it would quiet the angry spirit which had been at first aroused in Brazil by the conduct of the American consul at Bahia and the captain of the Wachusett. Reverting to our home affairs, the cardinal observed that the recent signal successes of the federal arms seemed to promise an early end to the war, which he most earnestly desired, and the re-establishment of the Union. He thought that the great difficulty now would be to arrange the terms of peace and the re-admission into the Union of the seceded States, as the violent passions excited by such a war as had afflicted our country for the past four years were not easily allayed. I remarked to his eminence that there was no angry spirit, no feeling of revenge, towards the people of the southern States among their brethren at the north; that we believed they had been misinformed and misled by a few ambitious and unscrupulous men, and that they would be welcomed back into the Union with open arms and in a forgiving temper, the moment they submitted themselves to the authority of the federal government.

I availed myself of the opportunity to mention to the cardinal a rumor which has been in circulation in Rome, that the Pope had written a second letter to Jefferson Davis, in the sense of encouraging him to persevere in his work of rebellion, and giving him the benefit of a papal recognition. The cardinal without any hesitation pronounced the report untrue. The Pope had written no second letter, he said, though he himself had addressed one, general in its terms and pacific in its spirit, to the southern "commissioners" who had addressed a circular to all the courts of Europe. This, the cardinal remarked, simply engaged the good offices of the Pope to bring about peace, whenever a fitting opportunity should offer itself for the exercise of his moral influence. Beyond this I do not think that the papal government will be in any more haste to interfere in our affairs than France or England.

I have the honor to be, with great respect, your obedient servant,

RUFUS KING.

Hon. WILLIAM H. SEWARD, *&c., &c., &c.*

Mr. Seward to Mr. King.

No. 24.]

DEPARTMENT OF STATE,
Washington, February 8, 1865.

SIR: I have received your interesting despatch of January 14, No. 31, and have read with much pleasure the account it gives of your conversation with various members of the diplomatic corps, on a recent occasion, at the residence of the Austrian ambassador to Rome.

Your proceedings, on receiving by telegraph the substance of the note of this department, relative to the capture of the Florida in the harbor of Bahia, are approved.

I am, sir, your obedient servant,

WILLIAM H. SEWARD.

RUFUS KING, Esq., *&c., &c., Rome.*

Mr. King to Mr. Seward.

No. 32.]

LEGATION OF THE UNITED STATES AT ROME,
February 11, 1865.

SIR: The intelligence of the sudden death of the lamented Edward Everett was received by the Americans in Rome with profound and unaffected regret.

Anticipating the wishes of the State Department, I have caused the rooms of the American legation to be draped in mourning, as a slight mark of respect to the memory of the departed statesman, orator, and patriot.

The unexpected departure of Victor Emanuel from Turin for the new capital of Italy—Florence—excites some effervescence in the political circles of Rome. The adherents of the papal government do not openly attach much importance to the change, but the liberal party build high hopes upon it. This party for several years past has kept entirely aloof from the carnival celebration customary at this season, but in honor of the Franco-Italian treaty, and, as they believe, the approaching realization of their darling wish—an united Italy, with Rome for its capital—they have resolved this year to participate in the carnival festivities, and do whatever they can to add to their gayety and splendor.

The health of the sovereign pontiff continues excellent, though the winter thus far has been an unfavorable one; and an unusual amount of sickness has prevailed in Rome.

The number of American visitors here has largely increased within the past few weeks, and I am happy to say that, with very rare exceptions, they are earnest and ardent supporters of the government of the Union.

I have the honor to be, with great respect, your obedient servant,

RUFUS KING.

Hon. WILLIAM H. SEWARD,
Secretary of State.

Mr. King to Mr. Seward.

No. 33.] LEGATION OF THE UNITED STATES AT ROME,
March 4, 1865.

SIR: I am reminded by the date of my letter that on this day our honored President renews his vow of devotion to the Constitution and laws of our country, and enters upon the second term of his administration. I desire to offer to him and to the faithful counsellors who form his cabinet my heartfelt congratulations on the events of the past few months and the happy auspices under which he resumes his good work, as well as my earnest wishes that, by the blessing of God, he may realize, within a brief period, his ardent hope for peace, liberty, and union.

Nothing has transpired in Rome since my last despatch calling for special comment. The carnival passed off without any disturbance, and was very generally participated in, as well by foreigners as by Romans.

I had an official interview with Cardinal Antonelli a few days since, and a very frank talk about affairs in America. His eminence seemed to appreciate fully the events of the late campaigns, and to look forward hopefully to the speedy cessation of hostilities and the submission of the insurgents to the constituted authorities of the country.

I availed myself of an opportunity during the current week to converse with the French ambassador, the Count de Sartiges, about affairs in Mexico and the rumor, very current in Europe, that Maximilian had ceded certain provinces to Napoleon as security for material and financial aid, of which ex-Senator Gwin was to be viceroy, and which was to form the nucleus of a "confederate" colony. The count treated the story as an absurdity, and repeated what he said to me some months ago, that the Emperor of the French would withdraw all his troops from Mexico at the earliest opportunity.

Bishop Lynch is still in Rome, though in no accredited official position. I hear, however, that he and those who sympathize with him profess confident hopes of some European demonstration in behalf of the so-called Confederate States on or immediately after this the 4th day of March. I do not myself entertain any apprehensions on the subject. Europe has enough to do at home, while the United States of America have abundantly proved that they can take care of themselves, and neither ask nor fear any foreign intervention.

I have the honor to be, with great respect, your obedient servant,

RUFUS KING.

Hon. WILLIAM H. SEWARD,
Secretary of State.

Mr. King to Mr. Seward.

No. 34.] LEGATION OF THE UNITED STATES AT ROME,
March 11, 1865.

SIR: I have the honor to acknowledge the receipt of despatches Nos. 23 and 24, from the State Department, under date of February 8, in reply to mine, Nos. 30 and 31, of January 7 and 14.

The news of the fall of Charleston, which left New York on the 22d of February, Washington's birth-day, arrived in Rome on the 4th of March, the first day of President Lincoln's second term. The coincidence added not a little to the pride and satisfaction with which the glad tidings were hailed by the loyal Americans, as well as all others in this imperial city, who look forward hopefully to the progress of civil and religious liberty throughout the world.

The rumor to which I referred in a previous despatch, about the Pope's probable departure from Rome in the event of the withdrawal of the French garrison, has been revived during the past week, and is quite current in diplomatic and other circles. It is added that, in the case that he leaves Rome, the Holy Father will take up his residence, temporarily, at least, in the island of Malta, where an asylum is understood to have been offered him some time since by the British government. My information upon the subject is not yet sufficiently reliable to enable me to form a definite opinion as to the authenticity of this report. I hope, however, to obtain ere long precise and trustworthy intelligence in the premises.

I am, sir, with great respect, your obedient servant,

RUFUS KING.

Hon. WILLIAM H. SEWARD, *&c., &c., &c.*

Mr. King to Mr. Seward.

[Extract.]

No. 35.] LEGATION OF THE UNITED STATES AT ROME,
March 25, 1865.

SIR: * * * * * The relations between the French and papal courts continue to engross attention in Europe, and many rumors are circulated as to the conversation between his Holiness and Count Sartiges, to which I adverted in my last communication. From what I can learn, I am inclined to believe that the French ambassador simply called the Pope's attention to the fact that the Emperor intended to carry out the Franco-Italian treaty, by withdrawing his troops from the Roman states, and suggested the advisability of organizing a sufficient force to preserve the peace and to maintain the papal authority. It is generally believed that the Pope, in reply, declined to increase the number of his troops, as not warranted by the resources at his command, or by the necessities of the case. I adhere to the opinion, heretofore expressed, that notwithstanding the treaty, in the possible event of the Pope's authority being threatened in Rome, there will be no lack of French bayonets to sustain it, and no transfer of the military protectorate to any other European power.

The recent intelligence from the United States has wrought a marked change in the public opinion of Europe. The belief that the war is nearly ended and peace, liberty, and union assured to our country is becoming very general. The idea of any foreign intervention in behalf of the so-called Confederate States is well nigh abandoned.

I am, sir, with great respect, your obedient servant,

RUFUS KING.

Hon. WILLIAM H. SEWARD, *&c.*, *&c.*, *&c.*

Mr. King to Mr. Seward.

No. 36.] LEGATION OF THE UNITED STATES AT ROME,
April 22, 1865.

SIR: I have the honor to acknowledge the receipt of despatch No. 26, from the State Department, under date of March 7, in reply to mine of February 11, and expressing satisfaction with the contents thereof.

The imposing ceremonies of Holy Week and Easter Sunday passed off this year with unwonted eclat. The weather was uncommonly fine, the concourse of visitors from all parts of the civilized world unprecedented, and the health of the Sovereign Pontiff so good as to admit of his officiating in person on the days appointed. To the Americans in Rome our Easter was a scene of special rejoicing, for the eve of Paschal Sunday brought us the glorious tidings of the defeat of Lee, the capture of Richmond, and, as we trust and believe, the final overthrow of the wicked and wanton rebellion. The intelligence was received with the sincerest gratitude and delight, and almost all the members of the diplomatic corps at the papal court offered me their hearty congratulations on this happy issue out of our national difficulties.

The Franco-Italian treaty continues to excite lively discussions in the diplomatic and political circles of Europe. It is not easy, in the midst of the varying opinions expressed and the conflicting rumors circulated, to predict with confidence the results of that convention. The chief interest hinges upon the future status of the Pope, and the probabilities of his leaving or remaining in Rome, in the event of the withdrawal of the French troops. I had a long conversation with the French ambassader, Count Sartiges, on this topic a day or two since. The count expressed the belief that matters were approaching a crisis; that the Pope was pressed by conflicting counsels, one party (the ultra-montane) urging him to abandon Rome, and the other opposing such a step as suicidal; that the issue was with the Holy Father himself, who thus far, at least, was strongly disinclined to leave the Vatican. That in his, the count's judgment, the departure of the Pope from Rome would be the signal for a general convulsion in Italy, if not throughout Europe, and that the peace of the world might depend upon the Pope's remaining in the imperial city, where he thought his person would always be secure and his authority respected. Count Sartiges further informed me that the Pope had addressed an autograph letter to Victor Emanuel, with a view to bring about a conference touching the questions of church and state, in issue between the papal and Italian governments, and that within a few days an accredited representative had arrived in Rome from Victor Emanuel, charged with a reply to the papal missive. He regarded this, he added, as a very important step in the right direction, for that would be the happiest possible solution of the problem, which, leaving the spiritual power of the Holy

Father unquestioned, should sustain his temporal authority by Italian bayonets. I have given quite fully the substance of the French ambassador's remarks, as I thought them very significant and based upon intimate knowledge of the facts.

Passing from Italian topics we conversed briefly about American affairs. The count said that he regarded the last news as entirely conclusive and the war as substantially at an end. His apprehension then was that some trouble might grow up between the United States and Maximilian. He did not fear any hostile or aggressive action on the part of our government, certainly not—he said, so long as the State department continues to be managed by the same able statesman, who had presided over it during the past four years; but there was danger that forty or fifty thousand desperate or adventurous men, thrown out of active service by the return of peace, might, at any moment, cross over from the southwest into Mexico, while there never would be wanting a Juarist chief to issue a pronunciamento and give to the movement the color of a revolution. I assured the count that peace once restored, the aim and policy of our government and people would be to cultivate friendly relations with all mankind, and that so long as our rights were respected and fair treatment extended to us we should be the last power to resort to war.

I cannot close this despatch without tendering to our honored President and his faithful cabinet my heartfelt congratulations upon the glorious successes which have crowned the Union arms and cause. "Thanks be to God who giveth us the victory!"

I have the honor to be, with great respect, your obedient servant,

RUFUS KING.

Hon. WILLIAM H. SEWARD, *&c., &c., &c.*

Mr. King to Mr. Hunter.

No. 37.] LEGATION OF THE UNITED STATES AT ROME,
April 29, 1865.

SIR: The appalling intelligence of the assassination of President Lincoln and the attempt upon the lives of the Secretary and Assistant Secretary of State, which reached Rome on the morning of the 27th instant, excited the most profound and universal sentiment of horror and indignation among men of every class, condition, and nation. The first account represented that the Assistant Secretary of State had also fallen a victim to the assassin's knife, and that the life of the Secretary was despaired of, but we are at least spared this aggravation of horrors, the latest despatch reporting that "Secretary Seward is out of danger," and that his son, though in imminent peril, is still alive. As the tidings spread the Americans in Rome gathered together at the rooms of the United States legation, and held a meeting to give utterance to the feelings which the news had excited in every loyal breast. I transmit herewith, as requested, a copy of the resolutions adopted. They but feebly express the intense emotions which the dastardly crime of the southern conspirators has everywhere aroused. Nor is this confined only to our own countrymen. From the cardinal secretary of state, the ambassadors of France, Spain and Austria, the representatives of Russia, and Brazil, and others, members of the diplomatic corps, and from some of the principal Roman nobility and citizens, I have received assurances of the utter detestation with which they regard the crime, and of their profound sympathy with the government and people of the United States in the hour of terrible trial and affliction. May Almighty God safely guard and guide our country through the surging waves of trouble into the calm sunshine of peace and public order.

In token of respect for the memory of the great and good man, who died as he had lived, faithful to his trust and at the post of duty, I have caused the rooms of the United States legation to be draped in mourning. The loyal Americans in Rome have all assumed the usual badges of mourning as a slight manifestation of their sorrow for the lamented death of our President, and of regard for his memory.

I need scarcely add that we await with trembling anxiety further news from America, and that it is the devout prayer of all true-hearted Americans in Rome that the lives of the Secretary and Assistant Secretary may be spared to their country.

I am, sir, with great respect your obedient servant,

RUFUS KING.

Hon. W. HUNTER,
Acting Secretary of State, &c., &c., &c.

(For enclosure see Appendix, separate volume.)

Mr. King to Mr. Hunter.

[Extract.]

No. 38.] LEGATION OF THE UNITED STATES AT ROME,
May 6, 1865.

SIR: The terrible catastrophe of the 14th of April, at Washington, still occupies all thoughts and tongues on this side of the water, and has called forth from the courts and people of Europe an expression of heartfelt sympathy and sincere sorrow unparalleled in history. Appropriate religious services were held in the United States legation rooms here, which were largely attended by Americans and others. * * * * * *

Our latest advices from home to the 22d of April encourage the belief that both the Secretary and Assistant Secretary of State have escaped the fate designed for them by their brutal and cowardly assailant, and still live to serve their country. I need not say with what unfeigned gratitude and joy this news has been received, not only by the Americans, but by men of all nations in Rome.

I had an official interview with Cardinal Antonelli a day or two since. His eminence embraced the opportunity to express to me, for himself and for the Holy Father, the horror with which they regarded the bloody act which had struck down the head of the American republic, and aimed a like blow at the life of his chief counsellor, and of their earnest sympathy for the American government and people in this hour of trial and affliction. His eminence further begged that I would make known these sentiments to the authorities at Washington.

In my despatch of April 22 I mentioned the arrival in Rome of an accredited representative of Victor Emanuel, charged with the reply of that monarch to the autograph letter addressed to him some weeks since by the Pope, in reference to certain matters at issue between them. This gentleman, Mr. Vegezzi, has been in Rome upwards of a fortnight; has held several conferences with the Pope and with Cardinal Antonelli; has received visits from the French ambassador and other members of the diplomatic corps, and only left on his return to Florence yesterday. I have very good reasons for believing that he is greatly content with the issue of his mission, and goes back in high hope that a reconciliation between the Pope and Victor Emanuel, which would bring with it peace and union throughout the peninsula, will ere long crown the ardent wishes of the friends of a united Italy. Such a result, it cannot be doubted, would be hailed with delight by the mass of the Italian people. On the other hand, it is wholly repugnant to the views and wishes of that formidable body in the Catholic church known as the ultra-montane party, and they, of course, will oppose in all possible ways the desired consummation.

I have the honor to be, with great respect, your obedient servant,

RUFUS KING.

Hon. WILLIAM HUNTER,
Acting Secretary of State, &c., &c.

Mr. King to Mr. Hunter.

No. 39] LEGATION OF THE UNITED STATES AT ROME,
May 13, 1865.

SIR: I duly received a copy of the circular from the State Department under date of April 17, directing all officers and others subject to its orders to wear crape upon the left arm for the period of six months in honor to the memory of our late illustrious Chief Magistrate. Anticipating in this respect the wishes of the department, I had already caused the United States legation rooms here to be suitably draped, and, in common with all loyal Americans now in Rome, had assumed the customary badge of mourning, which will be worn during the time prescribed. It is a melancholy satisfaction to know that the grief we feel at the bereavement the republic has sustained meets with general and earnest sympathy in all parts of the Old World, and that in Europe, as in America, enlightened public opinion has already inscribed among the most illustrious names on the roll of fame that of our martyred President.

The intelligence from home, to the 29th of April, bringing details of Johnston's surrender, seems to remove all doubt as to the complete and final overthrow of the slaveholders' rebellion. The four years ordeal through which our country has passed has proved indeed a fiery one, but, thank God, it has been bravely, unflinchingly, and triumphantly encountered. The latest advices as to the steadily improving condition of the honorable the Secretary and the Assistant Secretary of State have given wide-spread satisfaction. We cherish the hope that a few weeks will restore them to their wonted health, and once more insure to the country the benefit of their counsels and services.

In my despatch of May 6 I mentioned the recent visit to Rome of M. Vegezzi, an accredited agent from King Victor Emanuel, and spoke of the current rumors and conflicting hopes as to the progress and probable issue of his mission. The subject excites very general and lively interest in political circles, and forms one of the chief topics of conversation. It is not supposed that much has yet been accomplished towards effecting a complete reconciliation or establishing cordial relations between the Pope and the King of Italy, but at least a step has been taken in the right direction, and this of itself affords great encouragement to the friends of Italian unity. There can be no question, in my judgment that the Holy Father is sincerely anxious to bring about such a result, and is prepared to make liberal concessions in furtherance of so desirable an object. The advisers of Victor Emanuel and the body of the Italian Pope, in the papal as in the royal dominions, look forward hopefully for the same end. But, as I mentioned in a previous despatch, a very strong body in the church are wholly opposed to it, as are the radical or Mazzinian party among the people, though for very opposite reasons. It seems, indeed, to be a contest between extremes and means, the result of which is still very doubtful. The counsels of the French Emperor, I have reasons to think, are all in the sense of peace and unity between church and state in Italy, and everything seems to indicate his settled purpose to carry out the Franco-Italian treaty, and withdraw his troops from Rome at the time fixed upon. This, however, as I have before remarked, is contingent upon the maintenance of peace and public order here; for the Emperor will not permit the person or authority of the Pope to be molested or assailed for the want of adequate protection.

I called yesterday upon the cardinal secretary of state to communicate to him the latest tidings received from America. He fully concurred with me in regarding the intelligence as decisive, and the war as practically at an end, and he freely avowed his satisfaction at the auspicious result.

The cardinal inquired particularly as to the state of Mr. Seward's health, and again expressed for himself and the Holy Father their earnest hopes for his speedy recovery, and their sincere condolence with the American people in the loss of their lamented President.

I have the honor to be, with great respect, your obedient servant,

RUFUS KING

Hon. WILLIAM HUNTER,
Acting Secretary of State.

Mr. King to Mr. Seward.

[Extract.]

No. 40.] LEGATION OF THE UNITED STATES AT ROME,
May 24, 1865.

SIR: Since my despatch of May 13, nothing has transpired in Rome calling for special mention. The discussion to which I referred in my last, as to the result of the pending conference or correspondence between the Pope and Victor Emanuel, is still going on in diplomatic and political circles. It is doubtful, however, whether any material progress has yet been made towards a solution of the different questions involved. The return of M. Vegezzi, the envoy of Victor Emanuel, is daily looked for here, and it is generally supposed that he will bring with him some definite proposals on the part of the King of Italy. The feeling of opposition to any compromise or reconciliation between the Pope and the King does not seem to abate either with the ultra-montane party in the church or the radicals among the people, and the hope of a favorable issue to the negotiations appears to be less strong than it was a fortnight since.

Among the rumors received from America by the last arrival was one which has created some excitement and elicited a variety of comments on this side of the Atlantic. It is that which refers to the proposed "emigration" of many disbanded officers and soldiers of the federal army to Mexico, with the view of taking service under Juarez. The course which Maximilian has pursued towards the church since he ascended the throne of the Montezumas has cost him a large share of the popularity which he enjoyed at Rome a year ago, and there were not a few of the Catholic dignitaries who expressed the hope that the Austrian archduke may speedily find it advisable to return to Europe. Some of the French journals, accepting the rumor as a fact, see in it a threat against France, and seek to hold the federal government responsible for any movement of the kind. In conversing, however, last evening on this subject with the French ambassador, Count Sartiges, I was glad to hear him express the utmost confidence that, so long as the State Department at Washington continued to be guided by the same able hands and wise counsels which had controlled its action during the past four years, there need be no fear of any difficulty or misunderstanding between the United States and France.

* * * * * * * *

I have the honor to be, with great respect, your obedient servant,

RUFUS KING.

Hon. WILLIAM H. SEWARD, *&c.*, *&c.*, *&c.*

Mr. King to Mr. Hunter.

No. 41.] LEGATION OF THE UNITED STATES AT ROME,
June 2, 1865.

SIR: I have the honor to acknowledge the receipt of the circular from the State Department, under date of May 16, enclosing two copies of the President's proclamation of May 10, relative to insurgent cruisers, one of which I am directed to communicate, without delay, to the government to which I am accredited. In accordance with these instructions, I this morning presented to the cardinal secretary of state a copy of the proclamation in question, with a brief explanation of its contents.

I availed myself of the opportunity to converse with his eminence on the subject of American affairs. He rejoiced, he said, to see that the war was entirely over, and that the questions remaining to be disposed of were of trifling importance compared with the great one which had been so effectually settled. Alluding to the capture of Jefferson Davis, the cardinal expressed the hope that the government might find it consistent with its views of duty to spare the life which he had forfeited to the outraged laws of his country. I remarked to his eminence that of one thing at least he might rest assured—that no feeling of vengeance would dictate the course pursued, and that fewer victims would fall at the close of our great civil war than in any other similar struggle recorded in history.

The cardinal adverted to our existing relations with England and France, and the causes which might disturb them. Of these he seemed to think that Mexico was the most prominent. I assured his eminence that the American government would not permit any "filibustering" expedition to be fitted out in the United States, with a view to upset Maximilian and expel his French protectors from Mexico. At the same time I expressed the belief that the Austrian archduke could not maintain his authority there without foreign help, and when that was withdrawn—as it shortly must be—he would probably follow in their footsteps. The cardinal coincided in this opinion, and added that when consulted on the subject by Maximilian, upwards of a year ago, he had cautioned the Austrian prince against undertaking the enterprise. All that his eminence said, indeed, confirmed the view taken in my last despatch, as to the feeling now entertained by the papal court towards Maximilian and his projected empire on the western continent.

I mentioned to the cardinal that, within a few days past, Bishop Lynch, of Charleston, South Carolina, a reputed confederate agent, had applied to me, through a friend, to know upon what conditions he would be allowed to return to South Carolina and resume his clerical functions. The cardinal remarked, in reply, that the bishop had never been received or recognized in any way as an accredited representative of Jefferson Davis, and that, like every other good Catholic, resident in the United States, it was his bounden duty to honor, respect, and obey the constituted authorities of the government under whose protection he lived.

The envoy of Victor Emanuel, M. Vegezzi, is expected to return to Rome on Monday next. This is another step forward in the pending negotiations between the Pope and the King of Italy; but no prediction can yet be safely hazarded as to the final result.

I am, with great respect, your obedient servant,

RUFUS KING.

Hon. W. HUNTER,
Acting Secretary of State.

Mr. King to Mr. Seward.

No. 42.] LEGATION OF THE UNITED STATES AT ROME, *June* 24, 1865.

SIR: I have received from the State Department copies of the presidential proclamations of April 11, and May 2, 9, 10, and 22, as also of the notification issued by the Secretary of State, dated June 2, relating to foreign passports.

The festival of Corpus Domini was celebrated in this city on the 15th instant, with all the pomp and ceremony with which the church of Rome is accustomed to surround its public observances. The sovereign pontiff, whose health continues excellent, bore a conspicuous part in the imposing pageant, and was welcomed with every outward demonstration of affection and respect by the multitude assembled in the great square of St. Peter.

The anniversaries of the election and coronation of the present Pope, occurring on the 17th and 21st instant, were duly honored in Rome. In accordance with custom, all the members of the diplomatic corps now here called to offer to his Holiness their congratulations upon the happy return of these (to him) memorable days. During my interview with the Holy Father, he spoke with much feeling about American affairs, expressed the sincere pleasure which it gave him to learn that the war was ended, and desired me to convey to the President his best wishes for the success of the administration and the complete restoration of peace, prosperity, and public order. He asked several questions about our national debt, remarking, in the connexion, that ours was a country of wonders and of resources apparently so vast that even a debt of such magnitude need cause no disquiet. His Holiness seemed greatly interested in the probable fate of the leaders of the great rebellion, and especially of Jefferson Davis, expressing the hope that his life might be spared, and no victims offered up on the altar of the restored Union. But as for the conspirators and assassins who had struck down President Lincoln and attempted the murder of the Secretary of State, he was entirely content that, in their case, justice should do her perfect work. I repeated to his Holiness the assurance which I had heretofore given to Cardinal Antonelli that no life would be wantonly, vengefully, or unnecessarily taken, and that the greatest civil war the world had ever seen would close with the smallest number of victims recorded in history.

After taking leave of the Pope, I proceeded as usual to make a formal visit to the cardinal secretary of state, and conversed for some time with his eminence about American affairs. He, too, manifested great interest in the progress and results of the American state trials, and warmly congratulated me upon the final and happy termination of our great struggle.

M. Vegezzi, the representative of Victor Emanuel, has been in Rome, on his second visit, for two or three weeks past. He is here, however, in no recognized official capacity, but rather as a private and confidential messenger; and thus far his mission has been without any actual practical result. The influences for and against his success seem so nearly balanced that, as yet, it is difficult, if not impossible, to predict which way the scale will turn.

The papal court is about breaking up for the summer. Early next month his Holiness goes to his favorite retreat in the Alvan hills, Castel Gandolfo, and the diplomatic corps have already commenced dispersing. After St. Peter's day, the 29th instant, very few will be left in Rome.

Bishop Lynch, of Charleston, South Carolina, late confederate agent, is still here. I had an interview with him at his request a short time since. He admitted that the cause of the south was hopeless, expressed a wish to return to his home and post of duty, and asked me on what terms he could be re-admitted into the United States. I told him that the first thing to be done was to take the oath of allegiance, and make his peace with the federal government. This he was willing and ready to do, if that would suffice; but he seemed apprehensive that if he returned to America he might be proceeded against criminally. I told him that the President's proclamation, which was daily expected, would no doubt contain full information on this point. The proclamation has since arrived, and Bishop Lynch, I understand, considers himself included in the list of exceptions. His present purpose, as I learn from a mutual friend, is to proceed to Havana, and thence make his appeal to the federal authorities. I judge that he is effectually cured of his secession folly.

I have the honor to be, with great respect, your obedient servant,

RUFUS KING.

Hon. WILLIAM H. SEWARD, &c., &c., &c.

Mr. Seward to Mr. King.

No. 27.] DEPARTMENT OF STATE,
Washington, June 29, 1865.

SIR: Your despatches from number 33 to number 39, with the exception of number 35, have been received, and have been read with much interest. Your account of the feeling excited in Rome, and of the proceedings which took place there, on the reception of the news of the assassination of President Lincoln, are very gratifying.

I am, sir, your obedient servant,

WILLIAM H. SEWARD.

RUFUS KING, Esq., &c., &c., *Rome.*

Mr. King to Mr. Seward.

[Extract.]

No. 43.] LEGATION OF THE UNITED STATES AT ROME,
July 4, 1865.

SIR: I have the honor to acknowledge the receipt of the circular from the State Department, under date of June 7th, relating to the order issued to Rear-Admiral Goldsborough, then about to sail in the United States steamer Colorado for European waters. I believe that nearly all the maritime powers of Europe have now withdrawn their recognition of the insurgent States as belligerents, and no longer accord to rebel vessels-of-war any privileges as such, or withhold from the flag of the United States the customary naval courtesies. The government to which I am accredited possesses no navy, nor any ports likely to be visited by American ships-of-war, and has not taken any action in the premises to which the United States could object. When I mentioned to Cardinal Antonelli this morning the substance of the circular above referred to, he at once replied: "We, at least, have never recognized the southern belligerents."

St. Peter's day, the 29th ultimo, was duly honored in Rome. It was the great festa of the church, and nearly the whole population of the city seemed to take part in the ceremonies. The Pope officiated in person at the celebration of the mass in the morning, and a vast and perfectly orderly crowd enjoyed the magnificent display of fireworks on the Pincian hill at night. His Holiness, whose health continues excellent, takes his departure for Castel Gandolfo in a few days.

M. Vegezzi, the special messenger from the King of Italy, left Rome, on his return to Florence, last week. Thus far nothing has been accomplished, nor does the prospect of an ultimate agreement between the Pope and Victor Emanuel seem at all flattering. * * * * *

The few Americans remaining at this season in Rome, though far away from their native land, do not forget that this is the nation's birthday, and they honor it accordingly. They may be pardoned for repeating, with conscious pride, in the ancient capital of the world the old Roman boast, "I am an American citizen."

I have the honor to be, with great respect, your obedient servant,

RUFUS KING.

Hon. WILLIAM H. SEWARD, *&c., &c., &c.*

Mr. King to Mr. Seward.

[Extracts.]

No. 45.] LEGATION OF THE UNITED STATES AT ROME,
November 10, 1865.

SIR: * * * * * * * *

Two events have occurred in Rome, since my last despatch, of more than ordinary interest. The retirement of Monsignor de Merode from the papal cabinet, and the commencement of the evacuation of the papal territory by the French troops. The explanation given by the press of M. de Merode's withdrawal vary according to the political bias of the parties making them. Those who wish to attach but little consequence to the change attribute it to M. de Merode's failing health, while a much larger party see in it an important step in advance, and think that it augurs favorably for the reconciliation of Rome and Italy. M. de Merode was understood to reflect the sentiments of the ultramontane party, in church and state, and a marked antagonism existed between himself and Cardinal Antonelli, which threatened at times to disturb the harmony of the papal council. Now, however, that M. de Merode has retired, the influence of the distinguished secretary of state has become all paramount, and will, it is confidently hoped, be wisely and faithfully employed.

The evacuation of the French troops, in pursuance of the treaty between the Emperor of France and the King of Italy, commenced on Monday last, two batteries of artillery having left Rome that day to embark on French transports now lying at Civita Vecchia. Other bodies of troops will follow at brief intervals, and there seems no reason to doubt that the whole movement will be completed within the period stipulated, to wit, two years from September 15, 1864. To replace the soldiers thus withdrawn by Napoleon, the papal government is recruiting and organizing a considerable force; and the belief gains currency that, before the final evacuation of the French, an arrangement will be entered into between the Pope and Victor Emanuel which will secure to the Holy See all the protection it needs.

The cholera still lingers at different points along the Mediterranean coast, and, within the past few days, has been quite fatal in Naples. Thus far the pontifical states have escaped, comparatively unscathed, though it is hardly to be expected they will go entirely free. Meanwhile very rigid quarantine regulations are enforced all along the frontier, and the result is that, as yet, but few Americans or other foreigners have come to Rome. Should the sanitary condition of the Italian peninsula improve, however, there is every prospect of a large influx of Americans during the coming winter.

Within the current week I have enjoyed two interviews with the cardinal secretary of state, and conversed at some length on topics connected with American affairs. His eminence expressed his sincere gratification at the rapid progress towards peace and union which our country was making, and spoke in terms of very warm praise of President Johnson's plan of reconstruction, and of the merciful and magnanimous course which had been pursued towards the vanquished rebels. * * * * * *

The Pope, I am happy to say, is in the enjoyment of excellent health and spirits. He passed, Thursday, along the whole length of the Corso on foot, meeting everywhere, from the crowds who thronged that thoroughfare, unequivocal demonstrations of affection and respect.

I have the honor to be, with great respect, your obedient servant,

RUFUS KING.

Hon. WILLIAM H. SEWARD,
Secretary of State.

Mr. King to Mr. Seward.

No. 46.] LEGATION OF THE UNITED STATES AT ROME,
November 18, 1865.

SIR: I had the honor, yesterday, of an interview with the Holy Father, and enjoyed a long and interesting conversation with him about American affairs, as well as the condition of things in Italy and Europe. The Pope had many questions to ask about the progress of events in the United States, and expressed great satisfaction at the return of peace and the reconstruction of the Union. He inquired particularly as to the health of the President, whose life, he trusted, would be spared, that he might finish the work he had so well begun. He warmly approved the clemency which had been shown the rebel leaders, and hoped, he said, that Jefferson Davis would also receive the executive pardon. The most difficult problem he thought for the United States to solve was the proper disposition of the negroes; and he seemed to apprehend that we should find the question a troublesome one. Passing to European affairs, his Holiness remarked that there was great political agitation all over the continent; not in Italy only, but in Germany, Spain, France, and England, there seemed to be trouble brewing. Ireland was restless and discontented, and Fenianism uttered ominous threats. He had no idea, he said, that this movement would affect British rule in Ireland, for the ocean which rolled between the United States and Great Britain forbade the idea of invasion. But Canada, with its extensive and exposed frontier, offered an easier prize, and thither, he thought, the Fenians might turn their arms. It would be for the advantage of all parties, the Holy Father remarked, that the United States should take Canada and incorporate it into the American Union, rather than allow the Fenians to possess themselves of it. Better that it should be done by a regularly constituted government than by a revolutionary and irresponsible organization subject to no control, and liable to every excess. His Holiness spoke, I thought, despondingly of the aspect of affairs in Italy. Within another fortnight, he said, Saxony and Bavaria would reorganize the kingdom of Victor Emanuel. The Emperor of France was about to withdraw from Italy, and "the poor Pope would be left all alone in his little boat in the midst of the tempestuous ocean." What would happen God alone knew, and to His will and protection the Holy Father committed himself. I expressed the hope that no serious trouble would occur in Rome, and reminded his Holiness that it was the duty of the diplomatic corps to share his fortunes and remain near his person. Yes, he said, and during the revolutionary movement of '48, when he had sought refuge in the palace of the Quirinal, the diplomatic corps all hurried thither and formed, as it were, a cordon around him, so that, in the midst of the tumult and firing, he remained calm and tranquil. His Holiness adverted to the concessions which the different governments of Europe seemed to be making "to the revolutionary spirit of the age." They would not, he said, satisfy those who were clamoring for change, but only encourage them to make further demands until they would finish by telling the governments themselves that they could dispense with their further services. Evidently the Holy Father looked upon the condition of affairs in Europe as anything but satisfactory, and it was with deep and manifest emotion that he referred to the Supreme Ruler of the universe as his only guide and refuge in the apprehended troubles.

After taking my leave of his Holiness, I paid the customary visit to the cardinal secretary of state, and was received by him with his wonted kindness and courtesy. His eminence, who watches with close attention the progress of events in America, referred with great satisfaction to the reported interview of a delegation from South Carolina with the President of the United States, and to the language used and the sentiments avowed by Mr. Johnson on that occasion. His eminence cordially assented to the justice of the President's views, and expressed his warm and earnest approval of the course pursued by the federal authorities in re-establishing law, order, and civil government among the people of the States so lately in rebellion against the Union. A policy at once so wise and so humane deserved, as it could not fail, he thought, to secure complete success.

The cholera still prevails with great severity at Naples, but, as yet, there has not been a case in Rome, and the authorities here hope to escape the visitation of the pestilence, at least during the present season. Meantime very stringent quarantine regulations continue to be enforced all along the papal frontiers, and the result is that Rome is comparatively deserted; though at this period of the year it is usually crowded with visitors from all quarters of the globe.

The French troops continue to leave Rome by detachments, and Count Sartiges, the ambassador of France, remarked to me a few days since, that within a year there would not be a single French soldier left in the papal territory.

I have the honor to be, very respectfully, your obedient servant,

RUFUS KING.

Hon. WILLIAM H. SEWARD,
Secretary of State, &c., &c.

DENMARK.

Mr. Wood to Mr. Seward.

No. 182.] LEGATION OF THE UNITED STATES,
Copenhagen, February 6, 1865.

SIR: On the 4th instant, having received a communication from Mr. Bigelow, the United States chargé d'affaires at Paris, I addressed to the minister for foreign affairs the accompanying note, No. 47, and interrogatories, and to-day have addressed another note to him, No. 48, a copy of which is also herewith enclosed. Some time last autumn an iron-clad brig-rigged steam ram arrived at this port from France. I was informed, in answer to my inquiries, that she was for the Danish government. I was subsequently informed that she did not pass inspection, and would be returned to the builder, in France, as unfit for the Danish navy. I was also informed by a Danish naval officer that she was rudely and badly built, as he knew by inspection, and that her bolts had no heads to them, and she was in other respects defective. After lying here some three months, and having had several inspections, none of which, as I was informed, was satisfactory, she, with a crew of some thirty men, (as I was also informed,) was sent back to Bordeaux, and of which Consul Hansen duly apprized our consul at that place. She is a formidable and dangerous-looking craft, and is said to be heavily armed with Armstrong guns. I await the answer to my inquiries. It is possible this government may have been deceived, as there is a rumor of one "De Reviere," who once offered to make cannon for us and was refused, being concerned in the affair.

I remain, very respectfully, your obedient servant,

B. R. WOOD,
Minister Resident.

Hon. WILLIAM H. SEWARD,
Secretary of State.

Mr. Wood to Mr. Blumhe.

No. 47.] LEGATION OF THE UNITED STATES,
Copenhagen, February 4, 1865.

SIR: From authentic information this day received from the legation of the United States at Paris, there is reason to fear that one or more vessels-of-war built in France, but carrying the Danish flag, have recently passed into the hands of the so-called confederates of North America. Though I do not suppose that his Majesty's government has sanctioned or will sanction such a use of that flag, yet it is very desirable that the government which I have the honor to represent should be in possession of all the facts connected with this transaction, with a view to obtain such information, (if in the possession of his Majesty's government.)

I take the liberty of herewith enclosing to your excellency certain inquiries which, when answered, will put me in possession of the desired information. May I ask of your excellency as early an answer as will be convenient.

With renewed assurances of distinguished consideration, I have the honor to remain your excellency's obedient servant,

BRADFORD R. WOOD,
Minister Resident.

His Excellency Mr. BLUMHE,
Minister of Foreign Affairs, &c.

1st. How many vessels has the Danish government purchased in France?

2d. What are the names they bore before and after their purchase by the Danish government?

3d. Were they, or either of them, afterwards sent back to France, and what were the orders given their captains in respect to their delivery?

4th. When and where were they delivered, into whose hands, and what became of their equipage?

5th. Were they sold before their redelivery; and if so, to whom, and what were the terms of sale?

6th. Was any notice given to the French government that the vessels were not accepted by the Danish government before their sale and delivery to the new purchasers; if so, when and to whom?

7th. What was the name, rank, and nationality of the officer who took command of them, or either of them; and where and how were they, or either of them, named after the departure of their Danish equipage?

8th. Had they any armament on board when they were delivered; if so, in what did it consist?

9th. Were any arms or munitions of war taken on board while the Danish equipage was being transferred; if so, of what did they consist?

Mr. Wood to Mr. Blumhe.

No. 48.]

LEGATION OF THE UNITED STATES,
Copenhagen, February 6, 1865.

SIR: In addition to the inquiries I had the honor to address to you on the 4th instant, I would suggest, inasmuch as I learn from Paris that the French government say the Danish government bought the Staerkodder *absolutely*, that his Majesty's government furnish me with a certified copy of the contract and any other papers that passed between the two governments, and I would also respectfully inquire under what permission and other circumstances the Staerkodder left Copenhagen, whether under the command of an officer of the Danish navy, and whether she was fully coaled and armed. I assure your excellency that in seeking this information, I do it to exculpate his Majesty's government from any censure in the transaction.

With renewed assurances of high consideration, I have the honor to remain your excellency's obedient servant,

BRADFORD R. WOOD,
Minister Resident.

His Excellency Mr. BLUMHE,
Minister of Foreign Affairs.

Mr. Wood to Mr. Seward.

No. 183.]

LEGATION OF THE UNITED STATES,
Copenhagen, February 14, 1865.

SIR: Since my last despatch I have had several interviews with the acting minister for foreign affairs, Mr. Quaade, (Mr. Blumhe being ill,) and the director general of the ministry, Mr. Vedel. The affair of the Staerkodder, the iron-plated ram to which I referred in my last, is undergoing an investigation, and I have an assurance that the whole matter will be placed in my hands. From these interviews with the minister and the director general, I learn that the Staerkodder never belonged to the Danish government. Some time last winter or last spring they made a contract with one Arman, of Bordeaux, to build an iron-plated ram, carrying three heavy Armstrong guns, but as she did not fulfil the contract, she was rejected. Notwithstanding this she was sent to Copenhagen under the French flag, without guns; the guns following subsequently in an English ship. The ram, after arriving here, was again inspected and again rejected. In the mean time, or on her first arrival, she discharged her French crew. After lying here from the first of November until some time in January, either the agent of Arman, De Riviere, or Mr. Puger, a Danish merchant to whom she was consigned, applied for liberty to ship a crew, and permission to take her back to Bordeaux, under the Danish flag, inasmuch as she could not be taken back under the French flag, as two-thirds or three-fourths of the crew were not French; the French law, it was alledged, requiring it. This permission was conceded, and the Staerkodder, with a crew of forty-five Danes and Swedes or less, set out for Bordeaux, with De Riviere, the agent of Arman on board, and under the command of a Danish merchant captain. After passing into the Cattegat, for some cause or other, perhaps an alleged storm, she returned to Elsinore, and landed De Riviere. She again put to sea, but was compelled to put into Norway and coal, De Riviere having furnished the money. From thence she proceeded to the coast of Holland and took on board De Riviere and another man, and proceeded to Quiberon or Nantes, and, when anchored in French waters, De Riviere informed the Danish captain that he had sold the ship and he need go no further. The Danish captain and crew, (with, perhaps, the exception of two or three, said to be engineers or firemen,) left the ship, taking the Danish flag with them.

I should state that the Armstrong guns were placed in the hold of the Staerkodder when she left here. I must confess that the whole matter looks very much like a French trick on the part of Arman and his agent De Riviere, in which, perhaps, Puger had a hand, and in which the Danish government were the unsuspecting dupes. I have written Mr. Bigelow, our chargé d'affaires at Paris, but fear, from the state of the mails, the Baltic being closed, that he has not received my letter. We have communicated by telegraph.

I remain your obedient servant,

BRADFORD R. WOOD,
Minister Resident.

Hon. WILLIAM H. SEWARD,
Secretary of State.

Mr. Wood to Mr. Seward.

No. 184.] LEGATION OF THE UNITED STATES,
Copenhagen, February 20, 1865.

SIR: I herewith enclose a note I addressed the director general of the ministry on the receipt of a letter from Mr. Bigelow, our chargé d'affaires in Paris. I have seen him this morning, and he reiterates the assertion that the Sphinx or Staerkodder, or Stonewall, never belonged to the Danish government. I read in Galignani of the 12th instant, from the index, "That a secret negotiation is progressing between the United States government and the Danish government for the purchase of the Clyde-built iron-clad, of the Warrior model, belonging to the latter, and now lying at Copenhagen."

This ship is undoubtedly for sale, for, learning last autumn that negotiations for this purpose were pending, I made inquiry and was confidentially informed that the negotiations were with a power friendly to us. I understood from outsiders that the negotiations were with Spain. I repeat an opinion made some two years ago, that we should have a man-of-war in the North German ocean, and, commanding the Baltic, we can be our own best police.

I remain, &c., your obedient servant,

BRADFORD R. WOOD,
Minister Resident.

Hon. WILLIAM H. SEWARD,
Secretary of State.

Mr. Seward to Mr. Wood.

No. 103.] DEPARTMENT OF STATE,
Washington, February 21, 1865.

SIR: It is with sincere regret that I find myself obliged to call your attention to a serious cause of complaint against the government of Denmark.

Certain vessels were building at Bordeaux for the insurgents of the United States. This government remonstrated. The French government interdicted the departure of the vessels. One or more of them was reported to have been sold to Denmark. It is certain that one of them went to Copenhagen. Recently, that vessel is reported to have come, with a Danish crew and a Danish flag, to the island of Houat, on the coast of France, and to have there received an equipment and crew from an English vessel, and coals from a French vessel, and then to have put to sea as an insurgent vessel. There is much confusion in the reports of the transaction which have reached the United States. It is even doubtful whether there are not two vessels concerned in the transaction, instead of one. Again, we hear of one such vessel as having put into Ferrol for repairs; and again, of the same vessel, or another, having put into Corunna for repairs.

Mr. Raasloff here, and the Danish minister in Paris, deny that the Danish government have owned or sold the vessel which is reported to have been brought to Houat. The French minister of finance is understood to affirm that the vessel was so sold. Even the fact of the transfer to the insurgents is not yet clearly established. There is, however, too strong a presumption of the fact to allow this government to remain idle or unconcerned.

You will, therefore, ask for explanations of the Danish government, and in doing so you will not omit to inquire how it happened that, if that government intended to divest itself of responsibility, it caused or suffered the vessel to go into Houat, an unarmed place, not within the surveillance of the French government, instead of Bordeaux.

In every case, and speaking only upon the condition that the facts reported are true, you will inform the Danish government that this government cannot be expected to submit uncomplainingly to apprehended invasions of piratical vesels coming from European ports. We shall expect that Denmark will do whatever is necessary to prevent such acts, if the responsibility shall be traced to the government or to the subjects of Denmark.

You will say, moreover, that this government deems the time to have come when the maritime powers of Europe ought to withhold all protection and shelter from enemies of the United States who proceed from countries with which they are at peace.

I am, sir, your obedient servant,

WILLIAM H. SEWARD.

BRADFORD R. WOOD, Esq., *&c., &c., Copenhagen.*

Mr. Seward to Mr. Wood.

No. 104.] DEPARTMENT OF STATE,
Washington, March 2, 1865.

SIR: I have the honor to acknowledge the receipt of your despatch of the 6th of February, which contains an account of the representation you have made to the Danish government concerning the transfer of the ram Oliude, otherwise called the Stonewall, to pirates engaged in hostilities against the United States.

While it seems to me possible that your representation might properly have been made in a form more acceptable to that government, yet I approve of the proceeding in its general effect, and I authorize you to state to his Majesty's government that the subject is regarded by the President as one which it is hoped will receive the serious attention of the government of Denmark.

The inquiries which have been made in France leave it doubtful whether the Danish authorities have exercised that vigilance and that regard to the rights of the United States, in the transaction referred to, which, as a friendly nation, they had a right to expect. It must be apparent that this government cannot rest content if a naval war is waged against us, under a piratical flag, from any of the maritime states of Europe.

I am, sir, your obedient servant,

WILLIAM H. SEWARD.

BRADFORD R. WOOD, Esq., *&c.*, *&c.*, *Copenhagen.*

Mr. Seward to Mr. Wood.

No. 105.] DEPARTMENT OF STATE,
Washington, March 3, 1865.

SIR: Herewith I enclose, for your information, a copy of a despatch of the 9th ultimo, (No. 23,) from Mr. Bigelow, chargé d'affaires of the United States at Paris, in which he communicates a transcript of a note addressed to him by Mr. Drouyn de Lhuys, relative to the steam ram Olinde, otherwise Stonewall, together with several other papers upon the same subject.

I am, sir, your obedient servant,

WILLIAM H. SEWARD.

BRADFORD R. WOOD, Esq., *&c.*, *&c.*, *Copenhagen.*

(For enclosures see despatch No. 25, from Mr. Bigelow.)

Mr. Wood to Mr. Seward.

No. 185.] LEGATION OF THE UNITED STATES,
Copenhagen, March 3, 1865.

SIR: I herewith enclose copies of notes to the director general of the foreign ministry, of the dates of 25th, and to the minister for foreign affairs on the 28th February, ultimo. The letter to the foreign minister, who is still confined to his house by illness, was written after my interview and a full understanding with Mr. Vedel, the director general of the ministry. I yesterday had an interview with Mr. Quaade, minister without portfolio, and he assures me the fullest investigation shall be had in the matter; that my note of the 28th ultimo had been laid before the minister of justice, and that I might expect a speedy answer. I have to-day had an interview with Mr. Vedel, who submitted to me the contract with the French builder of the Olinde, *alias* Sphinx, *alias* Staerkodder, *alias* Stonewall, and other papers, which show that the ship never belonged to the Danish government. Copies of these will be placed in my hands. While I acquit the Danish government of an intentional breach of neutrality, yet we may suffer just as much as if they had intended it. I await the evidence now being taken, and to be taken, before presenting the whole case.

I have the honor to remain your obedient servant,

BRADFORD R. WOOD,
Minister Resident.

Hon. WILLIAM H. SEWARD, *Secretary of State.*

Mr. Wood to Mr. Blumhe.

LEGATION OF THE UNITED STATES,
February 28, 1865.

SIR: From information I have received from Mr. Hansen, the American consul, communicated to him by one of the crew of the Sphinx, or Staerkodder, and now the Stonewall, I learn that when this ship left Copenhagen she had on board another passenger beside De Riviere, a confederate officer, passing under an assumed name, and who took command of the ship after she arrived in French waters, (or when she met another steamer,) or when the Danish captain ceased to command. I am also informed that the French engineers who had brought the ship from France were kept on board this ship (the Staerkodder or whatever name) until the Danish engineers went on board, or until the day before, or a short time before she left Copenhagen; and that she had her guns in position when she left, and coal sufficient for the voyage to Bordeaux. That when she put back to Elsinore she landed De Riviere, and a Mr. Puggard brought her another engineer. After leaving Elsinore, and, as alleged, on account of bad weather, she put into Christiansand or some other port in Norway, coaled and remained there four or five days, three of which were pleasant, and went to sea in weather more boisterous than when she entered that port; the ship being a good seaboat, but leaky. About thirty-six hours after leaving Norway the ship altered her course for Nieu Dieppe, in Holland. One of the engineers remonstrated with the captain, as the weather was fine and the ship had plenty of coal.

At Nieu Dieppe she again took on board De Riviere and another man, (Waddell,) also a confederate officer, known to one of the engineers, and who informed the Danish captain who he was, and who subsequently became the second officer, or an officer on board the Staerkodder after she passed into confederate hands.

On the 21st January the Staerkodder arrived off Quiberon, or in French waters, and came to anchor. Here a man representing himself as the brother of De Riviere came on board and soon after left. The next morning the Staerkodder got under way, and was shortly after met by a ship under English colors, with coal, munitions of war, and a new crew, and soon after meeting with her was met by a French steamer. The Danish captain then informed his crew that the ship was sold, and tried to induce his crew or some of them to enlist and to remain on board, and which they refused to do, and insisted on being put on shore. They were set to work by the Danish captain to coal from the British steamer under the promise of eight francs per man for doing it. One of the engineers protested against this delivery of the ship, and insisted that the captain should go into port and the crew be properly discharged. They were finally landed by the French steamer, leaving the Danish captain on board and the Danish flag still flying.

I would request of your excellency that the Danish captain be examined as to his knowledge or belief as to the truth of the above, and particularly as to his knowledge or belief of the real names, character and business of the passengers who left Copenhagen with him, and of those who came on board in Holland, and what has become of them, and where he last saw them. And, further, that such of the engineers and crew be examined as shall be indicated by Mr. Hansen, the American consul; and, further, that the Mr. or Messrs. Puggard be examined as to their knowledge or belief of the character of the Staerkodder, or any of the particulars in the foregoing statement. And I would further request that inasmuch as Mr. Hansen understands the Danish language he may be present at such examination, and be permitted to suggest such questions as may occur to him bearing on this matter. I need not suggest to your excellency that if the captain and the agent or agents of this ship are innocent, the more searching the investigation the better for them. I do not believe that his Majesty's government has intentionally departed from the strictest neutrality; but if it should appear that Danish citizens have used the Danish flag for a fraudulent or piratical purpose, I am confident that his Majesty's government will vindicate its neutrality.

With renewed assurances of high consideration, I remain your excellency's obedient servant,

B. R. WOOD, *Minister Resident.*

Mr. BLUMHE, *Minister for Foreign Affairs.*

Mr. Wood to Mr. Seward.

No. 187.]

LEGATION OF THE UNITED STATES,
Copenhagen, March 14, 1865.

SIR: Your despatch, No. 103, of the 21st ultimo, was received yesterday. From the despatches and copies of letters received ere this, and those I now send, you may perhaps think I have more than anticipated my instructions.

I am very glad to receive and communicate to this government your last despatch, as the director general of the ministry informed me, a few days since, that the court intrusted with the investigation of the affair of the Staerkodder had discovered "it had not sufficient jurisdiction" to make the examination I desired. I have but recently discovered that the Staerkodder was originally intended for the confederates, and I am credibly informed that the Mr. Puggard I have already mentioned, a Danish merchant in this city, the consignee or correspondent of the ship, and the man who procured her crew and liberty to leave the port under the Danish flag, and whose re-examination I have asked, advanced large sums of money for the building of the Staerkodder, knowing that this vessel was being built for the confederates. I have informed both the minister for foreign affairs and the director general of the ministry of this.

To prevent all laches I again send a copy of my note to the director general, of the 25th ultimo. From a translation of Mr. Blumhe's note to me, enclosing copies, &c., of the contract with Arman, the French builder, and other papers, you will see what he says of the affair. I am still of the opinion that the Danish government was practised upon by the Frenchmen and one or more of its own subjects, and how far it will screen the latter remains to be seen.

I have the honor to remain your obedient servant,

BRADFORD R. WOOD,
Minister Resident.

Hon. WILLIAM H. SEWARD,
Secretary of State.

Mr. Wood to Mr. Blumhe.

LEGATION OF THE UNITED STATES,
March 12, 1865.

SIR: On the 25th and 28th ultimo, I respectively addressed notes to the director general of the ministry for foreign affairs and to his excellency the minister for foreign affairs in relation to the Staerkodder, and requesting an examination of the captain and some of the crew of that ship, as well as of Mr. Puggard, who, I have since learned, advanced money to build that ship when orignally intended for the so-called confederate insurgents. In a recent conversation with Mr. Vedel, the director general of the ministry, I expressed my fears that the crew of the Staerkodder would be dispersed before any examination of them could be had on the points I had presented. I am now informed that one Bolling, an engineer on board of the Staerkodder, will soon leave Copenhagen, he being engaged on a steamer running between Cursoe and Keil. I am also informed of some difficulty in the constitution of the court before which the examination is being held to obtain the investigation I have requested. I shall very much regret should there be no examination of the men I have designated.

With renewed assurances of high consideration, I remain your excellency's obedient servant,

BRADFORD R. WOOD, *Minister Resident.*

His Excellency Mr. BLUMHE,
Minister for Foreign Affairs.

Mr. Wood to Mr. Blumhe.

LEGATION OF THE UNITED STATES,
March 13, 1865.

SIR: I have this day received a despatch from the Secretary of State of the United States, in which, speaking on the condition that the facts reported are true, I am instructed to inform the Danish government, "That the government of the United States cannot be expected to submit uncomplainingly to the apprehended invasion of piratical vessels, coming from European ports, and that it is expected that Denmark will do whatever is necessary to prevent this, if the responsibility shall be traced to the government or to the subjects of his Majesty, the King of Denmark." I am also instructed to ask an explanation of his Majesty's government, and in doing so to inquire how it happened that, if his Majesty's government intended to divest itself of responsibility, it caused or suffered the Staerkodder to go into Houat, an unarmed place, not within the surveillance of the French government, instead of Bordeaux. I am also instructed to say, "That the government of the United States deems the time to have come when the maritime powers of Europe ought to withhold all protection and shelter from enemies of the United States who proceed from countries with which they are at peace."

With renewed assurances of high consideration, I remain your excellency's obedient servant,

BRADFORD R. WOOD, *Minister Resident.*

His Excellency Mr. BLUMHE,
Minister for Foreign Affairs.

Mr. Wood to Mr. Vedel.

DEAR SIR: From information I have received to-day, I have no doubt that the Danish captain of the Staerkodder knew the destination of that ship when she left Copenhagen, and that an examination of some of the crew will implicate him. I think it can be shown, beyond a doubt, that he knew the ship belonged to the confederates when he went into or when he left Nieu Dieppe. I have reason to believe that Mr. Puggard also knew the character of the ship. If this should prove true, and the Danish captain has used the Danish flag as a cloak, does it not only require his arrest and punishment, but also a request from the Danish government to the Spanish government not to consummate the fraud, but to retain the Staerkodder or Stonewall in the Spanish port, where she now is? I will see you at the earliest convenience, and fully explain.

I have the honor to remain, very truly, your obedient servant,

B. R. WOOD.

Mr. VEDEL,
Director General of the Ministry for Foreign Affairs.

Mr. Blumhe to Mr. Wood.

[Translation.]

COPENHAGEN, *March* 8, 1865.

SIR: In the note you have done me the honor to address to me the fourth of last month, you have called my attention to the circumstance that one or more vessels-of-war built in France, but bearing the Danish flag, have passed into the hands of the so-called Confederate States; and while entirely dismissing the supposition of any connivance whatever on the part of the government of the King in this transaction, you have asked of me some explanations upon certain points set forth in the appendix to your note.

Being sincerely desirous of removing any suspicion which could attach to the government of the King, under these circumstances, I have endeavored to collect all authentic information upon the negotiations which have taken place between the government of the King and Mr. Arman, shipbuilder of Bordeaux, relative to the iron-clad vessel Sphinx, alias Staerkodder, for it is evidently to this ship that your note alludes.

In sending you, sir, the enclosed documents, marked by letters A to F, I permit myself to accompany them with as succinct a narrative of the principal points as these portions admit of.

On the 31st day of March last, a contract was signed by which Mr. Arman engaged to deliver on the 10th of June, 1864, an iron-clad vessel of 300 horse-power, with guns and munitions. The vessel, which was already upon the stocks, was to be finished under the control of an officer of the Danish navy, who, in accordance with articles IX to XI of the contract, was charged with inspecting and accepting the vessel before she could leave Bordeaux to go to her destination. The conditions of the contract were not fulfilled by Mr. Arman. The ship was only finished on the 21st of October, and she neither realized the promises made as to her speed nor as to her draught of water.

The Danish officer, Mr. Shonheyder, consequently could not accept her. Nevertheless, Mr. Arman, hoping to succeed by a direct negotiation with the minister of marine, in causing the ship to be accepted, sent her the last of October to Copenhagen. The refusal of Mr. Shonheyder was, however, repeated to Mr. Arman during an interview which he had at Paris with the director of the ministry of marine, Mr. Eckildsen, and the Danish official added expressly that the ship having left Bordeaux without the authorization of the proper officer, she could only have been sent at his own risk and peril as well as at his own expense. The vessel, which arrived at Copenhagen in the middle of the month of November, was inspected here, but the minister of marine persisted in refusing to accept her; consequently the contract was annulled, and Mr. Arman understood expressly that the Danish government was freed from every obligation to him under the contract.

The ship must then return to France, but, from motives of economy, the builder had dis missed his captain and French crew upon the arrival of the vessel at Copenhagen. He thus found himself under the necessity of engaging here, through the intervention of his correspondent, a merchant of Copenhagen, a Danish merchant captain and a crew composed of Danish and Swedish sailors in order to carry the vessel back to Bordeaux; which rendered it necessary for him to ask a special permission of the department of customs, in order that the vessel, though French property, should be able to leave the port of Copenhagen under conditions so unusual. Being no longer able to demand assistance of French consuls in the ports where the severity of the season might, perhaps, force the ship to seek refuge, Mr. Arman likewise asked for a letter of recommendation to the Danish consuls as well as permission to make the voyage under Danish colors. This permission and this letter of recommendation were given to him, but I need not add that all the advances the captain should ask for in the ports were to remain entirely unconnected with the government of the King, and that it was expressly enjoined upon the Danish captain to strike the Danish flag as soon as he entered the port of Bordeaux.

I hope, sir, that these explanations will serve to answer the questions which you have addressed to me. They prove that the government of the King has been entirely unconnected with the transaction which appears to have taken place, and that it regrets it sincerely. I am engaged in taking some steps in order that, with the help of depositions made before the tribunal by persons belonging to the crew, there may be drawn up some "proces verbaux" upon everything which has taken place during the voyage of the vessel since her departure from Copenhagen, and I wait in order to send you this intelligence as soon as it reaches me.

Accept, sir, renewed assurances of my most distinguished consideration.

BLUMHE.

Mr. Wood,
Minister Resident of the United States of America.

Mr. Wood to Mr. Seward.

No. 188.] Legation of the United States,
Copenhagen, March 22, 1865.

Sir: I herewith enclose my last notes to Mr. Blumhe, the minister for foreign affairs. My information as to the confederate officer was received from Mr. Bigelow, our chargé in Paris. So far, I cannot learn of any suspicious arrivals in this city. Consul Hansen says he has been informed of enlistments for the confederates, forwarded to Hamburg by a Danish confederate agent. We have a detective on the lookout. I have written Consul Andersen.

I remain your obedient servant,

BRADFORD R. WOOD,
Minister Resident.

Hon. William H. Seward,
Secretary of State.

Mr. Wood to Mr. Blumhe.

Legation of the United States,
March 20, 1865.

Sir: I have just received information that two or three confederate insurgent officers, of the names of Doty, Bishop, and Thomas, were to leave London on the 10th instant, for Copenhagen, to purchase and equip a vessel for the confederate service. They doubtless expect to get this vessel to sea as a private commercial enterprise. Should these men, or any of them, succeed in their attempt, and by the complicity of subjectsof the King, as in the case of the Staerkodder, I can merely refer your excellency to the last despatch I have received from the Secretary of State of the United States, and which I have already communicated. As the French government are throwing on the Danish government the responsibility of the escape of the Staerkodder, and as neither the government of France nor England have permitted such a ship to leave their ports, and the English government are now prosecuting those engaged in assisting the confederates, may I hope his Majesty's government will be equally prompt in this matter with those Danish citizens who pay no regard to the neutrality of their country. I must again ask that Mr. Poggard be re-examined as to the facts I have hitherto presented, as well as the Danish captain of the Staerkodder, and especially whether they did not know, or have reason to believe, before that ship left Copenhagen, or before she left Elsinore the last time, that she belonged to or was intended for the so-called confederates. I have already asked for the re-examination of some of the crew, to be designated by the American consul, Mr. Hansen, and particularly of the engineers, only one of whose names, Belling, I have learned. I would also request that the Danish minister in Paris be permitted to furnish the American chargé de affaires, Mr. Bigelow, with the proofs that the Staerkodder did not belong to the Danish government.

With renewed assurances of distinguished consideration, I have the honor to remain, your excellency's obedient servant,

B. R. WOOD, *Minister Resident.*

His Excellency Mr. BLUMHE,
Minister for Foreign Affairs.

Mr. Wood to Mr. Blumhe.

LEGATION OF THE UNITED STATES,
March 22, 1865.

SIR: Consul Hansen informs me that one Block, No. 6 Hyskenstrade, is enlisting men for the confederate services and in some instances paying their expenses to Hamburg.

With renewed assurance of distinguished consideration, I have the honor to remain your excellency's obedient servant,

B. R. WOOD, *Minister Resident.*

His Excellency Mr. BLUMHE,
Minister for Foreign Affairs.

Mr. Seward to Mr. Wood.

No. 107.] DEPARTMENT OF STATE,
Washington, March 24, 1865.

SIR: Your despatch of the 20th of February, No. 184, has been received.

As the case of the Stonewall or Staerkodder stands at present, the proceedings of the Danish government, in connexion therewith, appear in an unfavorable light. A despatch, dated the 27th ultimo, has been received to-day from Mr. Hansen, our consul at Elsinore, communicating facts which painfully confirm our apprehension that the government of Denmark has not exercised in the matter such diligent care as the occasion required. We do not learn that it has addressed remonstrances either to Spain or to France, or that it has taken any interest in the subject, or even answered the inquiries you have made.

I do not doubt that Mr. Hansen has fully acquainted you with the facts which he has communicated to the department, nor that you will exercise proper vigilance in your efforts to collect further information upon the subject.

I am, sir, your obedient servant,

WILLIAM H. SEWARD.

BRADFORD R. WOOD, Esq., *&c., &c., Copenhagen.*

Mr. Wood to Mr. Seward.

No. 189.] LEGATION OF THE UNITED STATES,
Copenhagen, March 29, 1865.

SIR: The director general of the ministry called on me yesterday with copies of the testimony already taken, (in Danish,) and said they would allow any further examination of the witnesses desired. I shall look them over with Consul Hansen, (whose Danish makes him very useful,) and supply any deficiencies. I have requested this government to inform officially the French and Spanish governments that the Staerkodder, now Stonewall, never belonged to the Danish government, and the director general assures me it shall be done. But as with men, so with governments, who have little to do, they are forever doing it. I have sent to Mr. Bigelow the copies of the original contract between this government and Arman for the building of the Staerkodder, and of other documents, verified, and the Danish are translated into English.

Learning that a man by the name of Block was enlisting sailors for the confederates, and soldiers for the north, whom it seems he literally sold or forced to enlist, I have made complaint against him, and he is (the director general informs me) to be proceeded against criminally.

We are still blocked up by ice.

I remain, &c., your obedient servant,

BRADFORD R. WOOD,
Minister Resident, &c.

Hon. WILLIAM H. SEWARD,
Secretary of State.

Mr. Wood to Mr. Seward.

No. 191.] LEGATION OF THE UNITED STATES,
Copenhagen, April 14, 1865.

SIR: I herewith enclose a translated copy of the minister of foreign affairs, Mr. Blumhe's, reply to my note of the 3d instant, a copy of which I duly forwarded to you.

For obvious reasons I withheld communicating your despatch or circular, No. 106, until I had received the minister's reply to that note, as I knew you could not have been aware of the activity of the rebels in these waters. I also enclose you a note addressed to the minister of foreign affairs of the 12th instant, enclosing a copy of Mr. Consul Dudley's note to me. The Denmark is the same iron-clad I referred to in despatch No. 184, (20th February last,) built by Messrs. Thompson, on the Clyde, originally for the confederates. It seems the Danish government have employed (as Mr. Dudley informs me) the Messrs. Thompson, or an Englishman by the name of Watson, of Liverpool, to sell her. She is now lying in the harbor of Copenhagen. On the 8th instant—the King's birthday—the diplomatic corps waited upon him. He took the occasion to thank me for the kind manner which I had conducted in the affair of the Staerkodder, Sphinx, or Stonewall. I think I have balked the rebels in enlisting men here, and I have advised Mr. McDonald, the vice-consul at Hamburg, who is on the lookout for them.

I remain, &c., your obedient servant,

BRADFORD R. WOOD,
Minister Resident.

Hon. WILLIAM H. SEWARD,
Secretary of State.

Mr. Blumhe to Mr. Wood.

[Translation.]

COPENHAGEN, *April* 8, 1865.

SIR: I hasten to inform you that in regard to the information you have been kind enough to furnish me by your letter of the 3d instant, I have taken some steps in order that any attempt in the direction of enrolling Danish subjects for the service of the so-called confederates shall be put down.

I ought to add that the existing laws inflict very severe punishments not only on the recruiting agents, but also on those allowing themselves to be enlisted.

Be pleased to accept, sir, the assurances of my most distinguished consideration.

BLUMHE.

His Excellency Mr. WOOD, *Minister Resident.*

Mr. Wood to Mr. Blumhe.

LEGATION OF THE UNITED STATES,
April 12, 1865.

SIR: I have this morning received a letter from Mr. Dudley, the United States consul at Liverpool, (a copy of which I herewith enclose,) informing me of his apprehensions that the Denmark may be so sold as to pass into the hands of the so-called confederates, and which I have every reason to believe his Majesty's government does not intend.

With renewed assurances of high consideration, I remain your excellency's obedient servant.

B. R. WOOD, *Minister Resident.*

His Excellency Mr. BLUMHE,
Minister for Foreign Affairs.

Mr. Wood to Mr. Seward.

No. 192.]
LEGATION OF THE UNITED STATES,
Copenhagen, April 15, 1865.

SIR: The director general of the minister for foreign affairs, Mr. Vedel, has just called to say that the police have written assurances that the sailors enlisted here were for the merchant service in Mechlenburg. I had just received your despatch No. 107 of the 24th March, ultimo, and which I read to him as well as the material parts of despatch No. 106, and which I was prevented from reading to the minister on conference day, that day (Thursday as well as Friday) being a holiday. Do not these despatches rather conflict, at least in tone? The director general informed me that the government, immediately on my request, instructed Captain Fobby, the Danish minister at Madrid, to put himself in communication with the American chargé d'affaires and to act in concert with him with the Spanish government. The Danish government early informed the French that the Olinde, or Staerkodder, now the Stonewall, never belonged to the Danish government. You do not seem to have received my despatch No. 183, of the 14th February last, in which, after giving you a history of the affair of the ship as I then understood it, I expressed my belief that the whole matter looked like a French trick on the part of Arman, and in which he was assisted by Puggard the Dane. As this was some thirteen days before the date of Mr. Hansen's letter, I must confess I do not understand the delay.

I remain, &c., your obedient servant,

BRADFORD R. WOOD,
Minister Resident, &c.

Hon. WILLIAM H. SEWARD,
Secretary of State.

Mr. Wood to Mr. Seward.

No. 193.]
LEGATION OF THE UNITED STATES,
Copenhagen, April 24, 1865.

SIR: I should have stated, in connexion with your despatch No. 106, that this government never acknowledged the belligerency of the confederate rebel States, would never have permitted the Staerkodder, or Stonewall, to leave this port had her character been known, and never would have permitted her to coal in a Danish port. It was on my suggestion that Consul Hansen put himself in communication with some one or more of the former crew of that ship, though the information thus elicited and communicated has not been wholly borne out by the judicial investigation and examination. I believe now that the department has all the facts of the case, if my despatches have been duly received.

I remain, &c., your obedient servant,

BRADFORD R. WOOD,
Minister Resident, &c.

Hon. WILLIAM H. SEWARD,
Secretary of State.

Mr. Wood to Mr. Seward.

[Extract.]

No. 194.] LEGATION OF THE UNITED STATES,
Copenhagen, May 1, 1865.

SIR: There was but one feeling of horror here, on learning the assassination of President Lincoln and the attempt on your life. As soon as it was authoritatively known, the diplomatic corps and the minister of state called to express their sympathy, and the King, in a note from Mr. Blumhe, the foreign minister, (who is still confined to his house from illness,) feelingly expresses his; and this on the day of the funeral services for the deceased Czarowitch, his intended son-in-law, and at which all the foreign ministers assisted. I congratulate you on your narrow escape. I hope I can on your son's, but the news is contradictory, and I fear the worst. This terrible tragedy at Washington is a natural sequence of this rebellion and in keeping with the murder of Union prisoners by starvation. It is a consequence of slavery. Well, if the nation now rouse to the conviction, (as I have long since had, as you well know) that there is a class at the south, (of whom Booth was one,) the plotters of this rebellion and their brigands, who must, as a political necessity, be expatriated or in some way annihilated from our soil, if the freedman and the northern emigrant are to dwell in peace and safety at the south. The future of the south demands this * *

I remain, very truly, your obedient servant,

BRADFORD R. WOOD,
Minister Resident, &c.

Hon. WILLIAM H. SEWARD,
Secretary of State.

Mr. Wood to Mr. Hunter.

No. 195.] LEGATION OF THE UNITED STATES,
Copenhagen, May 8, 1865.

SIR: Your despatch No. 108, of the 12th of April, in relation to the closing of certain ports in the United States by a proclamation of the late President, and your circular of the 17th of April, ultimo, advising me of the assassination of President Lincoln, and of the accession of Mr. Johnson, the Vice-President, to the presidential chair, have been received and their contents communicated to Mr. Blumhe, the minister for foreign affairs. By a reference to my despatch No. 194 of the 1st instant, you will see that I had communicated the sad news of the murder of President Lincoln, and that this government had addressed, through Mr. Blumhe, a kind and sympathizing letter of condolence.

I have the honor to remain, your obedient servant,

BRADFORD R. WOOD,
Minister Resident, &c.

Hon. W. HUNTER,
Acting Secretary of State.

Mr. Wood to Mr. Hunter.

No 197.] LEGATION OF THE UNITED STATES,
Copenhagen, June 6, 1865.

SIR: I herewith enclose a copy of my note to Mr. Blumhe, minister for foreign affairs, on transmitting him the President's proclamation of the 10th of May, ultimo, in relation to the national ships of other powers. By reference to my despatch No. 193, you will see that that proclamation is not applicable to this government.

I remain, &c., your obedient servant,

BRADFORD R. WOOD,
Minister Resident, &c.

Hon. W. HUNTER, *Acting Secretary of State.*

Mr. Wood to Mr. Blumhe.

LEGATION OF THE UNITED STATES,
May 31, 1865.

SIR: The within proclamation of the President of the United States I am instructed by the Acting Secretary of State to communicate to his Majesty's government.

With renewed assurance of distinguished consideration, I have the honor to remain, your excellency's obedient servant,

BRADFORD R. WOOD,
Minister Resident, &c.

His Excellency Mr. BLUMHE,
Minister for Foreign Affairs.

Mr. Wood to Mr. Hunter.

No. 198.] LEGATION OF THE UNITED STATES,
Copenhagen, June 13, 1865.

SIR: I herewith forward a copy of a note I have received from Mr. Blumhe, the minister for foreign affairs, in answer to mine of the 31st ultimo, enclosing a copy of the President's late proclamation. From this you will see that this government has never acknowledged the so-called Confederate States as belligerents, having, as I think, a better record towards us than any other European power.

I remain, &c., your obedient servant,

BRADFORD R. WOOD,
Minister Resident.

Hon. W. HUNTER, *Acting Secretary of State.*

[Translation.]

Mr. Blumhe to Mr. Wood.

COPENHAGEN, *June* 9, 1865.

SIR: In answer to your letter containing the proclamation of the President of the United States of the 10th ultimo, relative to the American insurgent cruisers, I hasten to inform you that the government of the King has never recognized the so-called Confederate States as a belligerent party, and consequently that proclamation will not affect the conduct hitherto observed by the Danish authorities towards their cruisers. On mentioning that this fact is well known to the cabinet in Washington, which has often expressed satisfaction for it, to the minister of the King in that city, I accept the occasion to repeat the assurance of my most distinguished consideration.

BLUMHE.

Mr. BRADFORD R. WOOD,
Minister Resident of the United States.

Mr. Wood to Mr. Seward.

No. 203.] LEGATION OF THE UNITED STATES,
Copenhagen, September 18, 1865.

SIR: I am aware that it has often been said that the Prussians and Austrians waged war against the Danes for (among other things) their oppression of the inhabitants of Sleswig.

A delegation of some 2,500 from different towns in that duchy were here last week the guests of this city. They were most enthusiastic in their declared attachment to Denmark, asserting that, come what might, they would never cease to be Danes. At the banquet which took place at Klampenburg, near Copenhagen, and where some 50,000 people were assembled, and tables spread for 4,000, telegrams were being constantly exchanged between the towns in Sleswig, responsive to and in approbation of the speakers. The Sleswigers availed themselves of the last days of their liberty, before passing under the Prussian yoke, to make known their views and feelings towards Denmark, and their hatred of Prussia, and should the opportunity ever present itself they would be the first to rise and throw it off.

We should covet these men for emigrants. The King was absent in Jutland, but among the speakers at the banquet was Mr. Lehman, a former minister under the late King and a thorough republican.

I remain, sir, your obedient servant,

BRADFORD R. WOOD,
Minister Resident, &c.

Hon. WILLIAM H. SEWARD,
Secretary of State.

Mr. Wood to Mr. Seward.

No. 204.] LEGATION OF THE UNITED STATES,
Copenhagen, October 3, 1865.

SIR: The proclamation of the President removing all restrictions on the trade of the insurrectionary States has been received and communicated to this government. I have also this day received your despatch No. 111, of the 19th ultimo, giving me the agreeable information that Mr. Yeaman has accepted this mission. I will await his coming and shall be happy to render him all the assistance in my power, and which, as a stranger, he may need. I hope soon to receive my official letter of recall from the President to enable me to make my *cogné* to the court preparatory to leaving a country in which I have taken a great interest.

I remain, &c., your obedient servant,

BRADFORD R. WOOD,
Minister Resident.

Hon. WILLIAM H. SEWARD,
Secretary of State.

Mr. Seward to Mr. Wood.

No. 115.] DEPARTMENT OF STATE,
Washington, November 4, 1865.

SIR: I have to acknowledge the receipt of your despatch No. 205, of October 16th. Your announcement of the liberty which has been granted to the American Methodist Episcopal Church throughout the kingdom of Denmark is received with great satisfaction.

I am, sir, your obedient servant,

WILLIAM H. SEWARD.

BRADFORD R. WOOD, *Minister Resident.*

Mr. Wood to Mr. Seward.

No. 209.] LEGATION OF THE UNITED STATES,
Copenhagen, November 11, 1865.

SIR: I herewith enclose a copy of my note to the new minister of foreign affairs, Count Trys. I attended his first conference on the 9th instant. He is evidently a gentleman of culture and is of good address. The proposed amendments to the constitution rejected by the ministry have been accepted. I called the attention of Count Trys to the application of the American and Brazilian Steam Navigation Company, and which I had placed before the late minister, Mr. Blumhe. He referred me to Mr. Vedel, the director general of the foreign ministry. From him I learn that the government will wait the report of the governor of St. Thomas.

I remain, &c., your obedient servant,

BRADFORD R. WOOD,
Minister Resident.

Hon. WILLIAM H. SEWARD, *Secretary of State.*

Mr. Wood to Mr. Seward.

No. 211.] LEGATION OF THE UNITED STATES,
Copenhagen, November 18, 1865.

SIR: I have had audience with the King, delivered my letter of recall, and assured him (as directed) of the sincere desire of the President to maintain unimpaired the friendly relations so happily existing between the two countries. His Majesty reciprocated this assurance in the kindest and most cordial manner, and requested me to convey to the President the high estimation and regard in which he held him, and (as by the tenor of my instructions I am requested to communicate what was said, or I should not do it) he also requested me to convey to the President his thanks for my having been appointed a minister resident near this court, and for the kind and considerate manner in which I had discharged my official duties. He was evidently solicitous about our anomalous relations with Great Britain, and wished to know my opinion.

I have yet to have audience with some of the members of the royal family.

I remain, &c., &c., very respectfully, your obedient servant,

BRADFORD R. WOOD,
Minister Resident.

Hon. WILLIAM H. SEWARD, *Secretary of State.*

Mr. Yeaman to Mr. Seward.

No. 2.] LEGATION OF THE UNITED STATES,
Copenhagen, November 20, 1865.

SIR: I have the honor to state that I arrived here on the 12th instant, and, as soon as practicable, (on the 15th,) announced my arrival and mission to Count E. Juel Wind Frys, minister for foreign affairs, enclosing to him a copy of the President's letter to his Majesty Christian IX, accrediting me as minister resident here, and asking for an audience with the King to present the original as early as convenient. On the 18th I was advised by a note from the grand marshal that his Majesty would give me a special audience at half past one o'clock to-day, at the Christianburg palace. At the appointed time I repaired to the palace designated and was received and presented by the grand marshal. The King's deportment and conversation manifested the most marked friendship and regard for our government, inquiring with earnestness for the President's health and the peace of the country. In presenting the President's letter I addressed to the King a few observations about the friendly relations subsisting between the two governments, and also the conclusion and results of our late civil war, the substance of which and of the King's remarks in response will be found in the annexed paper marked A. The interview was eminently satisfactory and agreeable.

I am, sir, very respectfully, your obedient servant,

GEORGE H. YEAMAN.

Hon. WILLIAM H. SEWARD,
Secretary of State.

A.

MR. YEAMAN'S REMARKS.

I have the pleasure and the distinguished honor of presenting to your Majesty the letter of your friend, the President of the United States of America, accrediting me as minister resident of that government to reside near the government of your Majesty. In doing this, I beg to assure your Majesty that to me it is cause of extreme self-gratulation to have been designated as the representative of my government to a power which has always manifested so much friendship towards the American republic, and which has especially tendered so many proofs of that regard entirely through the terrible ordeal to which the union of the States was exposed for four years. I am happy to say that that contest has been decided in favor of the government, and its success has not been merely a triumph of arms. That success and its consequences are valuable in other and more important lights. It has demonstrated and secured in matter of fact and practice what was always true in law, that the Constitution of the United States is the framework of a government, a political nationality, invested with the most important attributes of sovereignty erected by citizens, and to which the citizen in turn owes allegiance and obedience, and that the Union is not merely a league or confederation of separate and independent sovereignties, from which any State or local government may retire at its own discretion or caprice. Happy it is, in this sense of our nationality, that all parties with us, even the lately insurgent forces and people, now accept the solution of the issue submitted by them to the arbitrament of the sword. The States which assumed to go out are rapidly and voluntarily resuming their places in the Union and under the Constitution; and those who were brave soldiers against the republic are promptly returning to their allegiance and to the walks and pursuits of private life, becoming loyal citizens under the wise policy adopted by the President. Your Majesty will excuse me for dwelling so long on these points, when you reflect that they are matters about which there has been so much misunderstanding in Europe.

Another result of that contest, and in which both parties to it seem to concur as a fact, is, that a race of some four millions of people recently held in slavery have been freed from bondage. The system of unpaid coerced labor is come to an end with us, and this change, in fact, will probably soon be incorporated as a declaration in the Constitution, the supreme law of the Union, so that the relation of master and slave may never again exist within the jurisdiction of the republic. In this particular, I am persuaded, we will secure the congratulations of nearly all governments, since there is no point of political economy and the morals of natural right upon which Christian people and the lessons of modern civilization are more nearly agreed than that it is not well that any man should be a slave and his labor the property of another.

With profound wishes for the continued health and happiness of your Majesty, and for the success and prosperity of your government, and with the hope, well assured, that no circumstance may ever occur to mar the very cordial relations subsisting between your government and my own, I thank you for the polite and friendly attention bestowed on me, a personal stranger, in consideration of the power which I am deputed to represent in your presence.

THE KING'S REMARKS IN RESPONSE.

To the observations upon the friendly relations subsisting between the two governments, and the hope that they may be perpetuated, the King responded at that moment with the most earnest and kindly reciprocation. Of the views expressed as to the result of the war, in establishing our nationality and bestowing freedom on a race, he manifested a clear appreciation and approval, and further remarked that the contest had been very deplorable, and, for so great a one, very protracted; that it had cost us innumerable and very valuable lives, and he hoped we would now forever remain one people and one nation. He expressed the surprise and horror he felt on hearing of the assassination of President Lincoln, and spoke of him as a very great and a very kind man. He spoke of the agreeable and satisfactory relations that had existed between himself and my predecessor, Mr. Wood, and wished me an equally agreeable residence. He then asked in a most friendly way about my family, if we were comfortably situated, hoped we could stand this northern climate, and concluded by asking me to express his thanks to the President.

SWEDEN

Mr. Campbell to Mr. Seward.

[Extract.]

No. 2.]

LEGATION OF THE UNITED STATES,
Washington, September 20, 1864.

SIR: I have the honor to inform you that I arrived here on Saturday, the 17th instant, by the way of Cologne and Lubeck. Upon my arrival I found my predecessor, the honorable Jacob S. Haldeman, with the books, papers, and archives of the legation in charge. I will take an early opportunity to examine the archives and property of the United States at the legation, and to prepare and forward a copy of the inventory thereof, properly verified, to the Department of State.

Having secured suitable apartments for myself and family, I hope within a short time to give my entire attention to the business and duties of the legation. In this connexion it affords me pleasure to add that I have received from the honorable Jacob S. Haldeman every kindness and attention necessary to secure individual comfort or to facilitate official duty.

Yesterday, the 19th instant, I had the honor to be received by his excellency Count Manderstrom, his Majesty's minister for foreign affairs, in company with Mr. Haldeman, upon which occasion I presented my open letter of credence from the President of the United States, and requested an audience with his Majesty for the purpose of delivering the original. His excellency, who received me very kindly, remarked that his Majesty was at the island of Ouland, on the Swedish coast, with a hunting party, and would return before Thursday, the 22d instant, and that he had no hesitation in saying that an early day would be fixed for my official reception.

* * * * * * * *

In the interview referred to Count Manderstrom further read a telegram received by him during the day, announcing the avacuation of Atlanta by the so-called confederate forces, under Hood, and their defeat by the federal army, with heavy loss. As he appeared desirous of ascertaining my views in relation to the effect of this success of the Union arms, I took occasion to explain the importance of the capture of Atlanta, and expressed the opinion that it would have a very material influence upon the ultimate triumph of federal authority. He paid strict attention to my suggestions, and then observed that both sides seemed equally confident. Thereupon I took occasion to suggest that the vaunted confidence of the so-called confederates could by no means be admitted, and pointed out facts to establish a contrary opinion, and remarked that even if the correctness of the position assumed by Count Manderstrom was admitted, still it was obvious that the more rapidly increasing weakness of those in rebellion must yield to the superior strength of governmental authority.

Count Manderstrom further informed me that the Prince and Princess of Wales were expected to visit Stockholm the latter part of the present month.

I have the honor to be, with great respect, your obedient servant,

JAMES H. CAMPBELL.

Hon. WILLIAM H. SEWARD,
Secretary of State, &c., &c.

Mr. Campbell to Mr. Seward.

[Extract.]

No. 3.] LEGATION OF THE UNITED STATES,
Stockholm, September 27, 1864.

SIR: In my despatch of the 20th instant I had the honor to inform you of my arrival here, and of an interview with Count Manderstrom, his Majesty's minister of state and of foreign affairs. Upon the return of the King from Ouland, on the 23d instant, I received a note from Count Manderstrom informing me that my audience with his Majesty would take place at the palace on Saturday, the 24th instant, at three-quarters past one o'clock p. m., and a subsequent note informing me that on Sunday, the 25th instant, I would be presented to her Majesty the Queen at the royal palace of Ulriksdale. At the appointed time on Saturday I was accordingly taken in charge by the grand master of ceremonies and King's chamberlain, and conducted in the King's carriage, with the usual ceremonies, to the palace. My interview with his Majesty, after the customary salutations, was cordial and unceremonious; I could not have been received more kindly by any gentleman in Europe. In delivering my letter of credence, I assured his Majesty that I was charged to convey to his Majesty the distinguished consideration and personal regards of the President of the United States, and to express the earnest desire that the amicable relations, both commercial and political, existing between the government of the United States and that of his Majesty, might be perpetuated. I took occasion to say during the interview that the President of the United States felt assured that the same enlightened judgment and experienced statesmanship that so ably directed affairs in his Majesty's kingdoms, secured to the Executive and people of the United States, engaged in sustaining an established and Christian government, his Majesty's profound sympathy. The King reciprocated my friendly expressions, and avowed himself sincerely desirous of continuing amicable relations with the government of the United States.

My subsequent interview with the Queen at Chateau Ulriksdale was as agreeable as interesting. Her Majesty was pleased to make many inquiries about the productions, climate, and people of my country, and appeared well informed concerning the United States. A note from Count Manderstrom informs me that the Queen Dowager Josephine will grant me audience at her country-seat of Drottingholm on the evening of, and immediately before, the ball to be given by her to their royal highnesses the Prince and Princess of Wales. On that occasion I will probably be presented to to the other members the royal family, thus completing the ceremony of reception.

In this connexion I may with propriety state that in my audiences with their Majesties I was preceded by Mr. Mora, envoy extraordinary and minister plenipotentiary of the emperor of Mexico. At a dinner given by Count Manderstrom, minister of state and of foreign affairs, the various honors which Swedish etiquette permits upon such occasions were bestowed upon the representatives of the continent of America, being distributed between the Mexican envoy, the retiring American minister, and his successor. The reception of Mr. Mora in his official capacity by the king will, it is believed, be followed by the establishment of a minister plenipotentiary of Mexico near his Majesty, unless circumstances of marked significance mar the plans of the emperor of that country.

* * * * * * * * *

The Swedish military and naval departments having in charge the subject of military mining, have of late been making a series of experiments under the direction of Colonel J. P. Shaffner, who claims to be a loyal citizen of Kentucky, in the Malar lake. Colonel Shaffner claims to be able to explode a mine in water, or in earth at any distance, say within twenty miles, with fuzes so constructed that there cannot be a failure of explosion instantaneously. The apparatus, or battery, is so portable that a youth can carry it from point to point, and so simple that it is always ready for use. He can explode one mine or one hundred at the same time or consecutively. I have seen the wrecks of the gunboats destroyed by Colonel Shaffner experimentally. Their destruction was complete. He has been able to explode a mine here at the distance of one and one-half mile, want of additional wire having limited the experiment to that distance, while the military authorities here having the subject in charge were only able to pass a spark over six hundred feet of wire.

Military men have informed me that during the battle of Alsen Colonel Shaffner, at 5 a. m., was ordered to mine a narrow strip of land, having the sea on both sides, over which the Danish army was obliged to retreat. Before 9 o'clock a. m. the mine was finished, and for a period of three days fifteen thousand Prussians remained in sight of the Danish army, not daring to traverse the mined territory. When the royal commission shall report upon the invention and experiments of Colonel Shaffner, I shall take pleasure in forwarding a copy to the Department of State.

I have the honor to be, with great respect, your obedient servant,

JAMES H. CAMPBELL.

Hon. WILLIAM H. SEWARD,
Secretary of State, &c., &c., &c.

Mr. Campbell to Mr. Seward.

[Extract.]

No. 4.]

LEGATION OF THE UNITED STATES,
Stockholm, October 3, 1864.

SIR: * * * * * * * * * *

In an interview with Count Manderstrom this afternoon, he informed me that the prevailing rumor that the conference at Vienna relating to the Danish question had closed abruptly without a satisfactory result, was unfounded so far as he could learn, and that in his judgment the termination of that conference would be pacific. There is, however, much anxiety here, if not apprehension, in relation to existing complications between the German powers and the Danish government, and the general opinion is that Prussia is exacting and illiberal in her demands, and that her course, if persisted in, will lead to further and unpleasant complications.

Count Manderstrom made many inquiries in relation to the progress of the war in the United States, as well as to the probable result of the approaching elections. I took the liberty of stating, in reply, that I had no hesitation in saying that, from all the information in my possession, and particularly in view of recent events, which I explained to his excellency, the administration, its views and policy, would be sustained by the American people, and that the rebellion was evidently tottering to its final and complete overthrow.

The Prince and Princess of Wales will leave Stockholm for England on Tuesday next. The festivities in honor of their visit to Sweden, particularly the journey to and banquet at the historical palace of Gripsholm, were well sustained throughout, and beautiful as interesting.

I have the honor to be, with the greatest respect, your obedient servant,

JAMES H. CAMPBELL.

Hon. WILLIAM H. SEWARD,
Secretary of State, &c., &c., &c.

Mr. Campbell to Mr. Seward.

[Extract.]

No. 7.] LEGATION OF THE UNITED STATES,
Stockholm, November 5, 1864.

SIR: I have to acknowledge the receipt from the department of despatches of October 5, No. 2; October 10, No. 47, (addressed to Mr. Haldeman;) October 13, No. 3, and October 17, No. 4.

An early opportunity was embraced by me to say to Count Manderstrom, in pursuance of instructions contained in your despatch No. 2, that the appointment of Baron Nils de Wetterstedt as envoy extraordinary and minister plenipotentiary to Washington was duly appreciated as a mark of the friendly regard of his Majesty towards the United States; and I further assured Count Manderstrom that the Baron de Wetterstedt would be cordially welcomed by the President as the representative from the King of Sweden and Norway.

Count Manderstrom expressed much gratification at the intelligence, and remarked that the Baron de Wetterstedt was well known at Washington.

Count Platten, minister of marine for his Majesty's government, meeting me at the palace, requested, in an informal way, that I would convey his acknowledgments to the Secretary of the Navy of the United States for the courtesy extended in permitting a Swedish captain of marine to take passage on board one of our monitors to New Orleans, thus enabling him to make report upon its construction and qualities. The Swedes are building three monitors after American models. I assured the Count Platten that the courtesy he referred to was a pleasure, and that the authorities of the United States would lose no opportunity of strengthening the friendly relations existing between the governments and peoples of the two countries.

The 4th instant having been the fiftieth anniversary of the union of Sweden and Norway, was celebrated in the capitals of the respective kingdoms with unusual splendor. The crown prince, Oscar, journeyed to Christiana to assist in the Norwegian observances, while a deputation from Norway was received at Stockholm by his Majesty King Charles. The ceremonies at this capital consisted of tedeum, anthems, and solemn discourse in the royal chapel; ode, music and oration in the hall of state; state dinner at the palace, and a grand illumination of the city in the evening. The following night the rejoicings were continued by a gala spectacle of a national character in the theatre, which was filled by his Majesty's guests. At all of these ceremonies and festivities I had the honor of attending in an official capacity. It is with diffidence that I offer a suggestion to so close an observer of European politics as yourself, but I have been forcibly impressed with the fact that the recent rejoicings of the *court* were without sympathetic response from the *people*. The national jealousies are great, and render impracticable the grand dream of Scandinavian union indulged in by a party of which Prince Oscar is the head. Warned by the fate of Denmark, the disposition of European governments seems towards strong alliances.

* * * * * * * * *

I have not been able to learn, after diligent inquiry, that the insurgents are making any efforts at present to purchase vessels or ordnance within the limits of this legation.

I have the honor to be, with great respect, sir, your obedient servant,

JAMES H. CAMPBELL.

Hon. WILLIAM H. SEWARD,
Secretary of State, &c., &c., &c.

Mr. Campbell to Mr. Seward.

[Extracts.]

No. 8.] LEGATION OF THE UNITED STATES,
Stockholm, December 6, 1864.

SIR: * * * * * * * * *
Permit me to tender my congratulations on the decisive result of the presidential election. It virtually ends the rebellion by depriving it of hope. It has been worth many victories in the field, and as a moral triumph, rising above the terrible sacrifices of civil war, reaches a sublime altitude. I have felt its influence in the changed political atmosphere around me. By reanimating our friends, and creating respect and fear among our enemies, it gives assurance of future unity and greatness. The telegram from Hamburg announcing the result was received here on the 22d ultimo and published in the evening papers. It was of the most satisfactory character, stating, as it did, that Mr. Lincoln had a majority of 400,000 on the popular vote, and in an electoral vote of 234 he would receive all but 13, and that all the States voting had cast their ballots for Mr. Lincoln save Kentucky, New Jersey, and Delaware. This despatch, written by a friendly hand, created surprise in some quarters, and I received congratulations from others. It was not what the "governing classes" expected or desired. They preserve "friendly relations," but would prefer the dismemberment of a power jealously regarded as too great, and the success of the aristocratic rebellion. Our safety consists in the strength they deprecate and the ability with which that strength is guided at home and directed abroad.

* * * * * * * * *

I have the honor to be, with great respect, your obedient servant,

JAMES H. CAMPBELL.

Hon. WILLIAM H. SEWARD, *&c., &c., &c.*

Mr. Seward to Mr. Campbell.

No. 9.] DEPARTMENT OF STATE,
Washington, December 13, 1864.

SIR: Information has been communicated to this department by the Secretary of the Navy that the steamer Wachusett, commander N. Collins, on her recent passage home from the coast of Brazil, had occasion to touch at the island of Saint Bartholomew, in the West Indies, for supplies. Commander Collins reports that every facility was afforded for the accomplishment of the object, notwithstanding the Wachusett at the time had a case of varioloid on board. The civility and courtesy of his excellency the governor of the island are highly appreciated, and it is deemed proper that you should make suitable acknowledgments therefor to the Swedish government.

I am, sir, your obedient servant,

WILLIAM H. SEWARD.

JAMES H. CAMPBELL, Esq., *&c., &c., Stockholm.*

Mr. Campbell to Mr. Seward.

No. 9.] LEGATION OF THE UNITED STATES,
Stockholm, December 13, 1864.

SIR: I have the honor to acknowledge the receipt, on the 11th instant, of your despatches No. 7, of the 18th November, and No. 8, of the 19th November last.

In accordance with instructions contained in despatch No. 8, I sought an early interview with Count Manderstrom, minister of state and of foreign affairs. His excellency received me with his usual cordiality, and hastened to communicate the contents of depatches announcing the progress and success of our armies in Georgia, under General Sherman. I then opened the business with which I was charged, by saying that my government had learned with regret that the Baron Nils de Wetterstedt had been despatched to Mexico, on business of a diplomatic nature, as the envoy of his Majesty; that while on a recent occasion it had afforded me great pleasure to express on the part of my government sentiments of appreciation and welcome, in accordance with the high official and private character of Baron Wetterstedt, I was now pained to say to his excellency that his official errand to Mexico was far from being satisfactory to the United States, and that if it did not prevent his official reception, it would certainly impair the cordiality of his welcome; that in thus speaking I did not exceed the letter or spirit of my instructions.

Count Manderstrom here expressed regret that the mission of Baron Wetterstedt should be thus regarded by the United States; and argued that not having reached Washington, or been officially received by my government, he could not be considered as minister to the United States while on his errand to Mexico.

To this I answered, that the note of his excellency, on file in the Department of State at Washington, announcing the diplomatic trust confided to the Baron Wetterstedt, and the reply of welcome on the part of the United States, certainly established inchoate relations in the contemplation of both governments.

Count Manderstrom then assured me that the fact complained of did not originate in any want of respect to the government of the United States; that it had not been practicable or desirable for the governments of Europe to maintain relations with Mexico in her former disturbed condition; that the empire of Mexico was now the only government in that country; that it had, through diplomatic agencies, claimed, and received, recognition of most of the powers of Europe, and he did not think the United States could complain of Sweden adding her recognition to that of her neighbors.

I rejoined, that the United States maintained amicable and full relations with the republic of Mexico, and knew no other government in that country; that she regarded with disapprobation the attempt to establish on her borders institutions inimical to her own; that while the right of recognition, claimed by all sovereign states, involved responsibilities, I was not instructed to make that the ground of complaint in this instance. But it must be apparent to his excellency, in view of the distinctly enunciated sentiments of my government, that any intercourse with the so-called empire, through the envoyé to the United States, must be regarded by them with displeasure.

Count Manderstrom then remarked, he understood, and thought he was not mistaken in saying, that Russia and Belgium had directed their respective representatives at Washington, Mr. Stoeckl and Mr. Blondeel von Ceelebroeck, to proceed to Mexico on similar errands. I contented myself with observing, that upon this fact, or the consequent action of my government, I was not informed.

The minister of foreign affairs then, with great earnestness and warmth, repeated his assurance that no disrespect to the United States had been intended. He reminded me of the long-established friendship of Sweden for the United States, and her consistent avoidance of recognition, or assistance to the confederate rebels, and the frequent aid his Majesty's subjects had rendered in our armies, thus showing the sympathy which our cause received here, and he sincerely hoped the good understanding heretofore existing might not be interrupted. I expressed the appreciation of the government of the United States for the friendship of Sweden and Norway, and assured him I should take pleasure in conveying the sentiments declared by him to my government, and rose to leave. Count Manderstrom accompanied me to the door, hoping that I would convey the full import of his expressions of respect and amity to my government, and with much frankness added, taking my hand in his, "My dear sir, it was simply a question of economy; Russia has done the same thing, and you know," said he, laughingly, "you are very good friends with Russia." "Not better than we have been with Sweden," said I, and took my leave.

In the course of the conversation Count Manderstrom remarked that Baron Wetterstedt would only remain in Mexico about five days.

I have the honor to be, your obedient servant,

JAMES H. CAMPBELL.

Hon. WILLIAM H. SEWARD,
Secretary of State, &c., &c., &c.

Mr. Seward to Mr. Campbell.

[Extract.]

No. 10.]

DEPARTMENT OF STATE,
Washington, December 17, 1864.

SIR: Your despatch of the 5th ultimo, No. 7, has been received, and so much of it as relates to Count Platten's request concerning the courtesy extended by the Secretary of the Navy, on a late occasion, to a Swedish captain of marine, has been communicated to the Navy Department. I thank you for the information you have given me relative to the anniversary of the Swedish union.

* * * * * *

I am, sir, your obedient servant,

WILLIAM H. SEWARD.

JAMES H. CAMPBELL, Esq., *&c., &c., Stockholm.*

Mr. Campbell to Mr. Seward.

No. 10.]

LEGATION OF THE UNITED STATES,
Stockholm, January 3, 1865.

SIR: I have the honor to acknowledge the receipt of your despatch No. 9, of December 13, 1864, relative to the courtesy extended to Captain Collins, United States navy, commanding United States steamer Wachusett, by his excellency the governor of the island of St. Bartholomew, on her recent passage home from the coast of Brazil.

I enclose a copy of a note addressed by me to Count Manderstrom, minister of state and of foreign affairs, on the subject.

I have the honor to be, your obedient servant,

JAMES H. CAMPBELL.

Hon. WILLIAM H. SEWARD, *&c., &c., &c.*

LEGATION OF THE UNITED STATES,
Stockholm, January 2, 1865.

SIR: The United States steamer Wachusett, on a recent passage home from the coast of Brazil, found it necessary to touch at the island of St. Bartholomew for supplies. Her commander, Captain Collins, United States navy, subsequently made report to the honorable the Secretary of the Navy of the United States, that the kindest consideration was bestowed upon him, and every facility extended for the accomplishment of his object by his excellency the governor of the island. Although there was a case of varioloid on board the Wachuset at the time, the knowledge of which might have restrained authorities less kindly disposed, yet the civility extended was as marked on the part of his excellency the governor as beneficial and grateful to the recipients.

I beg leave to assure your excellency that this courtesy was highly appreciated by my government, and, on behalf of the President of the United States, I most cordially thank his Majesty for this new assurance of friendship.

Permit me to renew on this occasion the assurance of my highest consideration.

JAMES H. CAMPBELL.

His Excellency COUNT MANDERSTROM,
Minister of State and of Foreign Affairs, &c.

Mr. Campbell to Mr. Seward.

No. 11.]

LEGATION OF THE UNITED STATES,
Stockholm, January 9, 1865.

SIR: I have the honor to enclose a reply to my note of the 2d instant, addressed to Count Manderstrom, minister of state and of foreign affairs, in relation to the recent visit of the United States steamer Wachusett to the island of St. Bartholomew.

A copy of the reply and of the translation thereof are herewith enclosed.

I have the honor to be, sir, your obedient servant,

JAMES H. CAMPBELL.

Hon. WILLIAM H. SEWARD, *&c., &c., &c.*

Count Manderstrom to Mr. Campbell.

[Translation.]

STOCKHOLM, *January* 4, 1865.

SIR: I have had the honor to receive the communication dated the second of this month, in which you express to me, by direction of your government, the satisfaction which it has experienced from the friendly treatment which the steamship Wachusett, of the United States navy, had received during a recent visit to the colony of St. Bartholomew.

In acting thus, the governor has only fulfilled the intentions and instructions of his government. The ships of the United States can always rely upon the most cordial reception in the ports of the united kingdoms and their dependencies.

In having the honor to offer you the assurance of this, I seize the occasion to add thereto, sir, that of my most distinguished consideration

MANDERSTROM.

Mr. CAMPBELL, *Minister Resident of the U. S. of America, &c.*

Mr. Seward to Mr. Campbell.

No. 11.]

DEPARTMENT OF STATE,
Washington, January 10, 1865.

SIR: Your despatch of the 13th of December, No. 9, has been received. Count Manderstrom must have been misinformed. Russia has not directed Mr. Stoeckl to leave his mission here to perform a duty in another quarter—such as the court supposes. The United States acknowledge with pleasure the relations of cordial friendship existing between themselves and Russia. But this friendship is neither more intimate nor more cordial than that which the United States desire to preserve with Sweden. They would deeply regret any occurrence that should show that this desire is not reciprocated on the part of Sweden.

I am, sir, your obedient servant,

WILLIAM H. SEWARD

JAMES H. CAMPBELL, Esq., *&c., &c., Stockholm.*

Mr. Campbell to Mr. Seward.

No. 12.] LEGATION OF THE UNITED STATES,
Stockholm, January 12, 1865.

SIR: I had the honor to receive your despatch No. 10, of the 17th ultimo.

Enclosed you will please find the translated copy of a note, No. 1, received by me from Count Manderstrom, of the 27th ultimo, as well as a copy of my reply, No. 2, relating to an international exhibition to be held at Bergen, Norway, next summer.

This exhibition, to which the Foreign Office calls my "special attention," will embrace fish of all kinds, from the whale to the minnow; fishing tackle; products and preservatives of fish; models of ships, boats, barrels, boxes, &c., &c.

This subject cannot fail to prove interesting to the fishing and trading communities of New England, and I trust the enterprise and ingenuity of my countrymen will contribute to the attraction of the occasion.

It is desired by those having the matter in charge that public attention in the United States may be called to their enterprise. I enclose copies of the programme, with a translation of the same.

I have the honor to be, with great respect, your obedient servant,

JAMES H. CAMPBELL.

Hon. WILLIAM H. SEWARD,
Secretary of State.

No 1.

Count Manderstrom to Mr. Campbell.

[Translation.]

STOCKHOLM, *December* 27, 1864.

SIR: I have the honor to call your special attention to the international exhibition of the products of fish and fishing tackle, as well as other objects employed in fishing, which will take place at Bergen, Norway, from the 1st of August to the 16th of September, 1865; an exhibition of which I have the honor to transmit you herewith the programme.

Be pleased to accept, sir, the assurance of my most distinguished consideration.

MANDERSTROM.

Mr. CAMPBELL,
Minister Resident of the United States of America, &c., &c., &c.

No. 2

Mr. Campbell to Count Manderstrom.

LEGATION OF THE UNITED STATES,
Stockholm, January 11, 1865.

SIR: I have the honor to receive the note of your excellency of the 27th ultimo, calling my attention to an international exhibition to be held at Bergen, Norway, in the course of next summer, relating to fish and fisheries.

The branches of industry embraced within the purview of the programme you did me the honor to enclose have added much to the wealth and prosperity of the New England States of my own country, as well as to the United Kingdoms of Sweden and Norway.

The exhibition cannot fail to be of importance and interest to the peoples of both countries, and I shall take pleasure in calling the especial attention of my government to a purpose so interesting.

This occasion is embraced by me, sir, to present the assurance of my most distinguished consideration.

JAMES H. CAMPBELL.

His Excellency COUNT MANDERSTROM,
Minister of State and of Foreign Affairs, &c., &c., &c.

Mr. Seward to Mr. Campbell.

No. 13.] DEPARTMENT OF STATE,
Washington, February 13, 1865.

SIR: Your despatch of the 12th of January, No. 12, has been received.

In order to make the request of a friendly state as widely known as possible throughout this country, the President has communicated to Congress a copy of your despatch and its accompaniments, relative to the proposed international exhibition to be held at Bergen, in Norway, during the coming summer.

The subject, as well on account of its novelty as its general importance, will no doubt attract the attention here which it so eminently deserves.

I am, sir, your obedient servant,

WILLIAM H. SEWARD.

JAMES H. CAMPBELL, Esq., *&c., &c., Stockholm.*

Mr. Hunter to Mr. Campbell.

[Extract.]

No. 16.] DEPARTMENT OF STATE,
Washington, May 9, 1865.

SIR: Your despatch No. 15, of May 8, has been received. The prompt measures adopted by you to thwart the supposed schemes of rebel emissaries in Sweden, to which your attention had been called by Mr. Wood, are approved and commended.

* * * * * *

I am, sir, your obedient servant,

W. HUNTER, *Acting Secretary.*

JAMES H. CAMPBELL, Esq., *&c., &c., Stockholm.*

Mr. Campbell to Mr. Seward.

[Extract.]

No. 15] LEGATION OF THE UNITED STATES,
Stockholm, April 8, 1865.

SIR: Your despatch of the 13th of February, No. 13, has been received.

I took occasion to communicate to Count Manderstrom the action of my government on the subject of the Bergen international exhibition, with which he expressed himself much gratified.

A letter from Mr. Wood, United States minister resident at Copenhagen, of the 1st instant, and received by me on the 6th instant, informed me that "confederate agents" were prowling around that city in search of a vessel that would answer for piratical purposes, and that he (Mr. Wood) understood that "Waddell, the captain of the late Florida," who was there, had said that he might go to Sweden, &c.

I immediately took the necessary steps to place the consuls of the United States at the Swedish and Norwegian ports on their guard against the supposed purposes of these rebel emissaries, and requested careful watchfulness of their operations.

I enclose a copy of Mr. Wood's note, (No. 1,) and of my reply, (No. 2,) as well as a copy of a letter addressed by me to the consul at Gothenburg, Mr. Thomas, on the subject, (No. 3.)

Preparations for the resumption of commerce with the Baltic ports are now being made. It is supposed the navigation will be free from ice after the 15th or 20th instant. The winter has been one of unusual severity, but the snow and ice are now fast disappearing.

* * * * * *

I have the honor to be your obedient servant,

JAMES H. CAMPBELL.

Hon. WILLIAM H. SEWARD, *&c.*, *&c.*, *&c.*

No. 1.

Mr. Wood to Mr. Campbell.

LEGATION OF THE UNITED STATES,
Copenhagen, *April* 1, 1865.

DEAR SIR: Confederate agents have been prowling around this city, and, I suppose, looking out for some vessel that will do for a pirate, and which they would expect to get out as a merchant vessel and arm at sea.

I have been informed that Waddell, the captain of the late Florida, is here, and that he has dropped the remark that he might go to Sweden; in other words, go where he could find such a ship as he wanted.

I am not sufficiently acquainted with Swedish ports or Swedish commerce to indicate what place he would go to, but have thought it advisable to apprise you of what I have heard. As it is no longer as easily as formerly to equip pirates in England, the confederates are now, I think, turning their attention to the smaller maritime powers.

I remain, very truly, your obedient servant,

BRADFORD R. WOOD.

Hon. Mr. CAMPBELL,
United States Minister, Stockholm.

P. S.—I should think Gothenburg a port, or one of the ports, most likely to be visited by the confederates. W.

No. 2.

Mr. Campbell to Mr. Wood.

LEGATION OF THE UNITED STATES,
Stockholm, *April* 6, 1865.

SIR: Yours of the 1st instant was received this morning, and I thank you for the information thus promptly given. We have been out of the track of rebel operations here, and, with the exception of a person calling himself William L. Preston, C. S. A., who left this place about the time of my arrival, I have not heard of any one within the jurisdiction of this legation who might fairly be suspected as a spy or agent of the insurgents.

I can understand the value of your suggestions, and will immediately take the necessary steps to place our consuls on the alert, and if, or when, necessary, will call the attention of the Swedish and Norwegian officials to the subject.

With thanks for your suggestions, and in the hope that we may meet in Europe, I have the honor to be, very respectfully, your obedient servant,

JAMES H. CAMPBELL.

Hon. BRADFORD R. WOOD,
United States Minister Resident, Copenhagen.

No. 3.

Mr. Campbell to Mr. Thomas, Jr.

LEGATION OF THE UNITED STATES,
Stockholm, *April* 6, 1865.

SIR: The following extracts are made from a letter received this day from Hon. Bradford R. Wood, United States minister resident, Copenhagen, and dated April 1, 1865, viz:

"Confederate agents have been prowling around this city, and, I suppose, looking out for some vessel that will do for a pirate, and which they would expect to get out as a merchant vessel and arm at sea. I have been informed that Waddell, the captain of the late

Florida, is here, and that he dropped the remark that he might go to Sweden; in other words, go where he might find such a ship as he wanted. I am not sufficiently acquainted with Swedish ports or Swedish commerce to indicate what place he would go to, &c. As it is no longer as easily as formerly to equip pirates in England, the confederates are now, I think, turning their attention to the smaller maritime powers, &c. I should think Gothenburg a port, or one of the ports, most likely to be visited by the confederates."

As the operations of the insurgent's agents may extend to your neighborhood, I have deemed it advisable to call your attention to this information, and to request of you (that which I know the interests of the United States will always receive at your hands without any request of mine) especial care and watchfulness in this regard. If necessary, my aid with the government officials here can be invoked by telegraph or otherwise, as you may deem best. I have written to the consuls of the United States at Bergen and Porsgrund on this subject.

What is the prospect of emigration to the United States from your part of Sweden for the approaching season? Be pleased to let me know.

I have the honor to be your obedient servant,

JAMES H. CAMPBELL.

WILLIAM W. THOMAS, Jr., Esq.,
United States Consul, Gothenburg, Sweden.

Mr. Campbell to Mr. Seward.

No. 16.] LEGATION OF THE UNITED STATES,
Stockholm, April 25, 1865.

SIR: Your despatch of the 24th ultimo, No. 14, has been received. I will give attention to the selection of proper consular agents at Hammerfast and Tronso.

It is abundantly evident that immigration from Sweden and Norway to the United States will be larger this season and probably in excess of any former year. It is accelerated by the now universal conviction that the rebellion has been subdued, and that there will be a great demand for labor in the United States in all branches of industry. In addition to ordinary inducements, it is thought extraordinary ones will arise in repairing the waste and destruction of war. On all sides we hear of families and individuals leaving for America, and reports from the various consulates indicate increased activity in the same direction. It is said that the Swedish foreign office issued one hundred and seven passports during the first few days of last week for persons intending to leave for the United States; and when we take into consideration the fact that emigrants are not obliged to take out passports, and probably not one in three does take out one, the conclusion points to a large immigration. The subject has created alarm among landed proprietors and governing classes. In the country meetings have been held by employers, complaining that young laboring men are leaving the country, and insisting that government should take steps to prevent an exodus of the people, so detrimental to landed and productive interests. They charge that the government of the United States, engaged in a great war, are inducing and aiding the able-bodied men to immigrate, and this idea obtaining among the people causes one class to regard its officers with jealous distrust, while another class daily seek at the doors of the legation and consulate the means to reach American shores. Again, political partisans seize the occasion to turn the feeling to their own account. Those who may be styled liberals insist that the cause of the immigration is to be found in the laws of the country, which they urge, among other things, obliges the citizen to pay taxes to support a state religion his conscience does not approve of, and that while the country is poor and wages low public burdens are onerous.

But I imagine the true reason is obvious. Receiving through letters from friends and relatives in America accounts of improved condition, and liberal institutions of homestead bills and fertile soil, the Swedish and Norwegian peasant believes he can better his condition in life, not for himself only, but for his children, and up to this better condition his desire reaches, as plants to the sun. The railings of government organs, and the publications, as the denunciations of interested classes, are vain. He has faith in the statements of his own class, and go he will, if he can provide the means. And that is the great impediment. The land is poor. Thousands would go if the means were provided. The doors of the legation have been besieged by persons inquiring whether the minister of the United States was not sending emigrants to America, and the same inquiry has been so constantly made of the consul (Mr. Ieefft,) that he felt called upon to insert a notice in one of the newspapers of the city to the effect that the government of the United States was not paying the passage money of immigrants, and that he had nothing to do with immigration companies. Among those who made the inquiry referred to at this legation, I recognized one or two with whom the object was simply to ascertain whether the current reports were true or not. To one and all the answer was returned that whilst I would furnish information to any one who desired to proceed to America, where all good men would be welcome who chose to go, yet that the government of the United States, its ministers, consuls and agents, had nothing to do with sending emigrants to the country, much less with furnishing funds for that purpose.

The news received within the last twenty-four hours of the surrender of Lee's army, as well as of the capture of Richmond and Selma, has developed a feeling of satisfaction among commercial and laboring classes of which I have sometimes doubted the existence. Swedish merchants are anxious to resume the exchange of iron for cotton, whilst the laboring classes have an impression that the war was in the interest of free labor and liberal institutions, and peace will stimulate both commerce and immigration.

Congratulating you upon the triumph of our arms, and the suppression of a causeless but gigantic rebellion,

I have the honor to be, your obedient servant,

JAMES H. CAMPBELL.

Hon. WILLIAM H. SEWARD, *&c., &c., &c.*

Mr. Campbell to Mr. Seward.

[Extract.]

No. 17.] LEGATION OF THE UNITED STATES,
Stockholm, April 30, 1865.

SIR: On the evening of the 26th of April a telegram from the embassy of the United States in London was received at this legation, announcing the death, by assassination, of Abraham Lincoln, President of the United States; also, an attack upon the life of the Secretary of State, resulting in injuries so severe as to render his recovery doubtful.

Overwhelmed with horror by this woful news, which was already in circulation in Stockholm, inspiring grave misgivings and vague fears in the minds of the friends of the republic, who but imperfectly understood its organization, I deemed it proper, on the following morning, to announce to the department of state and of foreign affairs of Sweden and of Norway, the facts of the death of the President of the United States of America, and the installation of his constitutional successor in executive office. (A copy of my note is herewith enclosed, No. 1.) At the same time, I communicated to Count Manderstrom the afflicting intelligence of the condition to which you, sir, had been reduced by a murderous attack, (No. 2.)

The prompt and sympathetic response of his excellency displays a warmth of emotion unusual in official papers, and is in harmony with the reputation and horror-felt by all classes of the Swedish people, (enclosures Nos. 3 and 4.)

These sentiments have sought expression at this legation in such varied forms as have deeply touched my heart, and caused me to feel that the blow dealt my beloved country by an assassin's hand is resented by all Christendom.

I have the honor to report the direct and marked action of the King, who commissioned the Count Axel Cronheilm, an officer of the royal staff, to visit the legation of the United States with messages of condolence, coupled with the strongest possible terms of detestation for the parricide, and assurances of the admiration entertained by him for the personal character and attributes of our lamented Chief Magistrate. These sentiments of sympathy for a mourning people, and reprobation for the crime by which they have been bereaved, were expressed in such earnest and feeling words as were worthy of the noble heart of his Majesty, and must prove acceptable to the nation in whose behalf they were uttered.

It was also the desire of the King that I would convey to him the earliest intelligence of your health, sir, as his Majesty felt the deepest interest in the preservation of a life so eminent and valuable.

In addition to the official communication from the department of state of Sweden and Norway, that most excellent gentleman, Count Manderstrom, in a personal visit, and private notes, (Nos. 5 and 6,) evinced such feeling as commands my gratitude.

In some of the ports the flags were at half-mast for the death of the President; the public journals spoke with appreciation of his life and death.

* * * * * *

The Swedish court has worn mourning for several members of royal houses in Europe, during the past winter, but in no instance have I observed a popular tribute comparable with this. The members of the diplomatic corps in Stockholm have been instant in their tokens of sympathy, and the American residents here have sought at the legation such comfort and information as might soothe their grief and allay their fears. The Baron Feysack, and Lieutenant Anderson, gallant officers of Sweden, whose swords have been drawn in the service of the United States, came to offer their condolences to the country they had defended, as did, also, the Count Piper, formerly minister resident at Washington, and other distinguished Swedes.

If the transmission of these details appears unnecessary, I find my excuse in the conviction that such tokens of sympathy in a remote land, for their national grief, must be as acceptable to the American people as they have been to their representative.

I may be suffered here to give utterance to my own emotions upon the dire calamity which has visited my country. The hand raised against the life of the President has inflicted a grievous wound upon every American heart, and, in common with millions bereaved of their Chief, I deeply feel the outrage perpetrated upon sacred national rights.

With regard to Abraham Lincoln, whom I knew and loved as a personal friend, I recognize with awe that God's instrument has been laid away in heaven's armory. Remembering how, in the raging of political tornadoes, he bore himself with the passionless calm of some grand abstraction, and, divested of prejudice or favor, devoted himself to the large ends of human freedom and national life, I feel that his death was the seal to the deeds of his life, and he closed his eyes on great purposes achieved, to open them upon the immortal crown. To his country he leaves the rich legacy of a beneficent government preserved; the American ideal of liberty attained; and the noble record of the Christian life he lived, the patriot's ends he wrought, and the martyr's death that he died to embellish her story.

Allow me to tender you, sir, my respectful sympathy for the mental and physical sufferings you have sustained, and to express most fervent thanksgiving to God, who, in His mercy, has spared a life so valuable to our country.

Praying for your speedy restoration to health and usefulness, I have the honor to be your obedient servant,

JAMES H. CAMPBELL.

Hon. WILLIAM H. SEWARD,
Secretary of State, &c., &c., &c.

No. 1.

Mr. Campbell to Count Manderstrom.

LEGATION OF THE UNITED STATES,
Stockholm, April 27, 1865.

SIR: It becomes my painful duty to inform his Majesty's government of the United Kingdoms of Sweden and Norway of the contents of a telegram received by me last night, from the honorable Charles Francis Adams, envoy extraordinary, &c., of the United States of America near her Britannic Majesty.

Mr. Adams announces to me the melancholy intelligence that his excellency Abraham Lincoln, President of the United States of America, was assassinated whilst in his box at the theatre, in Washington.

To my country this is a terrible catastrophe, for the President was enshrined in the hearts and shared the confidence of his countrymen in a remarkable degree. The nature of the crime by which he perished shocks civilization, as it outrages humanity; but his death will not retard the restoration of national authority, nor arrest the functions of the government.

The Vice President, the honorable Andrew Johnson, has assumed the functions of President in accordance with the provisions of the Constitution of the United States of America.

Official despatches, containing the details of this most abhorrent crime, have not yet reached this legation.

Permit me to renew to your excellency on this sad occasion the assurance of my most distinguished consideration.

JAMES H. CAMPBELL.

His Excellency COUNT MANDERSTROM,
Minister of State and of Foreign Affairs.

No. 2.

Mr. Campbell to Count Manderstrom.

THURSDAY MORNING, *April* 27, 1865.

MY DEAR SIR: Whilst writing to inform you of the national calamity which has smitten my beloved country, the kind note of your excellency was handed me. My London telegram, elsewhere communicated, forbids indulging in the hope expressed by you that the facts are exaggerated.

A simultaneous attack was made upon the President at the theatre, and Mr. Seward in his sick-room, where he was confined by serious injuries occasioned by a fall from his carriage. His recovery is doubtful, but I trust that God in his providence will spare to his country this eminent statesman, who, in her season of tribulation, has served her with ability, and guided her with wisdom.

No further details of these sad events have reached me.

For the prompt communication of the Swedish telegram, and the ready sympathy accompanying it, receive my warmest thanks. I can well understand how the intelligence of this enormous crime will shock the Christian people of Sweden.

Repeating my grateful appreciation of the sentiments expressed by your excellency, I have the honor to be, your obedient servant,

JAMES H. CAMPBELL.

His Excellency COUNT MANDERSTROM,
Minister of State and of Foreign Affairs.

No. 4.

Count Manderstrom to Mr. Campbell.

[Translation.]

STOCKHOLM, *April* 27, 1865.

SIR: I have received the official communication by which you have confirmed this morning the melancholy intelligence already in circulation yesterday evening, of the odious outrage to which the President of the United States fell a victim, on the evening of the 14th of this month.

I have thought it my duty to bring this overwhelming news immediately to the knowledge of my august Sovereign, and it is by his express order that I hasten to convey to you, sir, all the horror and profound regret with which it has inspired him. Not only the old and excellent relations which existed between the two governments, but the high esteem and the sincere consideration professed by the King for the noble character, and eminent qualities of the illustrious President who has been taken from a country to the welfare of which he was devoted, by the most atrocious crime, may easily explain the sentiments of just grief and sad sympathy with which the King is penetrated, and the reprobation with which his Majesty stamps a shameful assassination, directed by a parricidal hand against that good man.

This crime is aggravated by the infamous attack made upon the distinguished statesman confined to his bed of suffering, and who, wounded also in his most cherished affections, seems to leave us little hope of seeing him recover from his physical and mental anguish.

The King has charged me to beg you, sir, to testify to your government the sentiments entertained by him, and which, be assured, are shared by the two peoples united under his sceptre.

In giving utterance to the most sincere wishes that this frightful misfortune does not injure the United States of America, the government of the King expresses the hope of continuing with President Johnson the same relations of confidence and amity which have been maintained under the government of the illustrious President whose loss we so bitterly deplore.

In begging you, sir, to accept the expression of my most profound personal regret, I permit myself to add the assurance of my most distinguished consideration.

MANDERSTROM.

Mr. CAMPBELL,
Minister Resident of the United States of America.

No. 5.

Count Manderstrom to Mr. Campbell.

WEDNESDAY EVENING.

MY DEAR SIR: It is with the utmost dismay I find in the evening papers a telegram from New York, of the 15th instant, to the following purport:

"President Lincoln has been shot by an assassin. He died to-day. A murderous attempt has been directed against Mr. Seward. His recovery is doubtful."

This news is from Hamburg. I have received nothing to confirm them up to this hour. I hope it is an untrue, or at least exaggerated, report. Of course I will communicate to you what I receive.

You cannot doubt, my dear sir, the general sentiments of horror and indignation by which this awful news will be received in my country, and I beg to express to you the feelings of my most cordial sympathy.

I remain, my dear sir, with great truth and regard, yours, very truly,

MANDERSTROM.

Mr. CAMPBELL,
Minister Resident of the United States of America.

No. 6.

Count Manderstrom to Mr. Campbell.

APRIL 27, 1865.

MY DEAR SIR: I hasten to communicate to you the following details transmitted from London yesterday evening, but which reached me only this morning.

It appears that President Lincoln was murdered in his box at the theatre; the assassin, whose name is Booth, jumped down from the box on the scene and effectually escaped. He went directly to Baltimore, and was apprehended there. It was the brother of Booth who made the attack upon Mr. Seward in his sick-room and wounded him dangerously. His son, Mr. Frederick Seward, hastening to help his father, was murdered on the spot.

General Grant was to have assisted at the play, but was prevented by official business; this being mentioned, I suppose there was some plan laid against him.

Such a shocking series of atrocious crimes, up to this day never witnessed in your country, cannot fail to impress the minds of all good citizens and make them rally round the banner of order.

I reserve myself to answer officially to your note, but thought it my duty not to lose time in giving you all the details I have received.

I am, my dear sir, your very obedient servant,

MANDERSTRÖM.

Mr. CAMPBELL,
Minister Resident of the United States of America.

Mr. Campbell to Mr. Seward.

No. 18.]

LEGATION OF THE UNITED STATES,
Stockholm, May 3, 1865.

SIR: I thought proper to make a suitable acknowledgment for the note of Count Manderstrom, minister of state and of foreign affairs, of the 27th ultimo, enclosed in my despatch of the 30th ultimo, No. 17, and therefore note a reply, of which the enclosed is a copy.

I have the honor to be, your obedient servant,

JAMES H. CAMPBELL.

Hon. WILLIAM H. SEWARD,
Secretary of State.

Mr. Campbell to Count Manderstrom.

LEGATION OF THE UNITED STATES,
Stockholm, May 3, 1865.

SIR: I had the honor to receive the official communication of the 27th ultimo, whereby your excellency conveyed to me the detestation and horror entertained by his Majesty the King of Sweden and Norway for the infamous crime whereby the late President of the United States of America lost his life, coupled with sentiments of profound regret and personal admiration for the character of the illustrious dead, as well as sympathy and condolence for a bereaved people. I observed with unmingled satisfaction that his Majesty was pleased to refer to the excellent relations existing between the two governments, connected with the hope that these friendly relations may be continued under the President of the United States of America, the successor of the late President.

With a mind deeply penetrated by the noble sentiments of his Majesty, and the gracious manner of their expression, I hasten to convey to the President of the United States their full import, and to assure your excellency his Majesty's abhorrence for a crime that deprived a people of their chosen ruler, and sorrow for their loss, will be acceptable to, and fully appreciated by, the government and people of the United States, and will form a new tie between the governments and peoples of the two countries.

For the sympathy manifested by the Christian and law-abiding people of the united kingdoms of Sweden and Norway for your excellency's personal sentiments of condolence, not only for the loss of our beloved President, but for the terrible injuries inflicted upon the person of the very eminent Secretary of State of the United States, for his suffering heart, wounded in its most tender affections, I am deeply grateful.

To these assurances of profound appreciation on the part of my government suffer me to add, sir, that of my most distinguished consideration.

JAMES H. CAMPBELL.

His Excellency COUNT MANDERSTROM,
Minister of State and of Foreign Affairs, &c., &c., &c.

Mr. Campbell to Mr. Seward.

No. 19.]

LEGATION OF THE UNITED STATES,
Stockholm, May 5, 1865.

SIR: In my despatch of the 25th ultimo, No. 16, I called the attention of my government to the subject of emigration from Sweden and Norway to the

United States. Since that time the official newspaper, published in Stockholm, called the "Post och Surikes Tiedmingar," of the 26th ultimo, contains an order issued from the civil department of his Swedish Majesty's government, in relation to emigration to America, a copy of which order, together with a translation thereof affixed, (No. 1,) is herewith enclosed.

I feel very certain that Congress has not, and will not adopt any proposition to "subject emigrants to a loss of freedom for a certain period," however State legislatures may establish laws to enforce contracts in the forms and ways known to most civilized nations. Yet, I have not thought proper to protest against what appears from the order itself to have been a report from a Swedish consul, that such an act "was being drawn up to be laid before Congress," when no official character is assigned it. In fact, the Swedish authorities are sorely perplexed at the threatened loss of numerous of their most valuable artisans and laborers, and the order in question shows the extent to which they feel themselves obliged to go to arrest emigration.

We might join issue with the assertion contained in the order, that "experience has shown that many of those who have in former years emigrated to the United States have been disappointed in their hope of obtaining a better subsistence." This is doubted by the class which supplies emigration, for they know, from public and private channels, that experience, in most instances, points to a directly opposite conclusion. It is also well understood here that the governing classes in Sweden and Norway are interested in throwing every possible barrier in the way of depopulation, and, unless the department shall direct otherwise, I propose to leave the order in question to the press, to emigration societies, and to private correspondence.

I have the honor to be, sir, your obedient servant,

JAMES H. CAMPBELL.

Hon. WILLIAM H. SEWARD,
Secretary of State, &c., &c., &c.

[Translation.]

[Published in the official Gazette of the 26th of April, 1865.]

SWEDEN.—CIVIL DEPARTMENT.

It having been represented to his Majesty, on the basis of a report from the consul of the United Kingdoms at New York, that a company formed in that city, under the name of the American Immigration Company, with a view to promote immigration from other countries to the United States of America, had appointed a special agent at Gothenburg for the purpose of endeavoring to obtain emigrants from various parts of Sweden, and especially from the manufacturing towns and the iron districts, to which end the said agent is empowered to enter into an agreement with those who wish to emigrate, relating to the provision of employment for them on their arrival, and the payment of their passage; and, also, that an act is being drawn up in the United States to be laid before Congress, providing that emigrants who have had the expense of their passage to America advanced by the said Immigration Company shall be liable to be subjected to a loss of freedom for a certain period, in the event of their refusing, on their arrival, to fulfil the provisions of the said agreement; and, further, it having been proved by experience that many of those who, during previous years, have emigrated to the United States have been disappointed in their hopes of obtaining a better subsistence there than in their own country:

Therefore, his Majesty has been graciously pleased, on the 11th day of April, to prescribe that the grand governor of Stockholm, and the governors of those provinces from which emigration takes place, shall warn, by public proclamation, those who are tempted to such emigration not rashly to abandon their native land, in order to seek an uncertain existence among strangers, speaking a strange language, and separated from their relations and countrymen, while easier means of subsistence are continually being provided at home for the industrious workman.

In fidem.

STOCKHOLM, *April* 27, 1865.

Mr. Campbell to Mr. Hunter.

No. 20.] LEGATION OF THE UNITED STATES,
Stockholm, May 8, 1865.

SIR: Despatch No. 15, of the 13th ultimo, was received at this legation.

I enclosed copies of the three proclamations of the President of the United States, dated, respectively, April 11, 1865, contained in that despatch, to the Foreign Office of his Swedish Majesty, accompanied with a note, of which enclosure No. 1 is a copy.

I have the honor to be your obedient servant,

JAMES H. CAMPBELL.

Hon. W. HUNTER,
Acting Secretary of State, &c., &c., &c.

Mr. Campbell to Count Manderstrom.

LEGATION OF THE UNITED STATES,
Stockholm, May 8, 1865.

SIR: I have the honor to call the attention of his Majesty's government to several proclamations issued by the President of the United States of America, dated, respectively, on the 11th ultimo, and each herewith enclosed, in print, and attested by the undersigned.

The first (enclosure No. 1) relates to the closing of certain ports of entry of the United States; the second (enclosure No. 2) relates to the port of Key West, in Florida; and the third (enclosure No. 3) has reference to the exchange of reciprocal hospitalities between war vessels of the United States of America and similar vessels of foreign powers in the ports of their respective countries.

In the language of the proclamation last referred to, (enclosure No. 3,) it is believed by the President that, "whatever claim or pretence may have existed heretofore, the United States are now, at least, entitled to claim and concede an entire and friendly equality of rights and hospitalities with all maritime nations."

In requesting the attention of his Majesty's government to the proclamations enclosed, I seize the occasion to assure you, sir, of my most distinguished consideration.

JAMES H. CAMPBELL.

His Excellency COUNT MANDERSTROM,
Minister of State and of Foreign Affairs, &c., &c., &c.

Mr. Campbell to Mr. Hunter.

No. 21.] LEGATION OF THE UNITED STATES,
Stockholm, May 8, 1865.

SIR: I had the honor to receive your circular of the 17th ultimo, announcing to me, officially, the assassination of our revered Chief Magistrate, the President of the United States of America.

The melancholy tidings reached this legation in a semi-official character, on the night of the 26th ultimo, from the embassy of the United States in London; and the action taken in relation thereunto, and the reasons therefor, will be found fully set forth in my despatches No. 17, of the 30th ultimo, and No. 18, of the 3d instant.

The order from the Department of State, of the 17th ultimo, relating to wearing crape in honor of the memory of our late illustrious Chief Magistrate, was received and duly made known to the several consuls within the jurisdiction of this legation; but, immediately upon the receipt of the disastrous news, I took measures to pay that tribute of respect to the departed President.

In the midst of unfeigned sorrow at the death of the late President, I learn with much satisfaction of the improved condition of the Secretary of State and the Assistant Secretary of State, and trust that their valuable lives may be spared to their family and the nation.

I have the honor to be your obedient servant,

JAMES H. CAMPBELL.

Hon. W. HUNTER,
Acting Secretary of State, &c., &c., &c.

Mr. Campbell to Mr. Hunter.

No. 22.] LEGATION OF THE UNITED STATES,
Stockholm, May 12, 1865.

SIR: I have the honor to enclose a copy of the reply of Count Manderstrom, his Swedish Majesty's minister of state and of foreign affairs, to my note of the 8th instant, (see despatch No. 20,) conveying to him three proclamations issued by the President of the United States.

I have the honor to be your obedient servant,

JAMES H. CAMPBELL.

Hon. W. HUNTER,
Acting Secretary of State, &c., &c., &c.

Count Manderstrom to Mr. Campbell.

[Translation.]

STOCKHOLM, *May* 12, 1865.

SIR: I have the honor to acknowledge the reception of the note addressed to me by you, dated the 8th of this month, announcing three proclamations, published a few days before the detestable crime which put an end to his life, by the late President Lincoln: The first on the closing of certain ports of the United States; the second relating to the port of Key West; and the third concerning the treatment accorded in ports of the United States to the ships-of war of foreign nations.

I have not failed to observe them with the interest due their contents, and am happy to say, in regard to the last of these proclamations, that the restrictions which may be imposed upon the vessels-of-war of foreign nations in the ports of the United States will not be applicable to those of the King my august sovereign, the government of his Majesty having never refused to the ships of the United States the most favorable treatment, while it is a duty to acknowledge that such has also been the reception accorded to its own in the ports of the United States.

I avail myself of this occasion to renew to you, sir, the assurance of my most distinguished consideration.

MANDERSTROM.

Mr. CAMPBELL,
Minister Resident of the United States of America, &c., &c., &c.

Mr. Campbell to Mr. Hunter.

No. 23.] LEGATION OF THE UNITED STATES,
Stockholm, June 13, 1865.

SIR: Your circular of the 16th ultimo, enclosing two copies of the proclamation of the President of the United States relative to insurgent cruisers, was received.

I communicated the proclamation to his Swedish Majesty's government, and herewith enclose a copy of my note to Count Manderstrom on the subject.

Your despatch, No. 16, of May 9, 1865, was received.

I have the honor to be your obedient servant,

JAMES H. CAMPBELL.

Hon. W. HUNTER,
Acting Secretary of State.

Mr. Campbell to Count Manderstrom.

LEGATION OF THE UNITED STATES,
Stockholm, June 13, 1865.

SIR: Herewith I have the honor to enclose a copy of the proclamation of the President of the United States relative to insurgent cruisers, under date of the 10th day of May, 1865.

I am pleased to believe his Majesty, King of the United Kingdoms of Sweden and Norway, will concur in judging, with the President of the United States of America, in the necessity and propriety of the course taken by the President as indicated in this proclamation.

I embrace the occasion to renew to you, sir, the assurance of my most distinguished consideration.

JAMES H. CAMPBELL.

His Excellency COUNT MANDERSTROM,
Minister of State and of Foreign Affairs, &c., &c., &c.

Mr. Campbell to Mr. Seward.

[Extract.]

No. 25.]

LEGATION OF THE UNITED STATES,
Stockholm, September 14, 1865.

SIR: * * * * * * * *

The Russian squadron, of some twenty-five sail, including nine monitors and several iron-clads, with the Grand Duke Constantine on board, paid this capital a visit within the last fortnight, and shortly before my return from the international exhibition at Bergen. One monitor was lost and one damaged by striking a rock in the Bothnian gulf before the squadron reached Stockholm.

The visitors were received by the people with marked coldness or indifference, and by the King and officials with formal politeness. The Swedes say they are indebted for the visit to the fact that the Russians wish to show they are masters of the Baltic.

Russia is Sweden's chronic dislike. The loss of Finland has not been forgotten nor forgiven. The Grand Duke is proud of his ship, the General Admiral, built by Mr. Webb, of New York; he declared at Copenhagen that she was "the best ship in the world."

In the absence of Count Manderstrom, the minister of marine, Count Platen, has discharged the duties of the Foreign Office. A note from Count Manderstrom informs me that he has returned, and will this morning resume his post. Stockholm is exceedingly dull. The King is passing the season at the palace of Ulricksdale.

I have the honor to be your obedient servant,

JAMES H. CAMPBELL.

Hon. WILLIAM H. SEWARD,
Secretary of State, &c., &c., &c.

Mr. Campbell to Mr. Seward.

[Extract.]

No. 26.]

LEGATION OF THE UNITED STATES,
Stockholm, September 26, 1865.

SIR: * * * * * * * *

I had the honor to receive copies of the proclamation by the President of the 29th of August last, removing all restrictions on trade with the States recently in insurrection, including articles contraband of war, and in an interview had yesterday with Count Manderstrom, placed one of the copies in his hands. He remarked that it was very gratifying to observe that order had been restored in the United States, and full foreign and domestic commercial relations re-established, and that Swedish iron and other articles of export could now go freely forward. He further observed that the disturbances in the United States had been severely felt in Sweden by diminishing the export of iron, and reducing the receipt of cotton, as well as in the high prices of tobacco, &c., and ended by congratulating me upon the restoration of authority in and through the national domain. I assured Count Manderstrom that Americans valued Swedish congratulations, and that, in a very little time, my countrymen would furnish the markets of the world with cotton and tobacco, &c., as they had done heretofore, and in increased quantities. * * * * *

I have the honor to be your obedient servant,

JAMES H. CAMPBELL.

Hon. WILLIAM H. SEWARD,
Secretary of State, &c., &c., &c.

Mr. Hunter to Mr. Campbell.

No. 20.] DEPARTMENT OF STATE,
Washington, October 17, 1865.

SIR: Your despatch No. 26, of September 26, has been received. It is gratifying to hear of the friendship of Sweden and Norway for this government, as expressed by Count Manderström at your last interview.

I am, sir, your obedient servant,

W. HUNTER, *Acting Secretary.*

JAMES H. CAMPBELL, Esq., *&c., &c., Stockholm.*

Mr. Campbell to Mr. Seward.

No. 28.] LEGATION OF THE UNITED STATES,
Stockholm, November 4, 1865.

SIR: Herewith I enclose a copy of the opening address of the King of Sweden and Norway, read to the Norwegian Storthing at the recent meeting of that body, and which was transmitted to this legation by the Swedish Foreign Office, together with a translation of the same.

No question of more than ordinary local interest is pending or will be laid before the Storthing at its present session, with the exception of a military measure intended to give the King more immediate control of the Norwegian troops, a proposition which, in my judgment, the careful and jealous Norwegians are not prepared to adopt.

Since the separation of Norway from Danish authority, the former has gradually and steadily increased in material prosperity. Last year the fisheries yielded abundantly, and the export of lumber and cattle showed considerable improvements over former years. The country gives manifest evidence of progress in various directions, and under a system of government which allows great freedom to the Norwegian, its continued well-doing may be expected.

I have the honor to be your obedient servant,

JAMES H. CAMPBELL.

Hon. WILLIAM H. SEWARD,
Secretary of State, &c., &c., &c.

Discourse of the King at the opening of the eighteenth Storthing of Norway, 5th October, 1865.

[Translation.]

SIRS: In regretting that circumstances do not permit me to assist in person at the commencement of your labors, I transmit to you the expression of my royal good will, and I wish you all prosperity in the accomplishment of your important work.

During the epoch which has passed since the assembling of the last ordinary Storthing, our industry, notwithstanding partial reverses, has prospered to such an extent that the state revenues have flowed abundantly into its coffers. The extraordinary expenses for our system of defence, caused last year by political circumstances, have thus been able to be met without creating any embarrassment in the administration of the finances. The projects communicated by me to the last ordinary Storthing on the subject of several questions relating to a more satisfactory organization of the army, were only partially adopted. After the dissolution of the Storthing, I announced my intention of submitting them to a further examination. This work being finished, I submit to you the projects based on its results. I rely upon your enlightened love of country in nourishing the hope that the Storthing, while the general situation admits of a calm and deep reflection, will arrive at a result which I consider as answering the urgent necessity of a satisfactory military organization.

The debates which took place at the last ordinary Storthing concerning the reform of the judicial procedure in criminal matters has shown that there exists a great difference of opinion, not only respecting the necessity of such a reform, but also respecting the principles on which it should be based and the extension which should be given to it. It appeared to me that all these opinions agreed in recognizing the fact that the time for placing in execution a thorough principal reform has not yet arrived. But this should not prevent the reform of these acknowledged partial defects of the mode of judicial procedure, and a legal project tending to this end will be submitted to you.

A commission of Norwegians and Swedes has been formed to take into consideration the ameliorations that could be introduced into the compact of union between the two kingdoms. This commission commenced its labors in the spring of the present year, but several of its members finding themselves unable to continue them, on account of their labors as members of the Storthing and of the Diet, the commission has been obliged to adjourn during the reunion of the national representatives, and cannot reassemble until a later period. The documents relative to the formation of this commission will be communicated to you.

Treaties of commerce and navigation have been concluded with his Majesty the Emperor of the French. The United Kingdoms have by these treaties acquired the same advantages for commerce and navigation with France that that country had accorded by analogous treaties to other powers of Europe. In taking into consideration the importance of our commercial relations with France, and that of navigation between the two countries, I look at the reductions obtained by these treaties as being of essential worth, and I have learned with sincere satisfaction of the favorable reception that this measure has met with in Norway. Concessions have been exacted from us of the same kind as have been accorded to other powers who have concluded treaties with France. Several of them assuming the concurrence of representation, the validity of the treaties has been submitted, in that which concerns Norway, to the approval of the Storthing. The project relative to this question will be submitted to you.

The exhibition of articles belonging to the industry of fishing, which took place during the course of the summer at Bergen, and which is the first industrial international exhibition of Norway, has offered a satisfactory testimony of a tendency towards progress, and will aid to bring important and durable results for one of our principal branches of industry. The marked good will of several powers and foreign nations in favor of this enterprise has established their claims to our gratitude.

The Storthing will receive with satisfaction the communication of the happy increase of the royal house by the birth of a prince, with whom Providence has again pleased to bless the union of my well-loved brother, his royal highness Prince Oscar.

Our relations with all the foreign powers continue to be marked by confidence and friendship.

In calling the blessing of the All Powerful upon your labors, I renew to you, sirs, the assurance of my royal good will.

Given at the palace of Stockholm, September 30, 1865.

CHARLES.

SIBBERN.

Mr. Campbell to Mr. Seward.

No. 31.] LEGATION OF THE UNITED STATES,
Stockholm, November 15, 1865.

SIR: I have the honor to enclose the address of his Swedish Majesty to the Diet upon the assembling of that body on the 24th ultimo, with a translation thereof. Herewith will also be found a pamphlet copy of a proposition for the reform of the representation, which was laid before the Swedish Diet of 1863 and brought up for action at the present session.

According to usage, this proposition must be discussed and accepted or rejected without amendment at the present Diet.

The King, on the opening of the legislative chambers, called the attention of the members of the assembly to this project of reform, and urged its adoption with distinctness.

The proposition, embracing a radical change in the organization of the Swedish Diet, proposes to consolidate the four chambers of which the Diet is composed into two—a first chamber and a second chamber, the members of the first chamber to be elected by provincial assemblies and municipal authorities of the towns, for the period of nine years; the second chamber to be composed of members elected for three years by county jurisdictions, whereof those possessing a population under forty thousand shall elect one member, and those exceeding that number shall be districted by the King on the basis of one member to each forty thousand inhabitants.

These are the noticeable features of the project. It may readily be understood that so radical a change as the one contemplated in the organic law has given rise to much discussion and no little apprehension on the part of the public. It is urged by the friends of reform that the consolidation of the four chambers into two is necessary to meet the requirements of progress which the present cumbersome machinery retards, and that a privileged and numerous body, such as the present House of Nobles, looking more to the interest of their order, as well as to an obsolete past, than to necessary legislation, and drawing to their support the clergy on most questions of a vital nature, fail to meet the exigencies of an industrial and practical age. On the other hand, it is said the House of Nobles acts as a check upon what is termed the radicalism of the times, and is necessary under a monarchial form of government to the security of the throne itself.

The next month will probably determine the fate of the proposed measure, which at present is involved in much doubt, although the prevailing opinion is that it will be defeated. A modification by way of compromise may be agreed to and submitted to an extraordinary Diet convoked for its consideration.

There is apprehension on the part of the public that, in the event of the failure of the contemplated reform, indignation may be followed by revolution; but this I think improbable.

The government has presented the budget to the chambers for one year only, and not for three consecutive years, as has heretofore been the case. This departure from established rule may meet with opposition, as it is affirmed by many to be without precedent and unconstitutional. The explanation given by some of the friends of the government is, that they hope to carry the reform bill this session; hence the inutility of a further demand on the public purse at present.

I shall take care to keep the department informed on the subject as further developments occur.

I have the honor to be, very respectfully, your obedient servant,

JAMES H. CAMPBELL.

Hon. WILLIAM H. SEWARD,
Secretary of State, &c., &c., &c.

[Translation.]

Discourse of the King at the opening of the Diet, October 24, 1865.

SIRS: Grave interests and duties which impose a high responsibility call you to this session. May the All Powerful, whose divine protection we have just implored in the temple, preside over your works, and cause to issue from them the good of the country. We cannot but recognize with gratitude the happiness, without marked interruption, with which the roya house and Swedish people have been blessed. The union of my brother, the Prince of Dalcar lia, with the princess of the noble house of Saxe-Altenburg, and the birth of my nephew, the Duke of Noricia, form a happy increase of the royal family.

In the midst of disease and often alarming phases of the last five years we have constantly been blessed with the benefits of peace, and my relations with all foreign powers conserve the character of friendship and confidence.

The public enthusiasm which marked the celebration of the semi-centennial jubilee of the union of Sweden and Norway, in echoing equally from both sides of the mountains, proves that the ties which unite the people-brothers tighten more and more each day.

The commission of Swedes and Norwegians named by me to deliberate on the means of introducing ameliorations in the compact of union has commenced its labors.

The first of your duties will be to decide definitely, after conscientious examination, on the adoption of my proposition for a reform of the national representation. To ask an existing representation to renounce its rights, in full liberty of action and will, and to give up to others the glorious task of being the mandatories of the country, is to have a great confidence in his patriotism. I have thus a high idea of that with which you are animated in announcing the hope that you will accept this project, in the adoption of which I shall see a new guarantee of social progress.

In consequence of the decisions adopted by the general states at their last reunion, the new penal code, the maritime code, and the law on bankruptcies have received their application, (gone into effect.) In the conviction that the important changes introduced simultaneously to this effect should not be followed too rapidly by reforms in other principal branches of our legislation which should be revised, I will only propose to you during the present diet partial amelioration of existing laws.

I have concluded with his Majesty the Emperor of the French treaties of commerce and navigation, which, so far as they relate to Sweden, will be submitted in their entirety to your approbation. Those treaties have not only liberated our navigation from different changes, but have also facilitated the sale of several of our principal products. The concessions which, at the instance of other powers, we have made to France consist principally in a reduction justly due to the consumers of the duties attached to certain merchandise, at the same time maintaining a tax upon them which corresponds to the just measure of protection accorded to our national industries. By the treaties concluded in this regard with foreign powers considerable reductions have been made in the transmission of letters and telegrams abroad, and a new telegraphic cable between Skona and the island of Rugen offers us the certainty of not seeing ourselves deprived by sudden circumstances of this important way of communication with the continent. As the natioaal representation should meet annually according to the terms of the project on which you are called to decide, the budget which I will submit to you only contains the extraordinary expenses for the year subsequent to those for whose wants the last diet has already provided. If the provisions on which this proposition rests should not be realized, I have still the means of bringing before the general states in an opportune moment the necessary propositions for the following years.

Although important reductions have been made in the custom-house duties, and though the progress made in every sense by the country exact new allocations, you will be satisfied, by an examination of the calculations of the revenues of state, that they will amply suffice to cover the necessary expenses.

I have caused to be prepared complete plans for the organization of the army and the marine, calculated after the measure of our resources and the exigencies of our epoch, and I have approved of these plans in their principal parts. Your concurrence and also the allocations resulting from the adoption of these plans are indispensable to their being put in execution.

In reposing on the views manifested by the general states, I have accorded to industry an almost illimited liberty. The salutary influence that it will exercise in the future can be judged of with more certainty as its inauguration has not been accompanied with any sudden disturbance of existing relations. Liberal principles have equally received a more general application in other respects, for the facilities of distributing capital as well as for the conditions of the circulation of money, and for the establishment of institutions of credit.

Public instruction has been the object of my incessant solicitude. This work of the future becomes greater every day in importance as well as in extent. The number of pupils in the superior schools has been almost doubled during these last years; ameliorations have been introduced as much in the government of those schools as in the manner of teaching. I have united my efforts to yours to realize more and more the great idea of general primary instruction. I have at heart the desire of giving a solid and intelligent education to the population and to spread these benefits to the less fortunate classes.

Perfected institutions will equally furnish the best means of development to the national industry, and will place it on a basis more just, and more conformable to the interests of society, which restrictive laws and a system of onerous protection would fail to accomplish. I count with confidence on your co-operation for the encouragement of our industries; and in order to propagate the knowledge of their progress in all branches, I have decided that next summer a general exhibition of the products of the arts and industry of Sweden, and of the neighboring countries, will be opened in the capital.

The obstructions which arise at all times from great distances have been more and more overcome by the multiplied works which tend to facilitate in every sense communications between the different parts of the country. Our railroads have taken an extension which, seeing the population of Sweden and its financial resources, can be compared to that which has been executed in the richer and more populated countries. After having effected the junction of the two seas, and having brought ourselves nearer to the great European continent, I think it will be well to concentrate our forces on the accomplishment of railroads which are destined to connect the capitals of the two united kingdoms, in order to bring the people-brothers to each other.

Conforming to the tenor of the fundamental law, I declare the present session opened, in assuring you, sirs, of all my royal good will.

SWITZERLAND.

Mr. Seward to Mr. Fogg.

No. 66.] DEPARTMENT OF STATE,
Washington, February 8, 1865.

SIR: Mr. Hitz, the consul general of Switzerland, in this city, has transmitted to this department a communication from the federal council relative to the proposed introduction of the Swiss flag upon vessels navigating the high seas, and has solicited a favorable consideration of its contents. Mr. Hitz has been informed that the subject would receive attention, and that the views of the department thereupon would be communicated to you.

In order that you may fully understand the proposition, I herewith enclose a copy, in translation, of the paper submitted by Mr. Hitz.

Of its friendship for Switzerland, this government believes it has left nothing of doubt.

The United States are now engaged in a serious conflict with insurgents who, although they have neither ports nor coasts, are supplied by subjects of other powers, which powers recognize the insurgents as a naval belligerent. The United States deny that this recognition is just, or that it finds any warrant in the law of nations.

Moreover, the United States have for the present disallowed ship-building and armament here for foreign powers, because they need all the labor and skill of the country for the equipment of their own navy.

For these reasons you will seek an early opportunity to inform the Swiss minister for foreign affairs that the present time is not deemed a favorable one for considering the question which has been submitted by the federal council. You will make this communication in a confidential manner, if the President should prefer to receive it in this way, for the reason that this government, animated by the highest friendship for Switzerland, does not wish even to appear to be indifferent to a proposition that engages the attention of Switzerland.

I am, sir, your obedient servant,

WILLIAM H. SEWARD.

GEORGE G. FOGG, Esq., *&c., Berne.*

Mr. Hitz to Mr. Seward.

CONSULATE GENERAL OF SWITZERLAND,
Washington, D. C., January 31, 1865.

SIR: In compliance with the request of the federal chancery of Switzerland, this consulate most respectfully transmits to your honor the enclosed communication of the honorable federal council of Switzerland, relative to the proposed introduction of the Swiss flag upon vessels navigating the several oceans, and I would fain solicit a favorable consideration of its contents.

With assurances of high esteem, very obediently,

JOHN HITZ,
Consul General of Switzerland.

Hon. WILLIAM H. SEWARD,
Secretary of State, Washington, D. C.

The Federal Council to Mr. Hitz.

[Translation.]

BERNE, *December* 31, 1864.

In reference to petitions presented by a great number of Swiss citizens, the federal council has been occupied with the consideration of the question, whether Swiss citizens, owners of ships, should not also be admitted to the benefit of carrying the Swiss flag on the high seas.

Switzerland is assuredly on equality with any other nation in the right to use the free passage of the seas under her own name, and the circumstance that she does not border immediately on the seas cannot impair this right.

On the other hand, the federal council does not dissemble that, from the last circumstance, some difficulty may arise about the practical exercise of her right.

In consequence the federal council, before making a definite decision on this matter, takes the liberty to inquire of the general government of the United States whether it would be disposed to admit to its ports Swiss vessels expressly authorized by the federal council to carry the Swiss flag, and to assure to them like legal position as to vessels of other nations, as also to accord to Swiss, established in the respective states, authority to build Swiss vessels and to freight them.

The federal council can the better yield itself to the hope of a favorable answer, because the neutral flag of Switzerland might, according to conjunctures, become advantageous to all the states or to general commerce. The federal council, moreover, would not hesitate an instant in accepting all the obligations of international right which attach to that of carrying a flag.

The federal council has the honor to present to his excellency the assurances of its high consideration.

In the name of the Swiss federal council,

The President of the Confederation,
DR. T. DUBS.

The Chancellor of the Confederation,
SCHEISS.

Mr. Fogg to Mr. Seward.

No. 76.]

UNITED STATES LEGATION,
Berne, November 26, 1864.

SIR: I have the honor to transmit herewith the enclosed copy of a note from the federal council, inviting the adherence of the government of the United States to the convention concluded by the international congress, at Geneva, August 22, 1864, for the amelioration of the condition of sick and wounded soldiers.

By reference to article 9 of the convention—a copy of which convention I transmitted to you in my despatch of September 14, No. 70—you will perceive that the protocol was left open to enable those governments not there represented, or not represented by delegates empowered to sign the convention, to become parties to the same thereafter.

As it is provided in the convention that the ratification should be exchanged at Berne, the federal council deem it their duty to extend the invitation herewith enclosed.

I had hoped to receive, ere this, an acknowledgment of my despatch above alluded to, with the views of the State Department in relation to the convention. Thus far I have received nothing indicating that the despatch, copies of the convention and other papers, have ever been received by you. Mr. Miller writes me that the package containing them was forwarded by the steamer which left Liverpool on the 24th September. I cannot, therefore, suppose it failed to reach its destination, and can only explain to myself its failure to be acknowledged on the supposition of its having been reserved for examination, and subsequently laid by and forgotten. It may readily be supposed that I would like to be enabled to give some sort of response to the question: "Will the United States accede to the convention?" A question of no little interes among the people and in a country where the opinion and decision of the government of the United States are deemed of the very highest authority and importance.

As I indicated to you in my former despatch, I have in no manner committed the government, as, indeed, I had no authority to do, on this question. On the contrary, I have informally answered, when inquired of by the members of the federal council, or by my colleagues of the diplomatic corps, that it was very doubtful, by reason, if no other, of the present condition of our country, and of the impossibility of making the rebel authorities parties to the convention, or compelling them to respect its provisions.

Trusting soon to be in possession of your views in relation to this matter, and of the intentions of the government thereon,

I have the honor to be, with the highest respect, your obedient servant,

GEORGE G. FOGG.

Hon. WILLIAM H. SEWARD,
Secretary of State of the United States of America.

[Translation.]

BERNE, *November* 14, 1864.

In regard to article 9 of the convention concluded at Geneva, on the 22d of August, 1864, for the improvement in the condition of soldiers wounded in armies in the field, the Swiss federal council has the honor to invite the government of the United States also to assent to that convention, for which purpose the original draught has been left open for the governments of nations that have not yet assented.

As the management of the affair has been intrusted by the congress to the Swiss federal council, the latter hopes to receive an affirmative answer from the government of the United States, and willingly accepts this occasion of offering to the minister resident of the United States the assurances of high consideration.

DR. J. DUBS,
President of the Confederation.
SCHIESS, *Chancellor.*

Mr. FOGG, *United States Minister Resident, Berne.*

Mr. Fogg to Mr. Seward.

No. 78.]

UNITED STATES LEGATION,
Berne, January 2, 1865.

SIR: I have the honor to inform you that, in conformity with the Swiss federal constitution, which forbids that the same member of the federal council serve as president of the confederation two terms in succession, the national assembly, at its late session, made choice of Mr. Charles Schenk as president of the confederation, and of Mr. Martin Knüsel as vice-president, for the year ensuing.

Mr. Schenk served as vice-president during the past year, and Mr. Knüsel has been several times president—the last time in 1861. Yesterday the new president was inaugurated, and entered upon the duties of his office, remaining at the Palais Fédéral the greatest portion of the day to receive the New Year's greetings of the diplomatic corps, and such other officers or citizens as saw fit to call on him.

During my call the president expressed very earnestly and enthusiastically the deep interest which himself, personally, and the great body of the Swiss people feel in the contest going on in the United States. In common with the rest of Europe, Switzerland was suffering in her material interests by the long continuance of the war. But she was not blind nor indifferent to the great issues and principles involved in that war. Much as the struggle had cost in men and money, the United States and the world would be, in his judgment, amply compensated, if the result should be the extinction of slavery.

On parting, the president desired me to present his felicitations and those of the federal council to President Lincoln, on the result of the recent national election in the United States, and on the still more recent results of the Union military operations in Georgia and Tennessee. He expressed the hope that the next New Year's day might see the people and States of America once more united, happy, and free.

Joining heartily in this hope, and earnestly wishing the president and yourself a happy New Year, I am, with the highest respect, your obedient servant,

GEORGE G. FOGG.

Hon. WILLIAM H. SEWARD,
Secretary of State of the United States of America.

Mr. Fogg to Mr. Seward.

No. 82.]

LEGATION OF THE UNITED STATES,
Berne, March 4, 1865.

SIR: Your despatch dated February 8, No. 66, in regard to the communication from the federal council, asking the favorable consideration of the United States to the proposition to authorize vessels owned by Swiss citizens to sail under the Swiss flag upon the high seas, has been received.

In accordance with your suggestion, I yesterday had an interview with the president of the confederation, in which I explained to him the difficulties in the way of our government's considering that question at the present moment, when we are suffering from the recognition by other maritime powers of a belligerent flag, hailing from no accessible ports and owning allegiance to no maritime tribunals. I told the president, that for the United States to now give their assent to the proposition of Switzerland would be to abandon, in principle, the grounds upon which we rest our complaints against the course of England, France, and the other maritime powers who have conceded to the southern rebels the rights of naval belligerents, while such rebels were not in a condition to observe, nor disposed to hold themselves amenable to any recognized code of international maritime law. The rebel cruisers had assumed the right to burn our merchant vessels upon the ocean whenever and wherever met with, upon the very ground which, in our opinion, made them pirates, and not belligerents—that they had no ports into which to carry their prizes, and no prize courts to decide on the validity of their capture. Against this assumption by the rebels, and its practical recognition by several of the leading naval powers, the government of the United States had protested, and would continue to protest, reserving to itself the right to decide hereafter if it would not demand of these powers satisfaction and reparation for losses to our merchant navy, which only the unfriendly recognition of foreign governments and the active sympathies of the subjects of those governments could have enabled the rebel corsairs to inflict.

I added it was not impossible—perhaps not improbable—that, after the successful termination of our present struggle, and the settlement of the complications growing out of it, the United States might see fit to accept as law the new principles upon which the governments of England and France have acted towards us, and in that event the recognition of the Swiss flag upon the high seas, now asked of us, would be conceded as a matter of course.

In conclusion, I handed the president a French translation of your despatch, which he read with evident satisfaction, thanking me for the explanations I had given him, and wishing me to express his warm thanks to yourself for the cordial and friendly sentiments towards Switzerland contained in your despatch.

He saw plainly, he said, the present obstacles in the way of the United States taking immediate favorable action on the proposition submitted to them. But he hoped, as did the whole Swiss people, that an early day would see those obstacles removed by the suppression of the rebellion and the re-establishment of the Union. In this hope Switzerland could afford to wait, recognizing that the perpetuation of our great republic was of more importance, even to Switzerland herself, than any formal recognition of her flag either on land or sea.

I have the honor to be, with the highest respect, your obedient servant,

GEORGE G. FOGG.

Hon. WILLIAM H. SEWARD,
Secretary of State of the United States of America.

Mr. Fogg to Mr. Seward.

No. 84.] LEGATION OF THE UNITED STATES,
Berne, April 14, 1865.

SIR: At the request of a large number of the persons interested, I forward to you the enclosed letter from Professor J. Koronikolski to the President of the United States, in behalf of the Polish refugees now temporarily in Switzerland. The total number of these unfortunate men now within the limits of the Swiss Confederation is, I am told, about five hundred, mostly young men, and in many cases belonging to the best families in Poland. Having been engaged in the late unfortunate insurrection, they are unable to return to their native land, and are desirous to go to America.

Professor Koronikolski, whose letter I herewith forward, is the agent of these refugees, and is, I am assured, an honorable, patriotic and trustworthy man, and possesses the confidence of the federal council, who, as you will see by copy of a note addressed to him, (marked A,) takes a warm interest in the aspirations of these Poles to reach America.

Of course I have not felt at liberty to give any assurances of the government aid asked for in the enclosed letter, but I have assured them of the warm sympathy both of our government and people towards their brave and unfortunate nation.

Enclosed I send you, marked B, a copy of my note acknowledging reception of Professor K.'s letter to the President.

With the highest respects, your obedient servant,

GEORGE G. FOGG.

Hon. WILLIAM H. SEWARD,
Secretary of State of the United States of America.

A.

The Federal Council to Mr. J. Koronikolski.

[Translation.]

The Swiss federal council has resolved—

1st. To authorize the federal department of justice and police to give a contribution of one hundred francs each to such Poles as may desire to emigrate to the United States, provided that they find the other necessary means of transportation.

2d. To instruct the Swiss consul general at Washington to inform the government of the United States that a number of Polish refugees intend to emigrate to the United States with the purpose of founding a new home by the acquisition of lands, &c., and that the federal council requests the American government to facilitate to these unfortunate men the execution of their plan as far as practicable.

Given at Berne, April 10, 1865.

The Chancellor of the Swiss Confederation, SCHEISS.

Made out for communication to Mr. J. KORONIKOLSKI.

B.

Mr. Fogg to Mr. Koronikolski.

UNITED STATES LEGATION,
Berne, April 17, 1865.

MY DEAR SIR: Your letter addressed to the President of the United States in behalf of a portion of your unfortunate countrymen, Polish refugees now finding a temporary asylum in Switzerland, but wishing to secure a permanent home in America, has been received, and will be forwarded to Washington at the earliest moment.

Without being authorized to promise that all the prayers of your letter will be granted, I can assure you of the warm sympathy of the government and people of the United States for the sufferings and misfortunes of the brave patriots of Poland.

Wishing you, my dear sir, every possible success in your laudable efforts to ameliorate the condition of your countrymen, I am, very truly, your obedient servant,

GEORGE G. FOGG.

BERNE, *April*, 1865.

SIR: Animated by the desire to procure for his unfortunate countrymen, the Polish refugees, the best means of finding a new home, the undersigned, professor of gymnastics at St. Gall, Switzerland, has come to the conviction that by emigrating to the United States they would best secure a new civil existence, under the protection and laws of that country. The noble aspirations of the great republic are a pledge that its President will not withhold from them his generous support.

The Polish emigrants are scattered over a great many European states, where they have met with the most sympathetic reception, but no prospect of securing any durable futurity. The only hope left to them in Europe would be to see the regeneration of their country—a hope which, we must say, to our great pain, has vanished for a long time to come. We may therefore unhesitatingly say that, at present, we have no future in Europe.

Under these circumstances it is very natural that the Poles, like other political proscripts, should look towards America and seek to place themselves under the protection of the Union, which is assuredly the last and most secure asylum of the world, and in which they hope to become useful citizens under the star-spangled banner.

Far from it to be the intention to solicit from the Union the assistance usually accorded to the indigent. On the contrary, it is our purpose to establish a Polish colony, under the auspices, and, if possible, with the aid of our own resources—a colony which, at the same time, would have the means of being useful to all its countrymen emigrating thither.

Our principal purpose is to obtain assistance of the government at Washington in order that we may find on its hospitable soil some basis for the realization of our project and for keeping together our countrymen by a common tie. Besides, we would wish that the government would assign to us, for cash, lands in some part of the country where an extension of the colony according to its necessities would be practicable.

We can, of course, not know to what extent our request will be received by the government of the Union; considering, however, the facility with which colonization is going on in the Union, and in the conviction that the Union will receive the Polish proscripts as cheerfully as other emigrants, and that we will prove ourselves to be citizens equally useful, we take new courage in the certainty of success.

The undersigned takes the liberty respectfully and earnestly to entreat the American minister at Berne to forward this petition to his excellency the President of the United States, accompanied by his recommendation.

At the next meeting of Congress we, of course, reserve to ourselves to solicit the gratuitous cession of lands which, according to information given us by Minister Fogg, might be granted to emigrated American citizens. At the same time we desire, at a later period, to come to an understanding with the American committee of emigration as to the alleviation of the costs of transportation, although we do not venture to express the hope of being transported at the expense of the Union on board of its vessels. It may be the case that the government in its generosity will accord to us that favor spontaneously, in which case we would not consider it indiscreet to accept such favor from the hands of a great nation.

Flattering ourselves in the hope of a favorable response, we cannot conclude without urgently recommending the unfortunate homeless Polish proscripts to your generosity and to the sympathy of the brave and liberal nation.

I have the honor to be your excellency's most obedient servant,

J. KORONIKOLSKI.

His Excellency ABRAHAM LINCOLN,
President of the United States of America.

Mr. Fogg to Mr. Seward.

No. 85.] UNITED STATES LEGATION,
Berne, April 18, 1865.

SIR: The news of the capture of Richmond, which was received here by telegraph last Saturday, produced almost as much excitement as the same news must have produced in the various cities and villages of the United States. The enthusiasm of the people was nearly universal and quite irrepressible. Extras were issued from the offices of the leading journals, and within an hour the news was placarded all over the city. The satisfaction could hardly have been exceeded had the news been that of a great Swiss instead of an American victory.

The president of the confederation came to congratulate me on the great event. Other members of the government and leading citizens came. Telegraphic despatches came a little later from different and distant parts of Switzerland, from clubs, associations, and from individuals personally unknown to me, giving intelligence of the general joy at an event deemed of the greatest importance to the cause of liberty and liberal progress throughout Europe.

Up to this date we have few details, and know little beyond the general fact of "three days' severe fighting" and the occupation of Richmond by Union troops. Of course we wait with great interest the news by the steamer which left New York the 5th, hoping to hear of the submission or dispersion of Lee's army and a substantial close of the war. The event already announced is accepted in England and on the continent, equally by the enemies and friends of the American Union, as the end of the rebellion.

The same telegraph which brought the news of the fall of Richmond, fortunately for the financial interests of Europe, brought also the report of a "pacific" speech by yourself. For some cause not entirely easy to explain the idea had come to be almost universal among people, politicians, and journalists all over Europe, that the people and government of the United States, having got a taste of war, had become so in love with it, that as soon as they should have finished their own civil war, they would immediately pitch into England, a little later perhaps into France, and wind up by being ready to fight all the rest of the world.

People here in Europe, where armies are composed of trained soldiers, who are nothing but soldiers, cannot conceive what the United States can do with their immense military forces after the end of the present war, unless to employ them in a foreign war. Hence the feverish anxiety and general expectation to which I have alluded above.

The President's inaugural did something towards dispelling this "fearful looking for of judgment." But I would have been glad to hear him declare himself more explicitly; and I am glad to believe that you have done so.

Of all people in the world we shall, for a long time, have most need of peace with all nations, and least to fear from foreign aggression. With the immense exhibition of military and naval power we have made, we will be honored, feared, and respected as second to no nation on earth, and that without making any new demonstrations for one generation at least. And this fact of our pacific intentions cannot, in my judgment, be too promptly and emphatically declared.

Begging you to excuse this suggestion and congratulating the President, yourself, and the country on the great triumph that has been achieved, I have the honor to be, with the warmest esteem, your obedient servant,

GEORGE G. FOGG.

Hon. WILLIAM H. SEWARD,
Secretary of State of the United States of America.

Mr. Fogg to Mr. Seward.

No. 86] UNITED STATES LEGATION,
Berne, April 24, 1865.

SIR: By request of the writer and as an indication of the feelings and expectations produced by the recent successes of the Union arms, I send you a copy of the Bund, containing an elaborate editorial written directly on the reception of the first news of the capture of Richmond.

The Bund is the leading political journal of Switzerland, and the semi-official organ of the Swiss government, and is largely the exponent of the liberal sentiment of southern Germany.

Accompanying the Bund I send a translation of the article in question, which, as you will perceive, the editor wishes should be laid before the President. I will add that, in my judgment, the article does not overestimate the results likely to follow in Europe the re-establishment of the American Union, purified from the great evil which came so near destroying our national life.

Congratulating you with my whole heart on the capitulation of General Lee and his army, and the approaching return of peace, with liberty and union, I have the honor to be, with the highest respect, your obedient servant,

GEORGE G. FOGG.

Hon. WILLIAM H. SEWARD,
Secretary of State of the United States of America.

[Translation.]

BERNE, *April* 18, 1865.

SIR: As a token of sympathy for the cause for which the Union has fought and achieved with so brilliant success in the interest of democracy and humanity, the undersigned takes the liberty to send you the accompanying article on the fall of Richmond. According to the conviction at which I have arrived from the voice of the Swiss press, that article is the expression of the predominant public sentiment of Switzerland.

May the Union extend her military triumph to a complete civil regeneration of the United States and secure republican freedom upon firm ground forever.

With the most distinguished consideration, your obedient servant,

F. GEUGEL, *Editor of the Bund.*

His Excellency ANDREW JOHNSON,
President of the United States of America.

[Translation.—From the Bund of April 18.]

The Fall of Richmond.

Richmond has fallen, after three days' bloody fighting and the almost complete annihilation of Lee's army; under circumstances, therefore, which, in the main point, are equal to the termination of the American war! This is the news which Easter day has brought us—a bloody news, but grand and of the most auspicious portent in the history of the world.

Four years have already elapsed since the outbreak of the war. When it began, there stood the slave empire full of arrogance and confidence. It possessed an already formed army, nearly all the schooled officers having sworn allegiance to its star. Statesmen of reckless energy promised to lead it to victory. Upon its banner stood the motto of national independence and free trade, and it boldly denied, in Europe at least, that it was the slavery of the black race for which it had drawn the sword. All the mighty and rich men on its side, all the monarchs and aristocrats, all the material interests of Europe and their hosts of dependents, sympathized with it and made its cause their own. To its side at first inclined the fortune of war and victory, and with it the admiration of all who worshipped success. For a while, indeed, it seemed as if really the young glorious republic on the other side of the ocean must crumble into dust as a proof of the impracticability of popular self-government and see itself trampled upon by slave aristocrats, and soon, like the Roman republic, by absolute Cæsars.

Opposite to it stood, rich in resources, but hesitating and undetermined, indisposed to war, and without military organization, the democratic government of free labor. Unsuccessful as it was at first, the monarchists and materialists of Europe derided it, ridiculed its people as slaves of the dollar, just as if the dollar were not most almighty with the mockers themselves; they laughed satirically at the pretended abolitionism of the north; they desired and hoped from the bottom of their hearts that it would succumb, and that every hope of maintaining practical republican freedom would forever be destroyed for mankind. Even in our country (Switzerland) there were plenty of deluded people who would not see that the cause for which the Union fought was neither more nor less than the vital principle of their own existence.

And nevertheless there was a secret voice which whispered in all those hearts who love freedom that the people of the north were stronger than the slave-aristocrats of the south; and even when the wails of the defeats of Chickahominy, of Fredericksburg, and Chickamanga came across to us, the final triumph of the north was nevertheless considered certain.

How are matters standing now? Even in the worst epoch, when no military successes smiled on the north, when no able commanders had yet appeared, the enemy were never able to enter the soil of the Union without punishment. Mr. Lincoln, the head of the republic, plain, but of thoroughly balanced mind, remained firm. Even if he did not perform any brilliant exploits, so much the surer did he adopt the right, and, in truth, the grander and more successful policy, in which a genuine republican statesman is always superior to over-wise diplomatic demagogues. He declared the black race free, and the people of the north said amen. When the leaders in the south called, in the agony of despair, for arming the slaves, the slaveholders' congress struggled against it even in the last extremity, confessing openly that it was slavery for which the war had been waged. At the same time it was in the north that the most significant right was conferred upon a black man, to plead as an attorney before the highest courts of the nation.

The moral victory over the plague spot of slavery was followed at last by military success. Two years ago Vicksburg was conquered and the confederacy cut in two halves. There were two men who achieved this great feat by which the tide of victory was turned, namely, Grant and Sherman. The same men are now finishing the war. While Grant was approaching the rebel capital nearer than any one ever before him, and holding with iron grasp the principal army of the south, Sherman, by his march through Georgia, cut the eastern half of the rebel States again in two halves, exposing thereby the internal impotency of the rebel league. And at last, after Sherman had captured Charleston, the very cradle of the rebellion, and took his way northward towards Grant, Grant, at the right moment, grasped the rebel capital, already pressed from every side, and now crushed with one blow the organized power of the south.

The war is at an end. Even if Lee should escape from the hands of Grant and Sheridan and not run into the arms of Thomas, no more battles on a great scale need be expected. No more southern armies exist, but only bodies of from twenty to thirty thousand men, which, being without connexions between themselves, can, at the most, only carry on a guerilla war. The probability is that the moral power of the victory will prevent even this, and that the south will see that nothing is left it but submission.

Since October 19, 1781, when Cornwallis surrendered himself to the champions of liberty in North America, and by which event the existence of the Union was sealed, no day is more memorable than that on which Richmond fell. Eight years had not elapsed after the day of Yorktown when Europe witnessed the French revolution. As the victory of the American republic called forth then in Europe the greatest event which our continent has witnessed since the reformation, so will the present victory of the American republic send the surging waves over to Europe. We very much deceive ourselves if all the potentates of Europe have not felt a peculiar chill at the fall of Richmond. The people, on the contrary, feel in their hearts the exultation of beaming hope.

Of all the nations, however, the Swiss are the first to congratulate the Union on her victory—they, the only old republicans of Europe, surrounded on all sides by monarchies, and trusting their future only in the future of the democratic spirit of all the nations. Switzerland alone would be too weak to be the rock and champion of republicanism. Across the ocean, however, there stands now a great, firm republic, powerful enough to cope with any enemy and to maintain her position on the page of history. In the self-reliant power with which she has herself healed the cancer on her heart; in the fear which prevented even the mightiest monarchies of Europe, notwithstanding their most sincere desire, from troubling her convalescence, we draw the assurance of safety and the pledge that our republic will also not perish, but may, perhaps, at some future day, even take deeper root in Europe.

May the Union, noble and magnanimous towards the succumbed, but firm as a rock in her principles, follow up her victory, and as a fruit of it re-establish her national life, thoroughly healed from the former evil, in order that it may become and always remain true that "The cause of democracy and freedom must triumph!"

Mr. Fogg to Mr. Hunter.

No. 87.] UNITED STATES LEGATION,
Berne, May 3, 1865.

SIR: Your despatch of April 17, apprising me of the assassination of President Lincoln, is just received. The shocking intelligence has already been flashed by telegraph all over Europe several days earlier, as had also the scarcely less astounding news of the probably fatal attempt upon the lives of Secretary and Assistant Secretary Seward.

No words can convey any sort of idea of the excitement produced among all classes—rulers and people—on this side of the Atlantic. At first no one was willing to believe it. The news was too terrible for belief. But soon a despatch from Mr. Adams, in London, put an end to all doubts. The deed, terrible as it was, had been done, and the foremost man of all the world in the hearts of millions on both sides of the Atlantic lay stretched in death by the dastardly hand of an assassin.

The millions in America who loved Mr. Lincoln as a father, and revered him as the purest and greatest of patriotic statesmen, could scarcely have mourned him more profoundly than did the masses in Europe. Especially dear was he to the citizens of this little republic of Switzerland, where, from the beginning of our great struggle, his firm, true hand has ever been upheld by the warm sympathies and prayers of a free and gallant people, who had themselves not long since been called to strangle a somewhat similar, though far less iniquitous and sanguinary conspiracy against their nation's life.

You will have seen how all Europe is moved. I am able to do nothing but receive visits and letters of condolence from citizens, foreign ministers, and the members of the government. These last—some of them at least—I will send you with my next despatch.

Of my own personal grief over this great calamity, this is, perhaps, not the place to speak, but I cannot forbear. Few men out of his own family and neighborhood were so circumstanced as to know Mr. Lincoln better than myself up to the time of my leaving for my present post. He was kind to me, and I loved him as a father. I mourn him now as my dearest earthly friend.

I pray God that the blow of the assassin may not have proved fatal to Mr. Seward and his son. Asking you to express to them, if living, my most profound and heartfelt sympathy in their and our country's great suffering.

I have the honor to be your obedient servant,

GEORGE G. FOGG.

Hon. W. HUNTER,
Acting Secretary of State of the United States of America.

Mr. Fogg to Mr. Hunter.

No. 88.] UNITED STATES LEGATION,
Berne, May 4, 1865.

SIR: I herewith transmit, in copy and translation, the enclosed letter of condolence from the federal council on receiving intelligence of the assassination of President Lincoln and of the attempt upon the life of Mr. Seward.

Letters of a similar tenor are being prepared and forwarded to me from nearly all the cantonal governments and from the citizens of every portion of Switzerland. The mourning and regret for the death of our President are universal from the old men to the boys in the schools. I am convinced that no other man in any part of the world held such a place in so many millions of hearts.

Later I will forward to the State Department copies or the originals of the addresses now coming into the legation from the cantons, cities, and communes, near and remote, of Switzerland.

I herewith append also a copy of my note to the federal council in acknowledgment of theirs.

With the highest respect, your obedient servant,

GEORGE G. FOGG.

Hon. WILLIAM HUNTER,

Acting Secretary of State of the United States of America.

[Translation.]

BERNE, *April* 28, 1865.

The federal council have been apprised by the public papers of the horrible crime, the victims of which are two of the most worthy and most noble citizens and statesmen of the United States. One cry of horror and indignation at this act, inspired by the most brutal passion and the most heinous fanaticism, has resounded through the whole civilized world, and particularly through Switzerland, a country whose analogous institutions unite it so closely with its great sister republic.

The federal council hasten to address their most sincere condolence to the honorable minister resident of the United States in Switzerland, by expressing to him their profound grief over this shocking event, and the strong sympathy which they feel at this great calamity.

Free Switzerland, with similar institutions, will not cease to devote all her sympathies to free America and to her tendencies, inspired by truth and humanity—sympathies deriving new strength from this catastrophy.

The federal council cannot conclude without expressing the consoling hope that the new Union, reconstituted under the auspices *of fraternity* and *reconciliation*, will follow with increased energy the path which Providence has traced out for her, and erect before the eyes of the world the most sublime monument to the glory of the illustrious victim.

With those sentiments, the federal council have the honor to renew to Mr. Fogg the assurance of their high consideration.

In the name of the federal council.

The president of the confederation, J. SCHENK.
The chancellor of the confederation, SCHIESS.

LEGATION OF THE UNITED STATES OF AMERICA,
Berne, May 6, 1865.

The undersigned, minister resident of the United States of America in Switzerland, takes the earliest opportunity, after a return from a short journey, to acknowledge the receipt of the note of their excellencies of the high federal council, expressing their horror of the fearful act which has deprived his country of its great and wise chief, and plunged a whole great people in the profoundest grief.

This note will be forwarded without delay to Washington, where, if anything can alleviate the great national bereavement, it is the universal manifestation of regret with which all Europe, and especially Switzerland, share the grief of the American people, and mourn the great and good man, so suddenly struck down in the midst of his labors for the glory and regeneration of his country.

Among the incidents of his residence in Switzerland the undersigned will always remember, with the liveliest satisfaction, that in all the long struggle which, during four years, has developed the great qualities of President Lincoln, now recognized and honored by the whole world, the sympathies of Switzerland have never failed to be on the side of the government of the United States.

If other governments have sympathized with a rebellion against popular institutions and in favor of despotism, the government and people of the Helvetic republic have never wavered in their friendship towards a great sister republic and in fidelity to their own ancient traditions.

For this new testimony of friendship and warm wishes for the reconstitution of the American Union, expressed by the high federal council, as well as for their sympathy in a great national grief, the undersigned tenders to their excellencies his sincere thanks.

With the highest esteem and consideration,

GEORGE G. FOGG.

Mr. Hunter to Mr. Fogg.

No. 69.] DEPARTMENT OF STATE,
Washington, May 6, 1865.

SIR: Your despatch, No. 84, of the 14th, and No. 85, of the 18th ultimo, have been received. The subject to which that of the earlier date refers, namely, the proposed immigration hither of certain Polish refugees now in Switzerland, will receive proper attention. It has already been referred for consideration to the Secretary of the Interior.

I am, sir, your obedient servant,

W. HUNTER,
Acting Secretary.

GEORGE G. FOGG, Esq., *&c. Berne.*

Mr. Fogg to Mr. Hunter.

No. 91.] UNITED STATES LEGATION,
Berne, May 30, 1865.

SIR: Your circular, dated May 16, enclosing two printed copies of the President's proclamation of the 10th instant, relative to insurgent cruisers, is received, and, agreeably to your direction, I this morning waited upon the president of the confederation and placed one of said copies in his hands.

The president remarked that he had already perused a German translation of the proclamation, and that he thought it timely and just. If there was ever a justification for conceding maritime belligerent rights to the rebels, there could seem to be now no excuse for continuing such concession by any neutral or friendly power.

The president expressed himself enthusiastically, as he always does, in relation to the future of our great, free republic, which, with slavery destroyed, would leave no stain upon her escutcheon, at which the friends of liberty and popular institutions in other lands would be compelled to blush. He also asked particularly after the state of Mr. Seward's health, and in reply to my assurance of his steadily improving condition, he wished me to express to Mr. Seward the profound wishes of the entire government and people of Switzerland for his speedy and complete recovery, and to felicitate him, as also President Johnson, upon the end of the war and the near approach of a re-established Union, based on political equality and universal liberty.

With the highest respect, your obedient servant,

GEORGE G. FOGG.

Hon. WILLIAM HUNTER,
Acting Secretary of State of the United States of America.

Mr. Fogg to Mr. Hunter.

No. 93.] UNITED STATES LEGATION,
Berne, June 20, 1865.

SIR: I have the honor to forward herewith to the State Department, by the hand of Henry A. Smythe, esquire, of New York, appointed bearer of despatches to Washington, two bound volumes, containing over 300 original addresses of congratulation, sympathy, and condolence, from the various cantonal governments, municipalities, communes, associations, schools, and leading citizens of Switzerland, expressive of the universal joy occasioned by the triumphant suppression of the rebellion in the United States; the destruction of slavery, and the re-establishment of the American Union, and of the quite as universal sorrow over the assassination of the late President Lincoln, the events of whose life, and the moment and manner of whose death, will enshrine him in the Pantheon of history as the most illustrious character of modern times.

The volumes contain official addresses from the governments of twenty-one cantons, (all save one, Fribourg,) something more than 20,000 original autographs, comprising all the members of the federal council, members of the cantonal government, magistrates, clergymen, and military officers.

In truth, they comprise the aggregate and congregate voice of all Switzerland, whose heart, hopes, and prayers, have been with our government in all the long, and bloody, and sometimes apparently doubtful struggle, through which we have passed.

As these various addresses have been sent or brought to me by delegations or committees I have been obliged to make many brief speeches and write many letters, returning thanks in behalf of the government and people of the United States for a sympathy as sincere and deep as it was universal.

Trusting that these addresses and memorials will be sacredly preserved in the archives of the State Department as evidence of the solidarity of sentiments and aspirations between the people of Switzerland and those of the United States,

I have the honor to be your obedient servant,

GEORGE G. FOGG.

Hon. WILLIAM H. SEWARD,
Secretary of State of the United States of America.

(For the accompaniments see Appendix, separate volume.)

Mr. Seward to Mr. Harrington.

No. 2.] DEPARTMENT OF STATE,
Washington, July 25, 1865.

SIR: In presenting your letter of credence to his excellency the President of the Swiss confederation, it will be proper for you, while assuring him of the friendly sentiments of the government and people of this country, to state that the United States, during their recent struggle for unity and for the supremacy of their national government, have, among other adverse influences, had to contend with a disposition, at least on the part of some foreign powers, to interfere in the contest. In opposing this disposition they have not been unmindful that the integrity of the Swiss government was under similar circumstances externally threatened; but the Swiss nation, by prudence and firmness, successfully averted the danger. The recollection of that successful achievement of Swiss wisdom and virtue had no small effect in cheering us and enabling us to persevere in the same course.

I am, sir, your obedient servant,

WILLIAM H. SEWARD.

GEORGE HARRINGTON, Esq., &c., &c., *Berne.*

Mr. Fogg to Mr. Seward.

No. 102.] UNITED STATES LEGATION,
Berne, October 16, 1865.

SIR: I have the honor to inform you that my successor, Mr. Harrington, reached Berne last Friday, the 13th instant. The same day I called upon the president of the confederation to ask as early a day as convenient for the reception of the new minister. The president named Monday, the 16th instant, at noon, as the day and hour. Accordingly, precisely at noon to-day I accompanied Mr. Harrington to the executive chamber in the Palais Federal, where we were received by the president and the chancellor of the confederation.

On presenting my letter of recall I addressed some brief remarks to the president, agreeably to the general tenor of your instructions. I send you herewith copies of my address to the president and of the president's response. I also send, by permission of Mr. Harrington, copies of his remarks and of the president's response.

As the train is waiting which takes me to Paris on my way home, you will please excuse the brevity of this despatch.

Your obedient servant,

GEORGE G. FOGG.

Hon. WILLIAM H. SEWARD,
Secretary of State of the United States of America.

Mr. Fogg's address to President Schenk.

MR. PRESIDENT: I have the honor to present to your excellency the enclosed letter from Mr. Seward, Secretary of State of the United States, advising you of my proposed retirement from the mission with which I have been honored for several years near the government of the Swiss Confederation. In performing this duty it gives me pleasure to assure your excellency, as I am instructed to do, of the friendly sentiments of the President of the United States towards the government and people of Switzerland, and of his determination to lose no opportunity to improve and strengthen the relations of sympathy and good will so long and so happily subsisting between the two countries. I should do injustice to my own feelings, Mr. President, if I did not, in this hour of parting, say something more. When I entered upon my mission here, my country was just entering upon the most fearful crisis that can try a nation—a civil war—in which two diverse and hostile civilizations are contending for the mastery, and where, the sword once drawn, the one combatant or the other must perish. I need not tell you that this great crisis is happily passed, the government and republican institutions of the United States, emerging from their baptism of blood, stronger than ever. Slavery, our great national reproach, has perished in the conflict it provoked; and henceforth no incubus remains to cripple the influence or stay the advancement of liberal principles and popular government upon the American continent.

Many new and important questions will undoubtedly arise out of the armed conflict which has just closed, and whose solution will tax the wisdom of the wisest. Of their peaceable solution, however, in accordance with the demands of reason and justice, I have no doubt.

Mr. President, I have alluded to this subject because I know how profound is the interest which the republicans of Switzerland feel in regard to all that concerns their great sister republic on the other side of the Atlantic. I shall never forget the friendly sympathies with which our long struggle with rebellion was watched, and the joyful enthusiasm with which the triumph of the government was hailed in every portion of the Swiss Confederation. Still less can I forget the universal expression of indignation and mourning which followed the assassination of our great and generous President, whose fidelity, wisdom, and moderation had been so conspicuous as, even in a bloody war, to extort the admiration of the world.

Mr. President, I bid you, and through you, all your colleagues of the federal council, farewell. I return to my country to find it more happy than when I left it. I shall carry with me precious memories of your free and beautiful land, and of your people, whose independence and liberties may God preserve.

President Schenk's response to Mr. Fogg.

[Translation.]

MR. MINISTER: By the letter you have just now communicated to us, we have learned that you are going to leave our country, and to retire from the mission with which you were charged by your government near the Confederation during late years.

During this time the eyes of the Swiss people and of the whole world were fixed almost exclusively on the great events of your country. We saw—not spring into existence, for it existed and was in preparation through a decade of years—but burst into action, the rebellion, which tended to nothing less than to tear asunder the glorious Union of North America. We saw it suddenly plunged into a war, which became from year to year more vast and more formidable. We saw the star-spangled banner of the republic surrounded by enemies and by dangers; but we saw also that it was protected by a heroic nation, and that the greater the danger, and multiplied force of enemies, the more did strength, unity, confidence, and patriotism increase. During this time, the Swiss people—I dare will aver it—shared with you, Mr. Minister, in the sorrow, indignation, fears, hopes, trust, and, at last, also in the joy, when humanity triumphed over slavery, and the republic over its enemies within and without. The Swiss people felt only too well that the fate of the great republic involved also a portion of their own destinies. That period will remain inscribed with all those emotions on our memories, and we cannot remember them without calling to mind at the same time the worthy representative of the United States who has become so united in feeling with and so dear to us.

Carry with you, Mr. Minister, our thanks for the assurances of good will you have been pleased in the name of your government to renew to us, and please to say to your government how happy we are to witness the continuance and the strengthening of the relations of sympathy which so happily exist between the two republican nations.

Mr. Horrington's address to President Schenk.

Mr. PRESIDENT: In presenting to your excellency my letter of credence as minister resident of the United States near the Swiss Confederation, I am instructed by the Secretary of State to assure you of the friendly sentiments entertained by the government and people of the United States towards the Swiss Confederation.

I am further authorized to say that the United States in their recent struggle for unity and for the supremacy of the national government, have, among other adverse influences, had to contend with a disposition, at least on the part of some foreign powers, to interfere in the contest. In opposing this disposition they have not been unmindful that the integrity of the Swiss Confederation was under similar circumstances externally threatened, but the Swiss nation, by prudence and firmness, successfully averted the danger. The recollection of that successful achievement of Swiss wisdom and virtue had no small effect in cheering us and enabling us to persevere in the same course.

It will be my pleasure, Mr. President, as well as my duty, to preserve, and, if possible, to strengthen the friendly relations so happily existing between the two republics.

President Schenk's response to Mr. Harrington.

[Translation.]

On receiving the communication which you have just made to me, I must at once express our great satisfaction that the government of the United States has not allowed any interval in the representation in Switzerland. We see therein, with great pleasure, proof positive of the interest it feels for the Swiss people and government, of which we are happy now to receive new assurances. We also attach great importance to the continuance of this friendship, and will not forget on our part to do all that depends on us to keep up and add to the friendly relations which exist between the two countries. You have pleased to tell us that in the recent contest the government and people remember the partially analogous position in which Switzerland was placed some years ago, when a part of the cantons took arms against the confederation, and foreign powers menaced us with their interference. You remark that the people of the United States found encouragement in the recollection of the course which in that condition had been followed by the confederation, and the success which had crowned that course. Allow me to reply, Mr. Minister, that the encouragement which the United States may have found in our recent history is but little in comparison with the fresh impulse and additional strength which our thoughts and our republican convictions have drawn out from your magnificent history of recent years. When after the terrible assassination of President Lincoln, happening at a most critical moment, the republic, without being shaken for an instant, continued its course with a sure and firm step, that was for us, as for you, a triumph of republican institutions, and powerful strengthening of all hearts in the love of these institutions.

Accept, Mr. Minister, the assurance of our deep sympathy in the happiness of your country, for the President and his government who have sent you to us, and be convinced that we will endeavor to facilitate, as much as will depend on us, the accomplishment of the mission with which you are charged.

Mr. Seward to Mr. Harrington.

No. 3.] DEPARTMENT OF STATE,
Washington, November 1, 1865.

SIR: On the 20th of June last your predecessor, Mr. Fogg, transmitted to this department a despatch, No. 93, which was accompanied by two large folio volumes. The contents were in manuscript. These consisted of addresses and other communications from the government of Switzerland, the governments of its several cantons, the municipalities and corporations and the citizens of Switzerland, to the government and people of the United States. All of these had been elicited by some one or more of the great events which occurred in this country on or about the middle of April last, namely, the surrender of the insurrectionary armies, the realization of the abolition of slavery, the close of our civil war, the assassination of the late President, Abraham Lincoln, with combined conspiracies and assaults against the Vice-President and other persons connected with the government, the inauguration of the present Chief Magistrate, and the auspicious beginning of his administration.

These papers were from time to time delivered to and acknowledged by Mr. Fogg, and on their being received at this department they were immediately laid before the President of the United States, by whom they were read with feelings of profound and affectionate gratitude to the government and people of Switzerland. He remarked with especial satisfaction the unanimity of that people, the benevolent and fraternal character of their sympathies with the government and people of the United States, and the hopefulness of their sentiments concerning the prosperity and advancement of the free institutions of self-government. He was deeply affected also by the generosity of their tributes which the precious volumes contained to the memory of his predecessor, who had given up his life a sacrifice for the principles of this government, now so intimately connected with the great cause of humanity throughout the world.

It was the President's direction that the papers should be deposited as a perpetual memorial in the archives of the government, and that the sentiments they contained should be communicated in due season to the Congress of the United States. It was further his direction that an acknowledgment of the precious tributes should be promptly made. It devolves upon this department to execute this last direction. Casualties which occurred early in the year arrested the efficiency of the department, and caused the delay which I have now to excuse. You will read this despatch to the minister of foreign affairs of the republic of Switzerland, and give him a copy of it, if he will consent to receive the same and you will at the same time inform the minister that it will be deemed a favor if you shall be permitted to promulgate the despatch, and thus to make known, in the most effectual way possible the grateful sentiments which have been awakened in the government and people of the United States towards the government and people of Switzerland, by the manifestations they have thus given us of their sympathies and friendship.

I subjoin a list of the addresses and other papers received from Mr. Fogg, and venture to ask that it may be published together with this despatch, with a desire that the various parties therein named will be pleased to regard that publication as an acknowledgment made to themselves. It is confessed that in adopting this summary form of acknowledgment, I am unable to give full and discriminate expression of the sentiment of the United States; but proceedings on the part of the government of Switzerland vary so much, and so generously, from customary forms of national intercourse, that I have not been able to bring my response to them within any measure of acknowledgments heretofore adopted in international correspondence.

I am, sir, your obedient servant,

WILLIAM H. SEWARD.

GEORGE HARRINGTON, Esq., *&c.*, *&c.*, *Berne.*

Mr. Seward to Mr. Harrington.

No. 3.] DEPARTMENT OF STATE,
Washington, November 17, 1865.

SIR: Mr. Fogg's despatch bearing date October 16, and numbered 102, has been received. It gives an account of the ceremonies which occurred on taking his leave, and your presentation of your credentials to the President of Switzerland. The narrative is very interesting. Mr. Fogg's speech was proper in all respects, and your own was in accordance with instructions. The President's replies to Mr. Fogg and yourself have given especial satisfaction to the President of the United States.

Congratulating you upon so auspicious a beginning of you mission, I have the honor to be, sir, your obedient servant,

WILLIAM H. SEWARD.

GEORGE HARRINGTON, Esq., *&c.*, *&c.*, *Berne.*

JAPAN.

Mr. Pruyn to Mr. Seward.

No. 69.] LEGATION OF THE UNITED STATES IN JAPAN,
Kanagawa, December 6, 1864.

SIR: As you have been already advised by telegram of the 29th ultimo, via San Francisco, Major George Walter Baldwin and Lieutenant Robert N. Bird, officers of the 2d battalion, 20th regiment of British army, stationed at this place, were murdered on the 21st ultimo, by two yakunins, while in citizen's dress, near Kamakura, within the treaty limits. The murder was witnessed by several unarmed Japanese, who were laboring at a short distance from the place, and the assassins immediately fled.

Intelligence of this sad event was communicated to the foreign representation about midnight of that day, and it was stated one of the officers was still alive; but when the British officials and escort arrived at the place, about 3 a. m. the next day, both officers were found dead and the bodies placed on mats in the public highway, with a rough shed over them and fearfully cut to pieces, as has been invariably the case in all such assassinations.

I united with my colleague of France in commissioning the Abbé Mermet de Cachon, attached to his legation, to proceed to Yedo and represent to the Gorogio that the murder had caused great excitement in the regiment, as the officers were much beloved, and that it might be impossible to guard against retaliatory measures. We thought this suggestion might increase the desire and efforts for the arrest of the murderers. The Abbé Mermet on his return reported that the Gorogio very earnestly, and apparently with entire sincerity, promised that no effort should be omitted to bring the offenders to punishment.

I enclose Nos. 1 and 2, copy of my letter to the Gorogio, and translation of their reply.

I have not failed to give the British minister my hearty co-operation, having at his request been present at all the interviews he has had with the Japanese Vice-Minister Sakai Hida No Kami and the governors of foreign affairs associated with him. I have also at his request carefully examined the evidence taken by the British consul, with a view to such suggestions for further inquiry as I might deem necessary, and to such representations as the testimony already taken might render proper to be addressed to the Japanese government.

We have been forced to the painful conclusion that one of the officers, Lieutenant Bird, must have been put to death as late as 9 or 10 o'clock in the evening, the attack having been made on them between 4 and 5 o'clock in the afternoon; and if so, then by other than the two murderers, as they immediately left the place. One Japanese witness testifies that the younger officer, Lieutenant Bird, asked that a messenger should be sent to Yokohama to give intelligence of their condition; another that this officer asked for water and drunk it; two others that after the murderers escaped they saw one of the officers (identified, from his position when seen, as Lieutenant Bird) sitting up and then fall back. In short, eleven witnesses in some form or other testify to his having been alive after the escape of the murderers. And yet the post-mortem examination disclosed the fact, that the spinal chord had been completely severed, the wound being of a character which rendered it impossible for him to live after its infliction. Nor is it open to the explanation that the spinal column only was cut through, as found on the examination, and that the chord might have been ruptured by moving the body after death, as the surgeons who made the examination testify that the chord was severed by a clean cut; and further, it is not possible he could have sat up, even if it were not severed, with so fearful a cut through the bone alone.

This evidence made a profound impression on the vice-minister. The fearful suspicion excited, together with the tardiness of the governor of this place in making known to the foreign representatives the intelligence he had received, (a delay of nearly three hours being admitted, which he says, in excuse, were occupied in giving instructions to his officers, and with a report to Yedo,) induced me to concur with the British minister in his opinion that the governor should be dismissed from office. The vice-minister asked that no formal demand should be made, as that might embarrass the action of the Gorogio. The governor has been dismissed.

I hope that our improved relations and the increased power of the Tycoon's government will impart to it the desire and ability to bring the offenders to justice.

I have the honor to be, sir, very respectfully, your most obedient servant,

ROBERT H. PRUYN,
Minister Resident in Japan.

Hon. WM. H. SEWARD,
Secretary of State, Washington.

No. 1.

LEGATION OF THE UNITED STATES IN JAPAN,
Kanagawa, November 22, 1864.

The atrocious murder of two British officers has created so much feeling in this community, extending to officers and men of both the British land forces and fleet now at this place, as to induce his excellency the minister of France and myself to commission the Abbé Mermet to explain to your excellencies the critical situation of affairs, and the measures which, in our judgment, your excellencies should immediately adopt for the preservation of good faith, and in the interests of peace.

With respect and esteem,

ROBERT H. PRUYN,
Minister Resident of the United States in Japan.

Their Excellencies the MINISTERS OF FOREIGN AFFAIRS, *&c., Yedo.*

No. 2.

We have the honor to inform you that the intelligence of the murder of two Britsh officers in the vicinity of the town of Pruatsbee, in Soshu, (Sagami,) has filled us with pain and horror. Since the opening of the ports many deplorable events occurred, and we always did all in our power to arrest the culprits, but without success.

This makes us despair, and grieves us exceedingly. We must say, however, that although the troubled state of part of our country favors the rising of such banditti, we have better means than formerly of discovering them. We are aware that, should we fail to apprehend the murderers, our friendly relations might be jeoparded. This is a matter of the greatest importance. We have, therefore, sent the vice-minister of foreign affairs to your place to make an investigation, and direct the measures to be taken to insure a successful result.

We had a conference to-day with Mr. Cachou, who fully explained to us the impressions and observations of the ministers in regard to this murder, and feel convinced of the accuracy and great weight of his communication, which will stimulate our exertions to arrest the culprits. We have made it a point of absolute duty to come to a satisfactory conclusion before the departure of Sir Rutherford Alcock, the minister of Great Britain, which we state to your excellency with respect and esteem.

The 24th day of the 10th month of the first year of Gengi, (November 23d, 1864.)

MIDLUNO IDLUMI NO KAMI.
ABE BUNGO NO KAMI.
SUWA INABA NO KAMI.

His Excellency ROBERT H. PRUYN,
Minister Resident of the United States of America, &c.

Mr. Seward to Mr. Pruyn.

[Extract.]

No. 86.] DEPARTMENT OF STATE,
Washington, December 14, 1864.

SIR: Your despatch of October 12, No. 62, has been received, together with its voluminous appendix.

The questions you have been obliged to consider, and the measures which you have found it necessary to adopt in maintaining the treaty-guaranteed rights of the United States in Japan, were very grave and important. The difficulties of the case were greatly enhanced by the manifest need there was for intimate, cordial and hearty co-operation between yourself and the representatives of the other western powers. Having carefully examined the proceedings, I am authorized by the President to assure you they are fully approved. * * *

I am, sir, your obedient servant,

WILLIAM H. SEWARD.

ROBERT H. PRUYN, Esq., *&c., &c., Kanagawa.*

Mr. Pruyn to Mr. Seward.

[Extract.]

No. 71.] LEGATION OF THE UNITED STATES IN JAPAN,
Kanagawa, December 29, 1864.

SIR: I have the satisfaction to inform you that Shimidzu Seigi, one of the murderers of Major Baldwin and Lieutenant Bird, has been arrested and beheaded, and that the same fate has befallen two of his comrades, who, though not present at the time of the murder, formed a part of the band associated for the destruction of foreigners.

The two latter were first arrested, having, in company with Seigi, made a forced levy on some Japanese farmers, claiming they should contribute to their support, as they, the Lronius, were combined for the purpose of exterminating foreigners. The farmers succeeded in effecting the arrest of all but the principal offender, though several were severely wounded, and two of their number have not survived their wounds.

The Lronius were brought to this place and publicly beheaded.

Some time after their execution Seigi, having been traced by means of the money taken from the farmers, among which were some old coins, was likewise apprehended. He was, after his trial at Yedo, brought to this place, confronted with the witnesses who saw the murder at Kamakura, and in the presence of the British vice-consul fully identified as one of the murderers. He was then paraded through the Japanese and foreign quarters of the town, preceded by a placard stating his crime and sentence, and the next day was beheaded in the presence of numerous spectators, including the battalion of the 20th regiment, the battalion of royal marines, the artillery, and a great number of naval and military officers. Thus for the first time has punishment been inflicted on Japanese for the murder of foreigners. The offenders were two-sworded men and said to be well educated. I saw the murderer Seigi as he was paraded through the streets. He appeared to be a resolute, desperate man, totally unaffected by his situation unless, indeed, glorying in it. He improvised a song as he was aken through the streets, and sang even up to the moment of his death.

The government have caused notices to be affixed at the places where public notices are put up at Kamakura, and at this place, of the sentence and punishment of Seigi; and his head was placed for five days near the bridge over the largest stream between this place and the Tokaido.

This energetic action of the government will probably afford greater protection to foreigners than has heretofore been extended, but it can scarcely be expected to put a stop to assassinations. Some desperate characters hearing of Seigi's bold demeanor and of his dying declaration that foreigners would be the ruin of Japan, may not be deterred from the commission of similar crimes, but rather inclined to covet his posthumous fame.

As stated above, the government have caused a proclamation to be placed at prominent points within the treaty limits, to insure more effectually the safety of foreigners.

This has been, perhaps, in consequence of a suggestion I made to the vice-minister, Sakai Hida no Kami, of the character referred to in my unofficial letter giving you an account of the murder, that the officers and inhabitants who should fail to warn foreigners of an apprehended attack, or to capture those engaged in it, should be punished. * * * * * *

I have the honor to be, sir, very respectfully, your most obedient servant,

ROBERT H. PRUYN,
Minister Resident in Japan.

Hon. WILLIAM H. SEWARD, *Secretary of State.*

Mr. Pruyn to Mr. Seward.

No. 72.] LEGATION OF THE UNITED STATES IN JAPAN,
Kanagawa, December 30, 1864.

SIR: While there can be no doubt that the Tycoon is far more powerful than the Mikado, and has at his command the wealth and military force of the empire, the influence of the latter has, of late years, been frequently and potentially exerted in controlling public affairs, and determining the policy of the empire.

Theoretically, the Mikado is the Emperor, and the Tycoon, though not nominally even next in rank, is clothed with the executive power of the empire. The Mikado confers all titles of nobility, and any edict issued by him must be obeyed. These orders may, however, be easily evaded and he kept in ignorance of such disobedience, in consequence of his seclusion, or, if openly disregarded, the Emperor is forced to submit, because destitute of means to enforce obedience.

As I have explained, this shadow of power may become real and formidable by the aid of Daimios, who, though nominally subject to the Tycoon, as well as the Mikado, may be emboldened to defy the Tycoon's power, especially if shielded by the orders of the Mikado, to whom fealty is first due.

I have felt, as I have on several occasions informed you, that it was of vital importance to obtain the sanction of the Mikado to the treaties. There can be no question that his public proclamation to that effect would contribute greatly to the peace of the empire, and to the improvement of its relations with foreign powers, by putting it out of the power of the hostile Daimios to justify their hostility, by the real or pretended opposition of the Mikado to the treaties.

I have, therefore, frequently urged upon the Tycoon's government that the Mikado's assent to the treaties should be obtained, in justice to the treaty powers, and as a measure of security and stability to his own government. In the numerous interviews before and consequent on the operations at Simonoseki, my colleagues and myself united in pressing this closely and energetically on the government of the Tycoon.

We have been assured that the Mikado and Tycoon were at length in accord on this subject, and that, as soon as the Tycoon had completed his preparations for the security of the Mikado, the latter would make public proclamation thereof; but that it would not be safe for him to do so at present, as he was surrounded by and under the control of powerful numbers of the Sako or hostile party.

The Gorogio finally agreed that the minister, one of their number who had represented them at Kioto, should address a letter to the ministers of treaty powers, stating that the Mikado had avowed his friendship toward foreigners, and that he would embrace the earliest safe opportunity to declare the same publicly. Letter No. 1 was thereupon sent to each of the ministers, but was returned, because not sufficiently explicit. It was again transmitted to us with a confidential enclosure, of which I now send translation. (Enclosure No. 2.)

This is an important paper, provided we are assured of the sincerity of the Tycoon's government, as conclusive upon the point that the Mikado, as well as the Tycoon, has abandoned all hope of closing the ports and all opposition to the treaties.

A large force has been sent from Yedo, well armed and disciplined, uniformed for the first time like foreign troops, to swell the numbers gathered and assembled at Osacca for the purpose of enforcing the sentence against Choshu. I have asked that information be given of the progress of events, but cannot, as yet, say whether this can be expected.

I also enclose No. 3, translation of a very able and interesting letter sent to the British minister before the expedition to Simonoseki, which you will see contains statements corresponding with items of information already transmitted, and which I am inclined to regard as a more satisfactory history of the intrigues caused by the treaties than we have hitherto been fortunate enough to obtain.

So many of the facts stated are known to be true as to justify the belief that the history of the secret conferences at Kioto may be regarded as reliable.

I have the honor to be, sir, very respectfully, your most obedient servant,

ROBERT H. PRUYN,
Minister Resident in Japan.

Hon. WILLIAM H. SEWARD,
Secretary of State.

No. 1.

[Translation.]

I have the honor to state in writing that, upon my arrival at Kioto, I fully represented the circumstances of the relations with the treaty powers, as previously stated to you at the interview with my colleagues—the meaning of all of which was understood—wherefore everything, as hitherto, will be strictly observed; but now an important opportunity is presented to tranquillize the public feeling—the order for despatching troops for the punishment of Choshu having been issued, it is, therefore, desirable that you will note this first.

With respect and esteem.

The 23d day of the 10th month of the first year of Gengi, (Né.) (November 22, 1864.)

ABE BUNGO NO KAMI.

His Excellency ROBERT H. PRUYN,
Minister Resident of the United States of America, &c.

No. 2.

[Translation.]

The present state of the relations of our government with the foreign powers has been well understood and acquiesced in at Kioto, as I stated in the accompanying letter of this date, the 23d: hence the sending of envoys to the foreign countries has been abandoned, and the closing of ports shall not be mentioned; but there still remains hostile persons, and the Choshu matter has not been disposed of, wherefore I cannot communicate this to you in an official letter; those hostile persons, and also Choshu, will soon be punished, however, and when his Majesty the Mikado shall have been informed accordingly, this will be settled definitely, and a communication again be made. As the secret meaning could not be made perfectly clear to you from the accompanying letter alone, I now state that meaning privately and in a friendly manner, and it is requested that you will keep this secret and not let it be known.

ABE BUNGO NO KAMI.

No. 3.

[Translation.]

A Japanese giving an account of the state of affairs at present existing in his country, with a glance at the unsettled and agitated feelings of its inhabitants, and wishing to learn by what means it may be possible to change or calm down these oppositions for some time prevailing.

A peculiar state of affairs exists in this country. The person who is [illegible] our Emperor we call Tenshi, Son of Heaven; he lives in Kioto, and for a long time (the length of [illegible] a cotton-thread) has reigned over us. The higher officers surrounding him, as his immediate ministers, we call Kangé. In olden times the Mikado governed by himself with the assistance of these officers. But now even centuries have elapsed since the government fell into the hands of a man of a military character, (Booké,) the Sai Shogung, (Tycoon.) By a state of confusion introduced into the government, by making small things large, and reducing large ones by bringing about violent and astonishing changes, the government assumed a new form and lapsed into the hands of the Tokugawa dynasty, whose reign has continued to the present day.

For more than three hundred years the government was carried on by the direct line of the house of Tokugawa, and during that period the country enjoyed profound peace.

The Mikado left everything in the hands of the Tycoon, and the power of the military, Booké, came far to exceed that of the officer of the Mikado.

At this period Japan was closed, and of all nations, the Dutch and Chinese alone were privileged to have trading relations with us. But Commodore Perry appeared, and at Uraga and Yedo insisted upon making a treaty of commerce and friendship. The Tycoon called a meeting of Daimios, and put before them the demands of Perry, and asked their opinion whether the ports should be opened for foreign intercourse, or whether they were prepared to engage in a war and commence hostilities.

For a long time the question was discussed, but no person of sufficient might and forethought was there to give good advice. Among those most opposed to the Daimios was the prince of Mito, but as they were not prepared for war, it was judged better to defer hostilities.

A member of the Gorogio, a very clever and far-seeng statesman, Abe Ise no Kami, knowing well all the merits and demerits of the question at issue, concluded a treaty, when Perry appeared a second time, without any further reference to the other Daimios and the national feelings, and consequently many nations came to Japan. But the people who were on the side of the prince of Mito, and desirous of making war with foreign countries, rather than submit to such a new order of things, have made of late years great disturbances, (like wasps disturbed in their nests,) retainers of Daimios, throwing up their masters and becoming Lronius, were going through the country assembling people of their own ideas, went to Kioto, and represented to the Mikado that foreigners should be driven out of the country. These ignorant people further represented to the Mikado that there is no better country in the world than Japan, producing everything good for man, and have, therefore, no wants from without to be supplied, and that now, for the first time, we have had intercourse with foreign countries—trade ruins the interest of Japan. All the articles of daily use have been scarce, and great is the suffering of the country people in consequence; this has been undoubtedly the fault of the government of Tokugawa.

The Tycoon has ignored the Mikado, and his authority does not obey his orders, but looks only to his own advantage.

From what these officers report to the Mikado he believes them, and had little idea of the strength of other countries; the retainers of Choshu also trusted in the Lronius, and came to the conclusion that foreigners ought not to be allowed to remain any longer in Japan.

Three traitorous officers of the Mikado, Sango, Anega Kojo, and Nakayama caused much difficulty by raising alarming reports and making false and unfounded representations to the Mikado. The power of the court of Kioto, however, waxed great and began to rise like the morning sun, in its strength, while that of Yedo was gradually declining like a setting one.

Thereupon, Satsuma, and other powerful Daimios, seeing the drift of things, assembled at Kioto, and took counsel together, with a view of discussing the errors of the government, and of applying some remedy to its weakness. Among these Daimios, some were foremost in proposing to put off the closing of Japan until the country should become sufficiently rich and powerful to accomplish it effectually, and without dishonor. But Choshu, backed in his designs by Anega and Sango, succeeded in influencing the Mikado, and making it falsely known that the Mikado had declared himself for the closing of Japan, to which he had only given a partial and undecided consent.

Accordingly, on the 10th of the fifth month, the order for the breaking off of all relations with the foreigners was on its way to Yedo. Although the Daimios did not approve of these proceedings, they were still obliged to yield to the order of closing, supposed to have emanated from the court of the Mikado. They regretted the fact, and left Kioto.

In the mean time, fruitless negotiations were going on in Yokohama with the foreigners.

But now, Choshu, exasperated at the issue of his favorite plans, fired upon the men-of-war and merchant vessels of France, Holland, and America, contrary to all existing laws or rules. Meanwhile, in Kioto, the ill-designing Sango, and Anega Kojo were in constant league with Lronius, and deceiving the Mikado; but at length the Koogay Anega Kojo fell by the hands of those in favor of the foreigners—he was murdered by a Daimio's retainer, in secret. But still the affairs were not settled, notwithstanding many consultations and discussions, which, although worth recording, I shall not now repeat.

Envoys were sent by the Tycoon to Choshu to examine into his conduct; they were murdered, and fell victims to the revenge of Choshu.

Satsuma's eyes were opened since the fight at Kagolima, and affairs appeared to him in a new light; he changed in favor of foreigners, and thought now of making his country powerful and completing his armaments. Many Daimios began to take serious thought at the battle of Kagolima and its results, and began to calculate the disadvantages of being hostile to foreigners.

Choshu's power was sinking fast, and the fire of his doings was burning itself out. One of the ministers of Choshu, called Masida Dango, a very cunning and designing man, sent for his retainers in all directions, assembled all the Lronius, and went to Kioto, and proposed to the Mikado and his officers that they should go to the god of Dai Sui Koo, in the province of Isi, in order to pray for the expulsion of the foreigners, his covert design being to carry him captive to Yedo, close Yokohama, and upset the dynasty of Tokugawa, and assume the Tycoonship himself. This was discovered in Kioto, and Choshu was expelled from the capital by the Daimios Aisoo, Satsuma, Yekamonno, Kami, Himesi, and Esteizen.

The Koogays concerned in the plot of Choshu, afraid that punishment might overtake them, threw up their appointments, left Kioto, and took refuge in the territories of Choshu The remainder of the Lronius went to the province of Yamato and raised a rebellion there, used violence, and murdered many unoffending country people.

The Mikado called a meeting of Daimios at Kioto, and they went there again last year, in the eleventh month. At this meeting much had been discussed about the foreigners trading in Japan, but without any definite resolution being come to.

After this Choshu fired upon a steamer at Satsuma at anchor at Tauonra, and burned also some cotton junks at Kamimoseka. This caused the Mikado to give an order to the Tycoon to punish Choshu. The Tycoon promised this, and called in secret upon Satsuma, Heigo and Kohula, Geshu, Unshu, and Inshu to carry the order into effect. Before punishment could be inflicted, Choshu got news of the intended expedition against him and gathered together many Lronires to defend him, and made them spread reports in his favor.

The following is a record of his misdemeanors and crimes:

First offence.—Choshu, Mito, Isihasi, Bisen, Inaba, and the Lronius informed the other Daimios that Satsuma, Higo, and Etiszen were friendly with foreigners and desire commerce and opening of the country, and that therefore their advice should not be accepted; they also informed the Koogays to the same purport.

Second offence.—Choshu, Mito, Isihasi, Bisen, Insha, and the Lronius told the merchants of Ohosaka that the reasons why all the articles of daily use had become so dear was that Satsuma, Higo, and Etiszen had sent them all to Nagasaki, and sold them there to foreigners, which caused great misery to the inhabitants of Japan. The merchants of Ohosaka believed these statements to be true and took great dislike to Satsuma, Higo and Etiszen.

Third offence.—Choshu burned a cotton junk belonging to Satsuma at Kaminoseki and murdered the officer on board the same, exposed his head at Ohosaka with the statement that Satsuma was desirous of foreign trade and was making large gain by sending the necessities of daily use to foreign countries, and that this man whose head was exposed was punished in obedience to the mandate of Heaven. Also some hundreds of people were murdered by Choshu in secret for trading with foreigners.

Fourth offence.—Last year, on the 8th month, Choshu, by intriguing through the Koogay Sango, tried to excuse himself to the Mikado by addressing him in writing. At present Sango is in Choshu and entertained under his protection.

Fifth offence.—Choshu tried to embitter the Tycoon against Satsuma by spreading reports that Satsuma tried to usurp the Tycoonship himself.

There are many other crimes and offences committed by Choshu which are too numerous to be recounted here.

For a third time the Daimois assembled in Kiota, but they were not clever and farseeing, so that they were nearly all for the closing of the ports. The only Daimios who were in favor of the opening were Satsuma, and Etiszen, and a few others of smaller importance. Therefore Satsuma and Etiszen were not admitted in the council of the Daimios, and the Tycoon, Isihatsi, Kawakai, Itakoosa and other Daimios were misled by Choshu and formed the resolution to close Yokohama and only allow trade to go on in Nagasaki and Hakodati.

This successful stroke raised Choshu again into further importance; so that the presence of Satsuma, Heigo, Geshu (Aki,) who were in favor of the opening, were no longer required in Kiota, which made them much regret the consequences of such ill-advised resolutions, and they returned to their respective provinces grieved and their influence much impaired. The remaining Daimios fixed upon the utumn of this year as the time for the closing of Yokohama.

Stotsbasi was appointed defender and commander-in-chief of the Ohosaka castle and defences of the seacoast. He is about to erect more than twenty batteries and arm them with some 3,000 cannon to be made with all speed in order to protect the county.

POSTSCRIPT.—I have heard that two Dutch men-of-war have arrived here with instructions from their king to obtain satisfaction for the insult offered to their flag and the injury committed last year at Simonoseki, and that the English ships are to accompany them to coöperate with them. I sincerely hope that this report may turn out to be true in the interest of my own county. Although I am a very ignorant person, it appears to me that from the Mikado down to the Lronius there is a considerable darkness and ignorance prevailing as to the progress of events and civilization of foreign countries, and that therefore they look down upon foreigners as brutal savages, believing themselves in their conceit to be wonderfully powerful, and to this ignorance can be traced the immoderate desire that exists for the closing of the country. Choshu looks upon his conduct as a great deed, as having been the cause of the closing of the ports. This shall cause also a general war with the whole of Japan, which shall not only cost the lives of many thousands and impoverish the empire, but also be bought by Great Britain with many lives, which is contrary to the rules of the gods. If now Great Britain would have mercy upon our uncivilized people and teach them the power of your government, and, together with Holland, destroy Choshu, in so doing showing the forces and power of war to the whole empire, this would open the eyes of the whole of Japan, and acknowledging their mistake, they would in future observe the treaties.

In case this could not be done speedily, it would be good then to go to Ohosaka to show the British forces to the Mikado and make a new treaty with him. This would have the desired effect without any loss of lives.

That I, a Japanese by birth, should request you to send ships to Chosu, must be viewed by you with astonisment and like a traitor to my country, but it is because our country-people being ignorant of the power of Great Britain are only desirous of closing Japan, in which case civilization would never spread over our country.

For many years I have contemplated and regretted the above state of things, but there is little help for it, and therefore I again beg, that in order to save and enlighten our country-people, you will kill the prince of Choshu, and then my wishes will be fulfilled.

Although I intended to enter further upon the particulars respecting the present state of affairs in Japan, it would not be ready for the departure of the Dutch ship-of-war, and therefore you will kindly take all that I have said in a favorable light.

[No signature and no date.]

Mr. Pruyn to Mr. Seward.

No. 7.] LEGATION OF THE UNITED STATES IN JAPAN,
Kanagawa, January 21, 1865.

SIR: Under the provisions of the various treaties with Japan, citizens and subjects of the several powers have been assigned land, subject to an annual rent payable to the government, without the payment of any sum by way of purchase money. When land was of merely a nominal value, this was productive of no mischief, but this settlement has increased with such rapidity, and the improvements are now of so substantial a character, as to have caused a great rise in property. The poorest lots in the settlement have been sold at from $4,000 to $5,000 each, and lots in more favorable situations have increased more than tenfold in value since I have been in Japan, so that the present annual rental may be regarded as fully equal to the price asked for lots on my arrival. It is obvious that a strong temptation is thus offered to adventurers in China and elsewhere to come to Japan, demand a lot, realize a handsome profit, and then leave the country for new-comers to repeat the operation. Another difficulty has arisen from claims being preferred that an assignment of lands should be made to the powers with whom treaties have more recently been made for their subjects, in the same proportion as already granted to those first on the ground.

My colleagues and myself have desired to remedy as far as possible those evils and to guard against speculation in lands (as heretofore) to be acquired from the government. With that view we have entered into an agreement, of which I enclose (No. 1) a copy, to which we have asked the assent of the government, and which they have promised to give as soon as they shall hear from the governors of the other ports. We also succeeded in making an agreement with the Japanese government, of which I send copy, No. 2, for the enlargement and improvement of this settlement and for the sale of the leases of the land to be assigned to foreigners at public auction at a minimum price to be fixed by the consuls, which I need not describe in detail, as it will sufficiently explain itself. Our object in providing for public rides, &c., was to encourage excursions in directions and to an extent where foreigners would not be exposed to collisions with Japanese, but would have exercise and pleasant rides on safer and better roads. I also enclose (No. 3) approval of agreement.

The block of land set apart for the consulate forms parts of the site where Commodore Perry's treaty was concluded.

I have the honor to be, very respectfully, your most obedient servant,

ROBERT H. PRUYN.

Hon. WILLIAM H. SEWARD,
Secretary of State.

No. 1.

Memorandum in reference to future allotments of land at the open ports.

It being desirable in the common interest to agree and determine upon some plan for the appropriation of all such land as may be required to enlarge the limits of existing foreign settlement at Yokohama, as also at the other open ports, in such manner as shall be equitable and fair to all, without favor or distinction to nationalities, and in order to put such plan in a clear and practical shape, the following bases have been accepted and approved by the

1. All land hereafter to be acquired by the filling up of the swamp at Yokohama, or recovered from the sea at Nagasaki and Hakodadi, to be allotted by the consuls in concert, and in such portions as the requirements of trade may, from time to time, suggest, at an upset price, to be regulated by the market value of land—this price to be set upon each lot by the said consuls, in common accord. If they do not agree, then the upset price to be determined by the vote of the majority.

2. These lots to be first offered to all those subjects of treaty powers who shall be, at the time, unprovided, and who, for legitimate purposes of trade and not for traffic in land, or as mere investments, shall have registered their names at their respective consulates, and each lot to be assigned in the order of date of registry, irrespective of nationality.

3. Any of these lots, if not accepted at the sale fixed, to be then put up to auction, with

a public notice of at least fifteen days, and particulars as to situation, dimensions, and upset price. If this price should not be offered, the lots to be withdrawn from the sale and reserved for subsequent sale or appropriation.

4. The title-deeds to be issued on the requisition of the consuls of treaty powers, by the governor of the port, and countersigned by the consul of the nation to which the lease-holder belongs.

5. The proceeds of any such sales shall constitute a municipal fund, under such conditions as the consuls may conjointly agree upon.

These rules to apply to any new extension of land that may be obtained in any other direction, except that, when the Japanese government will not be indemnified for the expense of improvements by rent on land before valueless, one half the proceeds derived from the sale thereof shall be paid to said government, and the remaining half retained for said municipal fund, and when the Japanese shall be dispossessed of any land, a reasonable compensation will be paid to cover the expense of the removal of their buildings to some other locality; and no allotment of land to any foreigner for private use or advantage shall be required or sanctioned by the consuls, and a communication to be made to the Gorogio to this effect.

For public purposes the undersigned have already in their memorandum of the 22d of July, 1864, formally disclaimed and renounced any title to exclusive advantage whatever in respect to concessions of land or territory, either in the open ports or elsewhere in Japan, as whatever is granted to one may, with equal right and justice, be claimed by all in virtue of the most favored nation clause in all existing treaties. It is to be hoped that the Tycoon's government, fully advised of this, will, in their own interest, avoid making exceptional grants of land to any one nation, minister or consul, or other authority, or without reference to the rest, and to the equal rights of all.

Finally, all past experience in China and Japan having shown that any appropriation of land or concessions to distinct nationalities is a fertile source of trouble and a grave disadvantage in the end to all, raising questions of diverse jurisdiction for municipal purposes, distinct bodies of police, and tending to produce conflicts of jurisdiction, increased expense, and imperfect results in order and security, besides perpetuating a mischievous error, that the interests of different nations in Japan are distinct and may be promoted at each others expense, whereas in truth they are identical, and are best promoted by union and common action, the undersigned have determined to make an official representation by a *note identique* to the government of the Tycoon, suggesting that upon no other bases should land be allocated for the occupation of foreigners at any open port in Japan, and pledging themselves to uphold this arrangement as the only one consistent with equity and the best interests of all the treaty powers without distinction.

YOKOHAMA, *December* 3, 1864.

ROBERT H. PRUYN,
Minister Resident of the United States in Japan.
RUTHERFORD ALCOCK,
H. B. M.'s Envoy Extraordinary and Minister Plenipotentiary in Japan.
LEON ROCHES,
Minister Plenipotentiary to his Majesty the Emperor of France in Japan.
D. DE GRAEFF VAN POLSBROEK,
H. N. M.'s Consul General and Political Agent in Japan.

No. 2.

Memorandum.

Certain proposals for the enlargement of the settlement at Yokohama, and other public objects connected therewith, having been discussed and generally agreed upon by the undersigned foreign representatives on the one part, and Shibata Hiung No Kami and Shirashi Shimosa No Kami on the other, on the 8th of September, 24th of October, and 8th of the present month, as recorded in minutes of each, signed by the aforesaid representatives, it has now been resolved to put on record, in a clear and practical shape, the bases and conditions of such improvements, extension, and public works, as now finally agreed upon, to which the signatures of the said foreign representatives and Japanese commissioners shall be appended for the ratification of the government of the Tycoon, at Yedo, within five days from the date of these presents.

It has accordingly been agreed and resolved as follows:

1. An allotment of ground, already marked out on the other side of the canal, giving a circuit of one English mile (eighteen Japanese chô) to be made and designed in perpetuity for a parade and exercise ground for all nations; also, for a race-course for the foreign community. The ground being now a marsh, to be filled up by the Japanese government at their own expense, and as it is for common occupation both by Japanese and foreigners as a place

of exercise, no rental to be claimed for the same, with exception of the outside circle destined for a race-course, for which rent shall be paid at a rate hereafter to be fixed.

2. A site and temporary huts having been provided for naval, military, and civil small-pox patients of all nations, it is understood that an addition of either one or two huts being essential to complete the accommodation, these shall be put up by the Japanese government in the first instance, at the requisition of the foreign consuls to avoid delay, on the latter undertaking to repay the cost of erection.

3. A further extension within the limits already defined, of the ground for a cemetery for all nations, to be granted contiguous with that already so appropriated on the joint application of the consul.

4. A site having been allotted by the sea-shore for the building of abattoirs, &c., necessary to relieve the settlement of a great nuisance, unsightly alike to Japanese and foreigners, and prejudicial to health, it has now been agreed that the necessary buildings, according to plans already furnished, shall be erected without delay by the Japanese government, to be let under the control of the foreign consuls only to such butchers as they shall duly license; the said butchers to rent the premises when completed, paying a yearly rental of ten per cent. upon the cost of erection. But it is distinctly understood that the total cost shall not exceed about $10,000, a little more or less, the exact amount to be settled with the consuls.

5. The whole of the swamp on this side of the canal to be filled up by the Japanese government, and at their expense. When this is effected the Kôsakimachi, now situated in the midst, to be removed to the end furthest from the foreign settlement. In the event of fire and the burning down of this establishment before the completion of this work, it is agreed that it shall not be built on the present site. Of this swamp ground, when filled up, the Japanese government shall reserve for foreign occupation, to be actually allotted to them from time to time, in such portions as may be required on the joint requisition of the consuls, the space lying between the Otamachi and the canal called Okagawa, on a line with the street between the custom-house and the consular lot, as marked in red in the plan annexed, No. 1; the proceeds arising from such disposal to be added to a municipal fund, which shall be employed for the making a drainage of roads, &c., and keeping them in a state of repair. It is understood that rents shall be paid as for all other allotments within the foreign settlement.

6. The location and site now being cleared and actually assigned for consular residences and offices, marked No. 2 in the annexed plan, the same to be cleared completely of all buildings or tenements, and delivered over to the consuls for appropriation to such uses and divided as heretofore agreed upon by the consuls among themselves, without further intervention of the Japanese authorities, rental being paid by the respective tenants as in the other portions of the foreign settlement.

7. The whole of the ground extending from the custom-house hatoba along the sea-front to the lot recently assigned to the French, at Bentong, and backward to the main street, (section No. 3 in the plan annexed,) to be held available for foreign occupation and appropriated at public sale, open to competition for foreigners and Japanese, in such proportions or quantity as, from time to time, may be found expedient.

The Japanese government undertakes, when these appropriations are in progress, to extend the present bounds of the foreign settlement from the custom-house hatoba to the French lot of Bentong. Toward the expense of this work, already agreed upon in former conferences of the 8th September and 24th October, and recorded in the memoranda before mentioned, of one-half the proceeds of sales or prices paid for right of location in this new extension of settlement along the sea-side, (after paying expenses and indemnities for loss or removal of the Japanese tenants,) to be paid to the governor of Kanagawa so long as the whole expense shall not have been reimbursed according to verified estimates and contracts for the work done. It is understood that the rent shall be paid the same as for all other allotments.

8. As the ministers of the treaty powers are not at present enabled to resume their residence at Yedo, it may be necessary to make provision for the temporary *location* of one or more at Yokohama. With this object in view, the French and Dutch representatives having already locations assigned at Bentong, (as also the Prussian consul,) it is expressly agreed and provided that the remaining portion of the sea-front of Bentong, extending from the Prussian lot to the western corner and marked No. 4 in the plan annexed, shall be reserved for the ministers of the diplomatic representatives of Great Britain and the United States, and if not immediately required shall not be otherwise appropriated for any use except as at present occupied without reference to them, and their consent obtained, the size of this location to be settled afterwards between the Japanese government and the representatives of the above named two nations.

9. An adequate site for a club-house for the united services of all nations having been promised, either on the site of the buildings now occupied by the British commissariat, marked No. 5 in the plan annexed, or in its close vicinity, it is agreed that quick possession shall be secured, and the trustees of the club shall pay the estimated value of any buildings thereon or pay all the expenses of their removal by the owners, and be subject to rental in like manner as all other foreigners holding land.

10. A conveniently situated market being a great desideratum for Japanese for the sale of provisions, it is agreed that the open space now in use for that purpose, and marked No. 6 in

the annexed plan, shall be further enlarged and levelled, and at one extremity a series of stalls erected under a piazza or covered-way for the sale of provisions.

11. As under the present state of affairs the Japanese government desire foreigners to ride on the Tokaido as little as possible, they undertake to make a good riding road for the exercise of foreigners four or five miles in extent, winding round and through the Mississippi valley, not less than twenty feet wide, to be made and kept in good order by the Japanese government in accordance with the plans agreed upon and already being put in execution under the direction and superintendence of Major Wray, a chief engineer officer.

12. Finally, in order to avoid all further discussion about the keeping of roads, drainage, cleaning of streets, and other municipal objects for which hitherto the Japanese local authorities have been held responsible in view of the high rental paid by all foreign leaseholders, it has been agreed that these objects shall henceforth be secured by the foreign land renters themselves, and towards the expenses that must be incurred annually there shall be a deduction of 20 per cent. from the yearly rent paid by all lands leased to foreigners, to be paid in a municipal fund.

In witness whereof we, the undersigned foreign representatives and Japanese commissioners duly empowered to that effect, hereto set our hands and seals this 19th day of December, 1864.

Done in quintuplicate.

ROBERT H. PRUYN,
Minister Resident of the United States in Japan.
RUTHERFORD ALCOCK,
H. B. M.'s Envoy Extraordinary and Minister Plenipotentiary in Japan.
LEON ROCHES,
Minister Plenipotentiary of H. M. the Emperor of France in Japan.
D. DE GRAEFF VAN POLSBROEK,
H. N. M.'s Consul General and Political Agent in Japan.
SIBATA HINGA NO KAMI.
SIRAISI SIMOSA NO KAMI.

We have to state that Sibata Hinga No Kami and Siraisi Simosa No Kami having under our instructions agreed with you about land for foreign settlement, we approve the same and will exchange ratifications accordingly.

The 23d day of the 11th month of the 1st year of Gengi (21st December, 1864.)

With respect and esteem,

MIDLUNO IDLUMI NO KAMI.
ABE BUNGO NO KAMI.
SUNO INABA NO KAMI.

His Excellency ROBERT H. PRUYN,
Minister Resident of the United States of America, &c., &c., &c.

Mr. Pruyn to Mr. Seward.

[Extract.]

No. 8.] LEGATION OF THE UNITED STATES IN JAPAN,
Kanagawa, January 27, 1865.

SIR: * * * * * * It is possible that the Tycoon will decide before I leave whether he will prefer to tender a port or to pay the money for indemnity and expenses. My impression is that he will not be disposed to open another port, though it is possible Simonoseki, after being occupied as imperial territory, may be opened to trade. I have the statistics of the commerce of that port, which show a very large trade, and I shall meanwhile endeavor to obtain information as to the trade of other ports favorably located.

It may not be impossible for me to remark that I think, even should a port be tendered, that a portion of the indemnity agreed to be paid should be exacted.

The governors for foreign affairs have replied to a note which I directed Mr. Portman to write, asking information as to the projects of the expedition against Choshu, that some of them would come to this place at an early day to make a detailed statement on the subject.

orces of the Daimios of Kin Sin gathered to subdue Choshu a
t Kokwea, on the south side of the straits. The Niphon Daimi
ed near Kioto; the troops of the Tycoon, 16,000 of whom are a
les and uniformed and equipped in foreign style, are commanded by
of Matsmai, of the island of Yesso. The whole army is commanded
ince of Owari, of the imperial family. Choshu will not resist. It is di
hear what has transpired, or, rather, to form a correct judgment, in cons
of conflicting statements. I am inclined to believe, however, that Mo
n, Prince of Choshu, has abdicated, and assumed, as is usual in such cases,
rb and character of a priest. One of his ministers, descendant of a fol-
of Taico Sama, has taken the direction of affairs, and the heads of Cho
chief minister and of five of his chief retainers have been successively sent
vari, who shakes his head and keeps silence, thereby intimating that atone-
has not yet been made for the sacriligious attempt of Choshu to seize the
ed person of the Mikado. This is the cause assigned to the Japanese for
crusade against Choshu, not his hostility to foreigners.

he best opinion I can form of the probable result is, that Choshu will be
of a part of his territory, probably the province of Suoro, and that, as his
ission has been prompt, and his humiliation deep, the province of Nagato
be ultimately left to his son, now called Nagato, who, though at present, like
ther, in priestly garb, may be spared to represent the ancient house—older
he family of the Tycoon, and, before the rise of his dynasty, supreme in
provinces of the Mikado's empire.

s is said to be the policy of the powerful Prince of Satsuma, and may be
ed by the other Daimios. The magnitude of the preparations is too
warrant the belief that the expedition will be abandoned without large
of territory and treasure by the refractory prince. This induces me to
hat it is intended to pay the indemnity, and thus provide for it, and
me to recommend that in any event payment of a portion of it should

e honor to be, sir, very respectfully, your most obedient servant,

ROBERT H. PRUYN,

Minister Resident in Japan.

&c., &c.

Mr. Pruyn to Mr. Seward.

LEGATION OF THE UNITED STATES IN JAPAN
Kanagawa, February 13,

SIR: I have the honor to inform you that I have received a letter f[illegible] inisters for foreign affairs, in which they state that they had determi[illegible] o send the embassy to the treaty powers, as previously announced.

In my despatch, No. 57, of the 3d September last, I informed you t[illegible] embassy would not go further than Shanghai, the appointment having made only for the purpose of gaining time, by inducing the hostile party lieve that the Tycoon had not abandoned the hope of obtaining from the powers the concession of the closing of this port.

The letter of the ministers for foreign affairs is only of importance as a[illegible] evidence of the increased strength of the government.

I have the honor to be, sir, very respectfully, your most obedient servan[illegible]

ROBERT H. PRUYN,
Minister Resident in Ja[illegible]

Hon. WILLIAM H. SEWARD,
Secretary of State, Washington.

Mr. Pruyn to Mr. Seward.

No. 12.] LEGATION OF THE UNITED STATES IN JAPAN
Kanagawa, March 16,

SIR: I have the honor to enclose copies of the minute of a confe[illegible] cently held with the Gorogio by her Britannic Majesty's chargé d'aff[illegible] the political agent of the Netherlands, and also of a memorandu[illegible] by them on that occasion, and of their letter to me communicating t[illegible] closures 1, 2 and 3.)

Two subjects of common interest were [illegible] alleged attempt to create a governm[illegible] reference to what they said they felt [illegible] their government as to the final disposi[illegible] Tycoon in and by the convention recentl[illegible]

I was at Yedo on the day the British [illegible] was not aware of his design [illegible] jects, which Mr. Winches[illegible] [illegible] the consul [illegible] [illegible] ut on t[illegible] the letter and copies above referred to, the minister of France proposed that we should answer the same jointly, though we agreed in considering the memorandum objectionable in itself, and also in regretting that separate action had been taken. I preferred not to do so, fearing it might create some serious differences, and might connect me with personal difficulties the issue of which I could not foresee and would be powerless to control.

I have reason to know that my representations and mediation have tended greatly to moderate the reply of the French minister and to soften the asperity of feeling which at one time appeared to threaten an interruption of our harmonious action.

I also enclose, No. 4, copy of my letter to Messrs. Winchester and Polsbroek in reply, and No. 5, copy of note verbale of the French minister in reply to the same.

I thought it best not to enter into any extended discussion of the memorandum, but will ask my colleagues to join in a note to the Japanese government, which shall be more precise, and which will not justify the adoption of measures by the Japanese government which the representatives of Great Britain and Holland have inadvertently conceded it may legitimately adopt, such as either the direct increase of export and import duties, which is declared to be the right of all governments on the indirect increase of the former by the imposition of transit duties, the exercise of both of which rights must be regarded as restrained by existing treaties, and to that extent extinguished. The papers transmitted require no further notice. I hope the President will think I hav[illegible] acted with discretion, and that it was well not to make this separate action [illegible] subject of more serious complaint. My letter was framed with the desig[illegible] permit such explanation as might re-establish harmony, though I was se[illegible] it was, to say the least, indelicate to forestall the action of the four po[illegible] reference to a convention, which may even now be under consideration[illegible]

I have the honor to be, sir, very respectfully, your most obedient[illegible]

ROBERT H. PRUYN[illegible]

Minister Resident in [illegible]

Hon. WILLIAM H. SEWARD, *Secretary of State.*

No. 1.

Mr. Winchester and Mr. Polsbroek to Mr. Pruyn.

KANAGAWA, *March* [illegible]

SIR: We have the honor to wait on you with copies of a minute of what to[illegible] interview we had with the Gorogio on the 6th instant, and of a memorand[illegible] thought it right to present to them, consequent on the reply to our request f[illegible] on the subject to which the said memorandum relates.

Copies of this document have been transmitted to our colleague, the mini[illegible]tiary of France.

Be good enough to accept the assurance of our highest consideration, wh[illegible] honor to be your most obedient, humble servants,

CHARLES A. WINCHEST[illegible]

Her Britannic Majesty's Chargé d'Af[illegible]

D. DE GRAEFF VAN P[illegible]

Political Agent and Consul General of [illegible]

His Excellency ROBERT P. PRUYN,

Minister Resident of the United States.

No. 2.

Minute of a conference held at Yedo on the 6th March, [illegible]

Present: Midsuno Idlumi No Kami and Suwa Inaba No Kami, mini[illegible] No Kami, vice-minister, on the part of the Japanese goovernment, [illegible] chester, her Britannic Majesty's chargé d'affaires, and D. de Graeff van Polsbroek, consul general and political agent of the Netherlands.

After the usual interchange of compliments, the British chargé d'affaires opened the conference by announcing the return of Sir Rutherford Alcock to Japan, and the approval by his government of the policy pursued by him with regard to the late Japanese affairs, which intelligence was received by the Japanese ministers with much appearance of interest, and inquiries were made as to the probable date of his return.

The British chargé d'affaires then, while thanking the Japanese ministers in the name of his government for the energetic steps taken by them in bringing to justice one of the principals in the murder of the two British officers at Kamakura, inquired whether any traces had been discovered of Sakabashi Togiro, the other assassin, to which the minister replied that Simidlu Seiji must have given a false name of his accomplice, as no such name as Sakabashi Togiro was known to them. No effort, they said, would, however, be spared to discover and punish this criminal.

The gold watch sent out by the British government for the Prince of Matsmai for services rendered to the British barque Egeria was then handed over to the Japanese minister, with some appropriate remarks as to the degree in which the British government appreciated the kind treatment which, on various occasions, had been received by shipwrecked crews on the Japanese shores.

Next came the Hakodate and Nagasaki complaints, respecting privileges enjoyed by the Chinese in purchasing and exporting anati, and irico, and other important articles, which could not be obtained, except with great difficulty, by the subjects of treaty powers. The foreign representatives present pointed out to the Gorogio the injustice of this monopoly which had been granted to subjects of a new treaty power, and stated that it created constant difficulties and led to an organized system of native smuggling. The Chinese, they said, were quite as well able to pay for such articles as they required as other nations. When Japan was opened by the treaty of 1858, the trade with Holland, which had formerly been one of government's, ceased to be so, and the continuance of a government contract [fa]vorable to the Chinese, but prejudicial to all other nations, was totally opposed as well to [the] principles embodied in, as to the express provisions of, the treaties. Representatives [prese]nt were ready to admit that immediate interests might require special consideration, but [they] would be better provided for out of the produce of a regular and authorized duty to be [levied d]uring transit of these articles, than by the continuance of a contract opposed to [po]licy and treaty rights.

[The min]isters stated in reply that the matter would be duly inquired into, and that instruc[tions woul]d be sent to the governors of Nagasaki and Hakodate to remove their cause of [complaint.]

[The r]epresentatives present, while declaring themselves satisfied with this reply, said [they had an]other and very important subject to bring under the notice of the Japanese gov[ernment, and] one which they considered of such importance that they now thought it their [duty to ask f]or information from the Gorogio. Certain rumors, which had caused much dis[quiet,] had reached them of a project having been formed for the consignment of large [quantitie]s of silk and ova to one market in Europe for the purchase of vessels, arms, ammu[nition, et]c.

[The Ja]panese ministers did not deny the existence of some such project, and said they [considered] that Japan was perfectly at liberty to make contracts with any nation for the [supply of v]essels-of-war, arms, and other warlike stores, and to pay such contracts by the [pro]duce not required for home consumption in the same manner as they formerly [had done w]ith the Dutch government.

[Th]e Dutch consul general observed that the ministers were in error, inasmuch as [since the conclusion o]f the present treaties Japan had never had any direct trade with the Dutch [governme]nt; [fo]r they must remember, he said, that even for the old contracts remittances [were made], not in produce but in dollars, through the Dutch Trading Company, and [since the tre]aties were in operation the trade had been given over to individuals. The [project] led to the idea virtually of a monopoly which Japan was going to establish [in one m]arket—a proceeding which he and his British colleague were bound to op[pose, as it] was of vital importance for the trade of the subjects of their Majesties the [Kin]g and all other treaty powers, and if the Gorogio could not give the as[surance that such p]rojects were not in existence, or would not be prosecuted, so as to guar[antee against a recur]rence of the silk restrictions of 1863 and 1864, they had no alternative but [to report it t]o their respective governments as inconsistent with the rights acquired [un]der treaties. As the time would not allow any lengthened discussion of [the subjec]t, his British colleague and himself had, in the event of receiving such an [evasi]ve from the Gorogio, drawn up a memorandum setting forth their views [...] The said memorandum, signed, in the Dutch language, with a Japanese [translation, was the]n delivered to the first minister, who, in the name of the Gorogio, replied [that he] understood what the two foreign representatives present had said, and [as]sured that the subject would receive the consideration it deserved.

[It was agree]d, on the other part, that a governor for foreign affairs should shortly [come to Yokohama i]n order to discuss the subject with the foreign ministers generally.

Subsequently the two representatives present informed the Gorogio that, though no instructions had been received as to the convention of October last, they had been made acquainted with the views of their respective governments as to the alternative condition which left to the option of the Japanese government the opening of Simonoseki, or some other eligible port in the inland sea, in lieu of indemnity money, and were justified in stating that the same was unobjectionable.

The Japanese observed, in reply, that this was a point which required consideration, and which should be deferred till the return of the two members of the Gorogio who had been sent by the Tycoon on a special mission to the Mikado.

In conclusion, the two representatives present remarked that the time had arrived for re-establishing foreign legations at Yedo, and that the government of the Tycoon was now considered strong enough to remove all obstacles to the permanent residence of foreign diplomatic agents in the capital.

The Japanese minister replied, this was another point which they could not undertake to discuss until the members of the Gorogio were complete; if the message to Kioto was successful, there should, on their part, be no difficulty in settling the question of the foreign legations. Representatives were aware that since the past year a good deal had been done towards tranquillizing the country, and if the treaty powers would only give them a few months' more time, order and peace might be sufficiently restored so as to afford better security to the foreign agents in the Tycoon's capital.

The conference ended by the presentation of Commodore Montressor, commanding British squadron, and Colonel Browne, commandant of the British troops, with their respective staffs.

As reported by me: MARTIN DOHMEN,
Acting Japanese Secretary to her Britannic Majesty's Legation.

YEDO, *March* 6, 1865.

Countersigned by—

CHARLES A. WINCHESTER,
Her Britannic Majesty's Chargé d'Affaires in Japan.

D. DE GRAEFF VAN POLSBROEK,
Consul General and Political Agent of the Netherlands in Japan.

True copy: MARTIN DOHMEN.

No. 3.

Memorandum.

The rumors which now prevail with respect to the existence of an extensive design for the purchase of the raw silk and silk-worms' eggs of Japan, and despatching these to one particular market, to lay down funds required for the completion of contracts entered into on behalf of the Japanese government in that country, are of a nature calculated to create anxiety.

These rumors have been steadily on the increase, though they have not assumed such shape as to require the use, in speaking of them, of individual names; still, from their character and persistence, the undersigned are justified in applying to the Japanese government for general information as to whether any projects of the kind have been formed, and their nature, because, if the Japanese government is not able to assure the undersigned that such designs have not been or will be formed, it would be the duty of the undersigned to point out the difficulties which such plans are certain to create, and adopt, in doing so, the weightiest form of remonstrance.

The silk restrictions of 1863 and 1864, which consisted in the detention of that article at Yedo, were clearly contrary to treaties, which provide that (Art. xiv, British treaty) foreign merchants shall be allowed to trade freely with Japanese merchants in all lawful articles according to the stipulations in the treaties and the regulations.

There is not the slightest disposition on the part of the undersigned to complain of the selection by the Japanese government of any partial country for the supply of its stores, ships, and munitions; neither of the bringing of silk into open markets at Yokohama and the other ports is not interfered with, is there any objection to the Japanese government sending home silk instead of dollars to pay for their contracts. The experience of all commercial countries proves, beyond doubt, that it is neither wise nor prudent in a government to make themselves merchants. Whenever a government is known to be in the market to buy anything, the price is sure to rise; if it wishes to sell, it is equally sure to fall, through the tricks of individual merchants, who are always jealous of government as competitors, and never think it any sin to fleece them. But both governments and individuals have to pay for their experience, and only learn to abide by true principles when they find it is more costly to deviate from than to adhere to them.

But this is not what the reports point to; they mean a repetition of the restrictions of these last years, namely, that the native merchants are not to be allowed to bring their silk to Yokohama till they have first sold as much as the government wants at a lower price. Now this is simply a repetition of the silk restrictions of 1863 and 1864, with the single difference that its effect is to create a *total* or *partial* monopoly in favor of the country to which the silk is destined.

The effect on the merchants of other foreign countries settled in Japan is the same. There is no free market for the purchase of silk to which the Japanese traders are permitted to bring produce, on payment of the customary and regular transit dues. The price of any silk which is then brought into the market is heightened, because the supply has been diminished in proportion to the amount of the quantity brought through this forced reduction.

Naturally, if, after the communication of the views of the undersigned, they find from actual experience that there is a repetition of the restrictions alluded to, the government of the Queen and King will look to that of the Tycoon for explanation of designs which prevent British and Dutch subjects from trading in the open markets provided by treaty. On such a point they will make no question with any other party than the Tycoon's government.

But there is another point of view in which it is the duty of the undersigned to invite a consideration of these projects as rumored, which appear to them to rest on an unsound basis, and they believe are supported by false arguments. It is said there would be presumably greater profits on Japanese produce if consigned abroad for sale, in furtherance of these designs, and not sold in Japan. Why should not Japan, therefore, keep to herself the profit that lies between the foreign purchaser of the silk in Yokohama and the manufacturer in the foreign country?

This is true in a way, but not in the manner represented.

If the Tycoon's government were to encourage Japanese merchants and commercial agents to settle abroad in the great marts of the world—as London, Paris, Manchester, Lyons, Amsterdam, Hamburg, New York, &c.—there to receive the produce of Japan on consignment, and thence send back as returns such articles as are wanted, and, when sold in Japan, will fetch a profit, the profit both ways would be saved, minus the outlay involved in these foreign Japanese mercantile establishments. Nothing would give the governments of their Majesties the Queen and King greater pleasure than to witness such a step on the part of the government of the Tycoon. Already have numerous youths from the estates of the Tycoon and the princes been sent to Europe for instruction in sciences and arts. Why not send abroad the sons of Japanese merchants and commercial agents also to be instructed in the counting-houses of these great trading cities, and afterwards form in these countries establishments of their own? Such a step would be, indeed, the true reunion of Japan to the world.

But the mere consignment of whole or part of the available produce not required for consumption in Japan to one foreign mart will not secure a higher price. The essence of high price is competition. There are in Yokohama merchants from England, France, Holland, Switzerland, Germany, America, competing keenly with each other, face to face, with equal or greater number of Japanese merchants; whereas, if a particular market belonging to one of these nations is chosen, the competitors are in effect restricted to one section of the six or seven now to be found in Yokohama, so far as the side which will correspond to the foreign side of the Yokohama market is concerned, while the Japanese side must, as things now stand, be entirely represented by foreign agency. The eminent statesmen who govern Japan will, if they weigh such considerations, have no difficulty in arriving at the conclusion that the best market for Japanese produce is to be found in submitting it to the greatest amount of competition. It is by steadily adhering to true commercial principles that the financial operations of a government are best conducted. Every government does wisely, without foreign interference, to levy such steady and equitable taxes on its exports, imports, and produce as are requisite to supply the wants of the state, but the sudden creation of monopolies, and the imposition of restrictions to effect particular objects, is wasteful and improvident; a nation may be great and powerful for other reasons in spite of them, but never by reason of them.

YEDO, *March* 6, 1865.

CHARLES A. WINCHESTER,
Her Britannic Majesty's Chargé d' Affaires in Japan.
D. DE GRAEFF VAN POLSBROEK,
Consul General and Political Agent of the Netherlands in Japan.

No. 4.

Mr. Pruyn to Mr. Winchester and Mr. Van Polsbrock.

LEGATION OF THE UNITED STATES IN JAPAN,
Kanagawa, March 14, 1865.

GENTLEMEN: I have the honor to acknowledge the receipt of your joint letter of the 11th instant, with its enclosures, consisting of a minute of what took place at your recent conference with the Gorogio, and of a memorandum which on that occasion you presented to them.

The rumors to which you therein refer had not escaped my notice, but the project which they indicated was so manifestly in violation of existing treaties, and so incapable of execution, as to have failed to induce me to seek a conference with my colleagues, much less make it the subject of a formal note. I understood you, however, to say, when you verbally communicated to me the result of your conference, that they had assumed such shape and consistency as not to permit you to pass them by unnoticed. I should not have been indisposed, therefore, in conjunction with my colleagues, to have made them the subject of a joint memorandum, in which we should have declared to the Japanese government that the treaties contemplated only trade between the citizens and subjects of the different powers, and that any governmental interference, either by a purchase of the surplus products of the country or any part of them, or by preventing their reaching the open ports, or by sending them beyond those ports, would be justly regarded as an infraction of those treaties.

The signal success which has attended the cordial co-operation of the representatives of the four powers in matters of common interest, induces me to regret that there should have been an interruption of joint action, which I am disposed, however, to attribute rather to the suddenness of your determination while in Yedo to seek the interview, than to any want of courtesy to your colleagues, or of desire to obtain their concurrence. Apart from the necessity of manifesting to the Japanese government the continuance of this purpose of concerted action, I regret it the more as it deprives me of an opportunity of suggesting an important modification of your memorandum, to which I directed your attention at our interview immediately on your return from Yedo. I cannot admit "that there is no objection to the Japanese government sending abroad silk to pay for stores, ships, and munitions." The Japanese government would necessarily be the sole judge of the extent to which such right should be exercised. My objection extends to the principle, and any violation of it should meet with immediate and strong remonstrance. I was not aware till after the receipt of your letter that you had made the convention of October last the subject of any remark at that interview. In the absence of any despatches from my government since the receipt of the convention in the United States, I am unable to say what its decision or preference will be if the alternative of some eligible port shall be offered for the acceptance of the four powers. I cannot doubt, however, that our governments, when the proper time arrives, will act in concert after full consultation. While disposed to interpret your remarks at the recent conference to be such as it was declared to be by the convention—the establishment of better relations with Japan, and not the receipt of money—I would have suggested and counselled, had opportunity been afforded, that no communication should have been made in reference thereto, in the absence of positive instructions, until the representatives of the four powers were able to unite therein.

I embrace this opportunity to renew the assurance of my desire to cultivate and maintain unimpaired that perfect accord on the part of the representatives of the treaty powers which has been so happily established, and which has been productive of so much good, as most agreeable to my own wishes and the instructions of the President of the United States, and as the best security for the preservation of our common treaty rights.

I have the honor to be, gentlemen, your most obedient servant,

ROBERT H. PRUYN,
Minister Resident of the United States in Japan.

Messrs. CHAS. A. WINCHESTER,
Her Britanic Majesty's Chargé d'Affaires.
D. DE GRAEFF VAN POLSBROEK,
Political Agent and Consul General of the Netherlands.

No. 5.

[Note verbale.—Translation.]

LEGATION OF FRANCE IN JAPAN.

The undersigned has the honor to acknowledge the receipt of the joint letter, dated the 11th March, addressed to him by Mr. Winchester, chargé d'affaires of her Britannic Majesty, and Mr. De Graeff van Polsbroek, political agent and consul general of his Majesty the King of the Netherlands, transmitting copy of minute of their conference with the Gorogio, and of a memorandum which they have deemed proper to present to them.

The undersigned has already verbally expressed to Messrs. Winchester and De Graeff van Polsbroek, when they came to communicate to him the object and the result of their proceeding with the Gorogio the painful feelings which he experienced when learning that his colleagues had acted without him in a matter which interested him personally. It was, indeed, publicly known that the rumors taken for basis of the memorandum addressed by them to the Gorogio clearly and solely pointed to France and its representative, who, it was said, had induced the Japanese government to send all the silk of Japan to the market of Lyons, &c., &c.

The undersigned will not repeat, now, his opinions on this subject, but contents himself with submitting the following remarks to his colleagues:

The representatives of America, England, France, and Holland, having succeeded in establishing among themselves a perfect understanding, which has so powerfully contributed to improve our political and commercial situation in Japan, and having engaged themselves to act in concert each time that the general interests of the foreign nations shall be threatened by measures emanating from the Japanese government, the undersigned thinks that both his colleagues, Messrs. Winchester and De Graeff van Polsbroek, might have come to an understanding with him previous to writing the memorandum which they presented to the Gorogio on the subject of a question so pointedly connected with the interests of the respective citizens and subjects of the four powers above named.

Her Britannic Majesty's chargé d'affaires and the political agent of his Majesty the King of the Netherlands, would then have convinced themselves that not only does the undersigned consider any commercial operation on the part of the Japanese government as opposed to the spirit and the letter of the treaties and of international laws, but also that he did not admit, as his colleagues have admitted in their memorandum, the right of the said government to send silk abroad in exchange for arms and munitions which it may have purchased there.

The commercial interests which the undersigned is sent to protect require that the Japanese government shall absolutely abstain from any commercial act whatever, either directly or indirectly.

The undersigned cannot explain the reply of the Gorogio, according to the minute written by his colleagues, in any other manner than as a misunderstanding or an error of translation, on many occasions, and recently again he has had similar commercial questions to discuss with the Gorogio or their envoys, and never has he been able to trace, in their replies, the slightest indication of intentions on their part such as are attributed to them.

The spread or the maintenance of such errors might affect the character of the representative of France, and he, therefore, considers it a duty to call, without delay, for a special statement on this subject on the part of the Gorogio.

The undersigned also believes that Messrs. De Graeff van Polsbroek and Winchester might have omitted, jointly and officially, to discuss with the Gorogio the question relating to the war indemnity granted by the Japanese government to England, France, America, and Holland. This question having been the subject of a convention signed by the representatives of those four powers, it seems more natural to the undersigned not to discuss it with the Gorogio until after a mutual understanding of the said representatives.

It is thus with profound regret that the undersigned now states facts which would be of a nature to affect the good understanding which, until now, has subsisted between the representatives of the four powers, if he had not, while dismissing any impression of personal feeling, resolved upon maintaining unimpaired the unity which is the essential condition of the strength they must oppose to the restrictive tendencies of the Japanese government.

LEON ROCHES.

YOKOHAMA, *March* 14, 1865.

Mr. Pruyn to Mr. Seward.

No. 16.] LEGATION OF THE UNITED STATES IN JAPAN,
Kanagawa, April 24, 1865.

SIR: I have the honor to enclose a copy of a letter received from the minister for foreign affairs, in which it is announced that his Majesty the Tycoon does not think it expedient to avail himself of the privilege conferred by the convention of tendering Simonoseki, or some eligible port in the inland sea, in lieu of the indemnity which he therein agreed to pay to the four powers. (Enclosure No. 1.)

A similar communication was at the same time addressed to my colleagues; but as the representatives of England and Holland had announced to the Japanese government that their governments preferred that another port should be opened, and the minister of France had been instructed that the government of his Imperial Majesty thought it better that the pecuniary indemnity should be paid, it was not thought we could frame a reply in which all could unite, I therefore transmitted a letter to the Gorogio, of which I send copy, (enclosure No. 2.)

As by the terms of the convention it was entirely optional with the Tycoon to open a port, and as the effect of the decision was to make the obligation to pay the indemnity absolute, it appeared to me that it was advisable to offer to receive the first instalment at the time named, as it was understood that the money was already in the treasury and appropriated for that purpose. I therefore suggested to her Britannic Majesty's chargé d'affaires that it would not be inconsistent with his duty, under the letters he had received declaring the preference of her Britannic Majesty's government, to unite in receiving the money provided the Japanese government paid it, with the understanding that such receipt should not be understood as committing our governments to the extension of the times of payment of the remaining instalments. We therefore had a conference and agreed to make that proposition; whereupon I addressed a letter to the Gorogio, of which I enclose copy, enclosure No. 3, which corresponds substantially with the reply sent in by each of my colleagues.

You will see the government wish an extension of the time of payment of the second instalment, leaving it only to be inferred, not expressed, that the remaining instalments will be hereafter paid agreeably to the terms of the convention. But they make no promise to do so, and it is more than probable that if this extension be granted similar efforts will be made to extend the time of payment of the other instalments, which will prove an embarrassment to trade for several years. I concur with my colleagues in the opinion that no such extension should be granted.

I have the honor to be, sir, respectfully, your most obedient servant,

ROBERT H. PRUYN.

Hon. WILLIAM H. SEWARD,
Secretary of State, &c., &c., &c.

[No. 1.—Translation.]

In order to arrange the difficulty caused by the hostile acts of Mori Daizen against the ships of various powers, an agreement was entered into by us with the representatives of the treaty powers on the 22d of the 9th month, (October 22, 1864,) providing that in view of the mutual interests of the governments interested, it is optional to open Simonoseki or another port in the inland sea, or to pay a sum of money as indemnity, as stated in that written instrument.

After having fully taken the present state of things in our country into due consideration, we have come to the conclusion that the opening of a new port is not only undesirable, in view of our internal affairs, but that it would also be attended with inconvenience for the several powers.

The real cause which involved the friendly intercourse between the two countries in great difficulties is the action of Mori Daizen; the money of the indemnity therefore should be demanded of him; but as one of the Daimios of our country, it is impossible to allow him to enter into negotiation on the subject with the several powers, and hence our government was compelled to assume the responsibility.

If a port be opened instead, the inconvenience of both countries will increase twofold, and therefore, after mature deliberation, we have decided to choose the latter alternative, to wit, the payment of the indemnity.

The Choshu difficulty is still unsettled. Yet one portion of the sum of indemnity to be paid in six instalments shall be delivered in the 6th month of this year, (August, 1865,) and because this Choshu difficulty has not yet been disposed of, it is desirable that for the payment of the balance an extension of one year be granted, and it is proposed that the second instalment be paid in the 6th month of next year, and further payment, as provided by convention, from the last named date.

As you are well acquainted with the state of affairs in our country, we do not doubt that you will fully comply with our desire.

Stated, with respect and esteem, the 10th day of the 3d month of the 2d year of Gongi, (April 5, 1865.)

MIDLUNO IDLUMI NO KAMI.
SUWA INABA NO KAMI.

His Excellency ROBERT H. PRUYN,
Minister Resident of the United States of America, &c., &c., &c.

No. 2.

Mr. Pruyn to the Gorogio.

LEGATION OF THE UNITED STATES IN JAPAN,
Kanagawa, April 8, 1865.

I have the honor to acknowledge the receipt of your excellencies' letter of the 10th day of the 3d month, (5th instant.)

It announces that the government of his Majesty the Tycoon has, after mature deliberation, decided not to tender Simonoseki, or some other eligible port in the Inland Sea, in lieu of the indemnity, the right of which was reserved by the late convention.

Your excellencies therefore propose to pay the first instalment of the indemnity in the 6th month of the year, the second instalment in the 6th month of next year, and the four remaining instalments at intervals subsequent to the second payment, as provided by convention.

Sufficient time has not elapsed to enable me to receive instructions on the subject of the convention from my government and to learn its preferences.

I feel assured, however, it would have cheerfully accepted a new port in lieu of all or part of the indemnity, had such been the wish of the Japanese government.

I sincerely hope that the decision which has been made, founded, as it is, on a more intimate knowledge of the commercial and political relations of the several parts of the Empire with each other, may be such as is best calculated to improve the relations with the treaty powers, and to insure internal peace and tranquillity.

Meanwhile I shall transmit to my government a copy of the letter of your excellencies. On the arrival of instructions from our respective governments, the ministers of the four powers will be in a position to take your excellencies' letter into full and friendly consideration, and give such answer as may be in our power, as to your proposal to extend the payment of the balance of the indemnity.

With respect and esteem,

ROBERT H. PRUYN,
Minister Resident of the United States in Japan.

Their Excellencies the MINISTERS OF FOREIGN AFFAIRS, *&c.*, *&c.*, *Yedo.*

No. 3,

Mr. Pruyn to the Gorogio.

LEGATION OF THE UNITED STATES IN JAPAN,
Kanagawa, April 17, 1865.

In continuation of my letter No. 36, in relation to your excellencies' announcement, that the government of his Majesty the Tycoon had resolved to pay the indemnity agreed on by the convention of October 22, 1864, renouncing the right reserved therein to tender in lieu thereof an open port, it becomes my duty to inform your excellencies, that at a recent conference between my colleagues and myself we arrived at the following conclusions, which harmonize with those contained in my said letter No. 36, (enclosure No. 2.)

The decision of his Majesty the Tycoon becomes now a part of the convention, and has the effect to make the obligation to pay the indemnity absolute.

The representatives of the four powers will therefore be prepared to receive the first instalment at the time mentioned by your excellencies, but only on condition that such receipt shall not be considered as binding their respective governments to the extension of the time fixed for the payment of the remaining instalments. The undersigned would be authorized, with his colleagues, to accept the further instalments as they successively become due under the convention. The convention having doubtless before this been ratified by the powers, parties thereto cannot be changed by their representatives. They must therefore make known your excellencies' wishes to their respective governments for their decision. It will be competent if they shall decide, in a friendly spirit, to comply in whole or in part with the request of his Majesty the Tycoon to propose such equivalent advantages as may be regarded as necessary and just.

Animated by the most friendly sentiments, I have transmitted a copy of your excellencies' letter to my government, which will, at an early day after an interchange of views with the governments of Great Britain, France, and the Netherlands, give instructions to its representatives, corresponding with the decision at which they shall arrive.

With respect and esteem,

ROBERT H. PRUYN,
Minister Resident of the United States in Japan.

Their Excellencies the MINISTERS OF FOREIGN AFFAIRS, *&c.*, *&c.*, *Yedo.*

Mr. Pruyn to Mr. Seward.

No. 21.] LEGATION OF THE UNITED STATES IN JAPAN,
Kanagawa, April 28, 1865.

SIR: It has long been my opinion, as you are aware, that internal troubles in the empire are occasioned by the struggles of the Daimios to share in the profits of foreign trade, now wholly monopolized by the Tycoon, and I have reason to believe that the true sentiments of the Daimios, if not systematically misrepresented by this government, are at least withheld from our knowledge.

The Prince of Satsuma, once represented to be the head of the Sako or anti-foreign party, is now known to favor an extended trade. I believe such has already been his preference. When Nagasaki was only open to a very restricted trade with Holland, Satsuma imported largely from China through his princely domain, the Lew Chew islands. The highest-priced and most largely used cotton fabric is called Satsuma, partly manufactured in and partly received through his dominions.

Letters from Nagasaki now represent it as undoubtedly true that Choshu was equally favorable to an enlarged trade with foreigners, and is determined to participate in such trade, even if obliged to do so clandestinely.

These letters are simply confirmatory of what we have otherwise learned of his purpose, and every Daimio in Kin Sin and Sikoku, save one, openly advocate the immediate opening of ports in the Inland Sea.

The ports now open are in imperial territory, where the retainers and merchants of Daimios are subject to arbitrary arrests. Toguno Sagonou, one of Satsuma's physicians, has been confined in prison nearly three years, because a letter was found in his possession from a foreign merchant to his Daimio, advocating the policy of trade with foreigners.

At Osacca, the Daimios of the empire enjoy privileges of trade, secured to them by ancient laws and customs, which would enable them to meet the foreign merchants on a footing of great equality with the Tycoon. The many vexatious restrictions on trade which can be maintained in the now open ports would be loosened in that city, and another advantage, equally important, can be only secured in that commercial centre of the empire. The great merchants and the bankers can be met face to face. Here, irresponsible men are the factors. Advances cannot be safely made on produce to be delivered. Large sums have thus been lost. At Osacca they could be safely made, if needful, and with the enlargement of trade at this great entrepot of manufactured goods and native produce, attended as it will be by more intimate relations with a better class of Japanese, a more friendly feeling will prevail, and greater security be obtained for life and property.

I have the honor to be, sir, very respectfully, your most obedient servant,

ROBERT H. PRUYN.

Hon. WILLIAM H. SEWARD,
Secretary of State, &c., &c., &c.

Mr. Portman to Mr. Seward.

No. 27.] LEGATION OF THE UNITED STATES IN JAPAN,
Kanagawa, May 16, 1865.

SIR: It has been officially announced to me that, at an early day, his Majesty the Tycoon will leave Yedo to place himself at the head of the army which is to act against the Prince of Choshu.

In view of the profound peace which has uninterruptedly prevailed in Japan for more than two centuries, the Tycoon's government declared that they felt disposed to deal leniently with the Prince, and facilitate by every means his return to his allegiance; but his recent proceedings led to the suspicion that he had met with some support. It was at first believed that Choshu would comply, instead of which his resistance is now more marked than ever. Prompt action, had, therefore, been resolved upon to carry out the sentence by which he is to be shorn of all power hitherto possessed.

The Tycoon's government felt confident of the result of this military expedition, and added, that, when their internal difficulties shall have been disposed of, it will be easier faithfully to observe the treaties and cultivate friendly relations with the treaty powers.

I have the honor to be, sir, very respectfully, your most obedient servant,

A. L. C. PORTMAN,
Chargé d'Affaires ad interim in Japan.

Hon. WILLIAM H. SEWARD,
Secretary of State, Washington.

Mr. Portman to Mr. Seward.

No. 32.] LEGATION OF THE UNITED STATES IN JAPAN,
Yedo, June 9, 1865.

SIR: I have the honor to transmit herewith, No. 1, translation of a letter from the minister of foreign affairs, informing me of the departure, this day, of the Tycoon, for the purpose of placing himself at the head of his army, which is to suppress the rebellion of the Prince of Choshu.

This army is to gather contingent forces from various Daimios on the way, and, on arrival on the scene of action, it is estimated, will fully muster one hundred thousand fighting men.

There appears to be much uncertainty in regard to the attitude of several Daimios in the vicinity of Nagato, whose position as yet is not sufficiently defined; but there appears, also, to prevail an impression that the presence of so large a force will, by itself, be found sufficient to overawe not only the Prince of Choshu, but also such other Daimios who are now more or less wavering in their allegiance, and that the solution of all internal difficulties is now near at an end.

I have the honor to be, sir, very respectfully, your most obedient servant,

A. L. C. PORTMAN,
Chargé d'Affaires ad interim in Japan.

Hon. WILLIAM H. SEWARD, *&c., &c., &c.*

The Gorogio to Mr. Portman.

A. L. C. PORTMAN, Esq.,
Chargé d'Affaires of the United States of America, &c., &c., &c.:

We have to inform you that to-morrow, the 16th day, (9th June,) his Majesty the Tycoon will leave Yedo by land, for the purpose of punishing the Prince of Nagato and Suwo, and that Bungo No Kami, Suwo No Kami, and Satsibana Idlumo No Kami will leave at the same time, in his Majesty's suite.

Stated, with respect and esteem, the 15th day of the 5th month of the 1st year of K. U., (8th June, 1865.)

MIDLUNO TOLUNI NO KAMI.
ABE BUNGO NO KAMI.
MATSUDAIRA SUNO NO KAMI.

Mr. Portman to Mr. Seward.

No. 33.] LEGATION OF THE UNITED STATES IN JAPAN,
Yedo, June 10, 1865.

SIR: As soon as intelligence was received here that the President had approved the Pacific Mail Steamship Company bill, I united with the minister of France and chargé d'affaires of Great Britain in applying to this government for a lot of land suitable for a coal depot for each of the three steamship companies.

It is expected that, at an early day, the French company of the Messageries Imperiales will, like the British Peninsular and Oriental Steamship Company, make Yokohama the terminus of their line.

I have now the honor to inform you that I received a letter from this government to the effect that the governor of Kanagawa has been authorized to grant a lot for that purpose.

I am aware that our Pacific Mail Steamship Company is not expected to go into operation before 1867, but in view of the increasing prosperity and commercial importance of Yokohama, a suitable lot might not then be procurable, except at a heavy outlay.

I hope you will be pleased to approve of my action in this matter.

I have the honor to be, sir, very respectfully, your most obedient servant,

A. L. C. PORTMAN,
Chargé d'Affaires ad interim in Japan.

Hon. WILLIAM H. SEWARD,
Secretary of State, Washington.

Mr. Portman to Mr. Seward.

No. 35.] LEGATION OF THE UNITED STATES,
Yedo, June 20, 1865.

SIR: I have the honor to transmit, herewith, No. 1, copy of a letter from her Britannic Majesty's chargé d'affaires, and No. 2, copy of my reply, in reference to the atrocious assassination of Mr. Lincoln.

The extreme fiendishness of that deed, and of the attack on yourself, paralyzes the judgment, and I can only pray that you may have entirely recovered.

I have the honor to be, sir, very respectfully, your most obedient servant,

A. L. C. PORTMAN,
Chargé d'affaires ad interim in Japan.

Hon. WILLIAM H. SEWARD,
Secretary of State, Washington.

(For enclosure No. 1 see Appendix, separate volume.)

No. 2.

Mr. Portman to Mr. Winchester.

LEGATION OF THE UNITED STATES IN JAPAN,
June 20, 1865.

SIR: I have the honor to acknowledge the reception of your letter of yesterday, expressing the sentiments of profound pain and regret which, in common with all Englishmen in Japan, you felt at the intelligence of the atrocious assassination of Mr. Lincoln. I shall transmit a copy of your communication to my government.

Expressions like these, of the enormity of the crime committed, and the immensity of the loss sustained, will be received, in their affliction, by the people of the United States in the same spirit in which they are tendered, and cannot fail, under Providence, to contribute in cementing those feelings of good will which I sincerely trust and pray may forever subsist between our respective countries.

I have the honor to be, sir, your most obedient servant,

A. L. C. PORTMAN,
Chargé d'Affaires ad interim of the U. S. in Japan.

CHARLES A. WINCHESTER, Esq.,
Her Britannic Majesty's Chargé d'Affaires ad interim in Japan.

Mr. Portman to Mr. Seward.

No. 36.] LEGATION OF THE UNITED STATES IN JAPAN,
Yedo, June 24, 1865.

SIR: I have the honor to transmit herewith, No. 1, copy of a memorandum, signed on the 21st instant by the representatives of the four powers who, in September last, adopted the policy of reopening the Inland Sea, closed against foreign vessels by the aggressions of the Prince of Choshu, at Simonoseki, which policy was crowned with success, and met with the approval of their respective governments.

The present memorandum is in continuation of that policy, in view of the approaching operations of the Tycoon at the head of his army for the suppression of the rebellion of the Prince of Choshu, and with the object of securing the observance of strict neutrality.

I trust you will be pleased to approve of my action.

I have the honor to be, sir, very respectfully, your most obedient servant,

A. L. C. PORTMAN,
Chargé d'Affaires ad interim in Japan.

Hon. WILLIAM H. SEWARD,
Secretary of State, Washington.

No. 1.

Memorandum.

Choshu, Prince of Nagato, being in a state of overt insurrection against the Tycoon, and his Majesty the Tycoon having resolved to march himself at the head of an army, intended to reduce his contumacious vassal to obedience, civil war is imminent, and from the situation of its theatre may, to a certain extent, compromise the interests of the treaty powers by impeding the free navigation of their vessels through the straits of Simonoseki.

In presence of this state of things, the representatives of the four powers subscribing the convention of the 22d October, 1864, have met for the purpose of consulting as to the measures it may be convenient to adopt for protecting the interests of their countrymen, and securing the results contemplated by the expedition successfully directed by their respective naval forces against the batteries of Simonoseki in September, 1864.

This meeting took place on the 21st June, 1865, and the following is the result of the joint deliberations of the undersigned:

Considering that the batteries erected by the Prince of Nagato, in the straits of Simonoseki, were employed to prohibit the free navigation of the inland sea to foreigners, and were disarmed by the commanders of the allied forces, who imposed upon the prince the formal obligation not to re-arm them:

Considering that the allied forces have not renounced the obligation of a military position in the straits, save on a formal obligation accepted by the government of the Tycoon, to guarantee the free navigation of the straits to foreign vessels:

Considering, moreover, that while the rules of a wise policy require of the powers signing the convention to avoid every act of intervention in the conflict which has just commenced between the Tycoon and the Prince of Nagato, their treaty relations of friendship and commerce which exist only with the Tycoon require from them the moral support and facilities necessary to the exercise of the rights acknowledged by such treaties to belong to the Tycoon:

For these reasons the undersigned have adopted with one accord the following articles, and are agreed that a copy of this memorandum shall be addressed to the commanders of the naval forces of their respective nations now present or hereafter to arrive in Japan:

ARTICLE I.

In the interval which will elapse before the land and sea forces of the Tycoon shall present themselves in the straits of Simonoseki, the naval commanders of the powers, parties to the convention of the 22d October, ought, in virtue of that convention, to oppose the re-armament of the batteries of the Prince of Nagato in the said strait, or even to proceed to their disarmament if the Daimio should have re-armed them; but as the carrying these measures into effect might bring about conflicts and complications, which the undersigned wish absolutely to avoid, the commanders of the naval forces are requested, in this latter case, to make to the Prince of Nagato, or his representative, such remonstrances as they may deem appropriate, and in any event to ascertain the state of things, and to furnish the undersigned with an immediate report, in order that they may communicate with the government of the Tycoon thereon, and to place their respective governments in a position to give their instructions.

Article II.

Apart from the object of the preceding article, it is desirable that the commanders of the naval forces should be able to assure the free passage of the straits to foreign ships using it in regular trade with Japan, and to lend the aid required by treaty for repressing on the part of the merchant ships belonging to their respective flags in any part of the territories of Nagato, contiguous to the straits, trading operations, which, in terms of the treaties, are only authorized in the ports actually opened to foreigners.

Article III.

It is equally important to prevent the ships of the Tycoon, charged with the prevention of unlawful commercial operations with the insurgent prince, from going in such cases beyond the limits of right and humanity.

Article IV.

When hostilities shall commence in the straits between the Tycoon and Choshu, the commanders will warn foreign ships of the necessity of passing beyond the lines of fire, and should even require them to abstain from entering the straits if the passage at the time should bring them into actual danger.

Article V.

It is well understood that all the measures indicated by the undersigned shall be carried out in the manner which the naval commanders shall consider most fitting, and in any case that their desire is that the strictest neutrality should be observed in all that concerns the military operations between the Tycoon and the Prince of Nagato.

A. L. C. PORTMAN,
Chargé d'Affaires ad interim of the United States in Japan.
LEON ROCHES,
Minister Plenipotentiary of France in Japan.
CHARLES A. WINCHESTER,
H. B. M's. Chargé d'Affaires in Japan.
D. DE GRAEFF VAN POLSBROEK.
H. N. M's Political Agent and Consul General in Japan.

Mr. Portman to Mr. Seward.

No. 40.] Legation of the United States in Japan,
Yedo, July 5, 1865.

Sir: Late in the evening of the 3d instant, the day of the arrival of the mail at Kanagawa, I received a message from the Gorogio to the effect that s[illegible] officers of rank wished to visit me on this day. I was accordingly [illegible] by the governors for foreign affairs with a numerous suite, who, in the [illegible] his Majesty the Tycoon and his government, came to request me to convey to the President and yourself the sentiments of profound pain with which they had learned the assassination of Mr. Lincoln and the attack on yourself, and also their sincerest wishes for your speedy recovery. I assured these officers that I should not fail to comply with this request at the earliest opportunity.

I have the honor to be, sir, very respectfully, your most obedient servant,

A. L. C. PORTMAN,
Chargé d'Affaires ad interim in Japan.

Hon. William H. Seward,
Secretary of State, Washington.

Mr. Portman to Mr. Seward.

No. 44.] Legation of the United States in Japan,
Yedo, July 24, 1865.

Sir: I have the honor to transmit, No. 1, copy of a letter addressed by me to the Japanese government on the subject of an embassy which recently left for Europe.

Up to this date no reply has been received by me to that letter, and I have no doubt that the delay in giving me the information desired is owing to some secret agreement entered into some months ago with the representative of a treaty power in this country.

Although no engagement, either secret or otherwise, made on behalf of the Japanese government by this embassy with any European power, could in the slightest degree be binding on the United States, yet it might ultimately prove of an embarrassing influence.

I feel confident that at an early day I shall succeed in procuring a satisfactory reply to my letter from the Japanese government.

I have the honor to be, sir, very respectfully, your most obedient servant,

A. L C. PORTMAN,
Chargé d'Affaires ad interim in Japan

Hon. WILLIAM H. SEWARD, *&c., &c., &c.*

No. 1.

LEGATION OF THE UNITED STATES IN JAPAN,
Yedo, July 8, 1865.

I have to request your excellency to communicate to me the rank and names of the officers composing your embassy, which left by last mail steamer for Europe, and to inform me of the object of their mission.

Your embassy which left for Europe in 1862 concluded a secret convention with the governments of Great Britain and France, which was shown me by Colonel Neale, then her Britannic Majesty's chargé d'affaires, and the embassy which left subsequently concluded a convention in Paris, which latter convention was disapproved by his Majesty the Tycoon. In neither of these cases was any notice whatever given to the minister of the United States.

In the most friendly manner I now beg to submit that it is difficult to reconcile the conclusion of such conventions with a fair interpretation of the most-favored-nation clause, as contained in article 9 of the treaty concluded with Commodore Perry at Kanagawa on the 31st of March, 1854.

The President is animated with a most cordial friendship towards his Majesty the Tycoon and his government, which friendship, I am sure, is as cordially reciprocated, and I have therefore no doubt that your excellency will furnish me at an early day with the information desired.

With respect and esteem,

A. L. C. PORTMAN,
Chargé d'Affaires of the United States in Japan.

[illegible]llency MIDLUNO IDSUMI NO KAMI,
Minister for Foreign Affairs, &c., &c., &c.

Mr. Portman to Mr. Seward.

No. 47.] LEGATION OF THE UNITED STATES IN JAPAN,
Yedo, August 6, 1865.

SIR: I have the honor to transmit herewith, No. 1, translation of a letter from the Gorogio, informing me that two of the members at Osacca had commissioned two war steamers to cruise off the coast of Nagato, under instructions to seize all foreign vessels engaged in illicit traffic with the subjects of the rebellious prince of that province.

This letter was handed me with the request that the greatest possible publicity might be given to it.

I therefore addressed a letter to this effect to Mr. Seward, our consul general in China, at Shanghai, (enclosure No. 2,) and to the consular officers in this country, (enclosure No. 3.)

With my reply to the Gorogio (enclosure No. 3) I transmitted an authenticated copy, in duplicate, of my letter to the consuls above named, for each of those two war steamers, for the double purpose of enabling their respective commanders, in the probable absence of competent interpreters, to communicate with any American vessel, should any unfortunately be found engaged in such illicit traffic, and to show that both in China and Japan the consular officers of the United States have been informed of the presence of those steamers and the subject of their cruise.

On inquiry whether the commanders of those war steamers "would know how to act" in case of their meeting with any American vessel engaged in such illicit traffic, it was stated to me that the Japanese government were not quite prepared to discuss "any question of international law," but that I might rest assured that both commanders were cautious gentlemen, and that, moreover, they had been instructed to act with the greatest moderation, though it was hoped and believed that there would be no necessity for any action whatever on their part.

The mission of those steamers, though not fully disclosed, perhaps, is evidently the blockade of Simonoseki, to prevent supplies of arms, ammunition, &c., reaching the Prince of Nagato, now bolder than ever in his overt rebellion against this government.

I have the honor to be, sir, very respectfully, your most obedient servant,

A. L. C. PORTMAN,
Chargé d'Affaires in Japan.

Hon. WILLIAM H. SEWARD,
Secretary of State, Washington.

No. 1.

I have to inform you that, having learned that foreign ships are trading clandestinely at Simonoseki, in the province of Nagato, two ships-of-war, the Shokoku and the Kokurio, stationed at Osacca, have been sent, on the 25th of July, to cruise off the coast of Nagato for the purpose of seizing all vessels engaged in illicit traffic. This has been communicated to me by my colleagues then at Osacca.

I request you to make the foregoing known to all American ship-masters who may sail through the straits, and also to the commanders of American ships-of-war in the eastern seas, in order that a friendly understanding may exist when the officers of our respective nations shall meet each other.

With respect and esteem.

The 13th day of the 5th month of the first year of the Ke-M, (August 4, 1865.)

MIDLUNO IDLUMI NO KAMI.

A. L. C. PORTMAN, Esq.,
Chargé d'Affaires of the United States in Japan.

No. 2.

Mr. Portman to Mr. G. F. Seward.

LEGATION OF THE UNITED STATES IN JAPAN,
Yedo, August 5, 1865.

SIR: The Gorogio of Japan informed me that, on the 25th ultimo, two of its members at Osacca commissioned two war steamers, the Shokoku and the Kokurio, to cruise off the coast of Nagato, with instructions to seize foreign vessels engaged in illicit traffic.

In compliance with the desire expressed, I now have the honor to request you to make the foregoing known to the consular officers of the United States in China, for the information of all American citizens within their jurisdictions.

I have the honor to be, sir, very respectfully, your obedient servant,

A. L. C. PORTMAN,
Chargé d'Affaires ad interim in Japan.

GEORGE F. SEWARD, Esq.,
Consul General of the United States in China, Shanghai.

[Same, *mutatis mutandis*, to United States consuls at Nagasaki, Kanagawa, Hakodate, and Hong Kong.]

No. 3.

LEGATION OF THE UNITED STATES IN JAPAN,
Yedo, August 5, 1865.

I have the honor to acknowledge the receipt of your excellency's note of yesterday, stating that your colleagues at Osacca had commissioned two war steamers to cruise off the coast of Nagato for the suppression of illicit traffic, and, in reply, to inform you that I have this day given notice to that effect to the consuls of the United States in Japan, and consul general at Shanghai, for the information of the American consulates in China.

I transmit herewith a copy of that notice, and also an additional one, should you desire to send to each of the war steamers named in your letter a copy certified, and under the seal of this legation.

With respect and esteem,

A. L. C. PORTMAN,
Chargé d'Affaires ad interim of the United States in Japan.

His Excellency MIDLUNO IDLUMI NO KAMI.
Minister for Foreign Affairs, &c., Yedo.

Mr. Portman to Mr. Seward.

No. 48.] LEGATION OF THE UNITED STATES IN JAPAN,
Yedo, August 22, 1865.

SIR: On the morning of the 18th instant I was waited on by governors for foreign affairs, who came to inform me that the Japanese government was prepared to pay the first instalment of five hundred thousand dollars of the Simonoseki indemnity, according to the convention of the 22d October, 1864.

Aware that under article 2d of that convention the large sum of three millions (3,000,000) of dollars was payable quarterly in instalments of half a million (500,000) dollars each, "to begin from the date when the representatives of the powers signing it should make known to the Tycoon's government the ratification of the convention and the instructions of their respective governments," I only inquired whether similar announcements had been made to the representatives of the other treaty powers.

The governors then informed me that early on that day another governor for foreign affairs had gone to Yokohama for that purpose, and that such announcement would probably be made to the other representatives on the afternoon of that day.

In order that my absence might not embarrass the action of those representatives, I accordingly went down to Yokohama at once, with the object of ascertaining their views on this unexpected announcement.

The unanimous opinion was, in view of the decision taken and communicated to the Gorogio in April last, that no option was left but that the amount tendered should be received. I respectfully beg to refer you to the despatch No. 16, of this series, with its three enclosures.

I now have the honor to transmit herewith, No. 1, a copy of a memorandum dated the 21st August, 1865, agreeing to take delivery of the sum offered, appended to which is a copy of an order to the chartered Oriental Bank and chartered Mercantile Bank, to hold that money in equal sums of two hundred and fifty thousand (250,000) dollars each, to the conjoint order of the representatives of the four powers who signed the convention of the 22d October, 1864.

Your instructions as to the disposal of that money have no doubt been sent already. Their anticipated early arrival was an additional reason why I felt no hesitation in consenting to its being received. If the offer of the Japanese government had not been accepted at once when made, the payment of the first instalment might have been indefinitely extended, and the convention, as I learned, had already, in substance, been approved by the governments of Great Britain and France.

Should the whole amount of the indemnity, namely, three millions (3,000,000) of dollars, so much larger than originally intended, be deemed too large, which was Mr. Pruyn's opinion, as expressed in his despatch No. 65, of the 29th October, 1864, I beg respectfully to suggest, inasmuch as it is stated in article 3 of that convention that "the receipt of money has never been the object of the said treaty powers, but the establishment of better relations with Japan," &c., that a portion of that indemnity, say five hundred thousand (500,000) dollars, might be most advantageously employed in improvements in both the foreign and Japanese settlements, at the open ports, such as drainage, cleaning streets, &c. In no manner that I am aware of could any portion of such indemnity be employed to greater advantage and be of more lasting benefit to both our political and commercial relations with this country.

I have the honor to be, sir, very respectfully, your most obedient servant,

A. L. C. PORTMAN,
Chargé d'Affaires ad interim in Japan.

Hon. WILLIAM H. SEWARD,
Secretary of State, Washington.

No. 1.

Memorandum.

The government of the Tycoon having offered, in April last, to pay, in the course of the sixth month of the Japanese year of Gengi, (which terminated yesterday, Sunday, 20th August,) to the representatives of the foreign powers who signed the convention of the 22d October, 1864, a sum of five hundred thousand (500,000) dollars, as the first instalment of the indemnity stipulated for in the said convention, and the said offer having been accepted in April last by the representatives of the signing powers, and Taumra Higo No Kami having tendered, on the 19th instant, to the undersigned, on the part of the government of the Tycoon, the said sum of five hundred thousand dollars, the undersigned hereby record their agreement to take delivery of the said money, and with a view to its safe custody, to authorize, by the letter at foot, the deposit of the same in two equal sums of two hundred and fifty thousand (250,000) dollars in the chartered Oriental Bank and the chartered Mercantile Bank at Yokohama, each bank to receive one of the said sums and to hold the same subject to the instructions now expected from the respective governments of the undersigned as to the manner in which the said money is to be disposed of.

Signed at her Britannic Majesty's legation this 21st day of August, A. D. 1865.

HARRY S. PARKS,
H. B. M.'s Envoy Extraordinary and Minister Plenipotentiary.
A. L. C. PORTMAN,
Chargé d'Affaires of the United States.
D. DE GRAEFF VON POLSBROEK,
H. N. M.'s Political Agent and Consul General.
For the Ministre of France— P. CHEVEY RAMEAU,
Geiant du Consulat General de France.
COUNT DE TURENNE, *Attaché.*

You are hereby authorized to receive from the Japanese authorities the sum of two hundred and fifty thousand (250,000) dollars, and to hold the same subject to our conjoint order.

As the delivery of this sum may extend over several days, you will give a receipt at the close of each day for the amount received on that day, which will be countersigned by Mr. Eusden, Japanese secretary to her Britannic Majesty's legation.

H. S. P.
A. L. C. P.
D. DE GR. P.
P. C. R., (for M. Roches.)
C'T DE T.

S. G. RICHARD, Esq.,
Manager Chartered Oriental Bank.
R. BRETT, Esq.,
Manager Chartered Mercantile Bank, Yokohama.

Mr. Seward to Mr. Portman.

[Extract.]

No. 1.] DEPARTMENT OF STATE, *Washington, August* 31, 1865.

SIR: I have received your several despatches numbered and dated as follows: Nos. 29 and 30, June 1; No. 31, June 8; No. 32, June 9; No. 33 and No. 34, June 10.

The removal of the legation residence to Yedo is a gratifying circumstance, and it is hoped that the new building intended for the use of our minister there, which is now in course of preparation, may soon be completed.

The intelligence which you have communicated in your No. 32, relative to the Tycoon's imposing demonstration for the suppression of the rebellion of Prince Choshu, is very interesting, and it is sincerely hoped that the movement will speedily result in a satisfactory solution of the difficulties which now beset the empire. * * * * * * * *

I am, sir, your obedient servant,

WILLIAM H. SEWARD.

A. L. C. PORTMAN, Esq., *&c., &c., Yedo.*

Mr. Seward to Mr. Portman.

No. 2.] DEPARTMENT OF STATE, *Washington, September* 4, 1865.

SIR: A communication has been received from Mr. Pruyn, dated at London, July 31, transmitting the convention of January 28, 1864, for the reduction of import duties, concluded by him with the Japanese government, and also the convention entered into by and between his Majesty the Tycoon and the governments of the United States, Great Britain, France, and Holland, providing for the payment to said governments of the sum of three millions of dollars for indemnities and expenses. The latter instrument is accompanied by a memorandum executed by the ministers of said treaty powers, explanatory thereof and embracing returns of the forces employed in the recent operations in Japan.

These two conventions will, at the commencement of the next session of Congress, be submitted to the Senate for its consideration with a view to ratification.

I am, sir, your obedient servant,

WILLIAM H. SEWARD.

A. L. C. PORTMAN, Esq., *&c., &c., Yedo.*

Mr. Seward to Mr. Portman.

No. 3.] DEPARTMENT OF STATE, *Washington, September* 3, 1865.

SIR: Your despatch of the 5th of July has been received and submitted to the President of the United States. He is profoundly affected by the expressions of sympathy and condolence in the recent afflictions of our country which the Gorogio of Japan have authorized you to communicate to this government. We humbly trust that the dangers with which we have been threatened have been averted by an all-merciful Providence. But we are not, therefore, by any means less grateful to friendly powers for the good wishes they have expressed in our behalf. You are authorized to renew to the Gorogio the assurance of the friendship of the United States for the Emperor and people of Japan.

I am, sir, your obedient servant,

WILLIAM H. SEWARD.

A. L. C. PORTMAN, Esq., *&c., &c., Yedo.*

Mr. Portman to Mr. Seward.

[Extract.]

No. 50.] LEGATION OF THE UNITED STATES IN JAPAN,
Yedo, September 5, 1865.

SIR: I have the honor to transmit herewith a copy of a memorandum, signed yesterday, acknowledging the receipt from the government of the Tycoon of the sum of five hundred thousand (500,000) dollars, as the first instalment of the indemnity payable under the convention of the 22d October, 1864.

As stated in my despatch No. 48, of the 22d ultimo, this amount has been placed, in equal sums of two hundred and fifty thousand (250,000) dollars each, in the chartered Oriental and chartered Mercantile Banks, both at Yokohama, subject to the conjoint order of the four powers represented in the aforesaid convention. * * * * * * * *

I have the honor to be, sir, very respectfully, your most obedient servant,

A. L. C. PORTMAN,
Chargé d'Affaires ad interim in Japan.

Hon. WILLIAM H. SEWARD,
Secretary of State, Washington.

Memorandum.

AT YOKOHAMA, *September* 4, 1865.

The undersigned, representatives of Great Britain, France, the United States, and the Netherlands, hereby acknowledge to have received from the government of the Tycoon the sum of five hundred thousand dollars as the first instalment of the indemnity payable to the aforesaid four powers, under the convention of the 22d of October, 1864.

The government of the Tycoon having applied in April last to the aforesaid representatives for an extension of time in respect to the payment of the second instalment of the said indemnity, the aforesaid representatives have submitted that application to the consideration of their respective governments, and now await instructions on the point. The payment of the instalment is entirely independent of that application; but to prevent the possibility of misunderstanding it is hereby distinctly declared that the receipt of the aforesaid sum of five hundred thousand dollars does in no degree affect the right of the aforesaid four powers to require, if they see fit to do so, from the government of the Tycoon the punctual payment of the whole indemnity in quarterly instalments in the manner stipulated in the aforesaid convention.

HARRY S. PARKES,
H. B. M.'s Envoy Extraordinary and Minister Plenipotentiary in Japan.
LEON ROCHES,
Ministre Plenipotentiaire de sa Majestie France au Japan.
A. L. C. PORTMAN,
Chargé d'Affaires ad interim of the United States in Japan.
D. DE GRAEFF VAN POLSBROEK,
H. N. M.'s Political Agent and Consul General in Japan.

Mr. Portman to Mr. Seward.

No. 52.] LEGATION OF THE UNITED STATES IN JAPAN,
Yedo, September 13, 1865.

SIR: I have the honor to transmit herewith a copy of a correspondence on the subject of alleged interference in the purchase by American merchants of silk-worm eggs and cocoons at Kanagawa, and to inform you that all restrictions have been removed.

Enclosure No. 1, Mr. Fisher to Mr. Portman, August 14.
Enclosure No. 2, Mr. Portman to the Gorogio, August 15.
Enclosure No. 3, Mr. Fisher to Mr. Portman, September 4.
Enclosure No. 4, the Gorogio to Mr. Portman, September 7.
Enclosure No. 5, Mr. Portman to Mr. Fisher, September 7.
Enclosure No. 6, Mr. Portman to Mr. Fisher, September 9.
Enclosure No. 7, Mr. Fisher to Mr. Portman, September 11.

For several years the silk crops of France, Italy, and other silk-raising countries decreased, owing to a more or less alarming disease among the silk-worms. Renewal of the species thus became of the greatest importance; seed from China and Bengal failed, but the Japanese ova succeeded beyond expectation; and until such seed shall become acclimated in those countries they will be chiefly dependent upon Japan for a yearly supply of the same.

It would appear that the interference only complained of at Kanagawa, and not at the other open ports, was caused by the unauthorized action of the local authorities. Three American firms are alleged to have sustained losses in consequence of this interference, and their complaints are now being examined by Mr. Consul Fisher, in conjunction with the present governor of Kanagawa, whose predecessor was removed.

Should they have undoubted claims, I trust they will be of easy settlement at that port. I beg to assure you, however, that in no case shall I make any demands upon the Japanese government unless expressly authorized to do so.

I have the honor to be, sir, very respectfully, your most obedient servant,

A. L. C. PORTMAN,
Chargé d'Affaires ad interim in Japan.

Hon. WILLIAM H. SEWARD,
Secretary of State.

No. 1.

Mr. Fisher to Mr. Portman.

CONSULATE OF THE UNITED STATES OF AMERICA,
Kanagawa, Japan, August 14, 1865.

SIR: Serious complaints are made to me by the American houses of Messrs. Allmand & Co., and Messrs. Walsh, Hall & Co., of direct and indirect interferences in their trade, and thereby of positive daily violations made by the Japanese of article three of the treaty made with the United States, July 29, 1858, in regard to their freely buying silk-worm eggs and cocoons from the Japanese merchants who have them to sell, by the Japanese custom-house officials of this port, in that they only suffer certain named Japanese merchants to sell these important staples by their payment of a certain bonus or *leignorase* to other specially-licensed merchants of this port.

It is said this way of doing business has been ordered by the Gorogio, or government at Yedo, and I will be greatly obliged to you for the earliest possible denial of such interference, and for such information as you may be able to procure as to what, if any, instructions have been given to the custom-house officials of this port in regard to Japanese merchants selling silk-worm eggs and cocoons freely, and whether the government deliberately and openly intends its subjects, officials, or otherwise, to violate and set at naught our treaty-rights, and thus embarrass and restrict the lawful rights of our merchants, trade, and commerce at this port.

Your early attention and answer will greatly oblige our mercantile interests here, and enable me to communicate with them more intelligibly what steps are best to be taken in view of the damages they are now daily suffering in consequence of this official interference so justly complained of.

I have the honor to be, sir, very respectfully, your obedient servant,

GEORGE S. FISHER,
United States Consul.

A. L. C. PORTMAN, Esq.,
Chargé d'Affaires ad interim, Yedo.

No. 2.

Mr. Portman to the Gorogio.

LEGATION OF THE UNITED STATES IN JAPAN,
Yedo, August 15, 1865.

I have the honor to inform your excellency that I received this day a letter from the American consul at Kanagawa, containing serious complaints of interference in the purchase of silk-worm eggs and cocoons by American merchants at that place, in daily violation of article 3 of the treaty, and to request you to desire the governor of Kanagawa, with such officers who are well acquainted with the matter, to visit me at the earliest moment, for the purpose of examining those complaints in view of their prompt removal.

With respect and esteem,

A. L. C. PORTMAN,
Chargé d'Affaires ad interim of the United States in Japan.

His Excellency MIDLUNO IDLUMI NO KAMI,
Minister for Foreign Affairs, &c., &c., &c., Yedo.

No. 3.

Mr. Fisher to Mr. Portman.

CONSULATE OF THE UNITED STATES OF AMERICA,
Kanawaga, Japan, September 4, 1865.

SIR: As the season is rapidly advancing, and will soon draw to a close for the business of silk-worm eggs for this year, you will excuse me for recalling your attention to my No. 250, (enclosure No. 1,) of the 14th ultimo, in relation to the interference of custom-house officials in the purchase and sale of silk-worm eggs at this port, and request, if possible, that you will give me information in the course of this week as to what information you have obtained in relation thereto from the government at Yedo, that I may, without further delay, conclude what steps had best be taken in regard to the interests of American merchants and traders in that relation.

I have further to advise you that the American house of Messrs. Schultze, Reis & Co., of this port, have made the same complaint to me in regard to interferences and necessity for custom-house permits as Messrs. Walsh, Hall & Co. and Messrs. Allmand & Co.

I have the honor to be, sir, very respectfully, your obedient servant,

GEORGE S. FISHER,
United States Consul.

A. L. C. PORTMAN,
Chargé d'Affaires ad interim in Japan.

No. 4.

The Gorogio to Mr. Portman.

As it has been represented that foreigners meet with inconvenience in purchasing silk-worm eggs from our merchants, I have again instructed the governor of Kanagawa to allow this article to be as freely sold as any other article of commerce.

Stated for your information, in reply, with respect and esteem.

The 16th day of the 7th month of the year of Ke-U, (7th September, 1865.)

MIDLUNO IDLUMI NO KAMI.

A. L. C. PORTMAN, Esq.,
Chargé d'Affaires of the United States of America, &c., &c., &c.

No. 5.

Mr. Portman to Mr. Fisher.

LEGATION OF THE UNITED STATES IN JAPAN,
Yedo, September 7, 1865.

SIR: On the receipt of your letter No. 250, (enclosure No. 1,) of the 14th ultimo, I at once addressed the Gorogio on the subject, and, after several interviews with governors for foreign affairs, I was informed in reply that instructions had again been issued to the governor of Kanagawa to the effect that the trade in silk-worm eggs and cocoons should be as free as the trade in any other article.

Presuming that all cause of complaint for the future has thus been removed, it remains to ascertain the losses sustained by our merchants from this alleged interference in the purchase of silk-worm eggs, and I now have the honor to request you to transmit to me all such *bona fide* claims, in order that they may be presented to this government for examination without delay.

I have the honor to be, sir, very respectfully, your obedient servant,

A. L. C. PORTMAN,
Chargé d'Affaires ad interim in Japan.

GEORGE S. FISHER, Esq.,
United States Consul, Kanagawa.

No. 6.

Mr. Portman to Mr. Fisher.

LEGATION OF THE UNITED STATES IN JAPAN,
Yedo, September 9, 1865.

SIR: In amendment of the desire expressed in my letter to you, No. 90, (enclosure No. 5,) of the 7th instant, I now have the honor to request you to present the complaints of the American merchants for interference in the purchase by them of silk-worm eggs for examination to the present governor of Kanagawa, who, in conjunction with a governor for foreign affairs, if necessary, has been authorized to examine the same. In compliance with the suggestion made, it has been deemed necessary that an investigation of the said complaints at your port, where witnesses, if required, may be examined, would lead more promptly to the result desired.

I have the honor to be, sir, very respectfully, your most obedient servant,

A. L. C. PORTMAN,
Chargé d'Affaires ad interim in Japan.

No. 7.

Mr. Fisher to Mr. Portman.

CONSULATE OF THE UNITED STATES OF AMERICA,
Kanagawa, Japan, September 11, 1865.

SIR: Your communications Nos. 90 and 92, of the 7th and 9th instant, have been received, and will have my attention with the governor of Kanagawa, &c., as suggested, and I concur in opinion that this is the better plan than to refer these claims to Yedo in the first instance.

I have the honor to be, sir, very respectfully, your obedient servant,

GEORGE S. FISHER,
United States Consul.

A. L. C. PORTMAN, Esq.,
Chargé d'Affaires ad interim, Yedo.

Mr. Portman to Mr. Seward.

No. 54.]

LEGATION OF THE UNITED STATES IN JAPAN,
Yedo, September 22, 1865.

SIR: I have the honor to transmit herewith, No. 1, copy of a letter received from the Gorogio, in reply to representations made, informing me of the abolition of the regulations concerning the trade in irico, awabi, and sharks' fins, important articles of commerce, principally at Nagasaki, for the China markets.

I enclose, No. 2, copy of a letter addressed by me to Mr. Mangum, at Nagasaki; similar letters on the subject were addressed to the consul at Kanagawa and commercial agent at Hakodadi.

I can claim no credit for this important concession, which, like the removal of the restrictions on the purchase of silk-worm eggs and cocoons, the subject-matter of my despatch No. 52, of the 13th instant, is the result of prompt and united action under the perfect accord existing among the foreign representatives in this country.

I have the honor to be, sir, very respectfully, your obedient servant,

A. L. C. PORTMAN,
Chargé d'Affaires ad interim in Japan.

Hon. WILLIAM H. SEWARD, *Secretary of State.*

No. 1.

The Gorogio to Mr. Portman.

I have the honor to inform you that I have instructed the governors at the three opened ports to notify the consuls of the treaty powers at those places, respectively, that it has been decided to abolish the hitherto existing regulations concerning the trade in irico, dried awabi, and sharks' fins, and that from the 20th day of our ninth month (the 8th November next) the trade in those articles shall hereafter be as free as that in any other article of commerce.

The governors at the opened ports may possibly find it convenient to give effect to this decision at an earlier day, in which case the consuls of the treaty powers will be duly notified by them.

I have to request you to make the foregoing known to the consuls of the United States in this country.

With respect and esteem, the 2d day of the eighth month of the first year of Ke-U, (21st September, 1865.)

MIDLUNO IDLUMI NO KAMI.

A. L. C. PORTMAN, Esq.,
Chargé d'Affaires of the United States in Japan, &c., &c.

No. 2.

Mr. Portman to Mr. Mangum.

LEGATION OF THE UNITED STATES IN JAPAN,
Yedo, September 21, 1865.

SIR: I have the honor to inform you that this day I received a letter from the Gorogio, to the effect that the governors at the opened ports have been instructed to abolish the hitherto existing regulations complained of as restricting the trade in irico, awabi, and sharks' fins, and that from the 20th day of the 9th month (the 9th November of this year) the said articles may be as freely purchased as any other article of commerce.

The date as above mentioned has been fixed with a view of inaugurating this improvement at the opened ports on the same day, according to precedent, though it is optional with the governor at each port to allow it to take effect at an earlier day; and on causing inquiry to be made at the custom-house at your port, I trust you will find that the governor has availed himself of the privilege granted him, and that all the regulations of a restrictive character above referred to have been already abolished from the date of the receipt of his instructions.

Permit me to request you to make the foregoing known to all American merchants within your jurisdiction.

I have the honor to be, sir, very respectfully, your obedient servant,

A. L. C. PORTMAN,
Chargé d'Affaires ad interim in Japan.

W. P. MANGUM,
United States Consul, Nagasaki.

Mr. Portman to Mr. Seward.

No. 61.] LEGATION OF THE UNITED STATES IN JAPAN,
Yedo, October 20, 1865.

SIR: The Tycoon and his Daimios are still absent from this capital; troops are still going forward to Osacca, where the headquarters are established, and nearly all the available naval forces of this government are at anchor off Hiogo. Two armed Japanese vessels are constantly watching the Nagato coast, and occasionally other vessels are despatched on a cruise in the inland sea, for the purpose of preventing the landing of arms and munitions in Chôshu and the re-armament of the Simonoseki batteries.

The internal policy of this government is, as formerly, wrapped in almost impenetrable mystery, and, as usual, rumors are plentiful. It is with the greatest caution, therefore, that I approach the subject, experience having taught that rumors should not always be utterly disregarded, as they often form a clue to what is actually transpiring in this country.

Informal communications, from educated persons not in the employ of this government, in connexion with official statements I have been fortunate enough to elicit, lead me to interpret the present state of affairs in this country as in a fair way toward an early solution, in a form acceptable to our interests, of the hitherto existing internal complications.

It appears to be beyond doubt that the Mikado and Tycoon cordially agree upon all matters of internal as well as foreign policy. The Tycoon unquestionably commands the situation. With the two prominent members of the Gorogio who accompany him I am well acquainted, and I therefore feel quite confident that as vigorous a policy will be pursued by this government as circumstances will render advisable.

The Prince of Choshu still persists in his rebellion.

In most of the provinces of this empire there are, besides the Daimios of the province, so called because he either is the lineal descendant of the founder of the princely dynasty, or his legal representative by birth, other personages, also, more or less directly tracing their origin to the founder of such dynasty, many of whom, being Daimios, or members of the high nobility in their own right, often rank with Daimios of the first class, particularly if their wealth enables them to keep a princely state and retinue.

There are known to be Daimios nearly ranking with first-class noblemen in the provinces of Lewo and Nagato, and it is supposed that the pressure now being brought to bear upon them by the united influences of the Mikado and Tycoon will lead to their abandoning the cause of action which the Prince of Choshu, the senior Daimio of those provinces, apparently compelled them to adopt; and it is expected that, as soon as he shall find himself sufficiently isolated, the submission of this rebellious prince may be obtained without further resort to coercive measures.

It is as yet uncertain when the Tycoon and Daimios may be expected to resume their residence in this capital; this is not likely to take place for some time.

I have the honor to be, sir, very respectfully, your most obedient servant,

A. L. C. PORTMAN,
Chargé d'Affaires ad interim in Japan.

Hon. WILLIAM H. SEWARD,
Secretary of State.

Mr. Portman to Mr. Seward.

No. 63.] LEGATION OF THE UNITED STATES IN JAPAN,
October 30, 1865.

SIR: I have the honor to inform you that the accomplice to the murder of the two British officers, which took place in November of last year, has at last been apprehended. He confessed his crime, and was beheaded this day on the public execution ground, near Yokohama, in the presence of the British consul and other officers.

As in the case of Simidzu Seigi, the principal murderer, who was executed in December of last year, placards proclaiming his crime and sentence have been conspicuously posted at various places within the treaty limits of Kanagawa. This government, vigorously urged thereto by the foreign authorities, have evidently been untiring in their efforts to apprehend this criminal, and it is satisfactory to reflect that their admission of the atrocity of such assassins has again received a practical illustration.

I have the honor to be, sir, very respectfully, your most obedient servant,

A. L. C. PORTMAN,
Chargé d'Affaires ad interim in Japan.

Hon. WILLIAM H. SEWARD,
Secretary of State, Washington.

Mr. Portman to Mr. Seward.

No. 64] LEGATION OF THE UNITED STATES IN JAPAN,
Kanagawa, October 30, 1865.

SIR: I have the honor to transmit herewith, No. 1, copy of a memorandum, signed this day, setting forth the course of action unanimously adopted, in accordance with instructions received from their respective governments, by the representatives of Great Britain, France, and the Netherlands.

Similar instructions have, no doubt, been sent to this legation. I would have preferred to await their arrival, but I knew that a golden opportunity to place our political and commercial relations with this country on an improved basis had presented itself, and felt no hesitation, therefore, in cordially uniting with above-mentioned representatives in carrying out the instructions that had been received.

This action is unquestionably in continuation of the policy that was inaugurated with the successful expedition to Simonoseki, of which the President was pleased to approve, and which has been productive of so much benefit. It was, moreover, in harmony with Mr. Pruyn's views, as expressed in his several despatches with reference to the Simonoseki indemnity, and it was, also, well understood, though not frankly admitted, that the temporary transfer of the foreign legations to Osacca, at this juncture, could not but be highly acceptable to the Tycoon and his government, and, in all probability, would be the means of averting civil war, into which the hitherto existing civil commotion appeared likely to culminate at an early day.

The Tycoon, and four of the five members of which the Gorogio is composed, are now at Osacca.

I greatly regret that, on an occasion like the present, there is no national vessel in Japan. Very acceptable arrangements, however, have been made, by the vice-admiral commanding her Britannic Majesty's naval forces on this station for my accommodation on board her Britannic Majesty's frigate Pelorus, the largest ship in his squadron next to the Princess Royal line-of-battle ship, in which the British minister and staff have taken passage.

The French minister will take passage in the frigate Guerriere, and the Netherlands consul general and political agent in the Dutch sloop Tontinan, and at 10 o'clock to-morrow morning the squadron will sail for Hiogo and Osacca.

The mail closes this afternoon, and only a few hours are left me to complete all my preparations for this trip; I trust, therefore, that you will excuse me from sending a translation of accompanying memorandum by this mail.

I also transmit, No. 2, copy of my letter to the Gorogio, and No. 3, copy of my letter to the consular officers in this country, announcing the temporary transfer of the legation to Osacca.

I have the honor to be, sir, very respectfully, your most obedient servant,

A. L. C. PORTMAN,
Chargé d'Affaires ad interim in Japan.

Hon. WILLIAM H. SEWARD,
Secretary of State, Washington.

No. 1.

[Translation.—Memorandum.]

In virtue of the convention signed 22d October, 1864, the Japanese government engaged to pay to the governments of the United States of America, England, France, and the Netherlands, a sum of three millions of dollars, as indemnity for the expenditures made necessary by the expedition.

The representatives of the four powers above named, desirous of testifying to the Japanese government the disinterested views of their sovereigns, and of their sole desire to improve their relations with Japan, left to his Majesty the Tycoon the privilege of settling the payment of this indemnity by opening a new port to foreign commerce, required by the representatives of the said powers to declare whether he would or not avail himself of this privilege. The government of Japan declared about six months ago that it preferred to pay the indemnity, seeing that the state of the country caused it to regard the opening of a new port as impolitic; but at the same time requested the delay of a year to provide for the second instalment of the indemnity.

The representatives of the four powers, while acknowledging the right of the Japanese government to choose between the two conditions, did not consider themselves empowered to grant the postponement asked for, and had to refer to their respective governments. The instructions which they asked for on this subject have reached the undersigned representatives of France, England, and the Netherlands.

The right of the Tycoon to choose between the payment of the indemnity in the terms settled by the convention of the 22d October and the opening of a port on the Inland Sea, is naturally admitted by each of the said powers, but they differ in opinion on the subject of the postponement asked for by the Japanese government.

The cabinets of St. James and the Hague require either the strict execution of the articles of the convention of the 22d October in this respect, or, instead, consent to this postponement, and even to the abandonment of two-thirds of the indemnity on the three conditions following:

First, that the Japanese government open the port of Hiogo and the city of Osacca on the 1st January, 1866; second, that the Mikado ratify the treaties concluded with the foreign powers; third, and last, that the tariff of duties of import be fixed for the greater part of merchandise at five per cent., and can in no case exceed 10 per cent. The cabinet of Paris, on the contrary, would not see any obstacle to according the postponement to the Japanese government, if the latter should act in good faith in respect to the powers, signers of the treaties, and would perceive a danger in imposing on it the opening of Osacca before the epoch fixed by the additional convention of 1862. The cabinet of Paris declares, besides, formally, what is also admitted by the cabinets of St. James and the Hague, that the Tycoon being free to choose between the payment of the indemnity and the opening of a port, we would not have the right, if the prince execute one of these conditions, to exact the opening, by anticipation, of Hiogo and Osacca. The minister of the Emperor adds in recapitulation, in the despatch which his excellency addressed to the cabinets of London, of Washington, and of the Hague, under date of 22d July, 1865, that the imperial government is of opinion that the solution of this question may be devolved on the representatives of the four powers in Japan. In answer to this communication, Earl Cowley has informed Mr. Drouyn d'Lhuys that the government of her Britannic Majesty consented to this last proposition.

The representative of the United States of America has not received any instructions from his government; but the measures settled by the present memorandum being only the consequence of the policy which has been inaugurated between the four powers, signers of the treaties, Mr. Portman, chargé d'affaires ad interim, does not hesitate on this occasion to unite with his colleagues. Mr. De Graeff Van Polsbroek has received from his government identical instructions. In this state of things the undersigned, representatives of the United States of America, of England, of France, and of the Netherlands, have deemed it necessary to assemble for the purpose of a mutual understanding—First, on the means of reconciling the instructions of their respective governments, while preserving intact the union and community of purpose which have already given them such power; second, on the steps to be followed so as to make the best possible of the actual situation. After having examined the question in all its aspects; considering, on the one hand, that the proposition of the government of her Britannic Majesty to abandon a part of the indemnity in return, first, of the opening by anticipation of the port of Hiogo and of the city of Osacca; second, of the ratification of the treaty by the Mikado; and, third, of the revision of the tariff of duties, conforms with the spirit of the convention of the 22d October, 1864; considering, on the other hand, that the government of his Majesty the Emperor does not diverge from the propositions of the cabinet of St. James, except what there might be in them inopportune; considering the state of parties in Japan; considering that the conditions claimed by England and the Netherlands, if they were spontaneously granted by the government of Japan would no longer present the dangers which France apprehended, if such conditions should be imposed, and would be preferable for all interested in the payment of thier third of the indemnity, and that France would then have no objection to oppose to this new arrangement, which, is repeated, is in ful conformity with the spirit of the convention of the 22d of October; considering that the well-understood interests of the powers, signers of the treaties, and of Japan itself, require a prompt solution of questions depending, and that the abandonment of two-thirds of the indemnity might facilitate and hasten the ratification of the treaties by the Mikado, a ratification which is the best guarantee of the future good relations of the foreign powers with Japan, and that, moreover, the government of the Tycoon has engaged to obtain it from the Mikado; considering that the absence of the Tycoon and his principal ministers renders any negotiation at Yedo, if not impossible, at least illusory—that it is important, however, to affirm our right to obtain in due time the execution of an agreement and of a solemn convention, and to convince the Japanese government, as well as the Mikado and the Daimio, that the foreign powers have irrevocably determined to exact the opening of Hiogo and of Osacca at the time fixed by the treaties, if not obtained before in consequence of a mutual understanding—the representatives undersigned have agreed by common consent to transfer for the moment the seat of their negotiations to Osacca. This measure, which is in perfect conformity with the spirit of the treaties, because the said representatives are accredited to the Tycoon in person, will have, besides, in the eyes of the friends and enemies of the Tycoon, a signification which will singularly influence the happy issue of events which are in preparation.

In fact, the undersigned have been informed that the Tycoon, yielding to the instances of the Mikado and the Daimio who surrounded him, had consented to receive the Prince of Nagato as recipient in regard to conditions which this rebel Daimio had accepted some eight months before from Prince Owari, generalissimo of the Tycoon's army, but which, upon various pretexts, he had not complied with. But the Tycoon, distrusting, with reason, the real dispositions of his subject, fixed a period (the 13th of December) after which he would consider the favorable conditions which he was willing to have given the rebel Daimio as not having befallen, and would proceed at once to his chastisement.

The arrival at Osacca of the representatives of the powers, signers of the treaties, happening at this decisive moment, followed by a respectable naval force to treat amicably with the ministers of the Tycoon, will prevent, there is room to believe, the commencement of hostilities, which would, perhaps, be the signal for civil war, the consequences whereof, whatever they might be, could not but injure the political as well as the commercial interests of foreign powers in Japan; at all events, this arrival could not but give the Japanese government the moral support that would facilitate the results of its measures, to the effect of obtaining from the Mikado the ratification of the treaties.

In consequence the undersigned agreed immediately to address to the commanders of the naval forces of their respective countries, in order to have them understand the political situation, and to invite them to proceed to Osacca, where they would sojourn during the time necessary to lead to a good result the important negotiations which call them thither.

The undersigned take this determination, with the intimate conviction that it may lead to very fortunate results, and that in any event it is not of a nature to compromise the safe and conciliatory policy which their respective governments have ordered them to follow in respect to Japan.

Done at Yokohama, in quadruplicate, the 30th of October, 1865.

A. L. C. PORTMAN,
Chargé d'Affaires of the United States in Japan.
HARRY S. PARKES,
H. B. M.'s Envoy Extraordinary and Minister Plenipotentiary in Japan.
LEON ROCHES,
Minister Plenipotentiary of the Emperor of the French.
D. DE GRAEFF VAN POLSBROEK,
H. N. M.'s Political Agent and Consul General in Japan.

No. 2.

Mr. Portman to the Gorogio.

LEGATION OF THE UNITED STATES IN JAPAN,
October 30, 1865.

After conferring with my colleagues, the representatives of England, France, and the Netherlands, I have formed with them the unanimous opinion that the promptest mode to secure a solution, alike satisfactory to the Japanese government and to the treaty powers, of all that relates to the convention of the 22d of October, 1864, is to settle the important matter by negotiation with the ministers who are at present with the Tycoon.

I have, therefore, the honor to inform your excellency that I propose immediately to proceed to Osacca with my colleagues, the representatives above named.

The object, as above stated, is so eminently of a friendly character that it cannot fail to be productive of substantial benefit to the government and people of Japan.

With respect and esteem,

A. L. C. PORTMAN,
Chargé d'Affaires of the United States in Japan.

His Excellency MIDLUNO IDLUMI NO KAMI,
Minister for Foreign Affairs, &c., &c., &c., Yedo.

No. 3.

Mr. Portman to Mr. Fisher.

LEGATION OF THE UNITED STATES IN JAPAN,
October 30, 1865.

SIR: I have the honor to inform you that in concert with the representatives of Great Britain, France, and the Netherlands, I have determined upon temporarily transferring the legation to Osacca, at present the seat of the government of this country, with a view of bringing more promptly to a successful termination important negotiations that have been in progress for some time.

I am, sir, respectfully, your obedient servant,

A. L. C. PORTMAN,
Chargé d'Affaires ad interim in Japan.

GEORGE S. FISHER, Esq.,
United States Consul, Kanagawa.

Mr. Portman to Mr. Seward.

No. 65.] LEGATION OF THE UNITED STATES IN JAPAN,
Hiogo, November 18, 1865.

SIR: I have the honor to inform you that I arrived here on the 4th instant, and on that day addressed a letter to the Sorogio at Osacca announcing my arrival.

Since then two conferences have been held with the leading men of the Tycoon's government, minutes of which I herewith transmit, (enclosures Nos. 1 and 2.) I also transmit (No. 3) copy of the convention signed by Earl Russell and Japanese envoys in London on the 6th of June, 1862, as constituting, in connexion with the treaties, the groundwork for the negotiations now in progress. Having been made acquainted with the contents of your letter to Sir Frederick Bruce of the 15th of August, in which you announce your disposition in anticipation of the ratification by the Senate of the convention of the 22d October, 1864, to co-operate in the plans proposed by her Britannic Majesty's government, I feel assured that you will be pleased to approve of my action.

The information thus far elicited is of great importance, and in guidance in further negotiations I trust that it will be the means of leading to important results, which I shall, no doubt, be able to communicate *in extenso* at an early day.

I have the honor to be, sir, very respectfully, your most obedient servant,

A. L. C. PORTMAN,
Chargé d'Affaires ad interim in Japan.

Hon. WILLIAM H. SEWARD,
Secretary of State, Washington.

No. 1.

MEMORANDUM.

Minutes of a conference held on board her Majesty's ship Princess Royal, lying off Hiogo, on the 11th November, 1865, between the undersigned representatives of treaty powers and the undersigned members of the Tycoon's government.

Present: Sir Harry S. Parkes, K. C. B., her Britannic Majesty's envoy extraordinary and minister plenipotentiary; A. L. C. Portman, esq., chargé d'affaires *ad interim* of the United States; D. de Graeff van Polsbroek, esq., his Netherlandish Majesty's consul general and political agent; Vice-Admiral G. St. Vincent King, C. B., commander-in-chief; Abe Bungo No Kami, member of the Sorogio; Yamaguchi Suruga No Kami, ometske of the Tycoon; Inowuye Mondo No Sho, governor of Osacca.

The Japanese minister explained to the foreign representatives the circumstances that had prevented his meeting them on the 9th instant, as had been at first arranged.

An interview between the Mikado and Tycoon had been held on that day at Kioto, (Miaco,) and this necessitated his (the minister's) attendance in that city. He had left the following day and had travelled all night in order to be here this morning.

The British minister thanked Abe Bungo No Kami for his exertions, and explained the arrangements made for his reception, first by the representatives then present, and afterwards by the French minister, who was prevented by indisposition from leaving his vessel. As to the delay which had occurred at Kioto, it was hoped that this would in the end contribute to the despatch of business, and that it denoted that the foreign questions had been well considered at Kioto, and that the Mikado and Tycoon had arrived at a satisfactory understanding with each other on those points.

JAPANESE MINISTERS. The Tycoon's interview of the 9th was a very satisfactory one, and no effort is spared by him to effect a complete understanding with the Mikado on the subject of foreign relations. Unfortunately, this result cannot be immediately attained, in consequence of the evil influences which the Tycoon has to encounter.

FOREIGN REPRESENTATIVES. We hope, however, that the Tycoon has succeeded in obtaining that formal approval of the treaties which his ministers more than a year ago pledged themselves to the foreign representatives to procure. If this has been done, then, as observed in a letter of the 4th instant, our business may be greatly expedited.

JAPANESE MINISTERS. This official sanction of the Mikado is still withheld, in consequence of the intrigues with which the Tycoon has to contend. Choshu's affair is one of these.

FOREIGN REPRESENTATIVES. We regret to hear such a cause assigned, as it shows that the Tycoon's influence must be very limited if he cannot overcome such difficulties. As to Choshu, we have now reason to believe that he has become friendly to foreigners, and that the Tycoon no longer meets with opposition in that quarter to the execution of the treaties.

JAPANESE MINISTERS. It may be true that Choshu now appears to be friendly disposed toward foreigners; but he still retains his enmity to the Tycoon and seeks to complicate affairs at Kioto. The Tycoon's object has been to bring about an understanding with all parties by degrees, and thus gradually create a general opinion in favor of the treaties.

FOREIGN REPRESENTATIVES. We trust to hear from you that the Tycoon's efforts have been successful.

JAPANESE MINISTERS. Unfortunately, the result has not been entirely satisfactory. Considerable improvement has, however, been made, and the various parties in the country are beginning to understand that the treaties must be observed. It is very difficult, however, for a people like the Japanese to change an opinion they have so long held.

FOREIGN REPRESENTATIVES. We should feel obliged if you would describe definitely what difficulties are now experienced by the Tycoon's government in the execution of the treaties.

JAPANESE MINISTERS. The Japanese people, who do not understand the foreign question, are very slow indeed in comprehending the situation. When the Tycoon proposes amicable relations with foreigners, persons step in to make difficulties, and persuade the Mikado that Japan ought to have no foreign relations whatever. The Tycoon has great difficulty in controlling these people.

FOREIGN REPRESENTATIVES. Be so good as to give us the names of those obstructive parties.

JAPANESE MINISTER. I am unable to give you names, or to do more than refer in these general terms to the existence of unfavorable influences. There are people, however, who secretly complicate affairs and oppose foreign intercourse. Choshu is one of these.

FOREIGN REPRESENTATIVES. Choshu's hostility is an affair of the past, and the foreign governments cannot take into account those secret and indescribable hostile influences to which you so vaguely refer. If these exist, it is the duty of the ruling powers of the country to see that they are promptly suppressed. The governments of the treaty powers are at all events determined to insist upon the faithful execution of their treaties, and if the Tycoon wishes to be regarded as the governing power in Japan, he must be able to enforce their observance. The information we receive as to the feeling of the Daimios and influential people towards the treaties is of a very different kind to that supplied by the Tycoon's government. We find professions of friendship where the latter would lead us to expect direct hostility.

JAPANESE MINISTER. The Tycoon is exerting himself, and with success, to suppress all hostile action. Were the sanction of the Mikado to the treaties once obtained, everything would go on smoothly.

NETHERLANDS CONSUL GENERAL. I was at Simonoseki this year, and received earnest assurances from Choshu's officers that he is not unfriendly to the treaties. On the contrary, I was told that he was anxious to open Simonoseki to foreign trade. I was further told that the real reason of the breach between the Tycoon and Choshu was the convention he made with the admirals last year—in a word, Choshu alleges that he is attacked by the Tycoon, not on account of his previous hostility to foreigners, but because he has lately shown himself to be well disposed towards them.

JAPANESE MINISTER. Choshu's disloyalty to the Mikado has not yet been atoned for. He attacked the Mikado and is still his enemy. Choshu's friendly professions to foreigners are made solely with a view to his own interest.

NETHERLANDS CONSUL GENERAL. When Choshu fired on foreign vessels he did so in accordance with orders from the Tycoon, copies of which he furnished to the admirals. In these orders the Tycoon declared that foreign relations were to cease, and that foreigners were to be expelled from the country.

FOREIGN REPRESENTATIVES. We must now enter on the particular business that is before us. The Japanese minister is doubtless familiar with the convention of 1864, and also with the agreement made by the Japanese envoys with Earl Russell, in London, in 1862. By that agreement her Britannic Majesty's government consented that Hiogo and other places should remain closed for five years, on certain conditions which the Japanese minister must be aware have not been fulfilled. Therefore, in the terms of that agreement, her Britannic Majesty's government can insist upon the opening of Hiogo at once if they see fit to do so. According to the convention of 1864, the Tycoon bound himself to pay an indemnity of $3,000,000 or to open a port. The Tycoon, after considering the subject for nearly six months, decided upon paying the indemnity; but at the time that he informed the representatives of his choice, he applied for a considerable postponement of the date fixed for payment. This application has been communicated by the representatives to their respective governments, and instructions have now been received. They are to the effect that the governments of the four powers are not satisfied with these repeated delays and evasions on the part of the Tycoon's government, and they are determined upon requiring the punctual payment of the indemnity if the Tycoon should still prefer this condition to the alternative which we now have to propose. These are based on the desire of our governments to furnish another proof of their friendliness to the Tycoon, by convincing him that it has never been their wish to exact money from his government, but to improve our relations with Japan. These relations can be better promoted by the extension of commerce than by the payment of indemnities. Our governments are, therefore, willing to remit to the Tycoon two-thirds of the money stipulated in the convention of October 22, 1864, in return for the immediate opening of Hiogo and Osacca to trade, the formal consent of the Mikado to the treaties; and the regularization of the tariff on a basis of five per cent. In virtue of the London convention of 1862, the opening of Hiogo and Osacca might be demanded at any moment, and a revision of the tariff can be claimed under the treaty itself. A formal announcement by the Mikado of his approval of the treaties is, therefore, the only additional measure that is now asked, and this is simply a mark of friendship, which ought to be granted without hesitation, and which the Japanese ministers promised to obtain upwards of a year ago. We greatly regret to hear that this has not been obtained, and are naturally led to inquire why. We are justified in supposing that it is not withheld at the instigation of a strong hostile party, because we have received friendly assurances from some of the reputed leaders of that party, and also because the minister himself is unable to name a single Daimio or person of influence who takes a part against foreigners. At the same time it would not be surprising to find that foreign intercourse was regarded in a distasteful light by Mikado and Daimios, if it be true that the Tycoon, as is alleged, involves them in its burdens, and yet deprives them of participation in its advantages. It is possible that the disunion which is reported to exist between the Mikado and Tycoon, and between the Tycoon and certain of the Daimios, may be occasioned by disputes among themselves, in which foreigners have no concern. Such causes, however, cannot be allowed by the foreign governments to interfere with the exercise of the treaty privileges. In the proposed arrangements, which we have now met to discuss, an opportunity is offered to the Tycoon of proving whether he is really well disposed towards those governments with whom he has made treaties, and is willing to improve and extend his relations with them.

JAPANESE MINISTER. I am aware that the opening of Hiogo and Osacca was postponed on certain conditions. The Tycoon's government greatly regret that they have not been able to keep those conditions, but this result is not attributable to unfriendly feelings on their part towards the foreign governments, but to the obstacles they encounter among their own people.

FOREIGN REPRESENTATIVES. We should be glad if you would describe these obstacles.

JAPANESE MINISTERS. The Daimios were at one time hostile. They have ceased to be so now, in so far that they no longer wish to engage in open conflict with the foreigners; but their opinions are still divided on the subject of foreign trade, and they would be glad to see it stopped. I cannot give you, as you request, the names of any of the Daimios; indeed, the opinions I refer to are those rather of sections of the population than of individual Daimios.

FOREIGN REPRESENTATIVES. We are glad to gather from your remarks some confirmation of the statements we have heard elsewhere, that the Daimios are adopting more intelligent views respecting foreign relations, and are laying aside their old unreasonable hostility. This state of things should materially facilitate the adoption of a liberal policy by the Tycoon's government.

JAPANESE MINISTERS. But if Hiogo and Osacca were opened at this moment, the old feeling would return and the people's minds would be much disturbed.

FOREIGN REPRESENTATIVES. In our opinion, such an assertion cannot be maintained. We have never found the people unfriendly, and if the Daimios have ceased to be actively hostile, as the Japanese minister himself states is the case, we cannot see why the opening of the ports named in the third article of the treaty should be longer deferred. The foreign governments will not be content to go on waiting if they think that the delay is occasioned by faulty administration on the part of the Tycoon.

JAPANESE MINISTER. Affairs are by no means in a settled condition. The Mikado's approval of the treaties is still withheld, and must be obtained before any new ports can be opened. The Tycoon must proceed very gradually in this matter. If, in order to show his friendship to the foreign powers, he were suddenly to open new ports and cause fresh troubles to break out, neither foreign nor native interests would be benefited. I hope that the representatives will understand that the Tycoon's government has great difficulty to contend with.

FOREIGN REPRESENTATIVES. You keep us so entirely in the dark as to the nature of these alleged difficulties that it is not possible for us to understand them. On the other hand, the information that reaches us from other quarters is of such an opposite character that we may be excused from doubting whether these difficulties have any real existence. These indefinite statements have been so often repeated by the Tycoon's government during the last six years that we can no longer place any reliance on them. It is clear that the Tycoon's government either occasions these difficulties themselves or are powerless to prevent them. Do you wish us to understand that the Tycoon's government positively prefer punctual payment of the indemnity to accepting the alternative conditions now proposed?

JAPANESE MINISTERS. We are quite prepared to pay the indemnity in punctual quarterly instalments, as stipulated in the convention. We would rather pay this money, and even a much larger sum, than open new ports. This cannot be done while the present troubles continue, while Choshu remains unpunished, or until various improvements in our government are effected, such as the construction of a navy, better batteries, &c. We wish also to change the present wrong system in regard to the trade of the Daimios. At present a Daimio can only trade at the open ports through the custom-house officers, and not by means of his own agents. We are considering how an improved system can be introduced.

FOREIGN REPRESENTATIVES. The restrictions placed on the trade of the Daimios is one of the breaches of the treaty on the part of the Tycoon's government of which we complain. The treaty powers consider that the fulfilment of these treaties is the first duty on the part of the Tycoon's government, and should take precedence of the erection of batteries, &c., which are not needed to protect the country against a foreign enemy. When does the Tycoon's government propose to open Hiogo and Osacca?

JAPANESE MINISTER. Not before Choshu has been punished. We are aware that we are bound to open these and other ports in the beginning of 1868, and we trust to be able to do so about or possibly before that time.

FOREIGN REPRESENTATIVES. The foreign governments conceded the postponement of the opening of Hiogo and other ports on certain conditions. As these conditions have not been kept, the foreign governments have a perfect right to insist upon the opening of these ports when they think proper. (Paragraph in London convention referring to this point then read.) The Japanese minister will therefore understand that the period of the opening of these ports does not rest entirely with the Tycoon, and that it is quite within the competence of the foreign powers to withdraw the concessions made in 1862 whenever they see fit to do so.

JAPANESE MINISTERS. We regret that we have not kept all the conditions of the London agreement of 1862, but we trust that the foreign governments will indulgently consider the difficulties of our position.

FOREIGN REPRESENTATIVES. We cannot hold out the hope that the indulgence of the foreign governments in respect to Hiogo will be much longer continued. How can the foreign governments take into consideration the alleged difficulties of the Tycoon so long as it is impossible to understand in what these consist, and the Tycoon's ministers withhold all explanation respecting them? The reticence of the Tycoon's ministers is an old subject of complaint. Again, the foreign governments must be satisfied that their indulgence is not abused by the Tycoon's government. What good reason can the latter give for not having removed those restrictions on trade and intercourse which they are bound to do by the London agreement? The very first condition, the revocation of the old law outlawing foreigners, has not yet been complied with.

A discussion here arose among the Japanese as to the correct translation into their language of that passage in the London convention of 1862 which relates to the last-named subject. After advancing several contradictory statements, the Japanese minister finally declared that the law in question had been repealed twenty or thirty years ago, and that the revocation had again been repeated at a later date, which he could not remember. He would satisfy himself on that point, and inform the foreign representatives.

FOREIGN REPRESENTATIVES. The revocation of this old law is only one of the various conditions of the London agreement. Most of the restrictions on trade which should have been abolished both by the agreement and by treaty still exist, and I must repeat that on this ground alone the foreign governments can at any time claim the opening of Hiogo and Osacca irrespective of the payment of the indemnity of the convention of 1864.

NETHERLANDS CONSUL GENERAL. And I must distinctly remind the Japanese minister that the Netherlands government can demand the opening of Hiogo at any moment, as, although they gave their consent to the postponement agreed to by her Britannic Majesty's government, that concession was never formally communicated to the ministers of the Tycoon.

FOREIGN REPRESENTATIVES. We are anxious that the Japanese minister should carefully consider the proposals that have been made to him. If they are rejected by the Tycoon's government, and the speedy opening of Hiogo and Osacca refused, we shall have to represent to our respective governments our belief as to whether the Tycoon's government have good reasons for this refusal. Our governments will then consider whether they will insist upon their right to demand the opening of this and other ports on the ground of the non-fulfilment of the conditions of the London agreement of 1862. If, therefore, the Japanese ministers delay the opening of these ports, they may find themselves called upon to yield the point without being able to secure the advantage now offered them of a remission of two-thirds of the indemnity. The foreign governments can demand both the opening of Hiogo and Osacca and the payment of the indemnity, and yet are willing at the present time to forego the latter if the Tycoon's government will give a proof of friendliness and of their wish to encourage trade by voluntarily opening the ports themselves. The Japanese ministers should, therefore, clearly see that their advantage lies in giving favorable consideration to the proposals now made to them. We cannot perceive that the opening of Hiogo and Osacca, under present circumstances, can be either difficult or injurious to the Tycoon. On the contrary, by conceding this point promptly, he will strengthen the friendship of the foreign powers, may secure the remission of $2,000,000, and may avoid finding himself in the position of having to open the port unconditionally, upon the demand which the foreign governments, under the agreement of London, are entitled at any time to make. The foreign governments wish to support that of the Tycoon, but they expect to find their friendship and consideration reciprocated. They have reason to believe that this would be done by those Daimios who have expressed themselves anxious to cultivate relations; and the ministers of the Tycoon should bear in mind that there is nothing in the treaties which forbid intercourse with these Daimios at their own ports.

JAPANESE MINISTER. These arguments place the subject in a new light, and I shall be glad to give them my best consideration. To enable me to do this, I should wish to adjourn this conference until to-morrow at 10 o'clock.

The conference then terminated.

No. 2.

MEMORANDUM.

Minutes of a conference held on board her Britannic Majesty's ship Princess Royal, lying off Hiojo, on the 14th November, 1865, between the undersigned representatives of treaty powers and the undermentioned members of the Tycoon's government.

Present: Sir Harry S. Parkes, K. C. B., her Britannic Majesty's envoy extraordinary and minister plenipotentiary; A. L. C. Portman, esq., chargé d'affaires *ad interim* of the United States; D. de Graeff van Polsbroek, esq., his Netherlandish Majesty's consul general and political agent; Vice-Admiral George St. Vincent King, C. B., naval commander-in-chief; Idlumi No Kami, a vice-minister and member of the second council, accompanied by a Pometske of high rank.

The vice-minister stated that he had been sent by the Tycoon to meet the foreign representatives in the place of Abe Bungo No Kami, who was prevented by indisposition from keeping the engagement he had made with them on the 11th instant. O. Sasaware Ike No Kami, member of the Sorogio, had also been directed to accompany him, but was prevented, like Abe Bungo No Kami, by sickness, from doing so.

FOREIGN REPRESENTATIVES. It is unfortunate that we should have to deal on each occasion with a fresh envoy.

JAPANESE MINISTERS. The Tycoon received Abe Bungo No Kami's report of the conference, on the 11th, with the foreign representatives, and perfectly understood the arguments urged by the latter, and the justice of them. He had some idea of the foreign question before, but has now, for the first time, fully understood it, and is of opinion that it merits grave consideration. The Tycoon earnestly wishes a satisfactory adjustment, and will proceed to Kioto without delay to deliberate with the Mikado, whose sanction is necessary to the steps that have to be taken. Abe Bungo No Kami promised to bring to-day a decisive answer to the proposal of the representatives; but as the Tycoon is unable, himself, to come to a determination, without previously obtaining the approval of the Mikado, he will proceed to Kioto for that purpose. We hope the representatives will wait a few days to admit of our obtaining a final answer.

FOREIGN REPRESENTATIVES. Are we to understand these remarks to mean that the Tycoon has not yet explained to the Mikado the state of foreign relations, or applied for the approval of the treaties?

JAPANESE MINISTERS. The Tycoon may have spoken with the Mikado in general terms about foreign relations, but the difficulty as to the sanction of the latter to the treaties still exists. It is with the view of obtaining this sanction that the Tycoon now proposes to visit Kioto.

FOREIGN REPRESENTATIVES. But the Tycoon has only just returned from Kioto, where he staid a week, and his interview with the Mikado was assigned as the cause of the delay which occurred in sending Abe Bungo No Kami to meet the foreign representatives.

JAPANESE MINISTERS. That is true; but the late audience had more reference to the affairs of Choshu than to foreign relations.

FOREIGN REPRESENTATIVES. How long will it take to learn the result of this second audience?

JAPANESE MINISTERS. As the Tycoon will be unable to leave until the day after to-morrow, and will take two days to go up and the same time to return, and as the negotiations at Kioto will take some time, we wish you to delay your departure for fifteen days.

FOREIGN REPRESENTATIVES. As the Tycoon has so much difficulty in explaining matters at Kioto, perhaps it would be as well if the representatives were to accompany him there.

JAPANESE MINISTERS. That would seriously complicate matters; it would alarm the people and provoke the violence of the hostile party. The Tycoon himself will really proceed to Kioto for the purpose of fully explaining matters in person to the Mikado.

FOREIGN REPRESENTATIVES. Are we positively to understand that during the year that has elapsed since the Tycoon undertook to obtain the Mikado's sanction to the treaties he has done nothing to effect this measure?

JAPANESE MINISTERS. That is not so. The Tycoon has always been endeavoring to arrive at this result; but in consequence of the many difficulties he has had to contend with, he has not hitherto been able to succeed.

FOREIGN REPRESENTATIVES. Can the Tycoon himself secure the Mikado's sanction to the treaties, or does it depend on the Mikado's pleasure to give or withhold it?

JAPANESE MINISTERS. The Tycoon will explain the matter fully to the Mikado, and will use every endeavor to obtain this sanction.

FOREIGN REPRESENTATIVES. If the Tycoon represents matters clearly to the Mikado, will the Mikado then give his sanction?

JAPANESE MINISTER. The Tycoon will represent affairs in such a manner that the Mikado will be compelled to give his sanction to the treaties.

FOREIGN REPRESENTATIVES. As to Hiogo and the other ports and places named in the treaty, is it necessary for the Mikado's consent to be first given before these can be opened?

JAPANESE MINISTER. Yes, the Tycoon must first obtain the Mikado's consent.

FOREIGN REPRESENTATIVES. In the event, however, of the Mikado's consent being refused, can the Tycoon, in the exercise of his own authority, open these ports?

JAPANESE MINISTERS. The Tycoon will certainly succeed on this occasion in obtaining the Mikado's consent.

FOREIGN REPRESENTATIVES. On the subject of the revision of the tariff, must the Tycoon also first refer to Kioto for the Mikado's orders?

JAPANESE MINISTERS. Matters relating to the customs need not be referred to the Mikado, as they are not considered to be of sufficient importance. Formerly the Tycoon had the power as ruler of the empire to open ports, but now that the state of affairs has changed the Mikado's consent must first be obtained.

FOREIGN REPRESENTATIVES. You of course do not intend us to infer from these remarks any inability on the part of the Tycoon to give effect to the engagements he has contracted?

JAPANESE MINISTERS. The Mikado must first give his sanction to the treaties that have already been concluded. This is required to enable the Tycoon to faithfully carry out his obligations. It is to the absence of this sanction that any failure on the Tycoon's part to fulfil his obligations is to be attributed, and also all the troubles in respect to foreign relations which have hitherto occurred. I regret that formerly the sanction of the Mikado to the treaties was not required, because the Tycoon himself held sovereign powers, (literally, was the King Oi of the country;) but in the present state of affairs, he cannot enter into any new treaties or even carry out all the engagements of those already made without the approval of the Mikado.

FOREIGN REPRESENTATIVES. If that be the state of affairs it is of vital importance to the Tycoon to obtain the Mikado's approval. Unless he does so and proves to foreign governments that he is really charged with the conduct of foreign affairs, his position will become as subordinate as that of an ordinary Daimios.

JAPANESE MINISTERS. This is perfectly true, and it is precisely because the Tycoon understands this contingency, that he now intends to leave at once for Kioto in order to settle this point with the Mikado.

FOREIGN REPRESENTATIVES. The Tycoon, however, and the Mikado also, must clearly understand that whether the treaty powers have in future to deal either with one or the other, they will insist upon the strict fulfilment of the treaties. If the Tycoon wishes to be regarded as the governing power, he must be careful to take whatever steps are necessary to make his power complete. From what the Japanese minister says, this sanction of the Mikado to the Tycoon's past acts and his authority for the future control of foreign affairs appears indispensible, and we trust in his own interest that he will succeed in obtaining it. We wish to put a question as to that clause of the London agreement of 1862 which provides that the Daimios may trade at the open ports through their own agents. The necessary permission appears, however, to have been withheld. Is this attributable to the Tycoon's action?

JAPANESE MINISTER. The Tycoon can give this permission, but it would not be convenient to exercise his right in this respect as long as the Mikado withholds his consent to the treaties. So many complications are occasioned by the want of this consent, that we consider the time has come when it cannot longer be deferred, and the Tycoon will now come to a definite understanding with the Mikado.

FOREIGN REPRESENTATIVES. We do not comprehend the necessity for these repeated delays in effecting this understanding, or, considering the proximity of Kioto, why such a protracted interval as fifteen days should be required on the present occasion. We cannot consent to wait so long.

JAPANESE MINISTER. I am unable to state the exact time the Tycoon will require to obtain the Mikado's sanction to the treaties, but he is most anxious that no time should be lost. Matters have now been brought to a crisis, and your arrival with ships in these waters leads the Tycoon to suppose that you may wish to go on to Kioto yourselves unless he can effect a satisfactory arrangement.

FOREIGN REPRESENTATIVES. It is indispensable that we should ascertain what powers the Tycoon really possesses—whether the government of the country is in his hands, and whether he is the friend to foreign governments which he professes to be. If he cannot satisfy us on these points, we shall then have to consider how and where we are to seek the real government—whether at Kioto or elsewhere.

JAPANESE MINISTERS. The Tycoon, in order to keep up friendly relations with the treaty powers, and indeed to maintain the existence of his government, must obtain the Mikado's sanction to the treaties. If he fails in this, then he will lose his power and sink into a position something resembling that of a Daimio. I hope, therefore, that the foreign representatives will wait here for fifteen days, as that time is really necessary for the Tycoon's negotiations with the Mikado.

FOREIGN REPRESENTATIVES. We regret that the Tycoon has not made greater efforts during the year that has elapsed, since the foreign representatives in October last urged upon him, both in writing and through the Sorogio, the gravity of the situation.

JAPANESE MINISTER. The Tycoon, in consequence of internal dissensions, has hitherto been unable to direct his whole attention to foreign relations; but seeing that moderate measures are of no avail, he will now insist upon obtaining the Mikado's consent without further delay.

FOREIGN REPRESENTATIVES. We will consider the time that we will agree to wait for the Tycoon's reply, but as we have waited here ten days already, we certainly cannot consent to remain fifteen days more. We might possibly agree to a delay of eight or ten days at the outside, and in the interval we may find it convenient to visit Simonoseki or other places in the Inland Sea.

DUTCH CONSUL GENERAL. An agent of a Daimio called upon me in 1858 to inquire if his master could enter into direct trading relations with Holland, as he himself wished and was ready to do so.

JAPANESE MINISTER. There are other Daimios who would probably wish to do the same, but the Tycoon cannot give them permission to open their ports without the Mikado's consent.

FOREIGN REPRESENTATIVES. To judge from the representations said to have come from the several Daimios, they believe they can dispense with this permission and consider that they have the right to control their own trade, foreign or otherwise, in their own territories.

JAPANESE MINISTER. I am sorry to hear that such representations should have been made. It would be contrary to a mandate from Kioto, which forbids the Daimios to open their ports. Having informed you of the necessity the Tycoon is under to go to Kioto to discuss the confirmation of the treaties by the Mikado, I wish to take my leave.

FOREIGN REPRESENTATIVES. We cordially hope that success may attend the Tycoon's negotiations. The foreign governments will have to judge of his power and good will by his actions. Again, however, let us warn you that the treaties he has concluded must be faithfully kept by the ruling power of Japan, in whomsoever it may be vested.

The conference then terminated.

No. 3.

Memorandum signed by Earl Russell and the Japanese envoys, June 6, 1862.

It has been represented to her Britannic Majesty's minister in Japan by the ministers of the Tycoon, and to her Majesty's government by the envoys who have been sent to England by the Tycoon, that difficulties are experienced by the Tycoon and his ministers in giving effect to their engagements with foreign powers having treaties with Japan, in consequence of the opposition offered by a party in Japan which is hostile to all intercourse with foreigners.

Her Majesty's government having taken these representations into consideration, are prepared, on the conditions hereinafter specified, to consent to defer for a period of five years, to commence from the 1st of January, 1863, the fulfilment of those portions of the third article of the treaty between Great Britain and Japan, of the 26th of August, 1858, which provides for the opening to British subjects of the port of Neegata, or some other convenient port on the west coast of Nipon, on the first day of January, 1866, and of the port of Hiogo on the first day of January, 1863; and for the residents of British subjects in the city of Yedo from the first day of January, 1862, and in the city of Osacca from the first day of January, 1863.

Her Majesty's government, in order to give to the Japanese ministers the time those ministers consider necessary to enable them to overcome the opposition now existing, are willing to make these large concessions of their right under treaty, but they expect that the Tycoon and his ministers will in all other respects strictly execute at the ports of Nagasaki, Hakodadi, and Kanagawa, all the other stipulations of the treaty. That they will publicly revoke the old law outlawing foreigners, and that they will specially abolish and do away with—

1st. All restrictions, whether as regards quantity or price, on the sale by Japanese to foreigners of all kinds of merchandise, according to article XIV of the treaty of the 26th of August, 1858.

2d. All restrictions on labor, and more particularly on the hire of carpenters, boatmen, boats and coolies, teachers, and servants, of whatever denomination.

3d. All restrictions whereby Daimios are prevented from sending their produce to market, and from selling the same directly by their own agents.

4th. All restrictions resulting from attempt on the part of the custom-house authorities and other officials to obtain fees.

6th. All restrictions limiting the classes of persons who shall be allowed to trade with foreigners at the ports of Nagasaki, Hakodadi, and Kanagawa.

6th. All restrictions imposed on free intercourse of a social kind between foreigners and the people of Japan.

In default of the strict fulfilment by the Tycoon and his ministers of these conditions, which, indeed, are none other than those they are already bound by treaty to fulfil, her Majesty's government will, at any time within the aforesaid period of five years, commencing from the 1st of January, 1863, be entitled to withdraw the concessions in regard to the ports and cities made by this memorandum, and to call upon the Tycoon and his ministers to carry out, without delay, the whole of the provisions of the treaty of August 26, 1858, and specifically to open the aforesaid ports and cities for the trade and residence of British subjects.

The envoys of the Tycoon accredited to her Britannic Majesty announce their intention, on their return to Japan, to submit to the Tycoon and his ministers the policy and expediency of opening to foreign commerce the port of T'susima, in Japan, as a measure by which the interests of Japan will be materially promoted, and they engage to suggest to the Tycoon and his ministers to evince their good will to the nations of Europe, and their desire to extend commerce between Japan and Europe by reducing the duties on wines and spirits imported into Japan, and by permitting glassware to be inserted in the list of articles on which an import duty of five per cent. is levied, and thereby remedying an omission inadvertently made on the conclusion of the treaty. And they further engage to recommend to the Tycoon and his ministers to make arrangements for the establishment at Yokohama and Nagasaki of warehouses, in which goods coming from abroad may be deposited under the control of Japanese officers, without payment of duties, until such time as the importers shall obtain purchasers for such goods, and be prepared to remove them on payment of the import duties.

Her Britannic Majesty's principal secretary of state for foreign affairs and the envoys of the Tycoon have accordingly signed this memorandum, which will be transmitted by the former to her Majesty's representative in Japan, and by the latter to the Tycoon and his ministers, as an evidence of the arrangement made between them on the sixth day of June, 1862.

RUSSELL.

(Signatures of the three Japanese envoys.)

Mr. Seward to Mr. Portman.

No. 7.] DEPARTMENT OF STATE,
Washington, November 20, 1865.

SIR: I have to acknowledge the receipt of your despatch, No. 48, of August 22. The President sees no reason for disapproving your proceedings therein mentioned in regard to the receipt of indemnity money tendered and paid by the Japanese government for the use of the treaty-making western powers. For the present the subject of the disposition of the money is attended here by two difficulties. First, the treaty has not yet been approved by the Senate. Second, we are waiting an understanding with the interested

European powers. I hope that these difficulties will be removed in the course of the next month, (December,) within which Congress will have assembled, and I shall look for communications on the subject from the European states which I have addressed.

I am, sir, your obedient servant,

WILLIAM H. SEWARD.

A. L. C. PORTMAN, Esq., *&c., &c., Yedo.*

Mr. Portman to Mr. Seward.

No. 66.] LEGATION OF THE UNITED STATES IN JAPAN,
Yedo, November 30, 1865.

SIR: I have the honor to inform you that the Mikado's formal sanction of the treaties has been obtained; this is, in fact, the ratification of the treaties.

In preference to the opening of the port of Hiogo and the city of Osacca, on the 1st of January next, the Japanese government will pay the indemnity of $3,000,000, according to the convention of the 22d of October, 1864.

A revision of the tariff has been agreed upon.

It is also quite certain that civil war in Japan has now been averted.

I left Osacca bay on the 26th, and arrived at Kanagawa on the 28th instant. On my arrival I learned there was a rumor that I had been assassinated at Hiogo. I was immediately waited on by governors of foreign affairs, and received so many congratulations besides, that I could not leave for this place until yesterday in the forenoon.

This morning I communicated to the members of the government the Mikado's sanction, and also the instructions which they will soon receive from the Tycoon, with a view of arriving at a prompt amendment of the tariff so urgently needed.

I shall endeavor to prepare in time for this mail a detailed account of the successful negotiations and the results above mentioned, of which I have no doubt you will be pleased to approve.

I have the honor to be, sir, very respectfully, your most obedient servant,

A. L. C. PORTMAN,
Chargé d'Affaires ad interim.

Hon. WILLIAM H. SEWARD,
Secretary of State, Washington.

TURKEY.

Mr. Morris to Mr. Seward.

[Extract.]

No. 100.] LEGATION OF THE UNITED STATES OF AMERICA,
Constantinople, December 7, 1864.

SIR: * * * * * * * * *

I have translated the enclosed article from the Byzantes, a Greek paper published in this capital, which has a large circulation both here and among the Greek population throughout the empire.

It may be gratifying to the President to know how perfectly his character and actions are appreciated at this distant point by a foreign people, (for the editor but represents the sentiments common to all Greeks,) and how important his re-election is regarded by the friends of liberty in the east.

With great respect, your obedient servant,

E. JOY MORRIS.

Hon. WILLIAM H. SEWARD,
Secretary of State.

THE AMERICAN PRESIDENTIAL ELECTION.

[From the Byzantès, the leading Greek paper at Constantinople, of the 4th December, 1864.]

The news from New York announces the re-election of Mr. Lincoln, President of the United States. All the States, with the exception of three, cast their suffrage for this bold and energetic leader of the republic, who, long since, thoroughly cognizant of the ultimate aims of the southern secessionists, has inflexibly persevered in his efforts to preserve the Union at all hazards.

The event may be regarded as the beginning of the end. The war will be brought to an end, the Union will be saved, and foreign machinations will be foiled. Through the election of the peace candidate for the presidency foreign influence hoped to secure the success of the secession movement and the establishment of another power between the new empire of Mexico and the great democratic republic. If Mr. Lincoln had been defeated, the great undertaking which has been so long prosecuted, and at such immense sacrifices of blood and treasure, would have been frustrated, and before long the republic, through foreign intrigue, would have been dismembered, and the secession of the south recognized as a fixed fact. There would, no doubt, have been found in every State of the Union men lost to all patriotic instincts and animated exclusively by selfish ambition and monarchical sympathies, who would have played the same part in their respective States which the secessionists are now performing in regard to the Union. In confirmation of the truth of our remarks, we refer to the tone of the greater part of the French press. There is no mistaking it. The independence of the south is a question of life or death for the new dynasty in Mexico.

The secession movement is powerfully sustained from abroad by secret aid. The piratical cruisers of the disunionists find an asylum under the guns of Cherbourg, in France, and of Brazilian ships-of-war in the harbors of that country. Look at the affair of the Alabama and the Florida; look at the frenzied zeal of the French journalists for the election of anybody but Lincoln, and the false reports constantly published by them of reputed successes of the south, and their clamor for the cessation of the war and the intervention of European states, and it will be seen that we are not far from the truth. Lincoln has shown himself a man of superior intelligence; a consummate patriot, combining prudence with energy, and fertile, in an extraordinary degree, in expedients necessary for the successful prosecution of the great contest which he has in charge.

If America is indebted to Washington for one thing, it will ere long be made manifest that to Lincoln she owes all. Washington founded the Union; Lincoln will preserve it. It is undoubtedly a much more difficult task to preserve than to establish. Lincoln, as President of the United States, has become the providential savior of human liberty. His indomitable perseverance has stimulated the wonderful activity of the northern armies, given new life to the persistent energy of Grant and of the other generals of the north. Under his administration the American war approaches its end, and the south is sinking under exhaustion from the incessant attacks to which it is subject, the devastation of its chief cities, and the systematic siege of its capital. Lincoln has accomplished the programme of the Unionists. At first this programme embraced only the abolition of negro slavery at every cost; subsequently Lincoln added to it the maintenance of the Union at all hazards. Through the first the United States has shown itself consistent with the political principles to which it owes its origin; through the second, Lincoln has completely baffled the insidious schemes of the monarchists.

The enemies of the administration of Lincoln have denounced it in every way as factious, selfish, reckless, and improvident, and as leading the Union to ruin. One of the chief organs of the monarchical faction, the editor of the Courrier des Etats Unis, immediately after the election of Lincoln, left the State and transferred the seat of publication of his paper to Mexico. Despairing of sowing seeds of dissension in the republic, he has offered his services to the new empire. The enemies of Mr. Lincoln and the Union have endeavored to weaken the force of his re-election by asserting that it has been accomplished by illegal means. The result has, however, signally demonstrated that it is altogether owing to the unshaken confidence of the American people in the character and actions of the President. The enemies of the Union have not only sought to secure its dissolution by foreign intervention, but also in the protection which, openly and in defiance of law, they have afforded to the piratical vessels of the confederates, to involve the Union in war with foreign states, and to render Americans the instruments of America's ruin. The world has seen with what consummate skill Lincoln has navigated the ship of state through these perils by which it has been surrounded. Our readers recollect the manner in which Drouyn de Lhuys received the American minister, Mr. Dayton, on entering his office to express to him the views of Mr. Lincoln with respect to the new Mexican monarchy: "You proclaim war against us, then."

They who befriend the new Mexican empire, and who lavish their treasure for schemes of annexation and conquest in Cochin China, Africa, and America, to support the political system with which their interests are involved, are enemies of Lincoln. It is natural that the monarchical reactionists should denounce the republicans as demagogues, charlatans, *sans culottes*, revolutionists, &c., &c. They are called demagogues because they tell the people what their enemies do not wish them to know; charlatans, because they are frank and unreserved in their dealings with them; revolutionists, because they have the power to move the popular mind in the hour of danger. It is no wonder, indeed, that Lincoln is calumniated by these traducers of the friends of liberty. Despite this storm of calumny, and of the efforts of the enemies of the great American republic, the helm of state has been again committed by the suffrage of the people to the hands of this man of firm and inflexible purpose, and of indomitable perseverance. The war will soon terminate through the subjugation or the pacification of the south. The Jefferson Davis and Lee monarchical instruments cannot withstand the iron will of twenty millions of people, and the southern States will return within their proper orbit. And if Juarez, respecting the interests of the great democracy, may now be silent, he will again be heard when peace is made in the United States. The recent Union victories have given serious apprehension to the patrons of the new Mexican empire; they see in them the signs of approaching ruin to the cause of Jefferson Davis; and when that shall take place they know the road to Mexico will be opened.

The re-election of Mr. Lincoln to the presidency of the United States must be regarded as an event of signal historical import to the cause of liberty, and as a vindication of the superior intelligence of the American people. If ever there was a day in American history which required the practical exercise of legal liberty, it was the day of the recent election for the President of the United States. There can never be in the annals of the United States a more memorable day than that of the 8th of November, 1864. If the confederates make a great show of effort, and if Hood has entered Tennessee with 30,000 men, Sherman, according to the telegraph, having destroyed Atlanta, has abandoned it. Grant is erecting his winter tents in front of Richmond, and an extraordinary activity pervades all the armies of the north. The coming spring will, in all probability, finish a war which, on account of many difficulties, could not have been previously brought to an end.

Mr. Morris to Mr. Seward.

[Extract.]

No. 104.] LEGATION OF THE UNITED STATES OF AMERICA,
Constantinople, February 15, 1865.

SIR:

* * * * * * *

Having, in a previous despatch given some details in relation to the Turkish army, I deem it proper to furnish the following statements of the same, partly in correction of statements in that despatch, and for the purpose of approximating as near as possible to complete accuracy. At the death of Abdul Medjid, the Turkish navy consisted of 105 vessels of all sizes, 1,252 guns, and 8,314 horse-power. Of these, three were steam line-of-battle ships, carrying 86, 84, and 82 guns of 650 horse-power each, 5 frigates (steam,) each of 24 guns and 459 horse-power, 4 corvettes (steam,) mounting in all 68 guns and 600 horse-power, (total;) 13 sloops, mounting in all 73 guns and of (total) 1,560 horse-power; 19 steam transports, total horse-power 1,664. Of the sailing vessels, there were one line-of-battle ship of 428 guns; another of 64 guns; 1 frigate of 34 guns; 13 corvettes of 136 guns; total: 11 brigs, total 176 guns; 4 schooners, total 36 guns; 8 cutters, total 60 guns; 25 guns boats, total 85 guns. Grand total, 105 vessels of all sizes, 1,252 guns, and 8,314 horse-power.

Since the accession of the present Sultan there have been added to this force: one line-of-battle ship (steam,) 96 guns, 800 horse-power; 3 frigates (steam,) 60 guns, 600 horse-power; 7 corvettes, 52 guns, 1,080 horse-power; 9 transports, 970 horse-power; besides 4 iron-clad frigates in course of construction, mounting 136 heavy guns, and 8 sailing floating batteries, mounting 25 guns. Total 32 vessels, 490 guns, 4,500 horse-power, exclusive of the mailed frigates.

The present Sultan has increased the naval force by more than one-third of its artillery and almost double its steam power, raising the total to 1,742 guns, and about 15,314 horse-power.

Exclusive of the chief arsenal of construction at Constantinople, there are four other secondary arsenals: at Ismid and Ghemlek in the sea of Marmora, and Sinope and Eregli in the Black Sea, and two minor ones at Rhodes and Metelin. At all these places vessels are built.

The naval school is at Khalki, one of the Princes' islands in the sea of Marmora, where excellent instruction is given in nautical science to about 200 youths. General knowledge and the English language is also taught. The following is a table of the rank and monthly pay of the officers, including rations. The American gold dollar equals 23 Turkish piasters: Lieutenant, 500 piasters; captain of corvette, 700 piasters; captain of frigate, 1,200 piasters; commandant, 1,500 piasters; captain, 2,000 piasters; rear admiral, 3,000 piasters; vice-admiral, 10,000 piasters; admiral, 25,000 piasters. The number of men employed in the active service is 10,900; including the reserve force, it amounts to 33,000 men. The fleet is manned by conscription and by volunteers. The term of service is eight years, at the expiration of which period the men return to their homes, where they are divided into the first and second class reserve. During the present reign great zeal has been displayed in the perfection and increase of the navy, and new vessels are constantly being ordered in England and France, while the dock-yards of the empire are alive with unwonted activity. It is evident that the Sultan is fully aware of the peril to which the empire is exposed by the ambitious designs of Russia and France, and that he is determined to spare no expense or effort to meet the crisis which, constantly menacing the national existence, must sooner or later confront him.

In this connexion, I regret to announce the death of Mehemed Pacha, the minister of marine. I had the honor of his intimate acquaintance, and whenever we met he never failed to speak of the government and people of the United States in the kindest terms. He never forgot the courtesy exhibited to him in 1852, when on a visit to the United States.

* * * * * * *

With great respect, your obedient servant,

E. JOY MORRIS.

Hon. WILLIAM H. SEWARD,
Secretary of State.

Mr. Morris to Mr. Seward.

[Extract.]

No. 106.] LEGATION OF THE UNITED STATES OF AMERICA,
Constantinople, February 22, 1865.

SIR: * * * * * * As an example of the energy and zeal of the Sultan in military affairs, I may mention the fact that 40,000 Enfield rifles have recently been imported for the use of the army, and that within a short time 200,000 rifles of the best quality will be manufactured by the domestic arsenals and be placed in the hands of the troops. Five years ago the troops used only the flint-lock muskets, of a range of only 250 paces; now they are to be equipped with rifles carrying 3,300 feet. In addition to this, such improvements have been made in the imperial gun machine shops at Zeitun Bournon that 52,000 rifles of the Enfield system, called interchangeable, can be manufactured per annum. Active preparations are also making in the government machine shops for the manufacture of rifled cannon of iron and steel, of wrought iron of the largest calibre, for the arming of the new fortifications in construction on the Dardanelles and Bosphorus, and the frontiers of European and Asiatic Turkey, and for the iron-clad vessels under construction in England and at Constantinople. All these measures show a knowledge on the part of the Sultan of the perils of the empire, and his determination to meet them.

The recent series of Union victories have produced a general belief that the rebel cause is hopeless, and that the complete triumph of Union and liberty are near at hand. The liberal journals of Europe, almost without exception, are favorable to the success of the Union government, looking upon it as closely connected with the progress of civil and religious liberty in the Old World. The downfall of the Union would be the downfall of liberty in Europe and the herald of despotic reaction, and for this reason every friend of humanity on this side of the Atlantic rejoices in the victories that so signally prove the ability of the American republic to sustain its own existence, and in the mighty power it has displayed in the present struggle between the conflicting interests of freedom and slavery.

With great respect, your obedient servant,

E. JOY MORRIS.

Hon. WILLIAM H. SEWARD,
Secretary of State.

Mr. Morris to Mr. Seward.

No. 108.] LEGATION OF THE UNITED STATES OF AMERICA,
Constantinople, March 29, 1865.

SIR: I have the honor to acknowledge the receipt of despatch No. 86, of the date of February 11, and to transmit a translation of the note of Ali Pacha, minister of foreign affairs, to the Turkish minister in London, relative to the question of religious toleration in the Turkish empire.

It is important that the views of the Turkish government on this subject should be put on record among our own state papers, that the religious community in the United States may understand to what extent the free exercise and teaching of Christianity is allowed in the dominions of the Sultan, and to what restrictions it is subjected. As the American missionaries in Turkey have never made themselves amenable to any of the accusations of this note, it is unnecessary for me to repel them on their part.

In despatch No. 96 I mentioned that the government of the Sultan had appointed Haidar Effendi as special envoy to the government of the Emperor Maximilian, to reciprocate the complimentary mission of Martinez del Rio. It now appears that no minister will be accredited by the Porte, in any capacity, to Mexico.

The inauguration of President Lincoln for a second term has been to me, on the part of the minister of foreign affairs, the Grand Vizier, and other members of the imperial cabinet, a subject of the most cordial and friendly congratulation. His re-election is regarded by them as a just reward for the eminent services he has rendered, not only his own country but the world at large, in maintaining the integrity of the American Union and in promoting the progress of human liberty. Notwithstanding the burdens of debt and taxation, I find no one doubting our ability to discharge or sustain them, whilst our power and influence as a nation have been vastly increased by the formidable array of fleets and armies created by the war, and the science, skill and valor of our military and naval forces.

I have the honor to be, with great respect, your obedient servant,

E. JOY MORRIS.

Hon. WILLIAM H. SEWARD,
Secretary of State.

[Translation.]

His Highness Ali Pacha, minister of foreign affairs, to his excellency M. Musurus, ambassador of his Imperial Majesty the Sultan, at London.

SUBLIME PORTE, *November* 30, 1865.

MR. AMBASSADOR: I have received the two despatches addressed to me by your excellency on the 27th October and 3d of November last, together with the account of the interview held by Lord Russell with a deputation of the Evangelical Alliance.

My former communications have made you acquainted with the conduct of certain Protestant missionaries and the measures which the Sublime Porte was obliged to adopt. I now propose more particularly to enter upon the questions raised by the discussions which those measures have occasioned in England, and I feel sure that the same just and liberal appreciation, joined to the conciliatory spirit which I have been pleased to find in the language of the principal secretary of state of her Britannic Majesty, will aid us in dispelling all doubts and in annihilating all calumnies. It is, therefore, with unlimited confidence in the equity and friendly disposition of her Britannic Majesty's cabinet, and in the tried justice of the English nation, that I submit the following explanations to the enlightened judgment of his lordship:

The imperial government has established by the Hotti Humayun (Royal Rescript) of 1856 the free exercise of all forms of worship existing in the empire. The scrupulous accomplishment of this promise has been the more easy since the diversity of religious elements united under its protection imposed upon it the obligation to watch indiscriminately over the safety of all religious interests, and to guarantee each creed against the aggression of the other, by giving to all an entire liberty in their legitimate manifestations.

The Sublime Porte has acted in this spirit with the greatest sincerity. Not only has it recognized the jurisdiction and spiritual hierarchy of the different non-Mussulman creeds, but it has admitted them all to the same honors enjoyed by the established religion, and has spontaneously conceded to them equal prerogatives. Every one is now free to profess his own religion, and to follow his own form of worship. No law forbids religious communities of all the Christian rights to enter Turkey; their members are not subject to any restraints in the exercise of their spiritual ceremonies; all religious creeds erect their places of worship there, and enjoy full liberty, even in their outward forms and in their public ceremonies; and the sacred books of all religions are printed and published in different parts of the empire.

We can, therefore, affirm that Christians of all sects and Israelites enjoy in Turkey rights which they would be happy to possess in most Christian countries in Europe. It would be useless to enumerate the restrictions imposed on liberty of conscience in other countries, perhaps, without even excepting England itself, which in this respect is one of the most liberal nations, but whose legislature still preserves some restrictions of this kind. Among these, it will be sufficient to cite the severe penalties prescribed by a law in the reign of William III, for those who, by speaking, teaching, or writing, deny the truth of the Christian religion and the divine authority of the Holy Scriptures.

I do not contest that these restrictive enactments are in part modified in practice; but it is not the less true that the British legislature has recognized their necessity. In making these observations I have no other intention whatever than that of requesting a little more indulgence towards us. If, indeed, the British government, which is at the head of civilization, feels itself obliged in many cases to take account of the religious influence of a party, would it not be equitable to acknowledge that the Sublime Porte, also, could not but take into account the sentiments of her populations, and, above all, could not but seek to defend her religion within the limits of moderation and of justice against interested attacks?

The imperial government which has not admitted the free exercise of proselytism in favor of the religion of the state cannot admit it in opposition to that religion. The principle of religious toleration cannot, in our view, be reconciled with open aggression against any religion whatever.

Lord Russell has stated repeatedly in his speech the difficulties which arise in the application of the principle which is in question. His lordship declares that he cannot form a conception of the liberty of religious creeds without the freedom of recording in the ardor of conviction the arguments through which those ends have been adopted. The noble lord goes so far as to allow the attack in a private manner of a religion which is considered erroneous, but he sees offence in the act of publicly attacking and reproaching the religion.

Doubtless the liberty of opinion leads to that of wedding it; nevertheless, we believe that it is forbidden to employ other methods than that of persuasion. So far this mode of making known religious convictions is, we consider, justified on the principle of liberty of opinion. But his lordship, who condemns the aggression of religious convictions when they are made in broad daylight, will not dispute that there is a great step between a spontaneous and tolerant manifestation of convictions and a systematic propagandism, which makes use of powerful means, and acts with the settled purpose of effecting the subversion of other religions, which draws all its energy from the intolerance and the hatred of those religions, which speculates not only on the ignorance of the masses and the weakness of faith, but even upon political views, and, above all, upon motives of interest, which insults and reproaches instead of respecting the fears of others, and fears not to have recourse to corruption when it cannot obtain by persuasion. It would be vain to affect in practice all the considerations which the missionaries have too much neglected. Such a system would be none the less the contradiction of the principle of religious liberty, for by its very existence it attacks that liberty in others, and that respect for the conviction of others, without which religious tolerance would be but an empty form.

I do not think it necessary, sir, to insist upon the political consequences of this system. Lord Russell has established the necessity which presses upon every power to insure respect for itself and for the established religion of the country; and his lordship will not dispute the gravity which religious propagandism acquires, particularly from circumstances in Turkey, and the circumspection which the imperial government must use in all those questions which are of a nature to raise religious passions and to arm one race against another. The government of her Britannic Majesty, which has not forgotten either the religious disorders which have by turn covered every part of Europe with blood, nor the reserve which it has itself imposed upon Protestant missionaries in India, will willingly appreciate the respect due to the creed of a whole population, and the danger which would result from estranging it.

No European government, moreover, has sanctioned the principle of religious propagandism in England, in Prussia, and in Austria. Everywhere propagandism is subjected to the supervision of the authorities. The most liberal and the most tolerant governments have reserved to themselves the power to condemn it whenever it threatened public security and the interests of the religion of the state; and democratic Greece has just inscribed at the head of her constitution the prohibition of proselytism and of any other intervention contrary to the dominant religion.

But the missionaries, not content with accusing us of intolerance, would wish further to impute a violation of enjoyments solemnly contracted; they invoke in their favor the *Hatti Humayun*, and strive to give to their enterprise the sanction of legality. Now, the 6th article of the *Hatti Humayun* says, "Seeing that all creeds are and shall be fully exercised in my dominions, no subject of my empire shall be molested in the exercise of the religion which he professes, nor shall be in any way disturbed in that respect. No one shall be compelled to change his religion."

It would be truly difficult to draw from this text, which is so clear, an interpretation of a nature to justify the pretensions of the missionaries. The government of his Majesty the Sultan has spontaneously declared by the article I have just quoted that there will be secured to each community the free exercise of its worship, to each individual the power to profess and practice his religion without impediment; nothing more. Every other interpretation would lead to strange errors.

Can it be supposed that, whilst condemning religious persecutions, the Sublime Porte has consented to permit offence and insult to any creed whatever? That at the same time that she was proclaiming liberty to all non-Mussulmen creeds, she had given them arms against Islamism? That she had, in fine, destroyed at the same stroke the guarantees with which she surrounded the liberty of religious conviction? No one could for a moment insist on so unfounded an hypothesis without insulting the good sense of the Sublime Porte, and misapprehending the tact of the eminent diplomatist who pleaded with her the cause of liberty of conscience. But if the least doubt could be raised as to the spirit of the Hatti Humayun, he acts of the government of her Majesty the Queen would be sufficient to dissipate them. Your excellency is not unaware that an order in council of the Queen, addressed to the British embassy at the time of the formation of the high consular court, punishes with fine and even with hard labor every subject of the Queen who should render himself guilty of turning into derision or publicly insulting any religion established and professed in Turkey, or who should voluntarily commit any act tending to draw upon such religion or upon its ceremonies, upon its worship, or its practices, hatred, ridicule, or contempt.

If the imperial government, moved by a spirit of moderation—for which public opinion in England will assuredly give her credit—has tolerated the establishment of missionaries in Turkey, it could hardly recognize in any organized body the right of exercising a propagandism which the most civilized governments reject, which reason, the spirit and the letter of the Hatti Humayun, and the general interests of the empire equally repudiate. It could not sacrifice to the zeal of certain foreign missionaries the tranquillity of the empire. No one disputes the right of the missionaries to express, by the same title as every other person, their religious opinions with the respect due to those of others; but in every case where this expression assumes a character of publicity calculated to give rise to scandal to a part of the population, to wound the public conscience, and to disturb the tranquillity of the country, the imperial government is compelled to reserve to itself the right to act in conformity with the existing laws and public interests, which it is bound to protect.

It was my desire, sir, to expose without concealment our opinion upon a question which we grieved to see obscured by inexact or interested allegations, and to define the limits within which we think it right to reserve our action.

As I attach a high value to public opinion in England, I think it my duty to request you to make known to his excellency Lord Russell the foregoing observations, in order that his lordship may be in a position, when necessary, to cause their justice to be recognized, and in order that the British nation, after having heard both parties, should not allow itself to be influenced by gratuitous and unjust recriminations.

I think it my duty to add, in conclusion, that the free sale and circulation of the Bible continues, and will always continue, to be authorized by the empire.

ALI.

Earl Russell to Mr. Stuart.

FOREIGN OFFICE, *January* 21, 1865.

SIR: I send you a copy of a despatch of his Highness Ali Pacha to M. Musurus, which M. Musurus has just put into my hands.

I gather from this despatch that the Sultan will observe inviolably the 6th article of the Hatti Humayun of his late brother, which is in these terms:

"Seeing that all religions are and will be freely practiced in my states, no subject in my empire will be troubled in the exercise of the religion which he professes, or be in any manner disturbed on this account. No one will be compelled to change his religion."

I understand further, from the termination of the despatch, that the free sale and circulation of the Bible continues and will continue to be authorized in the Turkish empire. If these two declarations are maintained and acted upon, I am quite willing to close the controversy.

I have no desire to impugn the general spirit of toleration which animates the Sublime Porte, nor do I feel at all called upon to defend the laws and government of the British empire on the score of religious liberty.

I request you to give a copy of this despatch to his Highness Ali Pacha.

I am, &c.,

RUSSELL.

Mr. Morris to Mr. Seward.

No. 110.] LEGATION OF THE UNITED STATES OF AMERICA,
Constantinople, April 19, 1865.

SIR: I have the honor to transmit copies of a correspondence between his Highness Ali Pacha, minister of foreign affairs, and myself, relative to certain charges preferred by him against the American missionaries, and also a communication from the Rev. George Washburn, secretary of the American Board of Missions at Constantinople, upon the same subject.

A telegram of the 5th of April, from New York, was received here on the 16th instant, announcing the capture of Richmond and Petersburg, and the great victories of General Grant, which accompanied this glorious achievement.

The news created intense excitement, particularly among the commercial classes, and is regarded by all as a forerunner of peace and the re-establishment of the American Union in its pristine vigor. This event, and the victories of General Sherman which preceded it, have created a most salutary impression in relation to the strength of the government of the United States, and its ability to defend itself against domestic or foreign aggression. Never was the United States more feared and respected than it is now, in Europe, and never did our form of government more signally vindicate its self-sustaining power. The administration of President Lincoln extorts, even from its former most implacable enemies, the highest eulogies for its skill, energy, and consummate sagacity and wisdom with which it has conducted this gigantic war for the preservation of the Union.

To none, however, has this news of the successes of our arms given more gratification than to the members of the cabinet of the Sultan, who now, as during the whole progress of the war, have never failed to manifest their sympathy with the Union cause, and their wishes for its triumph. As I have related in previous despatches, the Sultan has himself personally, to me, before the diplomatic corps, on several occasions, given expression to similar sentiments.

I have been accustomed to say to foreigners that the maintenance of the Union was not exclusively an American question. It is one which interests mankind at large as much as ourselves, and, in pouring out our blood and treasure for its defence, we are only fighting a battle for the interests of universal humanity. Its overthrow would be a disastrous check to modern progress, while its maintenance upholds a government that stands as a pillar of light to guide mankind to the redemption of its usurped rights, and to encourage it in its struggles with those rulers who use power to found dynasties on the oppression of the masses.

This is the light in which the American question is regarded by all on this side of the Atlantic who have really any sympathy with the welfare of the human race, and the day is not distant when the United States, rising, phœnix-like, with renewed strength from the flames of war, will exercise a greater moral power over the civilized world than any of the great states of Europe.

I have the honor to be, very respectfully, your obedient servant,

E. J. MORRIS.

Hon. WILLIAM H. SEWARD,
Secretary of State.

Mr. Washburn to Mr. Morris.

CONSTANTINOPLE, *April* 5, 1865.

SIR: I beg to acknowledge, with thanks, the receipt of yours of this morning's date, with a copy of a despatch from his Highness Ali Pacha, of the 2d instant.

As it is plain that his Highness has been completely misinformed in regard to the relations of the American missionaries to the Protestant Christian community, it seems most desirable that I should state to you, briefly, but frankly, what these relations have been and now are.

His Highness himself cannot be more firmly persuaded than we are that foreign missionaries ought not to meddle with the civil affairs of this empire. We neither claim nor desire any such right. We are well aware that, should we meddle in civil or political affairs, we must identify ourselves with some personal or party interests, and thus destroy our proper influence as Christian teachers. We have, therefore, never sought to control the Protestant community, nor even to give advice, except when our advice has been formally asked. We have often collected from friends pecuniary aid from the community, but only when it has been officially asked for, and even then the money has been given under protest.

When this community was formed, in 1850, the Protestants were very few in number, and very poor. When Stepan Effendi was appointed their vehil, they were utterly unable to pay his salary, or even any great part of it. Under these circumstances they appealed to us, and we consented to become responsible for one year. We collected the money and paid the expenses, but distinctly disclaimed any desire to control the action of the vehil. From that day to this we have not ceased to urge upon the people the necessity of paying their taxes regularly. For some ten years we aided them every year with funds collected from friends, but about five years ago we gave them final and formal notice that we could furnish them with no more money, as we wished to have no connexion with their civil affairs.

Stepan Effendi, however, failing to understand the necessity of such action on our part, demanded that his salary should be paid in full by the missionaries; if it were not, he should cease to perform the duties of his office. We, of course, refused to do this, and continued to urge upon the people the necessity of supporting their chancery themselves.

Since that time, during these five years, the Protestant community has been almost destroyed by the efforts of Stepan Effendi to compel the missionaries to become responsible for his salary. Much of the time the business of the office has been neglected, and the people, suffering bitter wrong on this account, have refused to pay their taxes to him.

Some three years ago, however, he agreed to adopt a certain plan, proposed by the council of the nation, on condition of receiving arrears of salary. At the request of the Protestant council, the sum necessary was raised by the American and English missionaries; but, no sooner had he received the money, than, apparently under the influence of some evil adviser, he violated his word, and overturned the whole arrangement. Much of the time since that date his office has been closed.

But about three months ago Stepan Effendi came, *naslied* of his own accord, to several individuals, saying, "I wish very much to resign. I am old. I need my arrears of salary, and I wish to leave my post honorably. I beg you to see if there is no way to raise the money to pay me my dues. If it could be raised, I would gladly secure the appointment of some one else in my place. After this was finished I would take my money."

These persons came to me, and it appeared that the time had come when all the troubles of the community could be cleared away, once for all, by a friendly arrangement, equally pleasing to all parties.

I therefore replied: if all parties desire this, and request it, I think for once more, for a final settlement, I can find the money; but you must arrange it among yourselves.

They did arrange it fully among themselves. Stepan Effendi wrote a note to the notables of the community, of which the following is a translation:

"FEBRUARY 6, 1865.

"BELOVED BRETHREN: You are already well acquainted with the present condition of the Protestant chancery. I cannot endure that condition any longer. My debts are daily increasing, and in my present advanced stage of life I am in great distress. I therefore appeal to your brotherly kindness, that you would kindly undertake to deliver me from this condition. I inform you that I am ready to resign my office, and in my old age to retire to private life, if my claims upon the treasury are paid.

"With love,

"STEPAN SEROPIAN."

It was agreed by these notables that he should ask the appointment of Boghos Effendi, of Adrianople, in his place, as temporary caünaham, until the people could nominate some one to the Porte as permanent vehil.

Under these circumstances I was willing to advance the money necessary to secure this object, provided these changes could be actually accomplished before the money was paid. This was necessary, not from any desire on our part to control the Protestant community, but because Stepan Effendi had before violated his word under similar circumstances, and because I had the distinct declaration of the friends in England and America who had formally aided the community that they would not advance another *para* to the Protestant community until its affairs had been finally and satisfactorily arranged.

Stepan Effendi had proposed this condition in the first place. He still agreed to it, but he now insisted that the promise in respect to the money should be given to him in writing by a *rayah*. He suggested Mr. Haritun Minassian as satisfactory to him. Although this person had no connexion with and no interest in this money, he consented to act as a mutual friend in an arrangement which was certainly not less desirable for Stepan Effendi than for the community. The following papers were exchanged between them:

[Translation of a paper given by Stepan Effendi to Haritun.]

"FEBRUARY 15, 1865.

"I have summed up the claims of myself and Moses, my secretary, to February 28, 1865. The amount is 77,125 piastres. Of this I shall receive in gold 55,000 piasters, when, after having resigned my office, I shall have established Boghos Effendi as temporary caünaham of the Protestant community in my place, by order of the Porte. For 18,125 piasters I am to receive two bonds from Minassian Haritun, the printer. I am to receive a certificate for 21,000 piasters more, by which I can obtain this sum from the nation, and pay it to Ghazairs, as borrowed of him by me.

"STEPAN SEROPIAN,
"*Vekil of the Protestant Community.*"

[Translation of a paper given by Mr. Haritun to Stepan Effendi.]

"FEBRUARY 15, 1865.

"The subject of this paper is to state that on the 20th of Ramazan 1281, 55,000 piasters in coin, and two bonds—one for 9,237½ piasters, the other for 8,887½ piasters—in a bag, with Stepan Aghasscal, have been deposited with me, in behalf of the nation, and are in my possession, as a pledge for the claims of Stepan Effendi, Protestant vehil, and his secretary, Moses, for balance of salaries due them; subject to the agreement, that whenever, within six months from to-day, Stepan Effendi shall have resigned his office, and shall have caused Boghos Effendi, of Adrianople, to be appointed in his place, the 55,000 piastres and the two bonds in my possession shall, without fail, be delivered to him by me. If this agreement be not carried out, and the six months shall pass, then this money shall be restored to the individuals who have given it to me, and this paper will be void.

"HARITUN."

As Stepan Effendi expressed the wish to see and count this money and put his seal on the bag, he came to my office and did so, knowing that if the arrangements were complied with, this *moniuy* money was to be furnished by friends in England and America, as a free gift, to relieve the Protestant community of its embarrassments, and from all need of further aid.

That the money might be perfectly safe until Stepan Effendi had fulfilled the above conditions, I returned it to my safe whence it came, and gave to Mr. Haritun the following bond as security to him:

"CONSTANTINOPLE, *February* —, ——.

"Received from Haritun Minassian, printer, a deposit of 625 napoleons, (sealed by Stepan Effendi,) to be delivered to him whenever Stepan Effendi shall resign, and secure the appointment of Bogos Agha, of Adrianople, in his place as head of the Protestant community, provided that this be accomplished within six months of the above date. After that date this paper will have no value.

"GEORGE WASHBURN."

Up to this time it was supposed that Stepan Effendi was acting in good faith, as the arrangement had been originally proposed by him, and he had all along expressed his full satisfaction with it.

But it would appear that in his old age he must have become a tool in the hands of bad men, for, having secured the above bond from Mr. Haritun, he suddenly changed his mind, and declared that he had no intention of fulfilling these conditions of his own making, but would take the money in spite of us, without resigning at all. He declared in our bookstore that his Highness Ali Pacha had united with him to destroy the Protestant community, and drive the missionaries from the country. Of course this was as false as possible, and he appears to have told his Highness equally false stories in reference to us.

Stepan Effendi has since instituted the most oppressive and vexatious proceedings against Mr. Haritun, who is thus suffering as a perfectly innocent man for an act of friendship. If there has been any wrong done he has not done it. It rests either upon Stepan Effendi or upon me. I leave it to your judgment to decide between us.

His Highness Ali Pacha refers especially to a supposed purpose of ours to make a public demonstration against Stepan Effendi. I am happy to be able to assure you that his Highness has been deceived in this matter. We have never so much as dreamed of such a thing, and we consequently deny the charge as totally unfounded. The particular meeting to which he seems to refer, the only one I have heard of, was not planned by any missionary, nor was any foreigner present at it or in any way connected with it. We knew nothing of the meeting until we were informed by the Protestant notables that they had decided to hold such a meeting in the church in Stambool.

I am sure that if these facts are made known to his Highness he will rejoice in the opportunity of withdrawing the charge which he has been led, by incorrect information, to make against us.

It is our purpose so to conduct ourselves in this country, where we live under the august protection of his imperial Majesty the Sultan, that the Turkish authorities can have no occasion for complaint against us. We should regard any unfriendly controversy with the Porte as a positive calamity.

With your permission I shall send a copy of this letter to the Hon. Mr. Stuart, her Britannic Majesty's chargé d'affaires at the Porte, with whom also his Highness Ali Pacha communicated in reference to this question.

I remain, my dear sir, in behalf of the American missionaries, your most humble and obedient servant,

GEORGE WASHBURN.

[Translation.]

SUBLIME PORTE, BUREAU OF FOREIGN AFFAIRS,
April 2, 1865.

SIR: The Sublime Porte has just been informed that certain foreign missionaries are seeking to assemble the members of the American Protestant community with the view of causing a change of the civil organ of this community.

I need not remark to you, sir, that the interference of foreign priests in the affairs of a community exclusively composed of subjects of his Majesty the Sultan cannot be allowed by the Sublime Porte, and the object, purely civil or temporal, in question, can only be settled by the sole intervention of the authority of the country. Consequently I have to beg you, sir, to be so good as to recommend to the American Protestant missionaries to refrain from meddling with this question.

Accept, sir, the assurance of my highest consideration.

ALI.

Mr. MORRIS, *Minister Resident of the United States of America.*

Mr. Morris to Mr. Washburn.

LEGATION OF THE UNITED STATES OF AMERICA,
Constantinople, April 5, 1865.

DEAR SIR: I have the honor to enclose to you herewith a copy of a communication which I have received from the Sublime Porte on the subject of foreign Protestant missionaries in general, and the American in particular.

With much respect, your obedient servant,

E. JOY MORRIS.

Rev. GEORGE WASHBURN, *Pera.*

LEGATION OF THE UNITED STATES OF AMERICA,
Constantinople, April 7, 1865.

SIR: I have the honor to reply to your note of the 2d instant, relative to certain alleged proceedings of the American missionaries, and to enclose a communication from the Rev. George Washburn, on the subject.

The facts related in this paper exonerate the American missionaries from the charges preferred against them, and I hope they will be accepted by your Highness as a satisfactory refutation of the accusations of their enemies.

I avail myself of this occasion to renew to your Highness the assurance of my perfect consideration.

E. JOY MORRIS.

His Highness ALI PACHA,
Minister of Foreign Affairs.

Mr. Morris to Mr. Seward.

No. 111.] LEGATION OF THE UNITED STATES OF AMERICA,
Constantinople, May 1, 1865.

SIR: The receipt of a telegram from London on Friday last announcing the assassination of President Lincoln, and an attack on your own life, produced a great excitement in this country. A universal sentiment of indignation and of horror for such a crime against such a man as our late President, at the moment when the shouts of our victorious armies proclaimed that he had saved the country, and had won the respect and admiration of the world, by the successful issue of the struggle he had directed against that foe alike of humanity and American liberty and Union—southern slavery—was expressed by all the various nationalities of this capital.

The half-masted flag on the legation had hardly been raised before my colleagues of the diplomatic corps called to express their sympathies for our national loss. The society of Italian workmen delivered me the enclosed address of condolence, and the subjects of the Hellenic government in large numbers yesterday repaired to my residence to express their grief for such a calamity. Several of their number addressed the crowd in their native Greek, and in reply to a formal discourse from the chairman of the committee, I delivered to the assembled people the enclosed reply. In recognition of such a friendly act, I caused the Greek flag to be raised above the half-masted American flag. The spectacle of these two flags, of the two most intensely liberty-loving people in the world, floating together in kindred sympathy on the same staff, created a deep sensation among the passing crowds.

It gives me a melancholy pleasure to refer to these incidents as showing how widespread was the fame achieved by President Lincoln, and how earnest was the admiration felt for the services he had rendered to his race and to his country, even in this remote corner of Europe.

I cannot be mistaken, for I see and feel it all around me, in predicting that this assassination, be the motive what it may, will produce important political consequences throughout Europe, and will arouse and stimulate the friends of liberty to new efforts against despotism and arbitrary power.

The assassin's hand has consecrated the life and death of President Lincoln. He fell a victim to his devotion to the cause of liberty and human rights, and he will take his place in history among the martyrs whom universal humanity honors as its benefactor.

Lest there should be some apprehension relative to the qualifications of President Johnson to the high office, to the duties of which he has been called, I caused to be published in the journals of this city the excellent biographical sketch of his excellency contained in Appleton's American Encyclopedia. This memoir, reciting, as it does, in detail his public life—his long and honorable career as governor of Tennessee, and in the legislature of that State, and in both branches of the federal Congress, and his tried loyalty to the Union—made a most favorable impression on the public mind and gave a correct understanding of the capacity and services of the present head of the United States government.

I cannot conclude this despatch without expressing my fervent prayer that the life of Secretary Seward may be spared, and that by the favor of Almighty God he may recover from the wounds under which he is suffering. Never were his services to his country more evident than now, and never was there such a general concurrence in the opinion, both among strangers and Americans, of the immense importance of your excellency's life to the dearest interests of the American people.

I have the honor to be, with great respect, your obedient servant,

E. JOY MORRIS.

Hon. William H. Seward,
Secretary of State.

By this or the succeeding mail I will transmit the proceedings of the American residents, in meeting convened at my residence, relative to the death of President Lincoln.

N. B. The address from foreign bodies referred to in the above will be furnished in the next mail.

Mr. Morris to Mr. Hunter.

No. 112.] Legation of the United States of America,
Constantinople, May 3, 1865.

Sir: I have the honor to transmit enclosed copies of a correspondence between his Highness Ali Pacha and myself, relative to the late melancholy events at Washington.

Since the answer was written to the letter from the Porte, we have received the sad news of the death of Mr. Seward. This intelligence has caused a most painful impression through all circles, and particularly those of the government and diplomatic corps. He had won the admiration and esteem of all who are conversant with our politics, by his eminent ability as a diplomatic writer and by the rare skill and judgment with which he directed our foreign policy, in the most critical period of American history. His name and fame will be inseparably associated with the great events in which he was so conspicuous an actor.

I have the honor to be, very respectfully, your obedient servant,

E. JOY MORRIS.

Hon. WILLIAM HUNTER,
Acting Secretary of State.

Ali Pacha to Mr. Morris.

[Translation.]

SUBLIME PORTE, DEPARTMENT OF FOREIGN AFFAIRS, *May* 1, 1865.

SIR: The Sultan, my august sovereign, has learned with profound affliction the mournful news of the cruel death of President Lincoln, and of the wounding of the Secretary of State; and I have been commanded to convey to you an expression of the regrets of his imperial Majesty.

I need not state to you, sir, how much the imperial government, in its character of sincere friend of the United States, is interested in their prosperity, and how great has been the sorrow which this event has occasioned.

Be pleased, sir, to accept assurances of my high consideration.

ALI.

Mr. MORRIS,
Minister Resident United States of America.

Mr. Morris to Ali Pacha.

[Translation.]

LEGATION OF THE UNITED STATES OF AMERICA,
Constantinople, May 2, 1865.

HIGHNESS: I have had the honor to receive the letter which your Highness, by order of your august sovereign, addressed me on the 1st of May, in expression of profound grief of his imperial Majesty on learning the sad news of the cruel death of President Lincoln and the wounding of the Secretary of State.

I beg your Highness to be so good as to convey to his imperial Majesty my respectful thanks for this manifestation of his regrets on an occasion which has so deeply afflicted the hearts of a whole nation. This event is the more to be regretted as it came at a moment when a desolating civil war of four years' duration, involving alike the best interests of humanity and the American people, had been brought to a successful termination by the energy, wisdom, and firmness of purpose of President Lincoln, with the efficient co-operation of that accomplished statesman, Mr. Seward, and his colleagues in the cabinet, and by the valor and skill of our citizen soldiers and their commanders. It was hoped that these two distinguished men would have been permitted by Divine Providence to live to perfect in peace the re-establishment of that Union in defence of which so much blood had been poured out on the field of battle. In His inscrutable wisdom He has otherwise ordained.

I would also thank the imperial government for its sympathy in favor of the United States. During my residence at this court I have had frequent occasion to bear testimony to the American government of the earnest sympathy of the Ottoman government with the United States in the war for national existence in which it found itself engaged, and of the ardent desire of his Majesty the Sultan that it should terminate in the re-establishment of the Union in complete integrity, and on a firm and impregnable basis. In the hour of national calamity we have found in the Ottoman government a true and zealous friend. This new expression of its friendship only confirms its past acts, and will tend to strengthen yet more the good relations existing between the two countries.

I avail myself of this occasion to renew to your Highness the assurance of my most distinguished consideration.

E. JOY MORRIS.

Mr. Morris to Mr. Seward.

LEGATION OF THE UNITED STATES OF AMERICA,
Constantinople, May 4, 1865.

SIR: I have the honor to transmit enclosed two copies of the proceedings of a meeting of American citizens convened at this legation, relative to the assassination of President Lincoln and the attack on your own life. One copy is intended for the widow of the President, to whom I respectfully request that it may be forwarded.

Since the writing of my despatch of yesterday's date, we have been overjoyed to learn that the rumor of your death is not true, and that you are recovering from the dreadful wounds inflicted on you by the assassin. We humbly invoke an all-merciful God to restore you to health for the sake of the best interests of our beloved country. However variant may be the opinions of people in Europe as to the American war, they are accordant in the recognition of the consummate ability and sagacity with which you have directed our foreign policy. The preservation of your life is regarded as an event in which the world at large has a common interest with your fellow-countrymen. May Heaven prolong your useful life for new services to the American people!

I enclose the address of the Italian industrial society of this place, with a translation of the same; and also, as it was delivered in French, the original of my reply to the address of condolence of the Greeks, (Hellenics, subjects of George 1st,) from the Courrier d'Orient of this city of May 3, 1865.

I have the honor to be, with great respect, your obedient servant,

E. JOY MORRIS.

Hon. WILLIAM H. SEWARD,
Secretary of State

(For enclosures see Appendix, separate volume.)

Mr. Morris to Mr. Hunter.

[Extract.]

No. 114.] LEGATION OF THE UNITED STATES OF AMERICA,
Constantinople, May 11, 1865.

SIR: I have the honor to acknowledge the receipt of despatch No. 87, and the circular containing the official announcement of the assassination of President Lincoln. In a previous despatch I referred at large to the universal feeling of horror and indignation which such a monstrous crime had produced among all classes of the population of this capital. No human event, it seems to me, could inspire a deeper and more widespread sense of sorrow and abhorrence than such a crime against such a man. President Lincoln's course of action, during his four years' term of office, had been so honorable to himself and so useful to his country, that he had won even the respect of the enemies of the noble cause he championed. He lived long enough to refute the calumnies of his foreign assailants, and to confound the wicked schemes of domestic traitors. His steady perseverance in the course of right, his unshaken faith in ultimate success, and the stern loyalty he exhibited to the Constitution, astonished the European world, and enforced its admiration of one of the grandest exhibitions of moral courage and of the conscientious discharge of duty to be found in ancient or modern history. He has descended to the tomb with an untarnished fame, and honored alike by the kings and people of Europe, and the citizens of republican America.

Since my last despatch a deputation has called on me on the part of the

American church and nationality to express their condolence, and their hopes that slavery, the cause of all our woes, will be forever eradicated in the United States. This delegation consisted of three of the highest ecclesiastical dignitaries of the American church.

Enclosed will be found copies of despatches to the United States consuls at Beyrout and Smyrna, to which I respectfully call attention. Their main object is to disabuse the public mind of any erroneous impressions as to the character and qualifications of President Johnson. I am pleased to say that the elevated and rare traits of character which distinguished President Johnson, and his eminent capacity for the high trusts devolved upon him, are now beginning to be appreciated, and the European public are conscious that the destinies of the United States are guided by a firm and vigorous mind, which cannot be intimidated by any array of difficulties, and which is equal to any emergency. Energy, force of will, inflexible patriotism, and high moral courage, are the characteristics now ascribed to President Johnson, and they are producing a most salutary feeling of respect and regard for the nation over which he presides. Among Americans unlimited confidence is entertained in President Johnson, and the assurance is cherished that his administration will be a fitting sequel to that of his illustrious predecessor.

I respectfully suggest the propriety of giving publicity, through the press, to the addresses of felicitation and of sympathy made to me on the part of the Helenic Greeks of Constantinople. That of sympathy is full of eloquent feeling, and does such honor to the generous people for whom it speaks, that I venture to express the opinion that it ought be spread before the American republic. * * * * * *

I have the honor to be, very respectfully, your obedient servant,

E. JOY MORRIS.

Hon. WILLIAM HUNTER,
Acting Secretary of State.

(For enclosure see Appendix, separate volume.)

Address of felicitation of the Hellenic Greeks of Constantinople to Hon. E. Joy Morris, United States minister, April 27, on the victories which secured the overthrow of the pro-slavery rebellion and established the American Union.

[Translation.]

CONSTANTINOPLE, *April* 27, 1865.

Honored representative of the American people and government under the Presidency of the great citizen Lincoln:

The descendants of Plato have assembled before the residence of the respected representative of the glorious American republic to congratulate him on the victories which have saved his country.

When a hydra-headed rebellion was menacing the existence of the Union, with painful anxiety we watched the progress of the struggle, and our prayers were offered up to God for a brave people contending for national existence against domestic treason and foreign intrigues.

Fearful as was the conflict, our hopes of ultimate triumph for the cause of Union and liberty were based upon our confidence in the intelligence and patriotism of the descendants of Washington, and in the wisdom and heroic firmness of President Lincoln, who, at this critical period, directed the destinies of the nation.

We were not mistaken. The cause of humanity triumphed, because the American people appreciated the great issues at stake, and with a sacrifice of blood and treasure unparalleled in history, on the fields of battle saved their menaced institutions of free government from destruction. Noble example of patriotic devotion, worthy of honor wherever public virtue is esteemed and love of freedom is cherished!

The last American struggle must be inscribed with golden letters in the annals of history, for it was a battle for the dearest rights of man. All mankind participate in the benefits of the victory achieved, and from all parts of the world the thanks of sympathizing millions ar tendered to the American people for the constancy and valor through which the cause of right was finally crowned with success.

Accept, honored sir, the heartfelt congratulations of the Greeks of Constantinople, and may God inspire other nations to a similar exhibition of heroic virtue when their liberty and independence are assaulted.

Translation, from the original French, of the reply of Mr. E. Joy Morris, United States minister, to the above address of felicitation of the Hellenic Greeks of Constantinople.

With mingled emotions of joy and grief I receive this imposing manifestation of the Hellenics of Constantinople towards my country and its illustrious chief, the late President Lincoln. I rejoice that the character and actions of that great man are so justly appreciated and so affectionately revered by the intelligent community you represent. It is another proof of the fidelity of the Greek people to the glorious traditions of their history, that the same love of liberty which distinguished them in antiquity yet exists, and that everywhere, where there is a struggle between the spirit of liberty and despotism, their suffrages are on the side of those who are the champions of the natural rights of man.

It is from your ancestors, Hellenic Greeks, that we have inherited our passion for liberty. The history of Leonidas, with his three hundred Spartans, perishing willing victims for the safety of their country at Thermopylæ; that of Miltiades and Themistocles upon the plain of Marathon and the Gulf of Salamis, repelling the invaders of Greece, not by the force of numbers, but by the force of an invincible courage, is taught in our schools as a lesson of sublime patriotism.

Honor to a people who, after the lapse of twenty-five centuries, yet preserve in their hearts that sacred fire which rendered their ancient heroes immortal!

The terrible conflict which is about terminating in the United States was a struggle between the two opposite principles of liberty and slavery. To promote the interests of the latter, an attempt was made to destroy the American Union and to erect on its ruins a government the corner-stone of which was to be human slavery. By the favor of God, the man most capable of meeting such a crisis in this emergency was at the head of the nation. He was a man pure in his morals, of irreproachable integrity, and one who loved his race and country with equal affection. In defending the Constitution, he knew that he was defending an instrument of government in the preservation of which all mankind had a common interest with us. He comprehended in all its proportions the great part which God had given him to perform, and, before Heaven and earth, he proved that he was equal to the task imposed on him.

At the moment when the shouts of victory were rising from all the fields of battle, when the flag of liberty was again being raised on the towers and forts from which it had been sacrilegiously torn down four years ago, the President fell beneath the arm of an assassin. Fearful crime to kill such a man! Supreme folly, to choose such a moment for so infamous a deed. He had accomplished his mission; he had saved his country and had gained a place in the temple of glory where he will always be honored as one of the benefactors of humanity. The assassins of liberty and of its champions merit and receive in history an eternal execration.

The Secretary of State, Mr. Seward, who had so ably seconded the efforts of the President, and who, by his great capacity, had so wisely represented the nation abroad in his diplomatic writings, was also destined to be a victim. We implore an all-merciful God that his life may be spared, that he may contribute by his sagacious intellect to the consolidation of the republic which is now rising so majestically, unchanged in form and unharmed in strength, from so many fields of battle.

In the name of the American people, I thank you, Hellenics, for this enthusiastic demonstration of regard for my country and its savior, and for your wishes that the republic of the United States of America may continue to exist in the future, as in the past, the boulevard of modern liberty and the pioneer of human progress.

Adieu, Hellenics, and may the Greek and American flags which float united above our heads be a symbol of that fraternity of heart that exists between two people who have the same sympathies and the same aspirations.

Mr. Morris to Mr. Johnson.

UNITED STATES LEGATION,
Constantinople, May 10, 1865.

SIR: You have no doubt already received information of the assassination of President Lincoln, and of the attempt on the life of Secretary Seward, through the telegraph and the State Department. These dreadful deeds have aroused a feeling of horror and indignation throughout all Europe, and have betrayed to the world the fiendish passions engendered by the institution of slavery. It seems in the order of human events that no great humanitarian revolution can be accomplished without the sacrifice of some illustrious victim. Men offer up their lives on the scaffold for the benefit of their race, and others risk life and fortune, and all that endears them to existence, to further the cause of human rights. Great social and political evils cannot be uprooted without commotions that shake the world by their violence.

Certainly there never occupied the post of a ruler of a country a man who had less bitterness in his heart towards his fellow-men than President Lincoln, or one who was more genial in his nature, more tolerant to his enemies, and more just in his political conduct. The only offence he committed was that of being loyal to his country when others were false to her; of saving the republic when menaced by destruction. God, in his mercy, permitted him to live till he had baffled the schemes of the conspirators and had established the Union in its original integrity. His glory the dagger of the assassin cannot take away. It will live immortal in history and endear his name to the remotest generations of American freemen.

Had not the plans of the conspirators failed for want of unity of action, we should have had to mourn the deaths of the Vice-President and all the members of the cabinet. Their diabolical malignity aimed at paralyzing the government by a temporary anarchy of rule, thus hoping to create a widespread disorder and confusion.

President Johnson I believe you know. I knew him from six years since in Congress, when he was a member, and I know him to be a man of the utmost firmness of character and force of will, and to be possessed of a moral courage that renders him equal to any emergency. Amidst bad examples around him and the temptations incident to southern life, he has always been distinguished for exemplary habits of life. If there has been any deviation from these habits it is exceptional and not characteristic of the man, and no doubt induced by accidental causes. I have unlimited confidence in him from my own personal knowledge and observation, and I beg that you will refer to me when speaking to your colleagues of his capacity and character. How long I may continue to serve the government under him I know not, and shall take no steps to interfere with the free exercise of the judgment of the President in relation to the incumbent of this post; but as an American citizen I deem it my duty to aid in dispelling serious misapprehensions as to his character and capacity. He will be traduced and calumniated, as his predecessor was, because he is the President of a republic in the overthrow of which every enemy of human liberty has an interest, and every hour of whose existence gives the lie to the necessity of despotism and arbitrary power as instruments of government.

I rejoice to be able to inform you that the Secretary of State and his son are in a fair way of recovery, and that their assailant has been arrested with several of his accomplices.

Very respectfully, your obedient servant,

E. JOY MORRIS.

J. A. JOHNSON, Esq.,
United States Consul, Beyrout.

Mr. Morris to Mr. Hunter.

No. 115.] LEGATION OF THE UNITED STATES OF AMERICA,
Constantinople, May 18, 1865.

SIR: I have the honor to transmit, enclosed, addresses of condolence on the death of President Lincoln from the British residents of Constantinople and the printed account of the proceedings in connexion with the same, and from the native Protestant community of this place, through their head, Mr. Seropyan. That of the British residents represents almost the entire English colony of Constantinople, and contains very notable names belonging to it.

I beg that you will do the American community of Constantinople the honor to express to President Johnson their unqualified confidence in his ability to administer the government, and their assurance that through his firmness of purpose, energy and character, and long experience in public affairs, and his eminent capacity, the evils of the late civil war will soon be repaired, and the republic be restored to its pristine integrity and tranquillity. I venture also to express the remark that among foreigners the conviction prevails that the present head of the United States government is a statesman of unusual force of character and intellect. Whatever errors may have existed on this subject have already been dispelled.

I visited the grand vizier and minister of foreign affairs a fews days since and took occasion to give them a correct estimate of the public career, characteristics, and ability of President Johnson. They thanked me for the information, and assured me they would take great pleasure in communicating my statements to his Majesty the Sultan, who, as a sincere and undeviating friend of the Union, would be pleased to know that a statesman of such tried capacity, private worth, and elevated traits of character, now presided over the American republic.

General Marquez, a special envoy from the so-called emperor Maximilian of Mexico, has arrived here for the purpose of delivering to the Sultan the decoration of the Order of Guadaloupe.

I have the honor to be, very respectfully, your obedient servant,

E. JOY MORRIS.

Hon. WILLIAM HUNTER,
Acting Secretary of State.

(For enclosures see Appendix, separate volume.)

Mr. Morris to Mr. Hunter.

[Extract.]

No. 116.] LEGATION OF THE UNITED STATES OF AMERICA,
Constantinople, May 25, 1865.

SIR: I have the honor to transmit a letter of condolence on the part of the Shah of Persia and one from the Greek minister of foreign affairs to the Greek consul at New York. The letter has been communicated to me by the minister of Greece to the Porte, by order of his government, with the request that I should forward it to my government.

The object of the visit of General Marquez, the special envoy of the so-called emperor Maximilian, is limited to the purpose designated in my last despatch. The grand vizier declares to be without foundation the report that the Porte will give him its sanction of the incorporation of the Egyptian blacks into the imperial army, and of a further contingent of black troops from Egypt. He said, in reply to my inquiries on the subject, that the Porte would have nothing to do with such an affair. I learn, however, that General Marquez expects to receive at Vienna four battalions and a regiment for the service of Maximilian. The soldiers enlisted in Europe for this purpose are needy adventurers, whom necessity, and not sympathy with the imperial cause, has induced to accept the proffers of the agents of Maximilian. They are not such a class of men as can be relied on to support a government in the hour of adversity. The desire to get to America also is so great that men will embrace any pretext to compass their wishes in this respect. Never was there a time when the hearts of the million masses of Europe throbbed so warmly to the United States as now, and never was there less sympathy with any movements directed against the spread of our political principles on the American continent.

* * * * * * *

I have the honor to be, very respectfully, your obedient servant,

E. JOY MORRIS.

Hon. WILLIAM HUNTER,
Acting Secretary of State.

(For enclosures see Appendix, separate volume.)

P. S.—I beg to enclose a brief statement of the last financial scheme of the Turkish government.

The conversion of the home debt.

The following is an abstract of the statement issued in London by the contractors for thi operation:

"The great object of the scheme may be described as that of definitely transporting Turkish finance from the region of Oriental into that of European finance. Oriental governments invariably live from hand to mouth. They contract debts without forethought, are irregular in their payments, and as a consequence pay, in a long run, usurious rates in order to cover the risks. European governments, on the other hand, make the act of borrowing a deliberate and public act, surrounded by as many safeguards to the lender as possible, and they invest their public stocks with as many attributes of security and convenience to the holder as possible, so as to get money at the lowest rate which the intrinsic state of their credit admits of. Foremost among these attributes is the existence of one large, uniform stock, or consols, instead of various petty stocks of different denominations. Nor is it less important for countries where domestic capital is scarce and a large part of their national debt is raised abroad to make it payable in specie, at a fixed exchange, at all the principal monetary centres of Europe. A consolidated debt of this sort, payable at London, Paris, Amsterdam, and Frankfort, as well as at home, inscribed in a grand livrè, and charged on the general revenues of the empire, with due provisions against frittering these means away by hypothecations or raising further loans, except openly and under legislative authority, may be said to afford the maximum of security and convenience possible, and, consequently, to enable the state which adopts it to raise money at the minimum rate consistent with its intrinsic resources and credit. There is as much difference between this and the irregular expedients by which Oriental governments are accustomed to raise money as between the mortgage which a nobleman may give an assurance company on his estate, and the bills which the same nobleman, in the thoughtless days of his youth, may have given to some West End money-lender to meet a loss on the turf. The former is in some respects less convenient, for it must be paid punctually each quarter day in actual cash, while the latter may probably be stayed off for a term or two by signing a fresh piece of stamped paper; but then he pays the difference between 4 and 40 per cent. for the accommodation, and, what is even more important, he executes the mortgage deed only after due reflection and on some grave occasion, while, if once accustomed to it, he is apt to scatter about his signature to the looser sort of paper to meet every passing whim or inconvenience. These general principles apply peculiarly to the case of Turkey. The cause of her pecuniary embarrassments has been, not the deficiency of her resources to meet her necessary expenses, but the inveterate habit of borrowing from local money-lenders at Constantinople at 15, 20, and even 30 and 40 per cent., to meet arrears in the collection of taxes and irregular expenses incurred without any publicity or sanction.

"Again: punctuality in the payment of debts necessitates punctuality in the collection of revenue. Now, the want of this punctuality has been the want of Turkish finance. The revenue is ample to meet the expenditure, but practically from 20 to 30 per cent. of each year's collection is allowed to fall into arrear, and a considerable part of this arrear is never recovered. There is no reason why the whole revenue should not be punctually collected, as in India, where the arrears are inconsiderable. The necessity of paying half-yearly dividends punctually will soon bring about the administrative reforms which are alone necessary to make the collection of the very light taxation of Turkey prompt and regular. As regards the payment of a large part of her debt abroad, Turkey is also in an exceptionably favorable position. Turkey is like India, a country which habitually exports more than it imports, and this favorable balance of trade is certain to increase as roads and railways develop the resources of the interior. In the case of Turkey, therefore, as in India, a large amount of payment may be made abroad by the State without preventing the influx of a moderate amount of specie. If these payments ceased, the influx of specie would soon become excessive and raise prices to a point that would check exports."

"In addition to these general considerations, it is pointed out that the special advantages to the Turkish government of the present consolidation will be—

"1. That it enables them to raise a sum of £2,000,000 cash, without any increase of present burden on the budget, the saving by the reduction of the sinking fund from 2 to 1 per cent. on the capital covered being enough to pay 5 per cent. interest and 1 per cent. sinking fund on £4,000,000 of new stock.

"2. The new sinking fund being applied in the purchase of stock in the market at 55 or 60, instead of in drawings at 100, will go nearly twice as far, and, in addition to paying off the capital of the debt in 37 years, will accumulate a reserve fund equal to that capital in the same period.

"3. The existence of this reserve fund, and of a reserve of authorized inscription in the grand livre, will always enable the treasury to obtain such temporary advances as may be required to equalize the receipts and payments of different periods of the year, or to meet grave emergencies at a moderate rate of interest.

"As regards the present holders of the internal debt, the advantages are equally obvious. The holder of a six per cent. consolidé of 100 medjidies d'or, or £90 sterling, gets £110 sterling of new 5 per cent. consols, yielding a slightly better interest, with £20 more capital and all the vast improvements of security afforded by inscription in the grand livre and payment of interest in gold, at a fixed exchange, in all the principal places of Europe. For this great advantage he gives up nothing but the difference between the present two per cent. amortissement and the one per cent. new amortissement applied in purchasing the stock. As a question of figures, it is quite clear he gains greatly. The new consols are in all respects on a par, as regards security, with the existing six per cent. external loans, except as regards the special hypothecations of certain branches of revenue in favor of the latter, which are fast running off by the action of their sinking funds, and to which, with the exception of the special charge on the Egyptian tribute for the loan of 1854, no great value could be attached in the extreme and improbable case of Turkey becoming insolvent. But if a 6 per cent. stock with a 2 per cent. amortissement be worth 70, (and it is now quoted higher,) a 5 per cent. stock is worth 53 without any allowance for the 1 per cent. amortisation, which, being applied in purchase, tends to raise the average market price of the stock. And if £100 of the new consols be worth £53, a consolidé, which is exchanged for £110, is worth £58. But the market value of the same consolidé was not above £48 until the recent issue on the prospect of the conversion, and if the scheme for conversion had been defeated the price would in all probability have gone back to that figure, or lower. For the other classes of internal debt the advantage of conversion is equally obvious. Lastly, as regards the holders of the external debts, their position is improved by the general improvement of Turkish finance. Whatever improves the credit and adds to the borrowing power of a state, improves the security of previous debts. The holders retain all their special securities, whatever they may be worth, unaffected, and the only suspicion of an injury to them is that the superior attractions of the new stock may lead to competition with the old stocks in foreign markets. But this is by no means certain, as it is generally found that when a domestic stock rises in value the native holders buy rather than sell. This was strikingly the case in India with regard to the rupee paper, and there is every reason to believe that as Turkish stock rises and confidence is created, a larger, rather than a smaller, proportion of the whole debt will be held in Turkey. At any rate, the holders of the old external debts will always have the opportunity of converting, at a fair rate, if they desire it, into the new stock, as the policy of the Turkish government must always be anticipated by voluntary conversions, the period of the complete unification of the whole national debt, and discharge all special hypothecations. Supposing all debts converted into the new stock, the whole existing national debt of Turkey would only be about £60,000,000. Such a debt will be by far the smallest debt of any country of Europe in proportion to its population, revenue, and resources; and with a moderately good system of taxation and financial administration, which are now in the way of being carried out, the Turkish treasury would soon be in a state of prosperity.

"The following extract from a statistical return just published by the Foreign Office affords the best proof how light are the debt and taxation of Turkey compared not only with those of wealthy nations, such as England and France, but with the poorer countries of Europe, such as Russia and Austria, and even with the states of South America:

PER HEAD OF POPULATION.

	Annual revenue.			Public debt.		
	£	s.	d.	£	s.	d.
England	2	8	2	28	2	5
France	2	0	4	14	0	4
Russia	0	12	7	3	11	1
Austria	0	16	8	6	12	4
Italy	1	4	9	5	13	3
Spain	1	6	4	9	8	5
Portugal	0	17	1	8	7	1
Brazil	0	15	8	2	19	8
Chili	0	17	10	1	16	4
Peru	1	13	11	2	14	10
Turkey	0	7	9	1	3	1

Mr. Hunter to Mr. Morris.

No. 90.]

DEPARTMENT OF STATE,
Washington, June 27, 1865.

SIR: I have the honor to acknowledge the receipt of your despatches from No. 110 to No. 115, inclusive, the latter bearing date May 18. The accounts they furnish of the effect produced in the Turkish capital by the intelligence of the President's assassination and the attempt upon the life of Mr. Seward have been read with great interest and gratification. Your proceedings in connexion with this subject are fully approved.

I am, sir, your obedient servant,

W. HUNTER,
Acting Secretary.

E. JOY MORRIS, Esq., *&c., &c., &c., Constantinople.*

Mr. Morris to Mr. Seward.

No. 118.] LEGATION OF THE UNITED STATES OF AMERICA,
Constantinople, July 13, 1865.

SIR: I have the honor to acknowledge the receipt of the circular announcing the approaching departure of Rear-Admiral Goldsborough as commander of the United States squadron in European waters, and that he is instructed not to enter any port, unless absolutely necessary, where belligerent privileges may be extended to the United States rebels, &c. In this connexion I beg leave to refer to my despatch of May 6, 1862, enclosing a copy of the vizerial order addressed to all the public functionaries of the Sublime Porte on the sea-coast of the Ottoman empire. That order was to the following effect:

"SUBLIME PORTE, *Chiral* 24, 1278—(*April* 23, 1862.)

"EXCELLENCY: According to the principles of international rights established in the late treaty at the conference held in Paris, the use of ships-of-war and other vessels as privateers (Korsan) was entirely abolished by all the great powers therein represented.

"The legation of the United States of America has now requested that, conformably with the preceding, instructions be given by the Sublime Porte to its functionaries on the sea-coast of the empire, for the purpose of maintaining the principle adopted as aforesaid. As it has therefore been here deemed necessary, in view of said principle, that effectual measures should be taken to prevent vessels of the United States of America from being exposed to injury in any of the ports and waters of the Ottoman dominions by privateers such as those alluded to, your excellency will, in case any privateers or armed vessels preying on the commerce of the United States attempt to enter them, with or without prize, adopt such means as will prevent them from carrying the design into execution."

The above order was drawn up at my request, and with the understanding that it was intended to be a denial of belligerent rights to the United States rebels, and as a sign of the determination of the Turkish government to discountenance the hostile designs of the rebels against the integrity of the republic of the United States. The government of the Sultan never recognized the rebels as belligerents, notwithstanding the example of England and France, nor did it at any time, directly or indirectly, manifest any sympathy with their efforts for the destruction of the American Union. During the whole period of the war the war vessels of the United States enjoyed unlimited hospitality of the Turkish ports, and they were never put upon a level with the rebel cruisers, and subject to an odious and unjust restriction of twenty-four hours' stay in the harbors of this empire. The above order was issued in good faith, and it would have been enforced to its full extent had an occasion required it.

It gives me pleasure, now that the war is over, to refer to these facts. Considering the power of English and French influence at this court, it seems to me that the policy of the Ottoman government, with respect to the United States during the recent civil war, is one that does it infinite credit, and is a striking exhibition of political courage in behalf of a government whose friendship it has always cherished. There is no necessity, therefore, on the part of the Turkish government to issue a proclamation withdrawing belligerent rights from the United States rebels, for it never conceded any to them.

Rear-Admiral Goldsborough, should he honor the waters and harbors of Turkey with a visit of the squadron under his command, will be received with the highest honors, and with a cordiality of feeling indicative of the sympathy of this government with the cause he has so gallantly sustained in hostile waters during the last four years.

With great respect, your obedient servant,

E. JOY MORRIS.

Hon. WILLIAM H. SEWARD,
Secretary of State.

Mr. Morris to Mr. Seward.

No. 119.] LEGATION OF THE UNITED STATES OF AMERICA,
Constantinople, July 13, 1865.

SIR: I regret to be obliged to report that the cholera has made its appearance at Constantinople. It was introduced here by an Egyptian war steamer, on which several cases and deaths from this disease occurred. Thus far it has not spread much, it being confined chiefly to the arsenal to which the cholera patients of the vessel above referred to were transported. In all up to date not more than twelve deaths from cholera have occurred here. Sanitary measures are being taken to prevent it from extending among the population. I fear, however, that having made its entrance here, this capital cannot escape its ravages to a greater or less degree of intensity. The last reports from Egypt represent the deaths from cholera at almost 200 daily in Alexandria, and about 300 in Cairo. It was apprehended that in the hot months of August and September its ravages would be yet greater.

I have the honor to be your obedient servant,

E. JOY MORRIS.

Hon. WILLIAM H. SEWARD,
Secretary of State.

Mr. Morris to Mr. Seward.

No. 120.] LEGATION OF THE UNITED STATES OF AMERICA,
Constantinople.

SIR: I have the honor to acknowledge the receipt of despatch No. 90. I regret to be obliged to state that the cholera continues to extend its ravages, notwithstanding the efforts making by the government to arrest its progress. Whatever may be the opinion of medical men, it is evident that it is propagated by contagion, as it fixed itself in the locality where the first deaths from an Egyptian man-of-war took place, and has thence gradually extended itself over the Christian quarter of Pera, and through Stamboul, (Constantinople proper.) In the most infected region, Cassim Pacha, where it originally broke out—a quarter inhabited chiefly by workmen connected with the navy yard, and situated in a low valley encompassed by high hills, with imperfect drainage—it has been very fatal, having attacked almost the entire population. Such have been its ravages there that the government has ordered all the large khans and buildings occupied by many persons together to be vacated, and has provided tents for them on the heights surrounding the city.

Had proper quarantine measures been taken at first, the introduction of the cholera from Egypt might have been prevented. It seems to me, from our experience here, that it will be advisable in the United States to guard against it by the most rigid quarantine regulations. Otherwise, if it once enters the country it will be very fatal, in consequence of the great destitution prevailing in Virginia and other of the southern States, and of the diseases which always follow in the train of war.

The published number of deaths per day is about 160, but they are known to largely exceed that number. The whole number of deaths from the origin of the disease to the present time is about 2,000. A great panic prevails among the population, particularly the Christian portion of it, and people are fleeing by thousands in every direction from the city. It is to be hoped, however, that the sanitary measures adopted by the government and pursued with great energy will have the effect sooner or later to arrest the epidemic.

With great respect, your obedient servant,

E. JOY MORRIS.

Hon. WILLIAM H. SEWARD, *Secretary of State.*

THE CHOLERA.

To the Editor of the Levant Herald:

SIR: During the prevalence of the cholera morbus in the different ports of Turkey, any remarks that may tend to the better knowledge of the mysterious disease and its development may be acceptable, and I have, therefore, taken the liberty of addressing you the following—the result of my observations:

Cholera can be communicated—

1. By persons direct, who carry the seeds of the disease (or vitiated air) with them.
2. By clothes or other articles used by the sick.
3. By infected vessels or lazarettos, which, though isolated, are too near healthy towns, and these generating vitiated air, it soon passes the imaginary boundaries of quarantine.

In proof of these assertions I may remark:

1. The cholera in the present instance was introduced into Arabia by pilgrims from India, bringing with them the seeds of the disease. It did not develop itself until the period of the Courbarn-Baivam, when the thousands of animals sacrificed, of every size, from a camel downward, were left to putrefy; the effluvium, combined with the ascent of the holy hill by the pilgrims bear-headed in a burning, tropical sun, and the free use of all kinds of unwholesome fruits and vegetables, was immediately succeeded by the outbreak of the disease. At Djeddah it assumed a comparatively mild form, only ten per cent. of the cases proving fatal. The pilgrims in their passage through Egypt communicated the disease, which unfortunately proved to be of a much more fatal type.

The cholera was also introduced into Turkey at the commencement of the Crimean war by a French steamer with troops from Algiers. On her arrival at Gallipoli it was whispered a few cases had occurred during her voyage. The troops were, however, landed; in a few days cholera raged, and the French lost upwards of 2,000 men from the disease in this town alone. From Gallipoli the disease was introduced into the French hospital at Abydos by a few patients attacked with the malady sent from thence. Nearly the whole of the other patients were shortly after taken with the cholera.

2. The disease from the Abydos hospital was communicated to the Dardanelles. The first persons attacked were the washer-woman and her daughter, who washed the dirty linen sent to them from the hospital; they died, and the malady soon spread in the town.

3. During the present outbreak of cholera, the precaution of placing in quarantine vessels and passengers from Alexandria has not prevented the malady from spreading beyond the vessels and boundaries of the lazarettos, as instanced at Constantinople, Smyrna, and the Dardanelles, where it commenced chiefly in the immediate neighborhood of the lazarettos. It is certain the Egyptian frigate should never have been admitted into the vicinity of Constantinople, nor the steamer from Alexandria allowed to anchor near Smyrna or the Dardanelles, still less the passengers landed in the different lazarettos. Security, as far as we can judge of this mysterious malady, can only be attained by an early attention in preventing vessels from infected places performing their quarantine near healthy towns; for although the disease may not develop itself with the same intensity in one place as another, owing to atmospheric and other causes, still there is no doubt that cholera can be communicated (when the vicinity is too close) through the medium of the air, malgré quarantine and all its present regulations. Some distant point should have been chosen for the complete isolation of vessels coming from Alexandria, and there to perform their quarantine; for instance, one of the numerous islands of the Archipelago, far away from any of the thickly populated towns in Turkey.

I am, &c.,

F. C.

DARDANELLES, *July* 26.

Mr. Morris to Mr. Seward.

[Extract.]

No. 121.] LEGATION OF THE UNITED STATES OF AMERICA,
Constantinople, August 14, 1865.

* * * * * * *

SIR: I regret to state that the cholera still continues its ravages—the deaths for the last two weeks averaging, according to the official reports alone, about three hundred daily. The actual number is in excess of this estimate. It has spread over all the environs of Constantinople, and along both the Asiatic and European shores of the Bosphorus to the Black sea. Since the nights have grown cool, and the humidity has increased, it seems to have become more malignant, and to have assumed an almost contagious character.

Great consternation prevails among the population, and they are fleeing in all directions from the pestilence, many of them establishing themselves on remote mountain heights. The government has, at its own expense, transported over 80,000 of the laboring classes to ports on the Black sea, and it is safe to say that at least 150,000 people have left Constantinople. They seem to have carried the pestilence with them, for it has broken out at Trebizond, Sulina, at the mouth of the Danube, Salonica, Sansoum, and among the islands of the Grecian Archipelago.

Unfortunately, hardly any of the villages where Franks do not reside are provided with either physicians or pharmacies. In exclusively Mussulman villages, for want of medical aid, the mortality is very great and the epidemic has full sway. Apparently the weather is of the most salubrious character, the days being temperately warm, and the nights cool and refreshing, though humid. That the atmosphere is deranged, however, is evident from the fact that the slightest error in diet is sure to be followed by an attack of some of the premonitory symptoms of cholera. Vegetables, with the exception of potatoes, as well as fruits, are generally proscribed, and meats, such as beef, mutton, and poultry, constitute the staple food. These are the very articles, however, the most out of reach of the poor, and for want of means they are obliged to supply themselves with such cheap but pernicious food as melons, cucumbers, and other like vegetables.

Subscriptions have been raised on all sides to relieve the sufferings of the poor, many of whom, having lost the means of existence, actually perish with famine. The distress, destitution, and misery, is heart-rending and it is to be feared will be the prelude to yet sadder scenes in the coming winter.

It is generally supposed that the epidemic will prevail here, in a greater or less degree of intensity, to the month of October. It appears within the last few days to be very slowly declining.

Vessels arriving from any of the ports of the Ottoman empire are now released from quarantine restrictions.

With great respect, your obedient servant,

E. JOY MORRIS.

Hon. WILLIAM H. SEWARD,
Secretary of State.

Mr. Morris to Mr. Seward.

No. 122.] LEGATION OF THE UNITED STATES OF AMERICA,
Constantinople, August 28, 1865.

SIR: I have the honor to acknowledge the receipt of despatch No. 91.

The cholera is gradually disappearing. The number of deaths for the last week has been daily lessening, and the latest report exhibits a total of only sixty-nine fatal cases within the preceding twenty-four hours. Its decline was indicated first by the reappearance of other diseases which, according to physicians, cannot exist contemporaneously with cholera. In its last stages typhus, intermittent, and typhoid fevers have developed themselves, and are unusually malignant and fatal. A heavy storm of rain some ten days since seems to have a salutary influence on the atmosphere, and to have arrested the progressive tendency of the epidemic. The cool weather now prevailing, and the high winds, and great quantity of rain falling, will, no doubt, restore the atmosphere to its usual salubrious tone, and put an end to the disease.

The mortality, it seems, has been much greater than the official reports indicate. These did not include the deaths in the army and navy, and were imperfect, as a large number of deaths were not reported to the medical board, and that the authorities also suppressed a considerable portion of the known deaths, in order not to terrify yet more a panic-stricken population. I learn from a reliable source that in one day alone the actual number of deaths was 1,627, and that for a fortnight at least 1,000 persons died daily. Up to the present date, my family physician estimates the deaths to amount to 40,000; and this notwithstanding the flight of one-third of the population of Constantinople and its environs. From this point it has been carried by the fugitives to Trebizond and other ports on the Black sea, and to the towns on the lower Danube, in all which places it is very destructive.

The development of the cholera at Constantinople was very gradual and insidious. It was brought here by a Turkish war steamer from Egypt, June 26. This vessel violated the quarantine restrictions, and although two of the crew had died of cholera on the voyage, twelve sailors were landed at the naval hospital while suffering under the disease. For fourteen days the epidemic lay brooding in the hospital; on the fifteenth day it burst forth from the hospital and fell like a thunderbolt on the immediate neighborhood of Cassim Pacha and Hasskeni, sweeping away the population with irresistible havoc. From this region it made a leap over all the intervening localities to Yeni Keni, some ten miles distant on the Bosphorus, whither it was carried by a carpenter of the navy yard at Cassim Pacha. Thence it spread to the adjacent village of Theropea, where the mortality was so great that for a time the dead lay unburied in the houses. Subsequently it spread out on all sides until it enveloped the entire capital and its environs in its pestilential embrace.

It seems to have had its origin among the pilgrims to Mecca during the early spring months. The slaughtering of some hundred thousand sheep for sacrificial purposes, and the leaving exposed to decay in the open air the entrails and remains, infected the atmosphere, and caused the death, it is said, of 125,000 pilgrims. From Mecca to Djeddah the road was strewn with putrified corpses. Death and desolation were spread around by the tainted air, and the returning pilgrims carried the cholera to all parts of the East. No precautions were taken to prevent its introduction into Egypt, and multitudes of cholera-stricken pilgrims were permitted to enter the country and disseminate the pestilence. Egypt was already prepared for the reception of the cholera by the devastating cattle disease which, in the closing months of 1864, carried off 800,000 cattle, and as many sheep, goats, camels, &c. Three-fourths of these animals were thrown into the Nile, and in some places lay in such masses as to block up the stream, as at Damietta, where the dogs were able to cross the river (here about 2,700 feet broad) dry-shod on a bridge of carcasses. As the Nile affords the only drinking water, its infection from animal putrefaction must have already been the source of disease before the cholera made its appearance. In Egypt 82,000 persons died of cholera in forty days; in Alexandria, 12,000; in Cairo, 30,000; and in upper Egypt, 40,000.

Had not the most energetic and provident measures been adopted here by the government, after its first development, the mortality, great as it is, would have been far more extensive. A medical commission, composed of the chief physicians, was created at the outset, and invested with authority to enforce such sanitary precautions as they deemed necessary. Under their supervision, infection-breeding localities were purified, obstructed sewers cleansed, and those that were open covered over; all the quarters of the capital and its vicinity provided with physicians, whose attendance as well as medicines were furnished gratis to the poorer classes at the expense of the government; the sale of unwholesome food, and intramural interments, were prohibited; corps of fumigators instituted to disinfect the houses and streets; and hospitals, ambulances to carry the sick, and attendants, in requisite numbers, everywhere supplied. The progress of the epidemic was resisted by all the means of which the government could avail itself, and it is chiefly owing to its sagacious course of action, and to the untiring efforts of the medical staff and the practitioners in its employ, that we are indebted, under providence, for its final conquest. As a body, the medical fraternity of Constantinople has most honorably distinguished itself by its courage, devotion to professional duty, and scientific skill, during the last six weeks. The masonic lodge of "Italia" and the Italian Industrial Society deserve mention for the philanthropic spirit which induced their members to remain in the city in the midst of the pestilence, and to give their personal services to the care of the sick. Some of them fell victims to their noble-hearted zeal. No words of mine can do justice to the moral courage and self-sacrificing spirit which marked their conduct in a crisis when the boldest heart was appalled by the magnitude of the calamity, and which was so fearful in its nature as in many cases to render men insensible to the common impulses of nature, and to terrify parents into the abandonment of their children when attacked by the cholera.

I respectfully suggest that, if it shall be deemed necessary to take precautionary measures against the cholera in the United States, it will be advisable to establish the cholera quarantine quarters on islands at a distance from the mainland. It has been found to be invariably the case that the cholera communicates itself to adjacent localities when the lazarettos are on the mainland, and that such is the elastic nature of the miasma it cannot be prevented from propagating itself except by a wide mass of intervening water. It has thus far been prevented from penetrating continental Greece, and many of the islands in the archipelago, by the establishment of lazarettos on remote and distant islands.

With great respect, your obedient servant,

E. JOY MORRIS.

Hon. WILLIAM H. SEWARD,
Secretary of State.

Mr. Morris to Mr. Seward.

No. 124.] LEGATION OF THE UNITED STATES OF AMERICA,
Constantinople, September 4, 1865.

SIR: The official reports represent a rapid decline of deaths from cholera, and it is apparently nearly extinct at the capital. The number of deaths for August 29 was 33; August 31, 25; September 1, 15. In Smyrna the deaths were about five or six per diem. If, however, the mortality in the immediate environs was included with that of the capital, the total, correctly reported, would not be less, even now, than one hundred daily. The habits of the people, their poor food, for the most part of vegetables and fruits, and their wretched lodgings, render it very difficult to extirpate such a disease when it has once taken root in the country. It is only in the principal towns that physicians and medicines are to be found, and in localities not more than fifteen or twenty miles from Constantinople, numbers have perished for the want of any kind whatever of medical aid.

Unless rigid measures are adopted, the cholera will be revived here by the arrival of infected vessels from other ports of the empire. Within the last ten days, two Ottoman men-of-war, the Saadie and Medjidie, have entered the harbor with cholera patients on board, and on both of them several deaths occurred during the passage. As Constantinople is now in free pratique with all the ports of Turkey, unless such vessels are thoroughly disinfected, there is good reason to apprehend another outbreak of the epidemic.

Animal food being indispensably necessary as an article of diet at the present time, and the terror inspired by the ravages of the cholera having caused the flight of the drovers and butchers upon whom the capital chiefly depends for its supply, the government has been obliged to make up the deficiency. It has ordered the purchase of 70,000 sheep in the interior, and it has also fixed the price of the mutton at 5½ piasters the ohe, that it may be within reach of the poorer classes.

The cholera has recently invaded the imperial palace at Dolma Bagtche, where, after an illness of a few hours, it carried off the Hasnadar Ousta, or lady superintendent of the harem. Several other inmates of the harem having been attacked, the Sultan has been obliged to change his residence to another of the imperial palaces.

I should have mentioned that my authority for the number of cholera deaths in Egypt, reported in a previous despatch, was a Paris correspondent of the Free Press of Vienna, and that for the pilgrim deaths was the Courrier d'Orient of this city. As the figures given seem extravagant, I deem it proper to refer to the sources from which they were derived. While the deaths by cholera at Constantinople cannot be less than 30,000, all statements beyond that number must be merely conjectural.

I was not aware until recently of the personal exertions of a committee of the American missionaries among the cholera-stricken poor, many of whom have been saved from death by destitution and the epidemic through their humane efforts in their behalf.

Very respectfully, your obedient servant,

E. JOY MORRIS.

Hon. WILLIAM H. SEWARD, *Secretary of State.*

Mr. Seward to Mr. Morris.

No. 92.]

DEPARTMENT OF STATE,
Washington, September 5, 1865.

SIR: Your interesting despatches, No. 118 and No. 119, both dated July 13, and No. 120, without date, have been received.

Upon the recommendation of the Surgeon General, to whom was submitted, without loss of time, your No. 120, relative to the ravages of the cholera in the Turkish empire, the attention of the governors of the various States has been invited to the facts set forth by you, with a view to the prompt establishment of rigid quarantine regulations, to prevent, if possible, the introduction of cholera into this country. Herewith I enclose a copy of the accompaniment of the letter addressed by this department to the governors of States.

I am, sir, your obedient servant,

WILLIAM H. SEWARD.

E. JOY MORRIS, Esq., *&c., &c., &c., Constantinople.*

DEPARTMENT OF STATE,
Washington, September 1, 1865.

His Excellency the GOVERNOR OF THE STATE OF ——:

SIR: Your excellency's serious attention is invited to the accompanying letter of the acting Surgeon General of the army, to whom the despatch from the United States minister at Constantinople, which it mentions, was referred. The expediency of adopting quarantine measures for the purpose of preventing the introduction of Asiatic cholera into this country seems well worthy of consideration.

I have the honor to be your excellency's obedient servant,

WILLIAM H. SEWARD.

SURGEON GENERAL'S OFFICE,
Washington City, D. C., August 29, 1865.

SIR: In the absence of the Surgeon General, I have the honor to acknowledge the receipt of your communication of the 24th instant, enclosing despatch from Mr. Morris, minister resident of the United States at Constantinople, relative to the ravages of the cholera in that quarter, &c., and would most respectfully recommend that the attention of the governors of States be invited to the facts contained therein, with a view to the prompt establishment of rigid quarantine regulations to prevent, if possible, the introduction of cholera into this country.

The despatch from Mr. Morris and enclosed paper are herewith respectfully returned.

Very respectfully, your obedient servant,

C. H. CRANE,
Acting Surgeon General.

Hon. WILLIAM H. SEWARD, *Secretary of State.*

Mr. Morris to Mr. Seward.

No. 125.] LEGATION OF THE UNITED STATES OF AMERICA,
Constantinople, September 11, 1865.

SIR: The last bulletin of the medical commission reports but nine deaths by cholera. This is an indication that the epidemic is nearly extinct, but it is not reliable as a complete list of deaths, as a large proportion is unreported. It would be fair to estimate the daily mortality by cholera in Constantinople at, from eighty to a hundred even now, including, of course, the immediate environs. At no time has the official report been correct. The deaths, which at the maximum, according to this authority, reached four hundred in one day, are known to have been over two thousand. On the 14th of August the deaths reported to the grand vizier were eighteen hundred and ninety-seven. There is good reason to believe that for several days the mortality was considerably over two thousand, and I find, from inquiry among official sources, that the total deaths cannot be less than fifty thousand. Indeed the desolation has been frightful; in a single night, certain quarters of the city have been bereft of two-thirds of their inhabitants, and thus, it may be said, without almost any premonition. The attacks being generally in the night and sudden, death occurred in most cases before medical relief could be obtained. Although the poorer classes chiefly suffered, the greatest care in dietary regimen was required by all, the least excess being dangerous, and in many cases conducing to fatal results. The epidemic seems to be of a more malignant and contagious nature than its predecessors, to judge by the great mortality here and in Egypt, and Arabia, and its fatally rapid termination. It is to be hoped it will not remain with us for another year, as in 1846 and 1847.

I regret to report another terrible calamity to this already sorely afflicted capital. At about midnight, on the 5th of September, a fire broke out in Stambol, (Constantinople proper,) near the central police quarters, in the quarter of Demier Kapon. Under the influence of a violent north wind it soon spread with great fury, carrying everything before it. It reached the enclosure within which stand the government buildings known as the Porte, having levelled every intervening obstacle, but at this moment the wind changed, deflected the flames and they took a course around the wall, on the north of this enclosure, and rushed like a sea of fire on to the Hippodrome and the neighborhood of the mosque of Sultan Ahmet. Nothing could arrest the flames, not even the solid walls of the khans and mosques, and the pulling down of squares of houses. The fire raged until 6 p. m., on September [illegible] having, in this time, destroyed about eight thousand houses, ten mosques, twelve baths, twenty khans, two Greek churches, and one Armenian church. The length of the track of the fire is one and a half mile, and its breadth half a mile. Many palaces were destroyed; and among the rest one occupied by the Persian embassy. No such fire has occurred in Constantinople since the memorable one which happened in the time of the Crusaders, and which consumed one-third of the city. The present fire is the cause of immense distress; thousands of families are without homes and are reduced to helpless poverty, and many of them after having already lost valuable members from cholera. The losses from the destruction of property are immense, and at present beyond estimate. Generous as the government is disposed to be, it is almost beyond its power to afford relief to a population which is suffering so fearfully under the scourge of fire and pestilence. Private benevolence is taxed to its utmost to alleviate the misery which we everywhere see around us, but the affliction is so great that it will require some more abundant relief than has been yet devised.

I have the honor to be, very respectfully, your obedient servant,

E. JOY MORRIS.

Hon. WILLIAM H. SEWARD,
Secretary of State.

Mr. Seward to Mr. Morris.

No. 93.]

DEPARTMENT OF STATE,
Washington, September 21, 1865.

SIR: A despatch has been received at the department from Mr. Hale, agent and consul general of the United States at Alexandria, announcing that nine hundred negroes from the Soudan or upper country of Egypt, within the jurisdiction of the Pacha, were expected shortly to arrive at Alexandria to be embarked in French transports for Mexico, to relieve the contingent which was sent out in January, 1863. The latter proceeding, as you are aware, excited much comment at the time, but it passed unnoticed by this government, which was then seriously occupied with a peculiar condition of merely domestic affairs, and with the foreign embarrassments which grew out of that condition. Since then the United States have abolished slavery. The attention of Congress as well as that of the executive department and of the country has been very steadily fixed upon the course of events in Mexico, which I need not say form a subject of serious concern with regard to the safety of free republican institutions on this continent—an object with which we are accustomed to connect the desired ultimate consequence of the abolition of every form of compulsory civil or military servitude on this hemisphere.

You are instructed to bring this matter to the attention of the Turkish government, and to state that, in the opinion of this government, the renewal of the transaction referred to could not be regarded with favor, or even without deep anxiety by the people of the United States. It will be proper for you to inform the minister for foreign affairs that I have written upon the subject in the same sense herein adopted to the diplomatic agent of the United States at Paris, and to the consul general at Alexandria.

I am, sir, your obedient servant,

WILLIAM H. SEWARD.

E. JOY MORRIS, Esq., *&c., &c., Constantinople.*

Mr. Morris to Mr. Seward.

(Extract.)

No. 126.] LEGATION OF THE UNITED STATES OF AMERICA,
Constantinople, September 21, 1865.

SIR: I am happy to be ablo to inform you that the cholera as an epidemic has ceased to exist here. Such is the official statement of the board of health. It is still prevailing, however, with great intensity in Syria and Palestine, in Aleppo, Damascus, and other of the principal towns and villages of that part of the empire, and also along the Danube, and at Widden and other points in Bulgaria. It has thus far been excluded from those islands in the Archipelago belonging to the kingdom of Greece, by rigid quarantine regulations; but it has penetrated Candia and Cyprus, where it has committed great ravages. It was, at last advices, particularly malignant and fatal at Larnaca, the political capital of Cyprus. * * *

With great respect, your obedient servant,

E. JOY MORRIS.

Hon. WILLIAM H. SEWARD,
Secretary, &c.

Mr. Morris to Mr. Seward.

No. 127.] LEGATION OF THE UNITED STATES OF AMERICA,
Constantinople, October 9, 1865.

SIR: I have the honor to acknowledge the receipt of despatch No. 92, and to enclose a translation which I have made of a pamphlet in French by Dr. Bozzi, physician to the imperial arsenal, on the contagious properties of Asiatic cholera. The observations of Dr. Bozzi, being founded upon professional experience during one of the most fatal visitations of cholera on record, seem to me to be of sufficient importance to be communicated to the department for the instruction of the American public and medical authorities.

I have the honor to be, very respectfully, your obedient servant,

E. JOY MORRIS.

Hon. WILLIAM H. SEWARD,
Secretary of State.

Observations on the contagious properties of the Asiatic cholera, and of the absolute necessity of opposing its progress by the most rigid and perfect system of quarantine, suggested by professional experience at Constantinople during the summer of 1865, *by Dr. Bozzi, physician to the imperial arsenal; translated for the Department of State by E. Joy Morris, United States minister to Turkey.*

Whether the Asiatic cholera is to be contagious or not, is a question of the first importance to the public health of the world. Notwithstanding the many facts demonstrated of its contagious nature, the advocates of the contrary doctrine—and they have thus far been in the majority—have enforced their views in the discussion of measures of quarantine against the invasion of this disease; they have opposed every such measure, as not only incapable of preserving a country from this terrible scourge, but also as inflicting great damage on commercial and industrial interests. Even when quarantine restrictions have been adopted, no regard has been paid to the term of incubation of contagious maladies, nor to other circumstances equally important to be taken into consideration, in order that sanitary measures may produce their proper effect. This is the reason why the cholera has been imported into so many different countries.

The Asiatic cholera was confined for several centuries to its place of origin in Hindostan, and it was only when new and more rapid avenues of communication were opened, and commercial intercourse became more general and easy, that it was enabled to break through the limits imposed on it by nature. In its invading march it has followed with a wonderful fidelity the most frequented and the most convenient routes, turning aside from natural obstacles, and not penetrating where it was opposed by severe sanitary precautions. The German states, by extraordinary expedients, have preserved themselves from the cholera, although it has desolated neighboring countries, from which they are spared only by conventional lines of demarcation. Graves, a careful observer and profound savant, in reference to the invasions of Asiatic cholera, remarks that "it is a very striking fact, and which ought to have great weight in proving the importation of this terrible epidemic, that it has never appeared in any town until the time materially necessary for its arrival from the infected country had elapsed, and it would be easy to show that the facility of its propagation varies according to the rapidity of its means of communication."

It seems to me unnecessary here to cite the many facts which observers of great merit have published in proof of the contagious properties of Asiatic cholera. Those which have occurred during the present visitation of the cholera are more than sufficient to overthrow all the theories of the non-contagionists, and to remove all further doubt as to its truly contagious nature.

Carried to Mecca by infected pilgrims from India, the pestilence there made unparalleled ravages on account of the conjunction of extremely unfavorable hygienic conditions. It was imported into Egypt by infected Arab pilgrims; into Syria, Cyprus, and Smyrna by fugitives from Egypt, where the fury of the epidemic had caused such a panic among the inhabitants that the steamers were no longer sufficient for the transportation of an emigration which had suddenly taken the most extraordinary proportions.

The cholera was introduced into Constantinople by the Turkish steam frigate Monkbiri-Squrour, which arrived from Egypt the 28th of June, 1865, and from which several cholera patients were sent to the marine hospital. Before the debarcation of these cholera invalids there had not been a single case of cholera at Constantinople. Soon after this event, however, the disease communicated itself in the first instance to the hospital attendants, and subsequently to other soldiers or employés of the navy, who had frequent or constant intercourse with this locality. Following continually the same order of propagation, it extended its ravages into the different quarters of the capital. Thus the military operatives of the arsenal, and the marines, who occupied in common the same barracks, the sentinels, the crews of vessels at anchor before the arsenal, and the inhabitants of the adjacent quarter of Cassim Pacha, all in close proximity to the infected hospital; and in continual intercourse with the personnel of the same, were the first to be attacked by the cholera. Almost at the same time the disease broke out at Yeni-Keny, on the Bosphorus, separated from the first seat of the epidemic by several quarters and villages, and none of which had yet been visited by the cholera.

It was evident that the air had not borne it there; it was, on the contrary, proved that it was a civil operative of the arsenal who first carried the cholera to Yeni-Keny. Mr. Franceschini, of Bologna, has very properly observed that the cholera is introduced by infected persons, and that it does not fall from the clouds.

During the prevalence of the epidemic at Constantinople it was the poorer classes who, from their unwholesome manner of life, suffered most. At the cholera hospital of Connibe-hané all of the six military attendants died of the disease. The chief druggist of the engineer school, with his wife and four children, died of cholera. In my service in the two barracks of the Imperial Ottoman Maimé all the *infirmiérs* were attacked by cholera, but almost all were saved.

At the Princes islands an aged lady died of cholera in a chamber which contained several beds. The physicians prohibited the members of the family from sleeping in the chamber until it was disinfected. His injunctions were not heeded. What followed? The daughter of the deceased, her husband, a child, and a maid-servant all soon after also died.

An honorable family of Aleppo, residing at Pera, had given hospitality to a woman and her child; the last was carried off in a few days later by an attack of cholera. The head of the house begged the woman to leave the premises, and he caused the chamber where the child had died to be carefully closed up, but neglected to take the necessary preservative measures. A few days later his youngest son was attacked by cholera, and almost at the same time his wife also, and a domestic, who was employed in the house only during the day, fell ill of cholera. All the necessary hygienic measures were adopted to prevent the other members of the family from taking the disease, and they were successful. Thus this worthy family had the double satisfaction of being, in great part, preserved from the attacks of the epidemic, and of seeing cured all who had suffered from it.

Several philanthropic physicians fell victims to this fearful scourge; their names are engraved in the hearts of the poor, and they have done honor to humanity. In the city I have observed that when the disease broke out in a family the members of it generally were attacked; thus a number of families were entirely destroyed, and others have lost a great part of their members. In the space of a few days only about six hundred keys of houses, in which all the inmates had perished by cholera, were delivered to the authorities. One-quarter of the capital was almost entirely depopulated. The family and servants of a pacha, consisting of twenty-six persons, all died of cholera except three.

These are fearful facts. Do the non-contagionists require more conclusive proof of the contagious character of cholera? In many instances persons living near an infected locality were attacked by cholera when they were in anywise predisposed to the same. It has happened that families which fled from places of summer resort where the cholera was raging to their winter residences in quarters, where it had almost ceased to exist, except in isolated and insignificant cases, have been the first to be attacked by the malady, and these have communicated it to a great number of the inhabitants of the same street without spreading further. Two opposite extremities of Tataola were most singularly devastated by the cholera—Arkardja and Agio Athanassi. Arkardja was infected by the family of the engineer Kosti Kalfa, which had returned from Koulely, a village on the Bosphorus, where, the day before their departure, one of their children had died of cholera in a few hours after the disease manifested itself. Agio Athanassi was infected by the families which fled from Threpia, where the pestilence had displayed itself in all its fury. The village of Yeni-Keny underwent three successive invasions. The manner of the first invasion I have already explained; the second and third were produced by the return of the inhabitants of different parts of the town from the country, whither they had fled on the first appearance of the cholera.

In other quarters of the capital the reappearance of the cholera was due to the same causes. These facts again are an additional proof that the cholera does not travel of itself, but that it is carried from place to place by infected human agents, if no impediment be offered to its progress. The radius of action of a cholera centre does not extend very far; but when a number of localities are infected, the contagious miasma may be absorbed by a great number of individuals at the same time, and thus it may take the usual course of epidemic diseases. It is frequently objected against the contagious nature of cholera that many persons who have had constant relations with those affected by it have not been attacked. But did there ever exist a contagious malady which communicated itself to all who came in contact with it? Do not, also, according to general opinion, the most contagious diseases encounter constitutions either temporarily or absolutely refractory? Such immunity is to be explained by peculiar idiosyncrasies or other individual circumstances. The non-contagionists also insist if the cholera were contagious it would diffuse itself throughout the towns in which it has merely made its appearance. They ask, moreover, why it is that countries which it has traversed have remained exempt, notwithstanding their commercial relations with infected regions? It is easy to refute all these opinions: 1st, we repeat that there are permanent and temporary immunities dependent on the peculiar physical and moral characteristics of individuals which render them unsusceptible of the disease: 2d, the cholera which, it is pretended, was observed on a very small number of persons, was it really the Asiatic cholera? There is nothing to prove it. Is it shown that no measure was taken to prevent the importation of the epidemic? Or, if it was introduced because of the absence of opposition, was no precaution adopted against the first locality attacked? May it not be that the persons near these sites had not the constitutional predisposition to the disease? Is there evidence to show that a considerable number of persons of an uninfected region had frequent, and even constant, intercourse with cholera centres, without being attacked by the disease? No; absolutely no. Such a state of facts has no existence. And even admitting that the epidemic spared certain regions through which it passed, or that it merely manifested itself in them without exercising any ravages, must we necessarily conclude from this that it was not imported, and that it is not contagious? Certainly not; for it has been proven beyond doubt that such localities as are in an excellent hygienic condition are but slightly susceptible of cholera infection. Is it possible, also, that all countries present a combination of circumstances favorable to the propagation and intensity of the disease? When several cases of cholera have occurred in a particular spot, has it not been after the arrival of persons from some infected locality? It may be objected that cases of cholera have sometimes been observed where there was no communication with infected places. This is not satisfactorily proven; but even if it be admitted, it is not at all surprising, for, if isolated cases of cholera have been noticed in certain countries, it is because they have previously been visited by the cholera through importation. Why should we not admit the possibility of the seeds of contagion remaining in a dormant state? Numerous examples show that it is possible for them so to exist for a long period of time. Not a single case of cholera has ever been seen in any place which had not been previously visited by it. The fact of the importation of cholera by human beings being incontestable, its contagious properties follow as a necessary consequence.

Its mode of propagation has given rise to a quarrel of words among medical men. Some insist that Asiatic cholera is disseminated by miasmatic and contagious infection; others, by inhalation; and there are those who would have us believe that it is communicated by the immediate contact of cholera poison contained in the vomitings and evacuations, or by the absorption of a volatile poison emitted by them. (Bund.) Franceschi, of Bologna, is of the opinion that it is generated from cholera matter liable to fermentation, and which, brought into contact with the putrid atmosphere of an inhabited locality, produces there an analogous fermentation which gives rise to infection and the disease. Others finally regard it only as a spontaneous infection united with the local influences. All these different modes of accounting for the propagation of cholera are, I repeat, but a quarrel of words; but this quarrel may have very grave consequences. If we obstinately refuse to see in these facts anything else than evidences of spontaneous infection, we shall be disposed to abandon preservative measures, and the isolation which can alone prevent the introduction and extension of the Asiatic cholera.

Where a malady has manifested itself after the introduction into a country of an undeniable cause of miasmatic disengagement, (degagement)—if persons exposed have been immediately attacked, as facts have demonstrated, or if, transported and dispersed in various places, they have, in their turn, become the sources whence a malady of the same nature has diffused itself in such localities, can there be any doubt of the contagious nature of this kind of disease? To deny evident facts, and lose one's self in abstract explanations, is an abandonment of the only road which leads to the discovery of truth.

Thus the researches of Pettenkofer upon the influence of the sun, and the interpretations of Schoenheim, generalized by Stermer, having for an object to prove that the cause of the propagation of the cholera is the diminution of atmospheric ozone, are the product only of chimerical imaginations, and which cannot have any weight when confronted with the array of facts proving that the disease is introduced by importation.

From the preceding exposition the following inferences may be deduced:

1st. Asiatic cholera can only be produced spontaneously in Hindostan—its place of birth. It is only there that the special causes of soil and climate exist which periodically have developed it for several years.

2d. If Asiatic cholera makes its appearance in any other country, it is an evidence that it was brought there either by emigrants, pilgrims, or by passengers all alike infected. Certain matters, susceptible of impregnation by contagious miasma, and for its retention for a considerable period of time may also diffuse the disease, unless very strict measures of prevention are adopted against them.

3d. Asiatic cholera has always, in its march of invasion, followed the most rapid lines of communication, and those which render commercial intercourse men easy and frequent.

4th. Persons in the immediate vicinity of a cholera locality, and who are in constant intercourse with those under the influence of the disease, are much more liable to be attacked than those at a distance, or who, having but occasional relations with such a site, adopt the hygienic precautions which have a recognized efficacy.

5th. A grave responsibility in future must rest upon those intrusted with the quarantine services. It is desirable that sanitary physicians should be men of experience, and without preconceived ideas; such as have passed years in the practical observation of diseases, and not in meditating theories, and in losing themselves frequently in the field of illusions.

6th. With regard to the time of duration of the incubation of contagious maladies, it is indispensable that the quarantine isolation of persons should be fixed at twenty-four days, and the same term should be re-imposed again in cases of death. Inanimate and infected organic matter, and which may for a long time preserve the seeds of contagion, should be treated with extreme precaution, and efficient means be employed to destroy the seeds of disease with which it is impregnated. Too great rigor cannot be used in such cases.

Honor to the men who do not fear to sacrifice every possible interest in order to preserve the health and life of the nations.

To corroborate, in the most striking manner, what we have said on the advantages of rigid quarantine restrictions in resisting the invasion of cholera, we subjoin the following facts of recent occurrence:

Several maritime towns on the coast of the Ottoman empire having established strict quarantines against the recent cholera invasions, have been preserved from the epidemic, notwithstanding the extraordinary affluence of emigrants arriving from Turkish towns where it was raging. One of these exempted cities, Salonica, has had several mortal cases of cholera in its lazaretto, but the disease could not penetrate within the town, because of the wise and rigorous measures adopted against it. Greece has likewise been saved from the cholera by a similar course of action. In Italy also, wherever prudent and severe anti-cholera restrictions were established, the epidemic did not make its appearance, while in those towns where no such antagonistical measures were adopted this scourge of humanity has exhibited itself in its most desolating aspects.

Mr. Morris to Mr. Seward.

No. 130.] LEGATION OF THE UNITED STATES OF AMERICA,
Constantinople, October 29, 1865.

SIR: I have the honor to acknowledge the receipt of despatch No. 93, dated September 21, relative to the negro troops about to be sent from Egypt to Mexico. In conformity with the instructions from the department, I have made his Highness Ali Pacha, minister of foreign affairs, acquainted with the contents of the same. He informed me that the Ottoman government was in nowise connected with the sending of the original contingent of negro troops from Egypt to Mexico;

that it first became cognizant of the transaction through the public prints, and that at my request in 1863 it had addressed the late viceroy on the subject. He replied by telegram (and it was the last communication received from him, for he was then in a dying condition) that it was an inconsiderate act on his part, of which he deeply repented, but that it was then too late to recall the engagement he had contracted with the French Emperor. The affair was altogether surreptitious so far as the consent of the Porte was necessary to its authorization.

His Highness further observed that the present Pacha of Egypt, during his visit here last summer, had represented the great embarrassment he felt on this subject; that a request had been made to him by the French Emperor for a further contingent of negro troops to supply the losses occasioned by war and disease in the ranks of those originally sent, and that he deemed himself in some degree constrained by courtesy to a friendly sovereign and the example of his predecessor to comply with the request, and that he desired to know if the Porte would interpose any objections.

His Highness replied to this inquiry, after consultation with his Majesty the Sultan, that the Porte must not be considered as privy to the transaction; that it was originally entered upon without its knowledge or approbation, and that while, owing to the peculiar circumstances of the case, it would now insist on the cancelling of the obligations already contracted with the French Emperor by the viceroy, it must express the hope that this would be the last of such an impolite proceeding. The Pacha assured his Highness that the wishes of the Porte would, in this respect, be complied with. His Highness added that none of these negroes were slaves. He said that the minister of Maximilian at this court, General Marques, had never spoken to him on the matter.

In conclusion he remarked that the Porte entertained a sincere feeling of respect and friendship for the government of the United States; that it regarded it as its natural ally; that it admired the principles of equity and justice by which its intercourse with other nations was regulated, and, as he had often assured me, his Majesty the Sultan, and all the members of the Ottoman government, most cordially rejoiced in the re-establishment of the integrity of the American Union, and, as I was also aware, their sympathies during the late civil war had invariably been on the side of the constituted government of the United States. He begged me also to convey to the President of the United States the assurance that the government of his Majesty the Sultan desired to be understood as having no wish to interfere directly or indirectly against the interests of the government of the United States or of those of the American people, but that, on the contrary, it would be most happy to promote them whenever the occasion offered.

I have the honor to be, very respectfully, your obedient servant,

E. JOY MORRIS.

Hon. WILLIAM H. SEWARD,
Secretary of State.

Mr. Seward to Mr. Morris.

No. 99.] DEPARTMENT OF STATE,
Washington, November 17, 1865.

SIR: Your despatch of October 18, No. 129, has been received. It brings information of the very interesting fact that certain ecclesiastical estates within the empire have been secularized. I think that you very rightly anticipate, as fruits of this reform, a considerable augmentation of the national industry, with a very convenient and desirable increase of the public revenues. If it shall seem to you to be discreet, you will tender the President's congratulations to the Sultan upon that important event.

I am, sir, your obedient servant,

WILLIAM H. SEWARD.

E. JOY MORRIS, Esq., *&c.*, *&c.*, *Constantinople.*

Mr. Morris to Mr. Seward.

LEGATION OF THE UNITED STATES OF AMERICA,
No. 131.] *Constantinople, November* 22, 1865.

SIR: I have the honor to acknowledge the receipt of despatches Nos. 95 and 96. It is with pleasure that I find myself enabled to report another proof of practical progress in the interior of this empire. The isolation of the commercial centres from the marts of the interior, and the difficulties of transportation, as well as the great expense attending the movement of merchandise to the seaports, has induced the government, through its own resources and the aid of foreign capital, to engage of late in an extensive system of road-making. On the 5th of November last the macadamized road, which has been in construction for two years, between Ghemlek, on the sea of Marmora, and the city of Brusa, in Asia, was formally opened for travel. Brusa is about nine hours' travel from Constantinople, five of which are by steamers to Ghemlek. In the winter season this important city, which contains a population of 70,000 Mussulmen, Greeks, Armenians, Jews, and Franks, for want of a good road to the seaport, has been almost entirely cut off from communication with the capital. It is the seat of an extensive trade in raw silk, as well as manufactured silk and woollen goods, carpets, velvets, safran, turpentine, wool, wine, &c., and possesses an extensive trade with the chief towns of Northern Asia. The new road will secure an easy and more economical means of transportation of its rich and varied products, and will be serviceable at all seasons of the year.

A few weeks since a railroad has been completed from Smyrna to the city of Magnesia, (Manisa, in Turkish,) about forty miles in length. This is a flourishing city of about 35,000 inhabitants, about one-fourth of whom are Greeks and Armenians, and has largely engaged in the manufacture of cotton and silk stuffs and goat-hair shawls, and is on the great road between Smyrna and the most productive regions of Asia Minor. It is also one of the most ancient cities of this part of Turkey, and was a large and opulent city to the latest period of the Roman empire. It is intended to carry the road to Cassaba and Ala-Cheir, two important seats of trade further in the interior.

The railroad which has been in operation for more than a year from Smyrna to Ephesus, a distance of fifty miles, will be finished to Aidin, some thirty miles further, in the coming spring. Hitherto, the wool, silk, carpets, tobacco, &c., have been transported at such heavy rates from the interior, by the old route from Aidin to Smyrna, as to greatly enhance their cost price, the freight of a ton of tobacco costing about a dollar between these two points. The completion of the road to Aidin and of that to Magnesia will be the source of additional prosperity and commerce to the thriving city of Smyrna.

An active competition exists between Russia and Turkey to secure the transit trade from Persia to Turkey and Europe. The Russian government, taking advantage of the utter absence of serviceable roads between Trebizond and the Persian frontier, has recently commenced, with its usual vigor, the construction of a paved road from Poti, on the Black sea, *viâ* Tauris, Tiflis, &c., to the Persian frontier, and has built a port at Poti. A portion of this road is already in use, and has diverted such a large amount of trade from the old route between

Trebizond and Erzeroum and Persia as to oblige the Turkish government to enter upon the construction of a permanent and well-built road from Trebizond to the Persian confines, about thirty-five days distant by the existing route, and which is next to impassable in the winter. A corps of competent engineers and a large working force are engaged upon this road, the completion of which, some five years hence, will be of immense importance to both Turkey and Persia.

As the opening of new arteries of trade are of universal concern, I have deemed it proper to report the above details, as indirectly they have a bearing on our commercial relations with this empire, and it is also but just to the Turkish government that its enlightened efforts to develop the trade and improve the internal condition of the country should be officially made known.

With great respect, your obedient servant,

E. JOY MORRIS.

Hon. WILLIAM H. SEWARD,
Secretary of State.

EGYPT.

Mr. Hale to Mr. Seward.

No. 8.] AGENCY AND CONSULATE GENERAL OF THE U. S. OF AMERICA,
Alexandria, Egypt, November 25, 1864.

SIR: I have the honor to report that the President's proclamation of the 20th of October, appointing the last Thursday of November as a day of Thanksgiving and prayer, which he requested might be observed by all his fellow-citizens wherever they might then be, was received here on the 19th instant. The American citizens were accordingly assembled yesterday at the consulate general, where the President's proclamation was read, after which an interesting and impressive religious service was conducted by the Rev. Gulian Lansing, and the Rev. Andrew Watson, the American missionaries.

A telegraphic despatch announcing the re-election of President Lincoln had been received here the previous day, and in his very able discourse the Rev. Mr. Lansing did not fail to call attention to this wise disposition of their suffrages by the American people as a principal and conscientious cause of thanksgiving; a sentiment in which he had the cordial concurrence of all who were present.

I have the honor to be, sir, with great respect, your obedient servant,

CHARLES HALE.

Hon. WILLIAM H. SEWARD,
Secretary of State.

Mr. Hale to Mr. Seward.

No. 10.] AGENCY AND CONSULATE GENERAL OF THE U. S. OF AMERICA,
Alexandria, Egypt, December 22, 1864.

SIR: When the Sultan visited Egypt about two years ago, he made a number of donations for benevolent and charitable purposes, which the Pacha augmented in each case by a grant from his own purse. There were donations to the Greek, Coptic and Roman churches, and also one to the protestant community; the other donations were speedily applied, but that to the protestant community remained untouched in the hands of the bankers to whom it had been confided, from the obvious want of any organization to receive. Soon after my arrival in Egypt, I learned that the banker had proposed to deliver the grant to the consuls general of the United States, Prussia and Great Britain, acting jointly as the representatives of the protestant organizations under their respective jurisdictions, provided they would come to an agreement among themselves respecting a partition of the money.

Although the missionary and school establishments under the care of citizens of the United States in Egypt might perhaps claim a larger importance than those under other jurisdictions, the only possible basis of an agreement among the three consuls general was that of equality. I accordingly united with Mr. Theremin, the consul general of Prussia, and Mr. Reade, the acting agent and consul general of Great Britain, in an agreement for an equal division of the grant; we also joined in signing a power of attorney to Mr. Barthon, United States vice-consul at Alexandria, to draw the money from the banker's hands. I should mention that the arrangement for an equal division among the three consulates general had received the assent and the approval of Nubar, who had been appointed both by the Sultan and the Pacha to superintend the application of their bounty.

The exact amount of the Sultan's donation was not known until Mr. Barthon brought the sealed bag containing it to Messrs. Theremin, Reade and myself, who had assembled on the 17th instant to finish the business. On opening the bag it proved to contain two hundred and fifty new Turkish gold-pieces, probably coined for the purpose of these donations, each of the value of eighty-seven and three-quarter Egyptian government piasters. The value of the piaster, according to the official synopsis of foreign moneys prepared at the United States mint, is a very small fraction in excess of five cents, (namely 5.0067.) The Pacha's augmentation of the grant was fifteen thousand government piasters. The whole grant, accordingly, was thirty-six thousand nine hundred and thirty-seven and one-half government piasters; the share for each jurisdiction was twelve thousand three hundred and twelve and one-half government piasters, or six hundred and fifteen dollars in American gold.

Messrs. Theremin and Reade joined with me in a memorandum of the proceeding, which was prepared in triplicate, and signed on the principle of the alternate, each nation being named first in the copy of the instrument preserved by its representative.

There is fortunately no occasion for hesitating with regard to the disposition to be made of the share of this grant assigned to this consulate general, as the mission establishment of Rev. M. Lansing and his worthy associates was undoubtedly intended by the Sultan and the Pacha to be the recipient of their bounty, and is moreover an organization which is in all respects able to make a proper and fit use of the money.

It was of course a matter of gratification to me to be able to take part in the conclusion of an affair which has been pending unsettled nearly two years. In this country, where money commands a very high rate of interest, the grant might have been considerably increased, could it have been withdrawn from the banker's hands at an earlier date. It will now be made immediately available.

I have also to report another instance of the good will of the Egyptian government towards the American mission. The mission has recently purchased an estate in Alexandria, with a building thereon to be used for its schools in this town. Property held for religious purposes in this country, as in most others, is exempt from taxation; the schools of the missionaries are free; and the Pacha has in several instances manifested an enlightened interest in public instruction. I deem it not improper, therefore, to forward to the government the request of the missionaries that the government tax usually levied in all cases of transfers of real estate might in this instance be raised.

The minister for foreign affairs (who is also minister for public instruction) answered that the subject was one that could only be treated by the Pacha himself, and I accordingly mentioned the matter to his Highness, who immediately answered that he wished the missionaries to be free of the tax, but in order not to interrupt the regular course of proceedings, he would prefer that they should take out their title-deed and pay the tax in the usual manner, and that he would afterwards reimburse the whole expense of the transaction as a grant from his own purse.

The amount of the tax, with incidental expenses, proves to be about nine hundred dollars in American gold.

Many formalities are necessary to complete the legal title, involving delays, notwithstanding the zealous efforts of the officials to expedite the business. I detain the transmission of this despatch to be able to announce the completion of the affair.

[January 24, 1865.—The business is finished in a satisfactory manner, and the reimbursement of the tax has been paid into the missionaries' hands.]

It may be mentioned, as a proof of the progress of this country in civilization and of the enlightened regard of its rulers for the rights of foreigners, that a few years ago Franks were not allowed to hold real estate, and in cases of purchases were obliged to resort to some subterfuge in getting their title. Nothing of this sort is now necessary, and the title of the present estate is registered in the local court, in the name of the Rev. Mr. Watson, citizen of the United States, who holds it in trust for the mission. It is but a few years since our American States repealed their laws prohibiting aliens from holding real estate, and in some of the States I believe the disqualification still exists. In this particular, as in many others, moreover, it is to be observed that Egypt is far in advance of other parts of the Ottoman empire; and it is indeed ludicrous that Great Britain should make such persistent efforts to mark the Pacha of Egypt as a vassal of the Sultan.

These donations, although not very considerable in amount, are acceptable to the missionaries at the present time, when the high rates of exchange operate largely to diminish the avails of the remittances to them from America; and they are especially valuable as new evidences of the continued good will of the government, in which respect they are indeed significant. It may well be doubted whether there is any western nation whose rules, however tolerant of diverse religions, would make a money grant to a Mohammedan community.

The anniversary of the birth of Ismail Pacha, the present ruler of Egypt, was celebrated on the 15th instant. In the morning the consuls general and the high functionaries of state visited his Highness at his palace of Gazara and expressed their felicitations. In the evening a banquet was given by Ragheb, one of the Pacha's principal ministers, at the palace of Kasr-el-nil. The banquet was served in the European style, but with Oriental profusion and magnificence. The apartment in which it took place was lighted by at least a thousand wax candles. About eighty guests were present. When the cloth was removed, Ragheb made a brief speech of welcome and in honor of the Pacha, in the Turkish language. Mr. Testa, the consul general of Sweden and Norway, (who is the senior among those members of the consular corps here who are envoys of the nations they represent,) responded in a brief speech in French. The minister for foreign affairs next proposed in French the health of sovereigns and heads of governments friendly to the Pacha. It would have been proper that the former part of this toast should have been answered by the representative of some of the great European nations, but, from lack, I believe, of any understanding among them on the point, there was no response. As I was well aware that the language of the toast had been chosen expressly to compliment the President of the United States, I deemed it proper to make an acknowledgment of the courtesy. Beginning with an apology for my first essay at dinner-table speaking in French, (but no other language would have been understood by the greater part of those present,) I remarked that the President and people of the United States had observed with pleasure the progress made by Egypt under the enlightened rule of its present government. No doubt the staple agricultural productions of Egypt are the same as those of America—cotton, grain and sugar; and no doubt the present extraordinary prosperity of Egypt may be attributed in large degree to the American war; but our war is undertaken in the cause of humanity, and meanwhile we are not sorry that among all the countries of the world the greatest incidental benefit should have accrued to one like Egypt, whose rulers have always been friendly to us, have appreciated our position and respected our rights. I concluded by expressing a confident hope that the resources of Egypt, once ever developed, would promote a commerce of which all nations, our own included, would enjoy the advantage.

These remarks were heard with close attention by the company, and were well received. The ministers of state, and a few days afterwards the Pacha himself, expressed in cordial terms their gratification. The speech was taken down on the spot by a Turkish short-hand writer, and was printed in the official gazette in Arabic, in Turkish and French. The Italian and Greek newspapers also printed it in their respective languages.

The Pacha, in allusion to the grandeur of our war, and its probable result in the extinction of slavery, described to me in detail his efforts for the amelioration of the condition of the laborers in Egypt, and for the promotion of agricultural prosperity. He is himself one of the largest cotton-growers in the country, and enjoys a large profit from the high price of cotton; but the most abased fellah also partakes in the general prosperity, and in some of the villages the fallaheen have been strong enough to make a stand against the oppressions of the local magistracy; at any rate they are better able to put up with extortion, in cases where they do not choose to resist. In the large towns, and especially in Alexandria, however, the condition of the people is very different, as there has been an enormous advance in rents and in the prices of the necessaries of life.

Sir Henry Bulwer, British ambassador at Constantinople, arrived in Egypt last week. His presence here is believed to be distasteful to the Pacha, who has nevertheless placed one of his palaces at the ambassador's disposal. Mr. Colquhoun, the British agent and consul general, is expected to return to his post here by the packet to arrive to-morrow. Mr. Schreiner, the consul general of Austria, arrived the day before yesterday; Mr. Popolani, of Portugal, a few days earlier; and Mr. Ruyssenaers, of Holland, and Mr. Dumreicher, of Denmark, last month. The return of these gentlemen completes the consular corps, except that a successor has not yet been appointed for the Hanseatic towns to fill the vacancy caused by the death of Mr. de Rossetti. The unfitness of the climate for a summer residence makes the practice of the European governments nearly universal to give leave of absence to their representatives during the hot months, and it is only now that the climate is becoming agreeable. The number of travellers from all countries is much less than usual; from the United States only five have arrived, of whom one has gone up the Nile. Last year at this date I am told eighty parties had started for the Nile voyage; this year only eight.

I have the honor to be, very respectfully, your obedient servant,

CHARLES HALE.

Hon. WILLIAM H. SEWARD,
Secretary of State.

Mr. Hale to Mr. Seward.

No. 20.] AGENCY AND CONSULATE GENERAL OF THE U. S. OF AMERICA,
Alexandria, Egypt, March 4, 1865.

SIR: I have the honor to report that at midnight on the 26th February, being at Cairo, with all the other consuls general in Egypt, for the purpose of attending the official reception by the Pacha, appointed at the citadel at eight o'clock the following morning. I received by a special messenger from Alexandria a note brought by the English mail, arrived that afternoon, from Mr. Dudley, United States consul at Liverpool, of date of the 16th, informing me of the launch in the Mersey on the preceding day of a steamer, to which was given the Arabic name of Noor-el-Huda, and which was said to be designed for the Egyptian government, but which he feared was for the rebels. It was impossible to speak to the Pacha on the subject on the 27th, as his day was given to various formal receptions, but I saw his chief of ministers that day, and ascertained that they had no knowledge of the steamer; and on the morning of the 28th I obtained an audience of the Pacha, when he gave me full information to the effect that he had four steamers building in England, all with Arabic names, which he gave me, none of them resembling that given to the vessel launched at Liverpool Two of these vessels are building for his own use in the Thames, and the other two for the Azizieh company (a government establishment) by the English Peninsular and Oriental Company, also in the Thames, as I subsequently learned from the agent of the latter company. This full information from his Highness I was able to transmit to Alexandria by telegraph the same morning in season to be forwarded to Mr. Dudley by the British mail going out that day, the 28th, and thus the answer to Mr. Dudley's note left Egypt forty eight hours after the note came into the country.

I afterwards prepared a more formal memorandum, which I transmitted to Mr. Dudley by the next post. On account of the proof it affords of the friendly disposition of the Pacha towards the United States, I think proper to transmit to you herewith a duplicate of this memorandum. You will observe that to save future questions of this sort the Pacha has promised to tell me whenever he orders a new steamer.

I have the honor to be, sir, very respectfully, your obedient servant,

CHARLES HALE.

Hon. WILLIAM H. SEWARD,
Secretary of State.

Memorandum of a conversation had, this twenty-eighth day of February, in the year 1865, between Charles Hale, agent and consul general of the United States of America, and Ismail Pacha, Viceroy of Egypt, at his Highness's palace of Gazira.

The consul general said that he had been informed that a steamer had lately been launched at Liverpool, which was reported to be designed for the Egyptian government, or for an Egyptian company, but which he feared was for the use of the confederates, and he had come to ask his Highness if he had steamers building in England.

His Highness replied that he had four steamers building in England; that none of them are war steamers; that one of them, a yacht, for his own use, and one other, are building on the Thames, near London; that the two others are building by the Peninsular and Oriental Company for the Azizieh Company of Egypt. His Highness was unable to state where these two steamers are building.

The consul general inquired whether these steamers had names, and whether his Highness would give the names?

His Highness replied that the steamers had names; he stated the name of the yacht, and caused his excellency Fiki Bey to be summoned, who wrote all the names in Arabic characters on a paper now in possession of the consul general. His Highness repeated the names, and said they are the true and only names of his vessels, namely: for the yacht, Mahroussa; for the other steamer building at London, Bahira; for the two steamers building by the Peninsular and Oriental Company, Charkieh and Dacahlieh.

The consul general mentioned the name Noor-el-Huda, given to the steamer launched at Liverpool, and his Highness said he had no knowledge of that name.

In the course of the conversation his Highness remarked he had a frigate undergoing repairs somewhere, but she is an old vessel; and, further, that in view of the unauthorized use that had been of his name and that of his government; that he would not fail, if now informed that such course would be agreeable to the consul general, to give him information whenever he (his Highness) should have occasion to order any war steamer to be built; which the consul general accordingly requested, and his Highness thereupon promised.

The conversation was held in the French language. This memorandum faithfully gives its substance. Everything here set down was explicitly stated without reserve or hesitation.

In testimony of the truth whereof, the aforesaid Charles Hale, agent and consul general of the United States of America, and Victor Barthon, vice-consul for Alexandria, who [L. S.] was present during the whole interview, and heard the whole conversation, hereto set our hands at Cairo, Egypt, on the day first herein mentioned; and the said Hale hereto affixes his official seal.

CHARLES HALE.
V. BARTHON.

Mr. Hale to Mr. Seward.

[Extract.]

No. 24.] AGENCY AND CONSULATE GENERAL OF THE U. S. OF AMERICA,
Alexandria, Egypt, April 19, 1865.

SIR: Delegates of various chambers of commerce, to the number of about one hundred, assembled here about a fortnight ago, on the invitation of Mr. de Lesseps, for the purpose of visiting the works of the Suez canal. They set out on the morning of the 7th instant, and have this day returned.

The number of accredited members of the party was eighty-five, from fourteen different countries. There were ten official representatives of governments; sixty-two chambers of commerce, and eight other societies or organizations were represented by their delegates.

Of our own citizens among the party were Messrs. Cyrus W. Field, delegate of the Chamber of Commerce of the city of New York, and Washington Ryer, representing the State of California.

I enclose a translation of the report subscribed by the delegates. They speak of the completion of the work as merely a matter of time and money.

* * * * * *

I am, sir, very respectfully, your obedient servant,

CHARLES HALE.

Hon. WILLIAM H. SEWARD,
Secretary of State.

[Translation.]

CAIRO, *April* 17, 1865.

We, the undersigned, delegates of the chambers of commerce to the canal of Suez, after having examined the works already done, and having taken into consideration the possibility of the enterprise, report:

We started the 7th instant from Alexandria, by railroad, for Cairo, where we remained until the morning of the 9th. We then proceeded by railroad to Zagazig, where we embarked at 9 o'clock a. m., in boats drawn by mules and camels, on the fresh-water canal made by Mehemet Ali, and arrived the same day at Tel-el-Kebir, a station of the company.

The 10th, in the morning, we continued our journey in the same manner, and at noon we entered upon the fresh-water canal made by the company. At 5 o'clock p. m. we arrived at Ismailia, the central station on the Suez canal.

The 11th, we remained at Ismailia to examine the works there, as well as those of Serapium, the most elevated points of the isthmus.

The 12th, we started from Ismailia, by the sea canal, in boats of small draught drawn by mules and camels; we arrived at Kantara at 4 o'clock p. m, having visited the important workshops and works of El Gaisr and El Terdan. From this point, in many places, and for a length altogether of sixty kilometres, (about thirty-six miles,) the canal is already excavated to its full width. The portion previously traversed was only about one-third of the width proposed.

The 13th, we left Kantara, in the same way, for Port Said; twenty kilometres (twelve miles) before reaching this place we found five small steamboats, which brought us to the Mediterranean. There we examined the piers in course of construction.

The 14th, we remained at Port Said to visit the important buildings, workshops and materials which the company possessed in that town.

The 15th, we returned by boat to Ismailia, and the 16th, in the morning, we started for Suez by the fresh-water canal in boats drawn by mules and camels, arriving at Suez in the evening. The two locks, intended to connect the sea canal with the fresh-water canal in the course of construction at Ismailia, are not yet finished, and a transshipment here is now necessary.

Our passage from the Mediterranean to the Red sea was accomplished in twenty-seven hours, as follows: eleven hours from Port Said to Ismailia, and sixteen hours thence to Suez.

A telegraph wire extends the whole length of the canal, communicating with the wires of Cairo, Alexandria, and Suez.

During our voyage we had opportunity to observe the excavators and other machinery used for digging the canal. All the works belonging to the company appeared to us built and equipped in a solid and permanent manner. In our opinion, the construction of a ship canal across the Isthmus is only a question of time and money.

We are informed that the company has already made contracts with various contractors for the completion of the ship canal by the 1st of July, 1868, without exceeding the actual capital, including therein the indemnity due by the Egyptian government under the award of the Emperor Napoleon III.

During the whole of our trip we received the greatest hospitality from Mr. de Lesseps and the engineers of the company, and these gentlemen answered freely all the questions which we put to them.

[Signed by the delegates.]

Mr. Hale to Mr. Seward.

No. 25.] AGENCY AND CONSULATE GENERAL OF THE U. S. OF AMERICA,
Alexandria, Egypt, May 5, 1865.

SIR: I have the honor to report that his Highness the Pacha of Egypt has seized the earliest opportunity to express to me the pain with which he has heard the sad tidings of the assassination of the President of the United States; his detestation of the abominable crime, and his sympathy for our country in the grievous loss we have sustained.

I have the honor to be, sir, most respectfully, your obedient servant,

CHARLES HALE.

Hon. WILLIAM H. SEWARD,
Secretary of State.

Mr. Hale to Mr. Hunter.

No. 26.] AGENCY AND CONSULATE GENERAL OF THE U. S. OF AMERICA,
Alexandria, May 13, 1865.

SIR: I have the honor to acknowledge the receipt of your instructions, under date of the 17th of April, with official intelligence of the foul assassination of the President, and of the dastardly attempt, happily unsuccessful, to take the lives of the Secretary of State and the Assistant Secretary.

I have already, in my despatch No. 25, reported the cordial expressions of sympathy which his Highness the Pacha of Egypt hastened to make me, in an official interview, immediately after the sad news was known here.

I have since received and am daily receiving other expressions of the public feelings of all nationalities represented here, in respect for the memory of the late President, and of confidence in the administration of the government by his successor.

A special religious ceremony has been ordered by the Greek community, at the Greek church, and one will be held at this consulate general, conducted by the American missionaries, on the day appointed for the purpose in the President's proclamation.

I have the honor to be, sir, very respectfully, your obedient servant,

CHARLES HALE.

Hon. W. HUNTER,
Acting Secretary of State.

Mr. Hale to Mr. Seward.

No. 30.] AGENCY AND CONSULATE GENERAL OF THE U. S. OF AMERICA,
Alexandria, Egypt, June 3, 1865.

SIR: I have the honor to report that the religious services commemorative of the death of the late President, mentioned at the close of my despatch No. 26, took place as proposed on the 1st instant, the day appointed by the President's proclamation. It was conducted by the Reverend Messrs. Watson and Currie, the American missionaries. The service was largely attended, and the impressive discourse by the Rev. Mr. Currie upon the life and services of our late beloved President received an earnest and thoughtful attention.

I have the honor to be, sir, very respectfully, your obedient servant,

CHARLES HALE.

Hon. WILLIAM H. SEWARD,
Secretary of State.

Mr. Hale to Mr. Seward.

No. 32.] AGENCY AND CONSULATE GENERAL OF THE U. S. OF AMERICA,
Alexandria, Egypt, June 14, 1865.

SIR: I have the honor to report that on the 28th ultimo his Highness the Pacha came to Alexandria, and on the 31st I had a long interview with him at his palace of Ras-el-tine here. He expressed his cordial felicitations at the successful termination of our war.

He remarked that the discomfiture of the rebels had enabled him to make within a few days several advantageous purchases in England, among which he mentioned two war-vessels, and the complete machinery for the manufacture of small-arms, all of which had been destined for the confederates.

The Pacha takes much interest in his navy. A natural pride is felt in the safe arrival, a few days since, at Suez, of the Egyptian steam-frigate L'Ibrahimié, of four hundred horse-power, the first war-vessel bearing the Egyptian flag which has ever doubled the cape of Good Hope. She left Alexandria for Marseilles about eight months ago, and then passing the straits of Gibraltar proceeded to England, where some repairs were made to her machinery. In February, her commander, Mustafa Bey, having received the orders of the Pacha to proceed from England to Suez, the frigate started on her long voyage. Her first stop was at St. Helena, where, as afterwards at the cape of Good Hope, every attention was shown her by the authorities of the British government. From the cape of Good Hope she went to the Seychelles and Zanzibar, whence, touching only at Aden, she completed the voyage to Suez, the whole crew in perfect health and excellent spirits. The Pacha, who had previously ordered that the pay of officers and seamen should be augmented one-fourth for the period of the voyage, was so much pleased at its happy termination, that he also bestowed on all three months' additional pay, as a private gratuity.

The happy tidings of the end of the American war produced a fall in the price of cotton, from which resulted, here, a financial crisis. Several heavy failures occurred, and there were many instances of suffering and distress. From the greatly diminished value of the cotton crop, it has been apprehended that the fellahs or native cultivators would find themselves unable to pay the advances which had been made to them, generally by European capitalists.

Under these circumstances the Pacha has come forward with a comprehensive measure of relief. He proposes to furnish to the fellahs the means of paying their debts, securing himself by a mortgage on their lands.

The amount required for this purpose exceeds a million of pounds sterling, which is to be reimbursed by the fellahs in instalments extending over a period of fifteen years, with interest.

As the Pacha, notwithstanding his immense resources, is generally without ready money, he is negotiating a new loan for the amount required.

It is needless to remark that this measure is acceptable to all parties concerned. On the one hand, the capitalists are rejoiced to find provision made for the payment of their debts; while the fellahs obtain an extension of fiftten years' time, in the course of which they may reasonably hope to be able to cover their present losses.

On the part of the Pacha, moreover, the arrangement is not without its advantages. In the first place, his exchequer may gain something from the higher rate of interest charged to the fellahs above the rate necessary to be paid by him upon his loan. Next, he substitutes himself for European creditors, many of whom had mortgages upon the lands of their debtors, and prevents the possibility of the lands falling into the possession of aliens, which, although allowed in Egypt, is naturally distasteful. And, finally, he puts himself in the way of augmenting his own landed possessions, in cases in which the fellahs to whom this measure of relief is accorded shall fail in their payments. From the constitutional improvidence of these people this is not unlikely to happen in many cases, and the passion of the Pacha for the acquisition of land may thus be gratified. It has previously been computed that he is the owner of no less than one-sixth of the cultivable land within his dominions.

Without shutting our eyes to the force of these material considerations, which have no doubt had their share of influence in determining this measure, we must, nevertheless, give the Pacha full credit for it as an act of beneficent grace and timely relief which few rulers would have either the means or the inclination to accord to their subjects, in a time of financial distress.

I received on the 11th instant the instruction of the Acting Secretary, under date of the 16th May, covering the proclamation of the President, which I communicated without delay to his Highness's minister for foreign affairs, offering, at the same time, my congratulations that the Egyptian government four years ago assumed the position which the cabinets of London and Paris find themselves obliged to take now, in consequence of the President's proclamation.

I may mention without impropriety that both the Pacha and his minister, in my interview with them, have inquired about your health with much solicitude, and have expressed great satisfaction at the tidings I have been able to give them of the progress of your recovery.

I have the honor to be, sir, very respectfully, your obedient servant,

CHARLES HALE.

Hon. WILLIAM H. SEWARD,
Secretary of State.

Mr. Hale to Mr. Seward.

No. 33.] AGENCY AND CONSULATE GENERAL OF THE U. S. OF AMERICA,
Alexandria, Egypt, June 19, 1865.

SIR: I have the honor to report that the presence of cholera in this town was declared by the board of health on the 12th instant. The number of deaths reported on that day was three; on the next twelve; the next thirty-four; the next thirty-eight; the next thirty-four; the next fifty-three; the next sixty-one and yesterday, when the malady had prevailed a week, ninety-four. As Alexandria has a population of about one hundred and seventy thousand, these deaths are more significant from the rapid increase they exhibit than from their absolute number. The proportion of deaths to population at its highest is still very much less than one in one thousand.

The outbreak of the disease has nevertheless caused great alarm, and many persons have left the place. The regular steamships have been crowded, and several have been charted for extra trips. I learn that at the Greek, Italian, and Austrian consulates general, each of which has a very numerous colony here, hundreds of passports are signed daily (at the Austrian 400 in one day) for their subjects who are fleeing in dread of the disease.

I am happy to be able to report that thus far there has been no death in the American community.

His Highness the Pacha departed for a marine excursion in his steam yacht at the beginning of the last week, and is now reported to be at Scio.

I have the honor to be, sir, very respectfully, your obedient servant,

CHARLES HALE.

Hon. WILLIAM H. SEWARD,
Secretary of State, &c., &c., &c.

Mr. Hale to Mr. Seward.

No. 34.] AGENCY AND CONSULATE GENERAL OF THE U. S. OF AMERICA,
Alexandria, Egypt, June 27, 1865.

SIR: I have the honor to report that since the date of my last despatch the mortality by cholera at this place has increased.

The number of deaths since my last report, according to the daily official bulletins communicated to me by the *Intendance Sanitaire*, has been as follows:

19th, one hundred and one; 20th, one hundred and fifty-nine; 21st, one hundred and forty-five; 22d, one hundred and fifty-nine; 23d, one hundred and forty-one; 24th, one hundred and eighty-three; 25th, one hundred and ninety-three; 26th, two hundred and eight.

Many persons entertain the impression that the actual number of deaths exceed that thus reported.

The alarm is in nowise abated, and the outgoing steamers continue to be crowded with passengers.

The malady has made its appearance at Cairo. No official reports are made of the deaths there. We hear also of its ravages in the other inland towns and the villages.

There have been many deaths among the European shipping in the harbor.

When the disease first made its appearance there were two American vessels in port; one of them has since sailed. They have happily been spared, and I am glad to be able to say again, under this later date, that no case has occurred in the American community.

I have the honor to be, sir, very respectfully, your obedient servant,

CHARLES HALE.

Hon. WILLIAM H. SEWARD, *Secretary of State.*

Mr. Hunter to Mr. Hale.

No. 9.] DEPARTMENT OF STATE,
Washington, June 29, 1865.

SIR: I have the honor to acknowledge the receipt of your despatches, from No. 19 to No. 29, the latter dated May 27, and to thank you for the interesting and valuable information which they communicate.

I am, sir, your obedient servant,

W. HUNTER, *Acting Secretary.*

CHARLES HALE, Esq., *&c., &c., Alexandria.*

Mr. Hale to Mr. Seward.

[Extract.]

No. 35.] AGENCY AND CONSULATE GENERAL OF THE U. S. OF AMERICA,
Alexandria, Egypt, June 29, 1865.

SIR: I have the honor to report that intelligence was received here yesterday, from the Egyptian explorer, Baker, under date of Khartum, May 10, 1865. He reports that on the 14th day of March of the preceding year, (that is, eighteen hundred and sixty-four,) he discovered in north latitude 1° 14′ a lake, of which he had been in search; that he sailed in a canoe upon this lake 13 days to its junction with the river Nile, in north latitude 2° 16′; that he then ascended the river for a distance not stated, until he came to a fall through a gap one hundred and twenty feet higher. To the lake, which is two hundred and sixty miles long, he has given the name of "Albert Nyanza," and he regards this lake and the "Victoria Nyanza," of Captain Speke, as the two parents of the Nile. He reports that the lake "Albert Nyanza" receives the whole drainage of the Mountains of the Moon.

The explorer is expected here shortly, and upon his arrival in Alexandria further particulars may doubtless be obtained. * * * *

I have the honor to be, sir, very respectfully, your obedient servant,

CHARLES HALE.

Hon. WILLIAM H. SEWARD,
Secretary of State.

Mr. Hale to Mr. Seward.

No. 37.] AGENCY AND CONSULATE GENERAL OF THE U. S. OF AMERICA,
Alexandria, Egypt, July 7, 1865.

SIR: I have the honor to report that the number of deaths from cholera in Alexandria, according to the official reports for each day since my despatch No. 34, has been as follows:

27th June, two hundred and fourteen; 28th June, two hundred and nine; 29th June, one hundred and ninety-seven; 30th June, one hundred and eighty-four; 1st July, one hundred and ninety-five; 2d July, two hundred and twenty-eight; 3d July, one hundred and seventy-six; 4th July, one hundred and eighteen; 5th July, one hundred and thirty-two; 6th July, one hundred and forty-two.

It will be observed that the greatest mortality occurred on the second, when the number of deaths was 228, but that two days afterwards the number was reported 118, nearly one-half. This favorable change is due to a strong north wind which has prevailed during the week, and which it is earnestly hoped may continue. Moreover, the beginning of the rise of the Nile has been reported by telegraph from the upper country; a favorable effect is expected when the wave shall reach the Delta, now in about twelve days, by covering with water the low and stagnant places.

From the interior we continue to hear the most distressing reports. At Cairo the mortality is very great, as many as four hundred and fifty-seven deaths having been reported officially to have occurred in a single day, while private reports, perhaps exaggerated, estimate the deaths at twelve hundred daily. At Tanta, at Zagazig, at Damietta, Rosetta, and other places, the deaths are frightfully numerous. At most of these places there are no physicians, and the sufferers receive no assistance.

It is estimated that more than thirty thousand people have left Alexandria since the malady appeared on the 11th ultimo. It is ascertained that eighteen thousand passports have been granted; if it be assumed that an average of two persons travel under each passport, the number of departures has been thirty-six thousand.

For three weeks after the outbreak of the malady, the American community was happily spared; but it is my painful duty to report the death yesterday morning of Mr. A. C. Pangelaki, a citizen of the United States by naturalization. His father, I believe, was one of the victims of the massacre at Scio; the orphan boy was brought to the United States, and I have heard that he was employed in the Greek department at the University press in Cambridge, near Boston. After several years' residence in America he returned to the East, never forgetting, however, his adopted nationality. At Smyrna, in the year 1846, he published a little book of lessons designed to facilitate the study of the English language by foreigners. For at least ten years past he has been a resident of Alexandria, where his mild manners and blameless character have contrasted him favorably with some others of the same nativity who have sought to live here under the American flag. His age was fifty. I should mention that it is said by the physicians that the disease of which he died was congestion of the brain, not cholera; but as I met him in perfect health thirty-six hours before the sudden illness which in two days more ended with his death, I am still inclined to regard him one of the victims of the existing unhealthy state of the atmosphere.

The present is the sixth time Egypt has been visited by cholera, renewing in destructiveness the mortality of the ancient plague. The first outbreak of the cholera was in 1831, the next in 1838, the third in 1848, the fourth in 1850, the fifth in 1855; the period of exemption has never exceeded ten years, the term between the preceding and the present visitation.

It will readily be understood that in times like these no festivity was appropriate on the fourth of July; but I may report that on that day their excellencies Cherif Pacha, minister of foreign affairs, and Mourad Pacha, governor of Alexandria, notwithstanding their severe duties and anxieties, did not fail to visit me officially, and offered their congratulations on the happy recurrence of our national anniversary, and their best wishes for the prosperity of the Union. But one American vessel remains in port, and she clears to-morrow for England.

I have the honor to be, sir, very respectfully your obedient servant,

CHARLES HALE.

Hon. WILLIAM H. SEWARD,
Secretary of State.

Mr. Hale to Mr. Seward.

No. 38.] AGENCY AND CONSULATE GENERAL OF THE U. S. OF AMERICA,
Alexandria, Egypt, July 19, 1865.

SIR: I am gratified to be able to report that since my last despatch the mortality at this place has continued to diminish daily; the number of deaths from cholera reported yesterday was only eighteen; and there have been none in the American community since the two previously mentioned.

The number of deaths from cholera in Alexandria since the outbreak of the malady, until yesterday, inclusive—a period of thirty-seven days—according to the official bulletins, has been three thousand nine hundred and thirty-one. The number of deaths, from other diseases in the same period, has been one thousand three hundred and sixty-nine. The aggregate mortality within this period accordingly has been five thousand three hundred. The population of Alexandria may be estimated at one hundred and seventy-five thousand.

In Cairo the malady did not declare itself until eight days after its appearance at Alexandria. The number of deaths at that place to the 17th instant, inclusive, a period of twenty-eight days, according to the official bulletins, has been the following: From cholera, five thousand two hundred and forty-nine; from other diseases, two thousand three hundred; total, seven thousand five hundred and forty-nine. The population at Cairo may be estimated at four hundred thousand.

In Damietta, a place with a population of about forty thousand, the number of deaths from cholera between the 26th of June and 9th of July, inclusive, a period of fourteen days, was one thousand four hundred and eighty-five; and in the same period one hundred and three deaths from other diseases were reported.

Similar reports are received from many other places in lower and middle Egypt, but there have been very few cases at Suez, and none, it is believed, in upper Egypt.

The mortality obtained its maximum in Alexandria on the 3d instant, when the number of deaths reported from cholera was two hundred and twenty-eight; in Cairo on the 14th, when the number was four hundred and fifty-seven; in Damietta on the 5th, when the number was one hundred and seventy-two, a rate of mortality which, had it continued, would have wiped that town out of existence in eight months. Since these dates, happily, the amelioration has been constant and rapid.

The depth of water in the Nile was officially reported on the 10th instant to be eight pics and nine kerats. It had not been so low at the same date for four years certainly, and I believe for a much longer period. It has gained nearly two kerats each day since that date, or about eight inches in the space of a week. These measurements are made at the Nileometer near Cairo.

I have the honor to enclose tables showing the mortality, according to the official bulletins, for every day since the outbreak of the malady, both at Alexandria and Cairo, and a portion of a similar table for Damietta. It may be interesting to trace the progress of the disease at each of these places. In these tables the deaths are set down against the date when they were reported; in my previous despatches I have mentioned the same numbers with dates a day earlier. In point of fact, I believe the official bulletin each day includes the morning of the same day with the afternoon of the preceding day, and the night between.

I have the honor to be, sir, very respectfully, your obedient servant,

CHARLES HALE.

Hon. WILLIAM H. SEWARD,
Secretary of State.

A.

Number of deaths officially reported daily in Alexandria and in Cairo since the outbreak of the cholera in each place in the year 1865.

Date.	ALEXANDRIA.			Date.	ALEXANDRIA.		
	Cholera.	Other diseases.	Total.		Cholera.	Other diseases.	Total.
June 12	3	44	47	July 2	195	23	218
13	12	38	50	3	228	37	265
14	34	30	64	4	176	40	216
15	38	17	55	5	118	39	157
16	34	29	63	6	132	44	176
17	53	28	81	7	142	35	177
18	61	30	91	8	94	29	123
19	94	21	115	9	91	31	122
20	101	51	152	10	64	37	101
21	159	42	201	11	55	44	99
22	145	36	181	12	61	33	94
23	159	39	198	13	48	33	81
24	141	37	178	14	21	41	62
25	183	50	233	15	23	45	68
26	193	48	241	16	22	45	67
27	208	50	258	17	21	33	54
28	214	45	259	18	18	37	55
29	209	43	252				
30	197	40	237	Total.........	3,931	1,369	5,300
July 1	184	25	209				

Date.	CAIRO.			Date.	CAIRO.		
	Cholera.	Other diseases.	Total		Cholera.	Other diseases.	Total.
June 20	2	46	48	July 5	356	63	419
21	2	52	54	6	355	82	437
22	2	68	70	7	365	87	452
23	3	52	55	8	389	90	479
24	17	55	72	9	347	97	444
25	25	71	96	10	252	103	355
26	71	74	145	11	226	84	310
27	85	93	178	12	204	98	302
28	93	75	168	13	156	97	253
29	136	65	201	14	149	104	253
30	216	84	300	15	151	101	252
July 1	397	77	406	16	109	89	198
2	306	90	396	17	64	107	171
3	382	112	494				
4	457	84	541	Total.........	5,249	2,300	7,549

B.

Number of deaths officially reported daily in Damietta, Egypt, since the outbreak of the cholera there in 1865.

Date.	From cholera.	Other diseases.	Total.
June 26	1	1	2
27	10	7	17
28	35	4	39
29	54	4	58
30	67	8	75
July 1	93	6	99
2	107	8	115
3	141	7	148
4	157	8	165
5	172	6	178
6	171	11	182
7	169	13	182
8	166	11	177
9	142	9	151
Total to 9th	1,485	103	1,588

Mr. Seward to Mr. Hale.

No. 10.] DEPARTMENT OF STATE,
Washington, July 24, 1865.

SIR: Your despatches from No. 30, of June 3 to No. 35, of June 29, have been received, and I thank you for the interesting intelligence which they contain. The sagacious and beneficent measure devised by his Highness the Pacha for the relief of his people, to which you refer in your No. 32, shows him to be a wise and benevolent ruler. His expressions of kindness, as well as those of his minister for foreign affairs, which are personal to myself, are very highly appreciated.

I am, sir, your obedient servant,

WILLIAM H. SEWARD.

CHARLES HALE, Esq., *&c., &c., Alexandria.*

Mr. Hale to Mr. Seward.

No. 39.] AGENCY AND CONSULATE GENERAL OF THE U. S. OF AMERICA,
Alexandria, Egypt, August 7, 1865.

SIR: I have the gratification to report that the cholera has almost entirely disappeared from those parts of Egypt in which it has lately prevailed. For several days past no deaths from the disease have been reported in Alexandria, and by the latest daily report received, the number at Cairo was only five. From the villages the reports are equally favorable. There are, however, unhappily, rumors of the outbreak of the malady in upper Egypt which had previously been exempted. I shall take an early occasion to send you a completion of the tables of mortality enclosed in my last despatch.

His Highness the Pacha returned to Alexandria from his sea voyage, which has extended as far as Constantinople, on the 3d instant, and proceeded to Cairo the same day. On the 3d instant also arrived in Egypt Colonel Stanton, the successor of Sir Robert Colquhoun, as agent and consul general of Great Britain.

I have the honor to be, sir, very respectfully, your obedient servant,

CHARLES HALE.

Hon. WILLIAM H. SEWARD,
Secretary of State.

Mr. Hale to Mr. Seward.

No. 41.] AGENCY AND CONSULATE GENERAL OF THE U. S. OF AMERICA,
Alexandria, Egypt, August 26, 1865.

SIR: Nine hundred negroes from the Soudan or upper country of Egypt, within the jurisdiction of the Pacha, are expected shortly to arrive at Alexandria to be embarked in French transports for Mexico to relieve the contingent furtively sent out in the month of January, one thousand eight hundred and sixty-three. I must give the Pacha credit for putting me in possession of full and early information on the subject in the most frank possible manner. On this occasion, at least, there is nothing clandestinely about the proceeding. I told him that I regretted to hear of the movement, and wished, at least, that it might be delayed. He said that it was simply the execution of an agreement made between his predecessor, Said Pacha, and the Emperor of the French, three years ago; that the number of soldiers in service would not be increased by a single unit; that the number was inconsiderable, being only one battalion, or the fourth part of a regiment, and not exceeding nine hundred in all, officers included. He gave me the most positive assurance that it is not proposed to increase this number. The Pacha then fell into a line of conversation, which, especially as he expressed a wish that it might be regarded as confidential, it is not necessary to report in detail, more than to say that he expressed to me no interest, wish or expectation to see the successful establishment of an empire in Mexico under French auspices. He ridiculed the small effective results reached by the French in their efforts at colonization everywhere, and pointed with some pride to the small number of troops with which he keeps order in his own dominions compared to the great number of French troops always in service in Algeria, citing the recent pamphlet of the Emperor of the French for proof that, after all, that country is not well governed. He regards the sending out of this relief corps as a necessary act of humanity to the Egyptian negroes who are now in Mexico, while he thinks that he cannot in good faith escape the maintenance of a small force there in respect of the engagements entered into by his predecessor. The whole cost of the movement, which is "enormous," is paid by the French government. The Pacha made this point with emphasis, using the word "enormous" (or rather, its French equivalent) no less than three times, and betrayed evident satisfaction that the expenses do not come out of his own purse.

The circumstances of the original movement are described in the despatch of my predecessor No. 27, under date of January 18, 1865. Mr. Thayer addressed most energetic remonstrances to Said Pacha, and to his minister, and obtained a positive assurance that the number of the contingent should not be increased. Said Pacha was then actually on his death-bed, and his demise is reported in the same despatch. Of one ground of remonstrance to the movement suggested by Mr. Thayer, namely, the violation it implies of the suzeranity of the Porte, it may be remarked, in addition to the fact that it has heretofore proved futile, and to other reasons which exist for not pressing it at this time, that as the Pacha has just returned from Constantinople, it may not be improbable that he has prepared himself with the necessary permission.

In the course of the conversation the Pacha told me that the Egyptian army-list numbered about twenty thousand, of whom, as I understood, about eight thousand are in active service in various parts of the country. From other sources I have learned that the mortality in the army, from cholera, has been frightful. The Pacha, however, remarked that only one of his negroes had died from yellow fever in Mexico, saying that it appeared that the negro constitution was proof against such maladies. I hinted to him that if he can spare a few hundred soldiers peculiarly fit for service in Mexico, the United States have lately had under arms more than one hundred thousand of the same race. These men would be, in like manner, peculiarly fit for service in Egypt if the vicious principle of interference which supports the empire in Mexico, to which the Pacha lends his soldiers, should at any time be retaliated by us. Hitherto we have practiced the contrary principle, and have expected other governments to respect it, at least so far as America is concerned; and, without intervening ourselves in Oriental politics, "what the Pacha has done in Mexico at the request of another power, the United States might do in Egypt at the request of some friendly power."

These and other arguments, of course, might be pressed upon the Egyptian government, to prevent the departure of the relief. What I have already said to the Pacha will serve very well as a foundation for any formal communication in the way of an objection or protest that you may think advisable to instruct me to make; or, in case it is deemed best to let the matter rest without further remark, I think you need not hesitate to believe that, while the Pacha cannot very readily get rid of the subsisting engagement made by his predecessor, he has wit enough of his own to see that his sending troops to America, however inconsiderable in number, is a thing not particularly agreeable to the people of the United States, and that it would be very foolish for him to do anything more that might have the effect to provoke an intervention of the United States against him in some possible turn of Egyptian affairs.

No doubt you will regard the sending of this relief from Egypt, in connexion with the recruiting in Europe for the Belgian and Austrian legions for service in Mexico, the renewal of the French forces there, and other matters, of the views of the government with regard to which I am not apprized.

My audience with the Pacha took place at Cairo yesterday, and the overland mail which must take forward this despatch is already announced. But, unless upon reflection (for which as yet I have had little time) I should conclude to make a formal representation in writing to the Egyptian government, addressed to the minister of foreign affairs, I shall content myself for the present with the general remarks I have already made verbally to the Pacha, awaiting your further instructions.

Although the arrival of the negroes from the upper county may be expected at any time, everything moves so slowly in Egypt that it would not be at all surprising if it were to be considerably delayed.

I have taken advantage of the departure of one of the American missionaries for the upper country to arrange for timely confidential information of their coming.

I believe nothing is known of the matter in general circles here. It had not been mentioned to me by any of my colleagues.

I was gratified on the 19th instant by the receipt of your instruction No. 10, of July 24th.,

I have the honor to be, sir, very respectfully, your obedient servant,

CHARLES HALE.

Hon. WILLIAM H. SEWARD,
Secretary of State.

Mr. Seward to Mr. Hale.

No. 12.] DEPARTMENT OF STATE,
Washington, September 4, 1865.

SIR: Your despatches from No. 36 to No. 40, both numbers inclusive, have been received, and have been read with special interest. The department has promulgated the information communicated by you relative to the ravages of the cholera in Egypt, the violence of which, we are happy to learn, has sensibly abated. The completion of the tables of mortality already forwarded by you will be received with much interest.

I am, sir, your obedient servant,

WILLIAM H. SEWARD.

CHARLES HALE, Esq., *&c.*, *&c.*, *Alexandria.*

Mr. Seward to Mr. Hale.

No. 13.] DEPARTMENT OF STATE,
Washington, September 21, 1865.

SIR: Your despatch of August 26, No. 41, has been received. It announces that nine hundred negroes from the upper country of Egypt, within the jurisdiction of the Pacha, are expected shortly to arrive at Alexandria, to be embarked in French transports for Mexico, to relieve the contingent which was sent out in January, 1863. The latter proceeding, as you are aware, excited much comment at the time; but it passed unnoticed by this government, which was then seriously occupied with a peculiar condition of merely domestic affairs, and with the foreign embarrassments which grew out of that condition. Since then the United States have abolished slavery. The attention of Congress, as well as that of the executive department and of the country has been very steadily fixed upon the course of events in Mexico, which, I need not say, form a subject of serious concern with regard to the safety of the free republican institutions of this country, an object with which we are accustomed to connect the desired ultimate consequence of the abolition of every form of compulsory civil or military servitude in this hemisphere.

You are instructed to bring this matter to the attention of the Pacha's minister for foreign affairs, and to state to him that, in the opinion of this government, the renewal of the transaction alluded to could not be regarded with favor, or even without deep anxiety, by the people of the United States. It will be proper for you to inform the minister that I have written upon the subject, in the same sense herein adopted, to the diplomatic agents of the United States residing respectively at Paris and Constantinople.

I am, sir, your obedient servant,

WILLIAM H. SEWARD.

CHARLES HALE, Esq., *&c.*, *&c.*, *Alexandria.*

Mr. Hale to Mr. Seward.

[Extract.]

No. 44.] AGENCY AND CONSULATE GENERAL OF THE U. S. OF AMERICA,
Alexandria, Egypt, October 27, 1865.

SIR: I received on the 19th instant your No. 13, under date of 21st September, and lost no time in writing to the minister of foreign affairs, who is now in

Cairo, in the exact sense of your instruction. No answer has yet been received; but this is not remarkable, for the minister would naturally take the instruction to the Pacha, who has been making an excursion on the Nile so far as Minieh, from which he did not return to Cairo until the morning of the 25th.

Colonel Stanton, the British agent and consul general, to whom I had communicated the substance of my information at the end of August, and who had transmitted it to his government, called on me on the 20th instant (that is, the day after I had received your instruction) and informed me that he had the instructions of his government to remonstrate against any forcible and compulsory deportation of Nubians from Egypt to serve under the French flag in Mexico. I believe these are the exact words of his instruction.

I may mention that the British hold the Egyptian authorities to a very exact fulfilment of their promises for the abolition of slavery. It is certain that slavery still exists in Egypt; but any slave who can manage to get before the British consul is sent with the dragoman of the consulate to the local court where his free papers are demanded and are accorded. In this way Mr. Reade, British consul at Cairo, and Mr. Stanley, British consul at Alexandria, have secured the manumission of at least twenty each (probably a larger number) since I have been here. In one instance it was a slave woman who had escaped from a Pacha's harem, and fled to Mr. Reade's house. Her master followed and tried to persuade her to return. She was firm, and he was obliged to give her up, although, no doubt, she had cost him a large sum. Mr. Stanley, within a fortnight, has secured the freedom, in a similar manner, for two or three people escaped from the service of a high officer in the Egyptian navy.

It has, no doubt, occurred to Colonel Stanton, and the suggestion, no doubt, would be approved by Lord Russell, that the same principles which led Great Britain to object to forced labor on the Suez canal, and to involuntary domestic servitude in Egypt, apply to compulsory military drafts here for service in Mexico.

Soon after my despatch No. 41 was forwarded, one of the local papers here reproduced, in Italian, a letter, probably from the Independence Belge, connecting Nubra Pacha's visit to Paris with this business. It was stated in this letter that the Egyptian government would place several regiments at the disposal of France to re-enforce the army of occupation in Mexico, and that the question of money was all that remained to be settled between the Egyptian and French governments.

The French local paper printed the day before yesterday some extracts from a paper, by the Count de Kératry, in the Revue des Deux Mondes, extolling the good service of the Egyptian troops in Mexico.

* * * * * * * *

Meanwhile there is no intelligence of the coming of the negroes. A considerable body of Egyptian troops, perhaps as many as four or five thousand, have just come to Alexandria, and are quartered in the barracks at Ras-el-tin. These, however, are not negroes; a considerable portion of them are new recruits, and it is said they are brought here for purposes of drill.

A detachment of French soldiers, from Cochin China, has also just arrived from Suez at Alexandria, and is said to be waiting the arrival of transports to take them back to France. Meanwhile they are quartered on board the hospital ship, which is the only French government vessel now in this harbor.

Three Austrian men-of-war lately arrived and still remain in the harbor.

I shall keep this despatch open until the latest moment before the departure of the mail packet, in order to be able to send any additional information which I may be able to obtain.

I have the honor to be, sir, very respectfully, your obedient servant,

CHARLES HALE.

SUNDAY MORNING, *October* 29.

The mail packet is on the point of leaving. I have nothing important to add. I have as yet no answer from the minister of foreign affairs, and the position of things at the barracks of Ras-el-tin and in the harbor, according to reports received this morning, is not changed.

C. H.

Mr. Hale to Mr. Seward.

[Extract.]

No. 45.] AGENCY AND CONSULATE GENERAL OF THE U. S. OF AMERICA,
Alexandria, Egypt, November 13, 1865.

SIR: Although I have not yet received a formal answer from the minister for foreign affairs, there is no room to doubt that the proposed deportation of negroes from Egypt for military service in Mexico has been abandoned; and there is even some reason to believe that the trouble in the Soudan, which has been assigned in Paris as a reason for the abandonment of the expedition, was caused, if not wholly, at least in part, by the detestation entertained by the people, and especially among the men enrolled for military duty, for the distant service to which it was feared they were to be sent. His Highness the Pacha has not returned to Cairo, and has not remained in any one place more than one or two days since the date of my last despatch, and I must wait quite unwillingly, but probably not longer than the next post, before I can complete my report on this subject.

* * * * * * *

I have the honor to be, sir, very respectfully, your obedient servant,

CHARLES HALE.

Hon. WILLIAM H. SEWARD,
Secretary of State.

Mr. Hale to Mr. Seward.

No. 46.] AGENCY AND CONSULATE GENERAL OF THE U. S. OF AMERICA,
Cairo, Egypt, November 18, 1865.

SIR: On the 16th instant I called on his excellency, Cherif Pacha, minister for foreign affairs, having come from Alexandria for the purpose on the preceding evening.

The minister courteously made excuses for his delay in answering my note of 20th October, in which I had communicated to him the observations contained in your instruction to me, No. 13, of the 21st September. He told me that he was ready to give me an answer that would be in all respects satisfactory to my government.

I said that I was glad to hear this, and that if he could conveniently send me his answer that day or the next, I could communicate its substance by telegraph to Queenstown, in season to reach you, to be laid before the President before the opening of Congress. He said that he would do so.

We then dropped into a less formal conversation, when I was surprised to learn that the Egyptian government had not abandoned or even scarcely suspended the proposed expedition of negroes to Mexico. The minister expected that you would be entirely satisfied to have the expedition go on, if you were assured that the number of the force now in Mexico would not be increased, and that the soldiers were not slaves; and such was the substance of the formal answer he was about to send me.

As regards the first part of this answer, nothing else was ever proposed, and I told the minister that you could not have understood that anything else was proposed. His Highness had very clearly explained to me that the nine hundred negroes were to be embarked to relieve the contingent sent out in January, 1863; that I reported the proposition exactly in those words, although it was observed that nine hundred was the number given to me, while four hundred and fifty was the number stated to Mr. Thayer in 1863, and reported by him. No remarks had been made even upon this discrepancy. I spoke of the expedition in my despatch as a relief; you began your instruction by rehearsing the words of my despatch in the usual manner, and that your observations must be taken as based upon the distinct understanding that it was proposed to send out the negroes to relieve the contingent already in service.

The minister seemed to take it for granted that the compulsory service of the negroes not only formed the whole objection to the affair in the eyes of the people of the United States, but that if that objection were removed by assurances on his part they would be entirely satisfied to see the expedition go forward.

I told the minister that I knew nothing of personal knowledge of the circumstances of the embarcation of 1863, but I knew how it was described by Mr. Thayer, and what was the general opinion not only in the United States but in Alexandria, where the story of those days in January, 1863, when no black boas (door-keeper) could be persuaded to open a door at night for fear of being crimped, and when many black servants ran away to hide for a week in the desert, while the embarcation for Mexico was going on, was still familiar in many households; and I had supposed that there was no doubt of the furtive and secret character of the proceeding.

With regard to this last remark, the minister said, no doubt, the embarcation in 1863 was sudden and secret, but this was for a political reason, namely, that it was necessary to keep the thing from the knowledge of the Porte until it was all over; as the whole proceeding at that time was against the Sultan's will, it was arranged to have it finished before his remonstrance could arrive.

To conclude the conversation, however, I told the minister that his Highness had said to me expressly that he should not send the negroes except for the engagement of his predecessor to the Emperor of the French; that appreciating the position of his Highness, you had addressed your observations to the governments at Paris and Constantinople as well as to his own, and that I knew that the French government had been good enough, while assigning a special reason and reserving its general abstract right, to give up the affair on its part, after receiving your observations, and that I should be sorry if the Egyptian government, after receiving the same observations, found no reason to change the course that had formerly been proposed. I added that the announcement made by Mr. Drouyn de Lhuys to Mr. Bigelow to this effect was made independently of the matter of compulsory service, which had not been discussed between them until after this previous point had been disposed of, and then only as a matter of abstract interest; that Mr. Drouyn de Lhuys had expressly told Mr. Bigelow that the inquiries he proposed to set on foot here with regard to the nature of the service in the Egyptian army were to satisfy himself, and not as a matter of official concern to his government.

Cherif Pacha said this put an entirely new face on the affair, and could scarcely credit the accuracy of my information. To satisfy him I sent to my hotel for the copy which Mr. Bigelow had kindly transmitted to me of his despatch to you, No. 186, reporting his interview with the French minister. I read to Cherif Pacha the principal parts of this despatch, and afterwards, at his request, furnished him with a translation into French.

In sending to Cherif Pacha this translation, I wrote a note to express what was already understood between us, namely, that this was not precisely an official communication; that I was waiting his answer to my official note of the 20th October, and that meanwhile I was willing to add to his information upon the subject. I begged his particular attention to the fact that the note of the 20th October conveyed your observations upon understanding that the proposed expedition of negroes to Mexico, was to replace the contingent now in service there. I said that whatever reason might be assigned, the thing needed to tranquillize public opinion in the United States would be to hear that his Highness had been good enough to declare that he did not intend to renew the expedition of Egyptian soldiers to Mexico; that a replacement would be considered as a renewal; that if he liked to make a reserve of his rights in the manner pursued by the French minister, in saying that the proposed expedition was not abandoned, but that in effect it would not take place on account of domestic reasons, I should be satisfied with this, but that of course a definitive abandonment would give us great pleasure; that I believed France would make no objection to it; among our people in America it would be regarded as a new proof of the friendship of his Highness, and everywhere in the world it would be regarded as a proof of his noble wisdom in the interests of humanity, since, without giving to the service of the Egyptian negroes in Mexico the name of "slavery," it must be admitted would not be an agreeable thing for the soldiers, as his Highness himself had told me with all possible frankness when expressing his anxiety to replace the men now in that service by others.

The substance of the preceding paragraph, and nearly in the equivalent words in French, was written and sent to the minister, you will understand, with the view of influencing his answer to the note of the 20th October. He kept my messenger waiting a short time, however, and sent back by him his formal answer to that note, a translation of which answer is hereto appended and marked A.

As this formal answer to your observations will of course attract your particular attention, I make no remark upon it.

At the same time the messenger brought back a less formal note from the minister, in which he acknowledged the receipt of my last note, saying that for the present he could only refer me to our conversation of the morning, repeating that it gave the subject a new phase, of which the Egyptian government reserved for itself the examination, and that meanwhile he hastened to send me his official answer to your observations.

I believe that I have faithfully represented these communications, but for your greater assurance I transmit herewith, marked B, C, D, and E, copies of the originals of everything that has passed in writing, beginning with my note of the 20th October, in which I endeavored to give exactly the sense of your observations, continuing with the minister's official answer, (of which the translation is the piece marked A,) and concluding with our less formal correspondence of the 16th instant, already described.

The telegraph wire between Alexandria and Malta had just broken; but the steam packet to the latter port leaves to-morrow, takes forward to Mr. Bigelow, in Paris, a telegraphic message to the effect that the Egyptian government say the insurrection is suppressed, and that the expedition of negroes may go forward. I have also written to him fully.

A French transport has arrived in the harbor of Alexandria with troops for Cochin-China, who have been disembarked and have taken the railway for Suez.

With regard to the question of the compulsory service of the soldiers in the Egyptian army, and especially that of the blacks from the upper country, I hardly know what I may say with propriety in an official communication. I have reason to believe that Mr. Outrey, the agent and consul general here of France, was annoyed at being called upon by Mr. Drouyn de Lhuys to make a report upon this subject. Even to an entirely disinterested observer it might be difficult, in a country where the civil government is absolute, to distinguish between compulsory service in the army and military service everywhere; to distinguish between a levy in the Soudan and the conscription in France. It would remain to weigh the evidence in such cases as are reported to have occurred in filling the number of the contingent at Alexandria in January, 1863. If the object desired is merely to satisfy the private judgment of a candid observer, something might be learned from the various books of modern travel in Egypt. The difficulties which embarrass the subject when approached as a matter of discussion among governments are illustrated by the fact—reported in my last despatch but one—of the frequent release of negroes from slavery in Egypt by the interposition of the good offices of the British consulates. The Egyptian government may point to these instances as so many proofs in support of the assertion proudly made in the minister's answer to your observations, "Slavery no longer exists in Egypt;" for whenever the consulates bring forward an instance of the contrary, the man is immediately freed. Others would perhaps regard these instances as disproving the proposition insisted on, or at least as illustrating that it is not of universal application.

I shall endeavor to collect the most authentic and also the most available testimony within my reach, without loss of time, but should be glad of your instructions as to the manner and degree in which it may be advisable to push inquiries.

I have the honor to be, sir, very respectfully, your obedient servant,

CHARLES HALE.

Hon. WILLIAM H. SEWARD, *Secretary of State.*

A.

[Translation.]

MINISTRY OF FOREIGN AFFAIRS,
Cairo, November 16, 1865.

Monsieur l'Agent et Consul Général:

I have gladly received the despatch which you did me the honor to address me under date of the 20th October last, for the purpose of presenting in the name of your government the observations suggested to it by the expedition by his Highness of a battalion of negroes, of which the departure has been hitherto delayed by an insurrection in the Soudan, now suppressed, and who are destined to replace in Mexico those who were sent thither in 1863.

If your government had not thought proper to make any remark previously on this subject, you say this was because the government was too much occupied with internal affairs, and also because it had not then decreed the abolition of slavery. The government of his Highness, whose sympathies for that of the republic of the United States cannot be doubted for a moment, accordingly thinks it of the first importance to give explanations to the latter, which I take pleasure in believing will reassure it completely with regard to the bearing and the composition of the expedition in question. In fact, the situation of 1863 has not been modified; there has been no change to affect it. The Egyptian government, at the request of a friendly power, thought itself competent to make certain engagements in which its neutrality did not appear to be in any way compromised, and in which it was very far from thinking that it would ever incur the disapproval of the United States.

The French government, in making a request for the replacement of the contingent now in service by a new battalion, of which the composition remains exactly the same, and his Highness the viceroy, in agreeing to the request, do but obey the laws of the simplest humanity. It is three years, in fact, that these men have been living far from their country, where most of them have left their wives and children; home-sickness (la nostalgie) has made more gaps in their ranks than the climate or the fire of the enemy. In all countries of the world such considerations are thought worthy of regard, and the Egyptian government would have had a bad appearance not to accept their significance. Moreover, it would have been very difficult, not to say impossible, to escape the consequence of an agreement which put at the disposal of the French expedition to Mexico a certain number of men, strong and well-fitted for military service. The honor of the flag, and the respect due to its engagements then, united in requiring that the government of his Highness should receive with favor a request which had in its eyes the advantage of restoring, not only to their native country, but to their separate homes, a certain number of these men, who were chosen originally from the soldiers of the garrisons of Cairo and Alexandria, and who had a right to their discharge by reason of the expiration of the period of service due to the state.

In the material point of view, then, we have merely to deal with a simple substitution, and there is, in truth, no reason for anxiety at a situation which remains the same that has existed for three years past.

In the moral point of view, the objection appears to me still less well-founded. It is based on the fact that, at the date of the first expedition, the United States had not decreed the abolition of slavery.

Thus, in the opinion of the cabinet of Washington, the Egyptian soldiers who make part of the French expedition to Mexico are to be regarded as slaves, and their stay there as contradicting the great measure of humanity which has freed all their brethren in America.

Permit me, sir, to protest on my side against the expression of an error so clear. Slavery no longer exists in Egypt. It was abolished there long before it was abolished in the United States by the many sacrifices and glorious efforts on the part of the defenders of the Union. The negroes in the Egyptian territory are subjects of his Highness by the same title and with the same rights as the other natives of the country. In serving under our flag they obey a law of conscription equal for all. Regulations limit the period of service due by each man to the country, and the length of this period is proportioned to the number of the population.

This is not all. In virtue of a principle made applicable as long ago as the reign of our illustrious Mehemet Ali, all slaves enrolled under the flag become free in full right.

The good conduct of some of these soldiers since they have been in Mexico has been pointed out by the general-in-chief of the expedition to the French government, which has not hesitated to award to them crosses and medals of honor; others have been proposed to the Egyptian government by the same general-in-chief for similar distinctions, and even for promotion to the grade of superior officers, and the Egyptian government has made haste to recognize their merit.

I appeal to yourself, sir, is there a country in the world where soldiers who were merely slaves would be treated with so much regard and would enjoy so much consideration?

I rely, then, with all confidence on your co-operation to make known the details, to transmit these loyal explanations to the government of the United States, and to reassure it respecting the true condition of these Egyptian negroes. I take pleasure in hoping that, better informed than before, your government will be good enough to see nothing in this expedition but the simple replacement of one battalion by another in conformity with the terms of an understanding; a replacement of which the necessity is demanded by the laws of humanity and the rules of justice; at the same time that it is imposed upon his Highness by the benevolent interest which he feels for all his subjects without distinction.

Be pleased to accept, sir, the assurance of my high consideration.

The Minister of Foreign Affairs,
CHERIF PACHA.

B.

[Translation.]

AGENCY AND CONSULATE GENERAL OF THE
UNITED STATES OF AMERICA IN EGYPT,
Alexandria, October 20, 1865.

YOUR EXCELLENCY: At an audience which his Highness accorded me on the 25th of August last, he was so good as to give me some explanations about the circumstances under which the Egyptian government proposes to send nine hundred negroes to Mexico to replace the troops of the same kind which were sent there in the month of January, 1863.

Having thereupon made report to my government, without failing to set forth the noble frankness with which his Highness expressed himself in giving me on this subject all the details without reserve, I have just received instructions from my government.

I must say to you that the previous expedition in 1863, although it may have made room for many comments, was let pass by the government of the United States of America without remark, because it was at that time very much engaged with exceptionally complicated domestic affairs and with foreign difficulties. But since that epoch the United States have abolished slavery. Our attention is steadily fixed on the course of events in Mexico, a subject which seriously affects the security of republican institutions on the American continent, with which we are accustomed to connect the so-much-desired ulterior consequences of the abolition of all compulsory servitude, civil or military, in the western hemisphere.

I am therefore ordered, Mr. Minister, to bring the affair to your attention, and to say to you that, in the opinion of my government, the repetition of an expedition of Egyptian negroes to Mexico would not be regarded with approval, nor even without profound inquietude by the United States.

I must also inform your excellency that instructions of the same character have been sent to the diplomatic representatives of the United States at Paris and at Constantinople.

I have the honor to renew to your excellency the assurance of my high consideration.

Agent and Consul General,
CHARLES HALE.

His Excellency CHERIF PACHA,
Minister of Foreign Affairs.

D.

[Translation.]

AGENCY AND CONSULATE GENERAL OF THE
UNITED STATES OF AMERICA IN EGYPT,
Hotel des Ambassadeurs, Cairo, November 16, 1865.

YOUR EXCELLENCY: In submitting to you the translation, here enclosed, of a despatch from our minister at Paris, addressed to the minister of foreign affairs at Washington, you will readily understand that it is not precisely an official communication that I make to you.

I await your answer to my official note of 20th October, written under special instructions from my government; meantime I make known to you what has passed.

You will understand that I have only made mention to my government of a new expedition to replace the troops which are already in Mexico. The despatch of the 20th of September, of which our minister at Paris in the beginning of the letter here enclosed and also at the end under No. 1, was of the same purport with that addressed at the same time to me, and which I communicated to you under date of the 20th October. I pray you especially to take note of the language of my government.

I should say to you that, whatever may be the reason, that which is necessary to tranquillize public opinion with us would be to learn that his Highness has been pleased to declare that he does not intend to renew the expedition of Egyptian soldiers to Mexico. A replacing would be considered as a renewal.

If you wish to make a reserve in respect of your rights in the manner of Mr. Drouyn de Lhuys, by saying that the expedition is not abandoned, but that in effect it will not take place in consequence of interior events in Egypt, I would be satisfied, but naturally a definitive abandonment would give us great pleasure. France, as I believe, would not make objections; with us in America it would be considered as a fresh proof of the friendship of his Highness, and by all the world it will be deemed a noble proof of his wisdom in the interests of humanity.

Provided that the service of Egyptian negroes in Mexico is not slavery, it may be admitted that it is not at all agreeable to the soldiers, as his Highness told me with all frankness possible in expressing to me his wish to change the men sent by others.

I seize this occasion to renew to you the assurance of my high consideration.

CHARLES HALE.

E.

[Translation.]

DEPARTMENT OF FOREIGN AFFAIRS, CABINET OF THE MINISTER,
Cairo, November 16, 1865.

MR. CONSUL GENERAL: I have just received your despatch of the 16th, and the translation of the document therein referred to.

For the present I can only refer to our conversation of this morning in repeating that your despatch of to-day carries the question into a new phase, which the government of his Majesty reserves to itself to examine. Meanwhile I restrict myself to sending you my official answer to your esteemed despatch of 20th October last.

Please accept, Mr. Consul General, the assurance of my high consideration.

CHERIF PACHA.

Mr. HALE, *Agent and Consul General of the United States of America.*

Mr. Seward to Mr. Hale.

No. 16.] DEPARTMENT OF STATE,
Washington, November 27, 1865.

SIR: Your despatch of October 27, No. 44, has been received, and your proceedings in fulfilment of my instruction No. 13 are approved. We learn from Paris that the design which is referred to in that instruction concerning the deportation of Nubians in Egypt to serve under the French flag in Mexico will not at present be executed.

I am, sir, your obedient servant,

WILLIAM H. SEWARD.

CHARLES HALE, Esq., *&c., &c., Alexandria.*

Mr. Hale to Mr. Seward.

No. 48.] AGENCY AND CONSULATE GENERAL OF THE U. S. OF AMERICA,
Alexandria, Egypt, November 27, 1865.

SIR: The Ardeche, French frigate, which brought hither French soldiers for Cochin China, sailed out of the harbor on the 24th instant, having taken on board, according to all observations and reports, only the French soldiers who had previously arrived from Cochin China, and had been received on board the Sevres, as mentioned in my despatch No. 44.

The French soldiers brought by the Ardeche, of which the number is stated as one thousand and fifteen, were embarked at Suez on the 15th for their destination.

General de Marquez, accredited by Maximilian as Mexican envoy extraordinary and minister plenipotentiary to Constantinople, arrived at Alexandria on the 22d instant, and proceeded to Cairo, in company with Mr. Guiseppe Gogheb, accredited in the same way as Mexican consul general here, and also in company with Mr. De Maya, the Spanish consul general, an old personal friend.

I have not previously mentioned that, on Mr. Gogheb's hoisting his flag here, on the 2d instant, he sent to me, as well as to the other members of the consular corps, his circular intimating the day when he would be prepared to receive his colleagues. As I had met him previously in private circles, and also officially in his capacity as consul of Persia, (which commission he still retains,) I sent him a private note to intimate that I could not salute the flag or make him an official visit, but that I hoped to maintain friendly personal relations with him, and official relations with him in his capacity as consul of Persia.

Both Mr. Gogheb and Mr. Debhane, my Brazilian colleague, are natives of the East; they are estimable gentlemen, but naturally have little acquaintance with the governments whose commissions they hold, or with the condition of political society upon the American continent.

I have the honor to be, sir, very respectfully, your obedient servant,

CHARLES HALE.

Hon. WILLIAM H. SEWARD,
Secretary of State.

BARBARY STATES.

TUNIS.

Mr. Perry to Mr. Seward.

No. 58.] UNITED STATES CONSULATE,
Tunis, December 7, 1864.

SIR: I have had occasion in one of my despatches to speak of the support given to the cause of freedom, as opposed to slavery, by the official Arab journals of Tunis. In another despatch I spoke of a formal interview between an American slaveholder and one of the ministers of the Bey of Tunis, in which the former endeavored to impress upon the latter his ideas in regard to the advantages of slavery over free institutions. The Moslem minister of Barbary appreciated the zeal and eloquence of this propagandist of slavery, but having a practical knowledge of this institution, failed to be convinced by the arguments offered in its support.

Though piracy and slavery existed in this regency for centuries, they have disappeared with the advancing light of civilization. The former was abolished in 1816, when three thousand Christian captives (slaves) were released in one day; the latter was abolished in 1845, and on the 23d of January, 1846, Ahmed Bey, then upon the throne, addressed a letter to the resident consuls, in which he employed language to this effect: "We are all fellow-creatures of God, and as such have no right to enslave each other. I have long felt that human slavery is cruel, and have exerted myself for its eradication, and have given orders to my governors and deputies in all my provinces that no human being be henceforth recognized as a slave."

That the actual Bey entertains similar sentiments I have ample proof. During our interview with him, after some expressions on my part in favor of constitutional liberty, he replied: "I desire to extend the liberties of my subjects as fast as they are able to receive them;" and he closed his remarks by saying, as if for a delicate home thrust on me: "I see not how any just discrimination can be made in regard to these liberties on the ground of color or race; the privileges enjoyed should rather depend upon the intelligence and character of the subjects."

I now have the honor to lay before the department a more full, elaborate and authoritative statement of Tunisian sentiment in regard to the great question that agitates our country. It is a letter, already printed and circulated in the Arabic language, from one of the most respected and worthy men in this regency. It explains slavery from a Moslem point of view, quoting from the Koran and its acknowledged expounders, and showing from what motives the proclamation for the abolition of slavery was finally issued. In writing this letter, General Heussein, who has travelled extensively in Europe and is an accurate observer, had distinctly before him here the terrible evils consequent upon centuries of slavery. He saw here labor degraded by having been for so long a time regarded as the special and appropriate business of slaves; the public conscience deadened by familiarity with injustice and wrong; the principles of liberty uprooted, and supplanted by those of slavery, and the country impoverished to a fearful extent. With such a sad picture before him, he speaks his honest convictions as a Mussulman and as a man, and in the name of humanity exhorts Americans not to harbor an institution which produces such results.

This letter comes with the highest sanctions of the country, and the appeal which is made at the conclusion, to Americans, is but the utterance of a common sentiment in this region. General Heussein's negro Bona, who was pounced upon at Paris by a chivalrous southerner, still serves as his confidential companion; and should the general visit America, as he hopes to do at the conclusion of our pro-slavery rebellion, the question is asked whether Bona would be protected in his rights as a gentleman in the grand opera saloons of America, as he was at Paris.

Very respectfully, your obedient servant,

AMOS PERRY.

Hon. WILLIAM H. SEWARD,
Secretary of State, Washington, D. C.

Translation of a letter on Tunisian slavery, addressed to Mr. Amos Perry, consul of the United States of America at Tunis, first printed in the Arabic language and circulated in pamphlet form in the regency of Tunis by General Heussein, president of the municipal council of the city of Tunis and major general.

DJOUMADA ETHANNIA, 1281 *of the Hegira*—(*November*, 1864, *A. C.*)

SIR: I have been honored with a letter from you in which you state, that coming from a country where liberty and slavery for a long time existed and flourished side by side, and where they are at present involved in a death struggle for supremacy, you find many facts in the history of Tunis calculated to throw light on the legitimate influence of these two antagonistic principles. You ask me to explain Tunisian slavery, and to state what influence it has exerted on our institutions, and whether our people regret its abolition or rejoice thereat. You further wish to know whether our experience is favorable to servile and unpaid labor, or to that which is free and paid, and which the Tunisian government prefers as the basis of its social fabric, freedom or slavery.

1. Here is my reply. And I will first speak of slavery as modified by our laws and of the causes which led to its abolition in this regency.

Our government, like all Mussulman governments, is a theocracy, and its administration is consequently based upon laws which are in their nature both civil and religious. The Mussulman religion tolerates or permits slavery; and this it does because slavery is an institution anterior to the three revealed religions, Mosaic, Christian, and Mohammedan. In the time of Jacob, the Israel of God, the robber was doomed to suffer slavery for one year as punishment for his crime. Our religion substituted for the year of bondage cutting off the hand at the wrist. But it must be remarked that our religion authorizes slavery only on such conditions and under such laws as are very strict and difficult to be observed. One of these conditions is, never to injure or tyrannize over a slave. Nay, a slave who is ill-treated is declared thereby free. The words of the Prophets are: "Every slave ill-treated is free *ipso facto*." There are in our religious books innumerable precepts enjoining upon masters the exercise of benevolence toward their slaves; and the last words of our Prophet, on whom may the grace of God rest, were these: "I commend to you prayer and your slaves." He used to say also: "The men whom you possess are your brethren; it is God who has subjected them to you. Now he who has one of his brethren under his subjection should let him eat the bread of which he partakes, and should clothe him as he clothes himself, and should not over-work him." Oman Ben Alkatab, the second of the Califs, used to go every day where slaves were employed, and when he found any of them over-tasked, he diminished their tasks; nay, more, he went every Saturday to where beasts of burden were found, and if any of them appeared to him over-loaded, he ordered that their burdens be lightened.

It is a fact that our legislator infused into our laws the spirit of liberty, profiting from the least circumstance to favor personal freedom. Thus, if a master, by chance, let drop a word declaring one limb (for example, the arm) of his slave to be free, the law declares the whole body thereby freed from bondage. One of the eight objects for which expiatory alms are to be employed, as explained in the Koran, is the ransom of slaves. Thus we are bound to employ a part of our contributions for charity in purchasing slaves, with a view to their freedom. To be released from an oath inconsiderately taken, to atone for the crime of homicide and for the non-observance of a fast, and to be exonerated from the izhar,* the freeing of slaves is the prescribed means. Now, if the freeing of slaves had not been regarded by our lawgiver as a meritorious act, he would not have devoted to it the expiatory offerings otherwise given to the poor. Another proof of the liberal tendency of our laws is the recompense offered

---

* The izhar is the state into which a husband falls by the hasty utterance of a word, which, according to the Moslem law, makes it a sin for him longer to live with his wife. Thus, for instance, if he says to his wife in a fit of passion, "I shall not touch you any more; if I do may it be as I touch my mother or my sister," he must either divorce his wife, or, to live with her, must atone for that inconsiderate expression. By comparing his wife to his mother or his sister he loses his marital rights.

to those who free their slaves. Thus it is written: "If a Mussulman free a Mussulman slave, God shall redeem from the fire of hell as many limbs in the body of the former as there are in the body of the latter."

Now, since all these conditions and laws were difficult to be observed when our faith was yet lively and vigorous, how much more difficult must they be in these latter times, when our faith is chilled and our zeal repressed. And the enslavement of negroes, who are so different from the whites in their instincts and character, rendered the observance of these rules still more difficult. In fact, quarrels often occurred here between negroes and their masters, which had no other cause than the natural repugnance and antipathy that exist between the two races; and these quarrels were a source of unhappiness to slaves and of offence to masters, often giving occasion for the latter to violate the laws enacted for the well-being of the former.

Slavery becoming worse with time, at length attracted the attention of the Tunisian government, which finally advised, as a radical remedy for the existing evils, the complete abolition of slavery in the regency; for when a master could no longer treat his slave with the kindness prescribed by our laws, the slave had to be either sold or freed from bondage. The former course was scarcely a remedy; since the slave sold only changed masters, and the evil was likely to be repeated. The latter course was effectual and final, and hence its adoption by our government. The act of emancipation occurred in the month of Moharram, 1262 of the Hegira, (A. C. 1845,) during the reign of Ashmed Bey, of blessed memory. This prince addressed a letter to the religious tribunals on that occasion, in which he says: "It has been proved to us in a manner beyond question that our people are incapable of holding negroes as slaves in accordance with the conditions prescribed by our laws. We have, therefore, deemed it necessary, in order to ameliorate the condition of these unfortunate beings, to abolish slavery altogether. We have been influenced in adopting this measure by some political considerations," &c.

The political considerations here alluded to can be interpreted in different ways; but in my opinion our lamented sovereign had in mind the principles demonstrated by the great political economists of our age, that those countries where free labor exists, to the exclusion of that which is servile and forced, are thereby rendered more prosperous and happy. One of our distinguished writers and religious dignitaries, in a document issued to induce all those under his charge to comply with the requisitions of our late sovereign, employed the following language:

"O, generous souls, hearts full of compassion, your law is on the side of liberty; holding men as slaves is a misfortune and a disgrace; but God, who is the author of our being, can change the order of things, making slaves masters and masters slaves."

2. Another of your inquiries relates to the influence of slavery on our institutions and to the sentiments entertained by our people in regard to its abolition.

Since the holding of men in slavery was found to be neither necessary to supply the common wants of life, nor needful to the well-being of society, such a practice was, in general, abandoned here without pain, if not cheerfully; and, now, after nearly twenty years of experience, I am satisfied that this change is not regretted. And why should persons well to do in life, who have at heart the well-being of their fellow-creatures and the improvement of their country, regret liberating their slaves, when they can have in their stead the service of free men? And here the satisfaction of such persons was enhanced by their religious convictions that they would be rewarded before God in the final abode. But if there were persons who at first were disturbed by the abolition of slavery on account of changes introduced in their mode of service, or by reason of their selfishness and avarice leading them to prefer what was present and near to what was future and remote, these persons were at length consoled and satisfied, learning by experience the advantages of free and paid labor over that which is servile and unpaid—advantages which are appreciable alike in the light of reason and of general experience. Those who had employed slaves and could not afford to employ free servants readily returned to the order of nature, which is the best, doing their work with their own hands, so as to have the least possible need of their fellow-creatures. Indeed, when a person gets used to being served by others, he often becomes incapable of performing even the simplest duties of life; for man is more a slave of custom and habit than a follower of instinct. To gratify various wants of his existence, he is obliged to depend somewhat upon those around him; but in proportion as he is thus dependent, it is difficult for him to be gratified, and those things for which he is most dependent on others are most difficult for him to get.

Mankind may be divided in respect to labor into four classes. The first class comprises those who attend to their own business in person, working, and in general putting forth their utmost efforts. They perform the largest amount of labor. The second class comprises those who are out at service and are paid stipulated wages. Not putting forth, in general, their utmost efforts, they perform a smaller amount of labor, and though invaluable to society, are as a whole inferior to the first class. The third class comprises those who work by compulsion and without pay. To this class belong slaves and bondmen. Their inducements to labor being small, their amount of service is also small, and their rank as a producing class is very inferior. The fourth class comprises those who work neither for themselves nor for other people. They are the lazy and idle, whom God hates. Regarding labor as the part of slaves and slavish people, they would shun the very suspicion of belonging to such a class. Yet these persons, who stand lowest in the scale of the political economist and in the divine order, may not be lost beyond remedy. They may be benefited by seeing those of more intelligence and elevated station performing the offices which they regard with disdain. The idle and lazy need to be urged and encouraged by persons of influence and authority to pursue the path of usefulness. Man is more disposed by nature and the light of reason to love and do good than to approve and do evil. He is prompted to evil by his lower or animal instincts; but as a man, or rather as a reasonable being, he aspires to that which is good, and when he finds a physician skilful in overcoming the infirmities of his nature, he is put in the best moral condition. It is when men are thus treated and helped that general prosperity is secured; mutual assistance is afforded in the various occupations of life; all hands are employed for a common good; the sources of wealth are developed, and the country is enriched. It is thus that those countries are more prosperous where liberty exists to the exclusion of slavery, than where slavery exists to the injury of liberty and labor. The cause of this difference seems to me clear. The amount of labor voluntarily performed by free men is far greater than can be forced from wretched slaves, and is at the same time infinitely more satisfactory and advantageous to society.

3 It is my belief also that as liberty, unharmed by slavery, exerts an influence favorable to the material prosperity of a country, so it serves to elevate the character and sentiments of the people. There can be no permanent prosperity without justice, and justice results from freedom. If freedom be destroyed tyranny takes its place, disregarding the claims of justice and injuring the best interests of society. There can be no doubt that the prevalence of freedom tends to the elevation of the character of men, by leading them to reflect and reason in regard to general principles and their application in life. Men breathing the spirit of freedom are elevated and ennobled thereby, and are less likely to contract certain bad habits, such as vulgarity of manners, vanity, pride, and the like passions which often predominate in slave masters; for by habitually dealing with slaves these latter persons often become haughty in spirit and imperious and overbearing in manner. Nay, they often learn to regard other men, especially if they are black, as they regard their cattle. Slaves seem to them scarcely elevated above the brute creation.

In illustration of what I have here said, I will state an incident of which I was a witness. During the carnival of 1856, I went to the grand opera at Paris with a young negro. I had been in the saloon but a short time when an American gentleman sprang upon my companion, and, trying to seize him by his clothes, cried out with rage, "What is this negro doing in the saloon where we are? When has a slave ever been permitted to take rank with his masters?" The poor negro, not understanding what the American was saying, was astonished, stupefied at the scene. I immediately approached and said to the American, "Be calm, my friend; we are in Paris, and not at Richmond." Meanwhile, attracted by the noise, one of the guardians of the theatre hastened to the scene and informed the American that French laws give no preference to gentlemen on the ground of color or race, but much honor to character. In fine, the poor negro was delivered from the clutches of the American, not by the clearness of his white cravat and yellow gloves, but by the splendor of truth and the justice of freedom.

4. To return to our subject: The Tunisian government, deeming it needful for the harmony of society that slavery should be abolished, enacted the law of emancipation, regardless of the prophecies of those who maintained that slaves did not wish for their freedom, and that if emancipated they would prefer to return to a state of bondage. The poet says:

"Sore eyes shun the light of day."

"To the sick, pure water often has a bad taste."

But the instances of freedmen repenting that they were not again slaves occurred only immediately after the act of emancipation, when these poor creatures were thrown suddenly upon the world like cattle loosed from their stalls. They were ignorant and quite unprepared for the exigencies of their new life of freedom. But now that they have had experience, we find none of them with the slightest inclination to return to a life of slavery.

But passing by this objection, that falls to the ground of itself, I turn, in conclusion, to address myself to the people of your country.

O, inhabitants of America, ye are like that nation of whom Omar Ben Elaas, the friend of our Prophet, on whom be the grace and blessing of God, said: "They are the most compassionate people in times of war and domestic trouble; the quickest to recover from misfortunes; repulsed, they return to the charge; to the poor, the orphans, and the feeble, they are most charitable; and against the tyranny of kings they are most valiant." Such is the story of your character; and since God has permitted you to enjoy full personal liberty and to manage your civil and political affairs yourselves, while many other people are deprived of such distinguished privileges and blessings, it would not tarnish the lustre of your crown to grant to your slaves, as an act of gratitude for the favors God has bestowed on you, such civil rights as are not denied to the humblest and meanest of your citizens. You are too far advanced in civilization to imitate the example of those who, with bandaged eyes, ever turn in the same circle under the pretext of following in the footsteps of their fathers. Humanity invites you to eradicate from your Constitution all that can give countenance to the principle of slavery. Bity the slave. God loves the merciful among his worshippers. Be then ye merciful to those upon earth, that He who is in heaven may be merciful to you.

In concluding this letter, Monsieur La Consieur General, permit me to express my profoundest regrets for the war that afflicts and saddens your land, and my tenderest sympathies for the slaves there doomed to suffer.

You will please accept the assurance of my distinguished consideration.

Written with his perishable hand by the poor before the mercy-seat of his God,

GL. HEUSSEIN,
Major General and President of the Municipal Council of Tunis.

Mr. AMOS PERRY,
Consul of the United States of America at Tunis.

Mr. Perry to Mr. Seward.

[Extract.]

No. 60.] UNITED STATES CONSULATE,
Tunis, December 17, 1864.

SIR: The Bey of Camp, who is the presumptive heir to the throne of Tunis, set off from the Bardo on the 15th instant with an army of eight thousand men, composed of infantry, cavalry, and artillery. He is to collect taxes from the various tribes in the regency, extending his visit as far as the Gereed, and he is to be gone one year. Such has been the ordinary way of raising a revenue for many years past. Last spring the usual visit of the Bey's revenue agents was prevented by the rebellion.

The report of a battle between the Bey's troops and the rebels, near Kef, reached here yesterday. This difficulty occurred with the tribe that commanded the rebellion, by killing several of the Bey's most important officers.

The French consul made another visit to the Bey on the 10th instant, and as he held out his hand to the Bey the latter kept his hands firm in his side-pockets, as if not seeing the consul's movement. This was probably done as a return for the consul's previous act of disrespect to the Bey. * * * *

I am, sir, very respectfully, your obedient servant,

AMOS PERRY.

Hon. WILLIAM H. SEWARD,
Secretary of State, Washington, D. C.

Mr. Perry to Mr. Seward.

No. 66.] UNITED STATES CONSULATE,
Tunis, March 18, 1865.

SIR: I have the honor to report that the annual receptions by the Bey on the Little Byram have passed off with unusual harmony and good will.

The Arabs in the interior appear to be completely subdued, and peace exists throughout the regency.

Prince Arthur, third son of Queen Victoria, has visited Tunis this week, and was received and entertained by the Bey in a princely manner.

I am authentically informed that the cabinets of England, Austria, and Italy have expressed to the French cabinet the desire to come to a full understanding in regard to the status of Tunis. The French cabinet has replied in each case that this was an unfavorable time to discuss the Tunisian question.

The new French consul continues to pursue a conciliatory course towards the Tunis government.

I am, sir, very respectfully, your obedient servant,

AMOS PERRY.

Hon. WILLIAM H. SEWARD,
Secretary of State, Washington, D. C.

Mr. Perry to Mr. Seward.

[Extract.]

No. 68.] UNITED STATES CONSULATE,
Tunis, April 29, 1865.

SIR: The news of the downfall of Richmond was brought here from Malta on the 20th instant, by the commander of a Swedish sloop-of-war, and was by him communicated to the Bey. The Bey seized the occasion to congratulate me on this event. The news soon spread, causing much excitement and general satisfaction. Large numbers of natives and foreigners have sought entrance into this consulate, for the first time during my residence here, to felicitate me on this event in our history. The address of Secretary Seward, delivered on the 3d instant, has been printed and circulated in the Arab language.

The army of the Bey, commanded by the presumptive successor to the throne of Tunis, which left here last autumn to make a tour of the regency, has this week returned to the capital, enriched, it is said, with some millions in gold, and loaded with the products of the country, taken from the various tribes. While the Bey's treasury will be replenished by this act, his future resources will be diminished and the industry of the country discouraged. Such predatory excursions seem to be regarded as the legitimate exercise of governmental authority. It is an accepted maxim here that the masses can be controlled only by keeping them poor.

The visit of the Emperor Napoleon in Algeria seems to cause some discussion about the affairs of Tunis. No good understanding has yet been reached among the high powers of Europe in regard to the political status of this regency.

* * * * * * * * *

Very respectfully, your obedient servant,

AMOS PERRY.

Hon. WILLIAM H. SEWARD,
Secretary of State, Washington, D. C.

P. S.—The Bey has to-day reviewed his troops, and given a gold medal to each of his superior officers and a silver medal to his subordinate officers and privates. The effect of this presentation is said to be excellent. The zeal and fidelity of officers and soldiers are kindled anew, and the moral and physical condition of the troops is represented to be unusually good.

The prevalence of a strange and cruel rumor, of whose truth or falsity I have no knowledge, may illustrate the excitability of the Tunisian populace in regard to American affairs. "Peace proclaimed in America and President Lincoln assassinated at Richmond." These have been the words bandied through the city from noon to night. Great numbers have flocked to the door of this consulate to ascertain the truth or falsity of this report, and the dragomans were instructed to say that the consul has received no reliable information relative to the matter in question. The names of President Lincoln and Minister Seward have, by recent events, become almost as well known to the populace of Tunis as those of the Bey Mohammed and his minister Sidi Mustafa.

Mr. Perry to Mr. Hunter.

No. 70.] UNITED STATES CONSULATE,
Tunis, May 13, 1865.

SIR: I have the honor to acknowledge the receipt, on the 11th instant, of the two circulars of the 17th of April, 1865—one circular giving a statement relative to the assassination of our lamented President and the attempted assassination of our honorable Secretary of State, and the other circular naming the insignia of mourning to be adopted by those subject to the orders of the department.

All the national vessels in this harbor had their flags at half mast three days, commencing on the 8th instant, in honor of our lamented President, and within an hour after receiving your circular (on the 11th instant) circulars to the same effect as yours were in the hands of all my colleagues, and the flags of all the nations here represented were hung in mourning. Last week each of my colleagues did himself and our nation the honor to call upon me with expressions of sorrow for our deceased President and wounded statesman, of indignation against the perpetrators of those crimes, and of congratulation upon our glorious victories and our prospects of peace.

I deem it inadvisable to trouble you with detailed accounts of the interest and sympathy awakened in this place by the recent events in our country. The Bey's minister has replied to my circular with touching expressions of horror and sympathy. My colleagues have, most of them, written me long and interesting letters. A delegation from the Italian Masonic Lodge of this city waited upon me yesterday with an address, a copy of which I herewith enclose.

I have the honor to be, sir, very respectfully, your obedient servant,

AMOS PERRY.

Hon. WILLIAM HUNTER,
Acting Secretary of State.

(For enclosure see Appendix, separate volume.)

Mr. Perry to Mr. Hunter.

No. 71.]

UNITED STATES CONSULATE,
Tunis, June 17, 1865.

SIR: I have the honor to report a state of general tranquillity and good order in this regency. The domestic difficulties which were so serious last year seem to be fully overcome; and though the cause of jealousy and misunderstanding between several European governments that have a special interest here are not removed, there are fewer indications of irritation and bitterness now than usual.

A recent exchange of courtesies between the Bey and several European sovereigns has served to divert attention from the disagreeable scenes of last year. The Bey has recently sent missions to Paris, Stockholm, and Copenhagen, and decorations and presents have been exchanged between him and these several cabinets. The Bey sent a delegation to felicitate Napoleon III, at Bona, week before last; and there again a lot of decorations were exchanged, and reports were brought back of most cordial relations.

The Bey's portrait for our government is now completed, and other presents for the President and Secretary of State are spoken of as in a state of preparation. Though a mission to America is not yet formally announced, it is spoken of as a settled plan of the government, and I am waiting an announcement of the time and details. Our government is to be felicitated by the Bey on the abolition of slavery and on the establishment of peace, and the Bey's minister has requested me to inform him when the peace is restored in Texas as it is in the other States. I know the idea here is that whenever the mission takes place the American consul should accompany it. The mission may set out within a few weeks, or it may be deferred for some months. But to avoid embarrassing the Bey's well-intended efforts, I beg leave to suggest that if the mission be approved by the department, a conditional leave of absence be granted me at once, together with the authority to leave some suitable person charged with the duties of this office during my absence. I have specially in view for this charge the consul general of Sweden.

I may say that a deep interest is here manifested for the life, health, and long service of our experienced "prime minister," Secretary Seward, and of our new President. The war and the recent tragic scenes have served but to command additional respect for our government and heighten the interest in our country.

* * * * * * * *

The Bey is, I believe, sincerely interested for the abolition of slavery and for the establishment of peace in America, but in his expressions of interest he evidently avoids any expression that might prove distasteful to his neighbors.

Very respectfully, your obedient servant,

AMOS PERRY.

Hon WILLIAM HUNTER,
Acting Secretary of State, Washington, D C.

Mr. Perry to Mr. Hunter

No. 72.]

UNITED STATES CONSULATE,
Tunis, June 24, 1865.

SIR: The Bey has this day formally announced his decision to send an envoy to Washington with his portrait and with his felicitations on the abolition of slavery and the establishment of peace. The Bey expressed the hope that I would deign to accompany his envoy; to which delicate invitation I expressed a willingness to do all in my power to gratify his Highness. I stated that I could go only with the consent of my government. I assured his Highness that my government would do its utmost to gratify him, but that nearly two months would be required to communicate with it. He said his envoy would be ready to leave in three or four weeks, but could not well go without me.

As the telegraph is now complete from here to the continent, by way of Sicily, and as time is important, I suggest that a telegram be sent from Paris as early as possible. The expense of a short despatch does not exceed eight francs. If leave of absence is granted me, I will consider myself authorized to make the best arrangements possible for the discharge of the duties of this office during my absence.

* * * * * * * *

Very respectfully, your obedient servant,

AMOS PERRY.

Hon. WILLIAM HUNTER,
Acting Secretary of State, Washington, D. C.

Mr. Seward to Mr. Perry.

No. 14.]

DEPARTMENT OF STATE,
Washington, July 27, 1865.

SIR: Your despatch No. 72, of June 24, has been received. In it you announce that his Highness the Bey, having determined to send hither an envoy for the purpose of presenting his portrait and his felicitations to the government of the United States on the abolition of slavery and the restoration of peace, had expressed the desire that you should accompany his envoy. The leave of absence which you ask for that purpose is hereby granted.

I am, sir, your obedient servant,

WILLIAM H. SEWARD.

AMOS PERRY, Esq., *&c., &c., &c., Tunis.*

Mr. Perry to Mr. Seward.

No. 75.] UNITED STATES CONSULATE,
Tunis, July 29, 1865.

SIR: I have the honor to acknowledge the receipt of circular of May 15, together with copies of two proclamations by the President.

The announcement on my part that our country is now on a peace footing, so far as regards its relations to foreign nations, drew forth from the Bey and his minister warm expressions of gratitude.

On the 23d instant Admiral Yelverton, of the British navy, arrived in the harbor with a large iron-clad war-vessel, as a special commissioner from the Queen to invest the Bey with the Order of the Bath. On the 27th instant the ceremony of investiture was performed in the hall of state at the Bardo with great pomp, and in the presence of a numerous assemblage of Tunisians and foreign officials.

To-day a camp, or army of the Bey, has arrived at the Bardo, and its officers and soldiers have received their medals of honor.

The departure of the mission for America is delayed somewhat by the tardy arrival of the English admiral with the Order of the Bath. The plan seems to be for the same envoy to thank the Queen of England for this decoration and then to proceed to America with the portrait for the President. The time for the mission to set off has not been yet definitely named, though it will probably be in the course of two or three weeks from this date.

Very respectfully, your obedient servant,

AMOS PERRY.

Hon. WILLIAM H. SEWARD,
Secretary of State, Washington, D. C.

Mr. Perry to Mr. Seward.

No. 77.] UNITED STATES CONSULATE,
Tunis, August 30, 1865.

SIR: I have the honor to inform you that all the arrangements for the departure of the Bey's envoy, with the portrait for the President, seem to be completed. The chief of this mission is General Otman Hashem, who belongs to one of the most respectable families of Tunis, and has had considerable experience as a diplomatist. He has been the chief personage sent to Madrid and to Constantinople. He is to be accompanied by two aides-de-camp and by an interpreter. One aide-de-camp has the rank of colonel and the other of lieutenant. The general and one aide-de-camp speak only Arabic. The interpereter and one aide-de-camp speak French, Italian, and Arabic.

September 3, 1865.—The mission is thus far on its way to America. The Bey's portrait is a cumbrous article, and has to be sent first to Marseilles, and then by *grand speed* to Havre. We are to pass over Mount Cenis. As soon as I know by what steamer and what day we sail from Havre or Liverpool, I shall write.

The Bey, in his last interview with me, expressed the desire that we should return to Tunis as speedily as possible. On our arrival at New York or Boston we shall have to rest three or four days before proceeding to Washington. If we go by way of Halifax I will telegraph from there; if not, I hope I may find some expression of your wishes at New York. This will be the first time that any member of the Tunisian government has ever crossed the ocean; the visit is purely complimentary and diplomatic; the stay in America will be short. A pleasant welcome on the part of our government and people will do us no harm. On the contrary, there are diplomatic and commercial considerations, as well as those which pertain to civilization, that seem to me to favor a very cordial reception on our part. The red caps of these Tunisians will attract attention, and they have sufficient dignity and intelligence to command respect. I shall telegraph the department on my arrival.

Very respectfully, your obedient servant,

AMOS PERRY.

Hon. WILLIAM H. SEWARD,
Secretary of State, Washington, D. C.

Mr. Perry to Mr. Seward.

No. 78.] PARIS, *September* 13, 1865.

SIR: I have the honor to report our arrival here. We desired to sail as early as the 16th, but are delayed by the difficulties in securing berths. We have finally engaged passage in the Persia, which will sail from Liverpool on the 23d instant. I beg to recommend, with the sanction of our minister here, Mr. Bigelow, that the collector of our port at New York, or some other suitable person, be named to receive the Bey's envoy on his arrival at New York, and to conduct him to Washington in the course of three or four days. The envoy may thus receive informal official attention, and be gratified and instructed at the same time. If these Mussulmen ever attain civilization, it seems to me likely to be done through the light of our institutions. Our mode of treating religion may shock some of their prejudices, but it cannot encounter their hostility.

The envoy informs me that he has two letters from the Bey; one is addressed to the President and the other to Mrs. Lincoln, and he is directed to deliver them both in person. I presume the Bey supposed Mrs. Lincoln to be in Washington. The envoy is also instructed to express the gratitude of his sovereign that the life of our distinguished Secretary of State is spared for the service of his country and the world.

Two of the party speak French and Italian, but I am the only one that tries to use the English language.

The portrait was forwarded by express and expenses paid as far as Havre, and I have requested our consul there to forward it by a Cunard steamer to the care of the collector in New York or Boston. We leave to-morrow for London.

Very respectfully,

AMOS PERRY,
United States Consul at Tunis.

Hon. WILLIAM H. SEWARD,
Secretary of State.

Mr. Perry to Mr. Seward.

No. 79.] STEAMER PERSIA, NEAR NEW YORK HARBOR,
Evening of October 3, 1865.

SIR: I have the honor to report the arrival on our coast of the Tunisian embassy, accompanied by his aide-de-camp, secretary and servant. Enclosed are literal translations of three letters that are in the hands of General Hashem. They are copied subject to the influence of the turbulent waves. Letter No. 1 was first brought to my knowledge on the ocean. Tunisian appreciation of our country and its rulers, though expressed in flowery language, may be regarded as a reflection of European sentiments.

Our plan is to rest in New York two or three days, and then proceed to Washington. The portrait is on board the ship. It will afford me pleasure to receive instructions from the department as soon as possible.

Very respectfully,

AMOS PERRY.

Hon. WILLIAM H. SEWARD,
Secretary of State, Washington.

No. 1.

[Literal translation from the Arabic.]

Praise to the only God: To the excellency of him who has given distinction to the ministry, who has at the same time ordered and directed its affairs; to the excellency of him who is the glory of eminent ministers; whose renown is universal, and whose character and services are above all praise—Monsieur William H. Seward, minister of state and of foreign affairs of the United States of America: may he always be the head of the ministry and the director of eminent men. Rendering due honor to the distinguished office and to the high character of your excellency, we make known to you that his Highness, our august sovereign, ceases not to entertain for your government an abiding and ever-increasing friendship and regard, the cause of which is, your admirable conduct and your noble policy. His Highness has received the news of the re-establishment of peace and tranquillity in your great country. This news has afforded him unmeasured satisfaction; and sincere friendship makes him share with you the pleasure consequent upon this happy result and great event.

To this end, then, his Highness sends to your government the honorable, the beloved, the elect General Otman Hashem, to express to the President his sincere felicitations, and also to express to the President the heartfelt grief which his Highness experienced at the death of the lamented President, Abraham Lincoln, which sad event wounded all our hearts. We pray God that this may be the end of trials and misfortunes to your beloved country. His Highness also sends with his ambassador his portrait, to serve as a souvenir of his friendship, as stated in his letter.

His Highness looks with confidence to your excellency to arrange for an agreeable reception of his envoy, General Hashem, by his excellency the President.

We take this occasion, also, to inform your excellency that we have found in the conduct of him who is distinguished among his colleagues, Mr. Amos Perry, consul of your government at this court, the best disposition to maintain and strengthen the bonds of friendship which unite our two governments. His courtesy and honorable bearing merits and receives the approbation and the best compliments of his Highness, our august sovereign. We make this statement to bear our testimony to a worthy representative, and to show that your choice falls only on meritorious men.

Written by the poor before his God.

MUSTAPHA,

Major General, Prime Minister and Minister of Foreign Affairs of his Highness the Bey of Tunis.

Tunis, the 7th Rabi el tami, 1282—A. C., August 29, 1865.

No. 2.

[Literal translation from the Arabic.]

Praise to the only God: To the excellency of the eminent personage whose merits are celebrated and whose renown is universal like the light of the sun which cannot be hidden from the day; to the excellency of him who is the glory of great men—the cream of men of distinction—and whose virtues are above all praise, to our friend Andrew Johnson, President of the United States of America, may he always be exalted, and may his days be ever prospered.

Having rendered due honor to the elevated rank and to the eminent character of your excellency, we inform you that we have heard the agreeable news of the fruitful victory gained by your government, and of the consequent re-establishment of peace and tranquillity in your great country. This news has rejoiced us beyond measure, and has awakened our warmest sentiments of gratitude by reason of the great and sincere friendship which unites our two governments—which friendship has been bequeathed to us as a heritage by our ancestors to become stronger and stronger forever.

We were the more cheered by this news by having shared in the grief of the American people in the loss which they experienced in the death of their late President, Mr. Abraham

Lincoln, a loss which we keenly felt. This grief would have remained unalterably fixed in our hearts, but for the news of the re-establishment of tranquillity in your country, which news comes to moderate and assuage our affliction.

We desire to present to your excellency, and to your people, our best compliments, with expressions of condolence in your affliction and sorrow, and with expressions of felicitation in your prosperity and joy. We despatch our envoy, the honorable, the beloved, the elect, our son, General Otman Hashem, to be the interpreter of our sentiments in the presence of your excellency and in your country. We send at the same time with him our portrait, to be a souvenir of our friendship.

May God preserve your excellency, and perpetuate the happiness and prosperity of yourself and of your illustrious nation.

Written by him who has for your excellency the highest consideration, the slave of his God, the Mooshr Mohammed Essadek, Bashaw Bey, possessor of the Kingdom of Tunis.

The 7th Rabi el tami, 1282, A. C., August 29, 1865.

[LOCUS SIGILLI.]

No. 3.

[Literal translation from the Arabic.]

Praise to the only God: To the lady for whom we pray God that he would save her from trial and affliction, and protect her from dangers and sorrows both by day and by night: to her who is distinguished among ladies of distinction, the cream of elevated personages, and whose virtues are above all praise—to Madam Abraham Lincoln—may God shield her from every ill.

Acknowledging the honor due to your elevated character and position, we desire to express to you the pain inflicted on our heart by the sad death of your beloved husband. How cruel this fate, and how deep the wound inflicted by this terrible event! All hearts are put in mourning. The news of this catrastophe both plunged us into affliction and overwhelmed us with consternation. It turned our eyes upon the distressed of this earth, and our spirits were troubled.

Against death all effort is vain, and our sole remedy is to resign himself to the decrees of the Great God, and with Him to seek consolation. May the Great God then grant you patience and resignation, increasing your worthiness in proportion to the keenness and depth of your affliction and pain. May He order that this be the last of your trials, and that your days become long years.

Written by him who has for you the highest consideration, the slave of his God, the Moosher Mohammed Essadek, Bashaw Bey, possessor of the Kingdom of Tunis.

Tunis, 7th Rabi el tami, 1282, A. C., August 29, 1865.

[L. S.]

TANGIERS.

Mr. Hunter to Mr. McMath.

No. 14.] DEPARTMENT OF STATE,
Washington, November 7, 1864.

SIR: Your despatches, Nos 23 and 24, the latter dated the 6th ultimo, have been received, and the course pursued by you concerning the subject to which they refer, the erection of the new light-house on Cape Spartel, is approved. Pursuant to the request contained in your No. 23, a full power is herewith enclosed authorizing you to treat upon a footing with the representatives of other foreign powers at Tangiers with regard to the maintenance of the said light, &c. Notice of the time of illumination which had been agreed upon, the 15th ultimo, will be communicated to the Light-house Board, and will also be duly made public.

I am, sir, your obedient servant,

W. HUNTER,
Acting Secretary.

JESSE H. MCMATH, Esq., *&c., &c., Tangiers.*

Mr. McMath to Mr. Seward.

[Extract.]

No. 25.] CONSULATE OF THE UNITED STATES OF AMERICA,
Tangier, Morocco, July 8, 1865.

SIR: I have the honor to acknowledge the receipt of your despatches, Nos. 13 and 14, dated August 25, and November 7, 1864, respectively, the latter containing the full power authorizing me to treat upon a footing with the representatives of other foreign powers here with regard to the maintenance of the Cape Spartel light, &c. Circular letter dated 12th September last has been received. I had expected before this date to be prepared to forward the treaty to the President, but, as I informed you in my despatch No. 23, dated 2d September last, the Moorish minister for foreign affairs was ordered near his Majesty the Sultan, then at Rabat, and at this date has not returned to this place, although his Majesty left Rabat about six weeks since for Fez, the ancient capital of this country. We are daily expecting the return of the minister, and on his arrival no time will be lost in completing and forwarding the treaty. I cannot presume, however, that it will be forwarded in time for the President to submit it for ratification to the present, nor, perhaps, the extra session of the Senate that will probably be convened on or about the 4th of March next. I have been informally advised that ten powers will unite in maintaining the light, &c. The maximum sum fixed for the maintenance thereof is fifteen thousand francs per annum, fifteen hundred francs to each power, equal to $285. May I suggest that an appropriation be asked from the present Congress for that amount. By the regulations of the light-house council the cost of maintenance on the 15th of August last, two months previous to the illumination on the 15th of October last. For the present the expense is paid by the Sultan, but it is understood that the treaty powers will reimburse at the earliest moment after the completion of the treaty.

* * * * * * * *

I have the honor to be, sir, with great respect and esteem, your most obedient servant,

JESSE H. McMATH.

Hon. WILLIAM H. SEWARD,
Secretary of State.

Mr. McMath to Mr. Hunter.

No. 26.] CONSULATE OF THE U. S. OF AMERICA
FOR THE EMPIRE OF MOROCCO,
Tangier, May 4, 1865.

SIR: The lamentable news of the assassination of his excellency Abraham Lincoln, President of the United States, reached this consulate by telegraph, *via* Madrid, on the 28th ultimo. This intelligence has produced the most intense feeling of sorrow in the minds of all our populations, native and foreign. The event is so astounding that it is with difficulty I can bring myself to realize its occurrence, or estimate its consequences. The blow is sudden, horrible, and irretrievable. Never has a murder been committed more momentous in its bearing upon the time. A nation mourns the inestimable loss of one of the greatest and purest statesmen that ever lived. He dies surrounded with the brightest halo of glory that has ever crowned the labor of a statesman, and his work will survive him, and the greatest victory of liberty and humanity will not have been won in vain. I am, as yet, without details which can give me the slightest idea of the cause of so grave an event. However, it seems difficult to suppose that a crime committed on the President had not been dictated by a political motive; and I may say this crime is not only odious but useless, for Providence will not fail to raise up worthy successors of him who has fallen a martyr to liberty, humanity, and constitutional government. To my bleeding and grief-stricken country I offer my sincere sympathy and condolence.

This consulate has gone into mourning for thirty days.

Immediately upon the receipt of this distressing news I informed my colleagues that, as a mark of respect to the illustrious and unfortunate deceased, President Lincoln, the flag of the United States would be displayed at half mast for a period of three days at this consulate, and stated that, on this mournful occasion I would be pleased to see my flag accompanied with those of their respective nations. To this each of my colleagues assented; and at the same time expressed their sincere sympathy and condolence for the great national loss sustained in the untimely death of his excellency President Lincoln. I have also communicated this sad intelligence to my vice-consuls on the coast, and have requested them to display their flags at half mast for three days, and request their colleagues to accompany it with those of their respective nations.

The melancholy news of the attempted assassination of the honorable Secretary of State, and his son, the Assistant Secretary, reached me one day later than the former. Since then I have been advised by the latest news from London that there is a probability that both may recover from the wounds inflicted upon them. I sincerely hope and pray to Almighty God that both may be speedily restored to our common country, and to each my sincere sympathy is offered.

In profound grief for the events which have taken place, I have the honor to be, very respectfully, your obedient servant,

JESSE H. McMATH.

Hon. WILLIAM HUNTER,
Acting Secretary of State, Washington, D. C.

Mr. McMath to Mr. Hunter.

No. 27.]

CONSULATE OF THE U. S. OF AMERICA
FOR THE EMPIRE OF MOROCCO,
Tangier, May 15, 1865.

SIR: An incident has occurred at Tetuan which has caused a great sensation in this country. The facts which have come to my knowledge are as follows:

It appears that, according to an ancient custom, an old Moorish soldier acted as guard in the Jewish quarter and was paid out of the Jewish communal fund. This post had not been filled for four months, owing to the illness of the present guard. Some weeks previous to the 3d ultimo the Bashaw sent a message to the Jewish representative committee, claiming the guard's salary. The committee, in their turn, requested the Bashaw to relieve them of the expense, as the services of so old a man could well be dispensed with, seeing that the post had not been filled for four months. Moreover, owing to the late dearth consequent on a severe winter, the funds of the community were already in arrear, and they were not able to afford this charge. The Bashaw said nothing until the 3d of April, when he summoned to his presence the committee, composed of twelve persons. He told them he had received peremptory orders from the Sultan to place five soldiers as guards in the Jewish quarter instead of the one they formerly had, and to put in irons and send to the presence of the Sultan, at Meccanez, those members of the committee who were Moorish subjects, while those who were under foreign protection were to be banished from the country for the alleged crime of having rebelled against the Sultan's authority in refusing to keep the old Moorish guard. The vice-consuls were sent for to decide which of the members were under their protection, and they selected eight. The remaining four were immediately put in irons previous to being sent to Meccanez. Whereupon the vice-consuls energetically protested against banishing any persons under their protection, and appealed against the imprisonment of the four Jews. After expostulations with the Bashaw, the vice-consuls obtained from him the promise that he would postpone sending the persons to Meccanez for three days, that they might write to their chiefs in this city and obtain a reply. On the affair becoming known at this place no time was lost in drawing up a collective note, signed by all the foreign representatives, and addressed to M. Bargash, minister for foreign affairs, protesting, in the name of justice, against the arbitrary and tyrannical measure adopted. This note had due weight with the Moorish minister, who answered that he would order the Bashaw of Tetuan not to send the Jews to Meccanez, promising, also, to release them from their irons. Three days having, however, elapsed without any of these promises being carried into effect, the British minister, Spanish minister, the consul general of Portugal, and myself, not to be misled by promises, again took steps with the Moorish minister, which resulted in the removal of the chains from the prisoners and their transfer from their dungeons to more comfortable quarters; and hopes were entertained that as soon as the Sultan was made acquainted with the attitude of the foreign representatives his Majesty would order the men to be put at liberty. But before the return of the courier from Meccanez, the Bashaw again transferred the four Jews to their former dungeons. Thereupon each of the foreign representatives, except the minister for France, on the 28th ultimo addressed a note to the Moorish minister, demanding, in the name of justice and humanity, that the four persons be at once set at liberty; that if the four were guilty of any crime their colleagues must be equally guilty, and that steps had been taken by the vice-consuls at Tetuan to bring the eight persons, foreign-protected, before a proper tribunal for trial; that after a careful examination of all the facts and circumstances in the case, they had been adjudged not guilty of any offence, and therefore, as no further or stronger proof could be adduced against the four Moorish subjects who were imprisoned in irons on a similar charge, justice and humanity alike demanded that they at once be set at liberty; and I am glad to say this demand was at once complied with, and the four persons are now at liberty.

One of the eight Jews was American-protected—being the clerk of our commercial agent at that place—one Austrian and six Spanish-protected. The latter were brought to trial before the Spanish consul at Tetuan. My agent was ordered to be present, as well as the vice-consuls, and after a careful and impartial investigation the Spanish protégés were pronounced innocent of the violation of any law. My agent reported the evidence and finding of the tribunal, and I ordered him to take no steps against our protégé. The proceeding on the part of the Moors had its origin in a fanatical hatred for the Jews, and I am of the opinion, from many circumstances connected with this transaction, that the order for their arrest and imprisonment emanated from the Moorish minister, and that the Sultan knew nothing of it until the arrest was made and reported to his Majesty, who at once sent his order to the minister here to release the Jews. The Sultan is well disposed towards this part of his subjects, but his officers, wishing to show their authority, frequently manufacture the most unfounded accusations against them, and impose upon the Sultan by representations that have no foundation in fact.

I trust my action in this affair will meet the approval of the department.

I have the honor to be, sir, very respectfully, your obedient servant,

JESSE H. McMATH.

Hon. WILLIAM HUNTER,
Acting Secretary of State, Washington, D. C.

Copy of the note to Mr. Bargash, referred to in the previous despatch.

TANGIER, *April* 3, 1865.

The collective opinion of the representatives of foreign powers in Morocco upon the measure adopted by the Bashaw of Tetuan against certain respectable Israelites of that city, counsels, and views, communicated on this subject to Sedi Mohammed Bargash:

From the official reports of the vice-consuls at Tetuan, it appears that the Bashaw of that city has arrested some members of the Israelite community, with the exception of those who are foreign-protected. They have been charged with irons, and are to be carried to Meccanez. This severe measure has no other motive than that these Israelites have refused some months since to accept and pay, according to usage, a caid for the Israelite quarter of that city. Moreover, the Bashaw threatened the members foreign-protected of that community to expel them from the empire. We protest energetically against this last measure, which is contrary to existing treaties.

The undersigned desire to make known to his Majesty the Sultan the cruel manner with which his sovereign order has been executed. If all the accused are culpable, the undersigned are disposed to do justice concerning the complaint against the members foreign-protected; but as to the other members who are in irons, the undersigned consider it an act of unqualified cruelty to leave them in this dreadful situation until they be sentenced upon a cause in which these Israelites should all be equally bound. In consequence the undersigned demand, in the first place, that the persons incarcerated be freed from the irons until the Sultan shall be able to take into consideration the cause of their offence, and make known what shall be their condition in order not to incur this misfortune. The undersigned, persuaded that the Sultan, in his justice and wisdom, desires to preserve friendly relations with Christian powers, consider it their duty to inform his Cherifian Majesty of the acts of cruelty which have been perpetrated in his name. All are desirous not to see the authority of the Sultan set at naught; and they cannot help to inform him of certain energetic observations, that, undoubtedly, by the exaggerated zeal of his agents, a general cry of indignation from without may occur by a neglect of humanity, which is completely in opposition to the character for justice and generosity of his Majesty Sedi Mohammed.

E. DELUIN,
Consul General for Belgium.
F. MERRY Y COLON,
Minister for Spain.
JESSE H. McMATH,
Consul General for the United States.
AYMEE D'AGUIRE,
Minister for France.
J. H. DRUMMOND HAY,
Minister for Great Britain.
A. VERDINOIS,
Consul General for Italy.
JOSÉ CALASCO,
Consul General for Portugal.
G. D'EHRENHOFF,
Consul General for Sweden and Norway.

Mr. McMath to Mr. Bargash.

CONSULATE OF THE UNITED STATES OF AMERICA
FOR THE EMPIRE OF MOROCCO,
Tangier, April 28, 1865.

SIR: The undersigned, prompted no less by the feelings of humanity than by a sense of justice for unoffending Moorish subjects, is constrained to call the attention of the minister for foreign affairs to the very grave conduct of his Majesty's authorities with reference to the cruel treatment of the four aged and respectable Israelites again confined in a loathsome prison in Tetuan. The circumstances of the arrest and imprisonment of those persons are already well known to your excellency. It will also be borne in mind that the charge preferred against them was also made against eight other Israelites, equally respected, the latter being foreign-protected. I am officially advised by the vice-consul of the United States at Tetuan, who was ordered to be present and report the result of the inquiry of guilt against the Israelites Spanish-protected, and who were impartially tried before the Spanish tribunal at that place, that there was no evidence tending to criminate said Spanish protégés, and therefore they were dismissed. This, then, leads me to the conclusion that the four Israelites now imprisoned are innocent of any offence against his Majesty's authority, and their con tinued imprisonment upon unfounded charges will prove, if persisted in, highly scandalous to the Moorish government, and provoke the indignation of the friends of humanity throughout Europe and America. Therefore, I demand that said Israelites be at once set at liberty.

I avail of the occasion to assure your excellency of my high consideration and regard.

JESSE H. McMATH.

His Excellency SEDI MOHAMMED BARGASH,
His Majesty's Minister for Foreign Affairs.

Mr. McMath to Mr. Seward.

[Extract.]

No. 31.] CONSULATE OF THE UNITED STATES OF AMERICA
FOR THE EMPIRE OF MOROCCO,
Tangier, October 7, 1865.

SIR: * * * * * *

I presume the United States consul at Gibraltar has advised you of the appearance of Asiatic cholera at that place. It appeared there in July, but did not assume an epidemic form until about the 25th of August; and during September the mortality reached thirty per day, in a population of twenty-five thousand, civil and military. It is now declining gradually. I am glad to state up to this time it has not appeared either in this city or on our coast; and as the rainy season has commenced, it is not probable it will visit our coast this year. On the 25th of August our board of health, (composed exclusively of the diplomatic corps,) by a vote of four for and three against, cut the communication with Gibraltar, and thus prevented the English government supplying the garrison with bullocks from this empire. By reason of this measure, her Britannic Majesty's minister withdrew for the time from the board, and reported its proceedings and the vote of each member to his government. The French minister being one of the four, a few days since I was informed confidentially, by her Britannic Majesty's minister, that Earl Russell addressed himself to the French government, and asked that instructions might be given to the French minister to co-operate with her Britannic Majesty's minister, and on questions touching supplies for Gibraltar vote with the latter. To-day the board opened communication with the garrison, and established a quarantine of observation of six days on all vessels arriving from that port. On this measure the minister for France voted with the English minister. In consequence of the adoption of this liberal regulation, the Spanish chargé d'affaires *ad interim* withdrew from the board.

It affords me pleasure to inform you that our relations with his Majesty the Sultan continue to be of the most friendly and satisfactory nature.

I have the honor to be, sir, very respectfully, your obedient servant,

JESSE H. McMATH.

Hon. WILLIAM H. SEWARD,
Secretary of State, Washington.

MEXICO.

THE OCCUPATION BY FRENCH TROOPS OF THE REPUBLIC OF MEXICO, AND THE ESTABLISHMENT OF A MONARCHY THERE.

Mr. Dayton to Mr. Seward.

No. 442.] PARIS, *March* 25, 1864.

SIR: Mr. Drouyn de Lhuys informed me yesterday that the negotiation for a loan in behalf of Maximilian, as Emperor of Mexico, had been completed on favorable terms, and that he would sail for Mexico on Sunday next.

I regret to learn by the communication you enclosed to me that the power of Mexico is still further enfeebled by faction and division among themselves. There is nothing in the present condition of things there to justify a hope that the republicans of that country can successfully meet the French invading force, aided by factionists at home, and any action at present in that direction by the United States would be sure to embroil us with France. We cannot, under existing circumstances, afford a war with France for the Quixotic purpose of helping Mexico. "Sufficient unto the day is the evil thereof."

I am, sir, your obedient servant,

WILLIAM L. DAYTON.

Hon. WILLIAM H. SEWARD,
Secretary of State, &c., &c., &c.

Mr. Seward to Mr. Dayton.

No. 525.] DEPARTMENT OF STATE,
Washington, April 7, 1864.

SIR: I have received your despatch of March 25, No. 442, which informs me of the completion of the loan to the Grand Duke Maximilian, and of his anticipated embarcation for Mexico. In order that you may understand the condition of affairs in that country, as fully as they are understood here, I have given you a copy of a communication which has lately been received from our consul at Matamoras.

I give you also, for your information, a copy of a note which has been received from Mr. Geofroy on the subject of the protection which was extended to the consul at that place by Major General Heron, and of my answer to that paper. This correspondence embraces some other incidental subjects. It is proper to say that Mr. Geofroy proposes to communicate to me a statement of another distinct subject of complaint, in regard to proceedings on the frontier, under instructions from Mr. Drouyn de Lhuys, and that I have engaged to bestow due consideration upon it.

I send you a copy of a resolution which passed the House of Representatives on the 4th instant, by a unanimous vote, and which declares the opposition of that body to a recognition of a monarchy in Mexico. Mr. Geofroy has lost no time in asking for an explanation of this proceeding.

It is hardly necessary, after what I have heretofore written with perfect candor for the information of France, to say that this resolution truly interprets the unanimous sentiment of the people of the United States in regard to Mexico. It is, however, another and distinct question, whether the United States would think it necessary or proper to express themselves in the form adopted by the House of Representatives at this time. This is a practical and purely executive question, and the decision of it constitutionally belongs, not to the House of Representatives, nor even to Congress, but to the President of the United States. You will, of course, take notice that the declaration made by the House of Representatives is in the form of a joint resolution, which, before it can acquire the character of a legislative act, must receive first the concurrence of the Senate, and, secondly, the approval of the President of the United States; or in case of his dissent, the renewed assent of both houses of Congress, to be expressed by a majority of two-thirds of each body. While the President receives the declaration of the House of Representatives with the profound respect to which it is entitled, as an expression of its sentiments upon a grave and important subject, he directs that you inform the government of France that he does not at present contemplate any departure from the policy which this government has hitherto pursued in regard to the war which exists between France and Mexico. It is hardly necessary to say that the proceeding of the House of Representatives was adopted upon suggestions arising within itself, and not upon any communication of the executive department, and that the French government would be seasonably apprised of any change of policy upon this subject which the President might at any future time think it proper to adopt.

I am, sir, your obedient servant,

WILLIAM H. SEWARD.

WILLIAM L. DAYTON, Esq., *&c.*, *&c.*, *&c.*

Accompaniments:

Mr. Geofroy to Mr. Seward, April 3, 1864.
Mr. Seward to Mr. Geofroy, April 6, 1864.
Resolutions of House of Representatives, April 4, 1864.

Mr. Geofroy to Mr. Seward.

[Translation.]

LEGATION OF FRANCE TO THE UNITED STATES,
Washington, April 3, 1864.

SIR: As I have had the honor to inform you, I have transmitted to my government the documents which your excellency submitted to me, on the subject of the affair at Matamoras. The documents can scarcely have reached Paris at this moment.

While awaiting the answer they will occasion, I this morning received a second despatch from Mr. Drouyn de Lhuys, pointing to new facts on which I shall have the honor to confer with your excellency on the earliest day my health will permit me to go out; but there is a point which seems to be of importance to bring immediately to your notice. It would appear that on the news of the events of the month of January last, General Bazaine took the measures necessary to protect, in the direction of Matamoras, the Mexican territory against any further invasion. Whatever may be the opinion we may form upon past events, you will comprehend, sir, how necessary it is, to avoid all complication in the future, that General Banks, and the officers serving under his orders, may be again called to the strict observance of the instructions given the 23d November, 1863, from your excellency's department.

I should not, either, leave you in ignorance that the French troops must also have been directed to Sonora, where, according to reports, more or less founded, a very considerable number of emigrants from California must lately have disembarked at Guaymas, and have established themselves in the country in virtue of grants which were made to them by the ex-President, Juarez.

The mission of our forces is to prevent, in Sonora, all these takings of illicit possession, if they be really attempted; and, in any case, the lawfulness of concessions which shall have emanated from Juarez will never be admitted. Your excellency will probably judge proper to make this known to American citizens who might allow themselves to be drawn into such speculations.

I seize this occasion to renew to your excellency the assurances of my high consideration.

L. DE GEOFROY.

Hon. WILLIAM H. SEWARD, &c., &c., &c.

Mr. Seward to Mr. Geofroy.

DEPARTMENT OF STATE,
Washington, April 6, 1864.

SIR: I have the honor to acknowledge the receipt of your note of the 3d instant, in which you inform me that you have received a second despatch from Mr. Drouyn de Lhuys, pointing to new facts in relation, as I am left to infer, to the proceedings which took place at Matamoras in the case of Mr. Pierce, the consul at that place, and which have been made the subject of recent correspondence on your part with this department. I shall with pleasure receive the promised information, when the state of your health shall be such as to enable you to visit me, and I sincerely regret the cause by which such a visit is delayed. Since my last note to you on the Matamoras affair was written, I have learned that General Cortinas, with his forces, is certainly adhering to the government of the United States of Mexico. In view of this fact, it is not now apparent to this government that France, being, in our view, only a belligerent in Mexico, and having no forces at or near Matamoras when the transaction in regard to the consul occurred there, can reasonably expect explanations concerning it from the United States.

You inform me in the note now before me that, on hearing of that transaction, in January last, General Bazaine took the measures necessary to protect the Mexican territory, in the direction of Matamoras, against any further invasion, and you suggest that, in consequence of that proceeding, Major General Banks, and the officers serving under his orders, may be again called to a strict observance of the instructions which I gave to that general on the 23d of November last. Passing over the words "further invasion," as an accidental assumption of a fact which this government has not conceded, and is not yet prepared to concede, I have had no hesitation in informing Major General Banks of the purpose of General Bazaine, and enjoining the United States general to a strict and faithful observance of the instructions of November, which require him to forbear from any form of intervention in the war between France and Mexico.

You also inform me in your last-mentioned note that French forces have been directed towards Sonora, and you bring to my knowledge rumors that a very considerable number of emigrants from California have lately disembarked at Guaymas, and have established themselves in the country in virtue of grants which were made to them by President Juarez, whom you describe as ex-president. You further state that the mission of the French forces is to prevent, in Sonora, the taking possession of estates under such grants, the lawfulness of which you say will never be admitted, and you suggest to me the expediency of making this information known to American citizens who might be disposed to allow themselves to be drawn into such speculations.

While I appreciate the frankness and the good will which the Emperor's government manifest in thus communicating its views and purposes on the subject mentioned, it nevertheless remains my duty to say that this government has long recognized, and still does continue to recognize, the constitutional government of the United States of Mexico as the sovereign authority in that country, and the President Benito Juarez as its chief This government at the same time equally recognizes the condition of war existing in Mexico between that country and France. We maintain absolute neutrality between the belligerents, and we do not assume to judge, much less to judge in advance, of the effect of the war upon titles or estates. We have no knowledge of such an emigration from California to Sonora as you have described in your note. But if such an emigration has taken place, those persons who thus emigrate will, of course, be regarded as subjecting themselves to the authority and laws by which the rights of citizens of Mexico are governed; and while it seems unnecessary for the President to assume that such emigrants will claim the protection of this government for any estates, of whatever kind, they may attain, or attempt to attain, in Mexico, it would certainly be premature to attempt now to decide upon the validity of such claims.

Peaceful emigration from the United States is entirely free from restraint or influence of the government. Emigrants themselves are generally well informed concerning their rights. Under these circumstances, any interference of the government concerning such emigration would be as inexpedient as it would be without precedent. The case would be different if the act of emigration was attended with preparations and purposes hostile to Mexico, or to either belligerent party, or to any other nation, and, therefore, incompatible with the laws of the United States, or with the law of nations. It is believed that the government of the United States has sufficiently indicated the views it must take in such a case, if it should occur, which, however, there seems no immediate reason to apprehend.

Accept, sir, the renewed assurance of my high consideration.

WILLIAM H. SEWARD.

Mr. L. DE GEOFROY, *&c., &c., &c.*

Mr. Seward to Mr. Dayton.

No. 728.] DEPARTMENT OF STATE,
Washington, December 20, 1864.

SIR: I enclose a copy of a resolution which yesterday passed the House of Representatives by an almost unanimous vote, and may be supposed to have been occasioned by the instruction of this department to you, No. 525, of the 7th of April last.

This morning I was visited by Mr. Geofroy, who inquired as to the purport of the proceeding. I answered that the views of the administration in regard to Mexico are expressed in the President's message to Congress at the opening of the present session.

I am, sir, your obedient servant,

WILLIAM H. SEWARD.

WILLIAM L. DAYTON, Esq., *&c., &c., &c.*

Mr. Seward to Mr. Bigelow.

No. 1.] DEPARTMENT OF STATE,
Washington, December 21, 1864.

SIR: I enclose for your information a copy of a despatch of the 12th ultimo, No. 208, from Charles A. Leas, esq., the United States commercial agent at

Belize, in regard to a recent proclamation of Prince Maximilian affecting the British settlement in Honduras, and relating also to other features of political affairs in that quarter and the West Indies.

I am, sir, your obedient servant,

WILLIAM H. SEWARD.

JOHN BIGELOW, Esq.,
Chargé d'Affaires of the United States.

Mr. Leas to Mr. F. W. Seward.

No. 208.] UNITED STATES COMMERCIAL AGENCY,
Belize, November 12, 1864.

SIR: Great excitement is prevailing in the commercial and official circles of Belize in consequence of the appearance in the Mereda newspaper of an official proclamation, under the orders and by the authority of the emperor of Mexico, to the effect that the peninsula of Yucatan is, on and after the 1st of October last, to be governed or presided over by three prefects, and to be divided into three arrondissements, one of which is to be designated as the arrondissement of Mereda, the boundaries of which are to be as follows: Commencing at the mouth of the Rio St. Pedro y St. Pablo, on the Gulf of Mexico, and running up the centre of that stream to the Usumasinti; up the latter to a point where the Guatemala district of Peten is encountered; from thence along the line that divides Peten from Guatemala to the headwaters of the river Sarstoon; down the middle of the Sarstoon to the gulf or bay of Honduras, and from thence along the coast to the place of beginning; comprehending in this latter all the keys and islands contiguous to the main land. The same proclamation provides, further, "that there are a few Englishmen located at the mouth of the river Belize, or Wallis, who have had the permission, under the treaties with Spain, to cut wood, and that they are not to be molested," meaning that they are not to be disturbed in their wood-cutting operations.

Thus it will be seen that Maximilian has, by this proclamation, swept into his possession not only the district of country known as Peten, and which has always been claimed as being within the legitimate jurisdiction of Guatemala, but the whole of British Honduras, with all the keys and islands, thus ignoring entirely the idea of British sovereignty. These people are feeling themselves greatly insulted, as being designated as a few English wood-cutters, and are mustering up a large amount of bitterness of feeling against the emperor of Mexico, and, indeed, are preparing for dire vengeance against him. All the old and new guns, of a cheap character, are being purchased, with the view, I doubt not, to be sent for distribution among the Indians on the Yucatan side of the Rio Hondo, who are, and have been for some years, not only hostile to the Mexican government, but in open rebellion, having long since driven the Mexican authorities from the southern portion of Yucatan.

Though much real anxiety is being manifested among the better classes in Belize lest England will, without a struggle, succumb to the demand and assumption of Maximilian, more with the view of shaking off a dependency which has proved more burdensome than profitable, than from any belief that the latter can sustain his claim either by force of arms or peaceable arbitrament, yet I doubt not that England will resist the claim of Mexico with great tenacity. The old diplomatic battles will in every case, I doubt not, have to be again refought. I think I can see that Maximilian is disposed to take up the case where old Spain left it, namely, after the defeat of General O'Neil at St. George's key, at the close of the Pork and Doughboy war in 1798. If Mexico can evade or set aside her obligations as contained in her treaty with Great Britain of 1826, the question then of plenary sovereignty as the result of peaceable possession will be fairly opened, and the first necessity then created will be to determine as to what length of time should be considered sufficient, as between nations, to constitute a *de facto* claim; because, undoubtedly, England has remained in peaceable possession of this colony since the year 1798, without any practical objections from any quarter, unless, indeed, it can be believed that the treaties of 1809 and 1814 re-vitalized those of 1783 and 1786; and which, I think, might be believed without much damage to truth. However, I think the question is probably destined to be one of a somewhat vexed and litigious character; and the greatest barrier, in my opinion, to Mexico's claim will prove to be her treaty of 1826. But as this whole imbroglio is likely to be somewhat of the "dog-eat-dog" character, we have really nothing to do with it, particularly in view of the present arrangement of parties.

These people evidently have a great horror for Spanish rule and government, and from the intimations of some I infer that, if they are to be forsaken by the British government, they will, with uplifted, suppliant hands, implore the United States government to receive them under her capacious wings; and, indeed, some have interrogated me already as to the course we will pursue in case England relinquishes her claim to this colony, and my answer is "Sufficient for the day is the evil thereof." When the question demands a solution at our hands the government of the United States will doubtless treat it as its merits demand. But all this seems to look like a verification of the prophecy which I ventured to make some months ago to the effect that the full design of Napoleon would not be consummated until the New Mexican empire should be made to comprehend the ancient boundaries as governed by Iturbide; and, as a partial proof of this hypothesis, we have only to loop this effort of Maximilian with the attempt of the late French consul at Galveston to alienate the State of Texas from the American Union, and the case is fast being made out.

The same paper that contained the proclamation of Maximilian also contained a very inflammatory article against the English settlers in Belize, charging them with having furnished munitions of war to the Indians in rebellion against the Mexican authorities; also calling seriously in question their right to occupy this country. There is evidently a bad state of feeling existing on the part of the Mexican population of Yucatan, or the authorities thereof, against the English in British Honduras. Should you, however, find it desirable in the future to become thoroughly conversant with this entire question, so far as its historical bearings are concerned, I beg most respectfully to refer you to the manuscript which I had the honor to transmit to the department some months ago, and which, I think, is a faithful history of the country of British Honduras.

A rumor reached this place a few days ago through the newspapers that Denmark had proposed to dispose of her West India possessions to the government of the United States; and in a conversation with the governor the day following, I mentioned the fact of such a report being current, when he promptly replied that it would be the very best disposition that could be made of them. Whether or not he meant what he said is another matter. This afternoon I again met the governor, while taking his usual afternoon's ride, when he stopped me, inquiring the news. I informed him that information had just reached me that the Florida had been captured by a United States gunboat, and immediately the conversation changed to the proclamation of Maximilian. He said frankly that Great Britain would never relinquish the colony to Mexico; that the opinion is gaining popularity in England that it is not politic to hold so many dependencies at so great a distance: and hence, if it should be deemed desirable to relinquish this colony, it would be to the people themselves, so that they might either manage their own affairs or seek such affinities as would best suit their taste; and intimated, as he once before plainly observed, that the United States would be more suited to exercise jurisdiction in Central America than Mexico. Believing that his purpose was mainly to seek my opinion upon that subject, I remarked that while Cuba, from many considerations, might be desirable to the government of the United States, yet I was fully of the opinion that an extension of our territory upon the main land would neither be politic nor wise; that we now possess as much domain as could be well managed by one central power. But yet, nevertheless, the fact need not be disguised that we do feel a great concern that these Central American countries should have stamped upon them good stable governments of a republican character; and that we doubtless should not fail to lend our full moral influence, upon all proper occasions, to bring about and secure such a result, but that absorption, or annexation, is not any part of our present policy. Though I spoke thus to the governor as a man, and not by authority, and may or may not have reflected the national opinion, yet they are views I think highly conservative, and will, at least, tend greatly to smother up previous jealousies and assumptions in regard to our propagandism and cravings in Central America.

I understand that the commandant of Ysabel, in Guatemala, has arrived here in connexion with the proclamation of the emperor of Mexico.

With great respect, I have the honor to be your most obedient servant,

CHAS. A. LEAS,
United States Consul General.

Hon. F. W. SEWARD, *Assistant Secretary of State.*

Mr. Bigelow to Mr. Seward.

[Extract.]

No. 8.] LEGATION OF THE UNITED STATES,
Paris, January 20, 1865.

SIR: During an interview which I had yesterday with his excellency the minister of foreign affairs, and after disposing of some matters with which I have no occasion to trouble you at present, a conversation ensued, which I deem it my duty to report to you—part of it at his excellency's request.

I took the liberty of recalling a remark which his excellency made to me at our first interview, to the effect that the relations of France and the United States were, as usual, "friendly, though delicate—delicate." I asked him if he had any special source of anxiety in his mind when he made that remark, of which I or my government might be ignorant. He said promptly, "Oh, no; nothing. I only referred to the perplexities growing out of our neutral position." "No," he added, "if there were anything special I should have told you; you may always be sure that I shall speak frankly and freely with you." I thanked him for the assurance; said I should not have troubled him with the question, but I had already learned to know the value of his words, and had been struck by the somewhat emphatic repetition of the word "delicate," which led me to fear that something might have occurred since he last saw Mr. Dayton which had not been communicated to me.

I then said that, with the frankness which he invited by his example and promise, I would take the liberty of asking him another question, premising, however, that I did so without any special solicitude upon the subject, and of course without any instructions from my government. I referred him to reports quite current in the public journals, and at the clubs, that the Archduke Maximilian, the titular emperor of Mexico, had ceded or was about to cede Sonora to France. I told him that while I had no instructions to put such a question, I felt that I should neglect my duty if I failed to give my government the earliest information possible upon a matter in which the people of the United States would feel the liveliest interest.

His excellency replied that there had been no cession of terrritory, nor any question of such a thing; that it had been proposed to give the government of France a lien upon the mineral products of Sonora, in some way to secure the Mexican indebtedness to France, and an inquiry had been instituted to ascertain how far such a security could be made available, but nothing had been determined upon.

His excellency then said there was another report circulating in the papers, which he was glad of an opportunity of speaking to me about. He referred to the article of which I enclose a translation, copied from the *Epoca* of Madrid, and which I had already read and discussed with Mr. Barreda, the Peruvian minister, who had satisfied me that its material averments were entirely groundless. Mr. Drouyn de Lhuys stated that there was no foundation whatever for the story; that he did not know the motives of the Spanish journal for making such a statement, but he supposed the party in whose name it speaks were not indisposed to have it believed that France sympathized with Spain in her controversy with Peru.

I told him that I had seen the extract to which he had referred in an evening print, but was so entirely satisfied that there could be nothing in it, that I had not thought of troubling him with questions about it. I only wondered how such a paragraph could have found its way into the columns of the *Moniteur*. He asked if it was in the *Moniteur*. I said it was.

* * * * * * *

I am, sir, with great respect, your obedient servant,

JOHN BIGELOW.

Hon. WILLIAM H. SEWARD,
Secretary of State.

[Translation.]

At the risk of exposing ourselves to accusations, which, however, will not affect our enlightened patriotism, we believe it our duty to call public attention to the conduct of France towards Spain, in the Pacific, under circumstances in which it might have been put to the proof by our naval forces on the coast of Chili and Peru. According to statements made by semi-official journals and correspondents from Panama, it is certain, and proofs of these facts exist in governmental regions, that after the catastrophe which destroyed the frigate Triemfo, and when the attitude of the Peruvian congress threatened to lead to difficult complications for our flotilla, the commandant of the French naval forces in the Pacific put all his resources at the disposition of your navy; as also, several months previously, the French consul at Panama had exposed his life in order to save that of Mr. Salazar y Mazaredo, the Spanish representative. Four years ago France placed herself in the same way, and resolutely, on our side, in our African war. She has sustained us in Mexico, and has not made the least trouble on the subject of San Domingo. Of what importance is it that certain persons obedient to the unworthy prejudices of our epoch disregard these facts, which, nevertheless, evidence a profound respect for the independence of the Spanish nation, and prove sincere sympathy for the august sovereigns seated upon the throne of Castile? In our day public opinion does justice to whom it is due, and the passions of a party cannot succeed in misrepresenting the sentiments of a people as noble and as loyal as the Spanish people.—(*Epoca.*)

Letters from Guayaquil received by the Journal Las Noticias confirm the account published by *la Epoca* up to the 30th December. No demonstration or attempt of any kind had been made against our squadron in the Pacific, and according to the statement of its commandant he had no fears whatever of being attacked. The 16th, three days after the departure of the mail, the vessels destined to increase our force in those seas ought to arrive; and on the other hand, our vice-admiral had received from the commandant of the French fleet offers of service of every sort if he should have need of them.—(*Idem.*)

Mr. Seward to Mr. Bigelow.

No. 33.]

DEPARTMENT OF STATE,
Washington, February 7, 1865.

SIR: Your despatch of the 20th of January, No. 8, has been received, and your proceedings therein are approved.

You are very right in addressing to Mr. Drouyn de Lhuys the question about the reported cession of Sonora by the Archduke Maximilian to France. It is the opinion of this government that such a cession, or even the creation of a lien upon the mineral revenues of Sonora, would not be regarded with favor by the people of the United States. It would relieve the relations between this country and France very much if I am authorized to say that no such project will be adopted. No credit was given by this department to the story that France had put her naval force in the Pacific at the command of the Spanish admiral. We have every reason to be satisfied and gratified with the proceedings of the imperial government in regard to the suspected controversy which has arisen between Spain and Peru—a controversy which, I am happy to have reason to believe, is now in a way of amicable settlement.

You will read of projects on the part of our insurgents to suspend the present contest, or end it, by a combined war against France alone, or France and England. If they come in question, you may confidently say that this government prefers to fight this civil war out on the present line, if no foreign state intervenes in behalf of the insurgents.

I am, sir, your obedient servant,

WILLIAM H. SEWARD.

JOHN BIGELOW, Esq., *&c.*, *&c.*, *&c.*, *Paris.*

Mr. Seward to Mr. Bigelow.

No. 38.]

DEPARTMENT OF STATE,
Washington, February 7, 1865.

SIR: Mr. Etchison, recently for a brief period United States consul at Matamoras, a month or two since had an angry correspondence with General Mezia, the military commander there, on the subject of the arrest of fugitives from Texas who were claimed for the military service of the insurgents. Without expressing an opinion upon the chief points of the controversy, it may be acknowledged that on the part of Mr. Etchison it was conducted in a manner by no means likely to impress a military commander with the correctness of his views—was mostly officious, and entirely unauthorized by this department. You may communicate this information to Mr. Drouyn de Lhuys, should there be occasion therefor, and may add that at the very date of the correspondence referred to, instructions from this department were on the way to Mr. Etchison relieving him from his official functions.

I am, sir, your obedient servant,

WILLIAM H. SEWARD.

JOHN BIGELOW, Esq., *&c., &c., &c., Paris.*

Mr. Bigelow to Mr. Seward.

[Extract.]

No. 25.] LEGATION OF THE UNITED STATES,
Paris, February 9, 1865.

SIR: Reference had to my despatch No. 8, I desire to call your attention to the following official statement which I translate from the *Moniteur* of yesterday morning:

"All reports circulating in the journals relative to a cession made to France by the Mexican government of certain provinces of Sonora, Chihuahua, &c., &c., are absolutely unfounded."

The rumors which this paragraph is designed to put at rest have been widely circulated in Europe, and had begun to provoke discussion even in France, but in a tone uniformly unfavorable to the cession, the proximity of the new colony to the United States being always enumerated as its chief misfortune.

* * * * * * * * *

I am, sir, with great respect, your very obedient servant,

JOHN BIGELOW.

Hon. WILLIAM H. SEWARD,
Secretary of State.

Mr. Bigelow to Mr. Seward.

[Extract.]

No. 29.] LEGATION OF THE UNITED STATES,
Paris, February 14, 1865.

SIR: The Stonewall was yesterday afternoon lying at Ferrol. Mr. Perry states, upon the authority of the consular agent at Ferrol, that she stands in need of repairs before she can take the sea, and that the Spanish government will refuse her permission to make them.

Captain Craven is at Corunna with the Niagara. He exhibits impatience to have the Sacramento join him. Mr. Harvey informs me that the Sacramento is undergoing repairs also at Lisbon, but as far as I can gather from their despatches, she will soon be, if she is not already, on her way to Corunna. I doubt if Craven feels entirely confident of his ability to meet the Stonewall single-handed. He asked me, ignorant, I presume, of what I have already attempted, to solicit the intercession of France with the Spanish government to detain her Mr. Perry informs me, confidentially, that the fortifications of Ferrol are not strong enough to keep the Stonewall, if she is determined to go out. If so, the only effectual mode of detaining her is by sending vessels-of-war, and I doubt whether France has anything at hand that she would dare to expose to such an enemy.

I shall endeavor to shake Mr. Drouyn de Lhuys's determination when I see him on Thursday. I am unwilling to reply in writing to his letter of the 7th February, because I think it my duty to leave to you the selection of the ground upon which the controversy over this vessel, which is impending, shall be waged.

I have reason to believe that Slidell wrote home by the last mail that the Spanish government had sent to their minister, Mr. Mon, in Paris, to ascertain whether France desired the detention of the vessel. That Mr. Drouyn de Lhuys said they had nothing to do with her, and that Mr. Mon sent for Mr. Slidell, who satisfied him that the Stonewall was a regularly commissioned confederate vessel.

If Slidell is correctly reported—and I suppose he is—it only confirms me in the opinion towards which I have been steadily drifting since my interview with the minister of marine on Sunday week, that the depredations which the Stonewall may occasion us will be the least of the troubles of the government. They don't care how much these steamers wrong us, provided they do not give us an opportunity of fixing the responsibility for what occurs upon them.

* * * * * * *

Though I am unable to assign any very satisfactory authority for it, I am strongly impressed with the conviction that, but for the Mexican entanglement, the insurgents would receive very little further countenance from the imperial government, and that a reconciliation of the national policies of the two countries on that question would speedily dispose of all other sources of dissatisfaction.

I am, sir, with great respect, your very obedient servant,

JOHN BIGELOW.

Hon. WILLIAM H. SEWARD,
Secretary of State, &c., &c., &c.

Mr. Bigelow to Mr. Seward.

No. 35.] LEGATION OF THE UNITED STATES,
Paris, February 17, 1865.

SIR: The corps legislatif was opened by the Emperor on the 15th instant with customary impressiveness. I enclose a copy of his Majesty's discourse. He treated the discovery of Columbus with conspicuous reserve. As in a family of children the infant is apt to engross the parental attention, so, out of the large family of American States, the youngest born was the only one that cost his Majesty a remark. This silence in regard to the United States was natural. There has been, and from the nature of things there must continue to be while our war lasts, so much of menace in our attitude towards Mexico that the Emperor could hardly have pursued a course more consistent with his own dignity, or more satisfactory to his subjects on this occasion, than by observing an expressive silence. The tone of the discourse was eminently tranquillizing, and is greatly admired for the skill with which it disposed of several very delicate questions of foreign policy. The only feature of it that has provoked criticism is that which treats of the convention of the 15th September, 1864, and his language in that connexion is discussed, apparently, rather with the view of extracting interpretations and admissions from the official press, than from anything exceptionable in the tenor of the speech. The various allusions to his Galican ecclesiastical policy were received by his audience with strong marks of approbation. There was one paragraph of the speech to which I attach a larger meaning than perhaps it deserves. It was this:

"The convention of the 15th of September, disentangled from passionate interpretations, consecrates two great principles—the firm establishment of the new kingdom of Italy and the independence of the Holy See. The provisional and precarious state of affairs which excited so much alarm will soon terminate. It is no longer the scattered members of the Italian nation seeking to connect themselves by feeble links to a small state situated at the foot of the Alps; it is a great country which rises above local prejudices, despising the ebullitions of unreflecting agitations, which boldly transfers its capital to the centre of the Peninsula, and places it in the midst of the Appenines, as in an impregnable citadel. By this act of patriotism *Italy definitely constitutes herself*, and at the same time reconciles herself with Catholicity."

I have not been able to resist the suspicion that this language, coupled with the silence of the Italian and French press for some months about Venetia, imports some sort of a transaction in *esse* or in *posse* for a termination of the boundary quarrels between Italy, Austria and Rome, by common sacrifices, and by the adoption of the Appennines as one of the natural boundaries of Italy. The habitually practical character of the Emperor's statesmanship, and the almost equal necessity of these three powers to arrange their differences by some less expensive agency than the sword, may, however, have led me to attach more importance to these expressions than they really deserve.

What is said about the return of the army from Mexico is doubtless correct, so far as the wish and intention of the government is concerned, though it does not correspond with information which reached me a few days since of orders having been recently issued for more troops to be in readiness to leave for Mexico upon short notice.

The speech is received with great favor by the liberal press, while the domestic policy which is foreshadowed appears to have given universal satisfaction.

I am, sir, with great respect, your very obedient servant,

JOHN BIGELOW.

Hon. WILLIAM H. SEWARD,
Secretary of State, &c., &c., &c.

P. S.—I have no mail from Washington later than the 24th of January. I expect the Canada's mail through the despatch agency to-morrow morning.

5 p. m.—The Blue, or rather the Yellow Book, has just come in, but too late for this post. J. B.

Mr. Bigelow to Mr. Seward.

No. 36.] LEGATION OF THE UNITED STATES,
Paris, February 17, 1865.

SIR: One of the last communications which I had the honor to address to you from the consulate related to a scheme for enrolling Poles in this city, and in other parts of France and Europe, for the confederates. I am now able to give you some more definite information upon the subject.

The project had its origin with a Colonel Smolenski, a Pole by birth, who had resided many years in Texas, and who came out here to take part in the recent Polish revolution. He could not agree with the Polish commissioners here, abandoned their cause, and projected a scheme for the colonization of the northern frontier states of the confederacy with his unfortunate country people, who were to be supplied with a passage, a farm, and some other privileges, on condition that they would bear arms, if necessary, in defence of their new homes

The terms were framed under the direction of a Mr. Williams, an Englishman, of whom I can learn nothing precise, and a man named Bujnicky, refugeed from Russian Poland, whose property has been confiscated, and whose wife has been sent to Siberia. This man went, on the 26th of December last, to London for funds; he was here the other day, but without funds; his address there is Hotel Krall, John Street, American Square, London. Two Poles—one named Wilkiewiez, and the other Leongewski—were charged to receive the enrolments. When the number reached three hundred, they were to be sent on to the Confederate States; and it was to obtain funds to meet the expenses of their expedition that Bujnicky went to London. Three different recruiting stations were opened in Paris, and I am told that the number of three hundred would have been ready if the funds had arrived.

Before the affair, however, had reached this point, the police, whose forbearance had been counted upon, and not without reason, began to take a new interest in what was going on, and Mr. Boudeville, the head of the department of police, which is occupied with the movements of emigrants, sent his men and seized all the lists and documents in possession of the recruiting agents, and put an end, for the present at least, to the scheme.

He took exception to the clause of their articles about bearing arms; said he had no objection to their going as mere colonists where they pleased, but the conditions of their enlistment compromised the neutrality of France. They must find means to go somewhere else to enlist, if they wished to enter the confederate service. He then said, that *if they wished to enter the Mexican service, they might receive some encouragement.* Here the matter now stands. I presume if these men avail themselves of Mr. Boudeville's proposal, they will be used in aid of the Emperor's undertaking to bring back the French army from Mexico.

I learn from the same source which supplies me these details, that a Mr. Irwin S. Bullock and a Mr. Lewis were here, on the second of January, to confer with the recruiting agents about this business, and left on the fifth for Marseilles and Toulon. They have not returned so far as I can learn, though, as I was informed about that time, they were soon expected.

Two hundred and fifty Polish volunteers enlisted in London, and are expected to embark at Liverpool on the 25th of this month.

Some Polish refugees in Switzerland have written to a Mr. Teichman, also a Pole, acting for the confederates here, asking for aid to carry them to the confederate territory. It is also reported here among the Poles that Count Sabolewsky had been furnished with forty-five thousand francs to be used in collecting Polish recruits at Zurich and in Italy.

While applications from Frenchmen and Germans for service in our army have been constant for three years past, I do not remember to have received a half a dozen from Poles during my residence here.

This fact, taken in connexion with what seems a sort of combined movement among the refugees of that unhappy province, leads me to suppose that some means have been used to persuade them that they have common cause with the insurgents against us on the ground that the United States have made common cause with Russia against them.

I have here given you all the information I possess upon this subject up to date. I have not communicated these details as they reached me from time to time, because there seemed to be no occasion to trouble you with them.

I am, sir, with great respect, your very obedient servant,

JOHN BIGELOW.

Hon. WILLIAM H. SEWARD,
Secretary of State, &c., &c., &c.

Mr. Seward to Mr. Bigelow.

No. 48.] DEPARTMENT OF STATE,
Washington, February 21, 1865.

SIR: I transmit a copy of a letter of the 10th instant, and of the accompanying papers, addressed to this department by the Secretary of War, relative to the capture, in Mexican waters, by insurgents from Texas, of the steamer Ark, when on a voyage from New Orleans to Matamoras. The abuses of the rights of neutrals which, throughout the present war, have been committed by trade with the pretended neutral port of Matamoras, and the open intercourse and unfeigned good understanding between inhabitants of that port and enemies of the United States in Texas, have materially served to prolong the war itself, and, in our opinion, would perhaps have justified, if not the seizure, at least the blockade of Matamoras, as a measure of self-protection.

Please call the attention of Mr. Drouyn de Lhuys to the subject, with a desire that neutrality may be vigorously enforced there by the French troops in occupation, and so remove a source of embarrassment which seems to be quite annoying.

I am, sir, your obedient servant,

WILLIAM H. SEWARD.

JOHN BIGELOW, Esq., *&c., &c., &c., Paris.*

Mr. Stanton to Mr. Seward.

WAR DEPARTMENT,
Washington City, February 10, 1865.

SIR: I have the honor to transmit to you a report of Major General Canby, commanding the military division of west Mississippi, in relation to the seizure of a United States vessel at the mouth of the Rio Grande, together with certain official papers connected therewith, which accompany that report.

Your obedient servant,

EDWIN M. STANTON, *Secretary of War.*

Hon. WILLIAM H. SEWARD, *Secretary of State.*

NEW ORLEANS, *January 19, 1865.*

SIR: On the 16th of July last, the steamer Ark, Augustus Williamson, master, left this port laden with lumber, &c. She belonged to John Bochino, a citizen of the United States, entirely loyal, and a resident of this city for many years past. The value of this vessel was not less than $25,000, and her cargo was worth about $2,000. In proceeding up the Rio Grande, and when about twelve miles above Bagdad, her machinery became slightly disabled, and she ran aground from eight to ten steps' distance from the bank of the river on the Mexican side. While in this position and in Mexican waters, she was seized and taken possession of by the confederates, to wit, on the 7th of August, 1864, and carried to Brownsville, Texas. At this port she was condemned as prize, and subsequently sold as such to certain Mexican citizens, to wit, on the 23d October, 1864.

The steamer Ark cleared regularly at this port, receiving all essential documents, exemplifications of which are hereto annexed. She was also duly entered at the port of Bagdad upon arriving there.

The object of presenting this case to you, Mr. Seward, is to obtain restitution of this property, if possible. Mr. Bochino appears to have been divested violently thereof, in violation of the laws of nations, and in violation of the protection afforded our commerce in neutral waters, and Mr. Bochino has thought fit to lay this matter before you, sir, for such action as you may deem fitting in the premises.

Respectfully,

J. S. WHITAKER, *Attorney.*

Hon. WILLIAM H. SEWARD, *Secretary of State.*

John Bachino, the within named claimant, being duly sworn, deposes and says that all the facts set forth in the foregoing statement are true.

J. BACHINO.

Sworn to and subscribed before me this 26th day of January, 1865.

CHARLES CLAIBORNE,
United States Commissioner.

I, Charles Claiborne, United States commissioner for the eastern district of Louisiana, do hereby certify that John Bachino, the claimant herein, this day appeared before me at my office, and made oath to the facts set forth in this petition.

In faith whereof, I grant the presents under my signature and seal of office, at the city of New Orleans, this 26th day of January, in the year of our Lord 1865, and the eighty-ninth year of the American independence.

[SEAL.]

CHARLES CLAIBORNE,
United States Commissioner.

UNITED STATES OF AMERICA, EASTERN DISTRICT OF LOUISIANA,
City of New Orleans, State of Louisiana:

On this 21st day of January, in the year of our Lord one thousand eight hundred and sixty-five, before me, Charles Claiborne, a commissioner duly appointed by the circuit court of the United States for the eastern district of Louisiana, personally appeared at my office, in the city of New Orleans, in the said eastern district of Louisiana, Augustus Williamson, who, having been duly sworn, did thereupon depose and say: That on the 16th July, 1864, he left New Orleans in command of the steamer Ark, bound for Matamoras, with a cargo of lumber, say fifteen thousand feet, and three passengers. We arrived at Bagdad, Mexico, on the 29th day of July, 1864, and there entered the steamer at the custom-house. We laid at this port three days, and then on the 1st of August, 1864, left for our destination, Matamoras. At about 5 o'clock p. m. the machinery became so disabled as to prevent our further progress. I then threw out an anchor on the Mexican side, about twelve miles above Bagdad, say at about fifteen yards from the Mexican side of the river. I caused the vessel to sheer close in to the bank during the night, so as not to be in the way of other vessels that were passing. The river fell during that night about four feet, and the vessel was then left fast aground. I then found it impossible to get her off; went to Bagdad, and obtained a small vessel to take off her cargo, for the purpose of lightening her. On the 6th of August I carried in our yawl an anchor to the Texas side, and had intended to have used this, with a chain attached to the steamer, for the purpose of getting her afloat in deep water; but the chain not being long enough to reach the anchor, I was unable to use it as intended, to wit, to heave her off.

The steamer was not, therefore, attached to the Texas side of the river. On the 7th of August I got out a large portion of the cargo on the deck, for the purpose of putting it on board the vessel referred to. Before I could get any of this on board the small vessel, armed confederates came up in force, from two hundred to three hundred strong, on the Texas side of the Rio Grande, (at this point not over one hundred and fifty yards in width,) and required me to send my yawl-boat across for them, which I found it necessary to do. Twelve came over and took possession of the vessel, and made me and the crew prisoners, my passengers having already left me at Bagdad. On or about the 14th August they took us to Brownsville, the steamer being still left aground, with twelve soldiers on board; we were imprisoned up to the 27th of August, 1864, released then two days on parole, and then sent to Houston, being released eventually on the 8th day of December, 1864. I gave my deposition to the same facts herein stated, while in Brownsville, before the confederate authorities. I should have stated that some two or three days after the vessel was seized by the confederates, General Cortinas sent a courier on board the vessel to Colonel Ford, in command of the confederate force, demanding the vessel, because taken in violation of neutral waters; but the demand was disregarded. The confederates sold the steamer, after her capture, for the sum of thirteen thousand and fifty dollars in gold. She was sold at auction at Brownsville. I do not know who purchased her. Her name has been changed. She now is running on the river between Bagdad and Matamoras.

AUGUSTUS WILLIAMSON.

Sworn to and subscribed before me, this 21st day of January, 1865.

CHARLES CLAIBORNE,
United States Commissioner.

UNITED STATES OF AMERICA, EASTERN DISTRICT OF LOUISIANA,
City of New Orleans, State of Louisiana:

On the 21st day of January, in the year of our Lord one thousand eight hundred and sixty-five, before me, Charles Claiborne, a commissioner duly appointed by the circuit court of the United States for the eastern district of Louisiana, personally appeared at my office, in the city of New Orleans, in the said eastern district of Louisiana, Antonio Miguel, who, being duly sworn, did thereupon depose and say:

I left New Orleans on the steamer Ark on the 16th day of July, 1864. We left for Bagdad, Mexico, with the intention of going from that place to Matamoras. We reached Bagdad on the 29th July, 1864. We laid there three days, and then left for Matamoras; on the same day, when we were about twelve miles from Bagdad, the captain, with one of the deck hands, was at the helm; the captain was intoxicated and could not steer the steamer properly, and ran her aground on the Mexican side. He got her off, and backing her out she struck the Texan side; and when we had hardly started to go up the river the engineer cried out that the engine was disabled, and the captain then dropped anchor on the Mexican side, on the same place where we had been aground before. We remained there until the next morning. The water having fallen four feet during the night, the vessel was hard aground. Not being able to heave her off, the captain went down to Bagdad to see the owner. We remained there two days, and then returned to the steamer in the yawl. We took the cargo or a portion of the cargo from the hold and put it on deck, for the purpose of having it ready for a small steamer, the Valdez, which I understood had been chartered to take off the cargo of our steamer and transport it to Matamoras. The Valdez was alongside of us when a confederate force of two or three hundred men hailed us from the Texas bank and asked for the yawl, so that they could come on board. The yawl was sent to them. Twelve came on board and took possession of the vessel. They asked for her papers and for her American flag. The Mexican flag was flying at her masthead; it had been sent that very day by the owner to protect her. The papers and the American flag had been placed by the captain in a tin box and dropped in the water where they could have been found when necessary. The captain told the confederates that he had no papers on board, and that the only flag he had was the Mexican flag.

That same night the captain was drunk and told them that the steamer was American; that he had buried the American papers of the vessel and her American flag, and that he would get them and give them up. The next morning Colonel Ford came on board and told the lieutenant in command of the capturing force that the steamer could not be held; that she should be released. The lieutenant answered that she was a good prize, and gave to Colonel Ford the information he had received from Captain Williamson. Colonel Ford then told us that if the papers and flag of the steamer were delivered to him he would release us all. We were two or three days before making up our minds to deliver them up. After a consultation between the officers and crew, we all agreed to deliver them up and take their word that we should be immediately released. They did not keep their word; the flag and papers were delivered to them, and they took us prisoners to Brownsville, where we remained until the 1st day of September, 1864. We were carried to Houston and released on the 8th of December, 1864.

ANTO. MIGUEL.

Sworn to and subscribed before me, this 21st day of January, 1865.

[SEAL.] CHARLES CLAIBORNE,
United States Commissioner.

DISTRICT OF NEW ORLEANS,
Surveyor's Office, Port of New Orleans:

I do certify that the steamboat Ark, of New Orleans, is American built; that she has one deck; no masts; her length is eighty-two feet —— inches, her breadth seventeen feet —— inches, her depth three feet five inches, and measures *forty-four tons ninety-two feet*; has a round stern; has —— galleries and —— head; and that her name, and the name of the port to which she belongs, are painted on the stern in the manner required by the third section of the act for registering ships or vessels of the United States.

Given under my hand, at New Orleans, aforesaid, this twenty-eighth day of April, 1864.

J. P. TUCKER,
Acting Surveyor.

I, owner of the aforesaid, do agree to the foregoing description and measurement.

NEW ORLEANS, *April* 28, 1864.

I, J. C. Woolverton, of New Orleans, shipwright, do swear that the steamer Ark, having one deck, and being in length eighty-two feet, in breadth seventeen feet, in depth three and five-tenths feet, and measuring $44\frac{92}{95}$ tons, having one gallery and no head, was built by me, or under my direction, at New Canal, parish of Orleans, Louisiana, in the United States, in the years 1863 and 1864.

J. C. WOOLVERTON,
Shipwright.

Witness: P. E. HUGON.

No. 107.—PERMANENT.

In pursuance of an act of Congress of the United States of America, entitled "An act concerning the registering and recording of ships or vessels."

John Bachino, of New Orleans, State of Louisiana, having taken or subscribed the oath required by the said act, and having sworn that he is a citizen of the United States, and the only owner of the ship or vessel called the Ark, of New Orleans, whereof D. Bachino is at present master, and a citizen of the United States, as he hath sworn, and that the said ship or vessel was built at New Orleans, State of Louisiana, in the year one thousand eight hundred and fifty-four, as per enrolment No. 147, and documents on file in this office having certified that the said ship or vessel has one deck and two masts, and that her length is eighty-two feet —— inches, her breath seventeen feet —— inches, her depth three feet 5 inches, and that she measures 44 tons; and that she is a steamer, has a round stern and a plain head; and the said John Bachino having agreed to the description and admeasurement above specified, and sufficient security having been given according to said act, the said steamer has been duly registered at the port of New Orleans.

Given under our hands and seal, at the port of New Orleans, this 6th day of July, in the year one thousand eight hundred and sixty-four (1864.)

I do hereby certify that this is a true copy of the register of said steamer issued at this office July 6, 1864.

JOHN N. COLLINS, *Collector.*

Mr. Seward to Mr. Bigelow.

No. 49.]

DEPARTMENT OF STATE,
Washington, February 21, 1865.

SIR: I transmit, for your information, a copy of a letter of the 7th instant, and of the accompanying papers addressed to this department by the Assistant Secretary of War, relative to the surrender by General Mejia, at Matamoras, of refugees from Texas as deserters from the insurgents. This was the subject of the instruction to you, No. 38, of the 7th instant.

I am, sir, your obedient servant,

WILLIAM H. SEWARD

JOHN BIGELOW, Esq., *&c., &c., &c.*

Mr. Dana to Mr. Seward

WAR DEPARTMENT,
Washington City, February 7, 1865.

SIR: I am instructed by the Secretary of War to transmit, for your information, and for such action as you may consider appropriate and necessary, the enclosed communication from Major General Canby, with its accompaniments, in relation to the surrender by General Mejia, commanding at Matamoras, Mexico, of citizens of the United States, deserters from the rebel service, or refugees from the rebel territory.

I will thank you to return the enclosures, after having availed yourself of their contents.

I have the honor to be, sir, your obedient servant,

C. A. DANA,
Assistant Secretary of War.

Hon. W. H. SEWARD, *Secretary of State.*

General Canby to Mr. Stanton.

HEADQUARTERS MILITARY DIVISION OF WEST MISSISSIPPI,
New Orleans, La., January 27, 1865.

SIR: I have the honor to transmit, for the information of the Secretary of State, copies of certain papers, marked A, B, C, and D, in relation to the surrender by General Mejia, commanding at Matamoras, Mexico, of citizens of the United States, deserters from the rebel service, or refugees from the rebel territory, on the pretence that they are criminals and fugitives from justice.

The course of General Mejia, which, from his own statement, appears to be authorized by the Emperor Maximilian, is one of direct hostility to the government of the United States, and, in my judgment, should be so treated. For reasons that have been impressed upon me by the Secretary of State, I shall, until otherwise advised, take no further steps in this matter than to send an officer to the Rio Grande, for the purpose of ascertaining the extent of this *extradition*, and the names of the unfortunates who have been turned over to the vengeance of the rebels, and, by remonstrance with General Mejia, prevent any addition to the number of victims.

Very respectfully, sir, your obedient servant;

ED. R. S. CANBY,
Major General Commanding.

The SECRETARY OF WAR, *Washington, D. C.*

General Vile to Lieutenant Colonel Drake.

HEADQUARTERS UNITED STATES FORCES,
Brazos Santiago, Texas, January 12, 1865.

COLONEL: On assuming command at this place I immediately made such arrangements as greatly assisted deserters and refugees to reach my lines from Mexico.

This had the effect to increase the number of deserters very materially, and threatened to destroy the organization and efficiency of the rebel troops on this border.

Rumors have been reaching me for a month that the authorities of the Maximilian government were arranging to return deserters to the rebel authorities. During the last two days there has been a stampede among the very large number of these persons now on the Mexican side of the Rio Grande. As near as I can learn, some forty to sixty have been arrested by the Mexican authorities at Matamoras and delivered to General Slaughter.

I have not been able to hear from the United States consul at Matamoras for some days. If I had horses to draw the light artillery on the island I could easily drive Slaughter out of Brownsville. I have been over and felt of him sufficiently to satisfy me that he does not *intend to fight* in case we should advance. But it could not be held with the means of *this* command, and no material damage could be inflicted on him without a cavalry force.

No permanent relief can be given these destitute people without occupying and controlling the valley of the Rio Grande, which, of course, can best be done by going in from Matagorda bay and occupying San Antonio, which is the key to this whole valley and frontier.

These facts are stated for the information and consideration of the major general commanding department of the Gulf.

I have no doubt of the fact that deserters are being delivered on the claims of the rebel authorities. I shall learn more in a day or two in relation to the matter, and will report further.

I shall be glad to receive any instruction or orders deemed necessary (if any) in the case.

Very respectfully, your obedient servant,

WM. A. VILE, *Brigadier General*
Commanding military Division West Mississippi.

Lieut. Col. GEO. B. DRAKE,
A. A. General, Department of the Gulf.

Official copy:

C. G. CHRISTENSEN,
Lieutenant Colonel, Assistant Adjutant General.

General Mejia to Mr. Etchison.

[Translation.]

IMPERIAL ARMY OF MEXICO, MEJIA DIVISION, GENERAL IN CHIEF.

No. 852.] MATAMORAS, *January* 10, 1865.

MR. CONSUL: I have the honor to acknowledge the receipt of and to answer your official despatch of the 8th instant, containing a serious complaint in favor of the rights and liberties of American citizens residing in this city, and of those who, having escaped from the army of the Confederate States, have come seeking the protection of the government of Mexico.

You assure me that you have reliable information to the effect that the so-called authorities of Brownsville are daily carrying off American citizens, upon the pretext that they owe allegiance to their government, and that such abuses are committed by virtue of an agreement, made for the purpose, between the commander of the imperial forces at Matamoras and the confederate authorities at Brownsville. You conclude by stating to me that the government of the United States possesses the will and the power required to protect its citizens residing in foreign countries.

This last declaration, Mr. Consul, is an unseasonable threat, and the entire despatch is written under a strange hallucination of mind, entirely different from the measured language that is customary in the official intercourse between two countries, besides having no foundation in facts.

When you have deliberately considered their import, you will withdraw your words, or the government of the United States will do us justice by reproving the acts of its agent at Matamoras.

It is sufficient for me to state to you at present that it is untrue that any arrangement has been made by which American citizens are pursued, arrested, and conveyed to Texas, under the pretext that, owing allegiance to the confederacy, they have deserted from their army. Through private communications, the principal articles of the extradition treaty in regard to criminals, fugitives from justice, celebrated between Mexico and the United States during the ministry of Mr. Dobadao, have been agreed upon; from which slaves, also excepted by that treaty, are now expressly excluded, and deserters from the army who may seek refuge in Mexico; against these two classes of persons no claims can be attempted by the confederate authorities.

These private stipulations have been submitted for the approval of my sovereign, and, by his command, will be faithfully executed, as, being not only based on a pre-existing treaty, they attack the liberties of none others than criminals, but also in a sure manner expedite the ends of justice.

When the military commanders of the United States have pursued a course so diametrically opposed to humanity and civilization towards Mexico, as witnessed by the recent act of delivering Don Manuel de Regon, esq., a political exile, who sought refuge under the American flag, into the hands of his enemies, it appears incredible that an agent of that same government should not desire that at Matamoras, where the memory of that horrible violation is more indelibly impressed, the rights of citizens who are in no danger, and whose liberties no one pretends to attack, should not be protected.

The indecorous terms in which your note is couched authorize me, according to established custom, to return it without answer. I answer solely for the purpose of conveying the views herein expressed, but in future will limit myself to acting as is customary in these cases.

Accept the assurance of my particular regard.

THOMAS MEJIA,
Com'dg General of New Leon, Coahuila, and Tamaulipas.

The CONSUL OF THE UNITED STATES *at Matamoras, Present.*

I certify that the above is a true copy.

D. G. FENNO, *Lieut. and A. D. C.*

HEADQUARTERS DEPARTMENT OF THE GULF,
New Orleans, January 26, 1865.

Official copy:

C. S. SARGENT, *First Lieut. A. A. A. S.*

Mr. Etchison to General Vile.

UNITED STATES CONSULATE,
Matamoras, January 14, 1865.

SIR: I have the honor to acknowledge receipt of your letter of the 13th instant, in relation to the surrender of deserters and others from the so-called confederacy to the rebel authorities commanding at Brownsville, by the authorities of Matamoras.

I addressed a very severe letter to General Mejia on the subject, and a copy of his reply (translated) I enclose herewith.

It is reported in town that as many as twenty or more have been sent over, and without any trial or investigation being made. They are arrested, generally, very early in the morning, and are at once taken, with a file of soldiers, to the river, when they are delivered to the rebels. The whole proceeding is an outrage, as there can be no extradition treaty between two governments that have not in either case been recognized; and our treaty does not authorize the return of even criminals, until undoubted proof is shown that they are guilty. General Mejia's letter is a lame reply, and savors much of the pen of a rebel.

Referring to the cotton question, Dr. McManus requests me to say that, if you will have the kindness to send his cotton to the mouth of the Rio Grande, and have it surveyed and appraised, he will pay the salvage to you or your order.

I am, sir, very respectfully,

E. DORSEY ETCHISON,
United States Consul at Matamoras, Mexico.

Brigadier General W. A. VILE,
Commanding United States Forces, Brazos Santiago, Texas.

I certify that the above is a true copy.

D. E. FENNO,
Lieutenant and A. D. C.

HEADQUARTERS DEPARTMENT OF THE GULF,
New Orleans, January 26, 1865.

Official copy:

C. S. SARGENT,
First Lieutenant 2d La. Vols., A. A. D. General.

General Vile to Lieutenant Colonel Drake.

NEW ORLEANS, LA., *January* 25, 1865.

COLONEL: Since my communication of the 5th instant, in relation to the agreement between the Maximilian and confederate authorities, by which deserters from the rebel army are being surrendered to the confederate military authorities, I have received a letter from Hon. E. D. Etchison, United States consul at Matamoras, Mexico, enclosing copy of the reply of Brigadier General Mejia to the protest of the consul on this subject, copies of each of which are enclosed for the information of the major general commanding department.

I am reliably informed that these persons are being delivered to the confederate officers at various other points on the river.

From all I could learn, I think about seventy-five have been given up in this way.

I have the honor to be, very respectfully, your obedient servant,

WM. A. VILE,
Brigadier General Volunteers.

Lieut. Col. GEO. B. DRAKE,
Assistant Adjutant General, Dep't of the Gulf.

HEADQUARTERS DEPARTMENT OF THE GULF,
New Orleans, La., January 26, 1865.

Official copy:

JOS. HIBBERT,
Captain and A. A. General.

Mr. Bigelow to Mr. Seward.

[Extract.]

No. 44.]

LEGATION OF THE UNITED STATES,
Paris, March 6, 1865.

SIR: I send you some journals by this mail which may be worth your looking over; among others the last number of the Memorial Diplomatic, which is understood to be under the special inspiration of the ministry of foreign affairs.

You will find on page 157 confirmation of what I sent you by last mail about commissioners sent from Mexico to negotiate a concordat with the Pope. A translation of part of this article is enclosed. You will not fail to remark that the commission is charged to treat directly with the Pope, and that Maximilian has sent Velasquez, his minister of foreign affairs, as president of the commission.

The promulgation in Mexico of a decree from Maximilian imposing restrictions upon the publication of papal bulls, &c., simultaneously with the departure of this commission, leads me to suspect that the tone to be taken by the commissioners when they reach Rome will be quite as decided as represented in my private note of the 3d instant.

You will observe, by a paragraph on page 158 of the Memorial Diplomatique, that the government has found it convenient to attribute the delay to our government, in naming a minister to this court in place of the late Mr. Dayton, to another motive than a disposition on the part of the President to resent the long vacancy in the French mission at Washington, to which the delay is generally ascribed. It is one of many signs, becoming daily more common, that public opinion here begins to require of the government a conciliatory manner towards the United States.

* * * * * * * * * *

I am, sir, with great respect, your obedient servant,

JOHN BIGELOW.

Hon. WILLIAM H. SEWARD,
Secretary of State.

[Enclosure No. 44.—Translation.]

From the Memorial Diplomatique, March 5, 1865.

Our correspondent from Mexico informs us that, in accordance with the desire expressed by the Holy Father, and justified by the constant usage of the Roman court, negotiations for the definitive arrangement of the ecclesiastical questions in Mexico are about to be concentrated at Rome. With this view his Mexican Majesty has charged a special mission to go and treat directly with his Holiness; and as it was of importance to invest with this mission, as full of sharp points as it is delicate, men calculated to inspire a just confidence at the Holy See, the emperor Maximilian has designated his minister of state, Mr. Velasquez de Leon, as president of the commission, and first plenipotentiary of Mexico.

Mr. Velasquez de Leon is very favorably known at Rome for his devotion to the church. He will be aided by two councillors of state, charged more particularly to arrange the details of the execution of the concordat to be entered into between Rome and Mexico.

Mr. Velasquez de Leon and the two councillors of state who accompany him were to embark upon the French packet-boat which is expected about the 15th of March at Saint Nazaire.

Mr. Seward to Mr. Bigelow.

No. 62.] DEPARTMENT OF STATE,
Washington, March 7, 1865.

SIR: Your despatch of the 9th ultimo, No. 25, calling my attention to the official denial, in the Moniteur, of the truth of the report in circulation concerning the cession of certain provinces in Mexico to France, and to the communication of the Emperor to you upon the subject, has been received with satisfaction.

I am, sir, your obedient servant,

WILLIAM H. SEWARD.

JOHN BIGELOW, Esq., *&c., &c., &c., Paris.*

Mr. Bigelow to Mr. Seward.

No. 50.] LEGATION OF THE UNITED STATES,
Paris, March 10, 1865.

SIR: Referring to your despatch No. 48, relative to the capture of the United States steamer Ark by rebel Texans in Mexican waters when on a voyage from New Orleans to Matamoras, I have the honor to enclose a communication which I made upon the subject to his excellency the minister of foreign affairs yesterday.

I am, sir, with great respect, your obedient servant,

JOHN BIGELOW.

Hon. WILLIAM H. SEWARD,
Secretary of State.

Mr. Bigelow to Mr. Drouyn de Lhuys.

LEGATION OF THE UNITED STATES,
Paris, March 9, 1865.

SIR: On the 16th day of July last the United States steamer Ark, belonging to John Bachino, a citizen of the United States, and commanded by Captain A. Williamson, was cleared from the port of New Orleans for the port of Matamoras, in Mexico.

When about twelve miles above Bagdad, on the Rio Grande, in consequence of an accident to her machinery, she grounded within a few yards of the Mexican shore. While in this position, and in Mexican waters, she was seized, on the 7th of August, by insurgent enemies of the United States from Texas, taken to Brownsville, condemned with her cargo as lawful prize, and sold at auction to some Mexican citizens.

The constant abuse of the rights of neutrals by persons trading with the port of Matamoras throughout the present war, and the open intercourse and unfeigned good understanding between inhabitants of that port and enemies of the United States in Texas, have materially prolonged the war itself, and have provoked, if not the seizure, at least the blockade of Matamoras as a measure of self-protection.

In view of all these facts, I am instructed to express to your excellency the desire of my government that neutrality may be regularly enforced by the French troops in occupation of Matamoras, and thus a source of embarrassment may be removed which seems to be quite unnecessary.

I have the honor to renew to your excellency the assurance of my most distinguished consideration.

JOHN BIGELOW.

His Excellency Mr. DROUYN DE LHUYS,
Minister of Foreign Affairs, Paris.

Mr. Seward to Mr. Bigelow.

No. 65.]

DEPARTMENT OF STATE,
Washington, March 10, 1865.

SIR: I have the honor to acknowledge the receipt of your despatch of the 17th of February, No. 36, which gives me the information you have been able to acquire concerning the insurgent proceedings to enlist Polish subjects of Russia.

It is a pitiable result of the loss of national life that any of the children of Poland should, under influences of whatever form of demoralization, be disposed to pass into the military ranks of the army of disunion and slavery in the United States. Happily, the waning fortunes of the rebels seem likely to render the acceptance of such persons to the insurgent forces practically impossible, and so to prevent their incurring a disgrace to which we can only lament that they have so blindly consented.

I am, sir, your obedient servant,

WILLIAM H. SEWARD.

JOHN BIGELOW, Esq., *&c., &c., &c.*

Mr. Bigelow to Mr. Seward.

No. 52.]

LEGATION OF THE UNITED STATES,
Paris, March 10, 1865.

SIR: In consequence of a paragraph which I noticed in the Paris correspondence of a London journal, I asked the minister of foreign affairs yesterday whether he had any information of a circular issued by the minister of foreign affairs of the Archduke Maximilian to the maritime prefects of Mexico, in reference to consuls acting irregularly and without exequaturs from the imperial government, provoked, as was stated, by two recent appointments made by the government of the United States. His excellency replies that he had not heard of anything of the kind, but, if I desired, he would procure me a copy, if any had been issued. I said that as the circular purported, according to the newspaper reports, to have been provoked by the action of my government, I presumed it would interest them to know what it was, and said I would thank him to procure me a copy if he could conveniently. His excellency took a memorandum of my request, and said it should not be neglected.

This morning I received the first copy of a new journal, entitled the Epoque, established and conducted by M. Ernest Feydeau, in which the circular in question is given at length. Though I presume a copy has already reached you, there is a chance that it has not; I therefore enclose a translation, with the editorial paragraph which followed it.

In this connexion, I invite your attention to an article in the Constitutionnel of the 7th instant, signed Boniface, relating to the reciprocal relations of France, Mexico, and the United States, which is chiefly deserving of attention for the paragraph with which it closes, and which may be translated as follows:

"The work which France has undertaken in Mexico, *and which she will not leave unfinished*, moves, then, towards a happy and rapid accomplishment."

This article appeared nearly simultaneously, I am told, upon what I deem credible authority, with the declaration of the Emperor to his council that the honor of France was involved in the support of the new empire in Mexico. This declaration was followed by the issue of orders for the transport of 8,000 men—that is, eight regiments from Algeria—to the support of General Bazaine, who, as I have already advised you, lacks confidence in the mercenaries with whom the Emperor has attempted to replace the French soldiers in the archduke's service. Should this information prove correct, it will give to the approaching debates on the address, in the corps legislatif, unusual importance.

I am, sir, with great respect, your obedient servant,

JOHN BIGELOW.

Hon. WILLIAM H. SEWARD,
Secretary of State, &c., &c., &c.

[Translated from l'Epoque, March 9, 1865.]

The Minister of Foreign Affairs in Mexico to the Political Prefects of the Empire.

MEXICO, *January* 18, 1865.

It has come to the knowledge of this department that there are persons exercising the functions of consular agents in the territory of the empire without having received the usual *exequatur* either from the government of his Majesty or from that of the old republic, thus contravening established usage and the law governing this matter.

You will be pleased to invite, with all necessary managements, the persons exercising the above functions within your circonscription to present to you their brevet or their license. You shall give to understand to such as shall not be able to present such that they must henceforth abstain from the exercise of consular functions.

You shall see that these prescriptions be strictly carried out, and shall give an account to this department of the irregularities you may have discovered, or may discover hereafter, in these matters.

RAMIREZ.
Minister, Secretary of State for Foreign Affairs.

The circular derives a particular interest from the recent appointment of a new United States consul at Matamoras, and from the valueless exequatur delivered by Corona to the consular agent of the same country, residing at Mazatlan.

Mr. Seward to Mr. Bigelow.

No. 68.]

DEPARTMENT OF STATE,
Washington, March 13, 1865.

SIR: I have received your despatch of the 17th of February, No. 35, and I thank you for your careful comment on the Emperor's speech, which was delivered on the opening of the chambers.

I am, sir, your obedient servant,

WILLIAM H. SEWARD.

JOHN BIGELOW, Esq., &c., &c., &c., *Paris.*

Mr. Seward to Mr. Bigelow.

No. 70.]

DEPARTMENT OF STATE,
Washington, March 13, 1865.

SIR: I enclose for your information a copy of a despatch which has been received from Mr. Chase, our consul general for Mexico, residing at Tampico, and of my answer thereto. A word of frank explanation may now perhaps be fitly spoken to Mr. Drouyn de Lhuys concerning our consuls and commercial agents in Mexico.

I begin with saying that it is understood that a person authorized by the power now dominant in the capital of Mexico has arrived at New York and solicited an informal interview with me. The advance thus proposed has been declined, in conformity with the settled position of this government to hold no interview, public or private, with persons coming from any country, other than the agents duly accredited by the authority of that country which is recognized by this government. This government has insisted that the opposite position, which to some extent is held in other States, and under which Mason, Slidell, and Mann, insurgent emissaries from this country, are admitted to unofficial conferences, is unfriendly and injurious to the United States. Thus we govern ourselves in our intercourse with other states by the principles that we claim ought to govern them in their relations with the United States.

We have not, for political reasons, recalled, and we shall not recall, for such reasons, from Mexico, any of our agents who are accredited to the republican government in that country. On the contrary, we have not intended and we do not insist on their being allowed to remain there in the exercise of their functions by the authority which has displaced that government in the capital. If inhibited by these authorities, in places occupied by them, our agents are instructed to desist from their functions, and, if need be, to withdraw from the country. Thus, while abiding events, we shall not be found increasing the confusion of affairs in that unfortunate country. In the course we are thus pursuing in regard to consular and commercial agents, we do not understand that they will, by tolerating this course on our part in Mexico, make any political concessions to us. The matter is a purely commercial one, and has no political significance whatever.

It may be well, on the other hand, that the existing authorities in the city of Mexico should understand through the French government that no exclusion of our agents will have any influence whatever to induce a change of the political attitude towards Mexico which the government of the United States has hitherto maintained.

This government has learned something of the value of concentration of purpose. We are engaged in suppressing a dangerous rebellion, and we are not willing to be unnecessarily diverted from that special duty with any controversy with any party in Mexico or elsewhere concerning affairs in that state.

I am, sir, your obedient servant,

WILLIAM H. SEWARD.

JOHN BIGELOW, Esq., *&c., &c., &c.*

Mr. Chase to Mr. F. W. Seward.

No. 9.]

UNITED STATES CONSULATE GENERAL,
Tampico, February 16, 1865.

SIR: I have the honor to enclose herewith a copy of a note (No. 1) from the prefect of this city, and my reply thereto, (No. 2,) by which you will perceive that the imperial minister of foreign relations instructs the prefect to cause the commissions of all consuls to be presented to him, and, in the event of non-compliance, the offender is to understand that he is to abstain from all consular privileges.

You will doubtless recollect that I was recognized by President Juarez at San Luis Potosi, and as my commission will be examined in this office to-morrow, I shall withhold that recognition from the ruling authorities here, and I am apprehensive that difficulties may be thrown in my way to prevent the exercise of my consular prerogatives, and I beg that you will be pleased to instruct me as to the proper course to be pursued, so that I may carry out the views of our government should my fears be realized.

I have reason to believe that the whole force of the ministerial despatch upon this subject is aimed at this consulate, in order that the question of consular recognitions may be at once contested between the imperial government of Mexico and that of the United States.

I have the honor to be, sir, with great esteem and respect, your most obedient servant,

FRANKLIN CHASE.

Hon. FREDERICK W. SEWARD,
Assistant Secretary of State, Washington.

Mr. De la Serna to Mr. Chase.

No. 1.] TAMPICO, *February* 11, 1865.

MR. CONSUL: The political chief of this department, from the city of Victoria, advises this prefecture, in a note dated the 2d instant, as follows:

"His excellency the minister of state and foreign affairs advises this chief political prefecture, under date 18th January ultimo, what I here copy. 'It has come to the knowledge of the ministry that there are persons in the territory of the empire who are acting as consular agents without having obtained the customary exequatur, neither from his Majesty's government nor from that of the old Mexican republic, before its departure from this capital, contravening, by so doing, the established usages and violating the laws relative to this matter. Your honor will be pleased to invite, in a very attentive manner, the persons who are exercising those functions in the territory under your command, in order that they may present to you their patent or authorization, and after taking notice of the same you will give an account of its result. Those who do not present these documents, you will make them understand they have to abstain from all consular functions. Your honor will take care of the strict compliance of this ordinance, and you will give an account to this minister of the abuses of this kind which they may have committed or may commit.' And I enclose it to you, in order that in that district it may be strictly complied with, giving me an account of its results."

And I have the honor to communicate it to you for your knowledge and the end herein expressed.

God guard you for many years.

The Prefect, JESUS DE LA SERNA.

The Secretary, P. S. GARERA.

MR. CONSUL GENERAL
Of the United States of the North, Present.

Mr. Chase to Mr. Serna.

No. 2.] UNITED STATES CONSULATE GENERAL,
Tampico, February 13, 1865.

SIR: I have the honor to acknowledge the receipt of your note of the 11th instant, in relation to consuls, and in reply thereto I have to acquaint you that in the month of December, 1836, I took charge of this consulate as vice-consul, was promoted by the President to the rank of consul in August, 1842, and to the rank of consul general in the early part of June, 1863, and that the respective commissions are now filed in this consulate, subject to your inspection, should your honor deem such inspection necessary.

I have the honor to be, with the highest consideration, sir, your most obedient servant,

FRANKLIN CHASE.

Hon. JESUS DE LA SERNA,
"Prefecto Publico" of the Southern District of Tamaulipas, &c., &c., &c.

Mr. F. W. Seward to Mr. Chase.

DEPARTMENT OF STATE, *Washington, March* 13, 1865.

SIR: Your despatch No. 9 has been received. Your action in reply to inquiries of the prefect of police meets with the approbation of this department. Should it be required, you will exhibit both your commission and exequatur to the proper authorities. Your functions are not political, and consequently you have nothing to do with the recognition of any government, but must submit to the authorities *de facto* present, and if prohibited from discharging your duties, you will desist, and report at once to this department. In that case you will be at liberty to remain at your post without exercising your functions, or return to this country, as you may see fit.

I am, sir, your obedient servant,

F. W. SEWARD, *Assistant Secretary.*

FRANKLIN CHASE, Esq.,
United States Consul General, Tampico.

Mr. Bigelow to Mr. Seward.

[Extract.]

No. 55.]

LEGATION OF THE UNITED STATES,
Paris, March 14, 1865.

SIR: The sudden death of the Duke de Morny, and the prospect of an early termination of the war in the United States, has almost produced a panic in Paris. At no time since the Italian war have the French people appeared so concerned for the future. The markets have all been depressed, in spite of the efforts to sustain them.

To enable you the better to appreciate the influence and bearing of our late military successes upon public opinion, I enclose extracts from a series of journals, all more or less "officious," and all published at or about the same time. Enclosure No. 1 is an article from the Memorial Diplomatique on the "Monroe Doctrine." After giving an account of that doctrine, as he understands it, the writer proceeds to present additional reasons for feeling no disquietude about the French empire in Mexico, in consequence of unfriendly feelings in the United States.

Enclosure No. 2 is a report of some remarks made in the senate on the 10th by the Marquis de Boissy.

* * * * * * * *

Enclosure No. 3 is an extract from the reply of Chaix d'Est Auge to the Marquis de Boissy.

Enclosure No. 4 is an extract from an editorial article in the Avenir National of the 12th, commenting upon the article already cited from the Memorial Diplomatique.

Also extracts in same enclosure from the Patrié and the Presse and La France of the 13th.

These papers and proceedings will show that our attitude towards Mexico has been rendered much more disquieting to the people of France as our prospects of domestic peace have improved.

I am, sir, very respectfully, yours, &c.,

JOHN BIGELOW.

Hon. WILLIAM H. SEWARD,
Secretary of State.

[Enclosure No. 1.]

Translation from the Memorial Diplomatique, March 12, 1865, *page* 172.

* * * * * * * * *

Such, disengaged from the exaggeration of party spirit and political passions, is this famous Monroe doctrine, that certain journals seek to represent as the sword of Damocles suspended over the crown of Maximilian I.

Put forward in order to protect the sovereign independence of the state of the New World, it cannot be applied to the actual state of things in Mexico without treading under foot the principle of popular sovereignty upon which it rests. Nothing is more natural than that the United States should not be particularly pleased with the re-establishment of monarchy among their neighbors; but that, through pure sympathy for the republican form, they should believe themselves to possess the right to force upon Mexico the return of anarchy, is what simple good sense will ever refuse to admit.

In presence of the incessant approbation of an entire people, in presence of the daily increasing popularity of the imperial couple, the best accredited organs of the American press have been forced to acknowledge that the French expedition, far from having exercised an illegitimate pressure upon public opinion in Mexico, has, on the contrary, served to bring out in a wonderful manner the free expression of the national will.

"The end to be attained," said the Emperor of the French in the letter which he wrote to General Forey on the 3d July, 1862, "is not to force upon the Mexicans a form of government which would be disagreeable to them, but to aid them in their efforts to establish, according to their own wish, a government which may have some chance of stability, and which can insure to France redress for the wrongs of which she complains." And immediately afterward his Majesty adds:

"We have an interest that the republic of the United States be powerful and prosperous, but we have no interest that it should seize upon the whole of Mexico, control thence the Antilles, as well as South America, and be the sole dispenser of the products of the New World."

Hence we think that if the eventualities be considered not from a point of view purely hypothetical and conjectural, but in their practical and real aspect, we ought to take into account the letter of Napoleon III, which traces out distinctly the attitude of France in case the United States should depart from the Monroe doctrine, to such a point as to arrogate to itself the right of tutelage over a sovereign and independent state, as Mexico placed under the efficacious protection of the French flag.

It was with this object in view that, on the 10th of April, 1864, the convention of Miramar was signed, in the preamble of which is read:

"The government of his Majesty the Emperor of the French and that of his Majesty the Emperor of Mexico, animated by an equal desire to insure the re-establishment of order in Mexico, and to consolidate the new empire, have resolved to arrange by a convention the conditions of the stay of the French troops in this country.

"ARTICLE 1. The French troops which are now in Mexico will be reduced as soon as possible to a corps of 25,000 men, including the foreign legion.

"This corps, to protect the interests which have caused the intervention, will remain temporarily in Mexico, under the conditions arranged by the following articles:

"ARTICLE 2. The French troops will evacuate Mexico according as his Majesty the Emperor of Mexico shall be able to organize the troops necessary to replace them.

"ARTICLE 3. The foreign legion in the service of France, composed of 8,000 men, will, nevertheless, still remain for six years in Mexico after all the forces shall have been recalled, conformably to article 2. Dating from this moment, the said legion shall pass into the service and pay of the Mexican government. The Mexican government reserves to itself the faculty of shortening the duration of the employment of the foreign legion in Mexico."

In virtue of the stipulation which we have just cited, an army corps of 25,000 men remains in Mexico to protect the interests which have caused the intervention until the emperor Maximilian shall have organized the forces necessary to replace them.

Should, however, the reorganization of the Mexican army progress sufficiently rapid to render the complete evacuation possible at some not distant future, the foreign legion, which realizes an effective of 8,000 men, would still continue to unfurl the French flag in Mexico for six whole years after the departure of all the other troops, unless the emperor Maximilian should judge it expedient to shorten the duration of its employment. Thus imposing as seems the force of bayonets of which the United States will be able to dispose if they end the fratricidal war which at present divides them, there is very little fear that they will be disposed to make an attack upon Mexico, where, for eight or ten years still, they are sure to meet the French flag; and should they forget that it is to the generous co-operation of France that they owe their own independence, they could not be ignorant that the government of the Emperor Napoleon III does not compound in a matter of honor and dignity.

When Russia, confiding in the forbearance of which the other great powers had but too long time manifested in regard to her, attempted, in 1853, to fix forever her political preponderance in the east, imperial France did not hesitate an instant to draw the sword to maintain the independence and integrity of the Ottoman empire. Then pessamists were not wanting to spread alarm over the issue of a struggle entered into, at so great a distance, against the formidable colossus of the north. The British cabinet itself appeared at first frightened at the consequences of so perilous an undertaking, and was already disposed to subscribe to the wishes of the Czar; but imperial France having declared that were she obliged to sustain the war alone she would none the less take up the glove which the Autocrat of all the Russias had thrown down to Europe, England found herself drawn, in spite of herself, into the Crimean expedition.

It is principally to this glorious campaign that the government of Napoleon III owes the immense prestige which it now exercises throughout the whole world.

In revealing the power of his country in so striking a manner, he has, at the same time, delivered all Europe from the baleful terror which the Muscovite forces inspired, the exaggeration of which weighed upon her like a nightmare, paralyzing the regular development of liberal institutions in the centre of our continent.

As soon as the note of the notables of Mexico, conferring the crown upon the Archduke Ferdinand Maximilian of Austria, had by the subsequent adhesion of the *ayuntamientos* obtained the legal sanction of the country, the French diplomacy made it its duty to assure itself of the true dispositions of the American cabinet in regard to the new empire of Mexico. President Lincoln and Mr. Seward, at Washington, as well as Mr. Dayton, at Paris, did not cease to assert the well-defined purpose of the government of the United States to respect the results of the free vote of the Mexican people. They added, that out of regard to France, whose friendly sympathies for the Union were confirmed by her scrupulous neutrality in the war between the north and the south, President Lincoln, in case of re-election, formally promised to enter into diplomatic relations, with the government of Maximilian I if he was generally recognized by the other powers of Europe and America. The best-informed American journals agree in stating that President Lincoln only awaited the date of the renewal of his functions on the 4th of March to recognize officially the new Mexican empire; and this recognition, positively decided upon and making a part of the political programme of the government at Washington, will no doubt establish without delay between the two countries relations of perfect understanding and neighborliness.

Never in its discussions has the cabinet of Washington allowed to transpire the slightest allusion to the Monroe doctrine: still less has it from this leading point made reserves implying any right whatever in the internal affairs of Mexico. In effect the last attempt at conciliation between the confederates and the federals has revealed to us that the initiative tending to prop up the Monroe doctrine does not belong to the government of the north, but to that of the confederates, who, in a common undertaking based upon this doctrine, saw a means of bringing back the opinion of the population of the south to ideas of conciliation and federal unity.

It will be objected, perhaps, that if President Lincoln has preserved up to the present moment a wise and prudent attitude, it was to better cultivate the neutrality of France in the existing struggle between the north and the south, and that nothing could guarantee to us that, once a reconciliation made between the belligerents, he will not break through his promises, shielding himself behind the double pressure of Congress and the public opinion of the country.

The most efficacious guarantee for the ulterior conduct of the government of Washington lies, in our opinion, in the powerful interest which the United States have to entertain amicable relations with France. The notice to terminate the treaty stipulations of 1817 between England and the United States, relative to the *great lakes*, betrays in President Lincoln the presentiment of an inevitable rupture sooner or later between his country and Great Britain.

If peace is concluded between the north and the south, the armies at the disposition of the American Union will not be long in being used against Canada under one pretext or another. It would be the height of folly to irritate England, and at the same time to alienate the sympathies of France. The peace which would come to put an end to the war which the federals and confederates now wage will never be more than a truce. The schism between the north and the south is too deep to be entirely effaced, unless after several generations. Let the great powers coalesce against the north, and allow the south to have a glimpse of the perspective of a complete independence, they will at once find in the secession States an army ready to again take the field against a common enemy. Spain, on her side, will not ask better than to join her fleet to the naval forces of France and England, for more than Mexico, which is covered by the French flag, is the island of Cuba menaced by the United States.

If, after four years of bloody war, the government of Washington has not yet succeeded in subduing the confederates, can it for an instant remain under the delusion that it can make head against the formidable coalition of which France would necessarily become the soul? For in distorting the principle of the Monroe doctrine, in order to launch an army against Mexico, the United States would in consequence affect France as to her honor and as to her interests: as to her honor, because she could not leave unfinished the work which Napoleon III has called the *glorious page* of his reign; as to her interests, because, as Mr. Drouyn de Lhuys says in his despatch, addressed the 17th November, 1863, to the Marquis de Montholon, (page 182 of the Yellow Book,) the end of the expedition to Mexico would not be completely attained if it should not have for effect to create between two empires a close solidarity of interests.

LE CHEVALIER L. DEBRANEZ DE SOLDAPENNA.

[Enclosure No. 2.]

Extracts from the debate in the senate, March 10, 1865.

THE MARQUIS DE BOISSY. * * * * * * *

I return to the question of intervention. We intervene in China, and we are about to return. But I think we had better first return from Mexico. There are two large black points in the horizon—Mexico and Rome. With respect to Mexico, this is the sentimental wish I form. I wish that the American war may not end, but continue forever, even to the complete extermination of the contending parties, if necessary. If the war should unfortunately come to an end, our army would be taken prisoner. (Protestations on all sides.)

BARON DE HECKERIN. Such language cannot be used in such an assembly as the senate. (Adhesion.)

THE MARQUIS DE BOISSY. Why, you would have to deal with an army of 500,000 or 600,000 scoundrels. (Murmurs.)

THE PRESIDENT. Your suppositions are injurious to our soldiers, and the senate expresses its feelings by its murmurs.

THE MARQUIS DE BOISSY. I do not think so. (Affirmative signs.)

THE PRESIDENT. You see, M. le Marquis, that the senate does not agree with you.

THE MARQUIS DE BOISSY. Nevertheless, it is true that our army reduced to a total—— (Interruption and cries of Question! Question!)

THE PRESIDENT. The murmurs of the senate are the best reply to your observations.

THE MARQUIS DE BOISSY. Well, then, be it so. We shall triumph—20,000 men against 500,000 or 600,000. But how much will that cost us? (Enough! Enough!) Let us turn our eyes, then, to China.

[Enclosure No. 3.]

The Marquis de Boissy was followed by Chaix d'Est Auge.

The following is an extract from the reply of Chaix d'Est Auge to the Marquis de Boissy, *in the senate, March 10, 1865:*

* * * The speaker has trenched upon a number of questions, into which I shall hardly be expected to follow him. But the convention and the affairs of Mexico are two important questions every way worthy of attention. Those questions will be treated by other speakers, and this is not the moment to go very fully into them. Of the convention I beg leave not to say a single word. As to Mexico, I have at present not much to say. The Marquis de Boissy calls himself the friend of humanity; yet, when speaking of the fratricidal war which is ravaging the United States of America, he expressed a wish that the struggle, impious in its nature and its results, might never cease. That is a wish which I repel in the strongest manner. And if the interests of my country required the continuation of this conflict, I could never, without the most heartfelt repugnance, immolate humanity on the altar of my country. M. de Boissy fears that if the United States should become once more united, our army would be compromised, and possibly soon be made prisoners of war. Let him be reassured: the United States have too much good sense and reason to enter into such a war; they will not traverse deserts to add other provinces to provinces already too numerous. It is not because they are exhausted, but from a well-understood feeling as to their own interest, that they would not think of attacking us in Mexico. The same reasons prevailed with England when she declined to fortify Quebec, saying there was no reason to fear, and that Quebec was not threatened. I will briefly reply on a point to which I adverted last year, and in respect of which I thought I had given the Marquis de Boissy himself satisfactory explanation. The customs receipts of Vera Cruz, before our expedition to Mexico, were engaged to satisfy the claims of England, France, and Spain, and were divided monthly between them. On taking possession of that port, could we say to England and Spain, "the treaties are null and void; we tear them up and scatter them to the winds?" No; we regarded them as sacred, and respecting them was not giving way to England, but honorably fulfilling a contract which bore the signature of France.

[Enclosure No. 4.]

Extract from "L'Avenir National," Sunday, 12th March, 1865.

* * * * * * * *

The Memorial Diplomatique exerts itself to demonstrate that the Monroe doctrine is in no way applicable to the present situation. "The system," it says, "that President Monroe intended to combat was no other than that of legitimacy." This was, in effect, we concede, the first thought of Monroe at the moment when Spain thought of reconquering her former colonies. We have already said that the declaration of Monroe was made at the instigation of Canning, who was alarmed at the tendencies of the congress of Verona.

But now the Americans give to the principle a more extended interpretation. They see only in the words of Monroe the passage which is the solely important one for them: "We owe it to our good faith, and to the amiable relations which exist between the allied powers and the United States, to declare that we would consider any attempt on their part to extend their system to any part of this hemisphere as dangerous for our tranquillity and our security." This is the political evangel of the Americans, and one can foresee that upon the day when the south, at the end of its resources, will be obliged to submit, it will take as a pretext for reconciliation the necessary application of the Monroe doctrine.

We scarcely believe, with M. de Boissy, that as soon as peace is concluded there will be an invasion of Mexico of 500,000 to 600,000 *worthless scamps.* But this is an eventuality against which it would be prudent to guard.

It is wisdom in the French government to avoid a useless danger in foreign quarters. The convention with Maximilian of the 10th April, 1864, says well that 25,000 men, *including the foreign legion*, will remain temporarily in Mexico; but no minimum of sojourn is stipulated for—except for the foreign legion, which is to remain for six years—so all the other troops may be recalled from the present moment. We ought to wish that this may be at the soonest period possible.

Nevertheless, the Memorial Diplomatique, so reassuring in whatever concerns Mexico, is less incredulous in what regards the British possessions. "If peace," says it, "be concluded between the north and the south, the disposable armies of the American Union will not delay, under one pretext or another, to be used against Canada." What prevision is this which makes the Americans march rather towards the north than towards the south? We do not wish, like the Memorial Diplomatique, to give ourselves airs of prophesy, but we repeat that we would like for more than one reason to see our troops return from Mexico.

[Enclosure No. 4.]

Extracts translated from La France, (Reone financiere,) March 13, 1865.

Events have occurred, this week, which have reacted on the financial as well as on the political world. The illness and death of M. de Morny produced for a while a legitimate sensation among the financial men accustomed to identify the public credit with the statesman whose name is intimately connected with the institutions of the country. But this sensation could not be lasting; the present state of inactivity existed at the Bourse previous to the painful event which has so justly occupied public attention, and it will doubtless continue to exist after this sensation shall have passed away.

Attempts are also made to influence the market under pretence of the various vicissitudes of the war going on in America between the north and south; but the confederates are yet far from being conquered, and the fears expressed in relation to Mexico, in case of peace being restored in the United States, are singularly premature.

Why not ascribe the present situation to its general and real causes, instead of stopping at mere secondary considerations? The cause may be summed up in one word—distrust. How can those who have for so long a time sown the seeds of distrust wonder that they should now bear fruits? Every enterprise or institution of credit has been attacked, and we cannot be surprised that the public, having become suspicious of them, dares no longer venture upon a ground whose unsteadiness has so often been denounced.

CONTINUATION OF ENCLOSURE NO. 4.

[*Translated from the Memorial Diplomatique, March* 13, 1865.]

Besides the "Credit Mobilier," and its forthcoming dividend, which continues to be much talked about, the financial world appears greatly preoccupied concerning the future of the Mexican empire and the consequences which the approaching cessation of hostilities between the northern and the southern armies may have for that country.

The warlike tendencies evinced some time ago by certain members of the United States Senate were but disconnected facts, for which the government at Washington could in no wise be considered responsible. The initiative of the resolution adopted by that eminently deliberative assembly is not of a nature to justify the fear that, as some ceaselessly repeat it in the market, as soon as the fratricidal war which has for four years desolated that country [shall cease,] the Mexican empire will become, in the name of the Monroe doctrine, the aim of these tumultuous hosts, condemned by peace to an inactivity which would all at once become dangerous for Europe.

Shall the United States, after being reconstructed by peace, not have wounds enough of their own to bind up before attempting to quarrel with their neighbors? An empty treasury, a country laid waste, and a decimated population, are these not interior enemies with whom they shall also have to contend?

The work of regeneration so happily commenced and carried on by the emperor Maximilian, with as much firmness as success, may well be considered as a sure proof of the liberal views of civilization and progress which have so far inspired all the acts of the new Mexican empire. In our opinion the edicts of the emperor are in no ways inferior in reality to the principles of pretended equality of the United States of America.

Indeed, the ceaseless solicitude of the newly elected sovereign for the welfare of this people becomes every day more manifest in his incessant labors. Creation of railroad companies, contracts for marine transportation on the Pacific, everywhere, in short, does the emperor seek to simultaneously infuse activity and life into that country so favored by nature.

To demonstrate once more the value of these assertions, we give here the principal condition of a contract between the government of his Imperial Majesty, Maximilian I, and Mr. Edward Gautherin, ship-owner, having the contract for the Imperial Mexican Express Company:

The company is to be Mexican: foreigners becoming members shall have to renounce the rights they may possess as such.

The vessels on the Gulf lines shall carry the Mexican flag, and be nationalized according to the laws already in force.

The steamers of the Imperial Mexican Express shall run on the four lines of Vera Cruz to New Orleans, Vera Cruz to Havana, Vera Cruz to Campeachy, and along the whole coast from Taxpam to Coatzacoalcos.

The ships of the company shall be exempt from port and light-house duties.

The company receives from the government of his Imperial Majesty the monopoly for the construction of jetties and breakwaters in the stopping ports of its steamers, and is authorized to levy upon commerce a transit or storage duty on all goods shipped from or landed on these jetties or breakwaters.

This duty shall be equivalent to 80 centimes per ton for ordinary goods, and 80 centimes per two hundred pounds for such merchandise as iron, lead, rails, steam-engines, minerals, &c.

The government shall receive from the company 20 per cent. of the duties levied by it. The receipt of these duties shall be registered in two books, one of which shall remain in the office of the company and the other at the office of the custom-house.

The vessels of the company shall, on their lines, transport the employés of the preventive service and the mails. Besides the usual postage, the post office administration will take additional postage on the company's account, which it shall pay to it at the time of embarking the mail bags; and the amount due to the company shall vary according to the net weight of the bags and the nature of their contents.

Thus, for the mere transportation of letters the government shall pay one real per half ounce weight, being the price of a single letter from one point to another of the Gulf of Mexico. For letters to Havana the company shall receive two reals.

For carrying newspapers, pamphlets, and printed matter, the company shall charge two reals per *arrobe*.

The company engages to build its workshops, building docks, storehouses and yards on the grounds designated by his Imperial Majesty's government. The port of Vera Cruz is the point momentarily chosen as the centre of the lines of the Imperial Mexican Express steamers.

The company shall, as much as possible, employ the inhabitants of the country, as also the materials it furnishes, such as wood, copper, iron, coal, &c.

The grant is made for twenty-one years, and to the exclusion of any other Mexican company.

MAXIMILIAN.

CHAPULTEPEC, *January* 28, 1865.

[*Extract from La Presse, Monday, March* 13, 1865.]

* * * * * * * * * * * *

Money is abundant. The proof is seen by the state of the bank and by its rate of discount, which it has been obliged to reduce to 3½ per cent.; but this money does not want to be employed.

This feeling of distrust which the capital evidences is not peculiar to France; the English market proves it by the continuance of its feebleness. One cannot, then, without injustice attribute to the situation of a place, nor to noisily rumored proceedings, the dearth of our business and the weakness of our market. European politics leaves us in an absolute repose. From the American side it is not the same. It is a sad thing to say, but we fear for our cash boxes that peace may be made in America. The largest thorn that we have in our foot is, incontestably, the Mexican affair, which trammels our finances, and which causes lively apprehensions for the future. The equilibrium of our budget will feel for a long time, we think, the Mexican expedition. It allows to float incessantly the fear of a loan, which may be retarded by the aid of treasury means at the disposal of the minister, but the bankers think that it cannot be avoided. Italy herself threatens us with a loan.

[*From La Patrie, March* 13.]

Letters from New York, up to the 25th of February, brought out by the North American, arrived yesterday in London.

They contain no further military news, but there has been received in New York the text of an address of Juarez to the Mexicans, in which he says, "Faithful to my duty and to my conscience, I shall devote all my energy to the national defence, with the assistance and co-operation of the Mexican flag." He denounces emperor Maximilian as a usurper enslaving a free nation.

Houston papers publish a correspondence between the confederate Colonel Cyron and General Lopez, commanding the imperial troops on the Rio Grande. Cyron informs Lopez that the confederate government desires to cultivate friendly relations with the Mexican government. Lopez in return declares his sympathies for the southern cause. Named commander by emperor Maximilian, he says that the sons of the confederacy can rely on the complete security of their persons and interest, and on the fullest hospitality. He shall permit no expeditions to be fitted out against the confederates.

Houston papers also report that Matamoras has ceased to be a free port.

[*From La Patrie, March* 13]

However, in spite of all the elements tending to improve the condition of the market, the peaceful news from America has been made use of by the parties wishing to depreciate the stocks, who multiplied their offers, and sought to frighten their opponents by hinting at the complications which, according to them, might arise from a cessation of hostilities in the United States. From that moment the upward tendency of prices was not only completely paralyzed, but a retrograding tendency prevailed, and most stocks lost the advance they had previously obtained; some even descending below the previous fortnight's quotation.

Mr. Bigelow to Mr. Seward.

No. 59.] LEGATION OF THE UNITED STATES,
Paris, March 17, 1865.

SIR: Enclosed you will find a memorandum of a conversation which I had the honor to hold with his excellency Mr. Drouyn de Lhuys, on the 9th instant, in reference to the forcible surrender by General Mejia of refugees from the rebel army, referred to in your despatch No. 49.

The original of this memorandum was left yesterday with his excellency the minister of foreign affairs.

I have the honor to be, sir, your very obedient servant,

JOHN BIGELOW.

Hon. WILLIAM H. SEWARD,
Secretary of State, &c., &c., &c.

[Memorandum.]

LEGATION OF THE UNITED STATES,
March 15, 1865.

The undersigned, chargé d'affaires of the United States, had the honor to submit verbally to his excellency Mr. Drouyn de Lhuys, minister of foreign affairs, the following statement on the 9th instant:

It is stated upon official authority that General Mejia, commanding the Mejia division of the French army at Matamoras, had arrested between twenty and thirty refugees from the rebel army in Texas; conducted them, under the guard of a file of soldiers, to the banks of the Rio Grande and delivered them into the hands of armed enemies of the United States. The pretext assigned, I am told by General Mejia, for this procedure, was, that they were offenders against the laws of the confederacy, and, therefore, liable to extradition. If so, General Mejia appears not to have been aware that the alleged criminals had a right to a fair trial and conviction, which was denied them before they could be surrendered to any government, and that he had then authority to surrender them only upon the suit of a government recognized by the Emperor of France, and to which the right of extradition had been conceded by treaty.

The refugees in question were seized by Mexican soldiers, under the orders of General Mejia, and delivered without any trial into the hands of an armed band of conspirators from Texas, who represented no lawful government, and who could not, therefore, have any political status in any Mexican tribunal, civil or military.

The undersigned, while appreciating the difficulty of enforcing neutrality along the line which divides Texas from Mexico, where the temptations to violate it are so numerous, expressed the hope and expectation of his government that the government of France would not permit the conduct of General Mejia to pass without such instructions as would prevent the recurrence of a proceeding too liable to disturb the friendly relations of the two countries.

The undersigned availed himself of the same occasion to express to his excellency the minister of foreign affairs the regret of his government at the exceptionable tone of the correspondence, addressed by the United States consul at Matamoras to General Mejia, in reference to the surrender of these refugees, and to state that orders relieving the incumbent from his official charge were on their way to him at the time the correspondence was passing.

His excellency Mr. Drouyn de Lhuys stated, in reply to the undersigned, that he had received no information whatever upon the subject referred to by the undersigned, save what the undersigned had communicated; that the subject should be taken into respectful consideration, and that the officers of the imperial government in Mexico should be instructed to preserve a rigorous neutrality.

The undersigned avails himself of this occasion to renew to his excellency the minister of foreign affairs the assurances of his most distinguished consideration.

JOHN BIGELOW

Mr. Seward to Mr. Bigelow.

[Extract.]

No. 71.] DEPARTMENT OF STATE,
Washington, March 17, 1865.

SIR: I have now to recur to some suggestions contained in your despatch No. 29, the receipt of which I have already acknowledged, and also to acknowledge, in due form, the receipt of your despatch of February 14, No. 30.

The burden of these matters is an uneasy state of mind in the Emperor's government concerning our private relations with France, as affected by the war in Mexico.

This government foresaw the present embarrassment, and expressed itself frankly to the imperial government before it intervened in Mexico. It is that embarrassment which now affects the political situation in regard to that country. Even if it were necessary, on our part, to labor for its removal, the traditions and sympathies of a whole continent could not be uprooted by the exercise of any national authority, and especially could it not be done by a government that is so purely democratic as ours. The Emperor's persistence implies that he yet believes to be certain, what we have constantly told him that the people of the United States, reasoning upon preconceived sentiments and national principles, cannot even apprehend to be possible—namely, that a new European monarchical system can and ought to be permanently established on the American continent, and in territory bordering on this republic. It would seem that all parties must abide the trial of the experiment, of which trial it will be confessed that the people of Mexico must ultimately be the arbiters.

This government has not interfered. It does not propose to interfere in that trial. It firmly repels foreign intervention here, and looks with disfavor upon it anywhere. Therefore, for us to intervene in Mexico would be only to reverse our own principles, and to adopt in regard to that country the very policy which in any case we disallow.

* * * * * * *

I am, sir, your obedient servant,

WILLIAM H. SEWARD.

JOHN BIGELOW, Esq., *&c.*, *&c.*, *&c.*, *Paris.*

Mr. Seward to Mr. Bigelow.

No. 77.] DEPARTMENT OF STATE,
Washington, March 23, 1865.

SIR: I have received your despatch of March 6, No. 44.

Unemployed politicians can often raise vehement disputes upon mere surmises or accidents, as they can sometimes prohibit all debate upon the most questionable measures.

The French government can very well understand that our delay in filling the legation at Paris was involuntary, because that government has really found the appointment of a minister here was a duty attended by some embarrassment.

I thank you for the information you gave me concerning the negotiations of Maximilian at Rome for a concordat.

I am, sir, your obedient servant,

WILLIAM H. SEWARD.

JOHN BIGELOW, Esq., *&c.*, *&c.*, *&c.*

Mr. Seward to Mr. Bigelow.

No. 86.]

DEPARTMENT OF STATE,
Washington, March 27, 1865.

SIR: Your despatch of the 10th of March, No. 52, which is accompanied by a translation of a circular issued by the minister of foreign affairs of the Archduke Maximilian, relative to consuls in Mexico, who have no exequaturs from the imperial government, has been received. I have already sufficiently explained our position on this subject.

I am, sir, your obedient servant,

WILLIAM H. SEWARD.

JOHN BIGELOW, Esq., *&c.*, *&c.*, *&c.*

Mr. Seward to Mr. Bigelow.

No. 89.]

DEPARTMENT OF STATE,
Washington, March 27, 1865.

SIR: I have to acknowledge the receipt of your despatch of the 10th instant, No. 50, enclosing a copy of your note of the 9th instant to Mr. Drouyn de Lhuys, in regard to the capture of the United States steamer Ark by Texan insurgents in Mexican waters, and in reply to inform you that your note is approved.

I am, sir, your obedient servant,

WILLIAM H. SEWARD.

JOHN BIGELOW, Esq., *&c.*, *&c.*, *&c.*

Mr. Seward to Mr. Bigelow.

No. 94.]

DEPARTMENT OF STATE,
Washington, March 28, 1865.

SIR: Your despatch of the 14th of March, No. 55, has been received, and I have read with much interest the papers which accompany it, and which illustrate the disquietude now prevailing in Paris.

Fortunately, I have in my despatch of 15th instant, No. 71, explained to you the views and sentiments which our military and political situation suggests. We want our national rights. We are not looking for ulterior, national advantages, or aggrandizement, much less for occasions for retaliating in other forms of hostility against foreign states. We are not propagandists, although we are consistent in our political convictions.

I am, sir, your obedient servant,

WILLIAM H. SEWARD.

JOHN BIGELOW, Esq., *&c.*, *&c.*, *&c.*

Mr. Bigelow to Mr. Seward.

[With two enclosures.]

No. 66.] LEGATION OF THE UNITED STATES,
Paris, March 28, 1865.

SIR: I have received a "note verbale" from his excellency Drouyn de Lhuys, in reply to my note of the 9th instant, and in defence of the seizure of one hundred casks of powder in the gulf of La Paz, on board the United States schooner W. L. Richardson, by a French vessel-of-war. I enclose a copy and translation;

And am, sir, with great respect, your obedient servant,

JOHN BIGELOW.

Hon. WILLIAM H. SEWARD,
Secretary of State, &c., &c., &c.

Verbal note.

[Translation.]

MARCH, 1865.

The minister of foreign affairs has had the honor of receiving the note addressed to him by M. the chargé d'affaires of the United States, on the 9th instant, concerning one hundred casks of powder seized in the gulf of La Paz, on board of the United States schooner Wm. L. Richardson, by a vessel of the French division, on the Pacific station. The information received direct by the department of foreign affairs on this subject leaves no doubt that that seizure was made under the rule explained last year to Mr. Dayton. Circumstances were as follows:

A certain number of merchants at San Francisco had asked, through the medium of the legation of the United States, to be authorized to send every month to the ports of Chayatlan and La Paz powder destined for the working of the mines at Charique. Upon reflection the imperial government decided that it was the less disposed to depart from the rule, that so long as there is fighting going on at any point, it must consider any invoice of powder shipped to that point as essentially a contraband of war, inasmuch as it had ascertained that such operations had already been carried on for the benefit of its adversaries, from Mexican points on the Pacific coast. An answer to this effect was therefore returned to Mr. Dayton in May last by a verbal note, which is doubtless still to be found among the records of the legation.

The schooner Wm. L. Richardson having taken a cargo of powder to the port of La Paz, fell, necessarily, under the provisions of the rule recalled above, and there was all the less reason to depart from it, as reliable information had denounced this fresh invoice of powder to the French authorities as destined for the "guerillas" whom M. Veza was at the time endeavoring to raise in the States of Sonora and Sinaloa.

Mr. Seward to Mr. Bigelow.

No. 102.] DEPARTMENT OF STATE,
Washington, April 4, 1865.

SIR: Your despatch of the 17th ultimo, No. 59, together with its accompanying memorandum of a conversation that you had with Mr. Drouyn de Lhuys, upon the subject of the forcible surrender, by General Mejia, of refugees from the insurgent army to the armed enemies of the United States, has been received, and your proceedings are approved.

I am, sir, your obedient servant,

WILLIAM H. SEWARD.

JOHN BIGELOW, Esq., &c., &c., &c.

Mr. Bigelow to Mr. Seward.

[With two enclosures.]

No. 79.] LEGATION OF THE UNITED STATES,
Paris, April 18, 1865.

SIR : I have the honor to enclose a copy and a translation of a "note verbale," received from his excellency the minister of foreign affairs, in relation to the seizure of the United States mail at Acapulco by the French authorities.

I am, sir, with great respect, your very obedient servant,

JOHN BIGELOW.

Hon. WILLIAM H. SEWARD,
Secretary of State, &c., &c., &c.

[Enclosure No. 2.—Translation.]

Last November Mr. Dayton communicated to the Emperor's minister of foreign affairs a despatch in which the United States consul at Acapulco complained that the commander of the French forces in that city had ordered the seizure of the mail addressed to that consul. Positive information since received on the subject by the imperial government enables it to present this incident in its true light. It is necessary to state, in the first place, the exact position occupied by Mr. Ely, then consul of the United States, after the French troops had taken possession of Acapulco. That agent, by abstaining from any visit or official communication in writing asserting his quality to Admiral Bonet upon the latter's arrival, authorized the supposition that his exequatur having been granted not by Mexico, but by the local government of the state of Guerrero, he considered his mission to be interrupted by the new state of things. Admiral Bonet, therefore, considered Mr. Ely as having no longer any attributions beyond those of a purely commercial agent. Such was also the opinion of the commander of the United States sloop Narragansett, as evidenced in his search for a deserter from that vessel, as well as the opinion of Admiral Bell himself. This view of the subject appears to be also confirmed by the fact of the federal government giving only the title of commercial agent to the person appointed since as the successor of Mr. Ely. Here, now, are the facts concerning the seizure of the United States mails as they occurred:

Acapulco, previous to its being taken possession of by the French forces, had no regularly organized postal service. Letters from abroad were brought there by the packets of the Panama Steamship Mail Company in three separate bags. The one addressed to the company's agent contained letters relative to the affairs of that concern; the second, the mails intending to go on further; and the third, the correspondence for Acapulco and the interior of Mexico. This latter bag, for want of a regular postal agent, was addressed to the *American consul*, where the letters were delivered to the parties concerned and the postage collected. Complaints had occurred about deficiencies in the system of delivery of private letters, but, aside from that consideration, it was impossible to permit this state of things to continue from the moment that Acapulco was to follow the system adopted everywhere else by the Mexican government. Where taxes were to be levied it evidently belonged to a Mexican administration only to fulfil that office. The officer commanding at Acapulco had, therefore, decided on appointing a temporary postmaster, and his choice for this office fell upon the vice-consul of France, M. Dupuy. This gentleman, therefore, upon the arrival of the packet from San Francisco, on the 30th of September, caused the three mail bags, previously mentioned, to be delivered to himself. The one addressed to the *American consul* was open, and its contents proved that, as we have already stated, it was not a mail addressed by the government of the United States to their consul at Acapulco, but simply an ordinary letter bag. This decision, however, called forth some opposition at the hands of the commander of the federal sloop Cyane, who, whilst acknowledging that Mr. Ely no longer had any right to demand that the bag addressed to the *American consul* should be delivered to him, asked that it should be given to himself, who, as an officer of the United States navy, was the legal representative of his government. After explanations on the subject had passed between the commander of the Cyane and the commander of the French naval forces, these two officers, equally desirous of maintaining the friendly relations existing between the navies of the two countries, agreed that the bag should be delivered to the post office of Acapulco, and there opened in the presence of an officer of the United States sloop, who would thus ascertain that it was only a public mail, and not an official correspondence of the government of the United States.

This question had thus been disposed of in the most satisfactory manner, when subsequent events prevented this arrangement being carried out. M. Dupuy, the postmaster appointed, having seen fit to resign that office, and the evacuation of Acapulco having been resolved upon, things were put back in their former position. This, nevertheless, shows that the measures adopted at the time when the French forces took possession of Acapulco were fully justified both by the irregularity of the process of delivery of private correspondence and by the absence of any real right of Mr. Ely to demand that the system should be continued.

PARIS, *April* 12, 1865.

Mr. Bigelow to Mr. Seward.

No. 107.] UNITED STATES LEGATION,
Paris, May 26, 1865.

SIR: I fear our government will not succeed in giving entire satisfaction to the ruling classes on this side of the Atlantic, whatever we may do. They seemed very much dissatisfied, at the commencement of the war, that our armies were not more destructive; when they became more destructive, the same parties censured us for bloodthirstiness and insensibility to the blessings of peace. Now that peace has come, and we have reason to count upon a general jubilee in Europe, there appears to be more discontent than ever. The great grievances at present are, first, President Johnson's proclamation offering a reward for the delivery of Davis to the officers of justice; second, the reported emigration of discharged soldiers to Mexico; third, the trial of Booth's accomplices with closed doors.

The readiness with which all these prestiges are seized to weaken the impression which our unexpected triumph over what were deemed insurmountable embarrassments has a tendency to produce, shows how great is the importance attached here to our example.

The proclamation putting a price on Davis's head will be generally condemned by the Latin race, who are so accustomed to see a price put upon the heads of their most meritorious citizens that they feel an instinctive sympathy for any one who wears that flattering penalty. I think nothing that has happened during our war has produced so unpleasant an effect upon our friends here, though their impressions always yield to proper explanations when there is an opportunity of making them.

In regard to Mexico, the impression produced by the recent news from the United States has amounted to a panic. Some military successes of the liberals in Mexico are associated in the public mind with the emigration schemes advertised in the New York and Washington papers, which are supposed to respond to a public sentiment beyond the control of the government. The absence of the Emperor at the moment aggravates the alarm, and leaves the community a prey to rumors of the most disturbing character.

I dined with Mr. Fould on Tuesday evening. He sought several opportunities to talk with me of Mexican affairs. I assured him that he had nothing to fear from the United States; that the formidable enemies of the Archduke Maximilian were "those of his own household"—the Mexicans. He expressed a doubt whether our government and its friends would be strong enough to maintain our neutrality. I told him that so far as I could judge, there were not, nor were there likely to be, two considerable parties on our Mexican policy; that whatever the government decided to do would be pretty universally accepted by the people, because it would be likely to reflect their deliberate wishes, one of which I felt sure was to preserve friendly relations with France. He said he thought that the best way to remove all difficulty between the three countries, and to resolve all embarrassing questions, was for us to recognize the new government. This view he enforced with a few obvious remarks. I heard him through, and then remarked that he had opened a question which would require me, for its discussion, to go further back in the history of our respective countries than was possible on such a festive occasion, but I felt prepared to say to him that but for the unfriendly tone of the official press, and the abounding evidence of a willingness, if not a desire, on the part of influential classes in France to see our republic weakened by a permanent disunion, the Emperor would probably have experienced no difficulty in coming early to a satisfactory understanding with our government about Mexico. Unhappily, the impression had got abroad among our people that the Emperor had undertaken to build up an empire in Mexico upon the ruins of our republic, and it would take yet some time and some substantial proofs of good feeling on his part to remove this impression. His excellency arose from his seat at this remark, which I was preparing to elaborate a little, and said that was a subject that would take us too far to discuss on that occasion; and after a few more words our interview ended. It ended rather abruptly, because Mr. Fould is entirely of my opinion; he has been opposed from the outset to this expedition. He feels that he is gradually sinking, officially, under the weight of its burdens; and having no response to make to the view I presented, he did not wish to be betrayed into admissions unbecoming his position; at least such was my impression.

He introduced me, in the course of the evening, to Baron Dussin the elder, who is a very important arm of the government, though now eighty-five years of age, and whose sympathies have been rather with the insurgents than with the government during the late rebellion. He also showed great solicitude about Mexico, and seemed greatly relieved by my assurance that, regardless of the example set by other nations, and faithful to all our traditions, we should make our people, if any were otherwise disposed, respect our neutral obligations.

I mention these facts to show that the anxiety which is reflected by the press here and in England is not exaggerated, and as the foundation for a suggestion which I think it my duty to make to you. It is that, as far as possible, we avoid giving any pretext to this government upon which public opinion can be rallied against us. It is in a critical situation, and, I think, on the eve of a very important if not desperate step in reference to Mexico. Something must be done, and speedily. It is important that we neither do nor permit anything that will relieve the situation at our expense, for we now need all the good feeling in Europe that we can possibly inspire to repair the waste of our war. If we alienate France, or even establish an unfriendly feeling here, it will poison all the official journalism of Europe towards us, notwithstanding the universally acknowledged folly of the Mexican expedition. They all have less affection for the Monroe doctrine than they have for France or Mexico. I hope, therefore, that our government will protect itself by all dignified means from any suspicion of conniving at the military schemes, if there are any maturing in the United States, against Mexico, and show the old countries of Europe to how much better use we can put them than by fighting them. I would hardly trouble you with a suggestion apparently so superfluous as this, if I did not feel that, where men are in desperate circumstances, they may do desperate things, and sovereigns are but men.

I am, sir, with great respect, your very obedient servant,

JOHN BIGELOW.

Hon. William H. Seward,
Secretary of State, Washington, D. C.

Mr. Hunter to Mr. Bigelow.

Department of State,
Washington, June 5, 1865.

My Dear Sir: In compliance with the request of Mr. Seward, I have to acknowledge the receipt of your letter of the 19th of April last, relative to the support reported to be extended by the Emperor to Gwin, in Mexico, and the character of the new loan in aid of that country. In reply, I am directed to thank you for the interesting information.

I am, my dear sir, very faithfully yours,

W. HUNTER.

JOHN BIGELOW, Esq., &c., &c., &c.

Mr. Seward to Mr. Bigelow.

No. 167.]

DEPARTMENT OF STATE,
Washington, June 12, 1865.

SIR: Your despatch of May 26, No. 107, has been received. It treats only of familiar questions; but it treats of these with special earnestness. For this reason I reply in this communication to your suggestions, although I have considered the same subject so recently as the 3d of June, when I transmitted to you the views of the President.

You inform me that the proclamation putting a price on Davis's head has produced an unpleasant effect upon the friends of the United States, and that it is particularly condemned by the Latin race. Treason and the raising of civil war, in some European states, are, for obvious reasons, regarded by mankind as venial offences. In the United States they are looked upon with far greater severity, for reasons which it is not necessary that I should now explain. With such severity crimes of the present insurgents in the United States are regarded by the government and by the loyal portion of the people of this country. The time, indeed, is rapidly coming on when these crimes will be lamented with greater sincerity, and condemned with greater earnestness, in the region which civil war has left desolate, than any political crime or casualty which has recently occurred in Europe has been lamented or condemned on that continent. The United States are not in a temper favorable to the making of apologies or explanations to European statesmen and politicians for matters which do not affect foreign nations, and which relate exclusively to our domestic affairs. I have, therefore, to request that you will make no explanations or apology for the action which this government has hitherto pursued, and, as events shall transpire, may be found to be pursuing, in relation to rebels, who, without cause or necessity or excuse, have not only spread desolation and death throughout a large portion of the United States, but have employed energies of surpassing strength in the effort to invoke the intervention of foreign powers to make that desolation more ruinous, as well as perpetual. I state, however, for your own information, that the executive department has taken, as yet, no definitive action with regard to judicial proceedings against Jefferson Davis. Other subjects of greater urgency have, thus far, engaged its attention.

If it be true, as you have conceived, that France is likely to adopt some measure of hostility towards the United States on the ground of real or expected political complications in Mexico, the United States must wait the shock according to their ability. It is already known to the government of France that the United States are not prepared to recognize a monarchical and European power in Mexico, which is yet engaged in war with a domestic republican government and a portion of the Mexican people; but it must be acknowledged, on the other hand, that the United States have, from the first appearance of the shadow of that foreign domination in Mexico until its present stage of administration, expressed its views to France upon the subject in a perfectly direct, frank, and friendly manner. The sentiments of the people of the United States in regard to affairs in Mexico, which have been so often expressed in the manner to which I have referred, are natural and inextinguishable. It would be a new event in history if one nation can give cause of offence to another nation by declining to become the ally of that nation in a war for the overthrow of a state friendly to the power so refusing to become an ally. We shall not believe, until we have convincing proof, that France is to invade the United States on such a pretext. It is to this government a source of the highest satisfaction that, during the three years that the war has been carried on between France and the republic of Mexico, the United States have maintained the strict line of forbearance and neutrality which their relations to the several belligerent parties dictated. From time to time the French authorities have given notice to the United States of apprehended violations of neutrality by American citizens, and the government of the United States have promptly interposed and prevented the intrusions menaced. Here the United States must stand. Beyond this they cannot go. They desire peace, and would cheerfully restore their traditional relations with France. It will remain for France to say whether for these relations shall be substituted an alienation whose consequences might involve an arrest of the march of civilization throughout the world.

I am, sir, your obedient servant,

WILLIAM H. SEWARD.

JOHN BIGELOW, Esq., *&c.*, *&c.*, *&c.*

Mr. Bigelow to Mr. Seward.

[With one enclosure.]

No. 117.] LEGATION OF THE UNITED STATES,
Paris, June 13, 1865.

SIR: A statement of the minister secretary of state a few days since in the corps legislatif, and an article in the Moniteur of the 10th instant, have compelled me to break the silence I intended to have kept until I heard from you in reference to the grounds upon which the minister of foreign affairs placed his withdrawal of the proclamation of neutrality of June, 1865. I transmit herewith a copy of a note which I addressed this morning to his excellency the minister of foreign affairs, which will sufficiently explain itself, and my motives for not permitting the ministerial statements cited in it to pass in silence.

I am, sir, with great respect, your obedient servant,

JOHN BIGELOW.

Hon. WILLIAM H. SEWARD,
Secretary of State.

[Enclosure No. 1.]

Mr. Bigelow to Mr. Drouyn de Lhuys.

LEGATION OF THE UNITED STATES,
Paris, June 12, 1865.

SIR: In the official report of a speech made by his excellency the minister of state on the 9th instant, I find an erroneous statement, which, to prevent any possible misapprehension between your excellency and myself, I hasten to bring to your notice.

After speaking of the declarations made at Boston by General Rosecrans in reference to the alleged recruiting of American soldiers for the Mexican army, M. Rouher is reported to have said: "Pendant que ces declarations se faisaient à Washington et à New York, elles recevaient ici leur sanction et leur consecration formelle; le ministre des Etats Unis se presentait a notre ministre des affaires étrangères et lui disait: Sans doute nous ne voyons pas d'un œil favorable une monarchie s'etablir au Mexico. Sans doute nous preferons les formes republicaines; mais nous respectons la volontè des peuples et des nations; nous comprenons que le Mexique, qui a ètè longtemps regi par la forme monarchique veuille revenir à cet ètat de choses; il nous n'irons pas faire la guerre pour une question de forme de gouvernement."

[Translation.]

"While these declarations were being made at Washington and at New York, they received here their sanction and formal consecration. The minister of the United States presented himself also to our minister of foreign affairs, and said to him: Without doubt we do not behold with a favorable eye a monarchy established in Mexico. Without doubt we prefer the republican form, but we respect the will of peoples and of nations. We understand that Mexico, which had been long governed by the monarchical form, may desire to return to that state of things, and we are not going to make war upon a question of the form of government."

Mr. Rouher has probably misapprehended your excellency, for I am persuaded that you could never have so entirely misunderstood my language as to have reported me as saying that the people of the United States understand that Mexico, after having been so long subject to a monarchical form of government, may desire to return to it. What I stated that may have given the impression which has misled the minister of state was this, in brief: that now that the experiment had been begun, the Americans wished to be fully tried, under circumstances best calculated to determine, finally and forever, whether European systems of government suited the Mexican people best. If it should appear that they did, and public tranquillity was restored, no nation was more interested in such a result than her immediate neighbors. I added, that the success of republican institutions in the Spanish American states had not been such as to encourage us to attempt the propagation of them there otherwise than by our example, and that whatever government was acceptable to the Mexican people would be satisfactory to us.

I trust to your excellency's memory to confirm me in the assertion that I never expressed to you any opinion or impression importing that the Mexican people desired a monarchical government. In saying that the success of republican institutions in Spanish America had not been such as to justify us in becoming their armed propagandists, I did not countenance the inference that the Mexicans themselves were dissatisfied with the form of government under which they had been living prior to the occupation of their capital by French troops.

I beg your excellency will take such measures as may seem to you proper to correct the error into which the minister secretary of state, in common with his hearers, appears to have been betrayed.

I desire to avail myself of this occasion to correct another misapprehension which has become accredited by publication in the official journal.

The Moniteur, of the 10th instant, speaking of the neutrality of France between the United States and the late insurgents in the slave States, says:

"La situation étant aujourdhui changée et le gouvernement federal ayant fait connaître son intention de ne plus exercer à l'egard des neutres les droits qui resultaient pour lui de l'ètat de guerre, le gouvernement de l'Empereur n'a pas cru devoir plus longtemps reconnaître de belligerants dans les Etats Unis d'Amerique."

[Translation.]

"The situation being to-day changed, and the federal government having made known its intention no longer to exercise towards neutrals the rights which were imposed upon it as a consequence of the state of war, the government of the Emperor has not deemed it its duty longer to recognize belligerents in the United States of America."

I presume reference is here made to the communication which I had the honor to submit to your excellency on the 29th ultimo, extracts from which were quoted by your excellency in a subsequent communication to me, announcing the withdrawal of belligerent rights from the insurgents. Assuming such to be the authority from which the Moniteur makes the statement which I have cited, I feel it my duty to say that, thus far, the federal government of the United States has made no renunciation of any rights which belonged to it as a belligerent. It has ceased to exercise such rights, I presume, but I am not aware that it has renounced them.

The communication to your excellency of the 29th ultimo was in reply to a previous declaration of your excellency that a renunciation by us of the belligerent right of visit and capture of neutral ships must be a condition precedent to the withdrawal of belligerent rights from the American insurgents by France.

In arguing the inconveniences of making these measures dependent one upon the other, I stated that "the United states government, in applying for a repeal of the declaration of June, 1861, abandoned any of the rights of belligerent *which it is presumed to have claimed*, and became directly responsible for anything it might do in the character of a belligerent. If, after the withdrawal of the imperial declaration, it were to visit and search a neutral vessel, it would at once expose itself to reprisals, the same as for any other violation of international comity." That is to say, we abandoned any belligerent rights which, upon the theory of your excellency, we only shared in common with the insurgents, and, upon that theory, would be responsible for anything we might do in our proper character as belligerents.

These observations were based upon the doctrine of belligerent rights propounded in the communication to which I was replying without either admitting or denying its correctness.

Should my government be of the opinion that a nation may be entitled to the privileges of belligerent in suppressing a rebellion, without thereby conferring belligerent rights upon the rebels, it might not be prepared to renounce the practice of visiting and searching neutral vessels so long as that remedy was necessary for the national security. Your excellency will remember that I made no concealment of the fact that I had no instructions from my government to offer or accept any conditions to be attached to the withdrawal of the declaration of June, 1861. I merely argued the inconvenience and unreasonableness of the conditions attached to its withdrawal upon premises assumed by your excellency. The final suppression of the rebellion in the United States, of which intelligence has reached us since the correspondence under consideration took place, deprives the matter to which I have invited your excellency's attention of much of its practical importance, at the same time it is as well that the communications, both oral and written, which I had the honor to submit on the 27th ultimo, should not acquire in their re-statement any importance not properly belonging to them.

I beg, therefore, that nothing I have written or said to your excellency may be regarded as an acceptance of the principle that the assertion of belligerent rights by a nation against its rebellious subjects necessarily confers upon the latter belligerent rights.

I beg to renew to your excellency assurances of the very high consideration with which I have the honor to be your excellency's very obedient and very humble servant,

JOHN BIGELOW.

His Excellency Mr. DROUYN DE LHUYS,
Minister of Foreign Affairs.

Mr. Seward to Mr. Bigelow.

No. —.]

DEPARTMENT OF STATE,
Washington, June 17, 1865.

SIR: We have received a complaint from our commander at Brownsville, that General Mejia, the officer in command at Matamoras, had received from the rebel commander a quantity of cannon and other public property. It is understood that this complaint is to be followed by another, that the French authorities at Matamoras have also received into their service a large detachment of late rebel soldiers, with their arms. Circumstances indicate a growing disposition in some quarters of this country to find or make a *casus belli* with a view of the political situation of Mexico. I think it would be well for you, in an informal and confidential manner, to let the French government understand the great importance, as we think, of the practice on their part of the most just and friendly disposition towards the United States by the French authorities in Mexico, as well as in the shaping of French policies towards that country.

Prompt and punctual attention to this subject will be of most essential importance.

I am, sir, your obedient servant,

WILLIAM H. SEWARD.

JOHN BIGELOW, Esq., *&c., &c., &c.*

Mr. Bigelow to Mr. Seward.

No. 120.]

LEGATION OF THE UNITED STATES,
Paris, June 21, 1865.

SIR: I have the honor to transmit to you enclosure No. 1, a copy, and in enclosure No. 2, a translation, of a despatch received from his excellency M. Drouyn de Lhuys, in reply to my communication to him of the 12th instant, a copy of which was communicated to you in my despatch No. 117.

I am, sir, with great respect, your obedient servant,

JOHN BIGELOW.

Hon. WILLIAM H. SEWARD,
Secretary of State, &c., &c., &c.

[Enclosure No. 2.—Translation.]

Mr. Drouyn de L'huys to Mr. Bigelow.

PARIS, *June* 17, 1865.

SIR: I received the letter which you did me the honor of addressing me on the 12th of this month. You were so kind on the occasion of some remarks that were made in the corps legislatif, during the session on the 9th, by the minister of state, and of a note published in the Moniteur of the 10th, to recall to me the declarations which you had formerly made with regard to Mexico, and the withdrawal of the quality of belligerents from the seceded States.

"What I did write," you say respecting Mexico, "was that now that the experiment had been begun, the Americans wished it to be fully tried under circumstances best calculated to determine finally and forever whether European systems of government suited the Mexican people best. If it should appear that they did, and public tranquillity was restored, no nation was more interested in such a result than her immediate neighbors. I added, that the success of republican institutions in the Spanish American states had thus far not been such as to encourage us to attempt the propagation of them there, otherwise than by our example, and that whatever government was acceptable to the Mexican people would be satisfactory to us."

In the matter of withdrawing from the confederates the quality of belligerents, the following is, you tell me, the language which you employed in your letter of the 29th of May:

"The United States government in applying for a repeal of the declaration of June, 1861, abandoned any of the rights of a belligerent which it is presumed to have claimed, and became directly responsible for anything it might do in the character of a belligerent.

"If, after the withdrawal of the imperial declaration, it were to visit and search a neutral vessel, it would at once expose itself to reprisals, the same as for any other violation of international comity."

Feeling as you do, sir, that a theoretic discussion of these two points would now be of no practical interest, I thank you for having recalled to me the exact language of those declarations which you have had the goodness to make me.

Accept the assurances of the high consideration with which I have the honor to be, sir, your very humble and very obedient servant,

DROUYN DE LHUYS.

Mr. BIGELOW,
Minister of the United States at Paris.

Mr. Hunter to Mr. Bigelow.

No. 184.]

DEPARTMENT OF STATE,
Washington, June 26, 1865.

SIR: I have to acknowledge the receipt of your despatch of the 13th instant, No. 117, transmitting a copy of your note of the day before to Mr. Drouyn de Lhuys, correcting certain mistakes which had occurred in representing what you had said and written in regard, respectively, to the position of the United States as to the Mexican question and the revocation of the French decree concerning so-called belligerent rights of the insurgents.

I am happy to inform you that your note is fully approved.

I am, sir, your obedient servant,

W. HUNTER,
Acting Secretary.

JOHN BIGELOW, Esq., *&c., &c., &c., Paris.*

Mr. Bigelow to Mr. Seward.

No. 133.]

LEGATION OF THE UNITED STATES,
Paris, June 29, 1865.

SIR: In the course of an interview to-day with the minister of foreign affairs his excellency referred to reclamations made by our government of the arms and equipment of a fort in Texas, which had been bought by the Mexican

General Mejia from certain confederate officers after capitulation of the corps d'armée, to which the garrison of the fort belonged. Mr. Drouyn de Lhuys desired me to say to you that the information which had reached him led him to believe that Major General Mejia had committed an error, and that he had written in that sense to the French minister at Mexico.

I am, sir, with great respect, your very obedient servant,

JOHN BIGELOW.

Hon. WILLIAM H. SEWARD,
Secretary of State, &c., &c., &c.

Mr. Bigelow to Mr. Seward.

No. 134.] LEGATION OF THE UNITED STATES,
Paris, June 30, 1865.

SIR: In a recent conversation with the minister of foreign affairs, his excellency spoke of two subjects which I had instructions to bring to his notice some months since—the case of the federal steamer Ark, seized on the Rio Grande, within Mexican jurisdiction, by confederates from Texas, and sold at Brownsville to Mexicans; and the case of certain deserters from the confederate army, sent back by the Mexican general to the confederate authorities. His excellency then read to me a report on the facts of these two cases, which had been prepared for him in the bureaus of war and marine, to which it had been referred, and offered to send me a copy if I wished it. I said my government would, of course, like to know what defence could be made to its reclamations, that it might know whether they deserved to be prosecuted. He said I should have one to-morrow, with the understanding that it should only be taken for what it was, and not as an official communication of a final determination of the government on those subjects. I told him I would receive it, if he pleased, as a memorandum of a conversation. He said I should receive it to-day. If it comes in time for this mail I will enclose it.

I am, with great respect, your obedient servant,

JOHN BIGELOW.

Hon. WILLIAM H. SEWARD,
Secretary of State, &c., &c., &c.

Mr. Seward to Mr. Bigelow.

No. 187.] DEPARTMENT OF STATE,
Washington, June 30, 1865.

SIR: On my resumption of the conduct of this department, after a journey to Auburn, I find your despatch of the 13th of June, No. 117; and I find, also, that it was duly acknowledged by Mr. Hunter, then Acting Secretary of State, in despatch No. 184. So far as it relates to the misapprehension made by Mr. Rouher of your conversation with him in regard to the withdrawal of belligerent rights, there seems to be no reason for special remark. But so far as relates to the condition of affairs in Mexico, I think it important to notice the following passage in your despatch: "What I stated that may have given the impression which has misled the minister of state was this, in brief—that now that the experiment had been begun, the Americans wished it to be fully tried, under circumstances best calculated to determine finally and forever whether European systems of government suited the Mexican people best. If it should appear that they did, and public tranquillity was restored, no nation was more interested in such a result than her immediate neighbors. I added that the success of republican institutions in the Spanish American states had thus far not been such as to encourage us to attempt the propagation of them there, otherwise than by our example, and that whatever government was acceptable to the Mexican people would be satisfactory to us."

It is thought that the argument which you have recited in the passage thus extracted is not warranted by the instructions of this department. It will be well, at your convenience, to make this explanation to Mr. Drouyn de Lhuys. So far as our relations are concerned, what we hold in regard to Mexico is, that France is a belligerent there, in war with the republic of Mexico. We do not enter into the merits of the belligerents, but we practice in regard to the contest the principles of neutrality; and we have insisted on the practice of neutrality by all nations in regard to our civil war. Our friendship towards the republic of Mexico, and our sympathies with the republican system on this continent, as well as our faith and confidence in it, have been continually declared. We do not intervene in foreign wars or foreign politics. Political intervention in the affairs of foreign states is a principle thus far avoided by our government. I attach no great importance to this matter. It is right and proper, however, that the French government should not misunderstand the case, and so be suffered to fall into a belief that we have entertained any views favorable to it as an invader of Mexico, or that we at all distrust the ultimate success of republican systems throughout this continent.

I am, sir, your obedient servant,

WILLIAM H. SEWARD.

JOHN BIGELOW, Esq., *&c., &c., &c.*

Mr. Bigelow to Mr. Seward.

[Extract.]

No. 136.] LEGATION OF THE UNITED STATES,
Paris, July 6, 1865.

SIR: I have received from his excellency the minister of foreign affairs a statement, of which enclosure No. 1 is a copy, and No. 2 a translation.

* * * * * * * * *

This *résumé* is the promised communication referred to in my despatch No. 134.

I am, sir, with great respect, your very obedient servant,

JOHN BIGELOW.

Hon. WILLIAM H. SEWARD,
Secretary of State, &c., &c., &c.

[Translation.]

In a conversation of the 9th of March, and through two notes, one of the same date, and the other of the 15th of March, the minister of the United States pointed out to the minister of foreign affairs of the Emperor, as infractions of Mexican neutrality, in behalf of the confederates, two occurrences that had become known on the Rio Grande and at Matamoras. The steamer Ark, belonging to a citizen of the United States, having stranded in ascending the Rio Grande, above Bagdad, some yards distant from the Mexican shore, was seized, it is said, by the confederates, taken to Brownsville, condemned as a prize, with the cargo, and sold to Mexicans. Then it is asserted that more recently General Mejia, commanding the allied division, arrested at Matamoras thirty deserters of the south, and caused them to be taken under escort to the banks of the Rio Grande to be delivered up to a confederate corps.

The minister, without assuming to prejudge the accuracy of the above facts, replied to Mr.

Bigelow that, in principle, the government of the Emperor would always take into serious consideration any act pointed out as infringing on neutrality. The minister consequently comnicated the above information to his colleagues of the departments of war and marine, and requested them to beg the commandants in chief of our expeditionary corps and naval forces in Mexico to see, as far as it should depend upon them, that no act contrary to neutrality should take place on the Mexican frontier, bordering Texas. M. le Marechal Randon and M. le Marquis de Chasseloup Laubat sent at once to Marshal Bazaine and Commandant Clorié instructions in this sense.

Since then the commandant of our naval subdivision in the Mexican waters transmitted to the minister of marine precise information regarding the occurrences which Mr. Bigelow mentioned to the minister. They show, in the first place, and as we had reason to expect, that the French authorities had no part whatever in it; and further, that the facts did not exactly occur as was reported at Washington.

Thus, the steamer Ark was taken, as stated, by the confederates, but this seizure was effected before the expedition under the guidance of Marshal Bazaine, on the Rio Grande, last year, and when the disaffected under Cortinas were masters of Matamoras and Bagdad. When General Mejia afterwards took possession of Matamoras, in the name of the emperor Maximilian, the vessel was sold to one of its inhabitants, (a German, as we are informed,) but as the vessel was moored before Brownsville, General Mejia did not suspect what had passed in this matter, and that he would have to intervene with respect to the sale. The fact, therefore, could neither be laid to the charge of the Mexican nor of the French authorities.

In the case of the delivering up of southern deserters indicated by the United States minister, it is impossible, if it really did take place, to render any of the French authorities in the smallest degree responsible for it, considering that since the temporary occupation of Bagdad by the crews of the ships placed under the orders of the Admiral Rosse, there was positively no French military either at Bagdad or Matamoras until the second of last May, when the column of the Commandant de Brian was landed. A confederate leader announced that he was going to send back to the Mexican shore four deserters of the foreign legion. The Commandant de Brian could not return them to the Texan shore, after they had been brought over to the Mexican shore. He therefore consented to receive them, but without desiring to have an interview, on this occasion, with the authorities of Brownsville—a misconception of the orders of which they were the bearers having led the Mexican major and the French sergeant who were sent to meet these deserters to cross the stream in order to go in search of them. The sergeant suffered a month's imprisonment, and the major a month's arrest. M. le Commandant de Brian declared at the same time to General Mejia that neither of them should have any intercourse with the authorities of Brownsville; moreover, when the Commandant Florie was informed that they were also about to send back to him two of his sailors who had deserted, he refused to take any steps which should facilitate their delivery.

Mr. Seward to Mr. Bigelow.

No. 192.] DEPARTMENT OF STATE,
Washington, July 6, 1865.

SIR: I transmit a copy of a letter of yesterday, addressed by me to the Secretary of War, and of the telegraphic despatches therein referred to, from Major General Sheridan to Generals Grant and Rawlins; also a copy of a note of the same date, which I addressed to the Marquis de Montholon;* all of which papers relate to the fraudulent and illegal removal of a large portion of the property recently surrendered to the military forces of the United States in Texas, from that State to the Mexican side of the Rio Grande, including the steamer Lucy Given and eight hundred and twenty bales of cotton.

You are requested to make a representation of the facts to be gathered from these papers to Mr. Drouyn de Lhuys, and to protest against the reception within the military lines occupied by French troops in Mexico of any of the property above mentioned, expressing at the same time the expectation of this government that prompt satisfaction thereof will be made to the military authorities of the United States in that vicinity.

You will inform Mr. Drouyn de Lhuys that renewed instructions have been given to the general commanding the United States military forces in Texas to permit no aggressive movements of troops under his command within Mexican territory, unless special instructions to that effect from the War Department should be rendered necessary by a condition of affairs not now anticipated.

I am, sir, your obedient servant,

WILLIAM H. SEWARD.

JOHN BIGELOW, Esq., &c., &c., &c.

OFFICE U. S. MILITARY TELEGRAPH, WAR DEPARTMENT.

The following telegram received in cipher at Washington 5.30 a. m. June 30, 1865:

NEW ORLEANS, LA., *June* 28, 1865.

GENERAL: I have just returned from a hurried trip along the coast of Texas. The following is, to the best of my knowledge, the condition of affairs there: The Kirby Smith and Canby surrender was, for the most part, a swindle on the part of Kirby Smith & Co., as all the Texas troops had disbanded or had been discharged and gone home before the commissioners were sent to General Canby. Kirby Smith, Magruder, Shelby, Slaughter, Walker, and others, of military rank, have gone to Mexico. Everything on wheels, artillery, horses, mules, &c., have been run over into Mexico. Large and small bands of rebel soldiers, and some citizens amounting to about two thousand, have crossed the Rio Grande into Mexico, some allege with the intention of going to Sonora.

The Lucy Given, a small steamer, was surrendered at Matagorda, but was carried off and is now anchored at Bagdad, on the Rio Grande.

There is no doubt in my mind that the representatives of the imperial government along the Rio Grande have encouraged this wholesale plunder of property belonging to the United States government, and that it will only be given up when we go and take it. General Steele says the French officers are very saucy and insulting to our people at Brownsville.

Juarez does not appear to have any force of consequence on the Rio Grande. I cannot hear of any movements. The rebels who have gone to Mexico have sympathies with the imperialists, and this feeling is undoubtedly reciprocated.

I will direct General Steele to make a demand on the French authorities at Matamoras for a return of the property. The Lucy Given is a tangible case.

A Mexican steamer, loaded with cotton and flying the American flag, was captured a few days since between Rio Grande City and Brownsville. After the surrender eight hundred and twenty-six (826) bales of Confederate States cotton, stored at Rio Grande City, were crossed into Mexico, and this is only one item.

There is a good deal of irritation between French officials at Matamoras and our people, and the Maximilian party is getting nervous. My scouts report from Matamoras that seven thousand (7,000) troops are marching from the interior to that place; also that Mejia is working on the rifle-pits around Matamoras. This reported re-enforcement I give for what it is worth.

P. H. SHERIDAN,
Major General Commanding.

Lieutenant General U. S. GRANT,
Commanding Armies United States, Washington, D. C.

Mr. Seward to Mr. Bigelow.

No. 194.] DEPARTMENT OF STATE,
Washington, July 10, 1865.

SIR: Referring to previous instructions on the subject of the fraudulent and illegal removal of property belonging to the United States to the Mexican side of the Rio Grande, I now enclose for your information, and as illustrating the importance of the early attention of the imperial government being given to our demand for the restoration of that property to the authorities of this government, a copy of a telegram of the 6th instant from Major General Sheridan to General Rawlins, chief of staff of Lieutenant General Grant.

I am, sir, your obedient servant,

WILLIAM H. SEWARD.

JOHN BIGELOW, Esq., &c., &c., &c.

---

* This enclosure appears in the correspondence with the French legation.

OFFICE U. S. MILITARY TELEGRAPH, WAR DEPARTMENT.

The following telegram received in cipher at Washington, 3 a. m. July 8, 1865:

HEADQUARTERS MILITARY DIVISION OF THE GULF,
New Orleans, July 6, 1865.

GENERAL: Affairs on the Rio Grande frontier are getting beautifully mixed up. Cortinas has arrived, and now has his headquarters six miles from Matamoras, and has driven in Mejia's pickets. He also captured the steamer Senorita and took her over to the other side of the river for safety, and she was taken down to Rio Grande City and seized by General Brown. I do not know exactly how it is as yet.

Mejia replied to General Steele's demand for battery and other property taken across the Rio Grande, that he had no authority to comply with the demand, but would refer it to the imperial government. This is just what I expected, and only confirms my former impression, that the property can only be obtained when we go and take it.

General Steele says the French officers and soldiers are very bitter against our people, and writes me that a grandson of Marshal Ney, with two thousand French cavalry, is reported approaching Matamoras, and that he is very bitter, and says he is going to invade Texas. The feeling of the people in the interior of Mexico is very bitter, while the natives, soldiers and all, are said to be with our government, and want to get rid of French rule. Ringgold barracks is occupied by our troops.

P. H. SHERIDAN,
Major General Commanding.

General JOHN A. RAWLINS, *Chief of Staff.*

Mr. Bigelow to Mr. Seward.

No. 140.] LEGATION OF THE UNITED STATES,
Paris, July 11, 1865.

SIR: His excellency the minister of foreign affairs has sent me the accompanying correspondence between him and the late minister of war, in explanation of the alleged purchase by General Mejia of guns and munitions of war from the confederates at Brownsville after their capitulation.

I am, sir, with great respect, your obedient servant,

JOHN BIGELOW.

Hon. WILLIAM H. SEWARD,
Secretary of State.

[Enclosure No. 1.—Translation.]

The Minister for Foreign Affairs to his excellency Marshal Randon, minister of war.

PARIS, *June* 29, 1865.

MARSHAL AND DEAR COLLEAGUE: A despatch I received from our minister to the United States points out an incident which I hasten to mention to you. According to official intelligence received at Washington, at the time when the confederate corps which occupied Brownsville, in Texas, surrendered to the federal forces, the artillery and munitions shut up in the fort were in part clandestinely taken to the Mexican bank of the Rio Grande and delivered to the authorities of Matamoras. Informed to-day only of this fact, the government of the United States asks for the prompt restitution of material which should have been delivered to it at Brownsville; and the Secretary of State, Mr. Seward, has requested the Marquis de Montholon to engage himself in obtaining this restitution. Mr. de Montholon considering, very justly, that the reclamation was thoroughly well grounded, (if the facts are correctly stated,) promptly deferred to the request of Mr. Seward, and wrote about it to Marshal Bazaine, and to General Mejia, who was in command at Matamoras at the latest dates. This affair may, therefore, already have received, without further delay, a satisfactory solution. It might, however, be otherwise, and, on this supposition, I turn to you, asking you to send directly to Marshal Bazaine, by the courier of to-morrow, 30th, the necessary orders that he may contribute, if there still be need, and he has the means, to the prompt return of the *materiel* reclaimed. I write myself to our minister, Mr. Dano, that he may equally press upon the Mexican government the necessity of doing right, if satisfaction has not already been given to the request of the federal government.

[Enclosure No. 2.—Translation.]

The Minister of War to his excellency the Minister for Foreign Affairs.

PARIS, *July* 1, 1865.

MR. MINISTER AND DEAR COLLEAGUE: Your excellency has done me the honor to communicate to me, by your letter of June 29, last, the reclamation which the government of the United States set up on the subject of the artillery and munitions belonging to the fort at Brownsville, which were clandestinely transported to the Mexican bank of the Rio Grande by the confederates, with the purpose of keeping them from the federal forces.

I hasten to write by the courier of yesterday, June 30, to Marshal de Bazaine, to request him to give immediately instructions to General Mejia, commanding at Matamoras, to assure, if it has not already been done, the prompt return of the *materiel* reclaimed by the government of the United States.

Mr. Bigelow to Mr. Seward.

No. 145.] LEGATION OF THE UNITED STATES,
Paris, July 14, 1865.

SIR: I have the honor to enclose—

1st. A copy of the note by which his excellency the minister of foreign affairs acknowledged the receipt of the President's proclamation of the 23d of June last, terminating the blockade; and

2d. A translation of an article in the official paper in reference to the manner in which the withdrawal of belligerent rights from the confederates had been received in the United States, coupled with some remarks on the attitude of the United States towards France in Mexico. This article marks an important change in the tone of the Moniteur, and all the official press of the empire will feel the effect of it.

I am, sir, with great respect, your very obedient servant,

JOHN BIGELOW.

Hon. WILLIAM H. SEWARD,
Secretary of State.

[Enclosure No. 2.—Translation.]

We now know the impression produced in the United States by the decision of the Emperor's government to revoke the measures which had been adopted in our ports at the beginning of the insurrection of the south, in conformity with the ordinary rules of neutrality.

The Washington cabinet does full justice to the sentiments of which France has given proof in removing the restrictions upon the federal navy which resulted from those rules, and in ceasing to recognize in the confederate ships the character of belligerents. It has been pleased to see that the imperial government has been guided by a sincere desire to revive the ancient sympathies of the two peoples, whose reciprocal interests as well as their traditions invite them to cultivate the most cordial relations.

France, in her turn, finds nothing but what is praiseworthy in the attitude of the United States. The federal government has not hesitated to take the necessary measures to prevent the manœuvres of the agents of Juarez.

President Johnson shows himself resolved to enforce the loyal observance of the law relative to enrolments, and the instructions given on this subject to the judicial authorities are being executed.

So, as we said about two months ago, the Washington cabinet, a little before the death of Mr. Lincoln, had declared that it ought in no manner to create difficulties in the way of France in embarrassing the establishment of a regular government in Mexico.

Under the new President the American cabinet has remained faithful to these assurances, and its conduct, like its language, testify more and more strongly to its intention not to depart from them.

Mr. Seward to Mr. Bigelow.

No. 200.] DEPARTMENT OF STATE,
Washington, July 17, 1865.

SIR: I have to acknowledge the receipt of your despatch of the 30th ultimo, No. 134, relative to your conversation with the minister of foreign affairs upon the subjects of the steamer Ark and the deserters from the insurgent forces who were sent back by the Mexican general to the insurgents.

I observe that the paper, a copy of which was promised to you by his excellency, did not come. I understand from the Marquis de Montholon that he has papers on the same subject from Mexico. It is to be desired that there may be no unnecessary delay or controversy on the subject.

I am, sir, your obedient servant,

WILLIAM H. SEWARD.

JOHN BIGELOW, Esq., *&c., &c., &c.*

Mr. Seward to Mr. Bigelow.

No. 201.] DEPARTMENT OF STATE,
Washington, July 17, 1865.

SIR: I have to acknowledge the receipt of your despatch of the 29th ultimo, No. 133, informing me of the course pursued by Mr. Drouyn de Lhuys, in regard to the purchase by the Mexican General Mejia, from insurgent officers, of the arms and equipment of a fort in Texas.

I am, sir, your obedient servant,

WILLIAM H. SEWARD.

JOHN BIGELOW, Esq., *&c., &c., &c.*

Mr. Seward to Mr. Bigelow.

No. 205.] DEPARTMENT OF STATE,
Washington, July 22, 1865.

SIR: I transmit a copy of a letter of the 12th instant, and of the accompanying papers, addressed to this department by the Acting Assistant Secretary of War, on the subject of affairs on the Rio Grande.

You will bring to the notice of Mr. Drouyn de Lhuys the important statements contained in these papers, viz: the opinion expressed by General Mejia that there is a recognizable rebel party in Texas, and that a design is entertained in Mexico to produce an uprising against the United States in Texas, with a view to its annexation to Mexico, or at least to co-operate in maintaining the government of Maximilian. You ask the proper explanations on this subject without unnecessary delay.

I am, sir, your obedient servant,

WILLIAM H. SEWARD.

JOHN BIGELOW, Esq., *&c., &c., &c.*

Mr. Eckert to Mr. Seward.

WAR DEPARTMENT, *Washington City, July 12, 1865.*

SIR: I am instructed by the Secretary of War to transmit, for your information, copies of certain papers relative to the condition of affairs on the Mexican frontier, forwarded to this department by Major General P. H. Sheridan, commanding the military division of the southwest.

I have the honor to be, sir, your obedient servant,

THOMAS F. ECKERT,
Acting Assistant Secretary of War.

Hon. WILLIAM H. SEWARD, *Secretary of State.*

General Brown to Lieutenant Colonel Canby.

HEADQUARTERS UNITED STATES FORCES,
Brazos St. Jago, Texas, May 24, 1865.

COLONEL: I have the honor to report that I visited Bagdad, Mexico, yesterday, and had a personal interview with General Mejia, commanding the imperial forces on the Rio Grande. The General expressed a feeling of kindness towards the government of the United States, and a wish to preserve such a policy as would insure an impartial action upon the troops under his command, between the government of the United States and the rebels, or confederates, as he termed them. He still held to the opinion that, notwithstanding the surrender of the enemy on the east side of the Mississippi river, the rebels in Texas were a recognizable power. I had reliable information that the enemy had practically evacuated Brownsville, but General Mejia professed not to know anything about it, though the property of the confederate government had been sent over to Matamoras. I am informed, from a source I deem reliable, that General Slaughter has permission from General Mejia to cross into Mexico with his troops at any time when he may deem it necessary to do so; though this is not to be considered as being strictly official information. From all I can learn, the rebels, who intend to continue the contest against the government, are the friends, and are co-operating with the imperial government of Mexico. The peace party and friends of the government of the United States in Texas are the friends of the liberal government or party in that State. This confirms the information I had the honor to transmit in my despatch of the 23d instant.

On the 14th instant a body of troops from this post, who were marching up the east bank of the Rio Grande, were fired upon from the Mexican side. Upon its being reported to General Mejia he promptly disapproved of the act, and I am informed that he arrested three men who were reported to have been guilty of this breach of neutrality, and that he has ordered them to be shot to-morrow morning. An application to supply my command with beef-cattle and horses from Mexico has received the approval of the Mexican commander, but, notwithstanding these acts of apparent fairness, I am of the opinion that one of the strongest influences that are brought to bear upon the people of western Mexico, to induce them to support the imperial government, is that Texas is to be again annexed to that government, or that a protectorate is to be extended over it. I submit these facts for the consideration of the major general commanding.

I am, very truly, your obedient servant,

E. B. BROWN,
Brigadier General Volunteers, Commanding.

Lieutenant Colonel J. S. CANBY,
Assistant Adjutant General, Department Gulf, New Orleans.

General Brown to Colonel Crosby.

HEADQUARTERS UNITED STATES FORCES,
Brazos St. Jago, Texas, May 28, 1865.

COLONEL: I have the honor to report that I have received information that the rebels at Brownsville have broken up, after imprisoning their general (Slaughter) and forcing him to divide the money in his possession. Slaughter has sent the arms and ordnance stores into Matamoras and sold them to the imperial government. Such is the report.

I have ordered the 34th Indiana, and 62d A. D. C., with two pieces of artillery that I have fitted up in an imperfect manner, and to be drawn by mules, across the Boca Chica, and intend to move to White Ranche this evening, and to Brownsville to-morrow.

I shall increase the force, if I deem it necessary, and shall take the command in person.

I am, very truly, your obedient servant,

E. B. BROWN,
Brigadier General Volunteers, Commanding.

Colonel J. SCHUYLER CROSBY,
Assistant Adjutant General, Department Gulf, New Orleans.

General Brown to Colonel Crosby.

HEADQUARTERS UNITED STATES FORCES,
Brownsville, Texas, June 2, 1865.

COLONEL: I have the honor to trans[illegible] information of the major general commanding, the enclosed copies of a correspondence between General Mejia and myself. When the rebels evacuated this post the guard of citizens that was formed to protect their property was claimed to be a liberal company from Mexico, and, consequently, the representative of the imperial government was apprehensive of aggressive action on the part of my command.

The apprehension was increased by the menacing attitude of Negreta and Cortina, who are constantly harassing the imperial forces, and, probably, more from a feeling that the receiving artillery, marked U. S., from the rebel general Slaughter, and the extraordinary relations that have existed for the past four months between the rebels and the imperial government, had placed the representatives of that government in a questionable position. Under these circumstances, I thought proper to forward the letter enclosed, in order to allay the undue alarm that was manifesting itself at Matamoras.

I am, very truly, your obedient servant,

E. B. BROWN,
Brigadier General Commanding.

Lieutenant Colonel SCHUYLER CROSBY,
Acting Assistant Adjutant General, Department of the Gulf, New Orleans.

General Brown to General Mejia.

HEADQUARTERS UNITED STATES FORCES,
Brownsville, Texas, May 31, 1865.

GENERAL: In order that you may be informed of the desire on the part of the government of the United States to preserve amicable relations with the republic of Mexico, I have the honor to transmit the following extract from the instructions from the Secretary of State to the commanding officer of the department of the Gulf, and which has been furnished to me for my guidance while in command of the Rio Grande.

[Extract.]

"You have already found that the confusion resulting from civil strife and foreign war in Mexico offers seductions for military enterprise. I have, therefore, to inform you of the exact condition of our relations towards the republic at the present time. We are on terms of amity and friendship, and maintaining diplomatic relations with the republic of Mexico. We regard that country as the theatre of a foreign war, mingled with civil strife. In the conflict we take no part, and, on the contrary, we practice absolute non-intervention and non-interference. In command of the frontier, it will devolve on you, as far as practicable, consistently with your other functions, to prevent aid or supplies being given from the United States to either belligerent."

I am aware, general, that the fact that this town, immediately preceding its occupation by the troops under my command, was, in a measure, protected by persons inimical to the imperial government of Mexico, and the necessity that exists for the employment of men of this class in my operation against the bands of rebels in the country may be construed into a belligerent feeling towards your government.

I beg leave to assure you that such is not the case, and I repeat to you, formally, what I said in our conversation at Bagdad, that the troops under my command will not be permitted, in any manner, to interfere in the present relations of Mexico.

The same assurance has been given to members of the liberal party of Mexico, now residing at this post.

With considerations of respect, I am, general, your obedient servant,

E. B. BROWN,
Brigadier General Commanding.

Major General MEJIA,
Commanding Matamoras, Mexico.

General Canedo to General Osterhaus.

MATAMORAS, MEXICO, *June* 4, 1865.

GENERAL: In accordance with your instructions I arrived here a few days since, and have had but little of importance to communicate upon the L. S. project as yet. I would beg leave to recall to the recollection of the general-in-chief that I mentioned Mr. J. A. Quintero as one of the parties concerned in the affair, and that he had had an interview with Marshal Bazaine, in January last, in relation to it. Mr. Quintero was here last week in close conference with General Mejia, and returned again immediately to Monterey, and will be here again in a week. He is ostensibly enlisted in the imperial cause, but in reality is working for an uprising in Texas, the French and Mexicans to hold the frontier.

Of the other parties concerned in the enterprise two have gone to Europe, and one was heard of in Montgomery, two hours before General Wilson's entry into that place, endeavoring to purchase horses to go to Texas. One is now in San Antonio, and when I see Mr. Quintero I will know what is expected of me.

The citizens and foreign residents of this place are wholly enlisted in the imperial cause. Fortifications are being thrown up from bank to bank, encircling the city. There are thirty-five guns now here for defence. There are about six hundred Belgian troops and two battalions of Mexicans here. Four thousand infantry, artillery, and cavalry have just been sent off to Camargo, while two thousand French troops are looked for from the sea-board. A camp of instruction has been established at Monterey. An officer, formerly in the rebel service, is now here engaged in raising a regiment of Texans for service with the imperialists.

To sum up, it seems the enterprise I spoke of has received a sudden shock from the rapid successes of the federal arms, but is by no means extinct. What the delegation now gone to Europe may effect, with those who are to follow, remains to be seen; but certainly the feeling and spirit evinced by the confederates generally, and Texans in particular, is most decidedly in favor of an uprising in Texas, or at least assisting the imperialists against its enemies, particularly the United States.

Very respectfully, your obedient servant,

A. H. CANEDO.

Major General P. J. OSTERHAUS,
Chief of Staff, New Orleans.

Through Brigadier General BROWN,
Commanding United States Forces, Brownsville, Texas.

General Mejia to General Brown.

[Translation.]

No. 180.] MATAMORAS, *May* 31, 1865.

GENERAL: I have the honor to make answer to the note you have been pleased to address to me of this date, to inform me of the wish of the United States in maintaining friendly relations with the republic of Mexico. For this purpose you send me a copy of the instructions which the Secretary of State transmitted to the department of the Gulf, pointing out the neutral course he should observe, in view of the manner in which the United States consider the political situation of Mexico, and the state in which the relations of amity existing between both countries rest.

Allow me, general, to reply with my soldierly frankness. Although I ignore that there exists in Mexico the republic and foreign war, I regard with great interest the friendly sentiments of the United States towards my country, and I esteem at their just value the orders which in this sense emanate from your government.

And what wishes do the government of his Majesty the Emperor Maximilian foster in relation to the United States? I have the honor to transcribe here the following instructions which, in this respect, have been communicated to me by his excellency the marshal commander-in-chief:

"The government of Washington, explaining certain reports which gave room to believe that the authorities at New Orleans, or rather the federal forces in Texas, gave aid against us to some guerillas and dissident chiefs, has given assurance that the instructions sent to the federal authorities prescribed to them the strictest neutrality. It is, therefore, very proper, that in reciprocation we should use all the vigilance possible to prevent the confederates from making in Mexican territory or Mexican waters any attack or movement against their adversaries, or meeting any support, although indirect."

I think it useless to add, general, that I am disposed to comply exactly with the wishes of my government, and that I entertain sufficient confidence that the authorities of the United States will have the will and the power necessary to repress whatever act of hostility might be in preparation against my country within the territory of the Union.

Please accept, general, the assurances of my high esteem.

General MEJIA,
Commanding General, &c., &c.

Brigadier General E. B. BROWN,
Commanding U. S. Forces at Brownsville.

Mr. Seward to Mr. Bigelow.

No. 206.] DEPARTMENT OF STATE,
Washington, July 24, 1865.

SIR: Some observers who possibly are suspicious, but who certainly are known to be shrewd, infer from the tone of the ministerial press, and of that portion of the other press in Italy which more demonstratively sympathizes with the French government, that a project is on foot which contemplates an addition from Italy to the French army now engaged in Mexico, and with a view to hostilities against the United States. It is not believed here that either the Italian or French government entertains such a design. Nevertheless, existing circumstances render it important to the United States to know what measure of truth there is in statements of this character, and certainly it is only dealing justly and properly with the powers concerned, to bring the statements to their knowledge with a view to any explanations they may be prepared to give. I have, therefore, by the President's direction, taken measures to communicate with the government of Italy in an unofficial way, and will thank you to bring the same subject to the notice of Mr. Drouyn de Lhuys in a friendly manner.

I am, sir, your obedient servant,

WILLIAM H. SEWARD.

JOHN BIGELOW, Esq., *&c., &c., &c.*

Mr. Seward to Mr. Bigelow.

No. 207.]

DEPARTMENT OF STATE,
Washington, July 25, 1865.

SIR: Your despatch of the 6th instant, No. 136, with two enclosures, relative to the alleged infringements of neutrality in favor of the insurgents on the Rio Grande, in the case of the steamer Ark, and that of the delivery up of southern deserters to the insurgents, has been received, and will engage attention.

I am, sir, your obedient servant,

WILLIAM H. SEWARD.

JOHN BIGELOW, Esq., *&c., &c., &c.*

Mr. Hunter to Mr. Bigelow.

No. 213.]

DEPARTMENT OF STATE,
Washington, July 28, 1865.

SIR: Your despatch of the 6th of July, enclosing a copy and translation of a statement in regard to the case of the steamer Ark, and to the delivery up by the French troops of a party of insurgent deserters to the insurgent forces in Texas, has been received.

A further inquiry will be made in regard to the steamer, and the statement concerning the deserters will be communicated to the Secretary of War for his information.

I am, sir, your obedient servant,

W HUNTER, *Acting Secretary.*

JOHN BIGELOW, Esq., *&c., &c., &c.*

Mr. Hunter to Mr. Bigelow.

No. 214.]

DEPARTMENT OF STATE,
Washington, July 28, 1865.

SIR: I have to acknowledge the receipt of your despatch of the 11th instant, No. 140, transmitting a copy of correspondence between the minister for foreign affairs and the minister of war, in explanation of the alleged purchase of artillery and munitions by General Mejia from the insurgents at Brownsville, and showing the disapproval of the imperial government of any such transaction. These guns and munitions, probably, have been already restored to the United

States military authorities. Whatever may have been the facts of the transfer, it gives this government great satisfaction to find our confidence in the honorable disposition of France fully confirmed by the correspondence accompanying your despatch.

A copy of your communication has been sent to the Secretary of War for his information.

I am, sir, your obedient servant,

W. HUNTER, *Acting Secretary.*

JOHN BIGELOW, Esq., *&c.*, *&c.*, *&c.*

Mr. Hunter to Mr. Bigelow.

No. 215.] DEPARTMENT OF STATE,
Washington, July 31, 1865.

SIR: I enclose a translation of a note of the 4th instant,* and a copy of the accompaniments to which it refers, addressed to this department by Mr. Romero, the envoy extraordinary and minister plenipotentiary of the Mexican republic accredited to this government, relative to a supposed understanding between the insurgent commanders in Texas and the French commander in the adjacent quarter of Mexico, and to an alleged co-operation between them, for the purpose of preventing the recovery of Matamoras from its present possession. Supposing the papers referred to in Mr. Romero's communication to be genuine, they seem to require explanation to the French authorities, which you will consequently request of Mr. Drouyn de Lhuys.

I am, sir, your obedient servant,

W. HUNTER, *Acting Secretary.*

JOHN BIGELOW, Esq., *&c.*, *&c.*, *&c.*

Mr. Seward to Mr. Bigelow.

No. 216.] DEPARTMENT OF STATE,
Washington, July 31, 1865.

SIR: Your despatch of the 14th instant, No. 145, and its enclosures, have been received. The information which you give of the friendly change in the tone of the French journals is very satisfactory.

I am, sir, your obedient servant,

W. HUNTER, *Acting Secretary.*

JOHN BIGELOW, Esq., *&c.*, *&c.*, *&c.*

Mr. Bigelow to Mr. Seward.

No. 154.] LEGATION OF THE UNITED STATES,
Paris, August 5, 1865.

SIR: Referring to your despatch No. 192, I have the honor to transmit herewith, in three enclosures, copies of a letter upon the subject-matter of that despatch addressed by me to his excellency the minister of foreign affairs on the 26th ultimo, and a copy and translation of his reply received yesterday.

I am, sir, with great respect, your very obedient servant,

JOHN BIGELOW.

Hon. WILLIAM H. SEWARD,
Secretary of State, &c., &c., &c.

---

*For enclosures see Mr. Romero's note of the 4th of July.

[Enclosure No. 1.]

Mr. Bigelow to Mr. M. Drouyn de Lhuys.

LEGATION OF THE UNITED STATES,
Paris, July 26, 1865.

SIR: Referring to a conversation which I had the honor to hold with your excellency on the 6th instant, in reference to the delivery of cannon and other munitions of war by some of the rebel commanders in Texas to the Mexican general commanding at Matamoras, and referring also to the very satisfactory communication which I had the honor subsequently to receive from the Emperor's government upon the subject, it becomes my duty to invite your excellency's attention to the following supplementary representations.

Authentic information has reached my government that most of the rebel leaders of military rank in Texas, including Generals Smith, Magruder, Shelby, Slaughter, and Walker, together with numerous large and small bands of rebel soldiers and citizens, amounting to two thousand in number, crossed the Rio Grande and found asylum in Mexico after the capitulation of the insurgent commander; that everything on wheels, artillery, horses, mules, in fact all the public property that could be moved, were also carried over the border after the capitulation, but before the United States forces could occupy the country; that among other things thus carried away, of which information has reached me since I had the honor of bringing these border difficulties to your excellency's attention, was the steamer "Lucy Given," or "Gwin," which was surrendered at Matagorda and is now anchored at Bagdad, on the Rio Grande; and some 850 bales of cotton which were included in the capitulation and stored at Rio Grande City.

I regret to add that it is the impression of the federal general commanding that division of our army that persons calling themselves the representatives of the imperial government of Mexico have encouraged this extensive plunder of property belonging to the United States government, and also that the French officers in that vicinity have incurred the reproach of being very unfriendly and offensive in their bearing towards the citizens of the United States at Brownsville.

I hasten to bring these facts to your excellency's attention, in order, first, that the directions given by his excellency the minister of war, referred to in his communication to your excellency bearing date July 1st, may be extended, if not sufficiently comprehensive already, so as to insure the prompt restoration of the steamer "Lucy Given," or "Gwin," the 850 bales of cotton taken from Rio Grande City, as well as the artillery, carriages, horses, mules, &c., previously taken away by the rebels and their abettors; and, secondly, that all persons under the control of the Emperor's government may be instructed to avoid, as much as possible, a language or demeanor calculated to aggravate the difficulties of preserving peace on a frontier at the confluence of so many irritating influences. Animated by the spirt with which it is hoped this request will be received, my government has issued renewed instructions to the general commanding the United States military forces in Texas "to permit no aggressive movements of troops under his command within Mexican territory, unless under special instructions to that effect from the War Department, which shall be rendered necessary by a condition of affairs not now anticipated."

I pray your excellency to accept assurances of the high consideration with which I have the honor to be,

Your excellency's very obedient and very humble servant,

JOHN BIGELOW.

His Excellency Monsieur DROUYN DE LHUYS,
Minister of Foreign Affairs.

[Enclosure No. 3.—Translation.]

Mr. Drouyn de Lhuys to Mr. Bigelow.

PARIS, *August* 1, 1865.

SIR: I have received the note which you did me the honor to address to me on the 26th ultimo, concerning certain facts said to have occurred on the frontiers of Texas and Mexico, and to be of a nature to attract the attention of the government of the Emperor.

You recall on this occasion the communications which passed between us in reference to a similar incident, namely, the delivery of the artillery of Brownsville to the authorities at Matamoras. Information recently received in France, and which was reproduced in the newspapers, has made known to us the satisfactory solution given to that affair. Before our instructions, recommending the restoration of this property to the federal authorities, had time to reach Mexico, General Mejia had, of his own accord, ordered its surrender to the commander at Brownsville. This voluntary decision shows dispositions which, I doubt not, will be appreciated by the cabinet at Washington. The same information states, moreover, that the most friendly relations had been established between the military commanders of the United States and of Mexico in that part of the frontiers of the two countries.

You do me the honor to mention to me, in your communication of July 26, the passing over into the Mexican territory of a certain number of confederate generals, who, with some two thousand persons, soldiers, and others, are said to have, after the capitulation, crossed the Rio Grande, taking with them their artillery, horses, mules, &c., all of which were the property of the federal government.

I am not yet in a position to offer you any explanations on this point; but, from what we know of the views of the Mexican government, those proceedings would be entirely contrary to its intentions.

As for the steamer Lucy Given, or Gwin, and the 850 bales of cotton included in the capitulation, which are said to have been transferred to Mexican territory, I am also obliged to wait, before answering your demand, for the information which I have asked, both from the French military authorities and from the government of Mexico.

Accept assurances of the high consideration with which I have the honor to be, sir, your very humble and very obedient servant,

DROUYN DE LHUYS.

Mr. BIGELOW,
Minister of the United States, &c., &c., &c., Paris.

Mr. Seward to Mr. Bigelow.

No. 234.] DEPARTMENT OF STATE,
Washington, August 25, 1865.

SIR: I have to acknowledge the receipt of your despatch No. 154, of the 5th instant, which is accompanied by a copy of the correspondence which passed between yourself and Mr. Drouyn de Lhuys upon the subject of certain property, belonging to the United States, which was delivered by the insurgents in Texas to the general commanding at Matamoras. Your proceedings therein recited are fully approved. As far as relates to the affair at Matamoras, the action of the French government is satisfactory.

I am, sir, your obedient servant,

WILLIAM H. SEWARD.

JOHN BIGELOW, Esq., &c., &c., &c.

Mr. Bigelow to Mr. Seward.

No. 166.] LEGATION OF THE UNITED STATES,
Paris, August 31, 1865.

SIR: At my interview with Mr. Drouyn de Lhuys to-day, and after disposing of the matters referred to in my despatch of this date, marked "confidential," I alluded to the unhappy consequences of M. Rouher's attempt in the corps legislatif to quote from a conversation which had passed between Mr. Drouyn de Lhuys and myself in reference to Mexico. I expressed my regret that I had not then availed myself of his offer to make a correction in the Moniteur of the minister of state's statement, and then remarked that the speech in question had given such importance to our correspondence as to render it necessary for you to define with greater precision than I, in a somewhat desultory conversation, had deemed it necessary to do, the attitude which the United States occupied in reference to France and Mexico. I then read to him your despatch No. 187.

Mr. Drouyn de Lhuys said, by way of comment, that France neither asked nor expected from the United States anything more than neutrality in reference to Mexico—at least for the moment; that you had insisted that Mr. Davis, though occupying a large territory with a large army, was not a belligerent; and you now insist that Juarez, without an army and without a government that any one could find, represented the sovereign power of Mexico. He did not agree with you on either of these points, but he could not object to your holding these views. As long as we observed the neutrality promised in your despatch, he felt that we were doing all they had a right to require of us. In regard to your letter, he said he did not see that it differed materially from what I had represented; that I had never pretended that the people of the United States were not more partial to a republican than to a monarchical form of government, nor had he ever supposed the contrary, but he could not suppose that we would prefer to perpetuate brigandage and misrule, under the name of republicanism, rather than have order and security in Mexico, even under a monarchical form of government.

Here, owing to the lateness of the hour and an interruption, it was necessary to bring our interview to a rather premature close, to my regret. There were several points raised in the course of his conversation to-day on which I would have liked to return, but must trust to some future opportunity for that satisfaction.

Meantime I remain, sir, your very obedient and very humble servant,

JOHN BIGELOW.

Hon. WILLIAM H. SEWARD,
Secretary of State, Washington.

Mr. Seward to Mr. Bigelow.

[Extract.]

No. 259.] DEPARTMENT OF STATE,
Washington, September 6, 1865.

SIR: I have submitted to the President the letter which you wrote at Dieppe on the 21st of August, and which was marked unofficial. In that letter you discuss at large the present aspect of the relations between the United States and France as they are affected by the situation in Mexico.

On this subject this government does not think itself called upon to volunteer opinions, counsel, or advice, or gratuitously to offer explanations to the governments of Europe. On the contrary, we have been content to stand upon what we have already very frequently set forth, while every proper care has been taken to prevent or allay irritations which might tend to bring about unexpected and undesired collisions. It is possible, however, that the French government may think it proper to ask you for explanations to some extent of the President's opinions and policy.

This paper is intended to enable you, in such a case, to submit to the imperial government, in an earnest and yet altogether friendly manner, certain views which the President has taken of the political situation in Mexico. Those views are by no means new, and they are as distinct and full as the present condition of the question involved enables us to express.

It can hardly be deemed necessary to repeat on this occasion what has been so often and so constantly avowed by this government, namely, that the people of the United States cherish a traditional friendship towards France. We also habitually indulge a conviction that the existence of friendly relations between the United States and France is by no means unfavorable to the interests of that great nation. These sentiments have survived the many interesting national changes which, during the present century, have occurred in the two countries concerned, and they may therefore be deemed to be independent of all merely partisan or dynastic influences in the one country or in the other.

It is perceived with much regret that an apparent if not a real, a future if not an immediate, antagonism between the policies of the two nations seems to reveal itself in the situation of Mexico before mentioned. The United States have at no time left it doubtful that they prefer to see a domestic and republican system of government prevail in Mexico rather than any other system. This preference results from the fact that the Constitution of the United States itself is domestic and republican, and from a belief that not only its constituent parts ought to preserve the same form and character, but that, so far as is practically and justly attainable by the exercise of moral influences, the many American states by which the United States are surrounded shall be distinguished by the same peculiarities of government. I think it not improper to add, that although the Constitution of this government and the habits of the American people formed under it disincline us from political propagandism, and although they still more strongly disincline us from seeking aggrandizement by means of military conquest, yet that the nation has, at various times since its organization, found it necessary for expansion, and that the like necessity may reasonably be expected to occur hereafter. That expansion has thus far been effected by the annexation of adjacent peoples, who have come into the Union through their own consent as constituent republican States under the Constitution of the United States. To these two facts may be added the general one that peace and friendship between the United States and other nations on this continent, and, consequently, the advance of civilization in this hemisphere, seem to us more likely to be secured when the other American states assimilate to our own.

It is hardly necessary for me to indicate wherein the present attitude and proceedings of the French government in regard to Mexico seem to be variant from the policy and sentiments of the United States which I have thus described. I may remark, however, in general terms, that France appears to us to be lending her great influence, with a considerable military force, to destroy the domestic republican government in Mexico, and to establish there an imperial system under the sovereignty of an European prince, who, until he assumed the crown, was a stranger to that country.

We do not insist or claim that Mexico and the other states on the American continent shall adopt the political institutions to which we are so earnestly attached, but we do hold that the peoples of those countries are entitled to exercise the freedom of choosing and establishing institutions like our own, if they are preferred. In no case can we in any way associate ourselves with efforts of any party or nation to deprive the people of Mexico of that privilege.

Passing by all historical questions connected with the subject as not now necessarily requiring discussion, I have next to remark that this government finds itself neither less obliged nor less disposed at the present moment than it has hitherto been to adhere to its settled policy. Perhaps the French government may be supposed to have taken notice of the fact that, owing to the popular character of our government, our national policy is not adopted from the choice of any President or any particular administration, and that, on the contrary, every important or cardinal policy is a result of the determination of the national will legally expressed in the manner appointed and prescribed by the Constitution. Experience has shown that, in every case, any policy which has arisen from such popular sources, and which has been perseveringly supported by the general national conviction through a long series of years, has been found to be essential to the safety and welfare of the Union.

The intense popular interest which was awakened by the prevalence of a civil war of vast proportions during a few years past has tended in some degree to moderate the solicitude which the situation of foreign affairs was calculated to create; but that interest is now rapidly subsiding, and it may be reasonably anticipated that henceforth the Congress of the United States and the people in their primary assemblies will give a very large share of attention to questions of extraneous character, and chief among these is likely to be that of our relations towards France with regard to Mexico. Nor does it seem unwise to take into consideration the fact that the presence of military forces of the two nations, sometimes confronting each other across the border, has a tendency, which both of them may well regret, to produce irritation and annoyance. The French government has not shown itself inattentive to this inconvenience hitherto, while this government has been desirous to practice equal prudence But a time seems to have come when both nations may well consider whether the permanent interests of international peace and friendship do not require the exercise of a thoughtful and serious attention to the political questions to which I have thus adverted.

* * * * * * *

I am, sir, your obedient servant,

WILLIAM H. SEWARD.

JOHN BIGELOW, Esq., *&c.*, *&c.*, *&c.*

Mr. Seward to Mr. Bigelow.

No. 263]

DEPARTMENT OF STATE,
Washington, September 13, 1865.

SIR: I transmit a copy of a correspondence between this department and the minister of France, in regard to the case of the United States merchant steamer Sonora, now in the port of Tampico, in the hands of insurgents, and the restoration of which to her proper owner, Mr. F. Clavel, of New Orleans, is sought by this government.* I also transmit a copy of a despatch of the 24th of June last, No. 24, from Franklin Chase, esq., United States consul general at Tampico.

You will be pleased to lay the facts of the case before the imperial government, and to request that French agents at Tampico may be instructed to do what they properly can towards enabling Mr. Clavel to recover his property.

I am, sir, your obedient servant,

WILLIAM H. SEWARD.

JOHN BIGELOW, Esq., *&c.*, *&c.*, *&c.*

Mr. Chase to Mr. Hunter.

No. 24.]

UNITED STATES CONSULATE GENERAL,
Tampico, June 27, 1865.

SIR I have the honor to enclose herewith copies of the correspondence passed between this consulate and the prefecto politico of this district, in relation to the steamer Sonora, to which I beg to invite your attention.

The steamer Granite City, formerly belonging to our navy, which came into this port as a blockade runner, late in the month of March last, under the name of Three Marys, displaying the secession flag, is still in this port; also the steamer Jeannette, under British colors. These three vessels are the last of the arrivals from the coast of Texas.

Presuming that the movements of the Granite City might be of interest to our government, I reported her presence here to the honorable the Secretary of the Navy, in my despatches to that functionary, dated respectively 10th and 17th ultimo.

The feeling in this place is still so much in favor of the late southern insurrection, that I have but little or no hopes of anything favorable resulting from my interference in the case of the Sonora, and I would respectfully suggest that a vessel-of-war should be sent here forthwith, to demand her immediate restoration to her owner.

I am, with great respect, sir, your most obedient servant,

FRANKLIN CHASE.

Hon. WILLIAM HUNTER,
Acting Secretary of State, Washington, D. C.

---

*This enclosure appears in correspondence with the French legation.

No. 1.

Mr. Chase to the Prefecto Politico.

UNITED STATES CONSULATE GENERAL,
Tampico, June 20, 1865.

SIR: I have the honor to acquaint you that the steamer which arrived in this port on the 12th instant, from the coast of Texas, under the assumption of British nationality, is in reality the American steamer Sonora, belonging to Felix Clavel, esq., of the city of New Orleans, where she was duly and properly documented; but while in the prosecution of a legal trading voyage from New Orleans to Matamoras, she was unlawfully captured when at anchor in the waters of Brazos, by a boat with a crew of armed men, who overpowered the captain and crew, and escaped with her to the coast of Texas, then in possession of the so-called confederate forces.

As a matter of duty to investigate still further the character of the steamer in question, I have had an interview with Frederick Johnson, esq., her Britannic Majesty's consul at this port, upon this subject, who informs me that she is not entitled to the protection of his government, and that he has warned the captain of the consequences of making a false use of the flag of his country.

Although not officially, still I am credibly informed that all the so-called confederate forces west of the Mississippi, under the command of General Kirby Smith, were surrendered by that chief to Major General Canby, of the federal forces, on the 26th day of May last, thus giving the final blow to that insurrection which for a length of time had been so disastrous to the United States. I mention this circumstance to show that while in the confusion of the reoccupation of the ports of Texas by the federal forces the Sonora escaped, with a few bales of cotton, which have been landed in this port; consequently she did not depart from a port held in armed rebellion against the United States, because the whole State of Texas, by virtue of the above-mentioned surrender, has again come under the laws and the government of the said United States, and thus her departure therefrom cannot now be considered as from an enemy's port to any party or power. Hence the time seems to have arrived when those privileges which have been granted by foreign powers to a forced trade with the enemies of the United States have no further existence.

Under these circumstances, I beg to express the hope that your honor will be pleased to consider it an act of justice to detain the Sonora until her legitimate owner can have time to appear here, or to produce documentary evidence in reclamation of his property thus unlawfully wrested from him.

I improve this occasion to renew to your honor the assurances of my distinguished consideration and particular respect.

FRANKLIN CHASE.

Hon. JESUS DE LA SERNA,
Prefecto Politico, &c., &c., &c., of the Southern District of Tamaulipas.

No. 2.

[Translation.]

MEXICAN EMPIRE, POLITICAL PREFECTURE OF THE DISTRICT
SOUTH OF TAMAULIPAS, *Tampico, June* 23, 1865.

MR. CONSUL: The business relating to the steamer Sonora, of which you treat in your esteemed note dated 21st instant, has been transferred to the court of first instance of this district, that it may proceed in what may be needful pertaining to its exclusive jurisdiction, reserving to myself to send you the result when the judicial authority may determine what it considers to be proper.

The occasion, Mr. Consul, offers me that of protesting to you my distinguished consideration and esteem.

JESUS DE LA SERNA,
The Political Prefect ad interim.

P. S. GARCIA, *Secretary.*

CONSUL GENERAL *of the U. S. of America at this port, Present.*

Mr. Seward to Mr. Bigelow.

No. 264.]

DEPARTMENT OF STATE,
Washington, September 20, 1865.

SIR: At an early period of the war between France and Mexico a body of native negro Egyptian troops was put by the Pacha of Egypt at the service of the Emperor of the French, by whose direction they were conveyed from Egypt to Mexico, where they were incorporated in the French service. It has been represented that the embarcation of the negroes on that destination was involuntary, and was effected not without compulsion. I am not prepared to say that the statement is absolutely accurate in this latter respect. The proceeding excited much comment at the time, but it passed unnoticed by this government, which was then seriously occupied with a peculiar condition of merely domestic affairs, and with the foreign embarrassments which grew out of that condition. It is now represented to this government that a second embarcation of the same character and with the same destination and purposes is contemplated. Since the original transaction occurred the United States have abolished slavery. The attention of Congress, as well as that of the executive department and of the country, has been very steadily fixed upon the course of events in Mexico, which I need not say form a subject of serious apprehension with regard to the safety of free republican institutions on this continent—an object with which we are accustomed to connect the desired ultimate consequence of the abolition of every form of compulsory civil or military servitude in this hemisphere.

You are instructed to bring this matter to the attention of Mr. Drouyn de Lhuys, and state to him that, in the opinion of this government, the renewal of the transactions alluded to could not be regarded with favor or even without deep concern by the people of the United States or by their government. It is proper for you to inform Mr. Drouyn de Lhuys that I have written upon the subject in the same sense herein adopted to the diplomatic agents of the United States residing, respectively, at Alexandria and Constantinople.

I am, sir, your obedient servant,

WILLIAM H. SEWARD.

JOHN BIGELOW, Esq., &c., &c., &c.

Mr. Bigelow to Mr. Seward.

[Extract.]

No. 177.] LEGATION OF THE UNITED STATES,
Paris, September 21, 1865.

SIR: I profited by an opportunity which presented itself to-day at the reception of the minister of foreign affairs to recall what his excellency had said at our last interview about the gradual withdrawal of the French army from Mexico, for the purpose of mentioning a report which had reached me from our consul in Egypt, that six hundred of the Pacha's subjects of the Soudan were daily expected to embark for Mexico to re-enforce the invading army. I remarked that such a report was likely to provoke comment, and therefore I felt a desire to know, if he was disposed to tell me, how much foundation it had in truth. Mr. Drouyn de Lhuys said that he believed there were some troops raised some time ago in Egypt; he did not know how many, but he gave me the impression that he was not aware of anything on the way at this moment. Their capacity to resist the diseases of the Mexican coast led the government to look in that quarter for soldiers to garrison the unhealthy regions of Mexico. But he went on to add, that whatever may be the number of troops gone or going from Egypt to Mexico, what he had said about the actual reduction of the French army in Mexico was none the less true. Since seeing me, he had taken pains to verify in the proper quarter what he had stated to me as his conviction. The reduction, he added, would go on as fast as possible, for the Emperor was very anxious to get out of the country. How fast they could reduce, he said, would depend a great deal upon the United States. It was their wish to retire as soon as they could leave their interests in Mexico properly protected.

I said that his excellency surely could not have expected our government to go further than it had already gone to show its forbearance, or words to that effect. "No," he replied; "my last letters from Mr. Montholon are very satisfactory. So much so, that I sent a line yesterday to the Emperor on the subject." I told him, in substance, that he ought by this time to feel satisfied that our government had no disposition unnecessarily to embarrass the government of the Emperor.

* * * * * * *

I am, sir, with great respect, your obedient servant,

JOHN BIGELOW.

Hon. WILLIAM H. SEWARD, *Secretary of State.*

Mr. Seward to Mr. Bigelow.

No. 269.]

DEPARTMENT OF STATE,
Washington, September 25, 1865.

SIR: Your despatch of the 31st of August, No. 165, has been received. I have read carefully the account you have given therein of your conversation held with Mr. Drouyn de Lhuys on that day upon the special subject of the intercepted Gwyn correspondence and the general subject of Mexican relations. I agree with the minister for foreign affairs in his concluding suggestion, that, so far as possible, direct and verbal communications upon such delicate matters are to be preferred over formal ones. I am, moreover, well pleased with the general spirit and tone manifested by Mr. Drouyn de Lhuys in that conversation. Beyond these points he will hardly expect a minister of the United States to coincide. The unpleasant interpellation about Dr. Gwyn, as Mr. Drouyn de Lhuys calls it, was a consequence, a remote one indeed, but still a consequence, of the Emperor's giving private audience to Dr. Gwyn, a traitor acting in the interest of an insurrection against this government. Aware that such consequences must follow such suspected audiences, this department and this government decline in every case to give audience to such emissaries as Gwyn coming from states with which we are holding diplomatic relations.

It is well, I think, for both the French government and that of the United States, to avoid the giving and the unnecessary taking of offence. The object of each is to avert misunderstandings and not to make them. It is useless to try to do that unless we can successfully abstain from everything that might provoke irritation. It must be easy to see that the people of the United States have sensibilities as profound as those of the French people. The government of the United States may well be believed to have sensibilities as tender as those of France herself.

I am, sir, your obedient servant,

WILLIAM H. SEWARD.

JOHN BIGELOW, Esq., *&c., &c., &c.*

Mr. Seward to Mr. Bigelow.

No. 270.]

DEPARTMENT OF STATE,
Washington, September 25, 1865.

SIR: I acknowledge the receipt of your despatch of the 31st ultimo, No. 166, relative to your interview of that date with Mr. Drouyn de Lhuys, in regard to Mexican questions. Your proceedings on that occasion are approved. With regard to the views expressed by Mr. de Lhuys there is no occasion for special comment.

I am, sir, your obedient servant,

WILLIAM H. SEWARD.

JOHN BIGELOW, Esq., *&c., &c., &c.*

Mr. Seward to Mr. Bigelow.

No. 274] DEPARTMENT OF STATE,
Washington, September 25, 1865.

SIR: I have to acknowledge the receipt of your despatch of the 21st of June last, No. 120, giving me a copy of a note of the 17th of that month from Mr. Drouyn de Lhuys, in reply to yours correcting the statement made by the minister of state, concerning your representations upon the subject of Mexican affairs. You will pardon the delay which has occurred in making this acknowledgment, and which has been unavoidable.

I am, sir, your obedient servant,

WILLIAM H. SEWARD.

JOHN BIGELOW, Esq., *&c., &c., &c.*

Mr. Bigelow to Mr. Seward.

[Extract.]

No. 180.] LEGATION OF THE UNITED STATES,
Paris, October 6, 1865.

SIR: I had the honor yesterday to submit to the minister of foreign affairs your despatch of the 6th of September, defining the President's policy in reference to France as affected by her intervention in Mexico.

* * * * * * * * *

I am, sir, with great respect, your obedient servant,

JOHN BIGELOW.

Hon. WILLIAM H. SEWARD, *Secretary of State.*

Mr. Bigelow to Mr. Seward.

No. 181.] LEGATION OF THE UNITED STATES,
Paris, October 6, 1865.

SIR: Nothing has come from the other side of the Atlantic since my residence in France which has given more general satisfaction than the President's recent address to the delegates from the southern States. The Moniteur published it at length. The Constitutionnel of the 30th September devotes an article to the address, which commences as follows:

"President Johnson has set out boldly in a path whither the sympathetic encouragements of every sincere and enlightened friend of the United States cannot fail to follow him."

In the concluding paragraph the writer says, that "after the terrible trials which the United States have experienced, and which it was impossible for a nation always friendly as France has been not to feel, it is a special good fortune for the Americans, we might almost say providential, to be ruled by a man who has known how to withdraw himself so promptly from pernicious influences and to rise to the height of one of the greatest situations that can be imagined."

La France publishes the speech, and characterizes it as a very remarkable speech. I send by this mail a copy of The France of the 22d September, in which will be found an article devoted to our President, in which the writer says apropos of the President's speech, published in its columns the day previous, "It is a model of benevolence, uprightness, and good sense."

I also send a copy of the Avenir Nationale of the 2d October, which appreciates the speech in a like friendly spirit.

The Moniteur of the 30th says: "A Vienna correspondent announces that enrolments for Mexico would be resumed soon in Austria, but these enrolments would be made for the national (Mexican) army, and not for the foreign legion. A number of officers have already inscribed themselves. A knowledge of the Spanish language is required for admission. The troops will meet at Layback."

I yesterday met the Austrian chargé d'affaires at the ministry of foreign affairs, who told me that the soldiers who enlisted were expected to become Mexicans, but that the officers would not cease to be Austrians. He promised to procure for me copies of the articles which they respectively were to sign, if he could.

Your letter to Mr. Adams in reference to the debt of the Confederate States is also the subject of general discussion. In addition to what will be found in papers taken by the Department of State, I send you a copy of La France of the first instant, in which it is said that "the federal government in refusing to recognize this loan was incontestably in the right."

The Debats of the 1st instant, and in subsequent numbers, vindicates your course without reserve.

In the same spirit is an article in the Avenir Nationale, which I forward to-day, of the date of October 4.

I send these notes merely to aid you a little in gleaning such French newspaper impressions of our affairs as may interest you.

I have only to add that President Johnson's praises are now in every one's mouth here.

I am, sir, with great respect, your very obedient servant,

JOHN BIGELOW.

Hon. WILLIAM H. SEWARD,
Secretary of State.

Mr. Hunter to Mr. Bigelow.

No. 283.]

DEPARTMENT OF STATE,
Washington, October 9, 1865.

SIR: Your despatch of the 21st ultimo, No. 177, containing an account of your conversation with Mr. Drouyn de Lhuys in regard to the reduction of the French forces in Mexico, has been received, and will be taken into consideration. An instruction of the 20th ultimo, No. 264, will have placed you in possession of the views of this government in regard to the compulsory transportation of Egyptian negro troops by France to Mexico.

I am, sir, your obedient servant,

W. HUNTER, *Acting Secretary.*

JOHN BIGELOW, Esq., *&c., &c., &c.*

Mr. Hunter to Mr. Bigelow.

No. 285.]

DEPARTMENT OF STATE,
Washington, October 13, 1865.

SIR: Referring to your despatch of the 11th of July, No. 140, and to my reply of the 28th of that month, upon the subject of the alleged purchase by General Mejia of guns and ammunition from the insurgents in Texas, I have to state for your information, that in a letter of the 9th instant, from the Secretary of War, this department is informed that Major General Sheridan reports, under date of August 6, that the artillery in question was turned over to Brigadier

General Brown, United States volunteers, on the 8th of July, 1865, at Brownsville, Texas, by Major General Mejia.

You will avail yourself of a convenient opportunity to express to Mr. Drouyn de Lhuys the President's satisfaction at the honorable and friendly course of the French authorities in relation to this matter.

I am, sir, your obedient servant,

W. HUNTER, *Acting Secretary.*

JOHN BIGELOW, Esq., *&c., &c., &c.*

Mr. Bigelow to Mr. Seward.

No. 186.] LEGATION OF THE UNITED STATES,
Paris, October 18, 1865.

SIR: I waited upon his excellency M. Drouyn de Lhuys on Tuesday, the 17th instant, at his request, and among the matters brought under discussion was your despatch No. 264, of the 20th September, in reference to recruiting in Egypt for Mexico, which I read to him on Thursday last. His excellency said that the Emperor entertained no doubt of his perfect right to avail himself of the courtesy of an ally to strengthen his army, whenever and wherever he had occasion to do so; that the Pacha had placed at his disposition already some of his soldiers, who stood the climate of parts of Mexico better than Europeans, and had promised him more. There was no treaty nor written engagement between them on the subject—simply a verbal understanding. It so happened, however, that in consequence of an insurrection which has broken out in the Soudan, the Pacha has need of all his troops, and therefore the project of recruiting in his dominions is for the present arrested. His excellency repeated his previous statement that the Emperor did not mean by this explanation to countenance any doubt of his right to enter into any arrangements with any foreign power for military aid when he had need of it.

I then asked if the purpose of taking troops from Egypt was finally and definitively abandoned. He said no, he could not say it was definitively abandoned, though the government had no definite intention of renewing it. It was one of those prerogatives which, while they claimed the right, they had no present intention to exercise.

I then observed that the question raised by my government in your despatch was not the Emperor's abstract right to recruit his army from among the subjects of his allies, if they invited him to do so, but whether he would practically insist upon taking Egyptian slaves, in the uniform of soldiers, to do military or other service in Mexico. I remarked that it was represented to our government that the troops in question were not levied upon any equitable system of enrolment, but were seized by soldiers of the Pacha, dragged away so far from their homes as to be unable to find their way back, pressed into the army where they had no civil or political guarantees whatsoever, and, in point of fact, were taken for the Pacha's army in the same way, and by the same means, that the King of Dahomey uses to stock his slave market. Such, said I, is the popular impression, and such seems to be the impression left upon the mind of the President, as it certainly was on mine, by the communication received from our consul general at Alexandria. His excellency said that he did not know how the soldiers were levied by the Pacha, but should inquire about it; that his army was composed of men of different colors and nationalities; that all governments required more or less of involuntary military service in time of war, and that men thus impressed hardly deserved to be called slaves. I said that was a question of fact; that you did not say absolutely that the service of the Pacha's troops levied for Mexico was servile, but that such was reported to you to be the fact; and such, I added, was the presumption; that we, as a nation, had suffered bitterly from the institution of slavery, and that we naturally could not contemplate with composure the possibility of its being planted in a neighboring country, under any disguise whatever. Waiving, therefore, the abstract right asserted by the Emperor, which I had no occasion to discuss, even if I found myself unable to agree with his Majesty, I begged his excellency to inform me, in case it should appear that the troops levied by the Pacha for the Emperor were seized without any enrolment and without any recognition of their civil state and rights as citizens, whether France, the first to set the example to the world of emancipating her slaves, would accept them? He replied promptly, "By no means. The government of the Emperor will have nothing to do with the propagation or encouragement of slavery." He added that he should for his own information—the practical question you had presented to him having been disposed of by events, and therefore not requiring him to inquire officially—take steps to ascertain how the troops of the Pacha were levied for Mexico.

I said I would thank him to do so, and that I should also endeavor myself to obtain more precise information upon the subject. I concluded by saying that I should have pleasure in informing you—

First, that the levy of Egyptian troops referred to in your letter was not to be used in the re-enforcement of the French army in Mexico.

Second, that the Emperor at no time contemplated the enrolment of slaves into his army in Mexico, or elsewhere.

This communication will be submitted to Mr. Drouyn de Lhuys before it is posted.

I am, sir, with great respect, your obedient servant,

JOHN BIGELOW.

Hon. WILLIAM H. SEWARD,
Secretary of State.

Mr. Seward to Mr. Bigelow.

No. 293.]

DEPARTMENT OF STATE,
Washington, October 30, 1865.

SIR: I have your despatch of October 6, No. 180. While you have very properly given us the inferences which you drew from the conversation of Mr. Drouyn de Lhuys, which was elicited by the reading of my despatch of September 6, you have, at the same time, implied that he would probably return to the subject at a later day. The President waits with very considerable interest for the views of the French government. Whatever has occurred in connexion with the subject since my despatch was written has tended to enhance that interest.

I am, sir, your obedient servant,

WILLIAM H. SEWARD.

JOHN BIGELOW, Esq., *&c., &c., &c.*

Mr. Seward to Mr. Bigelow.

[Extract.]

No 300.]

DEPARTMENT OF STATE,
Washington, November 6, 1865.

MY DEAR SIR: * * * * * *

I will proceed to discuss the subject, and leave you to present the opinions of the President to such extent and in such manner as your own views of propriety shall suggest. The President feels himself bound to adhere to the opinion set forth in my despatch No. 259, which has, as we understand, been already read to Mr. Drouyn de Lhuys. The presence and operations of a French army in Mexico, and its maintenance of an authority there, resting upon force and not the free will of the people of Mexico, is a cause of serious concern to the United States. Nevertheless, the objection of the United States is still broader, and includes the authority itself which the French army is thus maintaining. That authority is in direct antagonism to the policy of this government and the principle upon which it is founded.

Every day's experience of its operations only adds some new confirmation of the justice of the views which this government expressed at the time the attempt to institute that authority first became known. The United States have hitherto practiced the utmost frankness on that subject.

They still regard the effort to establish permanently a foreign and imperial government in Mexico as disallowable and impracticable. For these reasons they could not now agree to compromise the position they have heretofore assumed. They are not prepared to recognize, or to pledge themselves hereafter to recognize, any political institutions in Mexico which are in opposition to the republican government with which we have so long and so constantly maintained relations of amity and friendship. I need hardly repeat my past assurances of our sincere desire to preserve our inherited relations of friendship with France. This desire greatly increases our regret that no communications, formal or informal, which have been received from the government of that country seem to justify us in expecting that France is likely soon to be ready to remove, as far as may depend upon her, the cause of our deep concern for the harmony of the two nations.

The suggestion which you make of a willingness on the part of France to propose a revision of the commercial relations between the two countries is not regarded as having emanated from the government of the empire. However that may be, it is hardly necessary to say that we should not be dwelling so earnestly upon the branch of political relations if it had not been our conviction that those relations at the present moment supersede those of commerce in the consideration of the American people.

Believe me to be always faithfully yours,

WILLIAM H. SEWARD.

JOHN BIGELOW, Esq., *&c.*, *&c.*, *&c.*

Mr. Seward to Mr. Bigelow.

No. 302.] DEPARTMENT OF STATE,
Washington, November 6, 1865.

DEAR SIR: I have just received your note of the 19th of October. I assume that your information in regard to the discontinuance of the project for Egyptian levies in Mexico is correct; it remains, therefore, for me to express the satisfaction of this government at that result.

I remain, dear sir, yours sincerely,

WILLIAM H. SEWARD.

JOHN BIGELOW, Esq., *&c.*, *&c.*, *&c.*

Mr. Seward to Mr. Bigelow.

No. 309.] DEPARTMENT OF STATE,
Washington, November 14, 1865.

SIR: I have received your despatch of the 18th of October, No. 186, in which you give me the substance of a conversation held between yourself and

Mr. Drouyn de Lhuys on the 17th ultimo, upon the subject of the re-enforcement of the French army in Mexico by recruiting troops in Egypt.

You are instructed to say to Mr. Drouyn de Lhuys that the disposition of this matter by the Emperor's government is received with sincere satisfaction by the government of the United States.

I am, sir, your obedient servant,

WILLIAM H. SEWARD.

JOHN BIGELOW, Esq., *&c., &c., &c.*

Mr. Montagnie to Mr. Seward.

No. 114.] UNITED STATES CONSULATE,
Nantes, November 16, 1865.

SIR: I have the honor to report that the ship which sailed yesterday from St. Nazaire to Vera Cruz carried four hundred soldiers for the so-called emperor of Mexico. One hundred and fifty were French; the rest belonged to the so-called "foreign legion."

I have the honor, sir, to remain, very respectfully, your obedient servant,

JOHN DE LA MONTAGNIE, *Consul.*

Hon. WILLIAM H. SEWARD,
Secretary of State.

Mr. Bigelow to Mr. Seward.

No. 199.] LEGATION OF THE UNITED STATES,
Paris, November 21, 1865.

SIR: I shall send you by this post a copy of La France of the 19th instant, containing an extraordinary article in defence of the French occupation of Mexico, from the pen of Lamartine. I should not trouble you to read this or anything else that Lamartine has written about the United States since his unsuccessful appeal to American charity some ten years since, but for its appearance in the columns of a *quasi* official journal, and for the comments which introduced it to the public. La France is edited by M. de la Guerrouière, a senator, who is supposed to enjoy in a special degree the confidence of his sovereign, and to be a perfectly legitimate aspirant to the portfolio of foreign affairs whenever it becomes vacant. The language of commendation, therefore, bestowed by La France upon "the masterly style," "lofty inspiration," and "strong thoughts" of Mr. Lamartine's rhodomontade gives it a certain importance which the effusions of his brain alone have long ceased to possess. The thesis which Mr. Lamartine attempts to elaborate, and which Senator La Guerrouière deems worthy of a conspicuous place in the columns of La France, is the following:

"The Globe is the property of man. The new continent, America, is the property of Europe."

In elaborating this doctrine in justification of "the generous and eminently civilizing purpose which has directed the imperial policy" of his sovereign in Mexico, Mr. Lamartine finds occasion to void all his ignorance and venom—and it is difficult to say in this case which most abounds—upon the people and government of the United States. Here is a specimen of both:

"We can easily understand that this people possess as yet hardly any elements of an American literature. The Mexicans before the conquest, the so-called savages of Montezuma, the Peruvians with their *quippos*, (poems,) were in this respect greatly in advance of them. The gigantic monuments left by the Aztecs give evidences of intellect and power far superior to those evinced in the purely utilitarian structures of the Americans of the north. Pioneers do not build for posterity; woodmen only know how to cut down those grand aristocratic trees of the forest to convert them into lumber, taking pleasure in falling them, as envy does in overcoming natural superiority. Their eloquence extends no further than the debates of their public meetings, where they bring the violence of their rude manners, and where brutal gestures and clenched fists take the place of that moral suasion which the great orators of ancient or modern Europe exert by means of argument and logic over distinguished men assembled for the purpose of seeking together for truth and right in all things.

"Their journals, innumerable because cheap, are but collections of the advertisements of quacks recommended by the Barnums of the press, compilations of slanders and invectives daily thrown to the different parties to furnish them with odious names or trivial accusations wherewith to discredit each other and gain subscribers. Their drawing-rooms are held at hotels; their gatherings of men, unsoftened by kindly feelings or female politeness, are but clubs in which eager traders avail themselves even of their time of rest to increase their fortune at the close of the day, proud of knowing nothing except that which pays, and conversing only on real or imaginary speculations in which to increase their capital a hundred-fold. Their liberty, which is entirely personal, has always in it something hostile to some one else. The absence of kindly feelings gives them in general the tone and attitude of a person afraid of insult or seeking to prevent insult by dint of an overbearing attitude. They are themselves aware of the habitual disagreeableness of their manners.

"One of the few political orators they possess, the most eloquent and the most honest, whom national jealousy has always prevented, on account of his superiority, from rising to the presidency, said to me one day: 'Our liberty consists in *doing everything that can be most disagreeable to our neighbor.*' The art of being disagreeable is their second nature. To please is a symptom of loving. They love no one; no one loves them. It is the expiation of selfishness. History furnishes no type of a nation like unto this people. Pride, coldness, correctness of features, stiffness of gestures, chewing of tobacco in the mouth, a spittoon at their feet, the legs streched on the mantel-piece or crossed, without regard for the decorum which man ought to observe towards man, a short, monotonous, imperious tone, a disdainful personality stamped upon every feature—such are these autocrats of gold.

"With a few shining exceptions, who suffer everywhere from the general pressure in an inferior atmosphere—exceptions which are all the more honorable as they are the more numerous individually, such is the American of the north, such is the air of his country, the pride of what he lacks. Such is this people to whom Mr. Monroe, one of its flatterers, said, in order to gain its applause: 'The time has come when you must not permit Europe to interfere in the affairs of America, but when you must henceforth assert your preponderance in the affairs of Europe.'"

While, as I have already intimated, the feebleness of Mr. Lamartine's character has long since made his talents as a writer a calamity to himself, and a source of mortification to his friends, it may be profitable for those who direct the government of the United States to know what sort of opinions about us are still most cheerfully propagated by journals deriving their inspiration from official sources.

In connexion with Mr. Lamartine's view of the Mexican expedition so cordially approved by Senator La Guerronière, I invite your attention to an extract from an article which appeared in the same journal only the day previous, the 18th instant, entitled "Les remaniements territoriaux." Its purpose was to show that if Prussia should persist in her design of annexing the duchies, France must look to her own safety, and seek a compensation by extending her frontier, it is to be presumed, on the Rhine:

"The Emperor's government, faithful to that spirit of moderation which France has shown, has no conflict to engage in, pretensions to support, or compromising questions to raise. But, if other great powers thought fit to give way to the impulses of an ambitious and turbulent policy, to rush into adventures, and to overthrow for their own profit the conditions of European order and equilibrium, France could not remain inert in the midst of that agitation more or less directed against her; she could not see aggressive forces increasing around her without thinking of fortifying her defensive positions; she would not feel bound to remain platonically quiet within her frontiers while other states had over-leaped the bounds fixed by treaties; she would regulate her conduct by the necessities of a situation which she has neither desired nor sought, but which had been created without her, in spite of her, and against her. She would do what the most simple common sense commands in such a case; she would in her turn take her precautions, and would think of her own safety by re-establishing an equilibrium which would restore to her the guarantees destroyed by the changes effected."

Should the time ever come when we need the counsel of older states to guide us in determining how to indemnify ourselves against the encroachments of European powers upon the territory of our neighbors, this paragraph may have a certain value.

I am, sir, with great respect, your very obedient servant,

JOHN BIGELOW.

Hon. WILLIAM H. SEWARD,
Secretary of State, &c., &c., &c.

Mr. Seward to Mr. Bigelow.

No. 316.] DEPARTMENT OF STATE,
Washington, November 23, 1865.

SIR: The Secretary of War yesterday informed me that he had just received intelligence from Major General Sheridan to the effect that, on the 7th instant, the republican forces in Mexico who were besieging Matamoras withdrew about six miles, but that they had again subsequently attacked the place; that our military officers in that vicinity have been subjected to most violent abuse by the newspaper which espouses the monarchical cause at Matamoras; that it constantly terms the President of the United States the murderer of Mrs. Surratt; that some of our soldiers who were visiting Matamoras were arrested and put to work upon their fortifications, and our officers and men fired upon by their gun-boats; that the most insulting letters from French officials have been addressed to General Weitzel and other officers; and that the consequence is much excitement on the part of our soldiers.

You are at liberty to make such use of that information as you may think proper, to show Mr. Drouyn de Lhuys the condition of irritability existing on that remote frontier.

I am, sir, your very obedient servant,

WILLIAM H. SEWARD.

JOHN BIGELOW, Esq., &c., &c., &c.

Mr. Bigelow to Mr. Seward.

No. 201.] LEGATION OF THE UNITED STATES,
Paris, November 24, 1865.

SIR: I received the following telegram yesterday from our consul general at Alexandria: "Le gouvernement dit insurrection supprimé expedition pourra se faire." I interpreted it to mean that the rebellion in the Soudan, referred to by his excellency Mr. Drouyn de Lhuys in our conversation referred to in my despatch No. 186, had been suppressed, and that the project of sending Egyptian troops to Mexico, suspended by the insurrection, was liable to be resumed.

In the course of an interview with Mr. Drouyn de Lhuys in the afternoon I showed him the telegram, and gave him my interpretation of it. His excellency promptly said that no change in the attitude of the imperial government on that subject had occurred since our conversation, nor was likely to; that it had signified no desire to have the troops, nor did he think it was longer in the contemplation of the Emperor to avail himself of aid from that quarter; and that, of course, the Pacha would not send troops without a new application. He closed by the more positive form of expression, that he knew the Emperor had no intention of renewing his application. I expressed my gratification at receiving from him such a satisfactory assurance.

I am, sir, with great respect, your obedient servant,

JOHN BIGELOW.

Hon. WILLIAM H. SEWARD, *Secretary of State.*

Mr. Bigelow to Mr. Seward.

No. 202.] LEGATION OF THE UNITED STATES,
Paris, November 24, 1865.

SIR: I have the honor to acknowledge the receipt of your instruction No. 296, covering the opinion of Mr. Attorney General Speed, in reference to certain decrees relating to emigration which have recently been promulgated from the city of Mexico, and to enclose a copy of a communication addressed by me, in compliance therewith, to his excellency the minister of foreign affairs, on the 22d instant.

I am, sir, with great respect, your very obedient servant,

JOHN BIGELOW.

Hon. WILLIAM H. SEWARD, *Secretary of State.*

[Enclosure to despatch 202.]

LEGATION OF THE UNITED STATES,
Paris, November 22, 1865.

SIR: Recalling the conversation which I had the honor to hold with your excellency on the 17th ultimo, in relation to the alleged levy of Egyptian troops for involuntary service in Mexico and the representations I then made in regard to the natural unwillingness of my government and country people to see slavery in any form replanted either within our territory or on our borders, I beg to invite your excellency's attention to certain recent decrees bearing upon the subject of emigration to Mexico, purporting to emanate from authorities acting in opposition to that republic. In the opinion of the law officer of my government, these decrees, if enforced, would inevitably reduce to the condition of peon slavery workingmen of the African race, and of course such of the freedmen of the United States as may have already been or hereafter may be seduced to go there without a full and intelligent comprehension of their liabilities. That your excellency may understand the grounds for this conclusion, I am instructed to transmit to your excellency a copy of the Attorney General's opinion, which will be found enclosed, and to invite the attention of the imperial government to the questions there discussed.

In complying with these instructions of my government, I avail myself of the language of the despatch containing them to say that, "If European opinion can be regarded as established in reference to any one political question, it is settled that African slavery in any form ought henceforth to cease throughout the world. We do not doubt that the Emperor of France cordially and fully concurs, as we do, in this humane sentiment."

I pray your excellency to accept assurances of the distinguished consideration with which I have the honor to be your excellency's very obedient and very humble servant.

JOHN BIGELOW.

His Excellency Monsieur DROYUN DE LHUYS,
Minister of Foreign Affairs.

Mr. Bigelow to Mr. Seward.

[Extract.]

No. 203.] LEGATION OF THE UNITED STATES,
Paris, November 24, 1865.

SIR: I have the honor to acknowledge the receipt of your despatch No. 300, in reply to my note of the 19th of October last, relating to Mexican affairs, and have given it very careful consideration. Yesterday I waited upon the minister of foreign affairs, and after disposing of some other matters, said to him that I had received no encouragement to continue the conversation which had occupied so large a portion of our interview on the 17th ultimo. I then added that I did not know that I had occasion to say anything more. His excellency asked if I had received any communication upon the subject. I said I had, and that the President did not at present see any prospect of the two governments being able to come to an understanding upon the basis discussed in our conversation.

* * * * * * *

I am, sir, your obedient servant,

JOHN BIGELOW.

Hon. WILLIAM H. SEWARD, *&c., &c., &c.*

Mr. Bigelow to Mr. Seward.

[Extract.]

No. 209.] LEGATION OF THE UNITED STATES,
Paris, November 30, 1865.

SIR: Upon reflection I concluded that I should be likely to leave more correct impressions, and perhaps exclude some erroneous ones from the mind of Monsieur Drouyn de Lhuys, by reading your despatch No. 300 to him, than by leaving him, after our interview on Thursday week, to imagine its contents. I accordingly called upon his excellency on Tuesday last, and after disposing of some other matters of less importance, told him frankly that I wished to read to him the despatch, to the contents of which I had referred at our last interview, to prevent his supposing it contained anything which I had thought proper or had been instructed to conceal from him.

* * * * * * *

When I had finished he thanked me for reading the despatch, though he felt obliged to say that he derived neither pleasure nor satisfaction from its contents.

* * * * * * *

I am, sir, your obedient servant,

JOHN BIGELOW.

Hon. WILLIAM H. SEWARD, *&c., &c., &c.*

Mr. Minor to Mr. Seward.

No. 153.] UNITED STATES CONSULATE GENERAL,
Havana, December 9, 1865.

SIR: The French packet steamer Nouveau Monde, from St. Nazaire to Vera Cruz, stopping at Havana, arrived here on the 6th instant, and left for Vera Cruz on the 7th instant, having on board nine hundred soldiers, re-enforcements for the French army in Mexico.

I have the honor to be your most obedient servant,

WILLIAM T. MINOR,
United States Consul General.

Hon. WILLIAM H. SEWARD,
Secretary of State, Washington, D. C.

Mr. Seward to Mr. Bigelow.

No. 327.] DEPARTMENT OF STATE,
Washington, December 12, 1865.

SIR: I enclose for your information a translation of a communication of the 29th ultimo* from the Marquis de Montholon, proposing, upon conditions, to withdraw from Mexico the French troops. A copy of my reply is also enclosed.

I am, sir, your obedient servant,

WILLIAM H. SEWARD.

JOHN BIGELOW, Esq., *&c., &c., &c.*

Mr. Seward to Mr. Bigelow.

No. 328.] DEPARTMENT OF STATE,
Washington, December 14, 1865.

SIR: I have to acknowledge the receipt of your despatch of November 24, No. 203.

While it is very interesting, it seems to discourage an expectation on our part of the early withdrawal of the French force from Mexico. It is to be remarked, however, that the opinions upon that subject which you have received from Mr. Drouyn de Lhuys were expressed by him, not only without the positive sanction of the Emperor, but also in the absence of knowledge on the part of the French government of the definitive conclusion of the President on the subject discussed.

It is desirable to leave no part of those conclusions open to misapprehension. And it is equally desirable that we shall be authorized to infer that such expositions of the imperial views as are given us in the name of the French government are made with the Emperor's approval. I trust that both these ends will have been accomplished before you receive this despatch. Your communication authorizes this expectation. For the present, therefore, I must be content with approving the tone, spirit, and substance of your explanations to Mr. Drouyn de Lhuys.

I have the honor to be, sir, your obedient servant,

WILLIAM H. SEWARD.

JOHN BIGELOW, Esq., *&c., &c., &c.*

Mr. Seward to Mr. Bigelow.

No. 329.] DEPARTMENT OF STATE,
Washington, December 14, 1865.

SIR: Your despatch of the 24th of November, No. 202, with its accompaniment, has been received.

The note you addressed to Mr. Drouyn de Lhuys on the subject of peon slavery in Mexico is approved.

I am, sir, your obedient servant,

WILLIAM H. SEWARD.

JOHN BIGELOW, Esq., *&c., &c., &c.*

---

* See letter of 29th November, its enclosure, and reply of Secretary Seward, December 6, 1865.

Mr. Seward to Mr. Bigelow.

No. 330.] DEPARTMENT OF STATE,
Washington, December 14, 1865.

SIR: Your despatch of November 24, No. 201, concerning the apprehended expedition of Nubian negroes against Mexico, has been received.

Instructions upon that subject will be given to you in another despatch.

I am, sir, your obedient servant,

WILLIAM H. SEWARD.

JOHN BIGELOW, Esq., *&c.*, *&c.*, *&c.*

Mr. Seward to Mr. Bigelow.

No. 332.] DEPARTMENT OF STATE,
Washington, December 16, 1865.

SIR: Your despatch of November 30, No. 209, was duly received, and it has been submitted to the President.

Your proceeding in reading my despatch, No. 300, to Mr. Drouyn de Lhuys is approved. The general tenor of the remarks made by you to the minister of foreign affairs on that occasion is likewise approved. It is not the executive department of this government alone which is interested and concerned in the question whether the present condition of things shall be continued in Mexico. The interest is a national one, and in every event Congress, which is now in session, is authorized by the Constitution and is entitled to direct by law the action of the United States in regard to that important subject.

It has been the President's purpose that France should be respectfully informed upon two points, namely:

First. That the United States earnestly desire to continue and to cultivate sincere friendship with France.

Second. That this policy would be brought into imminent jeopardy, unless France could deem it consistent with her interest and honor to desist from the prosecution of armed intervention in Mexico, to overthrow the domestic republican government existing there, and to establish upon its ruins the foreign monarchy which has been attempted to be inaugurated in the capital of that country.

In answer to an exposition of our views which was thus made, the suggestion was offered to you by Mr. Drouyn de Lhuys that the government of the United States might favor the express desire of the Emperor to withdraw from Mexico, by giving to him some formal assurance that, in the event of his withdrawal, this government would recognize the institution of Maximilian in Mexico as *de facto* a political power.

It was my desire, in framing the despatch No. 300, to express in behalf of the United States a decision that the recognition which the Emperor had thus suggested cannot be made, and to assign, by way of explanation, the grounds upon which that decision was based. I have carefully considered the arguments against that decision which were presented to you by Mr. Drouyn de Lhuys in the interview referred to, and I do not find in them any sufficient reasons for modifying the views which the United States have expressed.

It remains now only to make known to Mr. Drouyn de Lhuys my profound regret that he has thought it his duty to leave the subject, in his conversation with you, in a condition that does not authorize an expectation on our part that a satisfactory adjustment of the case can be effected on any basis that has thus far been discussed.

I am, sir, your obedient servant,

WILLIAM H. SEWARD.

JOHN BIGELOW, Esq., *&c.*, *&c.*, *&c.*

Mr. Seward to Mr. Bigelow.

No. 333.] DEPARTMENT OF STATE,
Washington, December 16, 1865.

SIR: Your despatch of November 21, No. 199, has been received. You have called my attention therein to a recent publication of Mr. Lamartine. The text of the publication is that America is the property of Europe. The publication has already attracted the attention of the American press. I think I can safely leave the debate where it has thus been taken up.

You direct my attention also to expressions made by the French press concerning apprehended conflict in the valley of the Rhine. It does not seem to me likely that France will, at one and the same time, occupy Matamoras and extend her sway into Germany. Political writers are not hindered by the material obstacles which military powers unavoidably encounter. Nevertheless, notwithstanding this incredulity, I thank you for your attention in these matters.

I am, sir, your obedient servant,

WILLIAM H. SEWARD.

JOHN BIGELOW, Esq., *&c.*, *&c.*, *&c.*

CORRESPONDENCE WITH FRENCH LEGATION.

Mexican refugees in New York and Washington preparing a movement in favor of Juarez.

Mr. de Geofroy to Mr. Seward.

[Translation.]

LEGATION OF FRANCE TO THE UNITED STATES,
Washington, January 12, 1865.

Mr. de Geofroy presents his compliments to his excellency Mr. Seward, and has the honor to transmit to him a note containing some information in which he requests he will have the goodness to fix his attention.

[Translation.]

It is believed to be known with certainty that the Juarist refugees at New York and Washington are preparing a movement in favor of the ex-President, and that they propose to stir up troubles simultaneously at Matamoras and in Sonora; that meetings have been held at lawyer Chamcey's, 243 Broadway, in the presence of some members of Congress. There Generals Doblado and Berriozobals, the intended leaders of the insurrection, must have stated the object, which would be to persuade the federal government that the people of Mexico are impatient of the new order of things; that everything is ready for action. The business houses of Ok, King & Mira, Fausto & Gorcouria, will take charge of the voyage for the partisans of Juarez on the eve of setting off from New York. Already those whose mission it is to rouse Sonora, seven in number, must be on their way to California.

Mr. Seward to Mr. de Geofroy.

DEPARTMENT OF STATE,
Washington, January 18, 1865.

SIR: Referring to previous correspondence between yourself and this department, relative to the construction in the ports of the United States of vessels destined to cruise against the commerce of France under letters of marque issued by President Juarez, of Mexico, I have the honor to enclose for your information a letter of the 3d instant, with the accompaniments from the Attorney General's office.

I have the honor to be, with the highest consideration, sir, your most obedient servant,

WILLIAM H. SEWARD.

Mr. L. DE GEOFROY, &c., &c., &c.

Mr. Pleasants to Mr. Seward.

ATTORNEY GENERAL'S OFFICE,
Washington, January 3, 1865.

SIR: By direction of the Attorney General, I have the honor to transmit you herewith a letter from the United States marshal for the eastern district of Louisiana, Cuthbert Bullitt, esq., in reply to instructions addressed to him by this office, relative to the alleged construction in New Orleans of vessels "destined to cruise against French commerce under letters of marque issued by Mr. Juarez, of Mexico."

Very respectfully, your obedient servant,

M. F. PLEASANTS,
Acting Chief Clerk

Hon. WILLIAM H. SEWARD, *Secretary of State.*

Mr. Bullitt to Mr. Speed.

OFFICE U. S. MARSHAL, EASTERN DISTRICT LOUISIANA,
New Orleans, December 23, 1864.

SIR: I have the honor to acknowledge the receipt of your esteemed favor of the 3d instant, with a copy of a letter from Mr. L. de Geofroy to the honorable Secretary of State, in which he alleges "that there are vessels being constructed in this port destined to cruise against French commerce under letters of marque issued by Mr. Juarez, of Mexico." I have made every effort to discover if there is any foundation for this report, and called on the commanding general as well as the French consul in regard to it. They agree with me that there is no ground for the complaint.

With much respect, your obedient servant,

CUTHBERT BULLITT,
United States Marshal.

Hon. JAMES SPEED,
Attorney General of the United States, Washington.

Mr. Seward to Mr. de Geofroy.

DEPARTMENT OF STATE,
Washington, January 21, 1865.

Mr. Seward presents his compliments to Mr. Geofroy, and has the honor to acknowledge the receipt of his communication of the 12th instant, relative to the supposed movement of Juarist refugees at New York and Washington.

In reply, Mr. Seward has the honor to state that the attention of the proper authorities has been called to the subject, with a view to the prevention of any violation of the neutrality laws of the United States.

Memorandum from French legation to Department of State.

[Translation.—Received February 4, 1865.]

MEXICAN ORGANIZATION IN NEW YORK.

It seems that several persons whose names are on the annex herewith are busied in New York in organizing an emigration which would be directed towards Mexico, with an object hostile to the government of the emperor Maximilian.

These individuals seem to be full of confidence in the success of their projects. They dispose apparently of funds considerable enough, and express themselves in a manner to allow the belief that the intrigue they are plotting in the United States has ramifications in Mexico.

The manner in which they speak of ex-President Juarez would lead to the thought that it is not on him they count, nor in his favor that they are agitating. Certain indications would lead rather to the supposition that the persons in question lend sympathies to General Santa Anna, which the event would develop. What they say of him would in any case be fit to compromise him, if the indiscretions which escape them were to be taken seriously.

It is said that Brooklyn, Cincinnati, and Santa Fé are the points of rendezvous for the emigrants that the favorers of the intrigue in question seek to gather in view of the disorders they meditate. It appears that a captain in the American army, whose name (Fichte) would indicate a German origin, set off five days ago for New Mexico, with the title of colonel and $7,500 in gold, given, it is said, by a New York banker (Berriozabul.) Santa Fé, whither he goes, will become a sort of recruiting depot for operations against Mexico.

Annex.—Colonel Flores, Colonel Bidal y Rivas, General Rivas, Captain Pelliteer, Marquis de Sard; an American officer of German origin, by name Fichte.

Mr. Seward to Mr. de Geofroy.

DEPARTMENT OF STATE,
Washington, February 7, 1865.

SIR: Referring to your communication of the 12th ultimo, relative to an alleged movement on the part of certain refugees to aid President Juarez, (a translation of which was communicated to the Secretary of the Navy,) I have the honor to state, in reply, that this department is informed, by a letter of the 2d instant from the Navy Department, that Acting Rear-Admiral Pearson has been apprised of the supposed movement, and that he, with those of his command in the Pacific squadron, have been instructed to use proper vigilance with the view of intercepting any expedition that may be fitted out in the United States in violation of its laws or international law, and which may embark from San Francisco, or other ports in California, to take part in the difficulties now existing in Mexico.

Accept, sir, the renewed assurance of my high consideration.

WILLIAM H. SEWARD.

Mr. L. DE GEOFROY, &c., &c., &c.

Mr. Seward to Mr. de Geofroy.

DEPARTMENT OF STATE,
Washington, February 11, 1865.

SIR: Referring to the correspondence which has occurred between the French legation and this department relative to the alleged construction, in the ports of the United States, of vessels-of-war intended to cruise against the commerce of France under letters of marque issued by President Juarez, I have the honor to enclose for your information a copy of a letter of the 7th instant, together with its accompaniment, from the War Department.

Accept, sir, the assurances of my high consideration.

WILLIAM H. SEWARD.

Mr. L. DE GEOFROY, &c., &c., &c.

Mr. Dana to Mr. Seward.

WAR DEPARTMENT,
Washington City, February 7, 1865.

SIR: Referring to your communication of the 25th, and to the reply of this department of the 26th of November last, relative to the alleged construction in United States ports of vessels intended to serve as privateers, under letters of marque from President Juarez, of the Mexican republic, I am instructed by the Secretary of War to transmit a copy of a communication on the subject from Major General McDowell, commanding the department of the Pacific, to whom a copy of your letter was sent with directions to take all necessary precautions to prevent the arming or fitting of vessels intended to be used in depredations on French commerce.

I have the honor to be, sir, your obedient servant,

C. A. DANA,
Assistant Secretary of War.

Hon. W. H. SEWARD,
Secretary of State.

General McDowell to Mr. Stanton.

HEADQUARTERS DEPARTMENT OF THE PACIFIC,
San Francisco, January 6, 1865.

SIR: I have the honor to acknowledge the receipt of a communication from the State Department to you, enclosing the translation of a note from the French minister, dated the 12th of November, 1864, relative to the alleged construction in United States ports, and especially in that of San Francisco, of vessels intended to serve as privateers under letters of marque from the President (Juarez) of Mexico; on which letter was indorsed your orders to take all necessary precautions to prevent the arming or fitting of vessels-of-war intended to be used in depredations on French commerce.

On the receipt of these orders I immediately sent for the French consul, and inquired of him whether he knew, or had any cause to believe or suspect, that any vessel was being constructed, armed, or fitted out in this port for the purposes before mentioned.

He replied that he knew of none, unless it was the Colon.

The Colon is a steamer, said to have been built by the Peruvian government, and which I have and have had under guard for several months past. The seizure was reported to you some time since.

I asked the consul in what way he connected the Colon with any operations against the French. He replied, only because the captain was a friend of the Mexican General Vega, and that he had every reason to believe that General Vega had in his possession letters of marque to be issued to parties in this place, but that he had been unable to fit out any vessels.

I have been and shall continue to be strict in everything concerning vessels leaving this place, or of being built in these waters, which can in any way be converted into privateers, either against our commerce or that of foreign nations.

I have the honor to be, very respectfully, your most obedient servant,

IRWIN McDOWELL,
Major General, Commanding Department.

Hon. E. M. STANTON,
Secretary of War, Washington, D. C.

Mr. L. de Geofroy to Mr. Hunter.

[Translation.]

LEGATION OF FRANCE TO THE UNITED STATES,
Washington, May 5, 1865.

SIR: It would follow, from reports worthy of credit, that certain persons propose to profit of the disarmament, and the order which takes off the prohibition of the exportation of munitions of war, by organizing expeditions to Mexico.

At New York, at Philadelphia, and even at Washington, they would recruit men, and prepare shipments of arms. I shall take care to communicate to you separately all the information I have received and which I shall receive in this respect.

I confine myself here to calling the most serious attention of the government of the United States to these manœuvres, and to the complications to which they would lead, in consequence of the presence of our troops in Mexico.

The legislation of the United States furnishes to the executive power not only the means to repress, but also to arrest any enterprise of a nature to disturb the good relations between the Union and friendly nations.

I pray you, therefore, sir, to be so good as to bring this condition of things as soon as possible to the knowledge of his excellency the President of the republic, who will determine what are the most efficient measures to be taken in order to remedy it.

I seize this occasion to renew to you, sir, the assurances of my most distinguished consideration.

L. DE GEOFROY.

Hon. WILLIAM HUNTER, *&c.*, *&c.*, *&c.*

Mr. Hunter to Mr. de Geofroy.

DEPARTMENT OF STATE,
Washington, May 6, 1865.

SIR: I have the honor to acknowledge the receipt of your note of the 5th instant, inviting the serious attention of this government to the reported propositions of certain persons to profit by the disarmament and the order which takes off the prohibitions of the exportation of the munitions of war, by organizing expeditions to Mexico, and to inform you that I have transmitted copies thereof to the Secretary of War and to the Attorney General, requesting them to give the matter their attentive consideration.

Accept, sir, a renewed assurance of my high consideration.

W. HUNTER, *Acting Secretary.*

Mr. L. DE GEOFROY, *&c.*, *&c.*, *&c.*

Memorandum from French Legation to Department of State.

[Translation.—Received May 6, 1865.]

A recruiting office for Mexico is established in New York, in Thirty-second street, near the Hudson river. There is also designated a house on the corner of Chatham and Pearl streets, as serving as a rendezvous for recruits. It is occupied by a person called Francis Laquer.

Mr. Ortega, lodging at the Barcelona hotel, Great Jones street, directs the operations. Mr. Ortega is at this moment in Washington. He would dispose of sums in coined silver and in ingots, parts of which is deposited in the safe of the Barcelona hotel.

Ortega, accompanied by the proprietor of the Barcelona hotel, should have bought within a few days past two thousand carbines—called Springfield rifles—at an armorer's named Stilwell, where they are still deposited, besides military cloths, &c.

The house should have sent twelve cases of arms to Philadelphia, where preparations for an expedition are also making. A brig would be armed at the foot of Congress street, New York, at Atlantic dock, intended to carry men and arms to Matamoras; and two other ships—two steamers—preparing at Atlantic dock, would be also destined to make part of the expedition.

Fifty-two men would have been sent from New York to Philadelphia.

Mr. Hunter to Mr. de Geofroy.

DEPARTMENT OF STATE,
Washington, May 10, 1865.

SIR: Referring to your note of the 5th instant, concerning the alleged employment of certain persons in endeavoring to organize an expedition to Mexico, I have the honor to inform you that it is stated in a letter of the 8th instant, from the War Department, that whenever authenticated facts are submitted to that department they will receive due consideration. It is presumed that at the time this letter was written the memorandum which you left with me containing further representation on the subject had not been received, and it is believed that the statement therein contained will engage the attention of the Secretary of War.

Accept, sir, a renewed assurance of my high consideration.

W. HUNTER, *Acting Secretary.*

Mr. L. DE GEOFROY, *&c., &c., &c.*

Mr. Hunter to Mr. de Geofroy.

DEPARTMENT OF STATE,
Washington, May 11, 1865.

SIR: Referring to your note of the 5th instant, relative to the organization alleged to be in existence within the United States, having for its object the completion of an expedition to Mexico, I have the honor to enclose, for your information, a copy of a communication of the 9th instant from the Attorney General.

Accept, sir, a renewed assurance of my high consideration.

W. HUNTER, *Acting Secretary.*

L. DE GEOFROY, *&c., &c., &c.*

Mr. Speed to Mr. Hunter.

ATTORNEY GENERAL'S OFFICE,
Washington, May 9, 1865.

SIR: I have the honor to acknowledge the receipt of your letters of the 6th and 8th instant, respectively, enclosing for my information copies of a note and memorandum addressed to your department by Mr. L. de Geofroy, relative to the alleged proceedings of certain persons, within the limits of the United States, to fit out expeditions to Mexico from our ports, and who may bring themselves within the provisions and penalties of the acts of Congress for the preservation of the neutrality of the United States. I thank you for this information, and will address, immediately, letters to the district attorney at New York, Philadelphia, Baltimore, and other places similarly situated, instructing them, in peremptory terms, to exercise the utmost vigilance in the detection and prosecution of persons who may be guilty of offences against the statutes referred to.

I enclose a copy of a letter on the subject, addressed to the district attorney at the city of New York.

A similar letter will be addressed to each of the law officers of the government in the other important districts.

I have the honor to be, very respectfully, your obedient servant,

JAMES SPEED,
Attorney General.

Hon. W. HUNTER,
Acting Secretary of State.

Mr. Ashton to Mr. Dickinson.

ATTORNEY GENERAL'S OFFICE,
Washington, May 9, 1865.

SIR: I have the honor to enclose you herewith copies of a note and memorandum received at the State Department from the legation of France, calling the attention of the government to certain proceedings alleged to be on foot in your district, and in other districts of the United States, for the purpose of fitting out expeditions to Mexico, with intent to violate the acts of Congress for the preservation of the neutrality of the United States. It is the desire of the government that you exercise proper vigilance and care in the detection and conviction of persons in your district who may bring themselves within the provisions and penalties of the statutes on that subject.

The enclosed documents may serve to indicate the movements of the persons alleged to be engaged in the fitting out such expeditions, with sufficient fullness and precision to enable you, and the marshal of your district, to obtain evidence that will warrant the arrest and binding over of the guilty parties to be of good behaviour, under the Constitution and laws, even if testimony sufficient to convict them cannot now be procured.

The Attorney General does not think it necessary to indicate the particular statutes on the subject of neutrality, with a view to direct you with regard to the means and methods of your procedure, in order to enforce the law and punish the guilty, with respect to the preservation of the neutrality of the government. He assumes that your acquaintance with the statutes, and zeal and fidelity in the execution of your office, will enable you, whenever a case fit for prosecution or conviction of the kind referred to is presented, to do all that a national sense of justice and dignity, or a foreign state interested in the subject, could require and demand of the executive department of the government of the United States.

You will please report the receipt of this letter, and the result of your investigation on the subject to which it relates.

Very respectfully, your obedient servant,

J. HUBLEY ASHTON,
Assistant Attorney General.

DANIEL S. DICKINSON, Esq.,
United States District Attorney, New York.

Memorandum from French Legation to Department of State.

[Translation.]

The enlistments continue at New York; the bounties are such as have been announced in the newspapers; the men are to take with them arms and munitions; a transport will be ready on Friday or Saturday for Tabasco.

Received May 16, 1865.

Attorney General informed May 17, 1865.

Mr. Seward to the Marquis de Montholon.

DEPARTMENT OF STATE,
Washington, June 12, 1865.

SIR: This department has official information that the insurgent commander at Brownsville, in Texas, after the surrender of his superior officer of the insurgent forces and public property in that quarter to the United States, clandestinely transferred to the authorities at Matamoras certain artillery and other articles, a part of those surrendered as aforesaid. As those articles became the property of the United States pursuant to the terms of the surrender, the authorities aforesaid could not acquire any title to them without the consent of this government; it is, consequently, expected that they will be restored. And you will oblige me, and may be instrumental in preventing further difficulties if you should request the officer in command at Matamoras, who may have received the articles, to restore them to the officer of the United States in command at Brownsville, without any delay which can conveniently be avoided.

I avail myself of this occasion, sir, to offer to you an assurance of my very high consideration.

WILLIAM H. SEWARD.

The MARQUIS DE MONTHOLON, *&c.*, *&c.*, *&c.*,

The Marquis de Montholon to Mr. Seward.

[Translation.]

LEGATION OF FRANCE TO THE UNITED STATES,
Washington, June 15, 1865.

SIR: I have received the despatch you did me the honor to write to me on the 12th instant, by which you inform me that the commander of the rebel troops at Brownsville (Texas) must have clandestinely sent to the authorities at Matamoras a certain quantity of artillery and material of war, notwithstanding the capitulations signed by his superior, one of the clauses of which implied the surrender to the federal authorities of the insurgent forces and of all public property.

I immediately brought the fact to the knowledge of the government of the Emperor, and believe it to be my duty at the same time to communicate it to Marshal Bazaine, commander-in-chief of the French forces in Mexico, so that he may inform himself without delay of the fact which gave cause to the reclamation your excellency has addressed to me.

Accept, sir, the assurances of my very high consideration.

MONTHOLON.

Hon. WILLIAM H. SEWARD, *&c.*, *&c.*, *&c.*

Mr. Hunter to the Marquis de Montholon.

DEPARTMENT OF STATE,
Washington, June 22, 1865.

SIR: I have the honor to acknowledge the receipt of your note of the 15th instant, informing me of the steps you had taken to bring to the knowledge of the Emperor's government, and also to acquaint Marshal Bazaine, commander-in-chief of the French forces in Mexico, with the circumstances attending the clandestine and improper transfer of men and arms by the insurgent commander at Brownsville to the authorities at Matamoras.

I beg that you will accept my thanks for your prompt action in the matter.

I have the honor to be, with the highest consideration, sir, your obedient servant,

W. HUNTER, *Acting Secretary.*

The MARQUIS DE MONTHOLON, *&c.*, *&c.*, *&c.*

Mr. Seward to the Marquis de Montholon.

DEPARTMENT OF STATE,
Washington, July 5, 1865.

SIR: It is not without a somewhat serious concern for the public peace that I bring to your notice the substance of information which this government has just now received, concerning the condition of affairs on the border which separates the United States from Mexico. This information is to the effect that all the public property belonging to the late insurgents in Texas, which could be removed, was subsequently to their surrender, but before the United States forces could occupy the country, transferred to the Mexican side of the Rio Grande; that the steamer Lucy Given, which was surrendered to the United States at Matagorda, was afterwards carried off, and, according to the latest intelligence, was anchored at Bagdad, in the Rio Grande, and that eight hundred and twenty bales of cotton, belonging to the insurgents, stored at Rio Grande City, were also carried across the river into Mexico.

I will thank you to call the attention of the military authorities of France in Mexico to this subject, in order that the property referred to may be restored, and that with a view to tranquillity on that frontier, no similar proceeding may be encouraged or authorized.

I avail myself of this opportunity to renew the assurance of my high consideration.

WILLIAM H. SEWARD.

The MARQUIS DE MONTHOLON, *&c.*, *&c.*, *&c.*

The Marquis de Montholon to Mr. Seward.

[Translation.]

LEGATION OF FRANCE TO THE UNITED STATES,
Washington, July 6, 1865.

SIR: I have received the despatch you did me the honor to address to me on the 5th of this month, in which you inform me that a great part of the public property of the insurgents of Texas would be, after the capitulation and before the federal troops could have occupied the country, transported across the Mexican river Rio Grande; that the steamer Lucy Given, surrendered to the government of the United States, must have been carried off, and be now at anchor at Bagdad; and lastly, that eight hundred and twenty bales of cotton, belonging to the insurgents and collected at Rio Grande City, must, in like manner, have been transferred to the other side of the river.

I will hasten, sir, to bring these facts to the notice of the government of the Emperor, and will at the same time make report of it to his excellency Marshal Bazaine, commander-in-chief of the French forces in Mexico.

As I had the honor to inform you on the 15th June, I have called the attention of his excellency Marshal Bazaine to the facts related in the despatch which you did me the honor to address to me under date of June 12th. Even before having received my letter the marshal had hastened to inform me of the latest events occurred on the Rio Grande.

It results, from the intelligence he addresses to me at date of June 19th, that a meeting had taken place among the confederate troops at the moment of disbanding them, and that one Colonel Fisher, who had served under Juarez, having tried to get possession of some part of the materiel of the place—that is, six cannon and two forges—to put them in the hands of the Juarists, General Stoughton, in order to stop this act from happening, sent this materiel across the Mexican river. Marshal Bazaine informs me that General Mejia immediately caused it to be inventoried and placed on deposit at Matamoras, so that it may be remitted to the disposal of the government of the United States.

Marshal Bazaine also apprises me that he has given the various columns which are operating in Mexico the most precise orders, for the purpose of avoiding all that might give umbrage to the government of the United States.

I hasten to bring these facts to your knowledge, as a fresh proof that the authorities are in no way disposed to encourage or authorize any act of a nature to compromise the good relations which they desire to maintain with the federal authority on the frontier of Mexico.

Accept, sir, the assurance of my high considerations.

MONTHOLON.

Hon. WILLIAM H. SEWARD, *&c.*, *&c.*, *&c.*

Mr. Hunter to the Marquis de Montholon.

DEPARTMENT OF STATE,
Washington, July 31, 1865.

SIR: I have the honor to enclose a copy of a letter of the 22d instant, from the Secretary of the Navy, and of that of the 10th instant, referred to therein, relative to the case of the United States merchant steamer Sonora.

I hope that you may deem it proper to take such steps as may be in your power towards securing the restoration of the steamer to Mr. Clavel or his agents.

Accept, sir, a renewed assurance of my highest consideration.

W. HUNTER, *Acting Secretary.*

The MARQUIS DE MONTHOLON, *&c.*, *&c.*, *&c.*

Mr. Welles to Mr. Seward.

NAVY DEPARTMENT,
Washington, July 22, 1865.

SIR: I have the honor to refer to you the accompanying letter, dated the 10th instant, addressed to this department by Mr. F. Clavel, of New Orleans, Louisiana, who appeals to the government to aid him in repossessing himself of the steamer Sonora, which he states formerly belonged to him; was captured by her crew, or a part of it, taken into an insurgent port, subsequently ran out, and is now, or was recently, at Tampico, where she appears to have been detained at the request of Mr. Chase, the United States consul general.

Very respectfully, &c.,

GIDEON WELLES,
Secretary of the Navy.

Hon. WILLIAM H. SEWARD, *Secretary of State.*

Mr. Clavel to Mr. Welles.

NEW ORLEANS, *July* 10, 1865.

EXCELLENCY: The undersigned respectfully begs leave to state that he is the owner of the steamer Sonora, belonging to the district of New Orleans, where she was registered on the 25th of February, 1864.

On the 16th of November, 1864, when on her way from Brazos Santiago to this port, she was forcibly captured by a part of her crew, who ran her into Aransas Bay, where they delivered her to the rebel authorities. She was condemned as being the property of a citizen of the United States, and sold for the sum of eleven thousand dollars in gold, which was divided among the captors. The crew had been shipped, and every one of them had taken the oath of allegiance to the United States.

Owing to the strict watch kept by the vessels of the western gulf blockading squadron, she did not leave Aransas bay before the 9th of June, 1865, after having learned the surrender of Texas, flying the rebel flag, bound to Tampico, where she arrived on the 12th of the said month.

The above stated facts will easily demonstrate that the capture of the steamer Sonora was a wrongful act of piracy, and her subsequent sailing from Aransas Pass, after the surrender of Texas, is another confirmation of the illegality of her capture.

The undersigned hopes that your excellency will afford him the protection of our powerful government to help him to recover his vessel. She is now detained in the port of Tampico by the demand made by Mr. Franklin Chase, United States consul, for her delivery to him, as being the property of an absent American citizen, piratically taken from him.

The undersigned, in a letter by him received from Mr. Chase, United States consul at Tampico, is advised by him to furnish your excellency with all the information in his power. The above statement is made to that effect.

Respectfully submitted:

F. CLAVEL,
77 Magazine street, New Orleans, Louisiana.

His Excellency the Hon. SECRETARY OF THE U. S. NAVY,
Washington, D. C.

The Marquis Montholon to Mr. Hunter.

[Translation.]

LEGATION OF FRANCE TO THE UNITED STATES,
Washington, August 4, 1865.

SIR: I hasten to let you know that I have just received from his excellency Marshal Bazaine a despatch announcing to me that the government of Mexico has decided that the American materiel unduly taken over to the Mexican bank on the surrender of Brownsville, to which the letter of your excellency addressed to me the 12th July relates, should be restored without delay to the federal authorities, and that orders were immediately sent to Matamoras to assure the execution of this decision.

Accept, sir, the assurances of my high consideration.

MONTHOLON.

Hon. W. HUNTER, *&c., &c., &c.*

Mr. Seward to the Marquis de Montholon.

DEPARTMENT OF STATE,
Washington, August 8, 1865.

SIR: I have the honor to acknowledge the receipt of your note of the 4th instant, in which you inform this department that, in compliance with the request contained in my note of the 5th ultimo, the French military authorities in Mexico have decided upon the restoration to this government of the public property which, on the surrender of Brownsville by the insurgents, was taken over to the Mexican banks of the Rio Grande.

Accept, sir, the renewed assurances of my high consideration.

WILLIAM H. SEWARD.

The MARQUIS DE MONTHOLON, *&c., &c., &c.*

The Marquis de Montholon to Mr. Hunter.

[Translation.]

LEGATION OF FRANCE TO THE UNITED STATES,
Washington, August 8, 1865.

SIR: I have the honor to acknowledge the receipt of your letter of date 31st July last, and also of the annexes which have relation to the affair of the merchant vessel the Sonora.

I will hasten, sir, to communicate the claim of Mr. Clavel to the competent Mexican authorities, and to testify to them the interest which the government of the United States takes in the adjustment of this affair.

Accept, sir, the assurance of my high consideration.

MONTHOLON.

Hon. WILLIAM HUNTER, *&c., &c., &c.*

Mr. Seward to the Marquis de Montholon.

DEPARTMENT OF STATE,
Washington, September 13, 1865.

SIR: Referring to my note of the 31st of July last, concerning the desired restoration of the steamer Sonora to her owner, Mr. F. Clavel, and thanking you for your reply of the 8th ultimo, I have the honor to enclose, in support of the claim, a copy of the letter of the 18th ultimo, from D. Lanzac, esq., of New Orleans, attorney for Mr. Clavel, and of the documents which accompanied it, from which it appears that Mr. Clavel has gone in person to Tampico, taking with him other documents bearing upon his claim to ownership.

The account of the transaction in regard to this vessel derived from the papers which have been laid before you is to the effect that the steamer Sonora was, on the 25th of February, 1864, duly registered in New Orleans, Louisiana, as a vessel belonging to the United States merchant service; that on the 16th day of November, 1864, when on her way from Brazos Santiago to New Orleans, she was forcibly captured by a part of her crew, who ran her into Aransas bay, where she was delivered by these piratical captors to agents of the insurgents, who are reported to have caused a pretended condemnation and sale of the vessel; the proceeds of which pretended sale, being the sum of eleven thousand dollars in gold, are said to have been divided among the capturing pirates, who had shipped on the Sonora as citizens of the United States, upon taking the oath of allegiance as such; that owing to the strict watch kept by the vessels of the United States blockading squadron, the Sonora was prevented from leaving Aransas bay before the 9th of June, 1865, when she sailed for Tampico, flying the insurgent flag.

Under these circumstances this government holds that the before-named steamer is the property of Mr. F. Clavel, and that the parties who navigated her to Tampico are trespassers and intruders, having no rights or authority in her; that the acts by which she came into their custody were piratical and fraudulent. It is therefore hoped that, so far as it might depend upon the agents of the imperial government, every facility will be afforded to Mr. Clavel to regain possession of the vessel.

Accept, sir, a renewed assurance of my high consideration.

WILLIAM H. SEWARD.

The MARQUIS DE MONTHOLON, *&c., &c., &c.*

Mr. Lanzac to Mr. Hunter.

NEW ORLEANS, *August* 18, 1865.

SIR: In reply to yours of 31st July, concerning steamship Sonora, I have to state that Mr. F. Clavel went to Brazos Santiago per schooner Mary Moulis, to have in the port of Matamoras, Mexico, an opportunity more easy than here to go to Tampico, as advised to do by the United States consul general, Mr. Franklin Chase.

Enclosed you will find copies of bill of sale by C. H. Delmater, in New York, to F. Clavel, and copy of register of custom-house in New Orleans.

Mr. F. Clavel took along to Tampico—

1. Log-book of steamer Sonora, brought back by Captain George M. Goodspeed.

2. Affidavits of T. Riondel and Thomas Delaney, firemen on board last trip the steamer made, stating the piratical capture.

3. Copies of register and bill of sale.

Since four weeks, about, Captain George M. Goodspeed, now commanding

United States quartermaster's department steamer Ruthven, plying between Galveston and Houston, Texas, is requested to send his affidavit and protest about the piratical seizure of the steamer by most of her own crew, but to this moment I did not receive any. As soon as to hand, I will send it to you.

Two firemen and the cook are in New Orleans at present.

If I could do anything in this matter during the absence of Mr. F. Clavel, you will be so kind as to advise me.

Most respectfully, I have the honor to remain your obedient servant,

D. LANZAC, 76 *Orleans street.*

W. HUNTER, Esq.,
Department of State, Washington, D. C.

Know all men by these presents, that I, Cornelius H. Delmater, of the city of New York, owner of the steamer called the Ouachita, of the burden of $79\frac{47}{100}$ tons or thereabouts, for and in consideration of the sum of ten thousand five hundred dollars, lawful money of the United States of America, to me in hand paid before the sealing and delivery of these presents by F. Clavel, the receipt whereof is hereby acknowledged, have and by these presents do grant, bargain, sell, assign, transfer, and set over unto the said F. Clavel, his executors, administrators and assigns, the said steamer, together with all and singular her masts, yards, sails, rigging, anchors, cables, boats, tackle, apparel, and appurtenances; to have and to hold the said steamer and appurtenances thereunto belonging, unto the said F. Clavel, his heirs, his executors, administrators and assigns, forever.

And I, the said Cornelius H. Delmater, for myself, my heirs, executors and administrators, do hereby covenant and agree to and with the said F. Clavel, his heirs, his executors, administrators and assigns, that at the execution of these presents I am the true and lawful owner of the said steamer Ouachita, appurtenances, and I now have full right and authority to sell and dispose of the same, freed from and cleared of all claims, incumbrances, or demands whatsoever.

In witness whereof, I have hereunto set my hand and seal, at the city of New Orleans, the fourth day of September, in the year of our Lord one thousand eight hundred and sixty-three.

C. H. DELMATER.

Signed, sealed, and delivered in the presence of—
A. C. WILMARTH.

STATE OF NEW YORK, *City and County of New York, ss:*

On the 4th day of September, 1863, before me personally came Cornelius H. Delmater, to me known to be the individual described in and who executed the foregoing instrument, and acknowledged to me that he executed the same.

A. C. WILMARTH,
Notary Public, New York, 41 *Chambers street.*

CUSTOM-HOUSE, *New Orleans, August* 10, 1865.

I do hereby certify that the above is a true copy of the record on file in this office.

S. A. STOCKDALE, *Deputy Collector.*

In pursuance of an act of Congress of the United States of America, entitled "An act concerning the registering and recording of ships or vessels," F. Clavel, of New Orleans, State of Louisiana, having taken or subscribed the oath required by the said act, and having sworn that he is a citizen of the United States, and the only owner of the ship or vessel called the Sonora, of New Orleans, whereof J. Hayes is at present master and a citizen of the United States, as he hath sworn, and that the said ship or vessel was formerly the British schooner Ouachita, captured and condemned as a prize, and sold by the United States marshal of the district of New York; and documents on file in this office having certified that the said ship or vessel has one deck, and two masts, and that her length is 116 feet, her breadth 16 feet, her depth 6 feet 6 inches, that she measures $116\frac{42}{95}$ tons, that she is a steamer, has square stern, and round truck; and the said F. Clavel having agreed to the description and admeasurement above specified, and sufficient security having been given according to the said act, the said steamer has been duly registered at the port of New Orleans.

WM. BULLITT, *Deputy Naval Officer.*

Given under our hand and seal at the port of New Orleans, this 25th day of February, in the year 1864.

JOHN F. COLLINS, *Deputy Collector.*

hereby certify the above is a true copy of original on file in this office.

S. A. STOCKDALE, *Deputy Collector.*

The Marquis de Montholon to Mr. Seward.

[Translation.]

LEGATION OF FRANCE TO THE UNITED STATES,
Washington, October 19, 1865.

SIR: I feel myself obliged to call the attention of your excellency to certain facts that occurred this year on the Rio Grande, and which seem to be in exact opposition to the repeated assurances your excellency has given me concerning the desire of the cabinet at Washington to preserve the most strict neutrality in the events now taking place in Mexico.

It is scarcely necessary for me to add, that I am convinced that the said facts occurred without the knowledge of the federal government, and that they must be the result of the negligence of subordinate agents. I do not hesitate, therefore, to inform you of them, convinced that it is only necessary to bring them to your notice in order to prevent their future occurrence.

The information conveyed to his Majesty's government states that the dissenting forces of Cortinas are recruiting many American colored persons, and that this partisan chief passes and repasses the Texan frontier whenever he pleases, going to Brownsville (Texas) to get whatever he needs.

About the end of July last Cortinas attacked the steamer Señorita on the river, loaded with cotton, taken on board at Camargo, and destined for Matamoras. The attack occurred on Texas ground, and the captured vessel was made fast to the Texan shore, where she has remained in possession of the dissenters since the 27th of July.

In the course of the same month a convoy of goods was to start for Monterey. Cortinas, who was in Brownsville, heard of it, and enlisted men publicly to attack it. His armed troops crossed the river, and the convoy would have certainly fallen into his hands but for the vigilance of the imperial authorities.

In fine, it is well known that Cortinas's men ride and walk armed in the streets of Brownsville, with ribbons on their hats, indicating the number of the guerilla band to which they belong.

It would be difficult for neutrality to be more openly violated, and that facts more grave should occur to contradict the assertions which your excellency has given me in the name of your government.

I will be very much obliged to you, then, if you will cause to be issued the orders necessary to prevent the renewal of any such acts in future.

Accept the assurances of my distinguished consideration.

MONTHOLON.

Hon. WILLIAM H. SEWARD, *&c., &c., &c.*

Mr. Seward to the Marquis de Montholon.

DEPARTMENT OF STATE,
Washington, October 31, 1865.

SIR: I have the honor to acknowledge the receipt of your note of the 19th instant in regard to violation of neutrality of the United States alleged to have taken place recently on the Rio Grande. In reply, I have the honor to inform you that I have requested the Secretary of War to cause the matter to be inquired into with a view to the adoption of such proceedings as may be called for.

Accept, sir, a renewed assurance of my highest consideration.

WILLIAM H. SEWARD.

The MARQUIS DE MONTHOLON, *&c., &c., &c.*

Mr. Seward to the Marquis de Montholon.

DEPARTMENT OF STATE,
Washington, November 10, 1865.

SIR: I have the honor to recur to your note of the 19th ultimo, in which complaints are made of violations of the neutrality of the United States on the Rio Grande, and to my note of the 31st of October, acknowledging the receipt thereof.

The first complaint is, that the "dissenting forces of Cortinas are recruiting many colored persons, and that this partisan chief passes the Texan frontiers whenever he pleases, going to Brownsville to procure whatever he needs." These representations were submitted to the Secretary of War for such information and such opinion as he might think proper to submit to the President.

It appears that upon these points the Secretary of War has no information. Major General Sheridan was instructed to preserve the same neutrality that had been observed towards the United States by the French or imperial party, when Brownsville and the greater portion of the Rio Grande was held by the rebels. If it should be ascertained that the insurgents had been able to cross and recross the Mexican frontier at will, and go into Matamoras with a view of obtaining what they required, then existing instructions might authorize a corresponding course on the part of this government towards the liberals. The Secretary of War is not aware of the existence of any regulation which prevents either imperialist or liberal from crossing the Texas frontier, or proceeding to Brownsville to make purchases; and if recruiting has been allowed by officers in command, it has been without the authority of the Secretary of War. I am of opinion that, American emigration having been invited to Mexico by the imperial party, there is neither law nor order preventing it; and that, as the republican government of Mexico is acknowledged by the United States, there can be properly no objection urged to such of their citizens as may choose going to Mexico, and taking, when there, whichever side they may prefer.

It is admitted that while the United States hold their present attitude towards Mexico, military commanders should not allow either party to recruit soldiers upon United States territory.

With regard to the second complaint, namely, that "about the last of July, 1865, Cortinas attacked the steamer Señorita on the river, loaded with cotton, taken on board that vessel at Camargo, and destined for Matamoras; that the attack occurred on Texas ground, and that the captured vessel was made fast to the Texas shore, where she has remained in possession of the dissenters since the 27th of July last; that in the course of the same month a convoy of goods was to start for Monterey, and that Cortinas, who was in Brownsville, heard of it, and enlisted men openly to attack the convoy; his armed troops crossed the river," &c., it is conceded that, if the facts were as represented, the conduct of the commander at Brownsville was entirely inexcusable. These complaints have been referred to Major General Sheridan, commanding the military division of the Gulf, with suitable instructions and directions to report the facts as to what had previously occurred.

It is stated by the Secretary of War that the United States have a long frontier upon the Rio Grande, where none of our troops are stationed; that either of the belligerents might easily commit acts of war upon the other from United States soil without such acts being known in time to prevent them.

Accept, sir, a renewed assurance of my very high consideration.

WILLIAM H. SEWARD.

The MARQUIS DE MONTHOLON, *&c., &c., &c.*

The Marquis de Montholon to Mr. Seward.

[Translation.]

LEGATION OF FRANCE TO THE UNITED STATES,
Washington, November 23, 1865.

SIR: Your note of the 10th November, in answer to mine of the 19th of October last, about events that had transpired on the Rio Grande frontier last year, informed me that the Secretary of War had ordered an investigation of some of the acts I complained of, particularly the capture of the steamer Señorita. You even added that if the facts were as you represented to me, it was evident the military commander in Brownsville was in the wrong.

I have just received from his Majesty's acting consul in New Orleans the annexed claim of the French commercial house of L. Mouler & Co., owner of thirty-five bales of cotton, part of the cargo of the steamer Señorita.

As your excellency will see by reference to the appended documents, Mr. Mouler's complaint coincides fully with others from a different source, and seems to confirm the verity of the first reports that reached me.

The house of Mouler & Co. now claims of the United States government, as indemnity, the sum of ten thousand and thirty-seven dollars ($10,037) for the loss of cotton, said to have been caused by the United States.

I will be very much obliged to your excellency if you will cause this claim to be put into the hands of the proper authorities, and let me know the result of the decision as soon as possible.

Accept the assurances of my high consideration.

MONTHOLON.

Hon. WILLIAM H. SEWARD, *&c., &c., &c.,*
Washington, D. C.,

[Translation.]

Claim of Mouler & Co.—The substance.

The French commercial house of Mouler & Co. sends a claim for $10,037 84 against the United States, for the loss of thirty-five bales of cotton, caused by act of the United States, to the consul.

NEW ORLEANS, *October* 27, 1865.

SIR: In June last Messrs. Maithes and Garza, of Camargo, Mexico, bought thirty-five bales of cotton on our account, and paid the duty to the imperial government of Mexico, and also to Juarez's agents, when they took possession of that port.

The house of Maithes and Garza shipped this cotton to us on the 21st of June, 1865, in the Mexican steamer Señorita, which was seized by the Juarist General Cortinas, and landed in the United States territory on the Texas side of the Rio Grande river.

We applied to the federal military authorities having the entire control of that part of the United States, but they showed no anxiety to return us our property, or even to order its sequestration, and sent us to the Mexican republican courts, which is a denial of justice or an act of derision.

Under these circumstances, all that remained for us to do was to request you to transmit to his excellency the minister of the Emperor in Washington the claim of $10,037 84 in gold, which we make against the United States government, and herewith send you, with all the corroborating evidence.

Accept, sir, our respectful salutations.

L. MOULER & CO.

STATE OF LOUISIANA, *Parish of Orleans:*

Before me, Pierre Coudrain, a notary public for the parish of Orleans, duly qualified and sworn, personally appeared Mr. Réné Dumestre, born at Siarrony, canton of Vis de Bigorre, (Upper Pyrenees,) one of the partners in the house of Mouler & Dumestre, established in this city of New Orleans, No. 109 Chartres street, and at Matamoras under the firm of L. Mouler & Co., who having been sworn according to law, says and declares:

1. That the house of Mouler & Co., established at Matamoras, is a French commercial house, and consists of Louis Mouler, Austin Caunere, Jules Desca, and this affiant, all French subjects; that none of its members have violated the neutrality commanded by the Emperor of the French in the conflict between the government of the United States and certain States assuming the name of Confederate States.

2. That on the 21st of June, 1865, Messrs. Maithes and Garza shipped at Camargo, Mexico, on the Mexican steamer Señorita, on account of L. Mouler & Co., of Matamoras, Mexico, thirty-five (35) bales of cotton, as shown by the original bill of lading, delivered by the captain of the said steamer, annexed to the present affidavit, and of which an authentic copy is annexed to the duplicates of this document.

3. That it is shown by a Spanish document, annexed to one of these patents, delivered by the custom-house collector at Camargo, Mexico, that the thirty-five bales of cotton shipped on the Mexican steamer Señorita had paid to the republican and also to the imperial government, at different times, (27th May, 1865, and 21st June, 1865,) its entry dues.

4. That the Mexican steamer Señorita, on the way from Camargo to Matamoras, was captured by General Cortinas, of the Juarist army, and a part of the cargo were the thirty-five bales of cotton shipped by the house of L. Mouler & Co., and belonging to them.

5. That the capture of this Mexican steamer Señorita is a fact too notorious to require proof of its seizure.

6. That these thirty-five bales of cotton were placed by the said General Cortinas on the farm of Mrs. Stephen Goseaseochea, who they say is Cortinas's mother, situated on the left bank of the Rio Grande, in Texas, and upon territory of the republic of the United States.

7. That the firm of L. Mouler & Co., on 15th and 22d of June, 1865, through its agent, Mr. Maithes, of the house of Maithes & Garza, tried to get the cotton from the federal military authorities, then controlling that portion of United States territory, exhibiting to them all proof of ownership.

8. That the federal authorities showed no inclination to do justice to the French commercial house of L. Mouler & Co., of Matamoras, and finally referred them to the *courts of the Mexican republic.*

9. That these thirty-five bales of cotton were sold by General Cortinas without opposition on the neutral territory of the United States, though they belonged to the French house of L. Mouler & Co., and the present affiant claims its value for his principal from the United States.

10. That these thirty-five bales of cotton intended to be shipped and sold in New York by the house of L. Mouler & Co., of Matamoras, where they would have probably arrived the 15th of July, 1864, was of the quality of good middling.

11. That these thirty-five bales of cotton averaged 475 pounds weight per bale, or sixteen thousand six hundred and twenty-five pounds, (16,625.)

12. That this affiant, in the name of L. Mouler & Co., will now fix the value of the said cotton in the New York market on the 15th of July, 1865, deducting the ordinary charges.

ACCOUNT OF THE VALUE OF THIRTY-FIVE BALES OF COTTON.

13. At the 15th July, 1865, good middling cotton was worth fifty cents a pound in New York, in United States treasury notes—that is, eight thousand three hundred and twelve dollars and fifty cents for the 16,625 pounds.

From this sum is to be deducted: 1. The insurance from Matamoras to New York, to have been paid by L. Mouler & Co., of five per cent. on the value of thirty-five (35) bales of cotton in Matamoras, which was thirty cents in gold per pound; that is, four thousand nine hundred and eighty-seven dollars and fifty cents ($4,987 50) for the sixteen thousand six hundred and twenty-five (16,625) pounds, making a sum of two hundred and forty-nine dollars and thirty-seven cents ($249 37) in gold, or at the premium in New York, (forty-two,) the sum of three hundred and fifty-four dollars, and eleven cents ($354 11) in United States treasury notes.

2. The freight to have been paid by this affiant to New York, at the rate of two cents a pound, in United States treasury notes, or $332 50 for the sixteen thousand six hundred and twenty-five (16,625) pounds, making $332 50.

3. The import duty at the rate of two cents a pound in gold, (act of Congress approved the 30th of June, 1864,) or two hundred and eighty-four thousandths (0.0284) of a dollar in United States treasury notes, or four hundred and seventy-two dollars and fifteen cents in United States treasury notes, for the sixteen thousand six hundred and twenty-five pounds, (16,625,) making $472 15. The total deduction will be $1,158 76, leaving the net profit on the thirty-five bales of cotton in United States treasury notes at $7,153 74.

14. That this sum of $7,153 74 cents in the United States treasury notes represents in gold the premium in New York on the 15th of July, 1865, being 42, the sum of five thousand and thirty-seven dollars and eighty-four cents, ($5,037 84,) what the cotton would have brought in New York at that time.

15. That this retention of property and denial of justice has caused the house of L. Mouler & Co. considerable damage, inasmuch as they have thus lost the use of that capital; and the affiant can adduce proof that the damage has amounted to five thousand dollars in gold

($5,000,) which sum the house of L. Mouler & Co., all the members of which are French subjects, claim in damages from the United States. 1. The sum of five thousand and thirty-seven dollars and eighty-four cents ($5,037 84) in gold, the value of the thirty-five bales of cotton of which the house of L. Mouler & Co., has been despoiled. 2. The sum of five thousand dollars ($5,000) in gold, as damages and interest.

In all, the sum of ten thousand and thirty-seven dollars and eighty-four cents ($10,037 84) in gold, for the reason and causes above mentioned.

R. DUMESTRE.

Sworn to and subscribed before me, in New Orleans, on the 21st of October, 1865.

[SEAL.] P. COUDRAIN, *Notary Public.*

[Translation.—No. 2.]

THE AUDITOR (CONDADOR) CHARGED WITH THE ADMINISTRATION OF THE FRONTIER CUSTOM-HOUSE OF THIS CITY.

I hereby certify that the importation No. 45, dated 29th of May last, made by Messrs. Lopez and Garcia, to the number of three hundred and fifty bales of cotton, has paid all expenses in this office, as appears from the proper day-book, page 72, policy No. 170; and at the request of those interested, and for legal purposes, I give this present copy in Camargo, the 3d of June, 1865.

Auditor in charge,

JESUS P. MARTE.

STATE OF LOUISIANA, *Parish and City of New Orleans:*

I, Pierre Coudrain, a notary public duly commissioned and sworn in and for this parish and city of New Orleans, do hereby certify that the above and foregoing is a true and correct copy of the original, produced and exhibited to me this day by Mouler & Co.; that I have signed said original "*ne varietur,*" at the date hereof, in order to identify it herewith, and delivered the whole to said Mouler & Co.

In witness whereof, I have hereunto signed my name and affixed the impress of my seal of office, at New Orleans, this second day of October, A. D. 1865, and the ninetieth year of the independence of the United States of America.

[SEAL.] P. COUDRAIN, *Notary Public.*

(Revenue stamp.)

[Translation.—No. 3.]

I, C. Whitaker, a citizen of Matamoras, and owner of the steamer Señorita, say it is true, and acknowledge to have received from Messrs. Maithes and Garza, merchants of this place, the following effects: thirty-five (35) bales of cotton, marked and numbered as in margin; entered, weighed, dry, and in good condition, to my entire satisfaction, to be carried to Matamoras in due time, and delivered in the same condition to Messrs. Mouler & Co.; and the faithful and legal delivery having been made, I am to be paid for the freight, at the rate of $8 per every bale; and to fulfil the same, I bind myself and my property, and sign these bills of lading, of the same tenor, and for a single effect.

M. & G.

Port of Camargo, June 21, 1865.

C. WHITAKER.

Amount of freight, $280.

(In margin: Not responsible for old damages.)

STATE OF LOUISIANA, *Parish and City of New Orleans:*

I, Pierre Coudrain, a notary public duly commissioned and sworn in and for this parish and city of New Orleans, do hereby certify that the above and foregoing is a true and correct copy of the original, produced and exhibited to me this day by Mouler & Co.; that I have signed said original "*ne varietur,*" at the date hereof, in order to identify it herewith, and delivered the whole to said Mouler & Co.

In witness whereof, I have hereunto signed my name and affixed the impress of my seal of office, at New Orleans, this 2d day of October, A. D. 1865, and the ninetieth year of the independence of the United States of America.

[SEAL.] P. COUDRAIN, *Notary Public.*

[Third class—two reals.—No. 1.]

Mexican empire—opened for the year 1864–'65, according to section 3d of act 41 of the law of February, 1856.

MATAMORAS, *May* 19, 1865.

Administrator, H. Galvan. Police prefect, Pedro de la Gazza.

THE ADMINISTRATOR OF THE FRONTIER CUSTOM-HOUSE OF CAMARGO.

I hereby certify that the steamer Señorita left the town of Camargo on the 21st of June, of the present year, with thirty-five (35) bales of cotton, the property of Maithes Mark, M. & G. and Garza, imported into said town by Messrs. Lopez and Garcia; and shipped to Matamoras, to the consignment of Messrs. Mouler & Co.; and at the request of persons interested, I give the present, at Matamoras, on the 21st of July, 1865.

The administrator, J. MA. ROSS.

STATE OF LOUISIANA, *Parish and City of New Orleans:*

I, Pierre Coudrain, a notary public duly commissioned and sworn in and for this parish and city of New Orleans, do hereby certify that the foregoing is a true and correct copy of the original, produced and exhibited to me this day by Mouler & Co.; that I have signed said original "*ne varietur*" at the date hereof, in order to identify it herewith, and delivered the whole to said Mouler & Co.

In witness whereof, I have hereunto signed my name and affixed the impress of my seal of office, at New Orleans, this 2d day of October, A. D. 1865, and the ninetieth year of the independence of the United States of America.

[SEAL.] P. COUDRAIN, *Notary Public.*

(Revenue stamp.)

The administrator and auditor of the frontier custom-house of Camargo certify that the custom-house of this city, under imperial orders, issued a permit, No. 26, for thirty-five (35) bales of cotton, shipped by Messrs. Lopez & Garcia to Matamoras on the steamer Señorita, and consigned to Messrs. L. Mouler & Co., import No. 45, date 27th instant, as appears from policy No. 170, folio 72, of the day-book in which the office accounts are kept, the duties having been paid to the liberal government at the time of importation.

The mark of the cotton is seen in the margin, and for the use of those interested I give the present in the said town of Camargo, on the 24th of July, 1865.

VIVIANO G. PERES.
V. FEJEDA.

STATE OF LOUISIANA, *Parish and City of New Orleans:*

I, Pierre Coudrain, a notary public duly qualified and sworn in and for the parish and city of New Orleans, do hereby certify that the above and foregoing is a true and correct copy of the original now produced and exhibited to me by Mouler & Co.; that I have signed said original "*ne varietur,*" at the date hereof, in order to identify it herewith, and delivered the whole to Mouler & Co.

In witness whereof, I have hereunto signed my name and affixed the impress of my seal of office at New Orleans, this 29th day of September, 1865, and of the independence of the United States of America the ninetieth.

[SEAL.] P. COUDRAIN, *Notary Public.*

(Revenue stamp.)

STATE OF LOUISIANA—EXECUTIVE DEPARTMENT.

BY J. MADISON WELLS, GOVERNOR OF SAID STATE.

To all who shall see these presents, greeting:

Know ye, that the document hereto annexed is in due form and made by the proper officer, and that Pierre Coudrain, whose name is subscribed thereto, was, at the time of subscribing the same, notary public for Orleans parish, duly appointed and commissioned, and full faith and credit are due and ought to be given to his official acts accordingly.

Given under my hand and seal of the State at the city of New Orleans, this twenty-eighth day of October, in the year of our Lord one thousand eight hundred and sixty-five, and of the independence of the United States of America the ninetieth.

[SEAL.] J. MADISON WELLS.

(Revenue stamp.)

By the Governor:
S. WROTNOWSKI, *Secretary of State.*

The Marquis de Montholon to Mr. Seward.

[Translation.]

WASHINGTON, *November* 29, 1865.

MY DEAR SIR: Conforming to the desire you expressed to me, I send you, herewith, a copy and translation of Mr. Drouyn de Lhuys's despatch, the contents of which I have had the honor to read to you.

With the highest regards, I remain, my dear sir, respectfully yours,

MONTHOLON.

Hon. W. H. SEWARD,
Secretary of State, &c., &c., &c.

Monsieur Drouyn de Lhuys to the Marquis de Montholon.—(Confidential.)

[Translation.]

MINISTRE DES AFFAIRES ÉTRANGERES,
Paris, October 18, 1865.

MONSIEUR LE MARQUIS: I have taken several occasions since two months to advise you of the dispositions of the imperial government concerning the duration of the occupation of Mexico by the French troops. I told you, in my despatch of August 17, that we called with our most sincere wishes for the day when the last French soldier should leave the country, and that the cabinet of Washington could contribute to hasten that moment. On the 2d of September I renewed to you the assurance of our strong desire to withdraw our auxiliary corps so soon as circumstances should allow it. At last, following the same ideas more fully, in a private letter of the 10th of the same month I added that it greatly depended upon the United States to facilitate the departure of our troops. If they would adopt toward the Mexican government an amicable attitude, which would aid to the consolidation of order, and in which we could find motives of security for the interests which obliged us to carry arms beyond the Atlantic, we would be ready to adopt without delay the basis of an understanding on this subject with the cabinet of Washington; and I wish to make fully known to you now the views of the government of his Majesty.

What we ask of the United States is to be assured that their intention is not to impede the consolidation of the new order of things founded in Mexico; and the best guarantee we could receive of their intention would be the recognition of the emperor Maximilian by the federal government.

The American Union should not, it seems to us, be kept back by the difference of institutions, for the United States have official intercourse with all the monarchies of Europe and the New World. It is in conformity with their own principles of public law to regard the monarchy established in Mexico as being, at least, a government "*de facto,*" without particular regard to its nature or its origin, which has been consecrated by the sufferings of the people of that country; and in thus acting the cabinet of Washington would only be inspired with the same feelings of sympathy which President Johnson expressed recently to the envoy of Brazil, as guiding the policy of the United States towards the younger states of the American continent.

Mexico, it is true, is still occupied at this moment by the French army, and we can readily see that this objection will arise. But the acknowledgment of the Emperor Maximilian by the United States would, in our opinion, have sufficient influence upon the state of the country to allow us to take into consideration their susceptibilities on this subject; and should the cabinet of Washington decide to open diplomatic relations with the court of Mexico, we would see no difficulty to enter in arrangement for the recall of our troops within a reasonable period of which we would—might—consent to fix the termination.

In consequence of the vicinage and immense extent of the common frontier, the United States are, more than any other power, interested to see their trade with Mexico placed under the safeguard of stipulations in harmony with the mutual wants of both countries. We would most readily offer our good offices to facilitate the conclusion of a commercial treaty, thereby cementing the political "rapprochement" the bases of which I have just made known to you.

By order of the Emperor, I invite you to make known to Mr. Seward the dispositions of his Majesty's government.

You are authorized, if you think it proper, to read him the contents of this despatch.

I remain,

DROUYN DE LHUYS.

The MARQUIS DE MONTHOLON, &c., &c., &c.

Mr. Seward to the Marquis de Montholon.

DEPARTMENT OF STATE,
Washington, December 4, 1865.

SIR: I have the honor to acknowledge the receipt of your communication of the 23d ultimo, in regard to the claim of Messrs. L. Mouler & Company, on account of their alleged loss of thirty-five bales of cotton in consequence of the seizure of the steamer Señorita by the Mexican General Cortinas, who is reported to have landed the cargo on the Texas side of the Rio Grande, and there to have disposed of it.

In reply, I have the honor to inform you that I have referred the claim to the Secretary of War for investigation.

Accept, sir, a renewed assurance of my highest consideration.

WILLIAM H. SEWARD.

The MARQUIS DE MONTHOLON, *&c.*, *&c.*, *&c.*

Mr. Seward to the Marquis de Montholon.

DEPARTMENT OF STATE,
Washington, December 6, 1865.

SIR: Having made known to the President the Emperor's views on Mexican affairs which you communicated to me on the 29th ultimo, I have now the honor to inform you of the disposition of this government in regard to the same subject. It seems proper, however, for me to say, in the first place, that what I have to communicate has been already fully made known to Mr. Bigelow, with authority, in his discretion, to impart the same to Mr. Drouyn de Lhuys.

The effect of the Emperor's suggestions when they are reduced to a practical shape seems to be this: that France is willing to retire from Mexico as soon as she may, but that it would be inconvenient for her without first receiving from the United States an assurance of a friendly or tolerant disposition to the power which has assumed to itself an imperial form in the capital city of Mexico. The President is gratified with the assurance you have thus given of the Emperor's good disposition. I regret, however, to be obliged to say that the condition the Emperor suggests is one which seems quite impracticable.

It is true, indeed, that the presence of foreign armies in an adjacent country could not, under any circumstances, but cause uneasiness and anxiety on the part of this government. It creates for us expenses which are inconvenient, not to speak of dangers of collision. Nevertheless, I cannot but infer from the tenor of your communication, that the principal cause of the discontent prevailing in the United States in regard to Mexico is not fully apprehended by the Emperor's government. The chief cause is not that there is a foreign army in Mexico; much less does that discontent arise from the circumstances that that foreign army is a French one. We recognize the right of sovereign nations to carry on war with each other if they do not invade our right or menace our safety or just influence. The real cause of our national discontent is, that the French army which is now in Mexico is invading a domestic republican government there which was established by her people, and with whom the United States sympathize most profoundly, for the avowed purpose of suppressing it and establishing upon its ruins a foreign monarchical government, whose presence there, so long as it should endure, could not but be regarded by the people of the United States as injurious and menacing to their own chosen and endeared republican institutions.

I admit that the United States do not feel themselves called upon to make a war of propagandism throughout the world, or even on this continent, in the republican cause. We have sufficient faith in the eventual success of that cause on this continent, through the operation of existing material and moral causes, to induce us to acquiesce in the condition of things which we found existing here, while our own republic was receiving its shape and development. On the other hand we have constantly maintained, and still feel bound to maintain, that the people of every State on the American continent have a right to secure for themselves a republican government if they choose, and that interference by foreign states to prevent the enjoyment of such institutions deliberately established is wrongful, and in its effects antagonistical to the free and popular form of government existing in the United States. We should think it wrong as well as unwise, on the part of the United States, to attempt to subvert by force monarchical governments in Europe for the purpose of replacing them with republican institutions. It seems to us equally objectionable that European states should forcibly intervene in states situated on this continent to overthrow republican institutions, and replace them with monarchies or empires.

Having thus frankly stated our position, I leave the question for the consideration of France, sincerely hoping that that great nation may find it compatible with its best interests and its high honor to withdraw from its aggressive attitude in Mexico within some convenient and reasonable time, and thus leave the people of that country to the free enjoyment of the system of republican government which they have established for themselves, and of their adherence to which they have given what seems to the United States to be decisive and conclusive, as well as very touching proofs. I am, sir, the more inclined to hope for such a solution of the difficulty for the reason that when, at any time within the last four years, the question has been asked of any American statesman, or even of any American citizen, what country in Europe was the one which was least likely to experience an alienation of the friendship of the United States, the answer was promptly given, France. Friendship with France has always been deemed important and peculiarly agreeable by the American people. Every American citizen deems it no less important than desirable for the future than for the past.

The President will be pleased to be informed of the reception which the Emperor gives to the suggestions which I have now made.

Accept, sir, the renewed assurances of my very high consideration.

WILLIAM H. SEWARD.

Marquis de Montholon to Mr. Seward.

[Translation.]

LEGATION OF FRANCE TO THE UNITED STATES,
Washington, December 9, 1865.

SIR: I hasten to acknowledge the reception of your excellency's note of the 6th December, in answer to my communication of the 29th ultimo.

I will not fail to transmit, without delay, this important document to the government of the Emperor.

Accept the assurances of my high consideration.

MONTHOLON.

Hon. WILLIAM H. SEWARD, *&c., &c., &c.,*
Washington, D. C.

Mr. Romero to Mr. Seward.

[Translation.]

MEXICAN LEGATION TO THE UNITED STATES OF AMERICA,
Washington, October 25, 1865.

MR. SECRETARY: Continuing my transmission to your department of the principal documents that can give the United States government an idea of the principal events now taking place in Mexico, I now have the honor of sending to you those mentioned in the enclosed index, some of which were brought by the last steamer from Vera Cruz, and others, although of older date, I think important.

As most significant, I must call your attention to the usurper's proclamation, dated in the city of Mexico, the 2d instant, and to his so-called decree of the 3d of the same month. In the first, the ex-archduke supposes, contrary to the fact, that the constitutional President of the Mexican republic had abandoned the national territory, and from this false hypothesis he concludes that the defenders of independence, whom he calls bandits, in obedience to orders received from the French, have no leader. It is nothing new for the usurper to call those patriots, who sustain the cause of independence and the institutions of Mexico, bandits; nor is it new for him to treat them as such, with a severity that would be called excessive if applied to criminals of the lowest order. He showed the same determination in his proclamation of the 3d of November last, of which I sent you a copy. Now Maximilian wishes to regulate this established system of assassination by a decree, issued on the 3d instant, creating most informal military tribunals, extending their jurisdiction to every person in the country found armed without license from his so-called government, regardless to the numbers and character of the party he belongs to. In this decree, excessively tyrannical, he condemns to death every armed man who is not a French soldier or a traitor; and even those who will proffer information which may aid the defenders of their country; and sanctions severe penalties for the mere act of concealing a patriot or circulating alarming news; and it has been carried out by his French directors, who have been, by the system of courts-martial, sending to the scaffold the captive patriots called *guerrilleros*, and even military officers of the national army, who could not be called so.

This extraordinary severity is in open contradiction to the studied mild promises made in his first proclamation on landing at Vera Cruz; which I also send to you, dated the 23d of May, 1864.

If the Mexican patriots have been waging a legitimate war during the existence of the national government on Mexican territory, in the usurper's opinion, what must be thought of his conduct in lending himself as a blind instrument in this war, and in declaring, when there is no change of circumstances, that those fighting in a legitimate war are bandits, and must be assassinated?

Under No. 10 I send a copy of the usurper's address delivered the end of last month, on the occasion of the erection of a statue to Morelos, in Guardiola square, city of Mexico. All the eulogies he makes upon that distinguished leader in the first war of independence are now literally applicable to the citizens defending the independence of their country in this second war of the same kind, and equally as just and sacred as the first. With unexampled inconsistency the usurper now declares those patriots bandits, and orders them to be assassinated within a certain time by means of courts-martial.

I also enclose two protests, made at Tacambaro on the 10th and 24th of May last, and signed by several French officers, prisoners of a republican force. In them you will perceive the generous and philanthropic conduct of the Mexican troops towards their prisoners, contrasting strangely with the decrees and barbarous conduct of their enemies.

I also enclose a general order from the army of the centre, showing the most recent organization of the national forces in that part of the territory of the republic.

In conclusion, you will see among these documents two acts: one passed by the town and county of Zongolica, in the State of Vera Cruz, and the other by the town and county of Juchitan, in the State of Oaxaca, in which the inhabitants declare their hostile sentiments towards the so-called empire, which takes place whenever the force of French bayonets is removed.

I take advantage of this occasion to renew the assurances of my distinguished consideration.

M. ROMERO.

Hon. WILLIAM H. SEWARD, &c., &c., &c.

A list of the documents sent by the Mexican legation, in Washington, to the Department of State of the United States, with his note of the 25th of October, 1865, on events recently taken place in Mexico.

No. 1. July 26, 1865. Act passed in the town of Zongolica, State of Vera Cruz, protesting against intervention and the empire, and offering obedience to the president of the republic.

No. 2. July 27, 1865. Act passed in Juchitan, State of Oaxaca, protesting against the establishment of an empire in Mexico by the French army, and acknowledging the republic.

No. 3. Order from general-in-chief of the army of the centre, regulating the first division of the army of the centre, operating in the State of Michoacan.

No. 4. April 11, 1865. Protest of an officer and several soldiers of the foreign legion, expressing their determination to remain as prisoners of war in Tacambaro, and not fight against the republic.

No. 5. May 24, 1865. Various French prisoners of war protest to remain in prison at Tacambaro until exchanged according to the laws of nations.

No. 6. May 28, 1865. Proclamation by the usurper to the Mexicans, published in Vera Cruz, on landing at that port.

No. 7. November 3, 1864. The usurper to Velasquez de Leon, declares that the people are in his favor, and his adversaries must be persecuted and punished as bandits.

No. 8. October 2, 1865. The usurper to the Mexicans. Proclamation asserting that President Juarez had quit the territory of Mexico, and all defenders of the republic were outlaws.

No. 9. October 3, 1865. The usurper to the Mexicans. Decree ordering prisoners of war to be executed within twenty-four hours, and those who aid the republicans or do not inform on them, &c., and imposing severe penalties on citizens who do not or cannot resist them.

No. 10. September, 1865. The address of the usurper on the erection of the statute of Morelos, in Guardiola square, city of Mexico.

IGNO. MARISCAL.

WASHINGTON, *October* 25, 1865.

[Enclosure No. 1.—Translation.]

In the town of Zongolica, chief town of the canton of the same name, in the State of Vera Cruz, on the twenty-sixth of July, one thousand eight hundred and sixty-five, in the room of the town hall, assembled the persons whose names are signed to this act, and presided over by Leandro Almador, who stated the object of the meeting.

Whereas the proposition of foreign intervention was accepted by some of the towns of the republic of Mexico in consideration of offers made to sustain the government legally established in the country, and this promise has not been kept, nor can it be, for the intervenors with their partisans, deceiving and imposing upon the people, have pretended to establish a monarchical government that can never be approved by any loyal Mexican, because it is not legitimate, and their emperor was elected by a small number of persons who met in the capital and determined upon his inauguration. This was called a meeting of *notables*, (and in fact they were all notable traitors to their country,) and was evidently illegal, for the states had not a single representative. Thus wrongfully established, this illegal government has given open evidence of instability, and the free children of Anáhuac will never permit a foreign despot, supported by bayonets, to control their destiny. But if the intervenors had allowed the Mexicans a free election, the government so constituted would have been considered legitimate, whereas it now wants every feature of legitimacy in its constitution.

Therefore, keeping in mind the sacred principles of the laws of nations, pertaining to a people who comprehend their duties and desire to shake off the yoke of tyranny, this assembly has resolved as follows:

1. The canton of Zongolica disavows the government of Maximilian as illegal, because it has not been rightfully established.

2. It acknowledges as legitimate the government of citizen Benito Juarez, wherever he may be, because he was lawfully inaugurated President according to the provisions of our Mexican codes.

3. These resolutions, intending to defend our independence, acknowledge as chief he who may be at the head of the national troops by legal appointment.

4. All urgent steps to be taken in our cause are left to the leader of the troops in this place, as he is rightfully entitled to authority.

Signed by Leandro Almador, Gumecindo Altemirano, Vicente Lebrija, Rafael Fuentes, Pedro Joaquin Cervantes, Teodoro Altamirano, Nicolas Tarvaleta, Pedro G. Telles, for the sergeants; Margareto Parrera and José Francisco Geria, for the corporals; Leandro Luna and Placido Gonzales, for the soldiers; José Maria Alfaro and Manuel Contreras. Luis G. Fuentes, Ygnacio Guevora, Goregorio Parra, Estanislao Altominano, José G. Como, Rafael Mendez, Santiago Galicia, José Maria Luna, José M. Vallejo, José Anto. Cal, José M. Tello, Luis Garcia, Cristobal Rosales, Miguel Martinez, Manuel Garcia, Lorenzo Cano, and Francisca Luna.

Before me,

YGNACIO S. MENDIZAVAL, *Secretary.*

A true copy.

YGNACIO MENDIZAVAL,
Secretray of the Command.

ZONGOLICA, *July* 26, 1865.

A true copy.

JOSÉ ANTONIO RUIZ, *Secretary.*

TLACOTALPAM, *August* 2, 1865

A true copy.

IGNO. MARISCAL.

WASHINGTON, *October* 25, 1865.

[Enclosure No. 2.—Translation.]

THE MILITARY COMMAND OF THE DISTRICT OF JUCHITAN.

In the town of Juchitan, on the 27th of July, 1865, the town council, the people, and the troops of Juchitan and San Blas, of Tehuantepec, having assembled in the hall of sessions, under the presidency of the citizen political chief, to consider the affairs of the country; having stated the chief objects of the meeting, after a short discussion, the following resolutions were adopted:

Whereas Juchitan has always been one of the most loyal districts in defence of the republic and of liberal institutions, and has been abused by a few persons who wished to sell their country to a bold adventurer, announcing falsely that this district was disposed to acknowledge the perishing empire now established in the city of Mexico, and upheld only by French bayonets:

Believing it to be the duty of every Mexican who loves independence and his country, and the government established by the spontaneous and free will of the citizens, to banish every suspicion of treachery imputed to him by miserable enemies, and to contradict them solemnly; to show their determination to defend the autonomy of their country at every sacrifice; and holding it a sacred obligation of every good citizen to let his country know what his sentiments are in regard to it, the people of Juchitan, fulfilling this duty, declare:

1. That they have not nor will they ever recognize the imperial government established by French bayonets in Mexico, taking advantage of its weakness, and imposing upon the people against their free will, depending only on the feeble support a few spurious Mexicans can lend them.

2. That they will resist that government by all means in their power, and oppose all authorities and decrees emanating from it.

3. They respect and observe the authorities and decrees ordained by the constitution of 1854 and the reformed laws, as whatever tends to national independence and territorial integrity.

4. They solemnly protest against all that has been said about their acknowledging the empire, as it is absolutely false, for this part of the country has always considered that form of government as illegitimate and opposed to national sovereignty.

5. Copies of these proceedings shall be transmitted to the governor and military commander of the free and sovereign State of Oaxaca, that by him they may be remitted to the

civil and military chief of the eastern coalition, as well as to other officers and military chiefs of the republic.

And so the meeting closed, with the following signatures to this document:

Signed by Cosme D. Gomes, 1st lieutenant; Luis P. Municipal; Feliciano Torres, mayor; José de Jesus Nicolas, Anastacio Giron, Pantaleon Jimenez, Mariano Martinez, Rufino Pineda, Mariano Guerra, Pedro Estoban, Pedro Vicente, Feliciano Castillo, Dionisio Torres, Colonel P. Gallegos, Apolonio Jimenes, Anastasio Castillo, Nazario de la Rosa, Augustin Gutierrez, Mariano Martinez, Albino Roblena, Miguel Varquez, Antonio Orozeo, Alexandro Lopez, Lieutenant R. Martinez, Manuel R. Ortiz, Gervacio Marin, Miguel Lopez, Regino Sanchez.

A certified copy:

GOMEZ

JUCHITAN, *July* 28, 1865.

[Enclosure No. 3.—Translation.]

General order of the central army—Distribution of its forces.

The citizen general-in-chief of the army has disposed that the first division be organized in the following manner:

Its commander-in-chief is citizen Brigadier General Vicente Riva Palacio; and its second, citizen General Nicolas Regules.

The first brigade, under the command of citizen General Regules, second in command of the division, shall be composed of the first, second, third, and fourth battalions of Michoacan, second corps of lancers of the regular army, second lancers of Toluca, and third of Michoacan, (formerly Caballos lancers,) and the Solorio section, with a half mountain battery.

The second brigade shall be formed by the fifth, sixth, and seventh battalions of Michoacan, the first corps of Toluca lancers, third of the same, (formerly the Pachuca squadron,) with a section of mountain artillery, the whole commanded by citizen Colonel Pedro Garcia.

The third brigade, under command of citizen Colonel Ignacio Zepeda, shall be formed of the eighth Michoacan battalion, the seventh corps of permanent lancers, the corps of active Jalisco lancers, with a section of mountain artillery.

The fourth brigade, under command of citizen General Estevan V. Leon, shall be composed of the Zitacuaro forces, the Guerrero lance corps, commanded by Colonel Castillo, and the southern expeditionary section of Toluca, with a section of mountain artillery.

The fifth brigade, commanded by citizen Colonel Leonardo Valdez, shall be composed of the Nuñez battalion, and the first and second squadrons of the Huetamo loyals, with a section of mountain artillery.

The Garnica section shall be composed of the tenth Michoacan battalion, and the first corps of lancers of the same State, formerly called the liberty lancers.

The Ronda section shall be composed of the ninth Michoacan battalion, and the second lancers of the same State, formerly the Puruandiro lancers.

Citizen Colonel José Maria Mendez Olivares shall be major general of the division.

Citizen Lieutenant Colonel Luis Santa Maria Cruzado shall be adjutant of the first brigade; citizen Squadron Commander, Lorenzo Contreras shall be adjutant of the second brigade; citizen Lieutenant Colonel José Maria Gomez Humaran shall be adjutant of the third brigade; citizen Lieutenant Colonel Carlos Castillo, of the fourth brigade; and citizen Squad Commander Jesus Barajas, of the fifth brigade.

Citizen Commander Fernando Gonzales shall be commissary of the first division: citizen Captain Miguel Alvarado, commissary of the first brigade; Trinidad Valdez, of the second; Simon Becerra of the third, and the fourth and fifth brigades shall retain their present purveyors.

By supreme command:

Major AGUIRRE.

Communicated:

F. G. AGUIRRE.

A true copy.

[Enclosure No. 4.—Translation.]

We, the undersigned, wounded in the battle of to-day, in this city, and accepting the offer of the commander-in-chief of the republican army of the centre to let us remain here on account of our condition, not being able to travel, and in accordance with the rules of war, promise upon our word of honor to remain here as prisoners of war to the said general-in-chief, and not to leave or take up arms against the forces of the republic, even when invaded or occupied by the enemy of that army.

The commander of the Belgian forces especially, who was in the place before the attack, binds himself by his word of honor, and the four soldiers attending him, to remain as prisoners under the same conditions as the other wounded Belgians who sign this protest with him and his attendants.

We also declare that we sign this protest without compulsion of any kind whatever, and only on account of the kindness of the commander-in-chief of the republican army of the centre, who respects the rights of humanity and the law of nations.

Done in Tacambaro on the 11th of April, 1865.

Signed by Major Teygad, Captain Schrimager, Lieutenant Carlot, soldiers; Pierre Schoos, Pierre Corthout, Delange, (sergeant,) Briart, Peters, Joseph Spenders, Frederick Frevens, Desmit, (musician,) Kaller, (corporal,) Ziffars, and many others.

A true copy.

TACAMBARO, *May* 24, 1865.

[Enclosure No. 5.—Translation.]

Protest made to General Salazar, at Tacambaro, the 10th of May, 1865, by Joseph Alfred Wanderbach. (sergeant,) Leopold Sueur, and François Ronchon, first regiment zouaves, and prisoners of war.

General Salazar, chief of the third division of the republican army, wishing us to be as comfortable as possible, being his prisoners, and thinking the town of Reyas would be a better place for us, has decreed as follows:

1st. That he has the best feelings for us, on account of the exchange proposed by Baron Neigre, commander of the French forces to which we belong, now in Morelia; that this exchange was delayed because they hoped to hear good news from commanders near our forces, and in case of captures there, it would be preferred to exchange them instead of others of more distant divisions.

2d. As General Salazar believes it will be better for us, he has had us brought to Reyes, requiring of us a protest, on word of honor, that when set at liberty we will consider ourselves as prisoners of war till exchanged. We make this protest in due form, binding ourselves not to violate it, but to regard it as a treaty made on our word of honor, to be confirmed by Baron Neigre, conformably to the laws of war.

3d. This protest shall be made duplicate, in French and Spanish, one copy to remain in General Salazar's hands, the other to be retained by us, the subscribers.

J. A. WANDERBACH,
Captain of Zouaves.
L. LE SUEUR.
RONCHON.

MILITARY COURT OF THE THIRD DIVISION.

The preceding protest was made before me, military judge of this division, and in the presence of the citizen secretary.

GUILLERMO SAMUDIO.

ROSENDO TAUREGUI, *Secretary.*

TACAMBARO, *May* 24, 1865.

A true copy:

J. MENDOZA, *Secretary.*

[Enclosure No. 6.—Translation.]

PROCLAMATION.

MEXICANS: You have longed for my presence. Your noble nation, by a universal vote, has elected me henceforth the guardian of your destinies. I gladly obey your will. Painful as it has been for me to bid farewell forever to my own, my native country, I have done so, being convinced that the Almighty has pointed out to me, through you, the great and noble duty of devoting all my might and heart to the care of a people who, at last tired of war and disastrous contests, sincerely wish for peace and prosperity—a people who, having gloriously obtained their independence, desire to reap the benefits of civilization and of true progress, only to be attained through a stable constitutional government. The reliance that you place in me, and I in you, will be crowned by a brilliant triumph if we remain always steadfastly united in courageously defending those great principles which are the only true and lasting bases of modern government, those principles of inviolable and immutable justice, the equality of all men before the law; equal advantages to all in attaining positions of trust and honor, socially and politically; complete and well-defined personal liberty, consisting in protection to the individual and the protection of his property; encouragement to the national wealth, improvements in agriculture, mining, and manufactures; the establishment of new lines of communication for an extensive commerce; and lastly, the free development of intelligence in all that relates to public welfare. The blessing of God, and with it progress and liberty, will not surely be wanting if all parties, under the guidance of a strong national government, unite together to accomplish what I have just indicated; and if we continue to be animated by that religious sentiment which has made our beautiful country so prominent even in the most troublous periods.

The civilizing flag of France, raised to such a high position by her noble Emperor, to whom you owe the new birth of order and peace, represents those principles. Hear what, in sincere and disinterested words, the chief of his army told you a few months since, being the messenger of a new era of happiness: "Every country which has wished for a great future has become great and powerful."

Following in this course, if we are united, loyal, and firm, God will grant us strength to reach that degree of prosperity which is the object of our ambition.

Mexicans! The future of your beautiful country is controlled by yourselves. Its future is yours. In all that relates to myself, I offer you a sincere will, a hearty loyalty, and a firm determination to respect the laws and to cause them to be respected by an undeviating and all-efficient authority.

My strength rests in God and in your loyal confidence. The banner of independence is my symbol; my motto you know already, "Equal justice to all." I will be faithful to this trust through all my life. It is my duty conscientiously to wield the sceptre of authority, and with firmness the sword of honor.

To the empress is confided the sacred trust of devoting to the country all the noble sentiments of Christian virtue and all the teachings of a tender mother.

Let us unite to reach the goal of our common desires; let us forget past sorrows; let us lay aside party hatreds, and the bright morning of peace and of well-deserved happiness will dawn gloriously on our new empire.

MAXIMILIAN.

VERA CRUZ, *May* 28, 1864.

[Enclosure No. 7.—Translation.]

MY DEAR MINISTER VELASQUEZ DE LEON: On returning from my laborious journey into the department of the interior, during which I have received in every city, town and village the sincerest proofs of sympathy and the most cordial enthusiasm, I have derived two important truths. The first is, that the empire is a fact firmly based upon the firm will of the immense majority of the nation, and that in it there is depicted a form of government of real progress, and one that suits best the wants of the people. The second is, that this immense majority is desirous of peace, tranquillity and justice—blessings that it expects and anxiously asks of my government, and which I, keeping in view my sacred duties to God and the people who have chosen me, am resolved to give them.

Justice will have for its foundation institutions suitable to the epoch, and in which I am laboring with unceasing zeal. To re-establish peace and tranquillity through all this fine extensive country, and to promote with speed its prodigious riches, my government is determined to employ all its efforts and energy. If until now it has shown forbearance to its political adversaries, to allow them time to know the national will and unite themselves to it, henceforth it is under the imperious obligation to combat them, for their banner no longer bears a political creed, but is only a pretext for robbery and slaughter. My duties of sovereign oblige me to protect the people with an arm of iron; and in order to correspond to the wishes loudly expressed from all parts, we declare, as head of the nation, with a full consciousness of our sacred mission and of the duty imposed upon us, that all the gangs of armed men who still infest some parts of our beautiful country, desolating it, disturbing and threatening the hard-working citizen in his labor and liberty, must be considered as bands of banditti, and fall, in consequence, under the inflexible and inexorable severity of the law. We, therefore, command all functionaries, magistrates and military commanders of the nation to pursue and destroy them with all their power. If our government respects every political opinion, it cannot tolerate criminals who break the first of liberties which it is called upon to protect—that of the person and that of property.

Given at the palace of Mexico, the 3d of November, 1864.

MAXIMILIAN.

[Enclosure No. 8.—Translation.]

PROCLAMATION.

MEXICANS: The cause which Don Benito Juarez upheld with so much valor and constancy succumbed some time since, not only to the national will, but to the very law which that leader invoked in support of his claims; and to-day even the bandits, into which the partisans of the cause have degenerated, have been abandoned by the departure of their chief from his native soil. The national government was for a long time indulgent, extending clemency so far as to give those misguided men who were ignorant of the facts an opportunity to join the great majority of the nation, and once more pursue the path of duty. In this the government was successful, and honorable men ranged themselves under its banner with confidence in the just and liberal principles by which its policy is shaped. The cause of disorder was sustained only by a few leaders, whose passions stifled their patriotism; by the most demoralized of the lower classes, too ignorant to comprehend political principles, and by a lawless soldiery, such as always remains the last sad vestige of civil war.

From henceforth the contest will be solely between the respectable men of the nation and bands of criminals and highwaymen. There can be no more leniency, as it will benefit only bands of men who burn villages and rob and assassinate peaceful citizens, decrepit old men, and defenceless women.

The government, strong in its power, will from this day forth administer punishment inflexibly, as called for by the laws of civilization, the rights of humanity, and the requirements of morality.

MAXIMILIAN.

MEXICO, *October* 2, 1865.

[Enclosure No. 9.—Translation.]

DECREE.

We, Maximiliano, emperor of Mexico, by the advice of our council of ministers and of our council of state, do decree as follow:

ARTICLE 1. All persons belonging to armed bands or societies not legally authorized, whether of a political nature or not, whatever be the number of those forming the band, or its organization, character, or denomination, shall be tried by a court-martial, and, if found guilty, if only of the act of belonging to such a band, they shall be condemned to capital punishment, which shall be executed within the twenty-four hours next ensuing after the declaration of the sentence.

ARTICLE 2. Persons belonging to the bands described in the foregoing article, when caught using arms, shall be tried by the commandant of the force making the capture, who, within twenty-four hours after such apprehension, shall cause the offence to be verbally investigated, hearing the offender in his own defence. A record of such investigation shall be written down, terminating with the sentence, which shall be to capital punishment should the offender be found guilty, if even solely of the fact of belonging to the band. The commanding officer shall cause the sentence to be executed within twenty-four hours, allowing the culprit to receive spiritual consolation; and after execution of the sentence the said officer will forward a record of the proceedings to the minister of war.

ARTICLE 3. Exemption from the penalty decreed in the foregoing articles shall be allowed solely to such persons as may be able to show that they were forcibly kept with the band, or that they met with it accidentally.

ARTICLE 4. If, upon holding an investigation, as prescribed by article 2, evidence should appear tending to the presumption that the prisoner had been forcibly kept with the band, without having committed any offence, or that, without belonging to such a band, he had accidentally fallen in with it, then in such case the commanding officer shall not pronounce sentence, but forward the presumed offender, together with a written statement of the proceedings, to the proper court-martial, in order that the latter may try the case in accordance with article 1.

ARTICLE 5. The following persons shall be tried and sentenced conformably to article 1 of this decree: 1. All who voluntarily assist guerillas with money, or give them any other species of material aid. 2. Those who may give them information, news, or advice. 3. Those who voluntarily transfer or sell to guerillas, knowing them to be guerillas, arms, horses, ammunition, provisions, or any other articles useful in warfare.

ARTICLE 6. The following persons shall also be tried in accordance with article 1, viz: 1. Those who maintain relations with guerillas indicating connivance with them. 2. Those who voluntarily or knowingly conceal guerillas in their houses or buildings. 3. Those who circulate orally or in writing false or alarming reports tending to disturb the public peace, and such as make any demonstration against the same. 4. All proprietors or administrators of country estates who neglect to give the authorities immediate information of the passage of any band through their property. The offenders mentioned in sections 1 and 2 of this article shall be punished by imprisonment of from six months to two years' duration, or with from one to three months' confinement with hard labor, according to the gravity of the offence. Any person alluded to in section 2, who may be a parent, child, husband, wife, brother, or sister of the party concealed shall not suffer the penalty above prescribed, but shall remain under the surveillance of the authorities during such a period as the court-martial may direct. All included in section 3 of this article shall be punished by the imposition of a fine of from \$25 to \$1,000, or imprisonment of from one to twelve months, according to the gravity of the offence. Those included in section 4 of this article shall be punished by the imposition of a fine of from \$200, to \$2,000.

ARTICLE 7. The local authorities in villages who fail to give immediate notice to their superior authorities of the passage of any armed body of men through their limits shall be punished gubernatorially by the said superior authorities, by the imposition of a fine of from $200 to $2,000, or with imprisonment from three months up to two years in duration.

ARTICLE 8. Any resident of a village or town who, after learning of the approach or transit of an armed body of men through the district, shall fail to notify the authorities of the same, shall be subjected to the payment of a fine varying from $5 to $500.

ARTICLE 9. All the male inhabitants of any town between the ages of eighteen and fifty-five, and free from physical disability, are required, in the event of the town being threatened by any hostile band, to come forward for its defence immediately upon being called upon; and should they refuse to act, they shall be punished by a fine of from $5 to $200, or by from fifteen days' to four months' imprisonment. Should the authorities deem it more advisable to punish the town for not having defended itself, a fine of from $200 to $2,000 may be imposed, and the same shall be paid jointly by those refusing to come forward for the defence of the place, as provided by this article.

ARTICLE 10. All proprietors or administrators of landed property who, although able to defend themselves, shall take no steps to prevent the invasion of guerillas or other outlaws, or who shall fail to notify the nearest military post without delay of such occupation, or who shall receive worn-out or wounded horses belonging to lawless bands upon their property, without informing the said authorities, shall be punished by a fine of from $100 to $2,000, according to the gravity of the offence; and if of sufficient gravity, they may be consigned to prison and handed over to the proper court-martial, to be tried in accordance with this law. The fine shall be paid by the offender to the revenue officer for the district wherein the property may be situated. The first provision of this article shall apply to villages.

ARTICLE 11. Any official, whether political, military, or municipal, who shall fail to proceed conformably to the provisions of this law against parties who may be charged with the offences mentioned, or against those suspected of having committed the same, shall be punished gubernatorially by a fine of from $50 to $1,000; and should it appear that such neglect arose from complicity with the delinquents, the said official shall, by order of the government, be handed over to a court-martial, in order that he may be duly tried and a penalty decreed suitable to the gravity of the offence.

ARTICLE 12. Robbers shall be tried and sentenced in accordance with article 1 of this decree, whatever may be the manner and circumstances of the robbery.

ARTICLE 13. The sentences of death rendered for the crimes described in this decree shall be executed within the periods stated, and no petitions for pardon will be received. When a sentence other than capital is rendered against a foreigner, after record has been made of the sentence, the government may use its privilege to expel all dangerous foreigners from the national territory.

ARTICLE 14. Full amnesty will be granted to all who have belonged or do now belong to armed bands, if they present themselves to the authorities before the 15th of November next: provided always that they have committed no other offence, reckoning from the date of the present decree. The authorities will take possession of the arms of such as present themselves for amnesty.

ARTICLE 15. The government reserves the right to declare when the provisions of this decree shall cease.

Our ministers are intrusted with the execution of this decree as far as each is concerned, and they will issue the necessary orders for its strict observance.

Given at the palace of Mexico on the 3d of October, 1865.

MAXIMILIAN.

The minister of foreign affairs, charged with the ministry of state,
JOSÉ F. RAMIREZ.

The minister of war,
JUAN DE DIOS PEZA.

The minister of improvement,
LUIS ROBLES PEZUELA.

The minister of the interior,
JOSÉ MARIA ESTEVA.

The minister of justice,
PEDRO ESCUDERO Y ECHANOVA.

The minister of public instruction and religious worship,
MANUEL SILICEO.

The sub-secretary of the treasury,
FRANCISCO DE P. CESAR.

[Enclosure No. 10.—Translation.]

ADDRESS.

MEXICANS: We celebrate to-day the memory of a man born in obscurity, from the lowest ranks of the people, and who occupies now one of the highest and most illustrious places in the glorious history of our country. A representative of the mixed races, to whom man's alse pride, outraging the sublime precepts of our gospel, refused to grant what is due to them, he has written his name in golden letters on the pages of immortality. How has he done it? With two qualities which are the virtues of a true citizen: the patriotism and courage of an indomitable conviction.

He wanted the independence of his country; he wanted it with the consciousness of the justice of his cause; and God, who helps always those who have faith in their mission, had gifted him with the peculiar qualities of a great leader. We have seen the humble son of the people triumph on the battle-field; we saw him, a poor curate, govern the provinces under his command in the difficult moments of their painful regeneration; we saw him die in shedding blood like a martyr to freedom and independence; but this man will live forever, for the triumph of his principles is the basis of our nationality.

As a free and democratic country, Mexico has the happiness to show the history of its regeneration and freedom represented by heroes belonging to all classes of human society, of all the races who form now an indivisible nation.

This happiness constitutes its futurity. Every one of them has worked with the same patriotic zeal for the good of the country. All of them have the same rights of enjoying the benefits of their arduous task, and thus to proclaim equality, which is the only and true basis of a nation which respects itself.

Let the movement which we inaugurate to-day for Morello's one hundredth anniversary be a stimulant to new generations, so that they learn from the great citizen the qualities which make the invincible strength of our nation.

True copy:

IGN'O MARISCAL.

WASHINGTON, *October* 25, 1865.

Mr. Corwin to Mr. Seward.

[Extracts.]

No. 14.] LEGATION OF THE UNITED STATES OF AMERICA,
Mexico, October 28, 1865.

SIR: I have to acknowledge the receipt of your despatches Nos. 105 and 106, dated, respectively, September 14 and 30. They were both received by me yesterday morning.

In my despatch No. 13, of September 10, I informed you that M. F. Maury, formerly of Washington, would probably be appointed by Maximilian "imperial commissioner of immigration." Since that time he has received this appointment, become a naturalized Mexican citizen, and been named honorary counsellor of state. J. B. Magruder, formerly an officer in the regular army of the United States, and lately a general in the confederate army, has also become a Mexican citizen, and been charged with the supervision of the survey of lands for colonization. Their scheme for bringing planters from the United States to Mexico promises even thus early to prove an almost complete failure. I mention these gentlemen on account of the prominent positions which one of them, at least, has held under the United States government.

* * * * * * *

On the 13th of this month Colonel Ramon Mendez, with four hundred infantry and three hundred cavalry soldiers, overtook and defeated, at Santa Ana Amatlan, the liberal forces, amounting to one thousand men, mostly infantry, under the command of General Salazar. The imperialists took prisoner Arteaga, general-in-chief of the army of the centre; Salazar, the general commanding and governor of the department; four colonels, five lieutenant colonels, eight captains, and many other subaltern officers. They also captured four hundred of the troop, the armament, horses and park.

It has been reported here for the last three days, and generally believed, that on the 21st instant Generals Arteaga and Salazar and the four colonels were shot in Uruapan. No official account of the disposition made of them has been published.

* * * * * * *

The second of this month, Maximilian issued an address to the Mexican people, which he begins by saying: "The cause which Don Benito Juarez sustained with so much valor and constancy has now fallen, not only by the national will, but before the law itself, which this chief invoked in aid of his titles. To-day even the little band into which said cause degenerated is abandoned by the departure of its chief from his native country." He then goes on to say that the national government for a long time has been indulgent and prodigal of its clemency, in order to allow those who had been misled, who did not know the facts, to unite themselves to the majority of the nation, and place themselves again in the path of duty; but that this indulgence now ceases, as those alone who burn towns and who rob and assassinate peaceable citizens, miserable old men, and defenceless women, would profit by it.

In accordance with the idea contained in the above-mentioned address, on the 3d instant a decree was published, the first article of which declares that all those who may belong to armed bands, which may not be legally authorized, whether they proclaim or not any political pretext, and whatever may be the number of those who form the band, their organization and the character and denomination which they may give themselves, shall be judged by courts-martial, and if found guilty, although it may be only of the fact of belonging to the band, shall be condemned to capital punishment and executed within twenty-four hours. Other articles provide for the punishment of those who may have corresponded with, secreted, or in any way aided those mentioned in article first; but I refer particularly to article first, as it shows that all those belonging to the armies fighting for the republican government will be shot if taken prisoners by the imperial troops. Article fourteenth grants an amnesty to all those who may have belonged or who may now belong to such armed bands, if they present themselves to the authorities before the fifteenth of next month.

* * * * * * * *

Some time next month, probably on the 5th, the emperor will leave this city to visit Yucatan; the empress will accompany him as far as Jalapa.

Your obedient servant,

WM. H. CORWIN.

Hon. WM. H. SEWARD,
Secretary of State of the United States, Washington.

Mr. Romero to Mr. Seward.

[Translation.]

MEXICAN LEGATION TO THE UNITED STATES OF AMERICA,
New York, November 20, 1865.

MR. SECRETARY: In my note of the 25th October last I sent you a copy of a decree dated 3d October, issued by the usurper who pretends to be the ruler of Mexico, authorized by his signature and those of his accomplices, members of his cabinet, in which all Mexicans defending the independence of their country, and even those who conceal or aid the patriots in any way, are ordered to be shot without trial or judgment of any kind.

This barbarous and bloody decree, the most cruel ever yet seen, has already begun to be executed. It is now my painful duty to inform you that on the 13th of October last the Generals Arteaga and Salazar, and Colonel Diaz Paracho, Villa Gomez, Perez Milicua, and Villanos, five lieutenant colonels, eight commandants, and a number of subordinate officers, were surprised and taken prisoners by the French forces in the town of Santa Ana Amatlan, State of Michoacan, as appears from the official despatch sent to the usurper, of which I enclose a copy in French.

These generals and colonels belonged to the regular army of the republic were officers of education and profession, and had fought for the independence of their country from the time the French first landed in Mexico.

General Arteaga had reached the highest rank in the Mexican army, and had recently succeeded ex-General Uraga in command in the army of the centre. He was thoroughly loyal, a patriot without blemish, and enjoyed a high reputation of honesty and probity among his fellow-countrymen of all political shades. His constancy and suffering in the campaign against the French, Austrian and Belgian invaders in the State of Michoacan, for the last two years, would suffice to give him great reputation if he had not already possessed one. His humanity was proverbial, as the French, Belgian, and Austrian soldiers who were taken prisoners by his forces at different times can testify.

The other chiefs and officers who were made prisoners with General Arteaga, though they had not arrived at the high position of their leader, were not less respectable and worthy.

These distinguished Mexicans were executed in accordance with the above-mentioned bloody decree of the usurper of Mexico. I have information, of the truth of which, unhappily, there is no doubt, that the two generals and four colonels were barbarously sacrificed, in flagrant violation of the laws of war and every principle of justice. But the consequences of these sanguinary murders must finally be favorable to the cause of Mexican nationality; for such acts of barbarism will not be tolerated by the Mexican people, who will punish the invaders and their instrument, so openly violating all the customs of nations and every principle of justice.

In communicating to you the news of these unpleasant events, I embrace the occasion to renew the assurances of my most distinguished consideration.

M. ROMERO.

Hon. WILLIAM H. SEWARD, *&c., &c., &c.,*
Washington, D. C.

[Enclosure No. 1.—Translation.]

From the "Estafette," a French paper published in the city of Mexico, of the 31st October, 1865.

Colonel Mendez made the following report to the War Department of his expedition against the disaffected of Michoacan:

On the 6th I left Morelia with the imperial battalion and two squadrons of the 4th regiment of cavalry, commanded by Colonel Wenceslaus Santa Cruz; and took the road to Patzcuaro, where I arrived on the 7th. The rest of my brigade joined me in the night, and on the 8th I started for Uruapan, where all the forces of the enemy, under Arteaga, were assembled.

I arrived in sight of Uruapan at three o'clock on the 9th, but a severe storm prevented me from entering the town. The streams had risen so high, my forces were separated into three sections. I could not cross the torrents till midnight. The enemy had several divisions. One of 700 men, under Ronda and Riva Palacio, started towards Paracho; another of 600 men, under Zepeda, Martinez, and Simon Guttierez, took the direction of Los Reyes; and the rest of the forces were commanded by Arteaga and his subordinates, Salazar and Diaz Paracho. He had many officers following his headquarters, and forces to the number of ten or twelve hundred men. This column marched towards Tancitaro.

On the 10th I rested awhile, intending to pursue Arteaga. It is useless to inform you that I flanked the enemy, instead of fronting them, so as to threaten both detachments and deceive Arteaga, who was my main object.

On the 12th I left San Juan and reached Tancitaro, where the enemy was posted. He left, and I pursued with my guerillas for three leagues. I was sure of overtaking him and whipping him before night, but that would not secure the leaders, so I made a halt at Tancitaro.

At 2 o'clock this morning I took 400 infantry with 300 cavalry and started for Santa Ana Amatlan, where I would wait for Arteaga and defeat him. In fact, the enemy could not believe it possible for me to march twelve leagues a day in such hot weather. It did cost me fourteen men, and most of the horses of the 4th regiment are foundered; but I attained my end: the enemy is completely routed.

Among my prisoners is the commander-in-chief, *Arteaga*, General Salazar, Colonel Diaz Paracho, Villa Gomez, Perez Milicua, and Villanos, five lieutenant colonels, eight commanders, and a large number of subordinate officers, a list of whose names I will send you. All the supplies, munitions of war and horses, mostly useless, have fallen into our hands. We have 400 prisoners, most of whom I will release, as they were enlisted by force along the line of march.

The government alone can appreciate this victory. I must make honorable mention of Lieutenant Rangel, of the 4th cavalry, whom I promised, in his Majesty's name, to promote to a captaincy, and for whom I solicit the cross of knight of the order of Guadalupe. This brave officer entered the city at the head of twenty men, and we are much indebted to him for the victory. Second Lieutenant Navia, of the imperial battalion, with only eight men, followed Rangel. I have made him no promises, because he belongs to my battalion. In due time I will make a proper report of the gallant conduct of these two officers, that the worthy may wear upon their breasts an honorable signal of their bravery, serving to encourage their companions.

I congratulate your excellency, and beg you to inform my august sovereign of this memorable day. God grant you many years.

RAMON MENDEZ, *Colonel.*

This achievement, one of the most glorious of the campaign, does the greatest honor to Colonel Mendez, and simplifies the task of pacificating Michoacan. Arteaga, without being a skilful general, is an honest and sincere man, who has distinguished himself more than once in his career by traits of humanity. Justice to the conquered.

CH. DE BARRES.

Mr. Seward to Mr. Bigelow.

No. 297.]

DEPARTMENT OF STATE,
Washington, November 3, 1865.

SIR: I am directed by the President to request you to ask the serious attention of the French government to the military proceedings in Mexico, by which native Mexicans taken captive while adhering in war to their own republican government are denied rights which the law of nations invariably accords to prisoners of war.

I am, sir, your obedient servant,

WILLIAM H. SEWARD.

JOHN BIGELOW, Esq., *&c., &c., &c.*

Mr. Seward to Mr. Bigelow.

No. 320.]

DEPARTMENT OF STATE,
Washington, November 28, 1865.

SIR: With reference to my despatch of the 30th instant, No. 297, it is now my painful duty to acquaint you that information has been received from the minister of the republican government of Mexico accredited to this government to the effect that the sanguinary policy referred to in the above-named despatch has actually been inaugurated by the execution of several distinguished officers of the liberal forces who had been surprised and captured by the imperialist forces in the town of Santa Ana Amatlan, namely, Generals Arteaga and Salazar, and Colonels Diaz Paracho, Villa Gomez, Perez Milicua and Villanos, five lieutenant colonels, eight commanders, and a number of subordinate officers.

It devolves upon me to instruct you again to call the serious attention of the imperial government to this subject, and to inform Mr. Drouyn de Lhuys that these reports have been received with the most profound concern by the government of the United States. If upon investigation they should prove, as there is too strong ground for believing, that they are well founded, we cannot suffer ourselves to doubt that, so far as the government of France is concerned, it can never countenance proceedings which are so repugnant to the sentiments of modern civilization and the instincts of humanity.

I am, sir, your obedient servant,

WILLIAM H. SEWARD.

JOHN BIGELOW, Esq., *&c., &c., &c.*

Mr. Bigelow to Mr. Seward.

[Extract.]

No. 209.] LEGATION OF THE UNITED STATES,
Paris, November 30, 1865.

SIR: * * * * * * * *

He (Mr. Drouyn de Lhuys) here referred to the representation I had made in regard to the shooting of the Mexican prisoners taken in war, and also to the case of Madame de Iturbide. Why, he said, do you not go to President Juarez? We are not the government of Mexico, and you do us too much honor to treat us as such. We had to go to Mexico with an army to secure certain important interests, but we are not responsible for Maximilian or his government. He is accountable to you, as to any other government, if he violated its rights, and you have the same remedies there that we had.

* * * * * * * * * *

I have the honor to be, sir, your obedient servant,

JOHN BIGELOW.

Hon. WILLIAM H. SEWARD, *Secretary of State.*

Mr. Seward to Mr. Romero.

DEPARTMENT OF STATE,
Washington, December 10, 1865.

SIR: I have had the honor to receive your communication of the 25th of October last, and the ten enclosures which accompanied the same, which you communicated for the information of the government of the United States.

You are pleased to call my particular attention to the most significant of these documents, namely, to a proclamation dated October 2, 1865, and to a decree of the 3d of the same month, issued by the so-called emperor of Mexico, in the latter of which the penalty of death is to be imposed upon all Mexicans who are in arms against his authority in that republic.

In reply, I have the honor to inform you that your despatch and its accompaniments, for which you will accept my thanks, have received the consideration to which they are justly entitled from this government.

You will accept, sir, the assurances of my renewed and very distinguished consideration.

WILLIAM H. SEWARD.

Señor MATIAS ROMERO, *&c., &c., &c.,*
Washington, D. C.

Mr. Romero to Mr. Hunter.

[Translation.]

MEXICAN LEGATION IN THE UNITED STATES OF AMERICA,
Washington, January 5, 1866.

MR. ACTING SECRETARY: On referring to my notes of the 25th of October and 20th of November last to your department, relative to the declaration of war to the death made by the French and their agents in Mexico against the citizens of that republic who are defending the independence of their country, and especially to the assassination of Major General Arteaga and several of his companions in arms, conformably to the spirit of that determination, I now have the honor to send you the copy of a letter from that general to his mother, written from Uruapan, dated October 20, 1865, on the evening of the day before his sacrifice.

This important document shows, in the first place, that the assassination of General Arteaga is an accomplished fact, notwithstanding the endeavors of the French to conceal it; and it shows, moreover, that it was premeditated and executed by orders from Mexico, or by command of the French general-in-chief of the invading army, or by the French agent in that city, on whom they try to lay the responsibility of their conduct.

It appears, in fact, as well from the letter I enclose as from the official report of the capture of those officers, which I sent you in my note of the 20th November last, that they were captured since the 13th of October, and it is inferred from the same letter that they were shot on the 21st of the same month, after a period of eight days. If they had been executed according to the usurper's sanguinary decree of the 3d October, without the interference of the superior French agents residing in the city of Mexico, they would have been tried by a court-martial within twenty-four hours after their capture, (art. 2,) and shot within the next twenty-four hours, (art. 1;) and, besides, the term of eight days was more than enough time to send from Uruapan to the city of Mexico and get an answer about the destiny of the prisoners.

The assassins have not had the manliness to assume the responsibility of their crime, but have tried to conceal it, or impose the guilt of it upon an unhappy traitor officer who has joined the conquerors of his country.

I accept this occasion to renew to you, sir, the assurances of my distinguished consideration.

M. ROMERO.

Hon. WILLIAM HUNTER, *&c. &c., &c.*

"URUAPAN, *October* 20, 1865.

"MY ADORED MOTHER: I was taken prisoner on the 13th instant by the imperial troops, and to-morrow I am to be shot. I pray you, mama, to pardon me for all the suffering I have caused you during the time I have followed the profession of arms, against your will.

"Mama, in spite of all my efforts to aid you, the only means I had I sent you in April last; but God is with you, and he will not suffer you to perish, nor my sister Trinidad, *the little Yankee.*

"I have not told you before of the death of my brother Luis, because I feared you would die of grief; he died at Tuxpan, in the State of Jalisco, about the first of January last.

"Mama, I leave nothing but a spotless name, for I have never taken anything that did not belong to me; and I trust God will pardon all my sins and take me into his glory.

"I die a Christian, and bid you all adieu—you, Dolores, and all the family, as your very obedient son,

"JOSÉ MARIA ARTEAGA

"DOÑA APOLONIA MAGALLANES DE ARTEAGA, *Aguas Calientes.*"

Mr. Romero to Mr. Hunter.

[Translation.]

MEXICAN LEGATION IN THE UNITED STATES OF AMERICA,
Washington, January 22, 1866.

MR. ACTING SECRETARY: In reference to my notes of the 25th of October and 20th of November last, and of the 5th instant, relative to the so-called decree of the usurper of Mexico, issued the 3d of October, ordering the assassination of all Mexicans defending the independence of their country, and especially to the assassination of General Arteaga and some of his companions-in-arms, I now have the honor to transmit to you various documents relating to this same subject, showing how far the barbarism of the usurper and his abettors is carried.

The first of these documents is a letter from General Don Carlos Salazar, of the national army of Mexico, who was captured and sacrificed at the same time with General Arteaga, to his family, a short time before his death. In it are found sentiments of the purest patriotism, and a consciousness of the fulfilment of duty. General Salazar suffered death with the resignation of a true martyr. These iniquitous assassinations occasioned an energetic protest, a copy in English of which is enclosed, of the Belgian officers who were made prisoners in the battle of Tacambaro on the 11th of April, 1865, and remained in General Arteaga's hands from that time, as prisoners of war, addressed to the usurper Ferdinand Maximilian.

You will here see the great contrast between the conduct of the Mexican authorities and the usurper's agents in the treatment of prisoners taken from the legion of mercenary adventurers, who even doubted whether the rights of war would be accorded to them or not; the usurper's agents, in violation of every principle of justice and every sentiment of humanity, assassinate every *Mexican* who defends the independence of his country.

It is not alone in Michoacan that these horrible crimes have been committed, but wherever French soldiers have dominion similar scenes are witnessed. There was a like case in Tamaulipas lately, the particulars of which you will find in the notes exchanged, at the beginning of this month, between General Weitzel, commanding the United States forces on the Rio Grande, who protests in the name of the civilized world against these excesses, and the traitor Thomas Mejia, the French agent at Matamoras, and a person calling himself R. Clay Crawford, general of division in the Mexican army.

These communications, of which I enclose copies, have been published by the papers of this country, and their authenticity is not doubted.

I profit by this opportunity to renew to you, sir, the assurance of my distinguished consideration.

M. ROMERO.

Hon. WILLIAM HUNTER, *&c., &c., &c.*

"URUAPAN, *October* 20, 1865.

"ADORED MOTHER: It is seven o'clock at night, and General Arteaga, Colonel Villa Gomez, with three other chiefs and myself, have just been condemned. My conscience is quiet; I go down to the tomb at thirty-three years of age, without a stain upon my military career or a blot upon my name. Weep not, but be comforted, for the only crime your son has committed is the defence of a holy cause—the independence of his country. For this I am to be shot. I have no money, for I have saved nothing. I leave you without a fortune, but God will aid you and my children, who are proud to bear my name. * *

"Direct my children and my brothers in the path of honor, for the scaffold cannot attaint loyal names.

"Adieu, dear mother. I will receive your blessings from the tomb. Embrace my good uncle Luis for me, and Tecla, Lupe and Isabel; also, my namesake, as well as Carmelita, Cholita, and Manuelita; give them many kisses, and the adieu from my inmost soul. I leave the first my silver-gilt watch; to Manuel I leave four suits of clothes. Many blessings for my uncles, aunts, cousins, and all loyal friends, and receive the last adieu of your obedient and faithful son, who loves you much.

"CARLOS SALAZAR.

"POSTSCRIPT.—If affairs should change hereafter—and it is possible they may—I wish my ashes to repose by the side of my children, in your town."

"URUAPAN, *October* 20, 1865.

"MY DEAR FATHER: I employ my last moments in writing to you. I would like to leave an honored name to my family; I have worked for it, defending the cause I embraced, but I could not succeed. Patience! But I believe you will not be ashamed to own a son who never left the path that you traced out for me so honorably, by precept and example. I have always acted honorably, and have no compunctions of conscience; I have behaved as a man of honor, and am not sorry for it; no one can complain of me, for I have injured no one. I hope this will be some solace to your sorrow, and will make you proud of my memory, ever pure and without a stain. I die content.

"Give my last adieus to my brother and all my friends, reserving for yourself the heart of a son sacrificed upon the altar of his country.

"T. VILLA GOMEZ.

"DON MIGUEL VILLA GOMEZ."

[Enclosure No. 3.—Translation.]

The *Republica*, a liberal journal representing the interests of the republican army of the centre, and issued at Nocupetaro, in the State of Michoacan, has published the following documents in French and Spanish:

To the General Commanding the Republican Army of the Centre:

GENERAL: Our hearts were filled with indignation upon learning the outrages committed upon officers of your army by Colonel Mendez; and we cannot do less than send the following protest to Maximilian, which we are convinced will be concurred in by all our brothers. We beg, therefore, general, that you will cause it to be sent to the other Zitacuaro prisoners, who will hasten to sign it, in order that it may be laid before Maximilian's cabinet as speedily as possible. Accept, general, the expression of the respect of your prisoners,

BREUER,
GUYOT,
FLACHAT,
VAN HOLLENBECK.

TACAMBARO, *October* 23, 1865.

SIR: We have learned with horror and dismay of the act committed by Colonel Mendez, who, in violation of all the laws of humanity and war, has executed a number of officers of the liberal army taken prisoners by him. In all civilized countries military officers respect prisoners of war. The liberal army—to which you refuse to accord even the name of army—pays a greater respect to those laws than the leaders of your forces; for we, who are prisoners, are respected by all, from generals down to private soldiers. Were we not with a genuine liberal force, the act of Colonel Mendez might provoke a bloody revenge; and we Belgians, who came to Mexico solely in order to act as a guard to our princess, but whom you have forced to fight against principles identical with our own, might have expiated with our blood the crime of a man who is a traitor to his country. We hope, sire, that this act of barbarity will not remain unpunished, and that you will cause the laws existing among all civilized nations to be respected. We protest most earnestly against this unworthy act, hoping that the Belgian name will not much longer continue mixed up with this iniquitous war.

BREUER,
GUYOT,
FLACHAT,
VAN HOLLENBECK,
and two hundred others.

TACAMBARO, *October* 24, 1865.

To the Representatives of the Belgian Nation:

GENTLEMEN: The Mexican question has frequently been discussed by you, but the chief point has been the legality or illegality of recruiting for the Belgian legion. Now, however, an event of great gravity obliges us to call your attention to it anew. The lives of two hundred Belgian prisoners are involved. Considering the question some time back, the force was intended solely as a guard of honor voluntarily offered for the protection of a Belgian princess. The emperor, disregarding the special service for which the legion was destined and the neutrality of the Belgian nation, ordered us to take the field, and being Belgian soldiers, we obeyed, and marched to the front cheerfully, animated by the love of war. Although we achieved triumphs, we also, unfortunately, sustained reverses, and two hundred of us Belgians are prisoners. Without taking our position into consideration, the emperor recently issued a decree which may cause terrible results. It announces to the republicans that after the 15th of November all persons caught with arms in their hands would be shot.

At the commencement of this month an imperialist colonel, named Mendez—an ex-republican, who sold himself to the empire—a man hating the Belgians, took a large number of prisoners from the republican army in a fight, including two generals and several officers of high rank, whom he caused to be shot, without regard to military law, and without waiting for the expiration of the period fixed by the decree, stating, after the execution, to persons who remonstrated with him upon the enormity of the deed, "What matters it? They can only revenge themselves upon the Belgians." This alluded to the fact that all the other (French) prisoners had been exchanged.

We expected that all the Belgian prisoners would be put to death; but the republic of Mexico being great and generous, like all free nations, deferred to act until after learning the action of the administration of the empire toward this Colonel Mendez.

The emperor is very fond of this man. He has already sacrificed our brave colonel, and he may sacrifice the lives of all the Belgian prisoners.

Gentlemen, it is incumbent upon you to intervene. The Belgian legion desired long since to return to its native country. It did not wish to take part in this iniquitous war, or to serve longer under an empire wherein such deeds are allowed to be committed.

Representatives of the nation, your duty calls you to act wherever the Belgian name is at stake. This is not a question of party, but of nationality.

Representatives of Belgium, remember our motto, "Unity and strength." It behooves you to speak. We call upon you in the name of Belgium, whose honest confidence has been abused. Representatives of Belgium, it behooves you to see that the blood of Belgians be not sacrificed. In the name of the country do your duty.

BREUER,
On behalf of the Belgian prisoners taken by the republican army.

General Crawford to General Weitzel.

BROWNSVILLE, TEXAS, *January* 1, 1866.

GENERAL: Information has just reached me that a number of soldiers belonging to the army of the republic of Mexico were this morning captured in battle by the soldiers of the so-called emperor of Mexico, and that, by the orders of the traitor Mejia, they are to be shot to death at daylight to-morrow.

I wish, general, to protest, in the name of humanity, against this violation of the usages of civilized warfare, and to request that you, on the part of the republic of the United States of America, prevent this atrocious murder of patriots in cold blood by the tools of the Austrian usurper.

The opinions of the people and of the government of the United States in relation to the inhuman orders of Maximilian are well known.

To permit the patriotic soldiers of a sister republic, with which we preserve diplomatic relations, to be butchered within sight of the flag of the United States, and within sound of an army of United States troops, is to prove false to every principle held dear by an American citizen.

As an officer of the army of the Mexican republic I earnestly ask, general, that you prevent the commission of this dreadful crime.

I have the honor to be, general, your obedient servant,

R. CLAY CRAWFORD,
General of Division, Army of Mexico.

Major General GODFREY WEITZEL,
Com'dg District of Rio Grande and 25th Army Corps.

General Weitzel to General Crawford.

HEADQUARTERS DISTRICT OF THE RIO GRANDE,
Brownsville, Texas, January 2, 1866.

GENERAL: I have the honor to acknowledge the receipt of your communication of yesterday.

I have notified General Mejia of the opinion which I firmly believe my government holds on that subject, and have entered solemn protest in writing against the act.

General Mejia replies that he is obliged to obey the orders of his government.

I will notify my superiors of this; but I have positive, written orders not to commence hostilities without instructions so to do.

I am, sir, very respectfully, your obedient servant,

G. WEITZEL, *Major General Commanding.*

R. CLAY CRAWFORD,
General of Division, Army of Mexico.

HEADQUARTERS DISTRICT OF THE RIO GRANDE,
Brownsville, Texas, January 2, 1866.

GENERAL: I understand that you have taken seventeen prisoners from the liberal forces, and that you intend to execute them.

In the name of the entire civilized world I protest against such a horrible act of barbarity. I believe it will stamp the power which you represent with infamy forever.

To execute Mexicans fighting in their own country, and for the freedom of their country, against foreign power, is an act which, at this age, will meet with universal execration.

I cannot permit this to be done under the eye of my government without, on its behalf, entering this solemn protest.

I am, sir, very respectfully, your obedient servant,

G. WEITZEL, *Major General Commanding.*

Major General TOMAS MEJIA,
Commanding line of the Rio Grande

IMPERIAL ARMY MEXICO, DIVISION MEJIA,
Headquarters Matamoras, January 2, 1866.

GENERAL: I acknowledge receipt of your communication dated this day.

I find myself under the necessity of repelling energetically the participation which you pretend to take in the internal concerns of this country.

The business to which the protest in your note refers has now been brought before competent tribunals, and no one has a right to suspend the proceedings.

For your individual cognition I will add that the persons in question are accused of having taken by force of arms thirteen wagons, twenty-six mules and horses, and robbed thirteen persons.

It would be very strange, general, if in the middle of this nineteenth century the bandits and fighting robbers were to receive help and protection from the civilized world.

By the same occasion I see myself obligated to remind you of the contents of the letter which I had the honor to address you on the 21st of last December. I shall return without answer all communications of the character and couched in the language of the one now before me.

Accept, general, my esteem and consideration.

TOMAS MEJIA,
General Commanding line of the Rio Grande.

Major General WEITZEL,
Commanding Western District of Texas, Brownsville.

The following is the letter of the 21st of December, referred to in the foregoing communication:

IMPERIAL ARMY MEXICO, DIVISION MEJIA,
Headquarters Matamoras, December 21, 1865.

GENERAL: I have received your letter dated 19th instant, transmitting me the instructions which you have received from New Orleans, and informing me that I must consider as belligerents the Juarist bands of Mexico, without applying to them the name of bandits, seeing that the government of the United States recognizes that of Juarez, for whom these forces are fighting.

Hereafter, general, I will not answer letters of the character and couched in the language of the one which now occupies me.

The Mexican authorities do not receive other commands, nor do they submit to any other will, than that of the government of Mexico. The conduct of the forces to whom you allude, and the decree of October 3 last, have defined uniformly the position of said forces in the country, and in that position will they now be considered in Mexico.

Accept, general, the assurance of my highest consideration.

TOMAS MEJIA,
Commanding line of Rio Grande.

Major General WEITZEL,
Commanding District Rio Grande.

Mr. Romero to Mr. Seward.

[Translation.]

MEXICAN LEGATION TO THE UNITED STATES OF AMERICA,
Washington, February 20, 1866.

MR. SECRETARY: I have the honor to enclose you two printed communications, of undoubted authenticity, which passed between General Riva Palacio, acting as commander of the army of the centre of the Mexican republic, and General Bazaine, commander-in-chief of the French army now invading that republic. The first is from Tacambaro, (State of Michoacan,) the 27th of November last, in regard to an exchange of prisoners, soon afterwards effected; and the second is from the city of Mexico, the 16th of the same month.

I also enclose a passport, in French and Spanish, given by the said General Bazaine to General Don Santiago Tapia, one of the prisoners exchanged at the time, who showed it to me in New York, on his way to the northern frontier, where he has gone to continue his duty as a soldier and patriot.

My object in sending you these documents is to keep the United States government informed of the conduct of the invaders of Mexico, and I now call your attention to the inconsistency of treating Mexicans as belligerents, after once having denied them that right. The French agent, Maximilian, after having denied all rights of belligerents to the soldiers of the republic, whom he proclaims as bandits in his decree of the 3d of October last, and shoots without trial, in conformity to his decree, even though they belong to regularly organized forces, now the commander-in-chief of the invaders, negotiates a formal exchange of prisoners with General Riva Palacio, whom he calls general and flatters with courteous language for his humanity to French prisoners. To say the least, this signifies an acknowledgment of the rights of belligerents to the forces of the republican army. The evident object of this inconsistency is to gain the release of the French prisoners; and it is an open confession, forced from the invaders of Mexican soil, that those forces defending the independence of their country are not disorganized bands of highway robbers, as they assert, and it is unjust and absurd to deny them the considerations usually extended to all belligerents throughout the civilized world.

I embrace the occasion to renew to you, Mr. Secretary, the assurances of my most distinguished consideration.

M. ROMERO.

Hon. WILLIAM H. SEWARD, *&c.*, *&c.*, *&c.*

[Enclosure No. 1.—Translation.]

No. 1403.]

EXPEDITIONARY CORPS OF MEXICO,
OFFICE OF THE MARSHAL COMMANDER-IN-CHIEF,
Mexico, November 16, 1865.

GENERAL: I received your favor through the politeness of Captain Miñon. I am pleased at the sentiments of humanity that have animated you in this affair. Anxious to assist you in this particular, I am disposed to do all I can to bring about a good understanding.

Therefore I have the honor to inform you that I have given orders for the exchange to take place in the town of Acuitzco, on the 2d of December, between 8 and 10 o'clock in the morning.

In this exchange, I place at your disposal—

First. General Canto and all the officers taken prisoners with him by Colonel Potier.

Second. All the officers taken prisoners in Tacambaro by Colonel Vanders Smissen.

Third. All the officers taken prisoners in Santa Anna Amatlan by General Mendez.

Fourth. All the soldiers taken prisoners in Morelia. And, finally, if you wish it, Generals Tapia and Juan Ramirez, taken prisoners in Oaxaca and kept in Puebla.

All the prisoners in Morelia will be delivered to you on the 2d. In regard to Generals Tapia and Ramirez, I give my word of honor to set them at liberty in Puebla, with safe conducts to go where they please, as soon as I hear that the exchange is made.

I have appointed Captain Bocarmé, of the Belgian regiment, to supervise the exchange of prisoners. Captain Antonio Salgado will accompany him, and he will be escorted to the town of Acuitzco by a Belgian company of 50 or 60 men and a few Mexican cavalry.

I hope, general, you will accept the good intentions offered you on this occasion.

The number of officers sent you from Morelia will be * * * *

I will not close this letter without thanking you for your kindness and attentions towards the prisoners.

Please accept the assurances of my distinguished consideration.

BAZAINE,
Marshal of France.

General RIVA PALACIO.

A copy of the original:

JESUS RUBIO, *Chief Clerk.*

TACAMBARO DE CODALLOS, *September* 27, 1865.

[Enclosure No. 2.]

REPUBLICAN ARMY OF THE CENTRE.—GENERAL-IN-CHIEF.—NO. 52.

HEADQUARTERS AT TACAMBARO DE CODALLOS,
November 27, 1865.

I have received, with much pleasure, through Captain Miñon, your proposals for an exchange of prisoners; and your excellency may rest assured that I will not oppose in any manner, but will do all I can to assist the exchange; and I will order all the prisoners in Zirandaro and Huetamo, Belgians and Mexicans, to be delivered to your excellency's commissioners.

Lieutenant Colonel Augustin Linarte, escorted by eighty cavalry, will attend to the exchange in Acuitzco.

I will, however, observe that Captain Miñon presented your communications to me last night; that from this place to the prisoners is a distance of forty-six leagues of very bad road, and from here to the place of exchange is twelve leagues, which united make a distance of fifty-eight leagues, and I think it hardly possible that the Belgian prisoners can make that distance in the few days your excellency has appointed. However, I have sent an express to start the prisoners to this city; and I take the liberty to request Captain Miñon to deliver a letter to Captain Visart Bocarmé, asking him not to start till I give the proper notice.

I am sure your excellency will not think I am to blame, if the exchange does not take place on the day you have fixed, and as I desire.

To prevent hostilities on the road from here to Morelia from interrupting the execution of this negotiation, I give orders that they be suspended along the line from Tacambaro to Acuitzco, and in case they are broken, I assure your excellency it will not be caused by the republican forces.

Before closing, I must thank your excellency for your kindness and civility in this business, a proof of your humane and noble sentiments.

I beg your excellency to accept the protestations of my distinguished consideration.

VICENTE RIVA PALACIO.

His Excellency Marshal BAZAINE,
Commander-in-chief of the Expeditionary Corps in Mexico.

A copy of the original:

JESUS RUBIO, *Chief Clerk.*

TACAMBARO DE CODALLOS, *November* 27, 1865.

[Enclosure No. 3.]

CORPS OF MEXICO.—OFFICE OF THE MARSHAL COMMANDER-IN-CHIEF.

Safe Conduct.

By virtue of the powers granted to me by his Majesty the emperor Maximilian, and in consequence of the exchange of prisoners effected the 5th of December, 1865, at Acuitzco, (Michoacan,) General Tapia Santiago, prisoner of war at Oaxaca, is set at liberty and authorized to return to Tacambaro to present himself to General Vicente Riva Palacio, or to follow him wherever he may be found.

The civil and military authorities are requested to let him pass freely, on his journey from Puebla to Tacambaro.

BAZAINE, *Marshal of France.*

MEXICO, *December* 8, 1865.

The present safe conduct allows General Tapia to remain only eight days in Tacambaro.

MARSHAL BAZAINE.

MEXICO, *December* 15, 1865.

[Translation.]

HEADQUARTERS OF THE REPUBLICAN ARMY OF THE CENTRE.

The citizen general, Santiago Tapia, presented himself at these headquarters on the 30th day of the past month, and, in compliance with the obligation referred to in the marginal note, returned to Mexico on the 4th day of the present month.

RIVA PALACIO.

TACAMBARO DE CODALLOS, *January* 2, 1866.

Mr. Romero to Mr. Seward.

[Translation.]

MEXICAN LEGATION TO THE UNITED STATES OF AMERICA,
Washington, March 10, 1866.

MR. SECRETARY: As a specimen of the manner in which the so-called decree of the usurper Maximilian, issued the 3d of October last, ordering the execution of all Mexicans who defend the independence of their country, is carried out, I have the honor to enclose to you with this note the death sentence pronounced against Colonel Carlos Garcia Cano, and the mode of its execution, contained in an extract from La Sombra, a paper published in the city of Mexico. The colonel was a young man of 25, who had once served in the ranks of the interventionists; but afterwards reflecting on his duty as a Mexican, he joined the defenders of independence.

He was subsequently taken prisoner, condemned and executed in the irregular manner shown by the annexed document.

I refrain from commenting on what is here improperly called trial, and which is nothing but real assassination. as it was done in accordance with the so-called decree, which is already known to the government of the United States.

I embrace the occasion to renew to you, Mr. Secretary, the assurances of my most distinguished consideration.

M. ROMERO.

Hon. WILLIAM H. SEWARD, *&c. &c., &c.*

[From "La Sombra," Mexico, February 4, 1866.]

Sentence and execution of Garcia Cano.

The following has been published:

WAR DEPARTMENT.—FIRST MILITARY DIVISION, FIRST SUBDIVISION.—NO. 36 OF THE SENTENCE.—DATE OF THE CRIME, 28TH OF DECEMBER, 1865.—COURT-MARTIAL.

Sentence condemning to the penalty of death the person named Carlos Garcia Cano, accused of rebellion against the imperial government, under aggravating circumstances, at the Pachuca Mines, on the 28th of December last, at eleven o'clock at night. On the 21st day of January, 1866, at 2 o'clock in the afternoon, the court-martial met, composed of Colonel Manuel Palomino, president; Captain Luis Alegre, judge; Captain Juan Dueñas, judge; Captain Nicholas Parra, reporter; 2d Sergeant Nicholas Salazar, notary—all appointed by the war department—and pronounced the sentence, from which we make the following extract:

"*Maximilian, emperor of Mexico, to all those present, and those to come, greeting:*

"The court-martial of Toluca has pronounced the sentence from which the following is extracted:

"The court-martial having heard the statement of the commissary reporter, has declared the named Carlos Garcia Cano, ex-colonel of cavalry—to the 1st question, guilty by unanimity; to the 2d question, guilty by unanimity; to the 3d, that he has commited the acts of which he is accused without palliating circumstances—according to the law, guilty by unanimity; to the 4th, the majority do not recommend him to pardon. Therefore the said court condemned the accused Carlos Garcia Cano, ex-colonel, 25 years of age, native of Jalapa, married and domiciled in Pachuca, to the penalty of death, in accordance with the law of the 3d of October, 1866, article first, which declares: that by virtue of article 139 of the code of military justice, the sum of five hundred dollars in gold and silver, cost of board deducted, shall go into the national treasury; the draft for five hundred and forty-nine dollars and twelve cents, and the pistol, which is the *corpus delicti* in another cause, shall be returned to the said Cano, together with the watch and chain, two diamond rings and the pocket-book, which is his property."

This day, the 21st of January, 1866, the present sentence was read by us, the notary undersigned, to the said Carlos Garcia Cano, in presence of the commissary reporter.

NICHOLAS SALAZAR, *Notary*.

NICHOLAS PARRA, *Commissary Reporter*.

This sentence began to receive its execution on the 21st, at 2 o'clock p. m. of the month and year mentioned; the watch and chain, the two diamond rings and the pocket-book, were returned to Cano. The execution was continued on the 22d, at ten minutes before ten, of the same month and year, Carlos Garcia Cano being shot in presence of the troops of the garrison. Finally, at five o'clock, the following sums were sent to the principal administration of revenues: 1st, 24 ounces, of $16 each, making $384; 2d, 3 idem, of $20, $60; 3d, 3 half ounces, $8, $24; 4th, in silver, $1 56½; a total of $469 56½; bill of the tavern for meals, $30 43½; making a total of $500; 5th, one pistol; 6th, a draft for $549 12.

Certified as correct:

NICHOLAS PARRA,
Commissary Reporter.

Countersigned—NICHOLAS SALAZAR, *Notary*.

A true copy:

J. M. MARQUEZ,
Under Secretary of War pro tem.

MEXICO, *January* 31, 1866.

Mr. Seward to Mr. Romero.

DEPARTMENT OF STATE,
Washington, March 14, 1866.

SIR: I have the honor to acknowledge the receipt of your communications of January 5 and 22, February 20, and March 10, 1866, with their enclosures, which relate to the decree issued on the 3d of October, 1865, by the so-called emperor of Mexico, and in which the penalty of death is declared against all Mexicans found in arms and defending the integrity and independence of their country, against the forcible intervention of France in that republic.

You further inform me that this penalty has actually been visited upon Major General José Maria Arteaga, and several of his companions-in-arms, recently made prisoners by the French.

In reply, it is scarcely necessary for me to assure you that the government of the United States deeply regrets the untimely fate which has overtaken these brave champions of the cause of liberty and republican institutions in Mexico; and fully deprecates the practice of a system of warfare so little in consonance with the usages of enlightened states.

I beg, in answer, to state that the subject will receive the attention to which it is so justly entitled from this government, and meanwhile have the honor to renew to you, sir, the assurances of my highest consideration.

WILLIAM H. SEWARD.

Señor MATIAS ROMERO, &c.,
Washington, D. C.

Mr. Corwin to Mr. Seward.

[Extract.]

No. 13.] LEGATION OF THE UNITED STATES OF AMERICA,
Mexico, September 10, 1865.

SIR: * * * * * *

The official paper published in this city, last evening, contained several important decrees issued by Maximilian on the fifth of the month, as it now appears. Among others is one in regard to colonization. As will be seen by a reference to the paper—a copy of which is sent enclosed herewith—this decree has been drawn up solely (though not ostensibly) with the view of inducing our southern planters to emigrate, with their slaves, to Mexico. Although the first article of the "reglamento" which accompanies the decree declares that "in conformity to the laws of the empire, all men of color are free by the simple fact of treading the Mexican soil," yet the remaining articles show clearly that the blacks who may come here under the contracts mentioned in the "reglamento" will be reduced to a state of peonage, which, in its practical workings, is but slavery disguised. The article third obliges the "patron" to maintain the children of his workmen. If the laborer dies the patron becomes the guardian of his children, who, until they attain their majority, are to remain in the service of the patron, under the same conditions as those agreed to by the father. In Mexico this majority is not reached until the man is twenty-five years old. If, in addition to this, it is considered how easy it is to bring the laborer into debt to the patron, and that, according to the system of peonage, the peon must remain with the master until he has paid the debt, and if it is considered also that but very small wages will be paid—as the patron is obliged to agree in the original contract (which is to be for a term of not less than five nor more than ten years) to feed, clothe, and lodge the workmen, and to provide for them in cases of sickness—it will be seen at once that in many, if not the majority of cases, the contract will be in reality a contract for life.

Thus Maximilian is proposing to inaugurate here a system which may, hereafter, give Mexico as much trouble as slavery has caused to the United States. Two considerations have led me to write on this subject. The first is, that only the best and most industrious negroes will come here with their old masters. The idle and the vicious will remain in our country. If I am correct in this supposition, the question is of some importance to our government. In the second place, I have thought you might deem it advisable to have the true nature of these contracts made clearly known to the black population of the south.

It is said that M. F. Maury, formerly in charge of the Washington Observatory, will be appointed imperial commissioner of immigration.

* * * * * * * *

I am, sir, your obedient servant,

WM. H CORWIN.

Hon. WILLIAM H. SEWARD,
Secretary of State of the United States.

Mr. Otterbourg to Mr. Seward.

No. 18.]

UNITED STATES CONSULATE,
Mexico, September 29, 1865.

SIR: I have the honor to inform the department that, in conformity with instructions received from our chargé d'affaires residing here, this consulate has been directed to issue passports when required.

Enclosed I have the honor to transmit the translations (No. 1) to which I referred in despatch No. 17.

I have the honor to be, sir, most respectfully, your obedient servant,

MARCUS OTTERBOURG,
United States Consul.

Hon. WILLIAM H. SEWARD,
Secretary of State of the United States of America, Washington.

No. 1.

DECREE.

We, Maximilian, emperor of Mexico, in consideration of the sparseness of the population in the Mexican territory, in proportion to its extent; desiring to give to immigrants all possible security for property and liberty, in order that they may become good Mexicans, sincerely attached to their new country, and having heard the opinion of our board of colonization, do decree as follows:

ARTICLE 1. Mexico is open to immigration from all nations.

ART. 2. Immigration agents shall be appointed, who will be paid by the government, and whose duty it shall be to protect the arrival of immigrants, and install them on the lands assigned them, and assist them in every possible manner in establishing themselves. These agents will receive the orders of an imperial commission of immigration, specially appointed by us, and to whom, through our minister of improvement, (Fomento,) all communications relating to immigration shall be addressed.

ART. 3. Each immigrant shall receive a duly executed title incommutable of landed estate, and a certificate that it is free of mortgages.

ART. 4. Such property shall be free from taxes for the first year, and also from duties on transfers of property, but only on the first sale.

ART. 5. The immigrants may be naturalized as soon as they shall have established themselves as settlers.

ART. 6. Immigrants who may desire to bring laborers with them, or induce them to come in considerable numbers, of any race whatever, are authorized to do so; but those laborers will be subject to special protective regulations.

ART. 7. The effects of immigrants, their working and breed animals, seeds, agricultural implements, machines, and working tools, will enter free of custom-house and transit duties.

ART. 8. Immigrants are exempted from military service for five years, but they will form a stationary militia, for the purpose of protecting their property and neighborhoods.

ART. 9. Liberty in the exercise of their respective forms of religious worship is secured to immigrants by the organic law of the empire.

ART. 10. Each of our ministers is charged with carrying out such parts of this decree as relates to his department.

Given at Chapultepec on the 5th day of September, 1865.

MAXIMILIAN.

By the Emperor:
The MINISTER OF IMPROVEMENT, (Fomento.)

MANUEL OROZCO Y BERRA,
Sub-Secretary, in the absence of the Minister of Improvements.

REGULATIONS.

Under article 6th of the foregoing decree we ordain as follows:

1. Under the laws of the empire all persons of color are free by the mere act of their touching Mexican territory.

2. They shall make contracts with the employer who has engaged or may engage them, by which such employer shall bind himself to feed, clothe, and lodge them, and give them medical attendance; and also pay them a sum of money according to whatever agreements they may enter into with them. Moreover, he shall deposit in the savings bank herein mentioned, for the benefit of the laborer, a sum equivalent to one-fourth of his wages. The laborer shall, on his part, obligate himself to his employer to perform the labor for which he is employed for a term of not less than five nor more than ten years.

3. The employer shall bind himself to support the children of his laborers. In the event of the father's death, the employer will be regarded as the guardian of the children, and they will remain in his service until they become of age, on the same terms as those agreed on by their father.

[illegible] Each laborer shall receive a book certified by the local authority, in which book his [illegible]tion, the statement of his place of labor, and a certificate of his life and habits will be [illegible] In case of a change of employer, the consent of the former employer shall be en-[illegible]

[illegible] of the employer, his heirs, or whoever may acquire his estate, shall [illegible] the same manner in which such employer was, and the laborer on [illegible] new proprietor on the same terms as in his former con-[illegible]

[illegible] arrested, shall be placed without pay on public [illegible] claim him.

[illegible] shall be brought before [illegible]

8. Special police commissioners will watch over the execution of these regulations, and officially prosecute all violators thereof.

9. A savings bank will be established by the government for the following objects:

10. The employers shall deposit in said bank every month, for the benefit of the laborers, a sum equivalent to one-fourth of the wages which each is entitled to under his contract of employment.

11. The laborers can deposit in addition, in the savings bank, in money, such sums as they may desire.

12. These deposits shall bear interest at the rate of five per centum per annum.

13. At the end of his engagement, and on the presentation of his book, the laborer shall receive the entire amount of his savings.

14. If at the end of his engagement the laborer wishes to leave his money in the savings bank, he can then receive the interest accrued; or if he wishes to leave this also, it will be added to his capital, and also draw interest.

15. In case a laborer should die intestate, or without heirs, his property shall pass to the treasury of the government.

Given at Chapultepec on the 5th day of September, 1865.

MAXIMILIAN.

By the Emperor:
The MINISTER OF IMPROVEMENT, (fomento.)

MANUEL OROZCO Y BERRA,
Sub-Secretary in the absence of the Minister of Improvement.

MAXIMILIAN, EMPEROR OF MEXICO.

Considering that there exist in the district of Cordoba, department of Vera Cruz, various rural estates which, in consequence of insolvency proceedings and other legal questions raised about the ownership of them, have been neglected in their principal parts, thereby depriving agriculture and the population of the fruits which they ought to produce;

Considering that said estates secure large sums of money by mortgage in favor of the clergy, which now belong to the public treasury by virtue of the laws of "desamortization;" and that, in consequence of the abandonment in which these estates have been left, their actual value does not, in any manner, suffice to cover these claims;

Considering that, notwithstanding the number of years that the said questions have been at issue, it has not been possible to terminate them, because the interest of the debtors is opposed to the clearing of the rights of their creditors, thereby doing much injury to the public treasury;

We decree:

ARTICLE 1. The rural estates designated as follows, and which are situated in the district of Cordoba, shall be taken possession of on the ground of public utility: Haciendas del Rosario, de San Antonio, de Ojo de Agua Grande, de Ojo de Agua Chico, de Santa Ana, de la Concepcion Palmillas, de San Francisco, de Toluquilla, rancho del Buen Retiro, hacienda de Guadalupe a la Punta, de Cacahuatal, and de San José del Corral and Venta Pasada.

ART. 2. Our minister of improvements (fomento) will order these estates to be appraised, in order that the interested parties shall receive the indemnity to which they may be entitled by the laws, as soon as it will be made clear, by legal process, what is due the public treasury upon the said estates for the mortgages of the clergy, and who are the legitimate proprietors of them.

ART. 3. The same minister will appropriate the said estates to colonization, dividing them into small lots, and taking care to secure their value, in order to pay it over, as part of the indemnity due for them, to those who may be entitled to it, when the investigations mentioned in the preceding article will have been made.

Given at Chapultepec on the 5th September, 1865.

MAXIMILIAN.

By the Emperor:
The Minister of Improvements: In his absence the sub-secretary,

MANUEL OROZCO Y B[illegible]

On the anniversary of the independence of Mexico, the 16th [illegible] emperor Maximilian delivered the following speech:

GENTLEMEN: This is a family festival, a festiv[illegible] this day under the folds of our glorious banner [illegible] elevating with unpreced[illegible] era, will be forev[illegible] the inauguration of our nationality, because every good Mexican must renew by an oath the promise to live for the greatness, the independence, and the integrity of his country, and show himself always ready to defend it with all his heart and soul. The words of that oath are the first uttered by a good Mexican. I solemnly repeat them now. My heart, my soul, my labor, and my lawful efforts belong to you and to our beloved country. No influence in this world can make me waver in my duty; every drop of my blood is Mexican now, and if God sends fresh dangers to threaten our country, you will see me fight in your ranks for its independence and integrity. I am willing to die at the foot of our glorious banner, because no human power can wrest from me the trust with which you have endowed me. What I say must be said by every good Mexican; it must efface past rancors; it must bury party hatred. Every one must live for the good of our beloved country. Thus united, and following the path of duty, we will be strong, and the principles which form the basis of our task will infallibly triumph.

Mr. Seward to Mr. Speed.

DEPARTMENT OF STATE,
Washington, October 2, 1865.

SIR: I have the honor to enclose herewith an extract from despatch No. 13, of September 10, 1865, received from William H. Corwin, esq., the chargé d'affaires of the United States in Mexico, and also translations of the decrees recently issued by the party exercising authority in the city of Mexico, in relation to the immigration and colonization in that country, referred to in that despatch.

I submit these papers with the view of ascertaining whether, under said decrees, peonage or any other form of slavery can be instituted in Mexico.

I will thank you for an opinion at your earliest convenience.

I have the honor to be, sir, your obedient servant,

WILLIAM H. SEWARD.

Hon. JAMES SPEED,
Attorney General of the United States.

Mr. Speed to Mr. Seward.

ATTORNEY GENERAL'S OFFICE,
October 21, 1865.

SIR: I have the honor to acknowledge the receipt of your letter of the 2d day of October, together with an extract from despatch No. 13, of William H. Corwin, chargé d'affaires of the United States in the city of Mexico, and also translations of decrees recently issued by Maximilian, now exercising the authority of an emperor in Mexico, in relation to immigration into and colonization in that country.

You ask me whether, under these decrees, peonage or any other form of slavery can be instituted in Mexico.

The decrees, of which you have sent to me copies, are, in substance, as follows:

It is recited that, considering the scant population of Mexican territory, it is desirable to give the fullest guarantees of property and liberty to immigrants; it is then decreed—

1. That Mexico shall be open to emigration from all nations.

2. Agents of emigration are to be appointed, and their powers and duties prescribed.

The 3d, 4th, 5th, 7th, 8th, and 9th articles set out and declare what shall be the rights and privileges of emigrants.

The 6th article reads thus: "Immigrants who wish to bring, or cause to come, working-men, in considerable number, of whatever race they may be, are authorized to do so; but these working-men will be the object of special protective regulation."

The second decree is supplementary, and in it are the special protective regulations for working-men referred to in the 6th article. These regulations read as follows:

1. In conformity with the laws of the empire, all men of *color* are free by the fact, alone, of having trod on Mexican territory.

2. They *shall* make with the patron who shall have engaged them a contract by which he shall bind himself to feed, clothe, lodge, and take care of them in their sickness, as well as pay them a salary, the amount of which shall be settled between them. The patron shall bind himself beside to deposit to the credit of the working-man a sum equivalent to one quarter of his salary in the savings bank, which will be further mentioned below. The working-man shall, at the same time, bind himself to his patron to execute the work to which he shall be set during the term of five years at least, and ten years at most.

3. The patron shall bind himself to provide subsistence for the children of his working-men; in case of the death of the father, the patron shall have the guardianship of the children, and they shall remain in his service until the age of majority, on the same condition that the father was.

4. Every working-man shall have a book, inspected by the local authority, on which shall be given his description, the indication of the place where he works, and a certificate of good life and conduct. In case of change of patron, the consent of the first patron shall be inscribed on the book.

5. In case of the death of the patron, his heirs, or the individuals who hav acquired his property, are bound toward their working-men on the same ter the patron was; and the working-man, on his part, is bound in respect to new proprietor in the terms of his first contract.

6. In case of desertion, the working-man apprehended shall be emp without any pay, on the public works, until he shall be reclaimed by his p

7. Every unjust act of the patron towards his working-man shall be over to the courts.

8. Special commissioners of the police shall watch over the execution present regulation, and shall, by virtue of their office, prosecute those c vening the same.

9. The government will establish a savings bank for the ends hereina mentioned.

10 The patron shall deposit in the bank every month, to the credit of the working-men, a sum equal to one-quarter of the salary to which they are entitled by reason of their contract.

11. The working-men may, besides, deposit in the savings bank the sum of which they shall have full credit.

12. The deposits shall have the advantage of five per cent. annual interest.

13. At the close of their engagement, the working-men, on the presentation of their book, shall receive their peculium integrally.

14. If, on the expiring of the contract, the working-men be disposed to leave their money in the savings bank, they can withdraw the interest due, or leave it on deposit; and in the latter case it shall be capitalized with the primitive capital, and shall also bear interest.

15. In case of death, intestate, or without heirs, the peculium of the working-men shall pass into the possession of the public treasury.

The sixth article of the decree and regulations is inconsistent and contradictory. Whilst the sixth article of the decree speaks of working-men of every race, the regulations under it seem to embrace men of color only.

Notwithstanding the broad declaration in the first regulation, that all men of color are free by the fact alone of having trod on Mexican territory, it is manifest that in the subsequent regulations a grinding and odious form of slavery is sought to be established.

Slavery is a law by which one man asserts dominion over the conduct of another, either for a specified time, or for life.

The law of slavery makes the man a mere machine, controlled and governed by another. The slave has but little occasion to exercise and use the noble faculties of his mind. The physical man is alone of value to the master or patron, and he, of course, looks only to the physical wants of the slave.

That the regulations make slaves of working-men and their families is evident.

1st. They are required to sell themselves for not less than five nor more than ten years.

2d. They are required by law, no matter how circumstances may change, or things may occur that were not reasonably within the contemplation of the parties, to specifically fulfil the engagement.

3d. They must execute every work to which they shall be set by their patron during that time.

4th. They cannot feed, clothe, lodge, or take care of themselves, either in health or in sickness.

5th. They cannot provide for the subsistence of their children, nor educate them, unless by permission of the patron; and in case of death, their children become the slaves of the patron until their majority.

6th. The patron or master can sell or dispose of them to whom he pleases.

7th. They may complain to the police of the harsh treatment of their master, but have no right to petition for or seek a change of any law which may be regarded as oppressive or unjust to them or to their class or country.

8th. If the police refuse to hear their complaints, or, hearing, deny interference, they are without redress.

9th. These regulations contemplate that the working-men require physical efforts only; their minds must remain uncultivated, their morals neglected, their religious training not cared for.

[illegible]h. There is no provision by which the working-man can purchase himself [illegible] time, or release or improve the condition of his children.

[illegible]th. What is to become of the working-man and his children after he shall [illegible]e faithfully served his term is not provided. Is he to be a free citizen, or [illegible]e still to be regarded as a working-man, and again compelled to sell himself and his family?

I have no hesitation in saying that these regulations constitute a law which deprives working-men of rights which we in this country regard, and which in every well-organized community should be regarded as inestimable, inalienable, and indestructible, and certainly makes them slaves. The history of this country, and particularly the history of the troubles from which we are just emerging, shows that no society can be organized permanently and remain at peace within its own borders, and with the outside world, where these great and important rights are denied to any considerable class of men.

I am, sir, very respectfully, your obedient servant,

JAMES SPEED, *Attorney General.*

Hon. WILLIAM H. SEWARD, *Secretary of State.*

Mr. Romero to Mr. Seward.

[Translation.]

MEXICAN LEGATION TO THE UNITED STATES OF AMERICA,
Washington, October 5, 1865.

MR. SECRETARY: I have the honor to remit to you, for the information of the government of the United States, a copy,* in English, of the so-called law

---

* For enclosure see despatch from Mr. Otterbourg, No. 18, of the 29th September, 1865.

which on the 5th of September last was issued at Chapultepec by the ex-archduke of Austria, Fernando Maximilian, so-called emperor of Mexico, in which, under pretext, apparently, of inviting foreign emigration to Mexico, he has adopted a plan which has for its purpose to call to that republic the disaffected citizens of the United States who are not disposed to acknowledge the authority of this government, nor to accept the consequences of the war, by admitting them with their prejudices and their peculiar system of labor, already well tried in the southern part of the United States.

According to the information I have received, founded on facts, and which I have communicated to your department, the Emperor of the French and his agent in Mexico, considering that in the country there were not elements sufficient to sustain them, have taken means to call to it all persons they supposed animated by any hostility against the United States.

The arrangements made with ex-Senator Gwin, of California, had that object, but as that individual was recognized as a declared enemy of the United States on the close of the civil war here, it was thought not advisable to irritate this country by carrying out the plans which had been agreed upon with him.

In place of them, there has been another combination, which, under a different form, it is hoped, may produce the like results. For this new plan they have gone to the extreme of practically re-establishing, in fact, in Mexico, the odious institution of slavery. The so-called law of the ex-archduke of Austria goes accompanied by a regulation signed by the same Maximilian, of which I also enclose a copy in English, whose first article, to cover appearances, declares that, "according to the laws of the empire, all men of color are free from the mere fact of stepping on Mexican territory;" but those following establish a slavery so much the more odious, because it is not restricted to color or dete[illegible]mination of caste.

The working-men—name they give to the slaves—will make, accordin[illegible] such regulations, a contract with their master, called *patron*, by which he [illegible] bind himself to feed, clothe, and lodge them, and support them in sickness[illegible] pay them a sum of money in conformity with the conditions agreed [illegible] between them. The fourth part of the sum will be lost to the working-[illegible] almost, because he cannot dispose of it nor of the interest while his contra[illegible] lasts, according to terms of articles 13 and 14. "The working-man will engage at the same time with his patron to do the work to which he may be assigned for the term of five years at least, and ten years at most." "The patron will engage to maintain the children of his working-men." This slavery is hereditary, because, according to article three of the regulations, "in case of the death of the father, (working-man,) the patron shall consider himself tutor of the children, and they shall continue in his service until majority on the same conditions as was the father." The heirs of the patron will hold, in their turn, these working-men in conformity with article 5. To complete the odious practices of the holders of slaves the regulation referred to contains (article 6) an article against fugitive slaves, [illegible] "in case of desertion, the workman, when caught, shall be assigned, w[illegible]es at all, to the public works until his patron comes to reclaim him. [illegible]ummate this work of iniquity, article 15 provides that in case of [illegible] intestate," or without heirs, the peculium of the working-man sha[illegible] the control of the public treasury.

It is really an extraordinary th[illegible]lmost incomprehensible, that when slavery has received a death-blow [illegible]y country that could revive it, and when it has been shown by facts [illegible]xistence is an evil, social, moral and political, there can be in the worl[illegible]er who, without having established his authority in the country he tri[illegible]minate over, should attempt to re-establish that odious system for the [illegible] of strengthening himself, and merely changing the name for the purpos[illegible]ding the world.

As this system of labor might b[illegible]r what in Mexico is called peonage, and as that may be considered here as an institution equivalent to slavery, I think it expedient to show to you that on some estates in the tierras calientes, to the south of Mexico, there has in fact been, through the abuses of the proprietors and the influence they enjoyed, something that might be compared in its practical effects with what the ex-archduke of Austria has now established in his aforesaid decree; but such abuses, besides being restricted to a very narrow district, were never sanctioned by the Mexican laws, and the national government of that republic has taken especial care to correct them and root them out. It was reserved for the ex-archduke of Austria to sanction such an abusive practice by a law which, if it goes into force, will be executed throughout the whole extent of the Mexican territory.

Before concluding this note, I think it proper to remit to you copy of the speech which was delivered in Mexico on the said 16th September by the said archduke of Austria, Fernando Maximilian, in which he expresses what he calls his irrevocable determination not to leave Mexico upon any consideration, whatever may be the circumstances. This is one proof more that the Emperor of the French is very far from desisting from his outrageous attempt to deceive the people of Mexico into acceptance of the yoke of a European monarchy.

It is satisfactory to me to avail of this opportunity to renew to you, Mr. Secretary, the assurances of my most distinguished consideration.

M. ROMERO.

Hon. WILLIAM H. SEWARD, &c., &c., &c.

Mr. Seward to Mr. Bigelow.

No. 296.] DEPARTMENT OF STATE,
Washington, November 2, 1865.

SIR: The condition of the emancipated slaves or freedmen within the United States is at this moment very properly a subject of deep interest. The establishment of the perfect equality of men of the African race with men of other races throughout the whole continent, is a policy which the United States may hereafter be expected to cultivate with constancy and assiduity. Certain decrees bearing on the subject of immigration which are understood to have been promulgated by authorities acting in Mexico, in opposition to that republic, have arrested the attention of this government. The law officer of the government has submitted to this department an opinion, that if those decrees were carried into execution, they would inevitably operate to reduce into a condition of peon slavery working-men of the African race, and, of course, such of the freedmen before mentioned as, with or without their intelligent consent, might be brought within the jurisdiction of Mexico.

If European opinion can be regarded as established in reference to any one political question, it is settled that African slavery in any form ought henceforth to cease throughout the world. We do not doubt that the Emperor of France cordially and fully concurs, as we do, in this humane sentiment. I have, therefore, to request you to place a copy of the opinion of the Attorney General, herewith enclosed,* in the hands of Mr. Drouyn de Lhuys, and ask that the attention of the French government may be directed to the question which the Attorney General has discussed with ability, and with an anxious desire to arrive at just conclusions.

I am, sir, your obedient servant,

WILLIAM H. SEWARD.

JOHN BIGELOW, Esq., &c. &c., &c.

---

* The opinion of the Attorney General referred to herein is that previously inserted under date of October 21, 1865.

Mr. Bigelow to Mr. Seward.

No. 202.] LEGATION OF THE UNITED STATES,
Paris, November 24, 1865.

SIR: I have the honor to acknowledge the receipt of your instruction No. 296, covering the opinion of Mr. Attorney General Speed in reference to certain decrees relating to emigration which have recently been promulgated from the city of Mexico, and to enclose a copy of a communication addressed by me, in compliance therewith, to his excellency the minister for foreign affairs, on the 22d instant.

I am, sir, with great respect, your very obedient servant,

JOHN BIGELOW.

Hon. WILLIAM H. SEWARD,
Secretary of State, Washington, D. C.

[Enclosure.]

Mr. Bigelow to Monsieur Drouyn de Lhuys.

LEGATION OF THE UNITED STATES,
Paris, November 22, 1865.

SIR: Recalling the conversation which I had the honor to hold with your excellency on the 17th ultimo, in relation to the alleged levy of Egyptian troops for involuntary service in Mexico, and the representations I then made in regard to the natural unwillingness of my government and country people to see slavery in any form replanted either within our territory or on our borders, I beg to invite your excellency's attention to certain recent decree bearing upon the subject of emigration to Mexico, purporting to emanate from authoriti acting in opposition to that republic. In the opinion of the law officer of my governm these decrees, if enforced, would inevitably reduce to the condition of peon slavery wor men of the African race, and of course such of the freedmen of the United States a have already been, or hereafter may be, seduced to go there, without a full and int comprehension of their liabilities. That your excellency may understand the grounds conclusion, I am instructed to transmit to your excellency a copy of the Attorney Ge opinion, which will be found enclosed, and to invite the attention of the imperial gover to the questions there discussed. In complying with these instructions of my governme avail myself of the language of the despatch containing them to say that, "If Europ opinion can be regarded as established in reference to any one political question, it is sett that African slavery, in any form, ought henceforth to cease throughout the world." We do not doubt that the Emperor of France cordially and fully concurs, as we do, in this humane sentiment.

I pray your excellency to accept assurances of the distinguished consideration with which I have the honor to be your excellency's very obedient and very humble servant,

JOHN BIGELOW.

His Excellency M. DROUYN DE LHUYS,
Minister of Foreign Affairs.

Mr. Seward to Mr. Romero.

DEPARTMENT OF STATE,
Washington, December 10, 1865.

SIR: I have the honor to acknowledge the receipt of your communications of the 5th October and 20th November last, with their several important accompaniments, which you were pleased to communicate for the information of the government of the United States. In reply, I have the honor to inform you that they have already received the consideration of this department, and that measures have been adopted which are deemed proper to meet the exigencies which they present.

I avail myself of this occasion to renew to you, sir, the assurances of my very distinguished consideration.

WILLIAM H. SEWARD.

Señor MATIAS ROMERO, *&c., &c., &c., Washington, D. C.*

Mr. Seward to Mr. Bigelow.

No. 329.] DEPARTMENT OF STATE,
Washington, December 14, 1865.

SIR: Your despatch of the 24th of November, No. 202, with its accompaniment, has been received. The note which you addressed to Mr. Drouyn de Lhuys on the subject of peon slavery in Mexico is approved.

I am, sir, your obedient servant,

WILLIAM H. SEWARD.

JOHN BIGELOW, Esq., *&c.*, *&c.*, *&c.*

Mr. Bigelow to Mr. Seward.

[Three enclosures.]

No. 243.] UNITED STATES LEGATION,
Paris, January 16, 1866.

SIR: Recalling my despatch No. 202, I have the honor to transmit a reply, received last evening, from his excellency the minister of foreign affairs to the note which I addressed him on the 22d of November last, in reference to certain decrees promulgated recently from the city of Mexico.

My letter acknowledging the receipt of his excellency's communication is also enclosed.

I am, sir, with great respect, your very obedient servant,

JOHN BIGELOW.

Hon. WILLIAM H. SEWARD,
Secretary of State.

Mr. Drouyn de Lhuys to Mr. Bigelow.

PARIS, *January* 15, 1866.

SIR: You did me the honor to communicate to me in the course of the month of November a letter addressed to Mr. Seward, the Secretary of State, by the Attorney General of the United States, on the subject of the decrees issued by the emperor Maximilian concerning immigration and colonization in Mexico. That document constituting a judgment upon interior acts of the Mexican government, I could only receive it as a piece of information. I was careful to point this out to you at the time, declining also any discussion upon measures to which the Emperor's government was absolutely foreign. In acknowledging receipt, therefore, according to your desire, of your letter of the 22d November, I consider myself bound to state the verbal reply which I had to make thereto.

DROUYN DE LHUYS.

Mr. Bigelow to Mr. Drouyn de Lhuys.

PARIS, *January* 16, 1866.

SIR: I have had the honor to receive your excellency's communication, dated the 15th instant, relative to certain decrees recently promulgated in Mexico upon the subject of immigration and colonization. Your excellency refuses all explanation of the inadmissible passages of one of these decrees, to which I had the honor to call your attention in a note of the 22d of November last, upon the plea that they relate to measures of internal administration, with which the Emperor's government had nothing to do.

Although the line separating the responsibility of the imperial government from that of the political organization it has planted in Mexico is traced with some indistinctness, I am certain my government will learn with satisfaction that France, which was one of the first powers to hold up slavery to the execration of mankind, declines all responsibility as to the attempt (although made under protection of her flag) to re-establish that institution in a country which had expressly stigmatized and abolished it.

I take this opportunity, &c.,

JOHN BIGELOW.

STEPS TAKEN BY MAXIMILIAN TO OBTAIN FROM THE UNITED STATES A RECOGNITION OF THE SO-CALLED EMPIRE OF MEXICO.

Señor Arroyo to Mr. Corwin.—(Confidential.)

[Translation.]

NEW YORK, *March* 2, 1865.

MY DEAR SIR: Under date of the 10th of January last his excellency Don José Ramirez, minister of state and of foreign affairs of the Mexican empire, authorizes me to address myself directly and confidentially to the honorable Mr. William H. Seward, Secretary of State, upon determinate points, which I will indicate to you when I may have the satisfaction of seeing you for the purpose.

The same Mr. Ramirez tells me the following: "You can see Mr. Corwin in my name and avail yourself of his influence, manifesting to him that I have regretted not to receive his reply to the letter which I addressed to him in August last." I therefore beg you to be pleased to aid me with your influence, in order to bring about and see whether the object of my commission can be obtained, not doubting that your kindness will cause you to assist me with your counsels and opinion.

I think that you will be of opinion that I should go to your city (Washington) to solicit, verbally, the two points to which my mission is concreted, and I will accordingly do so; but, before undertaking the journey, I would be pleased if you would do me the favor, if you have an opportunity, to indicate to Mr. Seward my expected journey, in order that, if he have no objection that I should see him extra-officially, he should so indicate it.

You can at once, if you think proper, intimate to Mr. Seward that one of the points of my commission is to see whether the habilitation (recognition) of our consuls can be obtained because of the embarrassments which exist in consequence of their non-habilitation (non-recognition;) and while in Mexico the exercise of their functions has been continued without embarrassment to the American consuls, and that the government, which was that of Don Benito Juarez, does not exist either de facto or de jure.

You will excuse me for writing to you in my own language, as I do not know the English with the requisite perfection.

I avail myself of this occasion to place myself at your disposition as your most obedient servant, &c., &c., &c.,

LUIS DE ARROYO,
Box No. 4202.

Mr. THOMAS CORWIN, *Washington.*

NOTE.—The foregoing letter was submitted to the Secretary of State by Mr. Corwin in the early part of the month of March, 1865.

Memorandum.

DEPARTMENT OF STATE,
Washington, March 13, 1865.

Mr. Seward read to Mr. Corwin as follows:

It is a fixed habit of this government to hold no official intercourse with agents of parties in any country which stand in an attitude of revolution antagonistic to the sovereign authority in the same country with which the United States are on terms of friendly diplomatic intercourse.

It is equally a fixed habit of this government to hold no unofficial or private interviews with persons with whom it cannot hold official intercourse.

For these reasons the overture, submitted by Mr. Corwin to the Secretary of State, is declined.

Memorandum by Mr. Seward.

On the 17th day of July, 1865, the Marquis de Montholon called at the Department of State, and said that a special agent had arrived at Washington from Mexico, and that he was the bearer of a letter signed Maximilian, and addressed to the President of the United States, a copy of which the Marquis submitted to the Secretary of State, saying that the agent was instructed to deliver the letter if it should be agreeable to the government of the United States. He also said that the agent brought papers to make explanations and adopt proceedings in relation to certain transactions on the Rio Grande, upon which the United States government had made representations to the imperial government of France.

The Secretary replied, that, inasmuch as the letter referred to was directly addressed to the President of the United States, the Secretary would reserve himself until he should have had a conversation with the President upon the subject.

On the 18th the Secretary of State delivered back the copy of the letter to the Marquis de Montholon, and said that the United States are in friendly communication now, as heretofore, with the republican government in Mexico, and, therefore, cannot depart from the course of proceeding it has heretofore pursued towards that country, and of course that the President declined to receive the letter, or to hold any intercourse with the agent who brought it.

WILLIAM H. SEWARD.

Mr. Romero to Mr. Seward.

WASHINGTON, *July* 31, 1865.

Mr. Romero presents his compliments to Mr. Seward, and has the honor to transmit to him a copy, in English, of a letter which he has received from the city of Mexico, dated the 8th of the month terminating this day, in which some truthful details are given of the efforts of the usurper of Mexico to obtain the recognition of the government of the United States.

Hon. WILLIAM H. SEWARD, *&c., &c., &c.*

[Translation.]

MEXICO, *July* 8, 1865.

* * * * * * * * * * * * * *

Up to a very recent period official circles here had been under the impression that President Johnson and Mr. Seward were great admirers of Maximilian, personally, and would be willing, at a proper time, to recognize him as the government of Mexico, but that they would prefer that some overtures should be first made to them, and that the affair should not be in any way pressed upon them as to time. Such has been for a long period the prevailing opinion with reference to the action of the United States government. This impression, it is said, has been largely supported by, if not mainly based upon, assurances which, it is asserted, have been communicated by Mr. Corwin, late minister here, in his correspondence from Washington, with Mr. Ramirez, Maximilian's secretary of state, and even with General Bazaine. Before Mr. Corwin left for home, he expressed himself in a way that led to the inference that he was disgusted with republics generally, and his relations with Mr. Ramirez and with General Bazaine, of whom he was a great admirer, were such as to be almost confidential in their character.

Since then Mr. Corwin has been considered here as the best friend of the empire in the United States, and great expectations have been based upon his supposed influence with the Washington government. That he has been lending his good offices and services to promote its recognition is unquestionably a fact.

Last winter he sought an interview from Mr. Seward in favor of Don Luis Arroyo, to obtain his recognition by our government as imperial consul in New York. In this attempt, however, he utterly failed. Mr. Corwin, it seems, recovered from that blow, and lately wrote a little more encouragingly to his friends. The news he sent was received with the greatest rejoicings at the palace. As the French, as well as Maximilian and everybody else here well understand that the empire only exists by the toleration of the United States, they thought at once of sending to Washington one of the highest officials, to pave the way for recognition, and, in justice to Maximilian, it must be acknowledged that he devised a very nice little intrigue. The grand marshal of the empire, General Almonte, was to be sent to Washington as ambassador extraordinary in special mission. He was to take among his suite Chamberlain Degollado, as attaché to the embassy. The general would carry with him an autograph letter of condolence from Maximilian to President Johnson upon the assassination of President Lincoln, and congratulating Mr. Johnson upon his elevation to the presidential chair. It was thought that Mr. Johnson could not be so rude as to decline receiving and answering such a letter, and giving a fair hearing to the grand marshal. Mr. Ramirez, the minister of foreign affairs, however, spoiled this little intrigue, either because he did not place entire confidence in the information he had received, or for other reasons. The fact is, he was unwilling to let the grand marshal go, for fear that he and his sovereign would be exposed to a grievous slight. He advised that the letter should be written and sent, but that it should be carried by Chamberlain Degollado, who would leave for the United States as if on private business. This plan was finally adopted. The French papers here denied it was ever thought to send General Almonte, and that Degollado left on private business alone. Degollado being married to a Virginia wife, was thought to be the person best fitted to go without attracting much attention, and to interest in his favor the United States government. Unfortunately for Maximilian, Degollado's wife has not and never had Union sentiments, and will not carry, therefore, much weight. Degollado was instructed to ask an interview from Mr. Seward or the President to deliver Maximilian's letter, through the French minister, M. Montholon, it being believed that there is nothing that our government could refuse when asked by such a source. You will be able to know better than we here what will be the result of this intrigue. Nobody believes here that it will succeed.

* * * * * * * * *

Mr. Romero to Mr. Hunter.

[Translation.]

MEXICAN LEGATION IN THE UNITED STATES OF AMERICA,
Washington, August 1, 1865.

MR. ACTING SECRETARY: I have the honor to enclose to you a copy of a note which the consul general of Mexico, residing in New York, addressed to me under date of yesterday, calling my attention to the annexed advertisement published in the World of the 29th of July last past, by Don Luis Arroyo, who calls himself the consul named for that city by the so-called Mexican empire.

I deem it proper to call to notice that Don Luis Arroyo, under the title of commercial agent, is about to exercise, as is advertised, all the functions to which he might be entitled if he were the true consul of Mexico, with the respective *exequatur* of the government of the United States. For this reason I beg you to have the goodness to communicate to me the views of the government of the United States upon two points, upon which I require to fix my ideas before adopting an opinion upon this matter. The first is, whether the government of the United States considers that the ex-Archduke Ferdinand Maximilian has the right to appoint in this country commercial agents who shall publicly exercise the functions of consul, or whether this right belongs solely to the governments whose existence is neither doubtful nor questionable.

According to my understanding, this government only sees in the republic of Mexico a war between it and France, without recognizing there Maximilian, not even as a government de facto.

The second point is, whether such commercial agents can exercise the functions of consuls, not only without a formal *exequatur*, but also without any other sort of permission or recognition from the government of the United States.

I must make known to you that up to this period the French consul in New York had been performing the functions which Don Luis Arroyo pretends now to exercise, which was perhaps more logical and manifested more consideration for the government of the United States, inasmuch as the French consul has an *exequatur* from this government, and re[illegible]ts more genuinely the order of things established in Mexico by the ar[illegible]oleon III. The change which is now made seems to be directed to man[illegible]at the government of the United States tacitly recognizes as a government[illegible]acto the work of the French intervention in Mexico.

I avail myself of this opportunity to reiterate to you, sir, the assurances of my distinguished consideration.

M. ROMERO.

Hon. WILLIAM HUNTER, *&c.*, *&c.*, *&c.*

[Enclosure No. 1.—Translation.]

CONSULATE GENERAL OF THE MEXICAN REPUBLIC IN THE U. S.,
New York, July 31, 1865.

In the number of the World dated the 29th instant a Mr. Arroyo, who calls himself the consul of the Mexican empire in the city of New York, has published an advertisement, of which I enclose you a copy, in which he gives notice to the merchants of this port who may send effects to Mexico, that all the certificates of invoices and manifests must be authorized by himself, and not by the undersigned.

As it is well known that the said Mr. Arroyo cannot exercise in this country consular functions, because he has not the *exequatur* of the government of the United States, a requisite which I alone possess, I have the honor to bring this fact to the knowledge of your legation, that you may, if you deem it proper, obtain from the cabinet of Washington a measure that will put an end to this abuse, through which the laws of this country are mocked, which provide that in order to be enabled to perform the duties of consul, the *exequatur* of the President is required.

I have the honor to protest to you on this occasion my most distinguished consideration.

Independence and liberty!

JUAN N. NAVARRO.

The Señor MINISTER PLENIPOTENTIARY
Of the Mexican Republic at Washington.

[Enclosure No. 2.—From the World, of July 29, 1865.]

Trade with Mexico.—Decree of Maximilian with regard to invoices and manifests of merchandise forwarded to Mexican ports.

NEW YORK, *July* 28, 1865.

To the Editor of the World:

SIR: Desiring that the commercial community may come to the knowledge of the adjoining decrees, I request your kindness to order its publication in the columns of your valuable journal, and oblige your most obedient servant,

LOUIS DE ARROYO,
No. 42 Broadway.

DEPARTMENT OF THE TREASURY,
Mexico, January 24, 1865.

(Section 1.—Circular No. 35.)

Consuls and vice-consuls from the empire of Mexico having been already appointed and residing in foreign countries, it appertains to them to legalize the invoices and manifests of merchandise forwarded to our ports, and also all documents required by the laws to be legalized. The agents appointed by the administration of Don Benito Juarez will cease in their functions, as such administration came to an end since the 31st of May, 1863.

Therefore, I would direct you, by order of his Majesty the emperor, to notify the commerce of that city that hereafter all such above-stated documents must be indispensably legalized by the agents of the empire. All invoices and manifests of vessels coming into the ports of said empire, certified by the former agents, whose appointments have not been renewed by the actual administration, shall be considered of no value, and shall not produce any legal effect or evidence whatever.

All which I communicate to you so as to have the same duly published, hoping that when you will acknowledge the receipt of this order you will inform me the day that the publication has been made, in order to advise it to the collectors of the custom-houses on the sea-ports.

M. DE CASTILLO.
Sub-Secretary of the Treasury.

LOUIS DE ARROYO,
Consul, acting as Commercial Agent, New York.

Mr. Seward to Mr. Romero.

DEPARTMENT OF STATE,
Washington, August 9, 1865.

SIR: Your note of the 1st instant has been received, in which you ask the attention of this department to an advertisement published in the New York World, of the 29th ultimo, by Don Louis Arroyo, in which that person gives notice that shippers to Mexican ports must have their invoices and manifests attested by him, as consul of the Mexican empire, in the city of New York.

In reply, I have to state that this department is not aware of any law of the United States which forbids a person claiming to be a consul of a foreign power from making on his own responsibility a publication of the character to which you refer.

It cannot be necessary for me to repeat what has uniformly been said by this government in all its official correspondence, that no other than the republican government in Mexico has been recognized by the United States. You are aware, however, that the party in arms against that government is, and for some time past has been, in possession of some, at least, of the ports of Mexico. That possession carries with it, for the time being, a power to prescribe the terms upon which foreign commerce may be carried on with those ports. If, as is presumed to be the case, one of those conditions is, that the invoices and manifests of vessels from abroad, bound to those ports, must be certified by a commercial agent of the party in possession, residing in the port of the foreign country from which the vessel may proceed, it is not perceived what effective measures this government could properly take in the premises. Such a commercial agent can perform no consular act relating to the affairs of his countrymen in the United States. To prohibit him from attesting invoices and manifests, under the circumstances referred to, would be tantamount to an interdiction of trade between the United States and those Mexican ports which are not in possession of the republican government of that country. The consuls of the United States in Mexico, who have their exequaturs from that government only, themselves discharge duties as commercial agents in the ports which are not under the control of that government in all respects like those which the person Arroyo, in the same way and to the same extent, claims to do at New York in respect to said ports.

I avail myself of this occasion to offer to you, sir, renewed assurances of my high consideration.

WILLIAM H. SEWARD.

Señor Don MATIAS ROMERO, *&c., &c.,*
New York City.

Mr. Romero to Mr. Seward.

[Translation.]

MEXICAN LEGATION IN THE UNITED STATES OF AMERICA,
New York, August 12, 1865.

MR. SECRETARY: I have had the honor of receiving your note of the 9th instant, in reply to mine of the 1st, asking questions of the department about the proceedings of Louis Arroyo, who has opened an office in this city, as commercial agent of the pretended Mexican empire.

As your note contains no positive answer to my interrogation, although it clearly indicates the steps to be taken by the United States government in the affair, I have thought it my duty, considering the circumstances of the case, to submit the question to the government of Mexico, and wait for instructions to direct me in regard to it.

I embrace this opportunity of renewing the assurances of my most distinguished consideration.

M. ROMERO.

Hon. WILLIAM H. SEWARD, *&c., &c., &c.*

Mr. Seward to Mr. Bigelow.

[Extract.]

No. 300.] DEPARTMENT OF STATE,
Washington, November 6, 1865.

MY DEAR SIR: * * * * * * *

I will proceed to discuss the subject, and leave you to present the opinions of the President to such extent and in such manner as your own views of propriety shall suggest. The President feels himself bound to adhere to the opinion set forth in my despatch No. 259, which has, as we understand, been already read to Mr. Drouyn de Lhuys. The presence and operations of a French army in Mexico, and its maintenance of an authority there, resting upon force and not the free will of the people of Mexico, is a cause of serious concern to the United States. Nevertheless, the objection of the United States is still broader, and includes the authority itself which the French army is thus maintaining. That authority is in direct antagonism to the policy of this government and the prin[illegible]ple upon which it is founded.

Every day's experience of its operations only adds some new confirmation of [illegible]stice of the views which this government expressed at the time the attempt [illegible]itute that authority first became known. The United States have hitherto [illegible]d the utmost frankness on that subject.

[illegible]till regard the effort to establish permanently a foreign and imperial [illegible]t in Mexico as disallowable and impracticable. For these reasons [illegible]not now agree to compromise the position they have heretofore as-[illegible]y are not prepared to recognize, or to pledge themselves hereafter [illegible] any political institutions in Mexico which are in opposition to the [illegible]overnment with which we have so long and so constantly main-[illegible]ns of amity and friendship. I need hardly repeat my past assu-[illegible] desire to preserve our inherited relations of friendship with [illegible] greatly increases our regret that no communications, for-[illegible]have been received from the government of that country, [illegible]pecting that France is likely soon to be ready to remove, [illegible]pon her, the cause of our deep concern for the harmony

The suggestion which you make of a willingness on the part of France to propose a revision of the commercial relations between the two countries is not regarded as having emanated from the government of the empire. However that may be, it is hardly necessary to say that we should not be dwelling so earnestly upon the branch of political relations if it had not been our conviction that those relations at the present moment supersede those of commerce in the consideration of the American people.

Believe me to be always faithfully yours,

WILLIAM H. SEWARD.

JOHN BIGELOW, Esq., &c., &c., &c.

Mr. Bigelow to Mr. Seward.

[Extract.]

No. 209.]

LEGATION OF THE UNITED STATES,
Paris, November 30, 1865.

SIR: Upon reflection I concluded that I should be likely to leave more correct impressions, and perhaps exclude some erroneous ones from the mind of Monsieur Drouyn de Lhuys, by reading your despatch No. 300 to him, than by leaving him, after our interview on Thursday week, to imagine its contents. I accordingly called upon his excellency on Tuesday last, and after disposing of some other matters of less importance, told him frankly that I wished to read to him the despatch, to the contents of which I had referred at our last interview, to prevent his supposing it contained anything which I had thought proper or had been instructed to conceal from him.

* * * * * * * *

When I had finished he thanked me for reading the despatch, though he felt obliged to say that he derived neither pleasure nor satisfaction from its contents.

* * * * * * * *

I am, sir, your obedient servant,

JOHN BIGELOW.

Hon. WILLIAM H. SEWARD, &c., &c., &c.

Mr. Seward to Mr. Bigelow.

No. 332.]

DEPARTMENT OF STATE,
Washington, December 16, 1865.

SIR: Your despatch of November 30, No. 209, was duly received, and [illegible] been submitted to the President.

Your proceeding in reading my despatch No. 300 to Mr. Drouyn de [illegible] is approved. The general tenor of the remarks made by you to the [illegible] foreign affairs on that occasion is likewise approved. It is not th[illegible] department of this government alone which is interested and conc[illegible] question whether the present condition of things shall be continue[illegible] The interest is a national one, and in every event Congress, whi[illegible] session, is authorized by the Constitution and is entitled to direc[illegible] action of the United States in regard to that important subje[illegible]

It has been the President's purpose that France should be [illegible] upon two points, namely:

First. That the United States earnestly desire to co[illegible] sincere friendship with France.

Second. That this policy would be brought into im[illegible]

France could deem it consistent with her interest and honor to desist from the prosecution of armed intervention in Mexico, to overthrow the domestic republican government existing there, and to establish upon its ruins the foreign monarchy which has been attempted to be inaugurated in the capital of that country.

In answer to an exposition of our views which was thus made, the suggestion was offered to you by Mr. Drouyn de Lhuys that the government of the United States might favor the express desire of the Emperor to withdraw from Mexico, by giving to him some formal assurance that in the event of his withdrawal this government would recognize the institution of Maximilian in Mexico as *de facto* a political power.

It was my desire, in framing the despatch No. 300, to express in behalf of the United States a decision that the recognition which the Emperor had thus suggested cannot be made, and to assign, by way of explanation, the grounds upon which that decision was based. I have carefully considered the arguments against that decision which were presented to you by Mr. Drouyn de Lhuys in the interview referred to, and I do not find in them any sufficient reasons for modifying the views which the United States have expressed.

It remains now only to make known to Mr. Drouyn de Lhuys my profound regret that he has thought it his duty to leave the subject, in his conversation with you, in a condition that does not authorize an expectation on our part that a satisfactory adjustment of the case can be effected on any basis that thus far has been discussed.

I am, sir, your obedient servant,

WILLIAM H. SEWARD.

JOHN BIGELOW, Esq., *&c., &c., &c.*

The Marquis de Montholon to Mr. Seward.

[Translation.]

WASHINGTON, *November* 29, 1865.

MY DEAR SIR: Conforming to the desire you expressed to me, I send you, herewith, a copy and translation of Mr. Drouyn de Lhuys's despatch, the contents of which I have had the honor to read to you.

With the highest regards, I remain, my dear sir, respectfully yours,

MONTHOLON.

Hon. WILLIAM H. SEWARD,
Secretary of State, &c., &c., &c.

Monsieur Drouyn de Lhuys to the Marquis de Montholon.—(Confidential.)

[Translation.]

MINISTÈRE DES AFFAIRES ETRANGÈRES,
Paris, October 18, 1865.

MONSIEUR LE MARQUIS: I have taken several occasions since two months to advise you of the dispositions of the imperial government concerning the duration of the occupation of Mexico by the French troops. I told you, in my despatch of August 17, that we called with our most sincere wishes for the day when the last French soldier should leave the country, and that the cabinet of Washington could contribute to hasten that moment. On the 2d of September I renewed to you the assurance of our strong desire to withdraw our auxiliary corps so soon as circumstances should allow it. At last, following the same ideas more fully, in a private letter of the 10th of the same month I added that it greatly depended upon the United States to facilitate the departure of our troops. If they would adopt toward the Mexican government an amicable attitude, which would aid to the consolidation of order, and in which we could find motives of security for the interests which obliged us to carry arms beyond the Atlantic, we would be ready to adopt without delay the bases of an understanding on this subject with the cabinet of Washington; and I wish to make fully known to you now the views of the government of his Majesty.

What we ask of the United States is to be assured that their intention is not to impede the consolidation of the new order of things founded in Mexico; and the best guarantee we could receive of their intention would be the recognition of the emperor Maximilian by the federal government.

The American Union should not, it seems to us, be kept back by the difference of institutions, for the United States have official intercourse with all the monarchies of Europe and of the New World. It is in conformity with their own principles of public law to regard the monarchy established in Mexico as being, at least, a government "*de facto*," without particular regard to its nature or its origin, which has been consecrated by the suffrage of the people of that country; and in thus acting the cabinet of Washington would only be inspired with the same feelings of sympathy which President Johnson expressed recently to the envoy of Brazil as guiding the policy of the United States towards the younger states of the American continent.

Mexico, it is true, is still occupied at this moment by the French army, and we can readily see that this objection will arise. But the acknowledgment of the Emperor Maximilian by the United States would, in our opinion, have sufficient influence on the state of the country to allow us to take into consideration their susceptibilities on this subject; and should the cabinet of Washington decide to open diplomatic relations with the court of Mexico, we would see no difficulty to enter in arrangement for the recall of our troops within a reasonable period of which we would—might consent to fix the termination.

In consequence of the vicinage and immense extent of the common frontier, the United States are, more than any other power, interested to see their trade with Mexico placed under the safeguard of stipulations in harmony with the mutual wants of both countries. We would most readily offer our good offices to facilitate the conclusion of a commercial treaty, thereby cementing the political "rapprochement," the bases of which I have just made known to you.

By order of the Emperor I invite you to make known to Mr. Seward the dispositions of his Majesty's government.

You are authorized, if you think it proper, to read him the contents of this despatch.

I remain,

DROUYN DE LHUYS.

The MARQUIS DE MONTHOLON, &c., &c., &c.

Mr. Romero to Mr. Seward.

[Translation.]

MEXICAN LEGATION TO THE UNITED STATES OF AMERICA,
Washington, February 11, 1866.

MR. SECRETARY: In corroboration of the reports I have already made to your department, on various occasions, concerning the plans of the French agents in Mexico to induce the discontented citizens of the south of the United States, who participated in the late rebellion against their country, to emigrate to that republic, I now have the honor to transmit to you a copy of a printed circular, containing the prospectus of the so-called "American and Mexican Emigrant Company," organized in St. Louis, State of Missouri, by virtue of a grant from the usurper, dated the 27th of April, 1865.

In this grant, to disguise appearances, it seems that general immigration is invited, while the prospectus plainly shows that it only relates to people from the south.

I embrace the opportunity to renew to you, Mr Secretary, the assurances of my most distinguished consideration.

M. ROMERO.

Hon. WILLIAM H. SEWARD, &c., &c., &c.

[Enclosure.]

Prospectus of the American and Mexican Emigrant Company.

The American and Mexican Emigrant Company is acting under a decree issued to it by the emperor Maximilian, on the 27th of April, 1865, a translation of which, from the Spanish, we give below:

This company is organized with the view of engaging in and developing the various enterprises of which Mexico is susceptible, and securing for Americans their natural and legitimate share of the profits and advantages arising therefrom.

The only practical way in which this can be effected is by a properly secured and organized system of American emigration.

The world has long been familiar with the inexhaustible mineral wealth, the rich agricultural resources, and the delightful climate of Mexico, but this wealth and these resources have remained so long hidden under the cloud of civil commotion, and other local causes, that the enterprising mind has been turned to other and more laborious fields of operation, until this country seemed, for the time, forgotten.

Circumstances have so conspired of late to force them afresh upon the public mind, until to-day Mexico fills the eye and is the theme of the civilized world. Capital from England, France, Austria, Spain, and the whole of Europe, is now finding its way into the country, building her railroads, buying her rich lands, carrying off her spices and precious woods, and digging her gold and silver.

The time, in our opinion, has at last come for the full development of Mexico; the world needs it, and she is about to respond to its necessities. She is our neighbor—her wealth, her resources, her commerce, are at our very doors, and would naturally be contributory to our own; but if Americans will not cultivate friendly relations with her, and will not take part in the enterprises of the country, we can expect but little or no profit from them.

We have now our agents in Mexico, who will keep us promptly and correctly advised of the condition of the country in all its aspects, and who will select the best agricultural and mineral lands in large quantities in the best parts of the empire.

All that an emigrant may want to know before he abandons his old home for a new one will be communicated through this company, by its agents in Mexico.

The climate on the table-lands is unequalled for its healthy character, and there being no frost or winter in that country, the poor man is relieved from the drudgery of working half of the year to provide clothing and fuel for the balance.

The soil, in many parts of the country, is the richest and most productive in the world, yielding all that can be raised in the United States, and in many parts much more abundantly with the same amount of labor, besides many other crops that will not mature here.

The unchanging spring-like character of the climate enables the inhabitants to plant crops in any season of the year, and the most luxurious pasturage is afforded at all times, thus saving the great expense and labor of laying up supplies for stock, as in cold countries.

Two crops of corn can be raised annually, and cotton, on account of the long seasons, will produce from one to one and a half bale to the acre. Coffee will begin to bear in from two to three years from the plant, yielding, for many years thereafter, an immense profit, with but little care, and no expensive machinery to prepare it for the market.

The luxuriant yield of the cocoa enables the farmer to realize as much as a thousand dollars per acre; sugar-cane produces from three to four thousand pounds per acre; tobacco arrives at a maturity and richness of flavor but little inferior to the best Cuban leaf; while hemp, wheat, barley, rye, oats and other small grain are successfully raised.

Mahogany, iron-wood, India-rubber tree, cedar-wood, and vanilla are abundant, which, with logwood and cochineal, and other dyestuffs, added to immense supplies of prime hides and wool, will constitute very important items of Mexican commerce.

In alluding to these productions we do not wish to be understood as saying that all of them can be found in *every* part of the country, but that each section possesses its own agricultural characteristics, the history and details of which will be part of the province of this company to acquire and communicate through its agencies.

The mineral wealth of the country is so well and widely known, that it would seem superfluous to say more than merely to refer to them. The gold mines are equal to those of California, and the silver leads have proven their richness beyond doubt, while platina, quicksilver, precious stones, iron and coal, have been discovered in liberal quantities; and from experiments already made, no doubt exists that coal oil abounds to a profitable extent; in short, it would seem that nature had emptied her richest stores into the lap of that country, and it requires but the provident and intelligent hand to develop her lavish gifts.

The company has already received offers of large grants of lands free of charge, but as we do not wish to be confined to any particular section of country by free grants, we are securing, and shall continue to purchase, large tracts in the most eligible localities, with particular reference to the wants and preference of the emigrant, which, whether from free grants or purchase, will be sold on such long time and divided payments that will, in the aggregate, amount to less than the annual *taxes* per acre in any other country.

These lands will be gotten in large quantities, at from 25 cents to $1 per acre; and will be resold in farms to the emigrant, at a less price than he could purchase for himself from the original proprietors, as there is no limit to the quantity which the company is allowed to purchase and improve.

A head of a family can go alone and locate his land, make his household arrangements, and, when he wants his family, he can, by communicating with our nearest agent in Mexico, have them brought to him by the company.

In order to obviate the difficulties and disappointments incident to a large emigration to a new country, lacking either information or material, the company will make known to its members, from time to time, as to what will be the best time and the best manner of going.

The company will see that houses suitable for the climate, &c., are erected for the emigrant at much cheaper rates than he can build for himself; and he can purchase his household effects, agricultural and mining implements, at designated and convenient localities, at prices shown him by schedule, before he leaves this country; and if he prefers to carry them with him, under the auspices of our company, he can do so free of duty.

The company's arrangements with passenger packets will enable them to procure tickets at reduced rates to the Mexican ports, where (upon presentation of certificate of honorary membership) he will find our agent, speaking his own language, ready to render all necessary facilities to reach the place he may select.

The proximity of Mexico to this country, and the facilities of communication of all kinds, which this emigration will create, will cause the American to feel that he has not sundered all the ties that bind him to his friends, but that, in reality, the advantages of travel and correspondence will be in favor of his new home, when compared to the distant parts of his own country. He will there find whole communities of the same race and language springing up around him, building up a homogeneous family, where churches, schools, and other civilizing institutions will exist, as he has been accustomed to since his youth, all protected by the well-settled principles of law and order; or, indeed, he can provide for all these advantages, before leaving, by associating with people of his own country or neighborhood, and going together, after selecting their farms in the same tract, as facilities will be afforded for this object by the company at their principal offices at home.

The mode adopted by the company for obtaining information will enable it to furnish those who shall connect themselves by honorary membership, on the payment of a fee of $10, all the facts relative to the industrial pursuits, agricultural, mining and manufacturing, with the nature of the country, its water-power, timber and climate, in every locality; which information will be derived from actual observation by our agents in the empire, and which will be transmitted regularly, and fresh from that country; in short, by our system of agencies and centres of intelligence we will be able to give to the honorary member, *upon any subject he may desire, all kinds of information* within the scope of our operations; and all this at an infinitely less cost than he could acquire by himself. This will obviate the expensive necessity of his travelling to, and over, a strange country, with a different language, where he would meet with vexatious annoyances in prosecuting his inquiries; and this fee for honorary membership is merely the basis of the fund upon which these agencies are established, and which fee is more than returned by the privileges it secures in the reduction of passage money, price of lands, and other general benefits.

These offices will be established at New York, St. Louis, Chicago, Charleston, New Orleans, Memphis, Galveston, Baltimore, Louisville, and all the principal cities of the Union, at which maps and plats of the country generally can be seen.

Honorary members will be furnished with information in reference to *all* lands in the empire of which we can get accurate accounts; they can go to Mexico under the auspices and benefits of this company, and be perfectly free to select any lands or occupation they may deem best after their arrival there; nor will our information be confined to lands alone, but to every branch of industrial life, so that our Mexican intelligence will be equally interesting to the merchant, the professional man, the manufacturer, the artisan, the miner, the contractor and the farmer, whether he desires to emigrate or to engage in these enterprises; and, after having aided the inquirer upon all points alluded to, we leave the matter entirely to his own self-interest or inclination to govern his future course.

This company will also make it their business to furnish correct and accurate information in regard to all lands which the government of Mexico may set apart for free grants to emigrants.

Printed circulars, containing an abstract of information received by the company from its agents in Mexico, will be sent to its local agent in each county where honorary members reside, at stated periods, (to be hereafter determined, as necessity may require,) and which will be open to perusal by honorary members.

Arrangements are being made with gentlemen of reliability in the southern States, who will be connected with this company, and whose names and offices will be announced in due time.

Members.—B. G. Caulfield, Chicago, Illinois; Wm. H. Russell, Lexington, Missouri: A. W. Arrington, Chicago, Illinois; R. O. Glover, New York; John Howe, St. Louis; James Rigney, Lexington, Missouri; John Scudder, Colorado Territory; Marshall O. Roberts, New York; Ed. P. Tesson, St. Louis; Charles P. Chouteau, St. Louis; Giovanni A. Bertolla, St. Louis; Gerard B. Allen, St. Louis; J. B. Wilcox, St. Louis; Charles S. Waller, Chicago, Illinois; Pierre A. Berthold, St. Louis; Daniel N. Carrington, New York; James Harrison, St. Louis; William L. Warder, Chicago, Illinois; B. P. Churchill, Cincinnati, Ohio; Lyttleton Cooke, Louisville, Kentucky.

Directors.—John Howe, D. N. Carrington, Gerard B. Allen, Hon. A. W. Arrington, Charles S. Waller, R. O. Glover, Charles P. Chouteau.

Officers.—James Harrison, president; Pierre A. Berthold, vice-president; Charles P.

Chouteau, treasurer; Bernard G. Caulfield, attorney; George Frank Gouley, secretary, office No. 18 Washington avenue, St. Louis, Missouri.

NOTE.—Clubs of honorary members may be made up, and the fees can be remitted to the nearest authorized office, or sent by express, or to some reliable friend who will receive the certificates, and return them as receipts for the money.

The decree.

MAXIMILIAN, EMPEROR OF MEXICO.

We grant to the American and Mexican Emigrant Company, represented by Bernard G. Caulfield, the concessions and exemptions which our secretary of internal affairs and improvements has advised us to make, so that said company may, by means of emigration, establish towns and agricultural communities, conformable to the laws of Mexico:

First. The American and Mexican Emigrant Company, represented by Bernard G. Caulfield, is authorized to acquire, for the purpose of emigration, any lands within the empire, be the same cultivated or not, which it may consider suited to the development of such mineral, agricultural, manufacturing, and industrial enterprises, as said company may see fit to establish. In developing the property which the company may buy or receive by grant from individuals, it will advise the government of its various enterprises within three months after they shall have been respectively entered into.

Second. Said company shall be exempt from the payment of the (five per cent.) tax attaching to all transfers of land in this empire on all property it may acquire, and the same privilege shall extend to emigrants who shall buy or acquire lands directly from the said company.

Third. Said company may introduce, free of duty, into the ports of this empire, all implements, machinery, houses and stock, which the necessity or convenience of emigrants may demand.

Fourth. Said company is authorized to build towns in such localities as it may select for that purpose, first advising the government, and obtaining recognition therefor.

Fifth. Said company is authorized to introduce emigrants into this empire from the United States, and also from Europe, and each resident of the empire, who shall make purchases of land from said company, or take part in its enterprises, shall have the same privileges as are hereby extended to emigrants: *Provided*, The purchase of land by each person shall not exceed one square kilometer.

Sixth. All contracts made with the emigrants, by or on behalf of said company, outside of the empire, and which are not repugnant to the laws thereof, shall be held, by the tribunals of the empire, of the same force as if made within the jurisdiction of the same.

Seventh. The government being now engaged in acquiring a knowledge of the lands of the empire, which are unsettled as to occupancy or title, is therefore not able at present to make a grant of lands to said company, but will do so as soon as the same can be conveniently done.

Eighth. The company will establish, in the capital of the empire, a general agency to superintend the development of its various enterprises, and to serve as a means of communication with this government.

Ninth. Said company shall be protected by the government in its operations, in order that it may accomplish the important ends it has in view.

Given at San Salvador, El Seco, the 27th of April, 1865.

MAXIMILIANO.

William H. Russell, general agent for New York and New England, office No. 17 Nassau street, New York.

Mr. Seward to Mr. Romero.

DEPARTMENT OF STATE,
Washington, March 15, 1866.

SIR: I have the honor to acknowledge the receipt of your note of the 11th ultimo, transmitting a copy of a printed circular containing the prospectus of the "American and Mexican Emigrant Company," organized in St. Louis, Missouri, by virtue of a grant from the so-called emperor of Mexico, dated the 27th of April, 1865.

Thanking you for your considerate attention, I avail myself of this occasion to repeat the assurances of my distinguished consideration.

WILLIAM H. SEWARD.

Señor MATIAS ROMERO, *Washington, D. C.*

MEXICAN LEGATION, WASHINGTON CITY, D. C.,
May 5, 1865.

SIR: My attention has been called to a statement made by M. Corta, a member of the French corps legislatif, in the sitting of that chamber of the 11th ultimo, while discussing the Mexican question, in which he, in conformity with the policy of his government, (whose agent he has been in Mexico,) tries to impeach the patriotism of the constitutional president of Mexico, using the most slanderous means, and averring that President Juarez has twice offered the State of Sonora to President Lincoln for seventy-five millions of francs.

M. Corta said (*Le Moniteur Universel* of April 12, 1865, page 433) as follows:

After these words of General Smith—(he has just quoted some words which he means to attribute to General Scott, calling him General Smith, as he names President Jackson where he means President Polk)—Sonora and the property confiscated from the clergy have been offered to the United States, to President Lincoln, for a sum of seventy-five millions. Well, the American government, the actual President of the United States, has refused this concession proposed by Juarez two different times.

I have been the only representative in Washington of President Juarez's government during the whole time of President Lincoln's administration, and I do not know of any such offer ever having been made to the United States through me or anybody else. Mr. Corwin, late United States minister, negotiated, it is true, in the city of Mexico, a treaty by which the United States were to loan to Mexico eleven millions of dollars, but no sale of Mexican territory was ever offered to this government, and only the guarantee of the product of some of the revenue of Mexico, to wit: the product of the sale of the national property lately in the hands of the clergy, and of the public unoccupied or vacant lands in the country, which are in Mexico a source of revenue as well as in the United States.

As for any previous offer of this kind by President Juarez, we have his statement denying flatly that he ever intended any such thing. I send you a copy of his statement making such denial.

It is my duty, as a Mexican and the representative of a government struggling for the independence of self, free, popular government and republican institutions, against foreign conspiracies and encroachments, to expose the intrigues of the enemies of my country, by which they expect to prejudice public opinion against us. Only this duty makes me intrude upon you, begging you to have this letter and its annexed published.

I would thank you for this favor, and remain, sir, your most obedient servant,

M. ROMERO.

President Juarez's letter.

NATIONAL PALACE, MEXICO,
February 22, 1863.

MY DEAR AND MOST ESTEEMED SIR: I have just read in the Monitor Republicano of to-day the speech which M. O'Donnell, president of the council of ministers of the Spanish government, has made in the discussion which took place with a view to answer the speech of the Crown, and I have seen with surprise, among several inaccurate assertions which M. O'Donnell has made about Mexican affairs, the following expressions: * * * "As for myself, Juarez, as a Mexican, has a stain which can never be washed away—that of having been willing to sell two provinces of that country to the United States." * * * This accusation, coming from a high functionary of a nation, and while an eminently serious and solemn act was taking place, when the statesman must be careful that his words are impressed with the seal of truth, justice, and good faith, is of the utmost importance, for one may be *led to think that* on account of the position he occupies he is in possession of documents which support his assertion—a thing which is not true. M. O'Donnell is authorized to publish the proofs he may possess concerning this affair. Meanwhile, my honor compels me to show that M. O'Donnell has made a mistake in the judgment which he has formed of my official conduct, and you are authorized, Mr. Editor, to contradict the imputation which has been made with so much injustice to the first magistrate of the nation.

I am, Mr. Editor, your humble servant,

BENITO JUAREZ.

EDITOR OF THE DIARIO.

Official.

RELATIVE TO PLANS TO INDUCE THE IMMIGRATION OF DISSATISFIED CITIZENS OF THE UNITED STATES INTO MEXICO, AND ESPECIALLY IN REGARD TO THE PLANS OF DR. WILLIAM M. GWIN AND M. F. MAURY.

Mr. Romero to Mr. Seward.

[Translation.]

MEXICAN LEGATION, *Washington, July* 9, 1864.

Mr. Romero presents his respects to Mr. Seward, and has the honor to enclose to him an extract taken from the New York Tribune, which contains the address which General Magruder, commander-in-chief of the insurgent army in Texas, made to Don Santiago Vidaurri, who was the governor of the states of New Leon and Coahuila, in the republic of Mexico, on solemnly receiving him at the city of San Antonio on the 21st May last, which address, no less than the answer of Vidaurri, demonstrates the existence of a perfect understanding between the traitors in Mexico and the insurgents in the United States, because both count on the aid of the French government to bring to a close, such as they desire, the enterprises in which they are engaged. This is the address to which Mr. Romero referred at the interview he had with Mr. Seward at the Department of State on the 20th June last past.

Hon. WILLIAM H. SEWARD, *&c., &c., &c.*

[Enclosure No. 1.]

AN INTERESTING PAIR OF REBELS.—VIDAURRI AND MAGRUDER COMPLIMENT EACH OTHER IN PUBLIC SPEECHES.

[*From the New Orleans Era.*]

The absquatulating ex-governor of the Mexican states of Coahuila and New Leon, Vidaurri, and the rebel commander-in-chief of Texas, General J. Bankhead Magruder, had an interesting meeting at Houston on the 21st May, a full account of which we give below, taken from the columns of the Houston *Telegraph* of the 23d. It was a solemn and impressive spectacle, the meeting of these two noble and devoted patriots, martyrs in the cause of liberty, who have fought and bled for their country, and made enormous fortunes by stealing cotton from defenceless citizens, selling it to meet the requirements of the public service, and pocketing the proceeds. Here is the way these disinterested, self-sacrificing men talk to each other for the benefit of the credulous and humbugged people:

Governor Vidaurri arrived in this city on Saturday, and was courteously received by General Magruder and his staff and a military escort. On meeting him at the depot of the Central railroad, General Magruder addressed him, in substance, as follows:

GENERAL VIDAURRI: I bid you welcome to this military district, not only as one who has been governor of neighboring and friendly states, those of Coahuila and Nueva Leon, but as an enlightened chief magistrate, who has established friendly relations with the confederacy, and has always appreciated the value of an uninterrupted commercial and amicable intercourse with the State and citizens of Texas.

I bid you welcome as one of those patriots who have wisdom to discern and nerve to execute whatever may be for the best interest of the country. In the wild storms which have swept over our native land you have exercised control to draw order out of chaos, and to secure the best interests of the people, even in spite of themselves.

For your noble efforts to serve the people of Coahuila and Nueva Leon you are now an exile. For your patriotic exertions to secure for them the blessings of a well-organized, regular, and just government, and to free them from any dependence on the most faithless and barbarous of all people, (those of the United States,) you have offered up yourself as a sacrifice. But the patriot will be rewarded; your sacrifices will be but temporary; and all wise and truly patriotic Mexicans will soon acknowledge the wisdom, as well as the patriotism, of your course, and, welcoming you back with open arms, will invite you to such a participation in the conduct of public affairs as your great ability and high character fairly demand.

Be assured, general, that we shall look with interest upon your future career, as we have done upon the past, and that we wish you health and prosperity as cordially as we bid you welcome.

[Enclosure No. 2.]

To this Governor Vidaurri replied, thanking General Magruder for the unexpected compliment he had paid him. He assured him that he had always felt the greatest sympathy for the Confederate States, as they had battled for their rights and for the poor privilege to be let alone. He was himself now an exile from his country for contending for the same rights that had been usurped by unprincipled men. He hoped soon that the Confederate States might reach the object for which they had long struggled.

The governor and General Magruder then took carriages, escorted by the general's staff. The *cortege* proceeded to the Fannin House, where it halted, and the distinguished stranger was waited upon by the military and civil authorities, his honor the mayor tendering him a welcome to the city.

It is a well-known fact that not two-thirds of the enormous sums of money derived from the seizure and sale of cotton by General Magruder and his emissaries was ever used for the benefit of the rebel government, but was invested in sterling bills and foreign loans, for the benefit of Magruder and the men connected with him in his swindling transactions. This is well known to hundreds of refugees from the State of Texas now in this city. Vidaurri, by levying heavy taxes upon the cotton transported through the territory over which he ruled, and by occasional seizure of a lot belonging to private parties, (against which there was no redress, owing to the lawless state of the country, and to the fact that the owners generally were rebels, and had no government that could or would protect them,) managed to feather his nest quite snugly. It is to be hoped, however, that when he decamped from Monterey, between the setting and rising of the sun, that he was compelled to leave behind all, or nearly all, of his ill-gotten gains.

Mr. Seward to Mr. Romero.

DEPARTMENT OF STATE,
Washington, July 27, 1864.

SIR: I have the honor to acknowledge the receipt of your verbal note of the ninth instant, enclosing an extract from the New York Tribune, which contains an account of the reception given to Don Santiago Vidaurri, late governor of the states of New Leon and Coahuila, (Mexico,) at San Antonio, on the 20th May last, by General Magruder, commanding the insurgent army in Texas.

While thanking you for that attention, I beg to renew to you, sir, the assurances of my high consideration.

WILLIAM H. SEWARD.

Señor MATIAS ROMERO, *&c.*, *&c.*, *&c.*,
Washington, D. C.

Mr. Romero to Mr. Seward.

[Translation.]

MEXICAN LEGATION TO THE UNITED STATES OF AMERICA,
Washington, December 3, 1864.

MY DEAR SIR: In the conversation we had on Thursday, 24th November last, I read to you extracts of a letter which a friend, resident in New York, had written to me in relation to the plans respecting Mexico which it is assured are entertained by many persons in the northern States, in concert with citizens of the south. You were pleased to ask me for a memorandum from this letter, and I offered to send it to you. I have not done so before now, because I expected to receive some advices from Mexico, and wished to see if the reports indicated were in any manner confirmed by the advices which should be received from that country. Those advices have now reached me, and I have the honor to send you the memorandum which you asked for, added to by the last news received.

I am, very respectfully, your obedient servant,

M. ROMERO.

Hon. WILLIAM H. SEWARD, *&c.*, *&c.*, *&c.*

[Translation.]

A friend of Mr. Romero writes to him from New York, under date of 22d November last past, informing him that from conversations he has had with an ex-general of the army of the United States, and an ex-governor and ex-senator of one of the States of the Union, he was convinced that there were serious intrigues on the part of many northern men, disgusted with the result of the late presidential election, in connexion with a considerable number of prominent men at the south, that in case—which is now considered probable—the south should have to yield to the armies of the north, they would go to Mexico and operate in the development of the mines and extension of agriculture, with the purpose, in the first place, of sustaining Maximilian, and for the purpose of occupying themselves afterwards in that country.

The number of persons dissatisfied at the north is large enough, and that of those who are disposed to venture on such an enterprise is altogether greater at the south, in the opinion of the person who communicates this information—being sufficient to give a great re-enforcement to Maximilian. This aid on the part of the south might assume the character of an armed immigration, which could take place before the forces of the United States could shut the door against them by taking the line of the Rio Grande.

The ex-general said, in the conversation referred to, that M. Montholon, French minister to Mexico, was working to this purpose, and that a full brigade would soon set off, as private individuals, from the Atlantic States for Vera Cruz, and others from California for the Pacific coast.

The ex-governor and ex-senator said that the French minister in Mexico had already concluded negotiations in respect of Sonora and Lower California.

These assertions agree entirely with the news received from Mexico by the last steamer from the Havana.

"The Estafette," which is the organ of the French policy in Mexico, has frequently made allusions to the convenience that Maximilian will cultivate the best understanding with the confederate authorities on the frontier, and to favor, in all modes, the immigration of citizens who have risen against this government.

A letter from Mexico, published by the "Courrier des Etats Unis," a French imperialist paper printed in New York, and which it is believed was written by M. Masseras, proprietor of that paper, who actually is in the city of Mexico, paves the way to prevent public opinion from being alarmed on learning that Maximilian thinks of aliening, or has aliened, a portion of the Mexican territory. The said letter appears to restrict itself to the Mexican financial question, and says that the budget of the so-called empire approaches forty millions of dollars, and the portions of Mexican revenue which are in the hands of the French are reckoned at four millions. To cover this deficit, says the letter, there is no other choice but to sell or mortgage the public domain. Various letters from Mexico, received in New York by different persons who are in communication with partisans of Maximilian, aver unanimously that he only exercises a nominal power, but that the real authority rests only in General Bazaine, who acts under instructions which he receives directly from the Emperor of the French, and of which even the Minister Montholon has no knowledge.

WASHINGTON, *December* 3, 1864.

Mr. Seward to Mr. Romero.

DEPARTMENT OF STATE,
Washington, January 7, 1865.

SIR: I have the honor to acknowledge the receipt of your note of the 3d of December last, communicating a memorandum of parts of a letter written to you by a friend in New York, under date of the 22d November, 1864, in reference to the plans of an armed emigration to Mexico contemplated by many disinterested persons in the northern States acting in concert with disloyal citizens of the United States.

In reply, I beg to express to you my appreciation of the information transmitted to this government, and to assure you that the subject of your communication will receive the serious attention to which it is justly entitled.

I avail myself of this occasion to renew to you, sir, the assurances of my very distinguished consideration.

WILLIAM H. SEWARD.

Señor MATIAS ROMERO, *&c., &c., &c.*

Mr. Romero to Mr. Seward.

[Translation.]

MEXICAN LEGATION TO THE UNITED STATES OF AMERICA,
Washington, February 6, 1865.

The undersigned, envoy extraordinary and minister plenipotentiary of the Mexican republic, has the honor to address himself to the honorable William H. Seward, Secretary of State of the United States, for the purpose of protesting in the most explicit and formal manner against the cession which the ex-Archduke of Austria, Ferdinand Maximilian, has made, or is about to make, to the French government of various states of the Mexican republic.

The undersigned permits himself to remind the honorable William H. Seward that at the interview which he had with him on the 19th January last past, he read to him a letter written at the city of Mexico on the 28th December previous, the latest date from that city received up to this date in this country, in which a person well-informed and entirely trustworthy communicated the news that French agents in that city had proposed to the deluded Mexicans who now encircle the usurper that the Emperor of the French has sent to Mexico a settlement, in virtue of which there is to be ceded to France the Mexican states of Tamaulipas, Nueva Leon, and Coahuila, parts of those of San Luis Potosi, Zacatecas, Durango, and Chihuahua, almost the whole of Sonora, and the peninsula of Lower California, the dividing line to be formed by the river Yaqui, on the Pacific, and Panuco, on the Gulf, to their sources, and a straight line drawn from one point to the other; that to make the cession of so considerable a part of the Mexican territory acceptable, assurance was made that France would establish in the ceded territory a military colony, which would be under its immediate protection, and which would place the rest of the country under shelter from filibustering attacks from the United States, which would produce the liquidation of the supposed debt which Mexico has with France, and which would facilitate the acquisition of three hundred millions to the treasury of the usurper. It is added, also, to make so considerable a loss less sensibly felt, that the states referred to have only belonged in name to Mexico, because they have been ruled by authorities which have not respected the orders of the central government of Mexico, and which were doomed to self-destruction, either because they might fall into the power of the French or of the United States, and that in such alternative there cannot be a moment's doubt of the preferable extreme. In the same letter assurance was given that such settlement had not been yet submitted to the usurper, and it was given out as understood that he would not fail to hesitate and even manifest opposition to it before his acceptance.

This circumstance signifies nothing, however; the usurper either has not his own will, or if he has, he cannot make it prevail when in contradiction to that of his protector. Besides, it is not to be presumed that he takes any interest in the destinies of a country which is not his fatherland, in which four years ago he was not known even by name to the vast majority of the nation, which he himself knew only by name, to which he has been brought and is sustained by foreign bayonets, and in which he is shedding the blood of patriotic Mexicans, who are maintaining their independence, to satiate a blind ambition for rule, which for his punishment he exercises only in appearance.

The undersigned always believed that the Emperor of the French would close up in this manner his interference in Mexico, when he should become convinced that it would not be possible for him to retain the whole republic as a French colony, and had the honor so to state to the honorable William H. Seward in the communication he addressed to him the 27th December, 1862, and which the President sent to the House of Representatives among the documents relating to Mexican affairs, transmitted with his message of 4th February, 1863.

That which then, however, did not exceed conjecture, although well founded, has come to be realized with the course of time and the development of events. News received from Mexico, from an entirely trustworthy source, has been confirmed by other advices received simultaneously from San Francisco, California, and from Paris; and such coincidences, combined with other antecedents which the undersigned is possessed of in this matter, do not leave him in the least doubt that if the settlement proposed has not been ratified, it is on the point of so being.

This conviction obliges the undersigned, in fulfilment of the duty which belongs to him as representative of the Mexican nation, to protest solemnly and energetically against any settlement made by the ex-Archduke of Austria in the name of Mexico, with the Emperor of the French, or with any other government, by which he alienes or hypothecates Mexican territory, or in any manner compromises the responsibility of the native country of the undersigned.

Addressing himself to the government of the United States, the undersigned does not think it necessary to halt to prove that the ex-Archduke of Austria only represents in Mexico the Emperor of the French, by whose army he was brought to that republic and is there sustained, and that therefore any settlement made between the ex-Archduke and the Emperor of the French would have the same obligatory force on the Mexican nation as one concluded between the said Emperor and General Bazaine, commanding in chief the French forces in Mexico.

The undersigned has not thought that he should await for official notice of the conclusion of such settlement in order to protest against it. It is of such gravity and transcendency, not only to the interests of Mexico, but to those of the whole American continent, that he would consider himself to be wanting to his most sacred duties should he for a moment delay to take this step.

The undersigned thinks fit, in justification of his conduct in this affair, to remind the honorable Secretary of State of the United States of a fact slightly resembling the present, when the representative of the French government in Mexico protested against a treaty concluded between Mexico and the United States of much less importance than the present, only because of the vague rumors, more or less founded, that they had received that it had been concluded, and before they had official notice of its execution.

After the rupture between the allied European powers at Orizaba, and when France alone continued making war on Mexico, the minister of the United States to this republic made a treaty with the Mexican government, in virtue of which the United States were to lend to Mexico eleven millions of dollars, Mexico hypothecating in payment for such amount the unoccupied lands of the republic, the unsold national property, previously called church property, and the unsatisfied bonds and promissory notes for national property already aliened. This treaty was signed in the city of Mexico the 6th April, 1862; but as it did not receive ratification by the government of the United States it was not officially published, and only mere rumors, more or less founded, were circulated about its object and stipulations; notwithstanding which the representatives of the Emperor of the French addressed to the Mexican government, under date of the 15th April aforesaid, a note in which they said to it that they had been informed that said government had concluded or was about to conclude a treaty with a foreign government by which were sold, ceded, transferred, or hypothecated thereto a part of the lands and public revenues of Mexico, to the whole of which lands and revenues France made claim of right, in virtue of the fraudulent claims of her subjects. With the note which the undersigned had the honor to address to the honorable Secretary of State on the 2d June, 1862, he remitted a copy of such protest.

The undersigned avails of this opportunity to renew to the honorable William H. Seward the assurances of his most distinguished consideration.

M. ROMERO.

Hon. WILLIAM H. SEWARD, *&c.*, *&c.*, *&c.*

Mr. Seward to Mr. Romero.

DEPARTMENT OF STATE,
Washington, February 25, 1865.

SIR: I have the honor to acknowledge the receipt of your communication of the 6th instant, in which, in the character of envoy extraordinary and minister plenipotentiary of the United Mexican States, accredited to the government of the United States of America, you enter your protest, in the most formal, energetic, and solemn manner, against any settlement or cession, either made or to be made by the ex-Archduke Ferdinand Maximilian, of Austria, in the name of Mexico, with the Emperor of the French, or with any other government, by which he alienates or hypothecates Mexican territory, or in any manner compromises the responsibility of the Mexican republic.

This measure you are led to take under the circumstances more fully detailed in your note, believing it to be in consonance with your most sacred duties as the representative of Mexico.

In reply, it affords me pleasure to state that the protest referred to will be placed upon file in the archives of this department, there to remain a testimony to your course in the premises, and as an additional evidence of the zealous and patriotic discharge of your functions as the minister of Mexico in the United States, and for such other uses and purposes as future events may render it necessary to apply it.

I avail myself of this occasion to offer to you, sir, the renewal of my very high and distinguished consideration.

WILLIAM H. SEWARD.

Señor MATIAS ROMERO, *&c.*, *&c.*, *&c.*,
Washington, D. C.

Mr. Romero to Mr. Hunter.

[Translation.]

MEXICAN LEGATION IN THE UNITED STATES OF AMERICA,
Washington, April 20, 1865.

MR. SECRETARY AD INTERIM: I have the honor to transmit to you, with this note, by instructions of my government, and for the information of that of the United States, a copy of a communication addressed on the 2d of December last by General Slaughter, who commands the insurgent forces in the western district of Texas, to Don Tomas Mejia, the commander of the forces of the intervention in Matamoras, in relation to the Mexican steamer Orizaba, captured by the insurgents under the plea that she was manned by citizens of the United States.

From this communication we may infer what are the relations that have existed between the insurgents of both republics, and what are the sympathies which those of the United States entertain for those of Mexico.

This same communication was republished in the Gazette of Monterey of the 18th December, referred to, preceded by an article, of which I also transmit a copy, in which the sentiments of sympathy expressed by General Slaughter are reciprocated, the interventionists of Monterey considering themselves satisfied with the explanations of the said general, and even praising his action in capturing the steamer Orizaba. The circumstance of the publication of such an article in the official paper of the so-called authorities of the intervention in New Leon is very significant.

These documents are an additional proof of the identity of political interests which exists between the insurgents of this country and the partisans of the French cause in Mexico, thus making manifest that which exists between the United States and the Mexican nation.

In confirmation of these impressions, I deem [illegible]roper to enclose the annexed slip from the Tribune, of New York, of the 13th [illegible]tant, which contains a letter written at the city of Mexico on the 29th of Ma[illegible] last, and in which important details upon the events which are occurring in [illegible]t country, and especially in that part occupied by the French, in alluding to [illegible]ourse of these latter towards the citizens of the United States.

I avail myself of this occasion to renew to y[illegible]ir, the assurances of my very distinguished consideration.

M. ROMERO.

Hon. WILLIAM HUNTER, *&c., &c., &c.*

[Translation.—Enclosu[illegible] 1.]

THE SOUTHERN CONFEDERACY [illegible] THE EMPIRE.

MONTEREY, *December* 18, 1864.

We insert in continuation a communication from G[illegible]l J. E. Slaughter, who is now in command of the confederate troops in the western dis[illegible]of Texas, which he addresses to General Don Tomas Mejia, in reference to the capture [illegible]he steamer Orizaba, which vessel was seized in the waters of said confederacy.

The Monitor of the Frontier, which has first publish[illegible]aid communication, says that the Orizaba was sailing under the flag of Mexico, and tha[illegible]erefore, the seizure of the vessel is illegal. It is known, however, that the Orizaba be[illegible]s to citizens of the United States; that her cargo, as General Slaughter assures us, also [illegible]gs to them, and that the crew of the vessel is composed of Yankees.

Will it be permitted to the Yankees under the shad[illegible] the Mexican flag to interfere with the operations of the war, and to mock with impunity [illegible]ights of a nation like the young confederated republic to which we are united by the [illegible]le tie of commercial relations and mutual interests?

However much the contrary may be alleged, we [illegible]eve that the interested parties will necessarily be compelled to have recourse to the adm[illegible]y court of the confederacy, which is the only competent one to decide whether or not t[illegible] is room for the restitution of the Orizaba.

[Enclosure No. 2.—Tra[illegible]tion.]

HEADQUARTE[illegible]F THE DIVISION OF TEXAS,
Brownsville, December 2, 1864.

GENERAL: I have the honor to acknowledge the rec[illegible]t of your communication dated November 30, *ultimo*, in reference to the capture of the [illegible]eamer Orizaba and the detention of her officers and crew by the authorities of the Confeder[illegible] States.

I understand that the Orizaba was built by citizens of the United States, and that she belongs to these; that her cargo also belongs to them; that, besides, her crew is of the same nationality.

These reasons compelled me to take the steamer, but the case will be adjudged by the court of admiralty, and if these points can be proven, it will be clear that her license to sail under the Mexican flag is a violation of the laws of that country, and consequently null.

The decrees issued by the courts of admiralty are a general rule respected by all nations.

Both the interested parties may recur to and have the right to prove by witnesses, either of themselves or by an attorney, before the court of admiralty, their respective assertions.

The captain and the owners have abused the Mexican flag to cover property which belongs to our enemies, and in such a case they will have to prefer a complaint to the court referred to, and not to the imperial government at Mexico.

I have replied to your note with all the frankness of a soldier and friend, and at the same time permit me, general, to assure you that the confederate government and authorities will use all their efforts to continue and perpetuate the most friendly relations with the imperial government, and whensoever my government shall promise it a thing, it will know how to comply with it, giving thus to it a loyal proof of true friendship.

Be assured, general, that any vessel which sails under the Mexican flag, and may be found in our waters, will be treated with every consideration.

Permit me, general, to repeat to you the assurances of my esteem and regard, and to subscribe myself, respectfully, your obedient servant,

J. E. SLAUGHTER,
[illegible]dier General Commanding Western District of Texas.

Señor Don TOMAS MEJIA,
General Commanding [illegible]oahuila, New Leon, &c.

A true copy:

JUAN VALDEZ.

[Enclosure No. 3.—F[illegible] the New York Daily Tribune, April 13, 1865.]

LATER FROM MEXICO.—DELIG[illegible]L COMPLICATION EXISTING AMONG THE DIFFERENT FOREIGN ELEMENTS COMPOS[illegible] THE MEXICAN GOVERNMENT.—MEXICO HOLDS THE TRUMP CARD.—FREEDOM OF [illegible] MEXICAN PRESS.—LATE RIOT AT PUEBLA BETWEEN THE FRENCH AND AUSTRIAN[illegible]NSULTS AND INDIGNITIES OFFERED TO AMERICANS.—DEPARTURE OF THE ARMY O[illegible]E NORTHERN CAMPAIGN.—GREAT REJOICING OF THE FRENCH OVER THE LATE RE[illegible]ED REBEL SUCCESSES.—EARTHQUAKE ON THE NIGHT OF MARCH 27.—ASCENT OF [illegible] VOLCANO OF POPOCATAPETL BY TWO AMERICANS — FROM OUR SPECIAL CORRESP[illegible]NT.

MEXICO, *March* 29, 1865.

The discords in the royal "ha[illegible]amily" continue to grow more and more interesting. Composed as it is of French, Bel[illegible], and Austrians, each striving for the ascendency, and neither being able to place any [illegible]ence in the other, the position of affairs can easily be imagined. At present, Elvin, t[illegible]ief of cabinet and confidant of the Empress Carlotta, seems to have the firmest hold, a[illegible] the Emperor's private counsellor. He was sent by the father of Carlotta to see that her [illegible]ests were not neglected, and plays his cards well. No communication can reach the E[illegible]or except through his hands, which gives him decided advantages over other members o[illegible] cabinet. All these strifes and bickerings in the imperial cabinet, in the end, amount [illegible]othing, as the decisions have all to be submitted to the approval of Marshal Bazaine, wh[illegible] moment undoes the work of days, and, as the head of affairs in Mexico, dashes in p[illegible] the fabrications of the imperial council. No appointments can be made, no decrees is[illegible], no sentences approved—in fact nothing done without being first submitted to this repre[illegible]tive of Louis Napoleon, who, in turn, is now ruled by a notorious Mexican prostitute, [illegible]gh whom important business is transacted, appointments procured, rights to property [illegible]ablished, &c., she, of course, requiring a *quid pro quo* for her services; so that, in the [illegible] Mexico is decidedly ahead, this second Cleopatra, by her charms, ruling the destinies o[illegible] nation.

Several of the editors of newspa[illegible] in this city, having indulged in rather severe criticism in regard to the trial and summary [illegible]ecution of General Romero, who was shot in this city on the 18th instant, (but eight ho[illegible]ntervening between the close of the trial and his execution,) they were by order of Gene[illegible]azaine called together on the 23d, and informed that the military order issued in 1863, [illegible]ring martial law throughout Mexico, had never been revoked; that the military power [illegible]ed supreme, and was above and beyond the criticism of the press, and from the decisio[illegible] this tribunal there was no appeal; that any criticism will be considered a military offen[illegible] for which the parties will be arested and tried by court-martial. After this rebuke to all [illegible]everal editors present were marched off under guard to await a hearing for past offences.

Bitter feelings exist between the French and Austrians now in Mexico. The memory of the battle-fields of Majenta and Solferino are too fresh in their minds to admit of other than unfriendly feelings, and the resu[illegible] is constant strife. Many of the French soldiers wear badges of honor awarded by thei[illegible]vernment for services on these hard-fought and victorious fields. A few days since so[illegible]ustrians were passing by the quarters of some French zouaves, and one of them wea[illegible] Austrian badge, for distinguished services at Solferino, was insulted by the zouave, and as[illegible]ed why he wore a Solferino badge. Without replying, the Austrian reached out his hand [illegible]nd tore the badge from the zouave and threw it on the ground. A general fight ensued, and each party receiving re-enforcements, it was feared it would lead to serious difficulty.

The late riot in Puebla is attribu[illegible]able to the same cause, notwithstanding the newspaper stories to the contrary. The French guards having charge of some Mexican prisoners, were maltreating them by beating them with their swords. The friends of the prisoners remonstrated against such treatment of unarmed men, and were sustained by the Austrians. Gaining courage, they made an attack upon the French, in which they were aided by the Austrians, and for part of two days the riot continued, in which fire-arms were used freely and a considerable number of lives lost. Business was entirely suspended, and the prefect of Puebla telegraphed to the capital for assistance.

The general feeling among the French officials is animosity to all Ame[illegible]ans, and knowing that they have the advantage of numbers and influence, they take every opportunity to show disrespect to them. Realizing "that every dog has his day," and that our day is not far distant, we show our contempt for their cowardly sneer by passing them by in silence. No justice can be had in Mexico for an American; so discretion is the better part of valor.

The late news received here, by way of Matamoras, of [illegible]efeat of Grant at Richmond, and the loss of eighty pieces of artillery, with a corresp[illegible] slaughter of federal troops, was received with great joy by the entire French concern [illegible]xico, from Maximilian down. The recent arrival of the steamer, however, has dispelled [illegible] happy illusion, and "Uncle Sam" again looms up before them as great a terror as t[illegible]ugman" is to the juveniles. The old adage "weary lies the head that wears a crown [illegible] never more fully realized in the history of any monarch than in the case of the pres[illegible]eror of Mexico. Seated on the apex of a volcano at home, ready at any moment to [illegible] forth and destroy him, and with a constant fear of American interference, and a co[illegible]nt withdrawal of his French supporters, leaving him at the mercy of a people whose [illegible]e has outraged by intruding himself upon them, the poor Maximilian begins to feel t[illegible] has been made the tool of France, and wishes for his old home, preferring to mee[illegible]emands of bailiffs for unpaid tailors' and grocers' bills to those that will be made of hi[illegible]he Mexican people.

The army is leaving the capital on the great northern [illegible]gn against Juarez, and the reported re-enforcements he has received from Califor[illegible]f the truth of this we know nothing, as but few American newspapers are allowed [illegible]ch here. Of the number of Americans that have joined Juarez, we have all kinds of [illegible] ranging from eighteen individuals to an army of ten thousand—the former being g[illegible]y believed to be nearest the truth.

On the night of the 27th an earthquake occurred. Th[illegible]k took place at 8½ o'clock, and was of very short duration, and not very severe, t[illegible] sufficiently so to be generally felt. The whole valley of Mexico is doubtless resting u[illegible]bed of volcanic matter, which will some day burst forth and destroy this *modern Sodom*, [illegible]quent earthquakes that occur being only warnings of the fate that will one day be he[illegible]

The ascent of the great volcano of Popocatapetl, the [illegible]t point of land on the North American continent, has recently been made by two Am[illegible]s—one a Californian, the other from Cumberland county, P[illegible]nsylvania; a full accou[illegible]which is being prepared for the press.

E. J. M'C.

Mr. Seward to Mr. R[illegible]o.

DEPART[illegible]T OF STATE,
Wa[illegible]gton, November 2, 1865.

SIR: I have had the honor to receive your n[illegible] of the 20th of April last, transmitting, by instruction of your government, [illegible]rrespondence which passed in December, 1864, between General Slaughte[illegible]rebel officer in Texas, and General Mejia, commanding the forces of the F[illegible]n at Matamoras, in Mexico, relative to the capture of the Mexican steamer O[illegible]ba, seized by the insurgents of the United States, and to the apparent goo[illegible]nderstanding then existing between said generals touching the relations [illegible]he two governments they claimed to represent.

You are also pleased to communicate an extr[illegible]om the New York Tribune of the 13th of April, 1865, giving important [illegible]ls of the events then transpiring in the Mexican republic.

Thanking you for the information thus comm[illegible]ated, I pray you, sir, to accept the assurances of my highest consideration.

[illegible]ILLIAM H. SEWARD.

Señor MATIAS ROMERO, *&c., &c., &c.,*
Washington, D. C.

Mr. Romero to Mr. Seward.

[Translation.]

MEXICAN LEGATION IN THE UNITED STATES OF AMERICA,
Washington, July 4, 1865.

MR. SECRETARY: I deem it my duty to call your attention to the printed documents which I have the honor to accompany with this note, and which show not only the friendly and cordial understanding which existed, to the injury of the United St[illegible]between the insurgents against this government, in Texas, and the French[illegible] are waging war against the government of Mexico in Matamoras, but al[illegible] measures taken in concert between the French and their agents on the one [illegible]and the insurgents of Texas on the other, to resist the forces of the natio[illegible]vernment of Mexico, sent with the view of recovering the port of Mata[illegible] from the possession of the French. These documents, which were foun[illegible] Brownsville at the time of the occupation of said city by the forces of t[illegible]ited States, have been recently published by a journal of New York, [illegible] have sufficient reasons to consider them authentic.

In the communication[illegible]h General James E. Slaughter, who commanded in Brownsville when Texa[illegible]n the possession of the insurgents, addressed on the 6th of April last to Col[illegible]Thomas M. Jack, assistant adjutant general of the military department of [illegible] it is stated that Don Santiago Vidaurri, who had been appointed a couns[illegible]o the usurper, had returned to Monterey and had written to him that he[illegible]nuch important information to give him, which he could not trust to the p[illegible]e also asserts that "the imperialist commander of the port of Bagdad, ([illegible]an,) recently assigned to that command, informed him that he had secret in[illegible]tions to permit the introduction of all kinds of arms and munitions of w[illegible]c., that might be desired, and that they should pass freely, for the use o[illegible]confederacy."

It is also mentioned th[illegible]re was in Monterey, accredited to the agents of the French, called the "[illegible]ial authorities," an agent of the said confederacy named Mr. Querentes. [illegible]ral Slaughter himself adds: "General Mejia, (the French agent in Ma[illegible]as,) who now commands here, promised me to do everything he could in ou[illegible]or;" and he can do no less than acknowledge that the Mexican people o[illegible]e frontier states, with the exception of the personal friends of Vidaurri, [illegible]pposed to the so-called empire.

In another communicat[illegible]which the said General Slaughter addressed to Don Tomas Mejia, under [illegible] of the 10th of May last, referring to the exportation of cotton from the s[illegible] which has been carried on through Matamoras, he says to him the follow[illegible] "The trade which the Confederate States are now carrying on through [illegible]thorized agents with Mexico and other countries through the ports of Mexi[illegible]as been carried on with the consent of the Mexican authorities." Genera[illegible]ughter means to say, *of the French agents in Mexico.*

Colonel J. S. Ford, wh[illegible]d, temporarily, the command in Brownsville, in the name of the so-called [illegible]deracy, communicated to Don Tomas Mejia, under date of the 28th of [illegible]last, that he was about to station some forces on the banks of the Rio Gran[illegible] attack a force "which was in communication with those of the United[illegible]tes, and which probably was acting in concert with it," and he recommen[illegible]o him to station other troops on the side of Mexico to act in concert with the[illegible]nfederates in the said attack, because "it is the duty and the interest of b[illegible]governments (the imperial of Mexico, and the confederated of the south) to[illegible]stroy and to disperse such bands," which shows that the French and the ins[illegible]ents have acted in concert against the forces of the United States.

They have done the same thing while treating of the forces of the M[illegible] government. The printed official communication, which I also enclose, on the 2d of March aforesaid, which was addressed to me by General N[illegible] commanding in chief the national forces of Mexico, shows, that having re[illegible] instructions to attack Matamoras, he saw, in approaching the city, th[illegible] artillery from Brownsville covered that post; that the confederates p[illegible] themselves to enter into the fight at the time he approached the city, a[illegible] they maintained a hostile attitude while he remained in its vicinity, thus [illegible] himself compelled finally to withdraw therefrom on that account.

Besides this statement of General Negrete's, which justifies (proves) t[illegible] nivance of the confederates with the French against the national gove[illegible] of Mexico, we have the testimony of General Slaughter himself, the com[illegible] in-chief of Brownsville, who, in the note which he addressed to the a[illegible] adjutant general, Colonel Jack, on the 18th of May, aforesaid, report[illegible] proceedings at the time General Negrete was pressing [illegible] Matamora[illegible] that said general knowing that he (Slaughter) was a [illegible]d imperia[illegible] fearing that his sympathies might influence his official [illegible]ct, he [illegible] commissioner to ask how he would act during the atta[illegible] reply, he said to him that the confederates recei[illegible] Matamoras, and that if the port was occupied b[illegible] blockaded by the French, for which reason it wa[illegible] remain in possession of the former. Further on, [illegible] the same time that I maintained a strict neutralit[illegible] such a manner that I obtained the same results w[illegible] if I had taken an active part in the contest. Ge[illegible] and retired; being fearful of the result should he b[illegible]

These are the principal facts, which are to be [illegible] nexed. In view of them, I think it would not b[illegible] say that they involved acts of hostility against th[illegible] French agents, who occupy the frontier, are resp[illegible] a question exclusively concerning the government [illegible] doubt not, will attach to it such importance as i[illegible] high dignity may induce it to regard as most ap[illegible] it if at the same time the facts mentioned did n[illegible] tility against the government which I have the [illegible] by armed citizens of the United States, whom, [illegible] aspirations, the Mexican government never c[illegible] nation, and did not even recognize in them the [illegible] for this reason, now, its clear right to ask repara[illegible] the government of the United States, within the [illegible] [illegible]ssors are.

[illegible]h the reservation, therefore, to again retu[illegible] [illegible]atter when I shall receive the instructio[illegible] [illegible]cate to me respecting it, to ask the repara[illegible] [illegible] may require, I deem it my duty to pr[illegible] [illegible]st the open hostility, with regard to [illegible] [illegible]nd his followers in Brownsville, saving [illegible] republic may have suffered, and ma[illegible] [illegible]tion for them at such time and in su[illegible] [illegible] of this opportunity to renew to [illegible] [illegible]nguished consideration.

[illegible]ARD, &c., &c., &c.

[Enclosure No. 1.]

NEW ORLEANS, *June* 17, 1865.

ices from the Rio Grande border are to the 10th instant. They contain the following ting account of the late revolution in northern Mexico, and the movement on Mata- It is in the form of a letter to citizen Matias Romero, envoy extraordinary and min- ienipotentiary of the Mexican republic to Washington. They call it here Negrete's report:

ing been invested by the citizen President of there public with extraordinary powers e war against the traitors and those who aid and abet them, I commenced operations the city of Matamoras, arriving in sight of it with my command on the 30th ultimo. n the march I learned that the traitor Mejia, in order to resist my attack, relied upon chants of said city who were armed, and the confederates of North America on the k of the Brazos.

information was confirmed by various reliable sources, from which I also learned illery belonging to the American troops of the south were in readiness in the main n Matamoras. From my own eyes I know that the confederates of North America l armed on the other side of the river since I approached the city, and that even to nent they ma[illegible] a hostile attitude, moving in my rear and compelling me to employ my cavalr[illegible] atch them. These facts agree fully and completely with the open wn by [illegible] federates toward the forces of Colonel Francisco Naranjo, when ued [illegible] tors who garrisoned the village of Piedras Negras. The latter with the anticipated consent and protection of the former.

I have determined to withdraw my troops, believing that k a city garrisoned by soldiers, re-enforced by merchants, numerical force superior to mine, and which, I have no federates in the storming of the place. The forces in the hich are now on the banks of the Bravo, have observed vernment of Mexico a conduct entirely opposed to the war king them accomplices of the vile attempt of Napoleon III ico, which is also a threat to the sovereignty of all the re-

r that the confederates, like the Mexican traitors, are allies h protect the enemies of the United States government, ours. The gravity of the case, and the importance that United States government, impel me to address you this ter of foreign relations.

consideration and esteem. Independence and liberty!

M. NEGRETE.

1865.

[Enclosure No. 2.]

HEADQUARTERS WEST SUB-DISTRICT, TEXAS,
Brownsville, January 10, 1865.

state, for your information, that a few days since the judge notified me of the possession of certain claims of citizens of ates, and that if payment was not made promptly he should f attachment in the case and to order the seizure of cott rnment, and to take such other steps necessary to s cumstances I feel it my duty to urge you, if in you his subject until the matter can be laid before th d decision.

* * * * * *

d on by the Confederate States, through the ntries through the ports of Mexico, was dou

* * * * * *

lient servant,

JAS. E. SLAU
Brigadier General

&c.

[Enclosure No. 3.]

HEADQUARTERS WES

state, for the information of means to retain and increa governments.

Governor Vidaurri has been appointed one of the "Council of the Nat turned to Monterey. I received a letter from him, in which he states he h tion to give to me which he cannot safely submit to writing. In view of Benavides has received a sick leave of absence from district headquarte mutual friend of Governor Vidaurri and myself, I have directed him to pr and place himself in personal communication with him. Upon his retur able to give more definite information as to the state of feeling towards o cause by the imperial government. I have made an arrangement with G mander of the imperial forces on this frontier, for the mutual rendition o of which has been forwarded to district headquarters. Its first practica return of three thieves, (who happened to be deserters from Jones's batter was great and pernicious. This course on the part of General Mejia, tog eral impression that the arrangement had been made between us for the r caused the United States consul to address a letter of protest, which wa satisfactory to him in its results, as he obtained in reply only a letter refle the acts and conduct of the federals in several instances in connexion wit am promised a copy of this correspondence, which, when obtained, I s ward.

The imperial commander of the port of Bagdad, (a Belgian,) lately as mand, informs me he has private instructions to permit all arms, ammunit of war, &c., to be introduced and passed for the use of the confederacy This is similar to the proposal privately extended to General Mejia, and to district headquarters. They show an evident feeling of friendship for

It is known by the Emperor, and strongly conjectured by myself, tha and the federals are in correspondence with each other. I received info since that a Mexican bearer of despatches from Juarez to the federals cro my district at Piedras Negras on the 17th ultimo. I have a large part deavoring to intercept him. If successful, I hope to be able, through thi cate matters between Mexico and the United States to such a degree as vantage.

The feeling of all the imperial officers on this frontier is strongly in our our cause strongly allied to their own in many respects, and are ready extend every possible aid which can be done without directly bringing th in contact with the United States.

We have already, in the person of Mr. Querentes, a commissioner of resident at Monterey. I do not think that any commissioner sent by th ing the department could be of any service in Mexico, as I presume M using every effort in his power to affect the new government.

Governor Vidaurri will, I feel certain, further our interest in every long as he retains his immediate position.

General Mejia, the present commander here, promised me to do all in I feel certain he entertains the kindest feelings for us all.

I may as well add here that the people on this frontier, with the excep party, are all opposed to the imperial government, and all look to federa

I am, colonel, very respectfully, your obedient servant,

JAS. E. S

Brigadier Ge

Colonel THOMAS M. JACK,

Assistant Adjutant General.

[Enclosure No. 4.]

HEADQUARTERS W

COLONEL: I have the honor to state, for the informatio during the late excitement in Mexico, arising from the app command of General Negrete before Matamoras, I was General Negrete to ascertain my policy. Knowing me to he feared it might influence my official acts.

I explained to him (through his agents) that we were Matamoras and its port for supplies for this country, and be blockaded by the French, and it would be impossible thing through that channel; hence it was to our interest f country.

I avoided committing myself by a direct or positive ans

While I maintained strict neutrality, I veiled my inte

hich would have been attained by actual assistance rendered. General siege and retired, being fearful of the result should he be compelled to

, very respectfully, &c., &c.,

JAS. E. SLAUGHTER,
Brigadier General Commanding.

M. JACK,
t Adjutant General.

[Enclosure No. 5.]

HEADQUARTERS WEST SUB-DISTRICT, TEXAS,
Brownsville, May 28, 1865.

* * I am satisfied that there is an organized band of robbers end to both sides of the Rio Grande, and who are in communication with ssibly act in conjunction with them.
ents render the conclusion inevitable that no organization connected in e government of the United States can be supposed to have much regard friendship of the imperial government of Mexico, and that it is the common interest of your government and of mine to break up and disperse I shall place troops on the river for that purpose, and should be pleased concert with yours.
o renew my assurance of regard and personal consideration. Your obe-

J. S. FORD, *Colonel Commanding pro tem.*

AS MEJIA, &c

Mr. Seward to Mr. Romero.

DEPARTMENT OF STATE,
Washington, November 4, 1865.

honor to acknowledge the receipt of your communication of ng my attention to the printed documents enclosed therein, correspondence between the insurgent leaders of the rebellion rders of Texas and the officers of the French army operating borhood in Mexico, manifesting a spirit of hostility, on the ent citizens of the United States, against the government you ist which acts of hostility you solemnly protest.
e to inform you that the matters referred to in your note, to onor of replying, shall receive the attention to which they

this opportunity to assure you of my distinguished consid-

WILLIAM H. SEWARD.

MERO, &c., &c., &c., *Washington, D. C.*

Hunter to Mr. Bigelow.

DEPARTMENT OF STATE,
Washington, July 31, 1865.

n of a note of the 8th instant, and a copy of the fers, addressed to this department by Mr. Romero, minister plenipotentiary of the Mexican republic relative to a supposed understanding between the as and the French commander in the adjacent leged co-operation between them, for the purpose of preventing the recovery of Matamoras from its present possessi the papers referred to in Mr. Romero's communication to be gen to require explanation from the French authorities, which you wi request of Mr. Drouyn de Lhuys.

I am, sir, your obedient servant,

W. HUNTER, *Acti*

JOHN BIGELOW, Esq., *&c., &c., &c.*

Mr. Romero to Mr. Sew d.

[Translation.]

MEXICAN LEGATION IN THE UNITED TATES OF A
Vashington,

MR. SECRETARY: Through an accident there have fallen int letters from Mr. William M. Gwin, formerly senator of California, at the present time in carrying into effect a plan of colonizatio states of the Mexican republic, which letters are dated at the on the 18th of March last, and directed one to Colonel John Wi York, in care of Mr. Royal Phelps, of the same city; and the o and daughters living at Paris. On one leaf of the latter is foun written by Mr. William M. Gwin, junior, to his mother, on the 1 said month of May. Although Mr. Gwin does not sign the let there is abundant reason for believing that they have been writ handwriting, the context, and more especially the circumstanc letter is signed, leave no doubt in regard to the authenticity of

Along with said letters there have come into my possession tw the mark "confidential" on it, signed by "Masse ," and direc Benjamin Wood, of New York, and the other a correspondenc same person and directed to the newspaper "The Daily New Both are dated at the city of Mexico, on the said 18th of May.

In the letter of which I enclose you a copy, an which was on the 1st instant by Colonel Don Enrique A. Mejia, of the Me will be informed of the manner in which those letters fell int For what it may amount to, I will state to you that the despat tion of the United States in Mexico for the department over wl referred to by Colonel Mejia, I placed in the hands of Mr. H of June last.

The importance of the documents adverted to has induce originals to your department, in order that the government of may take such steps in regard to them as it shall deem c safety and its interests. It appears from them that Mr. Gwin is in carrying into effect his project of colonization; so clearly, having written with much distrust, th letters might be intercepted, that project is kno States, since he proposes to take to the frontier o citizens of the United States living in the south, them there under the protection and with the ass also that he has, so far as the French Emperor is carrying into effect this undertaking, and that the to General Bazaine, commander-in-chief of the F to Gwin all the assistance which he may need i The sanction of Maximilian—the puppet whom t placed in Mexico in order that he might seem t try—which was the only thing wanted for the ained, but was on the eve of being obtained, as well because all f the usurper considered the plan referred to as the only salva-lled empire, as because the members of Maximilian's cabinet ed to the plan had left their places in order to be succeeded by favorable to it, and more especially because it is plainly to be Archduke of Austria has no will of his own in the affairs of having been placed in the country by the Emperor of the ng been sustained by him militarily and pecuniarily, in the part epublic occupied by the invading army, nothing is done but ommander decide to do of themselves or in virtue of orders nt, and ie ex-Archduke is only to keep up appearances, of eve ts to indicate to the Emperor of the French what ry be done finally in Mexico.

are corroborated in a letter from Vera Cruz of the "Times," at New Orleans, a copy of which I have

nt a copy of the enclosed letters, in order that on ary steps to frustrate the plans hostile to Mexico rench is endeavoring to develop in the republic. at such plans are equally hostile to the United letters, in order that you may make of them such

unity, Mr. Secretary, to renew to you assurances deration.

M. ROMERO.

&c., &c., &c.

[Enclosure No. 1.]

WASHINGTON, *July* 1, 1865.

business calls me to New York. I will explain in this s submitted to you came to my hands.

vas requested by Mr. Corwin, the acting chargé d'affaires of some despatches for the State Department, as he l been tampered with. As there was a probability that spatches by another conveyance to Vera Cruz, there to d this precaution, as I was arrested on arriving at Vera apers taken from me, including my passport as bearer e demanded of me, and as I denied having them, I was unicate with no one. Finding nothing to criminate me, nd allowed to embark for Havana. On board of the e French had been so anxious to procure.

d among them those now in your possession, probably ich being open I examined, and considered of sufficient

I was shown the original letter from Napoleon to Mar-vin's plan, as submitted to him, and directing the mar-l by Mr. Gwin. The object is to colonize Sonora and nfederates, as a barrier to any aggression of the United ays hostile, and, with the assistance of the French, suffi-nts against Maximilian.

ico for Sonora and the northern frontier in combination

nt servant,

ENRIQUE A. MEJIA.

[Enclosure No. 2.]

MEXICO,

MY DEAR MOTHER: Nothing has occurred since I last wrote; in fact tl occur; all business has come to a stand-still, because of the emperor's abs august Majesty has sufficiently amused himself with rural sports, he may return to his sleeping capital and wake us up from our present state of letha ing to exercise the admirable quality of patience, which means I begin to f sophical way of taking things coolly—the best thing a man can do in M object of the community is to approach as nearly as possible to a state of v imitate in all its lively peculiarities that interesting excrescence—a knot on Talcott arrived a day or two ago. He has been unwell in consequence of to and can scarcely walk, from having sprained his ankle. We breakfasted wi Saturday; the old man read them that part of your letter about Spiller. I little uneasy on account of his prolonged absence. The marriage, you kn taken place last month; now no one can say when it will come off. The o of the conviction that Spiller is going to act the dog. Your letters were an i tion. It was very consoling to hear you were in good spirits, although I still cherish in some small degree that pleasing reflection that, some day o ourselves a-starving. I am altogether opposed to ever being reduced to su and have determined, at the hazard of proving you a bad prophet, to make a fixed fact upon the principle, be there a will, then wisdom finds the way. and trust to luck for wisdom, and when that fortune is made, should you wanderer, I'll give you food and shelter.

May 18. The old man saw the marshal the other day, but nothing resulte view. He renewed his protestations of friendship, and declared he would ur claims to the utmost. We must content ourselves with an existence of longer, for no steps can be taken without the emperor. The old man saw he thinks there'll be no trouble, and so far as he himself is concerned, we ma support.

The minister of foreign affairs has gone to Europe, and every one says Al in. He will then be all-powerful, and with his favorable disposition towar are pretty certain to carry the day. Things are progressing as smoothly as provokes one to be detained when there is no sufficient cause. To think o here holding our hands, when those prodigious mines are inviting us to because the emperor will stuff birds! I feel very easy about Mexican affair fully blue about the south. Andy Johnson's speeches breathe such a hein can see nothing ahead but extermination. I shouldn't be surprised if there on the American continent the massacre and havoc of the French revolutio to contemplate the situation of the country. I am afraid they will commit all the horrors that have gone before will be as nothing. It's dreadful to it's ten times more dreadful to die on the scaffold. Johnson says treason c uation; it is a crime that merits the direst punishment. That's to say, be hung, and as we are all traitors there's nothing left for us but hanging me sick when I think of the bloody agony that awaits the southern peop learn to suppress our feelings; it may be, after all, that our only home wi people. If the old man shouldn't succeed, we shall have to live in Califor are fortunate to have even such a refuge.

I am very glad aunt Sue is going to Europe; she'll be a great comfort man wrote the judge from Havana, and said, when the time came and h he would let him know. He told the judge that uncle Alick must come w the necessary means, which should be paid on his arrival. Tell Carri lightful and to write me every mail. I promise to answer her every one. to write me, and not to get married. Love to all.

Your affectionate son,

W

NOTE.—On the same note-paper sheet appears the following:

[Enclosure No. 3.]

MY DEARLY-BELOVED WIFE AND DAUGHTERS: The States has made the blood of every southern sympathizer r be safe in our native country. How I thank Providence t and that very soon I will have a home for my wife and from oppression, and where we have every prospect of im My policy is on every man's lips as the only one that wi lingers most unaccountably away from the capital, but matter considers it so pressing that he has gone to him w one doubts that there will be an entire change of ministry, the emperor returns, and that his entire ministry will be ng this change in his absence, and that he remains away to accomplish it. I could give you names of persons who have approached me with this news no doubt on your minds that all of these things will happen, and that very y is unpleasant, but the certainty of success that will follow this delay is a , especially when everything is so dark for us everywhere else. Never have ccess. I have less now than ever. Willie is getting into heavy business. ng to him to give him the entire control of the richest gold mine in the , and he is one of three who have asked for the concession of all the rail-. He will succeed in both, and either of them will make a dozen fortunes. hole army will soon be in Texas. I will write more at large by British

yours, devotedly.

(No signature to this.)

osures No. 2 and No. 3 are written on the same sheet of note paper, and came addressed as follows:
M. Gwin, 55 Boulevard Malesherbes, Paris, France."
which is again enclosed in another envelope, addressed to—
den Broek & Co., 60 Rue de la Chaussee d'Antin, Paris, France."

[Enclosure No. 4.]

MEXICO, *May* 18, 1865.

LONEL: The news from the United States appals every one here, and paralyzes What will happen next is the constant inquiry. The emperor's absence must at a distance extraordinary, but it is now developing itself that he is bringing change in his counsels, and there will be an entire change of policy on his of the ruling men in his counsels have been displaced since he left, and two most obnoxious to my ideas of government, and most opposed to my project) abroad, if not in banishment, equivalent to it. No one here doubts but Al- s into power, and from the first he has declared that my plan of colonization ation for the empire. The same sentiment is uttered by every one in favor of fact, if anything in the future can be certain in this country, at an early day ecree opening North Mexico to the enterprise of the world. What a people e there if this policy is adopted. What a country it will be in a very few ent startling events, and the policy I have indicated, causes delay that is un- doubt of ultimate success. I have never been so confident as at present. and highly-valued friend, Mrs. W., that we will very soon meet again in the pot on the globe, and there will not be a cloud to obscure the future. She stmas dinner in the palace, to a certainty, and what a time we will have ere I will send an order to France for a large supply of the best wines in will be mellow to the taste by Christmas. This is not romance. The confronts every one of my sentiments banishes all romance. I must have usades will be surpassed in the emigration to the country of my future people never moved from one country to another. You and your wife are w that gave me a cheer of success, and that success will be marred if you in it. But, like me, you must be patient for a time; it may be but for a I confess I chafe at every hour's delay, but I do not permit this to depress nergies. I have to deal in generalities, for fear of accidents, but you may home where you will not only be prosperous and happy, but honored as first, had faith. your name in some important concessions that may be necessary to se- of my policy, but you may rely on it, if I do, benefits of no equivocal it to you. Every one with a particle of enterprise in his composition have the north, but I will be first on the ground. I shall open new books, and had better wait coming events before they venture their money. When , bring as many millions as you please, and they will soon turn into tens keptical here now acknowledge that no such country exists on e to write so obscurely, for fear of accidents, that you may h that I know what I am about.

I remain very truly yours.

(No signature.)

nvelope addressed as follows: "Colonel John Winthrop," ope addressed to: "Royal Phelps, esq., 22 East Sixteenth f America."
evidently in the same handwriting, which is believed to be

[Enclosure No. 5.]

Mr. Massey to Mr. Wood.

Private.] MEXICO, *May* 18, 1865.

DEAR SIR: Just on enclosing the within very hastily written communication, I hear of
person to leave in the morning for New York, and I avail myself of the opportunity to se
by him. You see I have been cautious but positive about Doctor Gwin. He, my famil
General Stone, and two others *mess* together; they are all in my rooms several times a da
or I or we in theirs. I see Mr. Soulé daily, all in the same scheme—Sonora, Sinaloa, Ch
huahua, and Durango; they have *all they want* from the French Emperor; the approval o
Maxamilian is *desired*. *Marshal Bazaine* has certain orders anyhow; the thing will be carrie
out, and Gwin will go out as director general, &c. Stone's project was distinct, as I hav
stated, and accidental. They harmonize, however, admirably. I am distinctly *pledged*, i
presence of witnesses, to have *any* scheme of mine carried out; I shall have them. There ar
fortunes in it, and a very peculiar kind of colonization alone permitted. I am too much hurried to say more; I must say, however, that *our* affair is the largest, and best, and most rapid
ever conceived or granted in any country. I dropped a line to the Empress the other day,
and in two hours had an answer entirely satisfactory. Nothing will be finished till the Emperor returns—said now not till 3d or 4th of next month; and when he does return he has
weighty matters awaiting him, so that I fear a still longer delay. Hence I cannot get through
in time for the next (British) steamer of the 1st. Nothing is being finished in his absence. I
do trust that, in the midst of the turbulent times about you, you have sequestered ample means
for our project; if I knew otherwise I would be off on another thing. But *with* ours, other
"*big things*" follow. I am sorry you have not written to me; I know not your hopes or
wishes. You *ought* to have sent me some money. It is hard to financier on nothing *indefinitely*, and I have concentrated my whole strength on our scheme. I enclose a letter for my
daughter—please mail it to her; and also, as I am delayed about making money, I want and
particularly request, you to send to her address a *draft* r $200 *in gold;* she needs it; he
term is out, and I have written that you will send it to he; don't neglect it—that is, if yo
and I are ever to have anything in common, and your fortune is secure if you will attend t
me a little. God knows what I will do about money if I don't get our scheme through quick
Have never seen a copy of the "News."

Your friend,

MASSEY.

HON. B. WOOD.

[Enclosure No. 6.]

CITY OF MEXICO, *May* 19, 186

Editor N. Y. Daily News:

The "*government*" is still on its travels; that is, the Emperor continues his recrea
about Orizaba; consequently, civil events make no progress—everything apparently w
for the Emperor's return. His absence has been, and is, exceedingly unpopular. He s
nothing to be *finished* without him, and documents and messages sent to him are seem
shelved. In consequence of important news from France by the late French steame
changes are being effected, and great improvements expected. The loan of $50,00
sufficient, with the income of the country, to "run" the government for two years,
which time it is at leisure to "consolidate" itself. The vote in the French Chambers
ue French troops in Mexico was unexpectedly large in its favor, and guarantees
tection of governmental stability here. That an improvement in the administ
s foreshadowed is indicated in the very sudden removal of Eloin, (called chie
ly chief *clerk* of cabinet,) who has been reputed to have exerted an oversh
over the Emperor and Empress, and has been exceedingly unpopular with
oreigners. Eloin was with the Emperor on his trip; and some instruction
ce were evidently impressive, for he left on the steamer at once, without
ng to the capital for a "change of clothes." He is said to have been s
ssion to Belgium and France; so, also, Ramirez, the secretary of state,
mission, it is said, to London and Brussels. The Emperor has a conver
iting honors! The secretary of the interior has also been permitted to re
d why he, too, was not provided with a foreign mission, although it is k
"loyalty" questionable. All these cabinet vacancies are
so till the Emperor's return. It would be useless to g

om Havana and Mexico will have heralded the re
f Mexico. All manner of things will doubtless
d noble ex-senator know that he knows how to k
l your readers as many particulars as they are i
t the Dr. is not a man to fail. He comes bac

health and spirits. All misunderstandings have been cleared up. All talk of the Dr. being ade duke, viceroy, or anything of the kind, is all stuff; it never entered the brain of any- dy but scribblers. The Dr. has a higher, nobler ambition than that kind of nonsense smacks f. That he is in process of full success there can be no shadow of doubt. Soon a domain s large as France, and composed of four of Mexico's richest states, will be open to the most eautiful a species of immigration ever known—all to become and remain a part of the em- ire of Mexico. Soon after the Emperor's return I will be in a position to tell your readers nore. Those who are tired of revolutions, and of mobocracies, and political corruptions, nay look forward with hope.

By an accidental coincidence General Charles P. Stone got upon the same steamer at Havana upon which Dr. Gwin had taken passage for Mexico. I would scarcely allude to it were it not that letter-writers will probably indulge in a variety of speculations. General Stone was engaged in the survey of Sonora in 1859, under the celebrated Jecker contract. Some of Jecker's claims having lately been audited by the imperial government, General Stone came on to see about his own interests. He came with a practical experience, too, of infinite importance in the near development of Sonora. His purposes and plans in relation thereto were totally independent of and disconnected with the larger enterprise of Dr. Gwin; yet each will materially assist the other. Within a very few weeks I am sanguine that all will be in process of successful accomplishment. Till I write again, your readers must wait, and take anything said in other journals with a very large "grain of salt."

Military matters are not very exciting. Of course you have heard of the entry and temporary occupation of Saltillo and Monterey by the troops of Negrete. Upon getting over to Matamoras they met with Mejia, re-enforced by five hundred fresh troops, and the Juarists precipitately retired. It is expected that they will be surrounded and taken prisoners. This is the only band of any size known to be in an organized condition in Mexico. Of course, as I have repeatedly said, it will in all probability require many years to get rid of this guerilla business. Mexico *has been used to it* for these many years, under all forms and shapes of government, and such an inveterate habit of a people cannot easily be broken up. The state of Michoacan is greatly disturbed—there is nothing like repose in it. It is a large state, and mountainous. Small parties can make very destructive irruptions, and French and Belgian troops have both suffered severely by surprise. Re-enforcements are almost constantly arriving at Vera Cruz. The vomito has been playing sad havoc already in the unfortunate city *just mentioned. It is extremely dangerous* for any one unacclimated to pass a single *night there. It will be a great blessing* * * * * * * * *

[*Here a portion of the third page of the letter seems to have been either torn or cut off.*]

Mexico and the world. Fortunately, it is going on with all possible vigor. The company *nstructing it* have subleased eleven leagues of the most labor to a French and Belgian comny; the part which includes the mountains to be done in two years. One single bridge ll cost $2,000,000, and will be made in England. The other part of the route goes on. e iron will be hauled over the mountains. It is in contemplation to finish this end, from city of Mexico to Puebla, within two years.

he tragic events in the United States are, of course, the almost universal subject of conation. It might possibly come under the head of "news" to tell you some of the comts in the highest circles. But you must pardon my refraining, because they would be unced as "copperhead" representations. And the events have been too thick and fast proper reference to them in a brief letter. From the stand taken by Andy Johnson and torney General and Secretary of War, it is evident that they must have their hands too r years to come to permit his talk about the "Monroe doctrine" to be any more than Such vindictiveness in conquerors was never before seen in the world's history, and will bring the destruction of its authors is written in the book of destiny. Either re" or to "subjugate" is the dream of an inebriate, under the policy shadowed fo rriage of the remains of Lincoln through the cities of the country, the uses splay in exasperating the lowest passions of humanity, has afforded scand an name all over the world too glaring for remark.

Yours, truly,

JOUR

e.—This communication seems to be in the same handwriting as enclos ies.

[Enclosure No. 7.—From the New York World of Ju

EMIGRATION TO MEXICO.

nister of public works at Mexico also publishes a no Thomas C. Massey, has been allowed to estab *a private enterprise solely*, with no responsibili or Maximilian.

[Enclosure No. 8.—From Vera Cruz, June 1. Correspondence of the New Orleans Times.]

The Emperor is still on his travels, stuffing birds and shooting deer, while the Empress is at a standstill awaiting his return to the capital. The last news from the interior is of a serious nature. Count Pottier has been defeated by the liberals in the state of Michoacan, the count wounded and his troops badly beaten, though he, of course, claims a victory, only retreating for want of water, when he says in the first part of the report that the fight occurred by a lake and during two hours' rain.

The liberals, under Negrete, still hold Monterey, Saltillo, and all the country bordering on the Rio Grande, and though the attack on Matamoras failed, they have been able to hold all the rest. The state of Tamaulipas, with the exception of the ports of Matamoras and Tampico, are entirely held by the liberals. Everywhere in the country the people seem to be rising against the French. The only part of the country really held by the imperialists is the environs of the capital and the road to Vera Cruz.

In the capital things continue the same as ever. There is no accord between the French commander and the imperial government. Nothing has been done to recuperate the finances of the country, though the news by the last steamer seems to indicate that the great project of the imperial loan-lottery will meet with success. If an individual tried to raise the wind by such means he would be indicted for swindling. Imagine, for bonds whose face shows 500 francs, the lender pays 350 francs. They bear six per cent. interest. Every year 3,000,000 are to be raffled and prizes drawn varying from half a million to twenty-five thousand for the benefit of bondholders. Besides, after fifty years their capital is to be doubled—that is to say, they receive one thousand francs with the interest payable semi-annually in Paris. The French government keeps the first amount paid in to cover the prizes and pay itself, and Maximilian only gets about two million. In one year he has spent $6,000,000, and is no nearer pacifying the country than he was six months ago. It is true he has in his cabinet some liberals, but the party will have none of him.

The confederates still continue to flock to Mexico. There is no doubt Dr. Gwin will get his project through. It only awaits the signature of Maximilian to become a law. He goes out as director general of emigration for the states of Sonora, Chihuahua, Durango, and Tamaulipas, with extraordinary powers and *eight thousand* French troops to back him. The emigration is to be strictly southern, or confederate. Ten thousand confederates are to be armed and paid by the empire, but kept in the above-mentioned states as protection to the emigrants. Strategical points are to be fortified and garrisoned on the frontier. Dr. Gwin's son has applied for and will get an exclusive privilege for all the railroads in Sonora. The southerners are elate, and golden visions float before them. The last news from the States has caused a panic, and every mail is anxiously expected. The Yankee invasion they consider as certain, but hug to themselves the idea that France, Austria, and Belgium will not allow the United States to invade the empire. Napoleon has sent out a director of police to Maximilian, Cappo d'Istri, who lately returned from organizing the police of the Celestial Empire. Persecutions immediately began, *a la* French. The first two imprisonments have caused great sensation.

It seems that Colonel Henry Mejia, of the liberal party, lately went to Mexico under a safeguard to attend to some valuable property he had inherited, and while in the city invented a rifle, of which much was spoken. It is said to shoot accurately sixty times in a minute. Finding it difficult to construct in Mexico, he decided going to the United States. By accident, in the same stage, there was Mr. Bay, ex-governor of Mexico, also of the liberal party. Two prominent liberals going to the States looked so much like conspiracy that on their arrival at Vera Cruz both were arrested and put in dungeons, their trunks broken open and papers seized. Unfortunately for Colonel Mejia, he had some despatches for the State Department at Washington, and also a model of his rifle, or, as the French called it, infernal machine. The despatches were opened and the rifle seized. As both these gentlemen had safe conducts, and really nothing could be proved against them, and as such imprisonments were in direct contravention of the provisional *statute*, they were released after eight days' close confinement. These arrests caused *intense* excitement, and the fears of an *emeute* induced, no doubt, their prompt release. The rottenness of the empire is beyond description. The lavish expenditures of Maximilian have no check, and nothing is done for the benefit of the country. If Maximilian lasts two years, the debt of Mexico would be increased $300,000,000. The roads are impassable in the rainy season. There is no security anywhere, no order, no system. The French loudly complain. They say something is due to France, which means that they are tired of the Austrians, and want Mexico for themselves; that if they must fight the United States, the prize must be for them. As for fighting the Americans, 40,000 French can easily rout an army of 100,000 Yankees. French vanity can admit no equality, as they say one shot, then a charge, and the poor Americans will be spitted on French bayonets. The confederates seriously proclaim that they only can save the empire by the emigration of southerners, who will rally by thousands at the call of Gwin, and raise an impassable bulwark against American aggression. This is seriously believed and circulated by the French commander-in-chief.

Mr. Seward to Mr. Romero.

DEPARTMENT OF STATE,
Washington, July 18, 1865.

SIR: I have the honor to acknowledge the receipt of your note of the 18th instant, with its several accompaniments, referring to the plans of Mr. W. M. Gwin, formerly a senator of the United States, for colonizing the frontier states of the Mexican republic.

Thanking you for your attention in communicating the important information contained in those papers to this government, I have, in reply, to inform you that the subject of your note will receive the prompt consideration of this government, and that proper measures will be adopted in reference to the same.

I have the honor to renew to you, sir, the assurance of my distinguished consideration.

WILLIAM H. SEWARD.

Señor MATIAS ROMERO, &c., &c., &c.,
Washington, D. C.

Mr. Seward to Mr. Bigelow.

No. 195.]

DEPARTMENT OF STATE,
Washington, July 13, 1865.

SIR: I give you a copy of three intercepted letters which have been submitted to this department: one letter, dated Mexico, 16th May, 1865, addressed by William M. Gwin (supposed to be junior) to his mother, followed by another letter on the same sheet, without date, in the handwriting of William M. Gwin, senior, well known to this department, addressed to his wife and daughter. The sheet referred to is directed to Mrs. William M. Gwin, No. 55 Boulevard Malesherbes, Paris, and is enclosed in another envelope addressed to Messrs. Van den Brock & Company, Rue de la Chausse d'Antin, Paris. Another letter, also in the well-known handwriting of William M. Gwin, dated Mexico, 18th May, 1865, is addressed to "My Dear Colonel." It is contained in an open envelope and addressed to Colonel John Winthrop. That envelope is contained in another to Royal Phelps, esquire, No. 22 East Sixteenth street, New York, United States of America. A third letter, dated at Mexico on the 6th of May, 1865, addressed to honorable B. Wood, and signed Massey, enclosing a communication to the editor of the New York Daily News, dated at the city of Mexico, 19th of May, 1865, upon the subject of Mexican affairs.

1st. They show that Dr. William M. Gwin and his family are disloyal.

2d. That they are engaged in obtaining from Maximilian, titular emperor in Mexico, grants of mineral lands in the states of that republic adjoining the United States, and that Doctor Gwin is to be the chief directing agent in working these mines.

3d. That a large accession of capitalists and emigrants into those states from the rebels against the United States is expected.

4th. That they assure the said Maximilian and the Emperor of France that their contemplated proceedings tend to promote Maximilian's success.

5th. That they regard their enterprise as injurious to the United States.

6th. That they claim to have the patronage of the Emperor of the French, with assurances of military aid.

I have to request that you submit a copy of this intercepted correspondence to Mr. Drouyn de Lhuys. You will frankly inform him that the sympathies of the American people are already considerably excited in favor of the republic of Mexico, and that they are disposed to regard with impatience the continued intervention of France in that country. That any favor shown to the proceedings of Doctor Gwin by the titular Emperor of Mexico or by the imperial government of France, with reference to those agents, will tend greatly to increase the popular impatience, because it will be regarded, perhaps justly, as importing dangers to, or at least a menace against the United States.

It is proper also that Mr. Drouyn de Lhuys shall be informed that if we could believe that the statements thus made by these speculators are true, it would necessarily seem to the President that the Emperor of France was proceeding in his war against Mexico in a course materially differing from that of neutrality in regard to the political institutions of that country, of which he assured the United States when the war was begun. The President, on the contrary, confidently and sincerely expects, in some form, an assurance that all the pretences of Dr. Gwin and his associates are destitute of any sanction from the Emperor of France. I do not enlarge on this subject, because the French government need not be informed of the susceptibilities of the people of the United States in regard to Mexico. Nor can it be necessary to say, that after having expelled insurgents from our own borders, the United States government could not look with satisfaction upon their re-organization as martial or political enemies on the opposite banks of the Rio Grande.

I regret to be obliged to offer such frequent suggestions of prudence for the consideration of the Emperor's government, but the course of events creates the necessity, and good faith prescribes the duty.

I am, sir, your obedient servant,

WILLIAM H. SEWARD.

JOHN BIGELOW, Esq., *&c., &c., &c.*

NOTE.—For intercepted letters see annexes to Mr. Romero's letter of July 8, 1865, to Mr. Seward.

Mr. Bigelow to Mr. Seward.

No. 157.] LEGATION OF THE UNITED STATES,
Paris, August 10, 1865.

SIR: I have the honor to transmit herewith copies of a letter addressed by me to his excellency the minister of foreign affairs, on the 1st instant, and of his reply, in reference to the schemes of Dr. Gwin and his associates in Mexico, referred to in your despatch No. 195.

The sensitiveness betrayed by his excellency upon this subject has determined me to defer any rejoinder until I have had time to hear from you. For that period, at least, silence will be the most effective rejoinder.

I am, sir, with great respect, your obedient servant,

JOHN BIGELOW.

Hon. WILLIAM H. SEWARD,
Secretary of State.

[Enclosure No. 1.]

Mr. Bigelow to Mr. Drouyn de Lhuys.

LEGATION OF THE UNITED STATES, *August* 1, 1865.

The undersigned, envoy extraordinary and minister plenipotentiary of the United States at Paris, has the honor to transmit to his excellency the minister of foreign affairs copies of four letters which have been recently submitted to the State Department at Washington.

The first, dated Mexico, May 16, 1865, is addressed by William M. Gwin, the son of Dr. and Mrs. William M. Gwin, followed by the second from Dr. Gwin himself, on the same sheet, without date, addressed to his wife and daughter in Paris. The third, in the well-known handwriting of the doctor, dated Mexico, May 18, 1865, is addressed to "My dear Colonel," and was contained in an envelope addressed to "Colonel John Winthrop." The fourth, signed "Massey," and dated Mexico, 18th May, 1865, was addressed "To the Hon. B. Wood," (now a prisoner of state for alleged treasonable practices,) enclosing a communication to the editor of the New York Daily News, dated at the city of Mexico, 19th May, 1865, upon the subject of Mexican affairs.

By these letters it appears—

First. That Doctor William M. Gwin and family, though citizens of the United States, are disloyal to its government.

Second. That they are engaged in obtaining from Maximilian, titular emperor of Mexico, grants of mineral lands in the states of that republic adjoining the United States, and that Doctor Gwin is to be the chief directing agent in working these mines.

Third. That a large accession of capitalists and emigrants into these States from parties in rebellion against the United States is expected.

Fourth. That they assure the said Maximilian and the Emperor of France that their contemplated proceedings will tend at once to promote the projects of Maximilian in Mexico, and inure to the injury of the United States.

Fifth. That they claim to have the patronage of the Emperor of the French, with assurances of military aid.

In submitting to his excellency, the minister of foreign affairs, copies of this correspondence, the undersigned is instructed frankly to state that the sympathies of the American people for the republicans of Mexico are very lively, and that they are disposed to regard with impatience the continued intervention of France in that country; that any favor shown to the speculations of Dr. Gwin by the titular emperor of Mexico, or by the imperial government of France, will tend greatly to increase the popular impatience, because it will be regarded, perhaps justly, as importing danger, or, at least, a menace to the United States.

Could the government of the undersigned be brought to believe that the state of these speculations were worthy of entire confidence, the President of the United States would be forced to the conclusion that his Majesty the Emperor of France was pursuing towards Mexico a policy materially at variance with that of neutrality in regard to the political institutions of the country, which he avowed at the commencement of his war with that republic. The President, on the contrary, confidently and sincerely expects in some form an assurance that all the pretences of Dr. Gwin, and of his associates, are destitute of any sanction from the Emperor of France.

It is unnecessary for the undersigned to say, that after having expelled insurgents from our own borders, the United States could not look with satisfaction upon their reorganization as martial or political enemies on the opposite banks of the Rio Grande.

The undersigned avails himself of this occasion to renew to his excellency the minister of foreign affairs assurances of the distinguished consideration with which he has the honor to be his excellency's most obedient and most humble servant.

JOHN BIGELOW.

His Excellency DROUYN DE LHUYS,
Minister of Foreign Affairs.

[Enclosure No. 2.]

Mr. Drouyn de Lhuys to Mr. Bigelow.

[Translation.]

PARIS, *August* 7, 1865.

SIR: I have received the letter which you have done me the honor to address to me, dated August 1. In it you mention to me some plans for the colonization of Mexico, deemed to have been conceived with intentions hostile to the government of the United States, and you desire to know if it is true that the emperor Maximilian and France lend their support to these undertakings.

We shall always be ready, sir, to respond frankly to demands for explanations coming to us from an allied nation when they are inspired by a conciliatory spirit, presented in an amicable tone, and based upon authentic documents or positive facts. But I must add that the Emperor is resolved to reject all interpolations which may come to us in a comminatory tone about vague allegations, and based upon documents of a dubious character.

You will understand, sir, that it is not for me to enlighten you concerning the speculations of such or such person who has emigrated to Mexico; but what I know of the intentions of the Mexican government enables me to say to you that it proposes to let the emigrants from the southern States enter upon its territory only individually, and without arms. They will receive such help as humanity requires, but will be immediately dispersed through the provinces of the empire, and bound to abstain, in their conduct, from everything which might awaken the just susceptibility of neighboring nations. I have, moreover, reason to believe that these dispositions of the emperor Maximilian are by this time as well known to the cabinet at Washington as they are to us.

As for France, she has on several occasions, sir, and with entire frankness, stated her resolution to observe in all the internal questions which may agitate or divide the Union an impartial and scrupulous neutrality. We have nothing to offer as a pledge of our intentions but our word, but we deem the word of France a guarantee which will satisfy any friendly power, as we ourselves are satisfied with the word pledged to us by the federal government, to remain strictly neutral with regard to affairs in Mexico. I take pleasure in recalling here, sir, the assurances which I had the satisfaction to receive from you on that subject, especially in your letter of the 12th of June last, and which I have stated in my answer, dated the 17th.

The Emperor trusts with confidence to the sentiments of which you were the interpreter, and although certain recent manifestations may seem difficult to reconcile with these declarations, his Majesty does not hesitate to rely always on the honorableness of the American people.

Accept assurances of the high consideration with which I have the honor to be, sir, your very humble and very obedient servant,

DROUYN DE LHUYS.

Monsieur BIGELOW,
Minister of the United States, &c., &c., &c., Paris.

Mr. Seward to Mr. Bigelow.

No. 231.]

DEPARTMENT OF STATE,
Washington, August 24, 1865.

SIR: Your despatch of August 10, No. 157, has been received. It is accompanied by a correspondence between yourself and Mr. Drouyn de Lhuys in relation to the alleged schemes of Dr. Gwin and his associates in Mexico.

It gives me pleasure to say, that information which was received from that country while that correspondence was going on, and which information seems to be authentic, induces the belief that the speculations referred to have altogether failed. I observe with still more pleasure that Mr. Drouyn de Lhuys, in the communication which he addressed to you of the 7th of August, authorized us to expect that those schemes and speculations, so far as they were hostile to the United States, would be disapproved by the authorities acting in Mexico under the direction of, or in co-operation with, the Emperor of France. It is perceived with regret that either in substance or in manner the representation which you addressed to Mr. Drouyn de Lhuys, and which elicited his communication, before referred to, in reply, was regarded by Mr. Drouyn de Lhuys as exceptionable. It becomes proper for me, under these circumstances, to say that your representation was made in conformity with instructions given you by this department, and that on reviewing these instructions we are not able to discover any ground for criticism. They were given under the belief that a seasonable attention to the reports and rumors that were in circulation in regard to schemes of Dr. Gwin and other rebel emissaries in Mexico was necessary to prevent difficulties and to allay apprehensions, the indulgence of which was prejudicial to a good understanding between the United States and France. The President is gratified with the renewed assurance which Mr. Drouyn de Lhuys has given us of the Emperor's resolution to observe an impartial and scrupulous neutrality upon all internal questions which may agitate or divide the United States.

I am, sir, your obedient servant,

WILLIAM H. SEWARD.

JOHN BIGELOW, Esq., &c., &c., &c., *Paris.*

Mr. Seward to Mr. Bigelow.

No. 390.]

DEPARTMENT OF STATE,
Washington, February 12, 1866.

SIR: Your despatch of January 16, No. 243, has been received. It was accompanied by a copy of a correspondence which took place between you and

Mr. Drouyn de Lhuys, on the subject of certain decrees which have been made by the authorities now existing in the city of Mexico, concerning emigration and colonization in that country. We are not able to agree with the French government in the opinion which it has expressed, that the subject does not fall properly within the province of the Emperor of France. The President hopes, however, that the anticipated relief of the embarrassing situation in Mexico, which is the subject of another correspondence between the two powers, will facilitate a solution of the special matter which has arisen out of the before-mentioned decrees. You may make this expectation known to Mr. Drouyn de Lhuys.

I am, sir, your obedient servant,

WILLIAM H. SEWARD.

JOHN BIGELOW, Esq., *&c.*, *&c.*, *&c.*

Mr. Seward to Mr. Romero.

DEPARTMENT OF STATE,
Washington, December 10, 1865.

SIR: I have the honor to acknowledge the receipt of your communications of the 5th of October last, with their several important accompaniments, which you were pleased to communicate for the information of the government of the United States.

In reply, I have the honor to inform you that it has already received the consideration of this department, and that measures have been adopted which are deemed proper to meet the exigencies which it presents.

I avail myself of this occasion to renew to you, sir, the assurances of my very distinguished consideration.

WILLIAM H. SEWARD.

Señor MATIAS ROMERO, *&c.*, *&c.*, *&c.*,
Washington, D. C.

Mr. Romero to Mr. Seward.

[Translation.]

MEXICAN LEGATION TO THE UNITED STATES,
Washington, October 20, 1865.

MR. SECRETARY: In addition to the intelligence I communicated to you in my note of 5th instant, relative to the plan adopted by French agents in Mexico for the purpose of uniting in that republic the discontented citizens of the United States who are not disposed to acknowledge the authority of this government, nor accept the consequences of the late civil war, I have now the honor to send you various extracts from the "Times," a paper published in English in the city of Mexico, in which you will see a list of prominent persons from the United States of the south, lately in insurrection against the federal government, and are now in the city of Mexico, and other details that are not without interest.

It seems also that the ex-archduke of Austria, Fernando Maximilian, now titular emperor of Mexico, already throwing aside all dissimulation, has made public his real plans, by appointing as agents of colonization Mr. Sterling Price, of Missouri, Mr. Isham Harris, of Tennessee, Mr. John Perkins, of Louisiana, and Mr. Wm. F. Hardeman and Mr. Roberts, of Texas.

Messrs. Price and Perkins have gone to the Gulf side, and Messrs. Hardeman and Roberts to the Pacific, in discharge of their trusts.

It seems Mr. M. F. Maury, ex-lieutenant in the navy of the United States, and afterwards agent in Europe for the insurgent States, is the person who directs this movement for emigration on foot. For this purpose he has been declared a subject of the usurper, and as it seems from the communication addressed to him on the 23d September aforesaid, of which I send copy, in which is granted to him the right to hold the offices reserved to the natural-born in the national territory, he has been appointed in addition, by the usurper, honorary councillor of state.

These facts indicate clearly what are the objects and the tendencies of the agents in Mexico, and I doubt not the government of the United States will attribute to them the importance they deserve.

I avail of this opportunity to renew to you, Mr. Secretary, the assurances of my most distinguished consideration.

M. ROMERO.

Hon. WILLIAM H. SEWARD, *&c., &c., &c.*

[Enclosure No. 1.—From the Mexico Times, September 23.]

COLONIZATION OF PUBLIC LANDS.

It is our pleasing task to state that the following gentlemen have been appointed agents of colonization by the imperial government: Señors Sterling Price, late of Missouri; Isham Harris, late of Tennessee; John Perkins, late of Louisiana; W. T. Hardeman and Roberts, late of Texas.

Señors Price, Harris, and Perkins left this city on the 19th instant for Cordova and the region of country bordering on the "tierra caliente." Señors Hardeman and Roberts left on the 20th instant for Tepic and the country bordering on the Pacific. Their duties are to examine the lands offered for colonization purposes, and to make their report to the proper authorities as soon as practicable. We look forward with the greatest interest to the report of these agents. They are men of the highest respectability. Their statements can be implicitly relied on. We beg our friends who have come to Mexico with the intention of seeking homes to wait with patience for the result of the labors of these gentlemen. We assure them that the government will act in the most liberal manner, and that in a very short time they will be amply repaid for the delays and privations to which many are at present subjected.

As Abraham said to Lot, the "whole land is before you where to choose," therefore be not impatient; God in his providence has so arranged it that you all will have good and comfortable homes in the dominions of the best of emperors. In a few weeks the report of the agents of colonization will be received, and good lands in healthy districts will be appropriated to every one who wishes to become a citizen of Mexico.

[Enclosure No. 2.—From the Mexico Times, September 30.]

American arrivals in Mexico.

Names.	When arrived.	Residence.
Sterling Price	August 9, 1865	Missouri.
J. B. Magruder	August 5, 1865	Virginia.
Isham G. Harris	August 9, 1865	Tennessee.
E. Clark	September 3, 1865	Texas.
Trusten Polk	August 9, 1865	Missouri.
Jo. O. Shelby	September 3, 1865	Do.
H. W. Allen	July 28, 1865	Louisiana.
H. Denis	do	Do.
W. A. Broadwell	September 7, 1865	Do.
M. F. Maury	June 1, 1865	Virginia.
J. Perkins	August 9, 1865	Louisiana.
Heber Price	do	Missouri.
H. M. Duncan	do	Do.
J. P. Tucker	do	Do.
W. T. Hardeman	August 20, 1865	Texas.

American arrivals in Mexico.—Continued.

Names.	When arrived.	Residence.
H. P. Bee	August 20, 1865	Texas.
M. W. Sims	July 22, 1865	Do.
George Young	August 20, 1865	Missouri.
R. J. Laurence	August 29, 1865	Do.
C. G. Jones	do	Do.
J. N. Edwards	do	Do.
D. C. Cage	August 9, 1865	Louisiana.
W. Yowell	September 3, 1865	Missouri.
George Hall	do	Do.
F. M. Kephart	do	Do.
R. A. Collins	do	Do.
Y. H. Blackwell	do	Do.
J. Terry	do	Do.
J. Moreland	do	Do.
T. Boswell	do	Do.
W. J. McArthur	August 20, 1865	Do.
J. C. Wood	do	Do.
Ras. Woods	August 25, 1865	Do.
M. M. Langborne	do	Do.
F. T. Mitchell and family	July, 1865	Do.
Señor Wood and wife	do	Do.
D. W. Bouldin	August 20, 1865	Do.
S. Hunkel	August 9, 1865	Do.
J. Beard	do	Do.
W. Skidmore	do	Do.
H. Thomas	do	Do.
C. M. Wilcox	July 16, 1865	Tennessee.
R. Joseph	September 3, 1865	Missouri.
T. Weston	September 12, 1865	Louisiana.
H. B. Acton	September 3, 1865	Missouri.
J. Donahoe	do	California.
I. Reed	In San Luis Potosi	Virginia.
T. J. Divine	In Monterey	Texas.
J. Brown	September 3, 1865	North Carolina.
Señor Conrow	In Monterey	Missouri.
Señor O'Bannon	In San Luis Potosi	South Carolina.
Señor Kimmel	August 9, 1865	Missouri.
D. Leadbetter	do	Alabama.
O. G. Jones	do	Louisiana.
S. Gregory	do	Texas.
Señor Thomspon	do	Do.
H. T. Chiles and family	September 11, 1865	Missouri.
M. L. Kritser	do	Do.
J. S. Kritser	do	Do.
T. Whalen	do	California.
J. M. Meador	do	Missouri.
T. Collins	do	Do.
W. Fell	do	Do.
B. F. Jones	do	Do.
J. B. Kirtley	September 3, 1865	Do.
J. D. Conner	do	Do.
G. M. Winship	do	Do.
J. Ward	do	Do.
E. Lilly	do	Texas.
N. T. Fincher	September 11, 1865	Do.
H. McNamee	September 3, 1865	California.
R. J. Flynn	do	Louisiana.
R. H. S. Thompson	August 6, 1865	Do.
Señor Bartlett	do	Mississippi.
G. Mitchell	August 9, 1865	Missouri.
J. N. Lane	do	Do.
B. H. Lyon	August 20, 1865	Kentucky.
J. J. Gaenslen	do	Virginia.
T. C. Hindman	September 10, 1865	Arkansas.

American arrivals in Mexico.—Continued.

Names.	When arrived.	Residence.
J. H. Brown and family	September 12, 1865	Texas.
J. Brown	do	Do.
P. M. Brown	do	Do.
H. C. Cook	do	Do.
Richard Taylor	August 25, 1865	Kentucky.
O. M. Watkins	August 8, 1865	Louisiana.
T. C. Reynolds	do	Missouri.
A. Ridley	do	California.
E. Kirby Smith	July 17, in Cuba	Florida.
J. N. Martin	July 25, in Cuba	Missouri.
E. G. Walker	do	Do.
T. O. Moore	July 25, in Havana	Louisiana.
W. Preston	July 25, in Canada	Kentucky.
Señor Roberts	August 25, 1865	Texas.
Alfred Mordecai	July 18, 1865	North Carolina.
Frank Moore	July —, 1865	Alabama.
A. W. Terrell	July 17, 1865	Texas.
George Flourney	do	Do.
Señor Lougnemare	do	Do.

MORE SOLDIERS FROM FRANCE.

Troops *are arriving in our city daily direct from France.* On yesterday a battalion of Turcos marched through the streets, exciting the admiration of all. They are a fine body of men, well drilled, and inured to every hardship and to all climates. We noticed they were commanded by native officers.

[Enclosure No. 3.—From the Mexico Times, September 30.]

GENERAL PRICE'S EXILE.—HIS EMPLOYMENT AS AN EMIGRANT LAND COMMISSIONER.

The Noticioso, of Vera Cruz, extracts the following from the New York papers:

The Brownsville correspondent of the New York Herald writes that from a conversation that took place between him and a confederate officer he learned that General Price, of Missouri, had taken service under Maximilian, who authorized the general to recruit a cavalry force of thirty thousand men from the late confederate army. He also learned that several other prominent rebels had received kind favors from the emperor, whose intentions are to collect a force of at least one hundred thousand rebels in less than one year in order to face General Sheridan on the Rio Grande.—*La Sociedad.*

[Enclosure No. 4.—From the Mexico Times, September 30.]

IMMIGRATION AND EMIGRANTS INVITED.

Open wide the doors to immigration. Encourage by the most liberal policy good citizens from Europe and the United States to come and settle upon the wild and uncultivated lands, and soon there will be seen an industrious and thrifty population, who will fully appreciate their new homes, and be ready at all times to defend them against domestic or foreign foes.

MEXICO, *September* 30, 1865.

His Majesty the emperor, being desirous of giving a signal proof of his estimation of the distinguished merit and eminent qualifications which adorn Don Mathew Fontaine Maury, and acceding to his application, has been pleased to concede to him papers of naturalization as a Mexican, with all the enjoyments and privileges which appertain to Mexican subjects, including the right of holding the public positions and employments reserved to those born on the territory of the empire.

The chief of the bureau of accountability in charge of the chancellorship,

IGNACIO M. DE CASTILLO.

Mr. Romero to Mr. Seward.

[Translation.]

LEGATION OF MEXICO TO THE UNITED STATES,
New York, November 4, 1865.

MR. SECRETARY: In confirmation of what I had the honor of communicating to you in my note of the 20th of October last, relative to the object of the colonization plan adopted by the usurper in Mexico, I now have the honor of transmitting to you a copy, in English, of the so-called five decrees of the ex-Archduke of Austria, promulgated in September previous, in which he names Mr. M. F. Maury, a declared enemy of the United States, as honorary counsellor of state, and imperial commissioner of colonization, and Mr. J. B. Magruder, also a declared enemy of this government, as chief of the colonization land office.

In the third of said decrees you will observe, in confirmation of what I communicated to your department, about the nature of the colonization to be made in Mexico, that Mr. Maury has been authorized to establish agencies in the States of Virginia, North and South Carolina, Texas, Missouri, and California, and in the cities of Mobile and New Orleans, which plainly shows they only think to get men from the south, and precisely from those States where they suppose there are most malcontents against this government. It is a very significant fact that not one single agency is established in the northern States, which were faithful to the Union of this government during the last civil war.

I also enclose a copy, in English, of the circular issued on the 5th of October, by Mr. Maury, as imperial commissioner of colonization.

I embrace this occasion of renewing to you, Mr. Secretary, the assurances of my most distinguished consideration.

M. ROMERO.

HON. WILLIAM H. SEWARD, &c., &c., &c.,
Washington City, D. C.

[Enclosure No. 1.]

MAXIMILIAN, EMPEROR OF MEXICO.

In consideration of his well-known capacity, I hereby nominate our honorary counsellor of state, M. F. Maury, imperial commissioner of colonization.

The minister of the interior is charged with the execution of this decree.

MAXIMILIAN.

For the Emperor:

LUIS ROBLES PEZUELA,
Minister of the Interior.

MEXICO, *September* 27, 1865.

MAXIMILIAN, EMPEROR OF MEXICO.

Our honorary counsellor of state, M. F. Maury, is authorized to establish the office of imperial commissioner of colonization at No. 13 San Juan de Letran street, and our minister of the interior is authorized to rent the said property at a sum not to exceed one hundred dollars per month.

MAXIMILIAN.

To the MINISTER OF THE INTERIOR.

For the Emperor:

MANUEL OROZCO Y BERRA,
Sub-Secretary.

CHAPULTEPEC, *September* 24, 1865.

MAXIMILIAN, EMPEROR OF MEXICO.

Our honorary counsellor of state, M. F. Maury, is authorized to appoint seven agents of colonization in the following States and cities of the United States: Virginia, North and South

Carolina, Texas, Missouri, California, New Orleans, Mobile. Said agents shall receive one hundred dollars per month as compensation, and the further sum of three hundred dollars per annum for necessary expenses.

MAXIMILIAN.

To the MINISTER OF INTERIOR.

For the Emperor:

LUIS ROBLES PEZUELA,
Minister of the Interior.

CHAPULTEPEC, *September* 24, 1865.

MAXIMILIAN, EMPEROR OF MEXICO.

The following sums are appropriated for the office of Señor Maury, honorary counsellor of state and imperial commissioner of colonization: Office furniture, $150; expenses of office, annually, $500; for one clerk, annually, $1,200; for one private messenger, annually, $300.
Our minister of the interior is charged with the execution of this order.

MAXIMILIAN.

To the MINISTER OF THE INTERIOR.

For the Emperor:

LUIS ROBLES PEZUELA,
Minister of the Interior.

CHAPULTEPEC, *September* 27, 1865.

The following is the decree of Maximilian appointing the rebel General Magruder as chief of the land office of colonization:

MAXIMILIAN, EMPEROR OF MEXICO.

Desiring to forward the object of immigration to Mexico, a land office of colonization shall be established in this capital, and J. B. Magruder is hereby appointed its chief. The following sums are appropriated for the expenses of this office: For salary of J. B. Magruder, annually, $3,000; for office furniture, annually, $150; for rent of office, monthly, $100; for office expenses, annually, $500; for pay of messenger, annually, $300.
Señor Magruder will report to us the number of engineers and surveyors which will be necessary to carry into effect the objects of his appointment, and also the amount which he recommends to be appropriated for their salary.
The minister of the interior is charged with the execution of this order.

MAXIMILIAN.

To the MINISTER OF THE INTERIOR.

For the Emperor:

LUIS ROBLES PEZUELA.
Minister of the Interior.

CHAPULTEPEC, *September* 27, 1865.

[Enclosure No. 2.]

The Mexico Times of October 14 prints the following circular:

No. 13 CALLE DE SAN JUAN LETRAN,
Mexico, October 5, 1865.

To the land-owners of Mexico:

All who desire to encourage immigration, and have lands to sell, are hereby informed that if they will make known to this office the terms and conditions upon which they are willing to dispose of them to actual settlers, this office, if the terms are favorable, will, without fee or charge of any sort, assist, through its agents abroad and by advertisements, such owners in bringing their lands to the notice of the immigrant.

It will also, in the case of lands which are offered upon terms that are sufficiently inviting to immigrants, cause them to be examined at the public expense. If found suitable as to health, quality, and location, it will have them surveyed and mapped, also without any expense to the owners, furnishing each with a copy of the survey of his own land.

The terms upon which offers are made will be regarded as confidential, if so desired; and in all cases the colonists and land-owners will be left free to make and consummate their own bargains according to the offers made through this office. In surveying and bringing these lands into market, preference will be given to those which, on account of terms, situation, and quality, offer the greatest inducements to immigrants.

M. F. MAURY,
Imperial Commissioner of Colonization.

Mr. Romero to Mr. Seward.

[Translation.]

MEXICAN LEGATION TO THE UNITED STATES,
Washington, December 12, 1865.

SIR: In confirmation of what I communicated to you in my notes of the 8th of July, 5th and 20th October, and 4th of November of the present year, relative to the efforts the French government is making, through its agent, Maximilian, to carry into Mexico the discontented citizens of the United States, and those who took a part in the late rebellion against this government, to which they are not disposed to submit, even after the end of the war, to organize them there and suffer them to give more trouble to their country, I have the honor to send you a copy, in English, of a letter written from Cordova, the 12th of November last, by Mr. Isham G. Harris, ex-governor of Tennessee, general in the confederate army, and a prominent person among the insurgents. The letter is directed to a Mr. George W. Adair, Atlanta, State of Georgia, and was published in the "New Era," of that city. It contains details and information positively confirming what I mentioned in my former notes respecting this important business.

I take this occasion to renew to you, Mr. Secretary, the assurances of my most distinguished consideration.

M. ROMERO.

Hon. WILLIAM H. SEWARD, *&c., &c., &c.*

[Enclosure.]

CORDOVA, MEXICO, *November* 12, 1865.

I lingered near Grenada, endeavoring to arrange some business matters, until the 14th of May. In the mean time I had a skiff built, and on the morning of the 14th I embarked, some six miles east of Greenwood, and set sail for the trans-Mississippi, the party consisting of General Lyon, of Kentucky, myself, and our two servants. We navigated the Backwater for one hundred and twenty miles, and on the morning of the 21st, just before daylight, I crossed over to the Arkansas shore. I crossed at the foot of Island No. 75, just below the mouth of the Arkansas river; proceeded westward as far as the Backwater was navigable, and on the morning of the 22d I left my frail bark, bought horses, mounted the party, and set out for Shreveport, where I hoped to find an army resolved on continued resistance to federal rule; but before reaching Shreveport I learned that the army of the trans-Mississippi had disbanded and scattered to the winds, and all the officers of rank had gone to Mexico.

Having no further motive to visit Shreveport, I turned my course to Red River county, Texas, where a portion of my negroes and plantation stock had been carried some two years ago. I reached there on the 7th of June; was taken sick and confined to my bed a week. On the 15th of June, with my baggage, cooking utensils, and provisions on a pack-mule, I set out for San Antonio, where I expected to overtake a large number of confederate civil and military officers en route for Mexico. Reached San Antonio on the 26th, and learned that all confederates had left for Mexico some ten days or two weeks before. On the morning of the 27th I started to Eagle Pass, on the Rio Grande, the federals holding all the crossings of that river below Eagle Pass. I reached Eagle Pass on the evening of the 30th, and immediately crossed over to the Mexican town of Piedras Negras. On the morning of the 1st of July set out for Monterey; arrived there on the evening of the 9th. Here I overtook General Price and ex-Governor Polk, of Missouri, who were starting to the city of Mexico next morning, with an escort of twenty armed Missourians. As I was going to the city, and the trip was a long and dangerous one to make alone, I decided to go with them, though I was literally worn out with over one thousand five hundred miles of continuous horseback travel. I exchanged my saddle-horse, saddles, &c., for an ambulance, put my two mules to it, gave the whip and lines to Ran, bought me a Spanish grammar and dictionary, took the back seat, and commenced the study of the Spanish language. We made the trip at easy stages of about twenty-five miles per day, and reached the city of Mexico on the evening of the 9th of August. The trip was one of the longest, most laborious, and hazardous of my life, but I will not tax your time or mine with its details, many of which would interest you deeply if I were there to give them to you.

Our reception upon the part of the government officials here was all that we could have expected or desired. We were invited to an audience with the Emperor at the palace, the far-famed halls of the Montezumas. At the time fixed we called, and were most kindly received by the emperor and empress, and were assured of their sympathy in our misfortunes, and of their earnest hope that we might find homes for ourselves and friends in Mexico. The empress was our interpreter in the interview. She speaks fluently the French, Spanish, German, and English languages, and is in all respects a great woman.

We overtook at the city of Mexico General Magruder, Commodore Maury, Governor Allen, of Louisiana; Judge Perkins, of Louisiana; Governor Reynolds, of Missouri, and Governor Murrah and Governor Clark, of Texas, with many other and lesser confederate lights. On the 5th of September the emperor published a decree opening all of Mexico to immigration and colonization, and Commodore Maury and myself and other confederates were requested to prepare regulations to accompany the decree, which we did, and which were approved by the emperor on the 27th. The decree and regulations offer very liberal inducements to immigration, among which are a donation of public lands at the rate of six hundred and forty acres to each head of a family, and three hundred and twenty acres to each single man; a free passage to the country to such as are not able to pay their own expenses, freedom from taxation for one year and from military duty for five years, religious toleration, &c., &c.

Commodore Maury has been appointed imperial commissioner of colonization, which makes his authority in the matter of colonization second only to that of the Emperor. General Price, Judge Perkins, and myself were appointed agents of colonization, and requested to examine the lands lying upon and near the line of railroad from the city of Mexico to Vera Cruz, for the purpose of determining whether they were suited to American colonization. We are engaged at this time in the discharge of that duty. We find in the vicinity of this place the most beautiful, and, all things considered, the best agricultural country that I have ever seen. The climate is delightful—never hot, never cold, always temperate, always pleasant. The soil richer and more productive than the best of the prairie lands of Mississippi in the Okolona country, yielding large crops of corn, barley, rice, tobacco, sugar-cane, and coffee, with all the fruits of the tropics, and the best that you ever tasted. You can raise two crops of corn on the same land each year. The usual mode of farming here is a crop of corn and a crop of tobacco on the same land, the corn ripening always before time to plant tobacco; and ten miles from here, in the direction of the coast, you strike as good a cotton country as can be found in the world.

The most profitable crop here is coffee; you plant about six or seven hundred trees to the acre; it begins to bear at two and produces a full crop at four years old. You can always calculate safely on an average of two pounds to the tree, though there are instances of a tree's bearing as high as twenty-eight pounds. The tree is hardy, and will live fifty or one hundred years. It costs about as much labor to cultivate and put into market an acre of coffee as it does an acre of corn in Georgia.

The coffee plantation, with its shade of bananas, figs, oranges, mangoes, and zapotes, with the walks fringed with pineapple, all in full bearing, is the richest and most beautiful spectacle upon which my eyes have ever rested. I have selected six hundred and forty acres about ten miles from here, where I propose to surround myself with the coffee plantation, in the midst of which I will nestle down, constantly inhaling the odors of the rich tropical fruits, and gaudy-colored and fragant tropical flowers, in an atmosphere of perpetual spring; yet turning the eye to the northwest, you constantly behold the snow-capped peaks of Orizaba and Popocatepetl, from which I can draw my ice at all seasons of the year.

There are about thirty confederates now here, all of whom will locate their lands and commence the work of settlement within a week or ten days

The place where we begin the first colony was highly improved and in a high state of civilization a hundred years ago. The extensive ruins of what were once magnificent structures show that the haciendas were highly productive, and the homes of wealth, luxury and refinement; but, about fifty years since slavery was abolished in the state of Vera Cruz, and the proprietors of these magnificent estates left the country with the large fortunes they had amassed. The church seized the lands and allowed them to lie idle and go to ruin. The buildings upon each of those places must have cost from $[illegible]00,000 to $500,000. The church held the property till about five years since, when it was taken by the government, and the government now sells it to us for colonization at $1 per acre, in quantities of six hundred and forty acres to each head of a family and three hundred and twenty acres to each single man, on a credit of one, two, three, four, and five ye[illegible] *This is the beginning of the first confederate colony in Mexico.* Among those who prop[illegible] to settle immediately are General Price and General Shelby, from Missouri, Judge Per[illegible] of Louisiana, and myself. The resources of this country are such as to insure fortune[illegible]he energy and industry that have usually characterized our people. The wonder is t[illegible]y have been permitted to remain undeveloped so long; but this is the most indolent, l[illegible]nd worthless population on earth.

* * * * * * * * * * *

Will many of the people of the southern States fe[illegible]ined to seek new homes; or will they follow the example of Lee, Johnston, and others [illegible]exico presents the finest field that I have ever seen for the enterprise of our people; an[illegible]w that slavery is abolished in the south, hired labor can be much more easily procured [illegible] and made much more profitable

34 D C **

than in any part of the United States. I do not propose, however, to urge or even advise any one to come; I only propose to give them facts, and leave them to decide for themselves, as I have done for myself. Such as feel inclined to come will be received with open arms and cordial welcome. But enough of this.

Where is Forrest, and what is he doing? and where and how is everybody else? for I have heard from none of our friends since I left Mississippi.

Give my kind regards to Mrs. Adair, Robin, Jack and Forrest, and kiss Mary for me, and tell her that it would give me great pleasure to have a romp with her this evening.

Write me fully, and do your best at penmanship, so that I may be able to read at least the greater part of the letter. I sent you a copy of the Mexican News, an English newspaper edited by Governor Allen about a month ago. I hope you received it, though there was very little of interest in it except that it shows the fact that *we had started an American newspaper at the city of Mexico*. I neglected to say to you that this place is situated on the line of railroad from Vera Cruz to the city of Mexico, seventy miles west of Vera Cruz. The railroad is now in operation to within eighteen miles of this place, and all the balance to the city of Mexico is under contract and the work rapidly progressing. It is a few hours' run by rail from here to Vera Cruz, from Vera Cruz it is three days by steam to New Orleans, and from New Orleans it is three or four days by rail to Atlanta. So you see that we are still neighbors, even if you should remain in Georgia. *The road is owned by an English company, but it is almost entirely in American hands.*

My health is excellent, and I feel that it cannot be otherwise in this charming climate. Direct your letters to me at Cordova, Mexico. And in conclusion let me beg you to excuse this horrid and disjointed letter, as it was written in the midst of a crowd, half of whom were continually talking to me and compelling me to talk to them.

Very truly your friend,

ISHAM G. HARRIS.

Mr. Seward to Mr. Romero.

DEPARTMENT OF STATE,
Washington, December 21, 1865.

SIR: I have the honor to acknowledge the receipt of your three notes dated, respectively, October 20, November 4, and December 12, 1865; which, with their several accompaniments, you have been pleased to communicate to me for the information of the government of the United States, touching the plan of colonization about to be inaugurated in the republic of Mexico, and in confirmation of your previous communications on the same subject to this department.

These very interesting documents, for the knowledge of which I am indebted to you, and for which I beg you to accept my thanks, have been duly considered by this government, and shall, hereafter, receive the attention to which they are so justly entitled.

I avail myself of this opportunity to renew to you, sir, the assurances of my very distinguished consideration.

WILLIAM H. SEWARD.

SEÑOR MATIAS ROMERO, &c., &c., &c.,
Washington, D. C.

Mr. Romero to Mr. Hunter.

[Translation.]

ME[illegible]N LEGATION TO THE UNITED STATES,
Washington, December 31, 1865.

MR. SECRETARY AD INTE[illegible] In addition to and in confirmation of the information I have already co[illegible]nicated to your department in various notes, relative to the efforts of the [illegible]ch government, and its agents in Mexico, to induce the malcontents of th[illegible]ited States who took part in the late rebellion against their government, and [illegible]not mean to submit now that it is over, to settle in Mexico and give afterw[illegible] new trouble to their country, I have the honor to transmit two documents, published by Mr. M. F. Maury, ex-confederate agent in Europe, and now termed "Imperial Commissioner of Colonization," in one of which he gives a special invitation to confederates who wish to settle in Mexico, and informs them that three hundred and fifty thousand acres of land are set apart for them in the States of Vera Cruz and Puebla.

I embrace the occasion to renew to you, sir, the assurances of my most distinguished consideration.

M. ROMERO.

Hon. WILLIAM HUNTER, *&c., &c., &c.*

[Enclosure No. 1.]

COLONIZATION OFFICE, NO. 13 CALLE SAN JUAN LETRAN, CITY OF MEXICO,
December 10, 1865.

SALE OF A FARM BY SUBSCRIPTION.

An offer of 350,000 acres of land is made to confederate settlers who wish to establish them selves in Mexico.

These lands, the most fertile of the empire, are intersected by three rivers. They are selected on the line of the railroad from Vera Cruz to the capital, and near the road from Vera Cruz to Jalapa. They are in the healthy part of the tierras calientes. They produce equally well coffee, cocoa, indigo, cotton, and sugar-cane, with all the tropical fruits and vegetables.

The proprietor will sell them to the settlers as soon as the latter have filed with the agents of colonization in the United States or Mexico, subscriptions for 200,000 acres, at the following rates:

The first 50,000 acres chosen, at	$1 75
The second 50,000 acres chosen, at	1 50
The third 50,000 acres chosen, at	1 25
The fourth 50,000 acres chosen, at	1 00

The first subscribers shall have the right to choose at the above rates, with the understanding that not less than 320 acres shall be sold to any one of them.

When the 200,000 acres shall have been subscribed for and chosen, the rest shall be sold at a price to be agreed upon between the seller and purchaser.

Payment shall be made in the following manner:

One-third of the amount is to be paid in cash at Mexico, Vera Cruz, or New Orleans. The rest thereof shall be paid in four years' time, causing the payment thereof to be effected in equal parts and yearly; that is to say, one-sixth per annum, adding thereto the interest at the rate of six per cent.

As villages and towns are established on the lands, a lot will be given gratis to each settler in said villages or towns. Said villages or towns shall be chosen and allotted by Mr. Maury, the imperial commissioner of colonization.

The surveying and the cost of the title of the property will be at the expense of the settlers.

The *hacienda* offered herewith is known to be one of the finest and most celebrated in Mexico. It presents, especially to the former planters of the south, a fine opportunity for establishing a flourishing American settlement. Those who are disposed to visit the country for the purpose of colonizing it under the imperial decree to promote immigration will receive every encouragement from this office.

The offer is made by respectable parties, and persons wishing to treat will be put in com munication by addressing the commissioner.

Apprentices, as per imperial decree of September 5, 1865, would do well here, though there is no lack of native labor.

M. F. MAURY, *Imperial Commissioner.*

[Enclosure No. 2.—Translated from "La Sociedad," Mexico, December 7, 1865.]

M. F. Maury, Imperial Commissioner of Colonization, to persons wishing to settle in Mexico:

The doors of the empire are wide open, and his Majesty the emperor has, in a most liberal decree, invited immigration from all quarters, and without distinction as to nationality.

Many people, both in the Old World and the New, having heard of this invitation, wish to change their skies and to avail themselves of its privileges. Gentlemen representing several thousand families in Europe, and hundreds in Tennessee, Missouri, Arkansas, Texas, the Carolinas, Alabama, Mississippi, and Louisiana, in the United States, are now anxiously seeking information in regard to the country, its condition and resources, with the view of making it their home.

Considering that almost the only source of information open to them upon this subject is to be found in anonymous contributions, made for the most part to a press by no means friendly to Mexico, I deem it proper to state for the information of all those, whatever be their nationality, who desire to renounce it and come to Mexico, with the intention, in good faith, of making it their home, and of planting their posterity here, that they would do well to come; for it is a land more blessed by nature in its soil and climate than any part of the United States, that great centre at present of human migration.

THE WEALTH OF THE SOIL.

The earth here yields to the care of husbandry with a profusion that would seem incredible there and fabulous in Europe. In some places it crowns the labor of the husbandman regularly with two and in others with three harvests annually; and in each one he gathers one hundred, two hundred, sometimes three hundred, and occasionally four hundred fold, and even more, according to his own skill and the kind of seed used.

Cotton and corn do well in almost all parts of the empire. But the cotton, especially of Tamaulipas, Matahuala, Fresnillo, Durango, Mazatlan, and the states north, is said to be of a better staple, save Sea-island, than any produced in the United States; indeed, the cotton of Yucatan is called Sea-island.

Under these fine climates, which give a purity and transparency to the atmosphere that makes existence itself an enjoyment, and invest the eye with the faculties of almost a new sense, the vegetable kingdom displays its wealth and its powers most gorgeously, and with the most marvellous vigor and concentration.

In chosen spots and upon a single hacienda may be seen crowded together, piled up in steppes one above another, in perfection, fruits, flowers, and products, which in less favored climes require as many latitudes, climates, and soils as can be found in the entire breadth of plain that lies between the sources of the Mississippi and the mouths of the Amazon.

Here, besides cotton and corn, the olive and the vine, we have the finest of wheat, with pulse and all the cereals in great perfection; also tobacco, coffee, sugar-cane, the cocoa plant, rice, indigo, cochineal, pimento, India-rubber, and henuquin, a peculiar and valuable fibre that answers many of the purposes of both flax and hemp, and, last of all, and what, moreover, no other country in the world can produce—Flora's feat and Bacchus's boast—the lordly maguey, or pulque plant of Anahuac.

I have seen some of the very best planters from Missouri, Tennessee, and the south, and I have conversed with the learned men from France and other parts of Europe, all of whom happen to have travelled through the northern and most healthy parts of Mexico. The Europeans report, on the one hand, an agricultural country superior to the best parts of France and Italy, and also of surpassing mineral wealth; while the Americans, on the other hand, pronounce it a grazing and cattle country to which even the blue-grass regions of Kentucky and Tennessee are not to be compared.

The mountains abound with minerals, the woods with game, and the forests with the finest of timber—with the most exquisite dye and ornamental woods, gums and spices, drugs, and medicinal plants of rare virtues.

SETTLEMENTS CONTEMPLATED.

Generals Price and Shelby, of Missouri; Governor Harris, of Tennessee, and Judge Perkins, of Louisiana, with a number of their friends, have gone to examine the country about Cordova. They are delighted with it; they intend to make it their home. The railway hence to Vera Cruz passes through it. The land is superb. It is sold by the government to immigrants at one dollar the acre, to be paid for in five equal annual instalments.

Generals Hardeman and Terry, with others from Texas, are equally well pleased with Jalisco. They are negotiating for the purchase of haciendas there sufficiently large to accommodate with land a settlement to be made up of themselves, their old neighbors and friends.

The Rev. Mr. Mitchell, of Missouri, has already commenced a fine settlement on the Rio Verdi, in San Luis Potosi. He and his comrades have gone into the cultivation of cotton, corn and tobacco.

The representative of large capital, M. Dousdebes, has a grant for establishing a colony from France and Spain on the shores of Matamoras.

Mr. Lloyd, of England, equally well supported, has engaged to establish a number of colonists between Vera Cruz and the capital, and a ship-load of European immigrants have just arrived in Yucatan to form the nucleus of a settlement in that fine peninsula. They have been received with ovations by the good people there.

A disposition equally favorable towards immigration is manifested in various other parts of the country.

Patriotic citizens have stepped forth at the call of his Majesty, and offered their own private lands, many of them upon the most favorable terms for colonization.

Mr. Jimires invites five hundred European families to his estates in Durango, offering them each a house andl ot, rent free, a weekly allowance of provisions without charge, and a guarantee of work at air wages for five years. At the end of that time he further promises a gratuity of $15,000 to the community, and a present to each family of a yoke of oxen.

Mr. Gil, of Guadalajara, invites twenty Belgian families to his highly improved and well-stocked hacienda, offering them one-half of it for cultivation on shares, he finding the stock, seed and cattle, and the colonists the labor. He offers also flocks and herds, from which to breed on halves.

Other enlightened and liberal-minded land-owners of the empire have offered their estates for colonization on terms equally liberal.

MISREPRESENTATIONS ABROAD CONCERNING MEXICO.

Many false impressions have taken root abroad about Mexico and the Mexicans. These operate greatly to our disadvantage, inasmuch as they are stumbling-blocks in the mind of the stranger, and tend to discourage immigration.

The world knows Mexico as a country that for the last half a century has been tossed by revolution. Many, listening to the stories of her troubles and the tales of her calamities as told by her enemies, have come to regard the whole land as a "God-forsaken country," inhabited by a bigoted, illiberal and inhospitable people, while, in fact, no part of the world can boast of a more refined society or a more elegant hospitality than that which is to be found in certain parts of the empire.

The Mississippi valley, even in its palmiest days, could not boast any plantation that could compare in baronial splendor, lordly magnificence and princely hospitality with your Mexican haciends that has escaped the ravages of war. The halls of some of them are large enough to entertain, and have entertained, several hundred guests for weeks at a time.

On some of these you will find well-appointed schools for the education of the children of the dependents at the expense of the proprietor; churches built and chapels maintained by the same munificent bounty; hospitals erected for the sick, the old servants pensioned, and all the operations of the estate carried on upon a scale and with expenditures followed by remunerative revenues such as but few farmers in Virginia or France can boast of.

But all parts of the country are not so.

For more than fifty years Mexico has been constantly torn by faction or scourged by war, and she has reaped abundantly of the harvests which always spring from such seeds—forced loans and contributions upon the rich, grievous burdens upon the poor, the spirit of enterprise in many departments of the empire well nigh crushed out of the people, the industrial energies of entire regions paralyzed, and capital itself frightened off into its hiding-places.

ABSENTEEISM.

Such a state of things long continued in any country is sure to be followed by a general absenteeism from their estates of the large land-owners. This is eminently the case in Mexico.

The effect of this absenteeism is expressed upon the landscape, and proclaimed by deserted mansions, neglected plantations, and other signs of ruin and decay, in tones that fall sadly upon many a heart. Many of these fine estates, with the walls of their noble old mansions still standing, are now offered for sale and settlement at prices varying from a few cents to a few dollars per acre. They are in the most choice parts of the country, and would, if restored to cultivation, embellish the land with a beautiful mosaic of the most lovely garden spots that the world ever saw.

With the immigrant coming to Mexico it is not as with the emigrant bound to the "far west" in the United States. There he goes to reclaim from the wilderness. Here he comes, for the most part, to reclaim from ruin and the ravages of war. Plantations that were once garden spots invite his coming. He may pitch his tent on the verge of highly cultivated districts from which he can draw his supplies until the bountiful earth, yielding to his own good husbandry, shall yield him of her increase. And this the soil of Mexico, under climates that have no winter, will do in two or three months.

One of the finest haciendas of the wasted districts is now on sale. It was abandoned some six or eight years ago in consequence of a revolution: the proprietor died, and it has not since been restored to cultivation. It yielded a regular annual profit of not less than $120,000. The dwelling-house alone cost $200,000. This hacienda is large enough to accommodate forty or fifty families with farms of one thousand acres each. It can now be had for less than five dollars the acre, and after the first payment, on long time to suit purchasers.

Other haciendas that are open to the choice and selection of the immigrant are much larger. Two, containing each more than three thousand square miles, have been offered by the proprietors for colonization.

I know of no country in which the land is held by so few and in such large tracts.

This also has produced marked effects upon the nation; it appears to have deprived Mexico entirely of what other countries consider their "bone and sinew"—their noble, enterprising, energetic, hard-working middle classes.

Some political economists divide society in Mexico into but two classes—the upper and lower; and out of a population of eight millions of people, more than seven millions are said to belong to the latter.

INDUCEMENTS OFFERED TO FOREIGN CAPITAL AND LABOR.

The statesmen of the country, with the emperor in their lead, desire to heal the breach rapidly. For this purpose, foreign labor, capital, and skill have been invited to our shores. Many good men of the country look upon immigration, on a large scale, as the readiest and best means of restoring the equilibrium of the classes, and of giving to this country and its institutions that stability and force which are so essential to the full development of its vast powers, capabilities, and resources. Hence the encouragement that is now offered to immigrants.

This country is now in a better state to receive immigrants than it has been for many years. The empire is daily gaining ground, strength, and support, and the armed organization against it is broken up into factions—its head and leader, ex-President Juarez, having left the country.

But now, with the dawn of a happy era of peace at last before her, Mexico, after half a century of continued change and revolution, finds herself in an exhausted state, and the immigrants who wish to cast their lot with her auspicious future must bring with them something more than brawny arms and stout hearts. They must not forget those appliances of industry, those labor-saving machines and improved modes of husbandry, which scientific skill and mechanical ingenuity, under the blessings of stable government and long-continued peace, have, in other parts of the world, brought to such perfection.

ROOM FOR ALL.

There is room, with encouraging prospects, for mechanics and artisans of all sorts, as well as for agricultural labor and scientific skill. Roads are to be repaired and made, bridges restored, mills—grist and saw—to be erected, dwelling-houses to be repaired or built, machine shops, and all those establishments which are so essential in the agricultural economy of other countries, will also be extensively required.

Immigrants who come to Mexico, from whatever country, will be warmly welcomed in many parts. They will meet with no open hostility anywhere, except from the hands of the lawless.

To resist them, and to have the full benefit of all those conveniences—such as mills and other establishments just alluded to, and which every well-ordered agricultural community requires—it is desirable that the immigrants should come in bodies and form settlements of their own.

Looking to this, the decree of September 5 invests them with a semi-military organization, and they are expected to be able to defend their settlements against robbers, who, however, rarely attack where resistance is expected.

Protestants will be drawn into communities also for the sake of schools and churches. Moreover, public interests require that each settlement should be large enough fairly to develop the whole system of domestic, social, and agricultural economy of the country whence the settlers came.

For this purpose, each settlement should be large enough to support saw and grist mills, tanyards, blacksmiths, wheelwrights, and the various other artisans and machinists who, in the pursuit of their calling, contribute to the requirements of modern agriculture, with all of its improvements.

ADVICE TO FOREIGNERS SETTLING IN MEXICO

There is still another reason why immigrants from all except Spanish countries should form themselves into settlements of their own, and that reason is one of language. A farmer coming to Mexico, ignorant of the language, ignorant of the customs of the country, and of the rate of wages, and settling down among neighbors all speaking in (to him) an unknown tongue, would find himself surrounded by embarrassments, none of which would exist in a settlement made up of his old neighbors, kinsmen, and friends. It would be well, therefore, for each colony to bring with it a large portion of its own labor.

The lands of Mexico have never been surveyed, nor has there been, until now, a land office. The consequence is that the government cannot tell which lands are public and which private; and though the chief of the land office is vigorously at work organizing surveying parties, and sending them forth into the field, it is found that lands sufficient to receive the coming tide of immigration cannot be surveyed, mapped, and brought into market for some time yet. Therefore, it is recommended to those, both in Europe and the United States, who desire to come now to Mexico, to form themselves into companies consisting of not less than twenty-five families each. Then, while those at home are making their preparations, let their pioneers come to Mexico for the purpose of purchasing a hacienda or other lands, and of making ready to receive the rest.

To those who will thus come now, with their families, and form settlements sufficient to call into play all the industrial appliances, consisting of machinery, shops, and implements connected with agriculture in its most improved state, and calculated to serve as so many centres of agricultural improvement in the country, special encouragement is held out.

They are invited to send forward their agents, who will receive all the information that the office of colonization can give, and every facility that it can throw in their way as to the most desirable parts of the country in which to settle, the choicest localities, and the cheapest and best lands, &c.

Having made their own selections, the government will then, in case they require it, lend them pecuniary assistance, sufficient to enable them to establish themselves in their new homes, and get fairly under way.

M. F. MAURY, *Imperial Commissioner.*

OFFICE OF COLONIZATION,
No. 13, *Calle San Juan Letran, Mexico, November* 18, 1865.

Mr. Hunter to Mr. Romero.

DEPARTMENT OF STATE,
Washington, December 31, 1865.

SIR: I have the honor to acknowledge the receipt of your note of this date, enclosing two documents, dated December 10 and November 18, 1865, issued by M. F. Maury, on the subject of the colonization of Mexico.

I avail myself of this opportunity to renew to you, sir, the assurances of my distinguished consideration.

W. HUNTER,
Acting Secretary of State.

Señor MATIAS ROMERO, *&c., &c., &c.,*
Washington, D. C.

NEGOTIATIÓN FOR THE TRANSIT OF UNITED STATES TROOPS, IN 1861, THROUGH MEXICAN TERRITORY.

Mr. Romero to Mr. Seward.

[Translation.]

MEXICAN LEGATION TO THE UNITED STATES OF AMERICA,
Washington, May 4, 1861.

MR. SECRETARY: The government of Mexico has been informed that there exists in this country a numerous combination of persons, who, whether guided by a fanatic spirit professed in good faith, or swayed by motives of pecuniary interest, are actively at work on the project of extending the institution of slavery, not merely within the limits of the United States, with which Mexico could have nothing to do, but also into Mexican territory, for which they propose the acquisition of the largest possible part of that territory.

You will comprehend, sir, that these apprehensions are very far from being unfounded. Their best justification would be in an impartial and minute glance over the public events which have occurred in this country within the last seven months. The facts which present themselves to view, and which would sustain such apprehensions, are so numerous, that there is really a difficulty, not in finding them, but in knowing which of them to overlook.

Without intending to mix myself up in the slightest degree with internal questions of this country, I pray you, sir, to permit me to refer to them, considering them only in the aspect in which they affect the dearests interests of Mexico, and the integrity of its territory.

Public opinion in this country regards as the principal obstacle which conflicted with an arrangement by means of a compromise at the last session of the Congress of the United States of the difficulties stirred up long ago, and recently renewed with fresh vigor, the persistent manner in which the representatives of propagandist ideas insisted that in the arrangement which should be agreed upon there should be an express clause recognizing slavery in the territory which the United States might in future time acquire at the south. You will recollect, sir, that this forethought, contained in the propositions presented to the Senate in

December of last year, by the Hon. J. J. Crittenden, senator from Kentucky, procured for them the acceptableness which they found among such representatives of propagandism.

If these recent events were not still fresh in the memory of all, I should be sustained in my assertion by the speeches delivered in the Senate by the Hon. Henry Wilson, senator from Massachusetts, on the 21st of February last, and in the House of Representatives, on the 31st of January preceding, by the Hon. Charles Francis Adams, representative from the same State.

If from the bosom of the national representation of the country I may be allowed to pass to the assembly called "the peace conference," gathered in this city in February last, on the proposition of the State of Virginia, to seek a pacific solution of the difficulties which disturbed the nation, I find on foot the same obstacle to the completion of an arrangement; and, thanks to the fact that the persons gathered in this assemblage were animated, apparently, by a more sincere desire of reconciliation, and that there were no representatives there from the States which, up to that time, claimed to have reassumed their sovereignty, which are precisely those which contain some citizens professing with most zeal propagandist ideas, an arrangement was arrived at, which, by not acknowledging slavery in express terms, in the territory which might in future be acquired, did not receive in Congress the approval of the representatives of propagandism.

Passing from the discussion of the deliberative assemblies to that which some States of the south at present consider the supreme law of the land, it appears that paragraph 3d, of section 3d, of article 4th of the Constitution, adopted on the 11th of March last by the congress assembled at Montgomery, and ratified by various States of the Union, authorizes "the Confederate States of America" to acquire new territory; providing expressly that "in all that territory (that acquired in future) the institution of negro slavery as it now exists in the Confederate States shall be recognized and protected by Congress and by the territorial governments."

The tone of the speeches which distinguished citizens of some of the southern States have delivered, as well in the halls of the Senate as in other places, and with different motives, the spirit of the publications by the press in the same States, and a multitude of other indications and demonstrations of great weight, which it would be prolix to refer to, manifest, in a manner which admits not the slightest doubt, that this combination of persons has a settled plan, well matured, thought over, and reckoned upon for a long time back, to acquire sooner or later, according as its possibility permits, all or a part of the territory of Mexico, for the purpose of introducing and developing therein what the said combination calls "its especial civilization," the base and foundation of which is the institution of slavery, if faith is to be given to what was said by a distinguished citizen of Georgia, who might consider himself authorized to speak in the name of the combination, in a speech which he delivered at the city of Savannah on the 31st March last.

You will consider, sir, how great has been the interest with which the government of Mexico has followed the course of the political events which have developed themselves in this country, and how great its regret on perceiving the rise and progress of a danger which threatens to disturb its tranquillity and to strike at its very existence as an independent nation.

Mexico does not desire to exchange its nationality for any other, however flattering might be the advantages which might result from such change. It has the elements necessary for a sovereign power. It conquered through the blood of its children its desired independence, and will maintain it to the last extremity against any invader who may attempt to take it from her. Whatever may have been the intestine difficulties which may have taken place up to this time, and have contributed to restrain its material progress, it has the consciousness of the important character it is to represent in future among the family of nations. It holds an absolute faith in its future, and believes that so soon as the beneficent shadow of peace and of democratic institutions may develop its immense resources, and the fabulous wealth which its soil contains, it will occupy in the world the important part to which it is called by nature.

Mexico will never consent that any human being shall be reduced to slavery within its territory. It is a free country, in which no man is born a slave; and in treading upon which, liberty returns to those who may before have had the misfortune to lose it. Its constitution forbids that any treaty be made in which the extradition of slaves is stipulated.

It has entered into treaty with Great Britain that it will contribute to the abolition of the slave trade, and that it will not allow of slavery in its territories; and these provisions of its fundamental laws, and of its international engagements, have an indestructible sanction in the hearts of all Mexicans.

The government of Mexico, which understands and estimates at its value the respect for the laws professed by the citizens of the United States, and the good faith and sound principles which guide the policy of their existing government, is very far from regarding the United States as authors and responsible for projects, in every view unlawful and unjust, which (although strenuous efforts have been made to bring proselytes to) as yet amount to only a small minority. But as such plans have been formed in this country, and as their authors are now, by force of late political events, in the way to attain the needful resources to take means to carry them into execution, the government of Mexico holds it to be its duty to denounce such projects to that of the United States, and, for the purpose of securing on a solid and stable basis friendly relations between the two countries, has authorized me to express to you the good disposition which it has to form a treaty which shall guarantee the boundaries of the Mexican republic as now agreed upon, to be marked out and recognized, and which shall prevent the introduction and spreading of slavery in Mexican territory.

In the opinion of the Mexican government, a treaty concluded upon the preceding basis would not be less favorable to the true interests of the United States than to those of Mexico. If the United States should succeed in establishing an insurmountable barrier which would remove all hope of extending slavery to the south of the Union, it will have attained a very important step in the definitive settlement of the question which has caused so many complications and difficulties to the country, and which now threatens to whelm it in a lamentable civil war; whilst in exchange for this advantage, it would only guarantee, in a manner more express, engagements already contracted with Mexico in the treaty of limits of 2d February, 1848, and of 30th December, 1853.

I have also instructions to state to you, sir, that in this or any other arrangement which may be made between the government of the United States and that of Mexico, it must be an indispensable condition that they are not to make participants thereto, in any way, the nations of Europe.

The government of Mexico considers that whatever inherence might be conceded to European powers in such conventions might be converted into a motive or pretext for the intervention of that continent in the affairs of the republic in particular, or of America in general, and desires, on its part, to avoid the possibility of such a thing happening, because it entertains the conviction that the intervention of Europe on this continent would be fatal to the preservation and development of democratic institutions, on which are founded the hopes of the progress and social welfare of humanity.

This opportunity is satisfactory to me to repeat to you, sir, the assurances of my very distinguished consideration.

M. ROMERO.

HON. WILLIAM H. SEWARD, *&c., &c., &c.,*
Washington, D. C.

Mr. Seward to Mr. Romero.

WASHINGTON, *May* 7, 1861.

SIR: I have received your communication of the 4th instant.

It would be unprofitable for this government to discuss with you the objects, purposes, and plans of that portion of the citizens of the United States who are engaged in the attempt to subvert the Constitution and effect a dissolution of the Union, even although it should be believed that beyond those designs, so injurious to our own country, they contemplate also aggressions against Mexico. At the same time I am free to say that it is an occasion of sincere satisfaction to learn that the government of Mexico is apprised of its own exposure to danger from the success of the revolution, and is resolved to avert it.

It should suffice for me to say that any designs of the insurgents here against your country cannot be carried into effect if their designs, aimed at the government of the United States, shall be effectually prevented. This government needs no additional incentive to perform its duty. It is taking all the care necessary to repress the revolution, and it has no doubt of its success.

The President receives with much pleasure the overtures of the government of Mexico for negotiating a new and beneficial treaty with the United States, and under other circumstances it would have given him pleasure to have considered them at large. But, as you are aware, Mr. Corwin has been appointed envoy extraordinary and minister plenipotentiary to represent this government at Mexico. He has very liberal instructions and ample power to negotiate a treaty which shall be equal and just and even liberal towards Mexico. Indeed, it is the desire of this government to establish such relations with Mexico, and with other American republics, as will strengthen the power of each, and enable them all to maintain a just and wholesome independence of the influences which come from the other hemisphere. You will be satisfied from this brief statement that Mr. Corwin will be able to give full consideration to the generous wishes of the government of Mexico. It is probable that he has already entered into the discussion of the question which the negotiation involves. He will immediately receive from this government instructions to meet with favor the enlightened views of the government of Mexico as you have communicated them to this department. Under these circumstances it would be inexpedient for us to engage in labors of the same kind and directed to the same end.

I shall, however, with great pleasure direct that this correspondence, together with your previous communication of the 30th April, 1861, in relation to the Indians of Yucatan, be forwarded to Mr. Corwin, and call his attention to the interesting subjects you have so fully and so ably discussed.

I avail myself of this occasion to renew to you, sir, the assurances of my high consideration.

WILLIAM H. SEWARD.

Señor MATIAS ROMERO, *&c., &c., &c.,*
Washington, D. C.

Mr. Seward to Mr. Romero.

DEPARTMENT OF STATE,
Washington, May 7, 1861.

SIR: The government of the United States contemplates the concentration of a body of troops from its Pacific possessions in the Territory of Arizona. This purpose can be most expeditiously accomplished if the government of Mexico will consent to their being landed at Guaymas, and marched by the most direct route to their destination. In this exigency I have the honor to request you to submit to the friendly consideration of the Mexican government the desire I have expressed, with a view to obtain the necessary permission; and I presume that in submitting the proposition there is scarcely any need that it should be accompanied with the assurance that in making the transit over Mexican territory the strictest regard shall be paid to the rights and authority of the government, and the persons, property, and interests of the citizens of the republic.

I avail myself of this opportunity to renew to you, sir, the assurance of my high consideration.

WILLIAM H. SEWARD.

Señor MATIAS ROMERO, *&c.*, *&c.*, *&c.*

Mr. Romero to Mr. Seward.

[Translation.]

MEXICAN LEGATION IN THE UNITED STATES OF AMERICA,
Washington, May 8, 1861.

MR. SECRETARY: I have had the honor to receive the note which you were pleased to address to me under date of yesterday, informing me that the government of the United States desires to concentrate in the Territory of Arizona a body of troops from its possessions on the Pacific by causing them to pass across the Mexican territory, and requesting me to submit that desire to the consideration of the government of Mexico with the view of its granting the necessary permission, to enable said troops to disembark at the port of Guaymas, and thence proceed by the most direct route to their destination. In reply, I have the honor to inform you that I have already transmitted your note to my government in which that request is solicited, and that so soon as I shall have received the decision of the President of Mexico I shall hasten to communicate it to you.

I avail myself of this opportunity to renew to you, sir, the assurance of my very distinguished consideration.

M. ROMERO.

Hon. WILLIAM H. SEWARD, *&c.*, *&c.*, *&c.*,
Washington, D. C.

Mr. Romero to Mr. Seward.

[Translation.]

MEXICAN LEGATION IN THE UNITED STATES OF AMERICA,
Washington, August 26, 1861.

MR. SECRETARY: Referring to my note of the 8th of May last, I have the honor to transmit to you a copy of a communication which I have just received from the department of foreign relations of Mexico, to which is annexed the permission granted by the sovereign congress of the republic on the 20th of June last to the troops of the United States to pass across the Mexican territory of Gauymas to Arizona, in the terms in which you requested it in the note you were pleased to address to this legation under date of the 7th of May referred to. I hope, sir, that the government of the United States will see in the grant of this permission a fresh proof of the sincere desire which animates that of Mexico to draw closer the relations of friendship which happily exist between the two countries.

I gladly profit by this opportunity to repeat to you, sir, the assurances of my highest consideration.

M. ROMERO.

Hon. WILLIAM H. SEWARD, *&c.*, *&c.*, *&c.*, *Washington, C. D.*

[Translation.]

No. 27.] MEXICAN REPUBLIC, DEPARTMENT OF INTERIOR AND FOREIGN RELATIONS
National Palace, Mexico, June 22, 1861.

As the consequence of your note relative to the permission that government asks from the government of this republic for the passage of American troops through its territory, I send you the annexed copy, containing the sovereign assent which has been given in the matter, in order that you may transmit it to the Department of State of the United States, and on the occasion I repeat to you the assurances of my consideration.

LUCAS DE PALACIO Y MAGAROLA.

The CHARGÉ D'AFFAIRES *of the Republic of Washington.*

WASHINGTON, *August* 26, 1861.

True copy: ROMERO.

OFFICE OF THE SECRETARY OF THE CONGRESS OF THE UNION.

The sovereign congress to which we made report of your note of the thirty-first last past, relative to the permission sought by the government at Washington for the passage of federal troops from Guaymas to Arizona, has pleased, at its secret session yesterday, to approve the following proposition:

First. The executive shall have power to grant the permission which the government of the United States has asked, to disembark at this time, at the port of Guaymas, a body of troops, under the assurance it has proffered that they shall march, by the most direct route, to the Territory of Arizona, and that in their transit they will observe the strictest regard for the rights and authority of the government of Mexico, and for the persons, property and interests of the citizens of the republic.

Second. The executive will issue suitable instructions to the government of the state of Sonora, and to the federal functionaries therein, that at the disembarcation and on the passage of that body of troops, no hindrance be in their way.

We send this to you for your information, and consequent effects, and as the result of the note referred to, to which we respond.

God and liberty!

MEXICO, *June* 21, 1861.

G. VALLE.
E. ROBLES.

The CHIEF CLERK *in charge of the Department of Foreign Affairs.*

MEXICO, *June* 22, 1861.

True copy:

JUAN DE DIOS ARIAS, *Chief Clerk.*

WASHINGTON, *August* 26, 1861.

True copy:

ROMERO.

Mr. F. W. Seward to Mr. Romero.

DEPARTMENT OF STATE,
Washington, August 27, 1861.

SIR: I have the honor to acknowledge the receipt of your note of yesterday, communicating a copy of a despatch just received from the Mexican government, transmitting to you the assent of the sovereign congress of the republic to the application of this government for permission to pass troops of the United States across the Mexican territory of Guaymas to Arizona, under certain pledges of security and non-interference with the persons or property of the territory to be traversed.

I beg you to convey to your government assurances of the high appreciation entertained by this government of the liberal, prompt, and magnanimous response which Mexico has made to the United States in this emergency. We are profoundly sensible that such a policy could be adopted only under the most exalted confidence in the integrity and good faith of this government, which will endeavor by every means so to excercise the privilege conceded, that neither the authorities nor the people of Mexico will have cause to regret the marked courtesy they have extended to a friendly power.

I avail myself of this occasion to renew to you, sir, the assurances of my highest consideration.

F. W. SEWARD,
Acting Secretary.

Señor MATIAS ROMERO, *&c., &c., &c.,*
Washington, D. C.

Mr. Corwin to Mr. Seward.

[Extracts.]

No. 2.] MEXICO, *June* 29, 1861.

SIR: I have the honor to acknowledge the receipt of your despatches Nos. 3, 4, 5, 6 and 7, with the papers referred to in them.

* * * * * * *

Congress has within the last week granted us the privilege of marching troops from Guaymas, through Sonora, to our possessions in Arizona. A leading member of Congress has kindly furnished me with a memorandum of what occurred when this question was up and acted on in secret session, a copy of which—with the decree—I send you, Marked D. This memorandum discloses the grounds upon which this concession was made, and the prevailing tone of public feeling here towards us at this time.

* * * * * * *

Very respectfully, your obedient servant,

THOMAS CORWIN.

Hon. WILLIAM H. SEWARD,
Secretary of State.

EXHIBIT D.

Memorandum of proceedings in the Mexican Congress with reference to the permission for transit of United States troops from Guaymas to Arizona, asked for by the Department of State, through the chargé d'affaires of Mexico in Washington.

The note from the chargé d'affaires of Mexico in Washington, accompanying a copy of the note from the department of State, in which permission was asked to land a body of United States troops at Guaymas and march them by the most direct road to the Territory of Arizona, was communicated to congress by the minister of foreign relations for the action of congress thereon.

On the reception of these notes by congress they were passed to the Committee on Foreign Affairs.

This committee reported unanimously in favor of conceding the permission referred to in the terms asked for by the Secretary of State of the United States.

On the presentation of the report, application was ordered to be made to the minister of foreign affairs that he state to congress what was the opinion of the executive in the premises. This was stated to be favorable to the permission solicited.

Several members then spoke upon the subject of the concession, setting forth that this permission which they were disposed to concede, although innocent in itself, might be taken by the States of the south as an offence, or used as a pretext to open hostilities against Mexico for the purpose of acquiring a part of her territory for the extension of slavery, and that the subject should therefore be treated as one of importance, but that they were, under all the circumstances, in favor of placing themselves on the side of the north.

One of the prominent deputies entered largely into a history of the causes which have produced the present struggle between the north and the south, and stated that from the knowledge he had of the tendencies and projects of the leading men of the south, he believed it inevitable, if the south separated from the north, that Mexico would find herself under the necessity of sustaining a war with the States of the confederation, and that while slavery existed there, no security could be felt that the territory of Mexico would not be invaded, either by means of open war or of fillibuster expeditions.

That in view of these circumstances it was clearly for the interest of Mexico to draw more closely its relations with the north by means of friendly acts and by a commercial treaty that would favor the interest of both countries, and even to celebrate a political treaty that would result in guaranteeing to Mexico in an absolute manner the integrity of her territory, or at least guarantee her against the introduction of slavery. These views were well received by the congress, and the permission for the transit of United States troops through Mexican territory was approved without opposition being offered by a single one of the members.

MEXICO, *June* 21, 1861.

EXHIBIT E.

[Translation.]

Confidential.] NATIONAL PALACE, *Mexico, June* 27, 1861.

MR. MINISTER: For the due information of your excellency I have the honor to enclose herewith the decree issued by the sovereign congress on the 21st instant, in which the executive is authorized to permit the transit of the troops of the United States across the territory of the Mexican republic.

By the steamer which will next sail the said decree will be communicated to the legation of Mexico in Washington, in order that it may be made known to that government.

While so informing you, it gives me pleasure to repeat to you that,

I am your very obedient servant,

LUCAS DE PALACIO Y MAGAROLA.

His Excellency THOMAS CORWIN, *&c., &c., &c.*

DEMONSTRATION OF HONOR BY THE UNITED STATES OF COLOMBIA TO PRESIDENT JUAREZ, OF MEXICO.

Mr. Romero to Mr. Seward.

[Translation.]

MEXICAN LEGATION IN THE UNITED STATES OF AMERICA,
Washington, July 22, 1865.

MR. SECRETARY: I have the honor to transmit to you, for the information of the government of the United States, a copy of a decree issued on the 2d of May last, by the congress of the United States of Colombia, in which it is declared that "in virtue of the self-denial and unconquerable perseverance which Señor Benito Juarez, in the character of constitutional president of the United Mexican States, has displayed in defence of the independence and liberty of his country," he has deserved well of America, and it is decreed, "as an act of homage to such virtues, and as an example to the Colombian youth," that the portrait of the president of Mexico be kept in the national library of Bogota, with an appropriate inscription.

This decree was published in the number 319 of the official journal of the United States of Colombia, corresponding to the 6th of May aforementioned, at page 1234, column fourth.

The government of Colombia has thus recognized the fact that the question which is being debated at present in Mexico affects all America.

I avail myself of this opportunity to renew to you, Mr. Secretary, the assurances of my most distinguished consideration.

M. ROMERO.

Hon. WILLIAM H. SEWARD, *&c., &c., &c.*

Decree of the 2d of May, 1865, in honor of the president of Mexico, Señor Benito Juarez.

The Congress of the United States of Colombia decrees:

ARTICLE 1. The Congress of Colombia, in the name of the people which it represents, in view of the self-denial and unconquerable perseverance which Señor Benito Juarez, in the character of constitutional president of the United Mexican States, has displayed in the defence of the independence and liberty of his country, declares that the said citizen has deserved well of America; and as an act of homage to such virtues, and as an example to the Colombian youth,

Resolves, That the potrait of that eminent statesman be kept in the national library, with the following inscription:

"BENITO JUAREZ, the Mexican citizen."

The Congress of 1865 offers him, in the name of the people of Colombia, this homage for his constancy in defending the liberty and independence of Mexico.

ARTICLE 2. The executive power will cause to be delivered into the hands of Señor Juarez, through the channel of the minister of Colombia, residing in Washington, a copy of the present decree.

ARTICLE 3. In the appropriation which is to be voted by the Congress for the ensuing year will be included the sum adequate to enable the executive power to give full compliance to the present decree.

Given at Bogota this first day of May, 1865.

VICTORIANO DE D. PAREDES,
President of the Senate of Plenipotentiaries.
SANTIAGO PEREZ,
President of the House of Representatives.
JUAN DE D. RIOMALO,
Secretary of the Senate of Plenipotentiaries.
NICOLAS PEREIRA GAMBA,
Secretary of the House of Representatives.

BOGOTA, *May* 2, 1865.

Let it be published and executed.

[L. S.] MANUEL MURILLO.

By the President:
ANTONIO DEL REAL,
Secretary of the Interior and Foreign Relations.

Mr. Seward to Mr. Romero.

DEPARTMENT OF STATE,
Washington, November 6, 1865.

SIR: I have had the honor to receive the copy of a decree, issued by the Congress of the United States of Colombia on the 2d day of May, 1865, which accompanied your note to me of the 22d of July last, expressive of their approbation of the conduct of his excellency Señor Don Benito Juarez, in the character of constitutional president of the United Mexican States, and as the champion and defender of their liberties, independence, and cherished institutions, in the ordeal through which Mexico is now passing.

This tribute to the patriotism and eminent virtues of President Juarez is indeed well deserved, and I am sure will be heartily indorsed by the people of the United States.

Thanking you for your kind attention in communicating so interesting a testimonial to this government, I avail myself of the occasion to offer to you, sir, the assurances of my most distinguished consideration,

WILLIAM H. SEWARD.

Señor MATIAS ROMERO, *&c., &c., &c.,*
Washington, D. C.

Mr. Romero to Mr. Seward.

[Translation.]

MEXICAN LEGATION IN THE UNITED STATES OF AMERICA,
New York, September 21, 1865.

MR. SECRETARY: I have the honor to send you a copy of No. 112 of the "official newspaper of the constitutional government of the Mexican republic," published at the city of Chihuahua the 29th of July last, in which you will see the report of the committee of the senate of the United States of Colombia, made on the 27th of February this year, respecting the decree in honor of President Juarez, approved by the Colombian Congress on the 2d of May following, and of which I had the honor to send a copy to the department with my note of 22d of July aforesaid. The fact that such report emanated from one of the respectable bodies of an American republic, and showing therein the manner in which the Mexican question is regarded, has decided me to send a copy of this document to the government of the United States. In doing this, I think it nevertheless proper to say to you, there is in it an inaccuracy resulting from mistaken information in Bogota respecting a letter which it was reported the ex-Archduke of Austria wrote to the constitutional president of the Mexican republic. The only document of this kind which has emanated from the ex-Archduke is a letter which Baron de Pond, counsellor of Maximilian, addressed from Brussels, under date of May 16, 1864, to a Mexican general resident in Europe, proposing to him an interview with the president of Mexico, of which letter I send a copy.

The constitutional president of the Mexican republic, to whose knowledge such letter came, did not think it decorous to occupy himself in answering it, in order not to enter into any relations with an usurper who was speculating on the misfortunes of Mexico. Nevertheless the contradictions between what the Archduke Maximilian asserted he would do in Mexico before he went to the republic, and what he has done since his arrival in Mexican territory, is noticeable. He then gave assurance "that he was far from imposing himself on the Mexicans by foreign force and against their will," and he was shortly afterwards sent there by the Emperor of the French, and since his arrival has been sustained in the places he has occupied by foreign bayonets. He made an appearance of respecting the right which every independent nation has of freely disposing of its destinies, whilst now he is busied in compelling the Mexican people to accept, by force of arms, a form of government entirely foreign to them, and to which they have clearly enough demonstrated that they will never submit. He then expressed the wish to call together all the strength of the country, without distinction of party, and to place himself in accord with the principal men of the liberal party, and afterwards he was converted into a blind instrument of the French to exterminate by means of courts-martial all the Mexican patriots who deemed it their duty to take up arms in defence of the independence of their country.

Lastly, it is to be noted that on the 16th of March, 1864, he still styled the constitutional president of Mexico the *legitimate chief of the country* when the French attempted to cause it to be believed that the national government of Mexico had disappeared a year previous—that is, since the 31st of May, 1863, when said government left the city of Mexico.

It is very satisfactory to me to avail of this opportunity to renew to you, Mr. Secretary, the assurances of my very distinguished consideration.

M. ROMERO.

Hon. WILLIAM H. SEWARD, &c., &c., &c.

[Enclosure No. 1.—Translation.]

From the official paper No. 112, of the constitutional government of the Mexican republic, published at Chihuahua, Saturday, July 29, 1865.

UNITED STATES OF COLOMBIA—SENATE OF THE PLENIPOTENTIARIES—REPORT OF A COMMITTEE.

CITIZEN SENATORS: The subject submitted to the discussion of this honorable assembly is that of the legislative body of the nation should offer a homage of admiration to the republican hero of Mexico—to the Señor Benito Juarez.

There it nothing more just, gentlemen, than this thought, nothing greater and more worthy of a generous people than to honor in men the noble sentiments which constitute virtue. If there be any merit in impugning vice and iniquity, it is almost obligatory upon us, proper to decorum, to bow down our heads before political honesty; yes, gentlemen, before the political probity which is the true phœnix of the age in which we live. It seems that Providence has created Europe to maintain in it the traditions of royalty and despotism, as it created America, with an intervening ocean, for democracy and republican institutions. But the proud despots of that Old World, with the mad design of changing that Divine law of the Creator, have overleaped the seas, and unfurled upon the virgin soil of America a monarchical banner; this duty has been assigned to the imperial house of Austria, which is most justly termed by the poets "the prison keeper of nations." A prince of that unfortunate house, backed by forty thousand French soldiers, and by a few hundred traitors, is he who has assumed upon the beautiful soil of the Montezumas the title of emperor. You, gentlemen, know very well, that in order to consummate so iniquitous an outrage it became necessary for three great powers of Europe—England, Spain, and France—to coalesce; and how, subsequently, in imitation of Pontius Pilate, the first two have washed their hands of it, without the certainty of their having washed them very clean, throwing upon the third the consequences of the treacherous crime of these three powers.

Mr. Thiers has stated, within the halls of the legislative chambers of France, during the session of the 26th of January, 1864, all that is desirable to say upon this subject He explains, in the clearest manner, the origin of this scheme, the diverse demands of the invading powers, and the results to be accomplished for the benefit of France. Time will tell us by and by whether the predictions of this statesman shall be realized or not, or whether the will of God shall permit that more shall be accomplished than what his voice could give utterance to, in the presence of the assembled Congress of his country. But, notwithstanding this great league, notwithstanding the veteran army of the Emperor Napoleon, notwithstanding the traitors and the new Franco-Austrian empire, a magistrate arises, sustained by loyal Mexicans, ready to bear aloft with firmness the standard of the republic, and to prevent the ruin of a legitimate government. This magistrate is the eminent American, Señor Benito Juarez.

Permit me, therefore, citizen senators, to dwell for a while upon the eminent personage whose name has already acquired a world-wide renown, and to whose solid virtues all elevated and just men, from every quarter of the globe, are compelled to do reverence.

Señor Juarez was born some fifty-eight years ago, in a humble village of the state of Oajaca, called Jatlan, and which to-day bears the name of its illustrious son. Even when a child, he one day bent his steps towards the gates of the capital of that state to solicit some occupation through which he might earn an honest living. He was at once admitted as a servant into the house of a wealthy gentleman, who, foreseeing his natural abilities and genius, caused him to be well educated. With the support alone of that kind friend he rises rapidly through his own merits, and attains the brilliant position of president of the supreme court of the republic—member of the national Congress—governor of his native state—secretary to the executive power—and of president of the republic. What were the distinguishing qualities of that American, that native, descended from the caciques, in his various situations of servant, master, lawyer, minister of justice, legislator, secretary of state, and of president? I will here state them: possessed of a pride which I shall call continental, or of that of race, they were loyalty, honor, and firmness.

At his present age, and in view of a situation the most difficult, complicated, and grave, which can be presented to the statesman, no one dares deny to him these high qualities, whether the judgment comes from his enemies or whether it originates from friendly pens. Mr. Thiers himself, who with such profound contempt speaks of the race from whom the worthy president of Mexico is descended, and to whom he says that it is only through complacency that the name of the "Latin race" is given—Mr. Thiers himself admits the probity, the force of character, the persistency, the patience, and the prudence of the Indian Juarez.

The celebrated writer Emilio Castelus, the most brilliant and wise apostle of democracy in Spain, while drawing a parallel between Juarez and Lincoln, the most conspicuous representative of the United States of America, gives vent to sentiments but too true, and but too flattering to the native magistrate of the unfortunate republic of Mexico. But why should I seek in foreign opinions the intrinsicment—the just meed of praise to the man who, himself, can even now see the position which history will award to him hereafter—that skilful sculptor which never errs. I shall now enter that field, though I may be deemed bold and irreverent.

He defends the capital, and causes Puebla to be defended to the utmost extent possible to human efforts; but Puebla succumbs to the necessities of the siege, to the number and resources of the enemy.

President Juarez then removes the seat of his government to San Luis Potosi, and thence still keeps alive in the hearts of the nation the holy love of country; thence he holds aloft to the Mexicans, and, within the grip of his strong hand, the banner of the constitutional government, pure, unsullied, and unconquerable; thence he proclaims to his fellow-countrymen, and to the people of the whole world, that the republic exists, that she struggles for the defence of her independence, and that she will, in the end, achieve it, because she disputes valiantly; thence he procures resources, he organizes forces, and directs the operations of the war; thence he keeps alive with his great example the sacred fire of the brave captains who sustain him; thence he holds out against the imperial hosts, which themselves prove their inability to conquer the country; thence he speaks to his friends in the United States these noble words: "but even as we are situated, we shall endeavor, with the help of God, to defend our beloved Mexico;" thence he manages and prepares the measures necessary to a vigorous, able, and determined defence, and in which it is impossible for us to say which is the greater—whether it be the efforts or the faith of this wonderful patriot; thence he gives to the oppressed peoples of the world living and speaking lessons, as to what they can and must do in order not to suffer their liberties to be wrested from them; thence he infuses into all noble minds this sublime hope, that, if Mexico falls entirely into the maws of wolves which have been sent to devour her, she shall fall as did Francis I, with her honor untarnished.

It is likewise from that same seat of government (and this is the measure which I consider the one, of all others, most worthy of his life (that Señor Juarez, in *his character as a courteous and polite gentleman*, replies to the tempting letter of Prince Maximilian without descending even in the smallest degree from his distinguished position as a republican representative. That document alone suffices to cover its author with glory, and to make his name immortal. But upon this brilliant reply I cannot pass a final judgment without quoting some of its passages; they are, gentlemen, as follows:

"The spirit of French fillibusterism is seeking to endanger our nationality; and I, who by my principles and my oaths am the one called upon to uphold its national integrity, its sovereignty, and its independence, must work incessantly, redoubling my exertions to fulfil the sacred charge which the nation, in the execise of her sovereign powers, has confided to me.

"I had previously noted, when the traitors of my country presented themselves as commissioners at Miramar with the view of tendering to you the crown of Mexico—sustained only by the treacherous proceedings of ten towns of the nation—that you had not seen, in all these proceedings, anything more than a ridiculous farce, unworthy totally of being seriously considered by an honorable and decent man. You replied to these frauds by demanding the will of the nation, freely expressed, as the result of its unanimous vote. Why, therefore, should I not be surprised to see you come upon the Mexican soil when no measures have been adopted respecting the conditions exacted? Why should I now *not* be astonished when I find you accepting the deceits of the traitors, adopting their language, decorating and placing in your service bandits like Marquez and Herrau, and surrounding yourself with that low class of the Mexican people? I have, frankly speaking, been greatly deceived. I believed you to be one of those pure organizations which ambition could neither reach nor corrupt."

What a lesson of decency and honesty thrown into the very teeth of a proud descendant of Charles V by an humble republican!

"You tell me that peace will result from the conference we may have, and with it the happiness of the Mexican people, and that the empire will hereafter, by placing me in an important position, have the benefit to be derived from my knowledge and the support of my patriotism. It is true, sir, cotemporaneous history registers the names of great traitors who have proved false to their oaths, their promises, and their words; who have betrayed their former history, and everything that is sacred to the man of honor; that in all these betrayals of all human relations the traitor has been guided by the infamous ambition of rule, and the vile desire of pandering to his own passions and vices; but the present incumbent in the presidency of the republic, *who rose from the obscure masses of the people*, shall bow poor and full of misery if, in the *arcana* of Providence, it has been decreed that he shall so succumb; but complying with his oaths, and meeting the hopes of the nation over which he presides, he will thus satisfy the inspirations of his own conscience." * * *

It is, gentlemen, impossible to speak more boldly or more worthily. It is not the pride of power which dictates these words, but the loftiness of a pure conscience, of an upright soul, and a calm heart. Juarez speaks to Maximilian as a sovereign to a sovereign; but the one uses the sovereignty of right, of reason, and of honor, while the other makes use of the measures of the corrupting sovereignty of kings. The one flatters with promises, and the other retorts upon him with the code of justice and of honor. The one proposes ignominious terms, the other repels infamy, and appeals to the judgment of history to decide between them. The one speaks like the serpent in paradise, with the view of seducing; the other, while retorting, expresses himself in the words of a Bayard or of an Armand Carrel.

The American statesman whom I have just described to you in a rapid and incomplete manner; the upright functionary who contrasts so strongly with so many others, traitors and perjurers; the honest man, who prefers misery and death to ignominy, because the word *duty* flatters him more than the bright decorations of a grand marshal; the Mexican who stood by the constitutional government at the time of the disloyal proceedings of President Comonfort; the genius who will allay—doubt it not—the fearful storm which has recently swept over the horizon of the New World, is he, citizen senators, to whom it is proposed to you to do honor by the enactment of a decree to that effect.

I cannot believe that there can be a single senator of Colombia who will not promptly concur, with his vote, to the consecration of a similar act which will do more honor to us than to the immortal Juarez. I also speak in the same terms with reference to members of the house of representatives.

The calm conscience of the president of Mexico needs no such incentives, we are perfectly sure, to induce him to continue fearlessly in the path of duty which he has followed to the present hour, and to the admiration of mankind. But the morality of the world must needs stamp upon its records this consolatory truth: that nations moving collectively, tending ever to the support of virtue, follow from afar—even though it be only with the eye—both the great men and the most noted criminals. Approve, therefore, gentlemen, of the decree which has been proposed to you by the two honorable senators from the sovereign state of Cauca, but approve it with the modifications which I have taken the liberty of indicating to you in a separate paper.

ALEJO MORALES.

BOGOTA, *February* 27, 1865.

[Enclosure No. 2.—Translation.]

GENERAL: After some conversation that his Imperial Highness the Archduke had with you in London and at Brussels, the thought struck him that a personal interview with President Juarez might assist in smoothing the difficulties and in enlightening him on the views of the Archduke for the good of the country he is called to rule over.

It has always been far from the thought of the Archduke to wish to let himself be imposed on the Mexicans by foreign force against their will. He has too much respect for the right which he acknowledges in every independent nation freely to dispose of its fate, ever to consent that any violence should be done to it as to the choice of its political institutions. Thus, the first condition attached by the prince to the acceptance of the crown has been the assent of the country; and if he is now ready to assume the reins of government, it is because the *acts* of adhesion, coming from the greatest part of the provinces of Mexico, authorize him to believe that the nation, regarded generally, is favorable to a change in its political forms, and to the establishment of a constitutional monarchy under the sceptre of his Imperial Highness.

If that monarchy is to be constituted, the Archduke is firmly resolved to base it on the concurrence of all the force of the country, without distinction of party. He wishes to labor sincerely to found, in the supreme interest of the well-being of the common country, political opinions which have too long divided a nation worthy of better destinies. A frankly-loyal effort on the part of the principal politicians of the liberal party, and especially with him who has been until now the legitimate head of the country, and whose political sentiments the Archduke has never failed to appreciate, would aid definitively in bringing about this end.

If Mr. Juarez shares this opinion, you might, general, by opening to him the ideas which you have yourself heard from the prince, and by reassuring the president on other points which are more readily discussed in conversation, convey to him the hope that his Imperial Highness would take care that it should be possible for him to go, in perfect security, to some point of the territory conveniently situated, there to meet with the Archduke.

In case the president should wish to have this interview, which would, without doubt, lead to happy results for the country, you might, general, have the goodness to send notice to his Imperial Highness through the medium of M. Jacques Kuhncherieb, his treasurer, who is always in attendance on the prince's person, and is a perfectly safe man.

Please accept, general, the assurances of my high consideration.

BARON DE PONT,
Counsellor of his Imperial Royal Apostolical Majesty.

BRUSSELS, *Hotel Bellevue,* 16*th March,* 1864.

Mr. Romero to Mr. Seward.

[Translation.]

MEXICAN LEGATION TO THE UNITED STATES OF AMERICA,
Washington, October 24, 1865.

MR. SECRETARY: Referring to the notes which, under date 22d July last and 21st of September following, I addressed to your department, remittng copy of a decree of the Congress of Colombia, approved 2d May of this year, in which it is declared that the constitutional president of the Mexican republic "HAS DESERVED WELL OF AMERICA, for the abnegation and unconquerable perseverance with which he has defended the independence of his country," I have now the honor to enclose to you a copy of No. 114 of the official paper of the Mexican government of the 21st September last past, in which is published the autograph letter that the president of the republic of Colombia sent with said decree to the constitutional president of the Mexican republic, the reply of this functionary, and the notes exchanged on the same subject between the minister of foreign relations of both governments.

I gladly avail of the opportunity to renew to you, Mr. Secretary, the assurances of my most distinguished consideration.

M. ROMERO.

Hon. WILLIAM H. SEWARD, &c., &c., &c.

[Enclosure No. 1.—Translation.]

From the official paper of Chihuahua No. 114, September 21, 1865.

Manuel Murillo, president of the United States of Colombia, to his excellency Señor Benito Juarez, president of the United Mexican States:

GREAT AND GOOD FRIEND: I have the honor to remit to you, in duly authenticated copy, the decree of the 2d May last, passed by the Congress of the United States of Colombia in your honor.

In sending you this legislative act, testimonial of the respect and consideration with which your conduct has inspired the people and the government of Colombia, let me be allowed to express to you my own admiration of your virtues, and of the good example which you have given.

You will see in this decree a pledge of the sympathies that this people has maintained for yours, and the fraternal interest with which it has watched every one of your efforts in favor of the dignity and autonomy of the United Mexican States.

Accept, sir, the sentiments of distinguished consideration and respect with which I am your good friend,

M. MURILLO.

The Secretary of the Interior and of Foreign Relations,
ANTONIO DEL REAL.

Given at Bogota, June 15, 1865.

[Enclosure No. 2.—Reply.]

Benito Juarez, president of the United Mexican States, to his excellency Señor Manuel Murillo, president of the United States of Colombia:

GREAT AND GOOD FRIEND: With your letter of 15th June of this year you have pleased to send me a copy of the decree of 2d May last, passed by the Congress of the United States of Colombia, making declarations of its kind sentiments in my favor, and directing a portrait of me to be placed in the national library of that republic.

This honor which the Congress of Colombia has designed to do me I receive with so much the more gratitude the more I think I do not merit it. I have done nothing but my duty, which for the public functionary, as for the private citizen, is the most sacred in periods of disaster to the country.

Inspired by their kind feelings, the Congress of Colombia has deigned to regard my conduct with kindness, and I ask you to please to manifest to it the sincere expression of my respect and profound acknowledgments. In high degree I thank you also for your own sentiments, in which you have assured me at the same time of the sympathy and fraternal interest of the people and government of Colombia with the cause of the Mexican republic. My gratitude will be a new motive to me ever to make the sincerest prayers for your welfare, and for the increasing prosperity of the people and government of the United States of Colombia.

Deign to accept, sir, the very distinguished consideration and respect with which I am your good friend,

BENITO JUAREZ.

The minister of foreign relations,
[L. S.] S. LERDO DE TEJADA.
PASO DEL NORTE, *September* 9, 1865.

[Enclosure No. 3.—Translation.]

U. S. OF COLOMBIA, DEPARTMENT OF THE INTERIOR AND FOREIGN AFFAIRS,
Bogota, June 15, 1865.

The undersigned, secretary of the interior and foreign affairs of the United States of Colombia, has the honor to transmit to your excellency an authenticated copy of the autograph letter which the citizen president of this republic addresses, under this date, to the most excellent Señor Benito Juarez, president of the United States of Mexico, transcribing to him the decree issued by the national Congress on the 2d of May last, and in compliance with which the portrait of the most excellent Señor Juarez shall be preserved in the national library as a homage to his virtues, and an example to growing generations of Colombia.

The undersigned avails himself of this occasion to present to your excellency the assurances of the very high consideration with which he has the honor to be your excellency's obedient servant,

ANTONIO DEL REAL.

His Excellency the SECRETARY OF FOREIGN AFFAIRS
Of the United States of Mexico, &c., &c., &c.

[Enclosure No. 4.—Translation.]

MEXICAN REPUBLIC, DEPARTMENT OF FOREIGN AFFAIRS AND OF GOVERNMENT,
Paso del Norte, September 9, 1865.

The undersigned, minister for foreign affairs of the Mexican republic, has the honor to communicate to his excellency Señor Antonio del Real, the minister of the interior and foreign affairs of the United States of Colombia, that he has received his note of the 15th of June of this year, with which he was pleased to transmit to him a copy of the autograph letter, and the despatch which contained it, addressed by the most excellent señor president of Colombia to the citizen president of the Mexican republic, transmitting to him the decree of the 2d of May last, which the Congress of Colombia passed in his honor. At the same time the undersigned has the honor to transmit to his excellency Señor del Real an authenticated copy of the letter of reply, together with the despatch which contains it, addressed by the citizen president of this republic to the most excellent señor president of the United States of Colombia.

The undersigned avails himself of this occasion to protest to his excellency the señor minister of foreign affairs of Colombia the assurance of his most distinguished consideration.

S. LERDO DE TEJADA.

His Excellency Señor ANTONIO DEL REAL,
Minister of the Interior and of Foreign Affairs of the U. S. of Colombia, &c.

Mr. Hunter to Mr. Romero.

DEPARTMENT OF STATE,
Washington, January 24, 1866.

SIR: I have the honor to acknowledge the receipt of your communications of September 21 and October 24 last, with their several accompaniments, all of which have reference to the decree issued on the 2d of May, 1865, by the Congress of the United States of Colombia, in honor of Don Benito Juarez, the president of the republic of Mexico.

You will be pleased to accept my thanks for the information thus kindly communicated by you to this government, and to receive the assurances of my very distinguished consideration.

W. HUNTER, *Acting Secretary.*

Señor MATIAS ROMERO, *&c., &c., &c.,*
Washington, D. C.

Mr. Seward to Mr. Romero.

DEPARTMENT OF STATE,
Washington, October 17, 1864.

SIR: I have the honor to transmit to you a small box to the address of the "Citizen Benito Juarez, President of the United States of Mexico," and also a copy of the despatch from Mr. Kirk, the United States minister to the Argentine Republic, under date of the 14th April, 1863, with the correspondence accompanying the same, received at this department some time since.

This box is said to contain a medal for the late Mexican General Zaragoza, presented to him by the citizens of Montevideo.

The delay in its delivery to you has been occasioned by the fact of your temporary absence in Mexico, and the forgetfulness of the clerk then in charge of the South American bureau to call the attention of his successor to the fact of its receipt, and which I trust you will consider an apology for this apparent but really unintentional oversight.

I avail myself of this occasion to renew to you, sir, the assurances of my most distinguished consideration.

WILLIAM H. SEWARD.

Señor MATIAS ROMERO, *&c., &c., &c.,*
Washington, D. C.

[Enclosure No. 1.]

Mr. Kirk to Mr. Seward.

No. 20.]
LEGATION OF THE UNITED STATES,
Buenos Ayres, April 14, 1863.

SIR: This box contains a medal of some value from the citizens of Montevideo, to the address of the president of Mexico. The consul of the "Oriental republic" called to see me, and requested me to send it to the United States minister in Mexico. I suggested the propriety of sending it to Washington, to be given in charge of the Mexican minister; and agreeably to that suggestion you will confer a special favor by sending it to the minister, and by acknowledging the receipt of the same.

I have the honor to be your obedient servant,

ROBERT C. KIRK.

Hon. WILLIAM H. SEWARD,
Secretary of State, Washington, D. C.

[Enclosure No. 2.—Translation.—Private.]

YOUR HOUSE, *April* 13, 1863.

SIR OF MY DISTINGUISHED ESTEEM: Having transmitted to the knowledge of the interested the answer that you had the goodness to give to the request that was made by my conduct, of encharging you to give sure direction to a medal dedicated by the people of Montevideo to the (now deceased) Mexican General Zaragoza, that precious object has just been sent to me to be placed in your hands with the indicated purpose.

In virtue of this, I have the honor to remit you a small package wrapped with cloth, waxed, sealed with the seal of the Oriental republic, and addressed to the citizen Benito Juarez, president of the United States of Mexico, in which the medal is found.

It is very grateful to me to be obliged for the participation that you have taken in this business; and on making it in the name of the people of Montevideo, and very particularly in my own, I am happy that an occasion presents itself to be able to prove the sentiments of the sincere respect and high esteem with which I have the honor to subscribe myself your very humble servant, who kisses your hands,

MARIANO DE ESPINA,
Oriental Consul General.

ROBERT C. KIRK, Esq., *&c., &c., &c.*

P. S.—I have to beg you will please acknowledge receipt of all, so that I may be able to satisfy the interested parties.

[Enclosure No. 3.]

LEGATION OF THE UNITED STATES,
Buenos Ayres, April 14, 1863.

SIR: I have the honor to acknowledge the receipt of a small package containing a testimonial of friendship from the good people of Montevideo to the address of his excellency the president of Mexico, with the request to transmit the same to its destination.

It will gives me much pleasure to comply with the request. You can inform the donors that I shall have an opportunity this week to send it by my friend, Mr. C. F. Perry, to the Hon. William H. Seward, Secretary of State of the United States, with the request to send it to his excellency the Mexican minister, at Washington.

I have the honor to be, your obedient servant,

ROBERT C. KIRK.

MARIANO DE ESPINA, Esq.,
Oriental Consul General, &c., &c., &c.

Mr. Romero to Mr. Seward.

[Translation.]

MEXICAN LEGATION IN THE UNITED STATES OF AMERICA,
Washington, October 18, 1864.

MR. SECRETARY: I have had the honor to receive your note of yesterday, with accompanying documents, and a small box covered with linen and sealed with the seal of the "Oriental republic of Uruguay," and directed to "Citizen Benito Juarez, President of the United States of Mexico," in which is a medal that several citizens of Montevideo wish to present to the late General Zaragoza, of the Mexican army. This box was sent to your department by the United States minister at Buenos Ayres, to be sent to its address by my legation.

I will send a copy of your note, together with the box and accompanying documents, to the Mexican government by the first safe opportunity. Meantime I ask you to accept my grateful thanks for your kindness in conveying this precious present from the people of a sister republic to a distinguished Mexican, who died defending the independence of his country.

With exceeding pleasure I embrace this opportunity to renew to you, Mr. Secretary, the assurances of my most distinguished consideration.

M. ROMERO.

Hon. WILLIAM H. SEWARD, *&c., &c., &c.*

Mr. Romero to Mr. Seward.

[Translation.]

MEXICAN LEGATION IN THE UNITED STATES OF AMERICA,
Washington, November 30, 1864.

MR. SECRETARY: Not having had a channel in every respect safe to transmit to the city of Chihuahua, the present seat of the supreme government of the Mexican republic, the box which you were pleased to send to me, with your note of the 17th of October last past, which contained a medal which the citizens of Montevideo intended to present to General Zaragoza, of the Mexican army, and which, after the death of that general, they determined to send to the president of Mexico, I made up my mind to send it to Madame Dona Margarita Maza de Juarez, the wife of the president of the republic, and who now resides in the city of New York, that she might preserve it as a family relic, or send it to her husband by a safe channel, as she might think most proper. Mrs. Jaurez has informed me that she has decided to accept the second alternative.

Deeming it proper to inform the Oriental consul general in Buenos Ayres of these facts, so that through him the citizens of Montevideo, who contributed to the medal contained in the box referred to, may be made aware of its present whereabouts, I have written to the said consul the communication which I enclose herewith, opened, requesting you to do me the favor to transmit it to its destination, through Mr. Robert C. Kirk, minister resident of the United States to the Argentine Republic, through whom the said box was sent to me.

Anticipating my acknowledgments for the forwarding of the enclosed communication, I avail myself of the opportunity to renew to you, Mr. Secretary, the assurances of my most distinguished consideration.

M. ROMERO.

Hon. WILLIAM H. SEWARD, *&c., &c., &c.*

[Enclosure No. 1.—Translation.]

MEXICAN LEGATION IN THE UNITED STATES OF AMERICA,
Washington, November 17, 1864.

I have the honor of transmitting to your excellency a package covered with canvas, with the seal of the Oriental republic in wax upon it, and directed, "To Citizen Benito Juarez, President of the United States of Mexico." This package was sent to me by the Hon. William H. Seward, Secretary of State of the government of the United States, with a communication apologizing for not having delivered it to me before, because of the negligence of some clerk in his department. It seems from that communication, of which I enclose a copy, that the package contains a medal of value, awarded by the people of Montevideo to General Don Ygnacio Zaragoza; and on learning the fate of that illustrious Mexican, it was determined to send it to the President of our republic, as was done through the Hon. Mr. Kirk, United States minister at Buenos Ayres, who sent it to the Secretary of State. As I have no safe means of conveyance for such a treasure, valuable in many respects, to Chihuahua, I beg you to receive it, to be sent to the President by the first opportunity, or to be kept for your husband when you meet again, whichever you think best.

I also request you to send me any papers the package may contain for the government, that I may forward them to the proper address.

I take this occasion to express my particular consideration and distinguished esteem.

M. ROMERO.

Lady MARGARITA MAZA DE JUAREZ, *New York.*

[Enclosure No. 2.—Translation.]

NEW YORK, *November* 28, 1864.

I have received your kind communication of the 17th instant, with a package sealed and addressed to my husband, by the republic of Buenos Ayres, through the Hon. W. Seward.

I will try to send it to my husband by the first safe opportunity that offers.

Independence and the republic!

MARGARITA MAZA DE JUAREZ.

C. MATIAS ROMERO,
Minister Plenipotentiary of the Mexican Republic, Washington, D. C.

[Enclosure No. 3.—Translation.]

MEXICAN LEGATION IN THE UNITED STATES OF AMERICA,
Washington, November 30, 1864.

I have the honor of transmitting to you the copy of a note addressed to me on the 19th of October last by the Hon. William H. Seward, Secretary of State of the United States, with a box to citizen Benito Juarez, constitutional President of the United Mexican States, containing a medal awarded to General Zaragoza, of the Mexican army, by certain citizens of Montevideo. In this note you will find an explanation of the long delay, on the part of the Department of the United States, in the delivery of the box.

The present condition of Mexico, caused by the war now sustained by the republic against the French invasion, and the distance of the present site of the national government, prevent frequent and safe communication. For this reason, and not wishing to run the risk of having such a valuable present lost, I have determined to send it to Mrs. Margarita Maza de Juarez, wife of the citizen President of that republic, now in New York. I did this on the 17th instant, as you will see from an accompanying copy of my letter to that lady. I also enclose you a copy of her answer, in which you will see what disposition she intends to make of it; and thus ends my connexion with the affair.

I beg you to make known these facts to the citizens of Montevideo who subscribed for the medal, and assure them that the people of Mexico will never forget that proof of sympathy and consideration given by a kindred nation in the time of our greatest adversity.

With pleasure I accept this occasion of offering you, Mr. Consul, the assurances of my distinguished consideration

M. ROMERO.

Señor DON MARIANO ESPINOZA,
Consul General, Buenos Ayres.

Mr. Seward to Mr. Romero.

DEPARTMENT OF STATE,
Washington, December 2, 1864.

SIR: I have had the honor to receive your note of the 30th ultimo, in reference to the box containing a medal intended as a present to the late General Zaragoza, of the Mexican army, from the citizens of Montevideo, and advising me of the disposition you have made of said box since it came into your possession, in October last.

The letter which accompanied your note, addressed to the consul general of the Oriental republic of Montevideo, Don Mariano de Espinosa, will, as you request, be transmitted to its destination, through the minister of the United States accredited to the Argentine Republic, with instructions to deliver it to that gentleman.

I avail myself of the occasion to renew the assurances of my very distinguished consideration.

WILLIAM H. SEWARD.

Señor MATIAS ROMERO, *&c.*, *&c.*, *&c.*,
Washington, D. C.

Mr. Seward to Mr. Kirk.

[Extract.]

DEPARTMENT OF STATE,
Washington, December 5, 1864.

SIR: Your despatches, Nos. 72, 73, and 74, dated, respectively, August 20, 21, and 22, were received on the 9th ultimo.

* * * * * * * * *

The enclosed communication is from Señor Romero, the minister of Mexico, who requests that you will be pleased to hand it to Señor Don Mariano Espinosa, at Montevideo, and has reference to the medal presented by citizens of that place to General Zaragoza, of the Mexican army.

I am, sir, your obedient servant,

WILLIAM H. SEWARD.

ROBERT C. KIRK, Esq., *&c.*, *&c.*, *&c.*,
Argentine Republic.

(For enclosures see Mr. Romero's note of 30th November.)

Mr. Romero to Mr. Seward.

[Translation.]

MEXICAN LEGATION IN THE UNITED STATES OF AMERICA,
New York, August 21, 1865.

MR. SECRETARY: I have the honor to remit you, for the information of the government of the United States, a copy of a communication addressed to me, the 22d of July last, by Mr. E. Coremaux, president of the Netherduitsche League, in Antwerp, enclosing an address of the said association, directed to the constitutional president of the Mexican republic, expressing, in the name of the Belgian people, the sympathy of that nation for the cause of liberty and independence in Mexico, and the regret at the conduct of King Leopold, for family reasons, in aiding the Emperor of the French in his endeavors to subjugate that republic.

I also enclose a copy of the above-mentioned address, together with my reply to Mr Coremaux, of the 9th instant.

I am gratified for this opportunity of repeating to you, Mr. Secretary, the assurances of my most distinguished consideration.

M. ROMERO.

Hon. WILLIAM H. SEWARD, &c., &c., &c.

[Enclosure No. 1.]

ANTWERP, *July* 22, 1865.

SIR: Enclosed we beg to hand you an address to the president of the republic, the honorable B. Juarez, voted to him by one of the most influential political associations of this country.

Being aware how difficult it is, under the present circumstances, to transmit an address to the legal government of Mexico, we should feel happy if, by your kind intercession, our letter should come to the hands of your president.

We are, sir, your obedient servants,

E. COREMAUX, *President.*
WM. HAGENAER, *Secretary.*

Honorable MATIAS ROMERO,
Ambassador of the Mexican Republic at Washington.

[Enclosure No. 2.]

ANTWERP, *July* 14, 1865.

The Netherlands League, a Flemish democratic association, counting its members by thousands, at its last general meeting, the 26th of May last, almost unanimously decided to address you, as the only legal representative of the Mexican nation, to congratulate you on your persevering resistance against a foreign usurper who is trying to rob the Mexicans of their liberty and independence; and at the same time this association protests against the impudent assent of the Belgian government to the recruiting of troops for the service of a foreign usurper, thus intervening in the domestic affairs of Mexico, in violation of all international law and of the laws of Mexico.

This address was about to be written, when a painful piece of news was received, causing anxiety, mourning, and unspeakable anguish in hundreds of families. It was, that your forces, Mexican soldiers, fighting for their independence, had gained a bloody victory over those that are endeavoring, by force of arms, to make an Emperor for Mexico out of an Austrian archduke. Those who perished so horribly in Tacambaro were mostly our countrymen. This association joined in the general mourning, and would probably have postponed acting upon the resolution but for the conduct of the Belgian government, which is contrary to the national will. We urgently desire that an energetic protest by us may convince you and the Mexican people that the people of Belgium take no part in these unjust proceedings, and are therefore free from all responsibility.

You know, Mr. President, that sixteen hundred Belgian young men left their country for Mexico. The way in which the Belgian government favored this expedition is no secret to you or to any one. The recruiting agents made believe everywhere that our young men were going solely to serve as a guard to the so-called empress of Mexico, daughter to the King of Belgium; and these men, thus deceived, continued to enlist, without reflecting that they were going to uphold principles of tyranny and oppression. But the whole Belgian nation, excepting a few interested individuals, condemns the proceedings in this affair. The people of Belgium are lovers of liberty, as zealous as any others, and the independence they want for themselves they desire for other nations. Belgians understand and admire the heroic resistance made by the Mexicans to the usurper, and they do not doubt but the country will finally be freed from foreign rule. Such also are the wishes of this association; for you know, Mr. President, that the few bewildered sons of this country among the Hapsburg forces is no reason, and never will be, for free Belgians to give up their sympathy for the good cause of which you are the worthy representative. However much our government, entirely influenced by France, may do, it will never persuade the people to favor the cause of a foreign usurper. The Belgian nation heard with sorrow the news of Tacambaro, and felt the greatest indignation and anger, not at Mexicans fighting for their independence, but against the really guilty who induced the enlistment of our youth, through deception. Let them bear the blame, and may the justice they deserve be meted out to them. This address of a democratic association, made to you in the name of thousands of free Belgians, is a proof that our people take no part in the preference of their government for the cause of a foreign usurper. Belgians will always follow the example of their ancestors, who ever devotedly loved liberty and hated foreign dominion.

In the name of the association, the Netherland League.

E. COREMAUX, *President.*
WM. HAGENAER,
J. LECLERC,
Secretaries.

Señor JUAREZ,
President of the Mexican Republic.

True translation from the original.

JOS. REFSELS, *Sworn Interpreter.*
NEW YORK, *August* 21, 1865.

A true copy:

IGN'O MARISCAL, *Secretary.*

[Enclosure No. 3.]

MEXICAN LEGATION IN THE UNITED STATES OF AMERICA,
New York, August 9, 1865.

SIR: I had the honor of receiving to-day, in this city, the communication you were pleased to direct to me in Washington, dated the 22d of July last, enclosing an address of the Netherlands League, a political association of Belgium, of which you are the worthy president, directed to Señor Don Benito Juarez, constitutional president of the Mexican republic, requesting mé to forward it to its destination.

I have the honor of informing you, in answer, that the document will be sent to-morrow by safe channel to the city of Chihuahua, the present seat of the government of Mexico, and as soon as the acknowledgment of its reception reaches me I will transmit it to the association over which you preside.

Permit me to say that this spontaneous demonstration of a body that represents the true popular spirit in Belgium, as yours, cannot fail to be received in the most cordial manner by the government and people of Mexico, and will contribute greatly to maintain the amicable disposition of the government and people of Mexico towards the enlightened inhabitants of Belgium in spite of all that King Leopold has done to destroy the friendly feelings and change them into sentiments of open hostility.

I take this occasion to offer you the assurances of my distinguished consideration.

M. ROMERO.

Mr. E. COREMAUX,
President of the Netherlands League, at Antwerp, in Belgium.

[Enclosure No. 4.]

Belgian sympathy for the Mexican republican cause.

An Antwerp paper of June 14 *(Escaut)* contains the proceedings of the Netherlands League *(Het Nederduitsche Bond)* at their recent meeting. The following we translate from the speech of Mynheer Vleeschouwer:

What have we in common with Mexico? Much, gentlemen. Not long ago Mexico was still a free and independent state, with her own government and laws. We Belgians, a people equally independent and free, formed a treaty of friendship and commerce with Mexico. The Mexicans were then our allies, were our friends. But the Emperor of France cannot tolerate liberty or independence anywhere. Even beyond the ocean he endeavors to murder liberty. He sent an army to subjugate the free Mexican people. By force he has imposed an emperor, and the Mexicans are now bending under the yoke of a foreign tyranny.

And we, the sons of free Belgium, what shall we do while we contemplate the oppression of our allies and friends? Shall we raise the voice, protesting against the shameful violation of the law of nations? No, no; we do not. We are forbidden to do it because we are a neutral nation. Our neutrality is guaranteed to us by treaties. We must be faithful to our neutrality, that we may be respected by other nations. This is the reason why we have not protested. This is the reason why we could not protest. But we have done something else. We have not done it ourselves: our government has done it by abusing our name. * * *

Belgium must make war on Mexico because our princess is married to the tyrant of Mexico. Frankly, what may such a policy lead us to? If the crowned heads should agree some day (the crowned heads are capable of everything) to make a kingdom in Switzerland, and wished to place our Count of Flanders on the new throne, should we not be obliged also to send an army to secure the submission of the Swiss to the Count of Flanders? And when the little princesses have grown up, the daughters of the Count of Flanders, and it is desired to convert them into queens and empresses of the regions now ultramarine republics, would it be necessary for us also, at the command of a foreign prince, to go and place them by force on their new thrones? Naturally, we could not act otherwise. There is a precedent which may always be appealed to against us. We have sent troops to Mexico to protect the daughter of Leopold I. Then you cannot appeal to your neutrality to refuse to send troops to protect the daughter of Leopold II. And you wonder, oh ye sublime statesmen, that the people murmur and feel no confidence in the future. Why do you not wonder more that the nation has had so much patience, and has not derogated all by means of the elections? Because everything in the state has become a lie. The representatives of the people no longer represent the people. They are only humble servants of a government composed of foreigners.

After other remarks in the same style, the speaker moved an address to President Juarez, which was adopted, expressing the strongest sympathy with the Mexican patriot cause, deep regret that the Belgian troops have been employed to oppose it and declaring that they were enlisted under false pretences only as a guard for the princess, now called empress.

The Mexican Club have passed a vote of thanks to the Netherlands "bond," and addressed to them a very well-written letter, in which they say: "The Mexican people have always believed they had an ally and brother in the enlightened Belgian people, and they have been painfully surprised at seeing the Belgian flag united with the flags of France and Austria in an enterprise to destroy the republic, to erect upon its ruins a throne as abominable as that which in past time oppressed Mexico and Belgium; but they understand that the Belgian people are strangers to that crime; they know that it has been born of the weakness of a government which humbles itself before the tyrant of France."

Mr. Seward to Mr. Romero.

DEPARTMENT OF STATE,
Washington, November 7, 1865.

SIR: I have the honor to acknowledge the receipt of your note of the 21st of August, 1865, transmitting to me, for the information of the United States, a copy of a communication addressed to you on the 22d of July last by Mr. Coremaux, president of the Netherlands League, in Antwerp, enclosing an address of the said association, directed to the constitutional president of the Mexican republic, expressing, in the name of the Belgian people, the sympathy of that nation for the cause of the liberty and the independence of Mexico, and their regret at the conduct of King Leopold, who, for family reasons, is aiding the Emperor of the French in his efforts to subjugate that republic. You are also pleased to transmit to me a copy of the address of the Netherlands League to President Juarez, dated July 14, 1865, and of your reply to Mr. Coremaux, dated New York, August 9, 1865, acknowledging the same.

Thanking you for your courtesy, in communicating this interesting correspondence to the government of the United States, I avail myself of this opportunity to assure you of my very distinguished consideration.

WILLIAM H. SEWARD.

Señor MATIAS ROMERO, *&c., &c., &c.,*
Washington, D. C.

Mr. Romero to Mr. Seward.

[Translation.]

MEXICAN LEGATION IN THE UNITED STATES OF AMERICA,
Washington, November 1, 1865.

MR. SECRETARY: On the 21st of August last I sent a note to your department, with the address made by the "Nederduitsche Bond," a democratic society of Antwerp, the 14th of July last, to the constitutional President of the Mexican republic, expressing the sympathy of the Belgian people for the cause of liberty and independence in Mexico, and their regret to see King Leopold, through personal and family motives, assisting the Emperor of the French in his efforts to conquer that republic. I now have the honor of transmitting to you No. 115 of the official paper of the Mexican government, dated 28th September following, containing the reply to that address of Mr. Lerdo de Tejada, minister of foreign relations, on the 23d of the same month, in the name of the President, showing how the Mexicans regard the unjustifiable conduct of the King of the Belgians.

Before concluding this note, I think it convenient to transmit you, for the information of the government of the United States, the English copy of a note which I addressed to my government, the 14th of November, 1864, in regard to the policy of the Belgian government towards Mexico, and of the answer of the minister of foreign affairs of the 27th of January last; which documents were published in the official paper of the Mexican government, about the end of January last, and re-published in English by the New York papers.

I am pleased with this occasion to renew to you, Mr. Secretary, the assurances of my most distinguished consideration.

M. ROMERO.

Hon. WILLIAM H. SEWARD, *&c., &c., &c.*

[Enclosure No. 1.—Translation.]

From the official paper of Chihuahua No. 115, September 28, 1865.

MEXICAN REPUBLIC, DEP'T OF FOREIGN RELATIONS AND GOVERNMENT,
Paso del Norte, September 23, 1865.

SIR: The citizen President of the republic received your letter of the 14th June of this year, addressed to him in the name of the Nederduitsche Bond, of which you are the worthy president, by a resolution in general meeting, and forwarded by the minister of Mexico in Washington.

The President has seen from your letter that an important political and popular association of Belgium, such as the Nederduitsche Bond, counting many thousand members, has considered and recognized it just to protest, in the name of the free Belgians, against the conduct and acts of its government in recruiting troops to support the wicked and passing pretensions of a foreign usurpation and despotism in Mexico.

You regret rightly that deceived Belgians should come to shed their own blood and that of Mexicans only for the interest of a stranger or a stranger's wife; and this consideration is more serious when we reflect that a Hapsburg and Orleans blot out the remembrance of their humiliation and family ruin, and offer themselves as servile instruments to another foreign power, for the reward of an empty title and a little money.

Free Belgians should only shed their blood for Belgium; they must not spill it, like slaves, to foster the family interests of a master; nor can they sell it, like mercenaries, for a handful of gold, without a patriotic sentiment. You regret rightly that a few deluded Belgians should come to shed their blood for a stranger, or the wife of a stranger, who are themselves the submissive slaves of another foreign power.

The Belgian government violated the vaunted neutrality of Belgium, and contemned the laws prohibiting its citizens from enlisting in a foreign service, when it acted for the personal interest of the King's daughter, who ceased to be a Belgian as soon as she became a stranger's wife, and thought to act with impunity when it became the accomplice of a strong nation in the perpetration of a crime against a weaker one.

The duties of the Belgian government towards Mexico, against whom she has never had, or pretended to have, the slightest cause of complaint; the principle of the law of nations requiring every nation to respect the independence and sovereignty of every other; and the eternal maxims of morality, condemning a causeless war, in which the principal and his accomplices are responsible for all the deaths and destruction, murders and robberies—were all disregarded by the Belgian government when it thought to take advantage freely of the misfortunes of a feeble nation, and had a private family interest in partaking of the fruit of crime.

But it is commendable in Belgium, as well as honorable for the progress of civilization and liberty, that compunctions of conscience have raised the voices of many of her free citizens, causing them to rebel and protest against that iniquitous conduct.

The Mexican republic is pleased with this protest, even amid her misfortunes and the struggles she is sustaining, and will sustain to the end; and the citizen President charges me to request you to express to the Nederduitsche Bond his great appreciation of its just and worthy sentiments.

Accept, sir, the assurance of my respectful consideration.

S. LERDO DE TEJADA.

Mr. E. COREMAUX,
President of the Nederduitsche Bond of Antwerp.

[Enclosure No. 2.]

No. 290.] MEXICAN LEGATION, UNITED STATES OF AMERICA,
Washington, November 14, 1864.

The enlistment in Belgium of a legion for the support of Maximilian and his wife in Mexico has encountered opposition among the people and even in the legislature of that country.

There having been published many advertisements in which recruits were called for to be enlisted under the direction of a retired lieutenant general, and other officers of the Belgian army, the ministers were questioned in the House of Representatives with reference to the participation of the government in such an enterprise, and several of the ministers, among them the minister of war, denied that the administration aided directly or indirectly in the project; but they confessed, however, that they had permitted Belgian subjects to enter upon this expedition without losing for this reason their nationality.

It is worthy of attention that notwithstanding this explicit confession, and the fact, which is well known, that the volunteers were rendezvousing in the city of Audimad, in an edifice which was in part a public building, as also that in the advertisements it was stated that the government permitted officers of the army to enlist, granting them for this purpose two years' leave of absence, in order to return to the country and still hold their positions if it did not suit them to remain in Mexico—it is worthy of attention, I repeat, that notwithstanding all this, the House of Deputies was apparently satisfied with the declarations of the ministers, and, taking note of the same, without further examination of the matter, passed to the order of the day, although not without several deputies manifesting their reprobation of all connected with the projected Belgian legion for Mexico.

A little before there had been in Brussels a meeting of the citizens, which condemned in energetic terms the enlistments alluded to, calling the attention of the Chambers to the same, and publishing in placards the resolutions they adopted with reference to the matter.

There have also been published two important pamphlets, which I have seen—the one entitled "The Belgian Expedition to Mexico—Appeal to the Chambers;" and the other, "General Chapellé—the Belgian Expedition to Mexico, and article 92 of the final code." Both are very well written, and are by distinguished members of the bar in Brussels.

In the first—after an impartial historical *résumé* of Mexico since the convention of London of October 31, 1861—it is demonstrated that the Belgian government, in its conduct with respect to the said expedition, has given offence to our country, and violated the neutrality which Belgium is always bound to observe with respect to all nations, in conformity with its political constitution.

By such conduct, says Mr. Demeur, Belgium has lost the right to invoke in the future that neutrality which is its principal protection, and has not only incurred the enmity of a feeble republic, such as Mexico will be for some time, but also that of the United States, which latter fact may have consequences the most ruinous.

The second pamphlet, written by Mr. Van Don Kerkoor, is a powerful demonstration by legal argument that the enlistments for Mexico, without previous and express authorization of the Belgian government, constitute a grave crime, that the penal code of that country punishes with death. It concludes with a vehement appeal to the attorney general, to whom the pamphlet is addressed, to indict and bring to trial the Lieutenant General Chapellé and his accomplices.

As soon as I have a secure opportunity, which I expect will be very soon, I will remit to the department both pamphlets.

I renew to you the assurances of my distinguished consideration.

M. ROMERO.

The CITIZEN MINISTER OF FOREIGN RELATIONS, *Chihuahua.*

[Enclosure No. 3.]

No. 86.] DEPARTMENT OF FOREIGN AFFAIRS AND OF GOVERNMENT,
National Palace, Chihuahua, January 27, 1865.

By your note No. 290 of the 14th of November last, the President has been informed of what you communicate with reference to the enlistments that have been taking place in Belgium for the purpose of forming a legion for the support in Mexico of the Archduke Maximilian and his wife, the daughter of King Leopold of Belgium.

There may be added to the observations you make with reference to this affair the fact that that government has never alleged, nor has it pretended, to have the slightest motive of complaint against the Mexican republic. Notwithstanding this, King Leopold has sought to take advantage of the misfortunes of a nation that has never done him an injury, and for the private interest of favoring his daughter, he has sought to give her the support of mercenary soldiers, whose purpose is to aid in overpowering the Mexicans and to shed still more the blood of a people who defend their independence and their liberty.

It is not strange, therefore, that King Keopold, from solely a private family interest, has been willing also to set aside the precepts of the constitution and the interests and the opinions of the people whom he governs.

I assure you of my most attentive consideration.

LERDO DE TEJADA.

The Citizen MATIAS ROMERO,
Envoy Extraordinary and Minister Plenipotentiary of the Mexican Republic in Washington.

Mr. Hunter to Mr. Romero.

DEPARTMENT OF STATE,
Washington, January 25, 1866.

SIR: I have the honor to acknowledge the receipt of your communication of the 1st November ultimo, with its three enclosures, consisting of the letters of Señor Lerdo de Tejada, the minister for foreign affairs of Mexico, to Mr. Coremaux, president of the "Nederduitsche Bond," of Antwerp, dated September 23d last, expressive of the appreciation of the Mexican government and people for the kind sympathies extended to them by that association in their letter to President Juarez, of the 14th of July last; also, of copies of your correspondence with Señor Lerdo de Tejada, in regard to the policy of the Belgian government towards Mexico, dated November 14, 1864, and January 27, 1865.

Thanking you for your attention in communicating these papers to this government, I have the honor to tender to you, sir, the assurance of my highest consideration.

W. HUNTER,
Acting Secretary.

Señor MATIAS ROMERO, *&c., &c., &c.,*
Washington, D. C.

Mr. Romero to Mr. Seward.

[Translation.]

MEXICAN LEGATION IN THE UNITED STATES OF AMERICA,
Washington, October 20, 1865.

MR. SECRETARY: As a proof of the feelings of the Belgian people in regard to the question now debating on Mexican soil, I have the honor of transmitting to you, for the information of the government of the United States, a copy of a communication I received from the Liberal Union of the Civic Guard of Liege, dated the 11th of August last, together with a copy of the resolutions passed the day before by that association, protesting against the proposal of Lieutenant General Pletincks, commander of the Civic Guard of Brussels, to erect a monument to the memory of the Belgians who fell in action at Tacambaro, in the Mexican republic, on the 11th of April, 1865, "because they lost their lives in a cause opposed to liberty, and in contradiction to the efforts the Belgians made in 1830 to gain their independence."

I also enclose a copy of those resolutions.

I accept this opportunity to renew to you, Mr. Secretary, the assurance of my very distinguished consideration.

M. ROMERO.

Hon. WILLIAM H. SEWARD, *&c., &c., &c.*

[Enclosure No. 1.]

LIBERAL UNION OF THE CIVIC GUARD OF LIEGE,
Liege, August 11, 1865.

SIR: We have the honor of transmitting to you, by another source, a copy of the deliberations of our association on the tenth of this month, and we respectfully request you to have them sent to the government of the Mexican republic.

Accept our distinguished regards.

The President, L. J. J. LEFEVRE.
The Secretary, G. CLERMONT.

The Secretary, G. CLERMONT.

Mr. MATIAS ROMERO,
Minister of the Mexican Republic in Washington.

[Enclosure No. 2.]

LIBERAL UNION OF THE CIVIC GUARD OF LIEGE.

The Liberal Union of the Civic Guard in general assembly convened, on the 10th of August, 1865, adopted the following resolutions:

Whereas Lieutenant General Pletincks, commander of the Civic Guard of Brussels, in a letter of the 1st of August, asked the concurrence of the civil militia in the erection of a monument destined to preserve the memory of the Belgians killed at Tacambaro; and

Whereas, although our fellow-citizens displayed incontestible courage and bravery, it is not less true that the cause for which they gave their lives is anti-liberal, and contrary to the efforts the Belgians made in 1830 to gain their independence; and

Whereas the Civic Guard, as protectors of democratic and constitutional institutions, cannot join in a manifestation that tends to glorify the subjugation of a nation:

Therefore, *The Liberal Union* protests against the idea of General Pletincks, and advises all the civic guards in the kingdom to reject it.

A true extract. By the committee:

The President, L. J. J. LEFEVRE.
Corporation Counsellor of the City of Liege.

The Secretary, G. CLERMONT,
Lieutenant, Quartermaster of the Third Battalion of the Civic Guard of Liege.

Mr. Hunter to Mr. Romero.

DEPARTMENT OF STATE,
Washington, January 24, 1866.

SIR: I have the honor to acknowledge the receipt of your note of the 20th of October last, transmitting, for the information of the government of the United States, a copy of a letter addressed to you by the Liberal Union of the Civic Guard of Liege, dated August 11, 1865, and also a copy of the resolutions adopted by that association on the 10th of the same month, in which the sentiment of the Belgian people in regard to the question now being debated on the soil of Mexico is manifested.

You will be pleased to accept my thanks for your courtesy in communicating these interesting papers to this department, while I avail myself of the occasion to renew to you, sir, the assurances of my very distinguished consideration.

W. HUNTER,
Acting Secretary.

Señor MATIAS ROMERO, *&c., &c., &c.,*
Washington, D. C.

THE IMPERIAL MEXICAN EXPRESS COMPANY IN NEW YORK.

Mr. Romero to Mr. Seward.

[Translation.]

MEXICAN LEGATION IN THE UNITED STATES OF AMERICA,
Washington, October 27, 1865.

MR. SECRETARY: It having come to my notice that the adventurer called Don Fernando Maximilian, of Hapsburg, who was Archduke of Austria, and who now pretends to exercise public authority in Mexico by right of conquest, has granted some so-called privileges to persons of this country, or who have come to it, to form here companies for the purpose of carrying them into effect, and that these persons assert, to gain buyers of shares, that the said privileges have been or will be sanctioned by the constitutional President of the Mexican republic, for which they have not the slightest foundation, it seemed proper to me, for the purpose of protecting the citizens of this country, who in good faith, and under that mistaken impression, might desire to take shares in such speculations, to recommend that the consul general of Mexico, in the United States, resident in New York, should make known to the public that it was not certain that the constitutional government of Mexico was disposed to sanction these grants, and sending to him the laws of the Mexican congress and the dispositions of the executive which declare null and void the acts of the invader. I have the honor to enclose to you copy, in English, of the note which, for this purpose, I addressed, under date of 18th current, to the consul of the Mexican republic at New York, accompanied by the dispositions which are quoted in it, (No. 1.) That functionary caused those dispositions to be published in the New York papers of the 23d instant, with the letter, of which I also enclose copy, in English, (No. 2.) On the same 23d day Mr. E. De Courcillon, titular president of the Mexican Express Company, formed in virtue of one of the spurious grants of the usurper, addressed to me the letter, of which I also enclose copy, (No. 3,) sending me a copy of that which, on the same date, he addressed to the New York press, (No. 4,) and another of the prospectus of his company, (No. 5.) I also send these two documents. To said letter I replied, on the 24th, in the terms you will see in the copy of my reply, which I also enclose, (No. 6.) The Mexican consul at New York replied, at the same date, to Mr. De Courcillon in the manner which appears in the copy annexed of his letter to the Herald of that city, (No. 7.)

I believe it to be my duty also to communicate to you, for the information of the government of the United States, the facts and documents to which I have made reference, to call your attention to an important point, which may affect not only the good relations which happily exist between the government of the Mexican republic and the United States, but even the duties which belong to this government as a neutral in respect to Mexico.

In my letter to Mr. de Courcillon, (No. 6,) in that of the consul of Mexico to the Herald at New York, (No. 7,) and in the memorandum which I transmit of the concession, so-called, of the usurper, (No. 8,) you will see that the company engages to transport all material of warfare of the invading army of Mexico. The reading of the prospectus of the company (No. 5) demonstrates this more plainly. Of the five agents the company has, there is one only in Europe, and he resides at St. Nazaire, which, as you know, is that port of France from which issues the material for war which the Emperor of the French sends to his forces in Mexico, and for which the French government has established a line of steamers between said port and Vera Cruz. Of the other four agents of the company, one resides at Vera Cruz, and the other at the city of Mexico, which are the stations held to prepare forcibly the material of war destined for the conquest of Mexico.

In article 7 of the so-called concession of the usurper (No. 8) you will see also that the agents of the company in Mexico, as well as abroad, are official agents authorized for colonization, and in that will be subject to the orders and instructions to one of the so-called ministers of the same usurper. The colonization which is here treated of is, as I have shown to your department in my notes of the 5th and 20th instant, eminently hostile to the United States as it is intended to be of citizens of the south who do not submit themselves to the authority of this government, and to whom invitations are held out to go to Mexico with their slaves, there to reorganize under the shadow of France. The president and the members of the junta of colonization established by the usurper are declared enemies of the United States, as I have shown to the department.

It is very satisfactory to me to avail of this opportunity to renew to you, Mr. Secretary, the assurances of my distinguished consideration.

M. ROMERO.

Hon. WILLIAM H. SEWARD, *&c.*, *&c.*, *&c.*

[Enclosure No. 1.]

MEXICAN LEGATION IN THE UNITED STATES OF AMERICA,
Washington, October 18, 1865.

It having come to my knowledge that certain speculators of this country have obtained pretended concessions from the French agents in Mexico—that is to say, from the so-called imperial government of Maximilian—for the establishment of an express company, proposed to be styled the "Imperial Mexican Express;" of a suburban railroad in the city of Mexico; of a line of steamers in the Gulf of Mexico, and another on the Pacific; of various lines of telegraph; to carry forward a contract for the survey of lands in the State of Sonora, and another with reference to lands and mines in Chihuahua, together with various projects of colonization in different parts of the Mexican republic; having also learned that the speculators to whom I refer, in order to induce persons of good faith to take part with them in such enterprises, have asserted that their so-called concessions will be ratified or hereafter respected by the national government of the republic, and there being not the slightest foundation for such assertions, I have to request you, in order that no one may be deceived, to cause to be published the annexed dispositions of the congress and of the supreme government of Mexico, which declare null and void and of no effect all acts of the usurping authorities.

I have also to add, that the sole fact of having so far recognized the said usurping authorities as to accept or solicit privileges or concessions from them, will be a circumstance which will not only redound to the prejudice and disability of all parties accepting or soliciting such concessions in any transaction which they may hereafter desire to have with the legitimate authorities of the republic, but will also subject them to all the responsibilities and penalties prescribed by law.

I renew to you the assurances of my consideration.

M. ROMERO.

The CONSUL GENERAL *of the Mexican Republic, New York.*

Decree of the Congress in Mexico.

[Translation.]

DEPARTMENT OF GOVERNMENT.

The citizen President of the republic has been pleased to direct to me the following decree:

Benito Juarez, constitutional President of the United Mexican States, to the inhabitants of the same:

Be it known that the congress of the Union has thought proper to decree the following:

ART. 1. The acts of the so-called authorities, imposed by the invaders and traitors, or which they may hereafter establish in the republic, are null and void, and can never be in any way approved.

ART. 2. All contracts celebrated by the said so-called authorities, or that may hereafter be celebrated, are also null and void; and all who take part in the same will incur civil responsibility, in addition to the criminal responsibility already prescribed by the laws now in force; and such contracts can never be regarded in any manner or taken into consideration by the supreme government of the republic.

ART. 3. The traitors cannot be considered under any aspect in the treaties which the government may celebrate with France.

Dated in the hall of sessions of the congress of the Union, in Mexico, the 13th of December, 1862.

PONCIANO ARRIAGA, *Vice-President.*

FELIX ROMERO, *Deputy Secretary.*
FRANCISCO BUSTAMENTE, *Deputy Secretary.*

Wherefore, I order that it be printed, published, circulated, and duly observed.

BENITO JUAREZ.

NATIONAL PALACE OF MEXICO, *December* 13, 1862.

To the citizen JUAN ANTONIO DE LA FUENTE, minister of foreign relations and of government:

I communicate the same to you for your intelligence and the consequent ends. Liberty and reform!

FUENTE.

MEXICO, *December* 14, 1862.
To the Citizen GOVERNOR *of the federal district.*

Circular from the Minister of Foreign Affairs.

[Translation.]

DEPARTMENT OF FOREIGN RELATIONS AND OF GOVERNMENT.

* * * * * * * * * *

The law of nations, in treating of *de facto* governments, presumes that they really exist, but it is an evident fact that the spurious authorities imposed by Napoleon III on the people now held or hereafter to be held in subjection by them are not and cannot be the government of the country, and much less when the legitimate government exists in reality. So much for the law of nations.

Now, as far as concerns our public law, those false authorities are nothing better than seditious and treasonable. Wherefore, the chief magistrate commands me so to declare and to protest, as in his name I do protest, that the republic does not and will not recognize in these supposed functionaries any power or authority whatever to bind it by their treaties, agreements, or promises, by their acts, omissions, or other means or manner whatsoever; and that those who execute any authority or commission conferred or consented to by the French will most assuredly be punished in accordance with the laws of the country.

Please to accept the assurance of my consideration and esteem.

Liberty and reform! FUENTE.

SAN LUIS POTOSI, *June* 10, 1863.

Protest of the permanent deputation of Congress.

[Translation.]

* * * * * * * * * * *

The permanent deputation, in the name of the congress of the Union, and as the faithful interpreter of the national sentiment so energetically and universally manifested, believes that it fulfils a most solemn obligation in reproducing, as by these presents it does reproduce, all the declarations and protests before made by the sovereign congress itself, by the executive, and by the other legitimate and loyal authorities of the country—declarations which disavow and declare null and of no effect, as against the sovereignty of the Mexican people, and without force or legal value, all acts done or which may be done by virtue of the power or under the influence of the foreign invader; and it declares that, in the constitutional orbit of its functions, remaining always at the side of the government which the nation, in the exercise of its sovereign will, manifested in conformity with its organic law, has freely established, until the next session of the national assembly shall take place, it will co-operate with all the energy and self-devotion inspired by patriotism in repelling force by force, and in using every means to disconcert and defeat the machinations of treason and of conquest, in order to maintain secure the independence, the sovereignty, the laws, and the perfect freedom of the republic.

FRANCISCO ZARCO, *President.*

IGNACIO POMBO, *Deputy Secretary.*
SIMON DE LA GARZA Y MELO, *Deputy Secretary.*

SAN LUIS POTOSI, *July* 22, 1863.

Letter from the Minister of Foreign Affairs.

[Translation.]

DEPARTMENT OF FOREIGN RELATIONS AND OF GOVERNMENT,
Chihuahua, March 23, 1865.

In the copy annexed to your note, No. 31, of February 6, of this year, the citizen President of the republic has seen the protest which you communicated under the same date to the honorable Secretary of State of the United States with reference to the report that the French government had resolved to order its agent, Maximilian, to sign a pretended cession of a large part of the territory of the Mexican republic.

The President approves your conduct, although in this matter the republic has already protested from the beginning, by means of its legitimate organs and of all its constituted authorities, against all the acts and consequences of the foreign invasion.

Neither the republic nor its government can ever be holden for the acts of the French agent Maximilian, whose only title to authority is that lent to him by the presence of the armed forces of France, and who could not sustain himself in Mexico for a single day without the support of foreign bayonets. * * * * *

I renew to you my attentive consideration.

LERDO DE TEJADA.

Citizen MATIAS ROMERO, *Envoy Extraordinary, &c., &c., &c.*

[Enclosure No. 2.]

CONSULATE GENERAL OF MEXICO,
New York, October 20, 1865.

To the Editor of the Herald:

For the information of the public, and in order to protect capitalists of this country against the misrepresentations of persons interested in sustaining the usurped authority of Maximilian, I have to ask the favor that you will publish in your columns the enclosed official communication from the Mexican minister, and annexed dispositions of the Mexican government, which declare null and void all acts or concessions emanating from the so-called imperial authorities now attempting to exercise power in Mexico, under the support lent to them by the protection of foreign bayonets, and which subject all persons lending aid and countenance to such usurping authorities to all the perils and penalties usual under such circumstances upon the restoration of the legitimate authority of the country.

I am, sir, very respectfully, your obedient servant,

J. N. NAVARRO, *Mexican Consul General.*

[Enclosure No. 3.]

OFFICE OF THE MEXICAN EXPRESS COMPANY,
No. 5 New Street, New York, October 23, 1865.

SIR: The New York journals of this morning contain your correspondence with Mr. Navarro, Mexican consul general, relating, among other matters, to the Mexican Express Company, with which we have the honor to be connected. It was our intention to have called upon you ere this in reference to the formation of this express company, but we were not able to do so. Our regret that we were not able to do so is increased by your correspondence with Mr. Navarro. We enclose to you a copy of a letter which has been addressed by us to the editors of the journals in which your correspondence appeared. The enclosure states the facts as represented to and believed to be true by the gentlemen who have become interested in the Mexican Express Company.

We did not and do not suppose that any American or Mexican citizen, having the interest of Mexico at heart, would object to having Mexico brought nearer to the United States by the formation of a company, composed of American citizens, for the purpose of facilitating commercial intercourse between Mexico and the United States. We fail to perceive how such a company, if organized in good faith, and prosecuting its business with enterprise, can be the subject of animadversion.

To assure you of the good faith of the company we enclose to you one of its prospectuses. We will afford to you such further explanations as you may desire; and we are authorized to state that any gentlemen in whom you have confidence may become shareholders in the company, upon the same terms as those who are publicly solicited to take an interest in it.

The enterprise and capacity of the company require time and effort for their development. The future will afford the time, and to accompany it by the proper efforts will be the undertaking of the company.

We trust that you will receive this letter in the same frank spirit which has dictated it, and that it will no longer seem improper to you that American capital and energy should be employed in developing the resources of Mexico.

We are, with great respect, your excellency's obedient servants,

By order of the board of trustees:

E. DE COURCILLON, *President.*
L. LE COUTEULX, *Agent, N. Y.*

His Excellency Señor ROMERO,
Mexican Minister Resident at Washington.

[Enclosure No. 4.]

To the Editor of the World:

SIR: I observe in your journal of this morning an article purporting to be signed by Señor Romero, as Mexican minister at Washington. Señor Romero states that it has come to his knowledge that "certain *speculators*" of this country have obtained pretended concessions from the French agents in Mexico,—that is to say, from the so-called imperial government of Maximilian—for the establishment of an express company, proposed to be styled the "Imperial Mexican Express," and that, in order that no one may be deceived, Señor Romero requests the publication of certain Mexican decrees made in December, 1862, and June and July, 1863.

In answer to so much of Señor Romero's article as relates to the express company now being formed for the transaction of express business between the United States and Mexico, I have to state, that in the month of May last Maximilian was pleased to grant to myself, and to such persons, American citizens, as might become associated with me, an exclusive privilege of carrying on an express business between Mexico and the United States, and guaranteeing, so far as he could do so, protection to the company and its business. After the grant of this decree I had an interview with President Juarez in Chihuahua, in which I stated to him, with entire frankness, that I had obtained a decree from Maximilian for the purpose of forming an express company to transact business between Mexico, the United States, and elsewhere, and that I proposed to interest therein American citizens and American capital. President Juarez advised me that he had no objection to the formation of such a company as I proposed, and that it was then and always had been his desire, knowing, as he supposed, the wishes and desires of the American people in regard to the form of government to prevail in Mexico, to have American citizens and American capital permanently transferred to Mexico. He remarked that this was the common-sense view of the matter, and that, certainly, there could be no objection to having American capital invested in Mexico for the purpose o conducting an express business.

I repeated these assurances from President Juarez to gentlemen in New York who have become interested with me in the formation of a Mexican express company. These gentlemen are too well known in the city of New York and in the United States, in connexion with expresses already in successful operation, to need any defence against a charge of "speculators."

I have sent copies of this letter to Mr. Navarro, Mexican consul, and to Señor Romero.

I am, very respectfully, your obedient servant,

EUGENE DE COURCILLON,
President of the Mexican Express Company.

No. 5 New Street, NEW YORK, *October* 23, 1865.

[Enclosure No. 5.]

Prospectus of the Mexican Express Company, organized October 10, 1865; *capital,* $2,000,000: *shares,* $100 *each.*

Trustees.—E. de Courcillon, city of Mexico; I. I. Hayes, 416 Broadway, New York; Clarence A. Seward, 29 Nassau street, New York; Henry Sanford, 59 Broadway, New York; L. W. Winchester, 65 Broadway, New York; Peter A. Hargous, 8 Pine street, New York; Henry B. Plant, Augusta, Georgia; John Hoey, 59 Broadway, New York; B. Haynes, San Francisco, California; Henry R. Morgan, 24 Broadway, New York; I. C. Babcock, 59 Broadway, New York.

President.—E. de Courcillon.

Vice-President.—I. I. Hayes.

Treasurer.—J. C. Babcock.

Secretary.—C. A. Seward.

Counsel of the company.—Blatchford, Seward & Griswold.

Agents.—Louis Le Couteulx, New York; J. P. Nourse, San Francisco, California; W. L. Benfield, Mexico; G. Guichene, Vera Cruz; Detroyat, St. Nazaire, France.

MEXICAN EXPRESS COMPANY.

The Mexican Express Company is organized under the laws of the State of New York, in conformity with a grant from the Mexican government. This grant is, in substance, as follows:

The company is exclusively authorized to carry on the express business throughout Mexico, and between Mexico and the United States and Europe. The government grants to the company the exclusive privilege of carrying mailable matter, and also of transporting all government property. It gives to the company the right to demand and obtain a military escort, when required, to fix its own tariffs, and to import all materials necessary for the express, free of duties. It also grants to the company the privilege of colonization, and the company's agents are recognized as official agents of colonization. It appropriates to the company, free of cost, four leagues of land, with the privilege of taking up, for the use of colonists, any of the unoccupied public lands, at a cost not exceeding one dollar per acre. The colonists, under the patronage of the company, are privileged to import all materials for their own use, free of duties.

The object had in view by the Mexican government in conceding these liberal privileges is to invite to the country American capital and energy, and it cannot be denied that the grant is very valuable. The banking and exchange business, and the transportation of specie and bullion from the city of Mexico, Guanhato, &c., and the mining districts, will be very large, while the distribution of imported articles of every kind throughout the country will furnish business only limited by the resources of the company.

The company will be patronized to the fullest extent by the Mexican government and people, and every facility will be afforded, consistent with the laws, for the transaction of its business. The faith of the government is pledged to protect the company's interest, and the merchants and citizens generally have signified their appreciation of the advantages to be derived from its successful working, and have proffered their co-operation. The business of the company is indeed ready made, and its immediate success is secured. Both government and people being united in their efforts to promote its organization and working, gives the strongest assurance that it is greatly needed.

The company will commence business at once, with a capital stock of two millions of dollars, one million of which will be sold, and the proceeds appropriated as a working capital. Only twenty per cent. of this will be required on subscription, and not more than ten per cent., in addition, will be called for within six months thereafter. This will furnish ample funds for placing the company in successful working order. Thirty days' notice will be given of any assessment. In the event of more capital being needed, as the business of the company is extended, the board of trustees have power, under the articles of association, to increase it as the necessities of the case may require, by their giving thirty days' notice to the original stockholders.

The books for subscription to the capital stock of the company are open at the banking office of Wilmerding, Cornwell & Heckscher, No. 5 New street, New York, where full explanations will be given by the undersigned.

I. I. HAYES, *Vice-President.*

[Enclosure No. 6.]

Unofficial.] WASHINGTON, *October*, 24, 1865.

SIR: Your favor of yesterday, relating to my correspondence with the consul general of Mexico in the United States, in regard to certain so-called grants given by the usurper of Mexico, and enclosing a copy of your letter to the press on that subject, has been received. I will answer it, in an unofficial manner, in the same frank spirit you say has dictated yours.

If you are an American citizen, and have at heart the broad interest of this continent, chiefly represented by the United States, I confess that I cannot understand why you, in your capacity of an American citizen, should so far recognize Maximilian as to ask for and receive grants from him, as if he represented the national authority of Mexico, and should afterwards organize a company in the leading city of this country of prominent and influential American citizens, which must, by necessity, give their support and throw all the weight of their influence towards the subjugation and enslavement of Mexico, and the consequent humiliation of their own country.

I confess that I cannot, either, understand how American capital transferred to Mexico, under the French and Maximilian, will be a support for the independent cause in that country. Were that so, the best policy for the United States, if they wish to defend the Mexican nationality and republican institutions on this continent, would have been to recognize at once Maximilian and establish friendly relations with him.

It has never seemed improper to me, sir, that American capital and American energy should be employed in developing the resources of Mexico, nor that companies composed of American citizens for the purpose of facilitating commercial intercourse between Mexico and the United States should be established. In several addresses that I have made in this country, all of which have been published, I have advocated that policy, not as my own only, but as the policy of the national government of Mexico. It is not generally known in this country that the present French intervention in Mexico has been due, in a great measure, to the very desire of the Mexican government of developing the country with American skill and capital, to the great regard it felt for the United States as a people, and to a wish to imitate their wonderful career by following in their footsteps. The French Emperor went to Mexico to overthrow the very government which was American at heart, and openly avowed that in doing so he intended to check the progress of the United States.

If Maximilian, who is, and has been, by his position, without will of his own, and reflecting only the Napoleonic policy, pretends now to encourage Americans to develop Mexico, his object is a very clear one, and that only to obtain support in this country, disappointing finally such persons as may in good faith accept his grants, even in case he could remain there long enough to have them developed.

I am sure there was some misunderstanding in what you state was your conversation with President Juarez on the subject of your company under Maximilan's grants. The President of Mexico is too much in earnest in the present war, too patriotic a man, and he has too much common sense, to encourage in any way an enterprise calculated to give aid and comfort to the enemies of his country with whom he is at war. Besides, he could not forget himself so far as to set aside the laws of Congress and his own, and recent official declarations on this subject. He will be, I am sure, as much surprised as I have been when he hears that his name has been used to induce American capitalists to embark in an enterprise which, of necessity, is, and cannot but be, inimical to himself and to his country.

There is another feature in your company which makes it still more inimical to the national cause of Mexico. According to article 1st of Maximilian's grants, and to article 1st of the first contract you signed with his so-called minister of fomento, your company "*binds itself to transport all the material of war of Maximilian* with a reduction of ten per cent. upon the prices adopted for the public," and by that provision you not only give moral aid and support to the invaders of Mexico, but also an effective material aid.

I am sorry I cannot avail myself of the opportunity to try the good faith of your company, by accepting the shares you kindly offer me for those persons in whom I have confidence and may designate, "to become shareholders of your company upon the same terms as those who are publicly solicited to take an interest in it." My duty and my sense of honor, besides other considerations of decorum and propriety, forbid me from aiding in any way an undertaking which I am sorry I cannot see in other light but as inimical to my country.

The French Emperor and his agents in Mexico, representing conquest and Cæsarism, are avowed and open enemies of the republic of Mexico and its defenders, representing American nationality and republican institutions. If you have been acting in good faith with the invaders, you certainly cannot be friendly to the republic; and, *vice versa*, if you act in good faith with the republic, you certainly cannot be a friend of Maximilian. It is for you to decide which is the wisest course to follow, but in either case you must accept the consequences.

I am, sir, very respectfully, your most obedient servant,

M. ROMERO.

E. DE COURCILLON, Esq., *New York City.*

[Enclosure No. 7.]

CONSULADO GENERAL DE LA REPUBLICA MEJICANA EN LOS ESTADOS UNIDOS,
New York, October 24, 1865.

To the Editor of the Herald:

Mr. Eugene de Courcillon, who signs himself "president of the Mexican Express Company," has addressed to me a communication, under date of yesterday, which I see also appears in your columns of this morning. I have to ask the renewed favor of the courtesy at your hands of space for a few words in reply.

Mr. de Courcillon states in his communication that in the month of May last Maximilian was pleased to grant to him and such persons (American citizens) as might become associated with him an exclusive privilege for carrying on an express business between Mexico and the United States, and guaranteeing, so far as he could do so, protection to the company and its business; that after the grant of this decree he had an interview with President Juarez in Chihuahua, in which he stated to him with entire frankness that he had obtained a decree from Maximilian for the purpose of forming an express company to transact business between Mexico, the United States, and elsewhere, and that he proposed to interest therein American citizens and American capital; that President Juarez advised him that he had no objection to the formation of such a company as he proposed, and that it was then and always had been his desire, knowing, as he supposed, the wishes and desires of the American people in regard to the form of government to prevail in Mexico, to have American citizens and American capital permanently transferred to Mexico; and that President Juarez remarked that this was the common-sense view of the matter, and that certainly there could be no objection to having American capital invested in Mexico for the purpose of conducting an express business.

These statements which I have quoted show very clearly the position of the "Mexican Express Company." They prove too much to be satisfactory either to President Juarez or to Maximilian.

It seems that after having obtained his grant from Maximilian, whom he fails to style "emperor," feeling somewhat doubtful about the future validity of concessions in Mexico from an Austrian archduke, he proceeded to "have an interview with President Juarez." What was the necessity or even propriety of this "interview," if Maximilian was and is to continue to be the government of Mexico? In this interview President Juarez advised him that it was then, and always had been, his desire to have American citizens and American capital permanently transferred to Mexico, and that there could be no objection to having American capital invested in Mexico for the purpose of conducting an express business. This is undoubtedly true. President Juarez has always been favorable to the introduction of American capital and American enterprise into Mexico, and every one of the boasted enterprises of material improvement, for the adoption of which so much credit is claimed by his partisans for Maximilian, had already been the subject of liberal concessions from his government long before even the name of Maximilian was known in Mexico. But it is not true that President Juarez desires that American capital shall be introduced into Mexico under concessions from the false and spurious government of Maximilian, which is sustained only by the presence of foreign bayonets, and which is shedding the blood of thousands upon thousands of Mexican citizens, whose only crime is that they are struggling to preserve the free institutions and the independence of their country. It would be an insult to the common sense as well as patriotism of President Juarez to suppose for an instant that he can look with favor upon enterprises which give their moral support to the invaders of his country by recognizing them as lawful and legitimate authorities and soliciting and accepting concessions from them. Were there no laws prohibiting such a course, the noble patriotism of President Juarez would alone render this impossible. He does desire to see American enterprises established in Mexico, but he does not desire that they should seek the auspices of the invaders of his country, who are attempting its life and to drive him, an exile, from his native land. I make these almost unnecessary explanations simply to call the attention of the public to a view of the questions which they may for a moment have overlooked. Republican institutions are not to be overthrown upon this continent, and it is therefore of interest to know on which side those who are about to invest their money in Mexico desire to place themselves.

But with reference to this express company there is a more serious view to take. Its sole title in Mexico is that contained in a so-called decree issued and signed by Maximilian, and dated May 15, 1865. Article first of this so-called decree is as follows: "It is conceded to Dr. de Courcillon, in conformity with an act of association presented to our minister of fomento, to establish throughout the empire, under the title of '*Expreso del Emperio Mexicano*,' a company for the transportation of travellers, merchandise, mails," &c. Article second is as follows: "Our government, in order to help and protect the said company, engages itself to use the services of the express for the transportation of all the civil and military freight of the said government, in conformity with a contract agreed upon between the company and our respective ministers." And article seven is as follows: "The agents of the company in Mexico as well as abroad are authorized as official agents of colonization, and in that capacity are subject to the orders and directions of our minister." Article first of the contract with the minister of fomento is in these words: "De Courcillon takes the obligation to transport the *materiel* of war and of administration with a reduction of ten per cent. from the prices adopted for the public, and otherwise with the same conditions and terms as for the public."

Does Mr. de Courcillon mean that he showed this so-called decree to President Juarez, and that President Juarez approved of the procuring of capital in the United States for the purpose of transporting the *materiel* for Maximilian with which he is waging war upon the Mexican people? Does he mean to say that President Juarez, or the legitimate authorities of the republic, will hereafter look with favor upon those who are associating themselves together to aid French and Austrian soldiers in their bloody work of slaughtering my fellow countrymen, of carrying desolation all over my country, and exterminating its inhabitants in the unholy attempt to force a European prince upon us as our ruler, to establish monarchical institutions where before a republic has existed? And is it citizens of this great, free republic of the United States, just emerged from the noblest struggle of all history in the support of those institutions, who are to join in this attempt? The question is not one of establishing useful enterprises in Mexico; it is whether American citizens will join in the perpetration of a crime—as Mr. Motley justly calls it—the crime of the destruction of a free republic.

My country was bare of arms when this unequal struggle with France commenced. We have as yet been unable to obtain them; the United States has been closed to us as a source of supply, and we have nowhere else to look. Yet the struggle is still carried on, and to-day in every part of the republic its citizens are spontaneously rising, and are offering resistance to the extent of their means against the invader. If the people of the United States will not aid the liberal side, can we not at least expect that they will refrain from giving their moral countenance and support on the side of the French? The brutal and bloody decree of Maximilian published to-day condemns to trial by court-martial and death within twenty-four hours every Mexican who continues to struggle for the freedom and independence of his country. Will Americans add their influence on the side of the invader? I am glad and proud to believe there are very few who, from motives of gain, can be so base.

I am, sir, very respectfully, your obedient servant,

J. N. NAVARRO,
Mexican Consul General.

[Enclosure No. 8.]

The concession is signed by Maximilian, and is dated May 15, 1865.

Article 1 is as follows:

"It is conceded to Dr. de Courcillon, in conformity with an act of association presented to our minister of fomento, to establish throughout the empire, under the title of 'Expreso del Imperio Mexicano,' a company for the transportation of travellers, merchandise, mails, &c., &c.

"ARTICLE 2. Our government, in order to help and protect the said company, engages itself to use the services of the express for the transportation of all the civil and military freight of the said government, in conformity with a contract agreed between the company and our respective ministers.

* * * * * * * * *

"ARTICLE 7. The agents of the company in Mexico, *as well as abroad*, are authorized as official agents of colonization, and in that capacity are *subject to the orders* and directions of *our minister*."

MAXIMILIAN.

MAY 15, 1865.

This is followed by three contracts—one for the carrying of freight, another for the mails, and another for colonization.

In article 1st of the first contract is the following obligation:

"ARTICLE 1. De Courcillon *takes the obligation to transport the materiel of war* and of administration with a reduction of ten per cent. from the prices adopted for the public, and otherwise on the same conditions as for the public."

The contract is for nine years.

Mr. Romero to Mr. Seward.

[Translation.]

MEXICAN LEGATION IN THE UNITED STATES OF AMERICA,
Washington, October 31, 1865.

MR. SECRETARY: In addition to what I had the honor to communicate to you in the note I addressed to you on the 27th of the month which ends to-day, in relation to certain pretended concessions made by the usurper Maximilian, and especially to the so-called company of the "Imperial Mexican Express," I have now the honour to send to the department an extract from the New York Herald, of said date, which contains a letter from Mr. Courcillon, president of such company, in which, laying aside his first idea of causing it to be believed that his pretended concession was sanctioned by the national government of Mexico, and even had been obtained to the advantage of said government, he shows what is and has been his real object.

I avail of this opportunity to renew to you, Mr. Secretary, the assurances of my most distinguished consideration.

M. ROMERO.

Hon. WILLIAM H. SEWARD, *&c., &c., &c.*

[Enclosure No. 1.]

THE MEXICAN EXPRESS COMPANY.

NEW YORK, *October* 26, 1865.

To the Editor of the Herald:

I do not propose to enter into any controversy with Mr. J. N. Navarro, consul general of ex-President Juarez at this port; but as I observe that his misinterpretation of my interview with the ex-President has been repeated in other quarters, I beg leave, through your courtesy, to say that, representing a business contract with the government of the emperor Maximilian, I simply wished to learn from ex-President Juarez whether the convoys of the Mexican Express Company passing through regions occupied by troops or guerillas acting under his orders would be molested. He assured me they would not be, and I consider the assurance creditable to his good sense. As he no longer, however, issues any orders on Mexican soil, the whole matter has ceased to have any importance for myself or my company.

I am your very obedient servant,

E. DE COURCILLON.

Mr. Seward to Mr. Romero.

DEPARTMENT OF STATE,
Washington, November 1, 1865.

SIR: Your communication of the 27th of October was received on the 28th of that month, and the one of the 31st on its date.

In relation to the operations of an express company which you represent as having been organized in this country, with views injurious to the republic of Mexico, I have the honor to inform you that this government has no knowledge on the subject otherwise than what is furnished by your note or derived from the newspaper press. If citizens of the United States, or other persons residing therein, shall, whether by virtue of any charter which that company may have or may pretend to have, in any way infringe the laws or treaties of the United States, or the law of nations, affecting the republic of Mexico, proper measures will be promptly taken to prevent or redress the wrongs which may be meditated or committed.

I shall deem it a favor to receive information on the subject from any quarter.

I avail myself of this occasion to renew to you, sir, the assurances of my most distinguished consideration.

WILLIAM H. SEWARD.

Señor MATIAS ROMERO, &c., &c., &c.,
Washington, D. C.

P. S.—Instructions to this effect have already been given to the prosecuting officers.

W. H. S.

Lieutenant General Grant to Mr. Seward.

HEADQUARTERS ARMIES OF THE UNITED STATES,
Washington, D. C., November 1, 1865.

SIR: I have the honor to forward for your perusal the prospectus of the Mexican Express Company, forming in New York city for the undoubted purpose of aiding the imperial government of that country, and also some slips taken from New York papers throwing some light upon the subject.

Your particular attention is respectfully called to the article taken from the New York Courrier des Etats Unis.

Very respectfully, your obedient servant,

U. S. GRANT,
Lieutenant General.

Hon. WILLIAM H. SEWARD,
Secretary of State.

[Enclosure No. 1.]

THE MEXICAN EXPRESS COMPANY.

NEW YORK, *October* 26, 1865.

To the Editor of the Herald:

I do not propose to enter into any controversy with Mr. J. N. Navarro, consul general of ex-President Juarez at this port; but as I observe that his misinterpretation of my interview with the ex-President has been repeated in other quarters, I beg leave, through your courtesy, to say that, representing a business contract with the government of the Emperor Maximilian, I simply wished to learn from ex-President Juarez whether the convoys of the Mexican Express Company passing through regions occupied by troops or guerillas acting under his orders would be molested. He assured me they would not be, and I consider the assurance creditable to his good sense. As he no longer, however, issues any orders on Mexican soil, the whole matter has ceased to have any importance for myself or my company.

I am your very obedient servant,

E. DE COURCILLON.

[Enclosure No. 2.]

THE MEXICAN EXPRESS COMPANY.

To the Editor of the Herald:

I observe in your journal of this morning an article purporting to be signed by Señor Romero as Mexican minister at Washington. Señor Romero states that it has come to his knowledge that certain speculators of this country have obtained pretended concessions from the French agents in Mexico—that is to say, from the so-called imperial government of Maximilian—for the establishment of an express company, proposed to be styled the "Imperial Mexican Express," and that, in order that no one may be deceived, Señor Romero requests the publication of certain Mexican decrees, made in December, 1862, and June and July, 1863.

In answer to so much of Señor Romero's article as relates to the express company now being formed for the transaction of express business between the United States and Mexico, I have to state that in the month of May last Maximilian was pleased to grant to myself and to such persons (American citizens) as might become associated with me an exclusive privilege of carrying on an express business between Mexico and the United States, and guaranteeing, so far as he could do so, protection to the company and its business. After the granting of this decree, I had an interview with President Juarez, in Chihuahua, in which I stated to him, with entire frankness, that I had obtained a decree from Maximilian for the purpose of forming an express company to transact business between Mexico and the United States and elsewhere, and that I proposed to interest therein American citizens and American capital. President Juarez advised me that he had no objection to the formation of such a company as I proposed, and that it was then, and always had been, his desire, knowing, as he supposed, the wishes and desires of the American people in regard to the form of government to prevail in Mexico, to have American citizens and American capital permanently transferred to Mexico. He remarked that this was the common-sense view of the matter, and that certainly there could be no objection to having American capital invested in Mexico for the purpose of conducting an express business.

I repeated these assurances of President Juarez to gentlemen of New York, who have become interested with me in the formation of a Mexican express company. These gentlemen are too well known in the city of New York, and in the United States, in connexion with expresses already in successful operation, to need any defence against a charge of "speculators."

I have sent copies of this letter to Mr. Navarro, Mexican consul, and to Señor Romero.

I am, very respectfully, your obedient servant,

EUGENE DE COURCILLON,
President of the Mexican Express Company.

[Enclosure No. 3.—Translation.]

From the "Courrier des Etats Unis," of New York, October 24, 1865.

Mr. Matias Romero has deemed it proper to revive a collection of decrees and laws from the so-called republican government of Mexico, which declare all the grants made by the legitimate government null and void. This confused heap of protests without force are reprinted in consequence of the establishment, in New York, of the "Mexican Express Company," to which capitalists and influential persons have subscribed, and among them Mr.

Clarence Seward, a nephew of the Secretary of State. The arrogance of the agents of Juarez agrees perfectly with the farce of their loan.

If thinking men, such as Mr. Clarence Seward, take part in enterprises patronized by the empire, it is because they believe in its stability; for the same reason no man of means will commit himself to this fancy loan. In order that this speculation should have any chances of success, it would be necessary that the United States should be determined to wage war against Mexico and France, and the most simple common sense, notwithstanding the ambiguous words of the Secretary of State, which people seek to interpret, and which were only spoken in order to partially satisfy the radical supporters of the Monroe doctrine—the most simple common sense, we repeat, indicates that the cabinet of Washington will not become the Don Quixote of a cause which numbers among its advocates so many competitors of Gines de Pasamonte.

Mr. Seward to Lieutenant General Grant.

DEPARTMENT OF STATE,
Washington, November 1, 1865.

GENERAL: I have the honor to acknowledge the receipt of your letter of this date, enclosing for my perusal the prospectus of the Mexican Express Company forming in New York city, and the three slips taken from New York papers, throwing some light upon the operations of that company, with the view of aiding the so-called imperial government of Mexico.

In reply, I have the honor to state that the proper measures have been adopted by this department to prevent a violation of the laws of the United States, and the existing treaty stipulations between the United States and the Mexican republic.

In this connexion, I transmit for your information a copy of my note to Señor Romero, of this date, upon the same subject, a copy of which has also been forwarded to C. A. Seward, esq., of New York.

You will be pleased to accept my thanks for the information communicated by you to this department.

I have the honor to be, general, your most obedient servant,

WILLIAM H. SEWARD.

Lieutenant General U. S. GRANT,
Commanding Armies of the United States, Washington, D. C.

Mr. Seward to Mr. Dickinson.

DEPARTMENT OF STATE,
Washington, November 1, 1865.

SIR: Information has been received at this department of the formation of an express company in the city of New York, styled the "Mexican Express Company," for the purpose of aiding the so-called imperial government of Mexico.

You will adopt prompt measures to prevent a violation, in this connexion, by citizens of the United States, or by other persons residing therein, whether by virtue of any charter which that company may have, or may pretend to have, in any way infringing the laws or treaties of the United States, or the law of nations, affecting injuriously the republic of Mexico.

You will diligently watch the operations of this Mexican Express Company, and act in the premises as your sound judgment and discretion shall dictate, with the view of preventing any violation of the just obligations of this government towards the constitutional and recognized government of Mexico.

I have the honor to be, sir, your obedient servant,

WILLIAM H. SEWARD.

DANIEL S. DICKINSON, Esq.,
U. S. District Attorney, Southern District of New York, N. Y.

The Secretary of State to Clarence A. Seward.

DEPARTMENT OF STATE,
Washington, November 1, 1865.

SIR: I transmit herewith, for your information, a copy of a letter addressed by me, to-day, to Señor Matias Romero, the envoy extraordinary and minister plenipotentiary of the Mexican republic, which relates to the formation of the Mexican Express Company, recently organized in the city of New York, and with which you appear to be connected.

I am, sir, your obedient servant,

WILLIAM H. SEWARD.

CLARENCE A. SEWARD, Esq., *New York.*

Mr. Romero to Mr. Hunter.

[Translation.]

MEXICAN LEGATION TO THE UNITED STATES OF AMERICA,
Washington, January 21, 1866.

MR. ACTING SECRETARY: In my note of the 27th of October, 1865, to your department, relative to grants made by the Austrian ex-Archduke Ferdinand Maximilian, to citizens of this country, to create some interest, among other objects in favor of usurpation, in the United States, and specially to the so-called "Imperial Mexican Express Company," formed in New York, by virtue of one of those pretended grants, I transmitted (No. 4) the copy of a letter addressed by Mr. de Courcillon, president of the said company, to the New York press on the 23d of October, and printed the next day, of which he sent me a copy, with his letter to me of the same date, and which I transmitted to the department, as No. 3. In the first of these letters Mr. de Courcillon, in order to induce citizens of this country to take part in his speculation, assured them it was sanctioned by President Juarez, and he used the following language:

"After the granting of this decree, (that of the usurper,) I had an interview with President Juarez in Chihuahua, in which I stated to him with entire frankness that I had obtained a decree from Maximilian for the purpose of forming an express company to transact business between Mexico and the United States, and elsewhere, and *that I proposed to interest therein American citizens and American capital.*

"President Juarez advised me that he had no objection to the formation of such a company as I proposed, and that it was then, and always had been, his desire, knowing, as he supposed, the wishes and desires of the American people in regard to the form of government to prevail in Mexico, to have American citizens and American capital permanently transferred to Mexico.

"He remarked that this was the common-sense view of the matter, and that certainly there could be no objection to having American capital invested in Mexico for the purpose of conducting an express business."

It immediately occurred to me that what Mr. de Courcillon had asserted could not be true, and I told him so in the letter I addressed to him on the 24th of October, a copy of which I sent to your department, No. 6, with my note above referred to. I communicated these facts to my government in due time, as was my duty, and to-day I received an answer from the President of the Mexican republic, dated El Paso, December 22, 1865, and enclose you a copy of it. You will see by it that President Juarez informs me that he has never sanctioned that project of Mr. de Courcillon, or anybody else, founded on the usurper's grants, nor could he do anything so contrary to the law and dignity of the Mexican nation, and that he never before heard of Mr. de Courcillon and his project.

I think proper to make you acquainted with this circumstance at the present time, as a future reference to this and similar affairs, intending at the same time to transmit the official answer of Mr. Lerdo de Tejada, Mexican minister of foreign affairs, to my communications of last October, as soon as it comes to hand.

I embrace this opportunity to renew to you, sir, the assurance of my distinguished consideration.

M. ROMERO.

Hon. WILLIAM HUNTER, *&c., &c., &c.*

[Copy.]

(Extract.)

CHIHUAHUA, *December* 1, 1865.

* * * * * * * *

I am much obliged to you for the information you have given me of Mr. de Courcillon's assumptions.

The gentleman is very much mistaken if he thinks I can approve of what has never come to my knowledge.

* * * * * * * *

BENITO JUAREZ.

Mr. JUAN N. NAVARRO, *New York.*

[Copy.]

(Extract.)

EL PASO, *December* 22, 1865.

MY DEAR FRIEND: * * * You did exactly right to deny the representation of Mr. de Courcillon that he had my sanction, or expected to have it, to carry out his Maximilian grant. Neither to him nor to anybody else have I offered things contrary to the law and the dignity of our country. Moreover, I had never before heard of the gentleman or his projects, * * * * *

Your affectionate friend,

BENITO JUAREZ.

Señor Don MATIAS ROMERO, *Washington.*

Mr. Romero to Mr. Hunter.

[Translation.]

MEXICAN LEGATON IN THE UNTED STATES OF AMERICA,
Washington, January 28, 1866.

MR. ACTING SECRETARY: I have the honor to inform you that I have just received the reply of my government to my communication of October, 1865, relating to the so-called grants of French agents in Mexico to citizens of this country, of which I spoke in my letter of the 21st instant.

In accordance with what I said on that occasion, I now have the honor to send to your department, for the information of the government of the United States, copies of two notes addressed to me on that subject by Mr. Lerdo de Tejada, minister of foreign relations of the Mexican republic, dated at Paso del Norte, the 26th of December last, and numbered 415 and 416.

I embrace this occasion to renew to you, sir, the assurances of my distinguished consideration.

M. ROMERO.

Hon. WILLIAM HUNTER, *&c., &c., &c.*

No. 415.]

DEPARTMENT OF FOREIGN RELATIONS AND GOVERNMENT,
OFFICE OF RELATIONS, AMERICAN SECTION,
Paso del Norte, December 26, 1865.

In your notes numbered 503, 516, 520, 523, 526, and 527, dated the 17th, 21st, 24th, 26th, and 27th of October last, and their enclosures, you informed me of the attempts of the usurper Maximilian to bribe persons of influence in that country, and even public men, by means of grants, particularly that for a company to establish a "Mexican express," in which company figures Mr. Clarence A. Seward, ex-Assistant Secretary of State, nephew of the Secretary of State, and a prominent citizen of New York, in the three-fold character of trustees, secretary, and counsellor.

You also informed me of the bad effect on the interest of our country this connexion of Mr. Clarence A. Seward's name with the said company had, causing light-thinking persons to believe that, because of his official and parental relations with the honorable William H. Seward, this circumstance interpreted the ideas and sympathies of that distinguished statesman, and even of the government of the United States, as in favor of Maximilian's usurpation.

You finally informed me of what you had said about the nullity of those grants, published in the newspapers of that country; and what you had said about them in various interviews with citizens of that republic, and the note you addressed to Mr. Seward on the subject on the 27th of October last.

I have given an account of all this to the citizen President of the republic, who approves of your diligent and enlightened zeal in this business, and has no doubt but you will continue to act with the same energy and interest.

I mentioned to you, in another note, that you could publish or not what I had communicated to you about the nullity of Maximilian's grants, and about the falsehood of Mr. Courcillon, who styles himself president of the company, in saying he had obtained the President's approbation.

I assure you of my attentive consideration.

LERDO DE TEJADA.

Citizen MATIAS ROMERO, *Envoy Extraordinary and Minister Plenipotentiary from the Mexican Republic at Washington City, D. C.*

No. 416.]

DEPARTMENT OF FOREIGN RELATIONS
AND GOVERNMENT, AMERICAN SECTION,
Paso del Norte, December 26, 1865.

In your note of the 24th of October last, No. 520, with its enclosures, you communicated to me what the consul general of the Mexican republic in New York had published in the papers of that city, at your request, about the nullity of the pretended grants of Maximilian to a company trying to be organized, to establish a "Mexican express," and what Mr. Eugene de Courcillon, as president of the above company, had published in the same papers in answer to the Mexican consul.

The declarations of the congress and government of the Mexican republic have been very frequent and explicit concerning the nullity of authoritative acts the French agent in Mexico and French intervention have pretended to enforce. In the war kept up by the intervention and Maximilian against the independence and sovereignty of Mexico, they can exercise no legitimate authority in the country because their acts have no foundation by right, and are only enforced by abuse of power and use of foreign bayonets. So the legitimate authorities of the republic have never recognized, nor will they ever recognize as valid, any acts whatever of the intervention and the French agent, Maximilian, because they have no principle of law nor any source of legitimate authority to pa[illegible]n.

In this publication Mr. de Courcillon says, that after obtaining the pretended grants from Maximilian, in May last, he had an interview with the President of the republic, at Chihuahua, and he said he had no objection to make to the formation of a "Mexican express" company, nor to its pretended grants.

It is to be presumed that this assertion of Mr. Courcillon would appear very unlikely at once to every person of common sense. The President has instructed me to tell you he said no such thing to Mr. Courcillon; that he did not speak with him in Chihuahua; does not know him; never spoke with him anywhere, nor ever had any intercourse with him by writing, nor in any other way, at any time or place, directly or indirectly.

I think I can also assure you, from reliable sources, that Mr. Courcillon has not been in Chihuahua since May last, and it appears, also, he never was in Chihuahua at any previous period.

I assure you of my very attentive consideration.

LERDO DE TEJADA.

Citizen MATIAS ROMERO, *Envoy Extraordinary and Minister Plenipotentiary of the Mexican Republic at Washington, D. C.*

Mr. Seward to Mr. Romero.

DEPARTMENT OF STATE,
Washington, January 31, 1866.

SIR: I have the honor to acknowledge the receipt of your two communications of the 21st and 28th instant, with their respective accompaniments, relative to the formation of an express company in the city of New York, under a grant emanating from the so-called emperor of Mexico, and which you are pleased to communicate for the information of the government of the United States.

Thanking you for your kind courtesy, I avail myself of this opportunity to renew to you, sir, the assurance of my very distinguished consideration.

WILLIAM H. SEWARD.

Señor MATIAS ROMERO, *&c., &c., &c.,*
Washington, D. C.

PRESENT CONDITION OF AFFAIRS IN THE REPUBLIC OF MEXICO.

Mr. Romero to Mr. Seward.

[Translation.]

MEXICAN LEGATION TO THE UNITED STATES OF AMERICA,
Washington, July 9, 1864.

MR. SECRETARY: At the interview with which, on my return from Mexico, you had the kindness to favor me on the 20th of November of the last year, you were pleased to communicate to me, while referring to what had occurred in relation to Mexico near this government during my absence from the United States, that ex-General D. José Domingo Cortes had presented himself at your department, calling himself the representative of the Mexican States of Sonora, Sinaloa, Chihuahua, and Durango, and the territory of Lower California, and had solicited the annexation of those States to the United States. As was my duty, I communicated such intelligence without loss of time to the Mexican government, and fearing that through the irregularity of the communications my correspondence containing it might miscarry, and desirous that those immediately interested should at once have notice of the steps which were taken in their name, I made the same communication directly to the governors of those States of which Cortes called himself the representative.

For reasons which I cannot understand, I have not yet received the instructions which I expected from my government on this important business, but I am sure that they can only come of the import which I had the honor to express to you at the interview referred to—that is, denying absolutely that Cortes represents, in whole or in part, the said States, and showing that the States themselves have no right, with reference to the constitution, to enter upon agreements of any kind with any foreign government, and that none are further than the people of the States mentioned (in view of the repeated proofs they have given of the purest patriotism through this period of trial) from desiring to annex themselves to any foreign country.

There have come to my hands, however, answers to my respective communications from the governors of the States of Chihuahua and Sinaloa, which corroborate in everything what I have verbally stated to the department. I was intending to transmit them to you, in conformity with the recommendations contained in them, when I should receive the instructions on this subject that I am awaiting from the federal government of Mexico; but having learned this morning that D. José Domingo Cortes has returned to the United States and is now in Washington, and has addressed your department in writing, I think it my duty, with the reservation of returning to occupy myself with this incident when I received the instructions referred to, to transmit to you a copy of the communications which are in this legation from the governors of Chihuahua and Sinaloa, and which show that Cortes is not in any manner authorized to speak in the name of those States, nor of any other in the Mexican republic, because they cannot be represented abroad except through the agents of the federal government of Mexico; that he is not known in the States whose representation he attempts to assume, and that the proposals he has allowed himself to make to this government are formally and solemnly rebuked and repelled by the legitimately constituted authorities thereof.

The confidence I have in the justice and sound judgment of the government of the United States induces me to address this communication to it, rather to enlighten its opinion than for any other purpose. If I had the least suspicion that Cortes would be received in this city as the duly authorized agent of any fraction of the Mexican republic, and that his proposals, whatever they are, might be taken into consideration, I should think it my duty to protest formally and without delay against such procedure and the arrangements Cortes might make.

I avail of this occasion to repeat to you, sir, the assurances of my most distinguished consideration.

M. ROMERO.

Hon. WILLIAM H. SEWARD, &c., &c., &c.

[Enclosure No. 1.—Translation.]

GOVERNMENT OF THE STATE OF CHIHUAHUA,
Chihuahua, January 11, 1864.

Your note, dated 20th November last past, which I have received to-day, and the copy you send me of what you addressed to the department of foreign relations and government, of same date, at the city of San Luis Potosi, have informed me of the unpatriotic steps taken with the minister for foreign affairs of that republic, Mr. Seward, by one D. José Domingo Cortes, about the annexation to the United States of this State and those of the Pacific coast, in order to free them from French intervention.

I at once approve the assurances you made to Secretary Seward, denying so calumnious an imputation, and repudiating it as unworthy of any good Mexican; and I assure you the government in my charge, and can also aver that the others in question, are very far from entertaining such wretched views, because, although it is sure they will as far as possible resist French intervention, it is no less sure that they pant for and will at all hazards secure the nationality of Mexico, and its existing institutions; being able to assure you, in fine, that not only is all news wanting here about the mission and character which the said D. José Domingo Cortes has attributed to himself, but that the existence even of such an individual is unknown, whose condign punishment you demand with so much justice from the supreme government of the nation, to which on the first opportunity I shall render an account of this incident, and of this present reply, in case the communication from your legation may have gone astray. It is gratifying to me to add to the previous explanations, and in reply to your note, the assurances of my very distinguished consideration.

God, liberty, reform!

LUIS TERRAZAS.

Citizen M. ROMERO,
In charge of the Mexican Legation to the United States of America, Washington.

[Enclosure No. 2.—Translation.]

MEXICAN REPUBLIC, GOVERNMENT OF THE STATE OF SINALOA,
AND MILITARY COMMANDANCY, MAZATLAN, *January* 24, 1864.

In La Libertad, official journal of Durango, of the 8th instant, I saw published the note which your legation addresses to the governor of that State, and the reply to it, both papers relating to the false mission upon which the Spaniard D. José Domingo Cortes presented himself to the Secretary of State of that republic, Mr. Seward, making proposals to annex to the North American confederation the States of Chihuahua, Sonora, Durango, this and the territory of Lower California. The adventurer D. José Domingo Cortes never has been a governor in this country, nor made representative of the States which he has been calumniating to the cabinet of the United States of the north, by describing them as discontented with the constitutional rule which governs them, and so false and faithless in the actual struggle with the invasion as to wish to throw themselves into the arms of a neighboring nation, rather than to seek safety in battle, as they have done in sending their contingents of blood to the interior, and preparing with men and *materiel* of war at their disposal to resist the French and traitors on their own territory, where, as yet, they have not gained in favor of intervention the vote of a single settlement, unless such as has been forced from them by the compulsion of brute violence. I fill my duty as representative of the State of Sinaloa by pointing out in this note, for the information of the government of the United States and confusion of the intriguer Cortes, the falsehood and calumny he used in his conference with Mr. Seward, in proposing to him, in the name of the States mentioned, annexation to that country. I send copy of this note to the supreme government of the nation for its proper application, and beg you to make it public, and to accept the assurance of esteem and consideration with which I subscribe myself your obedient servant.

Liberty and reform!

F. GARCIA MORALES.

P. HERREL, *Secretary.*

Citizen MATIAS ROMERO,
Mexican Minister to the United States of America, Washington.

Mr. Seward to Mr. Romero.

DEPARTMENT OF STATE,
Washington, July 15, 1864.

SIR: I have the honor to acknowledge the receipt of your note of the 9th instant, with its accompaniment, relating to the movements of ex-General Don José Domingo Cortes, of Mexico, and to assure you that its information and suggestions will receive my careful attention.

I avail myself of the occasion to renew to you, sir, the assurances of my distinguished consideration.

WILLIAM H. SEWARD.

Señor MATIAS ROMERO, *&c., &c., &c.,*
Washington, D. C.

Mr. Romero to Mr. Seward.

[Translation.]

MEXICAN LEGATION IN THE UNITED STATES OF AMERICA,
Washington, July 12, 1864.

MR. SECRETARY: I have the honor to transmit to you, for the information of the government of the United States, a copy of La Accion, No. 28, a paper published in the city of Saltillo, the capital of the State of Coahuila, under date of the 18th of June last, which contains an article written by Señor Zarco, a distinguished Mexican writer, in which he very clearly demonstrates the impossibility for the French agent in Mexico to comply with the pecuniary obligations he has contracted, even should his acts be binding upon the Mexican nation.

I do not doubt that the data and remarks contained in said article will be viewed with interest by the government of the United States.

I avail myself of this occasion to renew to you, Mr. Secretary, the assurances of my most distinguished consideration.

M. ROMERO.

Hon. WILLIAM H. SEWARD, *&c., &c., &c.,*
Washington, D. C.

[From La Accion, Saltillo, June 18, 1864.—No. 28.]

PRACTICAL DIFFICULTIES IN THE WAY OF THE ESTABLISHMENT OF A MONARCHY IN MEXICO.

ARTICLE I.—*The question of finance.*

From the rapid examination that we have made of the convention of Miramar, it appears that besides the humiliations, the dishonor, and the shameful pupilage which the inexperienced Austrian prince has taken upon his projected empire, he has imposed upon it a pecuniary burden of $126,580,000, which is required for the payment to France of the expenses of her piratical expedition, the hire of her soldiers in continuing the monarchical propaganda, the cost of the semi-monthly steamers which are to bring to the protecting army the orders of their government, and in making a small payment on ccount for the French reclamations, which are all admitted and recognized, and are to be paid.

The manner of revision adopted in the convention for these reclamations and certain antecedent circumstances give foundation to the belief that this last item is more expansive than any other, and that the archduke, whether from his ignorance of the facts or by reason of his profound gratitude to Bonaparte, has not ventured to offer even the slightest objection.

As reclamations have been the ostensible pretext of the war, and from them are to be satisfied the expectations of certain great personages about the court of the Tuilleries as well as enormous commissions, as has been seen in the private correspondence of Jecker, and as, since the time of the conferences of Orizaba, the French plenipotentiaries have constantly sought to state the amount of these reclamations only in round numbers and without any kind of examination, it is necessary to bear in mind that only on account of the Jecker affair $15,000,000 are claimed, and $12,000,000 on account of other reclamations which have never been even presented to any government of the country.

In order that the world may judge of the morality of these exactions, and that his Holiness Pope Pius IX, who condemns usury, should not hesitate to pronounce his blessing upon all these affairs, it is well to recall that the fifteen millions of Jecker proceed from a loan of $750,000, and that the twelve millions of other reclamations arise from a debt of only some hundreds of thousands of dollars.

This addition of $27,000,000 will probably bear an interest of six per cent. per annum, and thus in a term of twelve years it will amount, with capital and interest, to $46,440,000, making the total amount of the compromises of the convention of Miramar reach the sum of $173,120,000.

Supposing this debt to France is only paid, according to one of the articles of the convention, the sense of which is not very clear, in annual payments of five millions of dollars, it will result that the new empire will have to send this tribute during a period of thirty-five years, from which will result an enormous addition in the payment of interest.

We will now proceed to examine another financial transaction of the archduke, that is, the contract for the loan. After designing it for fabulous sums, after Minister Fould had refused France as a surety for it, after the Emperor of Austria had declared he would take no part in the business, and, finally, after the English bond-holders had refused to enter into the combination, the famous loan was reduced to the issue of titles for forty millions of dollars, that had to be disposed of in the markets of Paris, Brussels, Hamburg, and Amsterdam, at 63 per cent. Let us suppose that speculators take all these titles, Maximilian loses, or, more properly speaking, causes the empire to lose 27 per cent. by this issue, or, what amounts to the same thing, he only receives $27,200,000, acknowledges a debt of forty millions, and loses at once, on the principal alone, $12,800,000. But as he has to pay an annual interest of 6 per cent. for these forty millions, the loss in twelve years will be $28,800,000.

The result of all this is, that the contract and loan give the new empire only $27,200,000, and in twelve years cost $227,500,000. The calcul·tion is simple : a loss of $200,320,000. This is a magnificent first lesson in economy, order and foresight, given by the monarchy to the republic! Can a government thus beginning its existence keep up its credit to meet future obligations? It would be a phenomenon as new as it is incomprehensible. The empire, then, relies upon the sum of $27,200,000, hardly enough for the first year, to defray the expenses of its inauguration and future splendor; and after that, bankruptcy and poverty, as it is easy to demonstrate, and the gloomy conviction that Napoleon basely deceived the archduke, when he told him that he was going to seat him on piles of gold and silver instead of on a throne. Allowing that all the bonds find purchasers in European markets, Maximilian's private debts of eight millions of francs will have to be deducted from the $27,200,000, as well as the farewell presents made in Austria, alms left for the vagrants in Trieste, costs of the journey from Vera Cruz to Mexico, and the $10,000 pin-money renounced by the archduchess when she left Vienna.

The total yield of this great loan, a great portion of which remains in France, amounts to—as we commonly say—*a pie in the dog's mouth.*

The first days of jollity and frolic, of initiations and triumphal arches, of feasts and flattery, being over, we must look at the serious side of empires, to the question of finance, and then the eyes of the astonished Dutchman will see such a vortex before him he will miss his secondary position as kinsman of the Emperor Francis.

Let us now endeavor to estimate, as nearly as possible with the most authentic data, the annual expenses of the Mexican empire.

As a debt of honor, a sacred debt of gratitude, the cost of the crown, we have, in the first place, the tribute to France, giving the mildest interpretation to the contract, $5,000,000 ; interest on the loan, $2,400,000.

The financial question must be connected with the diplomatic, and as it is known that you can collect from a power *de facto* by force, without acknowledging it as a legitimate government, or having any intercourse with it, as the Penaud and Dunlop contracts made in Vera Cruz between the constitutional government and England and France prove, whether the new empire is acknowledged or not, we shall see these claims urged by the English, Spanish, and American creditors. This shows an interest to be paid on the English debt of $4,200,000.

As it is impossible to pay at once the $600,000 that Marquez robbed from the British legation, and as this is one of the archduke's debts of honor, an annual instalment of 6 per cent. will have to be paid upon it, making $36,000.

Interest on the Spanish debt, $605,000.

By virtue of the Mon-Almonte treaty, binding upon the empire, which must close its eyes to all kinds of frauds, an additional sum must be paid of $400,000.

Interest on the North American debt, at 6 per cent., estimating the principal at two millions, to say the least, $120,000.

The estimates of the empire, then, only for what may be termed international obligations, not including loss and damage claims by English, Spanish, Americans and Germans, will amount to, per year, $12,781,000.

Now, let us pass to the interior estimates. Keeping in mind the brilliancy of the throne necessary to lend charms and respectability to the empire, the great innovation of giving the clergy salaries, thus imposing the expense of public worship upon the treasury, and the difficulty of satisfying our priests for the loss of their titles, parish perquisites, mortgage rents, and the necessity of keeping a large army of Austrians or Mexicans, and the inexpediency of giving those soldiers less pay than the French, and remembering there can be no representative system till there is peace, we think this estimate not far from being correct, namely :

International obligations	$12,781,000
Interest of the home debt	1,200,000
The emperor's salary	1,500,000
Appropriation for the empress	100,000
Expenses of the imperial household	100,000
Worship and the clergy, at least	5,000,000
The army, 40,000 men, with the same pay as the French	8,000,000
The civil list, with pensions, rewards, annuities, secret service fund, &c., &c.	8,000,000
A total annual expense of	36,681,000

Relying upon the synoptical table of Mr. Miguel Arroyo, who estimates the number of imperial partisans at five millions, in order to supply the budget it would be necessary to establish a system of imposts, where every inhabitant would have to pay on an average a tax of more than seven dollars apiece.

But while Maximilian, counselled by Corta, Budin and Schergenbecher, is perfecting this prodigious invention, the empire would have to suffer a deficit of $24,681,000 in the second year of its establishment, as the revenue could not be more than sixteen millions annually, considering the state of war and other serious obstacles.

We must bow humbly to this wonderful result, and admire the genius and skill of Napoleon III, the great politician of our age, and the wisdom acquired by an Austrian visiting the holy places and mosques, and the foresight of the reactionary party.

How is this deficiency, threatening to increase from year to year, to be supplied? That is the question! It is the death of the empire in its cradle. How are you to extract gold and silver from the mountains offered by the perfidious Napoleon to the innocent archduke, instead of a throne? French generosity is not to be depended upon, further than fulfilling its good intentions and hiring soldiers. The Austrian brother will not spend a florin after he has robbed his pretty sister-in-law of her pin-money. The Pope's precious blessings may do well for eternal life, or help to make a passage through purgatory shorter, but nobody ever made a pot-pie out of them. The other powers will get their money, but no more, and loans will soon be shut out from governments born to bankruptcy. Outside of the empire they won't get a copper!

In the interior the disinterestedness of the opposition party and the clergy is not to be depended upon, because that party may be divided into two ranks: the hungry, who want to feed out of the public crib, and the avaricious, quick to receive and slow to give. There is no possible way to supply this deficiency, unless monarchical institutions can work a miracle and cause our fields to yield their crops monthly, make our cattle breed in geometrical progression, and increase the consumption of national and foreign produce one hundred fold.

They cannot now resort to the ingenious plan of selling a few of the border States, with the Juarists as chattels, because the United States do not desire an extension of territory, and the Confederate States cannot afford such luxuries; and France is not in a condition to accept Sonora or Tehuantepec in satisfaction of the Miramar contract.

But the mines remain, the mines of the whole country, the magnet of the expedition, the first cause of the intense interest Napoleon takes in Mexico, and the great argument of his ministers to justify his crimes before the legislative assembly. The archduke will have a bitter disappointment in this particular, if he expects to find the heaps of gold and silver with which his protector dazzled him through a distant perspective.

Mexico is, without doubt, the first mining country in the world, and much of its mineral wealth is yet to be explored; but if the imperial government undertakes these developments, it will require an enormous capital and a century of perfect peace. If it thinks more proper to profit by the mines alrealy discovered and worked, it will have to establish a mining monopoly, and sell the mines. All that is necessary to effect this is, to seize the property of all the mining companies, composed mostly of English, Prussians, Americans and Spanish stockholders. This difficulty, it will be seen, is not very easy to overcome.

The reactionary economists may advise the Austrian to raise the taxes and create others, on doors and windows for instance, to establish the monopolies of tobacco, salt, ice, powder, spirits and cards, to negotiate the sale of crusade bulls from the Pope; but the adoption of all these ways, in the present state of the country, would not raise two millions of dollars, when twenty-four millions are wanted to supply the deficit.

There is only one more miserable way *left*, and that is to impose high duties upon revived titles of nobility, and the grant of new ones, and on the grand crosses and little ones of the imperial order of Guadalupe. But this way, besides exposing the establishment of the monarchy to the jests of Barres, would not be very profitable, for the sale of titles of nobility never gave a great revenue to Spain, where the aristocracy has not become so contemptible as in Mexico.

The empire of the Austrian begins with a deficiency of twenty-four million six hundred and eighty thousand dollars annually; therefore it is born weakly, sickly and paralytic. It cannot live without continuous loans, which are impossible; it needs the pity of all powers to keep it in hopes; and if it does not keep its engagements, but violates treaties, it is in danger of being superseded.

Such is the state of the question of finance in the new empire. Sad will be the archduke's waking when his frolic is over, and, looking for the promised piles of gold and silver, he only sees his poor wife's dressing table!

FRANCISCO ZARCO.

Mr. Romero to Mr. Seward.

[Translation.]

MEXICAN LEGATION TO THE UNITED STATES,
Washington, July 15, 1864.

MR. SECRETARY: I have the honor to remit to your department, for the information of the government of the United States, copies in English and French of a protest which Don Jesus Escobar y Armendariz, agent of the Mexican government, made in the city of London, the 10th of June last past, against all the acts of French intervention in Mexico, and of the functionaries emanating therefrom, and principally against the loan which the Archduke Ferdinand

Maximilian of Austria decreed on the 10th of April previous, pretending by that act to commit the credit of the Mexican nation.

I avail of this opportunity to repeat to you the assurances of my very distinguished consideration.

M. ROMERO.

Hon. WILLIAM H. SEWARD, &c., &c., &c.

[Translation.]

Protest of Jesus Escobar y Armendariz, late secretary of the Mexican legation in Washington, and now agent of the constitutional government in Europe, against the last Mexican loan.

I, Jesus Escobar y Armendariz, agent of the constitutional government of Mexico, legally authorized, and in virtue of the divers protests made by the legislative and executive powers of the nation against all the contracts, and, in general, against all the acts of the French intervention, and of the functionaries emanating from it, protest anew that the Mexican nation and its constitutional government will never, at any time, recognize or admit the obligations which shall be contracted by any other functionaries than those who hold their authority from the constitution.

I protest especially against the Mexican loan which was decreed on the 10th of April last by the Archduke Ferdinand Maximilian of Austria, and against every species of obligation which shall be contracted at the charge of the Mexican nation by what person soever who shall not be authorized by the constitutional government, whether these obligations have for their object to create a fresh national debt or to augment the amount of that which already exists, or simply to introduce modification of the English debt, which the government considers sacred, or any other debt legally recognized; and although the protests of the supreme power of the nation have obtained, in Europe, all the publicity that was due to them, I now renew them in the interest of the public, and to affirm as much as possible the rights of the Mexican nation.

J. ESCOBAR Y ARMENDARIZ.

LONDON, *June* 10, 1864.

Mr. Seward to Mr. Romero.

DEPARTMENT OF STATE,
Washington, July 27, 1864.

SIR: I have the honor to acknowledge the receipt of your communication of the 15th instant, transmitting to me printed copies of a protest by Don Jesus Escobar y Armendariz, agent of the Mexican government, in the city of London, on the 10th of June last, against the acts of the French intervention in Mexico, and of the functionaries emanating therefrom, and principally against the loan decreed on the 10th of April previous by the Archduke Ferdinand Maximilian of Austria.

I avail myself of this occasion to renew to you, sir, the assurances of my very distinguished consideration.

WILLIAM H. SEWARD.

Señor MATIAS ROMERO, &c., &c., &c.,
Washington, D. C.

Mr. Romero to Mr. Seward.

[Translation.]

MEXICAN LEGATION TO THE UNITED STATES OF AMERICA,
Washington, February 6, 1865.

The undersigned, envoy extraordinary and minister plenipotentiary of the Mexican republic, has the honor to address himself to the honorable William H. Seward, Secretary of State of the United States, for the purpose of protesting, in the most explicit and formal manner, against the cession which the ex-Archduke of Austria, Ferdinand Maximilian, has made, or is about to make, to the French government of various States of the Mexican republic.

The undersigned permits himself to remind the honorable William H. Seward that at the interview which he had with him, on the 19th January last, he read to him a letter written at the city of Mexico, on the 28th December previous, the latest date from that city received up to this date in this country, in which a person well-informed and entirely trustworthy communicated the news that French agents in that city had proposed to the deluded Mexicans, who now encircle the usurper that the Emperor of the French has sent to Mexico, a settlement, in virtue of which there are to be ceded to France the Mexican States of Tamaulipas, Nuevo Leon, and Coahuila, parts of those of San Luis Potosi, Zacatecas, Durango, and Chihuahua, almost the whole of Sonora, and the peninsula of Lower California, the dividing line to be formed by the river Yaqui, on the Pacific, and Panuco, on the Gulf, to their sources, and a straight line drawn from one point to the other; that, to make the cession of so considerable a part of the Mexican territory acceptable, assurance was made that France would establish in the ceded territory a military colony, which would be under its immediate protection, and which would place the rest of the country under shelter from filibustering attacks from the United States; which would, besides, produce the liquidation of the supposed debt which Mexico has with France, and would facilitate the acquisition of three hundred millions to the treasury of the usurper. It is added, also, to make so considerable a loss less sensibly felt, that the States referred to have only belonged in name to Mexico, because they have been ruled by authorities which have not respected the orders of the central government of Mexico, and which were doomed to self-destruction, either because they might fall into the power of the French or of the United States, and that in such alternative there cannot be a moment's doubt of the preferable extreme. In the same letter assurance was given that such settlement had not been yet submitted to the usurper, and it was given out as understood that he would not fail to hesitate and even manifest opposition to it before his acceptance.

This circumstance signifies nothing, however; the usurper either has not his own will, or if he has, he cannot make it prevail when in contradiction to that of his protector. Besides, it is not to be presumed that he takes any interest in the destinies of a country which is not his fatherland, in which four years ago he was not known, even by name, to the vast majority of the nation, which he himself knew only by name, to which he has been brought and is sustained by foreign bayonets, and in which he is shedding the blood of patriotic Mexicans, who are maintaining their independence, to satiate a blind ambition for rule, which for his punishment he exercises only in appearance.

The undersigned always believed that the Emperor of the French would close up in this manner his interference in Mexico when he should become convinced that it would not be possible for him to retain the whole republic as a French colony, and had the honor so to state to the honorable William H. Seward in the communication he addressed to him the 27th December, 1862, and which the President sent to the House of Representatives among the documents relating to Mexican affairs transmitted with his message of 4th February, 1863.

That which then, however, did not exceed conjecture, although well-founded, has come to be realized with the course of time and the development of events. News received from Mexico, from an entirely trustworthy source, has been confirmed by other advices received simultaneously from San Francisco, California, and from Paris; and such coincidences, combined with other antecedents which the undersigned is possessed of in this matter, do not leave him in the least doubt that if the settlement proposed has not been ratified, it is on the point of so being.

This conviction obliges the undersigned, in fulfilment of the duty which belongs to him, as representative of the Mexican nation, to protest solemnly and energetically against any settlement made by the ex-Archduke of Austria, in the name of Mexico, with the Emperor of the French, or with any other government, by which he aliens or hypothecates Mexican territory, or in any manner compromises the responsibility of the native country of the undersigned.

Addressing himself to the government of the United States, the undersigned does not think it necessary to halt to prove that the ex-Archduke of Austria only represents in Mexico the Emperor of the French, by whose army he was brought to that republic and is there sustained; and that therefore any settlement made between the ex-Archduke and the Emperor of the French would have the same obligatory force on the Mexican nation as one concluded between the said Emperor and General Bazaine, commanding in chief the French forces in Mexico.

The undersigned has not thought that he should await for official notice of the conclusion of such settlement in order to protest against it. It is of such gravity and transcendency, not only to the interests of Mexico, but to those of the whole American continent, that he would consider himself to be wanting to his most sacred duties should he for a moment delay to take this step.

The undersigned thinks fit, in justification of his conduct in this affair, to remind the honorable Secretary of State of the United States of a fact slightly resembling the present, when the representatives of the French government in Mexico protested against a treaty concluded between Mexico and the United States of much less importance than the present, only because of the vague rumors, more or less founded, that they had received that it had been concluded, and before they had official notice of its execution.

After the rupture between the allied Europeans at Orizaba, and when France alone continued making war on Mexico, the minister of the United States to this republic made a treaty with the Mexican government, in virtue of which the United States were to lend to Mexico eleven millions of dollars, Mexico hypothecating in payment for such amount the unoccupied lands of the republic, the unsold national property, previously called church property, and the unsatisfied bonbs and promissory notes for national property already aliened. This treaty was signed in the city of Mexico the 6th of April, 1862; but as it did not receive ratification by the government of the United States it was not officially published, and only mere rumors, more or less founded, were circulated about its object and stipulations; notwithstanding which, the representatives of the Emperor of the French addressed to the Mexican government, under date of the 15th April aforesaid, a note, in which they said to it that they had been informed that said government had concluded or was about to conclude a treaty with a foreign government, by which were sold, ceded, transferred, or hypothecated thereto a part of the lands and public revenues of Mexico, to the whole of which lands and revenues France made claim of right, in virtue of the fraudulent claims of her subjects. With the note which the undersigned had the honor to address to the honorable Secretary of State on the 2d June, 1862, he remitted a copy of such protest.

The undersigned avails of this opportunity to renew to the honorable William H. Seward the assurances of his most distinguished consideration.

R. MOMERO.

Hon. WILLIAM H. SEWARD, *&c.*, *&c.*, *&c.*

Mr. Seward to Mr. Romero.

DEPARTMENT OF STATE,
Washington, February 25, 1865.

SIR: I have the honor to acknowledge the receipt of your communication of the 6th instant, in which, in your character of envoy extraordinary and minister plenipotentiary of the United Mexican States, accredited to the government of the United States of America, you enter your protest, in the most formal, energetic, and solemn manner, against any settlement or cession, either made or to be made by the ex-Archduke Ferdinand Maximilian of Austria, in the name of Mexico, with the Emperor of the French, or with any other government, by which he alienates or hypothecates Mexican territory, or in any manner compromises the responsibility of the Mexican republic.

This measure you are led to take under the circumstances more fully detailed in your note, believing it to be in consonance with your most sacred duties as the representative of Mexico.

In reply, it affords me pleasure to state that the protest referred to will be placed upon file in the archives of this department, there to remain a testimony to your course in the premises and as an additional evidence of the zealous and patriotic discharge of your functions as the minister of Mexico in the United States, and for such other uses and purposes as future events may render it necessary to apply it.

I avail myself of this occasion to offer to you, sir, the renewal of my very high and distinguished consideration.

WILLIAM H. SEWARD.

Señor MATIAS ROMERO, *&c., &c., &c.,*
Washington, D. C.

Mr. Romero to Mr. Seward.

[Translation.]

MEXICAN LEGATION IN THE UNITED STATES OF AMERICA,
Washington, February 17, 1865.

MR. SECRETARY: I have the honor to transmit to you, for the information of the government of the United States, a copy of the proclamation which the constitutional President of the Mexican republic addressed to his fellow-countrymen on the 1st of January last, manifesting anew his firm intention to continue without rest, to struggle, against the foreign invader, in defence of the liberty and independence of that republic.

I avail myself with much pleasure of this opportunity to renew to you, Mr. Secretary, the assurances of my most distinguished consideration.

M. ROMERO.

Hon. WILLIAM H. SEWARD, *&c., &c., &c.*

PROCLAMATION.

The Constitutional President of the United Mexican States to his compatriots:

MEXICANS: After three years of an unequal and sanguinary contest against the foreign legions which treason brought to our country, we are still firm and resolved, as on the first day, to continue the defence of our independence and liberty against despotism. We have been unfortunate it is true; fate has been adverse to us on many occasions, but the cause of Mexico, which is the cause of right and of justice, has not succumbed, has not perished, and will not perish, because there still exist valiant Mexicans, in whose hearts the holy fire of patriotism still glows; and in whatever part of the republic they may be carrying arms and the national standard in their hands, there, as here, will the country live; there, as here, will the living and energetic protest of right against might continue to exist. Let the incautious man, who has accepted the sad mission of being the instrument to enslave a free people, understand this well, and let him remember that treason, the failure to abide by plighted faith in the preliminaries of La Soledad, and the acts of recognition and of adhesion dictated by the foreign bayonets which sustain him, are the only titles through which he pretends to govern; that his tottering throne does not repose upon the free will of the nation, but upon the blood and corpses of thousands of Mexicans whom he has sacrificed without cause, and only because they were defending their liberties and their rights; that the traitors who have longed for and called him, and those who under the pressure of force tolerate his direful influence or render him vassalage, must recollect that they are Mexicans, and that they have children to whom they must not bequeath a legacy of infamy; and that, during a cruel and obstinate war of eleven years against a more powerful enemy and one more deeply rooted to the country, we have learned the manner of reconquering our independence, effecting it with the same means which our former rulers had at their command.

Probably the usurper may not be disposed to think of the false position he occupies, and instead of listening to the truths which our words contain, he may repel them with a smile of scorn and contempt. This matters not; conscience, which never forgets nor pardons, will cause them to prevail, and will avenge us. In the bustle and noise of the court, in the silence of the night, in the public festivities, and in the privacy of the domestic hearth—at all hours and in all places, it will pursue him, will importune him with the recollection of his crime, which will not permit him tranquilly to enjoy his prize, until the hour for expiation arrives; and then for the tyrant, for the traitors who sustain him, and for all those who to-day mock us and delight in the misfortunes of our country, will come their awakening from error with repentance; but these will then be fruitless, because then the national justice shall be inflexible and severe.

That hour will come, doubt it not, Mexicans, as that of our former conquerors came, in the year 1821. Let us wait, but let us wait while acting with the heroic resolution of Hidalgo and Zaragoza, with the activity of Morelos, and with the constancy and self-denial of Guerrero, by preserving and increasing the sacred fire which will produce the conflagration that will devour the tyrants and traitors who profane our land.

Mexicans! those of you who are so unfortunate as to live under the dominion of the usurpation, do not resign yourselves to bear the yoke of ignominy which weighs upon you. Do not delude yourselves by the perfidious insinuations of the partisans of accomplished facts, because they are and have always been the partisans of despotism. The existence of arbitrary power is a permanent violation of right and of justice, which neither time nor the force of arms can ever justify, and which it is necessary to destroy for the honor of Mexico and of the human race. This is our task; aid us, if you do not wish to bear the name of abject slaves to a foreign tyrant.

And you who, in these times of common danger, are contending against our oppressors, continue your task, working with the same heroism which you have shown up to the present moment, without being discouraged by misfortunes, terrified by dangers, and dismayed by the lamentable defections of some of our brothers. These, perhaps, may return to their ranks, to blot out, in defending their country, the infamous stigma of traitors which now degrades them; and should they not do it, if obdurate, they should continue in their degradation. Have pity upon them, because while in the midst of the enjoyments and distinctions they may possess, they are unfortunate. The remembrance that they are Mexicans and vassals at the same time of a foreign despot, will be the dreadful pang which shall wither and consume their miserable existence. Do not forget that the defence of our country and of liberty is for us an imperative duty, because it carries with it the defence of our own dignity, of the honor and dignity of our wives and of our children, of the honor and dignity of all men. Therefore have we generous colaborers within and without the republic, who, with their pens, with their influence, and with their means, are aiding us, and offer up fervent prayers for the salvation of our country. Redouble, then, your efforts, with the assurance that in due time our constancy, our union, and our activity will compensate our sacrifices by the final triumph of the holy cause we uphold. Mexicans! he who now addresses you these words, faithful to his duty and to his convictions, will continue to devote his vigilance to the national defence; he will further it by all the means which may be within his reach, and with your assistance and co-operation he will keep aloft and without humiliation the beautiful standard of independence, of liberty and progress, which Mexico has conquered by the heroic valor of her warriors, and through the precious blood of her sons.

Done at the national palace, in Chihuahua, January 1, 1865.

BENITO JUAREZ.

Mr. Seward to Mr. Romero.

DEPARTMENT OF STATE,
Washington, March 15, 1865.

SIR: I have the honor to acknowledge the receipt of your communication of the 17th ultimo, in which you are pleased to communicate, for the information of the government of the United States, a printed copy of the proclamation which the constitutional President of the Mexican republic, his excellency Benito Juarez, addressed to his fellow-countrymen on the 1st of January, 1865, and in which he renews his determination to continue the struggle in Mexico in defence of the liberty and independence of the republic.

Thanking you for your polite attention in communicating to me so interesting a document, I avail myself of the occasion to reiterate to you, sir, the assurances of my very distinguished consideration.

WILLIAM H. SEWARD.

Señor MATIAS ROMERO, *&c., &c., &c.,*
Washington, D. C.

Mr. Romero to Mr. Seward.

[Translation.]

MEXICAN LEGATION IN THE UNITED STATES OF AMERICA,
Washington, March 28, 1865.

MR. SECRETARY: I deem it proper to call the attention of the government of the United States to certain documents which have recently been brought to the public view, and which have reference to the events which are actually taking place in the Mexican republic, which documents, accompanied by an index, I transmit enclosed with the present note.

It is generally known that the Mexican clergy, who have taken so direct a participation in the civil wars of that republic, with the object of preserving the property, privileges, and influence which they enjoyed during the Spanish domination, upon finding themselves overcome, in 1860, by the public opinion of their country, and deprived of their wealth and influence, and having no longer the means in the country to incite another rebellion against the legitimately constituted government, conceived the project of intriguing in Europe in order to influence some of the powers of that continent, by availing themselves of the occasion of the breaking out of the civil war in the United States, brought about by a hierarchy similar to the ecclesiastical one of Mexico, to intervene in the internal affairs of my country, to overthrow the existing constitutional government, and to establish, by the force of arms, a European monarchy, with a Catholic prince upon the throne, who, agreeably to the official declarations of the French government, previous to the intervention and its subsequent acts, was to be the then archduke of Austria, Ferdinand Maximilian.

It was to be supposed that this monarchical government, which was to be established in Mexico, should follow a policy diametrically opposed to that of the republican government then existing. What was called the arbitrary acts, the excesses and errors of the latter, were painted in the darkest colors. Among those which occupied a very important place, were the laws of reform which had been decreed in Vera Cruz in July, 1859, establishing religious liberty, the supremacy of the civil authority, diminishing the privileges of the clergy, and declaring as the property of the nation the rich property which the former had until that period administered, and which was called the property of the church.

The clergy of Mexico who had intrigued to bring the intervention to their country, and who were lending to it their co-operation and their influence, were bound to believe, and with reason, and confidently expected, that so soon as the city of Mexico should fall into the power of the invaders, and there should be established in it the semblance of a government, they would begin by abrogating the laws of reform, which were the most conspicuous work of the national government, and which had so powerfully contributed to bring about the unjust war against which it was then defending itself.

Matters happened, however, otherwise, and after a series of events which it would be a long affair to relate, the usurper, who now calls himself the emperor of Mexico, and who has been placed and sustained there by the French bayonets, has just declared that he will carry into effect the laws of reform referred to, dictated by the government which he attempts to supplant; and he has thus in this manner given evidence, that in the opinion of the usurper himself, and of the Emperor of the French, whose instrument he is, the policy adopted by the said national government was both wise and prudent, and that the principal motive which was alleged for palliating the unheard of outrage of desiring to overthrow a national government is precisely what the usurper admires most, seeing that he has sanctioned it, notwithstanding his losing by it the support of the clergy; and it is also what it is being endeavored to present to the public opinion as his greatest merit, and the strongest proof of his ability, prudence, and energy.

With regard to the clergy of Mexico, to whom the same thing has happened as to the instigators of the southern insurrection, who, in their endeavor to save slavery, have seen it perish more speedily in the hands of the pretended government which they themselves created with the object of making it prevail, the protest which they have addressed to the usurper, and of which I accompany a copy among the documents annexed, (No. 3,) puts it out of all doubt that hereafter they will wage against the so-called empire the same war which they have made to the government of the republic, and that the phantom of a government established by France will lose, with the clergy of Mexico, the sole element of national support upon which it had relied up to this period.

It is very satisfactory to me to avail myself of this opportunity to reiterate to you, Mr. Secretary, the assurances of my most distinguished consideration.

M. ROMERO.

Hon. WILLIAM H. SEWARD, *&c., &c., &c.*

MEXICAN LEGATION IN THE UNITED STATES OF AMERICA,
Washington, March 28, 1865.

An index of the documents which this legation this day transmits to the Department of State of the United States, with a note of this date, in reference to the rupture which has occurred between the usurper and the clergy of Mexico:

No. 1. Rome, October 18, 1864.—Letter of Pius IX to Maximilian.

No. 2. Mexico, December 27, 1864.—Letter of Maximilian to his minister, Señor Escudero.

No. 3. Mexico, December 27, 1864.—Protest of the Archbishop of Mexico, and of the three principal bishops, in reference to the letter No. 2.

No. 4. Mexico, February 26, 1865.—Decree of Maximilian, declaring a state religion, and religious tolerance.

No. 5. Mexico, February 26, 1865.—Decree from same, confirming the laws of the government of the republic, called those of desamortization and reform.

IGNACIO MARISCAL,
Secretary.

No. 1.

[Translation.]

SIRE: When in the month of April last, before assuming the reins of the new empire of Mexico, your Majesty arrived in this capital in order to worship at the tombs of the holy apostles and to receive our apostolic benediction, we informed you of the deep sorrow which filled our soul by reason of the lamentable state into which the social disorders during these last years have reduced all that concerns religion in the Mexican nation.

Before that time, and more than once, we had made known our complaints in public and solemn acts, protesting against the iniquitous law called the law of reform, which attacked the most inviolable rights of the church and outraged the authority of its pastors; against the seizure of the ecclesiastical property and the dissipation of the sacred patrimony; against the unjust suppression of the religious orders; against the false maxims that attack the sanctity of the Catholic religion; and, in fine, against many other transgressions committed not only to the prejudice of sacred persons, but also of the pastoral priesthood and discipline of the church.

For these reasons your Majesty must have well understood how happy we were to see—thanks to the establishment of the new empire—the dawn of pacific and prosperous days for the church of Mexico; a joy which was increased when we saw called to the throne a prince of a Catholic family, and who had given so many proofs of religious zeal and piety. Equally intense was the joy of the worthy Mexican bishops who, on leaving the capital of christendom, where they had presented so many examples of their fidelity and self-denial towards our person, had the happiness of being the first to pay their sincere homage to the sovereign elect of their country, and of hearing from his own lips the most complete assurances of his firm resolution to redress the wrongs done to the church and to reorganize the disturbed elements of civil and religious administration. The Mexican nation also learned with indescribable pleasure of your Majesty's accession to the throne—called to it by the unanimous desire of a people who, up to that time, had been constrained to groan beneath the yoke of an anarchical government, and to lament over the ruins and disasters of the Catholic religion, their chief pride at all times and the foundation of their prosperity.

Under such auspices we have been waiting day by day the acts of the new empire, persuaded that the church, outraged with so much impiety by the revolution, would receive prompt and just redress, whether by the revocation of the laws which had reduced it to such a state of oppression and servitude, or by the promulgation of others adapted to the suppression of the disastrous effects of an impious administration.

Thwarted hitherto in our hopes by reason, perhaps, of the difficulties which attend the reorganization of a society long overturned, we cannot now refrain from addressing your Majesty and appealing to the uprightness of your intentions; the Catholic spirit of which you have given so many striking proofs on former occasions, and the promises made to us by your Majesty of protecting the church; and we confidently hope that this appeal, penetrating your noble heart, will produce the fruits we have a right to expect.

Your Majesty will undoubtedly perceive that if the church continues to be controlled in the exercise of her sacred rights, if the laws which forbid her to acquire and possess property are not repealed, if churches and convents are still destroyed, if the price of the church property is accepted at the hands of its unlawful purchasers, if the sacred buildings are appropriated to other uses, if the religious orders are not allowed to reassume their distinctive garments and to live in community, if the nuns are obliged to beg for their food and forced to occupy miserable and insufficient edifices, if the newspapers are permitted to insult the pastors with impunity, and to assail the doctrines of the Catholic church—if this state of things is to continue, then the same evils will certainly continue to follow, and perhaps the scandal to the faithful and the wrongs to religion will become greater than ever before.

Ah, sire, in the name of that faith and piety which are the ornaments of your august family; in the name of the church, whose supreme chief and pastor God has constituted us in spite of our unworthiness; in the name of Almighty God who has chosen you to rule over so Catholic a nation with the sole purpose of healing her ills and of restoring the honor of His holy religion, we earnestly conjure you to put your hands to the work, and laying aside every human consideration, and guided solely by an enlightened wisdom and your Christian feelings, dry up the tears of so interesting a portion of the Catholic family, and by such worthy conduct merit the blessings of Jesus Christ, the prince of pastors.

With this purpose, and in compliance with your own wishes, we send you our representative. He will inform you by word of mouth of the sorrow which has been caused to us by the sad news which thus far has reached us, and he will better acquaint you with our intentions and aims in accrediting him near your majesty.

We have instructed him to ask at once from your Majesty, and in our name, the revocation of the unjust laws which for so long a time have oppressed the church, and to prepare, with the aid of the bishops, and when it may be necessary, with the concurrence of our apostolic authority, the complete and definitive reorganization of ecclesiastical affairs.

Your Majesty is well aware that, in order effectively to repair the evils occasioned by the revolution, and to bring back as soon as possible happy days for the church, the Catholic religion must, above all things, continue to be the glory and the mainstay of the

Mexican nation, to the exclusion of every other dissenting worship; that the bishops must be perfectly free in the exercise of their pastoral ministry; that the religious orders should be re-established or reorganized conformably with the instructions and the powers which we have given; that the patrimony of the church and the rights which attach to it may be maintained and protected; that no person may obtain the faculty of teaching and publishing false and subversive tenets; that instruction, whether public or private, should be directed and watched over by the ecclesiastical authority; and that, in short, the chains may be broken which up to the present time have held the church in a state of dependence and subject to the arbitrary rule of the civil government. If the religious edifice should be re-established on such bases--and we will not doubt that such will be the case—your Majesty will satisfy one of the greatest requirements and one of the most lively aspirations of a people so religious as that of Mexico; your Majesty will calm our anxieties and those of the illustrious episcopacy of that country; you will open the way to the education of a learned and zealous clergy, as well as to the moral reform of your subjects; and, besides, you will give a striking example to the other governments in the republics of America in which similar very lamentable vicissitudes have tried the church; and, lastly, you will labor effectually to consolidate your own throne, to the glory and prosperity of your imperial family.

For these reasons we recommend to your Majesty the apostolic nuncio who will have the honor to present to you this our confidential letter. May your Majesty be pleased to honor him with your confidence and good will, in order that he may more easily comply with the mission that has been confided to him. Your Majesty will also be pleased to grant the same confidence to the worthy prelates of Mexico, in order that, animated as they are by the Holy Spirit, and desirous of the salvation of souls, they may be enabled to undertake with courage and joyfully the difficult work of restoration in all that they are concerned, and thus concur towards the re-establishment of social order.

Meanwhile we shall not cease daily to direct our humble prayers to the Father of light and the God of all consolation to the end that, all obstacles being overcome, the councils of the enemies of religious and social order turned to nought, political passions calmed, her full liberty restored to the spouse of Jesus Christ, the Mexican nation may be enabled to hail in the person of your Majesty its father, its regenerator, and its greatest and most imperishable glory.

Confidently hoping to see fully consummated these the most ardent desires of our heart, we send to your Majesty and to your august spouse our apostolic benediction.

Given at Rome, in our Apostolic Palace of the Vatican, the 18th of October, 1864.

PIUS IX.

No. 2.

[Translation.]

MEXICO, *December* 27, 1864.

MY DEAR MINISTER ESCUDERO: In order to smooth the difficulties which have arisen on account of the reform law, we propose to adopt a means which, while satisfying the just requirements of the country, shall re-establish peace in the minds and tranquillity in the consciences of all the inhabitants of the empire. For this purpose, when we were at Rome we opened negotiations with the Holy Father, as universal chief of the Catholic church.

The papal nuncio is now in Mexico, but to our extreme surprise he has declared that he is without instructions, and has to await them from Rome.

The unnatural situation in which we have continued, with difficulty, during seven months, admits of no more delay. It demands an immediate solution. We consequently charge you at once to propose suitable measures in order that justice may be administered without consideration of personal station; that legitimate interests created by these laws may rest secure; correcting the excesses and injustice committed in their name; to provide for the maintenance of public worship and protection of other sacred matters placed under the safeguard of religion; and, finally, that the sacraments may be administered and other functions of the sacred ministry be exercised throughout the empire without cost or charge to the people.

To this end you will, before anything else, propose to us the revision of the operations of the mortmain and nationalization of ecclesiastical property, shaping it on the basis that legitimate transactions executed without fraud, and according to the laws which decreed such amortization, shall be ratified.

Labor, in fine, according to the principles of free and ample toleration, keeping in view that the religion of the state is the Roman Catholic and apostolic.

MAXIMILIAN.

No. 3.

[Translation.]

SIRE: In fulfilment of the first and most sacred duty incumbent upon the prelates of the church, whenever the latter comes to be in conflict with the state, we are now placed under the painful but unavoidable necessity of raising our voice to the throne of your Majesty, and we are obliged to do so by the letter from your Majesty to the minister of justice, which has been published in the Official Gazette, and in which it appears that your Majesty has taken the resolution to decide by yourself the momentous questions which are pending between the church and the state with reference to the so-called laws of reform, and have instructed your minister to prepare the necessary measures in the premises without deeming it necessary to wait for the new instructions which the nuncio of his Holiness is about to ask on account of not having those demanded by the points proposed by the government of your Majesty.

Your Majesty is well aware that, during the thirty years which have elapsed since the month of December, 1833, when the laws regarding patronage, termination of civil coaction with reference to monastic vows, tithes, &c., were issued, to the same month of last year, when the two regents, Almonte and Salas, declared the said laws of reform to be still in force, the Mexican church has never ceased to oppose right to might against all the laws and measures which attack its doctrine, its jurisdiction, and its canonical immunities and privileges, protesting respectfully, but energetically, before the respective governments, carefully restraining and guiding the canonical conduct of the ecclesiastical authorities, and teaching and admonishing the faithful with reference to the obligations incumbent upon them under such circumstances as Catholics Apostolic Romanic.

Your Majesty also knows that neither the interests of party, nor the character of institutions, nor the political complexion of governments, have ever exercised the slightest influence with regard to this course of the church, which, faithful only to its mission of preserving pure and intact the doctrines of the faith, the rules of morals, and the authority of canonical discipline, has never taken any step, except in the nature of self-defence, when these principles have been assailed, and, in so proceeding, it has had in view no other end but the most worthy and holy purpose of saving intact the principles upon which the relations between church and state are based, and of re-establishing concord between the two powers, in order that, by means of this concord, the general peace of the nation should be preserved.

Your Majesty likewise comprehends, through your knowledge of our national history, that the principal, if not the only, cause of the civil wars that have devastated our unhappy country is the endeavor of an odious minority to assail religion and the church by means of laws which do violence to conscience.

Your Majesty knows, finally, that the arms which the Mexican episcopacy have employed in its defence have been only the *non licet* of the gospel, and that their earnest desire has constantly been that by means of an agreement between the national government and the Holy Apostolic See the unhappy necessity upon which their passive resistance is based should be made to disappear.

It is impossible to exaggerate, sire, the pain and unhappiness of the Mexican church on account of this persistent warfare, which, in the name of liberty, of progress, and of civilization, has been made upon it by this at once old and new revolution, that after having desolated Europe has come to combat its enemy—that is to say, Catholicism—in this part of the New World.

When, after so many vicissitudes, affairs arrived at the crisis produced in December, 1860, by the triumph of the democratic faction in the capital of the republic; when we saw consummated among us the work which the enemies of the church had labored so long to effect, we should have lost all hope whatever, had not our confidence been strengthened by our trust in Divine Providence, and also by our intimate knowledge of the Catholic character, which has always distinguished the Mexican people.

This hope gained new strength when the intervention, triumphing at last in this capital, made the declaration that nothing would be attempted against the independence, freedom, and rights of the nation, and that it would confine itself solely to the overthrow of the government of Don Benito Juarez, in order that Mexico should freely constitute itself; and it was still more increased, giving the greatest consolation to the church and the people, when it became known that your Majesty was the prince who was called upon to rule the destinies of Mexico. The tidings that we all had of your devout Catholicism, the sentiments manifested by your Majesty, both in your speeches and your writings, the highly significant step of not leaving Europe and sailing for this, your new country, without resorting to receive and bring with you the benediction of the common Father of the faithful; the readiness with which your Majesty sent a minister to Rome, and your earnest wish for the arrival of the apostolic nuncio, in order to enter upon the arrangements necessary for a happy termination of the terrible crisis into which this unfortunate country has been plunged on account of the questions raised by these so-called laws of reform ; all this, sire, had filled us with unspeakable consolation ; all this awakened in our hearts the most lively enthusiasm towards the august person of your Majesty, and diffused throughout all the country that extraordinary rejoicing which was universally and splendidly manifested from the moment your foot touched the shores of our country.

To no one did it then appear doubtful that these grave questions would be speedily and happily arranged, and we all expected that the day of true peace, the peace of conscience, terribly agitated by the laws and the measures of the government of Don Benito Juarez, would now arrive. That desired day appeared nearer and nearer to our sight when we learned that the apostolic nuncio had reached Vera Cruz ; because, it being impossible that the pending questions could be settled without the concurrence of both powers—that is, without the concert of the temporal and the spiritual sovereigns—the arrival of the nuncio was regarded by all as a pledge of that concert, especially considering the Catholic character of your Majesty, and the benevolent disposition and conciliatory spirit of the holy pontiff.

What must have been, therefore, our sorrow and our affliction when, instead of all that we had so earnestly desired, and with such good reason had confidently expected, we have seen all our hopes dissipated at one blow by the declarations and instructions embodied in the letter of your Majesty to the minister of justice? In this notable document we see that there has been no arrangement with the apostolic nuncio, on account of his instructions not embracing such points as have been raised ; that your Majesty has not been willing to await the arrival of further instructions, and that you have resolved by yourself alone to determine these grave questions, and have ordered that the necessary measures consequent upon this decision shall be prepared by the minister of justice.

Being ignorant of all that has transpreid in the secret conferences, as also with regard to the documents and instructions brought by the envoy of his holiness, we ought to respect the mystery in which the causes of what has passed, and the motives which have determined your Majesty to take a step of such grave importance, are involved. But as, in our humble opinion, whatever may have been these motives, we do not believe them capable of diminishing the sovereign power of the Catholic church, or of conferring upon the state a sufficient increase of power to enable it, by its decrees, to tranquillize the consciences of the faithful ; and as this circumstance, far from bringing about the desired end, will still leave on foot all the existing evils, because it is only the spiritual sovereign that can decide grave questions of moral import and tranquillize conscience, we are, therefore, compelled to approach your Majesty, and earnestly pray you to be pleased to suspend the operation of the declarations and orders contained in the above-mentioned letter of your Majesty.

In taking this step we feel ourselves sustained not only by the arguments and motives set forth in the manifesto issued by the Mexican episcopacy on the 10th of August, 1859, with reference to the so-called laws of reform promulgated by Don Benito Juarez at Vera Cruz, and in the expositions we addressed to Generals Almonte and Salas, as regents of the empire, in December of last year, in consequence of the circular issued by them on the 15th of that month, (copies of which documents we enclose to your Majesty herewith,) but also by the character of higher gravity which this question has now assumed by the fact of the intervention of the holy father, who has sent his nuncio at your Majesty's request.

The bases given by your Majesty to your minister involve, sire, the complete abrogation of all the privileges and powers of the church, the ratification of the laws of sequestration of ecclesiastical property, the confirmation of the interests created thereby, the authoritative intervention of the civil power in the maintenance of worship, the extinction of the canonical means of subsistence, upon which public worship and its ministers depend, and, finally, the sanction of free and ample tolerance for all religions, without other restriction than the declaration that the Roman Catholic apostolic is the religion of the state.

To none do we yield, or will we ever yield, sire, in our fidelity in the compliance with our strict duty towards the temporal sovereign ; but when, in order to obey him, it is necessary to fail in obedience to the law of God, or that of the church, and consequently to commit the sin of prevarication, passive resistance ought then never to be considered as an act of disobedience, because obedience is based upon the law of God, and ceases to be a duty when it is inconsistent with that law.

The article of our creed with reference to the Catholic church is a dogma of faith, and this dogma establishes a supreme right in matters of doctrine, of morals, and of canonical government, a supreme authority that cannot be subordinated to any other on earth, and it proclaims, as an unimpeachable principle for all Catholics, and as a rule of conduct, that whatever may be the power, rank, and position of those who exercise supreme authority in the state, they have absolutely no power whatever over these matters ; for it is only the visible head of the church—that is, the Pope—who can exercise this jurisdiction; it is only this power that binds and unbinds consciences; it is only this authority that is competent to proclaim dogmas of faith, to enlighten belief, to rule over morals, to decide doubtful questions, and to order all conflicts to cease by means of its sovereign declarations.

Your Majesty will permit us, protesting above all our most profound respect, to state that your sovereign resolution, with reference to the matters referred to in the letter addressed to the minister of justice, relates precisely to those very points of the struggle between the church and the state which would not be the subject of dispute did they not invade the spiritual power, as has been constantly demonstrated to the various governments by the Mexican episcopacy; that they are in open opposition to the social basis of the Catholic church, and directly opposed to positive provisions of the canons, and especially to those of the last general council; that they have been explicitly condemned by the apostolic see in pontifical allocutions; and that even the request and sending of an apostolic nuncio, for the definite settlement of these questions, proves that your Majesty has been of this same understanding, since it is clear that, had your Majesty not recognized the positive necessity for the concurrence of both powers in the settlement of these questions, your Majesty would not have made so great an effort to obtain the sending of the apostolic nuncio.

Besides, your Majesty, in referring to this step, characterizes it as "a means capable of satisfying the pressing necessities of the country, and of restoring peace to the minds and calming the consciences of all the inhabitants of the empire," which declaration, as true as precise and conscientious, renders unnecessary, sire, any demonstration on our part.

But we cannot omit to observe that these conceptions hold good, only supposing that the steps referred to had not been taken, and that, however grave other circumstances may be supposed to be, they cannot be sufficient to enable the resolution contained in your Majesty's letter to satisfy the exigencies of the country or to restore tranquillity to the consciences and establish peace.

Your Majesty is well aware that the temporal sovereign has no power over the conscience, except to retire its coaction over it, and that, therefore, while the Pope does not decide or the sovereign does not withdraw this coaction, conscience will continue to be agitated.

With regard to the just exigencies of the country, we do not know what other there can be if they are not those of conscience in its moral relations with interest. But, referring only to that other class of interest produced by the appropriation of ecclesiastical property in favor of the now unlawful holders of the property of the church, under the laws that have despoiled it, even referring to these, and bearing in mind that many of these holders seek in the solution of these questions, not the quieting of conscience merely, but the consolidation and restoration to value of their sudden wealth, your Majesty will allow us to state that even these persons will remain in the same condition as before, for the sovereign declaration of your Majesty will produce on their minds only the effect of adding the fear of new exactions and other burdens to the uncertainty which will continue to prevail so long as the concurrence of the holy pontiff shall not have been obtained.

We will not dwell, sire, upon what relates to the competent maintenance of public worship and the support of its ministers, because whatever the gratuitous enemies of the church may say, interest has never had the slightest influence upon the conduct of its pastors; nor will we state to your Majesty that civil coaction having ceased, only those contribute that are so disposed, and that the noble moral impulse that determines these gifts subsists independent of all human power. But we can assure your Majesty that all of us are ready to depend solely upon the piety of the faithful rather than upon any civil appropriation, because nothing is so dear to us, under these circumstances, as to sustain the dignity of the church and the independence of her priesthood.

With regard to religious tolerance, we can see nothing that renders it, not to say urgent, but even excusable. Mexico is exclusively a Catholic country, and the opposition of the people to religious tolerance has always been manifested in the most unequivocal manner. When the constituent congress of 1856 was discussing the fifteenth article of the project of constitution, which would have established religious tolerance, notwithstanding the assembly was made up of the most advanced partisans of what is called reform and progress, and in spite of their unanimous endeavor to secure the success of such an idea, they were obliged to give way under the irresistible pressure of public opinion, manifested as never before. The radical liberals were the masters of the situation—they had all power and controlled the public offices everywhere; yet, notwithstanding all this, and the slight influence of the opposite party, and particularly of the church, they were unable to stem the torrent. Addresses poured in from all parts of the country, municipalities, guilds, entire populations, men and women, all the community, pronounced against the article; and even the government of Comonfort, perceiving it was not wise to oppose the popular feeling so unanimously manifested, took its stand against religious tolerance, and the article was rejected by an immense majority.

These facts, sire, are eloquent indeed; and in seven years the character and will of a people are not changed.

It would have been very easy for us, in lightly touching upon the points to which this address relates, to make with reference to each one of those points, and in general with reference to the so-called laws of reform, more ample observations; but we have been desirous to confine ourselves carefully to the simplest indications, both in order not to exceed what our duty strictly requires, and not to distract your Majesty's attention; and finally, after so much that both ourselves and our predecessors have said, and have proved and demonstrated with all classes of arguments in our representations and protests to the different governments which have attacked the church, and very particularly in the documents which we enclose herewith, in order not to unnecessarily prolong this address, we do not feel that it is necessary for us to say anything more. We shall never, however, cease reiterating our supplications to your Majesty that you will cause an end to be put to the grave embarrassment that has arisen from the issuance, without awaiting the arrival of the new pontifical instructions, of a resolution that, not having the concurrence of the two powers, leaves still on foot, and even will largely augment, the evils already suffered, will aggravate each day more and more the situation and render it more critical; and we cannot say to what point will multiply the difficulties with which your Majesty is struggling for the re-establishment of peace and the consolidation of the empire.

PELAGIO ANTONIO,
Archbishop of Mexico.
CLEMENTE DE JESUS,
Archbishop of Michoacan.
JOSE MARIA,
Bishop of Oajaca.
BERNARDO,
Bishop of Queretaro.
IGNACIO MATEO,
Bishop of Zacotecas.

MEXICO, *December* 29, 1864.

No. 4.

[Translation.]

Maximilian, emperor of Mexico, having consulted our council of ministers, we have decreed and do decree the following:

ARTICLE 1. The empire protects the Catholic Apostolic and Roman religion as the religion of the state.

ART. 2. All forms of worship not contrary to morality, civilization, and good manners, shall have free and ample toleration in all the territory of the empire. No worship can be established without the previous consent of the government.

ART. 3 As circumstances shall demand, the administration, by police regulations, will arrange all that may concern the exercise of worship.

ART. 4. Abuses which may be committed by the authorities against the exercise of worship, and against the liberty which the laws guarantee to their ministers, shall be laid before the council of state.

This decree shall be placed in the archives of the empire and published in the official journal.

Done at the palace, at Mexico, February 26, 1865.

MAXIMILIAN.

By order of his Imperial Majesty.

PEDRO ESCUDERO Y ECHANOVE,
Minister of Justice.

No. 5.

[Translation.]

We, Maximilian, emperor of Mexico, having consulted our council of ministers, have decreed and do decree the following:

ARTICLE 1. The council of state shall revise all the operations of the amortization and nationalization of ecclesiastical property, executed in consequence of the laws of the 25th of June, 1859, and others agreeing therewith.

ART. 2. The council on making the revision shall remedy excesses and injustice committed by fraud, by violation of the said laws, or by the abuses of the functionaries charged with their execution.

ART. 3. The council will make the revision truly, openly, and in good faith, and with no more impediments than those which it may consider necessary in each case, for the manifestation and illustration of truth.

ART. 4. The resolutions of the council are irrevocable, and will be executed as they are, without exception of any kind.

ART. 5. Lawful operations executed without fraud, and in accordance with the laws already cited, will be confirmed. Those which do not come under this head will be annulled.

ART. 6. Irregular operations which may have been executed against the tenor of the said laws, with the approbation of the federal government, may be ratified, reducing them previously to the terms prescribed in the same laws, so long as there be no injury to a third party.

ART. 7. Transactions which may be declared null and void may be revised on condition that they be brought forward in accordance with the terms of the law of the 13th July, 1859; that there is paid into the treasury in money a fine of twenty-five per cent. on the total value of the estate or capital adjudged; and that no loss is caused to a third party by rights acquired previous to the revision of the claim.

ART. 8. Concessions made by the federal government, so that the part in money of the adjudication or redemptions should be covered with credits arising from the personal services of servants of the state, will not vitiate the operation so long as the concession is understood to be solely and immediately in favor of those who gave those services.

ART. 9. Lawful rights acquired by the law of the 25th of June, 1856, shall not be considered lost or extinguished, except by express renunciation or on proof of their having been executed simultaneously with the operation from which it is derived. The renouncements of women who may have no other right in property, or of the custodians or guardians of children, in the name of their pupils, will be of no effect.

ART. 10. To qualify the rights which are derived from the said laws and the effects which they must produce, the date of their publication will, in every instance, be considered according to the principles of legislation.

ART. 11. The transfer which the clergy made of property or estates in those places which were subjected to the administration of Generals Zuloaga and Miramon may be ratified, if there be no loss to a third party, by reason of any rights previously acquired. For the same reason the transaction executed by virtue of the laws of the 12th and 13th of July, 1859, shall also be ratified in subjection to them previous to their publication in their respective places.

ART. 12. In the case of operations on which the decrees have been executed, and judicial acts duly published, the revision thereof shall be limited to the reimbursement of the exchequer with regard to the enactments of this law, which may have been infringed or defrauded in the said transaction. The reimbursement of the exchequer must be made by the actual possessor of the estate or funds.

ART. 13. Whenever a transaction shall be declared null and of no effect, the sums advanced by the person executing it must be returned in coin, and the value which it may have, in the same manner, form, and terms in which it was originally made. The legal interest on these sums shall also be paid in cash, corresponding to the time which may have transpired and the actual value of the improvements which may have been made on the estates. These reimbursements will not take place in cases where it is known that the transaction had been fraudulently executed.

ART. 14. For the restitution of credits which do not exist in the public offices the council will issue a certificate, which will have the same legal effect as the replaced credit.

ART. 15. The restitution of estates or funds which may have been the object of invalid operations should be made with the proceeds or results which they may have realized.

ART. 16 There shall be established an office, to be called "The Administration of Nationalized Property." It shall have control over the administration of that kind of property which may not legitimately come under the head of private property; it shall copy the evidence which may be considered necessary for the revisions; it shall put into practice the administrative and economical operations contingent on each act of revision, or whatever may be deemed necessary for the council. And for the departments, wherever it may appear necessary, the council will propose to us the nomination of agents to discharge the functions with which they will be charged. A counsellor or auditor, appointed by us, on the proposal of the council, shall be inspector thereof.

ART. 17. All the funds or capital of nationalized property that may not have been transferred or redeemed, those which are recovered by revision, and those which proceed from the transfer of estates which were afterwards made, shall be in charge of the office of nationalized property, which will see that they are properly administered, and collect their rents while carrying out their functions.

ART. 18. No right which directly or originally proceeds from mortmain transactions or nationalization shall be exercised, or be made of any value, judicial or extra-judicial, while it is not shown in due and proper form that the operation whence it proceeded has been properly and correctly revised.

ART. 19. Although the revision may not be complete, if it be shown in due form that the process to obtain it has been presented, the rights to which the previous article refers may be exercised; but those who obtain it for them must give security to the satisfaction of the chief judge, (*Juez de primera instancia,*) or keep the matter in judicial course until the revision is complete.

ART. 20. Nor shall any right or privilege, judicial or extra-judicial, be exercised in relation to nationalized estates which may not have been included in operations of mortmain or nationalization, or which may have been returned to ecclesiastical corporations. The possessors or detainers of those estates must show cause within two months in the form prescribed by the enactments of this law.

ART. 21. Any person contravening the three last-mentioned articles, or their accomplices, shall incur a fine of from $1,000 to $15,000, or six months to five years' imprisonment. The penalty shall be applied openly and without reference to the nullity of the act or acts which may have been exercised.

ART. 22. The redemption of funds or capital must be shown within two months. If the manifestation be not made, the redemption will be considered null, and the deed of recognition will recover all its vigor and force.

ART. 23. Negotiations now pending in the tribunals in which there is a question of the validity or preference of rights acquired by the laws of mortmain or naturalization will pass the council and thus be disposed of.

ART. 24 Nationalized property which may not have been transferred in consequence of the laws already mentioned, and those which may be reclaimed by virtue of the revision, shall be transferred in the form and terms which the law provides for the sale of the estates of the exchequer, with due regard to the provisions prescribed by this law.

ART. 25. The cost of the transfers shall be placed at six per cent. per annum, with the hypothecation of the estate itself for a term of eighteen years, to be collected annually and in equal parts The diminution of the time of recognition and the payment in cash of the whole or part of the price shall not have any alteration.

ART. 26. Country property, in order to be transferred, shall be divided into parts, and the project of division which is formed in each case shall be presented to us for our approbation.

ART. 27. In every case of the transfer of country lands the preference shall be given to persons having no other landed property; and in no case shall more than two properties be transferred to a single person.

ART. 28. The transfer of agricultural lands shall only be made in favor of persons who have no other landed property.

ART. 29. All clerks, secretaries, notaries public, judges and others, shall, within two months from the publication of this law, remit to the minister of justice a circumstantial notice of all writings granted in their protocols from the 1st of June, 1856, with reference to nationalized property; with a statement of all notes in reference thereto. Those who do not exactly execute and punctually comply with this direction shall incur the penalty of deprivation of office and a fine of $500 to $3,000.

ART. 30. At the termination of the time specified in the last article our minister of justice shall name examiners of the protocols, to make examination as to the fulfilment of the aforementioned provision.

This decree shall be deposited in the archives of the empire, and be published in the official gazette.

Given in the palace of Mexico, February 26, 1865.

MAXIMILIAN.

By command of his imperial Majesty.

PEDRO ESCUDERO Y ECHANOVE,
Minister of Justice.

Mr. Seward to Mr. Romero.

DEPARTMENT OF STATE,
Washington, November 1, 1865.

SIR: I have the honor to acknowledge the receipt of your note of the 28th of March last, and of its enclosures, numbered 1 to 5, inclusive, calling the attention of this government to the said documents which refer to the events occurring in the Mexican republic, at their respective dates.

While thanking you for the information thus communicated, which is contained in your note and its interesting accompaniments, I avail myself of the opportunity to tender to you, sir, the assurance of my very distinguished consideration.

WILLIAM H. SEWARD.

Señor MATIAS ROMERO, *&c., &c., &c.,*
Washington, D. C.

Mr. Romero to Mr. Seward.

[Translation.]

MEXICAN LEGATION IN THE UNITED STATES,
Washington, April 7, 1865.

MR. SECRETARY: Pursuant to my intention to communicate to the government of the United States, through your respected channel, the principal documents which may come to my hands, and which may serve to give an idea of the policy observed by the forces and the agents of the French government in Mexico, I have the honor to accompany with this note some of those published in numbers 9 and 10 of "*El Correo de Mazatlan,*" the organ of the so-called government of the ex-Archduke Maximilian in the State of Sinaloa. I will take the liberty to briefly call your attention to these evidences brought to light by the agents themselves of the French intervention in my country.

The first is a decree from the French General Castagny, issued on the 25th of January last, in which, referring to another decree upon the same subject, from the general-in-chief of the French forces in Mexico, and to the instructions of Maximilian, a court-martial is established in Mazatlan, from which there is no appeal, to pronounce, at discretion, sentences which are to be executed within twenty-four hours against every republican guerilla, and even against any prisoner made from the regular forces who defend the independence of their country, for it is known that the former, and even in many cases the latter, are called by the invaders of Mexico "armed malefactors," against whom apparently the decree of which I speak is levelled. This barbarous system of trying by foreign courts-martial, and without subjecting to any law or rule, as they pass sentences at discretion, has already carried to the gallows hundreds of victims, among them many such as Señor Chavez, the constitutional governor of Aguas Calientes, and General Ghilardi, the companion-in-arms of Garibaldi. These are the "armed malefactors" whom the invader seeks to exterminate.

The second point in evidence, which I accompany with this note, is another decree from the same General Castagny, removing the political and civil authorities of Mazatlan, appointed by the French agent which preceded the said general at Mazatlan, and constituting other persons in their places, under the threat that, if any one of them should not accept the position to which he has been designated, he will suffer a penalty of imprisonment for six months, agreeably to the law issued upon the subject by the intervention.

The existence of this so-called law, and the necessity of threatening its execution in the decree to which I refer, are the best proofs which can be imagined of the want of popularity with which the cause of the intervention contends in Mexico.

The third evidence comprises several communications which have passed between the so-called political prefect of Sinaloa and the Licentiate Don Ladislao Gaona, from which it appears that this advocate did not immediately accept the appointment which was conferred upon him of judge of the first instance, and though he excused himself upon the plea of infirmity, he was ordered to be imprisoned, and compelled to accept the office.

The fourth and last evidence which I have the honor to transmit, although of a later date, constitutes from its tenor a very singular document. It is a proceeding subscribed by sundry persons of the city of Aguas Calientes, who were compelled by the political prefect to protest that they would not be hostile to the new order of things. But the fact is to be noted that the majority of the signers, not satisfied that it should appear in the instrument that they acted by order of the prefect, took care to set forth before each of their signatures that they complied with that act solely through the fear of the pains with which they were threatened. What is most singular in this document, which reveals what has taken place in drawing up all the acts of adhesion to the empire, should be brought to light as a proof of the spontaneity with which it is being accepted in Mexico. I forbear from the reflections which these documents suggest, because they cannot be concealed from the well-known penetration of the government of the United States, which I have no doubt will properly estimate them.

I avail myself of this opportunity to repeat to you, Mr. Secretary, the assurances of my very distinguished consideration.

M. ROMERO.

Hon. WILLIAM H. SEWARD, *&c.*, *&c.*, *&c.*

[Enclosure No. 1.—Translation.]

[From the Correo de Mazatlan, 28th of January, 1865—Volume 1, No. 9.]

Gregorio Almada, superior political prefect of the department of Sinaloa, to its inhabitants:

Know ye, that his excellency Major General De Castagny has directed to me the following decree:

"EXPEDITIONARY FORCE OF MEXICO, 1st DIVISION OF INFANTRY, GENERAL STAFF.

"General de Castagny, commanding the 1st division of the Franco-Mexican army:

"In virtue of the constituent decree of the general-in chief, issued the 20th of June, 1863, in virtue of the orders from his Majesty the Emperor Maximilian, and using powers conferred upon him, decrees as follows:

"ARTICLE 1. A court-martial is hereby established in Mazatlan.

"ART. 2. This court is invested with discretional powers to judge, without appeal, every person who belongs to the gangs of armed malefactors.

"ART. 3. This court shall pronounce sentence by a majority of votes and at one session.

"ART. 4. Sentences shall be executed within twenty-four hours, counting from the moment of their passage.

"*General Commanding the First Division*,
"DE CASTAGNY.

"MAZATLAN, *January* 25, 1865."

Therefore I order this to be printed, published and circulated, and that it be duly obeyed.

MAZATLAN, *January* 28, 1865.

Superior Political Prefect,
GREGORIO ALMADA.

Secretary General of the Prefecture,
GREGORIO MORENO.

[Enclosure No. 2.]

[Taken from the same paper as the preceding.]

Gregorio Almada, superior political prefect of the department of Sinaloa, to its inhabitants:

Know ye, that his excellency Major General de Castagny, has directed to me the following decree:

"EXPEDITIONARY FORCE OF MEXICO, 1st DIVISION OF INFANTRY, GENERAL STAFF.

"General de Castagny, commanding the 1st division of the Franco-Mexican army:

"Considering that the authorities of Mazatlan have been elected by a small portion of the population; and, moreover, have taken little pains to do their duty, it is decreed, that the following persons are provisionally appointed to office till their nominations are ratified by his Majesty the Emperor Maximilian:

"*Political prefect.*—Don Gregorio Almada.

"*Municipal prefect*—Don Francisco Gomez Flores.

"*City Council.*—President, Don Vicente Alvarez de la Rosa. Councilmen: 1. Angel Lopez Portillo. 2. Leon Villaseñor, (doctor.) 3. Manuel Hidalgo. 4. Miguel F. Castro. 5. Fortunato de la Vega. 6. Juan Ramirez. 7. Jesus Macias.

"*Syndics.*—1. Don Matias Acosta. 2. Don Santiago Rivero.

"*Alcades.*—1. Don Manuel Castellanos. 2. Don Francisco Muro. 3. Don Vicente Maldonado.

"Any of the persons above mentioned who refuse to perform the duties of the offices assigned to them shall suffer six months' imprisonment, according to the provisions of the law.

"*General Commanding the First Division,*
"DE CASTAGNY.

"HEADQUARTERS IN MAZATLAN, *January* 27, 1865."

Therefore I order this to be printed, published, and circulated, and command that it be duly obeyed.

MAZATLAN, *January* 28, 1865.

Superior Political Prefect,
GREGORIO ALMADA.

Secretary General of the Prefecture,
GREGORIO MORENO.

[Enclosure No. 3.]

[Taken from the same paper as the preceding.]

Gregorio Almada, superior political prefect of the department of Sinaloa, to its inhabitants:

Know ye, that his excellency Major General de Castagny, has directed to me the following decree:

"EXPEDITIONARY FORCE OF MEXICO, 1st DIVISION OF INFANTRY, GENERAL STAFF.—No. 1355.

"General Castagny, commanding first division of the Franco-Mexican army, considering it of great importance to organize the judicial power as soon as possible, and respecting the recommendations of the superior political prefect, decrees as follows:

"The persons mentioned below are hereby appointed to office till their nominations are ratified by his Majesty the Emperor Maximilian, as officers of the supreme court: Minister, Licenciado Don Jesus Betancourt; attorney, Licenciado Don José Maria Loreto Iribarren. The other officers required in the supreme court of justice shall be appointed by the political prefect, taking into consideration the minister's recommendations.

"The following persons are hereby appointed by the political prefect till their nominations are ratified by his Majesty the Emperor: First judge of first instance, Licenciado Ladislao Gaona; second judge of first instance, Licenciado Jesus Bringas.

"MAZATLAN, *January* 27, 1865.

"*General of the Division,*
"DE CASTAGNY.

"*Political Prefect,*
"DON GREGORIO ALMADA, *Present.*"

Therefore, I order this to be printed, published, and circulated, and command that it be duly obeyed.

MAZATLAN, *January* 28, 1865.

Superior Political Prefect,
GREGORIO ALMADA.

Secretary General of the Prefecture,
GREGORIO MORENO.

[Enclosure No. 4.]

[From El Correo de Mazatlan, the official paper of the department of Sinaloa, February 8, 1865, volume 1, No. 10]

Superior political prefecture of the department of Sinaloa.

As the same causes still exist that I explained to the superior political prefect of the department in my conference with him yesterday, why I should be excused from accepting the place of 2d judge of first instance, to which I have been appointed by General de Castagny; and as I am again suffering from another attack of malignant coast fever, from which I have already suffered much, making a change of air necessary to my recovery, as my physician says, I make known this to you that you may inform the superior political prefect of the department that, for reasons given, I cannot accept the aforesaid appointment.

L. GAONA.

To the SECRETARY *of the Superior Political Prefecture of the Department, Present.*
MAZATLAN, *January* 30, 1865.

[Enclosure No. 5.]

SUPERIOR POLITICAL PREFECTURE OF THE DEPARTMENT OF SINALOA,
Mazatlan, February 2, 1865.

EXCELLENCY: Your official letter of yesterday has informed me of the decree against Ladislao Gaona, who, despite his confinement, still refuses to serve as second judge of first instance for this port, to which he was appointed by your excellency's decree, promulgated the 28th of January last.

I now transmit the resolution to Mr. Gaona, and will see that it is enforced, and will recommend to you, when required, a person to fill his place in the above-mentioned office.

God grant you many years.

Superior Political Prefect,
GREGORIO ALMADA.

Secretary General,
G. MORENO.

His Excellency General of the Division,
DE CASTAGNY, *Present.*

[Enclosure No. 6]

SUPERIOR POLITICAL PREFECTURE OF THE DEPARTMENT OF SINALOA,
Mazatlan, February 2, 1865.

His excellency General De Castagny, of the division, informed me officially yesterday, that notwithstanding your disrespectful refusal of the second judgeship of first instance, to which you were called by a decree of the 28th of January, 1865, he will give a proof of his indulgence by granting you three days from yesterday to reflect upon the serious consequences of your resistance to the decree, and if you remain contumacious, to imprison you for six months for not respecting his commands as you ought.

I communicate this to you for your information.

Superior Political Prefect,
GREGORIO ALMADA.

Secretary General,
G. MORENO.

Licenciado Don LADISLAO GAONA,
Appointed Second Judge of First Instance at this Port, Present.

[Enclosure No. 7.]

SUPERIOR POLITICAL PREFECTURE OF THE DEPARTMENT OF SINALOA,
Mazatlan, February 2, 1865.

SIR: Don Ladislao Gaona writes me officially as follows:

"MAZATLAN, *February* 2, 1865.

"In reply to your note of to-day, I have the honor to say that I did not at first accept the judgeship offered me for the sole reasons given at the time, and not intended as contumacious. I now accept the place.

"L. GAONA.

"The SUPERIOR POLITICAL PREFECT *of this Department, Present.*"

I send you a copy of the above note, that you may order Mr. Gaona to be liberated and to take charge of the office to which he has been appointed.

God grant you many years.

Superior Political Prefect,
GREGORIO ALMADA.

Secretary General,
G. MORENO.

His Excellency General of the Division,
DE CASTIGNY, *Present.*

[Enclosure No. 8.]

MEXICAN EMPIRE, SECOND JUSTICE OF LETTERS,
Mazatlan, February 3, 1865.

I have this day taken possession of the second judgeship of first instance, by order of your note of the 29th January last, and have the honor to inform you of it.

L. GAONA.

The SUPERIOR POLITICAL PREFECT *of this Department, Present.*

[Enclosure No. 9.—Translation.]

[From the Pajaro Verde, Mexico, 25th day of August, 1864.]

PROTESTS.

We, the undersigned, in compliance with the order of the head prefect of the department that persons holding office under the constitution of 1857 shall present themselves at the prefecture and prove that they are not hostile to the imperial government, protest on our word of honor that we will behave like honest citizens, will live in a peaceful manner, and will engage in no act of hostility against the present government.

FELIX DE LA PAZ,
and twenty others.

I signed because the penalty established in the circular of August 10th last is very severe, and I am told that it will be enforced.

FRANCISCO B. JAYME.

I signed this protest for the same reason that the Licenciate Jayme did.

MIGUEL GUINCHARD.

I protest that I have been hostile to no government up to this time, and I sign the present protest because of the penalty imposed by the circular of the 10th of last August.

GUILLERMO R. BRAND.

AGUAS CALIENTES, *July* 18, 1864.

Although we have served none of the governments of the country, nor have joined any political parties, we sign this present paper to avoid the serious consequences that might occur in case of refusal.

J. REFUGIO GUINCHARD.

Although I never held any office, I have been summoned by the prefect to ask me to be neutral. I protest to be so to avoid me further troubles.

A. C. BERRUECO.

Not being employed by the government, but being partial to the liberals, I am called upon to make this protest that I will live in peace. I hereby declare to remain neutral under all circumstances.

TRINIDAD PEDROZA.
JESUS H. ASCON.

For the sake of suffering imprisonment or exile, I signed this protest.

BRUNO DAVALOS.

Although I am partial to the liberal party, I have never shown any hostility to the present government, and I sign this protest to save myself from banishment or worse evils.

LUZ G. BRAVO,
ANTONIO CORNEJO.
FRANCISCO ROSALES.

There are a great many other remarks like the preceding ones.

Mr. Seward to Mr. Romero.

DEPARTMENT OF STATE,
Washington, November 2, 1865.

SIR: I have the honor to acknowledge your communications of March 31, and April 3 and 7, 1865, with their respective enclosures, transmitting, for the information of this government, accounts of the condition of affairs in Mexico, and of the events occurring there connected with the operations of the forces contending in that republic.

You will be pleased to accept my grateful acknowledgments for the interesting information you have so kindly communicated, while I avail myself of the occasion to reiterate to you, sir, the assurances of my high consideration.

WILLIAM H. SEWARD.

Señor MATIAS ROMERO, *&c., &c., &c.,*
Washington, D. C.

Mr. Romero to Mr. Hunter.

[Translation.]

MEXICAN LEGATION IN THE UNITED STATES OF AMERICA,
Washington, May 10, 1865.

MR. ACTING SECRETARY: I have the honor to transmit to you, for the information of the government of the United States, a copy, in English, of a note which I this day received from Señor Lerdo de Tejada, the minister of foreign relations of the Mexican republic, dated from the city of Chihuahua, on the 23d of March last, and marked No. 102, in which the views of the Mexican government are communicated to me, with reference to the note which I had the honor to address to your department on the 6th of February previous, protesting against the acts of the French agents in Mexico, with which they are attempting to make the republic responsible.

I avail myself of this opportunity to renew to you, sir, the assurances of my distinguished consideration.

M. ROMERO.

Hon. WILLIAM HUNTER, *&c., &c., &c.*

[No. 102.—Translation.]

DEPARTMENT OF FOREIGN RELATIONS AND OF GOVERNMENT,
National Palace at Chihuahua, March 23, 1865.

In the copy annexed to your note No. 31, of February 6 of this year, the citizen President of the republic has seen the protest which you communicated under the same date to the honorable Secretary of State of the United States, with reference to the report that the French government had resolved to order its agent, Maximilian, to sign a pretended cession of a large part of the territory of the Mexican republic.

The President approves your conduct, although in this matter the republic has already protested from the beginning, by many of its legitimate organs, and of all its constituted authorities, against all the acts and consequences of foreign invasion.

Neither the republic nor its government can ever be holden for the debts of the French agent Maximilian, whose only title to authority is that lent to him by the presence of the armed forces of France, and who could not sustain himself in Mexico for a single day without the support of foreign bayonets.

The Mexican people, represented in the national congress, has solemnly declared its intention not to cede any part of the territory, whether large or small, to any nation. For this reason, in the laws enacted by congress, which conferred the most ample powers upon the government, even that of concluding treaties with foreign powers, the restriction was inserted that, in any treaty so concluded, the integrity of the national territory should be respected.

If Maximilian, in obedience to the orders of Napoleon, has signed or should hereafter sign a pretended cession of a portion of the territory, this should not be surprising, for, in order to do so, he must have set aside every consideration for the rights and will of the Mexican people, all respect for the national honor, and even for the sentiment of personal dignity, from the moment when, through of assumed authority, he determined to play in Mexico the part of the submissive agent of the French government.

I renew to you, sir, my very distinguished consideration.

LERDO DE TEJADA.

Citizen MATIAS ROMERO,
Envoy Extraordinary and Minister Plenipotentiary of the Mexican Republic, Washington, D. C.

Mr. Romero to Mr. Seward.

[Translation.]

MEXICAN LEGATION IN THE UNITED STATES OF AMERICA,
Washington, June 12, 1865.

MR. SECRETARY: There has come into my hands a memorandum which contains some considerations on the question about Mexico, treated from the point of view of the laws of nations in what regards the United States. Without expressing at present any opinion respecting it, much less asking it from the government of the United States, I confine myself to sending to you a copy of said memorandum.

I avail of this opportunity to renew to you, Mr. Secretary, the assurance of my most distinguished consideration.

M. ROMERO.

Hon. WILLIAM H. SEWARD, *&c., &c., &c.*

Memorandum.

Whatever were the causes which led to the war between France and Mexico, when it occurred it assumed the character of a war between two sovereign and independent nations. In *such* a war the United States had no right to interfere, for, in accordance with established principles of international law, the federal government was in duty bound to observe a strict neutrality. But after the occupation of the city of Mexico by the French, their real policy and intentions were unmasked. New tactics were at once adopted, which changed the entire aspect of affairs.

Former grievances were lost sight of; claims for indemnities and spoliations ceased to be the order of the day. Assisted by a few leading and influential Mexicans, France set to work to remodel the political status of the country, and succeeded in organizing an imperial party, representing the minority, in opposition to the republican party, representing the majority. Hostilities ensued between the two, and *civil war* was inaugurated. In his last annual message to Congress, President Lincoln, alluding to the situation of affairs in Mexico, took this view in declaring that *civil war* was still raging in that country.

This change of policy on the part of France changed the position of the United States in reference to the Mexican question. The war assumed a new form, and, from one waged between two nations, degenerated into a struggle for supremacy between two parties. If the French considered themselves justified in maintaining by force of arms one of these parties, the United States had undoubtedly the right to give their support to the other. International law no longer compelled them to observe a neutrality.

What was the result of this state of things? Simply that the imperial party, supported by French bayonets, and countenanced by other European governments, who suffered the newly-proclaimed sovereign of Mexico to contract loans and enlist soldiers in their midst, obtained the ascendancy over an adversary who was fighting, and still continues to fight, alone, unaided even with the moral support of the United States.

The United States have always proclaimed themselves to be the protectors of their sister republics on the American continent What hopes can the latter entertain of their future security when they see a great republic, of which they are the feeble imitators, assisting with indifference to the spectacle of a handful of foreign soldiers successfully progressing, on her very borders, in the work of erecting a government framed and fashioned on the European plan? What will be their reflections when they discover that the United States have nothing but words to offer to friends steadfast in their attachment from motives both of interest and sympathy?

If, through the instrumentality of the United States, a republic should be reared and fostered on the frontiers of France or of Russia, would these nations be indifferent to the event and accept the situation? Unquestionably not. For similar and more cogent reasons the United States cannot suffer the establishment, on the confines of their territory, of a monarchy created and maintained by foreign arms.

The United States have no more co-operated in safeguarding and perpetuating republican institutions in Mexico than the diminutive States of Central America, who have thought it sufficient to protest against this interference and encroachment on the part of European powers. But what may seem a matter of satisfaction to the pride of those states cannot be regarded in that light by so great and formidable a nation as the United States. The question at issue cannot remain in suspense; the United States must pursue one course or another—either to interfere actively in behalf of republican principles, and against the French occupation in Mexico, or to recognize Maximilian, and concede forever to European nations the right of an armed intervention in the domestic concerns of the republics on the American continent. Let the United States make this sacrifice, for they will then at least be spared, in the eyes of the world, the ridicule and mortification of not possessing the requisite energy to handle and settle a question of paramount interest to themselves, and in which the right is incontestably on their side.

Mr. Romero to Mr. Seward.

[Translation.]

MEXICAN LEGATION IN THE UNITED STATES OF AMERICA,
Washington, June 25, 1865.

MR. SECRETARY: Among the documents relating to Mexican affairs which I have neglected to transmit to your department, and which deserves the particular attention of the government of the United States, is a treaty, signed at Miramar, the 10th of April, 1864, between the Emperor of the French and the ex-Archduke of Austria, Ferdinand Maximilian, who assumed on that day the usurped title of emperor of Mexico.

In this treaty, of which I enclose you a copy in English, an alliance is agreed upon between the said ex-Archduke of Austria and the Emperor of the French.

I also enclose you a French copy, with English translation, of the address of Mr. Montholon, French minister near the said ex-archduke, when he was received by the latter on the 15th of June, 1864, and the usurper's reply.

I embrace this occasion of renewing to you, Mr. Secretary, the assurance of my most distinguished consideration.

M. ROMERO.

Hon. WILLIAM H. SEWARD, *&c., &c., &c.*

[Enclosure No. 1.—Translation]

TREATY.

The government of the Emperor of the French and that of the Emperor of Mexico, animated with an equal desire to secure the re-establishment of order in Mexico and to consolidate the new empire, have resolved to regulate by a convention the conditions of the stay of the French troops in that country, and have named their plenipotentiaries to that effect, viz:

The Emperor of the French—M. Charles Herbet, minister plenipotentiary of the first class, councillor of state, director of the ministry of foreign affairs, grand officer of the Legion of Honor, &c.; and the Emperor of Mexico—M. Joaquin Velasquez de León, his minister of state without portfolio, grand officer of the distinguished order of Our Lady of

Guadalupe, &c. ; who, after having communicated to each other their full powers, agreed on the following provisions :

ARTICLE 1. The French troops at present in Mexico shall be reduced as soon as possible to a corps of 20,000 men, including the foreign legion. This corps, in order to safeguard the interests which led to the intervention, shall remain temporarily in Mexico, on the conditions laid down by the following articles:

ARTICLE 2. The French troops shall evacuate Mexico in proportion as the Emperor of Mexico shall be able to organize the troops necessary to replace them.

ARTICLE 3. The foreign legion in the service of France, composed of 8,000 men, shall, nevertheless, remain in Mexico six years after all the other French troops shall have been recalled, in conformity with article 2. From that moment the said legion shall pass into the service and pay of the Mexican government, which reserves to itself the right of abridging the duration of the employment of the foreign legion in Mexico.

ARTICLE 4. The points of the territory to be occupied by the French troops, as well as the military expeditions of the said troops, if there be any, shall be determined in common accord, directly between the Emperor of Mexico and the commander-in-chief of the French corps.

ARTICLE 5. On all the points where the garrison shall not be exclusively composed of Mexican troops, the military command shall devolve on the French commander. In case of expeditions combined of French and Mexican troops, the superior direction of those troops shall also belong to the French commander.

ARTICLE 6. The French commanders shall not interfere with any branch of the Mexican administration.

ARTICLE 7. So long as the requirements of the French corps d'armé shall necessitate a two-monthly service of transports between France and Vera Cruz, the expense of the said service, fixed at the sum of 400,000 francs per voyage, (going and returning,) shall be paid by Mexico.

ARTICLE 8. The naval stations which France maintains in the West Indies and in the Pacific ocean shall often send vessels to show the French flag in the ports of Mexico.

ARTICLE 9. The expenses of the French expedition to Mexico, to be paid by the Mexican government, are fixed at the sum of 270,000,000 francs for the whole duration of the expedition down to 1st of July, 1864. That sum shall bear interest at the rate of 3 per cent. per annum. From the 1st of July all the expense of the Mexican army shall be at the charge of Mexico.

ARTICLE 10. The indemnity to be paid to France by the Mexican government for the pay and maintenance of the troops of the corps d'armé after the 1st of July, 1864, remains fixed at the sum of 1,000 francs a year for each man.

ARTICLE 11. The Mexican government shall hand over to the French government the sum of 66,000,000 francs in bonds of the loan at the rate of issue, viz: 54,000,000 francs, to be deducted from the debt mentioned in article 9, and 12,000,000 francs as an instalment of the indemnities due to Frenchmen in virtue of article 14 of the present convention.

ARTICLE 12. For the payment of the surplus of the war expenses, and for acquitting the charges in articles 7, 10, and 14, the Mexican government engages to pay annually to France the sum of 25,000,000 francs in specie. That sum shall be imputed : 1st, to the sums due in virtue of articles 7 and 10 ; 2d, to the amount, interest and principal, of the sum fixed in article 9 ; 3d, to the indemnities which shall remain due to French subjects in virtue of article 14 and following.

ARTICLE 13. The Mexican government shall pay, on the last day of every month, into the hands of the paymaster general of the army, what shall be due for covering the expenses of the French troops remaining in Mexico, in conformity with article 10.

ARTICLE 14. The Mexican government engages to indemnify French subjects for the wrongs they have unduly suffered, and which were the original cause of the expedition.

ARTICLE 15. A mixed commission, composed of three Frenchmen and three Mexicans, appointed by their respective governments, shall meet at Mexico within three months, to examine and determine these claims.

ARTICLE 16. A commission of revision, composed of two Frenchmen and two Mexicans, appointed by the same manner, sitting at Paris, shall proceed to the definitive liquidation of the claims already admitted by the commission designated in the preceding article, and shall decide on those which may have been reserved for its decision.

ARTICLE 17. The French government shall set at liberty all the Mexican prisoners of war as soon as the emperor of Mexico shall have entered his states.

ARTICLE 18. The present convention shall be ratified, and the ratifications exchanged as early as possible.

Done at the castle of Miramar, this 10th day of April, 1864.

HERBET.
JOAQUIN VELASQUEZ DE LEON.

[Enclosure No. 2.]

M. Montholon's speech.

SIRE: I have the honor to present to your Majesty the letters which accredit me to your Majesty in the quality of envoy extraordinary and minister plenipotentiary of his Majesty the Emperor Napoleon, my august sovereign.

It is with the most lively sentiments of gratitude towards Providence that, the first among the representatives of foreign powers, I approach the throne of your Imperial Majesty—that throne which has been raised amid the acclamations of an entire people, the assurance of a new future of power and of prosperity.

The work of restoration to which your Majesty has devoted yourself is one of those which could only have been undertaken by a great soul, animated by a spirit of abnegation and the desire to do good, and attracted even by the very difficulties that it presents. France, penetrated by the grandeur of the task and the immense advantages it will yield to the whole world, will follow with the most ardent solicitude the noble efforts of your Majesty, and will be always prepared to second them.

Already, sire, the Mexican nation experiences all the value of the generous thought which has guided your Majesties to these shores, and each day will be more and more appreciated all the extent of the benefits you have conferred upon them in responding to their appeal.

The noble companion whom God has placed at your side, sire, in view of the destinies reserved to you, will contribute, by her grace, by her virtues, by the high qualities of her mind and heart, to render unalterable the attachment of the Mexican people for your august persons.

Happy in having been selected by my sovereign to be his interpreter near your Imperial Majesty, my mission will be fulfilled according to the wishes of the Emperor and to the promptings of my own heart, if I shall be able to merit the confidence of your Majesty, and to contribute to render more and more intimate the fraternal relations of friendship which should exist between France and Mexico.

Established, both the one and the other, upon the basis of national suffrage, united for the future by the community of ideas, as well as by the reciprocal interest of commercial and industrial relations, the two empires will be drawn together by natural ties in the constant accord of a frank and loyal policy.

Be pleased, sire, to permit me to lay at the foot of the throne of your Majesties the sincere desires of the representative of France for the prosperity of your reign and the future grandeur of the Mexican nation.

[Enclosure No. 3.]

Maximilian's answer.

MONSIEUR LE MARQUIS: It is with sincere satisfaction that I receive from your hands the letters of credence by which his Majesty the Emperor of the French has accredited you near my person.

I am happy to see in you the representative of a sovereign who has done so much for the future of Mexico, and towards whom, as you have remarked, this country manifests sentiments of the most sincere gratitude.

I do not hesitate to believe that the bonds of friendship and the fraternal relations which unite France to Mexico will find in you a faithful interpreter; and, on my part, I will see with pleasure these ties drawn closer and closer between the two empires and the two peoples.

[Enclosure No. 4.—Translation.]

(El Iris, Tampico, June 9, 1864.)

DEPARTMENT OF STATE FOR FOREIGN AFFAIRS,
Imperial Palace, Mexico, May 19, 1864.

The regency of the empire has pleased to order the solemn publication of the act forwarded from Miramar by the Mexican commission charged to offer the votes of the Mexicans and the crown of the empire to his Imperial and Royal Highness the Archduke Ferdinand Maximilian of Austria, which says verbatim as follows:

At the palace of Miramar, near Trieste, on the tenth day of the month of April, 1864; being present in the reception room, his Imperial and Royal Highness the Archduke Maximilian of Austra and his august spouse, her Imperial and Royal Highness the Archduchess Carlota, accompanied by the Princess of Metternich, Countess Zichy, Lady of Honor to her Majesty the Empress of Austria, with the functions of Chief Lady of the Bedchamber of the Archduchess; the Countess Paula Kollatues, Canoness of the Chapter of Noble Ladies of Savoy; the Marchioness of Maria de Villa, Countess Zichy; his excellency M Herbet, minister plenipotentiary of the first class of his Majesty the Emperor of the French on mission from the Department for Foreign Affairs; his excellency Count O'Sullivan de Grasse, envoy extraordinary and minister plenipotentiary of his Majesty the King of the Belgians near the court of Vienna; M. Hypolite Morier, captain in the line of the French navy, and in command of the frigate Themis; and his excellency the Count Hadik de Tutak, actual privy councillor, Gentleman of his Imperial, Royal, and Apostolic Majesty, preceded by the grand-master of the ceremonies Marquis José Cerio, Gentleman of his Imperial, Royal, and Apostolic Majesty, and Gentleman on service of their Impérial Highnesses, who also were present at the audience; the president and other members present of the deputation charged to offer the vote of the Mexicans adopting monarchical institutions and inviting his Imperial and Royal Highness and his successors to occupy the throne, to wit: the most excellent D. José Maria Gutierrez de Estrada, Knight Grand Cross of the royal and distinguished Spanish order of Charles III, formerly minister for foreign affairs, and minister plenipotentiary of Mexico to various sovereigns of Europe; the most excellent Don Joaquin Velasquez de Leon, Commander of the imperial order of Guadalupe, former minister of finance in Mexico, and formerly minister plenipotentiary to the United States; Don Ignacio Aguilar, Commander of the order of Guadalupe, formerly minister of government and judge of the supreme court of the nation, and Don Adrian Woll, general of division, Commander of the orders of Guadalupe and the Legion of Honor, and M. de José Hidalgo, Commander with the decoration of the American order of Isabel the Catholic, of the Pontificate of Pio IX, and of that of Jerusalem, Grand Officer of that of Guadalupe, and Knight of that of San Silvestre; D. Antonio Escandon, Commander in the order of Isabel the Catholic, Knight of the order of St. Gregory, and of José Maria de Landa, Knight of the order of St. Gregory; and there were also introduced the Mexican gentlemen D. Francisco de Paula, Arrangoiz and Berzabel, Commander with the decoration of the royal American order of Isabella the Catholic, and of the Pontificate of St. Gregory, and Knight of that of Guadalupe of Mexico, formerly minister of the treasury; D. Tomas Murphy, Commander of the imperial and royal order of Francis Joseph of Austria, and formerly minister of Mexico to England; Colonel Don Francisco Facio, formerly chargé d'affaires at London, and consul-general at the Hanseatic Cities; D. Andrea Negrete, formerly chargé d'affaires at Belgium, and now chargé d'affaires and consul general at the Hanseatic Cities; D. Isidore Diaz, formerly minister of justice and of government; D. Pedro Escandon, Knight of the Legion of Honor, and formerly secretary of legation; Colonel D. José Annero Ruiz, Commander of the order of Isabella the Catholic, and Knight of that of Guadalupe, now consul at Marseilles; Doctor of Presbytery D. Ignacio Montes de Oca; Doctor D. Pablo Martinez del Rio, Knight of the order of Guadalupe; D. Fernando Gutierrez de Estrada, Knight of the order of St. Gregory; D. Ignacio Amor; D. Pedro Ontiveros, commanding battalion; D. Joaquin Manuel Rodriguez, commanding battalion. His excellency the president addressed to his Highness the Archduke the following allocution:

"Sir, the Mexican deputation has the happiness again to find itself in your august presence, and experiences unutterable gladness on reflecting on the motives which conduct it hither. In effect, sir, the good fortune falls on us to inform you, in the name of the regency of the empire, that the vote of the notables—by which you have been designated for the crown of Mexico—ratified this day by the enthusiastic adhesion of an immense majority of the country, of the municipal authorities, of the corporate bodies, consecrating that unanimous proclamation, has come to be, as well by its moral importance as by its numerical value, a truly national vote.

"By this glorious title, and sustained by the promises of the third of October, one thousand eight hundred and sixty-three, which have caused such well-founded hopes to spring up in the country, we now present ourselves to solicit from your Imperial Highness the full and definitive acceptance of the Mexican throne, which will become a bond of union and a source of prosperity to that people, subjected for so many years to very rude and terrible trials. So great have they been, that it would infallibly have succumbed beneath the burden of its calamities, without the aid of any one of the great empires of Europe, without the eminent qualities and admirable self-negation of your Imperial Highness, and lastly without the freedom of action which you are indebted for to the noble sentiments of your august brother, worthy head by a thousand titles of the illustrious house of Austria. Honor and gratitude to these two princes. Honor and gratitude also to the glorious nation which, at the call of its sovereign, has not hesitated to pour out its blood for our political redemption, thus creating between the one continent and the other a new fraternity in history, when until now this history has only shown to us in Europeans nothing but conquerors. Honor and gratitude to that emperor, great and generous, who, making a French interest of all the interests of the world, has in a few years, in despite of passing obstacles, had the glory and the fortune to raise the flag of France, always feared, but always sympathetic, on the confines of the distant empire of China, and on the remote frontiers of the far-off empire of Mexico. Honor and gratitude to such people and to such princes, is the cry of every true Mexican. By conquering the love of the people, you, sir, have learned the difficult art of governing them. Therefore it is that, after so many struggles, our country, which experiences an imperious necessity for union, will one day owe to you the inappreciable blessing of having conciliated the hearts of the Mexicans, whom public calamities and the blind waywardness of passion had divided and separated, but which only awaited your beneficent influence, and the exercise of your paternal authority, to show themselves animated by the same identical sentiments.

"A princess, who by her graciousness alone, no less than by her virtues and her high intelligence, is already queen, will without doubt understand, from the elevation of the throne, to draw together all minds into perfect union for the general improvement of the country. To see these benefits realized, Mexico with filial confidence places in your hands the sovereign and constituent power which must rule its future destinies, and assure its glorious hereafter, promising to you in this solemn moment of alliance a love with limit and happiness unchangeable.

"It is promised to you, sir, because, catholic and monarchic, through an uninterrupted tradition of ages, it finds in your Imperial Highness an offshoot worthy of the Emperor Charles the Fifth and the Empresss Maria Theresa, the symbol and the personification of those two great principles, bases of its primitive existence, and under whose protection, with institutions and appliances that the current of time has made necessary in the government of society, may some day be placed in the high position you are called to occupy among the nations—*in hoc signo vinces.*

"These two great principles, catholicism and monarchy, introduced into Mexico by the noble and knightly people who discovered it, eradicating the errors and dissipating the gloom of idolatry, to these principles, which trained us for civilization, we shall owe this time also our safety; revived as they have been by our independence, and, as they are now, by the smiling hopes bound up with the nascent empire. On this day, which would not be a day of happiness if it were not also a day of justice, our thoughts involuntarily turn to the historic times, and to the series of glorious monarchs, among whom excel in splendor the illustrious ancestors of your Imperial Highness. Nations as well as individuals should, in their hours of joy, salute with affectionate thankfulness the ancestors who no longer exist; and it is for us, sir, a glory we are ambitious of, to cause this just gratitude to shine forth at the very moment when our unhoped-for good fortune equally attracts to us the astonished regards of the world. In opening to you, sir, our wishes and our hopes, we do not say, we cannot say, that the undertaking is easy; the founding an empire never was so—never will be.

"The only thing we will assure you of is that the difficulties of to-day will to-morrow be your glory; and we will even add, that, in the work undertaken, the hand of God is manifestly revealed. When, with the progress of time, our hopes are satisfied and our predictions are verified, when Mexico appears prosperous and regenerate, then, reflecting that Europe sent to save us its brave battalions to the peaks of Anahuac and the shores of the Pacific, at a time when Europe itself was filled with apprehensions and danger, neither Mexico nor Europe, nor the world, nor that other world which will survive us, and which is called history, will doubt that our safety, procured contrary to all human probability, was not the work of Providence, and your Imperial Highness the instrument selected by it for its consummation. But not through thought of the hazarded fortunes of our country would it be possible for us to forget, sir, that in this hour of our rejoicing, the saddest gloom prevails in other places. We well understand, and our sympathies respond to the sense, that the Austrian land, and chiefly Trieste, your favored residence, will be inconsolable in your absence, but will be consoled by the recollection of your beneficence, and the splendid reflex of your glory.

"After having had the inappreciable fortune to hear from the lips of your Imperial Highness the words of hope that your definitive acceptance will become a reality, deign, sir, to grant us this distinguished and ineffable good fortune to be the first Mexicans who reverently greet you in the name of the country as the sovereign of Mexico, the arbiter of its destinies, and the trustee of its future; the whole Mexican nation, which waits with unspeakable impatience to possess you, will receive you on its privileged soil with a unanimous shout of welcome and of love. But for a soul like yours, sir, this brilliant spectacle, which would be a recompense to others, will only serve to inspire you with new spirit, and strengthen your confidence.

"The reward will come at a later day, and will be providential, like the undertaking achieved. There will be no reward more enviable than that your Highness will receive by coming boldly and respected to Mexico at no distant day; and in truth you could not experience a purer joy than to have founded on the voicanic soil of the Montezumas a powerful empire that will in a short time combine for its splendor and your glory the fruitful influence of that native genius with which Heaven has gifted our American land, with all of the perfection which the justly valued European organization can offer.

"The last conviction, sir, that with us crowns such happy presages, is that Mexico, that sends its acclamations to you from beyond the seas, and the whole world that gazes on you, will not long wait to learn that your Imperial Highness has not in vain had before your eyes, from your infancy, on the triumphal arch placed in front of the palace of your ancestors, that inscription, well worthy of them, and which takes by surprise the admiration of the traveller: 'Justitia regnorum fundamentum'—Justice the foundation of empire."

His Highness deigned to reply in these terms:

"GENTLEMEN: A deliberate examination of the acts of adhesion which you have come to present to me gives me confidence that the voice of the notables of Mexico, which brought you a short time since to Miramar, has been ratified by an immense majority of your countrymen, and that I can consider myself from this time by good right as the chosen one of the Mexican people. Thus is accomplished the first condition set forth in my reply of 3d of October last. I also indicated another to you at that time, to wit, that relating to securing the guarantees necessary, that the nascent empire should be able calmly to devote itself to the noble task of establishing on a solid basis its independence and well-being. We count to-day on those securities—thanks to the magnanimity of the Emperor of the French, who, in the course of the negotiations which have had place on this subject, has shown himself to be constantly animated by a spirit of loyalty and good-will, the record of which I shall always treasure in my memory.

"On the other hand, the august head of my family has consented to my taking possession of the throne which has been offered to me.

"Now, then, I can fulfil the conditional promise which I made you six months since, to declare here, as I do solemnly declare, that with the aid of the Almighty I accept at the hands of the Mexican nation the crown which it offers to me. Mexico, according to the traditions of that new continent, full of strength and of a hereafter, has exercised the right it has, thus to give to itself a government in conformity with its wishes and its wants, and has staked its hopes on an offshoot of that House of Hapsburg which, three centuries ago, established on its soil a Christian kingdom. I appreciate at its full value such a demonstration of confidence, and shall take care to respond to it. I accept the constitutional power with which the nation, whose organ you are, has seen fit to invest me; but I will only hold it for the time requisite to create regular order in Mexico, and to establish wisely liberal institutions; so that, as I announced to you in my address on the 3d October, I shall hasten to establish monarchy upon the authority of constitutional laws as soon as the pacification of the country may be completely effected.

"The strength of a power is, in my opinion, much better assured by the permanence than by the uncertainty of its limits; and I aspire to place in the exercise of my government those who, without detriment to its prestige, may guarantee its stability. We will prove, as I hope, that liberty well understood is perfectly reconcilable with the empire of order. I shall comprehend how to respect the first, and to cause the second to be respected. I shall exhibit no less vigor in ever maintaining the flag of independence, that symbol of future greatness and prosperity.

"Great is the undertaking confided to me; but I have no doubt of carrying it through, trusting in divine aid and the co-operation of all good Mexicans. I will conclude, gentlemen, by assuring you anew that my government will never forget the gratitude it owes to the illustrious and friendly monarch whose aid has made the regeneration of our beautiful country possible.

"In fine, gentlemen, I announce to you that, before setting off for my new home, I shall only remain long enough to go to the Holy City to receive from the venerable Pontiff the benediction so precious to every sovereign, but doubly important to me, who have been called to found a new empire."

The president replied, saying:

"Possessed by feelings that cannot be exceeded, and penetrated with delight ineffable, we receive, sir, the solemn YES which your Majesty has just uttered. This full and absolute acceptance, so ardently desired, and looked for with panting expectations, is the happy prelude, and must be, with God's help, the sure pledge of the salvation of Mexico, of its new birth, and of its future greatness. On the same day our sons will raise to Heaven offers of thanksgiving for this truly prodigious redemption. There remains to us one duty, sir, to fulfil—the duty of laying at your feet the love of the Mexicans, their gratitude, and the homage of their fidelity."

These last words spoken, the mitred abbot of Miramar and Lacroma, Monsieur George R.c.c., with mitre and crook, assisted by Friar Tomas Gomez, of the order of Franciscans, and Doctor D. Ignacio Montes de Oca, presented themselves to witness the oath which the emperor spontaneously took in these words:

"I, Maximilian, emperor of Mexico, swear to God on the Holy Evangels to promote by all means in my power the welfare and prosperity of the nation, to defend its independence, and maintain the integrity of its territory."

Their majesties were three times saluted with cheers: "Long live the emperor! long live the empress!" given by his excellency Señor Gutierrez de Estrada, and repeated with enthusiasm by the assemblage. They then retired to await the hour set for the Te Deum, which was solemnly chaunted in the chapel in presence of their majesties, the deputation and suite, at which act the emperor also wore the insignia of Grand Master of the Mexican order of Guadalupe. Meantime, at the moment the emperor took the oath, the imperial Mexican standard was hoisted on the tower of the castle, and the frigate Bellona, of the imperial and royal Austrian navy, gave a salute of twenty-one guns, which was repeated by the castle at Trieste, and by the French frigate Themis.

Thus closed the solemn act by which the Archduke of Austria, proclaimed emperor of Mexico by the free and spontaneous choice of that people, became invested with the sovereignty which he will transmit to his illustrious descendants, or to princes called to rule by the law of succession which his majesty may deign to sanction.

To perpetuate the memory of this great event, this act is extended, by order of his excellency the president of the deputation, in duplicate, and signed by him and other members of the same deputation before mentioned, and authenticated by me as secretary, and will be transmitted to the department of foreign affairs and to the archives of the imperial house.

J. M. GUTIERREZ DE ESTRADA,
President.

JOAQUIN VELASQUEZ DE LEON,
IGNACIO AGUILAR,
ADRIAN WOLL,
JOSÉ HIDALGO,
ANTONIO ESCANDON,
J. M. DE LANDA,
ANGEL YGLESIAS Y DOMINGUEZ,
Secretaries.

Mr. Romero to Mr. Seward.

[Translation.]

MEXICAN LEGATION IN THE UNITED STATES OF AMERICA,
Washington, 21st of July, 1865.

MR. SECRETARY: I have the honor to transmit to you, for the information of the government of the United States, a translation into English of the discussion which took place in the legislative body of France on the 8th of June last, in relation to the affairs of Mexico, and of extracts of the disposal of that discussion, which terminated on the 9th thereof. The said translation has been faithfully made from the official record of the proceedings of that assembly, published in the numbers 160 and 161 of the Moniteur Universel, of Paris, corresponding to the 9th and 10th days of June aforementioned, pages 766, 767, 768, and 776.

The Mexicans who defend the independence of their country against the colossal power of France, and who at the end of four years of an unequal contest maintain with the same undaunted courage and decision that holy cause, when neither misfortunes nor disasters nor treason can avail to intimidate them or to cause them to deviate by a single step from the path which they believe it to be their duty to follow, and through which they have already made themselves worthy of the respect of the world, now find themselves assailed by their enemies with the most opprobrious epithets, but which reflect dishonor upon those who so unjustly seek to tarnish the character of those whom they cannot conquer in a good fight. These Mexicans have now the satisfaction of seeing their conduct defended and vindicated by the independent orators themselves of the French assembly, and in the presence itself of the despot who does his utmost to bring discredit upon such noble patriots. Furthermore, this discussion contains other points of much importance, which I do not doubt will excite the serious attention of the government of the United States.

I avail myself of this opportunity to renew to you, Mr. Secretary, the assurances of my most distinguished consideration.

M. ROMERO.

Hon. WILLIAM H. SEWARD, &c., &c., &c.

[From Le Moniteur Universel, No. 160, June 9, 1865, page 766, volume —.]

Discussion in the French legislative body.

SESSION OF THURSDAY, *June* 8, 1865.

M. Schneider, vice-president, in the chair.

The session was opened at half past 3 o'clock. The minutes of the session of the preceding day were read by Count Le Pelletier d'Aunay, one of the secretaries.

* * * * * * * * * *

THE CHAIRMAN, M. SCHNEIDER. The Chamber stopped yesterday in the vote on bill F, annexed to article 7, at the sections relative to the ministry of war and of the general government of Algeria. I resume the reading of the bill:

EXPENSES OF THE MINISTRY OF WAR.

"Section 1, (division second)—Central administration, quartermaster's department, 12,500 francs." (Adopted.)

"Section 2, (division second)—General staff, police force, 1,357,000 francs." (Adopted.

"Section 3, (division second)—Pay and maintenance of the troops, 33,718,801 francs.'

M. Jules Favre is entitled to the floor.

M. JULES FAVRE. Gentlemen, in proposing to you to insert in the deficiency budget of 1865 a sum of thirty-five millions in round numbers to cover an excess of expenditures in the war budget, the government and your committee impose on us the duty of examining the particular items of these expenses, and you know the most important one, and that to which all the others may be referred, is that relative to the Mexican expedition.

It may be said that this year, in accordance with the mechanism of our financial system, this expedition exerts a double influence on it—passively in reference to the expense, actively in reference to the receipts; and these two particulars, by an inexorable degree of fate, are so indissolubly bound together that one governs the other; that, in order to recover a sum of twenty-five millions a year, which is carried to the credit side of the budget, it is at present indispensable to enter on the debit side a sum which, in the deficiency bill for 1865, exceeds thirty millions.

Such is, moreover, the calculation and the process to which we have been condemned from the very beginning of this Mexican expedition.

That expedition was undertaken for the recovery of an indemnity, of a debt, fixed at a sum less than a million; and if we estimate at the very highest figure the contingent debts claimed by the persons interested, they fluctuated between five and twelve millions. We have already devoted more than four hundred millions to this expedition, and as an indemnity for this outlay we have only a certificate of indebtedness from the Mexican government. It is therefore our duty to examine closely what our condition is, and what shall be the extent and the duration of our sacrifices.

I am well aware that I am here to meet with an objection that has been made to me several times, and which, at one of our recent sessions, was very precisely stated in the speech of the honorable minister of state. "These criticisms," said he, "are inoportune; they are contrary to prudence and even to patriotism. Our soldiers are now at work; France has accepted the conception and the execution of a great work beyond the Atlantic; and yet this is the very moment which is selected to examine and criticise the motives of that work; and so, at the time when the great interests of all dictate a concurrence of effort for its stable consummation, it is by such attacks enfeebled and ruined in advance."

Gentlemen, if such an objection as this could condemn us to silence, we might as well renounce forever the little share of power that has been left to us by the constitution. [Murmurs of disapprobation from several benches. Applause around the speaker.]

The initiative belongs not to us; especially in matters appertaining to our foreign relations we are called upon to consider resolutions already taken; and if we have not the right to examine them when they are submitted to us, we may as well abdicate our power entirely. [Renewal of similar demonstrations.]

That such is not your intention, gentlemen, I am fully convinced. Undoubtedly the spirit of abuse and passion is culpable; but that which is no less so, and which may be more dangerous, is the spirit of systematic illusion, and undiscriminating and predetermined confidence. The spirit of abuse and passion awakens the distrust of the government and places it on the defensive. On the contrary, the spirit of illusion, the spirit of systematic and predetermined confidence, encourages every species of rashness and folly; it is capable of precipitating rash undertakings from which it is impossible to withdraw.

It is therefore a very serious obligation upon us to examine the situation in which we are placed, whilst we strive, in truth, to avoid both those rocks, and for the decision of facts have recourse to a careful investigation of the truth, with the independence that appertains to this great assembly.

Well, you remember that when there was first question of this Mexican expedition, we entreated the government to be pleased to restrict it to the redress of the grievances of which our countrymen had to complain, and to abstain carefully from any interference with the internal affairs of the country. Then the language of the government was very different from that which we heard in one of your recent meetings. You may remember with what disdain they treated our anticipations; and when we spoke of a prospective emperor, to whose zealousness an appeal had already been made, how they treated all such ideas as chimeras, and how they loudly disavowed them; and when it was desirable to obtain the adhesion of the Chamber, and it was sought to specify the nature, the character, and the purpose of the expedition, they did not depart far from the system which we ourselves have always counselled to those in power.

They said, in fact, that it was for the redress of the grievances of our countrymen that we went to Mexico; only if the nation manifested a desire for a political change, we were to give them our assistance and we were to consult them; but it was from themselves and not from us that should emanate the final expression of will that was to decide as to their future government. Then the government very loudly proclaimed that it did not intend to allow itself any intermeddling in this regard; that it was a Mexican and not a foreign power that it intended to inaugurate. And on this point, here are the words uttered by the honorable minister of state, M. Billault, not on the occasion of the first debate between us, but the second, at the time of the debate on the budget in the month of June, 1862:

"When the French flag, an event which I hope will soon happen, floats over the walls of Mexico, we will not depart from this generous and protective policy; all, whether reactionists or liberals, violent or moderate, shall be equally admitted to participate in this general expression of the public will; there shall be liberty for all beneath the flag of France, and it will not be the first time, as you know, that it shall have thus sheltered under its tutelary folds the just manifestation of national desires.

"All will be allowed full and entire liberty of choice, and then if the tyranny of Juarez suits them—yes, if it suits them—well, they will say so!"

These, gentlemen, are the words that were received with almost unanimous approbation by the Chamber; these are the declarations that induced the resolution of the majority.

Now, I ask you, What have they in common with the lofty conceptions presented to you, at one of your recent meetings, by the minister of state? Ah! gentlemen, like yourselves, I am always touched by his talent; I am full of admiration for his eloquence; I am not astonished at the applause with which you receive his words; and if I have any regret, it is that I cannot join in it. Only let me be permitted to say to him, with all the deference which I entertain for him, that I find this eloquence often dangerous; that it inflames more than it enlightens; that it throws more brilliancy than light on the questions on which it is exercised; and, in my opinion, the minister of state, in treating of this Mexican question, has allowed himself to be carried too far by the dangerous seductions of oratory.

In any case, I assert that this grand idea of a regeneration of the Mexican nation, of the foundation of an empire which is to be, beyond the sea, the fruit of the power and protection of France, is the mere result of chance, of events; and that it has been developed by facts entirely unforeseen by those now advancing it. For this dilemma stands: either, as I am unwilling to believe, the truth has not been told to the Chamber, designs have been concealed from it before which it would have recoiled; or else these designs are merely the results of an afterthought. This great enterprise which it is now sought to glorify before you is only an idea that has been thrown into the scale of events by facts not sufficiently considered beforehand. All the difficulties, all the dangers, all the political inconveniences that such an idea might produce, were not taken into consideration; those who now entertain that idea gave themselves up to it as to a sort of necessity which it was impossible to foresee, and which became the pivot of the operations into which they were dragged, after having engaged in an expedition from which they should have refrained from the very beginning.

Thus, what I assert is, that this idea of the regeneration of the Mexican nation, which is now presented to us as one of the reasons for the continuance of our occupation, and the achievement of which alone can permit our flag to be withdrawn in an honorable manner, did not exist at the commencement. We went to Mexico to avenge our countrymen; we went to Mexico to interrogate the Mexican nation, and we solemnly declared to it that we would listen to its reply, and that we would conform ourselves to it.

Now the tone is somewhat changed. Hopes of a more lofty, but at the same time of a more deceptive character, are held up before your dazzled eyes; and, in order not to be led astray by them, we must examine them closely; we must not let olurselves be seduced by glittering words; we must not rely merely on the dedutions of eloquence; we must consult facts, and facts alone. [Manifestations of approbation around the speaker.]

Now, gentlemen, permit me to say that, if the transcendent talents and eloquence of the minister of state have oftentimes carried away the votes of the Chamber, they have not entirely mastered the prejudices of the committee; for the committee, even in view of these brilliant prospects held out, has given utterance to words of much wisdom—words, unfortunately, very useless, for they are incessantly repeated, and they are only a vain sound that moves the air; and I do not see, gentlemen, that the advice given to the government with so much deference is followed any more this year than in preceding ones.

Here is what the committee says: "In the course of these thoughts with which it has been deeply inspired, the committee could not refrain from directing its attention to the Mexican expedition. Less onerous since the return of our troops has commenced, the sacrifices which it has occasioned are, it is true, compensated by reimbursements; but political considerations combine with financial reasons to cause us to desire that the completion of the work of pacification and the definitive establishment of the Mexican army, which is in a good state of organization, should hasten the moment when the last soldiers of the expeditionary corps shall return to France."

And a little further on the same thought is again expressed, and it is peculiarly eloquent in view of the two numbers with which it is connected—41,342,470 francs on one side, claimed as the amount yet due for the expenses of our army, and 9,000,000 that are taken from the treasury of France to pay the Mexican army; certainly a very unpleasant innovation, and one which ought to be restricted within the narrowest limits.

So the committee adds, after having stated these facts: "We had in Mexico, at the beginning of last year, an army of 34,000 men; by the return home of various regiments its strength has been reduced to 28,000 men. It will be still further diminished from this time to the end of 1865 by the return to France of other regiments, which will embark at Vera Cruz as soon as the expiration of the sickly season will allow them to march towards the warm country without exposing the lives of our soldiers. Your committee on the budget cannot but repeat here the wish that the definitive organization of the Mexican army should contribute to facilitate this movement and hasten the moment at which the last detachments of our army are to return to their country."

Such, gentlemen, are the wishes that have been expressed by your committee, and I have the right to say—no one can contradict me—that herein the committee has spoken the sentiment of the whole country. Yes, it ardently desires that the last of our soldiers in Mexico should, as soon as possible, set foot on the soil of his native land, and that as soon as possible, also, we should disengage ourselves from this heavy and perhaps terrible responsibility that weighs upon us as long as our flag floats over a foreign land.

The committee lays down the period of the reorganization of the Mexican army as the fitting time for the withdrawal of the French forces.

We will soon have to ask ourselves whether, in a political point of view, not indeed permitting ourselves to be guided by mere theories, but seeking a solution from official documents, from those emanating from the government itself, from its despatches and its declarations, this is indeed the only condition that can allow the French army to withdraw and abandon Mexico.

But I will make this observation to the Chamber—that the language of the committee, which, in my opinion, is the sentiment of the whole country, is but the repetition of that used by all the committees before it that have examined our financial condition.

They have not failed to hold out the same warning to the government; they have not ceased to repeat to it, with all the energy which could be inspired into them by their ardent desire to maintain, as representatives of the majority, a good understanding with the government, while assuring it of their entire support, that it was necessary to put the earliest possible end to this Mexican expedition.

This is, also, what was said by our honorable colleague, M. Gouin, so well informed in such affairs, when, in his report, under date of December 25, 1863, he gave utterance to those words, which I cannot sufficiently urge the government to ponder, for they contain the secret of maintaining a true equilibrium in all budgets:

"We insist, on the contrary, with all our strength, that the government should confine itself within the ordinary resources of our budgets, and not enter upon a system of extraordinary expenses that may have the most serious consequences in the future. Let us learn, moreover, to resist the seductions of glory; let us enjoy that which we have acquired, and with which we can honorably desire a peace of which the nations have so much need. Let us have peace, and our finances will improve; we can then employ larger sums in our public works, which will prove an abundant source of wealth and prosperity for our people"

And none of you, gentlemen, have forgotten the remarkable report of our colleague, M. Larrabure, who not only repeated the wish expressed by the honorable M. Gouin, but also caused the government to adopt the declaration that had been made by him, that he hoped that by the end of 1864 our army should have quitted Mexico.

"At this moment," said the honorable M. Larrabure, "the Emperor's government declares that it has no engagements with any one, either to leave a body of French troops in Mexico, or to guarantee any loan whatever; it declares that it has no reason to think that it may be necessary to increase the number of the French troops now actually in Mexico; that any movements that may take place until their final withdrawal will be only for the purpose of replacing the sick and those entitled to discharge. Under present circumstances, as far as it can foresee, the government hopes that the end of 1864 will mark the term of the expedition."

And as the Chamber had participated somewhat in the feelings of the people in regard to an expedition that conducted our brave soldiers to the north of Mexico, the government deemed that it could give the committee the formal assurance that the expedition to San Luis Potosi should be the last.

"As to the expedition to San Luis Potosi in particular," said the report, "it has been judged necessary, in order to occupy the most important parts of Mexico. The country comprised between San Luis and the city of Mexico includes some important centres of population. Their occupation became useful solely in order to hasten the consummation of the work undertaken—the reparation of our grievances and the enabling Mexico freely to choose a new government. Being masters of the country as far as San Luis de Potosi, we can see these projects realized with more rapidity and success. The army will stop there."

Such, gentlemen, was the assurance of the government to the committee; such the engagement made by it; and the committee added these significant words, which I recommend to your kindly consideration, and from which I shall soon be entitled to draw their legitimate conclusions:

"The army will stop there; the method of universal suffrage, naturally set in motion in accordance with the usages or the institutions of the country, will be invoked for the selection of the system of government that may be best suited to it; whatever shall be its decision, France will respect it."

Thus, more than two years passed away; unforeseen obstacles presented themselves; the courage of our soldiers triumphed over everything, and the flag of France floated in triumph over the city of Mexico.

The government engages not to continue, for the advantage of a cause which cannot be that of France, an expedition that would conduct our armies into vast provinces where they would be exposed to fatigues, privations, and dangers, which they are not bound to undergo when it is not the cause of the nation that impels them.

This was the first declaration of the government. There has been a second one, which is no less important in a political point of view. It is that there would be no sort of pressure exerted on the Mexican nation. Not only will it be consulted, but it is indicated also how that will be done. It will be in the most liberal manner. Each and every individual will concur in the erection of this vast national edifice, from which only anarchy and evil passions will be excluded. Universal suffrage alone can have this secret and potency. If our troops have gone to Mexico to accomplish a stern duty, at least, after having stricken with the sword, they will give consolation by the introduction of civilization and its benefits, and universal suffrage will be the consequence of their descent on the Mexican territory. [Cries of good! good! around the speaker.]

This is what was said in the report, and I have bound myself to it. I will keep my word—I will cite only official documents—here is what was promised in the month of January, 1864.

And when, just now, I told you that the language used in 1865, and which comes from your committee, is only the echo of all these anterior declarations, and that it is in complete accordance with those of the various committees and of the government, you see that I was in the right.

But I ask you, my colleagues, of what use are all these declarations if they remain sterile? Why these promises if they are violated? Why these counsels given to the government if it takes no account of them? Has the army stopped at San Luis de Potosi? Not only you know that it has proceeded even to Durango and Monterey, but also—this is certain—a part of our troops have ventured, we know not why, into the deserts of Sonora, where there is nought but privations for our heroic soldiers, where they are condemned to transport their cannon on the backs of men, where they have to struggle against all the difficulties and all the unhealthiness of the climate.

Such is the language of the government and such its course of action. Can we continue? Is it wise to content ourselves with mere words like these? Is it well that a great assembly like yours, and the committees which are its expression, should continue this kind of misunderstanding between us and the government, while we say, "The expedition must be terminated," and the government says, "I wish to terminate it," and yet, in reality, continues and extends it?

Well, it must be said, the state of the case was defined with very great precision at our last meeting, with so much precision, indeed, that it is impossible now to take refuge behind the slightest equivocation.

In fact, gentlemen, when M. Thiers spoke upon this question, with his wonderful sagacity, he understood perfectly well that on that day when France took the Archduke Maximilian by the hand, placed him beneath the protection of her flag, and accompanied him with the aid of her armies to enthrone him in the city of Mexico, she espoused his cause and bound herself irrevocably to it.

And then, gentlemen, he put some very precise questions to the government, to which replies were given, and these questions and these replies it behooves you now to recall to mind. Here is what the honorable M. Theirs said in the session of January 26, 1864:

"I believe that when you shall have encouraged the government to persist in its purposes, which will depend on the tone which you may adopt, it will be very unseasonable and inappropriate for you afterwards to refuse it troops, sailors, and millions of money, in order to sustain to the end that which you are now about to undertake; for, reflect well on it, hitherto you have not committed yourselves, as an affair of honor, but on the day that the prince sails with your support, with your guarantee, you must sustain him at all hazards, whatever comes of it."

And our illustrious and venerable colleague, M. Berryer, insisting on these simple truths, added also, "Can the government assure France that it has resolved soon to quit Mexico? Or are we, on the contrary, to be told that it will prescribe as a preliminary, conformably to the instructions given to General Bazaine, the establishment of the monarchy of the Archduke Maximilian in Mexico?"

And behold, gentlemen, in what terms the honorable minister of state replied:

"The honorable M. Thiers has said to you, 'We wish to withdraw honorably from Mexico.' Yes, we wish to withdraw honorably. The Chamber has favorably received both of these declarations. In fact, these two declarations are the sentiment of the majority and the sentiment of the government."

You received these expressions, gentlemen, with marks of approbation.

"But the government does not deem it honorable to withdraw from it by negotiating with Juarez. The government does not consider it proper to treat with General Almonte, who represents no legally constituted authority. It can only negotiate with a government sprung from universal suffrage. When a contract shall have been made between the Mexican nation and the Archduke Maximilian, if he is elected, the French government, by negotiating with that sovereign, will not have thereby contracted a permanent and indefinite agreement for the maintenance of an empire in Mexico."

All this, gentlemen, is perfectly clear. The wish of the government is apparent to you. It does not wish to negotiate with Juarez, who is an enemy; it does not wish to negotiate with Almonte, who is the representative of a provisional government. It is necessary that it should meet the Mexican nation face to face, in the person of the chief, not who has been imposed upon it, but whom it has freely chosen through the medium of universal suffrage. And when this popular consecration shall have intervened to establish Maximilian on his throne, France will negotiate with him and will withdraw honorably.

This is, gentlemen, what was said by the government, and it was impossible, allow me to observe, for it to hold any other language. Precedents all pointed in that direction; the Emperor himself had already written:

"It is against my interests, against my origin, against my principles, to impose any government whatever on the Mexican people; let them select in full liberty the form that suits them best."

And M. Billault added, in the session of February 7, 1863:

"We appeal to the Mexican people. If its vote declares even for the government of Juarez, so be it; let its vote be allowed to take effect!"

And, under date of January 27, 1864, the minister of state gave utterance to words which do not much differ from them:

"The system of universal suffrage will soon perform its functions. If the Mexican nation adopts the republican form, we will respect its vote. If it prefers to establish a monarchy, we will likewise respect it. Now that seven-eighths of the Mexican people have been freed from the yoke of Juarez and from his exactions, universal suffrage will soon pronounce, and then the work of France will approach its completion."

Such words, it must be stated, are only the consequence of the original convention that united three powers to march against Mexico; for they had all mutually obliged themselves—they are the terms of article 2 of the treaty of October 31, 1861—"not to exert in the internal affairs of Mexico any influence of a nature calculated to injure the rights of the Mexican nation to choose the form of its government."

This, then, is perfectly well settled, and I do not believe it to be possible to deny that what the government has wished, what it yet recently wished according to its language last year, was to bring the Mexican nation freely to manifest its wishes by means of universal suffrage. It did not wish to impose on it any species whatever of form of government.

Only it has happened—and assuredly, in the career of a statesmen, such a good fortune is very rare—it has happened that the scheme which we had announced, and which, although it was denied, had been long beforehand prepared by diplomacy, namely, the advancement of the Archduke Maximilian, was what proved most agreeable to the Mexican nation. In one of our late meetings you heard the extremely interesting developments presented to you by one of our honorable colleagues just returned from Mexico He had therein superior advantages to us. He told us seriously that the Archduke Maximilian must succeed, because he had blue eyes and golden hair. [Laughter on various benches]

Yes, yes, this was one of the elements of success for him—this is what would cause him to be received with acclamation by the Mexican nation; and you will see that the Mexican nation did not even need to see him—his good qualities were foreshadowed to them; for, even before he had yet left Miramar, the announcement of his arrival had produced such an effect that a general enthusiasm was created in his favor. So we are told by the *Moniteur* of July 24, in which we read: "We call the attention of our readers to the correspondence from Mexico———."

And, in fact, in the session of January 26, the honorable vice-president of the council of state, M. Chaix d'Est Ange, entered into an enumeration of the adherents of the empire, and assuredly, gentlemen, nothing was more gratifying. He said:

"We have now five and a half millions of inhabitants out of seven millions adhering to us, yea, obeying our laws. There are not two millions outside of our circle of action, and on these, I believe, even the most ancient and best established governments of the country have never been able to lay their hands; even the Spanish government was unable to control them."

Thus, gentlemen, more than five millions out of seven millions adhered to the scheme proposed by France. The Archduke Maximilian had only to touch the soil of Mexico, triumphal arches were already prepared, and our honorable colleague has told us that from Vera Cruz to the city of Mexico it was but one long pageant; that at Vera Cruz they received him under a shower of flowers—always, it is true, excepting from these demonstrations the 1,500,000 Mexicans whom the honorable commissioner on the part of the government qualified as recalcitrant, incorrigible, and factious individuals. What is undeniable, at least, is, that they were men who defended their country and who desired no foreign domination. [Murmurs of disapprobation.]

This state of affairs is similarly set forth in the *exposé* of the condition of the empire which has been distributed among us.

Here, gentlemen, mention is made of the eagerness with which Maximilian was received. At page 174, towards the end, I read as follows:

"The results obtained in 1862 and 1863 by our expeditionary corps in Mexico, have, in 1864, received a solemn consecration. Under the protection of the flag of France, a regular government has been founded in that country, heretofore for more than fifty years delivered up to anarchy and intestine dissensions. In the beginning of the month of June the emperor Maximilian took possession of the throne, and sustained by our army, he inaugurates in all security an era of peace and prosperity for his new country."

And a little further on we find similar words of congratulation and confidence, and then we asked ourselves, on occasion of the address: "Since the Mexican emperor is established, since Maximilian is the messiah announced by all past times, since he is really the man both for the Indians and Spaniards, who receive him with acclamations, since he meets on his passage only the *bouquets* of the *señoritas*, let our soldiers return. What have they to do in Mexico? They are not needed; let them return. They would only mar by their presence the gaiety of such a universal holiday; they would only be an obstacle in the way of that entire unanimity of feeling that exists between the prince and the nation."

But between these words and the truth there is, unfortunately, gentlemen, a world of difference.

They have spoken to us of some Mexicans who were unwilling to take part with the new government; these they are occupied in pacifying. How is this pacification effected? Hear what we learn from the news published in the papers, and in reference to which the Moniteur has been vainly called upon for explanations. It has continued to keep silence. I regret it, gentlemen; for if these announcements are true, they are a stain upon the pages of the history of France. [Murmurs of disapprobation from several benches.]

Listen, gentlemen; here is what I read in a telegraphic despatch published by a Paris paper of the date of April 19, 1865, announcing that the pacification of Mexico is more and more complete, and that General Castagny has burned a city.

Do you know what San Sebastian is? It is a city of 4,000 souls; it has been given to the flames, and yet the Moniteur is silent.

I do not insist that such an announcement should be contradicted; only, until it is contradicted it stands; unfortunately, I have reason to consider it correct; and what induces me to believe that I am not mistaken is the proclamation issued by the same commander on entering one of the cities of Mexico, whereby he announced what fate was reserved for those who would not submit to his laws.

Listen, gentlemen, and ask yourselves, after having heard these words, whether mine are too severe:

"Mexicans! I have come, in the name of the emperor Maximilian, into the State of Sinaloa, to establish peace therein, to protect property, and to deliver you from the malefactors who oppress you under the mask of liberty."

Several voices: That is all right.

M. JULES FAVRE. How! protect property by burning a city of 4,000 inhabitants; to lay waste while declaring himself protector. [Interruptions and murmurs of disapprobation.]

A MEMBER. You have made no mention of the brigandage that has authorized such reprisals.

M. ROUHER, Minister of State. You are defending Romero, a robber and an assassin. [Confused manifestations.]

M. GARNIER PAGÈS. How! whole cities burned? It is only dens of thieves and brigands that have been destroyed.

THE MINISTER OF STATE. Be pleased to respect the French flag.

M. EUGENE PELLETAN. Burn a whole city! That is what they do in Poland.

M. GARNIER PAGÈS, in the midst of great confusion, utters some words that did not reach the reporters.

THE CHAIRMAN, M. SCHNEIDER. Assuredly, you cannot be well acquainted with the facts, to be so positive in your assertions. I request you to be pleased to permit M. Jules Favre to continue his speech.

M. JULES FAVRE. I proceed:

"Efforts have been made to distort the purpose of our intervention; many of you have been drawn into a false path, and they have allowed themselves to be blinded in regard to the veritable interests of their country."

It is we who have undertaken to teach the Mexicans what are the real interests of their country, and we have promised to consult them. [Disapprobation.]

That is not all: "The hour of justice has come." Listen to this, gentlemen, and I proceed to ask you whether there are two codes of morals—one for the use of the party that triumphs, and the other prohibited to the vanquished.

Listen to this: "The hour of justice has come. A rigorous sentence is being executed at this very moment against the district of Concordia." The sentence is the burnt city; and see how they reply to those who resist; the refuge of women and children, private property, everything is devastated, everything is destroyed. Mexico is enlightened by fire, and it is by the light of this fire that the proclamation which I read to you has been drawn up.

Listen: "The hour of justice has come. A rigorous sentence is being executed at this very moment against the district of Concordia. Let this example exert a salutary influence on your minds. Appreciate our course of action; to some protection, to others the chastisement which they deserve. You can choose between these two alternatives."

Several voices: Very well; that is all right.

M. JULES FAVRE. Listen; that is not all: "We are disposed to act with the greatest kindness towards those who honestly rally round the elect of the Mexican nation."

Numerous voices: Very good! very good!

M. JULES FAVRE. "But we are resolved to act with all necessary rigor against those who obstinately persist in sustaining the wretches who, usurping the glorious title of soldiers, dishonor the Mexican nation by their crimes.".

The same voices: That is very well said.

M. JULES FAVRE. We understand this language; you have only to open history; you will find there that the vanquished have been always calumniated. Words of a similar import were uttered against the vanquished of 1814 and 1815. [Loud manifestations of dissent and murmurs of disapprobation on a great number of benches.]

Permit me to speak, gentlemen; it is not only a right that I exercise; it is a duty that I perform. [Renewed disapprobation.]

HIS EXCELLENCY M. ROUHER, Minister of State. You injure the French army, the army of your country.

Numerous voices: Yes, yes; it is intolerable.

M. JULES FAVRE. That is what I ought to say, and that is what I say.

THE CHAIRMAN, M. SCHNEIDER. I pray you not to compare the French, overpowered by numbers in 1814, with men whom I do not wish to characterize and whom the French army has encountered in Mexico.

Numerous voices: Good! good!

M. LE MARQUIS DE PIRÉ. The brave men of 1815 had shed their blood for the defence of the country, and you have never shed anything but ink. [Confusion and noise.]

M. JULES FAVRE. I ask you, gentlemen, how such words can be reconciled with those that emanated from the Emperor, with those that have been uttered by the ministers in this hall, wherein it was declared that the Mexican nation was to be consulted, and that the Archduke Maximilian was to be of no account without his vote. Now it is declared that there are two camps in Mexico—the camp of the Mexicans who accept the empire, and these are protected.

Several voices: That is a duty.

M. JULES FAVRE. And the camp of the Mexicans who protest against the empire, and these are pillaged and shot down. [Confused manifestations of disapprobation.]

That is not all, gentlemen; these acts have been committed contrary to the law of nations, contrary to the laws of war, which require that neutrals should be respected; that private property should not wantonly and without cause be destroyed; that the sacking of cities should not be made a means of coercion in order to intimidate the minds of a people and inspire a salutary terror to insure the success of a pretender. Such are the principles laid down by all moralists and all who have written on the law of nations. [Discordant manifestations.]

THE CHAIRMAN, M. SCHNEIDER. M. Jules Favre, allow me one observation. I am an ardent partisan of liberty of speech, and I believe I have given proofs of it. The Chamber is no less anxious for it than I am, and it proves it at this moment; for, although it has already heard the Mexican question discussed several times, it is still willing to lend its attention. Yet, in the interest of your cause——

M. JULES FAVRE. It is not my cause; it is that of the law of nations.

THE CHAIRMAN, M. SCHNEIDER. I entreat you not to exaggerate anything, and to confine yourself to the use of such expressions as may not excite the legitimate sensibilities of the assembly. [Good! good!]

M. JULES FAVRE. In reply to the observation of the chairman, I thank the Chamber for having been pleased to hear me patiently. [Loud manifestations of disapprobation.]

Some voices: No, no—not very patiently.

M. DE GUILLONTET. The Chamber hears you with indignation.

M. JULES FAVRE. I address myself to the majority, and not to a few interrupters.

I have called the attention of the Chamber to some new facts—to facts which seriously compromise the policy of France, to facts that may compromise the future—and it is very important that the government should give precise explanations in this regard.

Now, gentlemen, I call your attention to another class of facts no less important. I refer to events that have excited, and very naturally, too, a strong degree of irritation in all minds in Mexico, and have given rise to hostile passions. Who can doubt it? That irritation, those passions, have found vent in certain writings. If those writings were culpable, why not bring them before the courts of justice? There is no better course. But that France, under the protection of its flag, should shelter a military council before which journalists are brought, and that in the name of the Emperor, who has proclaimed liberty and universal suffrage, these journalists should be delivered into the hands of the Archduke Maximilian—this is something that appears inconceivable to me, something that seems a great political fault. In this way we compromise—and here I avail myself of the expression just employed by the chairman—we compromise the cause that we wish to defend.

Yet, gentlemen, such things have come to pass in Mexico. Journalists have been brought before a council of war, and in the name of the Emperor and by French justice have been condemed to various punishments.

M. DE GUILLONTET. That is all very proper, for they were criminals.

M. JULES FAVRE. Is it by such means as this that you think you can bring about that pacification for which every one is anxious.

Gentlemen, a frank explanation is requisite here. You have been continually told of the possibility of withdrawing our troops, now at the end of 1864, now again at the end of 1865, and the minister of state, self-deluded, though, I am convinced, in good faith, told us, on the 23d of January, 1864, that it would be sufficient for our troops to remain a few months more in Mexico in order to consolidate the throne of the Archduke Maximilian and to give a proper impetus to the regeneration of that country.

It makes but little difference, gentlemen; and, as for me, I would very willingly consent that our troops should remain there not only some months, but even a year, provided that, at the end of that year, the promise of their return should be no longer an empty word. But if the programme of the minister of state is to be accomplished, do not delude yourselves; one year will not be enough; it will require ten years yet to establish firmly the throne of the emperor Maximilian; it will be necessary to sacrifice for that purpose 40,000 men a year, and 400 or 500 millions of money.

This is what I consider to be a truth now firmly established, and I ask your permission to prove it to you in a few words.

This regeneration of Mexico will bring complications of every kind in its train. Do you not believe it? Does not the present suffice to indicate what is to transpire in future? And if we were disposed to look over history, would we not find there eminent men, more eminent by far than those of the present day, men of genius even, who were led astray by ideas of this character?

What, in fact, happened to the first Emperor, to Napoleon? He, also, had an idea of regenerating a people. He then held forth to Spain such assurances as it would be well now to recall; for they teach a lesson, that princes who govern without any opposition before them—and, unfortunately for himself, Napoleon found none—princes who govern without any sort of control, may ruin their country while ruining themselves. In a proclamation which he issued to the Spaniards at the time that his troops were setting out for the peninsula, he said: "Your monarchy is old; my mission is to rejuvenate it."

I am distrustful of all self-imposed missions; and, for my part, I believe that it is the part of Providence to effect that there should be no more providential men, but nations governing themselves, and with power to direct their own destinies.

"I wish," added Napoleon, "that your latest posterity should preserve the memory of my name and say, 'He is the regenerator of our country!'"

Now that, thanks to God, she has been enabled to heal the severe wounds which we inflicted upon her, Spain has returned to us. But during the first years after our invasion, a violent hatred reigned in the heart of that nation towards those who had wished to protect and rejuvenate it.

And as to the mighty man who had conceived such projects, you know whither they conducted him! You have only to consult the deliberations of the senate, and you will see that his deposition was pronounced on the 14th of April, 1814, by the great legislative body of the state, which thus expressed its motives for the measure:

"Considering that Napoleon Bonaparte has undertaken a series of wars in violation of art. 50 of the constitution of the 22 Frimaire, year 8, which provides that declarations of war must be proposed, discussed, and promulgated like laws; * * * considering that the liberty of the press, established and consecrated as one of the rights of the nation, has been constantly subject to the arbitrary censorship of the police," &c., &c.

Such, gentlemen, is the answer of nations when they are unfortunate. [Tumultuous interruption.]

M. LE MARQUIS DE PIRÉ. The reply of France, in her misfortunes, has invariably been to turn republicanism out of doors. [Noise.]

THE CHAIRMAN, M. SCHNEIDER. In his retrospective review, the honorable M. Jules Favre has told you that there was no opposition under the first empire; there is certainly one under the second empire. [Laughter and applause.]

M. GLAIS-BIZOIN. That is not its fault.

M. EMILE OLLIVIER. Mr. Chairman, be pleased to permit freedom of discussion.

M. JULES FAVRE. What I wish to show is, that it is necessary, indispensable, that the position, which hitherto has been equivocal, should cease to be so; it is that it is necessary and indispensable that we should know what we have to do, and what the sacrifices are to which we are exposed. If the Chamber adopts the idea expressed by the minister of state; if, indeed, it wishes to establish the new Mexican government and the throne of the Archduke Maximilian on a firm basis, the majority is sovereign, and we will bow before it, while retaining our own opinion; but it must not be imagined that the achievement of such an undertaking can permit the return of our troops next year.

This is the delusion which I oppose, if in reality it exists, and I request your kindly attention for a few moments while I strive to combat it.

I am well aware of the truth of what was just said by our honorable chairman: the most of the points involved in this question have been already discussed. I shall call your attention only to such as are of present moment. Within these limits, gentlemen, I intend to confine myself, while investigating the events that have transpired since last year.

After a thorough study of all the facts in the case, political, military, and financial, it is impossible for any one seriously to believe that the government of Maximilian can exist without our army. With our army, I acknowledge, his throne would rest on an agreement; it would last as long as our assistance would be extended to it; but if you withdraw this assistance from it, it is evident that it will be overthrown. If, therefore, you wish to establish it firmly, our army must remain in Mexico. The Chamber should understand this thoroughly.

You remember what I said to you just now, namely, that the French government had obligated itself to consult the Mexican nation; that it had declared that its work would be finished as soon as universal suffrage should have pronounced, first, on this first question: "Is it a monarchy or a republic that is to be established in Mexico?" These are the words of the minister of state, not mine. Secondly, and on the supposition that a monarchy would be preferred, on this second question: "Will the monarch be the Archduke Maximilian?"

Now, gentlemen, not only did the minister of state use this language—and he spoke to you, with the preciseness which he usually exercises in his words, of the necessity of a formal contract between the Mexican nation and the sovereign, a contract without which the new government would be ephemeral, founded on force and not on right—but also the Archduke Maximilian himself entered into a similar engagement; and you remember the speech which he delivered to the Mexican deputation that came to bring to him the deliberations of the notables of Mexico. He said:

"I must, however, acknowledge, being herein fully of accord with the Emperor of the French, whose glorious initiative has rendered possible the regeneration of Mexico, that the monarchy of that country cannot be established on solid and legitimate foundations unless the entire nation, by a free manifestation of its will, confirms the wishes of the capital. On the result of the vote of the assembly of the country I must, therefore, in the first instance, make the acceptance of the offered throne depend."

And you remember also, gentlemen—you cannot certainly have forgotten it—that such were the instructions given by the minister of foreign affairs to Marshal Bazaine. I do not quote them in full to you; that would be an indiscretion. I content myself with reminding you that the minister had fully foreseen the distinction that was to be established between the deliberation of the notables and universal suffrage: "However," said he, "we can consider the votes of the assembly of the city of Mexico only as a preliminary indication of the disposition of the country."

And the minister enters, with minute care, into the details of the vote to which the whole Mexican nation should be invited, and without which the power of Maximilian could have no legitimate foundation.

Here, gentlemen, is what has been said by France, since it is from the Emperor's own mouth that these words have come. This is what has been repeated by his ministers in their diplomatic despatches. This is what has been asserted here in your presence. This is the condition of the agreement that has been made between the majority and the government. The Chamber has not been willing that the country should suffer violence, that the treasure and the blood of France should be employed in imposing on Mexico a government which it did not wish; a foolish and culpable enterprise if it were thus conducted; legitimate, on the contrary, if it were accepted by the unanimous will of the nation.

Now, I ask what has been done in this regard since 1864? If we choose to rely upon the passages which I have had the honor to quote to you a moment ago, it would seem that Maximilian had only to collect the votes. He was expected by a unanimous people, 5,500,000 Mexicans! The commissioner on the part of the government has counted them, and he is perfectly sure of the correctness of his calculations; 5,500,000 Mexicans were there, ready to place their votes in the urn! We demand nothing further: no more did Maximilian, probably!

What has been done with these 5,500,000 Mexicans? What political acts are there to which we can refer? For we are not called upon to inquire either into the resources of Mexico or into the number of its population. These are vague and confused questions, which it is easy to envelop in a pleasant mirage, to suit personal prejudices, but which must be set wholly aside. Let us look at facts.

What has Maximilan done? He was sincerely anxious, I am convinced, to inaugurate an era of prosperity in the country in which he was received, and for this purpose he had need of power. Nothing is possible without this vigorous instrument in a generous hand. But in order that this power should be useful, it was necessary that it should be well rooted in the heart of the nation. He has not dared to look in that direction, and the only act which we know of his is an act of good pleasure--a statute which, indeed, I have not now to examine, but which sufficiently testifies that there is yet between him and the nation some obstacle which prevents him from hearing its voice and consulting it. Nothing, therefore, has been done.

I have set before you the words uttered by the organs of the government, to the effect that the nation was to be consulted. If the nation desired to be republican, we would consent that it should be republican. They went even further, and said, "If the nation wishes to have Juarez, we will take Juarez." You have changed your ideas, then; you have changed your principles?

His Excellency M. Rouher, minister of state. Not at all.

M. Jules Favre. You have not changed your ideas?

The Minister of State. You have lost your memory. There have been two votes.

M. Jules Favre. You have not changed your ideas! I accept very willingly your declarations. I have said that I was convinced beforehand that the intentions were good; and when I just a while ago intimated, because—I say it once again—it is my duty, that the conceptions had been changeable, that they had changed with events, I said that the government had thereby undergone the fatal law of necessity imposed upon it.

Now, the government told us—look, now, gentlemen, and judge of its policy and its prudence, I entreat you—the government told us that if the Mexican nation was consulted, and if it accepted republicanism, the government would submit. And then what would it have to do? To assist Maximilian in packing up his baggage and crown. Gentlemen, do you understand such a policy? They proceed to consult the country in regard to a form of government, and they begin by proclaiming one, and declaring that all those who act against that government will be pursued as malefactors! This is the way in which they wish to consult universal suffrage. Assuredly, this is not in earnest; and in any case I have a right to say that, in a political point of view, nothing has yet been done; and as you have, with justice, attached all your hopes of the expedition to universal suffrage, and as, on account of circumstances which I have not to examine, it has not been possible to consult universal suffrage, you are still in a provisional state. You have not advanced one step; or, rather, if we may rely on your own official documents, you have recoiled; you have lost ground. For the enthusiasm of the people portended to us an easy election. The report sent to the minister of foreign affairs had this character. Otherwise, the minister of foreign affairs is a person of too grave a character to write to General Bazaine in phrases as inconceivable as this: "You have only to call the people together and take their vote." The minister must have received information that the vote was easy, and he must have believed it.

Now, at the present time, a vote is no longer possible. I say it is no longer possible, since it has not been taken. Otherwise, render an account to us of this delay in the accomplishment of your duty. Who prevents you from consulting universal suffrage, from causing the return of our troops?

Here is an important fact: Maximilian, very naturally, seeks to collect adherents around him. With whom did he arrive in Mexico? With the most powerful; with those who could insure success to his enterprise. I refer to our soldiers; for, whatever be the severity of certain chiefs, there is in the temperament of the French soldier, in his devotion, in his generosity, in his heroism, something that gains the hearts of the people.

This result was certain, especially in Mexico; and if we had not compromised all these advantages, the question would not be as melancholy as it now is. But, besides the French soldiers, there were auxiliaries who certainly did not participate in their sentiments. I refer—I wish to make use of a word that may offend no one—my honorable colleagues are fully persuaded that such cannot be my intention—[manifestations of disapprobation]—

A voice: Not so! [Exclamations.]

M. Jules Favre. He who says "Not so" assuredly says what the assembly is not willing to adopt as its own sentiment. It does not appertain to me to qualify it as it deserves; but I can say that if I had uttered it I should be profoundly sorry for it. [Signs of approbation.]

The Chairman, M. Schneider, I regret equally with you that the word should have been uttered. [Good! good!] Just a while ago I entreated M. Jules Favre to be more moderate, for the sake of his own cause. I also request the Chamber to listen to the speaker with more calmness.

M. Emile Ollivier. It is not the cause of M. Jules Favre; it is a question that appertains to the world in general.

M. Jules Favre. I would wish, I repeat, to make use of a word that would offend no one. It is certain that the party which accompanied Maximilian was the clerical party, the party that had opposed Juarez and the establishment of civil institutions, the party that had resisted the sale of the goods of the clergy. This is the party that constituted the escort of Maximilian. In it, gentlemen, he has found his most numerous and his firmest adherents.

I have no intention to entertain you with all the details of the quarrels that have taken place between him and that party. You know many of them, and I omit them. I proceed straight to the facts of most importance, which elucidate the condition of affairs.

Before his departure for Mexico, as all the world knows, Maximilian made a journey to Rome. No one has any right to qualify the motives of this journey; yet, when a person has charge of souls, when he is a prince, a prince presumptive, a prince that desires to be elected, everything becomes of importance in these various steps that are taken. It is plain enough that the newspapers have interpreted this one of Maximilian, and have seen in it a certain proof of an accordance between him and the views of the court of Rome.

Now, gentlemen, it is no secret to any one that the views of the court of Rome are diametrically opposed to the resolutions taken by the Mexican government in reference to the clergy; and, consequently, you will not be astonished that, in accounting for the journey of Maximilian to Rome, one of the best-informed journals in this country—I mean the Constitutionnel—should have said:

"Their Imperial Majesties have gone to pay a solemn visit to the Holy Father, in order to implore the benediction of the august chief of the church, and to place their future efforts under the ægis of his paternal intercession and of his powerful spiritual authority."

The conference between Maximilian and Pius IX appears to have been quite long. At its conclusion, the new sovereign had another one with Cardinal Antonelli:

"The next day, April 20, their Imperial Majesties assisted at the pontifical mass in the Sixtine chapel, at half past seven o'clock in the morning. After the gospel, Pius IX encouraged them, in a long sermon, to accomplish the designs of Providence, and represented to them their mission to Mexico as part of the grand scheme of Christian propagandism."

This visit must necessarily have excited attention. I desire to make no comments on it. It gave to the emperor Maximilian a certain kind of connexion with a well-known policy. The world was of opinion that it did not contribute naturally to weaken his relations with those who had been his first partisans.

Yet, what happened? In Mexico, the emperor Maximilian recognized the impossibility of governing by means of that party. He recognized, rightly or wrongly, I venture no judgment here, that that party was the most unpopular of all; that it compromised everything which he desired to effect; that it was impossible to abstain from proclaiming, what is contrary to the doctrines of the court of Rome, liberty of religious worship, toleration, and, to a certain extent, freedom of thought, and especially from giving his adhesion to the measures taken by President Juarez, whom our troops had expelled, relative to the alienation of the goods of the clergy; so that it has happened—no novelty, it is true, in history—that the successor, called in to do a very different thing, has been obliged to do what was done by his predecessor.

But what you can very easily conceive is that such a resolution was very ill received at the court of Rome; and it is well to point out to you, from the latest documents, what the actual condition of affairs is on this point, and consequently to what embarrassments and to what dangers the new empire and France—for France is inseparably bound up with it—find themselves at present exposed.

Here, gentlemen, is the manner in which the Holy Father expressed himself in this regard, in a letter addressed to Maximilian, under date of October 18, 1864:

"Heretofore, and on more than one occasion, we have made complaints on this point, in public and solemn acts, protesting against the iniquitous law called that of reform, which overturned the most inviolable rights of the church and outraged the authority of its pastors; against the usurpation of ecclesiastical property, and the plunder of the patrimony of the church; against the unjust suppression of the religious orders; against the false maxims which directly attacked the holiness of the Catholic religion; finally, against many other outrages committed not only against sacred persons, but also against the pastoral ministry and the discipline of the church."

And the Pope added: "Let no one obtain permission to teach and publish false maxims, subversive of morality; let instruction, public as well as private, be directed and superintended by the ecclesiastical authority; and, finally, let the chains be broken that have hitherto retained the church dependent on the arbitrary control of the civil government."

See, gentlemen, how the negotiation terminated which took place between the government of Rome and the emperor Maximilian. The latter did not choose to accept the conditions sought to be imposed upon him; he broke through them resolutely, it must be acknowledged. I shall not set before you the letter which he wrote to his minister; you know what wrath it aroused in the camp of those who suddenly became his adversaries. I am not at all disturbed thereat; I merely state the fact; I refer only to official documents. We first find a protest not very long delayed. The letter is of the date of December 27, 1864; the protest of the nuncio is of the same day. I shall not set it before you; I shall only say that if I qualified it as strong I should scarcely do it justice. But what was its echo at the court of Rome? We find it in a despatch from Cardinal Antonelli, which we may find exceedingly useful to consult. Here is what the cardinal says:

"The letter which his majesty, Maximilian I, emperor of Mexico, addressed, under date of December 27, ultimo, to Mr. Escudero, minister of grace and justice, and which was published the same day in the official journal of the empire, has caused the most painful surprise to all Catholic hearts, and has been a source of chagrin and regret to the Holy Father.

"Subsequent communications from the apostolic nuncio, and the note itself, which your excellency has been pleased to address, on the 8th of February last, to the cardinal secretary of state undersigned, have not been in the slightest degree calculated to diminish the serious apprehensions which the aforesaid act has produced in reference to the grave dangers to which the Catholic church is exposed in the empire of Mexico. The cardinal undersigned, in virtue of the orders of his Holiness, sees himself, therefore, obliged to call the serious attention of your excellency to an event so deplorable, and he hopes that the legitimate complaints and just remonstrances of the holy apostolic see will be favorably received by the new monarch."

Cardinal Antonelli concludes with these significant words:

"The Holy Father cannot admit that his majesty, raised in a Catholic family always so well disposed towards the church, can ever fail to recognize his own true interests and the real purpose of the mission which God has confided to him. He hopes, on the contrary, that his majesty will abandon the course marked out in his letter to the minister Escudero, and will thus spare the Holy See the necessity of taking proper measures to set right in the eyes of the world the responsibility of the august chief of the church—measures of which the last, certainly, would not be the recall of the pontifical representative in Mexico, in order that he may not remain there a powerless spectator of the spoliation of the church, and of the violation of its most sacred rights."

What is this despatch, gentlemen, if it be not a complete rupture, certainly according to the views of the court of Rome, but a rupture that shows that the archduke Maximilian can no longer rely for support on the party that called him to the throne? And as he cannot look for support to the liberals, you see in what a precarious condition he finds himself; and this explains perfectly why he has abandoned the idea of consulting universal suffrage.

At all events we must acknowledge that the situation has been completely changed since 1864. That the re-establishment of the Union in the North American States is not without danger to the French government and the Mexican government, no one can fail to recognize. That the condition of things should be developed in a manner least disastrous—thanks to the wisdom of both governments—I should be gratified; I hope it may be so. But you will admit with me that there is a certain degree of discouragement in the minds of the partisans of Maximilian, and a certain degree of elation in those of his adversaries; no one can fail to recognize the fact. On the other hand, it is undeniable that the American government has not recognized the empire of Mexico; and in a despatch recently published, and which bears the date of February 25, 1865, Mr. Seward, addressing himself to the representative of Juarez, acknowledges the receipt of his despatches, and expresses his desire for the welfare and success of the Mexican republic.

Thus, all that we said, all that we announced to you, from the month of February or March, 1862, when we entreated you not to engage in an expedition which would compromise our relations with our best allies—relations which permit us to preserve, on the sea at least, the peace of the world—all has been realized. That the government of the United States should not violate its treaties, I am anxious; but that a crowd of adventurers should not cross the frontiers, is something that I cannot, without difficulty, imagine.

Now, all these dangers, all these complications, all these compromises, explain how nothing can be effected in Mexico unless by force and a military establishment, and yet our military establishment is less solid and more precarious than it was last year.

On this point also I refer only to official documents. We have complained, and we yet complain, (I ask pardon of the minister of state,) that we have not had any kind of official statement whatever in reference to this most important question that so justly engrosses the attention of the country. The Moniteur has never published any official reports; only its editors have taken up the pen in unofficial statements.

In one of our former meetings the honorable minister told us that there were no other documents. I believe him; but in that case he is the least informed minister in the world, for we know what the Moniteur can do; we know what it did do on the occasion of a celebrated speech recently delivered, and which will leave a deep trace in history. The

Moniteur related only that the orator had made the circuit of the monument which he inaugurated, without saying one word of that which was most interesting to the reader. [Divers interruptions. Laughter and approbation around the speaker.]

Several members: The Moniteur did well.

M. JULES FAVRE. Now, relatively to Mexico, I ask myself how it is that the Chamber has received no communication of any official despatch whatever, and how it is that all that we have been told has come to us from the pens of the too skilful editors of the Moniteur. It is probable that the committee on the budget, which has the rare good fortune of receiving the intimate confidence of the government, which confidence it is utterly impossible for us to know, has been able to get a glimpse of the despatches. As to us, who are outside barbarians, who are reduced to the condition of the minister of state—that is, to have to study the state of our affairs in the Moniteur, and to be debarred from the knowledge of state documents—we who are, notwithstanding, the elect of the people, and who should debate on the affairs of the country, at least we will be allowed the right of consulting the Moniteur.

Well, I take up the last number that makes any mention of the affairs of Mexico. I do not find in it the report of Marshal Bazaine, a report which, notwithstanding, is the property of the Chamber, and which is refused to it; but I find in its stead some sort of a statement made by the official editors. Here is what I read in the Moniteur of May 15; the reports bear the date of April 28 and May 1:

"In the State of Tamaulipas, General Cortinas has fallen away from the imperial cause, with 750 men under his command."

Thus it is, gentlemen, that we form the Mexican army in order that it may pass over to the enemy. This is a Penelope's task assuredly that we are accomplishing, but with this difference, that Penelope was not killed by the fabric she wove. [Laughter.]

I resume. "In the State of Tamaulipas General Cortinas has fallen away from the imperial cause with 750 men under his command. General Mejia, who occupies Matamoras, has concentrated at that point the troops stationed in the surrounding districts. Foreigners, resident there, have spontaneously armed themselves in order to assist the garrison, which was to have been re-enforced on the 1st of May by the arrival of the third battalion of the foreign regiment, under the orders of the commandant, De Brian.

"The offensive movement undertaken by Negrete, from west to east, has induced the marshal commanding-in-chief to form two columns destined to cover the attacked territory. The one was to occupy Parras, fifty leagues west of Durango, over against the desert of Mapimi; the other, starting from San Luis, was to march upon Monterey, capital of New Leon, situated at an equal distance from Parras and Matamoras.

"If, contrary to all expectation, General Mejia, who commands in this latter city, should be obliged to yield to superior forces, he was to fall back upon Victoria, the capital city of the State of Tamaulipas, in such a manner as to cover the country in his rear, and to maintain his communications with Tampico, which was to become his base of operations.

"Finally, Marshal Bazaine announces his intention of proceeding in person to San Luis, where he is concentrating his reserves in order to be in a position to direct operations himself. Without mistaking the importance of the events that have transpired in the north, the marshal commanding-in-chief regards them only as among those incidents of war that can no more deceive his vigilance than shake his faith in success."

What success? That of battles? We have no doubt as to that; we are very sure that the French will succeed, on condition, however, that they be not overtasked; and if it be the desire that they should succeed we must resign ourselves to all the expenses, for without further expenses their situation in Mexico will become impossible to maintain.

You see now, all that has been said in regard to pacification is a mistake; we have been mistaken; we have been mistaken in good faith, I am willing to grant; we were entirely too credulous of success; we were told that all hearts flow to welcome Maximilian, yet here we see that the enemy assumes the offensive. I do not wish to remind you of any particular facts that have transpired; yet some weeks ago Marshal Bazaine besieged a city in person; in it he found a garrison of 8,000 men, and captured many hundreds of cannon. Now the enemy has assumed the offensive. Matamoras is threatened; General Mejia takes precautions for a retreat; Marshal Bazaine does not despair; neither do we despair; but we have arrived at a point where we are to ask ourselves whether, in a war so extensive, we should not take a great step at once, make war as it should be made, or abandon Mexico entirely—that is, according as the interests of France are or are not engaged in this affair. If they are engaged in it, be assured that by all, without any distinction of party, they will be sustained. But if, on the contrary, it is for foreign interests that we act, if it is for a foreign crown, if it is for the accomplishment of an impossible enterprise, if it is a phantom that we pursue, if the work to which the blood and the treasure of France are devoted is a work foreign to France, we will not continue it any further, and we will demand to have it abandoned.

Such is the conclusion at which we arrive from a consideration of the military occurrences.

And as a final and controlling idea, permit me to examine with you in a few words one of the most characteristic features in a question of this nature, and one of the most instructive. I refer to the financial aspect of the affair. The condition of the finances will teach us, and teach us beyond a possibility of doubt, the value of this Mexican business; for herein we are not dealing with contingencies. In the discussion of this point I do not wish to leave anything to uncertainty; I am going to state facts precisely as they are, in order that the discussion may be useful, and we may all of us be able, as we desire the welfare of our country, to arrive at conclusions favorable to it.

In order to estimate the worth of a private individual we have only to investigate what his credit is. If you desire to learn the worth of such and such a merchant, apply to those who have business transactions with him. If he pays badly, if he seeks to raise funds at the pawnbroker's, if he requests the signature of his wife or his family, you may be sure that this merchant is on the point of bankruptcy.

Now, Mexico has engaged in financial affairs and adventures without precedent, and I blush to see France assisting in them; to see that it is with the stamp of France, with the aid and under cover of her administration and of her public treasure, that those unexampled financial operations have been executed which I have to lay before the court. [Merriment]

You are a court of justice, gentlemen, in this affair; I am authorized, therefore, to use this word without offence to you.

A member: We recognize the lawyer in that.

M. JULES FAVRE. Yes, gentlemen, I am a lawyer, and I feel proud of it, for I have always exercised my profession conscientiously. [Cries of good! good! around the speaker.]

There are among us men of more or less lively imagination. I do not take offence at interruptions; I have a good right to be indulgent in regard to them. But when I am told that I have been a lawyer, I cast my eyes on the government benches and find there three illustrious confrères——

HIS EXCELLENCY THE MINISTER OF STATE. We are proud of it.

M. JULES FAVRE ——of whom some have been either my friends or my comrades, and I can only feel honored at the interruption. [Laughter. Cries of good! good!]

I said that we should know what the credit of Mexico is. On this point I asked my honorable colleague, M. Corta, permission not to accompany him on the peregrination, so interesting otherwise, and listened to with so much pleasure by the Chamber, which he undertook through Mexico. I am convinced that all his researches have been conscientious; that he has given them to us such as he himself conceives them to be; his intention has been to enlighten the Chamber. Only in place of this marvellous romance, which seems a page detached from some political Arabian Nights, written by some complacent historian anxious for a loan, [laughter,] I ask your permission to substitute the naked truth, namely, the loan itself; and we will proceed to see, from the conditions under which it is negotiated, what the worth is of the borrower.

Every one knows that Mexico borrowed last year a sum of two hundred millions of francs. No one knows it better than the minister of state, unless it be the minister of finance, who has in his portfolio fifty-four millions of this Mexican paper, which he would be very willing to convert into money; and at our last meeting you heard an honorable member of the government say, "But if we wished to realize, what would we lose? Ten millions! Ten millions at this time is a matter of no consequence to the government! Thus we can get out of the difficulty!"

Several members: Who said that?

M. JULES FAVRE. I, for my part, say that, if you look at the state of the market, it would not be ten millions, it would be more than twenty millions that you would lose, or rather the paper could not be disposed of at any price.

HIS EXCELLENCY M. ROUHER, minister of state. Will you please state the name of the speaker, the government member, who used that language?

A member: Is it not M. De Vintry? [Tumult and confusion.]

M. LE MARQUIS DE PIRÉ, in the midst of the confusion, utters some words which it is impossible to understand.

THE CHAIRMAN, M. SCHNEIDER. Please do not interrupt, M. de Piré, or I shall be obliged to call you to order. It is not the first time that you have interrupted with vehemence; I pray you not to renew the attempt. [Good! good!]

M. JULES FAVRE. At all events, the interruption of the minister of state would imply that the paper cannot be disposed of at any price, which is precisely my opinion. [Laughter and manifestations of approbation around the speaker.]

This being understood, after the two hundred millions had been borrowed by Mexico, Mexico very soon found itself completely short, and has been under the necessity of recurring again to credit; under what conditions? It must be stated, gentlemen, here once more, and I say it with extreme regret, it is with the assistance of the French government that the loan has been contracted and sent out—"subscription to 500,000 bonds of 500 francs each, authorized by his excellency the minister of finance."

What is the loan that is effected under the form of bonds? for it is not a consolidated loan that has been made by the Mexican government. It consists of bonds that are to be redeemed in fifty years and by annual instalments.

What is the amount of the loan? It is 500,000 bonds of 500 francs each; the calculation is very simple; that is 250 millions. The sum of 250 millions is therefore to be returned to the lender in the course of fifty years. But the bonds are issued only at the rate of 340 francs, and consequently Mexico, which is under the necessity of paying 250 millions, will only receive 170 millions.

M. Berryer. The bonds are for 310 francs, and not for 340

M. Jules Favre. I was just going to state that. On the 170 millions there is a commission. The notes, which are issued for 340 francs, are sold for only 310 francs. And truly I wonder at the minister of state who thought to overwhelm us when he told us in a speech recently delivered, "You speak of the contingency of a loan! The loan is already effected; the capitalists have been already found to take it."

Permit me, Mr. Minister! Capitalists! You mean those who get the 17 millions premium. We know too well that they have no money, and that they appeal to the public for it. They offered the bonds to the public, and we are to see with what allurements they seek to entice the people to take them, what immoral conditions have presided over this loan, and how afflicting they are, if not to our finances, at least to the morality which ought to direct the resolutions of a government.

The Mexican government is under the necessity of paying 250 millions; it will receive only 170 millions. It pays 17 millions premium to its agents, which reduces the real sum to 153 millions. 153 millions! I do not believe, gentlemen, that such a sum will ever go into the coffers of the Mexican government.

In order to obtain it, under conditions so unfavorable, and of such a nature that if an individual allowed himself to enter into them he would immediately be taken in charge by the courts, do you know what the Mexican government does? Do you know what the French government does, which authorizes it, patronizes it, takes it by the hand in order to introduce it to the financial market, as it has taken Maximilian by the hand in order to conduct him to the throne of Mexico?

Here are the conditions proposed to lenders. The bonds are to the amount of 340 francs, and they are to be redeemed in 50 years at the nominal rate of 500 francs, principal; that is to say, 5 millions a year, with an annual interest of 30 francs, which, on a principal of 340 francs, make 9½ per cent., nearly.

But this is not all. In order to obtain money that might otherwise never be forthcoming, so great is the confidence, so fully convinced are people of the solidity of the enterprise, it is not enough that 340 francs, or rather 310 francs, should produce an interest of 30 francs; that is, at the rate of 9½ per cent.—an appeal is made to what has been proscribed by our legislation; a revolt has been raised against it, and a deplorable and scandalous example given of laws trampled under foot, avaricious passions inflamed, most detestable passions that agitate the lowest classes of society, in order to bring into the coffers of the Mexican government the money that never would have found its way thither naturally. Here is what they have pressed into the service of the loan—a lottery. And then under what conditions?

The bonds shall entitle to chances in a lottery of 3 millions a year, of 1,500,000 francs every six months, divided in the following manner: There will be two semi-annual drawings. The first ticket drawn entitles the holder to 500,000 francs.

Thus the most obscure passer-by, the lowest citizen, the humblest and poorest, is called to give his 340 francs, and these 340 francs may produce him 500,000 francs! Who will resist this contagion, this seduction, this immoral perdition, this monstrosity, which is not only condemned by law, but by all honest hearts, and which is sufficient to demoralize the country? Who can resist it? [Sensation; "bravos" around the speaker.]

But there is not only a chance of 500,000 francs; there are other chances. The two following numbers are each 100,000 francs; the four following, 50,000; and then several other premiums.

I have referred to the morality of the affair; I have a right to speak of it thus in reference to the law, for there is one—there is none for the ministers: they set it aside whenever it impedes their schemes; they apply it to their fellow-citizens; they put them in prison, if it is necessary. [Manifestations of disapprobation.] As to themselves, they are above everything [Tumultuous interruption.]

Here is the law of which I speak. The date of its enactment is May 21, 1836. By this law lotteries are prohibited, for it says expressly: "Lotteries of all kinds are prohibited."

And in the commentary which is given of this law, by a man whom we all venerate as much as we love, and who is seated on the government benches, the honorable M. Duvergier, who has been a lawyer, who has been our leader, and whose name is inscribed at the head of the bar—I am only too happy to render him this homage without grudging it, although he is a counsellor of state——[Laughter and tumult.]

Well, here is what he says in his commentary: "When the epoch fixed at January 1, 1836, arrived, the royal lottery ceased to exist; but all the prohibitions issued against private and foreign lotteries have been maintained. It is evident that, in suppressing the lottery organized by the government, and which offered guarantees that no private enterprise could present, the legislature did not intend to permit the latter. Otherwise, it would be very absurd for the government to sacrifice an important branch of public revenue for the interest of public morality, and at the same time to leave a number of private enterprises to speculate"——

To speculate on what? It is not I that speak, it is the government—"on the credulity and cupidity of the lower classes."

Here is your lever; here is the instrument to which you have had recourse in order to obtain money, and you could not get any otherwise. Here is what was necessary for your enterprise, for the enterprise of the Mexican government is your enterprise. Here is what you have developed among the people. This is the detestable feverishness which the law condemns! [Confusion.]

And do you know what the Mexican government will have to refund? I do not speak here on suppositions; I have the figures before me.

Besides the obligations imposed on it by the loan, it will have to pay 3,000,000 a year. Whence it follows that, by adding 150,000,000 for premiums to the 250,000,000 at which the Mexican government is to pay off its bonds redeemable at par, we have thus a sum of 400,000,000 set down to the side of its indebtedness, in the face of a problematical credit of 153,000,000.

The scheme is wise—it is perfect; and the capitalists to whom appeal is made are treated by the borrower with so much distrust—so much fear is entertained of not obtaining their money, that after having granted them these conditional premiums they tell them: "When you shall have received back your 340 francs, or, rather, when you shall have received 500 francs, that is, when you shall have obtained 250,000,000 for the 170,000,000 that you advance, you shall also have refunded to you your entire capital!"

And they commence by raising in advance on the capital of the Mexican government a sum of 17,000,000 of francs, which is deposited in the treasury of France, the interest of which will be added to the principal, thus producing in fifty years a sum of 170,000,000. [Tumultuous demonstrations of various kinds among the members.]

So that in reality the Mexican government will only obtain a sum of 133,000,000. Such in reality is the sum that it will have in its hands, and yet it will be obliged to pay out 400,000,000. Where do you think it will obtain that amount?

Any man on the brink of ruin willingly exchanges some paper, to which he attaches his signature, for certain pieces of gold. [Confusion.] That is an operation as base as it is immoral. Now that is the very thing that is done; that is what you make the Mexican government do by causing it to borrow 133,000,000 against 400,000,000, which it will have to refund. It is impossible that such an operation should succeed. [Long-continued and noisy demonstrations of dissent.]

And yet you will be the persons who will have patronized it in the stock market. It will be in vain for you to say that you have not associated yourselves to it by giving it your guarantee; French capitalists will confront you by reminding you of the words uttered by you; they will tell you that on the very eve of the loan you pronounced here the eulogy of Mexico; that you have boasted of its resources; and then it will be your responsibility, and not that of the ephemeral name of Maximilian, that they will call up! [Disapprobation. Applause around the speaker.]

I have repeated the thing too often to be obliged to remind you of it once more. If the Chamber thinks that the interest of France is linked to the establishment of a great empire in Mexico, let it say so; but let it not delude itself with any of these declarations, which are mere mockeries—that our soldiers are returning to France, that they are on the point of setting out on their return.

If it is desirable that such an establishment should be prosperous and efficacious, in place of recalling our soldiers, let our fleets encircle Vera Cruz with new lines in order to carry re-enforcements thither; but let France be fully aware of what she does.

Already, gentlemen, there has been much money spent. If I wished to count it up, I should certainly exceed the sum of 400,000,000—400,000,000 that would now be so useful to France, when we are asked for an appropriation for our public works that would improve the national patrimony, when the employés of our institutions are not paid. [Enough of this! Enough of this!]

For my part, gentlemen, to establish at the distance of 2,000 leagues from my country an Austrian Rome, minus the glory, minus the grandeur of the idea, minus the prestige of historical recollections, I consider an act of folly in which I wish to have no part. And it is in the name of violated law and justice, in the name of the interests of France compromised thereby—of her patrimony spent in it, in the name of the generous blood of her children that has been shed to water that country, where we have constantly heard mention made of hopes where we have found only deceptions, that I loudly and explicitly condemn such folly. [Divers manifestations in the Chamber. Applause from some benches.]

(Continuation of discussion in the French legislative body —Speech of M. Chaix d'Est-Ange, in reply to M. Jules Favre.)

M. LE BARON DE BEAUVERGER. One word only, gentlemen. M. Jules Favre has said that he did not wish to offend any one here. I am willing to admit it. But it is impossible that M. Jules Favre should imagine that he offends no one when he compares our soldiers of 1814 to the Mexican brigands, when he compares our generals to incendiaries ——

(The interruptions and confused vociferations prevented the rest of the speaker's words from reaching us.)

THE CHAIRMAN, M. SCHNEIDER. M. De Beauverger, you are very wrong in assuming to speak, without being authorized by the chairman.

Moreover, I have not awaited your observation to address one to M. Jules Favre, and it was one of those observations that have no need of being made a second time. [Good! good!]

M. Chaix D'Est-Ange is entitled to the floor.

M. LE COMTE D'ORNANO. But, Mr. Chairman, a deputy has always the right of making an observation. [Divers manifestations.]

M. CHAIX D'EST-ANGE, vice-president of the council of state. Gentlemen——

Several voices: Let us adjourn till to-morrow.

Other voices: No, no! speak!

M. CHAIX D'EST-ANGE, vice-president of the council of state. I am at the pleasure of the Chamber. [Cries of go on! speak!]

Gentlemen, on commencing his speech the honorable gentleman who has just addressed you remarked as to the little power left to this great assembly. I confess that I do not comprehend either the sense or the occasion of such an observation. I know no other limit to this power than that which has been assigned to it by the constitution itself. I know no other limit to your liberty than that which propriety and your patriotism at the same time assign to it. Is the right of questioning denied to you? Is the independence of your votes clogged by anything whatsoever? And how can the honorable gentleman, who has used the liberty of speech in all its extent, speak of the little power left to this great assembly? How can he call you outside barbarians? I do not understand it.

However it be, he has been willing to resume this Mexican question, and to indulge in very diffuse observations upon it, to which I ask your permission to reply.

And in the first place, let us speak, since we must continually do so, of the origin of this quarrel and of the motives that induced France to take up arms. [Cries of no! no! to-morrow.]

A member: It is six o'clock.

M. THE VICE-PRESIDENT OF THE COUNCIL OF STATE. If the Chamber is annoyed and restless at the lateness of the hour, and fearful of a long speech, it is mistaken. I will be as brief as possible. [Go on! speak!]

The case is not one, as the honorable gentleman stated, of a quarrel entered into for a sum less than five millions, and which has led us into enormous expenditures, in a development of force entirely unexpected. The quarrel is one that rests on a very different basis and has a very different origin. Every one knows it, and the government has repeated it often enough to leave no one in ignorance of the facts. Our countrymen had been the victims of vexations, robberies, spoliations, assassinations. Reparation was demanded; it was impossible to obtain it. Must we have kept silence? No. We insisted on our demands, and then, on the refusal of any kind of satisfaction whatever, we were compelled to lay down an ultimatum. Finally, we came to what the honorable M. Thiers called, I think, the great argument of politics—war. This is how and why the war commenced; because the honor of the nation was interested in it; because the safety of our countrymen was involved in it; because there was at the time a reparation to be demanded for them on account of the material damage they had sustained, and a reparation of honor which France was entitled to exact.

Has France had—I proceed rapidly, I do not wish at this hour to abuse the patience of the Chamber—has France had any intention, as has been asserted, of imposing a government upon Mexico? On this point there is a reply which bears no contradiction—the letter itself read to the Chamber by the honorable M. Jules Favre, the letter written by the Emperor to General Laurencez:

"It is against my interests, against my origin, and against my principles, to impose any government whatever on the Mexican people; let it choose with full liberty the form that suits it."

This is the letter that was written; it bears no contradiction, and it is evident that in declaring war it was not sought to impose any government on Mexico, but to obtain the reparation to which we were entitled.

The same language, as the honorable M. Jules Favre can remember, was held in the tribune by M. Billault, speaking in the name of the government. He said—and I should be very far from contradicting his words—that entire freedom of voting should be allowed, that the Mexicans should be consulted as to the government that would suit them, and that their will should be rigorously respected and religiously executed. Was it the purpose to deceive the Chamber when such language was employed? Was it the intention really to impose a government on Mexico? On the contrary, has not every facility been afforded for the exercise of universal suffrage? Universal suffrage has been consulted, and has spoken with a unanimity almost complete.

Here, gentlemen, was the difficulty that was met with. The war must have been terminated by a treaty; a treaty must be made with some one. And Admiral Jurien, in a despatch which I find among the diplomatic documents, had excellent reason to raise the difficulty in the very outset of the proceedings, and to say: It is not treaties more or less advantageous that we need; we have already several with Juarez, but they have never been executed. We must be certain that the government which signs them should have power and will to maintain the execution of them It is under these circumstances that the Mexican people were consulted, and were told: Choose through the medium of universal suffrage whatever government suits you; be it a republic or a monarchy, your will shall be respected and carried into effect. If it be a republic, you shall have a republic; if it be the government of Juarez that you select, well; we will accept Juarez and treat once more with him. If it be a monarchy, it will be accepted and proclaimed by us.

Monarchy! As for me, said the honorable M. Thiers last year, my reason is confounded when I reflect that the idea has been entertained of establishing a monarchy in Mexico! Why, then, has the honorable gentleman been so much astounded? Monarchical government existed for 300 years quietly in Mexico. There are yet some men living, who, born at the commencement of this century, can remember that they lived under the vice-royalty, and that they lived peaceably, with few taxes, and in perfect security; that the *conductas*, so called, that is, the trains that conveyed the products of the mines from Potosi to Vera Cruz to be shipped at the latter place, could proceed freely, without any obstacle, without any danger of attack; that the Spanish flag was raised over the wagons, and that flag was respected by every one.

Some of these men there were who lived in their infancy and in their youth under the monarchical form of government, and who, comparing it with the republican form, said: We cannot take a single step without being attacked in our interests, in our liberties of every kind. We live under an anarchical government which, in the common opinion of nations, is a disgrace to Mexico.

In such a state of things there was reason to think that they might be entitled to have the liberty of choosing between a republican form of government, which they had the right to adopt, and a monarchical form, to which they had assuredly the right of returning.

That it should, forsooth, be a source of regret in the estimation of certain persons that they should have abandoned this republican form, under which Mexico lived so miserably for twenty years, in order to return to the monarchical form, under which it had lived so happily for three hundred years, I understand very well; the partisans of monarchy, however, are entitled to have their opinions as well as those of republicanism Now, the people have been consulted, they have been asked their opinion What action has been taken, and how? The same measures have been adopted that are always adopted in such cases. First, an executive junta was named. This junta was charged with the selection of an assembly, in the hands of which the legislative power should be deposited. This junta adopted a monarchical form of government and proclaimed the archduke. Addresses were signed in great number, and from all quarters adhesions poured in. Then it was that the result of these adhesions being thus collected together were carried to Miramar. What answer did the Archduke Maximilian return? I cannot, said he, I cannot go to Mexico, except in virtue of universal suffrage which will call me thither. I require that universal suffrage should be consulted, and consulted in the best possible way; that lists should be opened; that the result of the votes should offer all desirable guarantees; and when all these precautions shall have been taken, if universal suffrage calls me, I will go to Mexico.

Thereupon universal suffrage was consulted. What was the result? Here it is. Out of a population of 7,500,000 or 8,000,000 of inhabitants which Mexico contains, if we allow the very highest estimate, and include therein the remotest tribes, those which have hitherto escaped all dependence, and which have never been under the control of the central government, there have been 5,500,000 consulted, and they have cast their votes almost unanimously.

These 5,500,000 adhesions were carried to the Archduke Maximilian, who thereupon believed himself the choice of universal suffrage freely expressed.

But he was wrong, say they, to believe himself so. Why? Because there was a population of 1,500,000 persons outside of this vote; 1,500,000 incorrigible recalcitrants, who wished to have nothing to do with this government!

But the honorable M. Jules Favre is mistaken. These 1,500,000 individuals are the inhabitants of Sonora, savage Indians who have never recognized any government, and whose opinion it was impossible to consult. Now, from the fact that these 1,500,000 individuals have not contributed their vote to the universal suffrage, to draw the conclusion that there are yet 1,500,000 individuals who protest against the monarchy, who desire to have nothing to do with it, and wish the expulsion of the emperor Maximilian, is something that neither the Chamber nor any reasonable person will be willing to admit.

Therefore, when the honorable M. Jules Favre says that the Mexican people have been promised liberty and universal suffrage, and have not received them; that, consequently, the people should be consulted anew, I reply to him that universal suffrage is a great operation which cannot be repeated every year. When, after having consulted a people on the form of its government; when, after having asked it once, "What is your will? What form of government, a republic or a monarchy, suits you best?" it has with full freedom replied, "I wish a monarchy;" then, when after having consulted it in order to know who it should be that should govern them—who it was that had their confidence—for one reason or other it has repeatedly replied, "Here is the person for whom I ask!" then the trial by universal suffrage has been made, and you cannot, two or three years afterwards, come and ask us to have it renewed. [Cries of good! good!]

The emperor Maximilian has been consecrated by the will of the Mexican people. He is the choice of universal suffrage. It is an accomplished affair, and not one to be recommenced in this way from year to year. [Approbative laughter on several benches.]

M. Jules Favre has sought every possible means of attacking this rising government; he has taken it in its cradle, in the midst of difficulties of every kind and of every character that generally obstruct every new government, and especially a government succeeding an anarchy which had lasted for forty or fifty years; and then, magnifying these difficulties, he has sought to render its existence impossible and to prove to all that it was impossible. Has he succeeded?

He said, in the first place, that it had no credit. If we presumed to take the familiar comparisons that have been introduced into this debate by the honorable M. Jules Favre, that is to say, if we presumed to compare the credit of a merchant to the credit of a great state, we would ask you whether, whilst it would be repeated every morning that he was going to fail, whilst it would be continually stated in the greatest assembly in the world that he was unequal to his engagements, that he was on the point of bankruptcy, that he resorted to the pawnbroker's, it would not be necessary for this merchant to have the most firm credit in order to withstand such attacks? [Laughter.]

Now, such are the attacks to which the Mexican government has been subjected, a government which needed encouragement and sympathy; and they say that he has no credit!

No credit! In the first place, it is prompt and honorable with us. It carries out the treaty of Miramar with perfect exactness. It gives us securities; and how does it give them to us? It gives them to us at the market value, and we receive them at the same. I take up the last statement of the financial condition, and I find that the Mexican government was our debtor for all operations to the amount of 39,458,000 francs. It has paid us 38,838,000 francs. It owes us at present no more than 500,000 or 600,000 francs, a very small affair in a transaction of such a nature.

Meanwhile what is it doing in this new country—a country so long the sport of anarchy, where governments succeeded each other in some sort every day; where it was impossible to establish any system of taxation; where recourse was had only to the customs alone?

It makes loans, and it makes them under onerous conditions. Yes, that is true; but M. Juarez of whom you speak, M. Juarez who holds the country, who has armies, who has taken the field—I would like to know whether he could effect a loan at any rate at all, and whether he could obtain credit.

However it be, the Mexican government raises loans on conditions that make the honorable M. Jules Favre blush with shame, in the first place, because they are bad, onerous, ruinous; and secondly, because they are immoral and shameful.

Let us examine these different objections. They are ruinous! Pardon me. The nations that have the best credit have borrowed at rates that I do not care to specify, but with which the Chamber is well acquainted. It is an ordinary thing for a very regular country to borrow at 12 per cent. I might cite, for example, a loan that has, it must be said, the sympathies of the entire world, because it was contracted under sad circumstances. I refer to the federal loan. That great country, the United States, while it was divided, while it was delivered up to civil war, while it seemed that it must necessarily conquer or perish—that great country appealed to credit, which it had not previously known, and of which it seemed it would never have need, and it borrowed at rates more onerous, at rates much higher than the Mexican loan, rates which have been as high as $16\frac{27}{100}$ per cent. if my investigations are correct. Now, who could blame that great country, so straitened and hard pressed in its resources, for having borrowed at onerous rates, in order to sustain a war for the purpose and in the name of the preservation of its Union?

But, say they, if States can subscribe for loans on conditions more or less onerous--more or less ruinous--according to their embarrassments, according to the struggles which they have to maintain, these conditions are honorable or dishonorable according to the good or bad use that is made of the borrowed money. Now, the Mexican loan is, according to M. Jules Favre, a loan subscribed to under conditions that cause the blush of shame to mantle the cheek of my able and eloquent adversary.

M. Glais-Bizoin. Yes.

The Government Commissioner. What are these dishonorable conditions? They are premiums, chances, lottery—all those immoral things prohibited by the law of 1836.

Gentlemen, I do not approve of these conditions, if I may speak my personal sentiments on the subject; but it must be acknowledged at the same time that they have passed into customs, [protestations of dissent on certain benches,] into the customs of borrowers.

M. Jules Favre. You mean to say of emperors? [Laughter.]

The Vice-President of the Council of State. It is no estimate that I make; it is a fact that I relate; if it be not true, let it be contradicted. For fifty years Austria has been effecting loans by the offer of premiums. Prussia has effected loans by means of premiums. The provisional government, without deeming it an offence against morality—I am sure it did not wish to commit any such offence—[laughter]—the provisional government authorized the city of Paris to borrow by means of premiums, and it borrows yet by means of premiums.

I would be glad, in this regard, if no authorization of this kind were ever given; but it must be acknowledged that when we consult precedents, we find that such authorizations have been given, and that such premiums, I shall not say, have passed into public customs, but at least that they have accompanied many loans contracted under better circumstances, and by governments with greater credit.

M. Glais-Bizoin. Without lotteries?

The Vice-President of the Council of State. I beg your pardon; with lotteries, by means of lots, by means of premiums. Now, then, gentlemen, what are the resources that remain to the Mexican government in order to meet its engagements? Outside of loans has it any resources that it can present as a guarantee?

There is an assertion that has been made in some very authoritative works, and which, I believe, has been omitted by the honorable M. Thiers; it is, that under the ancient government, that is to say, under the vice-royalty, there were revenues by which the state supported itself, not by regular imposts, nor by duties on importations, which did not then exist, but from coinage and taxes on coinage, and from particular monopolies.

The illustrious and learned M. Humboldt, who passed five years in those regions, who studied the laws of the country, its resources, its means of advancement, writes that this country thus raised a revenue of twenty millions of piastres; that is to say, from one hundred to one hundred and ten millions of francs.

Mexico lived with ten millions of piastres. The rest it sent away either to the mother country—that is, Spain—or to Cuba, for the construction of fortifications there.

Such was the condition of affairs. It was, therefore—and you may form an idea as to what one hundred or one hundred and ten millions were worth at that time—it was, therefore, a country which had abundant resources for its existence.

Well, what are its resources now? The riches of the country are immense; that every one knows. The fertility of the soil is great; its productions are important, and present an excellent guarantee.

As to the amount of bullion extracted from the mines, it increases now; but the business of mining was ruined under the governments of Juarez and his predecessors. The working of the mines became an impossibility, when troops of bandits fell upon the miners, and seized and carried away the result of their labors. It is easy to understand that, in consequence, nearly all the mines were abandoned. But, at present, the working of them has been resumed with extraordinary activity, with new and more perfect processes, and the product is greater than ever.

As to the revenue from the customs, I have the statement of them, and I ask your permission to give you the data of two ports.

The customs at Tampico, during the first four months of 1864, yielded 96,000 piastres; in the corresponding months of this year they have yielded 431,000—that is, they have more than quadrupled.

At Vera Cruz the revenue from customs was from 800,000 to 900,000 piastres; it is now 1,645,000 piastres, or nearly double the former amount.

I do not wish, gentlemen, especially at this late hour, when I know how irksome it is for you to listen to a speech, I do not wish to have you enter on these calculations, and to show you how great are the resources that Mexico possesses, and how much more it has in imposts, which it is now proceeding to establish—such imposts as exist in all civilized countries—such, for example, as the land tax, so just and so natural, which he that owns the ground should pay to the state that protects him.

Such are the resources of Mexico And I should state that, at present, in spite of the prognostications of which it is the object, in spite of the evil auguries with which people seek to surround it, in spite of the threats that are directed against it, it assumes a new lease of life. What I have just said in a few words in reference to the revenue from customs sufficiently belies the fears that have been manifested, and proves that everywhere there is a total renewal of business. You see that by the increase of the custom-duties at Tampico and Vera Cruz commerce has received an important development.

The great line of railroad—that is, the line from Vera Cruz to Mexico—has been conceded to an Anglo-French company, that offers the most solid guarantees. This great line must be finished in five years; it will really be finished in three years.

There are, also, other lines of secondary importance capable of developing the resources of the country to a considerable extent, which, to the number of three, have been demanded and conceded already, and for the construction of which a capital has been subscribed of 4,500,000 piastres—that is, of 23,000,000 of francs.

Telegraphic lines are being constructed everywhere. In the notes which have been given to me in reference to the industrial development of the nation—that is to say, to the manifestation of the individual forces that attest the political life of a country—what do I see? Stage-coach enterprises, mines of coal, mines of petroleum, mines of gold, mines of silver; in a word, I see everywhere the development of all the resources of the country.

Now, gentlemen, we must come to the consideration of the desires of the Chamber, and see whether we can diminish the strength of our army in Mexico by causing the return of our soldiers to France as soon as possible. Be assured, gentlemen, that the government, in this regard, fully participates in your desire; that it is of the same mind with the learned authors of the reports laid before you, Messrs. Gouin, O'Quin, and Larrabure, and that it does all in its power to hasten the return of our troops to France. I have here a document, which, in this respect, can leave no doubt as to the intentions of the government.

Here are the sums of the numbers transmitted to the minister of war: The effective strength of our army on the 1st of January, 1864, amounted to 34,000 men; and on the 15th of January, 1865, it amounted to 28,000 men. As many as 8,000 men, therefore, have returned. And take notice that this is not all; for the order had been given for the return of a regiment now here—the second regiment of zouaves; but it was retained by Marshal Bazaine for the necessities of the siege af Oajaca, because he did not wish to strip other points. As soon, however, as the siege was finished, this regiment left Mexico; so that out of a total of 34,000 men, you see that more than a third has already returned to France.

This shows how the government yields to the just desire manifested by the legislative body to terminate this war as soon as it may be possible to terminate it.

In reference to this war, the honorable gentleman has given details, into which, especially at this moment, it is impossible for me to follow him otherwise than by a protest. He has said: "I have received news telegrams, and these telegrams inform me that a city has been burned; that Romero has been shot; that General Castagny has issued a proclamation—a proclamation," adds the speaker, "which I conceive myself required to read to you, for it is contrary to all military usages."

What, then, has General Castagny done? Whence comes it that he is denounced from this tribune? Whence comes it that for the benefit of those who are called the soldiers of Juarez, who are but miserable wretches, assassins, who disembowel women, who slay children, who commit nothing but pillages and conflagrations, whence comes it that for the benefit of such men an insult is offered to a brave French general, who nobly commands his men? [Cries of good! good!]

Whence comes it that amid the facilities of the tribune and far removed from the scene of events, in the impossibility of forming a correct judgment, on the faith of I know not what news, I know not what telegrams, a French general, present under his flag, in face of the enemy, is treated as a chief of bandits, a brigand, and a veritable vandal? It is against such imputations that we must protest. [Yes, yes! good, good!]

For the rest, gentlemen, there is nothing in the world more legitimate, more approvable, more honorable than this proclamation of General Castagny. Any soldier would have signed it.

How! He is there conducting his men against a ferocious enemy that flies before him; that always flies unless he be ten to one. He finds him committing atrocities and outrages, and yet you wish him to be treated as a soldier! How! Must we respect men who have committed such massacres; must we treat them as gallant men, as brave soldiers?

No; General Castagny has them shot, because he sees in them only wretches, bandits, all steeped in crime. [Good, good!] And here, gentlemen, General Castagny has certainly done his duty; he has acted as any one ought to act under such circumstances. [Yes, yes!] Not, indeed, as honor and the dignity of the flag demand when we fight with true soldiers, but as the security of men demands when they are opposed to a set of bandits. [Renewed manifestations of approbation. Cries of dissent from some benches.]

He merely sought to punish those who dishonored the name of soldier. Yes, I repeat it, his language was that of a soldier; his conduct that of a soldier; and it is for this that he must be treated as he has been here, in the midst of an assembly, all the words of which are repeated everywhere, repeated throughout the world.

I do not say that the general has any need of a vindication of his conduct, but the army which he commands needs a protest to be uttered in its name. [Good, good!]

M. JULES FAVRE. The honor of the French flag is involved in the burning and massacre of a city!

Numerous voices: Do not interrupt! do not interrupt!

THE GOVERNMENT COMMISSIONER. In the midst of this excitement I cannot hear what you say.

M. JULES FAVRE. It is because you do not wish to hear. [Cries of disapprobation.]

THE GOVERNMENT COMMISSIONER. No; I do not wish to hear. No, when I have the floor I do not allow any liberty of interruption. [Good!]

M. EUGENE PELLETAN. Has he or has he not burned a city?

Several members: Order! order!

THE CHAIRMAN, M. SCHNEIDER. You should not insist on such attacks upon a French general.

THE GOVERNMENT COMMISSIONER. I conclude in a few words. It has been sought to show the difficulties to be experienced by a new government. It is true such difficulties are experienced; but why come to its cradle to augment those difficulties, to raise up still more in its way, and to seek to render its task impossible; for, in brief, wars like this one which we have undertaken are not as the wars of other times, wars of devastation in which they carried murder everywhere. Here we have a war undertaken in the name of liberty, in order to restore that blessing to a people that has groaned for fifty years under an anarchy which all the world has pointed out to you; which President Buchanan, its neighbor, pointed out in his message, when he said that it was a disgrace to civilized countries to tolerate such a nation! Now, we are going to bestow civilization, liberty, order upon it, where disorder has hitherto reigned, as well as the most frightful slavery and the most complete anarchy. [That is true! Good! good!] It is, then, a noble enterprise. Why surround it with all those difficulties, all those evil auguries? Why seek to fetter this government in its progress? Why seek to cause its fall at every step which it takes?

Yes, we are aware it has difficulties with the court of Rome, but nations more ancient, more powerful, have them likewise.

There are there, face to face with each other, two powers charged with the care of souls. As has been said, the one is the minister of God upon earth, his most elevated servant; he answers in the name of religion. He is the minister of peace, of mildness, of reconciliation.

But by the side of this power which has charge of souls there is another which has charge of souls equally, and which says: "Here is a people that has been intrusted to me; in what ways must I conduct it?" In ways of progress, of civilization, of liberty.

Now, from this arise difficulties; that is very true; but such difficulties as the moderation of both powers will know how to smooth away.

The august chief of religion must persuade himself that the necessities of the times will no longer permit the world to remain in the ways in which it was two or three hundred years ago.

On the other hand, we must count upon the moderation of the sovereign who loves religion, who respects and venerates it, and who, before setting out for his new empire, and before placing his hand upon his new crown, wished in some sort to receive it from the hands of God, and went to ask it from the Holy Father. Between them everything will be arranged; there will be no possible difficulty; things will be established to the satisfaction of all; there is every reason to hope for such a consummation. [Sensation.]

There remains the last difficulty; this is the United States, with which we are incessantly threatened, or rather with which Mexico is incessantly threatened—the United States, jealous, impatient, and only awaiting an occasion.

In this regard, permit me to finish with a few brief words.

As to the United States, frequent mention has been made of the Monroe doctrine, though God knows I care not much to enter upon the subject. Much talk has been expended on it without any great knowledge of its nature. The honorable gentleman spoke just now of a letter of Mr. Seward. I merely ask his permission to reply by reading these few lines, only from the last message of Abraham Lincoln. It is in the nature of a last will and testament; it is not only an advice given to his own people, who have lost him by so frightful a misfortune, so horrible a crime, but it is also an advice given to the world in general, to whose admiration it is entitled.

Here is what he said in his message of the 4th of March, the last public document, I believe, which is known of his, speaking with a perfect humility in the midst even of his triumph:

"Without bitterness, without ill-will towards any one, with charity towards all, and with firm confidence in the right, as far as God permits us to see it clearly, let us finish the work in which we have been engaged, in order thereafter to heal the wounds of the nation, to take care of the soldier who has fought our battles, of his widow and his orphans, and to do all that lies in our power to attain a just and durable peace among ourselves and with all nations."

As to me, I know of no finer language than this. I was struck with it, even before it had been consecrated by the sad end of Abraham Lincoln, and before I could have thought it was his last will and testament and his last word in this world.

Now this last word is a word of mercy, a word of moderation, of peace and of clemency. Let us hope, gentlemen, that it will be understood by those who obey him no more, but who preserve his memory.

The blood shed in battle for a just cause, for the liberty of a great people, may be blessed by the God of armies; but the blood shed after anger has passed, in an unjust cause, perhaps for the purpose of invading the rights of an inoffensive neighbor, has never yet fertilized the earth that received it, nor ever brought good fortune to the hand that shed it. We must hope, therefore, that the United States will repair their losses; that they will carry out the programme left to them by Lincoln; that they will take care of the widows and orphans who are in such great numbers among them; and that, after a war so bloody and yet so just, they will not hasten to engage in new quarrels, especially when their interests are opposed to any such complications. [Good! good!]

From all sides: Let us adjourn! Let us adjourn!

THE CHAIRMAN, M. SCHNEIDER. To-morrow at 2 o'clock the public session will be resumed.

I propose to add to the order of the day, after the discussion of the deficiency bill, the bill relative to the cancellation of the rents of the bureau of liquidation, and to place the discussion of this bill before that of the regular budget for 1866. This order of discussion is necessary, because the arrangement of the items in the regular budget suppose the adoption of the previous measure.

To-morrow, therefore, the order will be: Continuation of the discussion on the deficiency budget for 1865; discussion of the bill relative to liquidation; discussion of the budget for 1866; discussion of bills of local interest.

(The Chamber adjourned at half-past 6 o'clock.)

[From Le Moniteur Universel, No. 161, June 10, 1865, page 776, vol. —.]

Debates in the French legislative body.

SESSION OF FRIDAY, *June* 9, 1865.

* * * * * * *

The discussion of the deficiency bill for 1865 was continued. The Mexican question was resumed and examined at some length by M. Ernest Picard, a member of the opposition, after which the minister of state, M. Rouher, addressed the Chamber on the same subject, in reply to M. Picard and to M. Jules Favre. The concluding portion of his speech, and a rejoinder from M. Jules Favre, are given as follows:

HIS EXCELLENCY M. ROUHER, minister of state. * * * * * In fact, the foolish hopes conceived by Cortinas, or by some few men who surrounded Juarez, have been dispelled; calm has succeeded agitation in the minds of men, and the authority of the American government has caused itself to be felt.

Enrolling offices were opened in New York and Washington; soldiers were invited thither to enlist under the flag of Juarez; large sums were offered as bounties to induce them to engage in the scheme.

The American government, adhering strictly and religiously to the duty of neutrality, closed these enrolling offices, in accordance with the law of April 20, 1818. And while this attempt was being essayed, a general, whose name had been freely mentioned in the papers in connexion with the scheme, and who was represented as intrusted with the duty of leading this army of filibusters to Mexico—General Rosecrans—in a speech delivered before the legislature at Boston, protested against the singular part which it had been sought to make him play, and said that he was not constituted or disposed by nature to be the leader of mercenary troops, and had no inclination to betake himself to Mexico to attack any government in that country; that the United States wished to respect the obligations of neutrality; that they would respect them with the greatest strictness and sincerity; and that the relations of friendship between France and the United States would not be, even in the slightest degree, compromised. [Good! good!]

While these declarations were being made at Washington and New York, they received a formal sanction and ratification here. The minister of the United States presented himself to our minister of foreign affairs, and said to him: "Undoubtedly we do not regard with any favorable eye the establishment of a monarchy in Mexico; undoubtedly we would prefer to see a republican form prevail in that country; but we respect the will of peoples and nations; we understood that Mexico, formerly for a long time governed by the monarchical form, desires to return to that state, and we are not going to make war on a mere question as to forms of government."

Such have been the formal declarations made by the minister of the United States to the French government, and thereupon all those spasmodic efforts very soon have failed that were manifested in the states of New Leon and Tamaulipas, and which, I have no hesitancy in asserting, were a deplorable and melancholy consequence of an odious crime committed in the United States; a consequence which is destined very soon to disappear; and the partisans that have been collected will quickly be dispersed by the battalions directed against them by Marshal Bazaine. Such is the real condition of the Mexican empire. [Good! good!]

They have called up here in this assembly—I know not for what purpose—the question as to the property of the clergy in Mexico, and they have said to you: "The Emperor Maximilian is deserted; abandoned by the very party that bore him to power!" And then they have deemed it their duty to parade before you the Pope's letter and the declaration of Cardinal Antonelli.

I do not feel myself called upon to make any reply to such assertions. The Emperor Maximilian attained his power by the will of the Mexican nation. He has called upon the parties to allow him to constitute a moderate party to assist him in the direction of public affairs. He has not sought for men in this or that faction; he has not required certificates as to antecedents from such as, abjuring evil passions, desired to subserve the interests of order and of civilization; and at the very moment at which I now address you, this prince, who is accused of quartering himself in the conservative party, counts among his ministers three former ministers of Juarez himself: the minister of the interior, the minister of public works, and the minister president of the council of state.

The Emperor Maximilian, without ill-feeling, without any party connexions, without any of those tendencies or any of those rancors which civil war leaves after it in a country, has appealed to all intelligent and well-inclined men, and has said to them: "Come to me, for I represent the cause of order, of security, of progress, and of civilization." [Loud manifestations of approbation.]

Now, gentlemen, permit me to address a request to the members of the opposition. [Hear! hear!] Permit me to tell them that they cannot exercise too much prudence and discretion in weighing the language which they use within this hall while yielding to the dictates of their convictions, the sincerity of which I have no disposition whatever to call in question.

If they could know, as the government knows, the detestable abuse that is made of their words, of their criticisms, of their charges against the government, within that empire of Mexico and in the midst of those very rebels whom we have to fight, I am deeply convinced that their voices would not be so loud on this question, and that they would regret the language which they have already used.

Numerous voices: Good! good!

The Minister of State. You would not believe the strange communications that reach the government in this regard. I have here the description of a banquet held in the United States by the friends of Juarez. Do you wish me to read to you the list of toasts that were offered? [Yes, yes! read them! read them!]

"The Mexicans of the party of Juarez, residing in New York, celebrated the other evening the anniversary of the independence of Mexico, by a grand banquet at Delmonico's. Among those present were remarked Messrs. Romero, Doblado, Juan Baz, Colombiez, Alatorre, and other personages more or less distinguished for various reasons. After the banquet, M. Romero gave the signal for the speeches, which, as usual, abounded in big words and high-sounding phrases. They drank '*to the death of Maximilian, tyrant of Mexico; to the death of the Pope, tyrant of consciences; to the death of Napoleon III, tyrant of the whole world.*'"

That is not all. They drank the health of the French deputies who oppose the tyranny of the Emperor! [Cries of indignation.]

Such are the sad abuses which wicked and fiery passions make of criticisms and oppositions even the most conscientious—such, I feel convinced, as these are.

But this is not yet all. Our soldiers, in the long and difficult marches to which their duty condemns them, often find documents traitorously scattered among them! Do you know their purport? "Juarez to the soldiers of France." I ask your pardon; do not hasten to cry out with indignation, "Juarez and his friend Jules Favre"

Several voices: That is true!

M. ROUHER, minister of state. To the French soldiers, proposing to them to desert the flag of that tyrant called Napoleon III! [Manifestations of indignation.]

What matter our previous differences of opinion? What matters it that you have approved or disapproved the Mexican expedition? Let such discussions be henceforward discarded.

Our flag now floats over far distant shores. Let us then have the same sentiments of patriotism; let us all desire the triumph of that cause which we have promoted in those regions! Let us hasten by the unanimity of our wishes, let us hasten the moment when the French troops, not humbled—that they cannot be—but triumphant, and having completed their work, shall return amid the applauses of all France, to receive the crowns which their courage will have merited. [Good! good! bravo! bravo! Prolonged and redoubled applause.]

M. JULES FAVRE. Mr. President, I rise to a personal explanation.

THE PRESIDENT, M. SCHNEIDER. I cannot very well see what can constitute the occasion for a personal explanation.

Several voices: Let him speak.

THE PRESIDENT, M. SCHNEIDER. I decide, then, that M. Jules Favre asks the floor for a personal explanation and not for a speech. If there be question of a speech, M. Emile Ollivier is entitled.

M. EMILE OLLIVIER. Oh, Mr. President, let M. Jules Favre speak.

M. JULES FAVRE. It is not, you may be sure, and the Chamber may feel convinced of it, to the last fact cited by the minister of state that I wish to make allusion. But in the explanations which he has made to you, there is one which is calculated to impress upon you the belief that on the part of the speakers of the opposition to the government, in the announcement of a fact recognized as very serious by all the members of the assembly, there might have been something of a surprise; and as such an insinuation affects my character for fair and open dealing, I ask your permission to reply to it.

I said, and you remember it perfectly well, that a corps commander, whose name it is unnecessary to mention——

Several members: Why so? Mention it.

M. JULES FAVRE. I said that General Castagny, at the head of a body of French troops, had recourse to a measure contrary to the laws of war and to the law of nations. [Denials.]

The minister of state says, in reply to me, that as yet there is something untimely and imprudent involved in the assertion, that as long as our troops are upon hostile territory, while they are exposed to death, we have no right to examine their conduct, and that it is proper for us to guard our expressions so that there might be no possibility of their doing any harm. [That is so.]

I ask you, then, why you applaud the words of the minister? What does he do?

Various voices: His language is patriotic; he is a Frenchman!

M. JULES FAVRE. As to me, I can admit no such argument; it is unworthy of any man of sense. [Murmurs and cries of disapprobation.]

I respect and honor the courage of our soldiers who brave all dangers, but I esteem not the less the courage of the statesman who, on the government benches, comes to sanction by his words the principles which he proposes to your votes. Each in his sphere fulfils a duty, and I cannot believe that one can be considered superior to the other. [Various manifestations.]

Now, if I render him this justice, I claim a similar one from him in regard to the part which we perform here. I ask, gentlemen, whether there can be a sort of infallibility, of inviolability, decreed by the danger which a general runs that would permit him to place himself above all laws. [Interruption.]

If it be so, it is undeniable that it would not be himself only; it would be the fate of the men whom he happened to command that he would succeed in endangering [Exclamations of indignation.]

As far as regards the fact which has provoked the discussion between the minister of state and us, nothing is more simple. That fact, gentlemen, is the burning of a city of four thousand souls. Before giving expression to it I took care to state that the fact had been announced a long time since that the Moniteur had been interrogated on the subject, and that the Moniteur had been silent.

Just a while ago, when the minister of state reproached me for not having asked him for explanations, he must have forgotten that from the 20th of April explanations had been asked by the press [Exclamations of disapprobation.]

Here is what the Journal des Debats said in its issue of the 20th of April last. [Oh! oh!—confusion.]

I am only replying to the reproach of the minister, which would seem to intimate that I announced a fact hitherto unknown; whilst, on the contrary, that fact was a public one, and several papers had called on the Moniteur for information in reference to it. [Interruption.]

M. ERNEST PICARD That is the very point in issue.

M JULES FAVRE. Here is what the Journal des Debats says:

"This despatch has been published by several journals, among others by the Constitutionnel, but we do not find it in the Moniteur of this morning. It is significant in its necessary brevity, for the telegraph does not indulge in long discourses; but we hope soon to find in the official organ the details and the documents which the despatch could not give, and which should serve to present under their true light the rigorous measures adopted by General Castagny against San Sebastian and against the four Juarist chiefs in question. San Sebastian counts, or rather once counted, since that city no longer exists, a population of four thousand inhabitants. Whilst allowing the greatest possible latitude to the cruel necessities of war, it behooves us to know the reasons that induced General Castagny to destroy by fire a centre of population of that importance."

There, then, was the question very distinctly made: Does the minister of state think that it is conformable to the law of nations, not to pursue a few brigands, not to shoot down some wretches who had assassinated our soldiers. These no one has ever defended within this hall—[So! so!]

The murmurs will not efface my words from the Moniteur; my words remain, and you cannot distort them.

Now, I assert that this fact was published in all the papers six weeks ago: A city of four thousand inhabitants, in which were peaceable and inoffensive inhabitants, women, children, and men of property, has been given to the flames. This act is contrary to the law of nations We have said so; we say so yet. Such proceedings might bring deplorable retaliations upon our soldiers I add that such violent proceedings, unless they are disavowed, compromise the honor of France to a most fatal extent. [Numerous cries of indignation. Cries of good! good! from some benches.]

THE CHAIRMAN, M. SCHNEIDER. I proceed now to put to the vote the third section of the article in reference to the war department, estimate marked F, and I announce in advance that there is a demand for the yeas and nays on the question.

"3d section. Pay and maintenance of the troops, 33,718,701 francs."

The demand for the yeas and nays is signed by Messrs Hénon, Carnot, Ernest Picard, Viscount Lanjuinais, the Duke de Marmier, Bethmont, Magnin, Jules Favre, Marie, Garnier Pagès.

A member: And Juarez! [Exclamations and laughter.]

A vote was then taken.

THE PRESIDENT, M. SCHNEIDER. The result of the vote is as as follows:

Number voting	245
Absolute majority	123
For	232
Against	13

The legislative body has adopted the section.

Mr. Seward to Mr. Romero.

DEPARTMENT OF STATE,
Washington, November 5, 1865.

SIR: I have had the honor to receive your note of the 21st of July, 1865, transmitting to me, for the information of the government of the United States, a translation into English of the discussion which took place in the legislative body of France on the 8th of June, 1865, in relation to the affairs of Mexico, and of parts of the disposal of that discussion, which terminated on the 9th of the same month.

Thanking you for this interesting document, I have the honor to renew to you, sir, the assurances of my high consideration.

WILLIAM H. SEWARD.

Senor MATIAS ROMERO, *&c., Washington, D. C.*

Mr. Romero to Mr. Seward.

[Translation.]

MEXICAN LEGATION IN THE UNITED STATES OF AMERICA,
Washington, 23d of July, 1865.

MR. SECRETARY: In virtue of the recommendation which you were pleased to make to me at the interview which we had yesterday at the Department of State, to the effect that I should state to you in writing what I verbally had the honor to represent to you, I now proceed to make to you the following statement:

You know very well with how much anxiety the government of Mexico has been awaiting the termination of the civil war in the United States—since our fate being identified to a certain extent with that of the Union, the success of the latter insured our own, whilst its overthrow would have made our situation more difficult. In fact, the French intervention in Mexico having been, as is already universally admitted, nothing else than a part of the conspiracy which was planned to subvert this government and to break up this country, nothing is more natural than that the principal question in the United States, when once decided in favor of republican institutions, the accessory one, which is being discussed in Mexico, should be decided in the same sense. The success, therefore, of the cause of the independence of Mexico is already beyond all doubt, even to the eyes of the most determined enemies of the republic, and it has now become only a question of time. The duty which the Mexican government has to shorten that time as much as may be possible causes me to address this communication to you.

We had believed that when once the civil war had terminated here, which from its magnitude and importance had absorbed the whole attention of the government of the United States, without permitting it to take the measures necessary to destroy those accessory to the rebellion which were developing themselves in foreign countries, the same government would have to pursue one of these two policies—either to take the steps it might deem proper in order that the French should withdraw themselves from Mexico, or to follow the same policy of neutrality observed up to this period, until peace is finally restored at home and the federal authority is established in the southern States, thus giving time to the Emperor of the French to the end that, reconsidering his measures, he may abandon an enterprise which is already without object, and which it is utterly impossible to realize, and which, should he persist in it, will involve him most certainly in future complications with the United States, which, when once at peace, will not be able to remain an indifferent spectator of the conquest by a European power of one of the principal regions of this continent in their immediate vicinity.

Upon the choice of these two policies I shall say nothing at this time, for I do not propose in this note to solicit from this government the adoption of the one or of the other. My object is solely to manifest that the time necessary having already elapsed to know which of them has been adopted, we have believed that it is the second; and in this belief, being unable to rely for the time being even upon the moral support of the government to put an end to the war carried on against us by the Emperor of the French, we deem it our duty to inform the government of the United States of what we desire to do in this country in the fulfilment of our duties as Mexicans.

In the first place, I deem it my duty to represent to you that, although the patriotism of the Mexican people is a sufficient guarantee to insure us success over our invaders, and although we have in our country sufficient elements to defend our independence—which elements have enabled us to resist during four years the most persistent efforts of the first military nation of Europe, and will enable us to prolong the contest to the point of compelling our enemies to leave our country—our situation is such that the French might be enabled to remain some years more in Mexico, if they persist in it and our condition does not ameliorate.

It is known that the people of Mexico is without arms.. As arms are not manufactured in the republic, we are compelled to use those which we may be enabled to import. The circumstance that some of our ports are occupied and others blockaded by the French, and, above all, the fact that this government had prohibited, to our prejudice, the exportation of arms from the United States, and that we could not obtain them in Europe, because almost all the governments of that continent are hostile to our cause, has caused the government of Mexico, from the commencement of the war, to find itself with a small quantity of muskets, and these in so bad a condition that it is really surprising how the resistance has been prolonged with implements so utterly worthless.

The principal, and almost exclusive, revenues of the Mexican government being derived from the yield of maritime custom-houses of the republic, and the most valuable of these being occupied or blockaded by the French, it follows that the government of the republic has found itself deprived of its revenues in times when it most required them to organize and sustain the armies which defend the independence of the country.

Our situation therefore is, to sum up, the following: with arms and means we can terminate in a few months the war which France is waging against us; and without these elements, we shall be obliged to limit ourselves to resisting the French, who will be enabled to remain in Mexico for an indefinite period, with great danger to the peace of this continent, until they find themselves compelled to quit that country through weariness, if not expelled by the force of arms.

You will understand, Mr. Secretary, that it is the duty of the Mexican government to shorten the war, and to do all that is incumbent upon it to procure the necessary elements to attain that result. The identity of interests existing respecting this point between the United States and Mexico, and, above all, the great sympathy which, with unparalleled unanimity, the people of the United States have manifested, even in the most unfortunate days of the Union, for the cause of the independence of Mexico, have led the Mexican government to believe that, by rendering this sympathy effective, those elements might be derived from it which are required to terminate immediately a war which otherwise might last for years, and all this without compromitting in any manner the government of the United States, and without causing it to deviate, by a single hair's breadth, from the duties incumbent upon it as a neutral power. Although in the realization of this idea we propose to ourselves to treat with the citizens of this country as individuals, without in any manner compromitting their government, and although what we think of doing is entirely lawful and compatible with the attitude occupied by the United States as a power neutral towards France, we deem it proper to submit our plans to the government of the United States, as a proof of our good faith, of our deference to this government, and with the view of receiving assurances, if this be possible, that no embarrassment will be placed in our way in the execution thereof, since a painful experience has taught us the necessity of taking this step. Reserving, therefore, the consideration of other matters, when circumstances shall require it, our wishes are limited for the present to the two following points:

1st. To negotiate a loan to the government of Mexico in this market, by disposing of bonds which shall contain the guarantees which we consider sufficient to induce speculators to purchase them, and which may make them acceptable to the people of this country. It is indubitable that the duties of a neutral power do not impose upon the United States that of preventing us from realizing our bonds, since this does not constitute the intervention of this government in our behalf. The market is as much open to us as to our enemies. If the French desire to negotiate a loan here upon the same basis as we—that is, as a private speculation, with which the government has nothing to do—evidently there would be no right to deny it the same. This same right is the one which we wish to exercise now. Our deference towards the government of the United States has reached the point that, notwithstanding we have had a pressing necessity for the funds which such a loan could have furnished us, and that there was a time which seemed most propitious for its realization, we preferred to await until the loan with the United States, which the house of Messrs. Jay Cooke & Co., of Philadelphia, is now selling, should be realized, in order not to appear to be acting in competition with the United States, and desirous of diverting the funds of its citizens to exterior objects while they were needed by their own government.

2d. To purchase arms and munitions of war, and to be enabled to export them to such places as may seem to us proper. After the order of the President of the 3d of May last, which rescinded the prohibition to export arms from the United States, and which has left in all their force the laws and traditions of this country respecting the commerce of belligerents in articles contraband of war, and, above all, after the precedent established by this government of permitting the French officers who arrived in November, 1862, to purchase the means of transportation for the invading army of Mexico, who purchased and exported the articles they needed to wage war against my country, as your department communicated to me in the note which it addressed to me upon this subject under date of the 24th of November aforesaid, it does appear that there cannot be the least cause that we should not be permitted now to do what the laws of this country declare in every respect lawful, and what this government has permitted to our enemies.

I do not doubt that the government of the United States will appreciate the sincerity of the motives which induce me to address it this note, and that it will favor me with a reply which will be entirely satisfactory to my government.

I avail myself with pleasure of this opportunity to renew to you, Mr. Secretary, the assurances of my most distinguished consideration.

M. ROMERO.

Hon. WILLIAM H. SEWARD, *&c.*, *&c.*, *&c.*

Mr. Seward to Mr. Romero.

DEPARTMENT OF STATE,
Washington, August 7, 1865.

SIR: Your note of the 23d ultimo, on the subject of the exportation of arms to, and the negotiation of a loan for, the Mexican republic, was duly received, and has been taken into consideration.

You are well aware that the government of the United States has official relations with the republican government in Mexico only, and heartily desires that that form of government may, by the unity, virtue, valor, and perseverance of the people in Mexico, be maintained in that country, as the United States earnestly desire that, in the same manner, it may be perpetuated in every other country in the American hemisphere where it has heretofore been established. Liberty and free institutions in any country are the rewards of the popular virtues I have named. They cannot be guaranteed by any one nation, however beneficent, to another, however well disposed to receive them.

I am not aware of any law or executive order which at present prohibits the exportation of arms, or of money, from the United States to Mexico, by either of the parties at war in that country, or by the individual citizens or subjects of the respective parties. Any proceedings for that purpose must, however, not be connected with proceedings which tend to infringe the impartial neutrality which this government has hitherto in every instance maintained. That neutrality is really the effect of existing municipal laws as well as of international law. It could, therefore, be deviated from by the executive government only when Congress should have directed it. To Congress alone belongs the constitutional power to declare war.

I avail myself of this opportunity to renew to you, sir, the assurances of my very distinguished consideration.

WILLIAM H. SEWARD.

Señor MATIAS ROMERO,
&c., &c., &c., New York, N. Y.

Mr. Romero to Mr. Seward.

[Translation.]

MEXICAN LEGATION,
New York, 12th of August, 1865.

M. Romero presents his compliments to Mr. Seward, and has the honor to transmit to him a printed copy, in English, of a treaty of alliance signed at Lima on the 23d of January last by seven of the American republics, which "desire to unite for the purpose of providing for their exterior security" against the aggressions of European powers.

M. Romero has also the honor to transmit to Mr. Seward a printed copy of another treaty, concluded on the same date and between the same contracting parties, with the object of completing the compact of alliance.

These two treaties constitute the principal result of the labors of the American congress which recently met at Lima, the capital of Peru.

Hon. WILLIAM H. SEWARD, *&c., &c., &c.*

[Enclosure No. 1.—Translation.]

In the name of God: The States of America which are hereinafter mentioned, desiring to unite in order to provide for their exterior security, to strengthen their relations, to maintain peace among themselves, and to promote other common interests, have determined to secure these objects by means of international compacts, of which the present is the first and fundamental one.

To that effect they have conferred full powers, as follows: By Salvador, to Don Pedro Alcantara Herran; by Bolivia, to Don Juan de la Cruz Benavente; by the United States of Colombia, to Don Justo Arosemena; by Chili, to Don Manuel Montt; by Ecuador, to Don Vicente Piedrahita; by Peru, to Don José Gregorio Paz Soldan; and by the United States of Venezuela, to Don Antonio Leocadio Guzman.

And the plenipotentiaries having exchanged their powers, which they found sufficient and in due form, have agreed herein to the following stipulations:

ARTICLE 1. The high contracting parties unite and bind themselves to each other for the objects above expressed, and guarantee to each other mutually their independence, their sovereignty, and the integrity of their respective territories, binding themselves in the terms of the present treaty to defend each other against any aggression which may have for its object the depriving any one of them of any of the rights herein expressed, whether the aggression shall come from a foreign power, whether from any of those leagued by this compact, or from foreign forces which do not obey a recognized government.

ART. 2. The alliance herein stipulated will produce its effects when there shall be a violation of the rights expressed in article 1, and especially in the cases of offences which shall consist—

First. In acts directed to deprive any one of the contracting nations of a part of its territory with the intention of appropriating its dominion or of ceding it to another power.

Second. In acts directed to annul or to alter the form of government, the political constitution, or the laws which any one of the contracting parties may give or may have given itself in the exercise of its sovereignty, or which may have for their object to change forcibly its internal system, or to impose upon it authorities in the like manner.

Third. In acts directed to compel any one of the high contracting parties to a protectorate, sale, or cession of territory, or to establish over it any superiority, right, or pre-eminence whatever, which may impair or offend the ample and complete exercise of its sovereignty and independence.

ART. 3. The allied parties shall decide, each one for itself, whether the offence which may have been given to any one of them is embraced among those enumerated in the foregoing articles.

ART. 4. The *casus fœderis* being declared, the contracting parties compromit themselves to immediately suspend their relations with the aggressive power, to give passports to its public ministers, to cancel the commissions of its consular agents, to prohibit the importation of its natural and manufactured products, and to close their ports to its vessels.

ART. 5. The same parties shall also appoint plenipotentiaries to conclude the arguments necessary to determine the contingents of the force, and of the land and naval supplies, or of any other kind which the allies must give to the nation which is attacked, the manner in which the forces must act, and the other auxiliary means be realized, and everything else which may be proper to the best success of the defence. The plenipotentiaries shall meet at the place designated by the appended party.

ART. 6. The high contracting parties bind themselves to furnish to the one which may be attacked the means of defence which each one of them may think itself able to dispose of, even though the stipulations to which the foregoing article refers should not have preceded, provided the case should, in their judgment, be an urgent one.

ART. 7. The *casus fœderis* having been declared, the party offended will not have authority to conclude conventions for peace or for the cessation of hostilities without including in them the allies who may have taken part in the war and should desire to accept them.

ART. 8. If (which may God avert) one of the contracting parties should offend the rights of another one of them, guaranteed by this alliance, the others will proceed in the same manner as though the offence had been committed by a foreign power.

ART. 9. The high contracting parties bind themselves not to concede to, nor to accept from, any nation or government a protectorate or pre-eminence which impairs their independence and sovereignty; and they likewise compromit themselves not to transfer to another nation or government any part of their territory. These stipulations do not hinder, however, those parties which are coterminous to make the cessions of territory which they may deem proper for the better demarcation of their boundaries or frontiers.

ART. 10. The high contracting parties bind themselves to appoint plenipotentiaries, who shall meet every three years, as nearly as possible, to adjust the conventions proper to strengthen and perfect the union established by the present treaty. A special provision of the present congress shall determine the day and the place at which the first assembly of the plenipotentiaries shall meet, which assembly shall likewise designate the following one, and thus thereafter until the expiration of the present treaty.

ART. 11. The high contracting parties will solicit, collectively or separately, that the other American states which have been invited to the present congress shall enter into this treaty; and from the moment the said states shall have made known their formal acceptance thereof, they shall have the rights and obligations which emanate from it.

ART. 12. This treaty shall continue in full force for the period of fifteen years, to be reckoned from the day of this date; and at the end of this period any one of the contracting parties shall have authority to terminate it on its part by announcing it to the others twelve months previously thereto.

ART. 13. The exchange of the ratifications shall take place in the city of Lima within the period of two years, or sooner, if it be possible.

In testimony whereof, we, the undersigned, ministers plenipotentiary, sign the present and seal it with our respective seals, in Lima, this twenty-third day of January, in the year of our Lord one thousand eight hundred and sixty-five.

P. A. HERRAN.
JUAN DE LA CRUZ BENAVENTE.
MANUEL MONTT.
JUSTO AROSEMENA.
VICENTE PIEDRAHITA.
JOSÉ G. PAZ SOLDAN.
ANTONIO L. GUZMAN.

[Enclosure No. 2.—Translation.]

In the name of God: The states of America, which, agreeably to the treaty of union and alliance of this same date, have allied themselves for sundry objects, being represented by the plenipotentiaries who subscribed the said treaty, and having exchanged their respective powers, found to be in due form, to wit: Salvador, by Don Pedro Alcantara Herran; the United States of Venezuela, by Don Antonio Leocadio Guzman; the United States of Colombia, by Don Justo Arozemena; Bolivia, by Don Juan de la Cruz Benavente; Chili, by Don Manuel Montt; Ecuador, by Don Vicente Piedrahita; and Peru, by Don José Gregorio Paz Soldan, have agreed upon the following stipulations:

ARTICLE 1. The high contracting parties solemnly bind themselves not to commit hostilities against each other, even by way of compulsion, and never to resort to the use of arms as a means of settling their controversies, which may arise from acts not comprehended in the *casus fœderis* of the treaty of defensive alliance signed on this date. On the contrary, they will employ exclusively peaceful means to terminate all these controversies, submitting to the decision of an arbiter, without appeal therefrom, when they cannot settle them in any other manner. The controversies respecting boundaries are included in this stipulation.

ART. 2. When the parties interested cannot agree upon the appointment of the arbiter, this will be done by a special assembly of plenipotentiaries named by the contracting nations, and equal in number, at least, to the majority of said nations. The meeting shall be held in the territory of any one of the nations nearest to the interested ones which the one which first solicited said appointment may designate.

ART. 3. Whenever, when the selection of the arbiter may be solicited, as provided in the foregoing article, the assembly of plenipotentiaries shall have met, in the number previously determined, of which article 10 of treaty of union and alliance speaks, and signed on this date, it will belong to said assembly to make the said appointment.

ART. 4. If one of the contracting parties should refuse or avoid the appointment of the arbiter, the other may have recourse to the other governments of the allied states, which will take into consideration, each one for itself, the interpretation of the case, and will endeavor to induce the resistant party to comply with the stipulation contained in article 1.

ART. 5. When the parties interested shall not have previously determined upon the manner of proceeding, in order to discuss their rights, it will be the duty of the arbiter to determine the procedure.

ART. 6. Each one of the contracting parties binds itself to prevent, by all the means which may be within its reach, the preparation or collection of materials of war in its territory, the enrolling or recruiting of persons, or the fitting out of vessels to operate hostilely against any one of the other powers which have subscribed and joined in this treaty. They also bind themselves to prevent the emigrants or political refugees from abusing their asylum by conspiring against the government of the country whence they came.

ART. 7. When the said emigrants or political refugees shall give just cause of complaint to the power whence they come, or to another bordering upon the one where they dwell, they shall be removed to a distance from the frontier sufficient to dispel every fear, whensoever the power thus threatened shall solicit the intervention of the latter, with documentary proofs.

ART. 8. The high contracting parties bind themselves not to permit the transit of troops, of arms, and of implements of war across their territory, when destined to operate against any one of them.

ART. 9. The contracting parties in the same manner bind themselves not to permit the vessels or squadrons of nations which may be at war with any one of those subscribing to the present treaty to provide themselves in their ports with articles which are contraband of war; nor to permit the repairing of their vessels-of-war, nor even that they shall establish themselves in the said ports to prey upon the nation with which they may be in a state of war or of open hostility.

ART. 10. The high contracting parties will solicit, collectively or separately, of the other states who have been invited to the present congress, their adhesion to this treaty; and from the moment the said states shall have manifested to all of them their formal acceptance thereof, they shall have the rights and obligations which emanate therefrom.

ART. 11. This treaty shall continue in full force for the term of fifteen years from the day of the date hereof; and at the expiration of that period any one of the contracting parties will be authorized for itself to terminate it, by giving notice thereof to the others twelve months beforehand.

ART. 12. The exchange of the ratifications of this treaty shall take place in the city of Lima within the period of two years, or sooner if it be possible, and it will have its effects among the parties who shall do so as soon as they shall have executed the same.

In testimony whereof, we, the undersigned plenipotentiaries, sign the present, and seal it with our respective seals, in Lima, on this twenty-third day of the month of January, in the year of our Lord one thousand eight hundred and sixty-five.

P. A. HERRAN.
ANTONIO L. GUZMAN.
JUAN DE LA CRUZ BENAVENTE.
MANUEL MONTT.
VICENTE PIEDRAHITA.
JOSÉ G. PAZ SOLDAN.
JUSTO AROZEMENA.

Mr. Romero to Mr. Seward.

[Translation.]

MEXICAN LEGATION TO THE UNITED STATES,
New York, September 14, 1865.

MR. SECRETARY: I have the honor to remit to you a copy of No. 95 of the "official newspaper of the government of the State of Tabasco," of the 20th July last, which came to my hands a short time since, in which you will see the congratulation which the governor of that State addressed on that same date of July to the consul of the United States at San Juan Bautista on the termination of the civil war in this country, manifesting at the same time his sorrow for the assassination of President Lincoln.

It is satisfactory to me to send you this communication, as proof of the sympathies which the Mexican people have for the people of the United States; of the sorrow with which they heard of their misfortunes, and of the rejoicing with which they celebrate their victories, well understanding that circumstances had become so complicated that the fate of the two peoples might be considered as identified, and that events favoring the United States could not be less than favorable to the cause of Mexican nationality.

I avail of this occasion to renew to you, Mr. Secretary, the assurances of my most distinguished consideration.

M. ROMERO.

Hon. WILLIAM H. SEWARD, *&c., &c., &c.*

[Enclosure No. 1.—Translation.]

[From the Boletin Official of Tabasco, vol. 1, No. 95, July 20, 1865.]

MEXICAN REPUBLIC, POLITICAL AND MILITARY
GOVERNMENT OF THE STATE OF TABASCO,
San Juan Bautista, July 4, 1865.

MR. CONSUL: The kindred people of this continent, united in the lovely bonds of democracy, ought to share mutually in its joys and its sorrows. For this reason Mexico will ever deplore the unfortunate event of the 14th of April last, the death of the illustrious champion of liberty, in the city of Washington. For this reason will Mexico forget her past misfortunes, in the midst of her present trials, and congratulate the great and heroic people of the United States on this day of glorious memory.

Accept, then, Mr. Consul, on this day—the anniversary of that auspicious day when your ancestors proclaimed their independence in the city of Philadelphia—my sincere congratulations, as a private individual, and as the representative of this State, of whose sympathies I believe myself on this occasion the most faithful interpreter.

Accept also, in the name of your government, the demonstrations of esteem and good will from the garrison of this place, who have kindred sentiments, and trust that Mexico in general, and Tabasco in particular, will be worthy members of the great democratic family that people the world of Columbus, in spite of the mean strategy now used to divide us.

I make vows to Providence for the happiness of the United States, and pray that the peace the great republic has just conquered at such a great sacrifice may last long, for the good of humanity.

You will please accept, on this account, the assurances of my personal esteem and consideration.

Republic and liberty! San Juan Bautista, 4th of July, 1865.

G. MENDEZ.

LEON ALEJO TORRE, *First Officer.*

B. N. SANDERS,
Consul of the United States at this port, present.

[Enclosure No. 2.—Translation.]

CONSULATE OF THE UNITED STATES,
San Juan Bautista, July 4, 1865.

SIR: As the accredited agent of my government at this capital, I give you my most sincere thanks for the eloquent and expressive homage offered in your communication of this morning to the memory of our deceased and patriot President, who fell beneath the hands of that most ignoble of criminals—an assassin; and at the same time, as a citizen of the United States, and in the name of that people, I give thanks to you, and through you to all the citizens of this State who may favor the democratic constitutional system, sincerely felicitating them on the anniversary of our national independence.

Let it be permitted to me to assure your excellency that with sentiments of the purest gratification and infinite satisfaction I will make known to the government at Washington that Mexico, forgetting on this day her misfortunes and calamities, sends her on the wings of the morning fresh proofs of her brotherly friendship, and reminds her once more, in the midst of her afflictions and calamities, of her eternal attachment to democratic principles.

It is very proper that two sister republics of the New World should rejoice on the happy termination of our giant war, as it must be admitted that if the integrity and unity of our republic had been destroyed, ten years would not elapse ere the new hemisphere would again fall under the domination of the Old World. This day, throughout all the circuit of the United States, the grandest spectacle ever witnessed by man is gazed on with admiration: a nation of thirty millions of inhabitants, who were yesterday at war among themselves, pardoning and forgetting the animosities engendered by civil war, this day reunite in their respective cities and districts, unanimously cheering in solemn utterances, which will resound forever; and as the rainbow is a witness of harmony between earth and heaven, so will this day be held by all the people of the United States as a guarantee of peace between east and west, north and south, by all generations to come.

Let us then rejoice on the complete restoration of the Union, which, by affixing the seal of experience to the declarations of the wise men who eighty-nine years ago laid the foundation-stone of the great transatlantic republic, demonstrates to the universe that our system of government can sustain, and remain unhurt, assaults which would destroy the very foundation of any nation not based upon democratic principles. Let us rejoice, therefore, in the triumph of the indestructible Constitution in its pristine vigor, for it has opened a new era in the history of republican government, vindicating it against the bitter jeering of the monarchists of the Old World, who idly hoped we would perish ignominiously in our civil war a short time ago raging with incomparable fury.

Let us thrice three times rejoice in the glorious proofs of the last years, because they, in union with the precious revolutionary memories of 1776, have added more splendor and fame to this day as one of those of jubilee for the defenders of liberty and of progress throughout the world; because another morning dawns, advancing towards high noon.

May God protect and defend the republics of the New World.

Please to accept the expression of my most distinguished consideration and respect.

B. N. SANDERS.

C. GREGORIO MENDEZ,
Governor of the State of Tabasco, present.

Mr. Romero to Mr. Seward.

[Translation.]

MEXICAN LEGATION IN THE UNITED STATES OF AMERICA,
Washington, 10th of October, 1865.

MR. SECRETARY: I have the honor to send you, for the information of the government of the United States, the documents, translated into English, mentioned in the index annexed, relating to public events which have taken place in Mexico. They relate to divers events, places, and times, and their reading contributes to give an idea of what is passing in that republic at different periods.

I avail myself of the occasion to renew to you, Mr. Secretary, the assurances of my most distinguished consideration.

M. ROMERO.

Hon. WILLIAM H. SEWARD, *&c., &c., &c.*

Index of the documents transmitted by the Mexican legation to the Department of State of the United States, and annexed to its note of October 10, 1865, *in relation to events which have occurred in Mexico.*

No. 1. Governor Ortega to the people of Puebla, February 18, 1864. Proclamation calling upon the people of the State to defend the State.

No. 2. General Alvarez to the people of the State of Guerrero, May 4, 1864. Proclamation.—Arrival of the French squadron at Acapulco.—Blockade of that port. (See for this proclamation No. 7, military operations in the southern division.)

No. 3. General Vega to Lozada Ampudia and Parrodi, May 15, 1864. Letters refusing to recognize the authority of Maximilian.

No. 4. General Lanberg to General Trias, and his reply, April 3, 1864. Letter inviting him to recognize the empire, and his reply in the negative.

No. 5. General Uraga to Messieurs Caserta and others, June 18, 1864. Letter declaring that he will always make war against France.

No. 6. The republican army to General Uraga, June 10, 1864. They tender him a vote of confidence and ask him to continue in command of the army as general-in-chief.

No. 7. General Riva Palacios to his army. Circular respecting the conduct of the French army, and ordering reprisals.

No. 8. General Cortinas to the people of Matamoras, August 22, 1864. Proclamation.—Attack upon Matamoras by the French forces.

No. 9. General Doblado to the *Courier des Etats Unis*, October 8, 1864. Letter giving the lie to reports published by said journal.

No. 10. General Doblado to the *New York Herald*, October 18, 1864. Letters explaining his pretended return to Mexico.

No. 11. General Garcia to his subordinates, July 30, 1865. Circular.—Depredations committed by the French on the east coast.

No. 12. The governor of Sonora to the people of that State, March 30, 1865. Proclamation.—Invasion of Sonora by the French, its enemies.

A true copy:

F. D. MACIN,
Second Secretary of Legation.

WASHINGTON, *October* 10, 1865.

No. 1.

[Translation.]

The governor and military commander of the State of Puebla to its inhabitants.

FELLOW-CITIZENS: I am sent among you by order of the supreme constitutional government, whose hope, as well as my own, is that you will shake off the foreign yoke which oppresses and humiliates you.

It was thought expedient that he who at a period of trial and peril wielded to your satisfaction the destinies of your State, and who received on a subsequent occasion your spontaneous suffrages for the same exalted position, should be the bearer of the mandate of the nation. You recognized in a becoming manner, in the midst of the fermentation of violent passions, that law, reason, and progress were the natural tendencies of humanity. He thus acquired a popular right to address you, and in virtue of that right I trust his words will have due weight; but more than this, he now addresses you in the name of truth, and leaves you to be the judges of his sincerity.

The two principles which were struggling for mutual destruction in the moral order of things came finally to establish their hostile camps on the soil of the country, and the partisans of progress and those of retrogression, each in defence of their opinions, appealed to arms to decide the contest. Various were the fortunes of war; but victory rested finally with the champions of reform. In their despair the vanquished sought refuge at the court of Napoleon, seeking assistance and laying at the feet of the Emperor the land of their birth and the government of their country. They sought to avenge themselves and to obtain possession, by the aid of a foreign power, of the control of the government. The clergy hoped by the same means to gain possession of the confiscated church property, and recover the prestige they had lost by the progress of reform.

This situation of Mexico, falsely represented to Napoleon, aroused his ambition, and the desire to gain in the territory of our country a compensation for those countries of Europe which he had failed to acquire from the neighboring States, and decided him to send an army of invasion, whose object was first concealed by the "convention of London," and subsequently by proclamations, in which his designs were veiled under the pretext of bringing about a moral reform and inaugurating a "humanitarian redemption" of the people of Mexico.

In this manner he opened a wide field to the hopes of the reaction party, of the clergy, and of a certain class of men disposed to receive with favor the unknown future, when it comes in the form of novelty and grandeur. Permit me, fellow-citizens, to make a comparison between the results of what is called intervention and its pompous promises.

The first act of the invading army was to break the engagements made solemnly in the "convention de la Soledad," "to retire to the post it occupied before the conclusion of that convention."

It lent its countenance to the *reactionestas* in inaugurating a provisional government in Orizaba, composed of partisans of that faction.

It admitted, but in a humiliating manner, the armed forces of this faction into its ranks, and keeps them there in the same humiliating subjection.

In the order of the day of the 17th May, after giving due praise to the garrison of Puebla, they obliged the staff and commissioned officers to march on foot as prisoners of war, and finally expatriated them.

On reaching the capital they caused two "juntas" to be formed, which, by superior order, declared that the country should constitute itself under the form of an empire, and that the emperor should be Maximilian, or such other as Napoleon should elect.

It established the pillory, to the disgrace of Mexico, of France, and of civilization.

It caused multitudes of Mexicans to be executed daily, under sentence of French court-martial.

It obliged the so-called "regency" of the empire to pass a decree declaring effective the laws of reform, and established a Protestant chapel, to wound more sensibly the interests of the clergy.

It kept the so-called regency in absolute "pupilage," and the participation of this "ally" is apparent in all the public acts of that body.

The clergy, wounded in its dearest interests, has withdrawn itself from the reactionistsc of which it was the principal nucleus. It has attempted to divide the great liberal part, by efforts to withdraw from it some of its most influential members. It cannot be denied that these are the most notable acts of the "army of invasion," which have placed it in the false position it occupies in the country it pretends to domineer over. It does not co-operate or sympathize with the tendencies of the principal factions or parties, and still less with those of the nation.

At short distances from the posts occupied by the French armies are found divisions of independent troops, or bands of guerillas; and such has become its impotency that it is unable to intimidate even the robbers who infest the vicinity of the garrison.

Persisting in their error, some men may continue to hope that in the course of time (an impossibility in the nature of things) the intervention will come to favor the national interests; but the address of the Emperor at the opening of the Chambers has destroyed the last and most distant hope of traitors. He has formally declared "that the sacrifices which France has made will be amply repaid," and "that the Mexican war, which was commenced to vindicate the honor of France, will end by insuring her interests." One must be deprived of common sense, and destitute of every noble and generous sentiment, to hope, after such a declaration of the French Emperor, that the intervention can ever be favorable to the true interests of Mexico, since the only object seems to be to secure the interests of France. On the other hand, when we examine the position of the "army of invasion," we at once perceive that it has no base in our country, for the reason that it favors no legitimate interests. Still less can it be said to have one in France, for the opposition which the Emperor has aroused by the war in Mexico has obliged him to declare his real intentions, as we have seen in that sentence just quoted. Least of all can there be found a base in the tendencies or interests of England, or Spain, or of the United States, for they are all in open opposition to the projects of the Emperor.

Notwithstanding the constant and cynical eagerness with which the imperialists seek to exaggerate the progress of intervention, with the intention of deceiving both France and the Emperor, and of asserting the intention of Maximilian to come to Mexico with the object of giving consistency to the imperial project, public opinion has pronounced its inexorable sentence against intervention and its agents, and this opinion will augment immensely the numbers of the defenders of independence. It will create new obstacles to the plans of Napoleon, and every hour as it passes is ringing the knell of the imperial cause. The sword has never vanquished public opinion—the sovereign of the world; as she vanquished the invaders in the mountains of Guadalupe and in the streets of Puebla, so shall she be victorious in a thousand battles. We will triumph to-day as we will triumph to-morrow, for the battle-field is now familiar to us, and we have learned, both morally and physically, how to endure the hardships of war, while we respect, amidst the thunder of arms and the din of battle, civil and individual rights. If every Mexican is bound to repel the stigma of treason, the noble sons of Puebla are doubly bound to do so from the gallant deeds of May 5 and April 25, which have raised within her territory lasting monuments to the glory of her citizens.

To arms, sons of Puebla! At the shout of Long live our constitution and independence! Long live the brave General Diaz, commander-in-chief of the line of the east! let us march to battle. God, reason, and justice defend our noble cause.

FERNANDO MARIA ORTEGA.

OAXACA, *February* 18, 1864.

(For enclosure No. 2 see No. 7, Mr. Clary's operations in the southern division.)

No. 3.

[Translation.]

Lozada to General Vega.

SAN BLAS, *March* 16, 1864.

MY DEAR GENERAL: I have just received, by the favor of General Don Romulo D. de la Vega, the enclosed letter from his excellency General Don Juan M. Almonte, to be forwarded to you in the safest manner.

I request, as a particular favor, that the reply to this letter, as well as that to the one enclosed, may be forwarded as early as possible, so that the letter to General Almonte may reach its destination without delay.

I beseech you give a favorable reception to the proposition of co-operation with the plans of General Almonte, for in so doing you will render a signal service to the country, and a very great one to me personally; for, in that event, I shall be spared the painful duty of commencing operations against your department, where I would prefer acting the part of a friend rather than that of an enemy.

Your obedient servant,

MANUEL LOZADA.

Senor General Don PLACIDO VEGA.

General Vega's reply to Lozada.

SAN FRANCISCO, *Alta California, May* 15, 1864.

SIR: Your letter, dated Tepic, March 16, was received three days since, covering several others—one, as you inform me, from Senor Almonte, &c., &c.

I believe you have been fascinated by the influence of certain men, who, to gratify their mean and contemptible passions, have involved Mexico in all the horrors of a national war—have given their countenance to a monarchy imposed on us by foreigners—and that this illusion alone has made you believe in good faith that the only object of the intervention is the happiness and prosperity of our people, without attacking our nationality and independence. But acts speak louder than seductive language and flattering theories, and they are in flagrant contradiction to the hopes you have been led to entertain.

To demonstrate this, I will only touch on two points, the appreciation of which is within the comprehension of all. The first of these treats of our material, the second of our religious interests. The first is the convention agreed to between the French government and the so called monarchical government of Mexico, by which it was stipulated that the latter shall pay to the former the monstrous sum of two hundred and seventy millions of francs, for expenses of administration to the month of July next, and from that time forward an annual allowance of one thousand francs for every French soldier. In addition to which, a further sum of twenty-five millions is made payable to France, with the understanding that that sum shall be an indemnity for twenty thousand French troops. Furthermore, and independent of the aforesaid sums, Mexico shall pay the expenses of the war, which will probably be made to amount to a fabulous sum, which is to be exacted from a government which will require many millions to keep up its magnificence and vain ostentation.

It is admitted, beyond doubt, that the basis of all monarchical institutions is the aggrandizement of the privileged classes, which constitute the nobility, and that this aggrandizement is at the cost of the masses—that is to say, by those who by their industry, by their obedience, by their poverty and their misery, constitute the people.

Can it be possible that you, a child of the people, identified with their griefs and their sufferings; that you, the natural protector of the indigenous races, the more worthy of interest that their sufferings are the greater—can it be that you have ranged yourself on the side of their enemies to add to the number of their oppressors? Do not, I conjure you, not in my own, but in the name of this despoiled race, disappoint, through a fatal error, the hope they cherished in confiding their interests to your keeping.

* * * * * * * * *

The judgment of the people, freely expressed, is rarely erroneous where their most vital interests are in question. Consult them, and I am convinced you will see things in a very different aspect from what you have seen them up to the present time.

There is no time for indecision. Let us unite as good Mexicans, and we shall save our country and the native rule, which has everything at stake in this formidable crisis.

This conviction is so profoundly rooted in my heart that no human power can change it, and for it I am ready to sacrifice my repose, my fortune, and my life. What I am and what merit I may possess I owe to my country. My love for it is a religious devotion. I have firm confidence that all those who, from an error of judgment, but with honest intentions, have given their adhesion to the intervention, will promptly abjure their errors, and, placing themselves under the flag of their country, will pledge themselves to its protection.

It is true that some incidents of the war have been unfavorable to our arms, but I assure you that the national party has great power, particularly among the native classes of all the frontier states. We have the sympathy of all civilized nations, including a considerable majority of the French themselves, and our cause will triumph, for justice and reason are the pillars of strength.

Convince yourself of these truths, reflect on them without prejudice, and I doubt not you will adopt my ideas. When that shall be the case I shall be very happy to hear from you again.

I have the honor to be your obedient servant,

PLACIDO VEGA.

Don MANUEL LOZADA, *Tepic.*

To a similar letter from Don José de Casanova we have a spirited reply from General Vega:

General Vega's response.

Señor JOSÉ CASANOVA, *Mexico:*

SIR: By comparing the dates you will perceive that there has been a delay in the reception of the letter of February 27, to which I now reply.

* * * * * * * * *

Once for all, I assure you that not even the eloquence of Cicero would suffice to eradicate from my breast my love of my country and of republican principles.

I pass over unnoticed your observations which refer to the intervention, as defined, according to your appreciation of it, with, perhaps, the pious desire of controlling your own services, rather than in the hope of leading me to drink of the fountain of treason; but I find myself compelled to refute certain assertions without foundation, and dispel doubts which might rise to imputations and illusions, either real or avowed, in contradiction with my true sentiments and derogatory to my public character.

* * * * * * * * * * *

When you admit that you knew my sentiments, I am surprised that, in the present state of things, you should urge me to accept the monarchical system, which you know I abhor; and, more than this, have the audacity to accuse me of the intention of segregating a portion of the country, and placing it under the dominion of a foreign government.

I never made use of language which involved such a thought, nor gave occasion to suppose that there existed in my bosom such a wish. My public life sufficiently proves this assertion, for never for a moment have I deviated from the principle that death was preferable to the loss of our nationality and independence; and that when all hope of saving the one or preserving the other should fail, better become a member of any of the American republics than be the vassal of a despot of decrepit Europe.

I doubt not that the constitutional governor of Zacatecas, General Gonzales Ortega, will be highly gratified at the contemptuous manner in which you speak of him, when aware that such language comes from an enemy of his country.

I conclude, assuring you that, as I had the honor and satisfaction of being one of those who filled the ranks of the army corps that marched on Puebla, now, more than ever, I will anxiously fly to unite myself to the corps that will take the initiative against the city of Mexico.

Your obedient servant,

PLACIDO VEGA.

General Ampudia, another traitor to anything just, honest or liberal, next tried his hand at gaining over the noble Vega. Among other arguments in favor of the empire he used the following: "What a glorious prospective for our country, so worthy, from its favored position, to rank among the greatest nations of the earth! Let us ask ourselves frankly, with our hands to our hearts, could we entertain such flattering anticipations, governed as we have hitherto been by men without antecedents deserving of respect, without wisdom, experience or probity, in the never-ending changes of scandalous revolutions."

General Vega's reply to Ampudia.

SIR: It would be vain for me to conceal the just and profound indignation I felt on reading your letter of the 27th of February, at the picture you draw of yourself in the character of the new ideas you have adopted. The republican general, the champion of reform, converted into a panegyrist of monarchical institutions! *and what is still more surprising, into a base adulator of the prince whom foreign bayonets are attempting to impose on Mexico! the soldier of the people bartering his sword for the toga of a courtesan!*

I will not attempt to refute, seriously, the theory you develop on the expediency of establishing a monarchy, not only in Mexico, but over all the American continent—a question which has exhausted the minds of politicians and writers of the first order. It is easy to see that you have undertaken this task, so much above your capacity, for the purpose only of giving proofs of your zeal in the service of your new master, and lessening the distrust there must be felt towards *an antiquated democrat aspiring to the post of equerry at the new court.*

As to this, however, the monarchy of Maximilian is worthy of partisans and champions like yourself.

I reject with indignation the position and the power you offer me. My honor and my conscience, which have never been sold or sacrificed, are above all the temptations which you can offer.

If I have derived satisfaction from the exercise of authority, it has only been from the reflection that this authority emanated from the popular voice, and implied an appreciation of my services on the part of my fellow-citizens, who have repaid with usury my devotion to the defence of their rights. *If you, on account of your advanced age and instability of your principles, have preferred comfort and repose, though on a dunghill, to the struggles, the sufferings and the privations consequent on the stubborn and prolonged contest which the great national party is determined to sustain against the foreign enemy, I, on the other hand, feel, in unison with my sense of dignity and the conviction of what is my duty, sufficient energy to combat these obstacles, and, if necessary, to lay down my life, provided I can carry to the grave a name unsullied by dishonor, and leave to my children a legacy untarnished by opprobrium.*

Should my language, at first sight, appear too virulent and depreciative, reflect that it has been provoked on your part by the flagrant insult implied in your contemptible proposition by which you attempt to dazzle me with treasonable offers of rank, office, and an elevated position.

Had there been any antecedents in my public life which could authorize your addressing me such dishonorable propositions, my reproaches would be less energetic; *but I pride myself that my past career is without blemish, and you were bound to respect it. It is evident that this is not the first occasion where you have shown a want of judgment.*

Your obedient servant,

PLACIDO VEGA.

This severe "settler" to Ampudia was not, it seems, sufficient to damp the imperial ardor of the miserable Parrodi, who was the next to send a friendly but very absurd invitation to General Vega to take side with Maximilian. We can only give the leading points of

General Vega's reply to Parrodi.

* * * * * * * *

But your criminal defection being confirmed by your own hand, I can only follow the inspirations of my own character and listen to the voice of duty *in striking your name from off the roll of men worthy of my esteem.* I deplore the error I have committed, in my estimation of you, in attributing to you civic virtues which you did not possess.

From this day forward I look upon you as a traitor and an enemy of my country.

Were there room for a belief that you had embraced in good faith the ideas which you now profess, there would be something worthy of respect in this change, but the language of your letter does not admit of that supposition.

* * * * * * * *

It belongs to history to qualify such conduct, and the judgment will be the more severe that the inconstancy of your conduct is the more flagrant.

As to myself, as a true lover of my country, and uncompromising on everything which may wound her dignity or be in opposition to her complete unity of action, *I shall struggle, without ceasing, in defence of our nationality, brutally and ignominiously attacked by France.*

Fortunately the elements to sustain the contest are every day becoming more considerable and more formidable, as also is the prestige of the constitutional government daily gaining ground; however much traitors may pretend to the contrary; but if, instead of this being the case, the national cause were weakened and on the point of succumbing, I feel within myself sufficient firmness of purpose to prefer being involved in the wreck of our political liberty to accepting the yoke of a foreign domination. My language, I acknowledge, is harsh, but it is the expression of my honest sentiments, and I should feel that I had been wanting in my duty to myself as well as to my country were I to attempt to conceal or extenuate them by words which expressed them with less energy. Should you, recognizing the error you have momentarily fallen into, rally to the side of all true Mexicans, and fulfil the sacred duty every man owes to the country of his birth, I shall have great satisfaction in recognizing in you a man worthy of my highest esteem. Until this shall be the case, there can exist between us no other relation than such as may occur between persons destined to battle for principles diametrically opposed to each other.

Your obedient servant,

PLACIDO VEGA.

No. 4.

[Translation.]

General Langberg to General Trias.

MEXICO, *April* 3, 1864.

MY DISTINGUISHED FRIEND AND COMPANION: In our last interview at Toluca we spoke at length concerning the dissatisfaction which was caused by the conduct of the constitutional government. We now see that we were right in deploring it, because your antecedents and mine were far distant from such intrigues. You, my friend, are a man educated in Europe, consequently you profess more intelligent ideas distinct from the general run of our army, and I have made this among other observations to the present general-in-chief of the Franco-Mexican army. The idea of the intervention and the near approach of the installation of a constitutional monarchy in Mexico are now inevitable, my friend, and you, being a man who, during the American invasion, knew how to sacrifice your interests and risk your life for the country, ought to take care that she does not now lose her blood uselessly. Besides, you ought to know the liberal tendencies and the intelligence of the man selected to sit upon the throne of the Aztecs, aided, as he is, by a nation like France, civilized by instinct, so that you need fear nothing for the principles which you conserve in your heart, and which are demanded by the age in which we live. It is an absurd thing to believe, as some do, that the conservative party is that which is going to rule in Mexico. I, who am here on the principal theatre of occurrences, guarantee to you and to every one that the political thought and the dominant idea of the men who are now at the front of public affairs are not either the enthronement of the ancient and recalcitrant ideas of times long past, or the proverbial disorder and anarchy which have just been overthrown. The principles of a government, liberal and moderate at the same time, are what must triumph in Mexico, having at its foundation a young monarch who in his early years has drunk in the inspirations of our century, and who from conviction holds ideas of true progress and intelligence.

Concerning yourself, I have already spoken to General Bazaine, and given him some details of the high qualities which adorn you. He is a gentleman of frank and sincere ideas; he aspires to nothing more than to be the faithful echo of the voice of his government; he desires nothing more than to see Mexico regenerated, free and happy. The truth of his words may be seen after the slightest interview with him, and I cherish the hope and conviction that France, represented by such a man, can have no other intention than the noble and humanitarian one to which I have referred.

In virtue of all these circumstances, and in use of the right which our sincere friendship gives to me, I invite you with all the sincerity of my soul to follow my example, hoping to co-operate with your prestige and influence in this State in establishing the good institutions which are recognized by the cities of most importance of your country. Those chiefs and old friends who may desire to second them you may assure of a most satisfactory and honorable result. Although unwell, I shall within a few days leave for Sinaloa, with the object of impressing Generals Placido Vega and Pesquiera with the same ideas.

You can send your answer to Mazatlan, directed to Colonel Aleman, of that port, and perhaps it will not be difficult for us to have an interview with those gentlemen. I beg, my friend, that you will meditate well over the contents of this letter, and be persuaded of my good and friendly intentions, &c.

EMILIO LANGBERG.

General DON ANGEL TRIAS.

General Trias's Reply.

SIR: The antecedents of your public and private life, combined with your foreign origin, ought to influence me so far as not to cause me any surprise at the contents of your letter, dated in Mexico on the 3d of April last. It ought not certainly to be surprising to any one that a man who has looked upon politics as the means of gaining his living, and to whom, having no fixed principles, it is all the same whether he sides with the Guelphs or the Ghibellines, so long as it does not lessen his profits and that he gets the best position possible, should sell, as you have done, the sacred cause of national independence, and should prostrate himself at the feet of a clown in the form of a monarch to receive the price of his crime in a handful of gold or a glance of favor, which flatters his vanity and tickles his hopes of reward; nor should the dishonorable and assiduous energy with which you seem to have embraced the propagandism of the wretched band to which you belong surprise me in the least, because in your earnest solicitude there is an end sought for, a result, however infamous and degrading it may be. But that which truly ought to surprise and astonish is the stupidity evinced in your selection of persons among whom you would pretend to make proselytes; for if the former act shows a man deprived of all virtue, the latter reveals the absence of even common sense. When you did me the justice to remember that I have sacrificed my interests and perilled my life for my country when I believed her nationality threatened, you ought not to have brought to mind these evidences of my strict and bounden duty in order to deduce from them the consequence that I should now be a renegade to my principles, set aside my dignity, and stain my character with a most hateful defection. From those premises arises a deduction diametrically contrary to that which you pretend to establish. If I had at any time in my life given the slightest proof of weakness in my principles or of lukewarmness in my patriotism, the insolent liberty which you have seen fit to take in addressing me your poor invitation would in a certain sense have been justifiable; but to pretend that I should be a traitor because I have been a patriot, to desire that I should be converted into a dishonest man because I have always been honorable, and to invite me to sell my country because I love it—these are contradictions which only the head of a madman and fool can conceive. Not wishing to go into the particulars of your letter, I limit myself to saying to you, after what I have already stated, that I am the same man of 1846 and 1847, to whom selfish interests and life itself are as nothing compared to the liberty of my country.

Yours, &c.,

ANGEL TRIAS.

Mr. EMILIO LANGBERG, *Mazatlan*.

No. 5.

[Translation.]

JUNE 18, 1864.

DEAR SIRS: I am satisfied that in addressing me your suggestions for avoiding the effusion of more Mexican blood—the sacrifice being barren, as you say—or, what is the same thing, that I should adhere to the order of things which the Emperor of the French is seeking to establish in the republic by the force of his bayonets—you did not conceive the slightest hope that I could yield to so mean a suggestion, but that you have sought for an opportunity of sowing discord in the minds of those worthy Mexicans who are so heroically struggling for the independence of their country, giving circulation to false, supposititious, and absurd comments respecting the power and the elements of the national party, *and to the vilest of calumnies concerning myself*. Fortunately these attempts are rendered abortive by the good sense and the patriotism of the nation, which knows its rights and has the will and energy to fulfil its duties.

I write these lines not to give an answer to those whom I consider unworthy, but to denounce their disgraceful machinations, in view of the wise judgment of my fellow-citizens.

As regards myself, I owe to the confidence of my government and the brave men who share with me the glory of fighting for the most sacred of causes, and, above all, to my patriotic conscience, the most solemn and explicit declaration that *I will never put arms out of my hands until the day in which I shall see the peace of my country solidly and effectually secured.*

Touching the details contained in your letter would be to mix one's self with nauseating filth. *I have no desire to bespatter myself in it.*

Besides, gentlemen, you are those who believe least in what you say.

To a soldier of the republic, mutilated for the cause of liberty, and trained up from infancy in the doctrines of political independence, no other motto is necessary than this: *War unto death to France; war unto death against those who, treacherous to the holy cause of the country, recognize or protect the foreign invader, or to the farce-making monarch which it is sought to enthrone on our soil. I have accepted war, and my country and the world may see in this the guarantee of my pledges.*

JOSÉ L. URAGA.

Señores DON JUAN J. CASERTA, DON JESUS L. PORTILLO, VICENTE ORTIGOSA, ANTONIO A. DEL CASTILLO, and RAFAEL JIMENEZ CASTRO.

No. 6.

[Translation.]

Some Franco-Mexican papers having circulated a report that General Uraga had given in his adhesion to the empire, after some preliminary business of the meeting, in which the general-in-chief showed the actual state of the army and the condition of those matters for which this meeting had been convened, the debate was terminated by the following resolutions being unanimously adopted:

1. The republican army, having to the present preserved and actually maintained the independence and integrity of its country, ratifies now the vote of confidence placed in its general-in-chief, citizen Lopez Uraga, so that he shall continue at its command and may direct its operations, and that he may support the cause of liberty and his country. The army trusts to his ability to maintain the honor of the republic, and to that of those under arms in the ranks of the army our honor, and that he will fulfil those solemn obligations which he owes to his country and to society.

2. That all bandits who have under all circumstances, and especially the present ones, endangered, by the reports they have circulated, the union of the defenders of the republic, shall be punished.

These resolutions, being submitted to a vote, were unanimously approved by the generals and officers present, the same who subscribe this act.

Residence of the general-in-chief of the republican army at Ciudad Guzman, June 10, 1864.

Signed—Miguel M. Echeagaray, Ramon Iglesias, Santiago Tapia, T. O'Horan, P. Rioseco, A. A. Guaderrama, Felix Vega, J. Diaz de Leon, L. Ornelas, Albino Espinosa, Augustin Iglesias, and Francisco Castillero, for the fourth division; José Linares, for the State of Queretaro; Francisco A. Ramos, for the Colima brigade; Antonio Neri, Miguel Garcia de Aguirre, Emilio Rey, Francisco O. Arce, Manuel Mariscal, Serapio Villalovos, Julio M. Cervantes, Simon Delgadillo, Maericio Casas, T. Romero, Francisco M. Villasenor, Manuel de Unzaga, M. Mena, Ciro Uraga, Guillermo F. de Unda, Antonio M. Jaurequi, Manuel Cevallos, Mateo Reyes, José G. Munoz, Marcos Villegas, army commissioner; Pascual Sepulveda, Salvador Brilmega, secretary of the treasury; M. R. Alatorre, commissioner of internal revenue; Francisco Hernandez Carrasco, Aristeo Moreno, secretary of the meeting.

A true copy: ARISTEO MORENO, *Secretary.*

CIUDAD GUZMAN, *June* 10, 1864.

No. 7.

Extracts from a circular addressed by General Riva Palacios, governor of the State of Michoacan, to his subordinate officers:

[Translation.]

"If the French general," he says, "wishes to bring civilization to this country, (Mexico,) he ought to commence by repressing the disorder of the troops under his command, who have traversed the ocean to show us that they have about them nothing of the soldier except the uniform and the arms. But in morality and discipline they are inferior not only to our organized corps, but even to guerillas of the worst kind known unto this day in the republic.

"The French wish to swim in the blood of our patriots, and authorize every expeditionary chief to murder and assassinate. They wish to convince the world of the justice of their cause, and to change their lies and calumnies into laws; and, in short, when the entire nation rejects their 'protection,' they seek to consummate a work of conquest by constructing the gallows and the guillotine for every man who will not consent to be placed under their ignominious yoke. * * * * * Inasmuch as the circular of the French general is a challenge of war without mercy and without quarter, we do not hesitate to accept it, because, in launching into the struggle for maintaining the independence and autonomy of Mexico, we have never counted on the clemency of Frenchmen. You will, therefore, apply in future to French prisoners who may fall into your hands and power the articles of the circular of the commander-in-chief of the expeditionary army; and, after having established their identity, all prisoners, civil or military, employed by the French, or the so-called empire, whatever may be their nationality, shall instantly be put to death. * * * * To shoot prisoners it is first necessary to make them; and never, at least as far as we know, has Riva Palacios been exposed to this good fortune. In regard to exploits, the French general has never, up to this time, done more than attack us with forces like three hundred to one. Before so easily disposing of the skin of the lion, they ought, I think, to try and capture the animal himself."

No. 8.

[Translation.]

Colonel José Maria Cortina, military commandant of the line of the Bravo, to the inhabitants of the heroic city of Matamoras:

FELLOW-CITIZENS: The French filibusters are invading this port; we will soon have occasion to show that, as sons of Mexico, we know how to repel force with force.

I appeal, then, to you to summon your patriotism, which has never been invoked in vain, in order that, sustained by it, you may defend the nationality menaced upon the frontier of the republic.

I solemnly call upon you to aid, to the extent of your abilities, the military authority in the endeavor to drive from the territory of Tamaulipas the foreign enemy, and especially to deliver this beautiful portion of the State from the calamity of invasion.

Remember that you first saw the light in this heroic city, and let it still preserve a glorious title accorded to its valor and its courage, which you are expected to illustrate on this occasion.

You will find at your head, defending the independence of the country and the integrity of Tamaulipas, your fellow-citizen and friend,

JOSÉ MARIA CORTINA.

MATAMORAS, *August* 22, 1864.

No. 9.

Letter from General Doblado.

To the Editor of the Courrier des Etats Unis:

SIR.: Referring to Mexican affairs in yesterday's number of your daily paper, you speak of me in terms so highly offensive to my honor that I feel compelled, in self-defence, to trouble you again for the publication of a few lines.

I repeat once more that I never did solicit anything at all of the so-called imperial government of Mexico, nor do I intend, returning there to submit to it; he who so states, falsely affirms that I have done so.

It is a most infamous calumny to insist upon saying that I pretended to make an arrangement with the invaders to save my private property. What I possess in the State of Guanajuato has been acquired just as legally as any property bought by any one else—politics having nothing to do with my fortune, which has been gotten by honest labor; for that very reason I need ask no guarantee at all of the so-called imperial government. My property, like every other person's, is guaranteed by the civil laws in vigor in Mexico long before the country was invaded. Of all the national property sold in Mexico, I bought but one single house, and that I paid for according to the regulations of the laws of reform, enacted there by the legitimate government of my country. The French intervention has never dared to derogate them, in spite of the exigencies of the clergy and traitors, because every one knows that owing to them the French resisting in Mexico have become possessors of more than one-third of the so-called church properties.

Therefore, that person asserts what is untrue who persists in affirming that I have endeavored to enter into any kind of arrangement with the usurper of Mexico to save my fortune, and I defy any one to show my signature affixed to any document of the kind.

I did pretend to save my fortune legally acquired, but by the only means honorable to a Mexican in these circumstances, viz: helping to keep up the war against the usurper, the French and traitors, and repelling force by force, to the utmost of my power. I think, by so doing, I have done my duty as a Mexican. I emigrated to this country after the fate of war had proved adverse to me, and after losing nearly all my soldiers.

As to my objection coming to this country, allow me to say, I do not consider myself bound to confide it to any one, and much less to writers who judge so lightly of persons whose present misfortune entitles them to the respect of all. I know, perhaps better than any one else, the little or no value of the guarantees the usurper's government might tender me, for I have not so soon forgotten the worth of Mr. Salign's signature at the preliminaries of La Soledad.

Your servant,

M. DOBLADO.

NEW YORK, *October* 8, 1864.

No. 10.

To the Editor of the Courrier des Etats Unis:

Through the correspondence I have just received from Mexico, by the steamer Eagle, I have been enabled to reach at last the true facts concerning the various statements and comments recently published by the press with regard to my returning to Mexico.

Being anxious to put an end to so many inaccurate rumors, I proceed to state the real facts of the case as they have taken place in Mexico.

A friend of mine, who was not acquainted with my present condition, nor with that of the new "empire," expecting, no doubt, though wrongfully, to do me a service, applied to General Bazaine and asked him for a safe conduct to protect my return to the country. He made his application without previously apprising me of the fact. The interventional authorities granted the request, and caused the safe conduct to be issued and sent to me here.

My friend notified me afterwards, as well of his steps as of the motives which guided him, in a letter I have received but to-day.

As it was my duty, I have immediately returned the safe conduct through the same medium it reached me, disapproving, in my answer to my friend, of his whole conduct, though thanking him for his good intentions.

I have, besides, written to some influential persons in Mexico, apprising them of what has taken place, and showing them how, in leaving my country, it was my fixed purpose to undergo ostracism and all its consequences rather than stain my public life by a dishonorable submission.

To leave my country, and to return to it after a few days' absence, would be indeed an inexplicable contradiction, as the causes which compelled me to abandon it are still existing. Who knows how long they will yet last?

I am confident that the persons in Mexico to whom I have written will give to my statement the required publicity, which, together with the undeniable fact of my remaining abroad, will be the best convincing argument against those who, in good or bad faith, endeavor to attack other persons for no other reason than that of differing with them in political opinions.

Being persuaded that what I have here stated is enough to satisfy all who judge and act in good faith, I shall no longer employ the public press in behalf of my person, this being, therefore, the last time I shall appeal to your kindness for the publication of my letters.

Yours, respectfully,

M. DOBLADO.

NEW YORK, *October* 13, 1864.

No. 11.

[Circular.—Translation.]

AMATLAN, *July* 30, 1864.

Yesterday the French invaders committed one of the most barbarous deeds which history can record.

Yesterday they stealthily approached our encampment at San Geronimo in one of their war steamers, they being covered by their bulwarks, from which protruded their rifle-guns. Our forces, a small number of which defeated them on the 14th instant at Garcia bridge, in order to prevent any injury which might arise to the farm of that name, were withdrawn to a convenient distance and beyond the reach of their artillery; but the French, under cover of the houses, landed, and, without seeking to engage us, gave themselves up to the most shameful and criminal pillage, and in the end set fire to the buildings of the farm. Subsequently they continued, torch in hand, upon the left bank of the river, protected meanwhile by their steamer, robbing everything on the rich farms in the vicinity and reducing them to ashes in the midst of their vandal rejoicings. All the sugar plantations and distilleries of brandy, all the sugar-cane fields and buildings on the bank of the river for the distance of three miles, were committed to the flames, and their owners, peaceful and hard-working men, who had given, after the labor of many years, an impetus to the industry of the country, and procured respectable comforts for their families, were in an instant reduced to poverty and compelled to seek shelter under the trees; thanks to the wantonness of the French and their traitor friends who reduced their splendid mansions to ashes, the value of which is estimated at no less than two hundred and fifty thousand dollars. This barbarous act, which I communicate to you without any exaggeration in its details, is an instance of what the people living on the leeward coast must expect from those who, contrary to common sense, proclaim themselves the propagandists of civilization, and calls for the most summary vengeance on our part. You must, therefore, cause copies of this official communication to be circulated and published in all the settlements and Indian towns of the country under your worthy charge, for the information of all the people of Mexico, and to the end that they prepare for war, some by personally volunteering, others by contributing their means, and all in every way possible to them; for it is clear that, from the measures adopted by our invaders, the question is no longer the defence of the country in its general acceptation, but that of defending, each one of us individually, our families, our interests, and our lives against the acts of barbarity practiced by the French and their traitor friends.

Independence and liberty.

ALEJANDRO GARCIA.

The COMMANDER OF THE CANTON OF ——.

No. 12.

[Translation.]

Proclamation of the citizen Ignacio Pesquiera, governor and military commander of the State of Sonora.

People of Sonora! The time for making sacrifices has come, inviting the patriot to crown himself with laurels, and to perform deeds which shall redound to the glory of his country. Guaymas, of Zaragoza, has been trodden under foot by the successors of Raousset, by the assassins of Cháves and of Ghilardé, by those who covet our territorial riches, and by those who intend to profane the honor of our wives and daughters, and to make us the slaves of a monarch, himself an adventurer. Though the invaders gave us no summons, but announced their arrival by acts of barbarity, they have not been enabled to prevent our brave defenders from withdrawing with their materials of war, and thus saving the honor of the national flag. They withdrew from the city in order not to expose it and the innocent families it contained to the calamities of war. Henceforth, however, they will continue to war upon the enemy; and they hope soon to punish him soundly on the battle-field. Thanks to their vessels, they have committed with impunity their first outrage; but outside of walls, in an equal fight, the smallest triumph to their cause will cost them much blood.

Fellow-citizens! Are we not the men who have been brought up in many contests for liberty and independence? Your noble pride and your holy enthusiasm, awakened by this cry of alarm, will be in keeping with that which our brothers, who have conquered in Sinaloa and who have immortalized themselves at Puebla, expect of you.

To arms, then, Sonorians! Let us raise aloft, and upon this frontier, the standard of our country, and to such a height that the nations of the earth shall contemplate it with applause. Henceforth the flag which shall be upheld by our arms is the only asylum for our individual guarantees, for the security of our families, and for the preservation of our national institutions.

The government has faith in the future of the state because its power is based upon your co-operation, and because Sonora has never wavered when danger threatened. Let us make one universal and spontaneous effort, and your beloved state will retain its supremacy; and then, rising above the weakness of our military resources, the world will look upon us as great in our honor and in our civic virtues.

Independence, liberty, and the Mexican republic.

IGNACIO PESQUIERA.

CAMP AT SANTA MARIA, *March* 30, 1865.

Mr. Romero to Mr. Seward.

[Translation.]

MEXICAN LEGATION IN THE UNITED STATES OF AMERICA,
New York, November 20, 1865.

MR. SECRETARY: I have the honor of transmitting to you, for the information of the government of the United States, the copy of a letter dated Berne, September 17, 1865, addressed by a Mexican citizen to a German baron, who is in the confidence of the ex-archduke of Austria, Ferdinand Maximilian, now called the emperor of Mexico.

This review of present affairs in Mexico is impartial, if not rather inclined to judge with too much kindness French intervention and its instrument, and plainly shows that the French Emperor's project to substitute an Austrian monarchy for a Mexican republic is entirely impracticable, and that, should it be insisted upon, it will only bring France into much trouble and expense, causing countless ills to Mexico.

As the monarchy, in fact, has no national support, it is impossible to conceive how it can be established or consolidated.

I am pleased with this occasion of repeating to you, Mr. Secretary, the assurances of my most distinguished consideration.

M. ROMERO.

Hon. WILLIAM H. SEWARD, *&c., &c., &c.,*
Washington City, D. C.

[Translation.]

BERNE, *September* 17, 1865.

SIR: I regret that I did not, at the time they took place, write down the conversations I had with the Archduke Ferdinand Maximilian and yourself when his highness first entered Mexico; and, for fear I may forget those between you and myself in the *imperial palace of that court*, I will note them in this letter.

I am not moved to this by the vanity of proving that my predictions have been fulfilled, or will be, but by the desire of recalling some important events to your mind, and enlarging upon others I barely mentioned in the course of our conversation.

It is now too late to discuss past events in Mexico, and the erroneous opinions formed of them in Europe. They belong to history; and, as to more recent deplorable events and grievous deceptions, they are attempted to be justified by saying that the present condition of Mexico is very different from what it was a year ago.

You are a friend of the archduke, and I am a friend of Mexico; so it is our duty to consider things as they are, and find the best remedy for them we can. In the first place, we must consider the very critical condition—more critical than is believed—not only of Mexico, but of the archduke, and examine the moral and physical support of the new empire, and the elements that are conspiring to destroy it.

The two principal parties in Mexico, the conservative and liberal, are subdivided into radical (or purist, as called there) and moderate.

The radical portion of the conservative party is composed of the higher clergy and a portion of the laical people, who, by education, prejudice, or perhaps by conviction, are forced to belong to it.

The moderate party is composed of persons of wealth, who, though partial to conservative principles, are always busy with the management of their own affairs, have, in reality, no political principles, and accept any form of government and liberal reform, provided the new government will let them enjoy their wealth in peace.

The radical fraction of the liberal party, purely republican, is composed of those who think it absolutely necessary to establish liberal principles (they made the reform) immediately, and at every cost, and the moderate fraction of those who are slow and measured in their steps towards the same end, for fear of convulsions and revolutions, and even social commotions.

When liberal principles are settled the moderate liberal party will cease to exist, as there will be no further cause for its existence, and its scattered members will have to be numbered with the conservatives.

In nationalizing church property and confirming other reforms made in the time of Juarez the archduke has made bitter enemies of the high clergy, and has alienated the lower priests, who were never hostile to Juarez, by depriving them of their old fees, and assigning them salaries which they will certainly never get. As to the persons in comfortable circumstances, that formed a portion of the moderate conservative party, and joined the imperialists for the sake of peace and quiet, they left it as soon as they found themselves in a more sanguinary and disastrous war than they had ever before seen. They found the empire more expensive than the republic, for it must be supported by enormous and continued foreign loans, that increase domestic taxes to pay them, and they find it does not protect them from guerillas; therefore, they desire a change, and want to try some other way to gain the security and peace their interests and inclinations require.

In regard to the liberal party, its moderate fraction no longer exists, as I have already said, and the pure radical party is the one that now keeps up the war against the empire. All the archduke has done by his personal influence is to persuade six or eight members of the moderate party to accept places in his cabinet; but this is very different from having the support of a political party.

We must conclude, then, that the empire has not the least moral support. As to physical support, all he has to depend upon are a few Mexican troops and the French army, with the Austrian and Belgian divisions. The archduke can place no confidence in the first, for many have already passed over to the republican side, and proposals from some of his generals are no secrets. As regards the foreign army, its insufficiency to subjugate the country is already proved: first, by the fact that it has fought four years in vain; second, that re-enforcements are now being sent to them; and third, in the opinion of their chief, who is the best judge, in a letter lately published, it is impossible to whip the guerillas, because they run off and disperse whenever attacked.

The elements that militate against the empire are also physical and moral. Among the latter, and in the first place, we may name the dislike to the archduke on account of his extravagance and immense and unnecessary debts with which he began to burden the country before he knew it; and for his inability to protect the Mexicans, as is seen by the shooting of General Romero; for the preference he shows to foreigners, putting them in office instead of the natives of the land; and finally, because he has established no good administration. A philosopher might excuse the archduke for these errors; but the people are not philosophers; they feel rather than reason, and they lack patience. A nation that has suffered so much from revolutions requires a long time to recover, and must have patience to suffer and wait. No Mexican has ever doubted but the country would be restored to peace in proper time without foreign intervention; and if a few decided for intervention, it was only because they thought it would restore peace at a more early day. As soon as they were undeceived they abjured their error.

In the second place we may mention the want of present and future means. The imperial expenses amount to forty millions of dollars annually; and every Mexican knows that the country, even in times of peace, could not produce the half of that sum. Let the French financiers who were sent to make their imaginary estimates say what they please: this is certain death to the empire. It cannot curtail its expenses, because a large army must be supported to defend it from the Mexicans; nor can the revenues be increased, because the situation of the country will not allow it. No resources are left then except temporary loans, and they will soon be exhausted.

To these opposing elements may be added that of the unpopularity of the Mexican war in France, because it embarrasses the French government. And we may include another reason why the empire in Mexico must end. The civil war in the United States is ended. This has discouraged the monarchists, while it has revived the hopes of the republicans.

Now for the physical elements that are hostile to the empire. I will only mention two: first, the constitutional forces, chiefly composed of guerillas; and second, expected aid from the United States. Guerilla warfare is not known in Europe, nor have they any idea how useful it is. The events in Spain at the beginning of this century have been forgotten, and they can only judge from recent events in Poland, a level and densely populated country, where the few guerillas formed were rather gangs of fugitives than organized guerillas, trying to escape from the immense armies that surrounded them. In countries like Mexico, mountainous and dry, with a mild climate, where horses abound, and inclemency of weather never prevents out-door movements; where food is found everywhere to supply the necessaries of life, guerillas always exercise a deciding influence. The chief difficulty is in a proper organization; but, this once acquired, they can defy the strongest powers in the world. This system is the stronger as its power is latent and deceptive; it gains time by sudden action, and you never know when it is defeated.

Mexico gained its independence of Spain by a series of sudden victories by guerillas, in eleven years. The reform was effected by the same means, in three years; and so must the second independence be achieved. The French army may triumph everywhere, just as the royalists did in the war of independence, and the clergy did in the reform; but, as the victories of all these parties were more expensive to themselves than destructive to the enemy, the latter finally triumphed.

For this very reason the national government need not be concerned about the rout of their guerillas—only a temporary dispersion, in fact—but may rejoice, because those defeats are only so many steps towards final victory. But to avoid the shedding of blood, danger, and expense, orders have been given to all the guerillas to annoy the enemy without offering battle, as that would cause the French to make fatiguing marches, at a great expense, without the least advantage, except a distant sight of their foes. Every late event in Mexico promises a repetition of the scene in San Domingo, where two hundred thousand inhabitants, with only six or eight thousand soldiers, have whipped Spain, and compelled her to a very mortifying retreat from that island.

I came from America in company with General Espinar, a gentleman of good judgment, who had served in San Domingo, and was then on his way to Spain to ask the evacuation of that island, for reasons very applicable to the French in Mexico. His proposal was shamefully received in Madrid, and, so far from listening to him, additional forces were sent to reduce the handful of opposing rebels in the colony.

Like the French leaders in Mexico, the Spanish generals in San Domingo continued to send despatches announcing victories, from day to day, until they declared the whole island subdued. The simple final result is just what General Espinar proposed, an abandonment of the island, under the most deplorable circumstances, after a great sacrifice of men and money. How much blood Spain would have spared, how much money she would have saved, and how great a shame to her reputation she would have avoided, if her government had done in time what she was compelled to do at last!

I see the French newspapers insist that the United States will remain neutral on the Mexican question, founding this argument on their conduct up to this time, and portions of public documents collected here and there; but they need put no trust in what a government says and does under certain political circumstances. What a government will do depends upon the natural inclinations of its inhabitants and the national interest of that government at the time.

If an American army were to dethrone Leopold of Belgium, and establish a democratic republic in that country, to exist under its immediate direction, would the Emperor Napoleon remain in quiet indifference? We guess he would try to save his throne in some way, even if he had to change political opinions in France. Well, the United States will act in exactly the same manner, and with greater reason, because the establishment of an empire in Mexico was a consequence of the southern rebellion; and did not the French Emperor declare publicly in a speech that his Mexican expedition was in defiance of the United States?

The present silence of that republic is a prudent consideration, as it must settle with England before it offends another great power. But if the British question is amicably settled by diplomacy, as is generally believed it will be, then we shall see the United States turn its attention to the empire. And even supposing it were prudent for the United States to keep at peace with France, it would still assist the constitutional government of Mexico in many ways without getting into war with other nations. It might not prevent private emigration to Mexico to aid Juarez, and arms, the great need, might be smuggled in from every quarter. Money they do not want; they can live upon the country, and they have always had enough men. Everybody knows the guns at Puebla were made of old muskets rejected, and unarmed bodies of men waited to use the guns of those who were slain. And even if the United States government refused to supply them with arms, individual interest would elude all prohibition and furnish them in any quantity, as was done in the late civil war. But we must not think that the exportation of arms will be prohibited, because the United States has adopted as a principle in neutrality that articles of war may be allowed in trade. If the exportation of arms was prohibited by the United States during the civil war, it was only because they were needed in the country—just as they prohibit the exit of corn in years of scarcity. So President Johnson, faithful to these principles, has revoked the prohibition to export arms and munitions of war. This recent act is a great benefit to Juarez—more beneficial, in fact, than if he had been aided by troops; and the fact of the United States constantly refusing to recognize the empire ought to convince Maximilian of the disposition and probable intention of the United States.

It is the policy now of the authors and aiders of intervention to say the republic of the United States will remain neutral; but they cannot believe it, for they would be the first victims of the error. In a nation where public opinion is all-powerful, and where it has been so often expressed against Mexican intervention, the President would run a great risk to proclaim neutrality in an affair of vital importance to his country Without debating this point to a greater extent, I will merely assure you that the United States will not remain neutral in the question of Mexico. And in giving you this assurance, do not believe, for an instant, that I am blinded by party zeal, for I consider it a disgrace to my country to ask for foreign assistance. I know how it lessens the sovereignty and independence of a nation. I think Mexico possesses all the necessary elements to regain her independence without foreign aid. I have faith in her future, and want her to act alone, that she may be indebted to no one for her success. One of the reasons (aside from duties and natural sentiments) why I have opposed European intervention so violently is precisely because it would compel us to call on the northern Americans for help. I believe, my dear Baron, that, as a sequel to what I have said, the time has come when the archduke will reflect seriously upon the precariousness of his position, and will take himself out of Mexico before the force of circumstances compels him to evacuate the capital. If he thinks his situation secure, I have nothing more to say; but if he doubts it, and should hereafter change his mind, and should need my assistance with Juarez and his cabinet, I will do all I can to get him out of trouble, and at the same time save my country from further misfortunes. I will try to induce Juarez to enter into a treaty honorable to both parties, showing the evils consequent upon foreign protection. He, as a true patriot, desires to see Mexico free from obligations to any foreign power, and I do not doubt but he can free it yet. But, I repeat, Maximilian must be quick in his determination, for if Juarez once appeals to the United States it will be too late to make treaties of any kind. In my opinion Maximilian already views affairs in Mexico in their proper light. The pleasant visions that beguiled his fancy at Miramar are gone, and he will now believe what I told him, when I assured him that the history of intervention in Mexico would be like that in France after the first revolution. The conquered party in both countries, filled with anger and thirsting for revenge, sought foreign aid by deceiving strange governments, exaggerating their sufferings and anarchy, declaring that the call for intervention was unanimous and very easy to be effected. When the people have made a reform—that is, when they have extirpated the cause of their displeasure—they are more proud and elated with hope than at any other time, and cannot bear the idea of a foreign yoke, and their patriotism is bold and exhibits its full strength on the least provocation. The prodigies of French patriots against combined Europe are well known. Mexico, feeble Mexico, will be satisfied with struggling within its own frontiers for its independence.

According to late news from Mexico a deep hatred to the French army is spreading throughout the country on account of its cruelty as conquerors; a dislike to Maximilian increases because he does not prevent these barbarities; he is blamed for not giving protection to persons and property; and the general want of confidence in the stability of the empire is increasing and becoming more general. The day is not far distant when this disaffection will pervade the whole nation, and a second of May, as in Madrid, will be the consequence—one of those sudden, spontaneous, and unanimous movements, of which we have seen several examples in Mexico to end Santa Anna's dictatorship. The French army is too small to resist such a movement; and if it cannot, what is to become of the archduke and his little band, unless France submits to new sacrifices? And supposing that Maximilian sustains himself for the present, what will support him in future? The French army cannot always remain in Mexico! Another army, composed of adventurers and volunteers from other countries, will not be sufficient to sustain him. What, then, must he expect? Just what I must repeat—sooner or later a defeat, or sudden expulsion. To retire quietly and decorously would certainly be far preferable, and he ought to know it better than we.

I will tell you how he could do it honorably, so as to raise himself much in the eyes of Mexicans and foreigners. Did Maximilian come to Mexico to secure the felicity of its people, or to sacrifice them and keep himself upon a throne? We must suppose the former case. Well, since he has not succeeded in this, he is in honor and duty bound to withdraw. Will any one blame him for doing his duty? Any other course of conduct would lessen him in the estimation of his peers, and ruin his former reputation. His grandfather, the Emperor Francis, declaring the German Confederation dissolved, on a similar occasion, thus gaining a great name in history, left him an example of abnegation and magnanimity he ought never to forget. If I were in his place, I would agree upon an armistice with the constitutional government; then I would conclude a treaty as advantageous as possible to myself, and send off the French army, in accordance with the treaty of Miramar; and lastly, I would publish a manifest explaining the object of my journey to Mexico, what I had done there, and finally withdraw from the country, agreeable to my promise to retire as soon as I found out that my presence was not pleasant to the people.

Such frank and loyal language would undoubtedly be more worthy of Maximilian than to involve his party in an unequal contest, turn the whole of Mexico into a battle-field, and drag France into a useless and expensive war to sustain him on a throne he could never hold. If a treaty could not be formed with the government, it would be honorable in Maximilian to withdraw at any rate, preferring peace in Mexico to personal interest, and saving France much trouble and expense. Maybe Maximilian might object to this manner of quitting Mexico! As unpleasant as it might seem to him, (but I see no reason why it should be,) he ought to remember that it is the best, and he cannot have choice. Later he might consider himself lucky to get off in a way he rejects at present. He now has a good chance to get away, and he will find danger in delay.

I have the honor to repeat, &c.,

JESUS TERAN.

Mr. Romero to Mr. Seward.

[Translation.]

MEXICAN LEGATION IN THE UNITED STATES OF AMERICA,
Washington, December 15, 1865.

MR. SECRETARY: I have the honor of transmitting to you, for the information of the United States government, the English translation of an article on French intervention in Mexico, written by that distinguished literary Frenchman Alphonse de Lamartine, and published at Paris last month, in his literary monthly magazine, entitled Literary Entertainments, (*Les Entretiens Littéraires.*)

The importance of this article is, that it expresses the real views of French intervention in Mexico, and is, in fact, more than anything else, a paraphrase of Emperor Napoleon's letter to General Forey of the 3d of July, 1862, pointing out briefly, but plainly, the objects of intervention. I sent you a copy of this letter among the documents annexed to my note of the 26th of January, 1864.

As a proof of this assertion I think it convenient to mention that the semi-official press of France has greatly lauded the article, considering it as the genuine expression of the Emperor's views.

With pleasure I accept this occasion to renew to you, Mr. Secretary, the assurances of my most distinguished consideration.

M. ROMERO.

Hon. WILLIAM H. SEWARD, *&c.*, *&c.*, *&c.*

M. Lamartine's article.

I am not afraid to say it boldly, notwithstanding the natural opposition which may exist between the diplomacy of the republic and that of the empire: against interests so French, so elevated, so European, as those we defend in Mexico, there is no patriotic opposition possible. The conception of the policy in Mexico is a sublime conception, a conception misunderstood, (I shall explain further on why,) a conception as just as necessity, as vast as the ocean, as new as all that which is apropos, a conception of a statesman, fecund as the future, a conception of safety for America and for the world.

We must here raise ourselves to a great height in order to comprehend the full force of this policy. The first empire, a purely military empire, and which sold Louisiana for a piece of bread to feed its armies, was never capable of a conception which equalled this.

The idea of a bold and efficacious position to be taken in Mexico against the usurpation of the United States of America is a new but just idea. *Europe has the right to take this position;* France takes the initiative. Let us examine this right from the elevated point of view from whence we distinguish the legitimacy of things, and let us start from this true but not radical position:

The globe is the property of man: the new continent, America, is the property of Europe.

In starting from this principle, which has become at this moment a fact, that the American continent has become the collective property of mankind, and not of the disrupted Union of a single race, without title and without right, at least over Spanish America, and over the Latin race, mother of all civilization—the principle that the protection of Europe, and of its independence, at least in the seventeen republican states of South America, belongs evidently to us and all the powers of the Old World—we must be prepared for events; we must protect the Latin race; we must, in the first place, take position at the point menaced by the United States.

We must do this, or else we must declare that the new continent, the property of Europe, is to belong entirely in twenty-five years, perhaps, to the armed pioneers who recognize no other title for their usurpation than their convenience, and who permit their citizens, like Walker, to raise, individually, fleets and armies against Cuba, while their federal general enters, in the name of the Union, into Mexico, and from there into all the civilized capitals of South America!

Why, therefore, should Europe or the Old World recognize these rights of piracy by sea and land for the United States, whilst in the Old World we recognize not only the right of protecting such property as is useful to all, but further, the right to expropriate with indemnity the right of all states and individuals in things useful to all?

This principle of the protection of interests useful to all, which applies to a commune, does it apply with less right to a continent entire? Evidently not. We do not say, expropriate the United States of Spanish America; their proper organic anarchy will expropriate them sufficiently! But we say Europe has the right, and, we add, the obligation, of not giving over to them the Latin race, Spanish America, the half which still remains free and independent of that magnificent part of the globe, more than half of the heaven, the earth, and the population of the New World!

What are the collective, sacred possessions, the necessities of mankind at large, that the policy of the Old World cannot and ought not to be delivered up to the mercy of the United States of English America? These things are the capital of the entire world, used by a few, necessary to all, in our state of civilization and in our system of exchange, which renders to us all moneyed gold as necessary as bread. The mines of gold are there!

In the second place, the food of the Old World—the wheat, flour, corn, potatoes, on which people subsist, and of which the privation in the years of famine might produce in Europe incalculable calamities and destructions of populations.

In the third place, the industries which have become in the last few years especially, by the salaries they assure to at least forty millions of workmen in cotton, the veritable and indispensable *stipendium* of wages and of life.

In fine, commerce, which compels us to maintain a navy and sailors, a floating population, incalculable as a number of men fed under sails, still more incalculable as an element of our national power. To permit the United States to renew the folly of the first empire, to establish an anti-European blockade, no longer on their ports alone, but on the world, as they have just proclaimed it, is no longer a poltroonery; it is to accept what New York offers us, it is to abdicate navigation, commerce, cotton, free trade, the marine of the Old World; it is not to live but on the death of life.

Thus, who does not know that the grain of America, of the valley of the Mississippi especially, does constitute the world's granary in case of famine, as Sicily was the granary of the Romans? Who does not know that the monetary capital of the universe is in the immense mines of Mexico, and Peru, and Sonora, and that these mines, given up to their natural productiveness by a good system of drainage, will place all the capital in gold and silver of the universe in the hands of the United States, masters of the two Americas? Who does not know that the master of capital is the master of interest, and that Europe, delivered up to this country of monopolies, will be forever subject to its despotism? Who does not know that, masters of the price of gold and silver, they will be masters also of our most vital industries, and that their coalition, already organized against our industry in silks, which rivals their industry in cotton, will ruin Lyons, the capital of tissues, and the second capital of France? Who does not know that in depriving us, or in depriving themselves by the extinction of the south, of the element of this industry in Europe, cotton, they will continue to starve, as they have already starved, eight millions of workmen in France, more than that in England, five millions in Austria, and thus take Europe by famine at every caprice of their arbitrary interests? Who does not know, in fine, that our commerce and navigation will be subject to the same destruction as our products?

In all this we discover evidently the secret thought which inspired the Mexican expedition, an expedition which bears the appearance of a temerity without compensation, and behind which I alone in France have seen the general utility.

France has not comprehended this expedition. Why? I will venture to reply: because on the commencement it was neither explained nor explainable. It was because this idea of taking a position in Mexico against the United States was not to be exclusively French, but European; it was necessary to consult together, to organize, to agree frankly on a common basis before acting, and this was not done. France, accused of secret intentions, was suspected by England and Spain. They believed that she simply desired to draw her two allies into a war of intervention for purely French and monarchical interests, instead of combining with London and Madrid an armed, disinterested, and European policy; and for this reason they suspected and at last abandoned France. But one of two things was true; either France was sincere and wished to act in the common interest, and in this case there ought to have been frank explanations in advance, and no action but after a diplomatic and military European agreement on an equal footing of force, which would thus give no motive for complaints of reticence or want of frankness against the intervention; or France, acting alone, ought to have acted with a force worthy of herself, and not commence by planting her protecting flag in Mexico with a handful of heroic men, abandoned by their auxiliaries, and insufficient for the accomplishment of the original conception.

In these facts lie the vice of the enterprise and the reasons why the people in France have not comprehended it, why Spain has had suspicions of it, and why England has abandoned it. France, when her loyalty in the matter is better understood, will bring back England and Spain to it, or she will act alone with preponderating forces. Spanish America will thus be protected, the United States will be repressed, Spain and England brought back, and this grand enterprise will turn out the honor of the century in Europe, and the honor of France in Spanish America.

One can easily understand that this people have yet scarcely any of the conditions of an American literature. The Mexicans before the conquest, the pretended savages of Montezuma, the Peruvians, with their poems of quippos, were in that respect much more advanced. The gigantic monuments of the Aztecs have left on the earth traces of intelligence and of force very much superior, thus far, to the exclusively utilitarian edifices of the Americans of the north. The pioneers of the north do not build for time; the log-splitters only know how to cut down in order to split up the grand aristocratic trees of the forests, which they see fall with the joy of men envious of the superiority of nature. Their eloquence is the struggle of their legislative assemblies, into which they carry the rudeness of their violent manners, and where brutalities of gesture and of the closed fist take the place of the beautiful moral violences which the great modern or ancient orators of Europe exercise by aid of persuasion or logic, or men of refinement assemble together for the purpose of seeking in common after the right and the justice of things.

Their journals, innumerable because they cost little or nothing, are only so many receptacles of advertisements of the charlatanisms recommended by the Barnums of the press—receptacles of calumnies and invectives thrown out daily to the various parties, in order to fasten upon them odious appellations or trivial accusations, so as to discredit one another, and to take away their subscribers. Their "salons" are held in hotels; their circles of men, which are tempered neither by good feeling nor by politeness toward women, are only so many clubs of eager tradesmen, utilizing even their hours of repose for their purses, proud to know only that which brings them in money, and entertaining each other only with real or illusory enterprises, by which they may centriple their fortunes. Their liberty, altogether personal, has always something about it hostile to some one; the absence of all kindness of manner gives them in general the air and the attitude of some one who is in the expectation of being insulted, or who seeks, by force of pride of manner, to prevent the insults that may be offered him. They have conscience themselves of the continual disagreeableness of their manners.

One of their rare political orators, (the most eloquent and most honest among them,) whom the envy of his fellow-citizens has always prevented from being elevated to the presidency of the republic, said to me one day: "Our liberty consists *in doing all that may be the most disagreeable to our neighbors.*" The art of being disagreeable is their second nature. To be willing to please is a symptom of love. They love no one; no one loves them. It is the expiation of egotists. History presents no parallel of such a physiognomy: pride, coldness, correctness of features, mechanism of gestures, munching of tobacco in the mouth, spit-box under the feet, legs perched against the chimney-jambs or doubled up on themselves without regard to the respect which man owes to man, an accent brief, monotonous, imperious, a disdainful air imprinted in every feature—this is the picture of one of these autocrats of money.

With few exceptions, which stand out and which suffer by the general pressure in an inferior atmosphere—exceptions so much the more respectable, inasmuch as they are more numerous in the individual—and there is the North American; there is the people to whom Mr. Monroe, one of their flatterers, said, in order to be applauded: "The time is come when you ought no longer to suffer Europe to mix in the affairs of America, and from which you ought to commence to exercise a preponderance in the affairs of Europe."

Mr. Romero to Mr. Seward.

[Translation.]

MEXICAN LEGATION IN THE UNITED STATES OF AMERICA,
Washington, December 24, 1865.

MR. SECRETARY: I have the honor of transmitting to you, for the information of the government of the United States, documents relating to Mexican affairs; and although some of them are of old date, I think them all of sufficient importance to be submitted officially to your consideration.

You will find among them several that manifest the atrocities of the European mercenaries sent to enslave the Mexican people, and to perpetrate all sorts of outrages upon them in the name of civilization, and in a country they already consider as conquered, and other reliable reports of the condition of things in the central part of Mexico and on the western coast of the republic.

I embrace this occasion to renew to you, Mr. Secretary, the assurances of my most distinguished consideration.

M. ROMERO.

Hon. WILLIAM H. SEWARD, *&c., &c., &c.*

No. 193.]

DEPARTMENT OF FOREIGN RELATIONS
AND OF GOVERNMENT, NATIONAL PALACE,
Chihuahua, May 17, 1865.

The citizen President of the republic has seen with pleasure what you have communicated in your note No. 137, of the 4th of April of this year, with reference to the demonstrations of public rejoicing which took place in Washington upon the reception of the news of the occupation of Petersburg and of Richmond by the troops of the Union.

The allusions of the Hon. Mr. Johnson, who at that time only had the character of Vice-President of the United States, and of the Hon. Mr. Seward, demonstrate that in that country the intrigues and the acts by which Napoleon has sought to injure the United States during its civil war have not been lost sight of. Napoleon has offended the people of the south by not favoring them, from fear of an open rupture of the government of the United States, as much as they expected and wished; and he has offended the north by clearly showing, so far as that fear would let him, how much he desired their downfall and the permanent destruction of the Union. Without doubt the terms of Napoleon's letter to General Forey have also been remembered, in which, without tact or prevision, he stated that the principal object of the intervention in Mexico was to oppose the United States, and to raise up against it the Latin race, as if it was possible to elevate a race by seeking to humiliate and degrade one of its members and foment forgetfulness of all of its sentiments of national dignity. In order to avert the effects of that stupid lack of foresight, the French senate has sought recently to record, in its answer to the address on the opening of the sessions, that the intervention in Mexico has not had any object in the antagonism of races, the senate thus pretending to deny the express terms of the letter of Napoleon.

In the allusions of Mr. Seward to the prudence of the Emperor of Austria, who has taken care to make known that he has no sympathy with rebellion anywhere, he assuredly had reference to what was manifested to his government with reference to the civil war in the United States, and also to what the government of the republic has reason to know was communicated to that of the United States at the beginning of last year with reference to the arrival of Maximilian in Mexico, explaining that it was his own personal affair, in which the government of the Emperor, his brother, had no part whatever. This was an act of prudence on the part of that sovereign, and at the same time of dignity; for he did not wish to take part in the unworthy enterprise of the archduke, his brother, who consented to come to Mexico to represent there the humble position of the simple instrument of a foreign government, and, in addition, the instrument of a government which had just, in Lombardy, been the means of conquering and humiliating his country and family; who consented also, at the call of a few Mexican traitors to their country, and reserving, in his turn, to deceive them and to prove false to them, when after a little he should be ordered by the French government.

I renew to you my attentive consideration.

LERDO DE TEJADA.

Citizen MATIAS ROMERO,
Envoy Extraordinary and Minister
Plenipotentiary of the Mexican Republic in Washington.

The following letter was written by a Mexican officer in the service of Maximilian, who was accompanying a detachment of Belgian troops sent into the State of Michoacan. It reveals a tale of horror that shows how utterly impossible it is for Maximilian ever to pacify that country except by the extermination of all its inhabitants. The civilization he is introducing is worse than that of the Goths and Vandals:

MARAVATIO, *April* 27, 1865.

MY DEAR UNCLE: Since I left Mexico this is the first opportunity I have had to address you a letter and communicate anything about our campaign, in which the fatigue is very great and the results next to nothing. For fifteen days we have been marching through mountains and deserts, behind an enemy whom we have not had the felicity of seeing even at a distance. We arrived at Zitacuro and found it deserted—the houses open but without inhabitants, nor even a sign that they had been occupied; for, all the inhabitants being enemies, they had retired some time since to the mountains and the most distant estates. Finding the place deserted in this manner, this circumstance, added to what had occurred some days before to the force of Lamabrid, caused the Belgian colonel, the sole commander of the expedition, to become very indignant, and to order the most severe measures yet necessary in such cases as this.

On the day following our arrival at this collection of houses—for it cannot be called a town where there are no inhabitants—we left for the neighboring villages and ranches with precise orders "to raze and destroy everything in them." In fact, on this day we burned the villages of San Francisco and San Miguel, leaving their inhabitants without property or home. It was a scene that would have filled with consternation even a Nero. Think of the families in the street, the children crying, some calling for their fathers, who had fled distracted to the mountains; others entreating in the most pitiful manner; and, accompanying all these laments, the echoes of the trumpet sounding without cessation the order to set fire. Everywhere was seen nothing but flames, which devoured everything. In fine, to relate to you all that I saw would be impossible. This operation finished, we scoured the fields and drove off the cattle, the horses, the mules, everything, in fact, which belonged to the miserable unfortunates who, in less than three hours, saw perish all their savings of many years. These operations we have repeated with two other villages and a hacienda belonging to one Arias, who is serving with Riva Palacios, and finally we left for this point, whence we proceed to Morelia.

Up to the present time I have only lost from my squadron two men and twelve Belgians, whom the Indians surprised in the mountains and whom they killed like dogs in the village of San Mateo, which also disappeared from the scene, thanks to the fire which consumed it.

I have met with no accident, and as I am more accustomed to active life than to quiet, I am well and in very good condition.

I trust that your health has also improved, and that everything is going on well, which I shall be much pleased to hear.

With great and sincere affection, your nephew, who hopes to see you soon,

SILVIANO NAVA.

General José Antonio Herredia.

Antonio Lopez de Santa Anna, well-deserving citizen of the country, and general of division of the national armies of Mexico, to his countrymen:

Mexicans: He who has always addressed you on solemn occasions, whether to explain to you his political conduct, or to give you advice, or to offer you his sword, is the same who now claims from you the greatest calmness and attention, in order that you may listen to him once more I speak to you from the heart. I have never deceived you, because truth has always been my rule.

The respect which in all times and under all circumstances I have paid the majority of the people, imposes upon me the duty to impress upon you that which you have already read in my manifesto, issued at Vera Cruz on the 27th of February, 1864.

I adhered to the system of government which appeared to be proclaimed by a considerable majority, in obedience to the principles which I professed, based upon submission to the national will, under the conviction that the Mexicans were those who, exercising their civil omnipotence, had given themselves new institutions, and were trying to find the way to conciliate order with liberty. But what a painful error! From this hospitable island I contemplate with increasing indignation the scaffold which the tyranny of a usurping people is raising in our beloved country to stain it with the blood of our brothers, and for the destruction of our people.

From this island I have contemplated also, with pride, your struggle for life with the invaders of your country, the soldiers called forth by the intervention, and the trumpet of the free has made my heart palpitate with joy, as in the happy days in which we combated together in defence of our firesides and our outraged rights. The hopes of those who sought in monarchy the repose which the republic denied them have been disappointed; the national dignity has been contemned, justice derided, our holy rights trodden under foot, thought enslaved, prostitution elevated and virtue vilified, the sanctuary draped in mourning, and the church afflicted with tribulations. Terror is seated upon the scaffold, brandishing over the patriots the knife of extermination. War to the invaders! Liberty or death should be the cry of every generous bosom in which honor has her home, independence her altar, and liberty her rites.

We thought that the Archduke Maximilian of Austria would restore to us peace, and he has been the new element of discord; that with wise laws he would enrich our treasury, and he has impoverished it in an incredible manner; that he would bring us happiness, and the misfortunes are innumerable which in so short a time he has heaped upon the ruins of ensanguined Mexico; that in fine he would be consistent in his principles and promises if he accepted the views of President Juarez in all that related to reform, at the same time that he persecutes him and gives him war to the knife.

European adventurers formed his guard of honor. The French bayonets are the foundations of his throne, and in the mean time so many see themselves condemned to oblivion, to the contempt of the veterans of independence, once the glory of our nation, and now objects of derision and mockery for the foreign soldiery. Such insults cannot be tolerated any longer. The hour has come in which we should exterminate from the sacred soil of the free the farcical rabble who profane the land with their feet, and insult us with their presence.

Liberals and conservatives, forget our fratricidal contentions, and advance to the rescue. Let us unite together against the common enemy. One banner covers us—the flag of liberty. One thought alone animates us—that of war and death to the invaders who destroy our towns and cities and behead our brothers. Eternal execration to the tyrants of our country!

Compatriots, if, on reading my manifesto of last year, your attention should be arrested by the expression that "the last words of my conscience and of my convictions is constitutional monarchy," remember that I also said on the same occasion, "I am not an enemy of democracy, but of its excesses;" and, above all, do not forget that I was the founder of the republic. A people is free, whatever be their form of government, when the head of the nation forgets that he is human. Let him remember only that he is the organ of the law. This, my belief, was also yours when the republic was changed to an empire.

But we have been mistaken. The prince whom you chose is not the organ of the law, but the usurper of our rights. He is not the defender of national independence, for if he were he would not cede Sonora. He is not the sovereign of the nation, but the humble vassal of a foreign potentate.

In order to inspire greater confidence in the new form of government which you have just adopted, and to carry to the throne for your benefit the advice of experience, I went to Vera Cruz to meet the proclaimed emperor, disposed to give him, without reserve, all my support; but his arbitrariness and discourtesy closed the doors of my country upon me. The decree of my expulsion was written in a language which our forefathers did not speak.

I owe you an explanation. The public journals of the capital published my recognition of the French intervention. This act of mine did not originate from my own will, but was imposed upon me by the force of circumstances.

Scarcely did the steamer that conducted me anchor in the port, ere a French commander presented himself before me on board of the vessel, as the chief superior of Vera Cruz, and made known to me that I would not be allowed to land, but, on the contrary, he should oblige me to return in the same vessel, if I did not immediately comply with the conditions which he presented to me written in French. These conditions required me to recognize the intervention and the monarch elect, and not to address the people.

Such quiet insolence could only excite my indignation. But the sufferings of my wife, caused by the painful journey by the sea, and the advice of some of my friends who came to meet me, inclined me to subscribe to these conditions, which, however, did not liberate me from the annoyances to which I was exposed.

All this proves that the intervention could not be supported without mistrust of the presence of the soldier who had always defended with energy the rights of his country, humbling on various occasions the flag of the haughty potentates and making their so-called invincible legions bow under the yoke of democracy.

My friends, in addressing you to-day, I am only inspired with the desire for your happiness and the glory of Mexico. No unworthy sentiments dictate my words. I have shed some drops of my blood in your defence, and I would shed it all, were it necessary, fighting in your armies, if not as your chief, then as a private soldier. In the mean time, while circumstances prevent me from joining your ranks, I wish you to know the sentiments with which I am animated.

Compatriots! on the memorable 2d of December, 1822, I adopted as my motto these words: "Down with the empire! Live the republic!" *Abajo el imperio! Viva la republica!* And now, from the foreign soil upon which I am exiled, I repeat that motto with the same enthusiasm.

A. L. DE STA. ANNA.

ST. THOMAS, *July* 8, 1865.

CITY OF MEXICO, *September* 19, 1865.

On the 16th of September last was the 44th anniversary of Mexican independence. Maximilian availed himself of that occasion to make a most remarkable speech, intended as a warning to the United States

If any one had been laboring under the idea that the Austrian archduke was about to leave Mexico, that impression must be dispelled. However great may be the complications that are to arise with the United States, he is committed irrevocably to remain in Mexico. His speech contains the following solemn and unmistakable words:

"No influence in this world can make me waver in my duty; every drop of my blood is Mexican now, and if God sends fresh dangers to threaten our country you will see me fight in your ranks for its independence and integrity. I am willing to die at the foot of our glorious banner, because no human power can wrest from me the trust with which you have endowed me."

No more direct reference or open defiance to the United States could be made. Now, after our war has terminated and time for reflection has been given, Maximilian, in defiance of the well-known views of the United States, deliberately takes his stand, and says: "I shall remain in Mexico." It is too late for him to say, as he might have done before, that he was mistaken and had been misinformed with reference to the views of the Mexican people; and that they do not desire an imperial form of government, and that in deference to their wishes he was willing to abdicate the throne. Now the die is cast, and the throne usurped through the aid of the arms of France is to be maintained at all hazards. This important step, however, had a higher origin than the vacillating purpose and feeble will of Maximilian. It emanates from Paris. Maximilian is the speaker, but the words are the words of Louis Napoleon. It is evident, from the advices that have reached here from France, that this speech, as well as the abandonment of the journey of Carlota, his wife, to Belgium, are the result of direct orders from Napoleon, who has decided to meet the issue, and he it is that is to be held responsible.

So strong has been the feeling of confidence here on the part of Maximilian and his advisers, since the receipt of recent advices from Paris, that he has gone further than anybody had dreamed he would, and has attempted, in order to encourage emigration from the south, to establish slavery in his dominions. Before entering on his edict upon this subject, I will refer for a moment to the colonization business and how it has been managed here.

It has always been the plan of Louis Napoleon and of Maximilian to rely in a considerable degree for the maintenance of their position here upon the support of discontented emigrants from the south who would seek refuge in this country.

In the Mexicans alone they saw no elements strong enough to oppose the United States, in the difficulties which they foresaw would arise upon the termination of our war. But they have calculated upon a large emigration from the south, and this explains their anxiety to receive with open arms all who harbored prejudice or had grievances yet to redress with the United States.

To secure this immigration they were willing, of course, to take them with all their prejudices of color, and, in fact, if necessary, indirectly to adopt, for a time at least, their well-tried system of labor.

The first plan was to have Duke Gwin, as commissioner general of emigration, to be located in the northern and frontier States, and there to build up a barrier against the encroachments of the United States. This plan would have been carried out had not the rebellion been crushed so speedily. That unexpected and undesired event deranged their plans and rendered more caution necessary. Duke Gwin was obnoxious to many of the leading rebels, who soon arrived in Mexico, and his name had been too prominently mentioned in connexion with the scheme, and its purpose was too well known, for it to be prudent to have him any longer at the head of it. Consequently Duke Gwin was unceremoniously thrown overboard, and a new plan has now, after much deliberation and study, been adopted. This plan, besides accomplishing all the purposes of the original scheme, has the merit of appearing not to be exclusive, and of presenting only the honest purpose of populating the country with laborers from abroad, whose presence all admit is so much needed.

The scheme is embraced in several decrees which have been recently issued. One issued on the 5th of September proclaims "that Mexico is freely opened to emigration from all countries," (which means southern emigration,) and is followed by certain "Regulations," signed by Maximilian himself, which, while declaring free, according to the laws of the empire, all who enter the Mexican territory, proceeds to establish certain rules and regulations by which the laborer is thrown really into a worse state of slavery than that of the southern States; and a slavery that is not confined to the colored man, but extends to all laborers alike.

The *peons*, or laborers, have to make a contract with their master, who is styled *patron*, by which they engage to work in his service for a period of not less than five nor more than ten years, which contract can be renewed at its expiration.

The *patron* is to engage himself to feed, clothe, and keep the serfs and to nurse them when sick, paying them also some nominal wages in money. The patron has also to feed his servant's children, and these, should the father die, are to remain in his service until they become of age. Fugitive serfs are condemned to the public works, without pay, until their master may demand them.

You have doubtless heard of the former peonage system of this country, of which scarcely a vestige has for many years remained, and that only in a limited part of southern Mexico, where it has existed in violation of law and only under an abusive practice of the land-owners, who have there a controlling influence. This system was equivalent to slavery, but the early legislation of Mexico and the constitution of 1857, in express terms, strictly abolished it and prohibited its exercise under severe penalties.

But it has remained for Maximilian, the Austrian, the docile tool of Napoleon, to attempt to re-establish this odious relic of the past, and deliberately to systematize by formal edict, and cover with the color of lawful right, this shameful practice of virtual human slavery. Can such things be allowed in the middle of this nineteenth century, and when in the United States that odious institution has just been abolished at the cost of the greatest war the world has ever seen? The object of this scheme is, while avoiding the use of the word "slavery," to establish a system in place of it which shall be equally satisfactory to southern men, and, while thus apparently drawing them in as emigrants, to strengthen their hands in the event of any movement by the United States. For the information of your readers I enclose a copy of the decree and "regulations" annexed

In addition to the evidence showing a design to secure the support of discontented people from the south, constant additions to the existing force in this country are being made from France. A French steam transport has just landed at Vera Cruz 800 men, and the last packet from St. Nazaire brought 500.

There are also on the way and expected soon to arrive 1,200 Egyptians, while the money remittances from France show that Napoleon is preparing to maintain a large army here.

The recent order of the Secretary of War disbanding a large part of Sheridan's army on the Rio Grande, has caused a great deal of satisfaction to the government here; and they assume that it is proof positive that the United States does not intend to disturb their possession of Mexico.

It is even asserted that the recognition of the United States will yet be obtained. Quite a number of agents of Maximilian are now at work in the United States, who are well supplied with funds for influencing popular opinion there through the press and other channels. The chief of these is an Austrian count, a personal friend of Maximilian, who was formerly acting as the assistant secretary of the yet to be created navy. Señor Arroyo is acting under him as so-called commercial agent, and Señor Degollado holds an inferior position subordinate to both. Encouraged by the reported withdrawal of our troops from the Rio Grande, these efforts will be redoubled; but it is to be hoped our government will in season appreciate how great an encouragement to Napoleon this measure will be, and suspend any further diminution of the forces at this most important strategic point.

The internal condition of affairs here could hardly be worse for Maximilian and the French than it is at present. The number of guerillas increases every day, and new leaders are coming into the field in every direction. They annoy and cut off the communication of the French, interrupt their mails, attack their convoys, prevent all travel except under strong military escort, stop the transit of merchandise, pick off the French pickets, and, whenever an opportunity is afforded them, swoop down upon and surprise some small outlying detachment. When pursued, they invariably disband and disperse in every direction, and are constantly always being pursued but never destroyed. As can easily be imagined, this kind of warfare is excessively annoying and unsatisfactory to the French. They are kept in a continual state of uncertainty and alarm, are constantly subjected to long and weary marches, and are fighting an enemy who is always before them but never overtaken, and is as intangible as a shadow, yet surrounds them and harasses them everywhere night and day. The Austrians and Belgians in considerable bodies have often been defeated by the guerillas, so that the former are no longer feared by the Mexicans, while the latter are even despised, and when taken prisoners are simply disarmed and let go at once. If I were to enumerate all the different encounters with the guerillas which are contained in the recent numbers of the Franco-Mexican papers, I should fill whole pages of the Herald. I will therefore content myself, as evidence, with translating a few items from La Sociedad, an ultra clerical paper of this city, and L'Estafette, the organ of General Bazaine.

The Estafette of the 7th of September comments upon the defeat at the Rio Florido, in the State of Chihuahua, of a *detachment* of French soldiers by the liberal General Patoni. The same issue has also the following:

"The neighborhood of Toluca has just been the scene of painful events. The 'dissidents' having surprised at San Felipe a detachment of the municipal guards, it was destroyed. This disaster costs the municipal guard of Mexico seventy men, and Captains Concha and Moncada, and Lieutenant Galindo."

The Sociedad of the 8th says:

"Figueroa took possession at Tecomovaca of a *conducta* of $200,000, proceeding from Oaxaca to Vera Cruz, the troops that escorted the money having been completely routed."

In the issue of the 10th the same paper adds:

"The Boletin of Tlaccotalpam publishes Figueroa's report of his engagement with the Austrians, after he left Tehuacan, at Trapichito, on the Rio Salado. Figueroa states that the enemy's losses were more than twenty killed and forty-eight prisoners, among them an Austrian lieutenant of cavalry." The same paper adds: "We are informed from a trustworthy source that Fragoso, who is again in the field, surprised, on the evening of the 2d instant, at the hacienda of San Antonio del Valle, an imperial force of ninety dragoons from San Juan del Rio. All were taken prisoners, except a few who escaped by scaling the walls of the hacienda. From the same source we learn that Ugalde, (another liberal chief,) coming from Huapango, crossed the national road to the interior on the 3d instant with a force of five hundred men on his way to Mezquital."

El Pajaro Verde of the 9th says:

"General Rueles (imperialist) is fortifying Tepeje del Rio, to await there the enemy, who is approaching that locality with upwards of twelve hundred men."

I should never finish were I to repeat all that is published of this character, and which is the staple of our daily news. "Tula, in the State of Mexico, has been captured by the republicans." "The republican forces have approached the outskirts of Orizaba." "The imperial General Tenajero has been defeated in Nuevo Leon." Such items fill the papers constantly. Maximilian, or rather General Bazaine, who is the real emperor, has abandoned the policy of conciliation heretofore pursued, and it is now a war of extermination against all who oppose them.

Here in the capital we have recently had an alarm, and some forty prominent Mexicans of distinction were arrested and imprisoned without trial or charge, and for no reason other than that they were known to be unfriendly to the empire in the opinions which they entertained, but without taking any part whatever in the struggle that is going on. No reason whatever has been assigned for their arrest and imprisonment, nor have they been brought before any tribunal for trial. Rumor says to-day that they are to be sent to Martinique, subject to hard labor. The outrages and atrocities that are being committed here by the French will, when known, shock the whole world and fill it with horror. Poland, even, has scarcely been the theatre of more iniquitous events.

The Sociedad of the 6th instant publishes the following, taken from an official report of an engagement in Aguas Calientes:

"According to orders, and with the greatest secrecy, without calling upon the authorities of the place, Don Manuel Lozano (a supposed republican) was arrested and immediately shot in his own house."

Speaking of French atrocities, the Sombra, a semi-liberal paper of this city, publishes the following:

"We have denounced before the nation many acts of cruelty of which the press of this city has taken no notice at all. We have also stated in our remarks addressed to the Estafette that it is impossible to consolidate peace in the presence of a power which, in utter disregard of the laws of nature, and stifling all feelings of humanity, decrees with profound secrecy and without any law but its own will the death of citizens. It is impossible, we repeat, to re-establish peace and public confidence by the use of such means."

In my next I will send you further extracts, which will unmistakably show the course of events. * * *

Mr. Romero to Mr. Seward.

[Translation.]

MEXICAN LEGATION IN THE UNITED STATES OF AMERICA,
Washington, February, 14, 1866.

MR. SECRETARY: I have the honor to transmit to you a copy of a French publication lately made in Paris, entitled "Mexico before the Chambers," and written by Mr. Georges Jauret. It is undoubtedly the most impartial article ever published in France on the Mexican question.

The importance of this publication is such that I cannot refrain from sending it to the department under your worthy charge, and recommending it to your particular attention.

I avail myself of this occasion to renew to you, Mr. Secretary, the assurances of my most distinguished consideration.

M. ROMERO.

Hon. WILLIAM H. SEWARD, *&c.*, *&c.*, *&c.*

[From La Presse, Paris, January 20, 1866.]

Mexico before the French Chambers.

I.

On the 5th and 6th of January, 1862, the first ships of France, Spain, and England appeared before the harbor of Vera Cruz. Spain had sent a large contingent of 7,000 men; The quota of France was much more modest, being only 2,500 men, and the English detachment amounted to little more than 700 bayonets.

The city was evacuated before any demonstration was made against the fort of San Juan de Ulloa, and the allies immediately took quiet possession.

Now a series of tedious negotiations began, and concluded with the convention of Soledad, on the 19th of February, 1862. But this convention was rejected at Paris, by a formal note in the Moniteur of the 2d of April; full diplomatic power was consigned to Mr. Dubois de Saligny; this disavowal became the pretext of a rupture between the allies, and very soon afterwards General Lorencez, at the head of the French corps, re enforced, was attacking the Monastery of Guadalupe, transformed into a citadel, at Puebla, on the 5th of May.

Thus at each step we took on Mexican territory we found ourselves more deeply involved. The skirt of a garment caught in a cog-wheel drags in the whole body. We begin by wishing to protect the interests of our countrymen; at Puebla it is the honor of the flag that demands vengeance; in Mexico we shall see the exigencies of national self-love determined not to give up a work once begun.

General Forey, taking re-enforcements with him, takes General Lorencez's place, and embarks at Cherbourg on the 30th of July. He organizes his columns, and on the 15th of February, 1863, nine months after the check at Guadalupe, he determines to take the offensive. He had twenty thousand men with him. The siege of Puebla commenced on the 18th of March, and on the 18th of May the city and its defences were taken. Finally, on the 10th of June, General Forey made his entry into the capital.

We now approach the decisive period. The meeting of notables is held, and on the 3d of October, 1863, a deputation starts for Miramar to offer the imperial crown to the Archduke Maximilian. The candidate for the restored throne of Mexico submitted his acceptance to the will of the people formally expressed, the result of this vote was communicated to him on the 10th of April, and he finally announces his acceptance to the Mexican delegates. On the 14th of April he embarked at Miramar for Vera Cruz. The lot is now cast; from this moment dates the decisive experiment and the commencement for France of the bitter fruits of intervention.

II.

Under this history of military incidents there is another profound one, diversified with confused and imperceptible accidents systematically dissembled by calculated reserves, and by what we are pleased to call diplomatic exigencies. This last is, however, the most interesting to learn; for it alone gives value to facts, in exposing the secret thought that has produced or directed them.

We must say now, as a preface to the work undertaken by our army, that Mexico is a country of a peculiar kind. It gets on, in opposition to its governments, by *pronunciamientos*, just like Spain, from which it has preserved certain political morals. At the time of our expedition, instability was the normal condition of the different powers that jostled, fought, and replaced each other.

It may be explained in this way: the Mexican people, without being brave, are restive. The wars kept up for independence have given them the habit of arms and the necessity of internal struggles.

In fine, Mexico extends over a vast territory, very poorly joined together in its parts. The absence of roads, the difficulties of communications make it a country very slightly connected federally, and so cut up that a victorious party must always find resistance in some remote quarter of the empire or republic, once headed by Santa Anna, then by Miramon, and now by Juarez.

Such were the difficulties we undertook to overcome when we signed the convention of the 31st of October, 1861.

III.

The idea of a French expedition first appeared in a despatch from Mr. Dubois de Saligny, dated in Mexico the 18th of April, 1861. The despatch was as follows:

"In the state of anarchy, we might say of social decomposition, in which we find this unfortunate country, it is very difficult to foresee the turn events will take. One thing seems certain to me: it is impossible to remain in *statu quo*. Everything indicates that we are approaching a new revolution. In this situation, it seems to me absolutely necessary for us to keep a material force upon the Mexican coast sufficient to protect our interests under all circumstances."

It is only a question of a protective demonstration, somewhat negative, as is plainly to be seen, that diverts intervention rather than invites it.

In his despatch of the 12th of June, 1861, Mr. Dubois de Saligny intensifies his thought, making it more decisive. It is no longer a question of simple *protection*, but one of *reclamations* by force. This despatch says:

"It remains for me to add, that I have little confidence in the new administration; that the position of this government appears to me so precarious that I believe more than ever in the necessity of taking immediate precautions to put ourselves in a condition to support by force, in case of need, the justice of our claims."

In his despatch of the 27th of July, Mr. de Saligny announced to Mr. Thouvenel that on the 23d, in accord with Sir Charles Wyke, he had broken his relations with the government of Juarez

As to Mr. Thouvenel, he admits the necessity of demanding satisfaction and indemnities; but he does not yet see, even in the most distant case, the project or thought to overturn the republican government of Juarez. See in what remarkably wise terms our minister of foreign affairs resumes his instructions in a despatch from Paris the 5th of September, 1861, addressed to Mr. Dubois de Saligny:

"The government of the Emperor entirely approves of your conduct, and protests in the most formal manner against that of the government of Juarez. That government must know the impression of the government of the Emperor, and must be instructed in regard to what we require of it. You must therefore declare to it that repudiation of the foreign debt, under any pretext whatever, is very unpleasant to us, and we demand the immediate repeal of the law of the 17th of July last. You will add, that we require the appointment of commissioners in the ports of Vera Cruz and Tampico, to be designated by us, and whose duty shall be to assure the deposit, in the hands of the powers entitled to them, of the funds collected for their benefit, in execution of foreign agreements, from the profits of the maritime custom-houses of Mexico. If the Mexican government refuses to accept these conditions, you will quit Mexico without delay, with all the *personnel* of his Majesty's legation."

At last, on the 30th of October, the day before the signature of the famous convention between France, England, and Spain, Mr. Thouvenel addressed Mr. Saligny another despatch, announcing in a positive manner the expedition, the conditions under which it was to be undertaken, and the object of the three powers in organizing it.

"The Emperor," said Mr. Thouvenel, "has decided that a naval division, under Rear-Admiral Jurien de la Gravière, shall be sent to the Gulf of Mexico to demand satisfaction, which must be given for insults to our dignity and injuries of all sorts to our citizens. The government of the Emperor will not act alone; the government of her Britannic Majesty and that of her Catholic Majesty propose to join their forces to ours in this expedition."

To explain clearly the situation, we are now forced to stop and ask Spain, in her turn, to allow a brief history of her projects in regard to Mexico. It will be seen here that French policy has only yielded to solicitations from Madrid. The wrongs to that power date back even further than ours. As early as the month of April, 1860, before the final triumph of Juarez, we find the first diplomatic protestations of Mr. Pacheco, the Spanish minister in Mexico. We will soon see what fatal fruit this early germ brought forth.

IV.

Let us proceed with the facts. In the month of April, 1860, as Mr. Calderon Collantes says in his despatch to Mr. Mon, on the 23d of October, 1861, Spain had conceived the project of a joint expedition, which would have terminated, according to the proposed plan, in the establishment of a *regular and durable government*, in the stereotyped language of diplomacy; but no definite resolution was taken till the end of August, 1861. As early as the month of September the government increases its communications with London and Paris; and on the 10th of December Mr. Isturiz writes from London to his government, "That there is nothing yet agreed upon between England and France about intervention in Mexican affairs." As I have observed, it was not till the 30th October, in Mr. Thouvenel's despatch to Mr. Dubois de Saligny, that French diplomacy reveals the existence of negotiations for the conclusion of a convention to be signed the next day, and on the 23d of the same month Mr. Calderon Collantes discusses the plan of it in a despatch to Mr. Mon, Spanish ambassador at Paris.

Let us now leave dates and hasten on to the instructive portion of this history. What matters it whether the expedition originated in Madrid, Paris, or London? This question was definitely settled when the three powers solemnly signed the convention October 31. From that day the responsibilities of the expedition ceased to be successive and personal; there is but one action and one responsibility. At present the situation has quite a different appearance. The convention has been given up, and France remains at Vera Cruz, in front of Mexico. We have nothing to say about the conduct of Spain and England after withdrawing from the convention of Soledad. What good would it do? But our expedition has gained its ends. It remains to be seen whether these ends were desired, sought for, or premeditated. And for the proper solution of the question it is certainly not without interest to discover what has been the French policy since the 31st of October, 1861, to the 10th April, 1864, and whether it has been constantly true to itself and constantly uniform.

In our mind there are but two orders of facts in the investigation of this question: apparent and tangible facts and those that escape vulgar comprehensions; there is the *letter* and the *spirit*.

V.

Consulting appearances, we easily conclude that France never had the idea, ostensibly at least, of exercising any force in the change of government in Mexico. The convention of the 31st October says, in article 1st:

"The commanders of the allied forces shall be authorized to carry out any other operations deemed necessary to enforce the specific aim stated in the preamble of this convention, and particularly to assure protection to foreign residents."

Mr. Calderon Collantes goes so far, on this occasion, as to demand, in his despatch of 23d October to Mr. Mon, the suppression of all of the article after the word "preamble." "Then," said he, "the intent of the convention cannot be doubtful."

Let us pass on to article 2d, certainly the most explicit:

"Art. 2. The high contracting parties bind themselves, in the coercive measures provided by the present convention, not to seek to acquire territory, nor take any private advantage, nor to exercise in the internal affairs of Mexico any influence of a nature to disturb the right of the Mexican nation to choose and constitute freely the form of its government."

This article is very explicit; and it appears much more so when we consider the commentaries made upon it by official declarations and facts. The first of these commentaries is certainly one of the most explicit. We find it in a diplomatic document from Washington, signed by Mr. Seward.

The three European powers in consort, moved by England, wished to have the co-operation of the federal government. The ministers of the three powers knocked at the door of the Washington cabinet, and the Secretary of State for foreign affairs answered in a despatch dated Washington, December 4, 1861; which despatch begins by giving almost the whole of the convention of the 31st October, and expresses the views of the United States upon each article.

What Mr. Seward says of article 2d is particularly interesting:

"The United States," says Mr. Seward, "take great interest—and they are happy to think that this interest is in common with the high contracting parties and other civilized nations—in believing that the sovereigns that have concluded the convention do not seek to obtain an enlargement of territory, or any other advantage not acquired by the United States, or any other civilized state, and that they do not wish to exercise any influence injurious to the right of the Mexican people to choose and freely establish the form of their government. The undersigned reiterates on this occasion the expression of his satisfaction, based on the declaration of the high contracting parties, that they recognize this interest, and he is authorized by the satisfaction of the President of the United States"

It is evident from these declarations of the American statesman that the three powers ought to have discussed the convention of the 31st October at Washington, in a sense altogether reassuring for the national sovereignty and the security of republican institutions in Mexico.

Mr. Seward adds these characteristic declarations:

"It is true that the United States also have causes of complaint against Mexico, as the high contracting parties suppose. After mature reflection the President is, however, of opinion that it is not proper at this time to demand satisfaction for these wrongs by an act of accession to the convention. Among the reasons for this decision, and which the undersigned is authorized to communicate, he will mention: 1st. That the United States prefer, as far as possible, to maintain that traditional policy recommended by the Father of the country, and confirmed by a happy experience, which forbids them to form alliances with foreign nations. 2d. Mexico being a neighbor of the United States on this continent, and possessing, as to some of its most important institutions, a system of government analogous to ours, the United States profess sentiments of friendship towards that republic and take a lively interest in its safety, its welfare, and its prosperity. Animated by these intentions, the United States are not disposed to have recourse to coercive measures to satisfy their wrongs at a time when the Mexican government is profoundly disturbed by internal dissensions and threatened by an external war. These same sentiments prevent the United States, with greater reason, from participating in an alliance in view of a war against Mexico."

The Secretary of State in Washington would have answered very differently if the three powers had allowed an afterthought of dynastic restoration to penetrate their communications. These afterthoughts have long existed, as we will soon see; but they are disguised, dimmed, and changed in the mystery of diplomatic conversations, waiting only the complaisance of facts and the attitude of the Mexicans to give them the right of publicity.

Mr. Calderon Collantes sends instructions to the captain general of Cuba There were but three points to impose on Mexico: 1st, solemn satisfaction for the expulsion of the Spanish ambassador; 2d, execution of the treaty signed at Paris between Mon and Almonte; 3d, indemnity. Nothing yet of the perspective of a monarchical restoration.

On his part, Mr. Thouvenel, on the 11th of November, 1861, sends instructions to Rear-Admiral Jurien de la Gravière. First, he is informed of the motives of the expedition; next, his duties are pointed out to him, and he is told what conditions he is to impose upon the Juarez government, with which the plenipotentiaries are still evidently authorized to treat. It is only later that Mr. Dubois de Saligny and Mr. Jurien de la Gravière will officially learn the irrevocable condemnation that threatens the Mexican republic.

"The combined forces of the three powers," says Mr. Thouvenel to Mr. Jurien de la Gravière, in his note of the 11th of November, "having arrived at the eastern shores of Mexico, you will, as I have said, claim possession of the ports of that coast. After this step, two alternatives may arise: either you will be resisted, and you will take these ports by force, or the local authorities will make no material opposition, and the Mexican government will refuse to enter into relations with you."

We here see that Mr. Thouvenel still admits the supposition of an arrangement with Juarez, and of course the maintenance of republican institutions. This does not certainly accord with the diplomatic conversations then taking place between Paris and Madrid, with the view of a monarchical establishment in Mexico; but we will have occasion presently to examine this discreet and mysterious phase of facts; we will continue for the present to look at the avowed aims and to expose appearances.

Mr. Thouvenel continues thus:

"Renewing a tactic used by one of his antecessors in the war with the United States, Juarez would retire to the interior. This expedient would not stop the allied powers. The interest of our dignity, and climacteric considerations, would determine us to act promptly and decisively. The government of the Emperor admits that whether it be to reach the Mexican government, or to render coercion more efficacious, you may be compelled to march into the interior, even as far as the city of Mexico itself." The march on Mexico is only regarded here as a possibility.

The conclusion of the despatch deserves to be given entire; we quote verbally:

"The allied powers, as I have said, have no other design than is expressed in the convention; they do not intend to interfere with internal affairs, nor to exercise any influence on the will of the people in their choice of a government. There are, however, certain contingencies we must be prepared for, and which we must previously examine. It might happen that the presence of the allied forces on the Mexican territory would induce the sensible portion of the population, weary of anarchy, and longing for order and repose, to try to form a government with the guarantees of strength and stability, that have been wanting ever since the independence of the country. The allied powers have a manifest common interest in ridding Mexico of the anarchy which has so long paralyzed its prosperity and annulled the riches bestowed upon it so bountifully by Providence, forcing it to change unstable and expensive governments for others of no better character. This interest ought to induce them not to discourage these attempts, and you will not refuse them your encouragement and moral support if they undertake to establish a government that will afford protection to strangers as well as to other residents. The government of the Emperor relies upon your prudence and discernment to appreciate, in concert with his Majesty's commissioner, (whose knowledge of Mexican affairs, from a long residence in that country, will be very useful to you,) the events that will come under your observation, and the part you will be called upon to take in them.

"THOUVENEL."

This is the first public appearance of the intentions of the French government on the restoration of royalty in Mexico But these intentions are so slightly developed, and so little encouraged, that the French plenipotentiaries, scarcely fixed upon Mexican soil, are authorized to send Juarez an ultimatum, comprehending all the wrongs against France, under the form of imposed conditions, concluding with an article 9, thus conceived:

"ARTICLE 9. As a guarantee for the fulfilment of the financial conditions and others, proposed by the present ultimatum, France shall have the right to occupy the ports of Vera Cruz, Tampico, and such other ports of the republic that seem proper, and to establish commissioners to be appointed by the imperial government, whose duty shall be to deliver funds collected in the maritime ports of Mexico, in execution of foreign contracts, into the hands of those powers to whom they are due, and to deliver sums due to France to the French agents.

"The said agents shall also be invested with power to reduce by half or in less proportion, as they please, the duties now collected in the ports of the republic.

"It is expressly understood that goods upon which importation dues have been paid shall be subjected in no case whatever to an additional tax of more than fifteen per cent. on import duties as internal tax or any other, neither by the supreme government nor by the state authorities."

This article shows that the French commissioners reject all projects of a nature hostile to the government, and are disposed to treat with Juarez.

VI.

The opening of the session of 1862 was impatiently expected. The imperial discourse would necessarily cast some light on this Mexican expedition, around which rumors from every quarter had cast so many shadows. At the opening of the session on the 27th January, 1862, the Emperor expressed himself thus on the Mexican question:

"We would be at peace with the world if the proceedings of an unscrupulous government in Mexico did not force us to join Spain and England in protecting our countrymen, and suppressing crimes against humanity and the laws of nations."

From the data of this imperial speech, then, it is only a question of one of those conflicts so frequent during the first half of the century across the sea. Citizens to protect, crimes to be suppressed—such is the wise, modest, and easy programme announced and avowed solemnly by imperial policy.

Next come discussions of the address. Strange rumors about Mexico circulate, and they find an echo in the centre of the legislature. Vague talks of monarchy in Mexico are heard; officious offers to a prince of the house of Hapsburg are hinted; the band of five bestirs itself, and presents this significant amendment:

"We see the beginning of the Mexican expedition with regret. Its aim seems to be to meddle with the interior affairs of a people. We advise the government to attend only to the reparation of wrongs."

Mr. Jules Favre gets up this amendment. He admits the reparation of wrongs; but he is alarmed when the name of Maximilian is pronounced, particularly in diplomatic circles. On the 24th of January, 1862, Lord Cowley wrote to Lord John Russell thus:

"I have heard it said so often that the officers going to Mexico with re-enforcements say they are going there to place Archduke Maximilian on the throne of that country, that I have thought it necessary to question Mr. Thouvenel on that subject.

"I asked him if negotiations were pending between France and Austria on the subject of the Archduke Maximilian. His excellency said no, but that negotiations had been commenced by Mexicans alone, who had gone to Vienna for that purpose."

We must confess that this affair, lately so much of a secret, was very suddenly developed; for only three days after Lord Cowley's despatch, Lord John Russell wrote, on the 27th of January, 1862, to the English minister in Mexico as follows:

"Sir: I have received your despatches of the 18th and 28th of November, and have placed them before the Queen. Since I last wrote to you the Emperor of the French has determined to send 3,000 more men to Vera Cruz.

"It is supposed these troops will march to the capital with the French and Spanish troops already in the country. It is said that the Archduke Ferdinand Maximilian will be invited by a number of Mexicans to ascend the throne of Mexico, and that the Mexican people will be rejoiced at this change in the form of their government.

"I have little to add to my instructions upon the subject. If the Mexican people, by a simultaneous movement, place the Austrian archduke upon the throne of Mexico, we have nothing to do with it; that is not in our convention.

"But we cannot forcibly interfere in this affair. Mexicans must consult their own interests."

And this was written in Europe, and talked of in diplomatic circles, two months before our plenipotentiaries tried to treat with Juarez and sent him the ultimatum. This is a mystery to be solved only by a contradictory study. Mr. Billault at this time undertook to quell the alarms of the opposition. The official orator is very plain, precise, and affirmative. Mr. Jules Favre dreaded the project of monarchical restoration. Mr. Billault answered him thus:

"England and Spain have joined us. The same offers have been made to the United States; but the United States, in regard to Mexico, do not seem to concentrate their views upon a simple reparation of damages suffered. Their policy views things differently, and we have decided to act without them. [Very well!]

"Does not this union of three powers fully satisfy you as to the private suppositions upon which your speech is founded? *You persist in seeing certain secret machinations of France, for the benefit of foreign interests, beyond open and avowed facts.* When such suppositions are affirmed, you ought at least to have some proof of them, and you have none!"

Mr. Jules Favre is afraid the convention of the 31st of October covers some ambiguity, and cannot give full faith to complaisant interpretations. Mr. Billault replies to him:

"The convention agreed upon by the three powers is plain and precise. The aim is to exact from Mexico :

"1. A more effectual protection of the persons and property of their subjects.

"2. The execution of obligations contracted towards them by that republic ; and article 2 of the convention adds :

"'The three contracting parties bind themselves to seek for themselves, in the use of coercive measures provided by the present convention, no acquisition of territory, nor any private advantage ; and to exercise in the internal affairs of Mexico no influence of a nature to trespass upon the right of the Mexican nation to choose and freely constitute the form of its government.'

"All that is plain and precise. It clearly explains what the three powers intend to do in common, and what they forbid each other to do. Against such solemn declarations what proofs have you to adduce?"

Mr. Jules Favre anxiously inquires why we should go as far as the city of Mexico. Mr. Billault answers:

"You ask why go as far as the capital? Gentlemen, the topographic and hygienic situation of the country commands it as much as political necessity. To take possession of the coast, and remain there, would be sacrificing our troops to the yellow fever. [That's so ! that's so !] It would be destroying ourselves ; anarchy would reign in the interior, and laugh at France and its futile efforts.

"The decisive blow must be struck at the heart of the power, and, leaving the yellow fever behind us, we must assault a less terrible enemy.

"There, and there only, can we force our rights to be respected, and command respect for our subjects, and the execution of obligations to our country too long delayed. [Good !] That is why our troops must go to the city of Mexico ; and as they left on the 20th of February, they ought to be there now."

Mr. Billault does not stop at these declarations. Urged on by the current of his eloquence and applause of his hearers, he becomes more explicit :

"This principle which we proclaim, this principle, the base of our public right—independence of the popular vote and national sovereignty—we will not violate it in the city of Mexico. We will leave these unfortunates perfectly free ; miserable people, oppressed by governments you praise, that never gave them the securities and blessings which are the rights of civilized societies. If they desire to continue that miserable existence, we will not force a better lot upon them ; but if they will accept a better condition, most certainly we will encourage them with all our sympathies, with all our counsel, with all our moral support."

It is still a question of moral support.

And, finally, to dispel all ridiculous rumors about the throne of Mexico and the Archduke Maximilian, to banish all fancies of idle imaginations, the minister makes this decisive argument to the Chamber:

"Such, gentlemen, is the situation, briefly explained ; and as to the rumors that gave umbrage to the ambassador of her Britannic Majesty, permit me to pass them by. Officers said they were going to put a foreign prince upon the throne of Mexico. What ! do you suppose a great diplomatic secret would be intrusted to the first army officer that might be sent to Mexico? Surely he was not serious!"

In the debate on the address of 1863, Mr. Saligny was accused of having instigated the French government to a monarchical restoration in Mexico. We will not undertake to defend our plenipotentiary against these imputations ; but we must defend truth against conjectures. Did not Mr. Saligny put his name, with that of Mr. Jurien de la Gravière, to the famous convention of Soledad, and thus give his support to the following articles :

"Art. 1. The constitutional government now in power in the Mexican republic having informed the commissioners of the allied powers that it has no need of the assistance so generously offered to the Mexican people, because it has the strength to preserve itself from internal revolt, the allies will resort to treaties to present the reclamations they are charged to make in the name of their respective nations.

"Art. 2. With this intent, the representatives of the allied powers protest that they have no intention to injure the sovereignty and integrity of the Mexican republic. Negotiations will be opened at Orizaba."

This was written on the 19th of February, 1862, over the signatures of the representatives of the allied powers. These principles were subsequently denied ; but the fact is not less serious, inasmuch as it reveals the nature of the instructions given to our plenipotentiaries. The preliminary convention of Soledad is the authorized and official commentary of the convention of the 31st of October.

VII.

The situation is now clearly established. It comes out as evidence, that until the official rejection of the Soledad convention, the French government did not acknowledge as an avowed object and aim the repression of the Mexican republic. The expedition is confined, ostensibly at least, to the prudent limits of a simple revindication. How, then, has it been brought to abandon that policy? By what intrigue has it been impelled to a monarchical crusade? By what association of ideas or facts has it been led to dream of a resurrection of an imperial crown for the benefit of the Archduke Maximilian?

Here we fancy that French policy has left its old initiation, yielded to the solicitations of the court of Spain, and suffered itself to be caught in a net of intrigues, woven for it by its refugees; but it is yet only an apprehension, and we leave it to facts that we are going to produce to contradict or affirm it.

Let us go back some years. As early as the 16th of March, 1860, the Spanish government began to propose its claims against a country "the situation of which could not be worse." Miramon then ruled the republic; but we must go back to the 24th November, 1858, to discover the first thought of a joint intervention in the affairs of Mexico. At that date Mr. Mon began to confer with Mr. Walewski on the necessity of establishing a government and a firm power in those countries.

On the 3d of January, 1859, Mr. Mon again wrote to Mr. Calderon Collantes in these terms: "The thought that I have not been able to make your excellency comprehend is to find out if it is not possible to aid in forming a government in Mexico, which, supported at first by the three powers, might afterwards exist without any assistance."

Would not any one say that this despatch was written the day before the convention of the 31st of October?

Mr. Mon continues: "Will your excellency inform me, if possible, what form is best, and what means most available, to attain this end? Count Walewski and myself have left this question here, in order to resume it at a more convenient season."

Mr. Calderon Collantes, minister of state, writes to Mr. Mon, on the 10th of January, that it is of the utmost importance to establish a strong and durable power in Mexico; but that to persuade Mexico to this, *moral suasion and purely diplomatic discussions are sufficient.*

As to the initiative taken in this grave question by Spain, it is indisputably affirmed in these few lines, borrowed from a despatch of Mr. Calderon Collantes, on the 18th April, 1860:

"Your excellency knows of the attempts made several times by the government of her Majesty to induce England and France to join in the adoption of measures to put an end to the anarchy now exhausting the Mexican republic."

The minister of state in Madrid continued in these terms: "I had a consultation sometime ago, on this grave affair, with Mr. Barrot, the French ambassador. Mr. Barrot transmitted my remarks to the department of foreign affairs of the Emperor, and recently he read me an extract from one of his despatches, which says that the governments of France and England are now disposed to combine their efforts to establish a government in Mexico, to be recognized by the whole nation, and put an end to the painful condition of that unfortunate country.

"Mr. Thouvenel thinks the best way would be to propose a constituent assembly to fix a permanent form of government, and settle all existing difficulties, whatever their nature or importance.

"Her Majesty's wish is that your excellency have an interview with Mr. Thouvenel, to try and contrive some way for the three powers to intervene in the disorders of the Mexican republic. Her Majesty's government thinks that the simple news of this resolution, and the first steps taken, will be enough to encourage the honest people of Mexico, and dispose them to act in favor of the establishment of a government which, without limiting the exercise of legitimate rights and guarantees enjoyed in other civilized countries, may suppress that spirit of rebellion that has caused so much harm to that unhappy country."

See the gentle approach. At first it is only a strong and durable power; nothing is said of a republican form. On the 18th of April, 1860, a republic was considered; two months after, Spain favored a monarchy; and lastly, when everything was ready, as she supposed, a Bourbon was proposed. And thus our policy has been insensibly seduced into the Mexican expedition.

Things were in this condition when Spain took the trouble to draw up a constitution for the reorganization of Mexico, and sent it simultaneously to London and Paris, on the 24th of May, 1860. What caused these plans of intervention, so actively caressed by Spain, so pleasantly received by France, to fail? It was their cool reception by England.

On the 27th of April, 1860, Mr. Isturitz wrote from London to Mr. Calderon Collantes: "In fact, on the 27th of April, 1860, Lord John Russell replied briefly to Mr. Isturitz, in regard to English co-operation, that he would not reject it, if it was 'understood that no force was to be used in the execution' of the projects. In a second interview, Mr. Isturitz insists on a more explicit answer from Lord John Russell. The secretary of state replies, that 'England will require protection to Protestant worship;' to 'which I replied,' adds Mr. Isturitz, 'in that case England cannot rely upon the co-operation of Spain.'"

After this reserved attitude of England, Mr. Thouvenel seems inclined to back out. On the 18th of May, 1860, he declared to Mr. Mon, "that as to force and coercive measures, he is by no means inclined to use them."

This is not all; on the 2d of June, 1860, Mr Barrot, our representative at Madrid, handed a despatch to the minister of state, in which the question of mediation is considered by data and instructions from Mr. Thouvenel.

"Moreover, it is understood," says that despatch, "that the steps to be taken must be of a friendly nature, to the exclusion of all forcible coercion."

This period of projected intervention may be considered as concluded, after the solemn declaration of Mr. Thouvenel.

Henceforth Spain hurries her military preparations, and sends *reserved* instructions to the captain general of Cuba.

Here the diplomatic history of the Mexican question has a large void; for a year passes before a Spanish despatch, of the 6th of September, 1861, revives diplomatic negotiations upon the Mexican question. A few days previous, Mr. Mon, alluding to the troubles in the United States, wrote to his government: "The government ought to know that this is a good opportunity to awaken old memories, and place upon the throne of Mexico a prince of the Bourbon blood, or intimately connected with that house."

We must pay strict attention to this despatch, because it will subsequently explain the sudden defection of the Spanish government.

On the 6th of September, 1861, the Spanish government instructs Mr. Mon to inform the French government that a Spanish expedition is fitting out against Mexico, and that special orders have already been sent to the captain general of Cuba. It was a sort of demurrer in the case, and Mr. Thouvenel, forgetting what he had said about coercive measures, is attracted within the orbit of Spanish policy. And it is not alone in regard to the expedition that this policy prevails, but also to its aim; and, in spite of the convention of 31st of October, in spite of instructions to Mr. Dubois de Saligny and Jurien de la Gravière, in spite of Mr Billault's declarations in the legislature, the Mexican republic is definitely condemned, and Spain's dream of monarchy is debated, not as a possible event, but as a project irrevocably determined on. On the 11th of October, 1861, Mr. Thouvenel wrote to our ambassador in London:

"I have told the English ambassador that I agreed perfectly with his government on one point. I agreed with Lord John Russell that our coercion of Mexico should be caused by our complaints against that government, and that the prevention of their repetition was the only ostensible excuse for a convention."

Is the word *ostensible* intentional? The minister continues:

"But it seems to me useless to object to legal participation in the events caused by our operations. * * * It is lawful to suppose that if the result of the American crisis should be a separation of the north and south, the two new confederations would seek compensations on Mexican territory, offered by anarchy to their rivalry. England would not remain indifferent to such an event, and the only thing, in my opinion, that could prevent it, would be the establishment of a new government in Mexico, strong enough to prevent its internal derangement."

It is evident from these declarations of Mr. Thouvenel, uttered twenty days before the convention, and five months previous to the solemn protestations of Mr. Billault, that it was no longer only to avenge our countrymen; and when we compare this declaration of Mr. Thouvenel with that of Mr. Mon on the crisis in the United States, which we have just quoted, we readily perceive the connecting link of the two kindred policies.

VIII.

We remember the clear, precise, and affirmative declarations of Mr. Billault. In 1864 the times and ministers have changed, and policy must change. The entire disinterested nature of the expedition must now be explained. As events have been hurried to the contradiction of Mr. Billault's declarations, Mr. Rouher must explain the unfailing unity of our policy in the Mexican question. Thus he is led, in contradiction to his eloquent predecessor, to prove that present facts were not unexpected, and that France foresaw them, if it did not will them, from the beginning of the expedition.

On the 12th of May, 1864, Mr. Rouher, in reply to Mr. Jules Favre, takes a retrospective observation, and lets a confession escape, in strong contrast to the previous declarations of Mr. Billault. He says:

"We did not stop at vain recriminations; we did not accept insignificant satisfaction, but we resolved from the first to march to Mexico, if our honor and the protection of our countrymen required it, in spite of temporary checks, of rude blame, and mean calumny; for after the situation was changed, despite the counsel of glory, we did not abandon the way we had traced out. We have neither been exalted nor discouraged. We came to Mexico to demand satisfaction of our honor, and overthrow a man who had dared to outrage France. We undertook to make peace in the country; we have reorganized the finances, the administration, and the army of that long unhappy nation, and we have invited it to choose its own government."

The expedition, then, according to Mr. Rouher, had started with the determination to overthrow Juarez, and substitute another government.

But that is not all.

Mr. Rouher expressed himself thus, in the house, on the 28th of January, 1864:

"We told the truth at first; it was satisfaction for our wrongs, protection to our countrymen, with the probable necessity of going on to the city of Mexico. If we go to Mexico, the Juarez government cannot be sustained; there must be a new one.

"The form and conditions of this government must be planned by prudent cabinets, determined to engage in a distant expedition."

Strange inconsistency!

The existence of a government with which our plenipotentiaries were to treat was doubted. There must have been a previous determination to transform the expedition into a crusade for monarchy, exclusive of outside machinations. In discussing the preliminaries of the expedition, Mr. Rouher quotes a despatch of Thouvenel to Count Flahault, on the 11th of October, 1861. Here it is:

"But the interest we have," says Mr. Thouvenel, "in the regeneration of this country does not allow us to neglect anything to insure its success. As to a form of government, any that would offer proper guarantees would suit us; and I believe England has no preference, and has come to no conclusion. But if the Mexicans themselves, weary of their former miserable governments, should return to the instincts of their race, and form a monarchy, I think we ought to aid them, yet leave them free to select whatever form of government they may think most conducive to their happiness.

"Continuing these ideas in the form of a confidential conversation, I added that in case of such an event, the government of the Emperor, entirely disinterested, did not propose a prince of the imperial family, but, willing to satisfy all parties, would be pleased to see the Mexicans select a prince of the house of Austria."

The proposal of the Archduke Maximilian for the restored Mexican throne is thus frankly made. Then, we ask, how could Mr. Billault, five months later, call the reports from America, about Maximilian's accession, ridiculous stories of silly officers?

Mr. Rouher next read a despatch from Mr. Thouvenel to Mr. Barrot, on the 15th of October, 1864, concerning the projects of monarchical restoration:

"In my despatch to Mr. Flahault, you will find the observations I made to Lord Cowley on this point, by which I have attempted to prove that though we assumed no direct responsibility in internal Mexican affairs, we would not discourage their efforts to form a regular and substantial government, and that the three powers ought to aid in this work of regeneration. In this way I was led to mention to Lord Cowley the possibility of a monarchy in Mexico, as you will see in my despatch to Mr. Flahault."

Mr. Rouher adds these characteristic details:

"Mr. Thouvenel continues. He relates his conversation with Mr. Mon, the Spanish ambassador in Paris; he acknowledges, in case of a monarchy in Mexico, France will accept the Austrian archduke, thus rejecting Spain's proposal to put a Bourbon upon that throne."

From that moment the zeal of Spain became less warm; her troops are already on the way to Vera Cruz; she is obliged to sign the convention then negotiating; but since she cannot slip a Bourbon prince upon the Mexican throne, she will withdraw from the business as soon as she can; and France, pushed forward and then abandoned by her two allies, will be left alone to pursue her solitary way to the city of Mexico with a crown in her knapsack.*

Such is history!

IX.

There was an unfortunate concurrence of circumstances to hasten the resolutions of our government. While Mr. Saligny was writing from Mexico, about the necessity of establishing a firm government there, a band of Mexican refugees, one of whom had served Miramon, began their monarchical campaign in Europe. Their part, even before the October convention, had assumed an official character. Almonte was the evil genius of our policy in this circumstance.

Mr. Billault was wrong to treat this band of refugees, on their way to Miramar or Vienna, so contemptuously in his speech in 1862, for not long afterwards, Almonte, their chief, appeared at Vera Cruz with a letter from Napoleon III, and made this celebrated declaration to the Mexicans:

"I have reason to know the desires of the allies, particularly of the French, to establish a firm government based upon peace and good morals in our unhappy country, and through our own instrumentality alone."

The refugees act with extreme prudence, but official documents contradict them. On the 9th of April, 1862, Mr. Saligny and Mr. Jurien de la Gravière addressed this note to General Doblado:

"When General Almonte left France, the government of his Majesty the Emperor of the French knew that hostilities had commenced in Mexico. General Almonte offered to conciliate his countrymen, and make them understand the benevolent intention of European intervention. His offer was accepted by the government of his Majesty, and the general was not only authorized but *invited* to repair to Mexico"

There is, then, no doubt about the official character of his mission.

On the 23d of March, 1862, General Prim wrote from Orizaba to Admiral Jurien de la Gravière about the refugees as follows:

"The act of introducing political refugees into the interior of the country, to plan a conspiracy that may destroy the existing government as well as its political system, while you pretend to be friendly and are waiting for a conference, is unexampled, and I am heartily astonished at it.

"If you have orders from your government, I must say I do not see the wisdom, justice, and grandeur of imperial policy; nor do I see any conciliation of the Emperor towards England and Spain in such a proceeding. I am sorry to say this, but your Mexican policy forces me to it, and I must also say it will cool the friendly relations of England and Spain towards France. I regret to say this, because nobody has more respect for the Emperor than I, and nobody loves France and Frenchmen more than I do."

General Prim writes to his government the 17th March in the same tone. General Lorencez had arrived with re-enforcements; there was a mutiny, and General Prim wrote:

"Articles in French papers announcing that the object of the imperial troops is to put Maximilian on the throne of Mexico, will not only cause a difficulty between France and Mexico, but a coolness between Spain and England and the imperial government. Almonte, Haro, Ramarez, and other monarch-makers arrived in Vera Cruz at the same time with General Lorencez. The Mexican government, knowing this, has sent me a note announcing its intention to prosecute these exiled enemies of the nation, who have returned to Mexico for criminal purposes."

The part played by these Mexican refugees in Europe, and their influence on French diplomacy, inducing a monarchical crusade beyond the ocean, are candidly expressed in a despatch of the Spanish minister to General Prim. We find the following lines in that despatch, dated Madrid, 22d of January, 1862:

"The Emperor of the French has informed the government of the Queen, by her ambassador, that he intends to increase the Mexican expedition by 3,000 men. The object of this seems to be to get enough men to march to the capital if necessary, to shorten operations and abridge the delay of troops in that country.

"As your instructions are clear and formal, I have no additions to make to them. But your excellency must know that the establishment of a monarchy in Mexico is daily increasing.

"Some of the natives of that country—and this deserves particular notice—now residing in Europe are engaged in that business."

All this while Mr. Saligny enters into the full spirit of the expedition in the part he has to play, and gets up a kind of side game with General Serrano against England. In a letter of the 24th of November, 1861, he speaks of the "incredible candor of perfidious Albion." The word *candor* is underlined. In a letter of the 39th of November he promises "proofs of the duplicity and stupidity of the British minister." He announces "curious revelations of a chimerical alliance between Mexico, England, and the United States against France and Spain;" and on the 23d he had already sent detailed accounts of the regular forces in Mexico. Alas! the 5th of May shows the result of all this; the blood of our soldiers who fell at Guadalupe will cry out against the advocates of Mexican emigration; and that order of General Lorencez, the betrayed and conquered general, will accuse the folly of ambition and the credulity of our policy.

On the 27th May General Lorencez said to his soldiers: "Your march on Mexico has been stopped by unforeseen obstacles, which we did not expect from what had been told us; they said Puebla invited you within its walls, and that its inhabitants would welcome you with flowers.

"With the confidence inspired by these assurances we appeared before Puebla; we found it bristling with barricades and commanded by a fortress armed with every means of de-fence."

This is the answer to the advocates of immigration; these sad lines dissipate the illusion and increase the bitterness of defeat.

We will now draw this first part of our labor to a close; we have pointed out the two currents that carried our policy into the dangers of the Mexican question; we have seen Mr. Billault reduce the expedition to a simple revindication of injured interests, and the secret conferences of diplomacy opening the doors to the projects of monarchical restoration. We have seen France first oppose the application of force in the restoration, and afterwards yield to the solicitations of Spain and the active manœuvres of Mexican immigration. Is that all? Alas! no. On the 9th of April, 1862, the alliance is broken at Orizaba. It is broken on account of the presence of the refugees who have already constituted a secret government; it is broken because Mr. Saligny wants to march on Mexico, when the Spanish plenipotentiary and the English minister declare that no deed "is of a nature to justify this resolution." (See report of conference held at Orizaba on the 9th of April.) It is broken, in fine, "because the three plenipotentiaries cannot agree upon the interpretation to be given to the convention of the 31st of October, 1861." (See note addressed by the plenipotentiaries to General Doblado on the 9th of April, 1862.)

X.

England never wanted the establishment of a monarchy, and Spain, after tugging France in by a Bourbon, was ready to quit on the first pretext.

Spain had long been preparing for a retreat, and General Prim was let into the secret. Saligny accuses him of wanting the crown for himself, and would not play Don Quixote for another's benefit. This was at the Orizaba conference on the 9th of April. General Prim, who must have known the Emperor's views in regard to Mexico when he met him at Vichy, wrote to Napoleon, from Orizaba, the 17th of March, the following letter:

"ORIZABA, *March* 17, 1862.

"SIRE: Your Imperial Majesty has deigned to write me an autograph letter, which, on account of the benevolent words it contains for my person, will be a title of honor for my posterity. ° ° ° ° ° ° ° °

"As to just reclamations, there can be no difference of opinions among the commissioners of the allied powers, and there will be less among the commanders of your forces and those of her Catholic Majesty. But the arrival of General Almonte, of the former minister, Haro, of Father Miranda and other Mexican refugees at Vera Cruz, with the idea of creating a monarchy in favor of Prince Maximilian of Austria, to be supported by the forces of your Imperial Majesty, tends to create a position difficult for all, and particularly hard for the general-in-chief of the Spanish troops, who, according to instructions from his government, will see himself obliged to refrain from contributing to the realization of the views of your Imperial Majesty if they are really to raise an Austrian archduke to the throne of Mexico.

"I have, moreover, the profound conviction that the partisans of monarchy are very few in this country, and it is reasonable, because this country has never known monarchy in the person of the Spanish monarchs, only in the viceroys, who ruled as they pleased in those distant times.

"Monarchy has not left here the immense interests of nobility, such as exist in Europe; it has not left moral interests nor anything to make the present generation wish for the re-establishment of monarchy, which it has not known. The vicinity of the United States, and their severe reprobation of monarchy, has contributed to create a hate for it here. In spite of constant disorder and agitation, the republic, which has existed more than forty years, has created habits, customs, and even a certain republican language hard to destroy.

"For these reasons and others that cannot escape the attention of your Imperial Majesty, you will understand that the general opinion of this country is against monarchy. If logic does not demonstrate it, facts prove it; for during the two months that the flags of the allied forces floated over Vera Cruz, and now that we occupy Cordoba, Orizaba and Tehuacan, important towns where there is no Mexican force, the partisans of monarchy have made no demonstrations to tell of their existence.

"Far be it from me to suppose that your Imperial Majesty has not the power to erect a throne in Mexico for the house of Austria. Your Majesty directs the destinies of a great nation, rich in brave and intelligent men, rich in resources, and that manifests its enthusiasm to second the views of your Imperial Majesty. You can easily carry Maximilian to Mexico and crown him King; but the King will find no adherents in the country but conservative chiefs, who had no thought of establishing monarchy when they were in power, but wish it now, when they are conquered, scattered and exiled.

"A few rich men are willing to receive a foreign monarch who comes supported by your Majesty's soldiers, but the monarch will have nothing to sustain him when the time shall come for your soldiers to withdraw, and he will fall from the throne, as others will fall, when the mantle of your Imperial Majesty shall cease to protect and defend them. I know that your Imperial Majesty, moved by a high sentiment of justice, will not force this country to change its institutions in such a radical manner unless the country desires it and requests it. But the chiefs of the conservative party, who landed at Vera Cruz, say it will only be necessary to consult the high classes of society and not mind the others; but that inspires a fear that violence may be offered to the national will.

"The English troops that were to come to Orizaba re-embarked as soon as they heard that a greater number of French troops were coming than had been agreed upon in the convention. Your Majesty will appreciate the importance of this withdrawal.

"I ask a thousand pardons of your Imperial Majesty for having dared to write such a long letter, but I thought the only true reply to your Majesty's kindness to me would be to tell the truth, and the whole truth, upon the political state of the country as I understand it. In doing this I have not only done my duty, but I have obeyed the great, noble, and respectful attachment I feel for the person of your Imperial Majesty.

"GENERAL PRIM, *Count Reuss.*"

The real design of the expedition, at first carefully concealed, afterwards timidly confessed, and now openly announced, comes out in relief. One remark, however, must be made before entering on the era begun by the accession of the Mexican Emperor. We did not go to Mexico only to put up a throne for an archduke; he is only the instrument of a theory, of a preconceived plan.

XI.

Mr. Billault was then near the truth when he insisted on reducing the expedition to mean proportions; when, in 1863, he mentioned the monarchy as an unexpected event, caused by a concourse of circumstances; and Mr. Larabure was true in his report of 1864, on supplementary credits, when he expressed himself thus:

"We must not conceal that these frequent expeditions disturb the nation. To be just, let us say at once, that the Mexican expedition now pressing most heavily upon our exchequer and public opinion grew to its present importance by a concatenation of unfortunate incidents which the government could neither foresee nor prevent."

When the Emperor himself said, in his discourse from the throne in 1863, "Distant expeditions, now so much criticised, have not been the results of premeditated plans; force of circumstances have brought them about, but they are not to be regretted;" he only half revealed his thought, for he destroyed his argument, *the force of circumstances*, in his famous letter to General Forey on the 3d of July, 1862:

"FONTAINEBLEAU, *July* 3, 1862.

"MY DEAR GENERAL: There will be people to ask you why we are going to waste so many men, and spend so much money, in establishing a regular government in Mexico.

"In the present state of the civilized world, the prosperity of America is not indifferent to Europe, for America supports our manufactories and keeps alive our commerce. We are interested in keeping the United States a powerful and prosperous republic; but it will not be interesting to us if it takes possession of the whole of the Gulf of Mexico, and governs the West Indies and South America, thus controlling the entire produce of the New World. We now see by sad experience how precarious an industry is that which is compelled to seek its raw material in a single market, the changes of which so seriously affect it.

"Now if Mexico preserves its independence and maintains the integrity of its territory; if a firm government be established there by the aid of France, we shall give to the Latin race beyond the ocean its ancient strength and power; we shall have guaranteed the security of our own and the Spanish colonies in the West Indies; we shall have extended our benevolent influence to the centre of America, and that influence, while it makes a market for our fabrics, secures us the material indispensable to our manufactures.

"Mexico, thus regenerated, will ever be favorable to us, not only from gratitude, but also because its interests will coincide with ours, and because it will find a support in its relations with European powers.

"NAPOLEON."

After examining attentively a file of the *Moniteur*, after having collated the documents and studied the evidence, we have come to the conclusion that the above letter contains the true secret of the Mexican expedition. The continued expansion of the United States towards South America has frightened Europe. We had to build a dike against it out of a restored throne in Mexico; and our wrongs furnished ample excuse for the expedition. The merit of the Emperor's letter to General Forey is the acknowledgment of a political theory, and the elevation of the expedition into a system.

XII.

The question becomes grand in this light. It is no longer a question of contest with the refractory population of Mexico; it is a rivalry, a contest perhaps, between the Old World and the New; so Mr. Berryer proclaimed prophetically in his speech on the supplementary credits of 1864:

"Nothing afflicts me more than the present strife in the United States. I desire peace with the least possible injury to each party in that great country. But in whatever way the civil war may terminate, we must not forget that the United States will be the ruling power in North America, and that we have offended her by our Mexican expedition. Those who deny this have not studied the documents under their eyes, and the historic facts of the last three years. I do not allude to that profound sentiment, the vital nerve of political existence in the United States, called the Monroe doctrine: a sentiment opposed to European intervention in American affairs. I do not speak of that. But how did you begin the Mexican expedition? With the convention of the 31st of October. And what did you say in that convention? Yielding to the wish of England, the United States are invited to join the convention. And in a letter of the 25th of July, 1862, I read that it was necessary to form a new government in Mexico, just to diminish the influence of the States of the north, and prevent them from trespassing upon South America. Thus the Mexican expedition was got up to oppose the United States.

"I exaggerate nothing; I simply tell the truth. Read the letter of July, 1862, and you will see that the development of the United States is to be arrested.

"Well, suppose you succeeded; when the civil wars in the United States are over, and that government saw a new nation by her side, sustained at an immense expense and sacrifice by a foreign power, hostilities would certainly break out. The northern republic would not tolerate an imperial monarchy in Mexico, and war would certainly be the consequence. This is the dangerous, impracticable situation to which you invite Prince Maximilian, and which will be ruinous to France if she persists in the enterprise. [Applause.]"

Thus the question is put upon new ground by the imperial letter and Mr. Berryer's eloquent commentary. These are the true conditions of the problem as France has propounded them by going to Vera Cruz, and as Mr. Seward has accepted them, when he wrote to the Spanish minister, at Washington, on the 14th of October, 1861, "That he acknowledged the right of Spain to make war on Mexico to defend her rights, and obtain satisfaction for injuries; but that, *as it was a question, in the eventualities of which entered the possibilities of a conflict with the United States and European powers*, he had carefully endeavored to avoid that possibility."

The manner in which the Mexican question has been officially laid down since General Forey's departure for Mexico, and Maximilian's accession, places France and the United States in new relations to each other. We must speak without circumlocution. The continuance of occupation is a political danger; is it a diplomatic duty?

XIII.

What are our obligations to the new empire? That is the interesting question now to French policy.

On the 10th of April, 1864, Archduke Maximilian received the Mexican deputation at his castle of Miramar, and announced his acceptance in these terms:

"Thanks to the magnanimity of the Emperor of the French, the necessary guarantees to fix the independence and prosperity of the country upon a solid basis are now given."

But, properly speaking, this is not an engagement; if we are bound, it is less by these vague effusions of a happy candidate, than by the precise terms of the diplomatic convention of the 10th of April, 1864. Now what does that convention say?

"The government of his Majesty the Emperor of the French, and of his majesty the emperor of Mexico, animated by a like desire to assure the re-establishment of order in Mexico, and to consolidate the new empire, have determined to settle by a convention:

"ART. 1. The French troops now in Mexico shall be reduced to 25,000 men, as soon as possible, including the foreign legion.

"That body shall remain temporarily in Mexico, to protect the interests for which intervention was instituted, under the conditions regulated by the following articles:

"ART. 2. The French troops shall evacuate Mexico in proportion as his majesty the emperor of Mexico can organize the troops necessary to replace them.

"ART. 3. The foreign legion in the service of France, composed of 8,000 men, shall remain in Mexico six years after all the other French forces are recalled, according to article 3. From that time the said legion shall go into the service and pay of the Mexican government. The Mexican government reserves the right of shortening the term of service of the foreign legion in Mexico.

"ART. 10. The indemnity to be paid to France by the Mexican government, for supporting the troops of the army corps from the 1st of July, 1864, is fixed at 1,000 francs per annum for each man."

At the time of the debate on the supplementary credits, 27th January, Mr. Berryer said:

"Has the government bound itself to furnish money or soldiers to that country? Are we bound, or are we not?"

Mr. Rouher answered: "If you had read Mr. Larrabure's report you would have known."

Now here is the report:

"The government of the Emperor declares at this time that it is under no obligation to leave a body of troops in Mexico, nor to guarantee any loan. It declares he has no reason to think it may be necessary to increase the French forces now on Mexican soil."

In the session of the 27th of January Mr. Rouher again said:

"In treating with the sovereign, the government contracts no permanent and indefinite responsibility for the maintenance of an empire in Mexico."

The convention of Miramar, the most important articles of which we have quoted, appeared officially in the papers of the 16th of April, 1864. It was quite natural for it to become the subject of an interesting debate in the discussion of appropriations. So on the 11th of May Mr. Berryer busies himself with the obligations and charges imposed by the convention in respect to the finances and military affairs of our army. Mr. Rouher answers him, but instead of sticking to the convention, he gives a brilliant picture of the condition of Mexico.

Let us listen to him a while.

Mr. ROUHER, minister of state, continues:

Mr. Berryer has discussed the whole Mexican question in his speech on the general appropriation. That question has caused many unfavorable apprehensions in this house.

When we debated it last year they said: Your San Louis Potosi expedition is madness. You are going to scatter the French army over four hundred square leagues. The Mexican army, under Juarez, Uragua, Doblado, will whip our scattered battalions.

M. THIERS, (interrupting.) They did not say that.

M. ROUHER. The honorable gentleman has only to refer to Mr. Jules Favre's speech, and he will see what has been said.

Mr. FAVRE. I have never doubted our military success.

Mr. ROUHER. They represented the expedition as marching contrary to the wishes of the Mexican people.

A voice, (interrupting.) And they were right.

M. ROUHER. You say they were right? Have you forgotten the triumphal march of General Bazaine over those four hundred leagues; our arrival at Guanahuato, Queretaro, and San Louis Potosi; the shouts of welcome wherever the French flag was seen? Some blind people can see no truth in historical facts. [Good, good.]

The San Louis Potosi expedition, that you blame, was a triumphal march. [Renewed applause.]

A little further on the minister exclaimed:

"Here is a new empire just beginning, a sovereign not yet seated on his throne, a government not yet organized, and capitalists have given it nine millions per annum, when old governments cannot negotiate their loans. Is not this a token of foreign confidence? There is no doubt that when Maximilian goes from Vera Cruz to Mexico, amid the enthusiastic demonstrations of the people" —— [Disturbance on some seats.]

Mr. PICARD. Then recall the army.

Recall the army! That was evidently the logical conclusion for peace.

Yet the convention existed; it was known; the government must explain its meaning officially. On the 12th of May Mr. Jules Favre grew urgent, irresistible:

"You know, gentlemen," said he, "what arrangement has been made. A new plan has been discovered to pay the expenses of the war; they must be paid by the victorious power, for France issues sixty-six millions in bonds, that are only notes of accommodation, over its signature. [Exclamations.]

"The convention of the 16th April, in the *Moniteur*, has regulated the stay of the French troops in Mexico. We are very far from the declarations of Mr. Larrabure's report: how long will our troops remain in Mexico? until the new empire shall be firmly established; that, in reality, is the business of France. Maximilian's empire must be consolidated. France is deceived when they tell her the expedition is over; it has hardly commenced.

[Confused noises.] We leave 25,000 men in Mexico for an indefinite time; political circumstances alone can fix the day for the recall of our troops. It is said they will be paid by the Mexican government—a deplorable thing for France. [Noise.] Our troops are thus put in the pay of a foreign prince; they will obey a foreign policy; they may be used in enterprises, in adventures, in perils."

Here Mr. Rouher takes the floor and gives the convention, and the interpretations it may provoke, their right place:

"We must once more consider the Mexican question. The honorable gentleman (Mr. Jules Favre) has told you that the treaty concluded with the emperor Maximilian violated engagements we had with you; he has spoken to you of the threats of American intervention, suspended, like the sword of Damocles, over the new Mexican empire.

"While I listened to the ironical eulogies given to the eloquence of the government orators, as they painted gay pictures of promised prosperity to Mexico, little moved by them, I was patiently reading the Mexican Courrier that I had just received; and here is what I read:

"'The general condition of Mexico is daily improving, as the masses comprehend and appreciate the generous views of the Emperor towards them. Resistance, now only local, has entirely lost its nationality. The bandits fly at the approach of our troops; and whenever they are caught they are cut to pieces. It has, in fact, relapsed into brigandage, very annoying to the inoffensive people who are the chief sufferers; but this will soon be suppressed by a well-organized police system.

"Confidence has greatly increased in the last month or two. People of all classes and all opinions come to the capital from every part of the country, meet and pass, forgetting their former hostility, and mingling in similar sentiments, with oblivion of the past and faith in the future. Under such circumstances, with the support of the government of the Emperor and the aid of European capital, Mexico cannot fail soon to enter into a way of national prosperity, by which Europe will be the first to profit.'"

Several voices: Who wrote it?

Mr. Rouher. It is signed by Mr. Montholon.

We will not spoil this brilliant picture by untimely reflections. He then continues:

"But they say the treaty contains promises contrary to our declarations. What does the treaty say? First, that the army shall be reduced to 25,000 men. The expedition is over, and 10,000 of our men will return by the 1st of January, 1865. As to the other 15,000 men, we declare they are to remain temporarily in Mexico to protect the interests of France, and the interests that induced the intervention."

Mr. Gueroult. Please read the treaty.

Mr. Rouher. I have not got it; but if the honorable gentleman will give it to me, I will read it to the house.

Mr. Gueroult. I have not got it either; but I think the time for the return of our troops was left to the emperor Maximilian.

Mr. Rouher. The honorable gentleman is mistaken; I will give the sense of the treaty from memory:

Article 1st says the army shall be reduced to 25,000 men, who will remain in Mexico to protect our interests there. So 25,000 men remain for no fixed time—till France chooses to recall them. Now, do you call this indefinite? No. The emperor of Mexico reserves the right to demand the return of our troops, in proportion as the Mexican army shall be organized.

Mr. Gueroult. But we can't stay so long.

A voice. No interruption!

Mr. Rouher. Does Mr. Gueroult know the facts? Does he know that there is already a national army of 25,000 men in Mexico, and does he not see that it is for the general interest to withdraw these troops, so expensive to the emperor of Mexico? A Mexican army is organizing. Mr. Berryer declared yesterday it would cost the Mexican government thirty-seven millions this year. A national army then exists. Our soldiers will return as soon as our interests no longer require their presence there. Each day brings this period nearer, and it will be equally welcome to both nations.

The treaty contains nothing contrary to the declarations of the legislature; and if some are pained at our stay in Mexico, I care little about them, for they are revolutionists, who would like to see the country again as it was in the time of Juarez. [Very good, very good.] The treaty is above criticism. It contains nothing but what conforms to the thoughts expressed by the legislative body in the address. [Good, good.]

Thus, in 1864, Mr. Rouher was sorry to see opposition to the prolongation of our stay in Mexico, because all who opposed it *were revolutionists, eager to deliver the country over to the agitations of the Juarez times*, which means that the prompt return of our army was impossible, in spite of the allay of passion and increasing prosperity of the Mexican empire; in spite of the brilliant picture he himself had drawn.

XIV.

The dark apprehensions of 1864 were fortunately dispelled by the bright prospects in the beginning of 1865. We find ourselves in presence of wishes, hopes, and promises. The good wishes are thus expressed in the address of 1865 :

"The legislative body believes with you, sire, that the most wisely governed nations cannot always avoid external complications; and when they do come, they must be met firmly and without illusion. The distant expeditions to China, Cochin-China, and Mexico, succeeding each other, have disturbed many people in France on account of their expense and sacrifice. We acknowledge that they are calculated to inspire respect for our subjects and our flag abroad, and tend to develop our commerce; and we shall be happy to see the good results realized that your Majesty has induced us to hope for."

This hope is explained in the *exposé* of the condition of the empire of that year, where we find the following lines :

"The emperor Maximilian has assumed the crown offered to him by the national will, and his arrival has happily put an end to the provisional situation of Mexico.. The emperor's reception in the capital, and all through the country, by all classes of people, and the support of influential men of all parties, leave no doubt about the wishes of an immense majority of the Mexican people.

"The new sovereign will gain strength and confidence by these manifestations, which will enable him to complete the great and generous mission he has so resolutely accepted. The pacification of an extensive country, where robbery was sheltered by the banner of a political party, could not be accomplished in a single day; yet, thanks to the soldiers of our expeditions who have penetrated every part of the country, this is being rapidly accomplished, and so the return of our forces from that country has already begun, and will continue, as the object of intervention permits. Functionaries from the different branches of our administration have been placed at the disposal of the Mexican government, at its request, to assist in the interior organization of affairs."

The promise offered is found in this solemn declaration of the imperial discourse for the session of 1865 :

"Thus all of our expeditions are drawing to a close; our land troops have evacuated China; the navy can protect our settlements in Cochin-China; our army in Africa is going to be reduced; that in Mexico is now returning; the Roman garrison will soon return; and when we close the temple of war, we can proudly inscribe these words upon a new triumphal arch :

"A la gloire des armées Francaises pour les victoires remportées en Europe, en Asie, en Afrique, et en Amérique.

("To the glory of the French armies for victories gained in Europe, Asia, Africa, and America.)

"Let us devote ourselves quietly to peaceful labors.

"The new throne is gaining strength in Mexico; the country is becoming quiet; its immense resources are being developed. This is the happy result of the bravery of our soldiers, of the good sense of the Mexican people, and of the intelligence and energy of the sovereign!"

GEORGES JAURET.

Mr. Romero to Mr. Seward.

[Translation.—Unofficial.]

WASHINGTON, *February* 21, 1866.

MY DEAR SIR: I have the honor to enclose you two extracts from a paper published in the city of Mexico, under the title of "*Diario del Imperio,*" the organ of the usurper Maximilian, in its numbers of the 20th and 22d of January last, containing four letters from Don Antonio Lopez de Santa Anna, who has several times been President of the Mexican republic, showing the part he has taken in the French intervention of that republic.

I am, sir, very respectfully, your obedient servant,

M. ROMERO.

Hon. WILLIAM H. SEWARD, *&c.*, *&c.*, *&c.*

[Enclosure No. 1.]

[From the Diario del Imperio, of January 20, 1866.]

DOCUMENTS FOR THE HISTORY OF MEXICO.

Antonio Lopez de Santa Anna, well-merited of the country, General of Division, Grand Master of the national and distinguished order of Guadalupe, Knight of the Grand Cross of the royal and distinguished order of Charles III, and President of the Mexican republic, to all who may see these presents greeting:

Being authorized by the Mexican nation to constitute it under the form of government I may think most convenient to assure its territorial integrity and national independence in the most advantageous and permanent manner, according to the full powers with which I am invested, and considering that no government is more suitable to a nation than that to which it has been accustomed for centuries and which has formed its peculiar customs;

Therefore, and to this end, placing full confidence in the patriotism intelligence, and zeal of Don José Maria Gutierrez de Estrada, I confer upon him, by these presents, the full powers necessary to enter into arrangements, and make the proper offers near the courts of London, Paris, Madrid, and Vienna, to obtain from those governments, or from any one of them, the establishment of a monarchy, derived from any of the royal races of those powers, under qualifications and conditions to be established by special instructions.

In faith whereof, I have caused these presents to be issued, signed by my hand, authorized by the seal of the nation and countersigned by the minister of relations, all under the proper reserve, in the national palace of Mexico, on the first of July, eighteen hundred and fifty-four.

A. L. DE SANTA ANNA.

[Enclosure No. 2]

ST. THOMAS, *November* 30, 1861.

MY VERY DEAR FRIEND: The news you have been kind enough to communicate to me, in your esteemed favor of the 31st October, received by the last mail, gave me very great pleasure, because it is so interesting that, if it can be realized, our country will be saved from ruin.

God grant that our dreams may come to pass as soon as possible!

The candidate you mention (his Imperial Highness Archduke Ferdinand Maximilian) is unexceptionable, and I therefore hasten to give my approbation. Do me the favor, then, to inform him of it, as well as our friends, but with all reserve, for you well know that in politics there are things that must not be published before the proper time, on account of the harm that might be caused.

I think the allied forces will reach Vera Cruz early in next January, and their arrival will be a cause of great rejoicing to all good Mexicans, because they will not be regarded as a threatening enemy, but as benefactors, to save them from the worst of tyrannies.

Public opinion will, undoubtedly, soon pronounce in favor of whatever suits the people.

Convinced that the time to act has come, I am ready to return immediately to my native land, determined to labor with all my strength till the realization of the undertaking is completed. I will let you know of my departure from this island by the mail of the 17th of December, and I will tell you where to address your letters to me.

Now you see, my friend, I am not dozing when the work is to be commenced, and my acts accord with my words.

If I am permitted to see my country constituted in a way to make it prosperous and happy in the future before I close my eyes in death, I shall be extremely gratified.

Don't fail to send me all the news you get.

Your most obedient servant,

ANTONIO LOPEZ DE SANTA ANNA.

His Excellency Don JOSE MARIA GUTIERREZ DE ESTRADA.

[Enclosure No. 3.]

[From the Diario del Imperio, of January 22, 1866.]

Santa Anna to Maximilian.

ST. THOMAS, *December* 22, 1863.

SIRE: When I heard that a considerable number of my fellow-countrymen, actuated by the purest patriotism, had fixed upon your Royal Highness to be called to the throne of

Mexico, my soul overflowed with pleasure. If it had been in my power to accompany the Mexican commission, your Imperial Highness would have heard from the mouth of one of the noblemen of independence, from one who held for many years the first place among his fellow-citizens, the ratification of what the worthy president of the country expressed with so much eloquence and sincerity.

Yes, sire, in having the honor to greet your Imperial Highness, with the rest of my countrymen, as the emperor of Mexico, and to offer you, respectfully, my humble services, I can assure you, without flattery, that my attachment to your august person is boundless; and since distance deprives me of the pleasure of appearing personally in your presence, my pen will do that duty from my present place of residence, hoping your Imperial Highness will receive the expression of my sentiments with your accustomed benevolence.

I may also assure your Imperial Highness that the voice raised in Mexico to proclaim your respected name is not the voice of a party. An immense majority of the nation desire to restore the empire of the Montezumas, with your Imperial Highness at its head, believing it to be the only remedy for existing ills, and the ultimate anchor of its hopes. Accept, then, in absolute confidence, the enthusiastic Mexican vote, and come courageously to the Mexican shores, certain of receiving the demonstrations of love and profound respect, believing, at the same time, that your agreeable presence will suffice to restore harmony throughout the land. The occasion is propitious. Your Imperial Highness can make the Mexicans happy by placing your name among those of the heroes blessed by posterity.

The vast, beautiful, and fertile soil of Mexico abounds in elements to form a first-class empire on the American continent; consequently it is no insignificant power that is offered to your Imperial Highness. True, the country has suffered from anarchy for half a century; but under the auspices of peace, with a paternal, just, and enlightened government, its resources will be restored in a few years, and it will be the admiration of the world. Would to Heaven I could see this before I end my days!

I hope your Imperial Highness will condescend to acknowledge, in the dean of the Mexican army, a devoted and disinterested friend, a very obedient servant, who wishes you the greatest happiness and fervently kisses the imperial hands of your Imperial Highness.

A. L. DE SANTA ANNA.

His Imperial and Royal Highness
ARCHDUKE FERDINAND MAXIMILIAN *of Austria.*

[Enclosure No. 4.]

ST. THOMAS, *15th of October*, 1861.

MUCH ESTEEMED FRIEND: In reply to your favor of the 15th of September, now before me, I must say to you that I had already received the news of the resolution adopted by the three maritime powers in regard to Mexico.

From what you tell me, there can be no doubt of a change of situation in a short time.

What remains to be done now is to take advantage of this propitious occasion to realize my long-cherished desires, remembering that such an opportunity never occurs twice.

What you have to do is to remind the governments near which you are accredited of your former petitions, insisting, especially, that Mexico cannot have a lasting peace until the disease is radically cured, and the only remedy is the substitution of a constitutional empire for that farce called a republic. Those nations can select one jointly. Remind them, also, that I am now, more than ever, disposed to carry out that idea, and that I will labor without ceasing to effect it.

I do not wish to depreciate the nationality of Mexico. My sole desire is to establish a government of order, to repair the damages of party strife, and to make the Mexicans contented by restoring the Catholic religion, now almost extinct, in a country that used to be famed for its respect and love for religion.

I beg you to communicate my resolve to our mutual friend Mr. ———, who I hope will use all his influence in aid of the triumph of correct principles.

In conclusion, I must say to you that since the profanation of our churches, I have determined to become the avenger of so many sacrilegious outrages, trusting that Providence will give me strength to carry out my resolution. * * * * I have improved much lately, and hope soon to be in Mexico.

Ever your affectionate friend and countryman,

ANTONIO LOPEZ DE SANTA ANNA.

Don JOSE MARIA GUTIERREZ DE ESTRADA.

Mr. Romero to Mr. Seward.

[Translation.]

MEXICAN LEGATION,
Washington, February 22, 1866.

Mr. Romero presents his respects to Mr. Seward, and has the honor to transmit to him a copy of extracts of a letter he has received from Paris, dated the 3d instant, and written by a reliable person, noticing the departure of forces from Oran for Mexico about the end of January last.

Hon. WILLIAM H. SEWARD, *&c., &c., &c.*

[Translation.]

PARIS, *February* 3, 1866.

MUCH ESTEEMED FRIEND: * * * * * * * * *

I must inform you that a regiment of the Foreign Legion, consisting of twelve hundred men, left Oran for Vera Cruz, seven days ago, in a vessel that came for them from Toulon, after taking on a quantity of ammunition there.

This was done in the greatest secrecy; even the newspapers do not mention it. It is likely the United States consul in Algiers or Oran has informed his government of it.

It is also certain that arrangements are pending between Paris and Vienna to send an army corps of Austrians to Mexico.

Señor Don MATIAS ROMERO, *Washington.*

Mr. Romero to Mr. Seward.

[Translation.]

WASHINGTON, *February* 26, 1866.

MY DEAR SIR: I have the honor to transmit to you a translation into English of the official documents relating to the affairs of Mexico, which were published by the French government on the opening of the sessions of the legislative body thereof, in what is called, in Paris, the "Yellow Book."

Desirous that this collection may be of some use to the department under your worthy charge, I transmit it to you, and avail myself of the occasion to repeat myself

Your obedient servant,

M. ROMERO.

Hon. WILLIAM H. SEWARD, *&c., &c., &c.*

THE YELLOW BOOK.

The Yellow Book, containing the diplomatic documents communicated to the Chambers, came out yesterday. These documents relate to the affairs of Italy and Rome; to the visits of the French and English squadrons; to the navigation of the Danube; to the Lebanon question; to the affair of Greece; to the United States; to the affair of Chili; to the affairs of the Plate; to the negotiations with Japan; to the extradition treaty between France and England; to commercial affairs—Sweden, Norway, Zollverein, Netherlands, Spain; to an international sanitary conference; in fine, to the United States correspondence relative to the affairs of Mexico.

Underneath this summary table we find the following note:

"As the publication of the correspondence on the subject of Mexico at this time might present some inconveniences on account of pending negotiations, the government of the Emperor reserves it for subsequent communication to the grand state bodies."

Further on, at the head of the correspondence relative to Mexican affairs, we find another note of this tenor:

"In postponing the publication of the papers relating to Mexico, the intention of the government of the Emperor was also to defer that of the United States upon the same question; but it is now thought unnecessary to delay the communication of that correspondence any longer, as publicity has been given in America to the documents presented to Congress."

It appears from this note that there are other documents relative to Mexico remaining to be published; in other words, the correspondence already published does not embrace all the Mexican documents, but only those documents relative to the reclamations of the United States.

UNITED STATES CORRESPONDENCE IN RELATION TO MEXICAN AFFAIRS.

The Minister of Foreign Affairs to M. Geoffroy, chargé d'affaires at Washington.

PARIS, *March* 23, 1865.

SIR: The United States chargé d'affaires has made the communication of which you gave me notice. Without formal instructions from his government, (so he said,) Mr. Bigelow read me Mr. Seward's despatch, the substance of which I will now give.

The people of the United States, said the Secretary of State, have now but one thought, from which no consideration can divert them, namely, the reconstruction of the Union. To effect this they are resolved to make every sacrifice, to recoil from no obstacle, and to triumph over every resistance.

They desire that the crisis through which they are now passing may not affect their relations with foreign states; but their sentiments towards them will chiefly be inspired by the dispositions they are supposed to have towards us in present circumstances. Sympathizing with those they think favorable to the end they wish to attain, the people, by the natural effect of the contest they are sustaining, are inclined to feel considerable irritation against those who encourage their adversaries, or who provoke by their wishes a result contrary to that which they are contending for at the price of so many sacrifices. Now it is generally believed in the United States, rightly or wrongly, that the French government would consider a definitive separation of the American Union into two distinct confederations as the most desirable consequence of the present war.

With the present state of mind in America, this opinion upon the tendencies of the French government might change the feelings of friendship so long entertained for France, and imbitter the relations between the two countries. The federal government, though not amenable to popular impressions, is obliged to regard them, and would be pleased to see the French cabinet take an occasion to manifest their sentiments towards the American Union; a manifestation of that nature would help to direct or reform the opinion, and prevent it from being perverted by thoughtless prejudices.

I told the United States chargé d'affaires that we might be excused from replying to suppositions that had nothing to justify them, and to which we are conscious of having furnished no pretext. I added, however, that I would have no hesitation to enter into frank explanations with the federal government of the attitude observed by us since the beginning of the American crisis, and to manifest once more our desire that no misunderstanding or equivocation should subsist between us. It is not necessary for France to recall the part she took at the founding of the great American republic. Still faithful to her sympathies, she has had the pleasure to see her interests accord with her sentiments in the continued development of the commercial relations of the two countries; and it is with sincere regret she has regarded the terrible conflict that endangered a state whose prosperity and grandeur she has always desired.

It is superfluous to say that we have remained absolute strangers to the circumstances, altogether internal, that have brought about the separation of the north and south, in the centre of the Union; but we may mention that we have not ceased to deplore the events that have been the consequence; that we had always expressed ourselves in regard to it in the most explicit manner, under all circumstances, even declaring ourselves ready to interpose our good offices if they should at any time be thought necessary to the success of an attempt at reconciliation.

Facts, however, strike everybody with incontrovertible authority. The war broke out, over an extensive territory, between the two factions of the Union, and has sustained an equilibrium for four years, kept up by large regular armies obeying constituted governments. It was impossible for foreign powers not to recognize the parties engaged in such a conflict as belligerents, and to grant them such characters allowed by the law of nations.

The government of the Emperor could not then hesitate to proclaim his consequent duty of strict neutrality. Held responsible for his deeds, he abstained from every resolution tending to prejudge the issue of a struggle to be decided by the force of arms and the will of God.

It was not his place to say, without meddling in affairs that concerned the people of the United States alone, what should be the terms of reconciliation, the object we so ardently desired. Without expressing any opinion on the subject, he has continued to maintain diplomatic relations with the federal government, and abstained from all official intercourse with the power existing in Richmond. The government of the Emperor has therefore conformed in all its acts to a strict and loyal observance of its declarations of neutrality by giving a friendly character, to its attitude towards the Union.

We do not doubt but the good sense of the American people, laying aside the passions of the struggle they are maintaining, will do justice to our intentions and our conduct towards them. It is the duty of the government to enlighten the people as much as possible, and direct their judgment. We, too, must beware of false impressions, and defend public opinion against ill-founded suggestions. While it is represented in the United States that France advocates disunion, it is repeated in Europe that the United States are only waiting for the end of their civil war to pounce upon Mexico and tear down a flag, the accidental vicinity of which, it seems to us, ought to inspire different sentiments in those who are now defending the work of the founders of the American republic. We reject such suppositions; we expect a complete reciprocity of amicable proceedings from the cabinet at Washington, and a similar observance of the rules of neutrality. We are pleased with the assurances that Mr. Seward has given us on that point. The exalted intelligence of that great statesman protects him, we are sure, from the prepossessions and prejudices that events in Mexico may have excited in some minds. We trust that these false impressions will disappear before a more calm and sound consideration of the true interests of the American people.

We went to Mexico to obtain redress and satisfaction for grievous wrongs, denying from the first, as we have always done since on all occasions, every intention of a settlement or of territorial acquisition. Our intervention has permitted reconstruction in that country, on conditions much more favorable than the former governments to the development of its social life and prosperity. We presume there is nothing in that to alarm the United States, and therefore we refuse to believe the designs attributed to them. Whatever may be the result of this struggle in the United States, we think the best employment the States of North America can make of their forces and available resources will be to repair the ravages of war. We cannot believe they are thinking of using them in an expensive and unjust war against a country that has never given them cause of complaint—in a war, in fact, (and we say it now because we do not wish to repeat it,) in which circumstances will force the United States to meet and oppose a power that was once their ancient ally.

We reject, then, these suppositions, condemned by our reason. We hope that the resolutions of the cabinet at Washington in regard to the Mexican government will continue to confirm our confidence in their wisdom. As we are neutral in the politico-military struggle in the United States, we expect their neutrality in our affairs in Mexico. As we will help to dissipate the doubts that exist in America in regard to our sentiments towards the United States, we would be pleased to see the federal government give us grounds to enlighten European opinion in regard to the intentions attributed to it by prejudiced minds.

Accept the assurances, &c.,

DROUYN DE LHUYS.

The Minister of Foreign Affairs to Marquis Montholon, French minister to the United States.

PARIS, *May* 2, 1865.

MARQUIS: In a conversation with the United States minister a few days ago, he made known to me the dispositions of his government in regard to Mexico, and read me several passages from despatches addressed to him by Mr. Seward, Secretary of State.

Mr. Bigelow said the people of the United States were attached to republican institutions, and, regarding them from their own experience as most suited to assure the prosperity and greatness of a nation, could not favorably look upon the establishment of a monarchy among their neighbors. The cabinet at Washington had to adopt the same opinion; yet they understood that peculiar conditions of races, climate, geography, past habits, and traditions, might incline another people to prefer for themselves a government different from that which was thought the best in the United States. But we must confess, added Mr. Bigelow, that the trial of democratic republican institutions for half a century in Mexico is far from being favorable, and has done more harm than good to that unfortunate country. The United States government, therefore, has no intention to oppose the experiment now to be made with full liberty there; nothing could be more contrary to its principles than to prevent a neighboring nation from choosing at pleasure any form of government. Resolved to observe a scrupulous and impartial neutrality in regard to what is passing in Mexico, we hope the attitude will prevent any difficulty between us.

The anxiety caused in America by our intervention originated from the fear to see us inaugurate a system of monarchical propagandism in the New World, and was increased by the idea that we entertained hostile feelings towards the cabinet at Washington during the dreadful crisis that was rending the United States. The federal government will not be deceived by these hypotheses, nor deviate from the line of conduct it has traced out, as long as the honor and interests of the republic are not injured.

I thanked the United States minister for the assurances he gave me in the name of his government, and, congratulating him on the wisdom of the act, I took a note of his declarations. I reminded him that our Mexican expedition was solely to sustain the just claims of our citizens, which the government then existing in Mexico had neither the will nor the power to sustain. That government, having really no foundation, though some provincial brigands carried its colors, fell at our approach.

With our assistance a new government has been formed, which is conscientiously laboring to effect a new political reorganization, promising protection to all interests, and a peace and security long unknown in that wealthy country. There was no absolute system of monarchical restoration in our conduct, nor the least shadow of intentions of conquest or propagandism. Towards the United States, during her four years of painful trials, we have constantly remained faithful to the duties of exact neutrality; and we have always shown our desire for peace in a country that has shown sympathy for us since its foundation. The few slight disagreements that have unavoidably risen, despite our scrupulous impartiality, show how hard it is in practice not to deviate from promised neutrality with the most loyal intentions.

We are pleased to hope, I said to Mr. Bigelow, that the government of the United States will soon be induced to establish friendly relations with the new government of Mexico. Commercial interests, moreover, require a closer relation between the two countries, and we hope this also will soon be accomplished in the political domain.

Such, marquis, is the substance of my answer to Mr. Bigelow's communications.

Accept the assurances, &c.,

DROUYN DE LHUYS.

The Minister of Foreign Affairs to the French Minister at Washington.

PARIS, *May* 30, 1865.

MONSIEUR LE MARQUIS: I have seen with pleasure the assurances which the President of the United States gave to you of his personal desire to keep the best relations with us. I am pleased in thinking that we shall find the proof of those sentiments, so conformable to ours, in the measures which the federal government will take in order to stop the announced enlistments in behalf of Juarez, and to discourage all attempts of that kind.

Accept, &c.,

DROUYN DE LHUYS.

The Minister of Foreign Affairs to the French Minister at Washington.

PARIS, *June* 1, 1865.

MONSIEUR LE MARQUIS: In the course of an interview which I had with Mr. Bigelow on the subject of raising the restrictive measures resulting from the neutrality of France, I reminded the United States minister that France had reason to reckon on the vigilance and firmness of his government to prevent or repress all acts which might, with respect to Mexico, weaken the cordiality of our relations. I also spoke to him of the reception accorded to you by President Johnson. I repeated, as I informed you on the 30th of last month, that we had heard with pleasure of the assurances given to you by the President of the friendly dispositions of the people of the United States towards us, and of the intention of that government to preserve the tradition of them. I added that the language addressed to you by Mr. Johnson, nevertheless, called for an observation on my part. I could not, indeed, abstain from expressing some astonishment at seeing the President inaugurate the relations of his government with the representative of the Emperor by referring to an anxiety about events of a nature calculated to disturb them. That concern to "anticipate beyond all ordinary prevision eventualities quite unlikely," and which might compromise *the good relations which, it is affirmed, there is a sincere desire to maintain, did not appear to me the best means of assuring their duration.* I could therefore but regret the expression of that excessive aforethought, especially in the circumstance when it had occurred. That portion of President Johnson's speech is no doubt addressed, as you remark, to a portion of the American public, and has been suggested by the desire of conciliating certain national susceptibilities. I understand it as such; but the fact must not be forgotten, as my duty was to remark it to Mr. Bigelow, that the French nation also has its susceptibilities, which are not less respectable, and to avoid wounding which is equally important.

Receive, &c.,

DROUYN DE LHUYS.

The Minister of Foreign Affairs to the French Minister at Washington.

PARIS, *July* 6, 1865.

MONSIEUR LE MARQUIS: I have seen with satisfaction, by your last despatches, that the efforts made in the United States to organize an armed emigration into Mexico continue to lose their importance, and I approve of the terms in which you proposed to treat that question with Mr Seward, when it shall be possible for you to open your relations with him in a regular and consecutive manner. It was a matter of great interest to us, in presence of the projected expeditions to Mexico so loudly announced in the United States, to remind the cabinet at Washington that the legislation of the country afforded it the means of opposing an obstacle, if such were its wish, to enterprises of that kind. But, having done this, our further measures must depend on circumstances, and you rightly thought the present moment inopportune for demanding that the federal government should publish a new proclamation in conformity with that of 1818.

The feelings with which the cabinet at Washington showed itself animated on this point, and of which I have recently received further proof, are moreover of a nature to satisfy us. On the 29th of last month Mr. Bigelow communicated to me a letter which he had just received from Mr. Seward, and the first which that minister had written, or rather dictated, since the events of which he was one of the victims. In it Mr. Seward protests against the apprehensions which the hasty language of certain American journals had given birth to in France. He affirms, in the most formal terms, that the existing government maintains the policy adopted by the previous administration relative to Mexico, and on which the representative of the Union had been many times charged to transmit explanations to me. The Washington cabinet is still resolved to observe neutrality in this matter. It is persuaded that the instructions given by the Attorney General to the district attorneys will suffice to prevent illicit armaments; and that if, in spite of the efforts of the government, some few irregular acts should occur, such acts would have no importance, and could not trouble either France or Mexico. I have received these declarations with pleasure, and I am happy to know that the facts related in your correspondence confirm the assurances which were spontaneously given by Mr. Seward.

Accept, &c.,

DROUYN DE LHUYS.

The Minister of Foreign Affairs to the French Minister at Washington.

PARIS, *July* 20, 1865.

MARQUIS: News from the United States shows us the particular importance attached to confederate emigration to Mexico in that country, and how much the public mind is now occupied with the pretended territorial or mining grants that the government of the Emperor seeks to claim.

The fall of the southern confederacy has hastened the time for the Mexican government to open relations of good fellowship with the cabinet at Washington. The very delicate question of confederate emigration is, in my opinion, the first step towards an alliance, if it be frankly and openly considered. It could not then fail to attract the attention of the emperor Maximilian. From what our minister in Mexico writes me, his Majesty intends to welcome emigrants to his territory under the following conditions: If they are armed and organized, they must lay down their arms at the frontier; they must take an oath of obedience to the Mexican government, with a promise not to engage in any attempt against a friendly or neighboring government. If they wish to settle as planters, they shall repair to designated localities, and not establish themselves upon the frontier of the United States, nor upon the isthmus of Tehuantepec. Generals Almonte and Robles are to be sent to the United States by the emperor to ask for the acceptance of these conditions.

According to my information, they will express themselves about in these terms at Washington: "We have," they will say to the federal government, "neither created nor desired the situation imposed upon us. Remnants of confederate armies or exiled citizens ask an asylum of us; the consequence for us is various obligations which we do not wish to avoid. We wish to fulfil the duties of humanity towards the conquered that the fate of war has compelled to quit their country. We wish to take advantage of this for ourselves and make Mexico profit by the activity and energy of men who come to seek a new country among us; in fine, we do not wish to quarrel with our neighbors, but our hope, on the contrary, is to form and keep up good and profitable relations with the American Union. To reconcile these different necessities, we will welcome the confederates; but we propose to disarm them on their arrival into Mexican territory, if they come with arms; to remove them from the frontier into the interior of the country, where we will give them lands and facilitate their definitive settlement according to their capabilities."

We can but approve of this conduct in general. It has suggested to me, however, one observation. If it is necessary to remove the Americans from the territory of the Union, it would not seem to me wise to interdict every American emigrant the faculty of establishing himself in the mining districts, and I do not think that the federal government, in case it did happen, should be offended at it. No matter about the details of the emperor Maximilian's plans; this seems to us the proper time to carry them out. Such language, clear, plain, practical, I think would be heard and understood at Washington.

As to the recent report, newly propagated in the United States, attributing to us the project of seeking territorial acquisitions or privileges for working mining districts, you know they have absolutely no foundation. You know better than anybody else what are our intentions in that particular, for it was to you I communicated them on the 30th of November last, and you gave notice of them to the Mexican government. The views of the government of the Emperor have not varied since that time. It is firmly resolved not to accept the cession of any portion of Mexican territory, and to decline all proposals for concession of mines in Sonora. You must say this openly everywhere, so as to leave no doubt in minds, and to remove every pretext for similar allegations.

Accept, &c.,

DROUYN DE LHUYS.

The Minister of Foreign Affairs to the French Minister in Washington.

PARIS, *August* 17, 1865.

MONSIEUR LE MARQUIS: The minister of the United States addressed to me on the 1st instant the note of which you will find a copy annexed. In the answer, of which a copy is also given, which I sent by the Emperor's command to this communication, I felt bound to declare to Mr. Bigelow that, always ready to reply to demands for explanations addressed to us in a friendly manner, *we could not think of responding to interpellations expressed in a threatening tone relative to vague allegations founded on equivocal documents.* At the same time I took the opportunity afforded by the communication of the minister of the United States, to remind him that, as observers of a scrupulous neutrality in all the internal questions which may agitate or divide the American Union, we were entitled to rely on the exact and loyal reciprocity promised to us on his part with regard to the affairs of Mexico. We do rely on it, in fact, and yet we are unable to conceal from ourselves that there is some difficulty in conciliating certain recent facts and manifestations, of which we cannot mistake the character, with the assurances we have received.

We know that our expedition, its consequences, the establishment of a monarchy in Mexico, have been viewed with displeasure in the United States; we have been told this, and we regret it. But a displeasure does not constitute a grievance, a sentiment does not create a right; and the peace of the world would be exposed to continual dangers if each State, in its relations with its neighbors, were to conduct itself solely to suit its own conveniences or preferences. In a free country *par excellence*, like the United States, it should be known that the liberty and the right of each—State or individual—have for limits the liberty and right of others.

I have not here to justify our expedition to Mexico. Obliged to do ourselves justice, we went to Mexico to seek the satisfaction which had been obstinately refused us. *We yielded to a necessity of the same nature as that which had, at another epoch, conducted the American arms to the capital of Mexico. The Union exercised the rights of victory in all their plenitude by annexing a new State. France does not go so far; we shall leave Mexico without acquiring an inch of soil,* and without reserving to ourselves any advantage not common to all other powers. After our formal declarations on this subject, and the categorical denials we have opposed to all contrary allegations, we are dispensed from replying to the persistent rumors of territorial cessions, by means of which endeavors are made to keep up irritation against us in the United States. The semblance of a government against which we made war disappeared at our approach. Far from pretending to dispose of the country, we invited and encouraged it to dispose of itself.

In a communication which Mr. Bigelow did me the honor to address to me on the 12th June last, he was pleased to acknowledge that the success of republican institutions in Spanish America had not been such as to encourage the United States to attempt propagating them otherwise than by example, and that, *in fine, any government which should be acceptable to the Mexicans would satisfy the United States.* There is no reason to be astonished, therefore, that Mexico, enlightened by disastrous experience, should endeavor, under a system better adapted to its instincts, to escape from the anarchical chaos into which it had been plunged by an interminable series of revolutions.

A movement took place in the sense of monarchical ideas in favor of a liberal prince, belonging to a dynasty certainly illustrious among all, but attached to us by no bond, and with which we had just been at war. The Archduke Maximilian, called by the suffrages of the country, and proclaimed emperor, now exercises the sovereign rights conferred on him by the Mexican nation. No other constituted power exists on Mexican soil. An ex-President, flying from village to village, is no more a head of a government than a few bands of guerillas, pillaging and infesting the high roads, are armies. Can the cabinet of Washington be ignorant of that state of things? It has itself, during four years, contested the character of a regular power to the government residing at Richmond. Are we not allowed to ask by what signs it recognizes in the person of M. Juarez the attributes of sovereignty?

Our right, resulting from injury done to our interests, took us to Mexico. We are unwilling to leave anarchy behind us, because we do not wish to have fresh wrongs to avenge, or interests again compromised to defend. We have already withdrawn some of our troops, and we shall recall them all gradually, according to the re-establishment of order and the pacification of the country. We look forward with the sincerest wishes to the day when the last French soldier shall quit Mexico. Those whom our presence disturbs or incommodes may contribute to the approach of that moment. There can be no doubt that excitements from outside keep up agitation. Let those encouragements cease; let them allow that unfortunate country, weary of anarchy, to become tranquil and organize itself under a government calculated to heal the wounds inflicted; order and tranquillity will soon be established, and the term assigned for our occupation will be greatly abridged. But the fact should be well borne in mind that we are not in the habit of hastening our steps on account of haughty injunctions or threatening insinuations.

You will have the goodness, Monsieur le Marquis, to take in the full meaning of this despatch, and to communicate those explanations to the federal government. They have for object, and we desire that they should have for effect, to clear up the situation and remove all doubts as to our intentions. We hope for a reply in the same spirit of frankness and conciliation that has dictated our own language. It is not worthy of two great nations to allow anything equivocal to subsist between them, and their governments would incur a severe blame in history, and a grave responsibility at the present time, if, in default of preliminary explanation, they were to abandon to the chance of circumstances and unforeseen incidents the maintenance of their good relations and the preservation of peace. Confident in the straightforward common sense of the American people and the enlightened sagacity of its government, we are unwilling to believe that temporary impulses can, against all that is common to us both in old reminiscences, against present interests and future prospects, prevent a truly solid and durable basis for the alliance between the two countries.

Receive, &c.,

DROUYN DE LHUYS.

The Minister of Foreign Affairs to the French Minister in Washington.

PARIS, *August* 17, 1865.

MONSIEUR LE MARQUIS: I have received the despatch which you addressed to me, dated the 18th July, informing me that the mission confided to M. Degollado by the Mexican government had completely failed, and that the President, on refusing to receive the letter of the emperor Maximilian, of which that emissary was a bearer, had declined all kind of relations with him. I have naturally noticed that the Secretary of State, on notifying you of this decision, took the occasion to declare that the intention of the cabinet of Washington was to continue their policy of not recognizing in Mexico but the Mexican republic and its president, Mr. Juarez. If this declaration of the federal government is to be regretted on every account, it is not less so to have it provoked by an attempt which was at least premature. The cabinet of Mexico, before engaging itself in such a course, should have been sure of the opportunity and probabilities of its overtures, and procure better information about the disposition with which they would be met in Washington. So it would have spared itself a disobliging reply, and prevented the occurrence of an incident annoying in every point of view.

DROUYN DE LHUYS.

The Minister of Foreign Affairs to the French Minister at Washington.

PARIS, *September* 2, 1865.

MARQUIS: I have had no official conversation with the United States minister since my answer of the 7th of August to his preceding communication. Mr. Bigelow did me the honor to call to see me yesterday. He did not come, he said, to answer my letter, leaving that case to his government if it thought proper to answer it; but he wanted to tell me personally that he desired to maintain friendly relations between the two countries, and avoid every cause of irritation; that, in showing me documents of the authenticity of which he had no doubt, he had only thought to elicit friendly explanations between us; and that he thought he had not departed from the regard that representatives of governments that respect and honor each other owe to each other in all discussions in the note he addressed to me on the 1st of August. I said to Mr. Bigelow that, doing full justice to his intentions, I had never intended to draw him personally into an official debate between our two governments. He had done his duty in transmitting to me the communication he was charged to deliver, and I had done mine by answering it in the name of the government of the Emperor. For my part, I was conscious of having assumed no exaggerated susceptibility on the occasion. As I had to place Mr. Bigelow's note of the 1st of August before the eyes of his Majesty and his ministers, my colleagues, it was their unanimous impression that I had translated in the answer I made to it.

We could not admit, in fact, that haughty demurrer, supported by documents I did not care to dispute, but whose diplomatic value I denied. I added that I would never refuse to take cognizance of all papers the United States minister would communicate to me as confidential, as means to explain facts concerning the relations of the two countries. He would find me, on the contrary, always ready to furnish him with any explanations he might desire or need, either from the minister of war or the Mexican government, as complementary of the information it would be necessary for me to have, in order to answer his questions.

The conversation on this point being exhausted, Mr. Bigelow spoke to me of the general disposition of opinion in the United States in regard to Mexico, and of the necessity of the federal government to leave the question till the meeting of Congress, the policy of which he could not determine beforehand. He read me some extracts from a despatch lately received from Mr. Seward. The Secretary of State approves of the language of the United States minister at Paris, as far as belligerents are concerned, but he does not find it explicit enough in explaining the dispositions of the American people in regard to Mexican affairs. Mr. Seward is afraid it will be inferred that the people and government are indifferent to the future of republican institutions in America, and particularly in Mexico.

Such is not the sentiment of the United States, and the Secretary of State expresses his confidence that American nations will continue to prosper under republican rule. He desires and hopes to see that form of government strengthened and perpetuated, particularly in Mexico. He recognizes no other, and in his eyes Juarez is the personification of it. He recognizes a state of war existing between France and the Mexican republic; he will not examine the causes, nor express an opinion upon the wrongs that have brought it on, and the federal government is resolved to observe a strict neutrality between the belligerents; but he hopes, when the war is over, republican institutions will be revived in Mexico.

I replied to the United States minister that I would not enter into a dogmatic dissertation upon the comparative merits of monarchical and republican institutions; but I was very much astonished to see existing and indisputable facts, recognized by legal authority and confirmed by the free suffrage of the Mxican nation, ignored by the United States. Time, good sense, and reflection, I had no doubt, would have their influence upon the American people, and banish their systematic prejudices. I could not refrain from entering a formal protest, however, against the persistence of the Secretary of State in considering Juarez and his wandering bands not only as belligerents, but as the recognized chief of a regular government.

I could not here refrain from quoting an example that came aptly into my mind.

When we recognized the south as belligerents, the federal government protested against it; and yet a constituted power resided in Richmond, was obeyed over vast territories, levied taxes, was defended by a large and valiant army, commanded by acknowledged chieftains; that was surely a belligerent; yet we only acknowledged the fact, and not the government that used these imposing forces, and we had no intercourse with it. Now I can find no similarity in the situation of Mexico. There I saw an ex-president flying from village to village, and I asked myself by what mistake they could suppose him to be invested with the rights of a belligerent and the attributes of a government chief.

But in this particular we are not to discuss the opinion and preference of the United States government; all we have to consider is, how the United States, acknowledging two belligerents in Mexico, can keep out of the quarrel and observe an exact neutrality between them. This is what I said to Mr. Bigelow. He, however, called my attention to the irritation caused to his government by the relation that he supposes has existed or does still exist between certain confederate chiefs and some of the Mexican authorities.

New attempts to trouble the American Union could only come now from Texas, and public opinion, already suspicious, could easily be deceived by simple appearances, if they thought that the attempts were organized in Mexico, where there is such toleration of government agents. It was, therefore, necessary to be very prudent on both sides, and to examine every incident in order to prevent bitterness and causes of serious conflict.

I answered Mr. Bigelow that the government of the emperor Maximilian had anticipated his wish, and had ordered the greatest circumspection and the strictest vigilance among his military authorities on the Texas frontier; that they must know that in Washington; and we advised the Mexican government to execute those provisions with vigor, promising to do all we could to assist them in it. I added that Mr. Bigelow's observations, the wisdom of which I recognized, gave me the occasion to repeat our recommendations and advice to Mexico on this important point.

In the course of our conversation Mr. Bigelow asked me of the state of affairs in Mexico, and if the results obtained augured favorably for the consolidation of the new government, and if we could foresee the time when we could withdraw our troops and leave her to attend to her own affairs. I told him we looked with confidence upon the future of the Mexican monarchy, but it was impossible to say when our assistance would cease to be necessary; power had been organized and order re-established, and we had actually withdrawn some of our troops. They must know that we wished to withdraw them all as soon as possible; but at the same time they must know that we were determined not to quit Mexico till we had secured the interests that had brought us there, and insured ourselves against the return of disorder and violence, for which we had, like others, to call the former government to account.

As I told you, marquis, in a previous despatch—and I repeated it to Mr. Bigelow—the federal government can contribute greatly to hasten the moment when the last French soldier is to quit the soil of Mexico.

Accept, &c.,

DROUYN DE LHUYS.

The United States Minister in Paris to the Minister of Foreign Affairs.

PARIS, *September* 12, 1865.

SIR: I have received the note which your excellency wrote to me on the 7th ultimo in answer to a communication I had the honor to address you on the 1st of said month, with respect to the alleged projects of Dr. Gwin and his associates in Mexico.

I have the honor to transmit to your excellency the enclosed copy of a despatch which I have just received from my government.

I avail myself of this occasion, &c.

JOHN BIGELOW.

For enclosure see Mr. Seward's despatch to Mr. Bigelow, No. 231, August 24, 1865, page ——.

The Minister of Foreign Affairs to the French Minister in Washington.

PARIS, *October* 18, 1865.

M. LE MARQUIS: The Emperor recommends to you very particularly the contents of my despatch to you of this date.

In writing to you this despatch I have entered upon a course which Mr. Bigelow himself inaugurated some days ago. At the end of a conversation upon other subjects, that minister asked me, in his own name and without prejudging the opinion of his government, if

I did not think that the recognition of the Mexican empire by the United States would facilitate and hasten the recall of our troops. The instructions which I forward you are the answer to that question.

Receive, &c.,

DROUYN DE LHUYS.

The Minister of Foreign Affairs to the French Minister at Washington.

PARIS, *November* 29, 1865.

M. LE MARQUIS: I have had a conversation recently with Mr. Bigelow, of which I think it well to give you the substance. In that conversation the United States minister enumerated the reasons the cabinet at Washington had for not establishing diplomatic relations with the Mexican government. The origin of that government, the antagonism between its form and the republican institutions of the neighboring country, and the small progress the emperor Maximilian would make in the affection and confidence of his subjects, these are the three motives that oppose, according to Mr. Bigelow, the relations we desire.

The representative of the federal government at the same time criticised certain measures adopted in Mexico. He quoted to me particularly the decree relative to the suppression of brigandage, and one other concerning the introduction of blacks; then he mentioned the sinister interpretations that might be given to the honors accorded to the Iturbide family, and expressed to me the unfavorable sentiments that all these resolutions would cause in the American people.

Although the greater portion of this question was not new, I thought I had better answer it. I will not return, I said to Mr. Bigelow, to the causes that determined the Mexican expedition. These causes are the same that carried the federal flag to Mexico some years ago. A double question of interest and dignity forced us to resort to arms, after uselessly exhausting all other means to have justice done to our citizens. Finding neither reparations for the past nor guarantees for the future in Mr. Jaurez's administration, we were happy to see the Mexican people assume a new government, and faithful to the maxims of our public law we applauded that manifestation of the national will. Our army has not exercised the least force upon that great act, and the new government once established, we have made ourselves an absolute law to respect its independence.

The monarchical form, far from constituting an innovation, is rooted in the traditions of the country, and the other system of government did not assure the Mexican nation enough strength, comfort, and stability to cause us to blame it for the resolution it has taken. We do not dispute the greatness and prosperity that republican institutions have given to the United States; but there is nothing absolute in politics, and a government that suits one country may not suit another. It is very certain that there was nothing but disorder and anarchy in Mexico previous to the new rule. Was not the cabinet at Washington the first to complain of that violent and troubled situation? Was not its interest, like that of all other powers, to see a more normal order of things, and more in harmony with the conditions of vitality of modern societies, established in that country? A monarchical form is certainly a menace to nobody. An empire in Mexico is certainly not more incompatible with the dignity of the United States than an empire in Brazil. There is, besides, in this affair a principle that governs all others—the privilege of every nation to choose its own political rule, and the United States have certainly too just a sentiment of their own independence to wish to control that of their neighbors.

As to the degree of confidence and affection that the Mexican nation feels for its sovereign, the reports that reach us do not agree with those received by the cabinet at Washington. I understand that the new government is daily growing stronger; that Jaurez, whose term has just expired, represents nothing, not even in the eyes of his few followers; that constantly changing his residence, having neither army nor finances nor administration, he is, in fact as well as in law, clothed with no characters that constitute the chief of a state. Can the emperor Maximilian, then, under these circumstances, accord the rights of belligerents to bands still in the field? Did not the federal government deny that quality to the confederates of the south? And yet the confederacy had a vast territory, powers obeyed everywhere, generals of rare talent, armies that the federal troops could only conquer by patience and courage. The pretended authority of Juarez, on the contrary, is but a fiction. Where is the seat of his government? Who knows the names of his functionaries or of his officers? What province or what city is subject to him? Where are the regular traces of his administration? What remains of it but undisciplined bands that live by robbery? If the remnants of the southern armies were to form to-day bands to overrun the federal territory, would the United States treat them as belligerents? In such a situation there is no question of international law, the question is internal, and the first duty of a government well organized is to maintain order in the country.

As to the Iturbide family, I have nothing to say to the reasons that influenced the spontaneous decision of the emperor Maximilian. He might have desired to raise the once illustrious name from obscurity, and his resolution might have been inspired by a sentiment of benevolence and respect for the historic recollections of the Mexican nation. I will say, by the way, that it is untrue that the rights of succession have been conferred upon young Iturbide

Moreover, if certain measures adopted in Mexico provoke the criticism of the cabinet at Washington, they ought not to call us to account for it. Autonomical and independent, the Mexican government is responsible for its own acts. True, our troops are still in Mexico; but the aid we lend to the emperor Maximilian constitutes in no manner a bond of vassalism.

In giving you this summary of my conversation with Mr. Bigelow, I desire, now that Congress is about to meet, to enable you to rectify the erroneous opinions that might be conceived around you, and I authorize you to make use of the present despatch in your conversations with Mr. Seward and the political personages of the Union.

Accept, &c.,

DROUYN DE LHUYS.

The Minister of Foreign Affairs to the French Minister in Washington.

PARIS, *December* 8, 1865.

MONSIEUR LE MARQUIS: I have received the despatch in which you relate me the conversation which you had with Mr. Seward in reference to the appointment of General Logan as minister of the United States to the Mexican republic, and the explanations which the Secretary of State thought necessary to give you concerning that measure in order to attenuate its disagreeable impression. We could not conceal our regret at the determination taken by the federal government, and the opinions publicly expressed by General Logan on our expedition to Mexico make it appear to us still more inopportune. The Emperor's government, in extending to Mexico the protection expected from him by all his subjects, has only pursued the fulfilment of an imperative duty; he ought to secure for the French subjects both legitimate reparations for the past and guarantees for the future. When this work is accomplished, his action will be withdrawn, for no second thought of conquest or domination will retain our arms beyond the ocean. It would then be painful to see, in the moment we look for the means of hastening the end of our expedition, some misunderstanding, endangering our traditional relations with the United States, and that from a situation essentially transitory there might grow a serious risk for the permanent interests which unite the two countries.

Receive, &c.,

DROUYN DE LHUYS.

The French Minister in Washington to the Minister of Foreign Affairs.

WASHINGTON, *December* 11, 1865.

MONSIEUR LE MINISTRE: On the 20th of November I transmitted to the Secretary of State a copy and translation of your excellency's despatch dated the 18th of October last. I have the honor now to make you know the note just addressed to me on that subject by the Secretary of State. I have confined myself to answer him that it had duly reached me, and that I should not fail to submit it at once to the appreciation of the Emperor's government, whose instructions I would wait to discuss its contents.

Please accept, &c.,

MONTHOLON.

(For note of Mr. Seward's to the Marquis de Montholon, dated December 6, 1865, see page —.)

The Minister of Foreign Affairs to the French Minister in Washington.

PARIS, *December* 20, 1865.

M. LE MARQUIS: I have read with interest the message his excellency President Johnson has addressed to the Congress of the United States, of which you have forwarded me a copy. My attention has been more especially directed to the portions of this document which might bear upon questions interesting at once the policy of the cabinet at Washington and ours. Mr. Johnson, in a passage which seems to allued to our expedition to Mexico, dwells upon considerations this is not the place to discuss—upon the vicissitudes of monarchical and republican constitutions in the two hemispheres. I will merely point out to you that the pursuit of our complaints against Mexico has no connexion with the existence in that country of this or that form of government, and that it did not any more depend upon a question of geography. If at the time we required just reparation for our fellow-subjects the power which had refused it had been a monarchy, that circumstance would certainly not have caused us to abandon claiming our right; and in whatever part of the world a nation might dwell which had injured French interests, the protection of the Emperor, due to all his subjects, would have been legitimately extended all the same. I cannot think that the Chief Magistrate of the Union has entertained an idea of raising doubts upon points so evident.

The same passage of the presidential manifesto speaks of the provocation which would compel the American people to defend republicanism against foreign intervention, "of designs hostile to the form of government of the United States," and lastly, of aggression upon the part of the European powers. We cannot feel ourselves affected by these expressions, for they in no way apply to the policy we have followed. It would be superfluous to remind you that the sentiments of constant friendship testified by the Emperor towards the United States exclude every supposition of provocation or aggression upon our part. As for threatening the form of government that country has adopted, and which France herself has contributed to establish at the price of her blood, nothing could be more foreign than such an undertaking to the traditions and principles of the imperial government.

I see, therefore, nothing in the language of Mr. Johnson really of a nature to arouse uneasiness as to the duration of friendly relations between France and the United States; and if some ambiguity prevails in terms employed with regard to the questions that preoccupy the two peoples, other portions of the message, by settling the bearing of the President's words, happily dissipate all uncertainty. The placing of the federal army upon a peace footing, and the considerable reduction of its *cadres*, at the same time with the diminution of the naval forces of the Union, prove the peaceful intentions of the cabinet of Washington, and the announcement of these measures by President Johnson is a pledge to us of the reciprocal confidence which must continue to animate our two governments.

DROUYN DE LHUYS.

The Minister of Foreign Affairs to the French Minister in Washington.

PARIS, *January* 25, 1866.

MONSIEUR LE MARQUIS: The United States minister desired that the communication which he made to me of the Attorney General's letter to Mr. Seward relative to the decrees of the emperor Maximilian concerning immigration and colonization in Mexico should be acknowledged in writing. I consequently addressed such an acknowledgment to Mr. Bigelow. He replied thereto by the letter of which a copy is appended. It would have been easy for me in my turn to continue the correspondence by discussing his reply. I did not consider it necessary to do so. I confined myself, in the verbal explanations which I had on this subject with the United States minister, to dwelling upon two points which I could not allow to pass without observation. I said, first, to Mr. Bigelow that I did not admit the expression "planted" applied to the part taken by the French government in the events which have modified the political system in Mexico. He was sufficiently acquainted with the causes which led us to that country to render it unnecessary for me to revert to them; and as to the present organization of that state, the Mexican people had themselves settled it according to their wishes and interests.

In the second place, I observed to the United States minister that I had declined all discussion with him upon the decrees of the emperor Maximilian in our interview, and that he was not, therefore, justified in attributing to me any opinion whatever upon the subject, as he appeared to do in the last sentence in his letter. I added that if he, however, wished to know my manner of viewing the question, I did not hesitate to say that the measures of the emperor Maximilian so strongly incriminated had not, in our opinion, the character and object attributed to them. It appeared to me advisable that you should not be ignorant of the manner in which this incident terminated.

Receive, &c.,

DROUYN DE LHUYS.

The Minister of Foreign Affairs to the French Minister in Washington.

PARIS, *January* 25, 1866.

MONSIEUR LE MARQUIS: The American newspapers bring us extracts from diplomatic documents published in the United States, in which are related some conversations that I have had with Mr. Bigelow on the subject of certain measures adopted by the emperor Maximilian's government. The observations of the United States minister, and my replies, relate particularly to the decrees of the Mexican government concerning the admission of blacks as colonists, to the suppression of brigandage, and to the position in which the Iturbide family were placed. I have not the official and complete text of the American documents before me, and it is therefore under the reservation of the ulterior reflections which they may suggest that I deem it expedient to define the sense of the explanations to which the questions I have just mentioned have given rise between Mr. Bigelow and myself. These explanations are, besides, stated in the despatch which I had the honor to address to you on the 29th of November last, and I shall confine myself, in my reference thereto, to reviewing that part of the despatch relative to these questions.

When the United States minister came to acquaint me with the opinions of the Washington cabinet, I had to state that I declined all official controversy upon the acts of a foreign government acting with full independence, and that I could only receive as simple information any communication he might wish to make on the subject.

It would not become us, in fact, to accept the responsibility for resolutions emanating from the free initiative of the Mexican government. To admit such a discussion would justify its being said, contrary to all our declarations and the attitude we have rigorously observed, that we consider ourselves invested in Mexico with sovereign rights. Now, the support we afford to the emperor Maximilian and the Mexican nation is precisely intended to aid them to constitute, according to their wishes, an independent power responsible for its acts. This reservation very clearly established, I observed to Mr. Bigelow, in the course of ordinary conversation, that the measures pointed out to him were of a purely administrative order, and did not appear to me to constitute any of those exceptional derogations from general principles which may sometimes, perhaps, authorize a government to intervene in the interior affairs of a neighboring country. Every State regulates as it thinks fit the admission of emigrants upon its territory, whether black or white, and the conditions of the colonization of its soil. It is evident that these conditions, offered to strangers, only apply to the persons who have freely accepted them. So also the Mexican government has only exercised a right incontestably belonging to it in declaring that in its eyes civil war no longer existed on its territory; and ceasing to recognize in wandering bands the character of belligerents, it has promulgated against them the severe penalties which have been applied in every country for the suppression of brigandage. Still less, in my opinion, can it be questioned respecting an act assigning in the state a particular rank to a particular family. In any case the effect of these measures did not go beyond the Mexican frontiers, and did not, therefore, appear to me to constitute any grievance of which a foreign government could complain. If, however, an opposite opinion should be entertained at Washington, I can understand that some uncertainty might be felt as to the means of causing the reclamations it might be thought proper to draw up to reach the right quarter. But, definitively, *because it does not suit the federal government to recognize the de facto government of the emperor Maximilian as existing by right*, and as, upon the other hand, it would seem to it ridiculous to address itself to the power it considers as legal, but which has in fact disappeared, I could not admit as a consequence that there was ground for finding fault with us to escape embarrassment, and for demanding at our hands explanations of acts emanating from the sovereign authority of a foreign government.

Receive, &c.,

DROUYN DE LHUYS.

MARQUIS DE MONTHOLON,
Minister of France at Washington.

Mr. Romero to Mr. Seward.

[Translation.]

MEXICAN LEGATION TO THE UNITED STATES OF AMERICA,
Washington, February 27, 1866

MR. SECRETARY: I have the honor to transmit to you a statement of the foreign debt of the Mexican republic, and the pecuniary responsibilities the French government wishes to impose upon that republic, as a consequence of its iniquitous intervention in the internal affairs of Mexico. This statement has been made out from correct data by an old employé of the Mexican treasury. It also comprises a comparison of the annual expenditures of the national government of the republic with those of the so-called empire of the usurper Maximilian.

I avail myself of this occasion to renew to you, Mr. Secretary, the assurances of my most distinguished consideration.

M. ROMERO.

Hon. WILLIAM H. SEWARD, &c.

AN IMPORTANT ASPECT OF THE MEXICAN QUESTION.

The following tables, compiled from authentic information recently received from the city of Mexico, show the following facts:

First. That the French government has charged Mexico for the expenses of invasion of her territory and other acts of intervention, up to July 1, 1864, the sum of *fifty millions of dollars.* Of this sum ten millions have been paid out of a loan subsequently made, and the remainder (forty millions) has been funded as a claim due by Mexico *to the French government itself.*

Second. That besides the above forty millions, loans have been negotiated for Maximilian, in France, to the amount of more than *one hundred and fifty millions of dollars,* which loans France is seeking to foist on the Mexican people as a legitimate debt, although every dollar realized therefrom has been used not for the welfare or benefit of Mexico, but to meet the expenses which have been incurred in this iniquitous attempt to overthrow republican institutions and establish a monarchy on American soil.

Third. That while the claims of France against Mexico, as admitted by the constitutional government before the intervention began, amounted to *less than three millions of dollars,* the claims of France as now put forward under Maximilian, and as recognized by him, already amount to *over one hundred and ninety-three millions of dollars.* This is apart from what may still be added under General Forey's recent and very significant reminder on the part of France, that it may be necessary "to make further pecuniary outlays in Mexico."

Fourth. That while the entire foreign debt of Mexico, before the French intervention commenced, amounted to but a little over *eighty millions of dollars,* that debt, if Maximilian is allowed to succeed, will be increased, even if no further addition is made to it, to over *two hundred and seventy millions of dollars.*

Fifth. That the annual expenses of Mexico under the republic were less than *twelve millions of dollars,* while under Maximilian they have already reached the sum of *forty-nine millions.* Of this sum over *ten millions* per annum is due for interest from Maximilian to France.

Comparative statement of the legitimate foreign debt of Mexico, as recognized by the constitutional government of the republic, with the annual expenditures, as established by act of Congress, August 16, 1861, and the debt which the French intervention seeks to impose upon the country, with the annual expenditures under the so-called empire of Maximilian.

FOREIGN DEBT AS RECOGNIZED BY THE CONSTITUTIONAL GOVERNMENT IN 1862.

To English subjects:

Funded debt.—Debts contracted in London £10,241,650, (interest at 3 per cent., at $5 per £)		$51,208,250
English convention debt, (interest at 6 per cent)		4,175,000
Pending claims.—Back interest unpaid and other acknowledged claims		13,231,793
Various reclamations		696,614
Total debt due to English subjects June 30, 1862		69,311,657

To Spanish subjects:

Funded debt.—Admitted convention debt	$4,205,481	
Additional amount in dispute	2,427,942	
(Interest at 3 per cent)		$6,633,423
Pending claims.—Back interest unpaid and other acknowledged claims		1,549,563
Various reclamations		1,278,000
Total debt due to Spanish subjects June 30, 1862		9,460,986

To French subjects:

Funded debt.—Balance of convention debt	$190,000
Pending claims.—To Juan B. Jecker for capital expended in his scandalous claim, and interest	1,984,000
Other claims	685,917
Total debt due to French subjects	2,859,917

RECAPITULATION.

Debt due to English subjects	$69,311,657
Debt due to Spanish subjects	9,460,986
Debt due to French subjects	2,859,917
Total foreign debt as recognized in 1862	81,632,560

ANNUAL INTEREST.

On debt contracted in London	$51,208,250 at 3 per cent.	$1,536,247
On English convention debt	4,175,000 at 6 per cent.	250,500
On other English claims, if capitalized	13,928,407 at 3 per cent.	517,852
On Spanish convention debt	6,633,423 at 3 per cent.	199,002
On other Spanish claims, if capitalized	2,827,563 at 3 per cent.	84,826
On French claims, if capitalized	2,859,917 at 6 per cent.	171,595
Total debt	81,632,560	2,760,022

Total interest t[illegible]	$2,304,599
Total interes[illegible]	283,828
Total inter[illegible]	171,595
T[illegible]	2,760,022

ANNUAL EXPENDITU[illegible] OF THE REPUBLIC, AS ESTABLISHED BY CONGRESS [illegible] 16, 1861.

Interest on the foreign deb[illegible]		$2,760,022
For foreign relations	$210,340	
For home departments	1,798,059	
For finance	1,573,624	
For war	4,745,395	
		8,327,418
Total annual expenditures of the national government		11,087,440

The interior debt of Mexico has been nearly extinguished by sales of church property made under the constitutional government.

UNDER MAXIMILIAN.—DEBT WHICH THE FRENCH INTERVENTION SEEKS TO IMPOSE UPON MEXICO.

Indebtedness acknowledged to France by Maximilian, as part of the expenses of the intervention, to July 1, 1864, 270,000,000 of francs, or $50,000,000, of which $10,000,000 were paid out of the first loan, and the balance funded at 3 per cent., viz	$40,000,000
First loan put out for account of Maximilian, 216,000,000 of francs, at 6 per cent. interest	40,000,000
To pay France the above $10,000,000, or 54,000,000 of francs, and 12,000,000 of francs more on account of reclamations to French subjects, further bonds, as an additional loan, were put in circulation to the amount of 110,000,000 of francs, at 6 per cent	20,370,370
Second loan put out for account of Maximilian in Paris, being the *lottery loan* of two series of bonds at 6 per cent. interest, amounting to 500,000,000 of francs, negotiated at 340	92,592,592
Total debt recognized by Maximilian in favor of France	192,962,962

Brought forward	$192,962,962
The debt in favor of France as recognized by the constitutional government is	2,859,917
Amount that Maximilian desires to augment the debt to France	190,103,045

The debt to English subjects remains the same under Maximilian as before, the back interest only having been capitalized.

The debt to Spanish subjects remains nearly as before, the interest unpaid.

ANNUAL INTEREST UNDER MAXIMILIAN.

On the debt to the French government for account of intervention, $40,000,000 at 3 per cent	$1,200,000
On the first loan, $40,000,000 at 6 per cent	2,400,000
On additional amount issued to pay French government and claims, $20,370,370 at 6 per cent	1,222,222
On second loan put out in Paris, or *lottery loan*, $92,592,592 at 6 per cent	5,555,555
Total annual interest on French claims under Maximilian	10,377,777
Interest on debt due to English subjects, same as under the constitutional government	2,304,599
Interest on debt due to Spanish subjects, same as under the constitutional government	283,828
Total annual interest on the foreign debt under Maximilian	12,966,204

ANNUAL EXPENDITURES OF THE [illegible]

Interest on his foreign debt, (of which $1[illegible]	[illegible]2,966,204
Annual cost of his lottery scheme in Paris. [illegible]	[illegible]391,237
Personal expenses and civil list of Maximil[illegible]	[illegible]332,500
25,000,000 francs per annum on account e[illegible] cording to treaty of Miramar [illegible]	4,629,[illegible]
400,000 francs per voyage subvention to the [illegible]eam-ers from St. Nazaire [illegible]	888,888
Ministers, legations, consulates, agents, employ[illegible]s, travelling expenses, military and civil expenses, and charges of his foreign armed force	26,220,868
Total annual expenditures under Maximilian	49,929,326

COMPARISONS.

Foreign debt as attempted to be recognized by Maximilian	$271,735,605
Foreign debt as recognized by the constitutional government	81,632,560
Attempted increase by Maximilian	190,103,045
Annual interest required to be paid by Maximilian	$12,966,204
Annual interest under the government of the republic	2,760,022
Attempted increase by Maximilian	10,206,182
Annual expenditures under Maximilian	$49,929,326
Annual expenditures as fixed by the national congress under the republic	11,087,440
Annual increase under Maximilian	38,841,886
Annual salary of Maximilian, so-called emperor of Mexico	$1,500,000
Annual salary of the President of the republic	30,000

WASHINGTON, *February* 27, 1866.

Mr. Seward to Mr. Romero.

DEPARTMENT OF STATE,
Washington, March 14, 1866.

SIR: I have the honor to acknowledge the receipt of your several communications, dated, respectively, July 12, 1864; May 10, June 12, 25, and 28; August 12, October 10, November 20, and December 7, 15, and 24, 1865; also of those of February 14, 21, 22, 26, and 27, and March 9, 1866, with their accompanying documents, all of them relating to the political condition of the Mexican republic, and which have contributed largely to my knowledge of the events transpiring in that country.

Thanking you for the information thus imparted, I beg to assure you of my high appreciation of the zeal and ability with which, from time to time, you have impressed this government as to the actual condition of affairs in the Mexican republic.

I avail myself of this occasion to renew to you, sir, the assurances of my highest consideration.

WILLIAM H. SEWARD.

Señor MATIAS ROMERO, *&c.*, *Washington, D. C.*

Mr. Romero to Mr. Seward.

[Translation.]

MEXICAN LEGATION TO THE UNITED STATES OF AMERICA,
Washington, March 12, 1866.

MR. SECRETARY: I have the honor to send you the annexed copy of a convention signed in the city of Mexico, on the 29th of September last, by the so-called assistant secretary of the treasury of the usurper Maximilian and M. A. Dano, minister of France, for the purpose of fixing the condition of the French officials sent to Mexico.

Two important facts are shown by this document:

1st. That the so-called government of Maximilian is not at all a national one, but essentially French, inasmuch as it is not only sustained by French bayonets and money, but even the minor officials are French; and they are so numerous that it has been thought necessary to secure their interests by means of a diplomatic convention.

2d. That the arrangements made by the French government with its agent in Mexico, embracing several years to come, show it is not disposed to withdraw its forces nor its influence from that republic, as it seems to wish the United States to believe.

I avail myself of the opportunity to renew to you, Mr. Secretary, the assurances of my most distinguished consideration.

M. ROMERO.

Hon. WILLIAM H. SEWARD, *&c.*

CONVENTION.

The Mexican and French governments, desiring to fix the position of the French officials placed at the disposal of his majesty the emperor Maximilian, the following diplomatic convention has been agreed upon between Don Francisco de P Cesar, under secretary of the treasury and public credit, and his excellency Don Alfonso Dano, envoy extraordinary and minister plenipotentiary of France to Mexico, commander of the imperial order of the Legion of Honor, &c., &c., both duly authorized by their respective governments:

ARTICLE 1. Those agents of the administrations of the French empire who are or may be placed at the disposal of the government of his majesty the emperor Maximilian shall be assigned to the offices and grades in which the minister under whose direction they may serve may think them most useful.

ARTICLE 2. The government of his majesty reserves the right of determining the number and the qualifications of the French officials he may need in the different public departments.

ARTICLE 3. The said agents shall have the right to a salary equivalent to that which they receive in France, and to a daily compensation at the following rates: Three dollars per day to those who receive fixed salaries of fifteen hundred francs a year; four dollars to those who get from sixteen hundred to twenty-four hundred francs; five dollars to those who have from twenty-five hundred to five thousand francs; six dollars to those who get from five thousand one hundred to eight thousand francs, and so on, increasing one dollar a day for every two thousand francs of fixed salary; but the French agents employed in Mexico previous to the first of January, 1865, shall continue to receive the salaries and perquisites they had before that date.

ARTICLE 4. The official Mexican salary is considered as composed of the European salary and the compensation mentioned in article 3. The payment of the ordinary salary proper is charged upon the Mexican treasury, as well as the contingent expenses mentioned in articles 8, 10, and 12.

ARTICLE 5 Whatever position the French agents may have in Mexico, they shall continue to belong to their former administrations. They shall be entitled to gradual promotion, according to the rules of the service to which they belong. In case an agent is promoted in France, he shall immediately enjoy the emoluments corresponding to his new rank in Mexico, according to article 3 of the present convention.

ARTICLE 6. The commission or patent granted to a French agent by the Mexican government shall give him no right of merit in France.

ARTICLE 7. To entitle him to a pension his term of service in Mexico shall be increased fifty per cent. above its actual duration.

ARTICLE 8. French agents sent to Mexico shall only receive their European salary from the time they leave off duty in France till they land in Mexico; but they shall receive for travelling expenses a sum equal to half of their year's pay in Europe; and in no case shall it be less than one thousand francs. The half of this sum shall be paid him before he embarks, and the other half after his arrival in Mexico. The government shall also pay his travelling expenses from the landing place to his place of residence in Mexico. The Mexican government reserves the mode of recompensing the services of the French agents, by increasing their salaries, or by honorific distinctions, as it finds most convenient.

ARTICLE 9. The salaries of the French agents, according to their grade in Europe, shall be subject to the discounts ordered by the law of the 9th of June, 1853, on civil pensions in France. The Mexican treasury shall have charge of the sums discounted in the offices at the time the salaries are to be paid, and shall deliver the amount to the French treasurer at the end of each month, together with a minute account, certified by the chief agent appointed for that purpose, by the minister of the Mexican treasury.

ARTICLE 10. After three years' residence in Mexico the French agent shall have a right to six months' leave of absence and a free passage to and from France. During the time of the leave of absence and the voyage he shall only receive the salary of his office in Europe.

ARTICLE 11. The agent who wishes to return to France before the completion of his term of five years shall contribute to the expenses of his return in proportion to the remaining term of service, except in case of delicate health or for other reasons independent of the agent's will.

ARTICLE 12 The Mexican government shall place at the disposal of the French government those agents it deems unfit for the service in Mexico, in which case they shall have their travelling expenses back to France paid by Mexico, together with their European salary, from the day of their embarcation to their arrival in France. And they shall also have a right to compensation equivalent to three months of their pay in Europe.

Done in duplicate, in Mexico, on the 29th of September, 1865.

F. DE P. CESAR.
ALFONSO DANO.

[A wax seal with the motto, "French legation in Mexico."]
[Another seal with the legend, Department of the treasury and public credit.]

Mr. Seward to Mr. Romero.

DEPARTMENT OF STATE,
Washington, March 17, 1866.

SIR: I have the honor to acknowledge the receipt of your note of the 12th instant, transmitting a copy of a convention concluded at the city of Mexico on the 29th of September, 1865, between the minister of France and the assistant secretary of the treasury of the so-called emperor of Mexico, for the purpose of fixing the position and pay of such French agents as may hereafter be employed in Mexico.

In reply, I have to inform you that the subject will receive the attention of this department, and, while thanking you for your courtesy, I avail myself of the occasion to renew the assurance of my high consideration.

WILLIAM H. SEWARD.

Señor MATIAS ROMERO, *&c., Washington, D. C.*

Mr. Romero to Mr. Seward.

LEGATION OF MEXICO IN THE UNITED STATES OF AMERICA,
New York, November 14, 1865.

MR. SECRETARY: I have the honor of transmitting a copy of a note from the consul of the Mexican republic in San Francisco, dated on the 17th of October last, which I received to-day, with the annexed documents.

It appears from these that General McDowell, commanding the military department of California, issued a General Order, No. 17, on the 11th of last October, containing a declaration in regard to the exportation of arms that will certainly cause a violation of the neutrality the United States wishes to observe in the present war on Mexican territory. The order is contrary to the laws of this country, which allow the export of arms and munitions of war for belligerent nations, when the United States are neutral; and you sent me these laws in your communication of the 24th of November, 1862, in reply to mine of the same month, informing your department that several French officers had visited New York and New Orleans for the purpose of purchasing articles contraband of war for the French army invading Mexico. And, moreover, I have no doubt that these laws or declarations are the only ones now in force, as applicable to the exportation of arms from this country to Mexico, since the revocation of the order prohibiting the exportation of arms from the United States; for Mr. Hunter, in charge of the Department of State, told me so in the President's name, in his note of the 12th of May last.

Now, the instructions given by the Secretary of the Treasury, Mr. Hamilton, the 4th of August, 1793, of which you sent me a copy with your note before mentioned, authorize the *exportation* of those articles, and I understand *exportation* to mean sending out of the country, whether by land or sea. So, if any distinction is made in the interpretation of this law to the injury of Mexico, I sincerely hope the government of the United States will remove it, so as to preserve the *bona fide* neutrality it intends to maintain in this war, of which the Mexican republic is now the stage.

As General McDowell did not deem it proper to revoke his order on the representations of the Mexican consul in San Francisco, I am compelled to appeal to your excellency, and ask you to forward to that general the necessary instructions for the preservation of the neutrality proclaimed by his government in the department consigned to his command.

This appeal to you is the more urgent, as the papers of to-day publish a telegram, apparently from good authority, asserting that the United States government will extend the effect of General McDowell's order, intended only for his department, along the entire frontier.

I cannot for a moment believe that this is true; and I hope you will enable me to give my government the necessary explanations to quiet apprehensions in this particular, and not shake the confidence it has in the honest intentions of the United States as a neutral.

I embrace this occasion of renewing to you, Mr. Secretary, the assurances of my distinguished consideration.

M. ROMERO.

Hon. WILLIAM H. SEWARD, &c.

[Enclosure No. 1.]

CONSULATE OF MEXICO IN SAN FRANCISCO,
San Francisco, October 17, 1865.

SIR: After calling twice at General McDowell's office, I had the good fortune to meet him yesterday.

I told him his order of the 11th instant, published with evidences of displeasure in the city papers, had attracted my attention; that the order disturbed (violated) the strict neutrality proclaimed by the President of the United States between belligerent parties in Mexico, as it favored the French, now holding the Pacific ports.

General McDowell said, as he always has done, that he felt the profoundest sympathy for Mexico; that he wanted the republic to triumph in this struggle; but the neutrality laws compelled him to act in the manner he did. He said I might complain to his superior. I then told him I thought it best to apply to him first, before writing a note about the affair, and learn the reasons he had for issuing the order in question; and afterwards I would appeal to General Halleck, his superior, as he advised me.

In accordance with this understanding with General McDowell, who, during our interview, was most polite and courteous, I addressed him yesterday the note of which I send you a copy, and also a translation of the order referred to; and I now await his reply to forward it to you.

I protest my esteem and distinguished consideration.

JOSÉ A. GODOY, *Consul.*

Citizen MATIAS ROMERO,
Envoy Extraordinary and Minister
Plenipotentiary of Mexico in Washington.

[Enclosure No. 2.]

CONSULATE OF MEXICO IN SAN FRANCISCO,
San Francisco, October 16, 1865.

The undersigned, consul of the Mexican republic in this port, has the honor of calling he attention of General Irvin McDowell, commander-in-chief of the department of California, to his order of the 11th instant, published in the papers of this city. By that order the sending of arms and munitions of war into Mexico across the United States border is prohibited, in regard to the neutrality towards the belligerents in Mexico.

As the exportation of arms is now allowed by the government in Washington, that order seems to the undersigned to favor one of the parties—namely, the French; for, as the ports on the Pacific are held by the invader of Mexico, the constitutional government, the only one recognized by the United States, has no other way than the frontier, which is now closed. Thus, general, the strict neutrality, so often announced by the government at Washington, ceases; and the consequence is, the usurping party, which the brave people of this great republic are endeavoring to drive out, is favored.

The consul undersigned hopes General McDowell will please revoke his order of the 11th instant, in conformity with the declaration of the President of the United States, permitting the export of arms and munitions of war. This is what the undersigned told General McDowell in the interview to-day.

The undersigned assures General McDowell of his esteem and distinguished consideration.

JOSÉ A. GODOY.

General IRVIN MCDOWELL,
Commander-in-chief of the Department of California.

SAN FRANCISCO, *October* 16, 1865.

A true copy:

JOSÉ A. GODOY.

[Enclosure No. 3.]

CALIFORNIA NEUTRALITY IN MEXICAN AFFAIRS.—A SPECIMEN OF BRITISH NEUTRALITY ON THE PACIFIC.—THE UNITED STATES AUTHORITIES CONNIVING AT THE FURNISHING OF ARMS TO MAXIMILIAN.—THEY REFUSE TO ALLOW ANY TO PASS THE FRONTIER TO THE LIBERAL PARTY, &c.

[Our San Francisco correspondence.]

SAN FRANCISCO, *October* 13, 1865.

I have already informed you of some of the measures taken by the liberalists of Mexico to supply themselves with arms from San Francisco. It would seem that the proclamation of the withdrawal of the prohibition of the shipment of arms to other countries by the United States government was to be twisted, after all, so as to mean really nothing, the benefits being all given to the French, who are allowed to carry away what they please, while the Mexicans are, as usual, to have no chance to help themselves The western coast being in the hands of the French, of course no more arms can be introduced by the Mexicans by water, and the overland route was the only one left them. The presence of Juarez at El Paso was favorable to their plan of introducing arms through Arizona, but it would seem that the commander of the department of California, to which the district of Arizona is attached, has arrived at the conclusion that it is his duty to interfere and negative the orders of the War Department, a course of action highly beneficial to the French and ruinous to the Mexicans. His order, which I have been permitted to copy from the official document, is as follows:

[General Orders No. 17.]

HEADQUARTERS DEPARTMENT OF CALIFORNIA,
San Francisco, California, October 11, 1865.

It is made the duty of the officers commanding the districts of Arizona and southern California—while keeping in view the recent orders allowing the exportation of arms and munitions of war—to instruct the commanders on the southern frontiers, within the department, to take the necessary measures to preserve the neutrality of the United States with respect to the parties engaged in the existing war in Mexico, and to suffer no armed parties to pass the frontier from the United States, *or suffer any arms or munitions of war to be sent over the frontier to either belligerent.* This is not to prevent individuals from passing with arms for their personal protection.

By command of Major General McDowell.

R. C. DRUM,
Assistant Adjutant General.

The words of the order are copied *verbatim*, the italics only being mine.

It will be seen at once that this order strikes directly at Juarez and *at no one else.* Maximilian can, of course, get all the supplies he wants by sea, and we have already had two of his ally's war steamers (the French frigate Victoire and armed steam transport Rhine) fitted up and furnished throughout with everything required for immediate service at the United States navy yard at Mare island.

Mr. Romero to Mr. Seward,

[Translation.]

MEXICAN LEGATION IN THE UNITED STATES OF AMERICA,
New York, November 18, 1865.

MR. SECRETARY: Referring to the note which I had the honor to address you on the 14th instant, in relation to General McDowell's order of the 11th of October last, prohibiting the exportation of arms over the California frontier, contrary to the laws of this country, I now find occasion to remit to your department the copy of a note I have just received from the Mexican consul in San Francisco, with six accompanying documents, that your department may take them into consideration while arriving at a determination upon the subject, agreeably to the request contained in my note of the 14th instant.

I avail myself, with pleasure, of this occasion to tender to you, Mr. Secretary, the assurances of my most distinguished consideration.

M. ROMERO.

Hon. WILLIAM H. SEWARD, *&c., Washington, D. C.*

[Enclosure No. 1.]

MEXICAN CONSULATE IN SAN FRANCISCO,
San Francisco, October 20, 1865.

SIR: I have the honor of sending you copies of the notes, from 1 to 6, written to me by General McDowell, commander of the department of California, in answer to one from me, of which I sent you notice, and my last, informing him that I had notified my government and your legation.

From the documents I enclose you will perceive that the order of the President of the United States prohibiting the exportation of arms and munitions of war has been disregarded by the subordinate authorities, to the incalculable injury of our cause.

Is it showing impartiality to belligerents when one is permitted to import all necessaries, by land or sea, and the other denied importations, even by land, the only way they can get them? The French, having possession of all the Mexican ports, can introduce arms, or whatever they please; we are denied the privilege of carrying arms across the frontier, to repel the invaders of our country.

As you are accredited to the government of the United States, you will act as you may deem it proper in this matter and to the greatest advantage to the holy cause which we defend.

Receive, sir, the assurances of my high consideration.

JOSÉ A. GODOY.

Citizen MATIAS ROMERO,
Envoy Extraordinary and Minister Plenipotentiary of Mexico in Washington.

[Enclosure No. 2.]

Consul Godoy to General McDowell.

MEXICAN CONSULATE AT SAN FRANCISCO,
San Francisco, October 16, 1865.

The undersigned, consul of the republic of Mexico at this port, has the honor to call the attention of General Irvin McDowell, military commander of the department of California, to the effect of the General Order issued by him on the 11th instant, which has been published in the city papers. The object of the order referred to is to prevent arms and munitions of war being sent through the United States frontier, in fulfilment, as it is expressed, of the duties of a neutral power towards the two parties that are now waging the war in Mexico.

As the government of Washington has permitted by official decree the exportation of arms, the undersigned begs to say that the order referred to, if carried out by General McDowell, must evidently work in favor of one of the two belligerents—that is to say, in favor of the French; for as the Mexican ports on the Pacific coast have been taken possession of by the latter, it closes the only channel through which the constitutional government of Mexico, the only one recognized by the United States, can now get arms.

Thus, general, the strict neutrality proclaimed by the government of Washington on different occasions ceases, and the usurping party, which the noble people of this great republic have no sympathy for, is directly favored.

The undersigned would suggest that General McDowell might withdraw his order of the 11th instant, if he thinks he could be justified in so doing, conforming to the decree of the President of the United States, which permits the exportation of arms and munitions of war.

At the interview he had with General McDowell the undersigned expressed the hope that his observations would be duly taken into consideration.

The undersigned protests to General McDowell the assurances of his most distinguished consideration.

JOSÉ A. GODOY.

General McDOWELL,
Commander Department of California, San Francisco.

SAN FRANCISCO, *October 20, 1865.*

A true copy:

JOSÉ A. GODOY.

[Enclosure No. 3.]

HEADQUARTERS DEPARTMENT OF CALIFORNIA,
San Francisco, California, October 18, 1865.

SIR: I have the honor to acknowledge the receipt of your note of yesterday, calling my attention to the effect of my General Order of the 11th instant with respect to the neutrality to be observed towards the two parties at war with each other in the republic of Mexico, and prohibiting the passage of arms and munitions of war across the frontier of the belligerents.

You conceive this order to be at variance with the orders from Washington, allowing the export of arms and munitions of war, and the effect of it to be advantageous to the French for the reason that they have possession of all the ports, and the Mexicans have no other channel by which to obtain arms than over the frontier, which channel this order now closes to them.

It is undoubtedly true that the possession of the seaports gives the French great advantage in the war; but this is a misfortune for Mexico for which the United States are not responsible, and it certainly could not justify them in sanctioning the use of their territory and frontier for the benefit of the Mexican government in a contest in which they have declared themselves neutral.

As it may be inferred from the tenor of your letter that you suppose that, under the order permitting arms to be exported from the United States, they could be sent to the French at any of the Mexican ports now in their possession, thus placing them on a more favored footing than the Mexicans, I beg to enclose you copies of my correspondence with the collector, by which you will see that it is not only by land that arms and munitions of war are not allowed to go to the seat of war, but by water as well; and that, so far as the United States authorities are concerned, the French in the seaports will be treated the same as the Mexicans on the frontier.

I regret deeply, señor consul, that any official act of mine should be thought by you or any one to work harm to your country, for which I have so warm a sympathy, and it is with real pain that I have to say that I do not feel that I would be justified in withdrawing the order of which you complain.

I have the honor to be, señor consul, with great respect, your most obedient servant,

IRVIN McDOWELL,
Major General, Commanding Department.

Señor J. A. GODOY,
Mexican Consul, San Francisco, California.

SAN FRANCISCO, *October* 20, 1865.

A true copy:

JOSÉ A. GODOY.

[Enclosure No. 4.]

HEADQUARTERS DEPARTMENT OF CALIFORNIA,
San Francisco, October 17, 1865.

SIR: I beg to ask if you would consider it your duty, under existing instructions, to permit arms and munitions of war to leave this port for a port of the republic of Mexico, such port being in the possession of the French forces, and you knowing that the arms and munitions of war were for the use of those forces in the existing war with Mexico, the United States being at peace with both belligerents.

Would you please let me know what has been your official action with respect to the neutrality of the United States in the existing war of the French against Mexico.

I have the honor to be, very respectfully, your most obedient servant,

IRVIN McDOWELL,
Major General, Commanding Department.

CHARLES JAMES, Esq.,
Collector of the Port of San Francisco, California.

SAN FRANCISCO, *October* 20, 1865.

A true copy:

JOSÉ A. GODOY.

[Enclosure No. 5.]

CUSTOM-HOUSE, SAN FRANCISCO,
Collector's Office, October 17, 1865.

GENERAL: In the case put in your note of this date, in respect to the shipment of arms and munitions of war to Mexico, I should refuse clearance, and submit the case to the Secretary of the Treasury.

I enclose copies of two orders, dated respectively the 15th and 26th ultimo, which indicate the policy which I have deemed it my duty to pursue in respect to the subject of your inquiries.

With great respect, your most obedient servant,

CHARLES JAMES, *Collector*.

IRVIN McDOWELL,
Major General, Commanding Department.

WASHINGTON, *November* 18, 1865.

A true copy:

IGNO. MARISCAL, *Secretary*.

SAN FRANCISCO, *October* 20, 1865.

A true copy:

JOSÉ A. GODOY.

[Enclosure No. 6.]

CUSTOM-HOUSE, SAN FRANCISCO,
Collector's Office, September 15, 1865.

SIR: I have information that a vessel will leave this port to-night with arms and munitions of war, in violation of the act of Congress of April 20, 1818. The vessel is described as a small coaster—name not reported. You will take an advantageous position, and bring to and search any suspected vessel, and if you find any arms and munitions of war on board detain her and report.

Respectfully,

CHARLES JAMES, *Collector*.

Lieutenant H. H. ANDREWS,
Commanding Revenue Cutter Shubrick.

SAN FRANCISCO, *October* 20, 1865.

A true copy:

JOSÉ A. GODOY.

[Enclosure No. 7.]

CUSTOM-HOUSE, SAN FRANCISCO,
Collector's Office, September 26, 1865.

SIR: You will be vigilant, and see that no warlike expedition or vessels laden with arms and munitions of war leave this port in violation of the neutrality law.

Respectfully,

CHARLES JAMES, *Collector*.

Lieutenant G. W. MOORE,
Commanding Revenue Cutter J Lane.

SAN FRANCISCO, *October* 20, 1865.

A true copy:

J. A. GODOY.

[Enclosure No. 8 —Translation.]

MEXICAN CONSULATE IN SAN FRANCISCO,
San Francisco, October 19, 1865.

The undersigned, consul of the Mexican republic in this port, has the honor of acknowledging the receipt of General Irvin McDowell's note of yesterday, with the accompanying documents.

He thinks proper to lay his correspondence with the commanding general of the department of California before his government and the minister plenipotentiary of Mexico in Washington, that both may know how to act in the case.

Before closing this note, the undersigned believes it his duty to inform General McDowell that he has never doubted for a moment his sympathy for the republic of Mexico, and for which he is thankful, as he told him at the interview on the 16th instant. The request for the repeal of the order of the 11th of this month was made because he believed it prejudicial to the national cause in Mexico.

The undersigned protests to General Irvin McDowell the assurances of his distinguished consideration.

JOSÉ A. GODOY.

General IRVIN McDOWELL,
Commander of the Department of California, in San Francisco.

SAN FRANCISCO, *October* 20, 1865.

A true copy:

JOSÉ A. GODOY.

[Enclosure No. 9.]

[From the New York Herald of November 16, 1865.]

SAN FRANCISCO, *October* 21, 1865.

The outrageous order issued by General McDowell, cutting off the last hope of the Mexican liberals for obtaining arms from this side of the continent, a copy of which I sent you last week, has called out a correspondence between Consul Godoy and General McDowell, copies and translations of which I enclose. What adds to the hardship of the case, although it does not appear on the face of the documents, is the fact that the arms which were to leave by the schooner referred to by Collector James were intended to be landed at a point on the lower coast not occupied by the French, and were for Mexican use, as the collector knew, so that his seeming impartiality is verily all on one side. You will see from the reading of this correspondence that the removal of the restriction on the exportation of arms has been practically nullified by the War Department as represented on this coast.

Mr. Seward to Mr. Speed.

DEPARTMENT OF STATE,
Washington, November 21, 1865.

SIR: I have the honor to submit for your consideration two notes, received from Señor Matias Romero, the minister of the Mexican republic, dated November the 14th and 18th instant, with their accompaniments, relative to the Order No. 17, October 11, 1865, issued by Major General Irvin McDowell, commanding the military department of California, prohibiting the exportation of arms or munitions of war, by the frontier, into Mexico.

I will thank you, as soon as practicable, for your opinion as to whether the Order No. 17, above referred to, is in conformity with any laws, regulations, or orders now in force, bearing upon the subject.

I am, sir, your obedient servant,

WILLIAM H. SEWARD.

Hon. JAMES SPEED,
Attorney General.

Mr. Speed to Mr. Seward.

ATTORNEY GENERAL'S OFFICE,
December 23, 1865.

SIR: I must ask pardon for my delay, occasioned by pressing engagements in court, in making reply to your letter of the 21st ultimo, enclosing for my consideration two notes received by your department from the minister of the Mexican republic, with their accompaniments, relative to an order, of date October

11, 1865, issued by General McDowell, commanding the military department of California, prohibiting the exportation of arms or munitions of war by the frontier into Mexico. The question asked by you is, whether, in my opinion, this order is in conformity with any laws, regulations, or orders in force, bearing on the subject.

No military officer has the right, in this country, to issue any order to which he cannot lawfully compel obedience by the forces under his command. The test, therefore, of the validity, in point of law, of this order of General McDowell, is, whether he could lawfully employ the military forces subject to his control to prevent American citizens, and other persons within our jurisdiction, from transporting arms and munitions of war, as merchandise, across the frontier into Mexico, in the present state of the affairs of that country.

The answer to be given to this question depends upon the character of the acts against which the order is directed—whether they are lawful or unlawful; and, if unlawful, whether the military authority can take cognizance of them and prevent or restrain their commission.

Some offences are cognizable exclusively by civil authority; others may lawfully be restrained or prevented by military power.

Counterfeiting the current coin of the United States is made criminal by statute, but the law leaves the offence to be dealt with by the civil authority of the United States. By the statute of 1818, the setting on foot any military expedition within the jurisdiction of the United States against the territory of a foreign state with whom the United States are at peace, is a high misdemeanor, but the statute expressly authorizes the President to employ the army and navy to prevent the carrying on of any such expedition from our territory.

It is plain that if it should be determined that it is not unlawful for American citizens, neutral people in the war now being waged on Mexican territory, to export articles contraband of war, by way of merchandise, to either of the belligerents, the inquiry as to the jurisdiction of the military authorities over the subject need not be pursued.

In that event any attempt on the part of those authorities to enforce obedience to rules or regulations of their own in regard to that subject would be clearly a usurpation of power.

Now, I apprehend it to be well settled that "neutrals may lawfully sell at home to a belligerent purchaser, or carry themselves to the belligerent powers, contraband articles, subject to the right of seizure *in transitu*. The right of the neutral to transport, and of the hostile power to seize, are conflicting rights, and neither party can charge the other with criminal act." (Kent's Com., p. 142.) I state the doctrine in the words of Chancellor Kent, "of whose writings it may be safely said," a late English author has remarked, "that they are never wrong."

In the case of the Santissima Trinidad, Mr. Justice Story, in delivering the opinion of the court, said, "There is nothing in our laws, or in the law of nations, that forbids our citizens from sending armed vessels, as well as munitions of war, to foreign ports for sale. It is a commercial adventure which no nation is bound to prohibit, and which only exposes the persons engaged in it to the penalty of confiscation." (7 Wheaton, 340.)

Without entering into an extended exposition of the law on this subject, I am of opinion that if the order of General McDowell was intended to interfere with such trade, conducted by our people, as the authorities to which I have referred have declared to be lawful, the order is not "in conformity with any laws bearing upon the subject."

I observe that a portion of the order to which my attention has been called was probably intended to be directed against military expeditions or armed enterprises carried on from this country against the belligerents contending in Mexico. Such expeditions and enterprises are, of course, violations of our statutes; and nothing in this opinion is intended to impugn the validity of the order in respect to them.

I have the honor to be, with the greatest respect,

JAMES SPEED,
Attorney General.

Hon. WILLIAM H. SEWARD,
Secretary of State.

Mr. Seward to Mr. Romero.

DEPARTMENT OF STATE,
Washington, December 24, 1865.

SIR: I have had the honor to receive your communications of the 14th and 18th of November last, with their respective accompaniments, which have reference to the order issued by Major General McDowell, commanding the military department of California, No. 17, under date of the 11th of October, 1865, prohibiting the exportation of arms or munitions of war into Mexico by the frontier.

Having submitted the subject to the Attorney General of the United States for his opinion on the 21st of November last, I have now the honor to transmit to you a copy of said opinion rendered on the 23d instant, and likewise to inform you that it will be officially communicated to the honorable the Secretary of War, with the request to give such instructions to Major General McDowell as shall conform to the decision of the Attorney General in the premises.

I avail myself of the occasion to reiterate to you, sir, the assurances of my highest consideration.

WILLIAM H. SEWARD.

Señor MATIAS ROMERO, *&c., Washington, D. C.*

Mr. Geofroy to Mr. Seward.

[Translation.]

LEGATION OF FRANCE IN THE UNITED STATES,
Washington, March 11, 1864.

SIR: According to information which has reached the Emperor's government, three regiments of the federal army have lately been sent to Matamoras, under pretext of protecting the consul of the United States at that point, and have there re-established the Juarist authority, by driving out therefrom General Cortinas, who had pronounced against it. This news, the official confirmation of which, however, it had not received, has fixed the attention of the Emperor's government. Such a fact would constitute a violation of the neutrality, on which the assurances of the cabinet at Washington have authorized it to rely, on its part, in regard to Mexico, and would also be entirely opposed to the instructions addressed by the Department of State to General Banks, who has been directed to favor neither of the two parties, and not to enter the Mexican territory, even to protect the American consul and citizens there. I therefore deem it my duty, sir, to point it out to you, and would be infinitely obliged if you could furnish me with explanations on this subject.

Be pleased to accept, sir, assurances of my high consideration.

L. DE GEOFROY.

Hon. WILLIAM H. SEWARD, *&c.*

Mr. Seward to Mr. Geofroy.

DEPARTMENT OF STATE,
Washington, March 12, 1864.

SIR: I have the honor to acknowledge the receipt of your note of the 11th instant, in which you state that, according to information which has reached the Emperor's government, three regiments of the United States army have lately been sent to Matamoras under the pretext of protecting the consul of the United States at that port, and have there established the Juarist authority by driving out therefrom General Cortinas, who had pronounced against it there. You proceed in your note to observe that this news, the official confirmation of which, however, had not been received by the French government, has fixed the attention of the Emperor's government; that the alleged proceedings constituted a violation of the neutrality on which the assurances of this government has authorized France to rely, and would also be opposed to the instructions which were addressed by this department to Major General Banks, who commands the United States forces on the borders of Mexico, and therefore you ask proper explanation thereupon.

In reply to your note, I have the honor to say that the attention of the President was first directed to the transaction you have mentioned by a note which was written to this department by Don Matias Romero, the minister plenipotentiary of the Mexican republic residing at this capital, on the 6th of February last. Mr. Romero, in that note, represented that the dispute at Matamoras, which was the occasion of the proceeding of General Herron, now complained of, was a dispute between two military leaders, each of whom acknowledged the authority and acted under the orders of the Mexican republic. Taking that view of the subject, Mr. Romero insisted that the proceeding of General Herron was a flagrant violation of Mexican sovereignty, as well as a violation of the before-mentioned instructions of this department to Major General Banks.

Upon receiving these representations of Mr. Romero, I called upon the Secretary of War for such information concerning this transaction as he possessed, and further requested that a full investigation thereof might be instituted. I have received from the Secretary of War certain papers which bear upon the transaction in question, but not yet the full report which has been requested. I have now the honor to place copies of these papers before you, namely, a report of Major General Banks, with the documents annexed, and to add to them an extract from a despatch of the United States consul at Matamoras, which has been received at this department.

A declaration of the views of this government upon the proceeding of General Herron is necessarily reserved until the result of the investigation which has been ordered shall have been ascertained. I shall be happy, in the mean time, to receive any information upon the subject which the government of France shall find it convenient and desirable to submit in support of the views of that government, which conflict with the representations of the Mexican government, as well as with the statements made by the military authorities and the consul of the United States.

I will add that General Banks has again been specially charged to do whatever is practicable to avoid any collision between the forces under his command and either of the belligerents in Mexico, and even to guard, so far as may be possible, against suffering any occasion to arise for dispute or controversy between his command or the authorities of Texas, and either or both of these parties.

Accept, sir, the assurances of my high consideration.

WILLIAM H. SEWARD.

Mr. L. DE GEOFROY, *&c., &c., &c.*

General Canby to Mr. Seward.

DEPARTMENT OF STATE,
Washington, February 10, 1864.

SIR: The Secretary of War instructs me to acknowledge the receipt of your letter of yesterday, transmitting a translation of a note addressed to you on the 4th instant by Señor Matias Romero, envoy extraordinary and minister plenipotentiary of the United Mexican States, inviting attention to a publication in the New York journals, during the month of January last, purporting to be a communication containing menaces, addressed from Brownsville, on the 26th of December last, by Major General N. J. T. Dana, then commanding the United States forces in Texas, to the governor of Tamaulipas, in the Mexican republic, and also to the Matamoras correspondence, published in the daily papers, in which it is stated that Major General Herron, now commanding United States forces at Brownsville, has sent troops into the city of Matamoras, during local disturbances in that city, in violation of Mexican sovereignty.

In regard to the alleged violation of the Mexican territory by United States troops acting under the orders of Major General Herron, the Secretary instructs me to transmit for your information the enclosed copy of a communication this day received, addressed to the general-in-chief by Major General Banks, commanding the department of the Gulf, with its accompaniments, which present a detailed account of the circumstances under which the temporary presence of the United States troops in Matamoras was deemed imperative for the protection of the United States consulate in that city.

On the subject of the alleged letter of menace addressed by Major General N. J. T. Dana, from Brownsville, to the governor of Tamaulipas, this department has at present no knowledge. As soon as any information on the subject is received it will be communicated to you.

I have the honor to be your obedient servant,

ED. R. S. CANBY,
Brigadier General, Assistant Adjutant General.

HON. SECRETARY OF STATE,
Washington, D. C.

General Banks to General Halleck.

[Extract.]

HEADQUARTERS DEPARTMENT OF THE GULF,
New Orleans, January 25, 1864.

GENERAL: I have the honor to transmit to you copies of despatches received from Major General F. J. Herron, commanding the forces of the United States on the Rio Grande, and giving in detail an account of affairs occurring on the 13th of January.

° ° ° ° ° ° ° ° ° ° °

The movement of troops into Matamoras seems to have been necessary to enable the consul to leave the city.

N. P. BANKS,
Major General Commanding.

Major General H. W. HALLECK,
General-in-Chief U. S. A.

Official copy:

J. C. KELTON,
Assistant Adjutant General.

General Herron to General Stone.

[Extract.]

HEADQUARTERS UNITED STATES FORCES ON THE RIO GRANDE,
Brownsville, Texas, January 16, 1864.

GENERAL: I enclose herewith my report in reference to sending troops to the other side of the river for the protection of the United States consulate, and believing it will interest you, I add some other facts in connection with the matter.

Upon arriving here I found Lerna established as governor of Tamaulipas, but Ruiz, who had been appointed military governor by Juarez, was moving on Matamoras with 600 men.

Colonel Cortinas was in command of the Lerna forces. Arriving near the town, commissioners from the two parties met and settled the matter in this way: Lerna to retire to his rancho; Ruiz to take his seat as governor; the troops of both parties to unite under General Cassistran, a Ruiz man, with Cortinas as second in command, and to march against the French at Tampico. Lerna at once vacated. Ruiz took his seat, and the troops of both parties were camped in the town.

As near as I can learn the agreement was violated in several particulars by both parties, and considerable feeling was created. On the afternoon of the 12th, about 4 o'clock, Cardenas, an officer of Colonel Cortinas, rode to Governor Ruiz's house and insulted him; was arrested by the guard, carried into a back yard, and shot within half an hour. This settled the matter, and at 8 o'clock the same evening the parties opened on each other with artillery in the plaza.

The fight continued throughout the night, and until 12 o'clock the next day. During the night, at times, the musketry was severe, and I should say 250 shots were fired with artillery. Mr. Pierce was satisfied that an attempt would be made to rob the consulate, and had great apprehension for his family. The governor having officially notified me that he could not protect him, and believing that I could remove him without complicating matters, I sent troops over, feeling satisfied that under the circumstances I was only doing my duty.

During the fight the town and the road leading to the ferry were filled with robbers doing a good business, and had Mr Pierce attempted to cross without a guard he would have been robbed, if not murdered. Both parties are perfectly satisfied with my action, although Ruiz complained somewhat that I did not aid him, claiming that the Mexican troops once aided the citizens of Brownsville in repelling an attack of this same Cortinas.

I have the honor to be, with great respect, your obedient servant,

F. J. HERRON,
Major General Commanding.

Brigadier General C. P. STONE, *Chief of Staff.*

HEADQUARTERS, *February* 3, 1864.

Official copy:

J. C. KELTON,
Assistant Adjutant General.

General Herron to General Stone.

HEADQUARTERS UNITED STATES FORCES ON THE RIO GRANDE,
Brownsville, Texas, January 15, 1864.

GENERAL: I have the honor to make the following report of circumstances that transpired on the night of the 13th instant:

About 8 o'clock in the evening we were startled by rapid cannonading and musketry firing evidently going on in the streets of Matamoras. just across the Rio Grande, which continued without cessation, spreading over the greater portion of the town, until 10 o'clock.

At this hour I received the following communication from Mr. L Pierce, jr., United States consul at Matamoras:

"UNITED STATES CONSULATE,
"*Matamoras, Mexico, January* 12, 1864—10 o'clock p m.

GENERAL: A battle is now raging in the streets of this city between the forces of Governor Manuel Ruiz and Colonel Juan N. Cortinas. My person and family are in great danger, as the road between here and the ferry is said to be infested with robbers. I have also about one million of dollars in specie and a large amount of valuable property under my charge in the consulate, and, from the well-known character of Cortinas and his followers, I fear the city will be plundered. I therefore earnestly request that you will send a sufficient force to protect myself and property, and to transport the money within the limits of the United States at the earliest moment possible.

"I am, sir, very respectfully, your obedient servant,

"L PIERCE, JR.,
"*United States Consul.*

"Major General F. J. HERRON,
"*Commanding United States Forces, Brownsville, Texas.*"

Within a very few moments the following, from Governor Manuel Ruiz, was handed to me:

"MATAMORAS, *January* 12, 1864—10 o'clock p. m.

"SIR: The forces commanded by Colonel Cortinas have attacked my positions in this place. As this town is very extensive, I cannot protect all, nor guarantee the United States consulate and the large property of American citizens, of different nations, living in this town. For this reason I shall endeavor to repulse the enemy, and ask you the favor to send some troops over to guard and protect the said property, which it is impossible for me to protect.

"I ask you, general, to take this application of mine in high consideration, and to admit my profound respect.

"Your obedient servant,

"MANUEL RUIZ, *Governor of Tamaulipas.*

"Major General F. J. HERRON."

I had, immediately after the firing commenced, despatched an officer (Colonel Black 37th Illinois infantry) to the United States consulate, with instructions to inform me at once of the condition of affairs, and hearing from him also that the road was infested with robbers, who were taking advantage of the fighting to rob and murder, and that the family of the consul could not get away without a guard, and the legal governor, recognized by President Juarez, having informed me officially that he could not protect him, I deemed it not inconsistent with my instructions to send a small force into the city of Matamoras for the purpose of removing the family of Mr. Pierce and the specie to this side of the river. I therefore ordered Colonel Henry Bertram, 20th Wisconsin infantry, to send forty men to take charge of the ferry, to put one regiment under arms and call at my headquarters for further orders. Upon reporting, I instructed him to take four companies of his regiment across the river, and proceed to the United States consulate, and there to make proper disposition of his force to protect the United States consul and his property, and to remove them at the earliest possible time to this side of the river; instructing him, at the same time, in the most positive manner, not to interfere in the fight. I then replied to Governor Ruiz as follows:

"HEADQUARTERS UNITED STATES FORCES ON THE RIO GRANDE,
"*Brownsville, Texas, January* 12, 1864—10½ o'clock p. m.

"SIR: Your note, dated Matamoras, 10 o'clock p. m., is at hand. Mr. Pierce, the United States consul, wrote at 10 o'clock, urging me to send a force to protect the United States consulate, and at his request I despatched Colonel Bertram, with a small force, to the consul's house, to protect him in moving to this side of the river.

"The troops have positive instructions not to interfere with either person or property, and to take no part in the fight. They will protect the consulate until safely removed.

"Regretting exceedingly the troubles which surround you, and with the hope that you may soon quiet matters, I have the honor to be, with great respect, your obedient servant,

"F. J. HERRON,
"*Major General Commanding.*

"Governor MANUEL RUIZ."

At the same time I wrote to Mr. Pierce, informing him of the instructions given to Colonel Bertram, and requesting him to prepare for removal at once.

I also sent the following notification to Governor Ruiz, sending a similar one to Colonel Cortinas:

"HEADQUARTERS UNITED STATES FORCES ON THE RIO GRANDE,
"*Brownsville, Texas, January* 12, 1864—10½ o'clock p. m.

"SIR: I have the honor to state that, owing to a battle now raging in the streets of Matamoras, between your troops and those of Colonel Cortinas, and the danger existing to the person and family of Mr. Pierce, United States consul, I have ordered Colonel Bertram, with four companies of United States troops, to proceed to the house of Mr. Pierce, at his request, for the sole and only purpose of conveying them within the territory of the United States. The dangers from assassins and robbers on the road between here and your city seem imperatively to demand this course, which I take reluctantly, with every assurance to you that I shall commit no hostile acts upon Mexican territory, nor interfere in any manner with the fight now going on in your city. I have instructed Mr. Pierce to remove as quickly as possible, that I may withdraw the troops.

"I have the honor to be, with great respect, your obedient servant,

"F. J. HERRON,
"*Major General Commanding.*

"Governor MANUEL RUIZ."

Colonel Bertram proceeded without delay to the other side of the river, marching by the shortest route to the consulate, and placing his troops within the yard which is attached to the house, and such arrangements were then made as would prevent any possibility of interference by our men.

At 12½ o'clock I received the following note from Colonel Bertram:

"AT UNITED STATES CONSULATE.
"*Matamoras, January* 12, 1864—12½ o'clock p. m.

"GENERAL: I have arrived at the consul's house, and assure you he was very happy to see us I marched the shortest route, the firing having stopped as soon as we appeared on the streets. The consul thinks Cortinas is gaining ground. I await further instructions.

"Very respectfully,

"H. BERTRAM, *Colonel Commanding.*

"Major General F. J. HERRON,
"*Commanding United States Forces.*"

To which I replied as follows:

"HEADQUARTERS UNITED STATES FORCES ON THE RIO GRANDE,
"*Brownsville, Texas, January* 12, 1864.

"COLONEL: Your note from the consul's is at hand. You will remain in your position, giving the consul sufficient time to remove his family and the valuables in the consulate to this side. Again let me state that you will interfere in no way with the fight, but keep your men at their posts for the duty assigned them. Send a good officer with the troops at the ferry, and issue the most positive orders prohibiting straggling from the ranks or interference of any nature whatever with either person or property. Should a stray shot come near or even strike one of your men, that will not be considered a sufficient reason for your firing. I have notified both Ruiz and Cortinas of your presence in Matamoras, and the purpose. Should you see either of the persons named, state fully what your instructions are.

"Your mission is a delicate one; be extremely careful.

"Respectfully,

"F. J. HERRON, *Major General Commanding.*

"Colonel H. BERTRAM"

At 12½ o'clock I received the following from Colonel Bertram:

"AT UNITED STATES CONSULATE,
"*Matamoras, January* 12—12½ o'clock p. m.

"GENERAL: I have received your letter. Your instructions are strictly obeyed, and I have sent the most stringent orders to Lieutenant Colonel Laughlin not to allow anything to be done that could be construed into a violation of your orders. Commissions from both Ruiz's and Cortinas's parties have been here to inquire into the object of our coming over. I told them what my instructions were, and both parties went away satisfied. The consul says he has about one million in specie in his possession, and that he cannot possibly remove it or his family until morning. I have not been able to learn positively which party is gaining. Ruiz still holds the plaza, and I think will hold it until morning.

"Respectfully,

"H. BERTRAM, *Colonel Commanding.*

"Major General HERRON,
"*Commanding United States Forces.*"

The fighting ceased for an hour after the appearance of my troops; but learning that there was to be no interference, both parties went at it again, taking care, however, to keep some distance from the United States consulate. Matters continued so until daylight, when I sent a sufficient number of wagons to remove the family of Mr. Pierce and property from the consulate. At 7 o'clock a. m. of the 13th they were safely landed on this side, and the troops withdrew. The fighting in the morning was carried on bitterly until 12 o'clock, when the Ruiz party retreated, and were scattered in every direction. The casualties on both sides were about fifty killed and one hundred wounded. Among the killed was ex-Governor Alveus López, a prominent Ruiz man.

Governor Ruiz's forces numbered 800 men and four pieces of artillery, while Cortinas's force was 600 men and six pieces of artillery. Considerable damage was done by the artillery to the town during the fight, and by lawless bands plundering, &c.

Colonel Cortinas has already announced himself as governor of Tamaulipas, while Governor Ruiz, General Rohes, and some other prominent officers, escaped and crossed to this side, and are now here refugees.

I have in this report given merely the facts in detail, and will not enter into any argument in justification of my course. Notified by the governor of the State that he could not protect the United States consulate, and with an appeal from the consul direct for protection for his family and property, I felt that it was unquestionably my duty to furnish a sufficient guard to remove him from the city, taking at the same time every precaution to prevent collision with either of the factions. I might here state that the English consul remained during the night at the United States consulate under our protection. * * *

In conclusion, I would say that Colonel H. Bertram, of the 20th Wisconsin infantry, who commanded the troops that crossed over, performed the delicate mission in an admirable manner, and proved himself an officer of more than ordinary judgment. His officers and soldiers are entitled to thanks for their conduct.

I have the honor to be, general, with great respect, your obedient servant,

F. J. HERRON, *Major General.*

Brigadier General C. P. STONE,
Chief of Staff, New Orleans.

HEADQUARTERS, *February* 4, 1864.

Official copy:

J. C. KELTON, *A. A. G.*

Mr. Pierce to Mr. Seward.

[Extract.]

UNITED STATES CONSULATE,
Matamoras, January 16, 1864.

SIR: Since the arrival of the federal troops (6th November) affairs on this side of the Rio Grande have been in a most complete uproar. Immediately upon the arrival of troops at Brownsville, General Cobos, the reaccionario, crossed over, and with a small force seized the governor (Ruiz) and other officials and placed them in confinement, making himself governor, R. Vila military commander, and Colonel Juan N. Cortinas, who created a disturbance and fight in Brownsville several years ago, second in command. After reigning twenty-four hours, Cortinas discovered that Cobos and Vila were endeavoring to get up a pronunciamiento in favor of the French, and he accordingly ordered his men to take them out and shoot them, which was done. Cortinas then proclaimed Jesus de la Lerna governor, and released Ruiz from prison, giving him two hours in which to leave town, referring the whole matter to the general government. In the mean time Ruiz went off to the interior, and as Lerna had been the cause of the revolution two years ago, Ruiz was sent back again to take his seat, with a large escort of regular troops. Lerna, who had arrived in town, supported by Cortinas, made preparations to defend the town, but after ten days' talk on the subject, on the first day of January it was agreed that Ruiz should take the chair, and the troops of both parties should go to Tampico to fight the French, and until they should be ready to start Ruiz should hold one side of the town and Cortinas the other. Everything remained quiet until the afternoon of the 12th, when Octiviano Cardenas, who belonged to the Cortinas party, went to the palace, in company with two other officers, and insulted the governor. In arresting him he fired his pistol off among Ruiz's soldiers. He was immediately seized, led out, and shot to death. This again started a correspondence between the contending parties, and at 9 p. m. the same evening the fighting commenced in the streets, one party using six pieces of artillery and Ruiz using two. The battle lasted until 11 a. m. on the 13th, when Cortinas took possession of the palace and town, and Ruiz and his friends fled to Brownsville, and at present we are without a governor.

During the night of the 12th, finding that robbing was being carried on in some parts of the town, and I having about a million of dollars in specie under my charge, at 10½ p. m. I applied to Major General Herron, commanding the forces on the Rio Grande, for sufficient men to protect our property from thieves and robbers, and he immediately crossed over a large force, who remained by us until morning, when I sent all the money to Brownsville, and the troops retired. * * * * * * *

I am, sir, very respectfully, your most obedient servant,

L. PIERCE, JR., *U. S. Consul.*

Hon. WILLIAM H. SEWARD,
Secretary of State, Washington, D. C.

Mr. Geofroy to Mr. Seward.

[Translation.]

LEGATION OF FRANCE TO THE UNITED STATES,
Washington, March 20, 1864.

SIR: I have received the note you did me the honor to write to me on the 12th of the month, with the various documents which accompanied it.

It seems, by these papers, that on the 12th of January last, a battle having been commenced in the city of Matamoras between the two Mexican chiefs, Ruiz and Cortinas, on the application of Mr. Pierce, consul of the United States there resident, who feared for his safety, Major General Herron, commanding the federal troops cantoned at Brownsville, Texas, sent across the frontier four companies of infantry, who came and took up a position in the vicinity of the consulate, and there remained until next day, the 13th; that they took back with them to the other side of the river Mr. Pierce, his family, and the valuables deposited at the consulate.

I remark that this temporary occupation had also been solicited by Ruiz, chief of the Juarists, who wrote at the same time as Mr. Pierce to General Herron, to declare to him that he was not in a condition to protect the United States consulate and the property of American citizens settled in the city, and who, under the pretence of providing for the safety of foreigners, wished probably to get for himself the support, at least apparent, of the federal troops.

On the morning of the 13th, when these were withdrawn, the Juarists disbanded, and Ruiz, with his principal officers, also crossed the river and took refuge at Brownsville.

In fine, it is evident it is General Banks whose charge it is to point it out that in taking possession of his command General Herron received a communication of the instructions prepared the 23d of November, 1863, by the Department of State, and that in consequence he acted, as also did Consul Pierce, in full knowledge of the subject.

Such are the facts established by the reports of the military commanders of the United States. It would be difficult not to recognize therein a violation of neutrality, and a positive breach of orders, although so clear, which had been given by the Department of State, precisely for the accordance of such eventualities.

I shall carry your excellency's note to the knowledge of the Emperor's government, and be prepared to transmit to it also the report of Major General Banks, which you are pleased to announce to me, as well as all other documents you may deem proper to complete the elucidation of the affair.

Please accept, sir, the assurances of my high consideration.

L. DE GEOFROY.

Hon. WILLIAM H. SEWARD, &c.

Mr. Seward to Mr. Geofroy.

DEPARTMENT OF STATE,
Washington, March 23, 1864.

SIR: I have the honor to acknowledge the receipt of your note of the 20th instant, in which you assume that the sending a few troops from Brownsville to Matamoras to protect treasure in the custody of the United States consul at the latter place, during the late civil conflict there, was contrary to the neutrality professed by this government, and which General Banks had been directed to observe in reference to affairs in Mexico. Without meaning to underrate the force of your remarks on this point, I deem it proper to postpone further discussion of this subject until such views of your government as may be formed, after a fair consideration of the correspondence which has already taken place, shall be made known to this department.

Accept, sir, the renewed assurance of my high consideration.

WILLIAM H. SEWARD.

Mr. L. DE GEOFROY, &c.

Mr. Geofroy to Mr. Seward.

[Translation.]

LEGATION OF FRANCE TO THE UNITED STATES,
Washington, April 3, 1864.

SIR: As I have the honor to inform you, I have transmitted to my government the documents which your excellency submitted to me on the subject of the affair at Matamoras. The documents can scarcely have reached Paris at this moment. While awaiting the answer they will occasion, I this morning received a second despatch from M. Drouyn de Lhuys, pointing to new facts, on which I shall have the honor to confer with your excellency on the earliest day my health will permit me to go out; but there is a point which seems to be of importance to bring immediately to your notice. It would appear that on the news of the events of the month of January last General Bazaine took the measures necessary to protect, in the direction of Matamoras, the Mexican territory against any further invasion. Whatever may be the opinion we may form upon past events, you will comprehend, sir, how necessary it is, to avoid all complication in the future, that General Banks, and the officers serving under his orders, may be again called to the strict observance of the instructions given the 23d November, 1863, from your excellency's department.

I should not, either, leave you in ignorance that the French troops must also have been directed to Sonora, where, according to reports more or less founded, a very considerable number of emigrants from California must lately have disembarked at Guaymas, and have established themselves in the country in virtue of grants which were made to them by the ex-President Juarez. The mission of our forces is to prevent in Sonora all these takings of illicit possession, if they be really attempted, and, in any case, the lawfulness of concessions which shall have emanated from Juarez will never be admitted. Your excellency will probably judge proper to make this known to American citizens who might allow themselves to be drawn into such speculations.

I seize this occasion to renew to your excellency the assurances of my high consideration.

L. DE GEOFROY.

Hon. WILLIAM H. SEWARD, &c.

Mr. Seward to Mr. Geofroy.

DEPARTMENT OF STATE,
Washington, April 6, 1864.

SIR: I have the honor to acknowledge the receipt of your note of the 3d instant, in which you inform me that you have received a second despatch from M. Drouyn de Lhuys, pointing to new facts in relation, as I am left to infer, to the proceedings which took place at Matamoras in the case of Mr. Pierce, the consul at that place, and which have been made the subject of recent correspondence, on your part, with this department. I shall with pleasure receive the promised information when the state of your health shall be such as to enable you to visit me, and I sincerely regret the cause by which such a visit is delayed. Since my last note to you on the Matamoras affair was written, I have learned that General Cortinas, with his forces, is certainly adhering to the government of the United States of Mexico. In view of this fact, it is not now apparent to this government that France—being in our view only a belligerent in Mexico, and having no forces at or near Matamoras when the transaction in regard to the consul occurred there—can reasonably expect explanations concerning it from the United States.

You inform me in the note now before me that, on hearing of that transaction in January last, General Bazaine took the measures necessary to protect the Mexican territory in the direction of Matamoras against any further invasion; and you suggest that, in consequence of that proceeding, Major General Banks, and the officers serving under his orders, may be again called to a strict observance of the instructions which I gave to that general on the 23d of November last. Passing over the words "further invasion" as an accidental assumption of a fact which this government has not conceded, and is not yet prepared to concede, I have had no hesitation in informing Major General Banks of the purpose of General Bazaine, and enjoining the United States general to a strict and faithful observance of the instructions of November, which require him to forbear from any form of intervention in the war between France and Mexico.

You also inform me in your last-mentioned note that French forces have been directed towards Sonora, and you bring to my knowledge rumors that a very considerable number of emigrants from California have lately disembarked at Guaymas, and have established themselves in the country in virtue of grants which were made to them by President Juarez, whom you describe as ex-President; you further state that the mission of the French forces is to prevent, in Sonora, the taking possession of estates under such grants, the lawfulness of which, you say, will never be admitted; and you suggest to me the expediency of making this information known to American citizens who might be destined to allow themselves to be drawn into such speculations.

While I appreciate the frankness and good will which the Emperor's government manifests in thus communicating its views and purposes on the subject mentioned, it nevertheless remains my duty to say that this government has long recognized, and still does continue to recognize, the constitutional government of the United States of Mexico as the sovereign authority in that country, and the President, Benito Juarez, as its chief. This government, at the same time, equally recognizes the condition of war existing in Mexico between that country and France. We maintain absolute neutrality between the belligerents, and we do not assume to judge, much less to judge in advance, of the effect of the war upon titles or estates. We have no knowledge of such an emigration from California to Sonora as you have described in your note; but if such an emigration has taken place, those persons who thus emigrate will of course be regarded as subjecting themselves to the authority and laws by which the rights of citizens of Mexico are governed; and while it seems unnecessary for the President to assume that such emigrants will claim the protection of this government for any estates of whatever kind they may attain or attempt to attain in Mexico, it would certainly be presumptuous to attempt now to decide upon the validity of such claim.

Peaceful emigration from the United States is entirely free from restraint or influence of the government. Emigrants themselves are generally well informed concerning their rights. Under these circumstances, any interference of the government concerning such emigration would be as inexpedient as it would be without precedent. The case would be different if the act of emigration was attended with preparations and purposes hostile to Mexico, or to either belligerent party, or to any other nation, and therefore incompatible with the laws of the United States or with the law of nations. It is believed that the government of the United States has already sufficiently indicated the views it must take in such a case if it should occur, which, however, there seems no immediate reason to apprehend.

Accept, sir, the renewed assurance of my high consideration.

WILLIAM H. SEWARD.

Mr. L. de Geofroy, &c.

Mr. Geofroy to Mr. Seward.

[Translation.]

LEGATION OF FRANCE TO THE UNITED STATES,
Washington, April 7, 1864.

SIR: About the end of December and beginning of January last, two bands, the one of 200 men, the second of 500, detached from the troops which are under the command of General Banks in Texas, went from Brownsville and Brazos Santiago, invaded the Mexican territory by taking advantage of the disorder which reigned at Matamoras, and went and carried off a considerable number of bales of cotton deposited at Boca del Rio Bravo by merchants of Monterey, on the pretence that this merchandise belonged to Americans of the southern States. The government of his Majesty has charged me to call the most serious attention of your excellency to these violations of territory, which, connected with that which I have already had the honor to point out to you previously, would constitute a combination of facts of which I have no need to develop the importance. I therefore beg your excellency to have the goodness to give me on this subject some explanations, and I take this occasion to offer to you the assurance of my high consideration.

L. DE GEOFROY.

Hon. WILLIAM H. SEWARD, *&c.*

Mr. Seward to Mr. Geofroy,

DEPARTMENT OF STATE,
Washington, April 9, 1864.

SIR: I have the honor to acknowledge the receipt of your note of the 7th instant, stating that about the end of December and beginning of January last, bodies of troops from the command of General Banks went from Brownsville and Brazos Santiago, in Texas, into Mexican territory, and carried off a considerable number of bales of cotton lodged at Boca del Rio Bravo. In reply I have the honor to acquaint you that this department has no knowledge, official or otherwise, of the proceeding referred to. Inquiry will, however, at once be made in regard to it, and such further proceedings will be adopted as the result may call for, it being the disposition of this government to maintain entire neutrality between the belligerents in Mexico, and its determination not to authorize or sanction any invasion of Mexican soil.

I have the honor to be, with high consideration, sir, your obedient servant,

WILLIAM H. SEWARD.

Mr. L. DE GEOFROY, *&c.*

Mr. Geofroy to Mr. Seward.

[Translation.]

LEGATION OF FRANCE TO THE UNITED STATES,
Washington, April 26, 1864.

SIR: Some months since a society was formed in the city of New Orleans the object of which is to make enrolments and purchases of arms and ammunition destined for Mexico. This association, openly avowed and known under the name of club of the Defenders of the Monroe Doctrine, D. M. D., has its regular meetings, duly announced by means of the newspapers, and employs all measures of propagandism for raising subscriptions and making proselytes. At its head are some Mexican refugees, and notably a Colonel de Borden. Some number of federal officers also form part of it, and Governor Hahn himself, whose opinions are known, has been received as a member. Already transmissions of arms and munitions have been directed towards the frontier of the Rio Grande, and I am assured, although I do not like to believe it, with the connivance of some of the authorities of the United States. It suffices me to point out such facts to your excellency. I have too many evidences of the scrupulous care you take to cause the observance of the most exact neutrality in the affairs of Mexico, not to feel certain in advance that the government of the United States will take the most effective measures to repress them, and that it will, in an exemplary manner, deal severely with those of its agents who shall be convicted of having taken part in this.

I seize this occasion to renew to your excellency the assurances of my high consideration.

L. DE GEOFROY.

Hon. WILLIAM H. SEWARD, &c.

Mr. Seward to Mr. Geofroy.

DEPARTMENT OF STATE,
Washington, April 30, 1864.

SIR: I have the honor to acknowledge the receipt of your note of the 26th instant, relative to the alleged formation of a society at New Orleans, the object of which is to make enrolments and purchase of arms and ammunition destined for Mexico, and stating that already transmissions of arms and munitions have been directed towards the frontier of the Rio Grande.

I have the honor to inform you, in reply, that letters have been addressed by this department to the governor of Louisiana and to Major General Banks, requesting an inquiry into the matters thus reported, with a view to insure a strict observance of neutrality on the part of officers and citizens of the United States.

Accept, sir, a renewed assurance of my high consideration.

WILLIAM H. SEWARD.

Mr. L. DE GEOFROY, &c.

Mr. Geofroy to Mr. Seward.—(Received May 27, 1864.)

[Translation.]

It seems that Brownsville, on the Rio Grande, is the very active centre of a traffic in articles contraband of war, a traffic which is carried on for account of the agents of Mr. Juarez, and that the federal authorities, who are accused of deriving large profits from it, favor, in place of hindering it; that General Herron, who commands at Brownsville, is on the best terms with Mr. Cortinas, whom he aids with all his power, by furnishing him arms, munitions, and even recruits, and that he loudly avows his sympathies with the pretended government which he still represents at Matamoras. The collector of the federal customs at Brownsville must be also, as it is given out, in connivance with Mr. Cortinas.

It seems that at this moment a ship is being laden near Boston, which is to carry to Mexico one or two batteries of artillery, carbines, swords, and bayonets. Contracts for these articles, contraband of war, have been made already, some weeks since, and the vessel which will carry them will, to turn aside suspicion, be cleared from some small port in New England. She will be given Brazos as her destination, which is at a short distance from the mouth of the Rio Grande, and from that locality the cargo will be sent on its way to a point occupied by the agents of Mr. Juarez.

Mr. Seward to Mr. Geofroy.

DEPARTMENT OF STATE,
Washington, May 28, 1864.

SIR: On the 30th of April last I had the honor to receive your note, written on the 26th of that month, in which you informed me that a society had been formed in the city of New Orleans, the object of which is to make enrolments and purchases of arms and ammunition destined for Mexico. You further informed me that this association, openly avowed, and known under the name of the club of the "Defenders of the Monroe Doctrine, D. M. D.," has its regular meetings, duly announced by means of the newspapers, and employs all means of propagandism for raising subscriptions and making proselytes; that at its head are some Mexican refugees, and notably a Colonel De Borden. Some number of federal officers also form part of it, and Governor Hahn himself, whose opinions are known, has been received as a member; that transmissions of arms and munitions have already been directed towards the Rio Grande, and that you were assured, although you did not like to believe it, that such transmission of arms and munitions were made with the connivance of some of the authorities of the United States.

I lost no time in bringing the complaints which you thus preferred, in their full effect, to the knowledge of Major General Banks, who is in command of the United States forces west of the Mississippi, and also to the knowledge of his excellency Michael Hahn, the governor of the State of Louisiana.

I have now the honor to inform you that I have received from the governor of Louisiana an official communication in relation to these complaints, of the effect following, namely: that there is a society or club in New Orleans under the name of the "Defenders of the Monroe Doctrine;" that his excellency Michael Hahn is not a member of the club, or of any similar association; that the presiding officer of the club is Colonel F. N. D. S. Borden, who is understood to be a loyal citizen of the republic of Mexico; that the only citizens of New Orleans who are known to the governor as belonging to the club are a few young men of no considerable influence; that the object of the club, so far as the governor has been able to ascertain it, is to bring moral influences to bear upon the government of the United States in favor of a maintenance of the Monroe doctrine, but not to act in violation of the law, or of the well-understood governmental policy of neutrality, in the war which exists between France and Mexico; that so far as the governor has learned, there has been neither any enrolment of men nor any subscriptions of money by the club, or by any other association, for the purposes of war in Mexico. Nor have any arms, ammunition, or men been sent there through any association of persons in the State of Louisiana, so far as the governor knows, or has even heard.

I am further assured by his excellency that he cordially co-operates with the other public officers in Louisiana in carrying out the known instructions and wishes of the President and this department, and in observing and enforcing the provisions of the law relating to the neutrality of the United States in the war between France and Mexico.

It remains only to assure your excellency that this department reposes implicit confidence in the statements of Governor Hahn, and, consequently, that there have been no such violations of the neutrality of the United States in New Orleans as, through misinformation, your excellency has been led to represent.

Accept, sir, a renewed assurance of my very high consideration.

WILLIAM H. SEWARD.

Mr. L. DE GEOFROY, *&c.*

Mr. Seward to Mr. Geofroy.

DEPARTMENT OF STATE,
Washington, June 21, 1864.

SIR: With reference to the memorandum, without date, relative to an alleged traffic in articles contraband of war, through Brownsville, on the Rio Grande, with the agents of President Juarez, which was received from the legation of France on the 27th ultimo, I have the honor to state, for your information, that Major General Banks, to whom a translation of that paper was communicated, has apprised me that the subject has received attention; that arrests have been made, and that goods have been seized upon the supposition that they were destined for a contraband trade with Mexico; that Major General McClernand, commanding the 13th army corps, being absent in consequence of sickness, has requested that Major General Herron will be assigned to the command of that corps, and his quarters will be established in the State of Louisiana.

Accept, sir, the renewed assurance of my high consideration.

WILLIAM H. SEWARD.

Mr. L. DE GEOFROY, *&c.*

Mr. Seward to Mr. Geofroy.

DEPARTMENT OF STATE,
Washington, June 22, 1864.

SIR: Referring to your note of the 26th of April last, and to my replies of the 30th of that month and 28th ultimo, in regard to the formation of a society at New Orleans, under the name of the club of the Defenders of the Monroe Doctrine, and to the alleged objects and proceedings of that association, I have now the honor to acquaint you that I have received information from Major General Banks corroborating the statements made by his excellency Governor Hahn, which were imparted to you in my note of the 28th ultimo. General Banks further reports that if there are any federal officers connected with the before-named society, they are not men of influence or character. Officers may have been led, in some instances, to associate themselves with it out of motives of curiosity, but have abandoned the organization as soon as its unlawful character and purposes became known; that a Colonel Van Zandt, one of the persons lately arrested, has been dismissed from the service. If enlisted men are connected with it, they are without influence, and in many instances of disreputable character; that as a combination this association is unimportant in its influence upon international relations, but that there are some dangerous men connected with it; that they had before and since the receipt of my communication to Major General Banks, of the 30th of April, been under close surveillance; that their objects are to enlist men, and, perhaps, to obtain arms and other materials for offensive demonstrations in Mexico or elsewhere; that it is quite as likely, however, to be intended to further their own ambitious personal projects and fortunes as to interfere in the affairs of Mexico or any other nation; that an arrest of these parties was made at the earliest moment when proof could be obtained of that purpose; that the steamer Crescent, upon which they had taken passage for Brownsville, was seized a few days since by Brigadier General Bowen, provost marshal general, and the departure of the expedition prevented.

In conclusion, Major General Banks reassures me that every precaution will be taken to avoid any unlawful interference with the affairs of Mexico, in violation of the policy of this government, as defined in my instructions to him.

Accept, sir, a renewed assurance of my highest consideration.

WILLIAM H. SEWARD.

Mr. L. DE GEOFROY.

Mr. Geofroy to Mr. Seward.

[Translation.]

LEGATION OF FRANCE TO THE UNITED STATES,
Washington, June 22, 1864.

SIR: I have received the note which you did me the honor to address to me yesterday, to announce to me that the memorandum which I remitted to your excellency on the 27th of last month, on the subject of shipments of arms and munitions to Mexico by the frontier of the Rio Grande, having been communicated to Major General Banks, that officer had just informed your excellency that he had given his attention to the affair, and in consequence had caused the seizure of some articles suspected of being contraband of war, destined to Mexico; and besides, that General Herron had been called to the position of General McClernand, in command of the 13th corps, who would have his headquarters in Louisiana.

I hasten, sir, to thank you for the news, and am going to communicate it to the government of the Emperor, which will appreciate, no doubt, as I myself do, both the promptitude of your excellency in sending these orders to New Orleans, and the diligence of Major General Banks in executing them.

Accept, sir, the assurance of my high consideration.

L. DE GEOFROY.

Hon. WILLIAM H. SEWARD, &c.

Mr. Geofroy to Mr. Seward.

[Translation.]

LEGATION OF FRANCE TO THE UNITED STATES,
Washington, July 8, 1864.

SIR: I have the honor to communicate to you the extract from the despatch of his Majesty's consul at San Francisco, which points out to me shipments of powder and arms to Mexico, which would take place from California, at the instigation of an agent of Juarez, named Vega, and I beg your excellency will be so good as to address to the authorities of that State orders analogous to those which stopped in Louisiana movements of the like nature.

Accept, sir, the assurance of my high consideration.

L. DE GEOFROY.

Hon. WILLIAM H. SEWARD, &c.

Mr. Cazotte to Mr. Geofroy.

[Translation.]

SAN FRANCISCO, *June* 10, 1864.

Since the departure of Mr. James, collector of the customs at San Francisco, the deputy collector, who replaced him, Mr. Cushman, has the air of receiving with great earnestness my communications for hindering the shipment of arms, gunpowder, and articles contraband of war, destined for Mexican ports, but the sum of it is, that he does nothing to stop them.

There is here a Mexican general named De Vega, who has come with money to get ready armaments in favor of ex-President Juarez; he purchases small vessels, loads them with arms and gunpowder, and applies at the custom-house, through his agents, to clear these vessels for the river Colorado, where there are several American settlements. In this manner the vessels get away with the permission of the custom-house, and under any pretext touch at some points on the Mexican coast, where they land their cargoes. Thus, quite lately, the American schooner Potter, cleared on these conditions, put ashore at

Guayamas 2,500 barrels of gunpowder and fire-arms. I complain bitterly of these subterfuges to the local authorities. I ask the deputy collector to exact security from the fitters out of vessels laden with articles contraband of war, and cleared for the American ports on the banks of the Colorado; he promises me mountains and miracles, but I do not obtain from him any positive result. The chief of police only, Mr. Burke, actively seconds my investigations.

CAZOTTE.

Mr. Seward to Mr. Geofroy.

DEPARTMENT OF STATE,
Washington July 9, 1864.

SIR: With reference to the memorandum, without date, which was received at this department from his Imperial Majesty's legation, and which related, among other things, to a trade in articles contraband of war between Brownsville and Matamoras, and with reference also to my reply of the 21st ultimo, I now have the honor to enclose, in further reply, a copy of a communication of the 8th instant from the Secretary of the Treasury, from which it appears that you have been misinformed.

Accept, sir, a renewed assurance of my high consideration.

WILLIAM H. SEWARD.

Mr. L. DE GEOFROY.

Mr. Fessenden to Mr. Seward.

TREASURY DEPARTMENT, *July* 8, 1864.

SIR: Your communication of May 28, enclosing translation of a memorandum from Mr. L. de Geofroy, chargé d'affaires of France, relative to "an alleged trade in articles contraband of war with Mexico, through the port of Brownsville, Texas," was duly received and referred to the officers of this department at Brownsville for report.

I now have the honor to transmit copy of the reports of the acting collector of the customs at Brownsville and the assistant special agent for the district of Texas.

Very respectfully,

W. P. FESSENDEN,
Secretary of the Treasury.

Hon. WILLIAM H. SEWARD, *Secretary of State.*

Mr. Breckinridge to Mr. Chase.

TREASURY DEPARTMENT,
Washington, June 2, 1864.

SIR: I have the honor to acknowledge the receipt of your favor of the 1st, enclosing a communication from the Hon. Secretary of State, together with the memorandum from the chargé d'affaires of France.

I left Brownsville, Texas, about the 7th ultimo. Up to that time no goods contraband of war had been sent into Mexico or sold to the agents of the Mexican government.

I do not know of a single article contraband of war having come to the port of Brazos de Santiago. and feel sure that trade in contraband goods could not exist, even to a very limited extent, without my knowledge.

Respectfully, &c.,

G. W. BRECKINRIDGE,
Assistant Special Agent.

Hon. S. P. CHASE, *Secretary of the Treasury.*

Mr. Worthington to Mr. Chase.

TREASURY DEPARTMENT, *June* 26, 1864.

SIR: I have the honor to acknowledge the receipt of communication dated May 28, Department of State, enclosing a memorandum from the French chargé d'affaires concerning a trade in munitions of war alleged to be carried on between Brownsville, Texas, and Matamoras, Mexico.

In reply to the surmise, I have only to report that till the last of May I was daily and constantly at Brownsville, in charge of the custom-house affairs, and I am certain that no such trade existed; in fact, the sole trade we had was with New Orleans, a city itself under martial law, and from whence no such supplies could be drawn.

As for the connivance of the collector of the customs, it is useless to refute, as he has no discretionary powers in such matters. Should munitions of war arrive at the port of Brazos de Santiago, they will come under the authority of the proper authorities; should they not have those authorizations they would, of course, be seized as contraband.

As regards the loading of a vessel or vessels near Boston with munitions for Mexico, I know nothing, nor have I ever heard of such a scheme.

I would also beg leave to refer you to the monthly reports of exports and imports, which show *all* the business of that department, to see how fallacious are any such reports.

With the most high respect, &c.,

CHARLES WORTHINGTON,
Special Agent and Acting Collector.

Hon. S. P. CHASE, *Secretary of the Treasury.*

Mr. Seward to Mr. Geofroy.

DEPARTMENT OF STATE,
Washington, July 14, 1864.

SIR: I have the honor to acknowledge the receipt of your communication of the 8th instant, reporting contemplated shipments of powder and arms from California to Mexico, and, in reply, to inform you that the attention of the proper departments will be immediately called to the matter.

Accept, sir, a renewed assurance of my high consideration.

WILLIAM H. SEWARD.

Mr. L. DE GEOFROY, *&c.*

Mr. Geofroy to Mr. Seward.—(Received August 27, 1864.)

[Translation.]

Recent advices, brought from Mexico to the government of the Emperor, have apprised him that very grave events, the responsibility for which would fall upon the government of the United States if it neglected to take them into serious consideration, would again be brought about at Matamoras. A great number of federals, after having evacuated Brownsville, have, as it seems, passed the Rio Bravo and put themselves at the disposal of Mr. Cortinas. This chief would also have received a considerable supply of arms and munition, despatched from American territory. If these advices are true, as it seems there is no ground to doubt, there must have been there a violation of neutrality, which of itself alone would give sufficient ground for reclamation on the part of the government of the Emperor. But the life of French subjects has ceased to be respected by the party dominant at Matamoras; two of them, as it seems, had been shot by order of Mr. Cortinas. It will, therefore, be the duty of the government of the Emper to protest the more energetically against the support given in this circumstance to its adversaries.

Mr. Geofroy to Mr. Seward.—(Received September 2, 1864.)

[Translation.]

A fraudulent shipment of arms, destined for Mexico, took place at San Francisco at the close of the month of July. A portion of it was seized through the efforts of Colonel James, collector of the customs at that city, upon the suggestion of his Majesty's consul; the residue, enumerated in the invoice annexed, was got out of the way and shipped on a small vessel, which, by the latest accounts, must be anchored, it is said, in one of the coves of the bay of San Francisco. When prescribing to Colonel James the most active search upon this subject, the Department of State is begged to recommend to him to cause constant watch to be kept on the conduct of a certain General Vega, who is at San Francisco, the agent for this sort of operations.

[Translation.]

Invoice of merchandise in the customs public store to my order, (order of General Vega.)

For the river Colorado:

Marked.	Package.			
Guadelupe Mining Co., Guayamas.	1 case of	Enfield rifles	77	120
	1 do.	do.	79	105
	1 do.	do.	76	76
	1 do.	do.	74	70
	1 do.	do.	75	70
	1 do.	do.	81	105
	1 do.	do.	82	50
	1 do.	do.	89	70
	1 do.	do.	91	70
	1 do.	do.	92	64
	1 do.	do.	93	120
	1 do.	do.	94	380
Esperanza Mining Co., Guayamas.	1 do.	do.	78	120
	1 do.	do.	83	100
	1 do.	do.	86	80
	1 do.	do.	87	370
	1 do.	do.	84	56
	1 do.	do.	85	100
	1 do.	do.	88	60
	1 do.	do.	90	114
	1 do.	heavy carbines equipped	106	400
	1 do.	do.	107	84
	1 do.	do.	108	59
	1 do.	Field rifles	95	100
	1 do.	do.	97	70
San Juan Mining Co., Guayamas.	1 do.	do.	98	70
	1 do.	do.	99	120
	1 do.	do.	100	119
	1 do.	do.	101	120
	1 do.	do.	102	100
	1 do.	do.	103	70
	1 do.	do.	104	70
	1 do.	do.	105	60
		Enfield rifle		40
	1 do.	do.	96	60
	34 cases.			

NOTE.—The packages above enumerated are now shipped on a small vessel moored at some point in the bay of San Francisco.

SAN FRANCISCO, *July* 21, 1864.

Examined:

CAZOTTE, *Consul of France.*

[L. S.].

Mr. Geofroy to Mr. Seward.

[Translation.]

MONTREAL, CANADA, *September* 23, 1864.

DEAR SIR: I have no other information in relation to that which has just occurred at Brownsville than what is contained in the paper. Whatever the causes which have led to it, it would seem, if we are to believe them, that the Mexican chief, Cortinas, has entered the territory of the United States with a corps of troops, to which, it is said, he has even given, of his own authority, the flag of the Union. This last act shows a boldness for which he, no doubt, will have to account to the federal government. That which interests me is that he be disarmed, and does never leave the American territory to make some incursion with his men on the right bank of the Rio Grande. I am sure, in advance, that upon the first intelligence of this affair you will have sent to Texas the strictest orders, in order that the duties which vicinage and neutrality require be strictly observed by the officers of the federal forces in that part of the country; and I have no need of insisting upon the grave responsibility which the latter might entail upon their government if, in contempt of their instructions, they should permit these refugees to station themselves upon the frontier, and there to commit acts of hostility, directly or indirectly; there to prepare expeditions, transfers of men and munitions; and, finally, there to render aid in any manner to the party in arms in the interior of Mexico against the troops of his Majesty. I will only remark to you that this recent act, when it shall be known in Paris, will make more pressing the demand for explanations, which I have recently been charged to address to you on the subject of the relations, not very intimate, which previously existed between Cortinas and some generals of the United States, from one bank to the other of the Rio Grande, and particularly upon the sale of arms belonging to the government of the United States which was made by these latter to that chief. I would therefore thank you to hasten the reply which you have been pleased to promise me upon this subject, at the same time that you will enable me to make known to M. Drouyn de Lhuys the measures you may have taken respecting Cortinas and his band.

If you should think that my presence should be immediately necessary at Washington, I would thank you to telegraph it to me at the consulate general of his Majesty at Quebec, as late as Tuesday next, the 27th, and after that at New York, at the Brevoort House, where I propose to remain until the 4th of October, and thence send off my mail.

Accept, dear sir, the renewed assurance of my high consideration, and of my devoted sentiments.

L. DE GEOFROY.

Hon. WILLIAM H. SEWARD, &c.

Mr. Seward to Mr. Geofroy.

DEPARTMENT OF STATE,
Washington, September 30, 1864.

SIR: Your note from Montreal, on the 23d, was received here on the 26th instant.

When I saw the earlier newspaper reports of an alleged entrance of General Cortinas within the territory of the United States, I deemed them improbable and unreliable. The only official information upon the subject which has been received is a statement contained in a report made by Major General Canby to the Secretary of War. Upon receiving that statement I immediately transmitted to Mr. Dayton a despatch containing the same statement, of which I now give you a copy for your information. Subsequent newspaper publications discredit the original rumors in the most essential parts; the latter, however, like the first, are vague and unsatisfactory. I have, therefore, addressed myself, through the War Department, to Major General Canby, and requested a full statement of the facts, and at the same time, although deeming it quite unnecessary, I have, by command of the President, renewed the injunction heretofore given, that the military forces of the United States must neither commit, nor suffer within the jurisdiction of the United States, any violation of the neutrality of this government in the conflict now going on in Mexico.

Accept, sir, the assurance of my very high consideration.

WILLIAM H. SEWARD.

Mr. DE GEOFROY, &c.

Mr. Seward to Mr. Geofroy.

DEPARTMENT OF STATE,
Washington, October 15, 1864.

Mr. Seward presents his compliments to Mr. Geofroy, and has the honor to communicate, for his information, a copy of a report of the 15th of September, and of its accompaniments, addressed to Major General Banks by Major General Canby, relative to the recent events which have taken place on the Rio Grande.

Mr. Dana to Mr. Seward.

DEPARTMENT OF STATE,
Washington City, November 1, 1864.

SIR: I transmit, herewith, by direction of the Secretary of War, the enclosed copy of the latest report received by Major General Canby, commanding the military division of the West Mississippi, concerning affairs on the Rio Grande frontier, and by him furnished, at your request, for your information.

I have the honor to be, sir, your obedient servant,

C. A. DANA,
Assistant Secretary of War.

Hon. WILLIAM H. SEWARD, *Secretary of State.*

General Canby to General Banks.

HEADQUARTERS MILITARY DIVISION OF WEST MISSISSIPPI,
New Orleans, Louisiana, September 15, 1864.

GENERAL: The correspondence of Colonel Day, in relation to the Mexican force under Cortinas, has been received. Colonel Day's action, so far as it is known here, accords with our neutral obligations, and is approved. The Mexican refugees are entitled to an asylum in our territory when they deliver up their arms and munitions, and restore any prisoners or booty that they may have taken from the French.

They will not be received into the service of the United States for service on the Rio Grande frontier, but may be enlisted for the general service. In this case they will be sent to this city, either before or after enlistment, to be organized, armed, and equipped. Their enlistment may be for one, two, or three years, but preferably for the shorter term, and their duty thereafter will be determined by the circumstances of the service.

As an armed enemy of France, this force will not be tolerated in our territory; and if this be the intention of Cortinas, the commanding officer will be instructed to regard, and, as far as his power extends, to treat his force as enemies of the United States.

You will please instruct Colonel Day, or the commander at Brazos Santiago, accordingly, and in the contingency of any of Cortinas's force entering our service, give the necessary instructions in relation to enlistment, transfer to this city, and the disposition to be made of private property. The public property of the Mexican government remains, of course, in the custody of the United States until disposed of by proper authority.

Very respectfully, your obedient servant,

ED. R. S. CANBY,
Major General Commanding.

Major General N. P. BANKS,
Commanding Department of the Gulf, New Orleans, Louisiana.

Official:

C. T. CHRISTENSEN,
Lieutenant Colonel, Assistant Adjutant General.

A copy was transmitted to the Adjutant General of the army, September 17, 1864.

Colonel Day to Major Drake.

HEADQUARTERS UNITED STATES FORCES,
Brazos Santiago, Texas, October 9, 1864.

MAJOR: I have the honor to transmit the following report of affairs at this post:

Everything has been quiet since the date of my last report—the enemy not having been seen. I have received information from Mr. Pierce, consul at Matamoras, also from other sources, that the rebels are greatly disappointed at the turn which Mexican affairs have taken at Matamoras. They had expected that they would be able to purchase or by some means obtain possession of a part of the artillery, which was at that place, from Cortinas. The surrender of Cortinas to Mejia, and his acknowledgment of the authority of Maximilian, of course destroyed all such anticipations. I have understood that many tempting proposals were made by Ford to Cortinas, with a view to obtain part of the artillery, all of which were steadily refused.

On the 29th of September Mejia took possession of Matamoras on the following terms:

No French were to be allowed to enter the city, and all French troops were to leave Bagdad, and the surrender made to Mexican troops alone. These terms were carried out. The French troops at Bagdad have been withdrawn to their vessels, and the place occupied by Mexican forces. I am unable to determine whether this state of affairs is favorable to the interests of the United States or not. I have been informed by some Mexican refugees, lately from Matamoras, that a confederate flag was flying at that place, and that confederate officers are received with great cordiality on the part of Mejia. The instructions received by me through the department headquarters with regard to Mexican refugees have been carried out. The refugees appear to be very well pleased with the manner in which they have been treated, and many are enlisting in the United States service for the period of one year. All the officers, and most of the men, however, have a desire to return to their homes as peaceable citizens of Mexico, and I anticipate a request from Mejia that they be allowed to do so. If such a request be made, I shall allow them to return unarmed, on condition that we secure some remuneration for the subsistence furnished.

The health of the troops under my command is steadily improving, and I am confident that ere long all symptoms of scurvy will disappear.

The steamer Alliance arrived here last Monday morning, the 3d instant. During the night of the same day she experienced a severe "norther," and was blown on shore. She not being able to get off until this morning accounts for the delay of my despatches.

Hoping that this will meet with your approval, I am, very respectfully, your obedient servant,

H. M. DAY,
Colonel, Commanding United States Forces.

Major GEORGE B. DRAKE,
Assistant Adjutant General, Department of the Gulf,
Brazos Santiago, Texas.

Official:

GEORGE. B. DRAKE,
Major and Assistant Adjutant General.

Mr. Geofroy to Mr. Seward.

[Translation.]

LEGATION OF FRANCE TO THE UNITED STATES,
Washington, October 17, 1864.

SIR: I have received the copy of the report addressed to Major General Banks by Major General Canby, which you did me the honor to send me the day before yesterday, and thank you for the communication.

It appears to me, from reading this document and accompanying papers, that, while recognizing and understanding from the outset what duties neutrality imposed on them, the military authorities of the Gulf have not, however, entirely resisted the application made by refugee Mexicans to be admitted into the army of the United States. It might even be inferred from the report of Colonel Day and Major George B. Drake, dated September 14, that the first idea of this enlistment came from him, and that it had been suggested to them by his orders. On his part, Major General Canby, thinking to remove all inconvenience by bringing to New Orleans these refugees, who are held under arms, has only succeeded in opening the way for greater difficulty.

New Orleans is (your excellency is not ignorant of the fact) the place where are prepared, and from which depart, clandestine expeditions bound for Mexico, which the United States government has been obliged to arrest not long since; no place could, therefore, be more ill chosen to keep together a body of Mexicans transformed into United States soldiers. The succor the federal government will derive from such recruits is, to my mind, problematical; the embarrassments they may occasion are much more plain.

I doubt not your excellency may be struck with these remarks, which the government of the Emperor has offered on its part to the envoy of the United States at Paris, and I am gratified to hope that you will advise the adoption, by the military commander in the Gulf, of measures which can give no room for any objection.

Accept, sir, the assurance of my high consideration.

L. DE GEOFROY.

Hon. WILLIAM H. SEWARD, *&c.*

Mr. Seward to Mr. Geofroy.

DEPARTMENT OF STATE,
Washington, October 24, 1864.

SIR: I have the honor to acknowledge the receipt of your note of the 17th instant, which relates to the proceedings of the military authorities of the United States in the department of the Gulf, in regard to the forces of Cortinas, and, in reply, to inform you that your comments and suggestions on the subject will receive due attention.

Accept, sir, a renewed assurance of my highest consideration.

WILLIAM H. SEWARD.

Mr. L. DE GEOFROY, *&c.*

Mr. Seward to Mr. Geofroy.

DEPARTMENT OF STATE,
Washington, October 25, 1864.

SIR: With reference to the informal memorandum, without date, which you left at this department on the 27th of August last, relating to reports that citizens of the United States, after evacuating Brownsville, have placed themselves at the disposal of the Mexican General Cortinas, and that arms and ammunition have also been furnished to the Mexicans, I have the honor to enclose, in reply, a copy of a communication on the 21st instant from the War Department, from which it would seem that, happily, the reports which had reached the imperial government, which gave occasion for the memorandum, were incorrect.

Accept, sir, a renewed assurance of my high consideration.

WILLIAM H. SEWARD.

Mr. L. DE GEOFROY, &c.

Mr. Dana to Mr. Seward.

WAR DEPARTMENT,
Washington City, October 21, 1864.

SIR: In reference to your communication of August 29, 1864, transmitting a complaint from Mr. Geofroy, chargé d'affaires of France, to the effect that citizens of loyal States have enlisted in the service of Cortinas, and that arms and ammunition have been furnished to the Mexicans, I am directed by the Secretary of War to respectfully call your attention to the report of Major General Herron, commanding United States forces on the Rio Grande, transmitted to this department by Major General E. R. S. Canby, commanding division of west Mississippi, and a copy which is herewith enclosed.

From this report it will appear that the statements referred to by Geofroy are entirely unfounded.

I have the honor to be, sir, your obedient servant,

C. A. DANA,
Assistant Secreta y of War.

Hon. WILLIAM H. SEWARD, *Secretary of State.*

General Herron to Lieutenant Colonel Christensen.

HEADQUARTERS DISTRICT OF BATON ROUGE AND PORT HUDSON,
Baton Rouge, Louisiana, September 24, 1864.

COLONEL: The letter of Hon. W. H. Seward, Secretary of State, to Hon. E. M. Stanton, Secretary of War, under date of August 29, 1864, covering translation of a communication received at Washington by the representative of the Emperor of the French, in regard to certain occurrences said to have taken place on the Rio Grande, and which has been referred to me for report, has been received. There is nothing specific in the charges and statements made upon which to make a detailed report.

With reference to the great number of federals said to have crossed into Matamoras after the evacuation of Brownsville, I would state that there were not six citizens of the United States left in Brownsville when I withdrew the troops from that place. I had sent all persons, men, women, and children, to New Orleans. Some few Mexicans, who had been living on the east side of the Rio Grande, may probably have crossed into Mexico, but I know the number must have been small, for I had previously shipped a great majority of even the Mexicans to New Orleans; I mean such as resided on our side of the river. I have been constantly in receipt of advices from Matamoras since the evacuation of Brownsville, and had such occurrences as the above taken place I would certainly have heard something of it.

With reference to the arms and ammunition said to have gone into Mexico from American territory, I would undertake to say, in the most positive manner, that nothing of the kind took place from January 1, 1864, to August 1, 1864, the period of my administration on the Rio Grande; nor did anything occur that would warrant even a rumor of such a thing.

It seems to me that when such charges are made, involving, as they do, the reputation of officers of the United States army, some kind of proof should accompany the charges; but these statements being so general, I can do nothing more than make a mere denial of the whole.

There is neither truth in the report nor ground for it.

I am, with great respect, your obedient servant,

F. A. HERRON, *Major General.*

Lieut. Colonel C. S. CHRISTENSEN,
A. A. G., New Orleans.

Mr. Geofroy to Mr. Seward.

[Translation.]

LEGATION OF FRANCE TO THE UNITED STATES,
New York, November 12, 1864.

SIR: It would appear, agreeably to the information which has reached the government of the Emperor from various quarters, that ex-President Juarez has not abandoned the project of issuing letters of marque against our commerce, and that there are being constructed in the ports of the United States, especially at New Orleans and at San Francisco, vessels destined to cruise for his account.

I bring this fact to the knowledge of your excellency, not supposing, however, that the federal government, had it learned it from another source, would not have immediately taken measures to prevent the departure of these vessels, which is announced as very near at hand.

If, however, the good faith of the authorities of the United States being overreached, these vessels should take the sea, I must inform you that the government of his Majesty could not, in any case, recognize in them the character of privateer.

Mr. Juarez cannot hereafter be seriously considered a chief of a government. The supreme authority in Mexico has no longer at this time, and for those who are the least impartial, any other real representative than the sovereign called by events to the head of that country. Mr. Juarez, whatever may have been his former position, has, therefore, to-day, neither the title nor the character to issue letters of marque. Those with which he should attempt to supply American or other vessels, being henceforth without value, would expose these vessels and their crews to be treated purely and simply as pirates.

In instructing me to make this declaration to your excellency, the government of his Majesty has, nevertheless, no other intention than that of enabling that of the United States to give this notice again, in due season, to those of its citizens who may have entertained, or who are ready to entertain, propositions of Juarez or those of his agents.

Accept, sir, the assurances of my high consideration.

L. DE GEOFROY.

Hon. WILLIAM H. SEWARD, *&c.*

Mr. Seward to Mr. Geofroy.

DEPARTMENT OF STATE,
Washington, November 18, 1864.

SIR: I have the honor to acknowledge the receipt of your note of the 12th instant, by which I am informed that the imperial government of France has learned from various quarters that the President of the United States of Mexico (by you described as ex-President) has not abandoned the project of issuing letters of marque against French commerce, and that there are being constructed in the ports of the United States, especially at New Orleans and at San Francisco, vessels designed to cruise for his account.

In reply, I am at liberty to inform you that this government has no knowledge of the design which is thus ascribed to the President of Mexico, nor has it any information that any such vessels are building, as is supposed, in either of the two ports you have specially designated, or in any other port of the United States. The vigilance of public officers is such as to inspire a confident belief that the information which the Emperor's government has received is erroneous. Nevertheless, for greater security of the present neutrality of the United States, that information will be specially submitted to the proper agents in New Orleans and San Francisco, with renewed injunctions for the discovery and prevention of the arming or fitting out of vessels-of-war to depredate on French commerce. Similar proceedings will be adopted in relation to other ports upon my receiving any information of unlawful designs or enterprises afoot therein.

It seems unnecessary to discuss the question you have raised, whether the President of Mexico has a right, by the law of nations, to grant letters of marque, inasmuch as this government peremptorily exacts perfect neutrality from citizens of the United States in the Mexican war.

Accept, sir, a renewed assurance of my high consideration.

WILLIAM H. SEWARD.

Mr. L. DE GEOFROY, &c.

Mr. Seward to Mr. Geofroy.

DEPARTMENT OF STATE,
Washington, November 26, 1864.

SIR: I have the honor to inform you that on the 3d of September last a translation of the memorandum and of the accompanying invoice, received at this department from the legation of France, on the 2d of that month, in relation to a fraudulent shipment of arms at San Francisco, California, which arms are said to have been destined for Mexico, was transmitted to the Secretary of the Treasury, who was requested to cause the matter to be investigated with a view to the adoption of proper proceedings in the premises.

It now appears as the result of the investigation, that early in August last the collector of customs at San Francisco was informed that the American schooner Haze, of about forty tons burden, had on board a quantity of arms, supposed to be four thousand stand, together with a large supply of munitions of war, soldiers' clothing, and other articles, and that she was moving from place to place, in the bay of San Francisco, apparently seeking an opportunity to evade the vigilance of the revenue cutter Joseph Lané, then on guard duty in that harbor, and get to sea, when she would transfer her cargo to the schooner San Diego, of about fifty-five tons burden. The collector thereupon immediately despatched two boats under the direction of Lieutenant Selden, the commander of the revenue cutter there, with a guard furnished by Brigadier General Mason, the provost marshal at San Francisco, in quest of the Haze. These boats returned on the 4th of August, after a fruitless search of twenty-four hours. At 9 o'clock of the evening of that day the collector was informed that a schooner resembling the Haze had been seen at anchor in Half Moon bay, about thirty-five miles south of the Golden Gate.

The San Diego having sailed on that day, pursued by the revenue cutter Joseph Lane, in obedience to the collector's orders, under the belief that the vessel reported as having been seen at the Half Moon bay was the Haze, he immediately despatched the steam-tug Merrimac, under the command of a revenue officer, with a guard from the provost marshal's office, in pursuit. They found the Haze at the place designated, with the arms, munitions of war, and soldiers' clothing on board. Having ordered her to be detained, the collector reported such detention to Major General McDowell, the commander of the military district in which San Francisco is situated, to whom the arms and munitions of war were delivered.

From this statement of facts you will clearly perceive that none of the arms referred to were exported from San Francisco.

Accept, sir, a renewed assurance of my very high consideration.

WILLIAM H. SEWARD.

Mr. L. DE GEOFROY, &c.

Mr. Seward to Mr. Adams.

No. 855.] DEPARTMENT OF STATE,
Washington, February 25, 1864.

SIR: I have before me your despatch of February 4, (No 590,) which speaks of the actual breaking out of hostilities between Germany and Denmark, and of the perplexities which that act produces in the British councils.

More recent information shows that Austria and Prussia have achieved a successful campaign, and are in possession virtually of all Schleswig. It remains to be seen whether a foundation can now be laid for a peace that will be satisfactory to the greater states, who charge themselves with the preservation of the balance of power in Europe. Without pretending to the knowledge necessary for the formation of a reliable judgment, I may, perhaps, be safe in believing that the present condition of things in the theatre of the war is very unsatisfactory to Great Britain.

I observe statements in the continental papers that emigrants have returned from this country with large promises to engage in the attractive conflicts of Europe. If this be so, and if these conflicts continue, this government will be summoned to new duties in maintaining neutrality. Our responsibilities in this way are already large enough. The war of France against Mexico wears upon the patience of the American people. Spain is watchful lest the insurgents of San Domingo receive aid from the United States; and their insurgents are here seeking recognition, at least as belligerents. If our own unhappy civil war should come to an end in the midst of a European war, it would be difficult to enforce upon citizens of the United States the performance of international obligations that Europe has refused to observe in regard to ourselves.

I am, sir, your obedient servant,

WILLIAM H. SEWARD.

Hon. CHARLES FRANCIS ADAMS, Esq.

Mr. Seward to Mr. Adams. (Same to Mr. Dayton, No. 501.)

[Extract.]

No. 868.] DEPARTMENT OF STATE,
Washington, March 8, 1864.

SIR: We hear that the Canada was partially disabled on her way to Halifax. Owing to this accident I am without any official information of European events of a date more recent than the 13th of February.

* * * * * *

The latest news received from Mexico gives us reason to believe that the already reduced forces of the government are to be further demoralized by faction. It is said that Vidaurri is disloyal to the republican government, and is demanding a resignation from the president, Juarez, with a view to the institution of General Ortega in his place, to be followed by a compromise with the French.

I am, sir, your obedient servant,

WILLIAM H. SEWARD.

CHAS. F. ADAMS, Esq.

Mr. Adams to Mr. Seward.

No. 630.] LEGATION OF THE UNITED STATES,
London, March 24, 1864.

SIR: The Archduke Maximilian came here for the purpose of getting a recognition of his new position. His father-in-law, Leopold, is here to favor his object. The government declined to act on the subject at present, but gave reason to hope that, so soon as the action in Mexico would appear to justify it, they would acknowledge him. It is understood that Spain and Belgium will follow in the wake of France, after which the other powers are expected to accede.

A loan has been negotiated for eight millions sterling, at 66 —, interest at 6 per cent, out of which a payment is to be made to France, in part, for the expense she has been at. The rest is to be used to organize a proper support for the archduke until he can get things going. The English creditors in the old loan, who have constituted the great support of this scheme, are greatly disturbed to find that no provision has been made for them.

I have the honor to be, sir, your obedient servant,

CHARLES FRANCIS ADAMS.

Hon. WILLIAM H. SEWARD,
Secretary of State, Washington, D. C.

Mr. Seward to Mr. Adams.

No. 937.] DEPARTMENT OF STATE,
Washington, May 3, 1864.

SIR: I thank you very sincerely for your despatch of the 15th of April, No. 669, which contains information particularly new and interesting in regard to the proceedings which have culminated in the departure of the Archduke Maximilian from Trieste, with the intention to establish an imperial monarchy in Mexico. Every thinking observer must be fully satisfied, even without special evidence, that those events had their origin in a conspiracy of Mexicans against the independence and freedom of their own country. Nevertheless, it will be fortunate for the future of Mexico, and for the cause of republican government there, if the history you have given me of the details of the conspiracy shall soon become generally known.

You have very clearly explained the motives and sentiments which have induced so many of the influential statesmen and authorities of Europe to favor the subversion of the Mexican republic. All these motives and sentiments resolve themselves into a jealousy of the advancement of the United States. Their great prosperity and progress have necessarily provoked this political antagonism. You very justly lament the pertinacity with which the American people continue their suicidal division in presence of the apparent overthrow of their influence in Mexico, but it is the same blindness of faction which led us into the civil war. Only time and events can cure it, and these we may well believe are doing their work. No appeal to the reason or to the patriotism of the insurgents is heard so long as they entertain hopes of success in their desperate enterprise. The loyal people of the United States seem to have no need for new or increased devotion to the national cause. At all events, considerations of foreign and remote dangers can scarcely be expected to gain serious attention, when the immediate domestic perils of the conflict absorb the popular mind. I know no other way for us than to contemplate the situation calmly, do our whole duty faithfully, meet every emergency as it arises with prudence, firmness, and force if necessary, and trust in God for a safe issue of the contest.

I am, sir, your obedient servant,

WILLIAM H. SEWARD.

CHARLES FRANCIS ADAMS, Esq., &c.

Mr. Dayton to Mr. Seward.

No. 380.] PARIS, *November* 27, 1863.

SIR: In the course of my conversation with Mr. Drouyn de Lhuys yesterday I referred briefly to what he had some time since said to me in reference to an early acknowledgment of the new government of Mexico. He said, pleasantly, that he feared he had been too sanguine. I told him that our kind relations with the Juarez government were unbroken, and that we did not anticipate an early and permanent establishment of a monarchy in Mexico. In the present condition of things, therefore, you did not feel at liberty to consider the question he had propounded. I do not think that he was either surprised or disappointed by this answer.

He informed me that the Emperor had been much gratified by your recent action in forbidding the recruitment of men in the United States for Mexico. This had been reported to him by Mr. Mercier. I reminded him, in passing, that this action seemed to contrast somewhat with that of the French authorities, in permitting the shipment of a crew for the Florida in a French port. It seemed to me that the allusion was *felt*. He made a note of it, as I supposed, and the conversation there dropped. I reminded him, however, that I had some time since sent him a copy of that despatch in reference to Russian privateers, sent to us at the beginning of the Crimean war. He said that, owing to his absence, he had not yet seen it, nor my communication which accompanied it.

I am, sir, your obedient servant,

WM. L. DAYTON.

Hon. WILLIAM H. SEWARD.

P. S.—The proposition for a congress yet engrosses all attention; but each of the great powers is distrustful of the others, and I am greatly mistaken if the proposition does not turn out an abortion.

Mr. Dayton to Mr. Seward.

No. 389.] PARIS, *December* 25, 1863.

SIR: I enclose a slip cut from a newspaper recently published here, the substance of which has made the round of the French and English journals, and will doubtless be re-copied in the journals of the United States. Mr. Drouyn de Lhuys says he knows nothing of it, and has never heard of the pretended envoy therein referred to. He says, further, that should he find that any such person has arrived, he will not fail to let me know it; but at present he supposes the paragraph to be like all the other "trash" of this character which is put in circulation.

I referred in this connexion to the supposed outline or schedule of a treaty alleged to have been agreed upon, some two or three months since, between his Majesty and the rebel agents abroad, and communicated to you by Mr. Morse, our consul at London, a copy of whose communication was enclosed to me in your confidential despatch, No. 438.

Mr. Drouyn de Lhuys says there is no truth whatever in this statement, and that the Emperor has no such negotiation whatever with the confederates on foot.

I am, sir, your obedient servant,

WILLIAM L. DAYTON.

Hon. WILLIAM H. SEWARD,
Secretary of State, &c.

[From a Paris paper.]

M Supervielle, who has just arrived in Paris, in the character of special envoy from the Confederate States, is a Frenchman by birth, who was formerly an advocate in the south of France, somewhere near Bordeaux. He has been living in Texas for the last seventeen years, and is now a naturalized American. He got away from Matamoras on board a French ship-of-war, which the admiral lent him to go to Vera Cruz, where he embarked in the transatlantic packet Florida for St. Nazaire. He is said to have a mission to notify to the French government the recognition by the Confederate States of the "empire" of Mexico, and also to try to persuade Napoleon III to recognize the south in return.

Mr. Seward to Mr. Dayton.

No. 466.] DEPARTMENT OF STATE,
Washington, January 26, 1864.

SIR: I enclose a copy of a despatch of the 31st ultimo, from Mr. M. D. L. Lane, the United States consul at Vera Cruz, and of the protest of José Wallace Smith referred to therein, containing a narrative of the treatment of which he alleges himself and others to have been the victims at the hands of the French authorities at Minatitlan. The case, as set forth, seems one of such excessive cruelty, that, without waiting further details, I have to request you to ask for an examination into the facts, and, if they are truly stated, to claim indemnity.

I am, sir, your obedient servant,

WILLIAM H. SEWARD.

WILLIAM L. DAYTON Esq., *&c.*

CONSULATE OF THE UNITED STATES OF AMERICA,
Vera Cruz, December 31, 1863.

SIR: I have the honor herewith to forward the protest of José W. Smith, a citizen of the United States, taken prisoner at Minatitlan, by French authorities, and sent to this place.

Mr. Smith leaves here for the States, per English steamer, to-morrow.

I have the honor to be, with great respect, your obedient servant,

M. D. L LANE,
United States Consul.

Hon. WILLIAM H. SEWARD,
Secretary of State, Washington, D. C.

[Protest.]

CONSULATE OF THE UNITED STATES OF AMERICA,
Vera Cruz, December 17, 1863.

By this public instrument of attestation, declaration and protest, be it known and made manifest to all whom it may concern, that on this 17th day of December, A. D. 1863, before me, M. D. L. Lane, consul of the United States of America for the port of Vera Cruz, and the dependencies thereof, personally appeared José Wallace Smith, who, being by me duly sworn according to law, did depose and say as follows:

When the French steamer under command of Commandant Conrad arrived at Minatitlan, February last, I was residing in that town and doing business there as a merchant. I was old regidor of the municipal body, enabled by a decree of the Mexican government to hold that position without infringement of my neutrality. The Mexican authorities, and most of the native inhabitants of the town, fled at the approach of the French, and I was left as the only neutral in office to represent the interests of the town, and if called upon, to deliver it over to the invading force. In this position I was recognized by Commandant Conrad, who, when I offered to resign my office, expressly desired me to retain it. The French did not occupy Minatitlan, but anchored their steamers at the mouth of the river, and for about two months I continued to act, by request of the French, as temporarily in charge of the town, and was recognized as such by both parties, and used as a means of communicating with each other.

Some time in May, in consequence of a want of confidence manifested in me by the Mexican authorities, arising from my connexion with Commandant Conrad, I resigned my position—a Captain Sanchez, of the Mexican army, being appointed as military commandant. From that moment my connexion with the liberal parties, innocent as it was, completely and entirely ceased. In July a French force took possession of the town, and with it came, as French political agent and collector of customs, one of "Walker's filibusters" - a man unfavorably known to the inhabitants, by name of Bruno Van Natzmer—who indirectly assumed and concentrated in himself all civil authority, and to a great extent the military also. This was easily accomplished with the former, on account of their ignorance and timidity, and it was yielded to him by the latter, on account of what they supposed to be his local knowledge and the soundness of his intentions; and immediately a system of persecution and personal vengeance was inaugurated such as people never thought to witness in this nineteenth century.

About the beginning of September, while at the American consulate on business, I was grossly insulted and threatened by one John Hume, a resident of the town. Among other things, he said he had me completely in his power, that he could count upon the influence and assistance of the principal authorities to carry out his threats, which were by any and every means to have me sent away from Minatitlan or shot, and if the authorities failed him, he would visit the latter fate upon me himself. At this time Natzmer was living at Hume's house, and on the most intimate terms with him. and there is every reason to believe they were conniving together against me, as will be proved by what took place afterwards.

A few days after the attack upon me at the consulate, Hume came to my house, and after repeating his insults and threats, struck me three times. I did not retaliate until he struck me the third time, and then I knocked him down; as he was rising he drew a revolver, four barrels of which were loaded, cocked and snapped it at me, whereupon I again knocked him down; the same thing was three times repeated. Some people now came up and put an end to the struggle, and the police arriving conducted us both to jail, where I was placed in close confinement, and Hume in a few minutes released by order of Natzmer, addressing him through the judge.

Natzmer then informed the judge that it was the order of the commandant that an official communication should be drawn up, and addressed to the commandant, stating that Hume had gone to my house in a state of drunkenness, and I availed myself of the fact to endeavor to assassinate him. The judge refused to make such a statement, unless it was first substantiated as the result of an examination, conducted in conformity to law; and, notwithstanding Natzmer threatened to send him to Martinique, the judge, fortunately for me, was not intimidated. The case was fairly examined and I was released, and the sentence that would have been otherwise passed on Hume was only withheld through fear of Natzmer; thus the case remains on the archives, if they are not destroyed or tampered with, with the exception of what I state as having passed between Natzmer and the judge, which took place before witnesses who will readily bear evidence, when they dare speak without fear of Natzmer's vengeance. His intentions towards me were thoroughly exposed, when he told the judge the next day, if he had done as he told him, by that time I should have been despatched.

On the 18th Lieutenant Rollin came to my house with two armed soldiers; he ordered me to put on my hat and follow him, and I was conducted to the public jail, where I found Nicholas Lopes, Albino Garcia, Luis Carimon. We were kept some four days *incommunicado*. On the evening of the fourth day the guard received an order from Lieutenant Rollin to take me out and shoot me at the sound of the morning bugle. I only knew the fate that was intended for me from the conversation of the guard, which I could not help overhearing, from their vicinity and the slight construction of the jail, which consisted of only one room. About fifteen minutes before the time appointed for my execution I heard that the order was suspended, but frequently during the next day I was led to believe, from the talk of the guard, that I had but a few hours to live.

On the afternoon of the fifth day we were marched off by a force under command of Lieutenant Rollin, and conducted to the river bank, where Natzmer was waiting with another force to receive us. We were placed by Natzmer on board the schooner Clara, put in the hold, our hands tied behind us, and our legs attached with iron rings to an iron bar of about five feet in length. To this bar five of us were chained. The hatches were then nailed down, and every aperture closed, except a hole about sixteen inches square, which had been sawed out of one of the hatches for the purpose of letting down provisions to us. From the extreme pain caused by the tightness of the bands and the constrained position of the arms, and all other physical and mental horrors of our frightful situation, I rapidly became delirious, and remained in that state eight or ten days. Under the influence of the delirium I used sometimes to cry out of a night, when the corporal of the guard would come down and stamp upon me, and beat me in a manner that has left marks upon my body that I will carry to my grave. This was an occurrence of every night during my delirium. The necessities of nature had to be relieved as we lay, and the filth was sometimes left to accumulate for days; we had no mosquito bars; our food was eaten amidst an amount of filth and stench and pestilent atmosphere that must be experienced to conceive. The band on our arms remained sometimes day and night; the effect on me has been to deprive me for life of the use of my left arm, and the right is seriously injured. In this state we remained thirty days—all except Albino Garcia, the previous collector of customs, about sixty-five years of age, who on the twenty-ninth day died from fever, superinduced by the horrors of our situation. The body, which was in a most filthy state, was allowed to remain from 8 a. m. to 5 p. m., still chained to the bar, and the hands still tied behind, and then it was drawn up by a rope passed under the arms like a sack of corn. During these dreadful thirty days Natzmer frequently came on board the vessel to see that his orders for our treatment were carried out, and it is to be presumed they were, for he gave no order for its alteration. On the 18th of November Natzmer came on board the schooner, and we were taken from the hold and delivered by him to the commander of the war steamer Fleche. I was in a wretched state of health—reduced in less than forty days from a strong, stout man to the merest shadow; and as I dictate this, unable to write myself, after nearly a month's rest, I am still the mere wreck of what I was before, and my constitution has received a shock that time can never cure.

On the Fleche we were again placed in irons, and forced to keep a sitting posture under deck for about sixty hours, until we arrived at Vera Cruz, during which time we were denied all nourishment excepting musty biscuit and water.

From the day of my arrest to my arrival in Vera Cruz I was in utter ignorance of the nature of the accusations, if there were any preferred against me, or upon what grounds I had been cruelly treated. On the 26th of November I was placed in custody of the United States consul at Vera Cruz, he becoming responsible for my appearance when called for, where I remained till December 14, when I was summoned before a court-martial, examined, and discharged On the 17th I was notified by the commandant superior at Vera Cruz that I was at liberty to go to the United States. Wherefore the said appearer, in his own name, hath declared to protest, as by these presents I, the said consul, at his special instance and request, do publicly and solemnly protest against the said Natzmer, as French agent and collector of the port of Minatitlan, against the French government, against the French commander of the French forces, on land and water, at Minatitlan and Vera Cruz, ruling in the name of France, against all and every person and persons, against all authorities and things, that have in any way occasioned or permitted my arrest, imprisonment, and cruel treament, holding each and all of them, in every matter, cause, or things concerned, liable and responsible for all costs, losses, damages, charges, and expenses already suffered, or that may be hereafter suffered, in my health or property, in any manner, shape, or form, on account of my said arrest and imprisonment and cruel treatment.

This done and protested at Vera Cruz the day and year first above written. In testimony whereof the said José W. Smith has hereunto subscribed his name, and I, the said consul, have affixed my hand and seal of office.

JOSÉ W. SMITH.

[L. S.] M. D. L. LANE, *U. S. Consul.*

Mr Seward to Mr. Dayton.

[Extract.]

No. 468.]

DEPARTMENT OF STATE,
Washington, February 1, 1864.

SIR: I have the honor to acknowledge the receipt of your despatch of January 15, No. 400. We learn from it the determination of the French government to permit the Rappahannock to be completed and prepared for sea, though not armed, at Calais.

* * * * * * * *

Yesterday information was laid before me of a design of an adventurous party, now beyond our jurisdiction, to obtain letters of marque from the republican government of Mexico to harass the commerce of France. This government is constantly called upon to give leave for the conveyance of arms into Mexico for the use of the Mexican authorities in the war with France. It stands firmly and faithfully upon its neutrality, but in doing this it wounds popular sympathies which no human power could repress. The Emperor's government has had abundant occasion to observe that the Executive of the United States has practiced prudence and forbearance in their relations with the maritime powers which were not expected from a government being so popular in its form as ours, because it seemed impossible. Is it not inexpedient for the government of France to continue indulgence towards our enemies such as we wholly refused to her enemies? The President thinks that you should invite Mr. Drouyn de Lhuys to bestow serious consideration upon the subject.

I am, sir, your obedient servant,

WILLIAM H. SEWARD.

WILLIAM L. DAYTON, Esq., &c.

Mr. Dayton to Mr. Seward.

No. 418.] PARIS, *February* 6, 1864.

SIR: During an interview with Mr. Drouyn de Lhuys, on Thursday last, he handed to me the memorandum of a contract, said to have been entered into between the Juarist authorities of the State of Tamaulipas and the federal authorities of the United States, in virtue of which the latter agreed to furnish a certain quantity of arms and munitions of war in return for delivery to them of many thousand Mexican mules. I herewith send you a translation of this memorandum, which is without signatures. Mr. Drouyn de Lhuys said he found the memorandum on his table, without recollecting exactly whence it came, and therefore called my attention to it. I told him that I had no knowledge on the subject, but from the orders which had been issued by my government forbidding the supply of arms to either belligerent in Mexico, and the fact that we needed arms ourselves, as I supposed, even more than mules, I did not believe such contract had been made. I promised, however, to take the memorandum, and call your attention to it, as I now do.

I am, sir, your obedient servant,

WM. L. DAYTON.

HON. WILLIAM H. SEWARD,
Secretary of State.

Memorandum.

[Translation.]

"It is affirmed that a contract has been entered into between the Juarist authorities of the State of Tamaulipas and the federal authorities, in virtue of which the latter were to furnish a certain quantity of arms and munitions of war in return for the delivery of several thousands of Mexican mules."

Mr. Dayton to Mr. Seward.

No. 423.] PARIS, *February* 19, 1864.

SIR: Your despatches, from No. 465 to No. 468, both inclusive, are duly received.

No. 466, enclosing the copy of a despatch from Mr. Lane, United States consul at Vera Cruz, and the protest of José Wallace Smith, referred to therein, were immediately communicated by me to Mr. Drouyn de Lhuys. These complaints, like that referred to in your No. 465, (the imprisonment of Mr. Mansfield, our consul at Tabasco,) he said must be referred by him to the French authorities in Mexico before he could give an answer. But he assured me these matters should be promptly investigated. It will, of course, be some considerable time before a report on these cases can be received from Mexico.

I am, sir, your obedient servant,

WM. L. DAYTON.

Hon. WILLIAM H. SEWARD,
Secretary of State.

Mr. Seward to Mr. Dayton.

No. 490.] DEPARTMENT OF STATE,
Washington, February 27, 1864.

SIR: Your despatch of February 9, No. 419, has been received. In this communication you mention that the Archduke Maximilian, of Austria, is expected in Paris, and that circumstances may arise in which it will be necessary for you either to attend or to decline to attend ceremonies which may be observed in his honor as a sovereign of Mexico, and you ask instructions. I have taken the President's directions upon the question. If the Archduke Maximilian appears in Paris only in his character as an imperial prince of the house of Hapsburg, you will be expected to be neither demonstrative nor reserved in your deportment towards him. If he appears there with any assumption of political authority or title in Mexico, you will entirely refrain from intercourse with him. Should your proceedings become a subject of inquiry or remark, you will be at liberty, in the exercise of your own discretion, to say that this government, in view of its rights and duties in the present conjuncture of its affairs, has prescribed fixed rules to be observed, not only by this department, but by its representatives in foreign countries. We acknowledge revolutions only by direction of the President, upon full and mature consideration. Until such regular authority for recognition, we do not hold formal or informal communications with political agents or representatives of revolutionary movements in countries with which we maintain diplomatic intercourse.

I am, sir, your obedient servant,

WILLIAM H. SEWARD.

WILLIAM L. DAYTON, Esq., &c.

Mr. Seward to Mr. Dayton.

No. 496.] DEPARTMENT OF STATE,
Washington, March 2, 1864.

SIR: Your despatch of February 6, No. 418, has been received, together with a copy of a memorandum which M. Drouyn de Lhuys has placed in your hands.

That memorandum is as follows: It is affirmed that a contract has been entered into between the Juarist authorities of the State of Tamaulipas and the federal authorities, in virtue of which the latter were to forward a certain quantity of arms and munitions of war in return for the delivery of several thousands of mules.

You very rightly expressed to M. Drouyn de Lhuys a disbelief of the fact stated in the paper I have recited. It is uncertain whether by the term "federal authorities" is meant the government of the United States, or only the agents of this government in the vicinity of Tamaulipas. If the former is intended, then you are authorized at once to declare that the allegation in the memorandum is without any foundation in fact. If the other condition is to be assumed, you will in that case inform M. Drouyn de Lhuys that, so far as the government, or any department of it, is informed, or has any reason to believe, the allegation is entirely untrue. That if it were true, the proceedings would be in violation of the instructions of this government, and would be denounced and censured. Although no evidence of the allegation is presented, the attention of the Secretary of War has been called to the subject and due inquiries will be instituted.

I am, sir, your obedient servant,

WILLIAM H. SEWARD.

WILLIAM L. DAYTON, Esq., &c.

Mr. Dayton to Mr. Seward.

[Extract.]

No. 430.] PARIS, *March* 11, 1864.

SIR: * * * * * * * *

M. Drouyn de Lhuys informs me that there is nothing in agitation here calculated to disturb the good relations between the United States and France. He says that the archduke has not asked the Emperor to acknowledge the south, nor does he believe that he has had anything of the kind on his mind. Certain English papers have been industriously propagating this idea, but there is, he says, nothing in it. He informs me that he believes certain English and French capitalists, already interested in Mexican loans, will, in the hope of saving a part, at least, of their existing investments, make a moderate advance in addition, and that the archduke will, from these sources, be able to raise a small loan to meet his existing wants; but it seems to me this cannot carry him far unless France shall stand security, or give other material aid.

I am, sir, your obedient servant,

WM. L. DAYTON.

Hon. WILLIAM H. SEWARD,
Secretary of State, &c.

Mr. Dayton to Mr. Seward.

No. 431.] PARIS, *March* 11, 1864.

SIR: I have again referred, in conversation with M. Drouyn de Lhuys, to the supposed negotiation reported by Mr. Morse, United States consul at London, for the cession of Texas to France for certain considerations. The supposed negotiation for the cession of Texas M. Drouyn de Lhuys assured me is without the slighest pretence of foundation. He said that France would not take Texas as a gift, even if it were accompanied with a handsome douceur besides; that she does not want it, and would not have it. That if the rumor were that she were about to part with some far-off or distant possession we might give it some credence, but never, while he was minister and his Majesty Emperor, need I trouble myself as to the truth of any report which looked to the acquisition of distant territory. Their policy, he said, looked directly in a contrary way. Whether this comports well with their existing action in Mexico may, perhaps, admit of a doubt.

I am, sir, your obedient servant,

WM. L. DAYTON.

Hon. WILLIAM H. SEWARD,
Secretary of State, &c.

Mr. Seward to Mr. Dayton.

No. 506.] DEPARTMENT OF STATE,
Washington, March 17, 1864.

SIR: I herewith transmit to you, for your information, the copy of a translation of a note of the 11th instant from Mr. L. de Geofroy, the chargé d'affaires of France, and of the reply from this department of the 12th instant, relative to the presence of United States troops in Matamoras.

I am, sir, your obedient servant,

WILLIAM H. SEWARD.

WILLIAM L. DAYTON, Esq., *&c.*

[For enclosure see correspondence with the French legation.]

Mr. Seward to Mr. Dayton.

No. 510.] DEPARTMENT OF STATE,
Washington, March 23, 1864.

SIR: For your information I give you a further correspondence between Mr. Geofroy and this department on the subject of the proceedings of General Herron. I give you also a copy of resolutions concerning the French in Mexico introduced into the Senate by Mr. McDougall, of California.

It is not easy to understand here how any earnest debate upon such a question as Mr. Geofroy has raised can promote the interest of either France or the United States, or contribute to a good understanding between the two countries.

I am, sir, your obedient servant,

WILLIAM H. SEWARD.

WILLIAM L. DAYTON, Esq., *&c.*

JOINT RESOLUTION in relation to the occupation of Mexico by France.

Be it resolved by the Senate and House of Representatives of the United States of America in Congress assembled, That the occupation of Mexico, or any part thereof, by the Emperor of France, or by the person indicated by him as emperor of Mexico, is an offence to the people of the republic of the United States of America.

SEC 2. *And be it further resolved,* That the movements of the government of France, and the threatened movement of an emperor improvised by the Emperor of France, demand by this republic, if insisted upon, war.

Mr. Seward to Mr. Dayton.

No. 519.] DEPARTMENT OF STATE,
Washington, April 4, 1864.

SIR: I transmit herewith for your information a copy of a despatch of the 4th ultimo, from the consul of the United States at Monterey, relative to the present difficulties in Mexico.

I am, sir, your obedient servant,

WILLIAM H. SEWARD.

WILLIAM L. DAYTON, Esq., *&c.*

Mr. Kimmey to Mr. Seward.

[Extract.]

UNITED STATES CONSULATE, MONTEREY, MEXICO,
March 4, 1864.

SIR: The difficulty between the general government and Governor Vidaurri is daily becoming more complicated. A decree from President Juarez, separating the States of Nuevo Leon and Coahuila, was given at Saltillo on the 26th ultimo. The following is a translation of the first article: "The State of Coahuila will immediately reassume its character as one of the free and sovereign States of the United Mexican States, separating itself from Nuevo Leon, in which it was incorporated." The separation of the two States gives President Juarez control of the Custen Heuse or Piedras Negras. Governor Vidaurri refuses to recognize the authority of the President, and has declared his intention of driving him from Nuevo Leon and Coahuila, and for that purpose is raising all the forces he is able to arm.

Another decree from the President deposes Governor Vidaurri, and declares this State in open hostility to the government of Mexico. Communication between this place and Saltillo is almost entirely cut off; no provisions of any kind are allowed to come this way. No mails pass either way, and it is only by foreigners coming in that we are able to learn of the movements of the government troops.

The President has now, in addition to the troops he left here, a force of about two thousand men from Durango, commanded by Governor Petona in person, which, with the volunteers from Saltillo and other points in the State of Coahuila, swells his numbers to not less than five thousand men.

Governor Vidaurri has about twelve hundred men, but, with the artillery he has belonging to the government, he will be able to protect himself in the citadel against a large force.

An order was issued here on the 1st instant to the troops to prepare themselves to march in two days for Saltillo. The time was, to-day, further postponed until the 7th instant.

A man just in from Saltillo represents the troops of President Juarez preparing to march on this place. An advance of five hundred men were twenty miles this side of Saltillo.

A despatch from General Bazaine, of the French forces, to Governor Vidaurri, was received a few days since. The following is its substance:

"In one hand peace is offered; in the other war. If you accept the former, you must adhere to the intervention, frankly recognizing the government which is established in Mexico. If, on the contrary, you decide for the latter, you must expect to suffer all the calamities incident to war."

The governor made, in substance, the following answer:

"I have not the power to choose between the two extremes which you propose; but will submit this vital question to the people, as I have always done on grave subjects, and their determination transmit to you as soon as obtained."

No advance of the French army has been made since my last communication; but, on the contrary, the report of their retreat to San Luis Potosi is quite generally believed.

The reoccupation of the Guadalajara by General Urega, and the taking by him of four thousand French and Reactienania prisoners, has given new heart to the Mexicans of the liberal party.

The French army in San Luis Potosi is levying contributions on the citizens for its support, and, instead of bringing peace, as they offer in every instance in advance, they bring misery on the people wherever their army goes.

* * * * * * * * * *

Your obedient servant,

M. M. KIMMEY,
United States Consul.

Hon. WILLIAM H. SEWARD,
Secretary of State, Washington, D. C.

Mr. Seward to Mr. Dayton.

No. 521.]

DEPARTMENT OF STATE,
Washington, April 5, 1864.

SIR: I have to acknowledge the receipt of your despatch of the 21st ultimo, No. 438, giving me a slip from Galignani's Messenger, reprinting from the "Globe," of London, a statement in regard to an alleged willingness of the

United States to accredit a minister to and receive one from the proposed emperor of Mexico. We are well aware that there was no foundation for the statement, and proper measures have been taken authoritatively to contradict it.

I am, sir, your obedient servant,

WILLIAM H. SEWARD.

WILLIAM L. DAYTON, Esq., &c.

Mr. Seward to Mr. Dayton.

No. 524.] DEPARTMENT OF STATE, *Washington, April 8*, 1864.

SIR: Your despatch of March 25, No. 440, has been received.

You allude therein to a report that reaches us through English journals of effect that it is arranged that the projected imperial government in Mexico shall soon extend a recognition to the insurgents at Richmond. The contradiction of this report, upon the authority of the Emperor of France, as you have communicated it to me, is gratifying, although no credit whatever has been given here to the statements referred to. On the contrary, it has not seemed probable that the Prince Maximilian could extend his guardianship to insurgents here while yet engaged in a struggle with the existing authorities of Mexico, unless, indeed, he was assured of support in that event by the government of France. Nor has it seemed probable, in view of previous explanations of M. Drouyn de Lhuys, that the Emperor of the French would be anxious to enlarge his responsibilities concerning American politics, at least before the Mexican problem should have definitely reached a solution.

I am, sir, your obedient servant,

WILLIAM H. SEWARD.

WILLIAM L. DAYTON, Esq.

Mr. Dayton to Mr. Seward.

[Extract.]

No. 449.] PARIS, *April* 11, 1864.

SIR: After sundry impediments, which, it would seem, have rendered the action of the Archduke Maximilian somewhat uncertain, and have much delayed his departure, it would seem he has at last accepted the offered crown of Mexico, and to-day he starts on his most adventurous career, going to that country by the way of Rome that he may receive the benediction of the Pope. I enclose you a slip, cut from Galignani, giving the substance of his speech to the Mexican deputation upon accepting the crown offered by them, and likewise another short slip, cut from the Moniteur, being its only comment of to-day on the subject. The French papers say that his government will not only be promptly acknowledged by the Catholic powers, but by all the leading governments of Europe, including England, Russia, Prussia, and France. For something like this you will, of course, be prepared.

I need not say what I have in substance said before, that I look upon this proceeding with intense anxiety. Nothing has occurred since my residence at this court which foreshadows future difficulty with France so probably as its action in this matter. God grant that it may be long delayed, and, if possible, avoided; but I fear. * * * * * *

I am, sir, your obedient servant,

WM. L. DAYTON.

Hon. WILLIAM H. SEWARD,
Secretary of State, &c.

"TRIESTE, 10*th*.—The emperor arrived at Miramar yesterday morning at eight o'clock. After signing the documents and taking breakfast, his majesty returned to Vienna, accompanied by the archdukes and Count de Rechberg. Their Mexican majesties will leave to-morrow at 4 p. m. The reception of the deputation takes place this day."

"TRIESTE, 10*th*.—This day, a little before noon, took place, at Miramar, the official reception of the Mexican deputation, and the acceptance of the crown of Mexico by the Archduke Maximilian. M Gutierrez de Estrada, the head of the deputation, delivered a long address, in which he dwelt on the importance of the national vote of Mexico. The archduke, replying in Spanish, said that he felt not the slightest doubt, from the act of adhesion just presented to him, that the immense majority of the country were in favor of the imperial form of government, and of himself as the head of the state. The choice of the country had been laid down in his reply of October 3 as one condition of his acceptance; and another was, that full guarantees should be given of his being able to devote himself peaceably to the task of advancing the prosperity of the country. Those guarantees were now fully assured, thanks to the magnanimity of the Emperor of the French, who, during the whole of the negotiations, had shown a straight-forwardness and kindness which he (the speaker) could never forget. 'The illustrious head of my family,' pursued the archduke, 'having given his consent, I now declare that, relying on the assistance of the Almighty, I accept the crown offered me by the Mexican nation. As I stated in my address of October 3, I shall endeavor to place the monarchy under the authority of the constitutional laws as soon as the pacification of the country shall be complete. The force of a government is, in my opinion, more assured by sound regulations than by the extent of its limits, and I shall be anxious for the exercise of my government to fix such bounds to it as may insure its duration. I shall hold firmly aloft the flag of independence, as the symbol of our future grandeur. I call for the co-operation of all the Mexicans who love their country, to aid me in the accomplishment of my noble but most difficult task. Never shall my government forget the gratitude it owes to the illustrious sovereign whose friendly support has rendered the regeneration of our noble land possible. I am now on the point of leaving for my new country, paying, as I go, a visit to Rome, where I shall receive from the holy father that benediction which is so precious for all sovereigns, but above all to me, called, as I am, to found a new empire."

[Translation.]

PARIS, *April* 10.

To-day, the 10th of April, at ten o'clock in the morning, the Archduke Maximilian received at his palace of Miramar the Mexican deputation charged with the duty of offering to him the crown. Mr. Gutierrez de Estrada, the head of the deputation, made a speech to his imperial and royal highness on presenting to him the vote of the people of the various localities.

The archduke replied by a formal acceptance.

The head of the deputation thanked his Majesty, and laid at his feet the testimonial of fidelity of the Mexican nation.

Immediately the Mexican flag was hoisted on the palace, and was saluted with twenty-one guns. A *Te Deum* was sung.

To-morrow, at four o'clock, the emperor and empress of Mexico will set out for their new dominions.

Mr. Dayton to Mr. Seward.

No. 450.] PARIS, *April* 14, 1864.

SIR: I herewith enclose to you a number of slips, cut from Galignani of the 12th, 13th, and 14th of this month, in reference to the Archduke Maximilian, and his acceptance of the throne of Mexico, which I have thought might be interesting to you.

I am, sir, your obedient servant,

WILLIAM L. DAYTON.

Hon. WILLIAM H. SEWARD,
Secretary of State, &c.

The *Memorial Diplomatique* gives a long account of the reception of the Mexican deputation at Miramar on Sunday. As the archduke always throws open his park to the public on holidays, an immense crowd collected to witness the arrival of the procession. The account says:

"Four carriages belonging to his imperial highness, preceded by outriders, went to convey the deputation from the hotel where they had lodged at the expense of the archduke. The deputation was composed of M. Gutierrez de Estrada, the president; Colonel Velasquez de Leon, ex-minister; M. Aguilar; ex-chargé d'affaires; General Woll; M. Esandon, banker; and M. Landa, merchant. A number of eminent Mexicans, among whom were M. Arrangoiz, ex-minister of finance; M. Murphy, formerly Mexican envoy at London; Colonel Fatio, M. Gutierrez de Estrada, jun., with several generals, colonels, and other officers, accompanied the deputation. All were in full uniform, as were also the officers of the household of the archduke, aides-de-camp, and the chamberlains. The deputation, after being received by Count Zichy, who filled the functions of grand master of the household of his imperial highness, were introduced into the grand drawing-room, into which the Archduke Maximilian, wearing the uniform of an Austrian vice-admiral, immediately afterwards entered. The French and Belgian ministers in Austria were present at the solemnity. M. Gutierrez de Estrada then delivered a speech in the Spanish language expressing the joy felt by the Mexican deputation in finding themselves in presence of his imperial highness; they had come in the name of the imperial regency to announce that the vote of the notables which had conferred the crown on him is henceforth ratified by the enthusiastic adhesion of the immense majority of the country; the unanimous acclamation of the notables of Mexico, of the municipal authorities, and of the popular corporations, has become a truly national vote."

The archduke then made the reply which has been transmitted by telegram. The account then goes on to say:

"As soon as the archduke had uttered the last word, the deputation and all the Mexicans present acclaimed their new sovereign by crying out three times: 'God save the emperor Maximilian I.' 'God save the empress Charlotte!' At the same instant, salutes of artillery, fired from the bastions of the castle, announced to the public the accession of the Archduke Maximilian to the throne of Mexico, and were immediately followed by other salutes from the port and town of Trieste. Then M. Gutierrez de Estrada, as president of the deputation, returned thanks to his majesty for his definitive acceptance of the Mexican crown. He said:

"'Sire, this complete and absolute acceptation on the part of your majesty is the prelude of our happiness; it is the consecration of the salvation of Mexico, of its approaching regeneration, of its future greatness. Every year, on this day, our children will offer up their thanksgivings to heaven in gratitude for our miraculous deliverance. As for us, sire, there remains a last duty to perform, and that is to lay at your feet our love, our gratitude, and the homage of our fidelity!'

"On saying those words the president of the deputation bent his knee and kissed the hand of the new sovereign according to Spanish custom, as a mark of homage. His example was followed by all the Mexicans present. A *proces-verbal* of the acceptance of the crown of Mexico having been drawn up, the emperor Maximilian first affixed his signature to it, after which the members of the deputation did the same, and lastly the notable Mexicans. That ceremony having been accomplished, the deputation proceeded into the apartments of the Princess Charlotte, whom they also proclaimed, and rendered homage to her in the same manner. While those things were taking place at Miramar, the news of the proclamation of the emperor of Mexico had already reached Trieste, and the bishop had a solemn *Te Deum* of thanksgiving celebrated in the cathedral of San Giusto, at which all the authorities of the town were present. Salutes from the batteries were fired at the same time. On the same day M. Zelasques de Leon, minister without portfolio, and General Woll, chief of the military household, took possession of their respective posts near the person of the emperor. In the evening there was to be a grand dinner at Miramar, when the new emperor was to appear for the first time in the uniform of a Mexican lieutenant general, modified on the model of the French army. His majesty Maximilian I will also wear the insignia of the order of the Virgin of La Guadalupa and of the national order of Mexico. A grand representation and a full-dress ball are to be given at the theatre at Trieste by the municipality."

The same journal likewise gives some information as to the settlement of the difference which has arisen concerning the Archduke Maximilian's position in the reigning family in Austria. It says:

"To avoid dynastic quarrels and obviate the partition of the patrimonial property of the house of Austria, a family law imposes on every archduchess contracting marriage the obligation of signing an act of renunciation. By this engagement she undertakes not to raise for herself or for her descendants of either sex any pretensions to the eventual succession to the throne, nor to any participation in either the endowments raised on the patrimonial property or the inheritances which might fall in *ab intestato*. The creation of the patrimonial property dates from the reign of Maria Theresa; a considerable portion of the family property was set aside for the extraordinary requirements of the different members of the family. The Grand Duke of Tuscany and the Duke of Modena, for example, now receive from that source incomes which could not figure on the budget of the state. Until now these acts of renunciation had only occurred on the marriage of archduchesses. The acceptation of a foreign crown by an archduke is a fact without precedent in the annals of the house of Hapsburg. Was it advisable to subject the archduke to the above-mentioned law? A family council, which assembled during the last stay of the archduke in Vienna, took the question into consideration. Different considerations caused the majority of its members to decide in the affirmative The Archduke Maximilian is the first agnate. As such, if (which Heaven forbid) the Emperor Francis Joseph should die without a male heir, he would be called on by right to the succession to the throne. There was so little time after the return of the archduke to Vienna from Brussels, where he received the final vote of the Mexican nation, that it was not possible to make all the family arrangements before the time first fixed for receiving the deputation. He was therefore called on to give his adhesion to a copy of the acts of renunciation which the archduchesses usually signed previously to their marriage, and which had always hitherto remained in the same form. In the precipitation which circumstances rendered necessary, the great difference between an archduke accepting a foreign crown and an archduchess marrying a foreign prince had been overlooked. Every princess by her marriage ceases to belong to the imperial family, and loses her quality of agnate to such an extent that her heirs are only entitled to the title of cognates. The Archduke Maximilian, on the contrary, still retained his title of first agnate, after accepting the sceptre of Montezuma. This consideration justifies the objections which the archduke raised against the document submitted for his signature. Negotiations were found necessary to bring matters to an arrangement. As regards the former, the wording of the act has been completely changed, in order not only to remove whatever might wound the prince's feelings, but also to mention the spontaneousness of his resolution. As regards the substance, the prince, having firmly resolved to devote himself to the destinies of the people which has chosen him, renounces for himself and his heirs, of both sexes, all right to the eventual succession to the throne of Austria *so long as the new Mexican dynasty shall continue to reign*. The renunciation is therefore not absolute. In declaring that the effects of his renunciation will continue so long as his dynasty shall reign, he implicitly deprives himself of the right of abdicating, except under the pressure of causes independent of his will. He also engages to respect accomplished facts in the interior of the Austrian monarchy. After leaving, if during his absence one of his brothers should be called on to succeed to the throne, he would recognize him as legitimate sovereign. We have no need to point out the extent of the concession at the point of view of Mexican interests. But that is not all: the archduke has made other sacrifices; he has abandoned the half of his appenage, and the whole of his rights of succession *ab intestato*. The future empress, as archduchess, received a sum of 20,000 florins (50,000 fr.) as pin money; wishing to join in the disinterestedness of her august husband, she has also renounced that income. Finally, the difficulties of which we have just pointed out the origin and the conclusion will have, on the whole, only served to place more in relief the noble and generous character of the archduke."

The late proceedings at Miramar and the acceptation of the Mexican throne by the Archduke Maximilian are remarked on by several of the Paris journals, which seem to draw a long breath of satisfaction at finding this apparently interminable affair at last brought to a close. The *Constitutionnel* has the subjoined observations:

"Every one is well aware to what a condition anarchy, under the form of a republic, had reduced Mexico. Both France and Europe knew only too well the deplorable state, as far as concerns both her material and her moral interests, into which that unfortunate country had fallen, in consequence of the ephemeral and spoliating governments, scarcely recognized at home and despised abroad. What is less known is that Mexico, already despoiled of half her territory, was the sure and speedy conquest of the United States. The word conquest, however, is too noble; for Mexico was put up to the highest bidder. If the disgraceful contract had been realized, the consequences of it would have been incalculable; the Latin races would have received a check from which they would with difficulty have recovered The principles of civilization, which constitute our moral influence in the world, would have been deeply interfered with; that is the idea which the Emperor Napoleon III expressed with extraordinary energy in his letter to the commander-in-chief of the French expedition. Mexico, by the re-establishment of the monarchy, returns into her traditional path, and again finds the true conditions of order and prosperity without sacrificing anything of her independence. What a noble mission for the young prince who accepts it so boldly, and comprehends it so well! France will thus have once more merited well from civilization. Once more short-sighted politicians will have been in the wrong, and, thanks to the great prudence which presides over our destinies, and to that perseverance which triumphs over obstacles and marches forward to its object with admirable calmness, this regeneration of Mexico which is being prepared will be one of the noblest pages of our civilizing mission in the world."

The France also has some remarks on the same subject, the following being an extract:

"The acceptance of the throne of Mexico by the Archduke Maximilian is for France a complete solution. Her task is finished. Her army will now return home in succession, with the prestige of a fresh glory and the consciousness of having performed one of the most considerable works of the present age. The expenses which that great expedition has entailed are about to be reimbursed with all the legitimate indemnities that French subjects can claim. We have in the face of history the honor of having constituted, alone, in spite of the desertion of our allies, and notwithstanding the difficulties and perils of the undertaking, in the regions of Central America, an empire, the stability of which is important to the interests of the whole world. It is not only a triumph for the French flag, but also for our principles. The Mexican empire is established on the basis of popular suffrage, which is, in the new right of which France is the expression, the only legitimate foundation of governments. It is also a triumph for that great policy which occupies itself before all with the general balance of power of modern nations, and which, in establishing in Mexico a strong, national, and regular government there, defends at once the interests of Europe and those of all the nationalities of South America. Lastly, French interests must there find guarantees and particular advantages, which cannot fail to excite attention. There has been created on the other side of the Atlantic, by the victories of our soldiers, an empire which owes its existence to us; which the bonds of the most cordial friendship and of the most legitimate gratitude must unite to us; which will give fresh strength and the straightforward influence of our policy in the New World, and open the unexplored treasures of its vast territory to French commerce and industry. The dignified and elevated speech delivered by the new emperor, on receiving the Mexican deputation, proves how highly he appreciates and how much he desires to second the generous views of France He twice expressed, in the warmest terms, his deep gratitude and his lively sympathy for the sovereign whose firm policy has conquered for him a powerful throne. The work of France has terminated. That of the emperor Maximilian now begins."

The Nation expresses itself in these terms:

"There is above all a fact which ought to be placed in the strongest light. In accepting the throne of Mexico, in virtue of popular right, the Archduke Maximilian renders to that source of authority a striking homage, which is the more precious that it emanates from a Hapsburg, and a member of that dynasty which thus far has the most openly disdained and outraged the principle of national sovereignty. We are about to witness the strange spectacle of two brothers, one of whom in Europe overrides that principle of nationality from which the other in Mexico demands the consecration of his sovereign power. We shall, no doubt, be permitted to invoke this precedent when we are contending against the policy of Austria in Italy, Hungary and elsewhere. The example of Maximilian I promises, besides, other arguments to the defenders of liberal causes. The prince proposes to inaugurate a constitutional *régime* which will soon replace, in his hands, the constituent power which has provisionally devolved on him. The fact must not be concealed that in a country disordered and ravaged by civil war the reign of liberty will be difficult to establish; in such a *régime* is, however, the only hope of safety. A system of government which has been preceded by a foreign rule should more than any other invigorate and strengthen itself by the employment of the national resources. An abuse of power could only give the prince a temporary authority; by a liberal government only can be effected a reconciliation and a pacification of all the opposing elements by which Mexico is disturbed. Arbitrary power will, besides, not be easily implanted in a country which has thrown off the yoke of its dictatorships, and which has before its around it, and everywhere, the example of nations governing themselves and prospering by liberty."

"Letters from Vienna," says the Patrie, "state that the parting of the Emperor from his brother, the Archduke Maximilian, was rather cool. The idea of a Mexican empire with an Austrian prince as sovereign met with decided resistance, up to the very last moment, in the official circles of the Austrian capital. The firmness of character of the archduke alone was able to triumph over that opposition, and now that the uselessness of all those efforts has been proved, the watchword in the regions of Vienna is: 'Mexico and its emperor are strangers to Austria and her interests.'"

THE EMPEROR OF MEXICO.—A telegram from Trieste to-day informs us that his Majesty is now much better, and intends to leave Miramar on Thursday next.—(Globe.)

The future empress of Mexico has just turned author, and issued privately "Souvenirs de Voyage à bord de la Fantasie," and "Un Hiver dans l'Isle de Madère."—(Reader.)

Mr. Dayton to Mr. Seward.

No. 452.] PARIS, *April* 18, 1864.

SIR: I herewith send you a printed translation of the "Convention concluded between France and Mexico, to regulate the conditions of the stay of the French troops in this last-named country for the purpose of establishing order and consolidating the new empire."

The convention explains itself.

I am, sir, your obedient servant,

WM. L. DAYTON.

Hon. WILLIAM H. SEWARD,
Secretary of State, &c.

[Enclosure.]

The Moniteur, in its official part, contains the text of the convention concluded between France and Mexico, to regulate the conditions of the stay of the French troops in this last-named country for the purpose of establishing order and consolidating the new empire. The convention runs thus:

The government of the Emperor of the French and that of the emperor of Mexico, animated with an equal desire to secure the re-establishment of order in Mexico and to consolidate the new empire, have resolved to regulate by a convention the conditions of the stay of the French troops in that country, and have named their plenipotentiaries to that effect, viz:

The Emperor of the French, M. Charles Herbet, minister plenipotentiary of the first class, councillor of state, director of the ministry of foreign affairs, grand officer of the legion of honor, &c.;

And the emperor of Mexico, M. Joaquin Velasquez de Leon, his minister of state without portfolio, grand officer of the distinguished order of our Lady of Guadalupe, &c.;

Who, after having communicated to each other their full powers, agreed on the following provisions:

ARTICLE 1. The French troops at present in Mexico shall be reduced as soon as possible to a corps of 25,000 men, including the foreign legion. This corps, in order to safeguard the interests which led to the intervention, shall remain temporarily in Mexico, on the conditions laid down by the following articles:

ART. 2. The French troops shall evacuate Mexico in proportion as the emperor of Mexico shall be able to organize the troops necessary to replace them.

ART. 3. The foreign legion in the service of France, composed of 8,000 men, shall nevertheless remain in Mexico six years after all the other French troops shall have been recalled, in conformity with article 2. From that moment the said legion shall pass into the service and pay of the Mexican government, which reserves to itself the right of abridging the duration of the employment of the foreign legion in Mexico.

ART. 4. The points of the territory to be occupied by the French troops, as well as the military expeditions of the said troops, if there be any, shall be determined in common concord directly between the emperor of Mexico and the commandant-in-chief of the French corps.

ART. 5. On all the points where the garrison shall be exclusively composed of Mexican troops, the military command shall devolve on the French commander. In case of expeditions combined of French and Mexican troops, the superior direction of those troops shall also belong to the French commander.

ART. 6. The French commander shall not interfere with any branch of the Mexican administration.

ART. 7. So long as the requirements of the French *corps d'armée* shall necessitate a tri-monthly service of transports between France and Vera Cruz, the expense of the said service, fixed at the sum of 400,000 francs per voyage, (going and returning,) shall be paid by Mexico.

ART. 8. The naval stations which France maintains in the West Indies and in the Pacific ocean shall often send vessels to show the French flag in the ports of Mexico.

ART. 9. The expenses of the French expedition to Mexico, to be paid by the Mexican government, are fixed at the sum of 270 millions for the whole duration of the expedition down to the 1st of July, 1864. That sum shall bear interest at the rate of 3 per cent. per annum. From the 1st of July all the expenses of the Mexican army shall be at the charge of Mexico.

ART. 10. The indemnity to be paid to France by the Mexican government for the pay and maintenance of the troops of the *corps d'armée* after the 1st of July, 1864, remains fixed at the sum of 1,000 francs a year for each man.

ART. 11. The Mexican government shall hand over to the French government the sum of sixty-six millions in bonds of the loan, at the rate of issue, viz: fifty-four millions to be deducted from the debt mentioned in article 9, and twelve millions as an instalment of the indemnities due to Frenchmen in virtue of article 14 of the present convention.

ART. 12. For the payment of the surplus of the war expenses, and for acquitting the charges in articles 7, 10, and 14, the Mexican government engages to pay annually to France the sum of twenty-five millions in specie. That sum shall be imputed, first, to the sums due in virtue of articles 7 and 10; and secondly, to the amount, interest and principal, of the sum fixed in article 9; thirdly, to the indemnities which shall remain due to French subjects in virtue of article 14 and following.

ART. 13. The Mexican government shall pay, on the last day of every month, into the hands of the paymaster general of the army, what shall be due for covering the expenses of the French troops remaining in Mexico, in conformity with article 10.

ART. 14. The Mexican government engages to indemnify French subjects for the wrongs they have newly suffered, and which were the original cause of the expedition.

ART. 15. A mixed commission, composed of three Frenchmen and three Mexicans, appointed by their respective regiments, shall meet at Mexico within three months, to examine and determine these claims.

ART. 16. A commission of revision, composed of two Frenchmen and two Mexicans, appointed in the same manner, sitting at Paris, shall proceed to the definite liquidation of the claims already admitted by the commission designated in the preceding article, and shall decide on those which have been received for its decision.

ART. 17. The French government shall set at liberty all the Mexican prisoners of war as soon as the emperor of Mexico shall have entered his states.

ART. 18 The present convention shall be ratified, and the ratifications exchanged as early as possible.

Done at the castle of Miramar, this 10th day of April, 1864.

HERBET.
JOAQUIN VELASQUEZ DE LEON.

Mr. Dayton to Mr. Seward.

[Extract.]

No. 454.] PARIS, *April* 22, 1864.

SIR: I visited M. Drouyn de Lhuys yesterday, at the department of foreign affairs. The first words he addressed to me on entering the room were, "Do you bring us peace, or bring us war?" I asked him to what he referred, and he said he referred more immediately to those resolutions recently passed by Congress in reference to the invasion of Mexico by the French, and the establishment of Maximilian upon the throne of that country. I said to him, in reply, that I did not think France had a right to infer that we were about to make war against her on account of anything contained in those resolutions. That they embodied nothing more than had been constantly held out to the French government from the beginning. That I had always represented to the government here that any action on their part, interfering with the form of government in Mexico, would be looked upon with dissatisfaction in our country, and they could not expect us to be in haste to acknowledge a monarchical government built upon the foundations of a republic which was our next neighbor. That I had reason to believe you had held the same language to the French minister in the United States. This allegation he did not seem to deny, but obviously viewed the resolutions in question as a serious step upon our part; and I am told that the leading secessionists here build largely upon these resolutions as a means of fomenting ill feeling between this country and some others and ourselves. Mr. Mason and his secretary have gone to Brussels to confer with

Mr. Dudley Mann, who is their commissioner at that place. Mr. Slidell, it is said, was to have gone to Austria, although he has not yet got off.

* * * * * *

I am, sir, your obedient servant,

WM. L. DAYTON.

Hon. WILLIAM H. SEWARD,
Secretary of State, &c.

Mr. Seward to Mr. Dayton.

No. 537.] DEPARTMENT OF STATE,
Washington, April 28, 1864.

SIR: I have the honor to enclose for your information a copy of a despatch of the 1st instant, No. 141, received at this department from Charles A. Leas, esq., our commercial agent at Belize, respecting the arrival at British Honduras of a number of southern refugees from Texas.

I am, sir, your obedient servant,

WILLIAM H. SEWARD.

WILLIAM L. DAYTON, Esq., &c.

No. 141.] UNITED STATES CONSULAR AGENCY,
Belize, April 1, 1864.

SIR: By an arrival from Matamoras we have added to the population of this colony a number of southerners, who escaped from Texas, and have determined to take up their residence within these possessions. They report that there is no hope left for the confederacy, and that there are thousands now in Texas who are anxious to escape, but cannot, in consequence of the stringency of the blockade. That is to say, these are parties who either cannot remain in the south after the rebellion shall be closed, in consequence of their not being comprehended in the amnesty proclamation, or from a deep-seated hatred and animosity will not again consent to reside among us as brother members of the same national family.

The individuals above referred to, as having just arrived here, are the second arrival of the kind within the past few weeks, all bringing the same report. Now, if these reports be true, (and I doubt not they are true,) then it seems to me that an important consideration is at once presented, namely, as to whether it would not be humane as well as politic to allow *some* door to be opened by which such persons may escape from our country. If their animosities are such that they are no longer willing to live with us in peace, then I argue that they are not worth having as citizens and residents. Their places can soon be filled by a better class of persons. When I write thus, it must not be presumed that I would have our government and nation ignore the punishing, even to the execution of a death sentence, the arch-traitors, and to accomplish that end to carefully close all the avenues by which such might escape. I refer more particularly to that class of persons who, from bitterness of feeling, are unwilling to take an oath of allegiance, or to longer live in peace with us, and hence prefer to seek a home in a foreign land. The fact is, that the authorities and large landed proprietors of this colony imagine that they can see in those persons the hope of this country; that, if they can be allowed to escape from the south, thousands would seek their homes in British Honduras, thus furnishing at once, an intelligent, experienced, and producing population, particularly in the cultivation of cotton, sugar, tobacco, &c., and I have made the suggestion herein contained at the direct request of some wealthy and influential gentlemen of this place. On yesterday Governor Austin gave his first dinner party, at which the subject was canvassed, and I there promised to communicate with the United States government in regard to the matter; hence, if you deem the suggestions worthy of consideration, I beg to ask, on behalf of the parties above alluded to, at the head of which may be considered the governor, that you will be pleased to communicate it to the honorable Secretary of State, through whom it may reach the President.

With great respect, I have the honor to be your most obedient servant,

CHARLES A. LEAS,
United States Consular Agent.

Hon. F. W. SEWARD,
Assistant Secretary of State, Washington.

Mr. Seward to Mr. Dayton.

No. 538.] DEPARTMENT OF STATE,
Washington, April 30, 1864.

SIR: Your despatch of April 11, No. 449, has been received.

I thank you for the information it brings concerning the acceptance of the tendered crown by the Archduke Maximilian, and his intended departure for Mexico.

Events which have recently occurred in the eastern section of that country, if they are correctly reported, show that the Mexican national authorities are not likely to be immediately suppressed. It is of course not impossible that new embarrassments for this government may grow out of the archduke's assumption of authority in Mexico. But we shall do all that prudence, justice, and honor require to avert them, at the same time we shall not forego the assertion of any of our national rights.

If such precautions fail to secure us against aggression, we shall then, I trust, be able to rise without great effort to the new duties which in that case will have devolved upon us. I remain now firm, as heretofore, in the opinion that the destinies of the American continent are not to be permanently controlled by any political arrangements that can be made in the capitals of Europe.

I am, sir, your obedient servant,

WILLIAM H. SEWARD.

WILLIAM L. DAYTON, Esq., *&c.*

Mr. Seward to Mr. Dayton.

No. 542.] DEPARTMENT OF STATE,
Washington, May 9, 1864.

SIR: Your despatch of April 22, No. 454, has been received. What you have said to M. Drouyn de Lhuys on the subject of the resolution of the House of Representatives concerning Mexico, as you have reported it, is entirely approved. The resolution yet remains unacted upon in the Senate.

Mr. Corwin was to leave Vera Cruz on the 3d instant under the leave of absence granted to him by this department on the 8th of August last.

I am, sir, your obedient servant,

WILLIAM H. SEWARD.

WILLIAM L. DAYTON, Esq., *&c.*

Mr. Dayton to Mr. Seward.

No. 465.] PARIS, *May* 16, 1864.

SIR: In a recent conference with M. Drouyn de Lhuys he complained seriously of your late action in refusing to the French navy a supply of coal bought by it in New York. He says France never has declared and never will declare coal contraband of war; that if the United States should do so, it would be a retrograde move, inasmuch as its traditional policy had always been in favor of neutrals and in limitation rather than in extension of the list of contraband. He hopes that we will not retrace our steps, but in this matter adhere to our past policy; that France has always gone with us, or we with her, on these questions of maritime law, and he does not think it for the interest of either country to part company; at least, that was the inference from his language.

He informed me, further, that your opinion was understood to be favorable to letting the coal go to the French vessels, but difficulty was made by the Secretary of the Treasury. I told him if this were so there might be some question connected with the revenue which had interfered, but he thought otherwise, and said that it was made to rest purely upon the question, is coal contraband of war? This is a question of deep interest to the French government—deeper, perhaps, than to us, she having a large navy and *little coal*, while Great Britain and the United States have an abundance of the latter article.

He said, further, that if the United States should declare coal a contraband of war, it would place France in a false position in reference to our country. That she, France, holding coal not to be contraband, would be compelled to supply it to our enemies in time of war, and to the confederates, while denying it to us because we denied it to them. That they would dislike much to be placed in a position indicating such apparent want of neutrality, yet that it would be inevitable if coal was declared by us contraband of war.

There is a good deal of sensitiveness manifested here upon this point. M. Rouher, minister of state, referred to it, I observe, in his late speech in the Chamber of Deputies.

I am, sir, your obedient servant,

WM. L. DAYTON.

Hon. WILLIAM H. SEWARD,
Secretary of State, &c.

Mr. Seward to Mr. Dayton.

No. 561.]

DEPARTMENT OF STATE,
Washington, May 21, 1864.

SIR: I have the honor to acknowledge the receipt of your despatch of May 2, No. 461, and to approve of your proceedings therein mentioned. We learn that Mr. Corwin, our minister plenipotentiary to Mexico, is at Havana, on his return to the United States, under leave of absence.

I am, sir, your obedient servant,

WILLIAM H. SEWARD.

WILLIAM L. DAYTON, Esq., *&c.*

Mr. Seward to Mr. Dayton.

No. 557.]

DEPARTMENT OF STATE,
Washington, May 23, 1864.

SIR: I enclose a copy of a despatch of the 27th ultimo, and of its accompaniments, addressed to this department by Mr. Chase, consul general of the United States at Tampico, from which it appears that that officer has been treated very rudely by the French military commandant there, and even threatened with imprisonment. You will make a proper representation upon the subject to the minister for foreign affairs of France, and will state to him that due reparation will be expected by this government. As the correspondence speaks for itself, no inquiry as to the facts of the case would seem to be necessary.

I am, sir, your obedient servant,

WILLIAM H. SEWARD.

WILLIAM L. DAYTON, Esq., *&c.*

Mr. Chase to Mr. F. W. Seward.

No. 18.]

CONSULATE GENERAL OF THE UNITED STATES,
Tampico, April 27, 1864.

SIR: I have the honor to enclose herewith a copy of a note (No. 1) addressed to me by the French superior commandant of this place on the 25th instant; also a copy of my reply thereto, (No. 3,) which was written and sent to that officer thirty minutes after the receipt of his first note, (marked No. 1,) although it was received at twilight.

My clerk went to and returned from the office of the commandant three times, without finding him, for the purpose of putting him in possession of the above-mentioned reply.

At the hour of 9.30 p. m. I received the second note, (No. 2,) menacing me with imprisonment, and, without knowing its contents, I sent him the reply, (No. 3,) after which I was not molested.

The opportune arrival of the United States steamer Kanawha, Captain Taylor, off this bar on the following morning, had the effect to soften the temper of this imperious superior commandant; still, I consider it my duty to submit this case to your decision, indulging the hope that redress for this outrage will be speedily demanded by my government.

I am, with great respect, sir, your most obedient servant,

FRANKLIN CHASE.

F. W. SEWARD, Esq.,
Assistant Secretary of State, Washington, D. C.

No. 1.

Commandant Givertoss to Mr. Chase.

[Translation.]

TAMPICO, *April* 25, 1864.

The commander-in-chief of Tampico begs the consul of the United States to be pleased to give him the names and Christian names of the individuals who have this day entered this city, and who have not reported themselves at our office. He will be pleased to guarantee, under his responsibility, the good conduct of these persons. In case he should not do so, the superior commandant will have them arrested as vagabonds. We require an immediate reply.

The superior commandant,

V. DE GIVERTOSS.

The CONSUL *of the United States.*

Commandant Givertoss to Mr. Chase.

No. 2.

[Translation.]

TAMPICO, *April* 25, 1864.

It seemed to me that I had asked of the consul of the United States what were the names of the Americans who had this day entered our city. Let him be pleased to answer immediately for the good conduct of those individuals; otherwise I shall find myself under the painful necessity of making him personally responsible therefor, and to make him my prisoner. Reply immediately.

The superior commandant,

V. DE GIVERTOSS.

The UNITED STATES CONSUL.

No. 3.

Mr. Chase to Commandant Givertoss.

CONSULATE GENERAL OF THE UNITED STATES,
Tampico, April 25, 1864.

SIR: In reply to your note of the present date, I have the honor to state to you that the only persons I am aware of who have arrived in this city are those that came in on yesterday, viz: Charles E. Johnson, William Garret, and Lewis Davison, seamen, and five passengers—the names of the latter I have not as yet ascertained—all of whom are from the

American schooner E. D. McClenahan, G. R. Edgett, master, which vessel was lately wrecked near Soto la Marina on her passage from New Orleans for this port.

These persons are doubtless peaceable; but if I should hear of anything to the contrary, they will not receive any countenance or protection from this consulate.

I have the honor to be, sir, most respectfully, your obedient servant,

FRANKLIN CHASE.

The SUPERIOR COMMANDANT *of this place, &c.*

Mr. Dayton to Mr. Seward.

[Extract.]

No. 484.] PARIS, *June* 8, 1864.

* * * * * * * * *

SIR: I thought M. Drouyn de Lhuys was rather disposed to find fault with late proceedings of our government. He referred again to your refusal of coal to their fleet, and to your giving up, as he said, to be hanged the secretary of Vidaurri, who had fled to Brownsville for protection, although now there was scarcely a war against France in Mexico—nothing against them but some roving marauding bands. He said, too, after their military officers were on the ocean to visit our country, with a view to examine what was to be seen there, and with our assent and assurance of welcome, they were then informed that *this line* or *that* could not be examined. M. Drouyn de Lhuys said it would have been more agreeable if notice had been sooner given, &c., &c. I could not but feel that this querulousness was in part the result of a consciousness that we, and not they, really had just cause of complaint. He was disposed to anticipate me in these matters—to complain rather than be complained of.

I am, sir, your obedient servant,

WM. L. DAYTON.

Hon. WILLIAM H. SEWARD,
Secretary of State, &c.,

Mr. Seward to Mr. Dayton.

No. 573.] DEPARTMENT OF STATE,
Washington, June 8, 1864.

SIR: Referring to my instructions of the 23d ultimo, No. 557, and to its accompaniments, relative to the rude treatment of Mr. Chase, the United States consul at Tampico, by the French military commandant there, I now transmit a copy of a further despatch from Mr. Chase of the 10th ultimo, No. 21, which gives a more detailed account of the matter. I need only to say that the aggression on the consul, for which you can ask reparation, is the menace contained in the second note of the French commandant to Mr. Chase.

I am, sir, your obedient servant,

WILLIAM H. SEWARD.

WILLIAM L. DAYTON, Esq., *&c.*

Mr. Chase to Mr. F. W. Seward.

No. 21.] CONSULATE GENERAL OF THE UNITED STATES,
Tampico, May 10, 1864.

SIR: On the 27th ultimo I had the honor to address a letter to you on the subject of two notes sent to me by the French superior commandant of this place, with which I enclosed copies of the said notes and copy of my reply to the first. A press of business on this consulate, and the prompt despatch of the British steamer's mail, prevented me sending a full report and the requisite translations, an omission which I now beg leave to supply, with the following explanations and enclosures.

From the outset of the French intervention with this country I have carefully pursued a strictly neutral course, and every American citizen residing in this place has followed my advice and example; and up to the present moment not one of them has been accused of meddling in the political or military affairs of the country. In the mean time I have firmly defended their just rights, but invariably manifesting a conciliatory disposition.

You will please perceive that in the first note of the French commandant he demands the names of certain individuals who, he alleges, entered this city on that day, (April 25,) and endeavored to hold me responsible for their moral conduct. That note was written in the French language, and not delivered to me until twilight on the day of its date; and, notwithstanding the unseasonable hour, I obtained a verbal translation, and sent my reply to it in thirty minutes after its receipt; but my clerk, not finding him in his office, went and returned with it three consecutive times without finding him. At 9.30 p. m. I received the second note, and, not knowing its contents, I again sent my reply to the first.

The second note was so written as to leave me in doubt whether the threat of imprisonment extended to me or not, and under that doubt I called at an early hour on the commandant, and pointed out the impropriety of his attempt to hold me responsible for the conduct of any persons entering this place. He excused himself on the plea of alarming reports there were in circulation.

In this state of affairs Captain Taylor, of the United States steamer Kanawha, happily arrived here, and, fearing that the appearance of that vessel might excite some real alarm, I lost no time in presenting that officer to the commandant, who courteously reported the presence of his vessel.

On my return to my office, I had a careful perusal of the second note, and ascertained that the threat of imprisonment was actually made against me, and I felt much regret that I had paid these visits.

The individuals who entered this city were those mentioned in my reply to the commandant, all of whom were duly reported to the captain of the port. Among the passengers there was only one American citizen.

I did not think it proper to reply to the second note from the commandant, but I expressed my astonishment at its contents to the acting French consul at this port remarking at the same time that no difficulty was pending between our respective governments, and that it behooved the authorities not to provoke any.

Shortly after that conversation the consul was sent to me with a message from the commandant offering to retire his notes. In reply, I stated that if the commandant felt any regret for his conduct towards me, and was willing to offer an apology in writing, I would take much satisfaction in forwarding it to my government, as the affair was now too serious to be decided by this consulate.

This offer was declined, and I now respectfully beg leave to submit this plain statement of the case to you, believing that you will consider it of sufficient importance to take measures for obtaining redress for this unprovoked wrong and in security for my future protection.

I have the honor to be, sir, with great esteem and respect, your most obedient servant,

FRANKLIN CHASE.

FREDERICK W. SEWARD, Esq.,
Assistant Secretary of State, Washington.

[The two notes and reply referred to in the above despatch, and which formed its accompaniments, are the same as those enclosed in Mr. Chase's despatch of the 27th of April last, No. 18, published in despatch of the 23d of May, No. 557, to Mr. Dayton.]

Mr. Dayton to Mr. Seward.

No. 489.] PARIS, *June* 13, 1864.

SIR: I have the honor to enclose herewith an *original letter* received a few days since from certain individuals, lately officers of the Mexican army, now prisoners of war in France, together with a copy of the answer returned acknowledging its receipt.

I am, sir, your obedient servant,

WM. L. DAYTON.

Hon. WILLIAM H. SEWARD,
Secretary of State, &c.

[Translation.]

TOURS, DEPARTMENT OF INDRE LOIRE, *May* 26, 1864.

SIR: As soon as the blind apologists of the sophisms and prejudices of another epoch roused the passions and interests of the government near which you are accredited, producing the unjustifiable invasion of which the Mexican territory is at present the theatre, we comprehended the new field which presented itself to the human race to continue its conquests of progress, of improvement, and of perfection, to which it incessantly aspires, in compliance with laws which nothing can impede.

Abstracting ourselves from selfish thoughts, we enter in good faith on the path of investigation, seeking the rules of morality, the dogmas of philosophy, the precepts of justice, on which might hang the pretext for overthrowing our independence, destroying our institutions, stifling our opinions, and casting around our necks the chains forged beforehand in the workshops of France. We must confess, Mr. Minister, that neither in morality, nor in reason, nor in justice, nor in history, nor in the annals of humanity, do we find a single word which can justify so vast an outrage, but without much effort we find that it rested on our wretchedness and on our weakness, because we have labored enough in demolishing the ancient edifice, whose social conditions were repugnant, to bury beneath its ruins the rights of the citizen, in order to build up a new edifice where might eternally dwell the rights of man There was, therefore, no room for hesitation; the sword is not argument. In this idea, grasping ours in one hand, and bearing aloft in the other the sublime tablet of the rights of man, convinced that an assault upon the nationality of one people is an assault upon that of every people, we gave a beginning to the struggle. Victory smiled on us awhile, notwithstanding that our adversary, to his indisputable knowledge in the art of war—knowledge very superior to ours—added deception and perfidy in order to conquer us. At length, at Puebla, we succumbed to the superiority of physical force, and came to this country in the character of prisoners of war of France.

We are in the firm conviction that, in proportion as we strip ourselves of our prejudices and of our privileges, reason resumes her place and civilization is aggrandized—not that civilization whose electric shock produces the shock of arms, but that whose torch is kindled in the conscience of the people. We, in consequence, think that wars of ambition and of conquest are no longer possible; those of emancipation and of liberty can alone take place, until the time arrive in which there can be no material forces which can contend with moral force. The enlightened and magnanimous American people thinks as we do, and, although tormented by a civil war whose end will be the security of the rights and immunities of man, does not, on that account, remain indifferent in a strife which affects its interests.

Even here we have heard its protest, and, considering it to be an unavoidable duty which gratitude counsels that your government should know the sincere and profound sentiments of admiration and respect with which we are inspired by the virtues of the people of the United States of America, our position obliges us to address the present letter to you, begging you to think proper to become the interpreter of our fraternal affection.

At the same time we ask you, Mr. Minister, to deign to accept the assurance of the very high consideration with which we are your very humble and obedient servants,

Colonel JESUS GOMEZ, *Portugal.*
Colonel JOSÉ MONTESENOF.
Colonel LEWIS LEGONETA.
Commodore JUAN URBINA.
Lieutenant Colonel V. H. RUNERAS.
Commandant PABLO REUTEVIA.
Commandant FRANQUITOM CORTEZ.

His Excellency Mr. DAYTON,
Envoy Extraordinary and Minister Plenipotentiary of the United States of America near the French government.

PARIS, *June* 7, 1864.

GENTLEMEN: As representative of the government of the United States at Paris, it is my pleasing duty to acknowledge the receipt of your letter of the 26th of May last, and to thank you for the kind sentiments and encouraging sympathies therein expressed.

It will give me much pleasure to forward your communication to the government at Washington.

Accept, gentlemen, the assurance of highest respect with which I have the honor to be, your very humble and very obedient servant,

WM. L. DAYTON.

Colonel JESUS GOMEZ, *Portugal*,
Colonel JOSE MONTESENOF,
Colonel LEWIS LEGONETA,
Commandant JUAN URBINA,
Commandant PABLO REUTEVIA,
Commandant FRANQUITOM CORTEZ,
Tours, (Indre Loire,) France.

Mr. Seward to Mr. Dayton.

No. 593.]

DEPARTMENT OF STATE,
Washington, June 27, 1864.

SIR: In your despatch of the 8th of June, No. 484, which has already been acknowledged, you remarked that you thought M. Drouyn de Lhuys was rather disposed to find fault with late proceedings of this government; that he referred again to our refusal of coal to the French fleet and to our giving up "to be hanged," as he said, the secretary of Vidaurri, who had fled to Brownsville for protection, although there now was scarcely a man against France in Mexico. You state that M. Drouyn de Lhuys further remarked, that after their military officers were on the ocean to visit our country with a view to examine what was to be seen there, with our assent and assurance of welcome, they were then informed that this line or that could not be examined, and that it would have been agreeable if notice had been sooner given. In your despatch No. 483 you intimate an apprehension that the French government may not be unwilling to find us acting so as to enable it to assume that it is put on the defensive, and entitled to vindicate its honor.

The remarks of M. Drouyn de Lhuys, although not intrinsically grave, derive importance from the peculiar position of the relations between France and the United States. The executive government of this country has no such susceptibilities as to make it desire or favor any misunderstanding with the government of France. On the contrary, it is an administration which, by its very constitution, would be pacific and friendly towards France, and towards all nations, even if it did not find especial and urgent persuasions to that policy in the distractions of our unhappy civil war. Nevertheless, it is not well to overlook the fact that a large mass of the American people, owing to the war of France against Mexico, are not less open to alienating influences in regard to France than the government of France can be in regard to the United States. It will be well, therefore, for you to let M. Drouyn de Lhuys understand that you communicated his complaints to me, and to give him my answer to them, which is as follows:

First. In relation to the supply of coals for the French fleet: the same practice was followed in regard to France in that case which is followed in regard to all other nations. Second. The restrictions on the supply of coals to foreign vessels were adopted for our own safety against a dangerous internal enemy, and for the guarding of our neutrality, as much in regard to Mexico as in regard to France. Third. That the difficulty about the exportation of the coals in question was accommodated to the satisfaction of the French government. Fourth. In regard to the delivery of the secretary of Vidaurri to the authorities of Mexico: the French government has not complained of that transaction, nor has this government been officially called upon to express itself concerning the affair. The proceeding was a military one; it occurred on a distant and disturbed frontier, without any knowledge on the part of the Executive, and, so far as this government has subsequently received any knowledge or information, the offending Mexican who was delivered up to his own government was an open enemy of the United States, and the general who delivered him up had no knowledge or reason to believe that the Mexican authorities would deal with him other than as a prisoner of war. Fifthly. As to the delay of the French officers on their way to the army of the Potomac, after this government had assented to their visit: the assent was given with no reservation, because no occasion for any was anticipated. A military exigency of extreme delicacy and importance subsequently occurred, and the commanding general of the armies of the United States deemed it important to exclude, for the time, all visitors from the army. Notice was given to the French as well as to the British commission at the first moment when this necessity was announced to this government. The French commission was received here with all the hospitalities of the government, and as soon as the exigency referred to had passed, they were sent forward to the field of observation. You may make these explanations to M. Drouyn de Lhuys. You may say to him that this government cannot admit that in either of the transactions I have thus reviewed, it has been either unjust, discourteous, or unfriendly to the government of France. This government avoids with equal care the putting unfriendly constructions upon the proceedings of the government of France and on other foreign states, and the giving of accidental offence on our own part to all foreign nations.

Pursuing this course, we calmly abide events which must determine whether, in spite of our devotion to peace, the field of war on this continent must be enlarged.

I am, sir, your obedient servant,

WILLIAM H. SEWARD.

WILLIAM L. DAYTON, Esq., &c.

Mr. Seward to Mr. Dayton.

No. 598.]

DEPARTMENT OF STATE,
Washington, July 2, 1864.

SIR: Your despatch of the 13th of June, No. 489, has been received, together with the papers annexed to the same. I have submitted to the President the correspondence which has taken place between certain Mexican prisoners of war and yourself, and have the pleasure to inform you that while your reply to these gentlemen is approved, the President is deeply affected by the sentiments of respect and affection for the United States which the Mexican officers have so thoughtfully and eloquently expressed in their communication.

I am, sir, your obedient servant,

WILLIAM H. SEWARD.

WILLIAM L. DAYTON, Esq., &c.

Mr. Dayton to Mr. Seward.

No. 515.]

PARIS, *July* 18, 1864.

SIR: Herewith I beg to enclose to you the translation of a note received from M. Drouyn de Lhuys in reference to the complaint by Mr. Chase, our consul at Tampico.

This note, like some others that M. Drouyn de Lhuys has written to me, is unsigned, and a mere substitute for an informal verbal communication, but, being in writing, is the more satisfactory as the less liable to be misunderstood.

Our consul in this case may be, and doubtless is, right in his complaint of rudeness on the part of French officials, but it does seem to me he would have shown more judgment if he had accepted the offered withdrawal of the notes complained of, (which was an implied apology,) rather than made this rudeness the subject of a serious diplomatic correspondence.

I am, sir, your obedient servant,

WM. L. DAYTON.

Hon. WILLIAM H. SEWARD, &c.

M. Drouyn de Lhuys to Mr. Dayton.

[Translation.]

Memorandum—July, 1864.

The minister of foreign affairs of the Emperor has examined the two despatches of the American consul at Tampico, relative to the threats of imprisonment to which he has been subjected—despatches which M. the minister of the United States has been directed to communicate to the government of his majesty. It is not possible to answer Mr. Dayton definitively upon this subject before receiving the explanations requested of the commander-in-chief of the French forces in Mexico. The attentive perusal of the second despatch of Mr. Chase cannot fail, however, to suggest to M. Drouyn de Lhuys some reflections, which it seems to him proper to offer at once to M. the minister of the United States. The circumstantial details given in regard to this affair by the American consul in his last report are in effect of a nature to lessen very much its gravity.

According to the declaration of Mr. Chase himself, he had already in his hands the two letters of the superior commandant of Tampico, which now cause his demand for satisfaction, when he went to this officer to represent to him that he could not answer for the good conduct of any one who might enter Tampico.

The commandant excused himself for having written as he had done, in alleging that he had been led into it by the alarming rumors which were at that time in circulation.

A short time afterwards Mr. Chase made a second visit to this same officer, to present, with a view to preventing any disquieting remarks, the captain of an American ship-of-war which had arrived, in the mean time, at Tampico.

The incident seemed then completely void, when the French commandant learnt from the manager of the imperial consulate that Mr. Chase, having re-read his second note, had manifested an extreme dissatisfaction with it. The commandant of Tampico hastened then to send back the French agent to the American consul to offer to withdraw the letters by which he felt himself wounded. Mr. Chase answered to this offer by requiring written apologies, in order to transmit them to his government, and the French officer refused them.

These are the facts, as Mr. Chase himself states them. Now it appears from this recital that the misdoings of the superior commandant of Tampico would consist in having written to the American consul in terms assuredly much to be regretted, but that he hastened, upon learning the impression which they had made upon this consul, to offer him spontaneously the withdrawal of his notes. He no doubt thought that would suffice Mr. Chase, since the two visits of the latter did not allow him to suspect the importance which the incident might take in the eyes of this agent. It is not to be admitted for an instant, as the latter gives it to be understood, that it was the appearance of a federal ship which brought the commandant of Tampico to the more correct proceedings, for he had, before the arrival of this vessel, very courteously received the observations of Mr. Chase, and, to speak the truth, it is rather singular that it was only after the satisfactory explanations exchanged, and after a second visit to the French officer, in order to present to him the federal captain, that Mr. Chase thought it useful to re-read more attentively, or to cause to be more faithfully translated, a note of six lines which had been the cause of all his previous proceedings.

So, by the very terms of the despatches of the consul of the United States, if there were for a moment a fault in the proceedings on the part of the superior commandant of Tampico, this officer seems to have wished, by his after conduct, to have effaced its impressions upon Mr. Chase.

Mr. Seward to Mr. Dayton.

No. 628.]

DEPARTMENT OF STATE,
Washington, August 8, 1864.

SIR: I have received your despatch of the 18th of July, No. 515, which gives me your views of the complaint of Mr. Chase, United States consul at Tampico, concerning certain notes addressed to him by a French officer on the entrance of a French military force at that place. Your despatch is accompanied by a memorandum concerning the case, which M. Drouyn de Lhuys has committed to you for the information of this government.

This memorandum is written in a candid and liberal spirit, and induces an expectation that, when the minister for foreign affairs shall have received the explanations which he has asked from the military authorities, he will relieve the case of all its gravity, by showing us that the French officer addressed his offensive notes to the consul without proper consideration of the respect due to that officer as an agent of the United States, and that the rudeness of the note is disapproved by his Imperial Majesty's government. I freely admit that I concur with you in the opinion that Mr. Chase might, with entire propriety, have consented to the proposed withdrawal of the note of which he complains; and I regret that he did not do so. You are quite at liberty to communicate this opinion of mine to M. Drouyn de Lhuys. This government attaches only as much importance to ceremonial questions as the prevailing state of public sentiment on this class of national issues requires. It has no desire to lift them to the dignity of diplomatic debate.

I am, sir, your obedient servant,

WILLIAM H. SEWARD.

WILLIAM L. DAYTON, Esq., *&c.*

Mr. Seward to Mr. Dayton.

No. 635.]

DEPARTMENT OF STATE,
Washington, August 18, 1864.

SIR: I enclose for your information a copy of a letter which I have received from his excellency Frederick F. Low, governor of California, relative to the rumor there that Mr. William M. Gwin is to be minister of finance under the new government of Mexico, and also concerning the supposed policy of the Emperor of France in regard to indemnity for the expenses of the war.

I am, sir, your obedient servant,

WILLIAM H. SEWARD.

WILLIAM L. DAYTON, Esq., *&c.*

Governor Low to Mr. Seward.

STATE OF CALIFORNIA, EXECUTIVE DEPARTMENT,
Sacramento, July 18, 1864.

SIR: I beg to acknowledge the receipt of your letter of the 20th June, enclosing copy of an extract from a letter received by you from Paris, giving information concerning the movements of Mr. William M. Gwin.

There is a rumor here that Gwin is to be minister of finance under the new government of Mexico, but I cannot vouch for the correctness of the report. My impressions are that the Emperor of France will require indemnity for the expenses of the war, and in the absence of any revenue which could be applied to that purpose, he will demand and receive from Maximilian certain territory which will comprise the States of Sonora and Sinaloa, probably in lieu of a money consideration.

Gwin has probably been sent as an emissary to shape the public mind for such a state of things. In any event, the ports in the Gulf of California will most likely be a sort of rendezvous for plotters of treason, bearing a similar relation to the Pacific coast that Nassau does to the Atlantic.

The Mexican question is one that is of especial importance to the people of this State, and for any information concerning it which you may think proper to communicate to me, I would feel especially obliged.

I have the honor to be your obedient servant,

FREDERICK F. LOW.

Hon. WILLIAM H. SEWARD,
Secretary of State, Washington, D. C.

Mr. Seward to Mr. Dayton.

No. 648.]

DEPARTMENT OF STATE,
Washington, September 15, 1864.

SIR: I give you for your information a copy of a despatch which has just been received from William H. Corwin, esq., our chargé d'affaires in Mexico. Later accounts than this despatch do not enable us to judge concerning the probable results of the military movements now going on in that republic. You will, of course, observe what Mr. Corwin relates of Dr. Gwin's purposes in Sonora. It is not to be doubted that they are unfriendly to the United States. But I think I hazard little in saying that they forebode even more of inconvenience to whatever government may exist in Mexico than of ultimate harm to our own country.

It is hardly to be apprehended that the insurgents will come out of the present civil war with any great capacity for establishing slavery in Mexico. It may, however, be well for you to ascertain how far such schemes of his find support in the councils of the Emperor of France.

I am, sir, your obedient servant,

WILLIAM H. SEWARD.

WILLIAM L. DAYTON, Esq., *&c.*

Mr. Seward to Mr. Dayton.

No. 656.]

DEPARTMENT OF STATE,
Washington, September 20, 1864.

SIR: I append, for such use as you may deem expedient, a copy of a letter of yesterday, addressed to this department by the Secretary of War, containing a despatch which has just been received from Major General Canby, who is commanding in the field west of the Mississippi.

The proceeding of Major General Canby has been approved. The despatch contains the official information this government has of the extraordinary events which have recently occurred on the Rio Grande.

I am, sir, your obedient servant,

WILLIAM H. SEWARD.

WILLIAM L. DAYTON, Esq., *&c.*

[Same to Mr. Adams.]

Mr. Stanton to Mr. Seward.

WAR DEPARTMENT,
Washington, September 19, 1864.

SIR: I enclose to you the following extract from a despatch from Major General Canby, received last night, dated at New Orleans, 3 o'clock p. m., September 12:

"Cortinas has crossed the Rio Grande to escape the French forces operating from Bagdad, and has been notified by the commanding officer at Brazos Santiago that, on surrendering his army and ammunition, his party would be received as refugees; and that his presence in the territory of the United States, as an armed enemy of a neutral power, would not be tolerated."

Your obedient servant,

EDWIN M. STANTON,
Secretary of War.

Hon. WILLIAM H. SEWARD,
Secretary of State.

Mr. Seward to Mr. Dayton.

No. 669.]

DEPARTMENT OF STATE,
Washington, October 3, 1864.

SIR: I transmit for your information a copy of a private note of the 23d ultimo from M. de Geofroy; of my reply of the 30th ultimo, and of a letter addressed by me to Major General Canby on the 30th ultimo, in regard to the alleged entrance of the Mexican General Cortinas, with an armed force, into the territory of the United States, with an assumption of military authority.

I am, sir, your obedient servant,

WILLIAM H. SEWARD.

WILLIAM L. DAYTON, Esq., &c.

For enclosures see correspondence with the French legation.

Mr. Seward to Major General Canby.

DEPARTMENT OF STATE,
Washington, September 30, 1864.

SIR: Unofficial newspaper statements concerning the alleged entrance of the Mexican General Cortinas, with an armed force, into the territory of Texas, within the United States, with an assumption of military authority, have attracted the attention of this department, as well as that of the minister of France at this capital. The reports are contradictory and apparently unreliable. The dignity of this government and its honor, as a neutral power in the conflict which is raging in Mexico, render it necessary that the President should be fully informed as early as possible of the proceedings to which I have thus referred. I have therefore to request that you will ascertain the facts and make a report thereon to the Secretary of War. In the mean time I have the pleasure to inform you that the proceeding is approved, by which, on the occasion referred to, you gave notice to the said Cortinas that his presence in arms within the United States, in an attitude of war against a friendly power, with which the United States are at peace, would not be tolerated. Although that proceeding indicates that you have faithfully adhered to the instructions given to your predecessors, yet I think it proper to renew the injunction that on no account, and in no way, must the neutrality of the United States in the war between France and Mexico be compromised by our military forces, or be suffered to be compromitted within your command by either of the belligerents.

I have the honor to be, general, your obedient servant,

WILLIAM H. SEWARD.

Major General E. R. S. CANBY,
Commanding Department of the Gulf, Headquarters, New Orleans.

Mr. Dayton to Mr. Seward.

No. 545.]

PARIS, *October* 7, 1864.

SIR: The copy of a despatch from General Canby in reference to Cortinas, crossing the Rio Grande with his forces into Texas, which you sent to me in your No. 656, to be used subject to my discretion, I read to M. Drouyn de

Lhuys. The facts had got into the newspapers with various comments, and as I well knew the attention of this government must have been called to the subject, I thought it safest at once to inform them of the prudent action of the government of the United States in the premises. M. Drouyn de Lhuys said this action of our government was a matter of interest, and begged me to let him take a copy of the extract, which I did. He remarked that it was important to him to have the means of explaining the facts at once, if the subject should be referred to by his Majesty.

I am, sir, your obedient servant,

WM. L. DAYTON.

Hon. WILLIAM H. SEWARD.
Secretary of State, &c.

Mr. Seward to Mr. Dayton.

No. 677.] DEPARTMENT OF STATE,
Washington, October 10, 1864.

SIR: I transmit a copy of a report of Major General Canby, and of the accompanying papers, relative to certain proceedings near Brownsville, in Texas, in connexion with the United States, Texan, and French forces in that quarter. The condition of affairs there does not seem to have been changed, but these papers will serve to explain it. To that end you may communicate them to M. Drouyn de Lhuys.

I am, sir, your obedient servant,

WILLIAM H. SEWARD.

WILLIAM L. DAYTON, Esq., &c.

Gen. Townsend to Mr. Seward.

WAR DEPARTMENT, ADJUTANT-GENERAL'S OFFICE,
Washington, October 4, 1864.

SIR: I am directed by the Secretary of War to transmit to you the enclosed documents in relation to the arrival in Texas of a Mexican force under Cortinas, with the request that after you have perused the same, they may be returned to this office for file.

I have the honor to be, sir, very respectfully, your obedient servant,

E. D. TOWNSEND,
Assistant Adjutant General.

Hon. WILLIAM H. SEWARD, *Secretary of State.*

General Canby to General Banks.

HEADQUARTERS MILITARY DIVISION OF WEST MISSISSIPPI,
New Orleans, La., September 15, 1864.

GENERAL: The correspondence of Colonel Day, in relation to the Mexican force under Cortinas, has been received. Colonel Day's action, so far as is known here, accords with our neutral obligations, and is approved. The Mexican refugees are entitled to an asylum in our territory, when they deliver up their arms and munitions, and restore any prisoners or booty that they may have taken from the French; they will not be received into the service of the United States for service on the Rio Grande frontier, but may be enlisted for the general service. In this case they will be sent to this city, either before or after enlistment, to be organized, armed, and equipped. Their enlistment may be for one, two, and three years, but preferably for the shorter term, and their duty thereafter will be determined by the circumstances of the service.

As an armed enemy of France, this force will not be tolerated in our territory; and if this be the intention of Cortinas, the commanding officer will be instructed to regard, and, as far as his power extends, to treat this force as enemies of the United States.

You will please instruct Colonel Day, or the commander at Brazos Santiago, accordingly, and, in the contingency of any of Cortinas's force entering our service, give the necessary instructions in relation to enlistment, transfer to this city, and the disposition to be made of private property. The public property of the Mexican government remains, of course, in the custody of the United States, until disposed of by proper authority.

Very respectfully, sir, your obedient servant,

EDWARD R. S. CANBY,
Major General, Commanding.

Major General N. P. BANKS,
Commanding Department of the Gulf.

Official:

C. T. CHRISTENSEN,
Lieutenant Colonel, Assistant Adjutant General.

Colonel Day to Major Drake.

HEADQUARTERS UNITED STATES FORCES,
Brazos Santiago, Texas, September 8, 1864.

MAJOR: I have the honor to transmit herewith a copy of a letter received by me from the commander of the French forces at Bagdad, also my reply to the same, in order that they may be considered at the same time with my report concerning the matter alluded to in each.

I am, very respectfully, your obedient servant,

H. M. DAY,
Colonel, Comd'g U. S. Forces, Brazos Santiago, Texas.

Major GEO. B. DRAKE,
Assistant Adjutant General, Department of the Gulf.

Official:

GEO. B. DRAKE, *A. A. G.*

[Indorsement No. 1.]

HEADQUARTERS DEPARTMENT OF THE GULF,
New Orleans, September 15, 1864.

Respectfully forwarded to Adjutant General of the army, through headquarters military division of West Mississippi, for information.

N. P. BANKS,
Major General, Commanding.

[Indorsement No. 2.]

HEADQUARTERS MILITARY DIVISION WEST MISSISSIPPI,
New Orleans, September 16, 1864.

Respectfully forwarded to the Adjutant General, with copy of my letter to Major General Banks, in reference to this matter.

EDWARD R. S. CANBY,
Major General, Commanding.

General Veron to Colonel Day.

COMMANDER-IN-CHIEF FRENCH FORCES,
Bagdad, Mexico, September 7, 1864.

COLONEL: Yesterday, the 6th of September, the hostile forces of General Cortinas displayed themselves before our lines and made a feint to attack the place which we hold. General Cortinas, who knows the march of our several columns made against him, managed to move without our knowledge, and with your powerful aid succeeded in passing his troops to your side of the river with arms and baggage.

The first squadron of cavalry afforded you immediate aid to fight the confederates.

This morning, the passing of all these forces being effected, you gave them provisions, all that they wanted. According to the facts, and according to the law of nations, which none can distrust, I am bound to consider the forces of General Cortinas as troops belonging to the United States government, which government now holds the responsibility for their future conduct. In any enterprise I might undertake I must be certain not to encounter them on my road, either now or later.

If perchance, colonel, you have some objections to propose to the view I have of the matter, be so good, colonel, as to make them known as soon as possible. With this intention I send you Captain Visconti, my aide-de-camp. The United States and France have been too long friendly *allies* for any uneasy or hostile feeling to be produced between them.

Please to accept, colonel, the assurance of my most distinguished consideration.

A. VERON,
Commanding French Forces, Bagdad, Mexico.

Official:

GEO. B. DRAKE, *A. A. G.*

BAGDAD, MEXICO, *September* 7, 1864.

Colonel Day to General Veron.

HEADQUARTERS UNITED STATES FORCES,
Brazos Santiago, Texas, September 8, 1864.

SIR: I have the honor to acknowledge the receipt of your communication, dated September 7, 1864, from the hands of Captain Visconti. In reply, I would respectfully state that you are laboring under an error with regard to the forces of General Cortinas receiving provisions from me on the morning of the 6th of September. Understanding that the enemy had a large drove of cattle at our front, I sent a small force of mounted men with instructions to capture and drive them into camp, if possible, for the sustenance of my command. I would further state that I have not as yet been officially informed that General Cortinas is within my lines, and that I will at once send an officer with a sufficient escort to him, and if he is within my lines I will demand that he shall surrender all arms and munitions of war to the United States.

I take this occasion to assure the commander of the French forces at Bagdad that I shall not for a moment countenance the occupation of United States soil by any armed force except our own, and especially by a force hostile to the French government, which has so long been on friendly terms with the United States. Desiring that this harmony may long continue to exist,

I have the honor to subscribe myself your most obedient servant,

H. M. DAY,
Colonel, Comd'g U S. Forces, Brazos Santiago Texas.

COMMANDER OF THE FRENCH FORCES,
Bagdad, Mexico.

Official:

GEO. B. DRAKE, *A. A. G.*

Colonel Day to Major Drake.

HEADQUARTERS UNITED STATES FORCES,
Brazos Santiago, Texas, September 8, 1864.

MAJOR: I have the honor to report that an armed body of Mexican troops have landed on the American shore of the Rio Grande river, about fifteen miles from these headquarters.

These troops are commanded by General Cortinas, governor of Tamaulipas, whom I have seen in person, and from him learn that it is his desire to receive protection from the United States authorities.

An order has been sent to him demanding an immediate surrender of his ordnance and ordnance stores to my command, after which I shall give him the protection that he desires. A copy of the order is herewith transmitted for your information.

This letter will be delivered by Major George A. Day, provost marshal of this district, who will give you any information you may desire, as he is in full possession of the facts in this case.

I respectfully request that instructions be furnished me for this class of refugees.

Very respectfully, your obedient servant,

H. M. DAY,
Colonel, Commanding Forces.

Major GEORGE B. DRAKE,
Assistant Adjutant General, Department of the Gulf.

Official:

GEO. B. DRAKE, *A. A. G.*

Colonel Day to General Cortinas.

HEADQUARTERS UNITED STATES FORCES,
Brazos Santiago, Texas, September 8, 1864.

GENERAL: It has come to my knowledge that you have landed on the territory of the United States with an armed force. I have no doubt but that you have done so on account of the concentration of the forces of the enemies of the Mexican Republic on Matamoras.

If that is the case, you are welcome, also your people that are with you; your arms, ammunition, and warlike stores must at once be surrendered to the United States forces.

When you have complied with the above requirements you can rely on being protected by the United States government. Any proposition you may desire to make will be cheerfully forwarded by me to my commanding officer at New Orleans.

Very respectfully, your obedient servant,

H. M. DAY,
Colonel, Comd'g U. S. Forces, Brazos Santiago.

General CORTINAS,
Commanding Mexican Forces.

Official:

GEO. B. DRAKE, *A. A. G.*

Colonel Day to Major Drake.

HEADQUARTERS UNITED STATES FORCES,
Brazos Santiago, Texas, September 8, 1864.

MAJOR: I have the honor to transmit herewith the following report of a slight engagement which took place at "Palmetto rancho," on the Rio Grande river, about sixteen miles from these headquarters. Learning from my scouts that the rebels had collected a large number of cattle which they intended to sell to the French troops at Bagdad, and that said cattle were in a bend in the river just above the "White rancho," I determined, after mature deliberation, to try and capture them, and at the same time drive back the rebels from their position, as they had been annoying us in various ways very much during the past few days. Accordingly, on the morning of the 6th I ordered a squadron of the 1st Texas cavalry and one piece of artillery (12-pounder howitzer) to proceed up the country and accomplish the object above named. Major E. J. Noyes commanded the expedition; Captain P. J. Temple the cavalry; Lieutenant A. Hills, 1st Missouri artillery, the artillery.

After crossing the Boca Chica Pass, skirmishers were thrown out to the right and left, and as they advanced the rebels slowly retired, until, reaching the "Palmetto rancho," a stand was made and brisk firing ensued. The main body arrived soon after, and a fair prospect of a heavy engagement was apparent, as the rebels were having reinforcements from above, but our artillery opened a very effective fire with shell, which had the effect to disperse the enemy, and the last seen of him he was flying in confusion in the direction of Brownsville.

Word being sent me by the major commanding of his position, I advanced three miles with a detachment of the 91st Illinois infantry volunteers to re-enforce him in case of necessity; it was not needed, however, and the whole force returned to camp on the morning of the 7th.

The expedition was successful in its results, for a lot of cattle were captured and brought in, and the rebels forced to leave this section of the country.

Hoping this report will prove satisfactory, I remain, very respectfully, your obedient servant,

H. M. DAY,
Colonel, Commanding Forces.

Major GEORGE B. DRAKE,
Assistant Adjutant General, Department of the Gulf.

Official:

GEO. B. DRAKE, *A. A. G.*

Colonel Day to Major Drake.

HEADQUARTERS UNITED STATES FORCES,
Brazos Santiago, Texas, September 14, 1864.

MAJOR: I have the honor to submit the following report of the action taken by me relative to the fact that an armed body of Mexican troops had crossed the Rio Grande, above our lines, of which I advised you in a recent report.

In the evening of the 8th of September, I ordered Major E. J. Noyes, commanding detachment 1st Texas cavalry, to move with his command up the Rio Grande, the point where the troops had crossed the river, and instructed him to demand of them the surrender of all arms and warlike stores, and to offer them the protection of the United States as refugees; I also instructed him that if he found it necessary, in order to defend himself against the rebels, to allow the refugees to temporarily resume their arms. Major Noyes proceeded agreeably to the above instructions, and the Mexicans willingly surrendered upon the demand being made. They were not commanded by Governor Cortinas, as I was at first informed, and hence reported to you, but Colonel Miguel Echazarretta, Cortinas not having moved his headquarters to this side of the river Shortly after the surrender had been effected, our forces were attacked by the rebels with nearly double their number, and, according to my instructions, the refugees were allowed to resume their arms, and fought bravely with our men. After a short engagement, in which one piece of Mexican artillery was used, the rebels were repulsed with great loss. They rallied and again attacked, and were again repulsed; so a third time; after which Major Noyes, being short of ammunition, fell back two miles and took a stronger position. Fearing that the rebels would receive re-enforcements from Brownsville, and would succeed in getting possession of the artillery which the refugees had surrendered to us, I advanced, on the 11th, with two hundred of the 91st Illinois and two pieces of artillery, as far as White's rancho, and ordered Major Noyes to fall back with his command to that place. The rebels followed with a force of about six hundred, but I soon routed them with my artillery. On the morning of the 12th I returned to camp, bringing with me all refugees who had crossed the river, their arms and warlike stores. Affixed to this report is a statement (which I respectfully submit as a part of the same) with regard to the number of refugees and the number and character of their arms. No casualties attended us in any of the above encounters except one United States soldier captured and several refugees. We took no prisoners, but the killed and wounded of the enemy must have been great. The refugees have been very quiet and orderly since their arrival in camp, and I understand that many of them evince a desire to enlist in the United States army.

Hoping that this will meet with your approval, I am, very respectfully your obedient servant,

H. M. DAY,
Colonel, Commanding U. S. Forces, Brazos Santiago.

Major GEORGE B. DRAKE,
Assistant Adjutant General, Department of the Gulf.

Statement of the number of Mexican refugees at Brazos Santiago, Texas; the number and character of their arms, amount of artillery, number of horses, &c.

Number of officers	13
Number of men	290
Muskets, calibre .69	27
Enfield rifles, calibre .58	195
Whitney muskets, calibre .58	24
Cavalry horses, with equipments	22
Mules	10
Six-pounder rifled brass guns	3
Rounds of cartridges, different calibre	1,200
Rounds of assorted ammunition	76

BRAZOS SANTIAGO, TEXAS, *September* 14, 1864.

I certify that the above statement is correct.

H. M. DAY,
Colonel, Commanding U. S. Forces.

Official:

GEO. B. DRAKE, *A. A. G.*

HEADQUARTERS MILITARY DIVISION WEST MISSISSIPPI,
New Orleans, September 14, 1864.

Respectfully forwarded to the Adjutant General of the army.
The action of Colonel Day is approved.

ED. R. S. CANBY,
Major General, Commanding.

Mr. Dayton to Mr. Seward.

No. 550.] PARIS, *October* 19, 1864.

SIR : I send you the enclosed slips, (one cut from a French paper of yesterday, and the other cut from Galignani of this morning,) the first of which announces the sailing of a first detachment of six hundred men of the Belgian legion destined to Mexico, and the other the contemplated conveyance to Vera Cruz of four thousand two hundred volunteers enlisted in Austria. The enlistments in Europe for service in Mexico, it would seem from this and other notices I have observed, are quite prompt.

I am, sir, your obedient servant,

WILLIAM L. DAYTON.

Hon. WILLIAM H. SEWARD, *&c.*

[Extract.—Translation.]

In a despatch from St. Nazaire we noticed that the Louisiana, of the General Transatlantic Company, went to sea yesterday at three o'clock. She took the first detachment of six hundred men of the Belgian legion enrolled for Mexico, one hundred and seventy-eight civilian passengers, and a full cargo of merchandise and material exported for carrying on of the war.

[Extract from Galignani.]

General Count de Thun has arrived in Paris, charged by the Mexican government to come to an arrangement with the Transatlantic Steam Navigation Company for the conveyance to Vera Cruz of four thousand two hundred volunteers, enlisted in Austria.

Mr. Seward to Mr. Dayton.

No. 685.] DEPARTMENT OF STATE,
Washington, October 20, 1864.

SIR: I have to acknowledge the receipt of your despatch of the 7th instant, in reference to Cortinas crossing the Rio Grande, with his forces, into Texas, and, in reply, to inform you that your action in laying before M. Drouyn de Lhuys an explanation of the attitude of the government of the United States in this matter meets my approval. No further information on the subject than that contained in my instruction No. 677, of the 10th instant, has yet been received.

I am, sir, your obedient servant,

WILLIAM H. SEWARD.

WILLIAM L. DAYTON, Esq., *&c.*

Mr. Dayton to Mr. Seward.

No. 552.] PARIS, *October* 21, 1864.

SIR: I yesterday transferred to M. Drouyn de Lhuys the answer of Mr. Bigelow, our consul at Paris, to the comments which his excellency had some time since addressed to me on the part of Mr. Bigelow, dated 6th of June last, on the movements of commerce between France and the United States. I do not append to this despatch a copy of this last communication of Mr. Bigelow, for the reason that you have, without doubt, received a copy of it from the consulate.

M. Drouyn de Lhuys, on receiving it, said he would examine it with great care. This is all I could expect of him, as there is nothing practical expected to grow out of this correspondence.

M. Drouyn de Lhuys took occasion, in the course of the interview of yesterday, to say he had received from Washington very satisfactory explanations in reference to the action of our government in regard to the Mexican troops under Cortinas which recently crossed the Rio Grande into Texas. That these explanations were confirmatory, as he said, of what I have already told him.

I am, sir, your obedient servant,

WILLIAM L. DAYTON.

Hon. WILLIAM H. SEWARD,
Secretary of State, &c.

Mr. Seward to Mr. Dayton.

No. 693.]

DEPARTMENT OF STATE,
Washington, October 31, 1864.

SIR: I enclose herewith a copy of a despatch of the 5th of October, and of its accompanying protest, from Lewis S. Ely, esq., our consul at Acapulco, relative to the seizure of the United States mail bag at that place, by order of the commandant of the French forces there, who, it appears, instructed the vice-consul of France to break the seal and take possession of the contents of said bag, which was done while in transit from the American steamer Golden City to the office of Mr. Ely. You will at once make known the facts of the case to the French government, and ask that an explanation may be given of this unusual proceeding.

I am, sir, your obedient servant,

WILLIAM H. SEWARD.

WILLIAM L. DAYTON, Esq., *&c.*

Mr. Ely to Mr. Seward.

CONSULATE UNITED STATES OF AMERICA,
Acapulco, October 5, 1864.

SIR: I have the honor to inform you that on the 30th day of September, A. D. 1864, the commandant of the French forces in Acapulco ordered the vice-consul of the French to seize the United States mail bag, and to break the seal and take charge of the contents.

The bag was taken while in transit from American steamer Golden City to my office. Had the commandant required the mail matter, after I had opened the bag and found a public mail therein, I should have given it to him without protest, notwithstanding I am acting under an arrangement between the French consul and our consul at Panama, which was that I should open all mails coming into Acapulco and distribute and forward to address, which arrangement has not been disturbed until this sudden seizure of our mail bag and the seal violated. Hence I deemed it my duty to protest against the proceedings.

No plea of contraband matter or anything improper passing through the mails was set up, but an assumed arbitrary power was exercised in demolishing the sacredness of a government seal for civil purposes.

I have the honor to be, sir, your obedient servant,

LEWIS S. ELY,
United States Consul.

Hon. WILLIAM H. SEWARD,
Secretary of State, Washington.

Mr. Ely to the French Commandant.

CONSULATE UNITED STATES OF AMERICA,
Acapulco, October 1, 1864.

SIR: I am informed, officially, that it was by your order that the United States mail, addressed under seal to the United States consul at Acapulco, was seized on the 30th day of September, A. D. 1864, the *seal broken*, and the contents removed beyond my reach.

As the land and naval forces of his Majesty the Emperor of the French here have no post roads or post routes, and as they perform no established postal service; and as the seizure of the United States mail was not done under cover of military surveillance, but by a civil officer of the French government, acting under your orders, and, more especially, as this mail service is performed by the United States of America, and the mails being forwarded to their legally constituted agent here, it becomes my duty to PROTEST, in the name of my government, and in this solemn manner, against the seizure, and against all and every person or persons whom it doth or may concern.

[L. S.] Given under my hand and the seal of this consulate the day and year above written.

LEWIS S. ELY,
United States Consul.

The COMMANDANT *of the Land Forces of his Majesty the Emperor of the French in Acapulco.*

Mr. Dayton to Mr. Seward.

No. 557.] PARIS, *November* 4, 1864.

SIR: I visited M. Drouyn de Lhuys on yesterday for the purpose of communicating to him more in detail the orders and proceedings of our government in reference to Cortinas and his force which crossed the Rio Grande into Texas. The papers which you forwarded to me on this subject were shown to him. They contained, in substance, little that I had not already said to him, and with which, when I communicated it to him heretofore, he seemed entirely satisfied. If, on reflection, he is disposed to complain, I suppose I will hear from him in writing.

I am, sir, your obedient servant,

WM. L. DAYTON.

Hon. WILLIAM H. SEWARD,
Secretary of State, &c.

Mr. Dayton to Mr. Seward.

No. 565.] PARIS, *November* 18, 1864.

SIR: Your despatch No. 693 enclosed to me the copy of a despatch of 5th October last, and its accompanying protest from Lewis S. Ely, our consul at Acapulco, relative to the seizure of the United States mail bag at that place by order of the commandant of the French forces there.

I have immediately called the attention of Mr. Drouyn de Lhuys to this subject, and asked the necessary explanations. He has received from me copies of the above papers, and says that he will at once take measures to ascertain the facts, or their view of them, and make the necessary answer to our demand for explanation.

I am, sir, your obedient servant,

WM. L. DAYTON.

Hon. WILLIAM H. SEWARD,
Secretary of State, &c.

Mr. Seward to Mr. Dayton.

No. 704.] DEPARTMENT OF STATE,
Washington, November 18, 1864.

SIR: I give you, for your information, a copy of a correspondence which has just taken place between Mr. Geofroy and this department.*

* See correspondence with the French legation.

You will perceive that in this correspondence I decline to discuss the question whether the President of Mexico, in his present reduced situation, has, by the law of nations, a right to issue letters of marque. I think the occasion a suitable one for bringing to the consideration of the imperial government the fact that it has now for three years and a half, against the constant protest of the United States, recognized as a naval belligerent an insurrection in the United States that has not only never had a recognized political existence, but also has never had a port in our country. It would simplify affairs very much, and contribute to the security of French as well as of American commerce, if the government of France should apply to our civil strife the principle it assumes in regard to Mexico, namely: that a military force which is destitute of ports or ships-of-war cannot rightly be deemed a naval belligerent.

I am, sir, your obedient servant,

WILLIAM H. SEWARD.

WILLIAM L. DAYTON, Esq., &c.

Mr. Seward to Mr. Dayton.

No. 705.]

DEPARTMENT OF STATE,
Washington, November 18, 1864.

SIR: Your despatch of the 4th instant, No. 557, relative to the result of an interview with M. Drouyn de Lhuys, in which you communicated in detail the order and proceedings of this government in reference to Cortinas and his forces which crossed the Rio Grande into Texas, has been received and is approved.

I am, sir, your obedient servant,

WILLIAM H. SEWARD.

WILLIAM L. DAYTON, Esq., &c.

Mr. Seward to Mr. Dayton.

No. 717.]

DEPARTMENT OF STATE.
Washington, December 4, 1864.

SIR: Your despatch of the 18th of November, No. 565, informing me that you had received assurances from Mr. Drouyn de Lhuys that the application of this government for explanation of the seizure of the United States mail-bags at Acapulco, by order of the commandant of the French forces at that place, would receive due consideration, has been received. Your proceedings in regard to the matter are approved.

I am, sir, your obedient servant,

WILLIAM H. SEWARD.

WILLIAM L. DAYTON, Esq., &c.

Mr. Seward to Mr. Pike.

[Extract.]

No. 151.]

DEPARTMENT OF STATE,
Washington, May 6, 1864.

SIR: I have the honor to acknowledge the receipt of your despatch of the 20th of April, No. 129. * * * * *

Recent advices from the eastern States of Mexico represent that the national cause has revived in that region since the flight of Vidaurri, the disloyal governor of Coahuila and New Leon. Our attitude in regard to the conflict in Mexico remains unchanged. We still continue to see there a war between France and Mexico, in regard to which we are, as in all other foreign conflicts, neutrals.

Our spring campaign is open, and it may be expected that its events and vicissitudes will for a time abate the interests with which we have been watching the commotion of Europe.

I am, sir, your obedient servant,

WILLIAM H. SEWARD.

JAMES S. PIKE, Esq., *&c.*

Mr. Koerner to Mr. Seward.

[Extract.]

No. 83.] LEGATION OF THE UNITED STATES,
Madrid, March 20, 1864.

SIR: * * * * * * *

The Archduke Maximilian has just returned to Miramar, and in a few days will formally accept the Mexican crown and assume the title of the "Emperor of the Mexicans." Ambassadors and ministers will be immediately sent to the European powers before he embarks. The name of the person designed to represent him here is already given in the papers. I would thank you for an intimation as to the manner in which you desire me to regulate my conduct towards him. He will, of course, make me an official visit. Shall it be returned officially, or only privately?

Your obedient servant,

GUSTAVUS KOERNER.

Hon. WILLIAM H. SEWARD,
Secretary of State, &c.

Mr. Koerner to Mr. Seward.

[Extract.]

No. 85.] LEGATION OF THE UNITED STATES,
Madrid, March 27, 1864.

SIR: * * * * * * *

It is stated here in various journals, which are likely to receive information from ministerial circles, that Mr. Preston has gone to Mexico to establish commercial relations with the new empire, and to procure its recognition of the Confederate States. It is also said in some of the papers that Spain has entered into a treaty with the new emperor, reserving the throne of Mexico, in case of failure of issue, to a Spanish prince. This would be an important fact if true, as it would secure the moral co-operation of Spain in the establishment of the new empire, and would have a tendency to place Spain in a somewhat antagonistic position to the United States. That Spain, in the end, would be cheated of her expectations I have no doubt; but still it is not altogether improbable that some inducements have been held out to her, which may have some present effect.

I have the honor to be, with the highest respect, sir, your obedient servant,

GUSTAVUS KOERNER.

Hon. WILLIAM H. SEWARD,
Secretary of State, &c.

Mr. Koerner to Mr. Seward.

[Extract.]

No. 90.] LEGATION OF THE UNITED STATES,
Madrid, April 2, 1864.

SIR: * * * * * *

The resolutions of the House of Representatives at Washington, protesting against a monarchy in Mexico, under European auspices, has caused surprise in diplomatic circles and a good deal of sensation in the press. It is generally supposed that the attitude assumed by the House will produce complications with France, and may lead to a war. As far as Spain is concerned, there are in fact very few persons in favor of the new empire under Maximilian; some, indeed, who would otherwise have been in favor of French policy in America, and who generally take their ideas from France, being disappointed in this instance because a Spanish prince was not selected.

I have the honor to be, with the highest respect, sir, your obedient servant,

GUSTAVUS KOERNER.

Hon. WILLIAM H. SEWARD,
Secretary of State, &c.

Mr. Seward to Mr. Koerner.

No. 81.] DEPARTMENT OF STATE,
Washington, April 7, 1864.

SIR: In your despatch of March 20, No. 82, you mention the probability that the Archduke Maximilian, on assuming the title of emperor over Mexico, will accredit a representative to the court of her Catholic Majesty, and you ask directions how to regulate your conduct towards the person who may be so accredited.

It is the policy of the United States to refrain from recognizing revolutionary governments. It has not recognized any revolutionary government in Mexico, while it has justly respected the belligerent rights of the parties engaged in war in that country. You will, of course, follow the policy which prevails here; and you will hold no official intercourse with any representative at Madrid of any revolutionary government that has been or shall be established against the authority of the government of the United States of Mexico, with which alone the United States are maintaining diplomatic relations.

I am, sir, your obedient servant,

WILLIAM H. SEWARD.

GUSTAVUS KOERNER, Esq., *&c., Madrid.*

Mr. Seward to Mr. Koerner.

[Extract.]

No. 82.] DEPARTMENT OF STATE,
Washington, April 18, 1864.

SIR: * * * * * * *

It is true that Mr. Preston has gone to Mexico, as a pretended legate of the insurgents to the so-called regency of the empire. They are very enterprising in diplomacy, but their success there is not greatly to be feared, unless they should retrieve misfortunes sustained on the battle-field. Spain has heretofore had opportunity to understand the slaveholders of the United States. It is not less her own interest than it is ours that she shall not suffer herself to be misled by them. What resistance could Mexico, now or at any future time, offer, with even European aid, against the slaveholding power of the United States, if it could escape destruction and attain independence in the present civil war?

I am, sir, your obedient servant,

WILLIAM H. SEWARD.

GUSTAVUS KOERNER, Esq., *&c., Madrid.*

Mr. Seward to Mr. Koerner.

No. 92.]

DEPARTMENT OF STATE,
Washington, May 17, 1864.

SIR: Your despatch of the 2d ultimo, No. 90, has been received, and that part of it which relates to the assumption of imperial authority in Mexico by the Archduke Maximilian has been read with much interest. For your information in regard to the course of the United States in connexion with this event, I herewith enclose a copy of an instruction addressed by me to Mr. Dayton, our minister to Paris, on the 30th ultimo.

I am, sir, your obedient servant,

WILLIAM H. SEWARD.

GUSTAVUS KOERNER, Esq., *&c., Madrid.*

Mr. Seward to Mr. Koerner.

[Confidential.—Extract.]

No. 95.]

DEPARTMENT OF STATE,
Washington, May 19, 1864.

SIR: * * * * * * *

This government, seriously preoccupied with domestic affairs, has deemed it prudent and just, and has found it possible thus far, to hold itself, as well as the whole American people, absolutely neutral in two wars, which are waged by European states in portions of America. I refer to the war of France against Mexico, and to the civil war to which Spain is a party in the island of St. Domingo. This government has been able to practice this neutrality and enforce its observance upon American citizens, because all the maritime powers of Europe, while they have constantly assured the United States of their purpose to maintain neutrality in our own unhappy civil war, have also disclaimed designs of political conquest in America. Several of the South American republican states, however, naturally sympathizing, as they must, with the republic of Mexico, and with the revolutionists of Spanish St. Domingo, allege, on the contrary, that several of the European states, which once had colonies here, are now seeking to reduce them again to the condition of dependencies. These apprehensions are not unlikely to be entertained by the whole people of the United States. The proceedings of Spain in Peru give them color, which is deeply to be regretted. Indeed, a general discontent with the forbearance of the government is already manifest. Should the sentiment of this country demand a reconsideration of the policy of neutrality which the government has hitherto maintained, it is very much to be feared that new complications might arise, which would not merely disturb the existing systems of commerce, but might endanger the general peace of nations. I need not enlarge upon the subject I have thus presented.

* * * * * * *

I am, sir, your obedient servant,

WILLIAM H. SEWARD.

GUSTAVUS KOERNER, Esq., *&c., Madrid.*

Mr. Seward to Mr. Motley.

[Extract.]

No. 66.]

DEPARTMENT OF STATE,
Washington, April 18, 1864.

SIR: After preparing for the outgoing mail very full despatches concerning Mexican affairs, I have just now received your confidential despatch of March 28, which informs me of the grave question that has arisen in the court of Vienna, concerning the effect of the Archduke Maximilian's acceptance of a crown in Mexico upon his presumptive rights to succeed to the imperial royal throne of Austria.

While I thank you very earnestly for this important information, I do not think it necessary to comment upon it. The question thus raised will probably have been in some way adjusted before this despatch will reach its destination. The present policy of this government in regard to Mexico would remain the same whether the archduke renounces or retains his claim to the succession in Austria; and it does not seem probable here that the ultimate destiny of Mexico can be influenced by anything so merely individual and personal as the character or relations of the person who at this new turn of the political wheel of that state may be lifted up by one of its factions, aided by foreign power, to the seat of Montezuma.

* * * * * * * *

I am, sir, your obedient servant,

WILLIAM H. SEWARD.

J. LOTHROP MOTLEY, Esq., *&c., Vienna.*

Mr. Seward to Mr. Motley.

[Extract.]

No. 78.]

DEPARTMENT OF STATE,
Washington, July 14, 1864.

SIR: * * * * * * *

I thank you for your suggestions concerning Mexico, and the probable influence of recent events in that country upon our relations with Austria. These are consequences of our civil war, and they cannot be controlled. All that can be done in regard to them is to practice prudence and good faith in our foreign relations, and at the same time make preparations for self defence, if, notwithstanding our best efforts, we shall find ourselves involved in new complications. Neither is our political system weak, nor does it stand on an uncertain foundation. We must, indeed, do all that we can to fortify, as well as to defend it; but we may not unwisely indulge an abiding confidence in its inherent strength and stability.

I am, sir, your obedient servant,

WILLIAM H. SEWARD.

J. LOTHROP MOTLEY, Esq., *&c., Vienna.*

Mr. Motley to Mr. Seward.

No. 34.] LEGATION OF THE UNITED STATES,
Vienna, September 21, 1863.

SIR: Since the date of my despatch of last week, No. 33, I have had an interview with Count Rechberg. Nothing, however, has up to this moment been decided in regard to the expected offer of the proposed Mexican throne to the Archduke Maxmilian. The affair, so far as the imperial royal government is concerned, remains as before. The deputation from Mexico is expected in the course of this week to arrive at Miramar, the archduke's residence, near Trieste.

I could not learn from the minister what conditions would be laid down by the archduke as necessary preliminaries to his acceptance of the crown, but I understood him to say that no binding arrangement would be concluded with this deputation, although it would probably be received.

I understood him, also, to repeat, as often before, that the Austrian government considered the matter as a purely personal one, regarding the archduke himself and his imperial brother only, and that the imperial royal government had not the means nor the inclination to send out forces to Mexico to maintain the new empire.

I do not think it worth while to report any of the observations which I unofficially made on the subject myself, and which were simply those which any loyal American, belonging to any section or party of the United States, would be always sure to make in regard to this overturning of a republic, and the substitution for it of a monarchical government on American soil, and upon our frontier, by means of foreign armies and navies.

It seems to me that public opinion does not need much enlightenment as to the effect likely to be produced upon the people of the United States by this European armed intervention in the affairs of an American republic. I suppose that the French Emperor is hardly acting in ignorance of American opinions and feelings, but in defiance of them, and that the archduke, in going forth upon this adventure to improve imperial institutions upon the ruins of a democratic republic, can hardly have failed of weighing all the possible consequences of such a step, and that he is not likely to have reckoned on the sympathy and support of the United States government and people.

I intimated to Count Rechberg that there were rumors of the impending recognition of the so-called southern confederacy by the provisional government now established in the city of Mexico. I understood him to reply that the Austrian government knew no such provisional government, and that a communication which had been received from that source had not been and would not be answered.

I alluded, also, to the daily rumors in the European journals of intrigues and secret understandings between the agents of the insurgent government in the seceded States and the Emperor Napoleon, in which recognition of that organization as an independent power by France was announced for the immediate future, coupled with cession of territory so far as such agents had the power to cede it to the new Mexican empire, as the price of French recognition and French alliance. He said that the archduke held himself aloof from all such intrigues. In regard to the expected recognition by the new Mexican empire of the so-called confederacy, he observed that it would be easy for the United States government in a moment to make such a step impossible.

If the United States should themselves recognize the new government of Mexico, of course such recognition by so important a power would be far more valuable than any political relations that might be established with the southern States. He observed that everybody knew that the previous attacks upon Mexico and the disposition to extend the United States dominion over the soil of that country had always proceeded from the South.

I answered, that the recognition by the United States government of this new empire seemed to me impossible. Instead, however, of saying anything more upon this topic myself, my personal opinions and feelings having been often enough and strongly enough expressed, I proposed reading to him your despatch to Mr. Dayton, of March 3, 1862, which, so far as I knew, had never been published, but of which a copy had been forwarded to me at the time, and which I had brought with me. He readily assented, expressing at the same time a strong respect for yourself and your character as a statesman. I thought it could certainly do no harm that the Austrian government should be in possession of, so wise and temperate a statement of American thought on that all-important subject, and accordingly, after reading the paper, I took the responsibility of promising a copy, which has subsequently been communicated to the imperial royal foreign office.

If I have done wrong in this you will let me know. I thought it might have some effect in causing reflection at this critical moment, and I relied on an observation in one of your despatches to me, that our government has no concealment in this matter.

I think you will hardly wish me to enter into academic or prophetic speculations upon this grave incident in our history. You are informed of the exact relations between the United States and France, while I am necessarily in the dark.

Rumors, suspicions, and threats, in regard to the attitude of that power towards us, fill the atmosphere of Europe. It seems impossible to doubt that the tendencies and sympathies of the French government are towards the slaveholders' insurrection, and that a recognition of the so-called confederacy is an ever-impending event.

Since the revelations of the British Parliament by Messrs. Roebuck and Lindsay, it would be folly to doubt the feelings of the ruler of France. At present the see-saw of his policy between Poland on the one side and Mexico on the other seems to incline towards our side of the world.

The Poles are left to fight, single-handed and naked as it were, against the whole power of Russia, for a winter's campaign in that direction on the part of France alone is hardly among the probabilities. The Gulf of Mexico seems more tempting at present, and you are better aware than I am how much or how little danger there is of that last chance of the insurgents, a foreign war against the United States. I am sure that the President will avoid such war with any power so long as the national honor and the national safety will permit.

I observe this morning a single paragraph in a widely circulated Vienna newspaper which is worthy of your attention. It is in an article defending the probable acceptance by the archduke of the Mexican crown: "According to latest accounts from Mexico it is hardly to be doubted that all inner discord in Mexico will come to an end so soon as the archduke shall tread its soil. * * * Also, the French government is supposed to have arranged with the American southern States for the cession of Texas. It is confidently assumed that the overwhelmingly German population of Texas would readily submit themselves to a German prince. It is apparently not feared that, in consequence of this cession, a war would arise between France and North America; should, however, the north of America, besides the still-continuing contest with the confederates, be willing to burden themselves with such a war in addition, then France would not object, perhaps even wish for it, in order at least to be able to interfere with armed force in favor of the south."

This is in a journal which is generally supposed—I know not how justly—to be "inspired" occasionally by government. Of what use, then, would be talk or argumentation on our side as to Mexican politics, if such views could find general acceptance?

Whether the Germans in Texas, who probably did not emigrate from their fatherland because fanatically attached to monarchical institutions, are grown so disloyal to their adopted country as is here represented, you can judge better than I can. My impression has been that they were not only strong and sincere democrats, but on account of their warm attachment to the United States government they had suffered much persecution from the insurgents. But under whose authority has Texas been ceded to France? Even were the insurgent government in as triumphant as it is really in desperate circumstances, on what theory and by what machinery is Texas to be ceded?

At least an ordinance of secession out of the confederacy, on the part of the State government, might be thought necessary; or is it supposed that the government at Richmond has spare troops enough at its disposal beyond the Mississippi to deliver over Texas, bound hand and foot, to the new emperor? Cessions in the Nice and Savoy fashion are not so easily accomplished in our hemisphere. Of course, the Emperor Napoleon, or any foreign potentate, is competent to attempt the conquest of Texas or of any other United States territory with or without "an arrangement with the southern States," but it would certainly be something new in the history of the world that the conquest of such a province, 237,000 square miles in extent, and with a population of 600,000, the acquisition of which has cost a war, besides $10,000,000 in money, should be effected without the inconvenience of a new war.

In conclusion, I should say, although I am unable to give you authentically the conditions to be laid down previous to the acceptance of the transatlantic crown by the archduke, that this will undoubtedly include a goodly number of French bayonets for a considerable number of years, a recognition of the throne by France and England at least, and some more substantial manifestations of Mexican opinion in regard to the proposed revolution of the government than the shadowy phenomena which have thus far been visible.

I should say, also, that this whole matter is an embarrassment to the imperial royal government. Offence might be given to France should her fatal present be refused, while acceptance can bring no possible good to Austria.

"Timeo Danaos etiam dona ferentes" is, I suspect, the secret thought of the government.

I have the honor to remain, very respectfully, your obedient servant,

J. LOTHROP MOTLEY.

Hon. WILLIAM H. SEWARD,

Secretary of State, Washington, D. C.

Mr. Motley to Mr. Seward.

[Extract.]

No. 36.] LEGATION OF THE UNITED STATES OF AMERICA,

Vienna, October 5, 1863.

SIR: I have the honor to acknowledge the receipt of your despatch, No. 41, of date September 11, marked confidential, in which information is conveyed to me as to the attitude of the United States government in regard to the war now existing between the empire of France and the republic of Mexico.

I understand from the latter portion of the despatch that the representatives of the United States abroad are instructed not to engage in the political debates which the present unsettled aspect of the war in Mexico has elicited. Hitherto I have occasionally deemed it my duty, in my private and unofficial capacity, to give expression to the almost universal American sentiment as to the events in question, and as to the misfortunes which have come upon a republic, our nearest neighbor, through the invasion of a distant and powerful nation. Of course, I have never engaged in any political debates, as I am fully aware that the United States government has never, directly or indirectly, authorized me to that effect.

I have thought, however, that it might be useful for the department to be informed, from time to time, of what might transpire as to the candidacy of the Archduke Maximilian for the throne which it is proposed to erect in Mexico, or in that part of the republic which has been subdued by the armies of the French Emperor.

I regret that my last despatch, No. 35, conveyed incorrect information. Although I stated that the source of that information was not official, nor such as I could vouch for, while I relied myself on its correctness, yet I should not have transmitted it at all, except for strong reasons for my faith, not now necessary to indicate.

At any rate, unless there has been some sudden change in the plans of the archduke, which I have no reason to suppose, it is obvious that the information was erroneous; for it now appears from the answer of his Imperial Highness to the deputation of "notables," a translation of which is herewith transmitted, that his ultimate acceptance of the offered crown is very problematical. The conditions laid down are such as have been intimated in all my previous despatches, except No. 35, and would seem very difficult of fulfilment. One would suppose, for instance, although it is not distinctly stated, that among the guarantees that of England would be included, and it is difficult to imagine that this could be obtained.

* * * * * * * *

I have the honor to remain, sir, your obedient servant,

J. LOTHROP MOTLEY.

Hon. WILLIAM H. SEWARD,
Secretary of State, Washington, D. C.

TRIESTE, *October* 3, 1863.

The Mexican deputation was received to-day by his Imperial Royal Highness the Archduke Ferdinand Maximilian. The archduke answered the address of the deputation:

GENTLEMEN: I am deeply touched by the wishes which were expressed by the assembly of notables at Mexico, at their sitting of the 10th of June, and which you have been charged to bring to me. It can only be flattering for our house that, at the first mention of the word monarchy, the eyes of your countrymen were at once turned to the race of Charles V. Although the task of assuring the independence and well-being of Mexico, by means of durable and free institutions, is a very noble one, still I must acknowledge, in full understanding with his Majesty the Emperor of the French, whose glorious initiative makes the regeneration of your beautiful country possible, that the monarchy cannot be restored, on legitimate and lasting foundations, unless the whole nation, of its own free will, ratifies the wish of the capital. Therefore, I must make my acceptance of the throne which is offered to me depend, first, on the result of a vote of the entire country. On the other hand, my comprehension of the sacred duties of the ruler over the restored empire makes it necessary for me to ask for those guarantees which are indespensable to protect it from the dangers which threaten its integrity and independence. Should the assurances of a well-grounded security in the future be obtained, and should the universal choice of the noble Mexican people fall upon me, I shall be ready to accept the throne, supported by the acquiescence of the high chief of my family, and confiding in the protection of the Almighty. In case that I should be called by Providence to the high mission of civilization connected with this crown, I must, gentlemen, declare to you, even now, my firm determination, following the wise example of my imperial brother, to open to the country the path of progress founded on law and order, by means of a constitutional government, and as soon as the whole realm has been restored to peace, to seal the fundamental fact with the nation by my oath. Only in this way could a new and truly national policy be called into life, in which all parties, forgetting their ancient enmities, would help to raise Mexico to that conspicuous rank among the nations to which she would seem to be destined under a government which held as its highest principle to let moderation and law govern

Gentlemen, will you communicate to your countrymen these resolutions, which I have freely imparted to you, and strive that it may be made possible to the nation to declare what government it wishes to see established.

Mr. Motley to Mr. Seward.

No. 38.] LEGATION OF THE U. S. OF AMERICA AT VIENNA,
November 24, 1863.

SIR: I have the honor to acknowledge the receipt of your despatches, Nos. 45, 46, 47, and 48, of dates October 9, 20, 23, and 23, together with a copy of your despatch of date 23d October, 1863, addressed to Mr. Dayton.

This paper I took the earliest opportunity to place in the hands of Count Rechberg, at an interview a few days ago. He read it through with great attention, and then observed that it seemed to him a very moderate and statesmanlike despatch.

He asked if I would leave it with him, but as you had only instructed me to "make the contents known" to him, I did not consider myself justified in so doing, because of the confidential nature of the document, and because it was addressed not to me, but to our minister in Paris.

Our conversation on the matter was brief. He repeated what he had often said before, that the imperial government held itself aloof from the whole affair. Austria was a continental power, not a maritime power of the first magnitude, and could, therefore, send no ships or armies to Mexico to sustain the proposed empire.

I understood him to remark that it was hardly to be expected that the people or government of the United States would regard with sympathy the reappearance of a monarchical form of government in their neighborhood, but that, on the other hand, the right of Mexico to decide as to its own form of government was not to be disputed.

I replied that this right was the leading principle of all our policy, but that a real decision of a nation as to its form of government could never be made in the presence of foreign armies and navies.

The conversation then passed to other topics.

I suppose that there is no doubt of the archduke's expectation to leave for Mexico before next summer.

I have the honor to remain, sir, your obedient servant,

J. LOTHROP MOTLEY.

Hon. WILLIAM H. SEWARD,
Secretary of State, Washington, D. C.

Mr. Seward to Mr. Judd.

No. 72.] DEPARTMENT OF STATE,
Washington, May 9, 1864.

SIR: I have to thank you for your despatch of April 16, No. 62, which contains a very interesting exposition of the political situation of western Europe. Since it arrived I have received news of the fall of Duppel, which, doubtless, lends a new complexion to the war between Denmark and Germany.

I am advised that Mr. Corwin, availing himself of a leave of absence granted in August last, expected to take his departure from Vera Cruz on the 3d instant. The late accounts from Mexico show that the French forces have encountered several reverses; but the statements are not very minute, and everything that comes from that quarter, in the interest of either belligerent, is believed to be much exaggerated. Nothing that has occurred there or in Europe has been thought to furnish sufficient ground for a change of the attidude which the United States has hitherto held in regard to Mexico.

I am, sir, your obedient servant,

WILLIAM H. SEWARD.

NORMAN B. JUDD, Esq., *&c., Berlin.*

Mr. Judd to Mr. Seward.

[Extract.]

No. 62.] LEGATION OF THE UNITED STATES,
Berlin, April 16, 1864.

SIR: Your despatches Nos. 69 and 70, dated 19th and 21st of March, respectively, as also circular 48, bearing date 6th February, are received.

* * * * * * * * *

The new empire of Mexico is established, so far as it can be done on this side of the ocean. Maximilian has accepted the crown and assumed all the trappings of royalty. He has organized his imperial and official household, appointed diplomatic representatives to the leading European courts, and sailed from Trieste in an Austrian armed ship, accompanied by French ships, and will call at Rome for a blessing on his way to his fancied empire.

The new Mexican loan has enabled Maximilian to pay his debts—he was hopelessly insolvent—has given him, in addition, a few millions of francs for travelling expenses, and put in the French exchequer the balance to pay past liabilities and guarantee future responsibilities. * * * *

I am, sir, your obedient servant,

N. B. JUDD.

Hon. WILLIAM H. SEWARD,
Secretary of State, Washington, D. C.

Mr. F. W. Seward to Mr. Sanford.

No. 148] DEPARTMENT OF STATE,
Washington, September 26, 1864.

SIR: I thank you for your interesting despatch of the 7th of September, No. 214.

The wisdom of allowing Belgian subjects to take military service against the republic of Mexico is the question which seems to be discussed in the Belgian legislature.

One important point was omitted, namely, how long the fidelity of a foreign legion employed in America in such a cause can be depended upon. It will be seen, I think, in the end, that European soldiers coming hither, ultimately become American republicans.

I am, sir, your obedient servant,

F. W. SEWARD,
Acting Secretary.

HENRY S. SANFORD, Esq., *&c., Brussels.*

Mr. Seward to Mr. Sanford.

DEPARTMENT OF STATE,
Washington, October 4, 1864.

SIR: I have the honor to acknowledge the receipt of your despatch of the 15th of September, No. 215, which mentions a probability that a special and extraordinary mission will be sent by the Belgian government to the so-called imperial government in Mexico. I have also received your private note, which mentions that Mr. Rondeel von Cuelebroeck, now minister plenipotentiary here, will likely be appointed to fill that extraordinary mission.

This government can have no right to question such a proceeding by the Belgian government, but it is easy to perceive that if the representative of Belgium shall be sent to Mexico to recognize a foreign imperial revolutionary government there, while the United States remain in treaty relations with the native republican government still existing in Mexico, and if that representative should, immediately after performing that function, be returned to the United States to renew his mission here, the transaction would then be liable to popular misapprehension, which, even though it should not impair his usefulness, might at least render his residence less agreeable than it is to be desired.

You may verbally and unofficially suggest these considerations to Mr. Rogier for his reflection.

I am, sir, your obedient servant,

WILLIAM H. SEWARD.

HENRY S. SANFORD, Esq., *&c., Brussels.*

Mr. Sanford to Mr. Seward.

No. 199.] LEGATION OF THE UNITED STATES,
Brussels, July 6, 1864.

SIR: Lieutenant General Chapelie, "charged by his majesty the emperor of Mexico with the mission of organizing a body of troops destined to form part of the imperial Mexican guard," has issued a notice under date of yesterday, which I enclose herewith, touching the condition, &c., of enlistment. The service is for six years, with a bounty of from sixty to one hundred francs, for non-commissioned officers and soldiers, and the same amount to be given at the expiration of their service, with return passage to Antwerp. Those who remain in Mexico as colonists will be entitled, the common soldier to about ten acres, the sergeant to about thirty acres of land, and to certain advances for its improvement; this grant of land to be doubled in the event of completing a second term of six years' service.

The pay while in Belgium is to be the same as that of the Belgian army. In Mexico it will be augmented in accordance with the needs of the soldier, and will be equal to that given to the best paid corps.

I have been told that the organization of this corps is complete, in so far as the officers are concerned, and that leave has been given to officers of the army who have joined this corps, which will number two thousand men.

I have the honor to be, with great respect, your most obedient servant,

H. S. SANFORD.

Hon. WILLIAM H. SEWARD,
Secretary of State, &c.

Mr. Sanford to Mr. Seward.

No. 214.] UNITED STATES LEGATION,
Brussels, September 7, 1864.

SIR: I enclosed to you on the 6th of July, in my despatch No. 199, a notice published by General Chapelie, inviting recruits for a Belgian legion to serve in Mexico.

Soon after, I called M. Rogier's attention, incidentally, to this notice, and asked him if the government was a party to this organization of troops. He replied that it was not; that, as a government, they had nothing to do with it; that they had, however, given permission to Belgians in their service, who desired to go, for without it they forfeited their nationality as Belgians. There was nothing in their laws, he continued, which prevented recruiting in Belgium for foreign service, provided it was not against a nation with which they were at peace.

This subject, coupled with the appearance in the streets of the recruits in Mexican uniform, has naturally excited public attention, and in the sitting of the 2d, on a motion by M. Coomans, he inquired of the minister of war if it was true that Belgian soldiers had received authorization from the government to take military service in Mexico, and upon what laws it was based. The minister replied that it was in accordance with numerous precedents, and he did not see why exception should be made against those Belgians wishing to serve a daughter of the King, who is a sovereign in another country.

An animated and interesting debate followed, which I enclose from the Moniteur, and which shows considerable embarrassment on the part of the government, and on the part of its friends, to defend its course, such as it is; for its effect would seem to tend to put the representatives of liberalism in Belgium in a false attitude before the liberal sentiment of Europe.

The motion of Mr. Coomans, expressing the regret of the house that the government had authorized the promotion in Belgium of a Belgian military corps for service in a foreign country, failed by a vote of 39 for and 53 against. A substitute, by M. Bara, declaring that "the house, in presence of the formal declarations that the government has remained and will remain completely aloof from the encouragement of a corps destined to serve in Mexico, proceed to the order of the day," passed by a vote of 50 for and 36 against.

I have the honor to be, with great respect, your most obedient servant,

H. S. SANFORD.

Hon WILLIAM H. SEWARD,
Secretary of State, &c.

Mr. Sanford to Mr. Seward.

No. 215.]

LEGATION OF THE UNITED STATES,
Brussels, September 15, 1864.

SIR: I have the honor to acknowledge the receipt of your despatches Nos. 142 and 143.

The Belge-Mexican corps which is organizing here, and to which reference has been heretofore made, seems to progress but slowly. I am informed that but about one-half the number contemplated (2,000) has been enlisted. The cause appears to be the want of funds to carry out the original plan. There seems to be a good deal of feeling against this expedition on the part of a portion of the population here, which I would not be surprised to see take the form of some public manifestation.

It is probable that this government will soon send an extraordinary mission to Mexico, and that M. Blondeel de von Cuelebroeck, the Belgian representative at Washington, will receive this temporary appointment.

I have the honor to be, with great respect, your most obedient servant,

H. S. SANFORD.

Hon. WILLIAM H. SEWARD,
Secretary of State, &c.

Mr. Sanford to Mr. Seward.

No. 220.]

LEGATION OF THE UNITED STATES,
Brussels, October 24, 1864.

SIR: I have the honor to acknowledge the receipt of your despatches from No. 144 to 149, inclusive; also, your circular despatch of 12th ultimo, and your communications marked "private," under date of September 17, 19, and of 4th instant. The latter, touching the appointment of the present Belgian minister to the United States on an extraordinary mission to Mexico, will be acted upon in accordance with your suggestion. M. Rogier is out of town, and will be absent for a week or so longer.

The King is absent on a visit to Germany and Switzerland, to return early the coming month.

A corps of Belgians, about 600, according to the journals, recruited here for service in Mexico as "Empress Guard," have left here for the country, *via* St. Nazaire, and sailed last week in the regular French packet for Vera Cruz. Want of funds will probably be an obstacle to the completion of the enlistment proposed here. Apart from the dissatisfaction which seems to be felt among the soldiers and officers as well, the debates in the Chambers reported to you, and which will doubtless be resumed at the next session, have also tended to make the service unpopular; and my impression is that the Mexican empire cannot safely count upon more soldiers from Belgium, even had it the funds to continue recruiting.

I have the honor to be, with great respect, your most obedient servant,

H. S. SANFORD.

Hon. WILLIAM H. SEWARD,
Secretary of State, &c.

Mr. Sanford to Mr. Seward.

No. 228.]

UNITED STATES LEGATION,
Brussels, November 21, 1864.

SIR: Another detachment from the depot of recruits for Mexico was despatched hence last week, *via* St. Nazaire, about 400 men, I am informed, and the remainder are to go forward, by the same route, by the steamer of December. As before stated, recruiting for Mexico has, since some time, been practically suspended.

The whole number recruited amounts, I believe, to some 1,400 men. How many have sailed or will sail from St. Nazaire, I know not. There has been considerable dissatisfaction manifested, and I suspect a good many desertions.

I have the honor to be, with great respect, your most obedient servant,

H. S. SANFORD.

Hon. WILLIAM H. SEWARD,
Secretary of State, &c.

Mr. Sanford to Mr. Seward.

No. 230.]

LEGATION OF THE UNITED STATES,
Brussels, November 28, 1864.

SIR: The budget of foreign affairs was discussed in the house of representatives on the 25th and 26th instant, and was voted without exciting any discussion of moment. The appropriation for the mission to Mexico was duly voted; one of the "liberal" members, M. Goblet, intimating, in reply to remarks of M. Kerryn de Lettenhove in favor of the Mexican empire, that it was not then the occasion to discuss that subject; that they would vote the appropriation asked for, and reserve the expression of their opinion upon the character of the intervention in Mexico. To an inquiry by one of the members why a full mission was provided for to Mexico and not to the United States and Brazil, the minister of foreign affairs replied that they but returned the courtesy which had been made to them. As an envoy extraordinary and minister plenipotentiary had been accredited to them by the emperor of Mexico, they proposed responding by the sending of one of the same grade to that country.

I have the honor to be, with great respect, your most obedient servant.

H. S. SANFORD.

Hon. WILLIAM H. SEWARD,
Secretary of State, &c.

Mr. Harvey to Mr. Seward.

No. 234.] LEGATION OF THE UNITED STATES,
Lisbon, October 17, 1863.

SIR: I have the honor to acknowledge the receipt of your No. 118, covering a copy of a confidential despatch to our minister at Vienna in regard to the proceedings of the French government in Mexico.

There can be no doubt of the prudence and propriety of your instruction that we should abstain from discussion of the important questions connected with the present situation of Mexico until a more appropriate time and opportunity shall be presented by events which are now fast taking shape and substance. In fact, the policy of our government in reference to the states of the American continent speaks so emphatically for itself, and is so generally known and understood in Europe, as to require little of either explanation or representation on the part of its diplomatic agents abroad.

That policy is founded upon justice and right, and involves various obligations and duties. If foreign powers deliberately assail and violate it, they cannot be ignorant of the results which must sooner or later attend any such infraction. It is only natural that the people of the United States should feel a deep concern for the fate of Mexico, from immediate neighborhood, from the nature of her political institutions, and from the common destiny which may be regarded, in the not far future, as the hope and aspiration of both.

An occasion may possibly happen when it will be proper for that feeling to be affirmed formally and distinctly, and we will be better prepared to exercise an effective influence at the opportune moment by a becoming reserve until it occurs. Intelligent and candid opinion will not misjudge us for avoiding unnecessary complications that might weaken our position, impair the value of our co-operation, and, perhaps, injure the rightful claim of Mexico to the sympathy and support of the friends of liberal institutions and constitutional government everywhere. Despotic rulers and the champions of absolutism have always regarded us with jealousy, disfavor, and distrust. Their instruments will be apt to pursue the work of misrepresentation until exhaustion succeeds to injustice. But if we continue wise in our conduct toward Mexico, experience may serve to correct some of these European errors, and to remove many delusions concerning the policy, purposes, and power of the United States.

I have the honor to be, sir, your obedient servant,

JAMES E. HARVEY.

Hon. WILLIAM H. SEWARD,
Secretary of State.

Mr. Seward to Mr. Wood.

No. 100.] DEPARTMENT OF STATE,
Washington, November 30, 1864.

SIR: Your despatch of the 24th ultimo, No. 173, was duly received. As you are aware that this government still maintains diplomatic relations with the re publican government of Mexico, I regret to learn from your despatch that you had thought it not improper to exchange visits with the envoy of the so-called imperial government of that country to the courts of St. Petersburg, Stockholm, and Copenhagen, on the occasion of his recent visit to the latter place. The error on your part is quite excusable, because you were without instructions upon the subject. You will be expected, however, hereafter to bear in mind that you can know no government of any state but the one which is recognized by this department, and that only agents of governments which are acknowledged here can be treated by you as representatives of foreign powers.

I am, sir, your obedient servant,

WILLIAM H. SEWARD.

BRADFORD R. WOOD, Esq., *&c.*, *Copenhagen.*

Mr. Seward to Mr. Campbell.

No. 8.]

DEPARTMENT OF STATE,
Washington, November 19, 1864.

SIR: It is understood here, with sincere regret, that Baron Wetterstedt has been ordered to Mexico on a mission of some character before coming to this country as the diplomatic agent of Sweden. It is proper that you should, without delay, inform the minister of foreign affairs that the proceeding referred to is, for obvious reasons, far from satisfactory to this government, and that if it should not prevent the baron's official reception here, it would certainly make him less welcome.

I am, sir, your obedient servant,

WILLIAM H. SEWARD.

JAMES H. CAMPBELL, Esq., *&c.*, *Stockholm.*

Mr. Fogg to Mr. Seward.

No. 50.]

UNITED STATES LEGATION,
Berne, October 2, 1863.

SIR: Your despatch No. 44, marked "confidential," of the date of September 14, and enclosing a copy of a despatch dated September 11, to Mr. Motley, United States minister at Vienna, is received.

Having carefully read your despatch to Mr. Motley, permit me to say that the suggestions therein contained, and which seem to be intended as directions for all the United States diplomatic agents abroad, commend themselves to my judgment as eminently timely and wise. I cannot doubt that our government looks with intense interest upon the proceedings of the French government in Mexico. There can for a long time have been no doubt, in the minds of intelligent observers of the events there transpiring, that the Emperor of France is *now*, at least, if not at the commencement of this invasion, bent on supplanting a republican form of government by an imperial one, and that without *really* consulting the Mexican people.

That these proceedings will at some not very distant day demand and receive the attention of the people and government of the United States, I firmly believe. That no recognition of, or consent to, those proceedings will ever be extorted from our indifference or weakness, I as firmly hope. Having, as that expedition against Mexico did have, its origin in a scheme against the peace and integrity of the United States, it is due, not less imperatively to a sister and neighbor republic than to the dignity and character of our own government, that the invaders receive no aid or countenance at our hands. Begun in conspiracy, and prosecuted under false pretences, I trust to see no concessions or recognitions on the part of our authorities interposing to save this Mexican enterprise from the disaster and disgrace it so ri hly merits.

But it is not necessary that we do more at present than maintain a "masterly inactivity" in view of events transpiring in Mexico. It may not be advisable that we *protest* even, except by our silence. Our nation has work of its own which cannot wait. Its *present* duty is to save itself. Its *future* may be to save its neighbor, and vindicate the supremacy of republican institutions upon the American continent. I trust in Heaven it will. But for that future we can afford to wait, while we cannot now afford to throw down the gauntlet to any new foe.

With the highest respect and esteem, your obedient servant,

GEORGE G. FOGG.

Hon. WILLIAM H. SEWARD,
Secretary of State of the United States of America.

EVACUATION OF MEXICO BY THE FRENCH.

Mr. Bigelow to Mr. Seward.

No. 228.] LEGATION OF THE UNITED STATES,
Paris, December 21, 1865.

SIR: The message of President Johnson at the opening of Congress has been received here with almost unanimous expressions of approval by the press, notwithstanding the wretched translation in which it was swathed at its birth into the French tongue. A desire to tranquilize the public mind at a moment when news from Washington was expected with great solicitude, no doubt, led many of the organs of public opinion to exaggerate a little the pacific and friendly tenor of the President's language. Every allowance made, however, for such considerations, you cannot fail to remark the unexceptionable tone with which it has been generally greeted. It has placed our government and policy, both foreign and domestic, before the world in an attitude which challenges universal respect.

I enclose extracts from the representative journals of Paris, by which you can judge the spirit of all. My impression is that the passage which refers to our relations with France and Mexico will involve an early change in the relations between those two countries, or else a still graver change in the relations of France with the United States; for, whatever may be the language held by the press upon the subject, it is impossible that the French government should not infer from the President's language that the policy of our government is not only unfavorable to, but inconsistent with, a long continuance of French authority in Mexico.

I am, sir, with great respect, your very obedient servant,

JOHN BIGELOW.

Hon. WILLIAM H. SEWARD, *Secretary of State, &c.*

[From the Constitutionnel of December 17, 1865—Administration.]

[Translation.]

Although we do not yet possess the text of President Johnson's message *in extenso*, the analysis of it furnished by the telegraph is sufficient to enable us already to appreciate its general character.

With regard to the European powers, in particular, the thoughts of the Chief Magistrate of the American Union are clearly set forth. Mr. Johnson declares that it shall be his constant aim to maintain peace and friendly relations with foreign nations; and he adds that he believes those nations to be actuated by a like disposition towards the United States.

The acts of the government at Washington had beforehand confirmed these declarations of the President. Since the close of the war the effective force of the army and navy of the United States has constantly undergone extensive reductions, and no later than yesterday the American news contained the announcement of the discharge of several volunteer regiments from the northern States, and of a decrease of two-thirds in the number of working-men employed in the naval arsenals These measures constituted in themselves an emphatic denial to the assertions of certain American journals, who have at all times made a trade of exciting public curiosity by means of sensation rumors. The language of the President, therefore, is but the official expression of a thought already manifested in acts.

Mr. Johnson has, moreover, seen fit to lay down, with regard to foreign nations, a rule to which none of the enlightened governments of Europe will refuse to subscribe. He has declared, as did most of his predecessors, his purpose of maintaining the traditionary policy of the United States, consisting in non-interference in the internal affairs of European nations, and demands that on their part European nations shall observe a similar conduct towards the American Union. He adds: "We should regard it as a great calamity to ourselves, to the cause of good government, and to the peace of the world, should any European power challenge the American people to the defence of republicanism against foreign interference." This passage was doubtless written with the sole object of giving some satisfaction to that over-excited portion of the American public who derive their political views from the newspapers above referred to. We would seek in vain, indeed, to discover which of the nations of Europe can ever have conceived the thought of interfering in the internal affairs of the United States. We know of none against which American citizens may one day be called upon to defend their institutions.

The President's message could not remain silent on the discussion created between England and the United States by the arming of vessels of English origin, which, after leaving English ports, hoisted the confederate flag, and inflicted serious damage upon the commerce of the United States. The President surrenders none of the claims set up by the cabinet at Washington on this point, but wisely contents himself with propounding a question of general interest, the solution of which he claims would be of importance for all nations. He acknowledges, moreover, that England entertains but kindly dispositions towards the United States, and declares to be himself actuated by a sincere desire to maintain peace between the two countries.

So far as the telegraphic analysis enables us to judge, the message of the President of the United States contains, therefore, none but the most reassuring declarations concerning the continuation of friendly relations between the great republic of the New World and the European powers. We shall soon have occasion to study this message in view of its internal policy, and of what is conventionally called in America *reconstruction*, viz: the position of the late Confederate States towards the States which have victoriously upheld the cause of the Union.

H. MARIE MARTIN.

[From the Journal des Debats of December 18, 1865—Orleanist.]

[Translation.]

The history of the United States since the civil war, and in consequence of that war, is destined to become more and more mixed up with that of Europe. The same force which has saved the Union has the power to make her expand by the unavoidable progress of its action and of its influence abroad. Before the war, no one would have dared to question the agricultural, commercial, and industrial prosperity in store for the American Union. Since the war, a still more important field appears to open before the nation of which M. de Montalembert said recently, "the American federation is, henceforth, replaced among the great powers of the world; all eyes will henceforth turn to it; all minds will be taught by the light of its future, for that future shall be more or less our own, and its destiny will perhaps decide ours."*

Let us not go so far. The rivalry of influence and the reciprocity of action between the American Union and Europe are not a new thing. On neither side have they yet assumed the character of a propagand. America has not sought to affect the customs or laws of

* La Victoire du Nord aux Etats Unis, by Count de Montalembert.

Europe, neither has Europe attempted to weigh upon the institutions of America. The famous declaration of President Monroe, whose true date (1823) has recently been restored to it by Mr. John Lemoinne, who also determined its meaning, was a purely defensive declaration, intended to assign a limit to the attempts at legitimist restoration then being carried out upon Spanish soil. To restore the divine right upon the throne of Spain was, of itself, a heavy undertaking; to restore it in Peru or Chili with the aid of French vessels was a pretension which no one would have thought of. President Monroe, nevertheless, laid down, in opposing visionary events, an international doctrine full of vitality.

France has always pretended to act abroad through the influence of her ideas and of her customs; this is right. The genius of France inclines to proselytism; it is generous, expansive, often disinterested. But in the present state of the world the door is everywhere open to liberal ideas, and contrary views obtain access but by force. The Americans of the north are the greatest producers of liberal ideas in the world, and therefore, in the noble interchange of them which is going on among nations, America seems called to a superiority which it will be easier to balance than to oppose. The generous emulation of liberty will do more towards it than overt force.

Those who, like us, bend under the weight of nearly the whole of the waning century, have but few lessons to receive from the American Union. What could they do with them? After being a sincere monarchist all through life, one remains so. It is too late to change one's ideas Constitutional monarchy, when one has placed in it one's confidence and faith, is, moreover, a great enough progress compared with the government by divine right, to permit one not to wish for more. There is, therefore, a whole generation whose political opinions remain uninfluenced by the spectacle of the triumph of the republican principle in the United States; but beware of the influence of such an example upon the generations which follow us; beware, especially, of its influence upon the masses, animated and sustained in their forward march towards the future by the stimulus of equality—a rail-splitter, as they say in speaking of Lincoln, a self-made man, who from being an obscure lawyer in Illinois, became a representative of his country, then President of the Union, *i. e.*, supreme chief of the executive power of the most powerful republic of the world; and once upon this summit, in the midst of the most formidable dangers, losing neither his coolness nor his foresight, nor his respect for legal restraints—perserving in spite of all attacks his stoical good temper and his resolute philanthropy—carrying on a desperate war upon an immense scale improvising armies provided with inexhaustible resources, and commanded by generals whose names are now among the greatest in the world. What a sight, even though death has by a felon's hand added to it its sting!

[From the Siecle of Tuesday, December 19, 1865—Democratic.]

[Translation]

Another discourse was not less impatiently looked for than that of the King of Belgium—we mean the message of the President of the United States. This document is usually very long. We hasten to the part of it which interests us the most—that relating to foreign affairs.

After referring to the good state of the relations subsisting between the American government and other powers, the message declares that since its foundation the republic of the United States has made it a rule not to interfere in the revolutions of which Europe was the theatre, and to follow the advice of Washington, "to commend the republic only by the careful preservation and wise use of its benefits." By their own moderation the United States have a right to expect that we should respond by a similar moderation. They will not deviate from the path which they have followed, unless they are forced to do so by the aggression of European powers. They count upon the wisdom and justice of these powers to respect the system of non-intervention, which during so long a period was sanctioned by time, and which, owing to its happy results, was approved on both continents.

This reciprocity, in truth, constituted the entire Monroe doctrine.

There is a passage in this part of the message which we will take pains to illustrate. It is that in which President Johnson—using a language which no one will think exaggerated—praises the results of American institutions:

"Here is the great land of free labor, where industry is blessed with unexampled rewards, and the bread of the workingman is sweetened by the consciousness that the cause of the country is his own cause, his own safety, his own dignity. Here every one enjoys the free use of his faculties, and the choice of activity as a natural right. Here, under the combined influence of a fruitful soil, genial climes, and happy institutions, population has increased fifteen-fold within a century. Here, through the easy development of boundless resources, wealth has increased with two-fold greater rapidity than numbers, so that we have become secure against the financial vicissitudes of other countries, and alike in business and in opinion are self-centred and truly independent. Here more and more care is given to provide education for every one born on our soil. Here religion, relieved from political connexion with the civil government, refuses to subserve the craft of statesmen, and becomes in its independence the spiritual life of the people. Here toleration is extended to every opinion, in the quiet certainty that truth needs only a fair field to secure the victory. Here the human mind goes forth unshackled in the pursuit of science, to collect stores of knowledge, and acquire an ever-increasing mastery over the forces of nature. Here the national domain is offered and held in millions of separate freeholds, so that our fellow-citizens, beyond the occupants of any other part of the earth, constitute, in reality, a people. Here exists the democratic form of government, and that form of government, by the confession of European statesmen, gives a power of which no other form is capable, because it incorporates every man with the state, and arouses everything that belongs to the soul."

Why should we be astonished if the American people be faithful to their institutions, and declare themselves willing to make every sacrifice to maintain them? This sentiment has no need of the name of any man; it is known throughout all time, and is everywhere called by the same word, patriotism.

[From the Epoque, 19th December, 1865—Liberal.]

The message of President Johnson to the Congress of the United States is to-day entirely known. Notwithstanding a translation hastily made, and in certain parts confused, as by design, the Havas agency has enabled France to read and to consider this long dissertation, in which the successor of Abraham Lincoln gives proof of the highest qualities of the statesman, and the grandest virtues of the citizen. If we may judge by what we have felt in reading this document, great must have been the emotion of the members of Congress assembled for the first time since the end of the rebellion, when they heard the words of the President. There are, indeed, ideas which can only be born and strengthened in certain lands, where liberty, so to speak, forms a part of the common air, and the members of Congress must have been justly proud at the thought that they lived in a medium so privileged.

What is especially striking in the message of Mr Johnson is the contrast between the President, as he appears to us, and the man of whom so repulsive a portrait was but recently drawn by certain sheets. We were shown a sort of demagogue, thirsting for absolute power, eager for vengeance, ready to plunge his country into all adventures; and now we see a citizen bearing, without seeming to bend beneath, the weight, the burden of a fearful responsibility, having accepted resolutely the heritage of Abraham Lincoln, and coming freely before the representatives of a free people to render an account of his stewardship.

He has but one ruling thought, which may seem strange in Europe, after having in less than one year restored the Union, reduced the war estimates from five hundred and sixteen millions of dollars to thirty-three millions, diminished in an equivalent proportion the navy estimates, provided for the extinguishment in thirty years of the public debt, amounting to $2,740,854,754, taken measures to withdraw rapidly from circulation the paper money; in one word, after having rendered immense services to the republic, he thinks of but one thing—to show that the honor of all these reforms is due to the law, which he has always respected.

The law and the Constitution: There is the proper, the just, the sovereign remedy. Four days before the opening of Congress, Mr. Johnson had restored almost everywhere the *habeas corpus;* and yet, as stated by a New York journal, one would scarcely have imagined that this guarantee was suspended. But it was still too much to have in possession an arbitrary instrument, even when no use was made of it, for Mr. Johnson thinks with the journal already quoted, "a free government is not defined by saying it is one which commits no act of tyranny. To complete the definition, it must be added that it is one under which tyranny is impossible."

The presidential message comprises three principal points of great interest for us. These treat of the reconstruction of the south, of the negro question, and of the foreign question.

In the first of these questions Mr Johnson maintains that those States included among the States that entered into secession were not in fact in rebellion as States, as, from the very first, the acts of secession of the States had been by the terms of the Constitution declared null and void. They should hence be considered as acts engaging only the responsibility of the individuals who had committed them. This theory, which takes up and resolves one of the most important questions of American constitutional law, explains why, as a skilful politician, Mr. Johnson has not wished to subject longer to the military rule the insurgent portions of the United States.

According to him, the military governments established in the States could only increase the discontent of former rebels, divide the people into conquerors and conquered, create a fatal precedent, be a source of ruinous expense to the Union, and, finally, arrest emigration towards the south, upon which the President greatly relies to heal the wounds of civil war; "for," says he, perhaps doing us too much honor, "what emigrant from abroad, what industrious citizen at home, would place himself willingly under military rule?"

He has, therefore, sought to reorganize the States on a constitutional basis, causing them to enjoy at once and anew the benefits assured by the Union. He recognizes that this policy is not without danger, as it implies the acquiescence of the States concerned, and the taking of a new oath of allegiance to the Union on the part of those States; but between two evils he has chosen that which may spring from the generosity of the conqueror. He expects, however, that the States shall give a pledge to the Union in consenting to ratify the project of amendment to the Constitution, which provides for the final abolition of slavery. He makes it known that the past can only be forgotten at that price.

The part of the message relative to the relations to be established between the freed blacks and the central government is not inspired by less sagacity and less respect for law. If by his words Mr. Johnson has indeed shown that he was favorable to the project of making electors of the freedmen, he has not been willing to violate the Constitution, and concede, by a presidential act, the electoral right to men of color. The Constitution prescribes that each State shall be the sovereign dispenser of its rights of suffrage; and it is only little by little, it must be remembered, that universal suffrage has become almost the general rule. It belongs, therefore, to each State, according to him, to resolve this question: and he hopes that this method will hasten the period of equality more than the intervention of the central government would do.

On this point, while rendering justice to the motives which have dictated the words of the President, and while approving his scruples, we cannot but form a wish. We hope that Congress, all-powerful in this matter, should do what the President has done well in not imposing. Two means, entirely constitutional, present themselves, in fact, for the attainment of the proposed end. 1st. Congress can amend the Constitution, and without occupying itself with the organic laws of each State, can declare by a vote, that no State can introduce into its laws distinctions based on race and color. 2d. It can refuse admission (under article four of the Constitution, which obliges the States to have a republican form of government) to the senators and representatives of those States which shall not, in their new Constitutions, have recognized the equality of the races; for if, in former times, the word "republic" has been coupled with the word "slavery," this monstrous confusion of terms is impossible to-day.

After the exposé of the domestic situation which we have been only able briefly to review, Mr. Johnson passes to the foreign question, and it is somewhat surprising to see him, by a trait of humor peculiar to the genius of American politicians, commence by congratulating himself upon the friendly relations entertained between the United States and the emperor of China. After the Son of Heaven came the Czar and the Emperor of Brazil. These are friends. As to England, the message does not conceal the fact that in recognizing the insurgents as belligerents, in furnishing to the rebellion vessels constructed in English ports, manned by English seamen, she has given occasion for serious complaints, further aggravated by her refusal to submit this question to international arbitration. The government of Washington, however, is not in pursuit of pecuniary reparation. It wishes to have discussed by a tribunal of nations the grave questions of the rights of neutrals. The message, however, does not counsel to Congress any demand for satisfaction; it limits itself to warning England that in future "the friendship between the two nations must repose upon the basis of mutual justice."

If the English journals have appeared satisfied with this part of the message, as the semi-official journals declare themselves no less delighted with the reserve of Mr. Johnson, in what concerns France and Mexico, we are less disposed, for our own part, to such rejoicing.

The message for any one who can read is a declaration very clear, very firm, although very moderate, of the will of the government of the United States to maintain its traditional policy—in other words, to sustain the Monroe doctrine. The translation given by the Havas agency contains in this part a mistake so much the more to be regretted, as it is of a nature to prevent the public opinion from being rightly informed. Thus this agency makes the President say that he would regard it as a calamity for the peace of the world "that any European power should throw the glove to the American people, as if for the defence of republicanism against foreign intervention," which signifies nothing at all; while the text reads, "should any European power challenge the American people, as it were, to the defence of republicanism against foreign interference." The formal reserves made by President Johnson take from this declaration little of its gravity.

This is not the language of a man who wishes to satisfy rancors, and achieve an easy popularity by flattering the bad instincts of national vanity. It is the grave and reserved utterance of the most authoritative representative of a people who wish not to embroil themselves heedlessly, but who are resolved not to see compromised in any case, a liberty so well conquered, so dearly preserved, and to which it owes its happiness and strength.

H. PENARD.

[From the Gazette de France, December 21—Legitimist.]

[Translation.]

The message of President Johnson begins with these words: "My first duty is to express, in the name of the people, my gratitude to God for the preservation of the United States"

This is a public prayer. It is a profession of religious faith in the power of God over earthly things. Atheists, free-thinkers, and doctrinaires of moral independence may say what they will on the usefulness of the people acknowledging a Supreme Being, just and good. This public acknowledgment by the head of a great people is of a nature to make a vivid impression on the mind of those to whom it is addressed, despite their railleries There is no more imposing spectacle than that of a sovereign bowing before the Majesty of God in the name of the entire people.

The chief of the republic of the United States did not believe himself guilty of a childish credulity in speaking as he did. On the contrary, he was convinced that he showed proofs of manliness of spirit in referring to the "intervention of Providence in human affairs" That which has frequently misled Europe in the predictions which she has formed of American affairs is, that in order to judge of the progress of events, she does not take into account the religious sentiment which animates the American people.

It was for this reason that so many in France believed that the reaction against the conquered would be followed up with an implacable and bloody spirit, and that liberty would succumb in the infinite calamity of civil war. The Americans possess passions more intense, perhaps, than ours, but they are certainly of a different kind

In Europe, the first movement of states, after a similar crisis, had been to constitute what is called a strong power, to surround it with all suitable material means to render it formidable, terrible. In the United States, the first duty of the head of the republic, who is called to the head of affairs by an odious assassination, was to reduce all the appurtenances of material force to their simplest expression, to re-establish the universal laws of liberty, to cause to disappear every symbol which would recall the existence of arbitrary rule in the minds of the people. What the President fears above all is, that the principles of liberty, upon which the Constitution rests, be undermined in the future. He vehemently recalls to mind the farewell which the Father of his Country gave to the people of the United States, when he was yet President, "the free Constitution, which was the one work of the nation, must be maintained inviolate and sacred" He saw in the maintenance of a strong army danger; he reduces it to 50,000 men. "Military governments," he says, "established for an indefinite period, would have offered no security for the early suppression of discontent; would have divided the people into vanquishers and the vanquished, and would have envenomed hatred, rather than restored affection. Once established, no precise limit to their continuance was conceivable."

"The wilful use of such powers, if continued through a period of years, would have endangered the purity of the general administration and the liberties of the States which remained loyal. Besides, the policy of military rule over a conquered territory would have implied that the States whose inhabitants may have taken part in the rebellion had, by the act of those inhabitants ceased to exist."

"But if any State neglects or refuses to perform its offices, there is the more need that the general government should maintain all its authority, and, as soon as practicable, resume the exercise of all its functions, On this principle I have acted, and have gradually, and quietly, and by almost imperceptible steps, sought to restore the rightful energy of the general government and of the States."

We see the President fears but one thing: it is, that the civic life be weakened, that the mind of the people, under the influence of excess of confidence caused by victories, should assign to the army a power which does not belong to it in a free country.

To reanimate the civic virtues and the energy of local governments, such is the work which the President of the United States assumes. And he presents this noble undertaking, very naturally, as the only means to revive prosperity in the republic He believes in the efficacy of liberty as a safeguard to order in a nation of freemen, just as he believes in God and the interposition of Providence in human affairs.

This is the striking character of this document, and it is most remarkable in that respect. Now, indeed, when the theory of right as the basis of order and progress are in such favor, it is interesting to reflect upon this noble defence of the contrary theory, and to carefully notice that these are not mere words, but that it is a man struggling with real facts, and in the face of one of the most formidable of political and social crises, who says that liberty is the best foundation for order, and asserts that when states lose that faith it is the duty of their chiefs to try to revive their energies.

GUSTAVE JANICOT.

[From Le Monde, December 19, 1865.—Ultramontane.]

President Johnson has treated at length the domestic question of the United States. The three serious points of this question are, the seceding States—the negroes—the finances. The seceding or rebel States have been received to pardon. It seems even that the intentions of the President were friendly. In his message he allows the partisans of the south to re-enter the Union, with all their rights; he details the inconveniences of perpetual military rule in a certain number of States; he prefers, in replacing these States under the law, to open the door to emigration, and thus to substitute successively free labor for slave labor. This passage of the message is a seductive appeal to emigration towards the southern States. It is to be regretted that in practice the southern people have not been treated so well as in words; the representatives of these States have not been admitted to Congress. The division which the President desires to obliterate by the exercise of his sovereign right of pardon exists in its entirety. Mr. Johnson may talk in vain of the Americans being brothers; they are divided into conquerors and conquered.

The blacks, on their side, are the object of the philanthropic theories of the President—theories which have scarcely any echoes in reality. We can hardly recognize in those famished gangs, wandering on the highways—in these houseless beggars whom our correspondents describe—free citizens of free America. One is led to doubt whether the dream of Mr. Johnson will ever be realized, when we see the contempt in which these proud republicans hold the African race. Free labor is not organized; empirical or radical projects gain favor—such as the expulsion of the blacks, their colonization, &c. The President is evidently disquieted by this question. It may be the cause of painful troubles; it may, by requiring severe measures, take from the United States a portion of their philanthropic prestige. In connexion with this question, the President makes an admission which is confirmed by a remark made by him in speaking of the finances. The southern States were, under the old arrangements, closed to northern emigrants: free labor found no access there—commercial transactions were greatly hampered. The northern States long before the war coveted these rich countries; they wished to farm them, as it were, for the benefit of their industrial properties; they intended to profit by that wealth, both to increase their revenues and to increase their markets. Slavery has been the flag that covered this traffic.

We will resume, in passing, the financial situation of the United States—a debt of two millions and a half of dollars (12,500,000,000fr.,) regular taxes; an organization of the debt so as to pay it in 30 years; a permanent army of 84,000 men, of whom 32,000 form a reserve; a fleet greatly increased; important naval constructions; a part of their territory held as unsafe—a part of the population deprived of its franchises and public charges—this is the general aspect. In what, let us ask, is this situation an enviable one? It is not like our old communities; still less is it free America. Debts, taxes, army privilege, internal dissensions: in spite of the cheerful tone of the President, there is more than one cloud upon the starry heaven that forms the banner of the Union.

The President has brought the same tone of moderation to the treatment of the foreign question.

This question has two objectives—England and France—*i. e.* the recognition of the belligerents and the Mexican expedition. On this last point the President says little—so little that it is disquieting. The generalities which he expresses are, in our opinion, an evident proof that there is something going on at Washington or Paris relative to the Mexican question. One does not speak so briefly of an expedition which operates at your very door, contrary to your proclaimed principles, unless there is something under the cards which it is desirable to hide.

The President is more explicit in regard to England, without being more threatening. He affects a still calmer tone, if possible, and contents himself with a sort of statement of facts. These facts, it is true, constitute, according to the interpretation of Mr. Johnson, a violation of neutrality. England, it is also true, has refused to bring them before an international commission. The President regrets this, but he does not hence conclude that good relations should cease between the two powers. For the rest, has Mr. Johnson a good right to demand to-day the assembling of an international commission to consider questions of the law of nations, when the United States have always hitherto claimed to hold themselves aloof from what Europe was doing in that sense? If our memory is exact, such was their attitude at the time of the congress of Paris, when the rights of neutrals were regulated.

The resumé of the exposition of the foreign attitude of the United States seems to us to be this.

The hour of action has not arrived.

H. VRIGNAULT.

Mr. Bigelow to Mr. Seward.

No. 235.] LEGATION OF THE UNITED STATES,
Paris, January 5, 1866.

SIR: I have received your instruction, No. 331, in relation to the levying of troops in Egypt to re-enforce the French army in Mexico. I invited the attention of Mr. Drouyn de Lhuys, yesterday, to the reports circulating in American papers in regard to the landing of large numbers of troops at Vera Cruz, and asked if the policy of the government had undergone any change, since my last conversation upon that subject, in connexion with the levy of Egyptians. He replied that it had not, so far as he was aware; that he believed the French force in Mexico had been undergoing a reduction, rather than an increase; but to make himself entirely sure upon the point, he would again make inquiries at the war office, and let me know their result as soon as possible. In reply to another question of mine, he said that the government had no intention to take Egyptian troops to Mexico, but that it adhered entirely to the policy heretofore announced to me on that subject. On receiving this assurance, I did not think it my duty to read to him the instruction to our consul general at Alexandria, which accompanied your despatch.

I am, sir, with great respect, your very obedient servant,

JOHN BIGELOW.

Hon. WILLIAM H. SEWARD,
Secretary of State.

Mr. Bigelow to Mr. Seward.

No. 240.] LEGATION OF THE UNITED STATES,
Paris, January 11, 1866.

SIR: I enclose a memorandum, received last evening from Mr. Drouyn de Lhuys, in pursuance of a promise which I have already reported to you. I called upon his excellency this afternoon for the purpose of getting clearer ideas upon some of its points, that no time should be lost by the two governments in securing an available basis of negotiation.

I read over to him the memorandum aloud, and as I proceeded, remarked that I presumed my government would not deny to France the sovereign right of making war, which, of course, belonged to all governments; that France would be singularly fortunate if the end for which she went to Mexico should be fully realized, for it always took two parties to make a war, and one must be in the wrong; and history had preserved the record of few wars in which either belligerent attained fully the end for which it took up arms. I asked him if he could give me an idea of the "guarantees" which he hoped to obtain from Mexico. He said they did not, of course, expect to get the money owing them, but they hoped for something which they might regard as an equivalent. That, however, was a matter of negotiation between them and Mexico. But he could not very well talk with me about those guarantees now, for they must depend upon the result of pending negotiations in Mexico, and were liable to be different from anything they might now be able to suggest. I then asked what form his excellency proposed that the "assurances" he asked from the cabinet at Washington should take. He replied that he had as yet given no thought to that subject.

I remarked that it seemed to me desirable, for obvious reasons, that our governments should appear to act as independently of each other as possible in this matter; that France could hardly enter with dignity into a formal covenant with us to make her retirement from Mexico depend upon our forbearance, neither could we covenant not to intervene without implying a disposition on our part to intervene but for such a covenant. I expressed a doubt, therefore, whether a formal covenant was consistent with the dignity of either nation, but I suggested that it would doubtless be perfectly agreeable to the Secretary of State at Washington to restate in a despatch to me the policy of non-intervention in the internal affairs of other independent states which we have hitherto pursued, and to which it is our purpose to adhere, in terms that would be perfectly satisfactory to the Emperor. A copy of such an opinion in his hands, I said, would possess all of the advantages and none of the disadvantages of a formal treaty.

I also expressed my belief that you would have no objection to make such a communication if it promised to favor an early and friendly solution of the questions pending between us.

Mr. Drouyn de Lhuys thought well of this suggestion; said he saw no need of a treaty; he preferred the separate and independent action of the governments, and he would be prepared, he said, in conformity with that policy, to show me when I could give him the assurance spoken of—the results of negotiations with Maximilian which were already going on quite independently of that assurance. I was glad to hear from his mouth this fact, glanced at in his memorandum, for it satisfied me that notice has already gone forward to Maximilian, probably by Mr. Hidalgo, that he must prepare to dispense with the French flag *avant peu.*

I then asked whether it would not be possible in some way to arrest the useless and demoralizing warfare that was carried on in Mexico between Maximilian and the Juarists, at least while these negotiations were going on, that is, while the French occupation should last. He said he wished there was; that the atrocities practiced there were really too dreadful to speak of, but he did not know that he could do anything to discourage them, and asked if I had anything to suggest. I said, I supposed that if the Juarists were sure that the French were intending to leave Mexico within a time which seemed reasonable to them, and that they would then have a fair chance of trying conclusions with Maximilian's party, they would be willing to leave him undisturbed, if undisturbed by him; and that if France or Maximilian had any indirect means of coming to such an understanding with Juarez, it might render the situation less embarrassing to all parties.

His excellency replied that he would be very glad if that were practicable, as it would enable them to leave the country so much the sooner; but they had no means of communicating with Juarez, and he asked me if I could suggest any mode of accomplishing what I proposed. I replied that we had relations, as he was aware, with Señor Romero, and anything that he would authorize me to say we should be most happy to say, of course, that would have a tendency to terminate this brutalizing strife.

His excellency promised to speak of this, and also of the form of the "assurance" which we had been discussing, to the Emperor.

I then asked his excellency if he had heard of Santa Anna's projects, of which I wrote you in my private note of the 8th instant. He seemed to be fully informed upon the subject.

My object in this conversation with Mr. Drouyn de Lhuys, as I have already stated, was to lose no time in getting our two governments to a point where they can begin to act in concert. How far I have succeeded I can better judge when I shall receive your reply to this account of it.

I remain, sir, with great respect, your very obedient servant,

JOHN BIGELOW.

Hon. WILLIAM H. SEWARD, *&c., &c., &c.*

[Translation.—Memorandum.]

The Washington cabinet recognizes the right which we have, like any sovereign nation, to make war on Mexico. On our side we desire to observe the principle of non-intervention. Does not the approximating of these two points offer the basis of a common understanding?

To make war is not only to overthrow fortifications, and kill a certain number of men; it is especially to assure a right infringed upon, the vindication of which has rendered necessary the employment of arms. Until this end is fully attained, the means of execution incident to war remain legitimate. In Mexico we hope to obtain before long the guarantees which we have sought, and which are to complete our final arrangements with the emperor Maximilian. At that moment the mission of our troops will be accomplished, and they can return to France. I write in this sense to Mexico, by order of the Emperor.

This will then be a case for the application of the principle of non-intervention. We will conform our conduct to it, and we are confident that the people of the United States who invoke this principle will respect it themselves, by observing towards Mexico a scrupulous neutrality. When we shall have received from the cabinet of Washington this assurance, we will be able to make known to them, in our turn, the result of our final negotiations with the empire of Mexico.

Mr. Hunter to Mr. Bigelow.

No. 369.] DEPARTMENT OF STATE,
Washington, January 15, 1866.

SIR: Your despatch of the 29th ultimo, No. 233, relating the substance of conversation reported to have taken place between Messrs. Forcade and Germigny upon the subject of the purposes of the Emperor in regard to the provision to be made for the payment of the Mexican bonds, should he conclude to withdraw his army from Mexico, has been received, and I have, in reply, to thank you for the information.

I am, sir, your obedient servant,

W. HUNTER, *Acting Secretary.*

JOHN BIGELOW, Esq., *&c., &c., &c.*

Mr. Bigelow to Mr. Seward.

[Extract.]

No. 248.] LEGATION OF THE UNITED STATES,
Paris, January 25, 1866.

SIR: The legislative chambers were opened by the Emperor on the 22d instant, with the usual ceremonies. The Prince Imperial, for the first time, asserted his hierarchical rank, by taking the seat on the right of the throne, the Prince Napoleon placing himself on the left.

A copy of the imperial speech is enclosed. The relations of France with the United States proved on this occasion a more fertile topic to his Majesty than on corresponding occasions heretofore. His language betrays his high appreciation of the value of our friendship, and a purpose henceforth to cultivate it assiduously. He says all that he could be expected to say about Mexico in the present state of his information. Resistance to the spread of the Anglo-Saxon race appears to have lost a portion of its importance in his eyes, and the world is distinctly notified that Maximilian must expect soon to rely upon his own resources if he remains in Mexico. The Emperor wisely left the time for withdrawing his army from that republic undefined. He is, therefore, at liberty to retire as soon as he pleases. Probably no part of the discourse gave such general satisfaction as that which held out hopes of an early release of France from her Mexican entanglement. The press of the metropolis reflects this feeling with singular unanimity. I enclose a few of the journals which are not habitually received at the State Department, containing articles of more or less significance upon this subject. In conclusion, let me say that the language of the Emperor, and the reception it has met with from his people, have left no doubt upon my mind of his intention to wash his hands of Mexico as soon as he possibly can. * * * * * * *

I remain, sir, with great respect, your very obedient servant,

JOHN BIGELOW.

Hon. WILLIAM H. SEWARD, &c., &c., &c.

The Marquis de Montholon to Mr. Seward.

[Translation.]

LEGATION OF FRANCE TO THE UNITED STATES,
Washington, January 29, 1866.

SIR: I have the happiness to hear of the return of your excellency to Washington at the very moment when I am in receipt of the note which Mr. Drouyn de Lhuys addresses to me, in answer to yours of the 6th December last, after having taken the orders of the Emperor in respect thereof. I hasten, Mr. Secretary of State, to place in the hands of your excellency the answer of Mr. Drouyn de Lhuys, praying you to be so good as to lay it before his excellency the President, Mr. Johnson.

Accept, Mr. Secretary of State, the assurances of my high consideration.

MONTHOLON.

Hon. WILLIAM H. SEWARD,
Secretary of State, &c., &c., &c.

Mr. Drouyn de Lhuys to the Marquis de Montholon.

[Translation.]

No. 2.] DEPARTMENT OF FOREIGN AFFAIRS, DIPLOMATIC BRANCH,
Paris, January 9, 1866.

MR. THE MARQUIS DE MONTHOLON: I have already charged you, by order of the Emperor, to make known to the cabinet of Washington the views of his Majesty's government on the affairs of Mexico, and you have, conformably with my instructions, made known to Mr. Seward the despatch I had the honor to write to you under date of 18th October. The Secretary of State has answered that despatch by a communication which he was pleased to address to you on the 6th of December, and from which I believe it to be my duty here to reproduce the leading points.

According to Mr. Seward, the presence of a foreign force in a country neighboring to the Union could not but be a source of uneasiness and disquiet. This state of things draws along with it on the federal government embarrassing outlays, and may lead to collisions. At all events, the principal cause of the dissatisfaction of the United States is not that there is in Mexico a foreign army; much less that such army is French. The cabinet of Washington recognizes in every sovereign nation the right to make war, provided the use of this right does not menace the security and legitimate influence of the Union. But the French army has gone to Mexico to overthrow a national republican government, and with the avowed aim of founding on its ruins a foreign monarchical government. Mr. Seward states, on this subject, how much the people of the United States are attached to the institutions they have given themselves, and, repelling any idea of propagandism in favor of these institutions, he claims for the various nations of the New World the right to secure to themselves this form of government at their convenience. He would consider as inadmissible that European powers should interfere in these countries with the idea of destroying the republican form in order to substitute kingdoms and empires. "Having thus frankly defined our position," adds Mr. Seward, "I submit the question to the judgment of France, sincerely hoping that great nation will find it compatible with its true interests, as well as with its so highly exalted honor, to abandon the aggressive attitude it has taken in Mexico."

Mr. Seward recalls in closing, as a reason for his hope of arriving at a happy solution, the ancient affection of the United States for France, and the value which every American citizen constantly attached in past time, and attaches in the future, to our friendship.

I have not failed to place this communication before the Emperor. After having maturely examined the considerations set forth by Mr. Seward, the government of his Majesty remains convinced that the divergence of views between the two cabinets is, above all, the result of an erroneous appreciation of our intentions.

Our expedition—need I say it?—had in it nothing hostile to the institutions of the nations of the New World, and assuredly still less to those of the Union. France could not forget that she has contributed with her blood to found them; and of the number of glorious memories which the ancient monarchy has bequeathed to us, there is not one of which Napoleon I showed himself more proud, and which Napoleon III can be less inclined to repudiate. If, moreover, we could have been influenced by a malevolent thought toward this republic, would we have sought in the beginning to obtain the concurrence of the federal government, which had, as well as ourselves, reclamations to make available? Would we have observed neutrality in the great crisis which the United States have passed through? And to-day would we be disposed, as we declare with the greatest frankness, to hasten, as much as it will be possible for us, the moment for the recall of our troops? Our only aim has been to follow up the satisfactions to which we had right, on recurring to coercive measures, after having exhausted all others. It is known how numerous and legitimate the claims of French subjects were. It was in presence of a series of flagrantly vexatious measures, and of glaring denials of justice, that we took up arms.

The wrongs to the United States were certainly less numerous and less important when they were led—they also—some years ago, to employ force against Mexico. The French army did not carry monarchical traditions in the folds of its flag.

The cabinet of Washington is not ignorant that there were in that country for many years a number of men of influence, who, despairing of obtaining order out of the conditions of the then existing rule, nourished the idea of falling back upon monarchy. Their thoughts were shared in by one of the last presidents of that republic, who even offered to use his power to favor the re-establishment of royalty.

On witnessing the degree of anarchy into which the government of Juarez had fallen, they deemed the moment had arrived to make appeal to the opinion of the people, tired out as they were with the state of dissolution in which their resources were being exhausted.

We did not think it a duty to discourage this supreme effort of a powerful party, the origin of which dates long anterior to our expedition; but faithful to the maxims of public right which we hold in common with the United States, we declared that question rested solely on the suffrages of the Mexican people.

The idea of the government of the Emperor has been defined by his Majesty in person in a letter addressed to the commander-in-chief of our army after the taking of Puebla. "Our object you know," wrote the Emperor, "is not to impose on the Mexicans a government against their will, nor to make our success aid the triumph of any party whatever. I desire that Mexico may revive to a new life, and that, soon regenerated by a government founded on the national will, on principles of order and of progress, on respect for the law of nations, she may acknowledge by her friendly relations that she owes to France her repose and her prosperity."

The Mexican people have spoken—the emperor Maximilian has been called by the will of the country. The government has appeared to us to be of a nature to restore peace to the interior and good faith to international relations. We have given it our support.

We went then to Mexico, there to exercise the right of war, which Mr. Seward fully recognizes in us, and not in virtue of any principle of intervention, about which we profess the same doctrine as the United States. We went there not to bring about a monarchical proselytism, but to obtain reparation and guarantees which we ought to claim, and we sustain the government which is founded on the consent of the people because we expect from it the satisfaction of our wrongs, as well as the securities indispensable to the future.

As we do not seek the satisfaction of an exclusive interest, nor the realization of an ambitious thought, our most sincere wish is to bring about, as soon as possible, the moment when we shall be able, with safety to our countrymen and with due respect for ourselves, to recall what remains in that country of the army corps which we have sent there.

As I have told you in the despatch to which the communication from Mr. Seward replies, it depends much on the federal government to facilitate in this respect the accomplishment of the desire which he expresses to us. The doctrine of the United States, resting as ours does on the principle of the national will, has in it nothing incompatible with the existence of monarchical institutions; and President Johnson in his message, as well as Mr. Seward in his despatch, repels all thought of propagandism, even on the American continent, in favor of republican institutions. The cabinet of Washington holds friendly relations with the court of Brazil, and did not refuse to form relations with the Mexican empire in 1823. No fundamental maxim—no precedent in the diplomatic history of the Union, therefore, creates any necessary antagonism between the United States and the form of government which has replaced in Mexico a power whose reign was nothing but a continual and systematic violation of its most positive obligations towards other nations.

Mr. Seward seems to make a double reproach to the government of the emperor Maximilian of the difficulties it encounters, and of the assistance it borrows from foreign forces, but the resistances which it has been obliged to wrestle with have in them nothing especial against the form of the institutions.

It undergoes the lot quite ordinary to new powers, and it is, above all, its misfortune to have to bear the consequences of disorders produced under previous governments, which lot is in effect that of those governments which have not found armed competitors and have enjoyed in peace an uncontested authority.

Revolts and intestine wars were, therefore, the normal condition of the country, and the opposition made by some military chiefs to the establishment of the empire is only the natural sequence of such habitudes of want of discipline and of anarchy of which the powers to whom this succeeds have been victims.

As for the support which the Mexican government receives from our army, and what is also lent to him by Belgian and Austrian volunteers, it causes no hindrance to the freedom of its resolutions nor the perfect independence of its actions. What state is there that needs not allies, whether to form it or to defend it? And the great powers, such as France and England for example, have they not constantly almost maintained foreign troops in their armies? When the United States fought for their emancipation, did the aid given by France to their efforts cause that great popular movement to cease to be truly national? And shall it be said that the contest with the south was not in like manner a national war, because the thousands of Irishmen and Germans were fighting under the flag of the Union? The character of the Mexican government, therefore, cannot be contested, nor the resistance which it must overcome to consolidate itself, or the foreign troops which shall have aided in bringing forth again safety and order in a country so long and deeply distracted, be considered a reason for disaffection toward it. Such an undertaking is surely worthy to be appreciated by a nation so enlightened as the United States, especially called on to gather the advantage.

In place of a country unceasingly in trouble, and which has given them so many subjects for complaint, and against which they have themselves been obliged to make war, they will find a pacific country, offering henceforth pledges of security and vast openings to their commerce. Far from injuring their rights or hurting their influence, they, above all, are those who must profit by the work of reorganization which is being accomplished in Mexico.

In recapitulation, marquis, the United States acknowledges the right we had to make war on Mexico. On the other part we admit, as they do, the principle of non-intervention; this double postulate includes, as it seems to me, the elements of an agreement. The right to make war, which belongs, as Mr. Seward declares, to every sovereign nation, implies the right to secure the results of war. We have not gone across the ocean merely for the purpose of showing our power, and of inflicting chastisement on the Mexican government; after a train of fruitless remonstrances it was our duty to demand guarantees against the recurrence of violence from which our countrymen had suffered so cruelly, and these guarantees we could not look for from a government whose bad faith we had proven on so many occasions.

We find them now engaged in the establishment of a regular government, which shows itself disposed honestly to keep its engagements. In this relation we hope that the legitimate object of our expedition will soon be reached, and we are striving to make with the emperor Maximilian arrangements which, by satisfying our interests and our honor, will permit us to consider as at an end the service of our army on Mexican soil.

The Emperor has given me orders to write in this sense to his minister in Mexico.

We fall back from that moment on the principle of non-intervention, and from that moment accept it as the rule of our conduct; our interest, no less than our honor, commands us to claim from all the uniform application of it. Trusting in the spirit of equity which animates the cabinet at Washington, we expect from it the assurance that the American people will themselves conform to the law which it invokes, by observing, in regard to Mexico, a strict neutrality. When you shall have informed me of the resolution of the federal government on this subject. I shall be able to indicate to you the results of our negotiations with the emperor Maximilian for the return of our troops.

I request you to remit a copy of this despatch to Mr. Seward, in answer to his communication of the 6th December last, begging him to have the goodness to lay it before President Johnson; and I rely with confidence for the examination of the consideration it embraces in the traditional sentiments recalled to notice in the note of the Secretary of State of the Union.

Accept, marquis, the assurances of my high consideration.

DROUYN DE LHUYS.

Monsieur le MARQUIS DE MONTHOLON,
Minister of France, near Washington.

Mr. Seward to Mr. Bigelow.

No. 378.]

DEPARTMENT OF STATE,
Washington, January 29, 1866.

SIR: I have to acknowledge the receipt of your despatch of the 5th instant, No. 235, relating to a recent interview between yourself and Mr. Drouyn de Lhuys upon the subject of levying of troops in Egypt to re-enforce the French army in Mexico. The views expressed by you on that occasion are approved.

I am, sir, your obedient servant,

WILLIAM H. SEWARD.

JOHN BIGELOW, Esq., *&c., &c., &c.*

Mr. Bigelow to Mr. Seward.

[Extract.]

No. 253.]

LEGATION OF THE UNITED STATES,
Paris, January 30, 1866.

SIR: I have still nothing later from the State Department than the 5th of January. France is a prey to the wildest rumors, and to a sort of solicitude which has been compared in my presence by French people to that which prevailed in 1789. This is partly owing to the ignorance of what has occurred between the two governments since the apparently critical moment at which the correspondence sent by the President to Congress closed.. In spite of the pacific and friendly tone of the Emperor's discourse, the public persist in believing that the actual situation is represented by that correspondence. To relieve this anxiety a little, the official press has announced the departure of M. Saillard to Mexico and Mr. Faverney to Washington with communications designed to prepare the way for the retirement of the French army from Mexico, and to satisfy President Johnson of the Emperor's loyal intentions towards the United States. You will find in the Paris correspondence of the London Times a curious account of Saillard's unsuccessful efforts to procure some letters of credence, first, from the Emperor, then the minister of foreign affairs, and finally from Walewski. Though his name is not given, he is the third party referred to. * *

To enable you to see how completely these relations of France with the United States have swallowed up all other questions, I send you a number of journals of a more or less representative character. You will be struck, no doubt, as I have been, by the fact that the propriety of our requiring the Emperor to withdraw his army from Mexico is not questioned by any of them; nor do I remember to have heard it questioned by any one with whom I have conversed. It is universally conceded that the moment the indemnity, for which the Emperor professes to have gone to Mexico, ceased to be attainable by arms, it was his duty to leave, in order not to have other motives, which could not be justified, assigned to his expedition.

I am, sir, with great respect, your very obedient servant,

JOHN BIGELOW.

Hon. WILLIAM H. SEWARD, &c., &c., &c.

Mr. Bigelow to Mr. Seward.

[Extract.]

No. 255.] LEGATION OF THE UNITED STATES,
Paris, February 1, 1866.

SIR: In the diplomatic circle last evening at the palace the Emperor asked me how my country people would like his speech at the opening of the corps legislatif. I replied that I had no doubt it would be read with general satisfaction. He then said he hoped we would soon have good news from the United States. I said I thought we might expect good news as soon as possible after your return to Washington. His Majesty asked if it was true, as the papers stated, that you would touch at Vera Cruz during your absence. I replied that I had not received a single line from Washington in reference to your trip, but that I had no reason to think it even probable that your voyage had any other purpose than recreation, which you could hardly obtain within reach of the telegraph, and that you probably thought the moment chosen the most propitious that was likely soon to offer for a brief absence.

* * * * * * *

I am, sir, with great respect, your obedient servant,

JOHN BIGELOW.

Hon. WILLIAM H. SEWARD,
Secretary of State.

Mr. Bigelow to Mr. Seward.

No. 257.] LEGATION OF THE UNITED STATES,
Paris, February 1, 1866.

SIR: I have the honor to transmit herewith a copy of the Documens Diplomatiques communicated to the corps legislatif on Monday, the 29th instant. You will learn from a note on the first page that it was originally intended, and so Mr. Drouyn de Lhuys stated to me this day week, to defer the publication of the correspondence relating to Mexico until the pending negotiations upon that subject should reach maturity. A subsequent note, at page 174, states that, in consequence of the communication to Congress of correspondence upon this subject by the President of the United States, it was thought best to withhold it no longer from the corps legislatif. The despatch on page 216 is in reply to your note addressed to the Marquis de Montholon, bearing date the 6th of December last, and gives an official version of the proposal which I had the honor to transmit to you in my despatch No. 240, of the 11th ultimo. I also invite your attention to the communication on page 223, addressed by Mr. Drouyn de Lhuys to the Marquis de Montholon, in reference to a note addressed by me to the former on the 16th ultimo. It is true that Mr. Drouyn de Lhuys did say, in conversation with me, laughingly, that he could have replied to me, if disposed, that France had not "planted" any political organization in Mexico, and that he did not believe Maximilian's decrees in reference to emigration contemplated any such purposes or results as I attributed to them, but he left me to understand that he did not think it worth while to write about it. I concluded that if he did not think it of consequence enough to answer in writing, he did not care to have a record made of his remarks. This will explain why you first hear of this conversation through a letter to the Marquis de Montholon.

I also send by the bag to-night a bundle of journals showing the impression left upon the public mind here by the appearance of this correspondence, and of that submitted to Congress by the President. It is easy to perceive that these publications have not been grateful to the government.

I am, sir, with great respect, your very obedient servant,

JOHN BIGELOW.

Hon. WILLIAM H. SEWARD,
Secretary of State.

Mr. Seward to Mr. Bigelow.

No. 382.]

DEPARTMENT OF STATE,
Washington, February 6, 1866.

SIR: I have received and submitted to the President your despatches of the 4th of January, No. 234, and of the 5th of January, No. 236, also your confidential despatch of January 11, No. 240. These papers contain much valuable information, and some useful suggestions concerning the mode of adjusting the difficulties of French intervention in Mexico. You will accept the thanks of the government. The Emperor seems to have matured his project on the 9th day of January. The Marquis de Montholon submitted to me an elaborate communication from Mr. Drouyn de Lhuys, which is supposed to have been prepared in execution of that project. My reply to Mr. Drouyn de Lhuys is now under consideration here. A copy of it will be sent to you for your information, at the same time that the paper itself is delivered to the Marquis de Montholon. The French government having transferred the discussion to this capital, you will be relieved of further direct action in the premises; but your advice and co-operation will be constantly desired, and when received will be highly valued.

I am, sir, your obedient servant,

WILLIAM H SEWARD.

JOHN BIGELOW, Esq., *&c., &c., &c.*

Mr. Bigelow to Mr. Seward.

[Extract.]

No. 264.]

LEGATION OF THE UNITED STATES,
Paris, February 8, 1866.

SIR: You will find in the Moniteur of the 7th instant the address reported by the senate commission in reply to the imperial discourse at the opening of the corps legislatif.

The passages of chief interest to the people of the United States are the following:

"You are, sire, the natural guardian of the interests of the army. It is not your Majesty who, after having led it to victory, would forget its glorious services on the return of peace. Besides, it is not always the safeguard of French honor and the bulwark of order and law? It is the army which now gives on the distant territory of Mexico an example of discipline, constancy, and of all military virtues, which it drops like a fruitful seed on its march.

"Your Majesty has announced that this memorable expedition to Mexico touches its term, and that you are coming to an understanding with the emperor Maximilian for the recall of your troops. That is the same as to say to satisfied France that the protection of her commercial interests will be assured in this vast and rich market made safe by our aid.

"As to the United States, if through any misunderstanding the presence of the French flag on the American continent appears to them less seasonable than it did at another very illustrious epoch in their history, the firm communications of your government have shown that it will not be imperious and menacing language that will determine us to return. France has not the habit of marching except to her own time. [Very well; very well.] But she loves to remember her ancient friendship for the United States. What you demand of them is neutrality and the right of nations. By this they may see that a war for the so often declared purpose of protecting our country people against a faithless government does not become, because successful, a war of conquest, of domination, or of propagandism."

* * * * * * * *

I am, sir, your very obedient and very humble servant,

JOHN BIGELOW.

Hon. WILLIAM H. SEWARD,
Secretary of State.

Mr. Bigelow to Mr. Seward.

No. 268.] LEGATION OF THE UNITED STATES,
Paris, February 9, 1866.

SIR: You will find at page 206 of the Documens Diplomatiques, transmitted with my despatch No. 257, a note addressed by Mr. Drouyn de Lhuys to the Marquis de Montholon, which is calculated to leave an incorrect impression of what passed at the interview to which it refers. For the purpose of rectifying that impression I addressed to Mr. Drouyn de Lhuys, on the 7th instant, a letter, which, with his reply, dated the 8th instant, I have the honor to enclose. It is at present my intention to request him to publish both letters in the Constitutionnel and La France, where the despatch in question has been reproduced.

I am, sir, with great respect, your obedient servant,

JOHN BIGELOW.

Hon. WILLIAM H. SEWARD,
Secretary of State.

Mr. Bigelow to Mr. Drouyn de Lhuys.

LEGATION OF THE UNITED STATES,
Paris, February 7, 1866.

SIR: I find at page 206 of the Documens Diplomatiques, for copies of which I have to thank your excellency, a letter to the Marquis de Montholon, bearing date October 18, 1865, in which your excellency says: "En vous écrivant," &c.

[Translation of extract.]

"In writing you this despatch I have entered into a path opened by Mr. Bigelow himself several days ago. In a conversation in relation to other matters, this minister asked me, in his own name, and without prejudging the opinion of his government, if I did not think that the recognition of the Mexican empire by the United States might facilitate and hasten the recall of our troops. The instructions which I send you are in answer to this question."

As neither the language which I remember to have used, nor the impression which I intended to convey in that conversation, correspond entirely with the version which your excellency has given of it in the foregoing citation, I desire to recall to your excellency the circumstances under which it occurred, for the purpose of showing that the confidence which I have in my own recollection, and in my memoranda made at the time, is not misplaced.

Your excellency, in reply to my inquiries, had been expressing your measure of faith in the ultimate consolidation of the power founded under the auspices of France in Mexico. And upon that faith rested your hopes of soon recalling your troops. You recapitulated some of the difficulties against which it would require a little time to provide; but all of which, you seemed to think, would diminish in magnitude, if the adversaries of the new order received no encouragement from the United States. It was in view of such representations that I asked whether, in your excellency's opinion, Maximilian would be able to sustain himself without the aid of France if his authority were recognized by the United States. That inquiry led to a conversation, in which I had occasion, at least twice, to state to your excellency that our recognition of any government in Mexico so long as it was sustained by foreign arms was impossible; that the logic of the situation required the independence of Mexico to be established by the withdrawal of all foreign soldiers before our government could formally recognize a government accused of owing its existence to their presence.

I am sorry to trouble your excellency with a rectification of a misapprehension which may seem trifling, but which also may acquire importance from the circumstances under which it has been submitted to the public.

I avail myself of this occasion to renew, &c., &c.

JOHN BIGELOW.

His Excellency Monsieur DROUYN DE LHUYS,
Minister of Foreign Affairs.

Mr. Drouyn de Lhuys to Mr. Bigelow.

PARIS, *February* 8, 1866.

SIR: I have received the letter which you have done me the honor to write me, dated the 7th February, on the occasion of a despatch recently published, in which I made allusion to a conversation which we had together upon the subject of Mexican affairs. Recalling that conversation, you have thought proper to define its terms. The report of it which you give is in consonance with my own recollection, and, as I construe it, does not contain any fact in contradiction to the despatch to which you refer. It is exact that, in the opinion which you then expressed, the recognition of the emperor Maximilian by the federal government should be preceded by the evacuation of Mexico by the French troops; while, according to my view, this evacuation should not take place until after the recognition of the Washington cabinet, which, by contributing to the consolidation of the new state of things established in Mexico, would have precisely the effect of facilitating and hastening the recall of our troops. You objected that your government could not decide to recognize an authority sustained by the presence of a foreign army, but, you added, it might be possible, on the one hand, that the government of the Emperor, seeing the United States ready to enter into regular relations with Mexico if that country were evacuated by the French troops, might determine to press the return of his soldiers; on the other hand, that the United States, being informed of the intention of the government of the Emperor, might show more disposition to entertain the idea of recognition. In thus associating the conditions from which an agreement might result, it was to be hoped that our cabinets might find in them the elements of a solution equally satisfactory to both.

I cannot but render homage, sir, to the spirit of loyalty and conciliation which dictated this language to you. But the hypothesis which we examined together remained subject to the appreciation of your government, whose judgment you reserved. The cabinet of Washington occupying a different point of view, the suggestions upon which our conversation turned have been without result.

Accept, sir, the assurances of my high consideration.

DROUYN DE LHUYS.

JOHN BIGELOW, Esq., *&c.*, *&c.*, *&c.*

Mr. Bigelow to Mr. Seward.

No. 270.] LEGATION OF THE UNITED STATES,
Paris, February 12, 1866.

SIR: The discussion of that portion of the senate address which related to the United States was disposed of on Saturday without debate. The paragraph relating to Mexico was voted after a brief speech from Marshal Forey, a report of which will be found in the *Moniteur* of the 11th instant. The part which the marshal took in planting the imperial flag in Mexico makes him its natural protector everywhere. He proved, however, rather more imperialist than the Emperior himself. He said that, instead of diminishing the French force in Mexico, it should rather be increased, in order to hasten the moment when the withdrawal of the French flag would be possible. When he had closed, the minister of state took occasion to say that the policy of the government, as given in the discourse from the throne, would not be modified by anything that had fallen from the marshal. There is either a difference of opinion among the intimate counsellors of his Majesty in regard to what is to be accomplished before the withdrawal of the French troops from Mexico, or there is a difference of opinion in regard to the means necessary for its accomplishment. Time will soon disclose which.

I am, sir, with great respect, your very obedient servant,

JOHN BIGELOW.

Hon. WILLIAM H. SEWARD,
Secretary of State, &c., &c., &c.

Mr. Seward to the Marquis de Montholon.

DEPARTMENT OF STATE,
Washington, February 12, 1866.

SIR: On the 6th of December I had the honor to submit to you in writing, for the information of the Emperor, a communication upon the subject of affairs in Mexico, as affected by the presence of French armed forces in that country. On the 29th of January thereafter you favored me with a reply to that communication, which reply had been transmitted to you by Mr. Drouyn de Lhuys, under the date of the 9th of the same month. I have submitted it to the President of the United States. It is now made my duty to revert to the interesting question which has thus been brought under discussion.

In the first place I take notice of the points which are made by Mr. Drouyn de Lhuys.

He declares that the French expedition into Mexico had in it nothing hostile to the institutions of the New World, and still less of anything hostile to the United States. As proofs of this friendly statement, he refers to the aid in blood and treasure which France contributed in our revolutionary war to the cause of our national independence; to the preliminary proposition that France made to us that we should join her in her expedition to Mexico; and, finally, to the neutrality which France has practiced in the painful civil war through which we have just successfully passed. It gives me pleasure to acknowledge that the assurances thus given on the present occasion that the French expedition, in its original design, had no political objects or motives, harmonize entirely with expressions which abound in the earlier correspondence of the minister of foreign affairs, which arose out of the war between France and Mexico.

We accept with especial pleasure the reminiscences of our traditional friendship.

Mr. Drouyn de Lhuys next assures us that the French government is disposed to hasten, as much as possible, the recall of its troops from Mexico. We hail the announcement as being a virtual promise of relief to this government from the apprehensions and anxieties which were the burden of that communication of mine, which Mr. Drouyn de Lhuys has had under consideration.

Mr. Drouyn de Lhuys proceeds to declare that the only aim of France, in pursuing her enterprise in Mexico, has been to follow up the satisfaction to which she had a right after having resorted to coercive measures, when measures of every other form had been exhausted. Mr. Drouyn de Lhuys says that it is known how many and legitimate were the claims of French subjects which caused the resort to arms. He then reminds us how, on a former occasion, the United States had waged war on Mexico. On this point it seems equally necessary and proper to say, that the war thus referred to was not made nor sought by the United States, but was accepted by them under provocations of a very grave character. The transaction is past, and the necessity and justice of the proceedings of the United States are questions which now rest only within the province of history. France, I think, will acknowledge, that neither in the beginning of our Mexican war nor in its prosecution, nor in the terms on which we retired from that successful contest, did the United States assume any position inconsistent with the principles which are now maintained by us in regard to the French expedition in Mexico.

We are, as we have been, in relations of amity and friendship equally with France and with Mexico, and therefore we cannot, consistently with those relations, constitute ourselves a judge of the original merits of the war which is waged between them. We can speak concerning that war only so far as we are affected by its bearing upon ourselves and upon republican and American institutions on this continent.

Mr. Drouyn de Lhuys declares that the French army, in entering Mexico, did not carry monarchical traditions in the folds of its flag. In this connexion he refers to the fact that there were at the time of the expedition a number of influential men in Mexico who despaired of obtaining order out of the conditions of the republican rule then existing there, and who, therefore, cherished the idea of falling back upon monarchy. In this connexion, we are further reminded that one of the later presidents of Mexico offered to use his power for the re-establishment of royalty. We are further informed that at the time of the French invasion the persons before referred to deemed the moment to have arrived for making an appeal to the people of Mexico in favor of monarchy. Mr. Drouyn de Lhuys remarks that the French government did not deem it a duty to discourage that supreme effort of a powerful party, which had its origin long anterior to the French expedition.

Mr. Drouyn de Lhuys observes that the Emperor, faithful to maxims of public right, which he holds in common with the United States, declared on that occasion that the question of change of institutions rested solely on the suffrages of the Mexican people. In support of this statement, Mr. Drouyn de Lhuys gives us a copy of a letter which the Emperor addressed to the commander-in-chief of the French expedition, on the capture of Puebla, which letter contained the following words: "Our object, you know, is not to impose on the Mexicans a government against their will, nor to make our success aid the triumph of any party whatsoever. I desire that Mexico may rise to a new life, and that soon, regenerated by a government founded on the national will, on principles of order and of progress, and of respect for the law of nations, she may acknowledge by her friendly relations that she owes to France her repose and her prosperity."

Mr. Drouyn de Lhuys pursues his argument by saying that the Mexican people have spoken; that the Emperor Maximilian has been called by the voice of the country; that his government has appeared to the Emperor of the French to be of a nature adequate to restore peace to the nation, and, on its part, peace to international relations, and that he has therefore given it his support. Mr. Drouyn de Lhuys thereupon presents the following as a true statement of the present case: France went to Mexico to exercise the right of war, which is exercised by the United States, and not in virtue of any purpose of intervention, concerning which she recognizes the same doctrine with the United States. France went there not to bring about a monarchical proselytism, but to obtain reparations and guarantees which she ought to claim; and, being there, she now sustains the government which is founded on the consent of the people, because she expects from that government the just satisfaction of her wrongs, as well as the securities indispensable to the future. As she does not seek the satisfaction of an exclusive interest, nor the realization of any ambitious schemes, so she now wishes to recall what remains in Mexico of the army corps which France has sent there at the moment when she will be able to do so with safety to French citizens and with due respect for herself.

I am aware how delicate the discussion is to which Mr. Drouyn de Lhuys thus invites me. France is entitled, by every consideration of respect and friendship, to interpret for herself the objects of the expedition, and of the whole of her proceedings in Mexico. Her explanation of those motives and objects is, therefore, accepted on our part with the consideration and confidence which we expect for explanations of our own when assigned to France or any other friendly power. Nevertheless, it is my duty to insist that, whatever were the intentions, purposes, and objects of France, the proceedings which were adopted by a class of Mexicans for subverting the republican government there, and for availing themselves of French intervention to establish on its ruins an imperial monarchy, are regarded by the United States as having been taken without the authority, and prosecuted against the will and opinions, of the Mexican people. For these reasons it seems to this government that, in supporting institutions thus established in derogation of the inalienable rights of the people of Mexico, the original purposes and objects of the French expedition, though they have not been, as a military demand of satisfaction, abandoned, nor lost out of view by the Emperor of the French, were, nevertheless, left to fall into a condition in which they seem to have become subordinate to a political revolution, which certainly would not have occurred if France had not forcibly intervened, and which, judging from the genius and character of the Mexican people, would not now be maintained by them if that armed intervention should cease. The United States have not seen any satisfactory evidence that the people of Mexico have spoken, and have called into being or accepted the so-called empire which it is insisted has been set up in their capital. The United States, as I have remarked on other occasions, are of opinion that such an acceptance could not have been freely procured or lawfully taken at any time in the presence of the French army of invasion. The withdrawal of the French forces is deemed necessary to allow such a proceeding to be taken by Mexico. Of course the Emperor of France is entitled to determine the aspect in which the Mexican situation ought to be regarded by him. Nevertheless, the view which I have thus presented is the one which this nation has accepted. It therefore recognizes, and must continue to recognize, in Mexico only the ancient republic, and it can in no case consent to involve itself, either directly or indirectly, in relation with or recognition of the institution of the Prince Maximilian in Mexico.

This position is held, I believe, without one dissenting voice by our countrymen. I do not presume to say that this opinion of the American people is accepted or will be adopted generally by other foreign powers, or by the public opinion of mankind. The Emperor is quite competent to form a judgment upon this important point for himself. I cannot, however, properly exclude the observation that, while this question affects by its bearings, incidentally, every republican state in the American hemisphere, every one of those states has adopted the judgment which, on the behalf of the United States, is herein expressed. Under these circumstances it has happened, either rightfully or wrongfully, that the presence of European armies in Mexico, maintaining a European prince with imperial attributes, without her consent and against her will, is deemed a source of apprehension and danger, not alone to the United States, but also to all the independent and sovereign republican States founded on the American continent and its adjacent islands. France is acquainted with the relations of the United States towards the other American States to which I have referred, and is aware of the sense that the American people entertain in regard to the obligations and duties due from them to those other States. We are thus brought back to the single question which formed the subject of my communication of the 6th of December last, namely, the desirableness of an adjustment of a question the continuance of which must be necessarily prejudicial to the harmony and friendship which have hitherto always existed between the United States and France.

This government does not undertake to say how the claims of indemnity and satisfaction, for which the war which France is waging in Mexico was originally instituted, shall now be adjusted, in discontinuing what, in its progress, has become a war of political intervention dangerous to the United States and to republican institutions in the American hemisphere. Recognizing France and the republic of Mexico as belligerents engaged in war, we leave all questions concerning those claims and indemnities to them. The United States rest content with submitting to France the exigencies of an embarrassing situation in Mexico, and expressing the hope that France may find some manner which shall at once be consistent with her interest and honor, and with the principles and interest of the United States, to relieve that situation without injurious delay.

Mr. Drouyn de Lhuys repeats on this occasion what he has heretofore written, namely, that it depends much upon the federal government to facilitate their desire of the withdrawal of the French forces from Mexico. He argues that the position which the United States have assumed has nothing incompatible with the existence of monarchical institutions in Mexico. He draws to his support on this point the fact that the President of the United States, as well as the Secretary of State, in official papers, disclaim all thought of propagandism on the American continent in favor of republican institutions. Mr. Drouyn de Lhuys draws in, also, the fact that the United States hold friendly relations with the Emperor of Brazil, as they held similar relations with Iturbide, the Mexican Emperor, in 1822. From these positions Mr. Drouyn de Lhuys makes the deduction that neither any fundamental maxim, nor any precedent in the diplomatic history of this country, creates any necessary antagonism between the United States and the form of government over which the Prince Maximilian presides in the ancient capital of Mexico.

I do not think it would be profitable, and therefore I am not desirous to engage in the discussions which Mr. Drouyn de Lhuys has thus raised. It will be sufficient for my purpose, on the present occasion, to assert and to give reassurance of our desire to facilitate the withdrawal of the French troops from Mexico, and, for that purpose, to do whatsoever shall be compatible with the positions we have heretofore taken upon that subject, and with our just regard to the sovereign rights of the republic of Mexico. Further or otherwise than this France could not expect us to go. Having thus reassured France, it seems necessary to state anew the position of this government, as it was set forth in my letter of the 6th of December, as follows: Republican and domestic institutions on this continent are deemed most congenial with and most beneficial to the United States. Where the people of any country, like Brazil now, or Mexico in 1822, have voluntarily established and acquiesced in monarchical institutions of their own choice, free from all foreign control or intervention, the United

States do not refuse to maintain relations with such governments, or seek through propagandism, by force or intrigue, to overthrow those institutions. On the contrary, where a nation has established institutions republican and domestic, similar to our own, the United States assert in their behalf that no foreign nation can rightfully intervene by force to subvert republican institutions and establish those of an antagonistical character.

Mr. Drouyn de Lhuys seems to think that I have made a double reproach against the Prince Maximilian's alleged government, of the difficulty it encounters and of the assistance it borrows from foreign powers. In that respect Mr. Drouyn de Lhuys contends that the obstacles and the resistance which Maximilian has been obliged to wrestle with have in themselves nothing especial against the form of the institutions which he is supposed by Mr. Drouyn de Lhuys to have established. Mr. Drouyn de Lhuys maintains that Maximilian's government is undergoing the lot quite common to new powers, while, above all, it has the misfortune to have to bear the consequences of discords which have been produced under a previous government. Mr. Drouyn de Lhuys represents this misfortune and this lot to be in effect the misfortune and lot of governments which have not found armed competitors, and which have enjoyed in peace an uncontrolled authority. Mr. Drouyn de Lhuys alleges that revolts and intestine wars are the normal condition of Mexico, and he further insists that the opposition made by some military chiefs to the establishment of an empire under Maximilian is only the natural sequence of the same want of discipline, and the same prevalence of anarchy, of which his predecessors in power in Mexico have been victims. It is not the purpose, nor would it be consistent with the character of the United States, to deny that Mexico has been for a long time the theatre of faction and intestine war. The United States confess this fact with regret, all the more sincere, because the experience of Mexico has been not only painful for her own people, but has been also of unfortunate evil influence on other nations.

On the other hand, it is neither a right of the United States, nor consistent with their friendly disposition towards Mexico, to reproach the people of that country with her past calamities, much less to invoke or approve of the infliction of punishment upon them by strangers for their political errors. The Mexican population have, and their situation has, some peculiarities which are doubtless well understood by France. Early in the present century they were forced, by convictions which mankind cannot but respect, to cast off a foreign monarchical rule which they deemed incompatible with their welfare and aggrandizement. They were forced, at the same time, by convictions which the world must respect, to attempt the establishment of republican institutions, without the full experience and practical education and habits which would render those institutions all at once firm and satisfactory. Mexico was a theatre of conflict between European commercial, ecclesiastical, and political institutions and dogmas, and novel American institutions and ideas. She had African slavery, colonial restrictions, and ecclesiastical monopolies. In the chief one of these particulars she had a misfortune which was shared by the United States, while the latter were happily exempted from the other misfortunes. We cannot forget that Mexico, sooner and more readily than the United States, abolished slavery. We cannot deny that all the anarchy in Mexico, of which Mr. Drouyn de Lhuys complains, was necessarily, and even wisely, endured in the attempts to lay sure foundations of broad republican liberty.

I do not know whether France can rightfully be expected to concur in this view, which alleviates, in our mind, the errors, misfortunes, and calamities of Mexico. However this may be, we fall back upon the principal that no foreign state can rightly intervene in such trials as those of Mexico, and on the ground of a desire to correct those errors, deprive the people there of their natural right of domestic and republican freedom. All the injuries and wrongs which Mexico can have committed against any other state have found a severe punishment in consequences which legitimately followed their commission. Nations are not authorized to correct each other's errors except so far as is necessary to prevent or redress injuries affecting themselves. If one state has a right to intervene in any other state, to establish discipline, constituting itself a judge of the occasion, then every state has the same right to intervene in the affairs of every other nation, being itself alone the arbiter, both in regard to the time and the occasion. The principle of intervention, thus practically carried out, would seem to render all sovereignty and independence, and even all international peace and amity, uncertain and fallacious.

Mr. Drouyn de Lhuys proceeds to remark, that as for the support which Maximilian receives from the French army, as well also as for the support which has been lent to him by Belgian and Austrian volunteers, those supports cause no hindrance to the freedom of his resolutions in the affairs of his government. Mr. Drouyn de Lhuys asks what state is there that does not need allies, either to form or to defend. As to the great powers, such as France and England, do they not constantly maintain foreign troops in their armies? When the United States fought for their independence, did the aid given by France cause that movement to cease to be truly national? Shall it be said that the contest between the United States and the recent insurgents was not in a like manner a national war, because thousands of Irishmen and Germans were found fighting under the flag of the Union? Arguing from anticipated answers to these questions, Mr. Drouyn de Lhuys reaches a conclusion that the character of Maximilian's government cannot be contested, nor can its efforts to consolidate itself be contested, on the ground of the employment of foreign troops.

Mr. Drouyn de Lhuys, in this argument, seems to us to have overlooked two important facts, namely: first, that the United States, in this correspondence, have assigned definite limits to the right of alliance incompatible with our assent to his argument; and secondly, the fact that the United States have not at any time accepted the supposed government of the Prince Maximilian as a constitutional or legitimate form of government in Mexico, capable or entitled to form alliances.

Mr. Drouyn de Lhuys then arranges, in a graphic manner, the advantages that have arisen, or are to arise, to the United States, from the successful establishment of the supposed empire in Mexico. Instead of a country unceasingly in trouble, and which has given us so many subjects of complaint, and against which we ourselves have been obliged to make war, he shows us in Mexico a pacific country, under a beneficent imperial sway, offering henceforth measures of security and vast openings to our commerce, a country far from injuring our rights and hurting our influences. And he assures us that, above all other nations, the United States are most likely to profit by the work which is being accomplished by Prince Maximilian in Mexico. These suggestions are as natural on the part of France as they are friendly to the United States. The United States are not insensible to the desirableness of political and commercial reform in the adjoining country; but their settled principles, habits, and convictions forbid them to look for such changes in this hemisphere to foreign, royal, or imperial institutions, founded upon a forcible subversion of republican institutions. The United States, in their customary sobriety, regard no beneficial results which could come from such a change in Mexico as sufficient to overbalance the injury which they must directly suffer by the overthrow of the republican government in Mexico.

Mr. Drouyn de Lhuys at the end of his very elaborate and able review, recapitulates his exposition in the following words: "The United States acknowledge the right we had to make war in Mexico. On the other part, we admit, as they do, the principle of non-intervention. This double postulate includes, as it seems to me, the elements of an agreement. The right to make war, which belongs, as Mr. Seward declares, to every sovereign nation, implies the right to secure the results of war. We have not gone across the ocean merely for the purpose of showing our power, and of inflicting chastisement on the Mexican government. After a train of fruitless remonstrances, it was our duty to demand guarantees against the recurrence of violence from which our country had suffered so cruelly, and those guarantees we could not look for from a government whose bad faith we had proved on so many occasions. We find them now engaged in the establishment of a regular government, which shows itself disposed to honestly keep its engagements. In this relation we hope that the legitimate object of our expedition will soon be reached, and we are striving to make with the emperor Maximilian arrangements which, by satisfying our interests and our honor, will permit us to consider at an end the service of the army upon Mexican soil. The Emperor has given an order to write in this same sense to our minister at Mexico. We fall back at that moment on the principle of non-intervention, and from that moment accept it as the rule of our conduct. Our interest, no less than our honor, commands us to claim from all the uniform application of it. Trusting the spirit of equity which animates the cabinet of Washington, we expect from it the assurance that the American people will themselves conform to the law which they invoke, by observing, in regard to Mexico, a strict neutrality. When you [meaning the Marquis de Montholon] shall have informed me of the resolution of the federal government, I shall be able to indicate to you the nature of the results of our negotiation with the emperor Maximilian for the return of our troops."

I have already, and not without much reluctance, made the comments upon the arguments of Mr. Drouyn de Lhuys which seem to be necessary to guard against the inference of concurrence in questionable positions which might be drawn from our entire silence. I think that I can, therefore, afford to leave his recapitulation of those arguments without such an especial review as would necessarily be prolix, and perhaps hypercritical. The United States have not claimed, and they do not claim, to know what arrangements the Emperor may make for the adjustment of claims for indemnity and redress in Mexico. It would be, on our part, an act of intervention to take cognizance of them. We adhere to our position that the war in question has become a political war between France and the republic of Mexico, injurious and dangerous to the United States and to the republican cause, and we ask only that in that aspect and character it may be brought to an end. It would be illiberal on the part of the United States to suppose that, in desiring or pursuing preliminary arrangements, the Emperor contemplates the establishment in Mexico, before withdrawing his forces, of the very institutions which constitute the material ground of the exceptions taken against his intervention by the United States. It would be still more illiberal to suppose for a moment that he expects the United States to bind themselves indirectly to acquiesce in or support the obnoxious institutions.

On the contrary, we understand him as announcing to us his immediate purpose to bring to an end the service of his armies in Mexico, to withdraw them, and in good faith to fall back, without stipulation or condition on our part, upon the principle of non-intervention upon which he is henceforth agreed with the United States. We cannot understand his appeal to us for an assurance that we ourselves will abide by our own principles of non-intervention in any other sense than as the expression, in a friendly way, of his expectation that when the people of Mexico shall have been left absolutely free from the operation, effects, and consequences of his own political and military intervention, we will ourselves respect their self-established sovereignty and independence. In this view of the subject only can we consider his appeal pertinent to the case. Regarding it in only this aspect, we must meet the Emperor frankly. He knows the form and character of this government. The nation can be bound only by treaties which have the concurrence of the President and two-thirds of the Senate. A formal treaty would be objectionable as unnecessary, except as a disavowal of bad faith on our part, to disarm suspicion in regard to a matter concerning which we have given no cause for questioning our loyalty, or else such a treaty would be refused upon the ground that the application for it by the Emperor of France was unhappily a suggestion of some sinister or unfriendly reservation or purpose on his part in withdrawing from Mexico. Diplomatic assurances given by the President in behalf of the nation can at best be but the expressions of confident expectation on his part that the personal administration, ever changing in conformity and adaptation to the national will, does not misunderstand the settled principles and policy of the American people. Explanations cannot properly be made by the President in any case wherein it would be deemed, for any reason, objectionable on grounds of public policy by the treaty-making power of the government to introduce or entertain negotiations.

With these explanations I proceed to say that, in the opinion of the President, France need not for a moment delay her promised withdrawal of military forces from Mexico, and her putting the principle of non-intervention into full and complete practice in regard to Mexico, through any apprehension that the United States will prove unfaithful to the principles and policy in that respect which, on their behalf, it has been my duty to maintain in this now very lengthened correspondence. The practice of this government, from its beginning, is a guarantee to all nations of the respect of the American people for the free sovereignty of the people in every other state. We received the instruction from Washington. We applied it sternly in our early intercourse even with France. The same principle and practice have been uniformly inculcated by all our statesmen, interpreted by all our jurists, maintained by all our Congresses, and acquiesced in without practical dissent on all occasions by the American people. It is in reality the chief element of foreign intercourse in our history. Looking simply toward the point to which our attention has been steadily confined, the relief of the Mexican embarrassments without disturbing our relations with France, we shall be gratified when the Emperor shall give to us, either through the channel of your esteemed correspondence or otherwise, definitive information of the time when French military operations may be expected to cease in Mexico.

Here I might perhaps properly conclude this note. Some obscurity, however, might be supposed to rest upon the character of the principle of non-intervention, which we are authorized to suppose is now agreed upon between the United States and France as a rule for their future government in regard to Mexico. I shall, therefore, reproduce on this occasion, by way of illustration, some of the forms in which that principle has been maintained by us in our previous intercourse with France. In 1861, when alluding to the possibility that the Emperor might be invoked by rebel emissaries from the United States to intervene in our civil war, I observed: "The Emperor of France has given abundant proofs that he considers the people in every country the rightful source of authority, and that its only legitimate objects are their safety, freedom, and welfare."

I wrote, also, on the same occasion, these words to Mr. Dayton: "I have thus, under the President's direction, placed before you a simple, unexaggerated, and dispassionate statement of the origin, nature, and purposes of the contest in which the United States are now involved. I have done so only for the purpose of deducing from it the arguments you will find it necessary to employ in opposing the application of the so-called Confederate States to the government of his Majesty the Emperor for a recognition of their independence and sovereignty. The President neither expects nor desires any intervention, or even any favor, from the government of France, or any other, in this emergency. Whatever else he may consent to do, he will never invoke nor even admit foreign interference or influence in this or any other controversy in which the government of the United States may be engaged with any portion of the American people.

* * * * * * * * *

"Foreign intervention would oblige us to treat those who should yield it as allies of the insurrectionary party, and to carry on the war against them as enemies.

"However other European powers may mistake, his Majesty is the last one of those sovereigns to misapprehend the nature of this controversy. He knows that the revolution of 1776, in this country, was a successful contest of the great American idea of free, popular government against resisting prejudices and errors. He knows that the conflict awakened the sympathies of mankind, and that ultimately the triumph of that idea has been hailed by all European nations. He knows at what cost European nations for a time resisted the progress of that idea, and, perhaps, is not unwilling to confess how much France, especially, has profited by it. He will not fail to recognize the presence of that one great idea in the present conflict, nor will he mistake the side on which it will be found. It is, in short, the very principle of universal suffrage, with its claim of obedience to its decrees, on which the government of France is built, that is put in issue by the insurrection here, and is in this emergency to be vindicated and more effectually than ever established by the government of the United States."

In writing upon the same subject to Mr. Dayton, on the 30th of May, 1861, I said: "Nothing is wanting to that success except that foreign nations shall leave us, as is our right, to manage our own affairs in our own way. They, as well as we, can only suffer by their intervention. No one, we are sure, can judge better than the Emperor of France how dangerous and deplorable would be the emergency that should intrude Europeans into the political contests of the American people."

In declining the offer of French mediation, on the 8th of June, 1861, I wrote to Mr. Dayton: "The present paramount duty of the government is to save the integrity of the American Union. Absolute, self-sustaining independence is the first and most indispensable element of national existence. This is a republican nation; all its domestic affairs must be conducted and even adjusted in constitutional forms, and upon constitutional, republican principles. This is an American nation, and its internal affairs must not only be conducted with reference to its peculiar continental position, but by and through American agencies alone."

On the first of August, 1862, Mr. Adams was instructed by this government in the following words: "Did the European states which found and occupied this continent almost without effort then understand its real destiny and purposes? Have they ever yet fully understood and accepted them? Has anything but disappointment upon disappointment and disaster upon disaster resulted from their misapprehensions? After near four hundred years of such disappointments and disasters, is the way of Providence in regard to America still so mysterious that it cannot be understood and confessed? Columbus, it was said, had given a new world to the kingdoms of Castile and Leon. What has become of the sovereignty of Spain in America? Richelieu occupied and fortified a large portion of the continent, extending from the Gulf of Mexico to the straits of Belle Isle. Does France yet retain that important appendage to the crown of her sovereign? Great Britain acquired a dominion here surpassing by a hundred-fold in length and breadth the native realm. Has not a large portion of it been already formally resigned? To whom have those vast dominions, with those founded by the Portuguese, the Dutch, and the Swedes, been resigned but to American nations, the growth of European colonists and exiles, who have come hither, bringing with them the arts, the civilization, and the virtues of Europe? Has not the change been beneficial to society on this continent? Has it not been more beneficial even to Europe itself than continued European domination, if it had been possible, could have been? The American nations which have grown up here are free and self-governing. They have made themselves so from inherent vigor and in obedience to absolute necessity. Is it possible for European states to plunge them again into a colonial state and hold them there? Would it be desirable for them and for Europe, if it were possible? The balance of power among the nations of Europe is maintained not without numerous strong armies and frequent conflicts, while the sphere of political ambition there is bounded by the ocean which surrounds that continent. Would it be possible to maintain it at all, if this vast continent, with all its populations, their resources, and their forces, should once again be brought within that sphere?

* * * * * * *

"On the contrary of all these suppositions, is it not manifest that these American nations were called into existence to be the home of freemen; that the states of Europe have been intrusted by Providence with their tutelage, but that tutelage and all its responsibilities and powers are necessarily withdrawn to the relief and benefit of the parties and of mankind, when these parties become able to choose their own system of government, and to make and administer their own laws? If they err in this choice, or in the conduct of their affairs, it will be found wise to leave them, like all other states, the privilege and responsibility of detecting and correcting the error, by which they are, of course, the principal sufferers."

On the 8th of May, 1862, Mr. Dayton was instructed to express to Mr. Thouvenel "the desire of the United States that peaceful relations may soon be restored between France and Mexico upon a basis just to both parties, and favorable to the independence and sovereignty of the people of Mexico, which is equally the interest of France and all other enlightened nations."

On the 21st of June, 1862, Mr. Dayton was authorized to speak on behalf of the United States concerning the condition of Mexico in these words: "France has a right to make war against Mexico, and to determine for herself the cause. We have a right to insist that France shall not improve the war she makes to raise up in Mexico an anti-republican or anti-American government, or to maintain such a government there."

Accept, sir, a renewed assurance of my high consideration.

WILLIAM H. SEWARD.

The MARQUIS DE MONTHOLON, *&c., &c., &c.*

Mr. Seward to Mr. Bigelow.

No. 388.] DEPARTMENT OF STATE,
Washington, February 12, 1866.

SIR: I enclose for your information a copy of a note of this date, which I have addressed to the Marquis de Montholon, in reply to Mr. Drouyn de Lhuys' communication of the 9th of January, upon the subject of the French intervention in Mexico.

I am, sir, your obedient servant,

WILLIAM H. SEWARD.

JOHN BIGELOW, Esq., *&c., &c., &c.*

Mr. Seward to Mr. Bigelow.

No. 390.] DEPARTMENT OF STATE,
Washington, February 12, 1866.

SIR: Your despatch of January 16, No. 243, has been received. It was accompanied by a copy of a correspondence which took place between you and Mr. Drouyn de Lhuys, on the subject of certain decrees which have been made by the authorities now existing in the city of Mexico, concerning emigration and colonization in that country. We are not able to agree with the French government in the opinion which it has expressed, that the subject does not fall properly within the province of the Emperor of France. The President hopes, however, that the anticipated relief of the embarrassing situation in Mexico, which is the subject of another correspondence between the two powers, will facilitate a solution of the special matter which has arisen out of the before-mentioned decrees. You may make this expectation known to Mr. Drouyn de Lhuys.

I am, sir, your obedient servant,

WILLIAM H. SEWARD.

JOHN BIGELOW, Esq., *&c., &c., &c.*

Mr. Bigelow to Mr. Seward.

[Extract.]

No. 272.] LEGATION OF THE UNITED STATES,
Paris, February 15, 1866.

SIR: I learn from an unofficial source that Gregorio Barandiran, the diplomatic representative of the Archduke Maximilian at Vienna, formerly secretary of legation under Señor Robles at Washington, is now at Paris, for money to fit out 10,000 Austrians, which, he says, are ready to embark from Trieste for Mexico. The Mexican commissioner informed him that there was no money in his hands. I am not sure of learning the result of the minister's suit here, as the money, if furnished, must come through indirect and concealed channels.

* * * * * * * *

I am, sir, with great respect, your obedient servant,

JOHN BIGELOW.

Hon. WILLIAM H. SEWARD,
Secretary of State, &c., &c., &c.

Mr. Seward to Mr. Bigelow.

No. 402.] DEPARTMENT OF STATE,
Washington, March 1, 1866.

SIR: Your very interesting despatch of the 1st of February last, No. 257, and its accompaniments, by which I am informed of the contents of the Documens Diplomatique, communicated to the corps legislatif on Monday, the 29th of January, by the French foreign office, and the popular impression in France concerning the Mexican question as affected by the publication of these papers, have been received. I thank you for the complete information you have placed at my disposal upon this important subject.

I am, sir, your obedient servant,

WILLIAM H. SEWARD.

JOHN BIGELOW, Esq., *&c., &c., &c.*

Mr. Seward to Mr. Bigelow.

No. 404.] DEPARTMENT OF STATE,
Washington, March 2, 1866.

SIR: Your despatch of February 8, No. 264, has been received. It recites the passages which are of chief interest to the United States in the reply proposed by the senate commission in France to the discourse which the Emperor pronounced at the opening of the legislature. Your comments upon those passages are deemed just and proper; nevertheless, the passages themselves are not regarded as requiring especial remark from this department at the present time.

I am, sir, your obedient servant,

WILLIAM H. SEWARD.

JOHN BIGELOW, Esq., *&c.*

Mr. Seward to Mr. Bigelow.

No. 405.] DEPARTMENT OF STATE, *Washington, March* 2, 1866.

SIR: I have received your despatch of the 9th of February, No. 268, and I have placed it with pleasure upon the records of the department. It shows that you have compromised no part of the position of this government in your conversation with Mr. Drouyn de Lhuys, and I notice with satisfaction the friendly spirit with which he accepts your explanation. It is hardly necessary to say that the misapprehensions which you have now corrected excited no particular uneasiness here.

I am, sir, your obedient servant,

WILLIAM H. SEWARD.

JOHN BIGELOW, Esq., *&c.*

Mr. Seward to Mr. Bigelow.

No. 408.] DEPARTMENT OF STATE, *Washington, March* 5, 1866.

SIR: I have the honor to acknowledge the receipt of your despatch of the 15th of February, No. 276, and I approve of the manner in which you have executed my instruction, No. 336. I feel, as Mr. Drouyn de Lhuys seems to feel, that it is a painful thing to contemplate even the possible occurrence of war between our country and France. Let us hope that the negotiations in which we are engaged will remove the ground for such apprehension. Should this hope fail, you may in your discretion revert to the matter of our special arrangement respecting postal steamers.

I am, sir, your obedient servant,

WILLIAM H. SEWARD.

JOHN BIGELOW, Esq., *&c.*

Mr. Seward to Mr. Bigelow.

No. 411.] DEPARTMENT OF STATE, *Washington, March* 5, 1866.

SIR: Your despatch of the 15th ultimo, No. 273, together with its accompaniments, a copy of your communication to Mr. Drouyn de Lhuys, and of his reply thereto, relative to the authenticity of the published letter of Marshal Bazaine to the republican general in Mexico, has been received.

Your inquiry seems to have been discreet, and it is approved.

I am, sir, your obedient servant,

WILLIAM H. SEWARD.

JOHN BIGELOW, Esq., *&c.*

Mr. Bigelow to Mr. Seward.

No. 282.] LEGATION OF THE UNITED STATES,
Paris, March 6, 1866.

SIR: On the 2d of March, in the corps legislatif, the president, Count Walewski, after reading the paragraph of the address to the throne relative to Mexico, gave the floor to Mr. Rouher, minister of state, who asked in behalf of the government that the paragraph should be voted without discussion, alleging that, considering the present state of diplomatic negotiations already initiated with the emperor Maximilian, the discussion of Mexican questions was at this time inopportune. This proposition was adopted, but not without a spirited debate, in the course of which Mr. Rouher repeated, in language rather more emphatic than the government has formerly used, that the French troops were soon to be withdrawn from Mexico; and, in addition, gave positive assurances that a future opportunity would be afforded for the thorough examination of the Mexican question in all its aspects.

The paragraph was then adopted, and the amendment of the minority rejected, the members of the opposition protesting that the opinion of the assembly was not to be prejudiced by this merely formal vote.

I transmit a copy of the paragraph adopted, the amendment of the opposition, and an extract from the remarks of Mr. Rouher.

I am, sir, with great respect, your obedient servant,

JOHN BIGELOW.

Hon. WILLIAM H. SEWARD,
Secretary of State, Washington, D. C.

[Enclosure 1 to despatch 282.]

"Our expedition to Mexico approaches its close. The country has received this assurance with satisfaction. Led to Mexico by the imperious duty of protecting our countrymen against odious acts of violence, and to obtain the redress of legitimate grievances, our soldiers and our sailors have worthily fulfilled the task which your Majesty has confided to their devotion. This expedition has attested once more, in those distant lands, the disinterestedness and the power of France. The people of the United States, who have long known the loyalty of our policy and the traditional sympathies by which it is inspired, have no cause to take umbrage at the presence of our troops upon Mexican soil. To wish to subordinate their recall to any other conveniences than our own, would be to attack our rights and our honor. You have these in charge, sire, and the legislative body knows that you will watch over them with a solicitude worthy of France and of your name." (Paragraph of the address to the throne, adopted 2d March, 1866.)

[Enclosure 2 to despatch 282.]

"We condemned the expedition to Mexico, at its outset, in calling attention to the embarrassments and sacrifices which it would impose upon France.

"Last year the return of our soldiers was solemnly announced; we regret that we should have encountered a delay not justified by French interests.

"The country has not forgotten the early declaration of the government in regard to the causes of the expedition. It is astonished to see our army devoted to-day to the defence of a foreign throne."

(Amendment proposed by MM. Bethmeout, Garnier-Pages, Jules Favre, Pelletan, Duc de Marmin, Picard, Glais-Bizoin, Javal, and others; rejected March 2, 1866.)

[Enclosure 3 to despatch 282.]

[Extract from the remarks of Mr. Rouher, minister of state, in the legislative body, on the 2d of March.]

"But the speech from the throne expressed to you a thought—that of the early close of our expedition; it declared that the expedition approached its termination. That thought is the common thought of the government and the corps legislatif, and here I have not to distinguish between the majority and the opposition. It is the thought of the public opinion. This thought is expressed in the project of the address.

"Is there a certain shade of differences? Be it so. Let it be reserved.

"What objection should there be, then, gentlemen, that the commission and the corps legislatif should express their sentiments immediately upon this great theme of the early (*prochain*) return of our troops from the shores of the Atlantic and of Mexico, making all reserves in regard to the conduct of the expedition, its results, and its relations with the United States, for a later discussion."

Mr. Seward to Mr. Bigelow.

No. 425.] DEPARTMENT OF STATE,
Washington, March 20, 1866.

SIR: I have to acknowledge the receipt of your despatch of the 15th ultimo, No. 272, in regard to the reports which have come to your ears concerning the attempts of the agents in Europe of Maximilian's government in Mexico to provide for the departure from Trieste of 10,000 Austrians for that country, and to enclose, for your information, a copy of a communication which I have addressed to Mr. Motley, the representative of this government at Vienna, upon the subject. I will thank you to apprise that gentleman of any further information that you may receive concerning this matter, in order that he may govern his proceedings accordingly.

I am, sir, your obedient servant,

WILLIAM H. SEWARD.

JOHN BIGELOW, Esq., *&c., &c., &c.*

Mr. Bigelow to Mr. Seward.

[Confidential.—Extracts.]

LEGATION OF THE UNITED STATES,
Paris, March 22, 1866.

DEAR SIR: The Moniteur of the 21st instant announces that a military convention was signed at Vienna on the 15th between the Austrian government and the representative of Maximilian—supplementary to a convention of the same nature which had been previously concluded between the same parties. The purpose of this engagement, says the Moniteur, is to insure the enrolments necessary to keep full the Austrian corps in Mexico.

In another journal, which I regret that at this moment I am unable to lay my hand upon, I have seen it stated that a line of steamers is to be started from Trieste to Vera Cruz, to ply regularly, from the 1st of April next. The Constitutionnel of the 21st contains also the following paragraph:

"We learn from the Freudenblatt, of Vienna, that the enlistments for Mexico will begin immediately; that the funds had been received from Paris two months since. In general," adds the Vienna journal, "our volunteers in Mexico seem to have made very fair savings, as Colonel Leiser has himself received more than 300,000 francs, to be sent to their friends in Austria. This proves that their wages are paid regularly, and that prices are not as high in Mexico as has been represented."

* * * * * * * *

The Paris correspondent of the London Post stated a few days since that Hidalgo, who is expected here in a few days, would bring the convention, signed by Maximilian, providing for the withdrawal of the French troops from Mexico. The paragraph was generally copied, but finally received a qualified contradiction in two or three of the *officious* journals, which stated that what Hidalgo would bring could not be known till he came, and that when he left, Mr. Salliard had not had time to communicate with Maximilian, &c.

* * * * * * * *

I presume the consul at Trieste and Mr. Motley will inform you of the objects had in view in the establishment of a line of steamers from Trieste to Vera Cruz. They certainly can hardly be of a commercial character.

I am, sir, with great respect, your obedient servant,

JOHN BIGELOW.

Hon. WILLIAM H. SEWARD,
Secretary of State, &c., &c., &c.

Mr. Seward to Mr. Bigelow.

No. 426.] DEPARTMENT OF STATE,
Washington, March 23, 1866.

SIR: Your despatch of the 6th instant, No. 282, informing me of the remarks of Mr. Rouher in the "corps legislatif" upon the amendment proposed by a minority to the address to the throne, has been received, and I have, in reply, to inform you that I consider it interesting, as information of a part of the legislative proceedings of France in regard to French intervention in Mexico.

I am, sir, your obedient servant,

WILLIAM H. SEWARD.

JOHN BIGELOW, Esq., *&c., &c., &c.*

Mr. Bigelow to Mr. Seward.

[Extract.]

No. 297.] LEGATION OF THE UNITED STATES,
Paris, April 6, 1866.

SIR: The Moniteur of yesterday morning announced that, as a sequence to communications exchanged between "M. Dana, minister of France, his excellency Marshal Bazaine, and the Mexican government, the Emperor has decided that the French troops shall evacuate Mexico in three detachments; the first to leave in November, 1866, the second in March, 1867, and the third in November, 1867."

At M. Drouyn de Lhuys' reception yesterday afternoon, I remarked that I supposed the paragraph in the Moniteur might be regarded as an official statement of the result of Baron Salliard's mission. He said it might, and then added that it was substantially what he had prefigured to me in our conversation last fall. He went on to say that the seasons for the debarking of the troops were selected from climatic and sanitary considerations.

* * * * * * * * *

I am, sir, with great respect, your very obedient servant,

JOHN BIGELOW.

Hon. WILLIAM H. SEWARD,
Secretary of State, &c., &c., &c.

The Marquis de Montholon to Mr. Seward.

[Translation.]

LEGATION OF FRANCE TO THE UNITED STATES,
Washington, April 21, 1866.

MR. SECRETARY OF STATE—SIR: I hasten to remit herewith to your excellency copy of a despatch which I at the moment receive from his excellency Mr. Drouyn de Lhuys, and which answers the despatch you were pleased to address to me, relative to Mexican affairs, on the 12th of February last.

Accept, Mr. Secretary of State, the assurances of my high consideration.

MONTHOLON.

Hon. WILLIAM H. SEWARD, *&c., &c., &c.*

Mr. Drouyn de Lhuys to the Marquis de Montholon.

[Translation.]

PARIS, *April* 5, 1866.

SIR: I have read, with all the attention which it deserves, the answer of the Secretary of State to my despatch of the 9th of January last. The scrupulous care with which Mr. Seward has pleased to analyze that despatch, and the extended considerations upon which he has entered to define, in regard to the exposé which I have made of the conduct of France in the affairs of Mexico, the doctrines which are the basis of the international policy of the United States, bear witness in our eyes of the interest which the cabinet of Washington attaches to putting aside all misapprehension.

We find therein the evidence of its desire to cause the sentiments of amity which the traditions of a long alliance have cemented between our two countries, to prevail over the accidental divergencies, often inevitable, in the movement of affairs and the relations of governments. It is in this disposition that we have appreciated the communication which the Secretary of State has addressed to you, the 12th of February last. I will not follow Mr. Seward in the developments he has given to the exposition of the principles which direct the policy of the American Union. It does not appear to me opportune or profitable to prolong, on points of doctrine or of history, a discussion, where we may differ in opinion from the government of the United States, without danger to the interests of the two countries. I think it better to serve those interests by abstaining from discussing assertions—in my opinion very contestable—in order to take action on assurances which may contribute to facilitate our understanding.

We never hesitate to offer to our friends the explanations they ask from us, and we hasten to give to the cabinet of Washington all those which may enlighten it on the purpose we are pursuing in Mexico, and on the loyalty of our intentions. We have said to it, at the same time, that the certainty we should acquire of its resolution to observe in regard to that country, after our departure, a policy of non-intervention, would hasten the moment when it would be possible for us, without compromising the interests which led us there, to withdraw our troops, and put an end to an occupation, the duration of which we are sincerely desirous to abridge. In his despatch of the 12th February last Mr. Seward calls to mind, on his part, that the government of the United States has conformed during the whole course of its history to the rule of conduct which it received from Washington, by practicing invariably the principle of non-intervention, and adds that nothing justifies the apprehension that it should show itself unfaithful in what may concern Mexico. We receive this assurance with entire confidence, and we find therein a sufficient guarantee not any longer to delay the adoption of measures intended to prepare for the return of our army.

The Emperor has decided that the French troops shall evacuate Mexico in three detachments: the first being intended to depart in the month of November, 1866; the second in March, 1867; and the third in the month of November of the same year.

You will please to communicate this decision officially to the Secretary of State.

Receive, Marquis, the assurance of my high consideration.

DROUYN DE LHUYS.

The MARQUIS DE MONTHOLON,
Minister of the Emperor, at Washington.

Mr. Seward to Mr. Bigelow.

No. 438.] DEPARTMENT OF STATE,
Washington, April 21, 1866.

SIR: I have the honor to acknowledge the receipt of your despatch of the 6th of April, No. 297. It is accompanied by a copy of the Moniteur, the official organ of the government of France, to the effect following: "That the Emperor has decided that the French troops shall evacuate Mexico in three detachments: the first to leave in November, 1866; the second in March, 1867; the third in November, 1867."

You inform me that you learn from Mr. Drouyn de Lhuys that the decision mentioned in the Moniteur may be regarded as an official statement of the result of Baron Salliard's mission in Mexico.

Presuming that we may expect very soon to receive a direct communication of the Emperor's views on the subject of the proposed evacuation of Mexico, I think a discussion on our part of the newly presented points in the subject of the French intervention would at the present moment be premature.

I am, sir, your obedient servant,

WILLIAM H. SEWARD.

JOHN BIGELOW, *&c., &c., &c., Paris.*

Mr. Seward to the Marquis de Montholon.

DEPARTMENT OF STATE,
Washington, April 23, 1866.

MY DEAR MARQUIS: I hasten, in advance of the departure of the mail, to acknowledge the receipt of your note of the 21st instant, together with the copy of a despatch you were pleased to give me, which was addressed to you on the 5th instant by Mr. Drouyn de Lhuys, in which the minister for foreign affairs of the empire of France replies to the communication I had the honor to address to you, concerning Mexican affairs, on the 12th of February last.

The subject will early receive the considerate attention of the President of the United States.

I am, my dear Marquis, very faithfully yours,

WILLIAM H. SEWARD.

The MARQUIS DE MONTHOLON, *&c., &c., &c.*

AUSTRIAN TROOPS FOR MEXICO.

Mr. Motley to Mr. Seward.

[Extract.]

No. 138.] UNITED STATES LEGATION,
Vienna, December 18, 1865.

SIR: I think it proper to send you herewith appended, marked A, a translation of a paragraph recently published in the semi-official papers and in the official Gazette of Vienna in regard to the enlistment in Austria for Mexico.

* * * * * *

I have the honor to remain your obedient servant,

J. LOTHROP MOTLEY.

Hon. WILLIAM H. SEWARD,
Secretary of State, Washington.

A.

Extract from the "General Correspondez," and copied into the Vienna Gazette (official) of December 15, 1865.

[Translation.]

We have already taken occasion long ago to contradict in the most decisive manner the reports, apparently spread with design, in regard to pretended agreements for the sending of troops to Mexico on the part of Austria and the arrangements thereto appertaining.

Similar reports are once more willingly spread, and may have originated in an article of the Patrie, which paper pretended to know that movements of imperial royal Austrian troops and subaltern officers to Mexico were impending, a fact which undoubtedly would have the character of a sending of Austrian auxiliary troops.

The manner in which this news has lately, and particularly by the Paris correspondent of the Cologne Gazette. been made use of against Austria, prompts us once more to refer to this affair, and to affirm in the most positive manner that these reports are nothing but inventions made for a purpose.

The truth in the whole question is limited to this, that it is proposed to permit such persons as have already fulfilled their military duty to Austria, but only such, to enlist in the Mexican service, in the same manner and with the same conditions as was the case when the last year's first enlistments for the Austrian-Mexican volunteer corps took place. The object of these newly permitted enlistments, as has already been explicitly stated, would only be to provide substitutes for the numerous vacancies in the Austrian volunteer corps serving in Mexico. The newly enlisted, like those who entered the volunteer corps in the year 1864, take the military oath to the emperor of Mexico, and pledge themselves to him for a six years' service. Their flag is not the Austrian, but the Mexican, and the power of Austria is in nowise engaged through them or for them. Also, it is entirely false when the Patrie puts the number of those volunteers at 10,000 men ; the latest enlistments in Austria for Mexico, concerning the permission for which negotiations are now in progress, would in any event not exceed yearly the total number of 2,000 men.

Whilst we are endeavoring to give a true and correct statement of this affair, we have to remark that no binding resolves have been taken in regard to this affair, but that, on the contrary, the negotiations on the subject have only just begun. But these may, however, very probably lead to the conclusion of a supplemental convention to the agreement entered into last year, of which the chief object was to place as securely as possible the rights of those enlisting, who, after all, remain at the same time Austrian subjects.

Mr. Motley to Mr. Seward.

No. 150.] UNITED STATES LEGATION,
Vienna, February 27, 1866.

SIR: I think it is well to state, referring to my confidential despatch No. 148, of date February 20, 1866, that I have been informed that efforts are making to induce the Austrian government to consent that 4,000 volunteers may be levied here this year for Mexico, on the ground that the supplementary article to the convention of Miramar permitted two thousand each year, and that none were forwarded in the year 1865.

I learn that this consent will probably be accorded, so that if the funds can be obtained for paying, equipping, and transporting them, 4,000 Austrian volunteers will be found and may be expected in Mexico this year. I believe that the funds have not yet been furnished.

I have the honor to remain your obedient servant,

J. LOTHROP MOTLEY.

Hon. WILLIAM H. SEWARD,
Secretary of State, Washington.

Mr. Seward to Mr. Motley.

No. 167.] DEPARTMENT OF STATE,
Washington, March 19, 1866.

SIR: Mr. Bigelow informs me, by a despatch of the 15th of February, that he learned from an unofficial source that "Gregorio Barandiran, the diplomatic representative of the Archduke Maximilian, formerly secretary of legation under Señor Robles at Washington, is now in Paris for money to fit out 10,000 Austrians, who, he says, are ready to embark from Trieste for Mexico. The Mexican commissioner informed him that there was no money in his hands. I am not sure of learning the result of the minister's suit here, as the money, if furnished, must come through indirect and concealed channels."

You are instructed to inquire concerning the facts, and if they justify the report, to bring it to the knowledge of the Austrian government seasonably, and say that the United States cannot regard with unconcern a proceeding which would seem to bring Austria into an alliance with the invaders of Mexico, to subvert the domestic republic, and build up foreign imperial institutions.

It is hoped Austria will give us frank explanations.

I am, sir, your obedient servant,

WILLIAM H. SEWARD.

J. LOTHROP MOTLEY, Esq., *&c., &c., Vienna.*

Mr. Seward to Mr. Motley.

No. 169.] DEPARTMENT OF STATE,
Washington, March 19, 1866.

SIR: I have your despatch of the 27th of February, No. 150, by which we learn that efforts are now made to induce the Austrian government to consent that 4,000 volunteers may be levied within that empire this year for Mexico, on the ground that the supplementary article of the convention of Miramar permitted 2,000 each year, and that none were forwarded in the year 1865.

Upon this statement of facts you express the opinion that the consent desired will probably be accorded by the imperial government, so that if the funds can be obtained for paying, equipping, and transporting 4,000 officers and volunteers, they will be found, and may be expected in Mexico this year. At the same time you state that it is your opinion that the funds have not yet been furnished.

The case thus presented renders it proper that I should call your especial attention to my despatch No. 167, which bears the date of, and is sent forward, this day.

In preparing that despatch I anticipated the case substantially which your communication now presents. You cannot, while practicing the courtesy and respect which are due to the Austrian government, be either too earnest or too emphatic in the protest you have been directed to make.

In performing this duty, you may be assisted by information of the actual state of the question concerning French intervention in Mexico at the present moment. With this view, I give you, confidentially, a copy of my note addressed to the Marquis de Montholon on the 12th day of February last. As yet, no reply has been received to this note, nor have its contents become public. You will, therefore, see the propriety of being discreet in such use of it as you may find it necessary to make.

After reading that paper you will be justified in saying that the American government and people would not be likely to be pleased with seeing Austria at this juncture assume the character of a protector to the foreign military power which, claiming the form of an empire, is attempted to be set up upon the supposed subverted foundations of the republic of Mexico.

I am, sir, your obedient servant,

WILLIAM H. SEWARD.

J. LOTHROP MOTLEY, Esq., *&c.*, *&c.*, *Vienna.*

Mr. Motley to Mr. Seward.

No. 155.] UNITED STATES LEGATION,
Vienna, March 27, 1866.

SIR: The military supplementary convention between that government of Mexico which is here recognized as the legitimate one and the Austrian government was signed on the 15th of this month.

As the nature and conditions of this agreement have already been fully stated in my despatches of January 8, February 20, and February 27, (Nos. 142, 148, and 150,) the matter can be no novelty to you, and there seems no necessity for repeating what has already been said.

It is expected that about 1,000 volunteers will be shipped very soon from Trieste to Vera Cruz, and at least as many more in the autumn.

I have the honor to remain, sir, your obedient servant,

J. LOTHROP MOTLEY.

Hon. WILLIAM H. SEWARD,
Secretary of State.

Mr. Seward to Mr. Motley.

No. 173.] WASHINGTON, *April* 6, 1866.

SIR: An informal note has just been received from Mr. Bigelow, the United States minister at Paris. In this note Mr. Bigelow writes, in substance, as follows:

"The Moniteur of the 21st of March announces that a military convention was signed at Vienna on the 15th, between the Austrian government and the representative of Maximilian, supplementary to a convention of the same nature which had been previously concluded between the same parties.

"The purpose of this engagement, says the Moniteur, is to insure the enrolments necessary to keep full the Austrian corps in Mexico."

Mr. Bigelow further writes as follows:

"I have seen it stated in another journal that a line of steamers is to be started from Trieste to Vera Cruz, to ply regularly after the 1st of April."

Again, Mr. Bigelow furnishes an extract from the Paris Constitutionnel of the 21st of March:

"We learn from the Freudenblatt, of Vienna, that the enlistment for Mexico will begin immediately; that the funds had been received from Paris two months since."

Your despatches of dates almost as late as that of Mr. Bigelow's note are silent upon the rumors which he brings to the notice of this government. It is possible that more authentic information which you may possess concerning the disposition and proceedings of the Austrian government may enable you to treat the matter mentioned by Mr. Bigelow with indifference.

Looking at the matter, however, from our point of observation, the rumors referred to are deemed sufficient to entitle us to ask a friendly and just exposition of the imperial royal government of the relations which it proposes to assume or maintain henceforth in regard to Mexico.

You are expected, therefore, to execute the instructions which have heretofore been sent to you to that effect; and it is thought proper that you should state that, in the event of hostilities being carried on hereafter in Mexico by Austrian subjects, under the command or with the sanction of the government of Vienna, the United States will feel themselves at liberty to regard those hostilities as constituting a state of war by Austria against the republic of Mexico; and in regard to such war, waged at this time and under existing circumstances, the United States could not engage to remain as silent or neutral spectators.

The President may desire to call the attention of Congress to this interesting subject. You will see the importance, therefore, of obtaining the information which is desired as early as may be practicable consistently with the courtesies due to Austria as a friendly government.

Should you, however, find important reasons, now unknown to us, for deferring the execution of this instruction, you will be at liberty to exercise your discretion and report those reasons to us.

I am, sir, your obedient servant,

WILLIAM H. SEWARD.

J. LOTHROP MOTLEY, Esq., *&c.*, *&c.*, *Vienna.*

Mr. Motley to Mr. Seward.

No. 158.] LEGATION OF THE UNITED STATES,
Vienna, April 6, 1866.

SIR: I had the honor to receive your No. 167, of date March 19. In this despatch it is stated that Mr. Bigelow informs you, under date of February 15, from an unofficial source, that "Gregorio Barandiran, the diplomatic representative of the Archduke Maximilian, formerly secretary of legation under Señor Robles, at Washington, is now in Paris for money to fit out 10,000 Austrians, which, he says, are ready to embark from Trieste for Mexico. The Mexican commissioner informed him that there was no money in his hands. I am not sure of learning the result of the minister's suit here, as the money, if furnished, must come through indirect and concealed channels."

In consequence of this information furnished by Mr. Bigelow, you instruct me to "inquire concerning the facts, and, if they justify the report, to bring it to the knowledge of the Austrian government seasonably, and say that the United States cannot regard with unconcern a proceeding which would seem to bring Austria into alliance with the invaders of Mexico to subvert the domestic republic and build up foreign imperial institutions. It is hoped that Austria will give us frank explanations."

In reply, I have to observe that Mr. Bigelow, in a private note to me of the same date as his despatch above cited, mentioned this report of the "10,000 Austrians ready to embark at Trieste for Mexico," but the story was so entirely at variance with everything well known to me here that I attributed very little importance to it. In order to make assurances more sure, however, I took pains instantly to verify the facts in the most exact and authentic manner. I learned, accordingly, that, instead of there being 10,000 Austrians at Trieste, there was not one Austrian soldier ready to embark at that port, or at any other point in this empire.

This intelligence, from the most unquestionable source, was transmitted by me in a private note to Mr. Bigelow, but I confess that I did not consider it worth while to trouble you with a matter which seemed to be mere newspaper gossip. I felt that, so long as I was deemed worthy of my present post, you would feel confident that I should always furnish you with accurate intelligence as to important events occurring in Austria, and that the concentration and embarcation for Mexico of 10,000 Austrians at Trieste were facts not likely to escape my notice.

You will doubtless remember that in my despatch of the 8th of January I stated, on official authority, that the Austrian government had consented that volunteers should be levied in this empire, from men who had fulfilled their term of service in Austria, in numbers sufficient to keep full the original legion in Mexico of 6,000 men.

As the supplementary convention to that effect had not then been signed, it was not possible to give you more definite information.

Subsequently, on the 20th of February, I informed you that the supplementary articles permitted the levy of 2,000 men each year for a certain period; and on the 29th of February I added that, as no volunteers had been sent in 1865, it was now permitted to send two quotas of 2,000 men each during the year 1866.

I also stated that the equipping and transporting of these troops, and all other expenses, were to be defrayed by that government at Mexico which has been recognized here as the legitimate one, and not in any proportion by the Austrian government. As you have especially instructed me not to engage in official or political discussions on the Mexican subject with the government to which I am accredited, and as that injunction, to which I have repeatedly and very lately alluded in this correspondence, has never been removed, I should have thought myself violating my duty had I taken the responsibility of entering any protest on the part of the United States government against these proceedings.

My personal opinions in regard to this attempt, by means of foreign armies and navies, to set up a foreign empire on the ruins of an American republic, are perfectly well known here and at home.

What is of infinitely more importance, every government in Europe, that of Austria included, knows the position of the United States government, and is aware that it will never, so long as a foreign power occupies the territory and waters of Mexico with its military and naval forces, recognize the existence of an empire which that power has sought to establish, nor accept it as the creation of the Mexican national will.

But I am now somewhat embarrassed by the instructions contained in your despatch No. 167.

It seems to me that if I should intimate now (as instructed by you, on receiving the rumors contained in Mr. Bigelow's despatch) that "Austria is in alliance with the invaders of Mexico," and should express the hope that "she will give us frank explanations," I should appear to suggest that the imperial royal government had not hitherto been frank in her dealings on this subject.

Now, it is my duty to say that I believe the imperial government has been perfectly sincere, straightforward, and loyal towards the United States in this matter, and in every other, since I have had the honor of holding my present post.

There have been no concealments, as I firmly believe, as to her position, in regard to what is called here the Mexican empire.

It has been uniformly stated by the imperial government that it had nothing to do with the attempt to establish that empire; that it had neither a military nor mercantile navy, nor superfluous land forces, adequate to sustain, by force, the government which the Archduke Maximilian sought to establish in Mexico; that his acceptance or rejection of the offer made to him in 1863 was a matter which personally concerned only himself and his brother, the Emperor of Austria, and that the imperial royal government was in no alliance, direct or indirect, with the proposed new government of Mexico.

The Austrian government had allowed a certain number of volunteers to be raised for service in Mexico by the Emperor's brother, a proceeding which would, of course, have been a violation of Austrian sovereignty, had it been done without permission.

What would have been the answer to a protest by the United States government against the original convention of Miramar granting that permission, or of a similar protest to the supplementary convention signed here on the 15th of last March, I cannot tell.

I suppose, however, that if the United States government had permitted, or were now to permit, the republican government of Mexico, recognized by the United States as the legitimate one, to raise volunteers within the territory of the United States, in whatever numbers, the Austrian government would not consider itself authorized to protest against such a measure, or to resent it.

It would, I suppose, consider that a measure incident to the sovereignty of the United States, and whatever might be the effect produced upon the various belligerents in Mexico by such a step, Austria, as a neutral, would not be affected by it.

My embarrassment is somewhat increased by the perusal of your No. 169, bearing the same date (19th of March) as your No. 167, both reaching me under the same envelope.

In this latter despatch, which acknowledges receipt of my No. 150, giving information that the supplementary convention thereafter to be signed would allow a double yearly quota, viz., 4,000 volunteers, to go to Mexico this year, on the ground that none were forwarded in the year 1865, you call my especial attention to your No. 167.

You observe that in preparing that despatch you anticipated the case substantially which my communication now presents. You instruct me further that while practicing the courtesy and respect which are due to the Austrian government, I cannot be either too earnest or too emphatic in the protest which I have been directed to make.

You further send for my guidance a copy of the note addressed to you by the Marquis de Montholon on the 12th of February, by which I learn the actual state of the question concerning French intervention in Mexico.

You also observe, that after reading that paper I shall be justified in saying that the "American government and people will not be likely to be pleased with seeing Austria at this juncture assume the character of a protector to the foreign military power which, claiming the form of an empire, is attempted to be set up upon the supposed subverted foundations of the republic of Mexico."

As a matter of fact, officially published here, only 1,000 volunteers are to go this summer. Whether this restriction is in order to avoid the unhealthy season in Vera Cruz, or because funds have not been provided for equipping and transporting a larger number, I know not.

As soon as the supplementary convention was signed last month, I instructed Mr. Thayer, United States consul at Trieste, to send me accurate intelligence as to the number of troops, dates of sailing, and other particulars of interest in this connexion, so that you may rely upon my keeping you duly informed on the subject.

It is my anxious desire to perform my duty to the United States government with the utmost fidelity in this most serious affair. I think that if I could have the advantage of direct conversation with you I should easily convince you that there is no intention on the part of Austria to succeed the French government in the position of protector to the foreign military power which it is attempted to set up in Mexico, and that it would be difficult for the imperial royal government to disavow any such intention more frankly and loyally than it has uniformly done.

If your efforts to bring about the evacuation of Mexico by the French army are successful, I do not think that the Austrian volunteers in that country will be sufficiently numerous to prevent a free expression of the national will as to the form of government thenceforth to be adopted. I also consider it indisputable that, whatever be the result, the Austrian government will never deem itself either directly or by implication called upon to sustain the cause which those volunteers have endeavored to support.

After making these preliminary observations, at no greater length, I trust, than is justified by the importance of the subject, I proceed to say that, in view of your decided and unequivocal instructions just received, I deem it, of course, my duty to break the official silence hitherto imposed upon me, and to bring the opinions of the United States government to the direct notice of the imperial royal government.

As, however, I consider frankness and sincerity the best rule in diplomacy, and especially on this occasion, I have decided to request the imperial royal minister for foreign affairs to read this despatch before I send it to you.

Should his excellency find in it any misstatements or wrong inferences, or if he should favor me with any suggestions or comments, I shall have the honor duly to notify you thereof in a subsequent despatch, probably by the same post that will take this one.

P. S.—The Moniteur of yesterday informs us as to the terms fixed for the evacuation of Mexico by the French army—whether to the satisfaction, or not, of the United States government I know not.

I have the honor to remain, sir, most respectfully, your very obedient servant,

J. LOTHROP MOTLEY.

Hon. WILLIAM H. SEWARD,
Secretary of State.

Mr. Seward to Mr. Motley.

No. 174.]

DEPARTMENT OF STATE,
Washington, April 16, 1866.

SIR: I have had the honor to receive your despatch of the 27th of March, No. 155, which brings the important announcement that a treaty, called a "military supplementary convention," was ratified on the 15th of that month between the Emperor of Austria and the Prince Maximilian, who claims to be an emperor in Mexico.

You inform me that it is expected that about one thousand volunteers will be shipped (under this treaty) from Trieste to Vera Cruz very soon, and that at least as many more will be shipped in the autumn.

I have heretofore given you the President's instructions to ask for explanations, and, conditionally, to inform the government of Austria that the despatch of military expeditions by Austria under such an arrangement as the one which seems now to have been consummated would be regarded with serious concern by the United States.

The subject has now been further considered in connexion with the official information thus recently received. The time seems to have arrived when the attitude of this government in relation to Mexican affairs should be once again frankly and distinctly made known to the Emperor of Austria, and all other powers whom it may directly concern. The United States, for reasons which seem to them to be just, and to have their foundation in the laws of nations, maintain that the domestic republican government with which they are in relations of friendly communication is the only legitimate government existing in Mexico; that a war has for a period of several years been waged against that republic by the government of France, which war began with a disclaimer of all political or dynastic designs; that that war has subsequently taken upon itself, and now distinctly wears, the character of a European intervention to overthrow that domestic republican government, and to erect in its stead a European imperial military despotism by military force. The United States, in view of the character of their own political institutions, their proximity and intimate relations towards Mexico, and their just influence in the political affairs of the American continent, cannot consent to the accomplishment of that purpose by the means described. The United States have therefore addressed themselves, as they think, seasonably to the government of France, and have asked that its military forces, engaged in that objectionable political invasion, may desist from further intervention and be withdrawn from Mexico.

A copy of the last communication upon this subject, which was addressed by us to the government of France, is herewith transmitted for your special information. This paper will give you the true situation of the question. It will also enable you to satisfy the government of Vienna that the United States must be no less opposed to military intervention for political objects hereafter in Mexico by the government of Austria, than they are opposed to any further intervention of the same character in that country by France.

You will, therefore, at as early a day as may be convenient, bring the whole case, in a becoming manner, to the attention of the imperial royal government. You are authorized to state that the United States sincerely desire that Austria may find it just and expedient to come upon the same ground of non-intervention in Mexico which is maintained by the United States, and to which they have invited France.

You will communicate to us the answer of the Austrian government to this proposition.

This government could not but regard as a matter of serious concern the despatch of any troops from Austria for Mexico while the subject which you are thus directed to present to the Austrian government remains under consideration.

I am, sir, your obedient servant,

WILLIAM H. SEWARD.

J. LOTHROP MOTLEY, Esq., *&c., &c., Vienna.*

Mr. Seward to Mr. Motley.

No. 181.]

DEPARTMENT OF STATE,
Washington, April 30, 1866.

SIR: I have the honor to acknowledge the reception of your despatches of the 6th of April, No. 158, and the 10th of April, No. 159.

These papers inform me that you have brought my despatches Nos. 167 and 169 to the notice of the imperial government, although not without some hesitation and embarrassment. Subsequently to the time when that duty was performed you must have received my despatch of April 6, No. 173, my further despatch of April 16, No. 174, and also my confidential despatch of April 16, No. 176, all of which despatches relate to the situation of Mexico.

I trust that these several communications will have cleared away whatever uncertainty you may heretofore have felt concerning the views of this government in regard to that subject.

In your No. 158 you have assumed that this government could not justly regard as a departure from neutrality by the Austrian government the authority which it has given by entering into a recent treaty with the Prince Maximilian for the recruiting of volunteers by him in Austria and their despatch by him to Mexico.

In support of this assumption you argue that the United States would not be willing to admit that it would be a violation of neutrality on their part to permit the recruiting of volunteers within their jurisdiction for military service under the republican banner in Mexico.

Your assumption, and the argument upon which you built it, were submitted by you to Count Mensdorff, and it is not unlikely that he may have inferred that the assumption is consistent with the views which are entertained by the United States, and would therefore be approved by them. It becomes necessary, for this reason, for me to say that I do not acquiesce in your position.

While any citizen of the United States is at liberty, under municipal and international laws, to expatriate himself unarmed, and to engage individually, when abroad, in any foreign service that he may choose, yet, on the other hand, the laws of the United States and the law of nations, as they are understood by us, forbid this government from authorizing or permitting the enlistment or organization on American ground, or the departure from our territory, of armed military forces to carry on hostilities against any foreign state, except in a war against that state duly declared by Congress.

The Prince Maximilian is either a principal or a subordinate belligerent in Mexico. The treaty which has been made between Austria and that belligerent, by which the former authorizes the organization within the Austrian dominions of two thousand or more volunteers, manifestly to be engaged in war against the republic of Mexico, is deemed by the government inconsistent with the principle of neutrality, and an engagement with Maximilian in his invasion of that republic.

I give you herewith a copy of a note which was received on the 21st of April instant from the Marquis de Montholon, together with a copy of the despatch which was addressed to that minister by Mr. Drouyn de Lhuys on the 5th of April instant.

I give you also a copy of the reply which I have made to the note of the Marquis.

These several papers, together with my aforementioned despatches, which you will now have received, will put you fully in possession of the opinions of this government, and of the duty which it has called upon you to perform.

It will be an occasion of sincere satisfaction if you shall be able to obtain from the imperial government an assurance that Austria will not hereafter intervene, by sending or by giving permission to the despatch of military forces from within her dominions to make or continue a war against the republic of Mexico.

I refrain from discussing the question you have raised, "whether the recent instructions of this department harmonize entirely with the policy which it pursued at an earlier period of the European intervention in Mexico."

Your despatch is calculated to produce an impression that, notwithstanding our protest, you expect the Austrian government will still permit the departure of the volunteers under the treaty, without waiting to give us an answer to that protest, and without affording us time to consider and reply to such answer as that government shall see proper and convenient to make. Should the Austrian government persist in proceeding in that manner, and to the extremity thus indicated, then this government will expect you to retire from Vienna, as directed in my aforesaid despatch No. 176.

I forbear also from discussing the question which you have raised of the propriety of some of the proceedings which have been taken by Mr. Bigelow in Paris, nor do I think it necessary to enter upon the consideration of the explanations which you have given of your own views in regard to these subjects.

The European war against the republic of Mexico has been from the beginning a continual menace against this government, and even against free institutions throughout the American continent. I feel very sure that no friend of such institutions, either at home or abroad, will ever well question the necessity, the wisdom, or the justice of the policy which we have steadily pursued and are still pursuing in regard to that war. It would be unprofitable for us, under such circumstances, to open personal discussions about that policy among ourselves.

I am, sir, your obedient servant,

WILLIAM H. SEWARD.

J. LOTHROP MOTLEY, Esq., *&c.*, *&c.*, *Vienna.*

Mr. Motley to Mr. Seward.

No. 167.] UNITED STATES LEGATION,
Vienna, May 1, 1866.

SIR: Many of the Vienna papers of last week published the following paragraphs, which I have reason to believe accurate:

"The shipment of the newly levied recruits for the Austrian volunteer corps in Mexico is fixed for the 15th May.

"According to an advertisement fastened to the council-house door, the last enlistments for Mexico take place on the 27th, 28th, and 30th April. As hand-money, 25, 30, and 35 florins are offered. According to telegraphic accounts received to-day at the war department, from the various districts, the recruiting for the Mexican volunteer corps is taking a favorable course. The greater part of the newly enlisted men have already arrived at the head depot in Laybach, and are fully uniformed.

"Some of them have received a furlough until the moment of sailing, and are seen in their new uniforms in Vienna.

"The number levied in Vienna, and in the provinces, up to yesterday, (26th April,) is 850 men."

I have as yet received no notification from Mr. Thayer, at Trieste, of the arrival of any of these volunteers in that city.

I have the honor to remain, sir, your obedient servant,

J. LOTHROP MOTLEY.

Hon. WILLIAM H. SEWARD,
Secretary of State.

Mr. Seward to Mr. Motley.

No. 182.] DEPARTMENT OF STATE,
Washington, May 3, 1866.

SIR: Your confidential despatch of the 17th of April, No. 161, has been received.

It is a matter of some relief that only so small a number of volunteers as six hundred have been gathered at Laybach, with a view to shipment from Trieste for Vera Cruz, and that the recruiting for that service is becoming very languid. It is to be hoped that a scheme obviously so unpopular in Austria will not be persisted in by the Emperor. My late communications leave no necessity for dwelling upon the subject at the present moment.

I am, sir, your obedient servant,

WILLIAM H. SEWARD.

J. LOTHROP MOTLEY, Esq., *&c.*, *&c.*, *Vienna.*

Mr. Motley to Mr. Seward.

No. 169.] UNITED STATES LEGATION,
Vienna, May 6, 1866.

SIR: I have the honor to acknowledge the receipt of your Nos. 173, 174, 175, and your 176, marked confidential, of dates April 6 and April 16, respectively, all reaching me under the same envelope on May 3, in the evening. No. 175 is in answer to my 156, and relates to the affairs of Austria and Prussia.

No. 173 contains certain extracts from Paris journals, and translations in Paris journals from Vienna newspapers, sent to you by Mr. Bigelow, United States minister in Paris. Such intelligence as was accurate in those extracts has already been indicated by me in advance from authentic sources in my despatches of January 8, February 20, and February 27.

The permission of the so-called imperial government in Mexico to levy troops to supply vacancies in the volunteer corps raised in this empire in 1864 was accorded in the beginning of this year, and mentioned in my despatch of 8th January. Of the signature of the supplementary convention I have subsequently apprised you. The statement that a line of steamers was to be started between Trieste and Vera Cruz, to begin to ply on April 1, has, I believe, no foundation in fact.

I have understood that Mr. Loosey, Austrian consul-general at New York, has long had the project of starting a line of steamers between Trieste and New York, and that latterly there had been some hope of causing such steamers to stop at Vera Cruz, but I have ascertained that the project has been for the present, at least, abandoned.

I sent this information to Mr. Bigelow, in reply to his inquiry made some five or six weeks ago.

The remainder of your No. 173 I shall have the honor to answer in connexion with your Nos. 174 and 176, in a separate despatch, which will go by the same post as does the present one.

Meantime I have the honor to remain, very respectfully, your obedient servant,

J. LOTHROP MOTLEY.

Hon. WILLIAM H. SEWARD,
Secretary of State.

Mr. Motley to Count Mensdorff.

LEGATION OF THE UNITED STATES OF AMERICA,
Vienna, May 6, 1866.

YOUR EXCELLENCY: It will be doubtless within your recollection, that on the 7th of April I had the honor to lay before you, for confidential perusal, a despatch of my own to Mr. Seward, Secretary of State of the United States.

This paper was in answer to a communication from the Secretary of State, instructing me to make as earnest and emphatic protest as was compatible with the profound respect entertained by the United States for the imperial royal government against the departure of any additional soldiers from Austria for Mexico.

The language of the protest which I was thus instructed to make was quoted at length in the despatch which I had the honor of submitting to your perusal before sending it to Washington. In returning that despatch, I understood your excellency to observe that it contained a just and explicit statement of the position of the Austrian government in regard to the affairs of Mexico, and that you had no further observations to make upon it.

Since forwarding that paper to Washington, I have received despatches of a grave nature from my government in regard to the same subject.

These despatches are not, of course, in answer to my communication abov mentioned. For this, sufficient time has not yet elapsed.

The instructions just received by me from Mr. Seward are in answer to my statement to him, under date of 27th March last, that the military supplementary convention between the Austrian government and the government of Mexico, recognized here as the legitimate one, had been signed on the 11th March, and that it was expected that about one thousand volunteers would be shipped very soon from Trieste to Vera Cruz, and at least as many more in the autumn.

An imperative duty is now placed upon me of again most respectfully calling your excellency's attention to the general and growing uneasiness throughout the United States on the subject of foreign troops in Mexico. In so doing, I wish to use the most courteous and becoming terms that are consistent with a faithful execution of the task just committed to me by my government.

Recognizing the right of one independent nation, for reasons deemed sufficient by itself, to make war upon another independent nation, and not feeling called upon to be a judge of the quarrel between the belligerents, the United States have scrupulously maintained neutrality in the war existing during the past few years between the empire of France and the republic of Mexico, with which power the United States government has not ceased to maintain friendly relations.

This preservation of neutrality has been rendered the more difficult in proportion to the growth of the conviction among the people of the United States that the war begun by France for the purpose of redressing grievances, and with a disclaimer of all political intentions on the part of France, was continued, as it were, indefinitely for the purpose of establishing and perpetuating on the borders of our own territory a foreign imperial government by means of European troops.

It is hoped that at last an arrangement has been effected by which the French troops, heretofore preventing a free expression of the national will in Mexico, are to be withdrawn.

The appearance of fresh troops arriving from Austria at exactly this moment, therefore, would almost inevitably increase the general excitement in the United States which the recent understanding with the French government had begun to allay.

It would be thought erroneous, as such a supposition really is, that the government of Austria was about to succeed that of France in an armed and protective alliance with the new government which it wishes to see established in Mexico.

A thousand volunteers, many of them, perhaps, veterans, having served their time in the Austrian army, will be regarded as the precursors of an indefinite number sufficient to supply the void left by the retiring French forces, and to overawe for a period of years the free action of the Mexican people in regard to their form of government.

The United States government has from the beginning neither acquiesced in nor intimated the possibility of a future acquiescence in the substitution of an imperial foreign and military government in the place of the national republic of Mexico, unless it should satisfy itself that such was unquestionably the will of the Mexican people.

That will, in the opinion of the United States government, can never be manifested in the presence of foreign fleets and armies. It has, therefore, during its very protracted diplomatic correspondence with the French imperial government, been unable to admit the validity of the revolution supposed to have been effected in the government of Mexico chiefly by the means of European forces.

In its last note addressed to the French government it expressed itself as understanding the Emperor of the French to announce to the United States his immediate purpose to bring to an end the services of his armies in Mexico, to withdraw them, and in good faith to fall back, without stipulation or condition on the part of the United States, upon the principle of non-intervention, as to which he is henceforth agreed with the United States.

The practice of the United States government, says the Secretary of State, is from its beginning a guarantee to all nations of the respect of the American people for the free sovereignty of the people in every other state. It is the chief element of foreign intercourse in our history.

Thus much of information I have thought it not superfluous to give of the latest expression by the United States government to that of France of its sentiments in regard to the affairs of Mexico.

I am now instructed to say to the imperial royal government of Austria, that, in the opinion of the United States, the time seems to have arrived when the position of their government in relation to Mexico should be frankly and distinctly made known to the imperial government, and to all others whom it may directly concern.

The United States, for reasons which seem to them to be just and to have their foundation in the laws of nations, maintain that the domestic republican government is the only legitimate one existing in Mexico. They cannot, in view of the character of their own political institutions, their proximity and intimate relations towards Mexico, and their just influence in the affairs of the American continent, consent to the subversion of that government by foreign armies. Having urged upon the French government their strong and, as they think, reasonable desire for the withdrawal of the French troops engaged in that objectionable invasion, it now becomes proper for the United States to announce that they are no less opposed to military intervention for political objects hereafter in Mexico with the sanction of the Austrian government than they are opposed to any further intervention of the same character in that country by France.

I am accordingly instructed to state that the United States sincerely desire that Austria may find it just and expedient to come upon the ground of non-intervention in Mexico which is maintained by the United States, and to which they have invited France. They could not but regard as a matter of serious concern the despatch of any troops from Austria for Mexico while the subject which I am thus directed to present to the Austrian government remains under consideration.

I have now faithfully laid before your excellency, as briefly as the importance of the subject would permit, the position of the United States in regard to Mexico.

Until recently I have been instructed by my government to abstain from formal political discussions here of the important events occurring in that country. On repeated occasions, however, I have felt it appropriate to express in courteous language, without formality, but in all sincerity, the opinions of the United States government and people as to the attempt to establish a foreign and imperial government by means of European military forces upon the ruins of an American republic.

Those opinions have been no secret to those with whom I have had the honor of conversing, but it is only now that I am instructed by my government to speak in its name, and with the whole weight of whatever influence it may be thought to possess over the general sentiment of the world. There has been no doubt, I suppose, as to the almost unanimous opinion of the American people on the subject.

From time to time it has been my duty to place before the imperial royal government documents emanating from the cabinet at Washington relating to the affairs of Mexico. The diplomatic correspondence of the United States government with that of France, from the beginning of the hostile expeditions against Mexico down to a very recent period, has been regularly printed, and within the reach of all who wish to read it.

Public sentiment in the United States as to intervention on the part of European governments and soldiers for the purpose of revolutionizing the polity, subverting the existing institutions, and controlling the destiny of American republics, has been manifested in every way in which it was possible to make it known, by solemn resolutions of Congress, by the utterances of great public meetings without distinction of party, and by the general voice of the American press.

The feelings of the American people and its successive governments, as exhibited through the whole of their national career, and publicly manifested on many solemn occasions, in regard to forcible and armed interference by European powers with established institutions on the western continent, are, whether they may be deemed reasonable or not, and whatever weight may be attached to them by European opinion, a matter of history and known to mankind.

Such interference was long ago proclaimed, on the highest official authority, as of necessity to be considered a manifestation of an unfriendly disposition towards the United States. It is hardly expedient, therefore, on this occasion, to consume more of your excellency's time by the exposition of a subject so familiar to you.

I beg your excellency to believe that the frankness and sincerity with which I have thus set forth, in obedience to the instructions of the President, the sentiments of the government which I have the honor to represent at the court of his imperial royal Majesty, are not incompatible with the most entire respect for the imperial royal government and with the Austrian nation, and with the warmest and most sincere desire for their welfare.

In conclusion, I feel it my duty, in this most grave aspect of affairs, to repeat the earnest hope that it may be found expedient to postpone the departure of fresh troops from Austria to Mexico until such answer to this communication as your excellency may be pleased to make shall have been candidly and deliberately considered by the United States government at Washington.

Meantime I pray your excellency to accept the expression of the highest consideration with which I have the honor to remain your excellency's very obedient servant,

J. LOTHROP MOTLEY.

His Excellency Count Mensdorff,
Imperial Royal Minister of Foreign Affairs, &c., &c., &c.

Mr. Canisius to Mr. Seward.

[Extracts.]

No. 57.] Consulate of the United States of America,
Vienna, May 8, 1866.

Sir: * * * * The news received here per telegraph that you have demanded of Austria the discontinuation of sending any more volunteers to Maximilian, of Mexico, has created here quite a sensation. The people of Austria feel now, in their distress, more than ever, that this enterprise of Maximilian, and the subsequent agreement made by this government to aid him by sending soldiers to that distant country, of no value to the people of this empire, was a great mistake.

I found in this morning's paper the following item:

[Translation.]

"LAYBACH, (near Trieste,) *May* 5.

"*The Mexican free corps.*—The recruiting for the Mexican free corps will definitely be closed to-day. All the recruits have to be ready on the 8th of this month at the principal depot at Laybach, as the embarcation commences in Trieste on the 10th instant. The Mexican Colonel Leissor will personally attend to the embarcation."

What the Austrian government will decide now, after your protest, will soon be seen, as the embarcation was to take place on the 10th of this month.

I have the honor to be, very respectfully, your obedient servant,

T. CANISIUS,
United States Consul.

Hon. WILLIAM H. SEWARD,
Secretary of State.

Mr. Motley to Mr. Seward.

No. 174.] LEGATION OF THE UNITED STATES,
Vienna, May 15, 1866.

SIR: Referring to my No. 173, of date May 12, I have the honor to state that I have received no answer as yet to my note to Count Mensdorff, of May 6, a copy of which was enclosed in my No. 170, of date May 8.

As I have already been informed officially, but confidentially, that the departure of the volunteers for Mexico has been prevented, (information which I immediately conveyed to you in my above-mentioned No. 173,) this delay has nothing in it surprising.

On the eve of a tremendous war, such as this, in which all Germany is almost immediately to be plunged, it is natural that there should be great press of business at the imperial royal foreign office. I have reason to suppose, moreover, that a desire on the part of the imperial royal government to know what reply you may be pleased to make to my despatch No. 158, confidentially communicated to the imperial royal minister of foreign affairs before it was forwarded to Washington, may, in part, account for the delay. I have, of course, not intimated that there was the slightest probability of any change having been effected in the emphatic opposition on the part of the United States government to the sending of volunteers from Austria to Mexico. On the other hand, I think that you may consider it certain, as a matter of fact, that no soldiers will sail again from Austria to Mexico.

I shall be glad to be informed officially of the state of the negotiations between the United States government and that of France.

From the American newspapers I gather that the decree of the French Emperor concerning the evacuation of Mexico had been communicated to the United States government.

I know not whether the United States government has expressed its concurrence with that decision.

My latest authentic intelligence as to the negotiations with France is contained in your note to the Marquis de Montholon of February 12.

I would also observe, in passing, that the two last published volumes of the Diplomatic Correspondence, parts 3 and 4, for the year 1864, containing the correspondence with France and all other countries excepting England, has never been sent to me.

Happening to be in London at the close of last year, however, I procured a copy at the United States legation.

I think it not superfluous to state that, according to information received from Mr. Thayer, United States consul at Trieste, the transport in which the volunteers were to have been conveyed from that port to Mexico was the French merchant ship Tampico.

I have the honor to remain sir, your obedient servant,

J. LOTHROP MOTLEY.

Hon. WILLIAM H. SEWARD,
Secretary of State.

Mr. Motley to Mr. Seward.

No. 177.] UNITED STATES LEGATION,
Vienna, May 21, 1866.

SIR: I have the honor to state that I have just received a note from Count Mensdorff, in answer to my note of date May 6, a copy of which was forwarded with my despatch No. 170, of date May 8.

I have prepared a careful translation of the minister's note, which, together with a copy of the original, I transmit with this despatch.

I cannot doubt that both the contents and friendly spirit of this communication from the imperial royal government will give sincere satisfaction to the United States government.

I have the honor to remain, sir, your obedient servant,

J. LOTHROP MOTLEY.

Hon. WILLIAM H. SEWARD,
Secretary of State.

Count Mensdorff to Mr. Motley.

[Translation.]

MINISTRY OF THE IMPERIAL HOUSE AND OF FOREIGN AFFAIRS,
Vienna, May 20, 1866.

The undersigned, minister of the imperial house and of foreign affairs, has had the honor to receive the note which the Hon. Mr. Lothrop Motley, envoy extraordinary and minister plenipotentiary of the United States of North America, addressed to him on the 6th of the current month, in which expression is given to the representations which his government has seen itself called upon to make in regard to the volunteers enlisted in the Austrian states for military service in Mexico.

The undersigned has already had repeated occasions to give verbal explanations to the envoy of the United States concerning the nature and extent of the enrolments in question which have taken place in very limited measures, both as to numbers and period of enlistment—explanations which were intended to remove every doubt which could have arisen in the eyes of the government of the United States in regard to the intentions of Austria in this matter. As, however, it appears from the latest communications of the envoy that the said explanations have not hitherto had the effect to entirely tranquillize the North American government in this respect; as that government feels obliged to see in the enlistments in question an exertion of influence on the part of Austria in the internal affairs of Mexico which might become a motive for the United States to come out of the neutral position which it has hitherto maintained in regard to those affairs; as, finally, according to the observation contained in the note of Mr. Lothrop Motley, the exertion of an influence of the above-mentioned character would be regarded as well by the government as by public opinion in the United States as an unfriendly proceeding towards them, which would be entirely out of harmony with the intentions of the imperial government, the undersigned finds himself in the position, without, therefore, being able to agree with all the views developed in the many-times cited note, to make known to the envoy that, in consideration of all the above-mentioned circumstances, the necessary measures have been taken to prevent the departure of the volunteers lately enlisted for Mexico.

In the confident expectation that the cabinet at Washington will feel itself on this account the more induced to allow no change to take place in the neutral position hitherto maintained by it towards Mexico, and that the government of the United States will recognize in this proceeding of the imperial cabinet a new proof of its sincere wish to remove everything that might be capable of exercising a prejudicial influence upon the relations between the two countries, the undersigned makes use of this occasion to renew to the honorable Mr. Lothrop Motley the assurance of his high and distinguished consideration.

MENSDORFF.

Mr. LOTHROP MOTLEY,
Envoy Extraordinary and Minister Plenipotentiary, U. S. A.

Mr. Seward to Mr. Motley.

No. 184.]

DEPARTMENT OF STATE,
Washington, May 26, 1866.

SIR: Your despatch of May 6, No. 169, has been received, and I thank you for the information which it communicates concerning the relations between Austria and Mexico.

I am, sir, your obedient servant,

WILLIAM H. SEWARD.

J. LOTHROP MOTLEY, Esq., *&c., &c., Vienna.*

Mr. Seward to Mr. Motley.

No. 185.]

DEPARTMENT OF STATE,
Washington, May 26, 1866.

SIR: I have the honor to acknowledge the receipt of your despatch of the 8th instant, No. 170, which paper is accompanied by a copy of a note which, on the 6th instant, you addressed to Count Mensdorff in execution of my instructions Nos. 173, 174, and 176.

I have great pleasure in saying that the President approves entirely of the proceedings on your part which are related in your despatch, and equally approves of your note to the Austrian minister for foreign affairs.

I am, sir, your obedient servant,

WILLIAM H. SEWARD.

J. LOTHROP MOTLEY, Esq., *&c., &c., Vienna.*

Mr. Seward to Mr. Motley.

No. 186.]

DEPARTMENT OF STATE,
Washington, May 30, 1866.

SIR: I have the honor to acknowledge the receipt of your despatch of the 15th instant, No. 174. In that paper I find the following paragraphs:

"As I have already been informed, officially, but confidentially, that the departure of the volunteers for Mexico has been prevented, (information which I immediately conveyed to you in my above-mentioned No. 173,) this delay has nothing in it surprising.

* * * * * * *

"I think that you may consider it certain, as a matter of fact, that no soldiers will sail from Austria to Mexico."

Your No. 173, referred to in the first paragraph, has not yet reached this department. The paragraphs extracted, however, are sufficient to satisfy the

President that our wishes in regard to the Mexican question are receiving just consideration by the imperial royal government.

If it shall seem to you to be expedient, you will say this to Count Mensdorff, and at the same time express to him our earnest and sincere wishes to remain always in peace and cordial friendship with Austria.

In compliance with your request, I send herewith, for your information, a copy of so much of the correspondence with France concerning Mexico as has not heretofore been furnished you.

I am, sir, your obedient servant,

WILLIAM H. SEWARD,

J. LOTHROP MOTLEY, Esq., *&c., &c., Vienna.*

Mr. Seward to Mr. Motley.

No. 189.]

DEPARTMENT OF STATE,
Washington, June 9, 1866.

SIR: I have the honor to acknowledge the receipt of your despatch of the 21st of May, No. 177. It is accompanied by a copy of a note which was addressed to you by Count Mensdorff on the 20th of May last.

Count Mensdorff announces to us in the said note that the departure of the volunteers lately enlisted in Austria for service in Mexico will not be allowed to take place. This decision of the imperial royal government is received by the President with sincere satisfaction. It is in harmony with the spirit which has governed the proceedings of Austria in her intercourse with the United States throughout the whole period in which political disturbances in America have been the subject of discussion between the United States and the Emperor.

You are authorized to communicate these sentiments to Count Mensdorff, and to assure him that the present just, liberal, and friendly proceeding on the part of Austria will not fail to enhance the good will and cordial friendship which the United States so habitually cherish for the government and people of Austria.

I am, sir, your obedient servant,

WILLIAM H. SEWARD.

J. LOTHROP MOTLEY, Esq., *&c., &c., Vienna.*

[From the Débats of the 18th May, 1866.—Forwarded by Mr. Bigelow.]

[Translation.]

We have good reason to call in question the news of the departure of Austrian volunteers for Mexico, published in the Memorial Diplomatique. Nothing, in fact, could be more unlikely after the despatches from the government of the United States which we have laid before our readers. Correspondents at Trieste announce not merely that the Austro-Mexican detachment has not embarked, but that it will be disbanded, and that the men who compose it have for the most part requested to take service in the corps of volunteers which is organizing in view of the approaching war. The Austrian government (they write from Trieste) was under the greater obligation not to withdraw its forces from the service of the country, because it at the same time avoided assuming an offensive attitude towards the United States of America. Thus our own previous impressions are confirmed, notwithstanding the pretended information of the Memorial Diplomatique.

Mr. Bigelow to Mr. Seward.

[Extract.]

No. 325.] LEGATION OF THE UNITED STATES,
Paris, May 25, 1866.

SIR: The following semi-official announcement appeared in La France last evening: "The return to France of Marshal Bazaine with the first detachment returning from Mexico is under consideration. In this case the marshal will turn over his command to General Douai."

Should nothing occur to change the present programme, I think Marshal Bazaine will return with the first detachment of French troops in October next. I am told that the contract with the Transatlantic Steamship Company, for their transport from Vera Cruz to St. Nazaire, was signed on Monday last.

I have as yet received no reply from Mr. Drouyn de Lhuys to my inquiry in reference to the contract supposed to have been signed at the ministry of marine for the shipment of troops from Trieste to Vera Cruz. His silence leaves little room to doubt that my suspicions were correct.

* * * * * *

I have, &c.,

JOHN BIGELOW.

Hon. WILLIAM H. SEWARD,
Secretary of State.

Mr. Seward to Mr. Bigelow.

No. 469.] DEPARTMENT OF STATE,
Washington, May 31, 1866.

SIR: I have to acknowledge the receipt of your despatch of the 16th instant, No. 320, containing a translation from La France of the 15th, in regard to the disposition of Austrian troops which had been intended for the service of the imperialists in Mexico, and enclosing translation of extracts from the Memorial Diplomatique and the Debats relating to this and other branches of the Mexican question.

I enclose, confidentially, for your information, a copy of an instruction of this date, which I have addressed to Mr. Motley.

I am, sir, your obedient servant,

WILLIAM H. SEWARD.

JOHN BIGELOW, Esq., *&c., &c., &c.*

Mr. Seward to Mr. Bigelow.

No. 474.] DEPARTMENT OF STATE,
Washington, June 4, 1866.

SIR: Your despatch of the 10th ultimo, No. 316, was duly received. The position which you inform me therein that you propose to take in regard to the forwarding of troops to Mexico is approved. Thanking you for your attention to the subject,

I remain, sir, your obedient servant,

WILLIAM H. SEWARD.

JOHN BIGELOW, Esq., *&c., &c., &c.*

Mr. Seward to Mr. Bigelow.

No. 476.] DEPARTMENT OF STATE,
Washington, June 6, 1866.

SIR: I have the honor to acknowledge the receipt of your despatch of May 25, No. 325.

The information which it contains seems to justify us in assuming that the French government has made arrangements for withdrawing one-third of its forces now in Mexico from that country in October. The knowledge of this fact will have a tendency to quiet the public mind in the United States.

I am, sir, your obedient servant,

WILLIAM H. SEWARD.

JOHN BIGELOW, Esq., *&c., &c., &c.*

EUROPEAN TROOPS IN MEXICO.

Mr. Bigelow to Mr. Seward.

No. 330.] LEGATION OF THE UNITED STATES,
Paris, June 4, 1866.

SIR: I waited upon his excellency the minister of foreign affairs on Saturday last, in pursuance of a previous appointment, to confer with him upon the subject-matter of your instruction, No. 459, marked confidential. As he had been already apprised of the contents of that despatch, through the French minister residing at Washington, I was spared the necessity of restating them. He said that the imperial government proclaimed its intention to retire from Mexico because it suited its convenience and interests to retire, and for no other reason. When, therefore, it announced formally, not merely to the United States, but to all the world, that the army would be withdrawn from Mexico within a specified term, he thought it should be deemed sufficient. The government made its declaration in good faith, and means to keep it. It means to withdraw its army within the time prescribed, and it does not intend to take one or two hundred troops in the first detachment, and one or two hundred more in the second, leaving the great body of them to the last; though it had not deemed it necessary to specify with minuteness details of this kind, which depend upon hygienic and climatic considerations, of which it was the best and the only competent judge. This, his excellency said, he wished I would say to my government.

I asked his excellency if I had ever intimated to him, whether in writing or orally, any suspicion of the Emperor's intention to withdraw his army from Mexico in unequal proportions. He replied that I had not. I then asked him if any other person authorized to speak in the name of my government had done so. He said no; but he had read imputations of that kind in one of our papers. I replied, in substance, that the press was a law unto itself, but that we had better not accept it as a law unto us; and as he asked me to communicate to my government a formal answer to what sounded like an accusation of insincerity and bad faith on the part of the Emperor, I wanted his authority for stating that no such accusation had reached him through any official channel. He replied that he only had read of it in a newspaper.

I then went on to say that the purpose of your instruction, as I understood it, was simply to obtain an explanation, which was sure to be required of you, of the shipment by France of large bodies of troops to Mexico after the purpose to withdraw her whole army had been officially proclaimed. To this his excellency replied, that since seeing me he had gotten from his colleagues of the marine and war departments information to the purport—

That no troops belonging to the *Corps Expeditionaire* had been sent to Mexico this year, unless for the sake of partly replacing soldiers missing, but at any rate without augmentation of the number of standing troops.

That the shipment of troops referred to in the public prints, and in your despatch, was most likely that made in the transport Rhône about the beginning of the year.

That this Rhône touched at Martinique, but not at St. Thomas, as was stated.

That she carried 916, and not 1,200, soldiers,

That they belonged to the Foreign Legion, and not to the Expeditionary Corps.

That they consisted of troops which had been waiting transportation a long time in France and in Algeria to join their regiments.

That no new troops had been enrolled for the Foreign Legion since the Emperor proclaimed his purpose to withdraw his flag from Mexico, and that no more, for what he knew, were intended to be enrolled.

In regard to the shipments of troops from Austria, he said that that was an affair entirely between that government and the Mexican, with which France had nothing to do; that since I had spoken to him upon the subject he had verified his own convictions by a reference to the ministers of war and of marine, and had ascertained that no engagements of any sort had been entered into by either for the enrolment or transport of troops from Austria to Mexico. He went on further to say, that it was the intention of the government to withdraw the army entirely from Mexico within the time specified in his dispatch to you at the very latest; sooner if climatic and other controlling considerations permitted, and it was not its intention to replace these with other troops from any quarter.

At the conclusion of a long conversation of which I have given the important results, I expressed my satisfaction with his excellency's explanations, and the pleasure I should have in communicating them to my government.

This despatch has been submitted to Mr. Drouyn de Lhuys, and the foregoing version of the results of our conversation has been approved by him.

I am, sir, with great respect, your obedient servant,

JOHN BIGELOW.

Hon. WILLIAM H. SEWARD,

Department of State, Washington, D. C.